Baseball America
2026
PROSPECT HANDBOOK

BASEBALL AMERICA INC. DURHAM, N.C.

Baseball America
2026 PROSPECT HANDBOOK

Editors
MARK CHIARELLI, CARLOS COLLAZO,
J.J. COOPER, MATT EDDY
AND JOSH NORRIS

Assistant Editors
BEN BADLER, JESÚS CANO,
PETER FLAHERTY, DANIEL MALONE,
GEOFF PONTES AND JACOB RUDNER

Contributing Writers
IAN CUNDALL, JON MEOLI,
BILL MITCHELL, NICK PIECORO,
ALEX SPEIER AND TAYLOR BLAKE WARD

Design & Production
SETH MATES

Cover Photo
KONNOR GRIFFIN BY
MIKE CARLSON/MLB PHOTOS VIA GETTY IMAGES

NO PORTION OF THIS BOOK MAY BE
REPRINTED OR REPRODUCED WITHOUT
THE WRITTEN CONSENT OF THE PUBLISHER.

FOR ADDITIONAL COPIES
VISIT OUR WEBSITE AT BASEBALLAMERICA.COM
OR CALL 1-800-845-7276 TO ORDER.

US $40.95, PLUS SHIPPING AND HANDLING PER ORDER.
EXPEDITED SHIPPING AVAILABLE.

DISTRIBUTED BY SIMON & SCHUSTER
ISBN: 979-8-9916170-1-7

STATISTICS PROVIDED BY MAJOR LEAGUE BASEBALL
ADVANCED MEDIA AND COMPILED BY
BASEBALL AMERICA

© 2025 by Baseball America Enterprises, LLC
All Rights Reserved. Printed in the USA.

Baseball America
ESTABLISHED 1981
P.O. BOX 12877, DURHAM, NC 27709 • PHONE (800) 845-2726

EDITOR-IN-CHIEF J.J. Cooper @jjcoop36
EXECUTIVE EDITOR Matt Eddy @MattEddyBA
CHIEF INNOVATION OFFICER Ben Badler @benbadler
VICE PRESIDENT, DESIGN & STRATEGY Seth Mates @sethmates
HEAD OF AUDIENCE DEVELOPMENT Mark Chiarelli @Mark_Chiarelli
DIRECTOR OF FINANCE AND REVENUE Mike Stewart
TECHNOLOGY DIRECTOR Steven Peters

EDITORIAL
SENIOR EDITOR Josh Norris @jnorris427
NATIONAL WRITERS Carlos Collazo @CarlosACollazo
Peter Flaherty @PeterGFlaherty
PROSPECT WRITER Geoff Pontes @GeoffPontesBA
NATIONAL COLLEGE WRITER Jacob Rudner @JacobRudner
STAFF WRITER Jesús Cano @Jesus_Cano88
SENIOR DIGITAL EDITOR Daniel Malone
SPECIAL CONTRIBUTOR Tim Newcomb @tdnewcomb

BUSINESS
MARKETING/OPERATIONS COORDINATOR Angela Lewis
CUSTOMER SERVICE Melissa Sunderman

STATISTICAL SERVICE
MAJOR LEAGUE BASEBALL ADVANCED MEDIA

BASEBALL AMERICA ENTERPRISES
CHAIRMAN & CEO Gary Green
PRESIDENT Larry Botel
GENERAL COUNSEL Matthew Pace
DIRECTOR OF OPERATIONS Joan DiSalvo
PARTNERS Stephen Alepa
Jon Ashley
Martie Cordaro
David Geaslen
Glenn Isaacson
Sonny Kalsi
Peter R. Riguardi
Ian Ritchie
Brian Rothschild
Beryl Snyder
Tom Steiglehner

PJL MEDIA
PRESIDENT Jonathan Segal
VICE PRESIDENT, OPERATIONS B.J. Schecter

BASEBALL AMERICA is published bimonthly, six double-issues per year, by Baseball America Enterprises, LLC, 650 Fifth Avenue, Suite 2400, New York, NY 10019. Subscription rate is $109.99 for one year; Canada $112.99 (U.S. funds); all other foreign $125.99 per year (U.S. funds). Periodicals postage paid at New York NY, & additional mailing offices. Occasionally our subscriber list is made available to reputable firms offering goods and services we believe would be of interest to our readers. If you prefer to be excluded, please send your current address label and a note requesting to be excluded from these promotions to Baseball America Enterprises, LLC, PO Box 12877, Durham, NC 27709, Attn: Privacy Coordinator. POSTMASTER: Send all UAA to CFS (See DMM 707.4.12.5); NONPOSTAL & MILITARY FACILITIES: send address corrections to Baseball America, P.O. Box 420235, Palm Coast, FL 32142-0235. CANADA POST: Return undeliverable Canadian addresses to IMEX Global Solutions, P.O. Box 25542, London, ON N6C 6B2. Please contact 1-800-381-1288 to start carrying Baseball America in your store.

© 2025 by Baseball America Enterprises, LLC. All Rights Reserved. Printed in the USA.

FOREWORD

When we rolled out BA Grades in 2012, we described the addition as the biggest change to the Prospect Handbook since we first published the book in 2001.

Now, it's time for a refresh.

This year, we're making the biggest tweak to the process since BA Grades debuted. Our goal? To reset the baseline for how we account for risk to more accurately reflect what we are attempting to convey.

We casually refer to them as "BA Grades," but in reality our grades have two vital components: a future role grade and the likelihood of achieving that grade.

The number component is an attempt to summarize the likely projected role of a prospect on the familiar 20-80 scouting scale. A role grade paints a picture of a player's upside, but it does not account for the likelihood of such an outcome.

Risk assessment is crucial when comparing, for example, a tooled-up Dominican Summer League star with a big league-ready Triple-A player. Or when comparing a position player to a pitcher. Or when comparing a player who missed a year to injury with one who has a long track record of health.

When BA Grades were introduced in 2012, we settled on "high" as the baseline risk for all players, because, well, prospects are risky when compared with major leaguers.

In many ways, that is accurate. It was our attempt to spell out just how difficult it is for even solid prospects to turn into MLB regulars. Prospects by their very nature are risky. But it also wasn't what we wanted to fully convey. Those prospects deemed "high" risk weren't riskier than the average prospect.

They were just risky, like all prospects.

We have always fused the BA Grade with risk to create what we call an adjusted grade. Different gradations of risk carry different penalties. For example, an "average" risk deducts 10 points from a player's BA Grade. (For much more on BA Grades and our revised risk scale, please see Pages 10-11.)

Now, for the first time, we are printing those adjusted BA Grades. They are designed to capture how different player types with different levels of experience can line up on an ordinal ranking, providing tiers of talent.

Changing our risk scale is a big adjustment for BA. We have maintained the same scale for more than a decade, with its roots tracing back to the prospect days of Mike Trout, Bryce Harper and Nolan Arenado.

But we don't want to let a reverence for history or tradition prevent us from making improvements. We always want to be striving to improve, and we hope this takes us forward.

J.J. Cooper
Editor-in-chief, Baseball America

ABOUT THIS EDITION

All BA Grades and scouting grades are projected to players' peak seasons and are assessed on the 20-80 scouting scale, where 50 is average.

Position players are graded on the five scouting tools.

HIT: hitting ability
POW: game power
RUN: speed
FLD: fielding
ARM: arm

Pitchers are graded on pitch types they throw and their control.

FB: fastball
CB: curveball
SL: slider
CH: changeup
CT: cutter
SP: splitter
SW: sweeper
CTL: control

All statistics generated in the affiliated minor leagues and major leagues in 2025 are presented for all players, along with their career minor league totals and career MLB totals, where applicable.

Age listed for players is their "baseball age," or age as of June 30, 2025.

EDITOR'S NOTE: The transaction deadline for this book was Dec. 15, 2025. You can find players who changed organizations by using the index in the back.

>> **A note about player eligibility for this book:** A prospect is any player who is signed with a major league organization as of our transaction deadline and who has not exceeded 130 career big league at-bats, 50 career big league innings or 45 career days of *active* major league service. Time spent on the injured list does not count as active service. The only exceptions to the rule are "foreign professionals" and other one-time affiliated players coming back from Japan or Korea. While these players are eligible to win the Rookie of the Year award, the fact that they signed major league contracts makes them more akin to major league free agents than true prospects.

L = Low. M = Mild. A = Average. H = High. X = Extreme.

TABLE OF CONTENTS

ARIZONA DIAMONDBACKS
STARTS ON PAGE 18

No. Player, Pos	BA Grade/Risk	No. Player, Pos	BA Grade/Risk	No. Player, Pos	BA Grade/Risk
1. Ryan Waldschmidt, OF	55/A	11. Cristian Mena, RHP	45/A	21. Dylan Ray, RHP	45/A
2. Kayson Cunningham, SS	55/A	12. Jansel Luis, 2B	50/H	22. Yassel Soler, 3B	50/X
3. Demetrio Crisantes, 2B	55/H	13. Kohl Drake, LHP	45/A	23. Ivan Luciano, C	45/H
4. Slade Caldwell, OF	50/A	14. Ashton Izzi, RHP	45/A	24. Yu-Min Lin, LHP	45/A
5. David Hagaman, RHP	55/A	15. LuJames Groover, 3B	50/H	25. Mason Marriott, RHP	45/H
6. Daniel Eagen, RHP	50/A	16. Brandyn Garcia, LHP	45/A	26. Jaitoine Kelly, RHP	50/X
7. Patrick Forbes, RHP	50/A	17. Druw Jones, OF	50/H	27. Dean Livingston, RHP	50/X
8. JD Dix, 2B	50/H	18. Mitch Bratt, LHP	45/A	28. Daury Vasquez, RHP	50/X
9. Tommy Troy, 2B	45/A	19. Carlos Virahonda, C	50/H	29. Yordin Chalas, RHP	45/A
10. Cristofer Torin, SS	45/A	20. Brian Curley, RHP	45/A	30. Chung-Hsiang Huang, RHP	45/H

ATHLETICS
STARTS ON PAGE 34

No. Player, Pos	BA Grade/Risk	No. Player, Pos	BA Grade/Risk	No. Player, Pos	BA Grade/Risk
1. Leo De Vries, SS	65/A	11. Shotaro Morii, SS/RHP	55/H	21. Yunior Tur, RHP	45/A
2. Jamie Arnold, LHP	60/A	12. Kade Morris, RHP	50/A	22. Ryan Lasko, OF	40/A
3. Gage Jump, LHP	60/A	13. Henry Baez, RHP	50/A	23. Breyson Guedez, OF	50/X
4. Wei-En Lin, LHP	55/A	14. Gunnar Hoglund, RHP	45/A	24. Corey Avant, RHP	40/A
5. Braden Nett, RHP	55/A	15. Mason Barnett, RHP	45/A	25. Clark Elliott, OF	40/A
6. Henry Bolte, OF	55/H	16. Steven Echavarria, RHP	50/H	26. Kenya Huggins, RHP	45/H
7. Edgar Montero, SS	55/H	17. Zane Taylor, RHP	45/A	27. Kyle Robinson, RHP	40/A
8. Joshua Kuroda-Grauer, SS	45/A	18. Gavin Turley, OF	45/A	28. Cole Miller, RHP	45/H
9. Devin Taylor, OF	50/A	19. Junior Perez, OF	45/A	29. Darwing Ozuna, OF	50/X
10. Tommy White, 3B/1B	50/A	20. Eduarniel Núñez, RHP	40/M	30. Chen-Zhong Ao Zhuang, RHP	35/M

ATLANTA BRAVES
STARTS ON PAGE 50

No. Player, Pos	BA Grade/Risk	No. Player, Pos	BA Grade/Risk	No. Player, Pos	BA Grade/Risk
1. Cam Caminiti, LHP	60/H	11. Herick Hernandez, LHP	50/H	21. Cedric De Grandpre, RHP	45/H
2. JR Ritchie, RHP	55/H	12. John Gil, SS	45/A	22. Jhancarlos Lara, RHP	50/X
3. Didier Fuentes, RHP	50/A	13. Tate Southisene, SS	55/X	23. Dixon Williams, 2B	45/H
4. Owen Murphy, RHP	55/H	14. Blake Burkhalter, RHP	40/M	24. Eric Hartman, OF	45/H
5. Briggs McKenzie, LHP	55/H	15. Conor Essenburg, OF	55/X	25. Isaiah Drake, OF	40/A
6. Alex Lodise, SS	55/H	16. Hayden Harris, LHP	40/M	26. Jim Jarvis, SS	35/M
7. Lucas Braun, RHP	45/M	17. Rolddy Muñoz, RHP	45/A	27. Patrick Clohisy, OF	40/A
8. Garrett Baumann, RHP	50/A	18. Landon Beidelschies, LHP	45/A	28. Blane Abeyta, RHP	35/M
9. Luke Sinnard, RHP	50/A	19. Cody Miller, SS	45/A	29. Owen Carey, OF	45/H
10. Diego Tornes, OF	55/X	20. David McCabe, 1B	40/M	30. Brett Sears, RHP	35/M

BALTIMORE ORIOLES
STARTS ON PAGE 66

No. Player, Pos	BA Grade/Risk	No. Player, Pos	BA Grade/Risk	No. Player, Pos	BA Grade/Risk
1. Samuel Basallo, C	65/A	11. Braxton Bragg, RHP	55/H	21. Joseph Dzierwa, LHP	45/A
2. Dylan Beavers, OF	55/H	12. Slater de Brun, OF	55/H	22. Wilfri De La Cruz, SS	55/X
3. Trey Gibson, RHP	55/A	13. Aron Estrada, 2B/OF	50/A	23. Jordan Sanchez, OF	50/H
4. Nate George, OF	55/A	14. Boston Bateman, LHP	55/H	24. Anthony Nunez, RHP	50/H
5. Luis De Leon, LHP	60/H	15. Nestor German, RHP	50/A	25. JT Quinn, RHP	50/H
6. Ike Irish, OF/C	55/A	16. Caden Bodine, C	50/A	26. Wellington Aracena, RHP	45/H
7. Esteban Mejia, RHP	65/X	17. Austin Overn, OF	45/A	27. Ethan Anderson, C	45/H
8. Michael Forret, RHP	55/H	18. Levi Wells, RHP	50/H	28. Stiven Martinez, OF	50/X
9. Enrique Bradfield Jr., OF	50/A	19. Juaron Watts-Brown, RHP	50/H	29. Joshua Liranzo, SS/3B	45/H
10. Wehiwa Aloy, SS	55/H	20. Thomas Sosa, OF	45/A	30. Vance Honeycutt, OF	50/X

BOSTON RED SOX
STARTS ON PAGE 82

No. Player, Pos	BA Grade/Risk	No. Player, Pos	BA Grade/Risk	No. Player, Pos	BA Grade/Risk
1. Payton Tolle, LHP	60/M	11. Henry Godbout, 2B	50/A	21. Harold Rivas, OF	50/H
2. Franklin Arias, SS	55/A	12. David Sandlin, RHP	50/A	22. Tyler Samaniego, LHP	45/A
3. Connelly Early, LHP	50/M	13. Eddy Azocar, OF	55/H	23. Hayden Mullins, LHP	45/A
4. Kyson Witherspoon, RHP	55/A	14. Anthony Eyanson, RHP	50/A	24. Hector Ramos, SS	50/X
5. Juan Valera, RHP	50/A	15. John Holobetz, RHP	50/A	25. Sadbiel Delzine, RHP	50/X
6. Jake Bennett, LHP	50/A	16. Shane Drohan, LHP	50/A	26. Gerardo Rodriguez, C	45/H
7. Justin Gonzales, OF	55/H	17. Tyler Uberstine, RHP	40/A	27. Allan Castro, OF	40/A
8. Yhoiker Fajardo, RHP	50/A	18. Miguel Bleis, OF	50/H	28. Blake Aita, RHP	45/H
9. Dorian Soto, SS	55/H	19. Mikey Romero, 3B	45/A	29. Johanfran Garcia, C	40/A
10. Marcus Phillips, RHP	55/H	20. Yoeilin Cespedes, 2B	50/H	30. Luke Heyman, C	45/H

L = Low.   M = Mild.   A = Average.   H = High.   X = Extreme.

CHICAGO CUBS
STARTS ON PAGE 98

No. Player, Pos	BA Grade/Risk
1. Moises Ballesteros, C	55/M
2. Owen Caissie, OF	55/M
3. Jaxon Wiggins, RHP	60/H
4. Jefferson Rojas, SS	55/A
5. Ethan Conrad, OF	55/A
6. Kane Kepley, OF	50/A
7. Kevin Alcantara, OF	50/A
8. Jonathon Long, 1B/OF	45/M
9. Cole Mathis, 3B	50/H
10. Pedro Ramirez, 2B/3B	45/A
11. James Triantos, 2B/OF	45/A
12. Josiah Hartshorn, OF	55/X
13. Dominick Reid, RHP	45/A
14. Brandon Birdsell, RHP	45/A
15. Jostin Florentino, RHP	50/H
16. Cristian Hernandez, SS	45/A
17. Kaleb Wing, RHP	50/H
18. Owen Ayers, C	45/A
19. Juan Cabada, 2B/3B	45/H
20. Angel Cepeda, SS/3B	45/H
21. Riley Martin, LHP	40/A
22. Ty Southisene, 2B	45/H
23. Will Sanders, RHP	40/A
24. Juan Tomas, SS	45/H
25. Erian Rodriguez, RHP	45/H
26. Pierce Coppola, LHP	50/X
27. Tyler Schlaffer, RHP	40/A
28. Brody McCullough, RHP	50/X
29. Ariel Armas, C	40/A
30. Nick Dean, RHP	30/L

CHICAGO WHITE SOX
STARTS ON PAGE 114

No. Player, Pos	BA Grade/Risk
1. Noah Schultz, LHP	65/H
2. Caleb Bonemer, SS	60/H
3. Braden Montgomery, OF	55/A
4. Hagen Smith, LHP	60/H
5. Billy Carlson, SS	60/H
6. Tanner McDougal, RHP	50/A
7. Jaden Fauske, OF	55/X
8. Christian Oppor, LHP	50/H
9. Sam Antonacci, 2B	45/A
10. Kyle Lodise, SS	45/A
11. Mathias LaCombe, RHP	50/H
12. William Bergolla, 2B/SS	45/A
13. Ky Bush, LHP	45/A
14. Mason Adams, RHP	45/A
15. George Wolkow, OF	50/H
16. Javier Mogollon, SS/2B	45/A
17. Jeral Perez, 2B	45/A
18. Aldrin Batista, RHP	45/H
19. Jedixson Paez, RHP	45/H
20. Alexander Alberto, RHP	45/H
21. Gage Ziehl, RHP	40/A
22. Blake Larson, LHP	50/X
23. Jairo Iriarte, RHP	45/H
24. Landon Hodge, C	50/X
25. Jacob Gonzalez, SS	35/M
26. Luis Reyes, RHP	45/H
27. Gabe Davis, RHP	45/H
28. Shane Murphy, LHP	35/M
29. Yobal Rodriguez, RHP	50/X
30. Matthew Boughton, 2B/SS	50/X

CINCINNATI REDS
STARTS ON PAGE 130

No. Player, Pos	BA Grade/Risk
1. Sal Stewart, 1B	55/M
2. Alfredo Duno, C	60/H
3. Rhett Lowder, RHP	55/A
4. Tyson Lewis, SS	55/H
5. Steele Hall, SS	55/H
6. Chase Petty, RHP	50/A
7. Edwin Arroyo, SS	45/M
8. Cam Collier, 1B	50/A
9. Hector Rodriguez, OF	45/M
10. Stharlin Torres, RHP	55/H
11. Aaron Watson, RHP	55/H
12. Julian Aguiar, RHP	50/H
13. Jose Franco, RHP	45/M
14. Adolfo Sanchez, OF	50/H
15. Sheng-En Lin, RHP	50/H
16. Leo Balcazar, 3B/2B	45/A
17. Mason Neville, OF	50/H
18. Tyler Callihan, 2B/OF	45/A
19. Zach Maxwell, RHP	45/A
20. Mason Morris, RHP	50/H
21. Jirvin Morillo, C	50/H
22. Liberts Aponte, SS	45/H
23. Eli Pitts, OF	50/X
24. Luke Holman, RHP	50/X
25. Arnaldo Lantigua, OF	50/X
26. Carlos Sanchez, 3B/OF	40/A
27. Edgar Colon, RHP	50/X
28. Trevor Kuncl, RHP	40/A
29. Carlos Jorge, OF	40/A
30. Connor Burns, C	40/A

CLEVELAND GUARDIANS
STARTS ON PAGE 146

No. Player, Pos	BA Grade/Risk
1. Travis Bazzana, 2B	55/M
2. Chase DeLauter, OF	60/A
3. Ralphy Velazquez, 1B	55/A
4. Angel Genao, SS	55/A
5. Parker Messick, LHP	50/M
6. Braylon Doughty, RHP	55/A
7. Jace LaViolette, OF	55/H
8. Khal Stephen, RHP	50/H
9. Jaison Chourio, OF	55/H
10. Cooper Ingle, C	45/H
11. Juneiker Caceres, OF	50/A
12. Joey Oakie, RHP	60/X
13. Dean Curley, SS	50/A
14. Jacob Cozart, C	45/A
15. Juan Brito, 2B	45/A
16. Welbyn Francisca, SS	45/A
17. Daniel Espino, RHP	55/X
18. Andrew Walters, RHP	50/H
19. Kahlil Watson, OF	45/A
20. Yorman Gómez, RHP	50/H
21. Nolan Schubart, OF	50/H
22. Aaron Walton, OF	45/A
23. Petey Halpin, OF	40/M
24. Alfonsin Rosario, OF	50/H
25. Josh Hartle, LHP	45/A
26. Dauri Fernandez, SS	55/X
27. Gabriel Rodriguez, SS	50/H
28. Doug Nikhazy, LHP	40/M
29. Rafe Schlesinger, LHP	45/A
30. Will Hynes, RHP	55/X

COLORADO ROCKIES
STARTS ON PAGE 162

No. Player, Pos	BA Grade/Risk
1. Ethan Holliday, SS	60/H
2. Charlie Condon, 1B	55/A
3. Jared Thomas, OF	50/A
4. Brody Brecht, RHP	50/H
5. Roldy Brito, OF/2B	50/H
6. Cole Carrigg, OF	45/A
7. Max Belyeu, OF	50/H
8. Jackson Cox, RHP	50/H
9. Robert Calaz, OF	50/X
10. Welinton Herrera, LHP	45/H
11. J.B. Middleton, RHP	45/H
12. Griffin Herring, LHP	45/H
13. Ethan Hedges, 3B	45/H
14. Wilder Dalis, 3B	45/H
15. Roc Riggio, 2B	40/H
16. Sean Sullivan, LHP	45/H
17. Carson Palmquist, LHP	40/A
18. Zac Veen, OF	40/A
19. Ashly Andujar, 2B/SS	40/A
20. Cristian Arguelles, OF	50/X
21. Sterlin Thompson, OF	40/A
22. Gabriel Hughes, RHP	40/A
23. Cole Messina, C	40/A
24. McCade Brown, RHP	40/A
25. Riley Kelly, RHP	45/H
26. RJ Petit, RHP	35/M
27. Derek Bernard, OF	45/H
28. Tanner Thach, 1B	45/H
29. Yujanyer Herrera, RHP	45/X
30. Sandy Ozuna, RHP	45/X

L = Low. M = Mild. A = Average. H = High. X = Extreme.

TABLE OF CONTENTS

DETROIT TIGERS
STARTS ON PAGE 178

No. Player, Pos	BA Grade/Risk	No. Player, Pos	BA Grade/Risk	No. Player, Pos	BA Grade/Risk
1. Kevin McGonigle, 2B/SS	70/M	11. Kelvis Salcedo, RHP	55/X	21. Jack Penney, SS	45/A
2. Max Clark, OF	65/A	12. Malachi Witherspoon, RHP	50/H	22. Jake Miller, LHP	45/A
3. Bryce Rainer, SS	65/H	13. Owen Hall, RHP	50/H	23. Nick Dumesnil, OF	45/A
4. Josue Briceño, 1B/C	60/H	14. Andrew Sears, LHP	45/A	24. Angel De Los Santos, SS	50/X
5. Jordan Yost, SS	55/H	15. John Peck, SS	45/A	25. Ty Madden, RHP	40/A
6. Hao-Yu Lee, 2B/3B	45/M	16. Ryan Hall, RHP	50/H	26. River Hamilton, RHP	50/X
7. Max Anderson, 2B	45/A	17. Trei Cruz, SS	40/M	27. Paul Wilson, LHP	50/X
8. Cris Rodriguez, OF	55/X	18. Ben Jacobs, LHP	45/A	28. Eduardo Valencia, C/1B	45/H
9. Franyerber Montilla, SS	55/X	19. Thayron Liranzo, C	45/A	29. Jackson Strong, OF	40/A
10. Michael Oliveto, C	55/X	20. Dylan Smith, RHP	40/M	30. Grayson Grinsell, LHP	40/A

HOUSTON ASTROS
STARTS ON PAGE 194

No. Player, Pos	BA Grade/Risk	No. Player, Pos	BA Grade/Risk	No. Player, Pos	BA Grade/Risk
1. Jacob Melton, OF	50/M	11. Ryan Forcucci, RHP	55/H	21. Jancel Villarroel, C	45/A
2. Xavier Neyens, SS	60/H	12. Miguel Ullola, RHP	50/A	22. James Hicks, RHP	40/A
3. Anderson Brito, RHP	60/H	13. Lucas Spence, OF	50/A	23. Jose Fleury, RHP	40/A
4. Ethan Frey, OF	50/A	14. Zach Cole, OF	50/H	24. Nick Monistere, 2B	40/A
5. Brice Matthews, 2B	50/A	15. Joseph Sullivan, OF	45/A	25. Alonzo Tredwell, RHP	45/H
6. A.J. Blubaugh, RHP	45/M	16. Anthony Huezo, OF	55/X	26. Nick Potter, RHP	40/A
7. Kevin Alvarez, OF	55/H	17. Jackson Nezuh, RHP	45/A	27. Hudson Leach, RHP	45/H
8. Ethan Pecko, RHP	50/A	18. Jase Mitchell, C	50/X	28. Cole Hertzler, RHP	45/H
9. Walker Janek, C	50/A	19. Parker Smith, RHP	40/A	29. German Ramirez, SS	45/H
10. Bryce Mayer, RHP	55/H	20. Will Bush, C/1B	40/A	30. Alimber Santa, RHP	40/A

KANSAS CITY ROYALS
STARTS ON PAGE 210

No. Player, Pos	BA Grade/Risk	No. Player, Pos	BA Grade/Risk	No. Player, Pos	BA Grade/Risk
1. Carter Jensen, C	60/H	11. Felix Arronde, RHP	45/A	21. Grayson Boles, RHP	50/X
2. Kendry Chourio, RHP	60/H	12. Ben Kudrna, RHP	45/A	22. Blake Wolters, RHP	45/H
3. David Shields, LHP	55/H	13. Carson Roccaforte, OF	45/A	23. Mason Black, RHP	40/A
4. Blake Mitchell, C	55/H	14. Steven Zobac, RHP	45/A	24. Hunter Patteson, LHP	40/A
5. Josh Hammond, SS/3B	55/H	15. Michael Lombardi, RHP	50/H	25. Cameron Millar, RHP	50/X
6. Sean Gamble, 2B/OF	55/H	16. Asbel Gonzalez, OF	50/H	26. Shane Panzini, RHP	40/A
7. Ramon Ramirez, C	50/H	17. Gavin Cross, OF	45/H	27. Dennis Colleran Jr., RHP	45/H
8. Drew Beam, RHP	45/A	18. Justin Lamkin, RHP	45/H	28. Frank Mozzicato, LHP	40/A
9. Luinder Avila, RHP	40/M	19. Warren Calcaño, SS	50/X	29. Freddy Contreras, RHP	50/X
10. Yandel Ricardo, SS	50/H	20. Ramcell Medina, SS	50/X	30. Henry Williams, RHP	40/A

LOS ANGELES ANGELS
STARTS ON PAGE 226

No. Player, Pos	BA Grade/Risk	No. Player, Pos	BA Grade/Risk	No. Player, Pos	BA Grade/Risk
1. Tyler Bremner, RHP	55/A	11. Talon Haley, LHP	55/X	21. Raudi Rodriguez, OF	40/A
2. Ryan Johnson, RHP	50/M	12. Chris Cortez, RHP	45/A	22. Joel Hurtado, RHP	40/A
3. George Klassen, RHP	55/H	13. Chase Shores, RHP	50/H	23. Xavier Mitchell, LHP	40/A
4. Nelson Rada, OF	50/A	14. Barrett Kent, RHP	50/H	24. Ubaldo Soto, RHP	45/H
5. Gabriel Davalillo, C/3B	50/H	15. Samuel Aldegheri, LHP	45/A	25. Marlon Quintero, C	40/A
6. Joswa Lugo, SS	55/X	16. Walbert Ureña, RHP	50/H	26. Yilver De Paula, SS	45/H
7. Johnny Slawinski, LHP	50/H	17. Juan Flores, C	45/A	27. Peyton Olejnik, RHP	40/A
8. Trey Gregory-Alford, RHP	50/H	18. Nate Snead, RHP	40/M	28. Austin Gordon, RHP	40/A
9. Denzer Guzman, SS	50/H	19. CJ Gray, RHP	50/X	29. Mitch Farris, LHP	35/M
10. Dylan Jordan, RHP	45/A	20. Hayden Alvarez, OF	45/H	30. Luke LaCourse, RHP	45/H

LOS ANGELES DODGERS
STARTS ON PAGE 242

No. Player, Pos	BA Grade/Risk	No. Player, Pos	BA Grade/Risk	No. Player, Pos	BA Grade/Risk
1. Eduardo Quintero, OF	60/A	11. Kendall George, OF	45/A	21. Zach Ehrhard, OF	45/A
2. Josue De Paula, OF	60/A	12. Christian Zazueta, RHP	50/H	22. Kyle Hurt, RHP	40/M
3. Mike Sirota, OF	55/A	13. River Ryan, RHP	55/X	23. Noah Miller, SS	40/A
4. Zyhir Hope, OF	55/H	14. Adam Serwinowski, LHP	45/A	24. Marlon Nieves, RHP	45/A
5. Jackson Ferris, LHP	55/H	15. Joendry Vargas, SS	55/X	25. Cam Leiter, RHP	55/X
6. Charles Davalan, OF	50/A	16. Kellon Lindsey, SS	55/X	26. James Tibbs III, OF	40/A
7. Alex Freeland, SS	45/M	17. Ching-Hsien Ko, OF	45/A	27. Landyn Vidourek, OF	45/H
8. Zach Root, LHP	50/A	18. Brendan Tunink, OF	50/H	28. Ronan Kopp, LHP	40/A
9. Emil Morales, SS	55/H	19. Aidan West, SS	50/H	29. Jose Rodriguez, RHP	40/A
10. Chase Harlan, 3B	55/H	20. Patrick Copen, RHP	50/H	30. Sterling Patick, LHP	40/A

L = Low. M = Mild. A = Average. H = High. X = Extreme.

MIAMI MARLINS
STARTS ON PAGE 258

No. Player, Pos	BA Grade/Risk	No. Player, Pos	BA Grade/Risk	No. Player, Pos	BA Grade/Risk
1. Thomas White, LHP	70/H	11. Fenwick Trimble, OF	50/H	21. Liomar Martinez, RHP	45/A
2. Robby Snelling, LHP	60/A	12. Luis Cova, OF	55/X	22. Grant Shepardson, RHP	45/A
3. Aiva Arquette, SS	60/A	13. Dillon Head, OF	50/H	23. Nate Payne, LHP	45/A
4. Joe Mack, C	55/A	14. Andrew Salas, OF/SS	55/X	24. Eliazar Dishmey, RHP	50/H
5. Kevin Defrank, RHP	60/X	15. Luis Arana, SS/3B	55/X	25. William Kempner, RHP	40/M
6. Kemp Alderman, OF	50/A	16. Esmil Valencia, OF	50/H	26. Kifraidy Encarnacion, LHP	55/X
7. Cam Cannarella, OF	50/A	17. Keyner Benitez, LHP	55/X	27. Jared Serna, SS/2B	40/M
8. Brandon Compton, OF	50/A	18. PJ Morlando, OF	45/A	28. Maximo Acosta, 3B/SS	40/M
9. Karson Milbrandt, RHP	50/A	19. Josh White, RHP	45/A	29. Jose Castro, OF	45/H
10. Starlyn Caba, SS	50/H	20. Noble Meyer, RHP	50/H	30. Deyvison De Los Santos, 1B	45/H

MILWAUKEE BREWERS
STARTS ON PAGE 274

No. Player, Pos	BA Grade/Risk	No. Player, Pos	BA Grade/Risk	No. Player, Pos	BA Grade/Risk
1. Jesús Made, SS	70/A	11. Tyson Hardin, RHP	50/A	21. Craig Yoho, RHP	40/M
2. Luis Peña, SS/2B	60/H	12. Luke Adams, 1B/3B	50/A	22. Frank Cairone, LHP	50/H
3. Cooper Pratt, SS	55/A	13. Brady Ebel, SS	55/H	23. Bryce Meccage, RHP	50/H
4. Logan Henderson, RHP	50/M	14. Robert Gasser, LHP	45/A	24. Tyler Black, OF/1B	40/M
5. Bishop Letson, RHP	55/H	15. Ethan Dorchies, RHP	55/H	25. Josh Knoth, RHP	50/H
6. Luis Lara, OF	50/A	16. Blake Burke, 1B	45/A	26. Jayden Dubanewicz, RHP	45/H
7. Jeferson Quero, C	50/A	17. Braylon Payne, OF	50/H	27. Handelfry Encarnacion, OF	45/H
8. Marco Dinges, C	50/A	18. Brock Wilken, 3B	45/A	28. Manuel Rodriguez, RHP	45/H
9. Josh Adamczewski, 2B/OF	50/A	19. JD Thompson, LHP	50/H	29. Daniel Dickinson, 2B	45/H
10. Andrew Fischer, 3B/1B	50/A	20. Eric Bitonti, 1B	50/H	30. Coleman Crow, RHP	40/A

MINNESOTA TWINS
STARTS ON PAGE 290

No. Player, Pos	BA Grade/Risk	No. Player, Pos	BA Grade/Risk	No. Player, Pos	BA Grade/Risk
1. Walker Jenkins, OF	65/A	11. Riley Quick, RHP	55/H	21. Marco Raya, RHP	45/A
2. Emmanuel Rodriguez, OF	60/H	12. Quentin Young, 3B/SS	60/X	22. Ryan Gallagher, RHP	45/A
3. Kaelen Culpepper, SS	55/A	13. Andrew Morris, RHP	45/M	23. John Klein, RHP	40/M
4. Connor Prielipp, LHP	55/A	14. Hendry Mendez, OF	50/A	24. Khadim Diaw, C/OF	45/A
5. Eduardo Tait, C	60/H	15. Brandon Winokur, 3B/SS/OF	55/X	25. Haritzon Castillo, SS/2B	50/X
6. Dasan Hill, LHP	60/H	16. Adrian Bohorquez, RHP	50/H	26. Geremy Villoria, RHP	50/X
7. Charlee Soto, RHP	55/H	17. Santiago Castellanos, RHP	55/X	27. Teilon Serrano, OF	50/X
8. Kendry Rojas, LHP	50/A	18. James Ellwanger, RHP	55/X	28. Kyle DeBarge, 2B/OF	40/A
9. Marek Houston, SS	50/A	19. Matt Barr, RHP	55/X	29. Enrique Jimenez, C/1B	45/H
10. Gabriel Gonzalez, OF	50/A	20. Jose Olivares, RHP	50/H	30. Kala'i Rosario, OF	40/A

NEW YORK METS
STARTS ON PAGE 306

No. Player, Pos	BA Grade/Risk	No. Player, Pos	BA Grade/Risk	No. Player, Pos	BA Grade/Risk
1. Nolan McLean, RHP	65/A	11. Mitch Voit, 2B	50/H	21. Randy Guzman, OF/1B	50/H
2. Carson Benge, OF	55/M	12. Elian Peña, SS	55/H	22. Franklin Gomez, LHP	50/H
3. Jonah Tong, RHP	55/A	13. Nick Morabito, OF	45/A	23. Jonathan Pintaro, RHP	40/M
4. Jett Williams, SS/2B	55/A	14. Chris Suero, C/OF	50/H	24. RJ Gordon, RHP	45/A
5. Brandon Sproat, RHP	50/M	15. Zach Thornton, LHP	50/H	25. Daiverson Gutierrez, C	45/H
6. A.J. Ewing, OF/2B	55/H	16. Will Watson, RHP	45/H	26. Trey Snyder, 2B/3B	45/H
7. Ryan Clifford, 1B/OF	50/A	17. Eli Serrano III, OF	50/H	27. Dylan Ross, RHP	40/H
8. Jacob Reimer, 3B	50/A	18. Marco Vargas, SS/2B	45/A	28. Jeremy Rodriguez, SS/2B	45/H
9. Jack Wenninger, RHP	50/A	19. Boston Baro, SS/3B	45/A	29. Peter Kussow, RHP	50/X
10. Jonathan Santucci, LHP	55/H	20. Antonio Jimenez, SS	50/H	30. Cam Tilly, RHP	45/H

NEW YORK YANKEES
STARTS ON PAGE 322

No. Player, Pos	BA Grade/Risk	No. Player, Pos	BA Grade/Risk	No. Player, Pos	BA Grade/Risk
1. George Lombard Jr., SS	55/A	11. Cade Smith, RHP	45/A	21. Henry Lalane, LHP	50/X
2. Elmer Rodriguez, RHP	55/A	12. Mac Heuer, RHP	45/A	22. Stiven Marinez, SS	50/X
3. Dax Kilby, SS	60/A	13. Brendan Jones, OF	45/A	23. Francisco Vilorio, OF	50/X
4. Carlos Lagrange, RHP	55/A	14. Brock Selvidge, LHP	45/A	24. Xavier Rivas, RHP	45/H
5. Ben Hess, RHP	50/A	15. Kyle Carr, LHP	45/A	25. Jace Avina, OF	40/A
6. Spencer Jones, OF	60/X	16. Kaeden Kent, SS	45/A	26. Dylan Jasso, 3B	40/A
7. Bryce Cunningham, RHP	55/H	17. Pico Kohn, LHP	45/A	27. Brando Mayea, OF	45/H
8. Dillon Lewis, OF	55/H	18. Cade Winquest, RHP	40/A	28. Allen Facundo, LHP	45/H
9. Thatcher Hurd, RHP	55/X	19. Jack Cebert, RHP	45/A	29. Jose M. Rodriguez, RHP	45/H
10. Chase Hampton, RHP	55/X	20. Harrison Cohen, RHP	40/M	30. Carson Coleman, RHP	45/H

L = Low. M = Mild. A = Average. H = High. X = Extreme.

TABLE OF CONTENTS

PHILADELPHIA PHILLIES
STARTS ON PAGE 338

No. Player, Pos	BA Grade/Risk	No. Player, Pos	BA Grade/Risk	No. Player, Pos	BA Grade/Risk
1. Aidan Miller, SS	65/A	11. Cody Bowker, RHP	45/A	21. Zach McCambley, RHP	40/A
2. Andrew Painter, RHP	65/H	12. Sean Youngerman, RHP	50/H	22. Jean Cabrera, RHP	40/A
3. Justin Crawford, OF	55/A	13. Ramon Marquez, RHP	50/A	23. Anderson Araujo, C	45/H
4. Aroon Escobar, 2B	50/A	14. Carson DeMartini, SS	45/A	24. Romeli Espinosa, SS	45/A
5. Gage Wood, RHP	50/A	15. Griffin Burkholder, OF	50/H	25. Keaton Anthony, 1B	40/A
6. Dante Nori, OF	50/H	16. Alirio Ferrebus, C	50/H	26. Saul Teran, RHP	40/A
7. Gabriel Rincones Jr., 1B/OF	45/A	17. Seth Johnson, RHP	40/M	27. Yoniel Curet, RHP	45/H
8. Matthew Fisher, RHP	50/H	18. Alex McFarlane, RHP	40/A	28. Casey Steward, RHP	40/A
9. Moisés Chace, RHP	50/H	19. Gabe Craig, RHP	40/A	29. James Tallon, LHP	40/A
10. Cade Obermueller, LHP	50/H	20. Devin Saltiban, OF/2B	45/H	30. Bryan Rincon, SS	40/H

PITTSBURGH PIRATES
STARTS ON PAGE 354

No. Player, Pos	BA Grade/Risk	No. Player, Pos	BA Grade/Risk	No. Player, Pos	BA Grade/Risk
1. Konnor Griffin, SS/OF	75/A	11. Esmerlyn Valdez, OF/1B	45/A	21. Duce Gourson, 2B	45/A
2. Bubba Chandler, RHP	65/A	12. Wyatt Sanford, SS	50/H	22. Jesus Travieso, RHP	50/H
3. Edward Florentino, OF	65/H	13. Omar Alfonzo, C	45/A	23. Levi Sterling, RHP	50/H
4. Seth Hernandez, RHP	65/H	14. Sammy Stafura, SS	50/H	24. Jeter Martinez, RHP	50/H
5. Jhostynxon Garcia, OF	45/A	15. Khristian Curtis, RHP	45/A	25. Zander Mueth, RHP	50/H
6. Rafael Flores, C/1B	45/M	16. Reinold Navarro, LHP	55/X	26. Easton Carmichael, C	45/A
7. Termarr Johnson, 2B	50/A	17. Darell Morel, SS	55/X	27. Murf Gray, 3B	45/A
8. Antwone Kelly, RHP	50/A	18. Thomas Harrington, RHP	40/M	28. Jack Brannigan, SS/3B	40/A
9. Hunter Barco, LHP	45/H	19. Nick Yorke, 2B/OF	40/M	29. Tony Blanco Jr., 1B	50/X
10. Wilber Dotel, RHP	50/A	20. Axiel Plaz, C	50/H	30. Johan De Los Santos, SS	50/X

ST. LOUIS CARDINALS
STARTS ON PAGE 370

No. Player, Pos	BA Grade/Risk	No. Player, Pos	BA Grade/Risk	No. Player, Pos	BA Grade/Risk
1. JJ Wetherholt, SS	65/H	11. Yairo Padilla, SS	55/H	21. Braden Davis, LHP	45/A
2. Liam Doyle, LHP	60/A	12. Ryan Mitchell, SS/OF	55/H	22. Jack Gurevitch, 1B	45/A
3. Rainiel Rodriguez, C	60/A	13. Tekoah Roby, RHP	60/X	23. Frank Elissalt, RHP	40/A
4. Joshua Baez, OF	60/H	14. Tink Hence, RHP	55/H	24. Nate Dohm, RHP	40/A
5. Quinn Mathews, LHP	50/M	15. Jesus Baez, SS/3B	50/A	25. Bryan Torres, 2B/OF	40/A
6. Brandon Clarke, LHP	60/X	16. Nathan Church, OF	40/L	26. Zach Levenson, OF	40/A
7. Tanner Franklin, RHP	55/H	17. Cooper Hjerpe, LHP	50/H	27. Chase Davis, OF	45/H
8. Ixan Henderson, LHP	45/M	18. Cade Crossland, LHP	45/A	28. Matt Pushard, RHP	40/A
9. Jimmy Crooks, C	45/A	19. Deniel Ortiz, 1B/3B	45/A	29. Travis Honeyman, OF	40/A
10. Leonardo Bernal, C	50/A	20. Brycen Mautz, LHP	45/A	30. Blaze Jordan, 1B/3B	45/H

SAN DIEGO PADRES
STARTS ON PAGE 386

No. Player, Pos	BA Grade/Risk	No. Player, Pos	BA Grade/Risk	No. Player, Pos	BA Grade/Risk
1. Ethan Salas, C	55/A	11. Jagger Haynes, LHP	45/A	21. Jhoan De La Cruz, SS	50/H
2. Kruz Schoolcraft, LHP	55/A	12. Tucker Musgrove, RHP	50/H	22. Deivid Coronil, 3B	55/X
3. Kash Mayfield, LHP	55/A	13. Braedon Karpathios, OF	50/A	23. Garrett Hawkins, RHP	45/A
4. Miguel Mendez, RHP	55/A	14. Lamar King Jr., C	45/A	24. Luis Gutierrez, LHP	45/A
5. Jorge Quintana, SS	50/A	15. Romeo Sanabria, 1B	45/A	25. Bryan Balzer, RHP	45/H
6. Humberto Cruz, RHP	50/A	16. Michael Salina, RHP	50/H	26. Tirso Ornelas, OF	35/M
7. Ty Harvey, C	50/H	17. Truitt Madonna, C	50/H	27. Francis Peña, RHP	40/A
8. Ryan Wideman, OF	50/H	18. Lan-Hong Su, RHP	50/H	28. Carlos Alvarez, LHP	50/X
9. Bradgley Rodriguez, RHP	45/A	19. Kavares Tears, OF	45/A	29. Rosman Verdugo, 3B	40/A
10. Kale Fountain, 1B/3B	50/H	20. Kannon Kemp, RHP	50/H	30. Victor Lizarraga, RHP	35/M

SAN FRANCISCO GIANTS
STARTS ON PAGE 402

No. Player, Pos	BA Grade/Risk	No. Player, Pos	BA Grade/Risk	No. Player, Pos	BA Grade/Risk
1. Bryce Eldridge, 1B	60/M	11. Argenis Cayama, RHP	55/H	21. Trent Harris, RHP	40/M
2. Josuar Gonzalez, SS	65/H	12. Blade Tidwell, RHP	45/M	22. Cam Maldonado, OF	45/A
3. Bo Davidson, OF	55/A	13. Carlos Gutierrez, OF	50/H	23. Diego Velasquez, 2B	40/A
4. Jhonny Level, SS	55/A	14. Trevor McDonald, RHP	40/M	24. Joe Whitman, LHP	45/H
5. Jacob Bresnahan, LHP	55/A	15. Parks Harber, 3B/OF	45/A	25. Carlos De La Rosa, LHP	50/X
6. Keyner Martinez, RHP	55/H	16. Daniel Susac, C	45/A	26. Alberto Laroche, RHP	50/X
7. Dakota Jordan, OF	55/H	17. Luis De La Torre, LHP	45/A	27. Reid Worley, RHP	45/H
8. Gavin Kilen, SS	50/A	18. Jesus Rodriguez, C	40/M	28. Yunior Marte, RHP	40/A
9. Trevor Cohen, OF	50/H	19. Josh Bostick, RHP	45/A	29. Yulian Barreto, SS	50/X
10. Carson Whisenhunt, LHP	45/M	20. Lorenzo Meola, SS	45/A	30. Gerelmi Maldonado, RHP	40/A

L = Low.   M = Mild.   A = Average.   H = High.   X = Extreme.

SEATTLE MARINERS
STARTS ON PAGE 418

No. Player, Pos	BA Grade/Risk	No. Player, Pos	BA Grade/Risk	No. Player, Pos	BA Grade/Risk
1. Colt Emerson, SS	65/A	11. Nick Becker, SS	55/H	21. Chia-Shi Shen, RHP	50/H
2. Kade Anderson, LHP	60/A	12. Yorger Bautista, OF	60/X	22. Jared Sundstrom, OF	50/H
3. Lazaro Montes, OF	60/A	13. Griffin Hugus, RHP	45/A	23. Rhylan Thomas, OF	45/A
4. Ryan Sloan, RHP	60/H	14. Korbyn Dickerson, OF	45/A	24. Marcelo Perez, RHP	45/A
5. Michael Arroyo, OF	50/M	15. Teddy McGraw, RHP	55/X	25. Victor Labrada, OF	45/A
6. Jonny Farmelo, OF	55/H	16. Brock Rodden, INF	45/A	26. Grant Knipp, RHP/C	50/H
7. Jurrangelo Cijntje, SHP	55/H	17. Michael Morales, RHP	45/A	27. Robinson Ortiz, LHP	45/A
8. Luke Stevenson, C	50/A	18. Mason Peters, LHP	45/A	28. Charlie Beilenson, RHP	45/A
9. Felnin Celesten, SS	55/H	19. Luis Suisbel, 3B/SS	50/H	29. Lucas Kelly, RHP	45/A
10. Tai Peete, OF	60/X	20. Leandro Romero, SS	55/X	30. Tyler Cleveland, RHP	45/H

TAMPA BAY RAYS
STARTS ON PAGE 434

No. Player, Pos	BA Grade/Risk	No. Player, Pos	BA Grade/Risk	No. Player, Pos	BA Grade/Risk
1. Brody Hopkins, RHP	60/A	11. Trevor Harrison, RHP	55/H	21. Jackson Baumeister, RHP	50/H
2. Theo Gillen, OF	60/H	12. Jadher Areinamo, 2B	50/A	22. Homer Bush Jr., OF	40/M
3. Carson Williams, SS	55/A	13. Dominic Keegan, C	45/M	23. Tre' Morgan, 1B	40/M
4. TJ Nichols, RHP	55/A	14. Jose Urbina, RHP	50/A	24. Alex Cook, RHP	45/A
5. Santiago Suarez, RHP	55/A	15. Adrian Santana, SS	45/A	25. Emilien Pitre, 2B	45/A
6. Daniel Pierce, SS	55/H	16. Ty Johnson, RHP	45/A	26. Taitn Gray, 1B/OF	50/H
7. Brendan Summerhill, OF	50/A	17. Cooper Flemming, SS	50/H	27. James Quinn-Irons, OF	50/H
8. Aidan Smith, OF	50/A	18. Dean Moss, OF	50/H	28. Gregory Barrios, SS	40/A
9. Xavier Isaac, 1B	55/H	19. Gary Gill Hill, RHP	45/A	29. Joe Rock, LHP	40/A
10. Nathan Flewelling, C	55/H	20. Brailer Guerrero, OF	55/X	30. Brayden Taylor, 3B	45/H

TEXAS RANGERS
STARTS ON PAGE 450

No. Player, Pos	BA Grade/Risk	No. Player, Pos	BA Grade/Risk	No. Player, Pos	BA Grade/Risk
1. Sebastian Walcott, SS	65/A	11. Leandro Lopez, RHP	45/A	21. Paxton Kling, OF	50/H
2. Caden Scarborough, RHP	55/A	12. Dylan Dreiling, OF	45/A	22. Elorky Rodriguez, 2B	50/X
3. Gavin Fien, SS	55/H	13. Alejandro Rosario, RHP	55/X	23. Seong-Jun Kim, SS/RHP	50/X
4. Josh Owens, SS/RHP	55/H	14. Yeremy Cabrera, OF	45/A	24. Maxton Martin, OF	40/A
5. Jose Corniell, RHP	45/M	15. Emiliano Teodo, RHP	45/A	25. Paulino Santana, OF	45/H
6. AJ Russell, RHP	50/A	16. Izack Tiger, RHP	50/H	26. Anthony Gutierrez, OF	45/A
7. David Davalillo, RHP	50/A	17. Malcolm Moore, C	50/H	27. Ben Abeldt, LHP	45/H
8. Devin Fitz-Gerald, SS/2B	50/H	18. Dalton Pence, LHP	45/A	28. Paul Bonzagni, RHP	45/H
9. Winston Santos, RHP	50/M	19. Carter Baumler, RHP	40/M	29. Cameron Cauley, SS	45/H
10. Yolfran Castillo, SS/3B	50/H	20. Jack Wheeler, 3B	50/H	30. Joey Danielson, RHP	40/A

TORONTO BLUE JAYS
STARTS ON PAGE 466

No. Player, Pos	BA Grade/Risk	No. Player, Pos	BA Grade/Risk	No. Player, Pos	BA Grade/Risk
1. Trey Yesavage, RHP	60/M	11. Yohendrick Pinango, OF	45/A	21. Jake Casey, OF	50/H
2. Arjun Nimmala, SS	60/H	12. Silvano Hechavarria, RHP	50/H	22. Spencer Miles, RHP	45/H
3. JoJo Parker, SS	60/H	13. Victor Arias, OF	45/A	23. Ryan Jennings, RHP	40/A
4. Johnny King, LHP	60/H	14. Blaine Bullard, OF	50/H	24. Charles McAdoo, 3B	45/H
5. Gage Stanifer, RHP	55/H	15. Tim Piasentin, 3B	50/H	25. Adam Macko, LHP	40/A
6. Ricky Tiedemann, LHP	60/X	16. Angel Bastardo, RHP	45/A	26. Brandon Barriera, LHP	50/X
7. Juan Sanchez, SS	55/H	17. Josh Kasevich, SS	50/H	27. Carson Messina, RHP	50/X
8. RJ Schreck, OF	45/M	18. Fernando Perez, RHP	45/A	28. Brandon Valenzuela, C	30/L
9. Jake Bloss, RHP	55/H	19. Micah Bucknam, RHP	45/A	29. Javen Coleman, LHP	40/A
10. Jake Cook, OF	50/H	20. Sean Keys, 1B/3B	45/A	30. Edward Duran, C	40/A

WASHINGTON NATIONALS
STARTS ON PAGE 482

No. Player, Pos	BA Grade/Risk	No. Player, Pos	BA Grade/Risk	No. Player, Pos	BA Grade/Risk
1. Eli Willits, SS	60/A	11. Landon Harmon, RHP	55/X	21. Ronny Cruz, SS	50/X
2. Jarlin Susana, RHP	60/H	12. Sam Petersen, OF	50/H	22. Christian Franklin, OF	40/A
3. Harry Ford, C	55/A	13. Ethan Petry, OF	45/A	23. Sean Paul Liñan, RHP	40/A
4. Luis Perales, RHP	60/H	14. Andrew Pinckney, OF	40/M	24. Yoel Tejeda, RHP	45/H
5. Travis Sykora, RHP	60/H	15. Jackson Kent, LHP	45/A	25. Riley Cornelio, RHP	40/A
6. Alex Clemmey, LHP	55/H	16. Yohandy Morales, 1B/3B	45/A	26. Andrew Alvarez, LHP	40/A
7. Seaver King, SS	50/A	17. Marconi German, SS/2B	50/H	27. Philip Glasser, OF/2B	40/A
8. Luke Dickerson, SS	55/H	18. Caleb Lomavita, C	45/A	28. Nauris De La Cruz, OF	50/X
9. Coy James, SS	55/H	19. Miguel Sime Jr., RHP	50/X	29. Brayan Cortesia, SS	50/X
10. Angel Feliz, SS	50/H	20. Jorgelys Mota, 3B	50/X	30. Griff McGarry, RHP	40/A

BA GRADES

For the 15th year, Baseball America has assigned Grades and Risk Factors for each of the 900 prospects in the Prospect Handbook. For the BA Grade, we used a 20-to-80 scale, similar to the scale scouts use, to keep it familiar. However, most major league clubs put an overall numerical grade on players, called Overall Future Potential or OFP. Often, the OFP is merely an average of the player's tools.

The BA Grade is not an OFP. It's a measure of a prospect's value, and it attempts to gauge the player's realistic ceiling. We've continued to adjust our grades to try to be more realistic, and less optimistic, and keep refining the grade-vetting process. The three most popular grades in this book are 45/Average, 50/High and 40/Average. That attempts to reflect the reality that the majority of prospects in this book are either players with a chance to be solid MLB regulars, but with plenty of risk of reaching that ceiling or less risky players who are also likely role players. Few future franchise players or perennial all-stars graduate from the minors in any given year, and players' role grades often decrease (along with their risk) as they climb the MiLB ladder. The goal of the Grade/Risk system is to allow readers to take a quick look at how strong their team's farm system is, and how much immediate help the big league club can expect from its prospects. Got a minor leaguer who was traded from one organization to the other after the book went to press? Use the player's Grade/Risk and see where he would rank in his new system.

It also helps with our organization talent rankings, but those will not simply flow, in formulaic fashion, from the Grade/Risk results because we incorporate a lot of factors into our talent rankings, including the differences in risk between pitchers and hitters.

ADJUSTED GRADES ARE INCLUDED FOR ALL PLAYERS UNDER "ADJ"

.isk: High. **Adj:** 40.

BA Grade Scale

GRADE	HITTER ROLE	PITCHER ROLE	EXAMPLES
75-80	Franchise Player	No. 1 starter	Shohei Ohtani, Aaron Judge, Tarik Skubal
65-70	Perennial All-Star	No. 2 starter	Kyle Tucker, Blake Snell, Jose Ramirez
60	Occasional All-Star	No. 3 starter, Game's best reliever	Bo Bichette, Luis Castillo, Mason Miller
55	First-Division Regular	No. 3/No. 4 starter, Elite reliever	Michael Busch, Jeremy Peña, Sonny Gray
50	Solid-Average Regular	No. 4 starter, High-leverage reliever	Masyn Winn, Mitch Keller, Tyler Soderstrom
45	Second-Division Regular/Platoon	No. 5 starter, Middle reliever	Caleb Durbin, Ernie Clement, Dean Kremer
40	Reserve	Fill-in starter, Low-leverage reliever	Paul DeJong, Adrian Houser, Eduard Bazardo

RISK FACTORS (WITH ASSOCIATED GRADE REDUCTIONS)

LOW (0): A player who is close to the majors, typically with little or no projection remaining and no pressing injury questions.

MILD (–5): Some work left to refine their skills, but a proven player.

AVERAGE (–10): The most common or median risk level for Top 30 prospects. The average prospect has significant risk or weaknesses in some areas of their game.

HIGH (–15): Injury or performance questions. Also, many teenagers in the low minors.

EXTREME (–20): The most acute durability or performance concerns.

BA GRADES

Explaining The 20-80 Scouting Scale

None of the authors of the Prospect Handbook is a scout, but we all have spoken to plenty of scouts to report on the prospects and scouting reports enclosed. So we use their lingo, including the 20-80 scouting scale. Many of these grades are measurable data, such as fastball velocity and speed (usually timed from home to first or in workouts over 60 yards). A fastball grade doesn't stem solely from its velocity—command and life are crucial elements as well. A 100 mph fastball with poor movement characteristics may grade below a 97 mph fastball with elite movement. Secondary pitches are graded in a similar fashion. The more swings and misses a pitch induces from hitters and the sharper the bite of the movement, the better the grade.

Velocity steadily has increased over the past decade. Not all that long ago an 88-91 mph fastball was considered major league average, but current data shows it is now well below-average. Big league starting pitchers now sit at 94-95 mph on average. You can reduce the scale by 1 mph for lefthanders, whose velocities are usually slightly lower. Fastballs earn their grades based on the average range of the pitch over the course of a typical outing, not their peak velocity.

A move to the bullpen complicates in another direction. Pitchers airing it out for one inning should throw harder than someone trying to last six or seven innings, so add 1-2 mph for relievers.

Hitting ability is as much a skill as it is a tool, but the physical elements—hand-eye coordination, swing mechanics, bat speed—are key factors in how it is graded. Raw power generally is measured by how far a player can hit the ball, but game power is graded by how many home runs the hitter projects to hit in the majors, preferably an average over the course of a player's peak seasons. We have tweaked our power grades based on the recent rise in home run rates.

Arm strength can be evaluated by observing the velocity and carry of throws, measured in workouts with radar guns or measured in games for catchers with pop times—the time it takes from the pop of the ball in the catcher's mitt to the pop of the ball in the fielder's glove at second base. Defense takes different factors into account by position but starts with proper footwork and technique, incorporates physical attributes such as hands, short-area quickness and fluid actions, then adds subtle skills such as instincts and anticipation.

Not every team uses the wording below. Some use a 2-to-8 scale without half-grades, and others use above-average and plus synonymously. For the Handbook, consider this to be the BA 20-80 scale.

20: As bad as it gets for a big leaguer. Think Chandler Simpson's power or Rowdy Tellez's speed.
30: Well below-average, but not unplayable, such as Ryan Yarbrough's fastball.
40: Below-average, such as Juan Soto's defense or Dylan Cease's control.
45: Fringe-average. Adley Rutschman's speed or Dansby Swanson's hit tool qualify.
50: Major league average, such as Bryson Stott's hitting ability.
55: Above-average. Randy Arozarena's power.
60: Plus. Marcus Semien's defense or Zac Gallen's control.
70: Plus-Plus. Among the best tools in the game, such as Freddie Freeman's hitting ability, Blake Snell's curveball and Matt Wallner's arm.
80: Top of the scale. Some scouts consider only one player's tool in all of the major leagues to be 80. Think of Aaron Judge's power, Bobby Witt Jr.'s speed or Devin Williams' changeup.

20-80 Measurables

HIT Grade Batting Avg	POWER Grade Home Runs	SPEED Home-First (In Secs.) RHH—LHH	FASTBALL Velocity (Starters) Grade Velocity	ARM STRENGTH Catcher: Pop Times To Second Base (In Seconds)
80 .... .315+	80 ....40+	80 ....4.00—3.90	80 ..... 99+ mph	80 .... < 1.86
70 ..... .295-.314	70 34-39	70 ....4.10—4.00	70 98	70 ......1.87-1.89
60 .... .275-.294	60 28-33	65 ....4.15—4.05	65 97	60 ......1.90-1.93
55 ..... .265-.274	55 23-27	60 ....4.20—4.10	60 96	55 ......1.94-1.95
50 ..... .255-.264	50 19-22	55 ....4.25—4.15	55 95	50 ......1.96-1.97
45 .... .245-.254	45 14-18	50 ....4.30—4.20	50 94	45 ......1.98-1.99
40 .... .235-.244	40 10-13	45 ....4.35—4.25	45 93	40 ......2.00-2.04
30 .... .215-.234	30 5-9	40 ....4.40—4.30	40 91-92	30 ......2.05-2.10
20 .... <.215	20 0-4	30 ....4.50—4.40	30 89-90	20 .... > 2.11
		20 ....4.60—4.50	20 ..... 88 or less	

MINOR LEAGUE DEPTH CHART

AN OVERVIEW

One key feature of the Prospect Handbook is a depth chart of every organization's minor league talent. This shows you at a glance what kind of talent a system has and provides even more prospects beyond the top 30 ranking.

Players are usually listed on the depth charts where we think they'll ultimately end up. To help you better understand why players are slotted at particular positions, we show you here what scouts look for in the ideal candidate at each spot, with individual tools ranked in descending order.

LF
Power
Hitting
Fielding
Arm Strength
Speed

CF
Fielding
Hitting
Speed
Power
Arm Strength

RF
Power
Hitting
Arm Strength
Fielding
Speed

3B
Power
Hitting
Fielding
Arm Strength
Speed

SS
Fielding
Arm Strength
Hitting
Power
Speed

2B
Hitting
Fielding
Power
Speed
Arm Strength

1B
Power
Hitting
Fielding
Arm Strength
Speed

C
Fielding
Hitting
Arm Strength
Power
Speed

STARTING PITCHERS

No. 1 starter
- Two plus pitches
- Average third pitch
- Plus-plus command
- Plus makeup

No. 2 starter
- Two plus pitches
- Average third pitch
- Average command
- Average makeup

No. 3 starter
- One plus pitch
- Two average pitches
- Average command
- Average makeup

No. 4-5 starters
- Command of two major league pitches
- Average velocity
- Consistent breaking ball
- Decent changeup

CLOSER
- One dominant pitch
- Second plus pitch
- Plus command
- Plus-plus makeup

SETUP MAN
- Plus fastball
- Second above-average pitch
- Average command

POSITION RANKINGS

Context is crucial to prospect evaluations. So, to provide yet another layer of context, we rank prospects at all eight field positions plus righthanded and lefthanded starting pitchers. The rankings go deeper at the marquee positions of shortstop and righthanded starter.

We grade players' tools on the 20-80 scouting scale, where 50 is average. The tools listed for position players are ability to hit for average (HIT), hit for power (POW), run (RUN), fielding ability (FLD) and throwing arm (ARM). The tools listed for pitchers are fastball (FB), curveball (CB), slider (SL), changeup (CH), other (OTH) and control (CTL). The "other" category can be a cutter, splitter or sweeper.

Included as the final categories are BA Grades and Risk levels on a scale ranging from low to extreme.

CATCHER

No.	Player	Org	HIT	POW	RUN	FLD	ARM	BA Grade	Risk
1.	Samuel Basallo	Orioles	55	70	40	45	70	65	Average
2.	Carter Jensen	Royals	55	60	40	50	65	60	Mild
3.	Rainiel Rodriguez	Cardinals	60	65	30	45	60	60	Average
4.	Moises Ballesteros	Cubs	60	55	30	40	50	55	Mild
5.	Joe Mack	Marlins	40	55	40	60	65	55	Average
6.	Alfredo Duno	Reds	40	60	40	45	50	60	High
7.	Ethan Salas	Padres	45	45	45	70	60	55	Average
8.	Harry Ford	Nationals	50	50	60	40	50	55	Average
9.	Eduardo Tait	Twins	40	60	30	45	60	60	High
10.	Caden Bodine	Orioles	60	40	40	60	45	50	Average

FIRST BASE

No.	Player	Org	HIT	POW	RUN	FLD	ARM	BA Grade	Risk
1.	Bryce Eldridge	Giants	40	70	30	40	55	60	Mild
2.	Sal Stewart	Reds	65	55	40	45	30	55	Mild
3.	Ralphy Velazquez	Guardians	55	60	30	45	60	55	Average
4.	Josue Briceño	Tigers	45	65	30	40	55	60	High
5.	Charlie Condon	Rockies	50	70	40	45	55	55	Average
6.	Ryan Clifford	Mets	40	60	50	50	60	50	Average
7.	Jonathon Long	Cubs	55	55	40	45	45	45	Mild
8.	Cam Collier	Reds	50	55	40	50	55	50	Average
9.	Luke Adams	Brewers	45	55	40	40	50	50	Average
10.	Blake Burke	Brewers	40	60	30	45	40	45	Average

SECOND BASE

No.	Player	Org	HIT	POW	RUN	FLD	ARM	BA Grade	Risk
1.	Travis Bazzana	Guardians	60	55	60	50	45	55	Mild
2.	Luis Peña	Brewers	55	50	70	40	60	60	High
3.	Jett Williams	Mets	55	45	65	50	60	55	Average
4.	Demetrio Crisantes	Diamondbacks	60	50	45	45	45	55	High
5.	Aron Estrada	Orioles	50	45	55	50	50	50	Average
6.	Josh Adamczewski	Brewers	55	50	45	30	40	50	Average
7.	Jadher Areinamo	Rays	60	45	45	60	50	50	Average
8.	Brice Matthews	Astros	30	55	60	60	45	50	Average
9.	Termarr Johnson	Pirates	50	50	45	45	40	50	Average
10.	Aroon Escobar	Phillies	55	45	40	40	50	50	Average

THIRD BASE

No.	Player	Org	HIT	POW	RUN	FLD	ARM	BA Grade	Risk
1.	Andrew Fischer	Brewers	50	60	40	40	55	50	Average
2.	Josh Hammond	Royals	50	55	50	55	60	55	High
3.	Jacob Reimer	Mets	50	60	40	45	55	50	Average
4.	Hao-Yu Lee	Tigers	50	50	50	45	45	45	Mild
5.	Chase Harlan	Dodgers	40	55	50	50	55	55	High
6.	Quentin Young	Twins	40	60	55	50	70	60	Extreme
7.	Tommy White	Athletics	55	55	30	40	50	50	Average
8.	Jesus Baez	Cardinals	50	50	40	45	60	50	Average
9.	LuJames Groover	Diamondbacks	60	45	40	45	50	50	High
10.	Brock Wilken	Brewers	40	60	20	40	45	45	Average

POSITION RANKINGS

SHORTSTOP

No.	Player	Org	HIT	POW	RUN	FLD	ARM	BA Grade	Risk
1.	Konnor Griffin	Pirates	60	70	70	60	70	75	Average
2.	Kevin McGonigle	Tigers	70	60	55	55	45	70	Mild
3.	JJ Wetherholt	Cardinals	70	55	55	55	55	65	Mild
4.	Jesús Made	Brewers	70	60	60	50	60	70	Average
5.	Leo De Vries	Athletics	60	55	50	55	60	65	Average
6.	Colt Emerson	Mariners	60	50	45	55	50	65	Average
7.	Aidan Miller	Phillies	55	55	50	60	60	65	Average
8.	Sebastian Walcott	Rangers	50	70	55	50	70	65	Average
9.	Caleb Bonemer	White Sox	55	60	50	50	50	60	Average
10.	Bryce Rainer	Tigers	55	55	55	55	70	65	High
11.	Josuar Gonzalez	Giants	50	45	70	70	60	65	High
12.	Eli Willits	Nationals	55	50	60	55	55	60	Average
13.	Aiva Arquette	Marlins	50	60	45	50	60	60	Average
14.	Franklin Arias	Red Sox	60	40	40	60	55	55	Average
15.	Arjun Nimmala	Blue Jays	45	55	55	55	60	60	High
16.	Cooper Pratt	Brewers	50	45	55	55	60	55	Average
17.	George Lombard Jr.	Yankees	50	55	60	50	50	55	Average
18.	Dax Kilby	Yankees	60	55	55	50	40	60	High
19.	JoJo Parker	Blue Jays	55	55	50	50	55	60	High
20.	Kaelen Culpepper	Twins	50	45	50	50	60	55	Average
21.	Carson Williams	Rays	30	60	60	65	65	55	Average
22.	Ethan Holliday	Rockies	50	65	40	50	55	60	High
23.	Billy Carlson	White Sox	50	45	50	70	70	60	High
24.	Kayson Cunningham	Diamondbacks	60	45	55	50	50	55	Average
25.	Angel Genao	Guardians	55	45	50	50	60	55	Average

CENTER FIELD

No	Player	Org	HIT	POW	RUN	FLD	ARM	BA Grade	Risk
1.	Walker Jenkins	Twins	70	50	55	60	55	65	Average
2.	Max Clark	Tigers	60	50	65	60	60	65	Average
3.	Carson Benge	Mets	60	55	50	55	65	55	Mild
4.	Eduardo Quintero	Dodgers	60	55	55	55	55	60	Average
5.	Mike Sirota	Dodgers	55	50	60	55	55	55	Average
6.	Theo Gillen	Rays	60	45	60	60	40	60	High
7.	Ethan Conrad	Cubs	55	55	55	55	50	55	Average
8.	A.J. Ewing	Mets	60	40	65	55	55	55	Average
9.	Nate George	Orioles	55	45	70	70	50	55	Average
10.	Bo Davidson	Giants	45	60	60	55	55	55	Average
11.	Justin Crawford	Phillies	55	40	70	50	50	55	Average
12.	Jacob Melton	Astros	50	55	60	55	50	50	Mild
13.	Slade Caldwell	Diamondbacks	55	40	60	60	45	50	Average
14.	Henry Bolte	Athletics	40	60	70	60	60	55	High
15.	Kane Kepley	Cubs	60	40	60	70	45	50	Average

CORNER OUTFIELD

No	Player	Org	HIT	POW	RUN	FLD	ARM	BA Grade	Risk
1.	Edward Florentino	Pirates	60	60	40	45	55	65	High
2.	Dylan Beavers	Orioles	55	50	60	50	60	55	Mild
3.	Josue De Paula	Dodgers	60	60	40	45	50	60	Average
4.	Chase DeLauter	Guardians	55	60	55	50	60	60	Average
5.	Owen Caissie	Cubs	50	65	45	45	60	55	Mild
6.	Ryan Waldschmidt	Diamondbacks	55	55	55	50	50	55	Average
7.	Joshua Baez	Cardinals	55	65	60	50	60	60	High
8.	Emmanuel Rodriguez	Twins	40	60	55	55	60	60	High
9.	Lazaro Montes	Mariners	40	70	30	40	60	60	High
10.	Zyhir Hope	Dodgers	40	60	55	50	50	55	Average
11.	Braden Montgomery	White Sox	50	60	50	50	70	55	Average
12.	Ike Irish	Orioles	55	50	45	45	65	55	Average
13.	Michael Arroyo	Mariners	60	50	50	40	45	50	Mild
14.	Jared Thomas	Rockies	50	50	55	50	50	50	Average
15.	Justin Gonzales	Red Sox	50	55	45	45	70	55	High

RIGHTHANDER

No	Pitcher	Team	FB	CB	SL	CH	CTL	OTH	BA Grade	Risk
1.	Nolan McLean	Mets	60	60	60	55	50	70*	65	Average
2.	Trey Yesavage	Blue Jays	60	—	55	—	50	70^	60	Mild
3.	Bubba Chandler	Pirates	70	45	55	60	50	—	65	Average
4.	Brody Hopkins	Rays	65	70	—	45	45	65#	60	Average
5.	Andrew Painter	Phillies	60	55	60	50	60	55*	65	High
6.	Seth Hernandez	Pirates	65	55	55	70	55	—	65	High
7.	Jonah Tong	Mets	65	45	40	60	45	—	55	Average
8.	Jaxon Wiggins	Cubs	70	45	60	50	50	—	60	High
9.	Rhett Lowder	Reds	50	—	70	50	65	—	55	Average
10.	Elmer Rodriguez	Yankees	60	55	50	—	60	55*	55	Average
11.	Jarlin Susana	Nationals	70	60	60	55	45	—	60	High
12.	Tyler Bremner	Angels	60	—	50	70	60	—	55	Average
13.	Kyson Witherspoon	Red Sox	60	45	55	—	50	60#	55	Average
14.	Trey Gibson	Orioles	55	60	60	40	50	55*	55	Average
15.	Braylon Doughty	Guardians	55	65	—	50	60	—	55	Average
16.	Ryan Sloan	Mariners	60	60	—	60	50	—	60	High
17.	Logan Henderson	Brewers	50	—	40	60	60	45#	50	Mild
18.	Kendry Chourio	Royals	60	55	—	60	60	—	60	High
19.	Caden Scarborough	Rangers	70	—	—	—	55	60*	55	Average
20.	Carlos Lagrange	Yankees	60	—	55	40	45	60*	55	Average
21.	Esteban Mejia	Orioles	70	—	60	40	45	—	65	Extreme
22.	JR Ritchie	Braves	50	50	55	50	55	—	55	Average
23.	Brandon Sproat	Mets	50	55	60	60	50	—	50	Mild
24.	Braden Nett	Athletics	60	60	45	45	45	55*	55	Average
25.	Ryan Johnson	Angels	55	40	60	45	60	60#	50	Mild
26.	T.J. Nichols	Rays	60	—	60	40	60	—	55	Average
27.	Travis Sykora	Nationals	65	—	55	55	50	—	60	High
28.	Luis Perales	Nationals	70	—	45	—	40	60#	60	High
29.	Anderson Brito	Astros	60	60	—	55	50	50*	60	High
30.	Santiago Suarez	Rays	60	50	—	30	70	60#	55	Average
31.	David Hagaman	Diamondbacks	60	60	50	55	55	—	55	High
32.	Tanner McDougal	White Sox	65	60	50	45	40	—	50	Average
33.	Gage Wood	Phillies	70	50	60	45	50	—	50	Average
34.	Charlee Soto	Twins	60	—	50	60	50	—	55	High
35.	Kevin Defrank	Marlins	70	—	55	60	45	—	60	Extreme
36.	Bishop Letson	Brewers	55	—	60	45	55	—	55	High
37.	Gage Stanifer	Blue Jays	55	—	60	45	45	—	55	High
38.	Khal Stephen	Guardians	55	40	50	—	55	50^	50	Average
39.	Didier Fuentes	Braves	60	45	50	40	55	—	50	Average
40.	Michael Forret	Orioles	55	60	50	50	50	55^	55	High

LEFTHANDER

No	Pitcher	Team	FB	CB	SL	CH	CTL	OTH	BA Grade	Risk
1.	Thomas White	Marlins	60	—	70	65	45	—	70	High
2.	Payton Tolle	Red Sox	70	—	50	45	50	50#	60	Mild
3.	Kade Anderson	Mariners	60	60	60	45	55	—	60	Average
4.	Liam Doyle	Cardinals	70	40	50	—	50	55^	60	Average
5.	Noah Schultz	White Sox	65	—	70	55	50	50#	65	High
6.	Jamie Arnold	Athletics	60	—	60	60	55	45#	60	Average
7.	Gage Jump	Athletics	60	55	55	50	50	—	60	Average
8.	Robby Snelling	Marlins	60	60	55	55	50	—	60	Average
9.	Cam Caminiti	Braves	60	—	55	55	55	—	60	High
10.	Connelly Early	Red Sox	50	50	40	60	50	55*	50	Mild
11.	David Shields	Royals	45	55	55	50	60	—	55	Average
12.	Wei-En Lin	Athletics	55	55	50	55	60	—	55	Average
13.	Connor Prielipp	Twins	60	—	60	60	55	—	55	Average
14.	Johnny King	Blue Jays	60	60	—	40	45	—	60	High
15.	Luis De Leon	Orioles	70	—	60	60	45	55^	60	High
16.	Parker Messick	Guardians	50	45	50	55	55	—	50	Mild
17.	Jacob Bresnahan	Giants	60	—	50	60	55	—	55	Average
18.	Quinn Mathews	Cardinals	50	45	55	60	50	—	50	Mild
19.	Dasan Hill	Twins	55	50	—	60	45	60*	60	High
20.	Kruz Schoolcraft	Padres	60	—	55	55	50	—	60	High

* Sweeper. ^ Splitter. # Cutter.

TALENT RANKINGS

Organization	2025	2024	2023	2022	2021
1. Pittsburgh Pirates	17	12	11	3	15

Having Konnor Griffin, the best prospect in baseball, is a great start, but the Pirates' depth of top-tier prospects, including Bubba Chandler, Edward Florentino and Seth Hernandez, puts them on top. The organization's second-tier depth is less impressive, but it's better to have a horde of elite prospects than a system filled with depth.

2. St. Louis Cardinals	19	20	9	18	12

Led by JJ Wetherholt, the Cardinals boast one of the most talented farm systems in the game. They have a good balance of impact position players, such as Wetherholt, Rainiel Rodriguez and Joshua Baez, and impact pitching, as exemplified by lefthanders Liam Doyle, Quinn Mathews and Brandon Clarke.

3. New York Mets	12	8	5	16	19

The Mets stand out for the depth and diversity of their prospect stock. Nolan McLean is the No. 1 pitching prospect, while the organization has top prospects at first, second and third base and center field. Every member of their top 10 played at Double-A or higher, with McLean, Jonah Tong and Brandon Sproat reaching MLB.

4. Baltimore Orioles	18	1	1	4	7

The Orioles had the largest bonus pool in the 2025 draft, and the products of that draft have restocked the depth of the system behind a still-impressive top. Samuel Basallo and Dylan Beavers give the team a pair of 2026 American League Rookie of the Year candidates, and there's a next wave behind them.

5. Milwaukee Brewers	8	2	13	25	28

The 2025 Organization of the Year, the Brewers are among the best in the game throughout all facets of scouting and player development. Four of their top 10 prospects are homegrown international signees, and they find late-round gems as well as any club. They have a system with impact talent at the top and depth at all levels.

6. Detroit Tigers	2	5	26	6	5

Few organizations can come close to matching the Tigers' top-end prospect talent, led by Kevin McGonigle, Max Clark and Bryce Rainer. The system drops off pretty quickly afterward, but the recent investments in high-ceiling pitchers could pay off in 2027 and beyond.

7. Cleveland Guardians	6	19	4	12	11

Cleveland's farm system is one of the deepest in the game, with a litany of hitting and pitching prospects and success stories from both the amateur and international markets. Heading up the ranking are Travis Bazzana, Chase DeLauter and Ralphy Velazquez, a trio of position players who could become lineup anchors.

8. Athletics	11	25	27	27	29

The A's have been team turmoil at the franchise level with their nomadic wanderings toward Las Vegas. On the field, however, the success of 2025 rookies Nick Kurtz and Jacob Wilson and the impressive pitching prospect depth the team has built has vaulted the organization into a top-tier farm system.

9. Seattle Mariners	4	16	22	1	2

Similar to 2025, the Mariners boast one of the league's most impressive Top 10s, headlined by Colt Emerson, Kade Anderson and Lazaro Montes. Beyond that, however, the talent drops off sharply beyond the top 10, though notable names in that range include Korbyn Dickerson, Leandro Romero and Teddy McGraw.

10. Minnesota Twins	7	14	21	14	8

The Twins' trade deadline sell-off added talent to an already promising system. It has depth and balance, but many of the players come with a fair amount of risk. The top trio of Walker Jenkins, Emmanuel Rodriguez and Connor Prielipp are all close to major league-ready, but all have lengthy injury track records.

11. Los Angeles Dodgers	10	3	3	8	9

The front of the Dodgers' system is led by a quartet of high-upside outfielders with contrasting skill sets. From there, a lot of the group's more intriguing prospects dealt with injuries in 2025. The system's pitching talent could use a boost.

12. Miami Marlins	25	27	20	20	10

The Marlins' progress is most evident on the mound, where top prospects Thomas White and Robby Snelling are nearing the major leagues. Position help is close behind, with catcher Joe Mack and outfielder Kemp Alderman approaching readiness, while the lower minors are stocked with upside on both sides of the ball.

13. San Francisco Giants	23	22	18	17	14

This system is in its best shape in years. Beyond top prospect Bryce Eldridge, the group has benefited from a bumper crop of young talent, including firecracker shortstop Josuar Gonzalez, undrafted outfield success story Bo Davidson and Arizona Complex League standout Jhonny Level. There's depth and upside in spades.

14. Boston Red Sox	1	13	10	11	21

Once a system dominated by high-end hitting talent, the Red Sox have seen things flip completely. Now, seven of their top 10 prospects are pitchers. They have enviable near-ready pitching depth, but their position player prospects after Franklin Arias face a lot of questions.

15. Toronto Blue Jays	22	24	15	19	4

It was a banner season in 2025 for the Blue Jays' farm. Their revamped pitching development yielded the gift of World Series hero Trey Yesavage. The righthander leads a loaded top 10 group at the head of the system, but a lack of depth in the 11-20 range drags the system down.

Organization	2025	2024	2023	2022	2021
16. Tampa Bay Rays	5	7	6	2	1

The Rays' system took a hit in 2025 because of injuries and some prospects taking a step back. The team still has plenty of pitching depth, and no organization has more slick-fielding shortstops across all levels of the minors. The question is: Will any of those shortstops will hit enough to fit as an MLB regular?

17. Chicago White Sox	3	18	28	30	20

The White Sox have made significant strides in player development in recent years, but the development of lefthanders Noah Schultz and Hagen Smith remains one of the big to-do items for 2026 and beyond. Shortstop Caleb Bonemer's emergence as a top prospect gives the team another potential long-term building block.

18. Cincinnati Reds	9	11	8	7	18

The Reds' farm has several prospects ready to help in Cincinnati. First baseman Sal Stewart should fit right into the middle of the lineup, while righthander Rhett Lowder should return the rotation at some point. Keep an eye on shortstop Tyson Lewis, who could make a big jump up the rankings in 2026.

19. Washington Nationals	15	15	7	26	30

Led by No. 1 overall pick Eli Willits, the Nationals' system leans heavily on shortstops and also boasts power arms aplenty in the top 10. Incoming head of ops Paul Toboni and his player development team now are tasked with coaxing more on-field production from key players. Trades for Harry Ford and Luis Perales enhanced the depth.

20. Philadelphia Phillies	16	21	19	23	27

Shortstop Aidan Miller, righthander Andrew Painter and outfielder Justin Crawford give the Phillies an enviable trio of near-at-hand talent, but trades have sapped the system of depth. They'll need to hit big on their draft picks to move back up the ranks.

21. Chicago Cubs	14	4	17	15	22

The Cubs have boasted a strong top of the system for the past several seasons, with a collection of Top 100-caliber prospects. Unfortunately, many of those players have not yet graduated despite significant upper-minors experience. The system is shallow after the top and has a real lack of impact pitching.

22. New York Yankees	24	10	16	13	16

After trading 16 prospects during the 2025 season, the Yankees' system is as fallow as it has been in years. Righthanders Elmer Rodriguez and Carlos Lagrange could see New York in 2026, and shortstops George Lombard Jr. and Dax Kilby both have high upsides and impact potential.

23. Texas Rangers	20	3	12	9	24

Sebastian Walcott is one of the game's elite talents, and righty Caden Scarborough was one of the game's bigger breakouts in 2025. Overall, the system needs major rebounds from its near-proximity prospects to supplement the big league roster. Bouncebacks from the 2024 draft class would go a long way, too.

24. Houston Astros	30	29	24	28	26

For the better part of the last decade, the Astros' system has ranked among the worst in the game. While no one is going to mistake this system for a top-15 collection of talent, it's deeper than it's been in a decade. Houston boasts two high-upside teenagers in shortstop Xavier Neyens and outfielder Kevin Alvarez.

25. Kansas City Royals	27	30	29	5	13

Catcher Carter Jensen's breakout gives the Royals another potential long-term regular to go with Bobby Witt Jr. and Maikel Garcia, but the Royals' misses on three straight top 10 draft picks—Asa Lacy, Frank Mozzicato and Gavin Cross—have left a lasting mark. 2024 first-rounder Jac Cagliano reached MLB.

26. Arizona Diamondbacks	21	2	10	17	10

Arizona has doubled down on solid hitters in recent drafts, a trend that should lead to a significant number of future big leaguer. Now, the organization is left to wonder: How many impactful big leaguers are currently down on the farm?

27. Atlanta Braves	28	26	30	22	6

The Braves targeted bats in the 2025 draft for the first time in years, but the system's strengths continue to revolve around its pitching depth, with lots of uncertainty in the hitting ranks. Few systems tilt as heavily toward pitchers. Eight of the top 10 prospects are pitchers, including the top five.

28. Los Angeles Angels	29	28	25	29	23

As has been the case recent years, the Angels have some intriguing prospects at the top, but the depth of the system remains far below-average. Some of that is because of the team's tendency to push players quickly to the majors, which means 2024 first-rounder Christian Moore doesn't qualify as a prospect anymore.

29. San Diego Padres	26	6	23	21	3

The Padres system would rank in a more prominent spot had the organization not traded a slew of prospects—headlined by Leo De Vries—at the deadline. Teen catcher Ethan Salas has re-assumed the top spot in the system, followed by a trio of intriguing arms. At this juncture, the system lacks depth and high-end talent.

30. Colorado Rockies	13	23	14	24	25

Paul DePodesta and the new Rockies front office regime have a steep mountain to climb, given the current state of the farm system and lack of impact big leaguers. Ethan Holliday and Charlie Condon are the organization's top prospects, and even they come with major questions.

Corbin Carroll

Arizona Diamondbacks

BY NICK PIECORO

With Jordan Lawlar's graduation from prospect status, the Diamondbacks suddenly lack—in the eyes of most evaluators—the sort of high-probability, high-ceiling player that their system has featured, sometimes in bunches, for most of the past decade.

What they do have is a web of intriguing talent scattered throughout the organization. Not many of these players are viewed with consensus in the scouting community. Talk to one evaluator and they might dream on half a dozen position players growing into everyday roles; talk to another and they'll identify a different group of five or six entirely.

Many of the Diamondbacks' best hitters come with profile questions that revolve around their future defensive home, such as Tommy Troy, JD Dix and LuJames Groover. Some lack the physicality that scouts like to see to safely project impact, like Kayson Cunningham and Slade Caldwell.

The same is true on the mound, where perhaps a dozen pitchers have a chance to stick in a rotation, depending on whom you ask.

Many of the Diamondbacks' best arms lean more toward deep repertoire and control than overwhelming pure stuff. And among those who do possess better raw material, several have not yet shown the ability to consistently command it.

Is it concerning that there aren't slam-dunk types? The Diamondbacks would certainly prefer more of them. But what they have—namely, upside in various forms—sure beats some alternatives.

Each of the organization's first five picks in the 2024 draft turned in encouraging seasons, led by outfielder Ryan Waldschmidt, who showed off his polished, professional game while reaching Double-A. His year puts him on the radar for a 2026 callup.

Moreover, the Diamondbacks bolstered their prospect depth at the 2025 trade deadline, landing

PROJECTED 2029 LINEUP

Catcher	Gabriel Moreno	29
First Base	Demetrio Crisantes	24
Second Base	Kayson Cunningham	23
Third Base	Jordan Lawlar	26
Shortstop	Geraldo Perdomo	29
Left Field	Ryan Waldschmidt	26
Center Field	Slade Caldwell	23
Right Field	Corbin Carroll	28
Designated Hitter	Ketel Marte	35
No. 1 Starter	Corbin Burnes	34
No. 2 Starter	Ryne Nelson	31
No. 3 Starter	David Hagaman	26
No. 4 Starter	Brandon Pfaadt	30
No. 5 Starter	Daniel Eagen	26
Closer	Justin Martinez	27

five pitchers who rank inside their Top 20—and another three, all relievers, who could pitch in the majors in 2026.

The most highly regarded of those arms was the most anonymous when he was acquired. Viewed as the third player in the Merrill Kelly trade with the Rangers in July 2025, righthander David Hagaman had a brief showing with his new organization—he made a month's worth of starts and mostly pitched three or four innings at a time—but immediately looked like a potential force.

Hagaman leads an unusually pitching-heavy top 30 for the Diamondbacks. The organization has always been more adept at churning out position players than pitchers, but if pitching is a numbers game, the Diamondbacks' odds look better than they have in a while.

At this point in time, the Diamondbacks mostly need their system to add complementary pieces—or to continue to churn out prospects who can be used as trade currency to fill holes. Their roster already includes high-upside, prime-age players like Ketel Marte, Corbin Carroll and Geraldo Perdomo.

Whether Waldschmidt, Cunningham, Demetrio Crisantes or someone else can turn into that kind of player remains to be seen. For now, they represent the best of a deep—but arguably low-ceiling—system. ∎

DEPTH CHART

ARIZONA DIAMONDBACKS

TOP 2026 ROOKIES	RANK
1. Cristian Mena, RHP	11
2. Kohl Drake, LHP	13
3. Brandyn Garcia, LHP	16

BREAKOUT PROSPECTS	RANK
1. Brian Curley, RHP	20
2. Jaitoine Kelly, RHP	26

SOURCE OF TOP 30 TALENT

Homegrown	24	Acquired	6
College	8	Trade	6
Junior college	0	Rule 5 draft	0
High school	7	Independent league	0
Undrafted free agent	0	Free agent/waivers	0
International	9		

LF
Ryan Waldschmidt (1)
Junior Franco
Mayki De La Rosa
Erick De La Cruz

CF
Slade Caldwell (4)
Druw Jones (17)
Jakey Josepha
Raily Liriano

RF
Gavin Conticello
Angel Ortiz
Adriel Radney

3B
LuJames Groover (15)
Yassel Soler (22)
Victor Santana

SS
Kayson Cunningham (2)
Cristofer Torin (10)
Jose Fernandez
Tytus Cissell

2B
Demetrio Crisantes (3)
JD Dix (8)
Tommy Troy (9)
Jansel Luis (12)

1B
Ivan Melendez
Ben McLaughlin
Manuel Pena
Enyervert Perez
Ruben Santana

C
Carlos Virahonda (19)
Ivan Luciano (23)
Christian Cerda
Alberto Barriga
Jose Urbina

LHP

LHSP
Kohl Drake (13)
Mitch Bratt (18)
Yu-Min Lin (24)
Blake Walston
Spencer Giesting
Caden Grice

LHRP
Brandyn Garcia (16)
Philip Abner
Grayson Hitt
Rocco Reid

RHP

RHSP
David Hagaman (5)
Daniel Eagen (6)
Patrick Forbes (7)
Cristian Mena (11)
Ashton Izzi (14)
Brian Curley (20)
Dylan Ray (21)
Mason Marriott (25)
Jaitoine Kelly (26)
Dean Livingston (27)
Daury Vasquez (28)
Chung-Hsiang Huang (30)
Junior Ciprian

RHRP
Yordin Chalas (29)
Yilber Diaz
Hunter Cranton
Andrew Hoffmann
Juan Burgos
Kyle Amendt
Christian Montes De Oca
Hayden Durke
Roman Angelo
Landon Sims
Jose Cabrera

ARIZONA DIAMONDBACKS

1 RYAN WALDSCHMIDT, OF

Born: October 7, 2002. **B-T:** R-R. **HT:** 6-2. **WT:** 205.
Drafted: Kentucky, 2024 (1st round supp.).
Signed by: Jeremy Kehrt.

BA GRADE
55 Risk: Average
Adjusted grade: 45

SCOUTING GRADES
Hit: 55. Power: 55. Run: 55.
Field: 50. Arm: 50.
Projected future grades on 20-80 scouting scale

TRACK RECORD: Lightly recruited out of high school in Bradenton, Fla., Waldschmidt started his college career at Charleston Southern before transferring to Kentucky, where he was a two-year starter. He turned in a strong junior year, hitting .333 with a 1.079 OPS and 14 home runs in 59 games. That performance came on the heels of a devastating injury suffered the previous summer in the Cape Cod League, where Waldschmidt blew out his left knee while making a play on a ball hit to left field. The injury ultimately required ACL surgery. The Diamondbacks saw no ill effects from the injury the following spring and were impressed by the quality of his at-bats, the consistency of his performance and his hard-working, energetic approach to the game. Using the Prospect Promotion Incentive pick they were awarded when Corbin Carroll took home National League Rookie of the Year honors in 2023, the D-backs selected Waldschmidt at No. 31 overall and signed him for $2.9 million. He more than lived up to expectations in his first full season, hitting a combined .289 with 18 homers and nearly as many walks (96) as strikeouts (106) in a year split between High-A Hillsboro and Double-A Amarillo.

SCOUTING REPORT: Waldschmidt has a wide base and barely strides with a minimal load, generating an aggressive but controlled, low-maintenance swing. He is extremely discerning when it comes to how often he swings. Not only did he run just a 15.7% chase rate in 2025, but he often opted not to swing at strikes that he perceived to be pitchers' pitches. That selectivity led to long, grinding at-bats, many of which began 0-2 or 1-2 but ended with a full count. He enters his at-bats with a good plan and stays committed to it. He has a steep bat path in which he is in and out of the zone quickly, leaving him with little margin for error. The uphill nature of his swing is a concern to some evaluators, who believe he will need to flatten it out or risk being exposed by tough righthanders. Others see it as less of an issue, trusting in his ability to hunt the pitches he will be able to get in the air. His build is more strong and sturdy than fluid and graceful, but he moves well enough and is an above-average runner underway. He surprised some in the organization with how competent he was in center field but likely will profile better on an outfield corner, particularly with the D-backs, who have a strong collection of center fielders. He has an average arm.

BEST TOOLS

BATTING
Best Hitter	Demetrio Crisantes
Best Power Hitter	Yassel Soler
Best Strike-Zone Discipline	Ryan Waldschmidt
Fastest Baserunner	Druw Jones
Best Athlete	Druw Jones

PITCHING
Best Fastball	Patrick Forbes
Best Curveball	David Hagaman
Best Slider	Daniel Eagen
Best Changeup	Dylan Ray
Best Control	Mitch Bratt

FIELDING
Best Defensive Catcher	Carlos Virahonda
Best Defensive Infielder	Cristofer Torin
Best Infield Arm	Cristofer Torin
Best Defensive Outfielder	Druw Jones
Best Outfield Arm	Druw Jones

THE FUTURE: Waldschmidt's year was impressive enough that club executives are talking about him as part of the 2026 outfield mix in Arizona. With left fielder Lourdes Gurriel Jr. expected to miss the first half of the year following knee surgery, Waldschmidt could come to camp with a chance to win a job on the Opening Day roster. It is more likely he starts in the minors, but he could force his way to the big leagues sometime during the year.

Year	Age	Club (League)	Level	AVG	G	AB	R	H	2B	3B	HR	RBI	BB	SO	SB	OBP	SLG
2025	22	Hillsboro (NWL)	A+	.268	68	235	57	63	13	1	9	43	51	53	10	.415	.447
2025	22	Amarillo (TL)	AA	.309	66	249	57	77	14	3	9	35	45	53	19	.423	.498
		Minor League Totals		.288	148	528	125	152	29	4	18	85	111	115	33	.426	.460

ARIZONA DIAMONDBACKS

2 KAYSON CUNNINGHAM, SS
HIT: 60. **POW:** 45. **RUN:** 55. **FLD:** 50. **ARM:** 50. **BA Grade:** 55. **Risk:** Average.

Born: June 25, 2006. **B-T:** L-R. **HT:** 5-10. **WT:** 182.
Drafted: HS—San Antonio, TX, 2025 (1st round). **Signed by:** Justin Seely.
TRACK RECORD: Cunningham was widely regarded as the best pure hitter among high schoolers in the 2025 draft. He also had another credit to his name: In a prep class loaded with shortstops, he was the starter at the position for Team USA in the 18U World Cup qualifier in Panama the summer before his senior year. While he was at it, he led Team USA with a .417 average. Because Cunningham fit the profile of many recent Diamondbacks draft picks—undersized frame, lefthanded hitter, strong contact skills, plays an up-the-middle position—it was no surprise when Arizona drafted him at No. 18 overall then bought him out of his Texas commitment with a $4.58 million bonus.
SCOUTING REPORT: Cunningham has a quick, efficient swing and excellent barrel control. He rarely swings and misses, recognizes balls from strikes and has shown average power, though some evaluators aren't confident the pop will get to that level in pro ball. While he can occasionally leave the yard to his pull side, he routinely sprays line drives to the gaps. Cunningham's hands, instincts and range, as well as his ability to make different types of throws, gave the D-backs confidence that he could remain at shortstop. Things seemed to be moving fast for him defensively in his 11-game pro debut for Low-A Visalia, but the organization plans to give him every chance to stick at the position. Some scouts who saw him post-draft wrote him up as a second baseman.
THE FUTURE: Cunningham's bat should play just about anywhere. D-backs evaluators saw shades of Kevin McGonigle in his game with his adaptable, contact-oriented, high-average swing along with a high probability to stick at an up-the-middle position. If he hits as expected, he should be an everyday player who fits anywhere in the top half of a lineup.

Year	Age	Club (League)	Level	AVG	G	AB	R	H	2B	3B	HR	RBI	BB	SO	SB	OBP	SLG
2025	19	Visalia (CAL)	A	.255	11	47	2	12	1	0	0	4	3	15	1	.308	.277
		Minor League Totals		.255	11	47	2	12	1	0	0	4	3	15	1	.308	.277

3 DEMETRIO CRISANTES, 2B
HIT: 60. **POW:** 50. **RUN:** 45. **FLD:** 45. **ARM:** 45. **BA Grade:** 55. **Risk:** High. **Adj:** 40.

Born: September 5, 2004. **B-T:** R-R. **HT:** 6-0. **WT:** 178.
Drafted: HS—Nogales, AZ, 2022 (7th round). **Signed by:** Mark Ross.
TRACK RECORD: Crisantes has been known as a prolific hitter with health concerns going back to his high school days in Nogales, Ariz. While he has continued to mash in pro ball, he also has continued to have trouble staying healthy. Crisantes required Tommy John surgery at age 15, followed by a revision TJ shortly after being drafted in the seventh round in 2022. He burst on the scene in 2024, when he hit .341 and compiled a 57-game on-base streak between the Arizona Complex League and Low-A Visalia. Just 34 games into his 2025 season at High-A Hillsboro, Crisantes needed surgery to repair a posterior labral tear in his left shoulder, costing him the remainder of the year. He had a .902 OPS in his final 20 Northwest League games prior to injuring his shoulder on a swing in mid-May.
SCOUTING REPORT: Crisantes has a simple, repeatable swing that allows him to generate hard contact at good angles. Though the raw thump he produces isn't plus, his tight launch angle distribution suggests a hitter who can maximize the power he has at his disposal. He rarely swings and misses and showed an improved approach in 2025 before his injury. Scouting looks were limited during his abbreviated season, but evaluators and D-backs officials said Crisantes' defensive play at second base has improved. His arm remains below-average but most see the total defensive package as good enough—assuming that he provides above-average production at the plate. He is a fringe-average runner.
THE FUTURE: Crisantes likely starts 2026 in Double-A and could move quickly from there. With Ketel Marte entrenched at second base, Crisantes might need a position change—potentially even to first base—to find his way to regular at-bats in the majors. First and foremost, he will need to get—and stay—healthy.

Year	Age	Club (League)	Level	AVG	G	AB	R	H	2B	3B	HR	RBI	BB	SO	SB	OBP	SLG
2025	20	Hillsboro (NWL)	A+	.252	34	123	18	31	8	0	4	29	21	19	6	.358	.415
		Minor League Totals		.323	155	594	131	192	38	7	12	103	87	109	38	.412	.471

ARIZONA DIAMONDBACKS

SLADE CALDWELL, OF

HIT: 55. **POW:** 40. **RUN:** 60. **FLD:** 60. **ARM:** 45. **BA Grade:** 50. **Risk:** Average. **Adj:** 40.

Born: June 18, 2006. **B-T:** L-L. **HT:** 5-9. **WT:** 182.
Drafted: HS—Jonesboro, AR, 2024 (1st round). **Signed by:** Nate Birtwell.
TRACK RECORD: One of the better hitters on the showcase circuit the summer before his senior year, Caldwell went off the board with the 29th pick in the 2024 draft. The Diamondbacks made the Arkansas prep the latest in a series of undersized position players they have selected high in the draft during the Mike Hazen era. The club signed Caldwell away from a Mississippi commitment with a $3.087 million bonus. In his first full season as a pro in 2025, Caldwell torched the Low-A California League through 48 games but initially struggled after an aggressive promotion to High-A. He and the Pirates' Konnor Griffin were the first 2024 preps to advance past Low-A.
SCOUTING REPORT: Caldwell's swing is short and compact by virtue of his short levers. He makes a lot of contact, though his swing can appear pushy or slappy, leading most scouts to project fringe-average power at peak. He has elite zone awareness with a 15% chase rate but appeared too passive at times, raising questions about whether his high walk rate was the result of him gaming the system against low-level pitchers. It also might have led to a higher strikeout rate as he occasionally took hittable pitches early in counts. Still, Caldwell has the look of a potential table-setting on-base machine. He has plus speed, though he is not yet a good basestealer. Evaluators were split on his defense, some seeing an average center fielder, others landing on plus. Caldwell is adored for the way he plays the game. Instinctual, gritty and tough, he routinely makes plays that help his team win.
THE FUTURE: Caldwell's hitting approach, speed and defense give him a high floor, but how much he hits—and for how much impact—will determine his future value. Even if his pure production is light, team officials believe his baseball IQ and tenacity will fit well as part of a winning core.

Year	Age	Club (League)	Level	AVG	G	AB	R	H	2B	3B	HR	RBI	BB	SO	SB	OBP	SLG
2025	19	Visalia (CAL)	A	.294	48	163	40	48	13	2	3	20	44	62	13	.460	.454
2025	19	Hillsboro (NWL)	A+	.238	66	244	43	58	16	1	0	18	47	76	12	.370	.311
		Minor League Totals		.260	114	407	83	106	29	3	3	38	91	138	25	.408	.369

DAVID HAGAMAN, RHP

FB: 60. **CB:** 60. **SL:** 50. **CH:** 55. **CTL:** 55. **BA Grade:** 55. **Risk:** High. **Adj:** 40.

Born: April 16, 2003. **B-T:** R-R. **HT:** 6-4. **WT:** 215.
Drafted: West Virginia, 2024 (4th round). **Signed by:** Chris Collias (Rangers).
TRACK RECORD: Hagaman redshirted his freshman year at West Virginia then worked mostly in relief each of the next two years before going down with an elbow injury in April 2024. He had Tommy John surgery a month later. Despite that, the Rangers drafted him in the fourth round and signed him for $515,000. Hagaman was eight outings into his return to the mound when he was traded to the Diamondbacks in July 2025 as part of the Merrill Kelly trade. Seen at the time as the third piece in the deal, trailing Kohl Drake and Mitch Bratt, he emerged as arguably the most electric arm in the D-backs' system.
SCOUTING REPORT: Hagaman has had loud stuff dating back at least to college, but he not only took it up a notch in 2025, he also paired it with a newfound ability to pump quality strikes. His fastball averaged 94 mph with 18 inches of carry and came at hitters from an elite extension of seven feet. He topped out in the 97-98 mph range, but evaluators said they wouldn't be surprised if he eventually sat in the upper 90s. Hagaman's curveball is hard, up to 86 mph, but maintains consistent depth. His mid-80s changeup has late movement like a hard sinker. He also throws a slider that is at least average. He attacked hitters and showed no fear of being in the zone. The 6-foot-4 righthander has a loose, stable delivery that allows him to get down the mound with ease.
THE FUTURE: Hagaman did not throw more than five innings or 65 pitches in an outing in 2025, so he will need to show he can maintain both his caliber of stuff as well as the same quality and quantity of strikes over a full season. If he can, the D-backs might have landed another building block for their rotation.

Year	Age	Club (League)	Level	W	L	ERA	G	GS	IP	H	HR	BB	SO	BB%	SO%	WHIP	AVG
2025	22	ACL Rangers	Rk	0	0	1.29	3	3	7	5	0	0	12	0.0	48.0	0.71	.200
2025	22	Hickory (CAR)	A	0	1	3.52	5	5	15	10	0	6	16	9.7	25.8	1.04	.182
2025	22	Hillsboro (NWL)	A+	1	0	3.15	5	5	20	11	3	4	27	5.3	35.5	0.75	.159
		Minor League Totals		1	1	2.98	13	13	42	26	3	10	55	6.1	33.7	0.85	.174

ARIZONA DIAMONDBACKS

6 DANIEL EAGEN, RHP
FB: 50. **CB:** 60. **SL:** 55. **CH:** 45. **CTL:** 50. **BA Grade:** 50. **Risk:** Average. **Adj:** 40.

Born: November 23, 2002. **B-T:** R-R. **HT:** 6-4. **WT:** 205.
Drafted: Presbyterian, 2024 (3rd round). **Signed by:** Jaren Shelby.
TRACK RECORD: Eagen has dealt with adversity since childhood. He needed surgery at age 4 to remove a cancerous brain tumor. He is now cancer-free. After a dominant 2024 season in which Eagen earned Big South Conference pitcher of the year honors, the Diamondbacks made him the highest-drafted player in Presbyterian history as a third-round pick. Eagen wasted no time delivering on his potential. He carved up the Northwest League for High-A Hillsboro in 2025, logging four double-digit strikeout outings, before a late-season promotion to Double-A, where he struggled in hitter-friendly Amarillo.
SCOUTING REPORT: Eagen checks all the boxes for a future starting pitcher. He has a strong, 6-foot-4 frame, a simple, repeatable delivery and a repertoire that looks like it should translate to the major leagues. His fastball sits at 93 mph and topped at 96 with nearly 20 inches of carry. His two breaking balls are both at least above-average. His big, 82 mph downer curveball had a 42% whiff rate, while his gyro slider—which at 86 mph sat between the heater and curve—got whiffs at a 54% clip. His split changeup remains a work in progress and was expected to be a focus for him in the offseason. Eagen is a good competitor and worker who takes his game-planning and prep work seriously.
THE FUTURE: Eagen should reach the majors as a starter, but whether he remains in that role could depend on any number of factors, including whether his stuff improves, his repertoire becomes deeper and how he commands his arsenal. He could have the ceiling of a No. 4 starter, though his stuff would profile in a late-inning role. Either way, he is looking like a nice scouting and player development success story for the organization.

Year	Age	Club (League)	Level	W	L	ERA	G	GS	IP	H	HR	BB	SO	BB%	SO%	WHIP	AVG
2025	22	Hillsboro (NWL)	A+	7	5	2.49	19	19	98	63	7	41	132	10.6	34.1	1.06	.184
2025	22	Amarillo (TL)	AA	0	3	5.49	4	4	20	16	5	11	21	12.9	24.7	1.37	.216
		Minor League Totals		7	8	2.99	23	23	117	79	12	52	153	11.0	32.4	1.12	.189

7 PATRICK FORBES, RHP
FB: 70. **SL:** 60. **CH:** 45. **CTL:** 40. **BA Grade:** 50. **Risk:** Average. **Adj:** 40.

Born: December 24, 2006. **B-T:** R-R. **HT:** 6-3. **WT:** 220.
Drafted: Louisville, 2025 (1st round supp.). **Signed by:** Christian Beal.
TRACK RECORD: Kentucky's Mr. Baseball in 2022, Forbes was a star shortstop at Bowling Green High but went undrafted in part because of his strong commitment to Louisville. A two-way player as a college freshman, he scaled back to pitching full-time during his sophomore year. A year later, in 2025, his draft stock skyrocketed after a dominant first month of the season, but he saw his control take a step back later in the year. He also dealt with a flexor injury. The Diamondbacks, betting on his premium athleticism allowing him to reach his high ceiling, drafted Forbes with the 31st overall pick and signed him for $3 million. He did not play in official games after the draft.
SCOUTING REPORT: Forbes unleashes an explosive fastball from a low release point. He averages 95-96 mph with the pitch, topping out in triple digits, generating both ride and run. He used it well at the top of the zone at Louisville. Forbes has a sweepy slider with good horizontal movement, a pitch with late break that holds the fastball tunnel well. The D-backs are hoping to develop both a gyro slider and a changeup to round out his arsenal. Forbes' command came and went at times at Louisville, with too many noncompetitive pitches over multi-batter stretches. He walked 10.7% of batters as a college junior. That represented an improvement over previous seasons, when he worked primarily in relief.
THE FUTURE: With a limited arsenal and a history of control issues, Forbes has obvious reliever risk. But given his high-end athleticism and newness to pitching, the D-backs are hoping he can make the same sort of development strides as Ryne Nelson, another successful two-way player the club drafted out of college. If he does, he could have at least midrotation upside.

Year	Age	Club (League)	Level	W	L	ERA	G	GS	IP	H	HR	BB	SO	BB%	SO%	WHIP	AVG
2025	20	Did not play															

ARIZONA DIAMONDBACKS

8 JD DIX, 2B

HIT: 55. **POW:** 50. **RUN:** 60. **FLD:** 50. **ARM:** 40. **BA Grade:** 50. **Risk:** High. **Adj:** 35.

Born: October 12, 2005. **B-T:** B-R. **HT:** 6-2. **WT:** 180.
Drafted: HS—Whitefish Bay, WI, 2024 (1st round supp.). **Signed by:** Nate Birtwell.
TRACK RECORD: A well-regarded high school player in Whitefish Bay, Wis., Dix saw his draft stock slip in 2024 due to a shoulder injury that ultimately required surgery for a torn labrum. The Diamondbacks, who liked him before the injury, drafted him anyway with the 35th overall pick with the hope that he fully recovers from the procedure. So far, that hasn't happened, but with his first full pro season under his belt, Dix looks intriguing anyway as an athletic, hitterish and hard-nosed player. He began 2025 in the Arizona Complex League before moving up to Low-A Visalia at the end of June.
SCOUTING REPORT: The switch-hitting Dix has pure, natural swings from both sides of the plate. He offsets long levers with good bat speed and solid bat-to-ball ability. His production in 2025 was just fair, but he has a strong hit tool foundation with few red flags. He sees and handles fastballs and offspeeds well, isn't too passive or aggressive, uses the whole field and doesn't hit too many balls on the ground. Those are the sort of attributes that, assuming Dix adds strength to his athletic-looking frame, suggest at least an above-average hitter with average power, if not more. His arm remains a concern. Some think it is fringy but playable at second base, others say it will force a position change, either to first base or the outfield. Dix is a good runner who stole 28 bases in 89 games in 2025. A confident and instinctual player, he is a gamer who makes winning plays.
THE FUTURE: Dix is an athletic, projectable player with a wide range of possible outcomes. If his arm improves, perhaps he becomes an offensive-minded second baseman. If not, his bat could still play at either first base, left field or even in center field, where some think his speed could give him plus range.

Year	Age	Club (League)	Level	AVG	G	AB	R	H	2B	3B	HR	RBI	BB	SO	SB	OBP	SLG
2025	19	ACL D-backs	Rk	.342	39	152	31	52	12	4	1	19	20	34	9	.421	.493
2025	19	Visalia (CAL)	A	.261	50	188	34	49	7	2	1	15	38	51	19	.391	.335
		Minor League Totals		.297	89	340	65	101	19	6	2	34	58	85	28	.404	.406

9 TOMMY TROY, 2B/OF

HIT: 50. **POW:** 45. **RUN:** 60. **FLD:** 40. **ARM:** 50. **BA Grade:** 45. **Risk:** Average.

Born: January 17, 2002. **B-T:** R-R. **HT:** 5-10. **WT:** 197.
Drafted: Stanford, 2023 (1st round). **Signed by:** Andrew Allen.
TRACK RECORD: After a three-year career at Stanford in which Troy showed improvement every season, the Diamondbacks drafted him 12th overall in 2023 and signed him for $4.4 million. He had a disappointing first full season in which he dealt with groin and hamstring injuries, then let a slow start put him in a bad headspace, causing him to press to get his numbers right. Instead, his struggles continued. He regrouped in 2025, taking far better at-bats and making better contact, primarily for Double-A Amarillo, and he looked more at home at second base than he did at shortstop in 2024.
SCOUTING REPORT: Troy has a compact righthanded swing with tight movements and fast hands. He made improvements across the board from 2024, cutting his chase rate, working more walks and making harder contact to spray line drives to all fields. He can struggle with righthanded spin on the outer half. Troy also has not looked like an impact bat, though his combination of raw power, pitch recognition and bat-to-ball ability suggest more power could be in the tank if he can do things like hit fewer ground balls or hit to his pull side more effectively. Troy looked capable of being a solid defender at second base, though he made enough mistakes that some wonder if his best fit might be in the outfield. In addition to second base, he played 20 games in center field, mostly while with Triple-A Reno. His plus speed raises his defensive floor as an outfielder.
THE FUTURE: Troy still has some steps to take to reach his ceiling as a solid everyday regular, but he made significant progress on both sides of the ball in 2025. Where he best fits defensively and how much impact he provides remain up for debate. His floor could be as an offensive-minded utility player.

Year	Age	Club (League)	Level	AVG	G	AB	R	H	2B	3B	HR	RBI	BB	SO	SB	OBP	SLG
2025	23	Amarillo (TL)	AA	.286	87	343	56	98	20	2	12	47	49	70	21	.382	.461
2025	23	Reno (PCL)	AAA	.295	38	156	23	46	8	2	3	19	18	28	3	.381	.429
		Minor League Totals		.270	224	868	138	234	49	7	24	112	114	197	49	.361	.425

ARIZONA DIAMONDBACKS

10 CRISTOFER TORIN, SS

HIT: 55. **POW:** 30. **RUN:** 40. **FLD:** 60. **ARM:** 60. **BA Grade:** 45. **Risk:** Average. **Adj:** 35.

Born: May 26, 2005. **B-T:** R-R. **HT:** 5-10. **WT:** 175.
Signed: Venezuela, 2022. **Signed by:** Cesar Geronimo/Didimo Bracho.
TRACK RECORD: When he signed out of Venezuela for $240,000 in January 2022, Torin was an advanced defender whose actions in the field were reminiscent of Javier Baez, who happened to be his favorite player as a kid. Torin is still regarded as a strong defender and a likely shortstop by most, but he also has shown a knack for putting together tough at-bats, making contact and making winning plays. After a rough season at the plate for Low-A Visalia in 2024, he bounced back in 2025, hitting .291, primarily for High-A Hillsboro, while adding nearly 50 points in slugging despite playing at a higher level.
SCOUTING REPORT: Starting with a slightly closed stance before striding to neutral, Torin generates a simple righthanded swing geared for contact. He has a low chase rate and a low whiff rate, particularly on pitches in the zone. He shows good game awareness at the plate with things like a two-strike approach and knowing when to sell out on an aggressive swing. Torin walks about as much as he strikes out, but he doesn't hit balls hard consistently, raising questions about his ultimate impact. He hit six home runs in 2025 and likely will struggle to reach double digits in the majors. Torin is a smooth shortstop with good hands and a strong arm. Evaluators were worried he might have to move off the position because of his short, thick build, but those concerns have quieted as he has stayed on top of his conditioning and looks more athletic. He also plays second base. Torin is a below-average runner.
THE FUTURE: Whether Torin hits enough to be a big league regular remains to be seen, but even if his outcome is more of a Miguel Rojas utility type, many evaluators see a decent likelihood that he enjoys a long career in the majors.

Year	Age	Club (League)	Level	AVG	G	AB	R	H	2B	3B	HR	RBI	BB	SO	SB	OBP	SLG
2025	20	Hillsboro (NWL)	A+	.287	122	467	78	134	22	3	6	57	66	78	15	.381	.385
2025	20	Amarillo (TL)	AA	.381	5	21	5	8	4	0	0	2	3	3	1	.440	.571
		Minor League Totals		.281	350	1309	253	368	61	10	14	159	222	224	73	.391	.375

11 CRISTIAN MENA, RHP

FB: 45. **CB:** 55. **SL:** 50. **CH:** 45. **CTL:** 50. **BA Grade:** 45. **Risk:** Average. **Adj:** 35.

Born: December 21, 2002. **B-T:** R-R. **HT:** 6-2. **WT:** 214. **Signed:** Dominican Republic, 2019.
Signed by: Marino De Leon/Ruddy Moreta/Marco Paddy (White Sox).
TRACK RECORD: Mena, who signed for $250,000 in 2019, rocketed through the White Sox system, then was traded to the Diamondbacks for outfielder Dominic Fletcher in February 2024. He has contributed in the majors in each of his two seasons with the Diamondbacks but finished on the injured list each time, first with a forearm strain in 2024, then a shoulder strain in 2025.
SCOUTING REPORT: Mena's velocity ticked up again in 2025, jumping about 1.5 mph from the previous year on both his four-seam (average 94.4 mph) and two-seam (93.6 mph). He uses his sinker more against righties and his four-seam to lefties, but the sinker tends to play better with his high release point. His hard, downer curveball is his best pitch, eliciting whiffs at a big 46.6% rate. He became more consistent with his sweepy slider and racked up whiffs (46%) on it, as well. His changeup rounds out his arsenal. He has had some control issues in the past but threw more strikes in 2025. He was an innings-eater, particularly considering his age, in the White Sox system, but durability issues the past two seasons raise concerns.
THE FUTURE: Depending on how the offseason unfolds for the Diamondbacks, they could enter spring training with a job available in their starting rotation. If they do, Mena figures to be in the mix for it. Otherwise, he figures to return to Triple-A Reno where he would be a top candidate once a need arose, assuming he can stay off the IL.

Year	Age	Club (League)	Level	W	L	ERA	G	GS	IP	H	HR	BB	SO	BB%	SO%	WHIP	AVG
2025	22	Reno (PCL)	AAA	2	3	4.84	9	9	45	52	6	16	52	8.3	27.1	1.39	.264
2025	22	Arizona (NL)	MLB	1	0	1.35	3	0	7	3	1	3	8	11.5	30.8	0.90	.130
		Minor League Totals		17	22	4.87	92	91	427	441	54	185	498	9.9	26.7	1.47	.267
		Major League Totals		1	0	4.66	4	1	10	7	3	6	10	14.6	24.4	1.34	.200

ARIZONA DIAMONDBACKS

12 JANSEL LUIS, 2B
HIT: 50. **POW:** 45. **RUN:** 60. **FLD:** 50. **ARM:** 50. **BA Grade:** 50. **Risk:** High. **Adj:** 35.

Born: March 6, 2005. **B-T:** B-R. **HT:** 6-0. **WT:** 170. **Signed:** Dominican Republic, 2022.
Signed by: Cesar Geronimo Jr./Pedro Meyer.
TRACK RECORD: Luis is an athletic, tooled-up switch-hitter who has shown some offensive potential in the four seasons since the Diamondbacks signed him for $525,000 in January 2022. He also has shown some flaws, namely an erratic approach at the plate that evaluators see as a potential stumbling block in his development. He is a relative of former big league infielder Pedro Ciriaco.
SCOUTING REPORT: Luis employs a simple swing from both sides of the plate and collects hits by virtue of his good hand-eye coordination. However, his propensity to swing does his production no favors. Not only does he run a poor chase rate, he also swings at a high number of pitches in the zone, including some that aren't in his best interest to attack. It winds up hurting his quality of contact, and his raw power might be a grade higher than what he exhibits in games. Still, he deserves credit for having hit .304 in High-A Hillsboro in 2025, which, considering he played the entire season at 20, suggests he has a strong base on which to build if he refines his approach. After playing primarily shortstop in previous seasons, he saw more time at second base, though some think his plus speed could translate to center field.
THE FUTURE: Still young, if Luis is able to tamp down his approach, he could unlock more offensive production and reach his ceiling of an everyday big leaguer.

Year	Age	Club (League)	Level	AVG	G	AB	R	H	2B	3B	HR	RBI	BB	SO	SB	OBP	SLG
2025	20	ACL D-backs	Rk	.500	4	16	5	8	2	1	0	2	0	1	2	.500	.750
2025	20	Hillsboro (NWL)	A+	.304	102	405	60	123	19	7	5	65	27	73	22	.342	.422
		Minor League Totals		.291	324	1304	210	380	69	23	20	162	96	257	69	.348	.426

13 KOHL DRAKE, LHP
FB: 55. **CB:** 50. **SL:** 45. **CH:** 50. **CTL:** 50. **BA Grade:** 45. **Risk:** Average. **Adj:** 35.

Born: July 17, 2000. **B-T:** L-L. **HT:** 6-5. **WT:** 230. **Drafted:** Walters State (TN) JC, 2022 (11th round).
Signed by: Tyler Carroll (Rangers).
TRACK RECORD: After winning NJCAA pitcher of the year honors in 2022, Drake was drafted that July by the Rangers in the 11th round and signed for $175,000. He struggled in his first full season, but he showed up the following spring with better stuff, more physicality and a cleaner delivery and turned in a breakout season. He had just reached Triple-A in July 2025 when the Rangers traded him to the Diamondbacks in the Merrill Kelly deal. He made four starts after the trade when his season ended due to left shoulder inflammation.
SCOUTING REPORT: Drake's fastball averaged 93.4 mph in 2025, up more than 3 mph since his first full season. The pitch doesn't come from a great attack angle, but at times averages 18-19 inches of induced vertical break and exhibits life in the form of armside run. His curveball produces whiffs at a 30% clip with its sharp, late, downward action. The changeup tunnels well with his fastball and gets fade and sink. His slider is sharp and tight when it is at its best. Starting his old-school delivery by bringing his glove over his head, he attacks the strike zone and generates good deception from his big frame, allowing him to get more whiffs than his pure stuff would suggest.
THE FUTURE: Drake might be one of those sum-is-greater-than-the-parts pitchers with a deep mix, an aggressive mindset and enough command to make it work. He profiles as a back-end starter and could reach the majors at some point in 2026.

Year	Age	Club (League)	Level	W	L	ERA	G	GS	IP	H	HR	BB	SO	BB%	SO%	WHIP	AVG
2025	24	Frisco (TL)	AA	4	3	2.44	12	12	55	32	5	22	70	10.0	31.8	0.98	.164
2025	24	Round Rock (PCL)	AAA	1	1	5.19	4	3	17	20	2	6	17	8.1	23.0	1.50	.294
2025	24	Reno (PCL)	AAA	1	2	9.18	4	4	17	24	3	8	19	9.8	23.2	1.92	.338
		Minor League Totals		10	12	4.17	44	29	179	166	16	65	232	8.5	30.5	1.29	.244

14 ASHTON IZZI, RHP
FB: 55. **CB:** 50. **SL:** 50. **CH:** 45. **CTL:** 45. **BA Grade:** 45 **Risk:** Average. **Adj:** 35.

Born: November 18, 2003. **B-T:** R-R. **HT:** 6-3. **WT:** 165. **Drafted:** HS—Oswego, IL, 2022 (4th round).
Signed by: Joe Saunders (Mariners).
TRACK RECORD: Seen as highly projectable coming out of the same high school team that featured Noah Schultz, Izzi was taken in the fourth round by the Mariners in 2022 and signed away from a Wichita State commitment for $1.1 million. After a couple of up and down seasons to start his career, he was having an uneven year in High-A Modesto when he was shipped to the Diamondbacks as part of the Josh

ARIZONA DIAMONDBACKS

Naylor trade. He fared well across six starts with his new organization, including a one-hit, nine-strikeout performance in his last outing of the season.

SCOUTING REPORT: Izzi sits 94 mph and tops at 97 mph with his fastball, averaging 17.2 inches of carry. He has a low-80s sweeper and a mid-80s gyro slider, both of which elicit whiffs. He also throws a power changeup with depth and run. Some see the delivery of a future starter while others believe he has a tendency to open his hips early in order to generate torque, which can hurt his command. Strong outings can go off the rails quickly, sometimes due to walks. He is still learning to sequence his pitches effectively.

THE FUTURE: Izzi's sometimes shaky command portends some reliever risk, but his arm strength and ability to spin the ball suggests a strong fallback option in relief. With a strong frame and deep pitch mix, he still has a chance to be a back-end starter.

Year	Age	Club (League)	Level	W	L	ERA	G	GS	IP	H	HR	BB	SO	BB%	SO%	WHIP	AVG
2025	21	Everett (NWL)	A+	2	4	5.51	12	12	47	53	8	21	54	9.7	24.9	1.56	.275
2025	21	Hillsboro (NWL)	A+	1	2	3.58	6	6	28	27	3	7	26	6.0	22.2	1.23	.250
		Minor League Totals		9	13	4.06	53	53	204	205	18	95	188	10.5	20.7	1.47	.257

15 LuJAMES GROOVER, 3B

HIT: 60. **POW:** 45. **RUN:** 40. **FLD:** 45. **ARM:** 50. **BA Grade:** 50. **Risk:** High. **Adj:** 35.

Born: April 16, 2002. **B-T:** R-R. **HT:** 6-2. **WT:** 212. **Drafted:** NC State, 2023 (2nd round).
Signed by: George Swain.

TRACK RECORD: Known prior to 2025 as "Gino," Groover spent a year at UNC Charlotte before playing two seasons at NC State, where he hit .332/.430/.546 with a team-leading 13 homers in 2023. Despite questions about his future defensive home, the Diamondbacks took him in the second round and signed him for $1.78 million. He missed three months with a broken wrist in his first full season, but stayed healthy in 2025, hitting .309 with a .399 on-base percentage in Double-A. His lack of power is a concern, particularly given his limited defensive profile.

SCOUTING REPORT: Groover has a clean, direct bat path and little wasted movement in his swing. He has low swing and chase rates and rarely swings and misses. His lack of impact has long been a concern for evaluators; those concerns were exacerbated after he slugged only .434 with just 12 homers in 470 at-bats at hitter-friendly Amarillo. Some in the organization trust more power will come as he adds strength and experience; others believe he needs to make trade-offs to create more leverage, possibly at the expense of batting average. He has improved at third but still projects as fringe-average there.

THE FUTURE: Groover needs to show he can hit for more power—and hit righthanded pitching better—in order to profile as an everyday player at a corner. But his hit tool gives him a good foundation and should earn him plenty of opportunities to improve.

Year	Age	Club (League)	Level	AVG	G	AB	R	H	2B	3B	HR	RBI	BB	SO	SB	OBP	SLG
2025	23	Amarillo (TL)	AA	.309	123	470	73	145	23	0	12	56	63	79	3	.399	.434
		Minor League Totals		.297	211	797	122	237	41	2	23	107	101	125	8	.384	.440

16 BRANDYN GARCIA, LHP

FB: 60. **SL:** 55. **CB:** 60. **CH:** 40. **CTL:** 45. **BA Grade:** 45. **Risk:** Average. **Adj:** 35.

Born: May 27, 2000. **B-T:** L-L. **HT:** 6-4. **WT:** 235. **Drafted:** Texas A&M, 2023 (11th round).
Signed by: Derek Miller (Mariners).

TRACK RECORD: After three years working mostly as a starter at Quinnipiac, Garcia landed at Texas A&M in 2023 and, thanks to added strength and a move to the bullpen, saw his stuff tick up, including a fastball that touched 97 mph. As the year progressed, he grew into a more trusted role out of the Aggies' bullpen. The Mariners, drawn to his power stuff, snapped him up in the 11th round—and immediately saw it pay off. Working as a starter in his first full season, Garcia emerged as one of the organization's better pitching prospects. He was traded to the Diamondbacks in July 2025 in the Josh Naylor trade and pitched well down the stretch out of the Arizona bullpen.

SCOUTING REPORT: Garcia has two legitimate weapons in his power sinker and depthy sweeper. The two-seamer gets above-average sink and averages 96-97 mph, topping out in triple digits. His mid-80s sweeper generated massive whiff rates in both the minors (51.7%) and majors (47.2%) and was particularly vexing to lefthanded hitters. He has a slider in the upper 80s that sometimes resembles a cutter and a changeup he barely throws. His strike-throwing game is just fair. Though he can dominate lefties, he might need another weapon to attack righties.

THE FUTURE: The Mariners shifted Garcia to relief in part based on the rotation depth ahead of him and need in the bullpen. Garcia threw well out of the bullpen in September for the Diamondbacks, who might just keep him in that role in 2026.

ARIZONA DIAMONDBACKS

Year	Age	Club (League)	Level	W	L	ERA	G	GS	IP	H	HR	BB	SO	BB%	SO%	WHIP	AVG
2025	25	Arkansas (TL)	AA	4	4	3.96	24	0	25	20	3	12	33	10.9	30.0	1.28	.215
2025	25	Tacoma (PCL)	AAA	1	0	2.16	8	0	8	9	0	5	9	12.8	23.1	1.68	.273
2025	25	Reno (PCL)	AAA	1	1	3.27	6	0	11	7	2	8	13	17.0	27.7	1.36	.189
2025	25	Seattle (AL)	MLB	0	0	4.50	2	0	2	4	0	3	1	27.3	9.1	3.50	.500
2025	25	Arizona (NL)	MLB	0	2	5.84	12	0	12	14	0	5	13	9.1	23.6	1.54	.286
		Minor League Totals		12	8	2.54	74	25	170	138	10	75	197	10.3	26.9	1.25	.223
		Major League Totals		0	2	5.65	14	0	14	18	0	8	14	12.1	21.2	1.81	.316

17 DRUW JONES, OF

HIT: 40. **POW:** 50. **RUN:** 65. **FLD:** 70. **ARM:** 60. **BA Grade:** 50. **Risk:** High. **Adj:** 35.

Born: November 28, 2003. **B-T:** R-R. **HT:** 6-4. **WT:** 180. **Drafted:** HS—Peachtree Corners, GA, 2022 (1st round).
Signed by: Hudson Belinsky.
TRACK RECORD: Jones, the son of 10-time Gold Glove winner Andruw Jones, has long reminded onlookers of his father. Taken by the Diamondbacks with the second overall pick in 2022 and signed for just shy of $8.2 million, Jones' pro career has been defined by injuries and lackluster production that belies his raw ability. Always an excellent defender, he showed prolonged flashes of standout offensive performance in 2025, hinting at what kind of player he could be if everything clicks.
SCOUTING REPORT: Jones has quick hands and excellent bat speed, and after cycling through a variety of tweaks and adjustments, he seemed to land on something that worked for a month-long stretch in Hillsboro. Standing right on top of the plate, he started taking more aggressive swings that not only generated hard contact but also fly balls to his pull side. He wound up reverting back to old habits, hitting more grounders to the opposite field over the final month of the season, but the power production he showed was the closest to what evaluators envisioned coming out of the draft. Defensively, he gets good reads, takes great routes with long, gliding strides and is hungry to catch everything within reach. He also has a plus arm.
THE FUTURE: Jones managed to produce for a short stretch last year; doing it for closer to a full season is his next challenge. If he can, he still might have some offensive upside he can deliver along with his plus defensive abilities.

Year	Age	Club (League)	Level	AVG	G	AB	R	H	2B	3B	HR	RBI	BB	SO	SB	OBP	SLG
2025	21	Hillsboro (NWL)	A+	.255	123	478	77	122	25	5	5	56	56	127	28	.335	.360
		Minor League Totals		.260	273	1003	179	261	43	15	13	133	167	304	58	.366	.372

18 MITCH BRATT, LHP

FB: 45. **CT:** 55. **CB:** 50. **SL:** 45. **CH:** 45. **CTL:** 70. **BA Grade:** 45. **Risk:** Average. **Adj:** 35.

Born: July 3, 2003. **B-T:** L-L. **HT:** 6-1. **WT:** 190. **Drafted:** HS—Statesboro, GA, 2021 (5th round).
Signed by: Takeshi Sakurayama (Rangers).
TRACK RECORD: Born and raised in Newmarket, Ontario, Bratt moved from Canada to Georgia in hopes of being scouted more extensively during the pandemic. The Rangers took him in the fifth round in 2021 and gave him an $850,000 bonus. He climbed steadily through their system before being included in the Merrill Kelly deal in July 2025. He was added to the 40-man roster in the fall.
SCOUTING REPORT: Bratt's fastball sat just 91.6 mph but he got a well above-average 31.8% whiff rate with it in 2025. He creates deception with the angles he throws from, and not only does he locate it well, but he is also fearlessly willing to attack hitters with it. He is just as aggressive with his mid-80s cutter, another pitch he uses to pound the zone and elicit whiffs (29.6%). He also throws a curveball and changeup, though the latter remains a work in progress, a tough pitch to master given his arm angle. He is an elite strike-thrower, issuing zero or one walk in 19 of his 24 outings in 2025. He earns high marks as a competitor and worker.
THE FUTURE: Bratt doesn't wow anyone—and likely will always have detractors because of his average stuff—but his excellent command and willingness to pump strikes could allow him to outperform the way Marco Gonzales did. Still, he is a divisive prospect; some see a back-end starter, others see a depth arm or long relief type, at best.

Year	Age	Club (League)	Level	W	L	ERA	G	GS	IP	H	HR	BB	SO	BB%	SO%	WHIP	AVG
2025	21	Frisco (TL)	AA	6	3	3.18	18	17	91	91	13	16	106	4.3	28.5	1.18	.259
2025	21	Amarillo (TL)	AA	1	1	3.98	6	6	32	31	5	7	42	3.8	31.6	1.14	.242
		Minor League Totals		22	18	3.27	87	78	380	348	38	94	450	6.0	28.5	1.16	.238

19 CARLOS VIRAHONDA, C

HIT: 50. **POW:** 45. **RUN:** 45. **FLD:** 55. **ARM:** 60. **BA Grade:** 50. **Risk:** High. **Adj:** 35.

Born: December 13, 2005. **B-T:** R-R. **HT:** 5-11. **WT:** 180. **Signed:** Venezuela, 2023.
Signed by: Cesar Geronimo Jr./Ronald Salazar.
TRACK RECORD: Arizona signed Virahonda for $200,000 out of Venezuela in January 2023 mostly because of their conviction in his defensive abilities, including good receiving skills and a powerful arm. But they also like his short, quick swing, and in his three seasons as a pro he has shown he has some offensive upside, as well. He bounced back from a miserable season in 2024 to put himself back on the map in 2025, performing well on the complex and holding his own in Low-A Visalia following a promotion.
SCOUTING REPORT: Virahonda has a stocky build with short levers, and all of his actions seem compact and quick as a result. He has a balanced, repeatable swing and a knack for making contact, particularly on fastballs. He has cut down on his chase rate each of the past two years but still needs to refine his approach. His raw power is average though it doesn't yet translate in games. It should improve as he gains strength and experience. His defense projects to be above-average, giving him a solid foundation as a prospect. He is a good receiver who posts excellent pop times thanks to a combination of a strong arm and a quick, compact throwing motion. He is a fringe-average runner.
THE FUTURE: Virahonda's strong season left some envisioning him as the club's catcher of the future. If it all comes together, he could be a contributor both at the plate and behind it.

Year	Age	Club (League)	Level	AVG	G	AB	R	H	2B	3B	HR	RBI	BB	SO	SB	OBP	SLG
2025	19	ACL D-backs	Rk	.347	37	121	30	42	8	1	1	20	14	18	3	.464	.455
2025	19	Visalia (CAL)	A	.256	33	129	13	33	4	0	3	14	13	34	1	.362	.357
		Minor League Totals		.257	157	522	78	134	34	3	6	69	47	100	9	.370	.368

20 BRIAN CURLEY, RHP

FB: 60. **CB:** 50. **SL:** 55. **CH:** 45. **CTL:** 50. **BA Grade:** 45. **Risk:** Average. **Adj:** 35.

Born: June 1, 2003. **B-T:** R-R. **HT:** 5-10. **WT:** 212. **Drafted:** Georgia, 2025 (3rd round). **Signed by:** Derrick Tucker.
TRACK RECORD: Undersized and lightly scouted out of high school, Curley ended up committing to Virginia Commonwealth, where he redshirted his freshman year as he recovered from Tommy John surgery. He pitched two seasons there, mostly in relief, before transferring to Georgia. He started the year as the Bulldogs' closer, worked his way into the rotation and ascended to the Friday night starter's role. The Diamondbacks, who took him in the third round and signed him for an under-slot $700,000, plan to give him a chance to start, knowing there is a fallback since his stuff would play well in short bursts.
SCOUTING REPORT: Curley sat 95-96 mph and touched 100 with his fastball. He gets above-average carry and it plays up further due to a low release height and unusual approach angle. His upper-80s slider has both depth and power. His curveball is more of a top-to-bottom offering, and he also threw a third breaking ball, a sweeper, though the three could blend together. He also has a fringe-average changeup. How the entire package, including his command, which is good enough when the stuff is loud enough, plays on a five-day pro schedule remains to be seen. He is inquisitive, coachable, hard-working and confident.
THE FUTURE: Curley's fastball and slider might jump a full grade in a relief role, so if starting doesn't work out he should have the stuff to pitch late in games out of the bullpen.

Year	Age	Club (League)	Level	W	L	ERA	G	GS	IP	H	HR	BB	SO	BB%	SO%	WHIP	AVG
2025	22	Did not play															

21 DYLAN RAY, RHP

FB: 50. **CB:** 45. **SL:** 45. **CH:** 55. **CTL:** 50. **BA Grade:** 45. **Risk:** Average. **Adj:** 35.

Born: May 9, 2001. **B-T:** R-R. **HT:** 6-3. **WT:** 230. **Drafted:** Alabama, 2022 (4th round). **Signed by:** Stephen Baker.
TRACK RECORD: Ray had Tommy John surgery his freshman year and was limited to only 31.1 innings in his collegiate career, but the Diamondbacks used a fourth-round pick on him anyway in 2022, a selection that amounted to a bet on his athleticism. He has steadily moved through the Diamondbacks' system, eating innings and improving his repertoire along the way.
SCOUTING REPORT: Ray sits 93.3 mph with his fastball, topping out at 96.7 mph, and gets about 16 inches of rise, a number that likely increases once he is out of the extreme elevation of Double-A Amarillo and Triple-A Reno. His changeup, which induces decent whiff (27.8%), is his best pitch. It gets solid armside run and limits hard contact. By the end of the year, he had both a depthy slider and hard cutter, and he rounds out his repertoire with an upper-70s curveball. He is a good competitor and isn't afraid to attack the strike zone.

ARIZONA DIAMONDBACKS

THE FUTURE: After being added to the 40-man roster over the winter, Ray is expected to return to Triple-A Reno in 2026. Viewed as either a depth starter or a back-end type at best, he has put himself in the conversation for a callup should the need arise.

Year	Age	Club (League)	Level	W	L	ERA	G	GS	IP	H	HR	BB	SO	BB%	SO%	WHIP	AVG
2025	24	Amarillo (TL)	AA	6	3	3.93	10	10	50	38	8	17	53	8.2	25.5	1.09	.205
2025	24	Reno (PCL)	AAA	6	3	6.30	18	18	90	107	18	38	70	9.4	17.3	1.61	.300
		Minor League Totals		22	22	5.05	78	78	341	341	58	132	352	9.0	24.0	1.39	.261

YASSEL SOLER, 3B

HIT: 50. **POW:** 55. **RUN:** 40. **FLD:** 55. **ARM:** 55. **BA Grade:** 50. **Risk:** Extreme. **Adj:** 30.

Born: January 26, 2006. **B-T:** R-R. **HT:** 5-11. **WT:** 185. **Signed:** Dominican Republic, 2023.
Signed by: Cesar Geronimo Jr./Peter Wardell/David Felida.
TRACK RECORD: Soler signed with the Diamondbacks for $425,000, then turned in a pair of strong performances in his first two seasons. But he ran into issues during his first full season at an affiliate, struggling badly to open the year. He finished on a solid note, but the season left many convinced he needs to make changes to both his approach and his swing.
SCOUTING REPORT: Soler has a loose, powerful swing, though he both chased and whiffed more than he had in 2024. He has always had a steep swing, but his sometimes overly aggressive approach seemed to amplify the flatness of it—and the small margin for error it creates. He can also tend to work around the ball, catching pitches too deep. He needs to find a way to get the ball in the air more often. His hands work fine at third, where his above-average arm plays well. He still has work to do there but has a chance to remain at the position. He has a thick frame and needs to stay on top of his conditioning to maintain his athleticism.
THE FUTURE: His strong finish was encouraging, but Soler will need to answer some of the questions his year raised if he hopes to reach his ceiling as a power-hitting third baseman.

Year	Age	Club (League)	Level	AVG	G	AB	R	H	2B	3B	HR	RBI	BB	SO	SB	OBP	SLG
2025	19	Visalia (CAL)	A	.240	92	342	42	82	13	2	12	46	42	90	5	.342	.395
		Minor League Totals		.260	184	691	101	180	35	4	20	98	73	151	12	.348	.410

IVAN LUCIANO, C

HIT: 50. **POW:** 45. **RUN:** 30. **FLD:** 50. **ARM:** 50. **BA Grade:** 45. **Risk:** High. **Adj:** 30.

Born: November 24, 2006. **B-T:** L-R. **HT:** 5-10. **WT:** 185. **Drafted:** HS—Dorado, PR, 2024 (2nd round).
Signed by: Pedro Hernandez.
TRACK RECORD: Going into his draft year, Luciano transferred to an academy in Puerto Rico that was 90 minutes from home, seeing his family only on weekends, in order to focus on baseball. The move paid off. Luciano kept getting better in all facets, prompting the Diamondbacks to jump the line to take him with their second-round pick in 2024. They signed him for $990,000. Staying at the spring training complex nearly all year, Luciano turned in a solid debut, putting together good at-bats and showing good leadership skills behind the plate.
SCOUTING REPORT: Luciano has a simple, repeatable swing with quiet hands and a small move. He takes quality at-bats—he had nearly as many walks as strikeouts—and he uses the whole field and finds the barrel often. He still lacks the strength and physicality to drive the ball with authority, no surprise given his age. His catching and throwing could be inconsistent, but he is smart and well-prepared and shows excellent leadership skills, giving him the right sort of makeup for a catcher.
THE FUTURE: Evaluators are split on whether they prefer Luciano or Carlos Virahonda as the organization's top catching prospect, but Luciano's offensive approach might give him a little higher floor. He will face a big test when he opens next year in full-season ball.

Year	Age	Club (League)	Level	AVG	G	AB	R	H	2B	3B	HR	RBI	BB	SO	SB	OBP	SLG
2025	18	ACL D-backs	Rk	.275	44	131	16	36	6	1	2	19	28	31	1	.398	.382
2025	18	Visalia (CAL)	A	.286	3	14	2	4	1	0	0	2	0	5	0	.286	.357
		Minor League Totals		.276	47	145	18	40	7	1	2	21	28	36	1	.389	.379

24 YU-MIN LIN, LHP

FB: 40. **CB:** 50. **SL:** 55. **CH:** 55. **CT:** 40. **CTL:** 50. **BA Grade:** 45. **Risk:** High. **Adj:** 30.

Born: July 12, 2003. **B-T:** L-L. **HT:** 5-11. **WT:** 160. **Signed:** Taiwan, 2021. **Signed by:** Tzu-Yao Wei/Peter Wardell.
TRACK RECORD: After signing for $525,000 in late 2021, Lin cruised through his first two professional seasons before battling adversity each of the past two. In 2024, he missed two months after being struck in the face by a line drive while in the dugout during a Double-A game. In 2025, he was knocked around in the Pacific Coast League, seeing his walk and homer rates spike while his strikeouts plummeted. In between, he helped his native Taiwan win the Premier12 tournament, working four scoreless, one-hit innings in the championship game.
SCOUTING REPORT: Lin averages just 90.9 mph with his fastball, topping out at 94.9 mph, and got very little whiff (9.4%) with the pitch in 2025. He used his four-seamer more than his sinker, a reversal from the previous year. He makes his living with his array of secondary pitches, which includes a slider, curveball and changeup. He also throws a cutter. Typical of starters in Reno, Lin appeared less aggressive with his stuff at times, seemingly pitching away from contact.
THE FUTURE: Lin's ability to generate tremendous spin on both his curveball and slider gives him a decent floor, but the lack of power in his repertoire limits his ceiling. He still has back-end starter potential but will need to get better results than he did in 2025.

Year	Age	Club (League)	Level	W	L	ERA	G	GS	IP	H	HR	BB	SO	BB%	SO%	WHIP	AVG
2025	21	Reno (PCL)	AAA	5	7	6.64	23	23	102	124	18	60	85	12.5	17.7	1.81	.303
		Minor League Totals		16	20	4.48	82	82	384	369	44	168	417	10.2	25.2	1.40	.256

25 MASON MARRIOTT, RHP

FB: 50. **CB:** 55. **SL:** 50. **CH:** 50. **CTL:** 50. **BA Grade:** 45. **Risk:** High. **Adj:** 30.

Born: August 14, 2002. **B-T:** L-R. **HT:** 6-0. **WT:** 198. **Drafted:** Baylor, 2024 (6th round). **Signed by:** J.R. Salinas.
TRACK RECORD: A well-known prospect during his high school days in the Houston area, Marriott's strike-throwing issues pushed him down draft boards and toward Baylor. He spent three years in Waco, getting better every season and earning the Friday night starter role his junior year. His improved command to go along with a solid array of pitches prompted the Diamondbacks to take him in the sixth round, where they gave him an under-slot $241,000. He opened eyes in his first spring as a pro, then turned in four strong starts in High-A before going down. He had Tommy John surgery in May 2025.
SCOUTING REPORT: Before the injury, Marriott sat 93.5 mph with his fastball and touched 96.6 mph with good carry. He racked up whiffs with his power curveball and his changeup had good depth and armside run. He continued to show improvement in filling up the zone, posting a mark of just 3.7 BB/9 before the injury. He has a fluid, athletic delivery.
THE FUTURE: Marriott likely won't be back until midway through 2026, but if he can pick up where he left off, he could show he has the makings of a starting pitcher. Failing that, with his mid-90s fastball and sharp breaking ball, he looks equipped to hold down a spot in a big league bullpen.

Year	Age	Club (League)	Level	W	L	ERA	G	GS	IP	H	HR	BB	SO	BB%	SO%	WHIP	AVG
2025	22	Hillsboro (NWL)	A+	1	0	2.29	4	4	20	13	0	8	25	10.4	32.5	1.07	.188
		Minor League Totals		1	0	2.36	7	4	27	19	0	9	31	8.7	29.8	1.05	.200

26 JAITOINE KELLY, RHP

FB: 60. **CB:** 45. **CH:** 55. **CTL:** 50. **BA Grade:** 50. **Risk:** Extreme. **Adj:** 30.

Born: June 29, 2007. **B-T:** R-R. **HT:** 6-3. **WT:** 257. **Signed:** Aruba, 2024.
Signed by: Peter Wardell/Craig Shipley/Randolph Oduber.
TRACK RECORD: The younger brother of Pirates prospect Antwone Kelly, Jaitoine threw mostly in the upper 80s with a raw delivery and underdeveloped secondary stuff when the Diamondbacks started scouting him in 2023. Liking his size and the way he moved—and the fact that his older brother threw significantly harder despite having a smaller, stockier build—the Diamondbacks signed Kelly for $70,000 on what was a deep projection play. A couple years later, it is looking like a sharp investment. Kelly's fastball made a big jump in 2025 and he looks like he could have the makings of a future starting pitcher.
SCOUTING REPORT: After averaging 88.3 mph and topping out around 91-92 mph in 2024, Kelly's fastball averaged 92.6 mph and touched 95-96 in 2025. He averaged 17.2 inches of carry and has been up to 7 feet of extension. His best secondary is a kick changeup with good fade that can resemble a splitter. He has a slow, sweepy curveball that grades as below-average; he might need to add a harder, shorter breaking ball that would pair better with his fastball. He has an above-average delivery and arm action and made huge strides in his strike-throwing. He will need to continue to work on his body to maintain athleticism.

ARIZONA DIAMONDBACKS

THE FUTURE: Kelly has a long way to go but has significant upside given his arm and frame. If it all comes together, he has the potential to be a midrotation starter.

Year	Age	Club (League)	Level	W	L	ERA	G	GS	IP	H	HR	BB	SO	BB%	SO%	WHIP	AVG
2025	18	ACL D-backs	Rk	1	1	4.81	5	4	24	24	1	7	15	7.4	15.8	1.27	.276
2025	18	DSL Arizona Red	Rk	0	0	4.66	3	3	10	11	0	3	11	7.1	26.2	1.45	.289
2025	18	Visalia (CAL)	A	0	0	6.00	1	1	3	4	0	1	2	7.7	15.4	1.67	.333
		Minor League Totals		1	5	5.47	20	18	74	75	4	44	63	13.5	19.3	1.61	.273

27 DEAN LIVINGSTON, RHP

FB: 60. **SL:** 55. **CH:** 50. **CTL:** 50. **BA Grade:** 50. **Risk:** Extreme. **Adj:** 30.

Born: September 7, 2006. **B-T:** R-R. **HT:** 6-4. **WT:** 205. **Drafted:** HS—Dacula, GA, 2025 (4th round).
Signed by: Derrick Tucker.
TRACK RECORD: The Diamondbacks under GM Mike Hazen don't reach for high school arms early in the draft often, but they did so with Livingston, giving him $1 million to keep him off campus at Georgia. A well-scouted name on the travel circuit the prior summer, Livingston showed improvement the following spring and opened eyes at the draft combine.
SCOUTING REPORT: With his strong, sturdy frame and quick arm, Livingston offers projection throughout his profile. He throws both a four-seam and two-seam fastball that sit in the mid 90s. He touched 98 mph at the combine. His ability to spin the ball was a question, but he flashed an above-average slider in the spring before the draft, a two-plane breaker up to 84 mph that resembled a power slurve. His changeup might be his best secondary pitch at present. He also tinkered with a cutter and curveball. Tall and lean, he has room to add strength and could stand to smooth out some delivery pieces in his lower half. An excellent athlete, he showed power as a hitter in high school and had plus run times from home to first.
THE FUTURE: Livingston shows a lot of inconsistencies, but his frame, athleticism and already-plus fastball gives him a foundation for a future rotation piece. If the fastball continues to get better, he could have a fallback as a late-inning reliever.

Year	Age	Club (League)	Level	W	L	ERA	G	GS	IP	H	HR	BB	SO	BB%	SO%	WHIP	AVG
2025	18	Did not play															

28 DAURY VASQUEZ, RHP

FB: 60. **SL:** 55. **CH:** 45. **CTL:** 45. **BA Grade:** 50. **Risk:** Extreme. **Adj:** 30.

Born: April 17, 2006. **B-T:** R-R. **HT:** 6-2. **WT:** 170. **Signed:** Dominican Republic, 2023.
Signed by: Cesar Geronimo Jr./Pablo Arias.
TRACK RECORD: Vasquez was skinny and athletic with a whippy arm when the Diamondbacks signed him in January 2023 for $50,000. A deeper projection prospect with an upper-80s fastball, it did not take long for Vasquez to start looking more like a potential impact arm. In three years in the system, his velocity has exploded into the mid-to-upper 90s and his strike-throwing has significantly improved, making him one of the organization's more intriguing young arms.
SCOUTING REPORT: Vasquez has a fluid, easy delivery and a quick arm that generates an electric fastball. He sits 95 mph and tops at 98 mph, averaging almost 17 inches of ride, and holds his velocity deep into his starts. His sweepy breaking ball averages about 79 mph, and while some believe he should throw it harder, he elicited a huge 60% whiff rate on it in 2025. His firm changeup has good armside run and had a 53.8% whiff rate. Vasquez is athletic and repeats his delivery well, signs that his below-average control could improve with time.
THE FUTURE: Vasquez has a wiry build with room to add some strength, but his remaining projection is mostly about command: If it improves, he will have a chance to start. Otherwise, he could be a power-armed reliever.

Year	Age	Club (League)	Level	W	L	ERA	G	GS	IP	H	HR	BB	SO	BB%	SO%	WHIP	AVG
2025	19	ACL D-backs	Rk	1	1	3.83	11	7	45	36	1	23	61	11.9	31.4	1.32	.218
2025	19	Visalia (CAL)	A	1	3	3.72	5	5	19	17	2	14	19	15.4	20.9	1.60	.227
		Minor League Totals		4	8	4.05	37	26	131	100	4	82	138	14.1	23.7	1.39	.209

ARIZONA DIAMONDBACKS

29 YORDIN CHALAS, RHP

FB: 60. **SL:** 50. **CH:** 45. **CTL:** 45. **BA Grade:** 45. **Risk:** High. **Adj:** 30.

Born: February 22, 2004. **B-T:** R-R. **HT:** 6-3. **WT:** 192. **Signed:** Dominican Republic, 2023.
Signed by: Cesar Geronimo Jr./Pedro Meyer.
TRACK RECORD: Already armed with a lively fastball that touched 94 mph, Chalas signed with the Diamondbacks for $10,000 in January 2023. At the time, he had no secondary offerings and little overall refinement to his game. In the time since, he has picked up even more velocity, added a weapon with his slider and shown potential with a split-change. Though he didn't exactly run with his opportunity the organization gave him to start in 2025, he did get a chance to log more developmental innings and work more in between-start bullpens. He finished the year working short relief stints in the Arizona Fall League.
SCOUTING REPORT: Chalas averages 95-96 mph as a starter but closer to 97 in relief. He throws both a four-seam and a two-seam fastball, the latter of which generates good armside run. His slider is his best secondary pitch; at its best it is short and tight in the 85-87 mph range. His split-change flashes plus but is inconsistent. His control is better than his command, though neither are average.
THE FUTURE: Chalas profiles best as a reliever. He figures to open 2026 in the Double-A bullpen, and if he is finding the zone often enough with his lively stuff, he could become a big-league option at some point.

Year	Age	Club (League)	Level	W	L	ERA	G	GS	IP	H	HR	BB	SO	BB%	SO%	WHIP	AVG
2025	21	Hillsboro (NWL)	A+	2	4	5.54	21	17	65	70	2	30	63	10.2	21.4	1.54	.269
2025	21	Amarillo (TL)	AA	0	0	11.37	5	0	6	9	2	8	5	22.9	14.3	2.68	.346
		Minor League Totals		7	12	4.92	87	17	146	147	11	75	167	11.4	25.3	1.52	.257

30 CHUNG-HSIANG HUANG, RHP

FB: 45. **CB:** 50. **SL:** 45. **CH:** 55. **CTL:** 45. **BA Grade:** 45. **Risk:** High. **Adj:** 30.

Born: October 26, 2005. **B-T:** R-R. **HT:** 6-0. **WT:** 175. **Signed:** Taiwan, 2025. **Signed by:** Tzu-Yao Wei/Peter Wardell.
TRACK RECORD: A product of the same Taiwanese high school program as fellow Diamondbacks prospect Yu-Min Lin, the Diamondbacks pushed to sign Huang after seeing him on a collegiate national tour in which he threw well against players in the 2025 MLB draft class. His fastball was up a bit from high school and he pounded the zone with an array of pitches. The Diamondbacks signed him for $210,000, then watched him turn in a season in which he pumped strikes and racked up whiffs at both the complex and Low-A levels.
SCOUTING REPORT: Huang sits 91-92 mph with his fastball, touching 95, and he gets both ride and run on the pitch. He throws both a splitter and a changeup, though the two can blend together. The splitter gets more vertical action while the change generates fade and run. The curveball and slider project as average pitches. He induced whiff rates in the 40-50% range on all of his secondary pitches, getting tons of chase (52.9%) on the splitter in particular. He has an athletic build and a frame with room to add strength. His command of the English language has improved significantly.
THE FUTURE: Huang has the ingredients that point to a back-end starter's ceiling. Adding strength and velocity would go a long way toward helping him reach it.

Year	Age	Club (League)	Level	W	L	ERA	G	GS	IP	H	HR	BB	SO	BB%	SO%	WHIP	AVG
2025	19	ACL D-backs	Rk	1	1	4.41	9	8	33	24	2	10	40	7.4	29.6	1.04	.200
2025	19	Visalia (CAL)	A	3	2	2.78	7	7	36	26	2	5	38	3.6	27.7	0.87	.200
		Minor League Totals		4	3	3.56	16	15	68	50	4	15	78	5.5	28.7	0.95	.200

Nick Kurtz

Athletics

BY MARK CHIARELLI

PROJECTED 2029 LINEUP

Catcher	Shea Langeliers	31
First Base	Nick Kurtz	26
Second Base	Max Muncy	26
Third Base	Jacob Wilson	27
Shortstop	Leo De Vries	22
Left Field	Tyler Soderstrom	27
Center Field	Denzel Clarke	28
Right Field	Lawrence Butler	28
Designated Hitter	Brent Rooker	34
No. 1 Starter	Jamie Arnold	25
No. 2 Starter	Gage Jump	26
No. 3 Starter	Luis Morales	26
No. 4 Starter	Wei-En Lin	23
No. 5 Starter	Braden Nett	26
Closer	Jack Perkins	29

For an organization best known for pioneering the advancement of sabermetrics at the turn of the century, the Athletics now find themselves at the forefront of another trend.

Teams across baseball are more aggressive than ever promoting their first-round picks to the majors within two years of the draft. Few clubs are as comfortable challenging their polished college bats as the A's, and they saw the payoff in 2025.

Nick Kurtz, the fourth overall pick in 2024, played just 33 minor league games before reaching the majors in late April. He promptly lit the league aflame, hitting .290 with 36 homers to win Baseball America's Rookie of the Year award. Jacob Wilson, the sixth pick in 2023, slashed .311/.355/.444 with 13 homers in 125 games, accounting for 3.5 fWAR at shortstop. Together, that duo gives the A's a foundational young core that could shepherd them into their next window of contention.

The A's finished fifth in baseball in average (.253), fifth in slugging percentage (.431) and seventh in homers (219). They locked up 25-year-old Lawrence Butler to a long-term extension and watched 2020 first-rounder Tyler Soderstrom belt 25 homers and emerge as a Gold Glove finalist in left field, a position he learned on the fly after Kurtz's arrival at first base.

Another gem could soon join them. The A's swung big at the trade deadline, prying teenage sensation Leo De Vries from the Padres in the Mason Miller deal. De Vries' arrival immediately replenished the top of the system, giving the club another infielder with all-star upside. The 18-year-old finished the year at Double-A Midland.

Still, 2025 wasn't perfect. The A's finished under .500 for the fourth straight year. They lost 20 of 21 games over one stretch from mid May to early June that buried their playoff hopes even despite a strong 41-34 finish from July 1 on.

Their offensive exploits were certainly aided by their temporary home in West Sacramento, Sutter Health Park. It also houses Triple-A Sacramento and is one of the majors' most extreme hitting environments. Unsurprisingly, A's pitchers finished with the fourth-worst ERA in baseball (4.71). The club's big-money offseason signing, Luis Severino, encapsulated the challenge: his ERA climbed from 3.02 in road games to 6.01 at home.

There's reason to believe the A's will achieve better balance in 2026 and beyond. They lost their pitching coordinator Mike McFerran, who they hired away from Wake Forest, to the Royals in December, but before he left he helped the club modernize its pitching development program, emphasizing acquiring and developing pitchers with outlier release traits.

Lefthander Gage Jump is one such example. The 2024 second-rounder was one of the bigger breakout arms in the minors in 2025, surging onto the Top 100 Prospects and positioning himself for a big league debut in 2026. The club's 2025 first-rounder, Jamie Arnold, is another polished college arm who could move quite quickly.

If they can solve their home-park pitching woes, the A's are primed to take a step forward behind a productive young position core, a revamped pitching pipeline and more reinforcements on the way, making them one of baseball's sneakier playoff threats in 2026. ∎

DEPTH CHART

ATHLETICS

TOP 2026 ROOKIES — RANK
1. Gage Jump, LHP — 3
2. Gunnar Hoglund, RHP — 14
3. Mason Barnett, RHP — 15

BREAKOUT PROSPECTS — RANK
1. Shotaro Morii, SS/RHP — 11
2. Zane Taylor, RHP — 17
3. Darwing Ozuna, OF — 29

SOURCE OF TOP 30 TALENT

Homegrown	21	Acquired	9
College	11	Trade	9
Junior college	0	Rule 5 draft	0
High school	3	Independent league	0
Undrafted free agent	0	Free agent/waivers	0
International	7		

LF
Devin Taylor (9)
Breyson Guedez (23)
Clark Elliott (25)
Cameron Leary
Darling Fernandez

CF
Junior Perez (19)
Ryan Lasko (22)
Nate Nankil
Rodney Green Jr.
Pedro Pineda

RF
Henry Bolte (6)
Gavin Turley (18)
Darwing Ozuna (29)
Jared Dickey
Carlos Pacheco

3B
Tommy White (10)
Ayden Johnson
Myles Naylor
Daniel Bucciero

SS
Leo De Vries (1)
Edgar Montero (7)
Joshua Kuroda-Grauer (8)
Shotaro Morii (11)
Bobby Boser
Ali Camarillo
Drew Swift

2B
Euribiel Angeles
Max Durrington
Colby Halter

1B
Brennan Milone

C
Davis Diaz
Dylan Fien
Logan Sauve
Cole Conn
CJ Rodriguez

LHP

LHSP
Jamie Arnold (2)
Gage Jump (3)
Wei-En Lin (4)
Grant Richardson
Alex Barr
Jackson Phipps
Corey Braun
Franco Zabaleta

LHRP
Will Johnston

RHP

RHSP
Braden Nett (5)
Kade Morris (12)
Henry Baez (13)
Gunnar Hoglund (14)
Mason Barnett (15)
Steven Echavarria (16)
Zane Taylor (17)
Kenya Huggins (26)
Kyle Robinson (27)
Cole Miller (28)
Chen Zhong-Ao Zhuang (30)
Samuel Dutton
Yordan Rodriguez
Donny Troconis
Tzu-Chen Sha
Ricardo Reyes

RHRP
Eduarniel Nuñez (20)
Yunior Tur (21)
Corey Avant (24)
Jefferson Jean
Jackson Finley
Jorge Marchecho

ATHLETICS

1 LEO DE VRIES, SS

Born: October 11, 2006. **B-T:** B-T. **HT:** 6-1. **WT:** 190.
Signed: Dominican Republic, 2024.
Signed by: Jonathan Feliz (Padres).

TRACK RECORD: A native of the Dominican Republic, De Vries grew up idolizing Manny Machado and Fernando Tatis Jr., and for a time looked destined to join them in San Diego. The Padres signed De Vries for $4.2 million, the second-largest bonus in the 2024 international class, and aggressively pushed him to Low-A for his pro debut. In 2025, he was the youngest player to open in the High-A Midwest League at 18. His season took a shocking turn at the trade deadline when the Athletics acquired him as the centerpiece of the Mason Miller deal. De Vries was promoted to Double-A Midland soon after and finished the year hitting .255/.355/.451 with 15 homers across two levels.

SCOUTING REPORT: De Vries is already one of the most polished teenage hitters in the minors, showing preternatural bat-to-ball skills, a mature all-fields approach and a knack for loud contact even without elite strength or exit velocities. His track record and advanced skills make it easy to forget he won't turn 20 until October. A switch-hitter, his lefthanded swing is more fluid and naturally geared for loft, producing line drives with carry, while his righthanded stroke remains less consistent and often pull-oriented. He's still learning to rein in his eagerness. He'll chase elevated fastballs and expand early in counts, but his hand-eye coordination allows him to get away with mistakes that would punish most hitters his age, and he rarely misses pitches over the heart of the plate. De Vries posted nearly identical exit velocities to 2024 and evaluators are split on his future power. Some see plus impact emerging as his body fills out, while others project solid-average pop that will play up through contact quality and timing. Defensively, De Vries shows the ingredients to stay at shortstop. He's smooth, instinctive and confident, with soft hands and a plus arm, though his footwork and pre-pitch positioning still require refinement. At times, he can rush routine plays or get showy, leading to unnecessary errors. The A's believe this can be cleaned up, and he has all the tools to become an above-average defender if he doesn't outgrow the position. De Vries can turn in above-average run times underway, though he doesn't always show it, and has good instincts on the bases. Evaluators were universally impressed by his innate feel for the game.

BA GRADE: 65 Risk: Average
SCOUTING GRADES: Hit: 60. Power: 55. Run: 50. Fielding: 55. Arm: 60.
Adjusted grade: 55
Projected future grades on 20-80 scouting scale

BEST TOOLS

BATTING
Best Hitter	Joshua Kuroda-Grauer
Best Power Hitter	Junior Perez
Best Strike-Zone Discipline	Brennan Milone
Fastest Baserunner	Henry Bolte
Best Athlete	Henry Bolte

PITCHING
Best Fastball	Gage Jump
Best Curveball	Braden Nett
Best Slider	Jefferson Jean
Best Changeup	Kyle Robinson
Best Control	Wei-En Lin

FIELDING
Best Defensive Catcher	CJ Rodriguez
Best Defensive Infielder	Drew Swift
Best Infield Arm	Leo De Vries
Best Defensive Outfielder	Junior Perez
Best Outfield Arm	Ryan Lasko

THE FUTURE: De Vries has one of the highest ceilings of any prospect in baseball, evoking comparisons to Francisco Lindor for his switch-hitting ability and two-way impact. His offensive profile will hinge on how much power comes as he matures, but he has all-star potential with a knack for maximizing his best-struck contact once he cleans up the finer points of his game. De Vries should return to Double-A to begin 2026, but the A's aren't afraid to push prospects aggressively.

Year	Age	Club (League)	Level	AVG	G	AB	R	H	2B	3B	HR	RBI	BB	SO	SB	OBP	SLG
2025	18	Fort Wayne (MWL)	A+	.245	82	310	46	76	19	4	8	46	52	72	8	.357	.410
2025	18	Lansing (MWL)	A+	.268	15	56	9	15	2	3	2	12	4	15	1	.338	.518
2025	18	Midland (TL)	AA	.281	21	89	17	25	7	1	5	16	10	20	2	.359	.551
		Minor League Totals		.248	193	754	135	187	50	11	26	112	116	191	24	.358	.447

ATHLETICS

2 JAMIE ARNOLD, LHP
FB: 60. **SL:** 60. **CH:** 60. **CT:** 45. **CTL:** 55. **BA Grade:** 60. **Risk:** Average. **Adj:** 50.

Born: March 21, 2004. **B-T:** L-L. **HT:** 6-1. **WT:** 192.
Drafted: Florida State, 2025 (1st round). **Signed by:** Jemel Spearman.
TRACK RECORD: After striking out 159 batters over 105.2 innings to lead Florida State to the College World Series as a sophomore, Arnold entered 2025 as the top-ranked pitching prospect in his draft class. He was a touch less crisp as a junior yet still matched his 2.98 ERA from the prior season. Fellow college lefties Kade Anderson and Liam Doyle leapfrogged him in the draft, and the Athletics were thrilled he fell to them at No. 11 overall.
SCOUTING REPORT: Evaluators struggle to find many comparisons for Arnold because of his combination of a low three-quarters arm slot, low release height and explosive, athletic delivery. The most common is Chris Sale, though the 6-foot-1 Arnold is five inches shorter. He attacks hitters with a plunging arm stroke and uncoils down the mound quickly, producing impressive extension and deception. His best pitch is a plus mid-80s sweeping slider that he landed for strikes more than 70% of the time as a junior and can manipulate against both righties and lefties. Arnold's fastballs average 93 mph: a four-seamer with a flat approach angle and a two-seamer to rack up ground balls. He overhauled his mid-80s changeup before the 2025 season, creating a pitch with unusual action more typical of a righthander's breaking ball. It flashes swing-and-miss movement with inconsistent results. He'll also sprinkle in a mid-to-upper-80s cutter. Arnold's unique release makes hitters uncomfortable, but his success will hinge on consistently commanding his fastball and honing his unusual angles and movement patterns into consistent strikes.
THE FUTURE: Arnold may not have explosive velocity, but his stuff plays up thanks to his outlier traits. The A's hope they'll be able to maximize Arnold's stuff in much the same way they did with Gage Jump and Jacob Lopez in 2025. He projects as a midrotation starter with some volatility tied to his command.

Year	Age	Club (League)	Level	W	L	ERA	G	GS	IP	H	HR	BB	SO	BB%	SO%	WHIP	AVG
2025	21	Did not pitch															

3 GAGE JUMP, LHP
FB: 60. **CB:** 55. **SL:** 55. **CH:** 50. **SW:** 55. **CTL:** 55. **BA Grade:** 60. **Risk:** Average. **Adj:** 50.

Born: April 12, 2003. **B-T:** L-L. **HT:** 6-0. **WT:** 197.
Drafted: LSU, 2024 (2nd round supp.). **Signed by:** Kelcey Mucker.
TRACK RECORD: Jump ranked No. 57 in the 2021 draft out of high school but instead went to UCLA, where he had Tommy John surgery in 2023 before transferring to LSU and making 15 starts in 2024. The Athletics selected him 73rd overall that summer and signed him for $2 million. Jump made his pro debut in 2025 and quickly became a breakout pitching prospect. The A's managed his workload carefully, yet he still reached Double-A Midland and finished with the second-most strikeouts in the system (131) while earning a Futures Game nod.
SCOUTING REPORT: The 6-foot, 197-pound lefthander knows how to use his size and dogged mentality to his advantage. Jump weaponizes the top of the strike zone with a riding mid-90s fastball that touches 97 mph from a low arm slot, missing bats with its uphill life and deception, then he layers in the rest of his arsenal. His low-80s curveball tunnels well off his fastball, and he features two distinct sliders: a firmer mid-80s version with late tilt and a low-80s sweeper added in 2025 that misses bats to his glove side. The changeup lagged behind early but improved as the year went on, flashing above-average depth. Jump repeats an unorthodox, high-effort delivery better than expected and fills the zone, walking just 7.4% of hitters in 2025, yet it also raises some durability questions with evaluators, given his college elbow surgery. Some also see home run risk against major league hitters, though he allowed just seven in 112.2 innings in 2025.
THE FUTURE: Jump profiles as a midrotation starter with the fallback of a high-leverage reliever, which the A's may have considered down the stretch in 2025 if they were in contention. He's a candidate to join their rotation at some point in 2026, with an outside shot of doing so out of spring training.

Year	Age	Club (League)	Level	W	L	ERA	G	GS	IP	H	HR	BB	SO	BB%	SO%	WHIP	AVG
2025	22	Lansing (MWL)	A+	4	1	2.32	6	5	31	21	1	5	45	4.1	37.2	0.84	.186
2025	22	Midland (TL)	AA	5	6	3.64	20	19	82	69	6	29	86	8.5	25.3	1.20	.224
		Minor League Totals		9	7	3.28	26	24	113	90	7	34	131	7.4	28.4	1.10	.214

ATHLETICS

4 WEI-EN LIN, LHP

FB: 55. CB: 55. SL: 50. CH: 55. SP: 45. CTL: 60. BA Grade: 55. Risk: Average. Adj: 45.

Born: November 4, 2005. **B-T:** L-L. **HT:** 6-2. **WT:** 179.
Signed: Taiwan, 2024. **Signed by:** Adam Hislop.
TRACK RECORD: Lin signed for $1.3 million out of Taiwan in June 2024. A year later, he turned in one of the best seasons of any teenage pitcher in pro ball. The 19-year-old bypassed Rookie ball, then struck out 24 batters over his first 12 innings for Low-A Stockton without issuing a walk. Lin never slowed down from there, scaling three levels to finish at Double-A Midland. His 117 strikeouts were second-most among teenage minor leaguers, while his 33.4% strikeout rate led all Athletics farmhands with at least 50 innings, and he walked just 6.3% of batters.
SCOUTING REPORT: Despite modest velocity, the 6-foot-2 lefthander fearlessly pounds the strike zone with a polished four-pitch mix that overpowered inexperienced hitters. His 91 mph four-seamer tops out at 95 mph and could gain more power as he fills out his broad-shouldered frame. Even now, it's effective thanks to its ride-run characteristics from a lower release height with above-average extension. Lin landed it for strikes at an astounding 78% clip through August, with hitters chasing more than 44% of the time. His deceptive 83 mph cut-slider shows impressive induced vertical break, while his mid-70s curveball gets plenty of whiffs. The A's may explore adding a sweeper in 2026. Lin ties everything together with an upper-70s Vulcan-grip changeup that flashes plus and a separate splitter. Some evaluators are bullish on Lin's changeup progress, while others are more skeptical about how it will fare against better hitters. He repeats his quick, loose delivery with ease.
THE FUTURE: After a revelatory 2025, Lin is one of the Athletics' more intriguing young arms. He would benefit from added power and more chase from his secondary pitches, and he must prove his stuff plays against upper-level hitters, but his pitchability gives him a high floor and midrotation upside.

Year	Age	Club (League)	Level	W	L	ERA	G	GS	IP	H	HR	BB	SO	BB%	SO%	WHIP	AVG
2025	19	Stockton (CAL)	A	1	4	3.96	13	10	50	49	5	6	69	3.0	34.0	1.10	.253
2025	19	Lansing (MWL)	A+	3	1	3.26	11	1	30	17	3	12	40	10.1	33.6	0.96	.163
2025	19	Midland (TL)	AA	0	0	4.05	2	2	7	4	1	4	8	14.3	28.6	1.20	.167
		Minor League Totals		4	5	3.72	26	13	87	70	9	22	117	6.3	33.4	1.06	.217

5 BRADEN NETT, RHP

FB: 60. CB: 60. SL: 45. CH: 45. SW: 55. CT: 55. CTL: 45. BA Grade: 55. Risk: Average. Adj: 45.

Born: June 18, 2002. **B-T:** R-R. **HT:** 6-3. **WT:** 192.
Signed: St. Charles (MO) JC, 2022 (UDFA). **Signed by:** Kurt Kemp/Chris Kemlo (Padres).
TRACK RECORD: A Missouri native, Nett attended St. Charles Community College but never appeared in a game. He was working a shift at Home Depot when the Padres called with an undrafted free agent offer in 2022 after they were intrigued by his 16.2 innings in the MLB Draft League that summer. That decision looks wise. Nett blossomed under pro instruction and spent all of 2025 in Double-A—first with San Antonio, then Midland after joining the Athletics in the Mason Miller-Leo De Vries blockbuster.
SCOUTING REPORT: Nett forces hitters to contend with premium velocity and a dizzying array of up to seven pitches, including three fastballs. The headliner is his mid-90s four-seamer, which touched 99 mph in 2025 with solid carry, though his command of it backed up slightly from 2024. He leaned more heavily on a low-90s cutter in search of a way to get lefthanded hitters out more consistently, and he also mixes in a mid-90s sinker that generates grounders and functions as a strike-stealing efficiency pitch. Nett's preferred breaking ball is a 78 mph curveball with big shape and more than 3,000 rpm of spin, complemented by a tighter mid-80s slider and a low-80s sweeper with 15 inches of break. After previously using a splitter, Nett shifted to an upper-80s changeup in 2025 seeking more consistent strikes. He's a dynamic athlete with a compact arm stroke and impressive arm speed, but he remains a fringy strike-thrower who walked 10.3% of Double-A hitters in 2025 and too often fell behind early in counts.
THE FUTURE: Given his limited college track record and deep arsenal, the 23-year-old might require some patience as he seeks a consistent combination of pure stuff and strikes, but there's midrotation upside if he can strike the right balance.

Year	Age	Club (League)	Level	W	L	ERA	G	GS	IP	H	HR	BB	SO	BB%	SO%	WHIP	AVG
2025	23	Midland (TL)	AA	1	3	4.60	7	7	31	36	3	14	30	9.9	21.3	1.60	.293
2025	23	San Antonio (TL)	AA	5	4	3.39	17	17	74	71	5	34	86	10.4	26.3	1.41	.247
		Minor League Totals		8	9	3.93	41	35	149	137	8	87	166	13.0	24.9	1.50	.243

ATHLETICS

6 HENRY BOLTE, OF

HIT: 40. **POW:** 60. **RUN:** 70. **FLD:** 60. **ARM:** 60. **BA Grade:** 55. **Risk:** High. **Adj:** 40.

Born: August 4, 2003. **B-T:** R-R. **HT:** 6-3. **WT:** 205.
Drafted: HS—Palo Alto, CA, 2022 (2nd round). **Signed by:** Troy Stewart.
TRACK RECORD: Bolte has steadily climbed the rungs of the Athletics' minor league system since signing out of a Bay Area high school for $2 million as a second-rounder in 2022. Along the way, he made a series of mechanical tweaks in search of more contact. He split his age-21 season in 2025 between Double-A and Triple-A, batting .284/.385/.427 with nine home runs and 44 stolen bases over 114 games before a nagging wrist injury ended his year and required September surgery.
SCOUTING REPORT: Bolte is a player of extremes. He produces some of the best exit velocities of any A's minor leaguer, runs the bases as well as any player in the system and is a potential plus outfield defender. Bolte has been quite productive in the minors and, on the right weeks, scouts see massive upside. In other weeks, they wonder if he'll ever hit enough to piece it all together in the majors. The righthanded-hitting Bolte has smoothed out his swing and improved pitch recognition to trim his strikeout rates, yet still ran a 33% whiff rate in 2025 with holes up in the zone against velocity and down and away versus breaking balls. He also pounds too many balls into the ground, and his 59% groundball rate limits his in-game impact, though the A's believe his lingering wrist woes contributed to that result. Bolte oozes athleticism on the bases and at all three outfield spots, and his frenetic play style can also lead to some erraticism.
THE FUTURE: There's boom-or-bust risk with Bolte, whose power-speed profile is not far off from current A's outfielder Colby Thomas. The organization remains encouraged by Bolte's intangibles and year-over-year progress, and he has the upside of an everyday outfielder who hits .240 with 25-30 homers and steals bases—if he can find a way to optimize his swing and approach to make better contact.

Year	Age	Club (League)	Level	AVG	G	AB	R	H	2B	3B	HR	RBI	BB	SO	SB	OBP	SLG
2025	21	Midland (TL)	AA	.278	80	295	43	82	14	4	7	42	41	95	31	.378	.424
2025	21	Las Vegas (PCL)	AAA	.300	34	120	23	36	6	2	2	14	16	46	13	.404	.433
		Minor League Totals		.268	360	1336	240	358	69	19	38	199	185	513	122	.369	.433

7 EDGAR MONTERO, SS

HIT: 50. **POW:** 60. **RUN:** 45. **FLD:** 50. **ARM:** 55. **BA Grade:** 55. **Risk:** High. **Adj:** 40.

Born: November 21, 2006. **B-T:** B-R. **HT:** 6-2. **WT:** 190.
Signed: Dominican Republic, 2024. **Signed by:** Juan Carlos De La Cruz.
TRACK RECORD: The switch-hitting Montero signed for $1.2 million out of the Dominican Republic in 2024, tying Jose Ramos for the largest bonus in the Athletics' international class, then produced a .773 OPS in 54 Dominican Summer League games in his pro debut that year. His production surged after returning to the DSL in 2025. He was one of the league's most productive hitters, slashing .313/.484/.580 with nine homers, and his walk total (60) surpassed his strikeout total (54) in 55 games.
SCOUTING REPORT: The 6-foot-2, 190-pound Montero remade his body and arrived for his second tour in the DSL in much better shape and with more twitchiness. His exit velocities made a corresponding leap, and his 90th percentile 104.7 mph EV at 18 years old was a 3 mph jump from the previous season. Scouts saw potentially plus impact from both sides of the plate, though Montero's lefthanded swing is a bit more advanced right now. He also showed a patient, advanced approach with impressive spin recognition. He'll need to answer some questions about his pure feel to hit against better pitching after he whiffed on nearly 28% of pitches in 2025. He offset that swing-and-miss with an advanced feel to find the barrel and pull his best-struck contact. Defensively, Montero is an energetic player with sound hands, footwork and above-average arm strength that can fit at shortstop. Whether his body allows him to is another question. He could ultimately move to third base if he continues to get bigger and stronger.
THE FUTURE: Montero has an enticing blend of potential impact and a sound plan of attack at the plate, and that could carry him through the system even if he one day shifts off shortstop. He will come stateside in 2026 with a chance to skip the Arizona Complex League and open the year with Low-A Stockton.

Year	Age	Club (League)	Level	AVG	G	AB	R	H	2B	3B	HR	RBI	BB	SO	SB	OBP	SLG
2025	18	DSL Athletics	Rk	.313	55	176	47	55	14	3	9	50	60	54	11	.484	.580
		Minor League Totals		.276	109	352	82	97	23	6	12	74	108	104	22	.443	.477

ATHLETICS

8 JOSHUA KURODA-GRAUER, SS
HIT: 60. **POW:** 30. **RUN:** 55. **FLD:** 55. **ARM:** 50. **BA Grade:** 45. **Risk:** Mild. **Adj:** 40.

Born: January 31, 2003. **B-T:** R-R. **HT:** 6-0. **WT:** 190.
Drafted: Rutgers, 2024 (3rd round). **Signed by:** Ron Vaughn.
TRACK RECORD: The Athletics' third-round pick out of Rutgers in 2024 lived up to his reputation as a contact maven in his first full professional season. Splitting time between High-A Lansing and Double-A Midland, he led all A's minor leaguers with 147 hits and posted an exceptional 87.4% contact rate. The tradeoff was almost no power. Kuroda-Grauer went homerless over his first 143 professional games before launching two in one week in mid September.
SCOUTING REPORT: Kuroda-Grauer's advanced contact ability and zone coverage allow him to touch nearly any pitch in any location, filleting line drives and grounders all around the field. He rarely misses in zone but can sometimes trust his bat-to-ball skills to his detriment, chasing nearly 30% of the time and quite frequently with two strikes. His swing produces virtually no impact or pull-side damage—he had the third-lowest pull percentage among qualified A's minor leaguers—but he will sting the occasional higher-end exit velocity, which suggests there could be a bit more oomph under the hood, especially if he gets better at not decelerating through contact and recognizing which pitches he can damage. Defensively, Kuroda-Grauer adds significant value. He's an above-average shortstop with sure hands, a quick exchange and an accurate arm, and he adapted seamlessly to second and third base after Leo De Vries' promotion to Double-A. The A's were particularly impressed by his early work at third and even tried him in the outfield in the Arizona Fall League. He's an average runner but a savvy baserunner with excellent instincts who swiped 27 bases while earning high marks for leadership and competitiveness.
THE FUTURE: In the absence of more power, Kuroda-Grauer might be best suited for a super utility role in which he can provide contact and on-base skills at the bottom of a lineup and add value defensively.

Year	Age	Club (League)	Level	AVG	G	AB	R	H	2B	3B	HR	RBI	BB	SO	SB	OBP	SLG
2025	22	Lansing (MWL)	A+	.293	80	334	38	98	21	1	0	26	26	37	26	.353	.362
2025	22	Midland (TL)	AA	.301	41	163	25	49	9	0	2	21	14	12	1	.372	.393
		Minor League Totals		.301	149	605	81	182	32	1	2	55	52	58	32	.371	.367

9 DEVIN TAYLOR, OF
HIT: 55. **POW:** 55. **RUN:** 40. **FLD:** 40. **ARM:** 40. **BA Grade:** 50. **Risk:** Average. **Adj:** 40.

Born: January 6, 2004. **B-T:** L-R. **HT:** 6-1. **WT:** 215.
Drafted: Indiana, 2025 (2nd round). **Signed by:** Rich Sparks.
TRACK RECORD: Few college hitters in the 2025 draft were more accomplished than Taylor. He hit .350 with a program-record 54 homers over three years at Indiana, surpassing the likes of Hoosiers alum Kyle Schwarber, played for USA Baseball's Collegiate National Team and produced a .907 OPS on the Cape in 2024. The Athletics selected him 48th overall and signed him for $2.5 million, and he debuted with Low-A Stockton, where he slashed .264/.388/.481 with six homers in 28 games.
SCOUTING REPORT: Taylor could become a well-rounded, above-average hitter because of his disciplined line-drive approach that extends all the way from his diligent pregame work in batting practice to game action. He rarely expands the strike zone. Instead, he works the whole field, deftly using his barrel skills to his advantage. Taylor's above-average power tends to materialize more often in games, especially to center and left-center field, where he did most of his damage in his brief stint in Stockton, though he can get a bit pushy at times and he whiffed on pitches 30% of the time in his limited pro look. There's considerable pressure on Taylor's bat to perform because of his limited secondary tools, which was magnified early in his junior spring when he got off to a slow start at the plate. He's a below-average runner and thrower with a bit of a cavalier approach in the outfield, where he's likely limited to left field in the long run. The A's think they can coax better defense, footwork and throwing mechanics out of Taylor in pro ball.
THE FUTURE: Even if it's unlikely he provides much value elsewhere, Taylor could develop into a second-division regular in left field on the strength of his advanced offensive chops. He's ready for High-A Lansing in 2026.

Year	Age	Club (League)	Level	AVG	G	AB	R	H	2B	3B	HR	RBI	BB	SO	SB	OBP	SLG
2025	21	Stockton (CAL)	A	.264	28	106	25	28	5	0	6	18	21	37	2	.388	.481
		Minor League Totals		.264	28	106	25	28	5	0	6	18	21	37	2	.388	.481

ATHLETICS

10 TOMMY WHITE, 3B/1B

HIT: 55. **POW:** 55. **RUN:** 30. **FLD:** 40. **ARM:** 50. **BA Grade:** 50. **Risk:** Average. **Adj:** 40.

Born: March 2, 2003. **B-T:** R-R. **HT:** 6-1. **WT:** 228.
Drafted: LSU, 2024 (2nd round). **Signed by:** Kelcey Mucker.
TRACK RECORD: White has excellent amateur bona fides. He played at IMG Academy, became college baseball's 2022 Freshman of the Year at North Carolina State, then transferred to LSU, where he won a national championship and earned first-team All-America honors in 2023. He hit 75 career college home runs before the Athletics drafted him in the second round in 2024. So far, White's pro career hasn't ignited in quite the same fashion. He hit .275/.334/.439 with 12 homers in 93 games in 2025, primarily at High-A Lansing, while missing time with minor knee and hamstring injuries. He also received a 2025 Futures Game nod.
SCOUTING REPORT: For all of his aluminum bat power prowess, White has looked more hitterish as a pro. He's especially tough to beat in the strike zone and made contact at an 82% clip in 2025 with notable bat speed and plate coverage. Sometimes, his ability to reach almost any pitch can work against him. White's ultra-aggressive approach leads him to expand the zone and hit his way into outs, limiting how often his above-average raw power shows up in games. White's approach and power plays best to right-center field. Evaluators noted that White can get caught guessing and his footwork mechanics can vary. It's not uncommon to see him ditch his toe-tap entirely with two strikes. Defensively, White has solid hands and arm strength, yet his mobility is tested at third base, where he made 18 errors in 77 games in 2025. White began to see more time at first base upon reaching Double-A Midland and in the Arizona Fall League, and it's likely a better fit for him.
THE FUTURE: If he can dial in more patience to better channel his impact potential, White's combination of bat-to-ball skills and power could support a second-division regular role, most likely at first base.

Year	Age	Club (League)	Level	AVG	G	AB	R	H	2B	3B	HR	RBI	BB	SO	SB	OBP	SLG
2025	22	Lansing (MWL)	A+	.260	66	254	38	66	18	0	11	36	22	37	3	.326	.461
2025	22	Midland (TL)	AA	.311	27	106	11	33	5	0	1	15	7	17	0	.354	.387
		Minor League Totals		.263	118	467	64	123	25	0	14	65	38	75	3	.327	.407

11 SHOTARO MORII, SS/RHP

HIT: 50. **POW:** 50. **RUN:** 45. **FLD:** 50. **ARM:** 55.
FB: 50. **SL:** 45. **SP:** 45. **CTL:** 55. **BA Grade:** 55. **Risk:** High. **Adj:** 40.

Born: December 15, 2006. **B-T:** L-R. **HT:** 6-0. **WT:** 190. **Signed:** Japan, 2025. **Signed by:** Toshiyuki Tomizuka.
TRACK RECORD: The two-way talent eschewed a path to the Nippon Professional Baseball League and instead signed with the A's for $1.51 million in 2025 out of high school in Japan. Morii debuted in the Arizona Complex League and slashed .250/.399/.384 with three homers over 43 games. His pitching ramp-up was delayed, and he didn't appear on the mound during the regular season, though he logged innings in instructional league after the year.
SCOUTING REPORT: For an 18-year-old with little experience against premium pitching, Morii adapted quickly and showed surprising physicality. He has a discerning eye—sometimes overly so—and combines bat speed with barrel accuracy to pepper line drives to all fields. While he only hit three homers, Morii's underlying exit velocities were above-average for his age, though scouts don't see a ton of physical projection remaining, which could also impact his defensive home. He has an above-average arm but fringy range at shortstop that could one day push him to second or third base. On the mound, Morii is more raw. In limited looks, he showed a three-pitch mix fronted by a low-90s fastball along with decent feel for a splitter and a slider that acts more like a curveball, plus a smooth and repeatable delivery.
THE FUTURE: There's virtually no modern precedent for a two-way player who regularly spends time in the field. The A's plan to let Morii continue both roles in 2026 with Low-A Stockton, where he could rotate between infield duties, DH and a weekly mound appearance, though his long-term future is likely to come at the plate.

Year	Age	Club (League)	Level	AVG	G	AB	R	H	2B	3B	HR	RBI	BB	SO	SB	OBP	SLG
2025	18	ACL Athletics	Rk	.258	43	151	39	39	8	1	3	27	36	47	4	.399	.384
		Minor League Totals		.258	43	151	39	39	8	1	3	27	36	47	4	.399	.384

ATHLETICS

12 KADE MORRIS, RHP
FB: 55. **CB:** 45. **SL:** 55. **SW:** 55. **CH:** 45. **CTL:** 45. **BA Grade:** 50. **Risk:** Average. **Adj:** 40.

Born: June 21, 2002. **B-T:** R-R. **HT:** 6-3. **WT:** 190. **Drafted:** Nevada, 2023 (3rd round). **Signed by:** Rich Morales (Mets).
TRACK RECORD: Morris was a steady performer at Nevada before the Mets drafted him in the third round in 2023 and traded him a year later to the A's for Paul Blackburn. Morris has logged at least 135 innings in each of the past two seasons. He split 2025 between Double-A Midland, where he posted a 2.79 ERA in nine starts, and Triple-A Las Vegas, where he recorded a 5.22 ERA across 98.1 innings.
SCOUTING REPORT: Lithe and athletic at 6-foot-3, Morris pounds the strike zone with arm speed and a deep arsenal that works primarily east to west from a lower arm slot. He upped the usage of his mid-90s sinker in 2025, generating a groundball rate above 50%, and pairs it with two distinct sliders: a harder mid-80s version with tilt and depth, and a newer low-80s sweeper. He'll also mix in an average upper-70s curveball and a fringy upper-80s changeup. Lefthanded hitters fared considerably better against Morris, especially if his arm slot wandered too low and his secondaries flattened out. A softer changeup may help keep them more honest. Morris is more control over command and has the feel to fill the strike zone, but is still learning how to sequence his deep mix. Without a true plus putaway offering, he sometimes gets himself into trouble by overthrowing in search of strikeouts.
THE FUTURE: Morris profiles as a back-of-the-rotation option who leans on his pitchability and generates quick groundball outs. He's among several A's upper-minors arms who could reach the majors in 2026.

Year	Age	Club (League)	Level	W	L	ERA	G	GS	IP	H	HR	BB	SO	BB%	SO%	WHIP	AVG
2025	23	Midland (TL)	AA	2	3	2.79	9	9	52	42	2	11	48	5.3	23.1	1.03	.221
2025	23	Las Vegas (PCL)	AAA	7	7	5.22	19	19	98	112	14	37	80	8.5	18.4	1.52	.289
		Minor League Totals		13	17	4.19	50	47	251	247	28	84	228	7.8	21.1	1.32	.255

13 HENRY BAEZ, RHP
FB: 55. **SL:** 50. **CH:** 45. **CT:** 40. **CTL:** 50. **BA Grade:** 50. **Risk:** Average. **Adj:** 40.

Born: October 12, 2002. **B-T:** R-R. **HT:** 6-3. **WT:** 199. **Signed:** Dominican Republic, 2019.
Signed by: Bill McLaughlin/Emmanuel Rangel/Trevor Schumm/Chris Kemp (Padres).
TRACK RECORD: Baez signed with the Padres for just $125,000 in 2019 and developed into a steady strike-thrower who consistently kept the ball on the ground. He benefited from low batting averages on balls in play in both 2024, when he broke out with a 2.99 ERA over 126.1 innings, and then again upon returning to Double-A in 2025. Baez was acquired by the A's at the trade deadline as part of the Mason Miller-Leo De Vries blockbuster. He logged just 12.1 innings with his new organization before a forearm injury ended his season.
SCOUTING REPORT: At 6-foot-3 and 199 pounds, Baez consistently generates groundball rates above 50% with an arsenal that works best moving laterally to stay off barrels. He leans on a mid-90s sinker that touches 98 mph and doesn't miss many bats but he can climb the ladder for some whiffs to his arm side. His best secondary is a low-80s slider that replaced his curveball in 2025 and serves as both his best swing-and-miss and chase offering. He'll also mix in a fringy upper-80s changeup with modest fade and a seldom-used upper-80s cutter. Baez has solid control and works from the first base side of the rubber with a quick tempo to the plate.
THE FUTURE: Baez is unlikely to ever post gaudy strikeout totals, but he could carve out a role at the back of a rotation as a groundball specialist who efficiently turns over lineups. He's expected to be healthy for spring training in 2026.

Year	Age	Club (League)	Level	W	L	ERA	G	GS	IP	H	HR	BB	SO	BB%	SO%	WHIP	AVG
2025	22	San Antonio (TL)	AA	4	2	1.96	20	20	97	66	2	31	89	8.1	23.4	1.00	.195
2025	22	Midland (TL)	AA	1	1	5.84	3	3	12	13	1	4	11	7.3	20.0	1.38	.260
		Minor League Totals		20	16	3.21	91	84	400	328	18	147	386	8.7	23.0	1.19	.222

14 GUNNAR HOGLUND, RHP
FB: 45. **SL:** 55. **CH:** 55. **CT:** 45. **CTL:** 60. **BA Grade:** 45. **Risk:** Average. **Adj:** 35.

Born: December 17, 1999. **B-T:** L-R. **HT:** 6-4. **WT:** 235. **Drafted:** Ole Miss, 2021 (1st round).
Signed by: Don Norris (Blue Jays).
TRACK RECORD: Hoglund's pro career has been defined by stops and starts since needing Tommy John surgery just before the Blue Jays drafted him 19th overall in 2021. He never threw a pitch for Toronto before being dealt to Oakland in the Matt Chapman trade, and further setbacks limited him to 69 professional innings through 2023. Finally healthy in 2024, Hoglund reached Triple-A Las Vegas and entered 2025 spring training showing a notable velocity bump. He made his major league debut and logged 32.1

ATHLETICS

innings with a 6.40 ERA before right hip labral surgery ended his season in June.
SCOUTING REPORT: Before his injury, Hoglund had emerged from a healthy offseason with his best stuff in years after making significant changes to his pitch mix. His 93-94 mph four-seamer added roughly 1.5 mph and three inches of extension, touching 96-97 with improved shape and separation from his sinker. He also added more sweep to his low-80s slider, which joined his bread-and-butter mid-80s changeup as a legitimate whiff offering. Hoglund's firmer 90 mph cut-slider gives lefties a different look. His hallmark precision has also remained intact. Yet for all his alterations, Hoglund's big league debut showed his ceiling may be capped by a lack of premium bat-missing stuff, especially with his fastball.
THE FUTURE: Durability remains the main concern, as Hoglund must show he can sustain both health and his improved stuff. If he does, his pitch mix and control give him the foundation of a back-end starter.

Year	Age	Club (League)	Level	W	L	ERA	G	GS	IP	H	HR	BB	SO	BB%	SO%	WHIP	AVG
2025	25	Las Vegas (PCL)	AAA	1	2	2.43	6	6	30	24	3	7	30	6.1	26.1	1.04	.226
2025	25	Athletics (AL)	MLB	1	3	6.40	6	6	32	38	10	11	23	7.9	16.5	1.52	.299
		Minor League Totals		12	15	3.89	49	48	229	201	29	57	203	6.1	21.8	1.13	.235
		Major League Totals		1	3	6.40	6	6	32	38	10	11	23	7.9	16.5	1.52	.299

15 MASON BARNETT, RHP
FB: 50. **CB:** 55. **SL:** 50. **CH:** 45. **CTL:** 50. **BA Grade:** 45. **Risk:** Average. **Adj:** 35.

Born: November 7, 2000. **B-T:** R-R. **HT:** 6-0. **WT:** 227. **Drafted:** Auburn, 2022 (3rd round). **Signed by:** Will Howard (Royals).
TRACK RECORD: The Royals drafted Barnett in the third round in 2022 out of Auburn, and two years later he became the centerpiece of the deadline deal that sent Lucas Erceg to Kansas City. Barnett made a strong first impression on his new organization, helping Double-A Midland make a deep postseason run in 2024, but struggled to follow it up in 2025. He posted a 6.13 ERA over 119 innings in the hitter-friendly Pacific Coast League, and was similarly roughed up in 22.1 major league innings after a late-season callup.
SCOUTING REPORT: At his best, Barnett works with a lively mid-90s fastball that misses bats at the top of the zone and sets up a four-pitch mix. In 2025, however, a series of adjustments dulled the pitch's impact. The 6-foot righthander raised his arm slot, creating one of the more vertical release angles in baseball, and the change reduced his fastball's vertical approach angle and upper-end velocity. Combined with Triple-A's automated challenge system that made it tougher to steal strikes at the top of the zone, Barnett's whiff and strike rates slipped as he fought to recalibrate. His mid-80s sweeper and changeup generated above-average miss rates in the minors but were punished in his brief big-league sample, while his upper-70s curveball showed better results in a limited showing.
THE FUTURE: Barnett's pitch mix, feel for spin and competitiveness provide the floor of a back-of-the-rotation starter. Restoring his fastball's hop and reclaiming more quality strikes will determine whether he reaches that ceiling.

Year	Age	Club (League)	Level	W	L	ERA	G	GS	IP	H	HR	BB	SO	BB%	SO%	WHIP	AVG
2025	24	Las Vegas (PCL)	AAA	6	2	6.13	25	23	119	125	17	65	124	11.9	22.8	1.60	.265
2025	24	Athletics (AL)	MLB	1	1	6.85	5	5	22	26	3	11	18	10.6	17.3	1.66	.286
		Minor League Totals		22	17	4.44	78	72	375	332	35	165	434	10.3	27.0	1.33	.235
		Major League Totals		1	1	6.85	5	5	22	26	3	11	18	10.6	17.3	1.66	.286

16 STEVEN ECHAVARRIA, RHP
FB: 55. **CB:** 45. **SL:** 60. **CH:** 45. **CTL:** 45. **BA Grade:** 50. **Risk:** High. **Adj:** 35.

Born: August 6, 2005. **B-T:** R-R. **HT:** 6-1. **WT:** 182. **Drafted:** HS—Millburn, NJ, 2023 (3rd round). **Signed by:** Ron Vaughn.
TRACK RECORD: The A's went well over slot to sign Echavarria for $3 million as a third-round pick in 2023. He skipped rookie ball and endured growing pains in his 2024 pro debut, posting a 6.55 ERA over 57.2 innings with Low-A Stockton. His follow-up season with High-A Lansing in 2025 was smoother. Echavarria threw 104 innings, the sixth-most of any teenager in the minors, with a 4.59 ERA, 19.5% strikeout rate and 9.3% walk rate.
SCOUTING REPORT: Echavarria's raw stuff is impressive for his age. The athletic 6-foot-1 righty works with a mid-90s fastball that touches 99, and pairs it with a potentially plus mid-80s slider that flashes wicked two-plane break. He's still working on turning his raw tools into consistent results. Spotty command, especially with the heater, is one reason why, though his strike rate climbed from 59% in the first half of 2025 to 65% in the second half. Despite its velocity, his fastball doesn't generate many swings and misses due to ordinary shape, so he may ultimately rely more on his secondaries. He reintroduced a low-80s curveball in 2025 and mixes in an upper-80s changeup with promising movement but scattered location.

ATHLETICS

THE FUTURE: Echavarria's combination of arm talent and athleticism gives him some of the highest upside among A's starting pitching prospects. The A's are hopeful his second-half strides set up a breakout 2026, and he could open the season with Double-A Midland at 20 years old.

Year	Age	Club (League)	Level	W	L	ERA	G	GS	IP	H	HR	BB	SO	BB%	SO%	WHIP	AVG
2025	19	Lansing (MWL)	A+	3	7	4.59	26	25	104	106	8	42	88	9.3	19.5	1.42	.268
		Minor League Totals		3	12	5.29	45	44	162	180	12	78	147	10.6	20.1	1.60	.284

17 ZANE TAYLOR, RHP

FB: 55. **CB:** 50. **SW:** 50. **CH:** 55. **CT:** 50. **CTL:** 60. **BA Grade:** 45. **Risk:** Average. **Adj:** 35.

Born: June 1, 2002. **B-T:** R-R. **HT:** 6-0. **WT:** 200. **Drafted:** UNC Wilmington, 2025 (5th round). **Signed by:** Rich Sparks.
TRACK RECORD: Taylor was a great strike-thrower over his first three seasons at UNC Wilmington, then his stuff took a leap in 2025 while maintaining pinpoint control. The result was an 11-2, 1.98 season and second-team All-American honors. Taylor then went to the draft combine, where he threw the hardest four-seamer (97.3 mph) of any pitcher, before the A's drafted him in the fifth round. He impressed them enough to warrant a two-inning spot start with Triple-A Las Vegas in September.
SCOUTING REPORT: After previously sitting in the low 90s, Taylor's fastball averaged 93.6 mph and touched 98 as a senior with a 73% strike rate, the fourth-best mark among college arms who threw at least 500 four-seamers in 2025. To hitters, the pitch appears to have dead-zone shape, but it avoids barrels because of its carry-run characteristics from an extremely low release height. Taylor doesn't have a clear plus secondary, but he throws plenty of them. His 83 mph changeup might be the best of the bunch, and he also works in a mid-80s cutter that looks like a gyro slider, an 82 mph curveball, and the A's taught him a sweeper in pro ball. Taylor has impressive command and his 3% walk rate in 2025 was eighth-best among Division I pitchers with 50-plus innings.
THE FUTURE: Taylor has a great sense of how his arsenal and arm slot work together. If he can sustain his velocity gains, he has back-of-the-rotation upside with a chance to move quickly through the A's system.

Year	Age	Club (League)	Level	W	L	ERA	G	GS	IP	H	HR	BB	SO	BB%	SO%	WHIP	AVG
2025	23	Las Vegas (PCL)	AAA	0	0	0.00	1	1	2	1	0	2	4	25.0	50.0	1.50	.200
		Minor League Totals		0	0	0.00	1	1	2	1	0	2	4	25.0	50.0	1.50	.200

18 GAVIN TURLEY, OF

HIT: 40. **POW:** 55. **RUN:** 55. **FLD:** 50. **ARM:** 60. **BA Grade:** 45. **Risk:** Average. **Adj:** 35.

Born: November 12, 2003. **B-T:** R-R. **HT:** 6-2. **WT:** 200. **Drafted:** Oregon State, 2025 (4th round). **Signed by:** Jim Coffman.
TRACK RECORD: The A's haven't shied away from using early draft picks on toolsy college outfielders with contact questions like Colby Thomas, Denzel Clarke and Rodney Green Jr. in recent years. Turley is the latest of that ilk. They signed him for $600,000 in the fourth round of the 2025 draft after he hit 53 homers over three seasons at Oregon State. Turley debuted with Low-A Stockton and hit .243 with four homers in 21 games along with a 27.2% strikeout rate and 11.2% walk rate.
SCOUTING REPORT: Turley is a great athlete with explosive bat speed, and he knows how to utilize his leveraged swing to create loud contact to his pull side. There's also room on his 6-foot-1, 196-pound frame for more muscle. Turley steadily cut his strikeout rate from 32.4% as a freshman to just 22.1% in his junior spring all while maintaining impressive walk rates. Still, there are questions about how much contact Turley will make as a professional—especially against breaking balls—because of how his swing works in the zone and his pitch-recognition skills. Turley's also a lively baserunner and defender. He's an above-average runner with a plus arm who may be best suited for a corner outfield spot and played mostly right field in Stockton.
THE FUTURE: Turley must prove he can make enough contact in pro ball. If he does, there's a path to an everyday corner outfield role in the mold of one-time Oregon State commit Tyler O'Neill.

Year	Age	Club (League)	Level	AVG	G	AB	R	H	2B	3B	HR	RBI	BB	SO	SB	OBP	SLG
2025	21	Stockton (CAL)	A	.243	27	107	15	26	8	0	4	20	14	34	0	.336	.430
		Minor League Totals		.243	27	107	15	26	8	0	4	20	14	34	0	.336	.430

ATHLETICS

19 JUNIOR PEREZ, OF

HIT: 30. **POW:** 60. **RUN:** 55. **FLD:** 60. **ARM:** 60. **BA Grade:** 45. **Risk:** Average. **Adj:** 35.

Born: July 4, 2001. **B-T:** R-R. **HT:** 6-1. **WT:** 200. **Signed:** Dominican Republic, 2017.
Signed by: Felix Perez/Trevor Schumm (Padres).
TRACK RECORD: Perez signed with the Padres for $300,000 in 2017 and was traded to the A's two years later for Jorge Mateo after an impressive Arizona Complex League stint. He has since taken a winding path up the ladder, which included briefly becoming a minor league free agent before returning to the A's in 2025. That reunion paid off. In his age-23 campaign, Perez hurtled back onto the organization's radar, hitting 26 homers between Double-A and Triple-A—eight more than any other A's minor leaguer.
SCOUTING REPORT: Perez is a toolshed whose strength, speed and athleticism stand out immediately. He produces top-end exit velocities and is an above-average runner who impacts games on the bases and in the field. Perez has impressive speed in the outfield even when he doesn't get the best jumps and is a potentially plus defender and thrower at all three spots. But Perez has long run hot and cold offensively because of his below-average hit tool. Despite rarely expanding the zone, Perez still missed nearly a third of the time and ran a contact rate below 70% in 2025. His leveraged swing is susceptible to plenty of in-zone whiff and to spin away. Perez closed the year on a hot streak with Triple-A Las Vegas, cutting his strikeout rate to 26.9% while blasting 12 homers in 42 games.
THE FUTURE: After an unlikely resurgence, Perez played his way back into 40-man roster consideration. He profiles as a toolsy fourth outfielder who could provide power, speed and defense off the bench.

Year	Age	Club (League)	Level	AVG	G	AB	R	H	2B	3B	HR	RBI	BB	SO	SB	OBP	SLG
2025	23	Midland (TL)	AA	.201	95	339	50	68	15	5	14	53	57	116	16	.318	.398
2025	23	Las Vegas (PCL)	AAA	.298	42	151	37	45	14	1	12	34	30	49	11	.412	.642
		Minor League Totals		.229	674	2405	402	550	137	21	83	345	378	885	175	.336	.407

20 EDUARNIEL NUÑEZ, RHP

FB: 60. **CB:** 45. **SL:** 60. **CTL:** 30. **BA Grade:** 40. **Risk:** Mild. **Adj:** 35.

Born: June 7, 1999. **B-T:** R-R. **HT:** 6-2. **WT:** 170. **Signed:** Dominican Republic, 2017.
Signed by: Mariano Encarnacion/Gian Guzman/Jose Serra (Cubs).
TRACK RECORD: Nuñez spent seven years in the Cubs system after signing in 2017, reaching Triple-A Iowa while flashing premium stuff and erratic control. The Padres signed him as a minor league free agent before the 2025 season and helped him throw enough strikes to finally reach the majors. The A's acquired him at the trade deadline in the Mason Miller-Leo De Vries deal, and he split time between Triple-A and the majors, issuing as many walks (11) as strikeouts in 12.2 big league innings across both organizations.
SCOUTING REPORT: Nuñez's electric arm talent gives him one of the best fastball-slider pairings in the organization. He has plus-plus fastball velocity at 97-99 mph and reaches 101 from a low release height that adds deception despite below-average extension. Nuñez went to an upper-80s slider entering 2025 that was a better fit for his arm slot, and it's a plus pitch that minor league hitters missed more than half the time. He relies almost entirely on those pitches, rarely using a curveball that was once a bigger part of his arsenal. Corralling his arm speed and finding consistent control remains his biggest challenge. Nuñez made progress after slightly closing off his delivery in 2025, throwing more strikes in the minors, but his strikes were more scattered in the majors.
THE FUTURE: The 26-year-old is a pure reliever with late-inning upside and up-down volatility depending on how the strikes net out.

Year	Age	Club (League)	Level	W	L	ERA	G	GS	IP	H	HR	BB	SO	BB%	SO%	WHIP	AVG
2025	26	San Antonio (TL)	AA	2	1	3.57	18	0	23	17	1	11	38	11.8	40.9	1.24	.210
2025	26	El Paso (PCL)	AAA	2	0	0.00	11	0	12	2	0	6	18	14.0	41.9	0.65	.054
2025	26	Las Vegas (PCL)	AAA	1	0	3.09	10	0	12	8	1	8	15	16.3	30.6	1.37	.205
2025	26	San Diego (NL)	MLB	0	0	3.86	4	0	5	4	1	4	2	19.0	9.5	1.71	.250
2025	26	Athletics (AL)	MLB	1	0	9.00	6	0	8	9	1	7	9	17.9	23.1	2.00	.310
		Minor League Totals		26	23	3.86	229	24	345	285	21	227	394	14.7	25.5	1.48	.224
		Major League Totals		1	0	7.41	10	0	13	13	2	11	11	18.3	18.3	1.89	.289

ATHLETICS

21 YUNIOR TUR, RHP
FB: 60. **CT:** 55. **SL:** 50. **SP:** 55. **CTL:** 40. **BA Grade:** 45. **Risk:** Average. **Adj:** 35.

Born: August 9, 1999. **B-T:** R-R. **HT:** 6-6. **WT:** 193. **Signed:** Cuba, 2022. **Signed by:** Juan Carlos De La Cruz.
TRACK RECORD: The A's signed Tur for $100,000 at the tail end of the 2022 period after a tryout out of Cuba. After spending parts of two ensuing seasons in Low-A, he broke out in 2025 when moved primarily into a starting role, climbing three levels to finish at Triple-A Las Vegas. He logged a career-high 125.2 innings with a 3.29 ERA, 24.5% strikeout rate and 11.3% walk rate.
SCOUTING REPORT: A gangly 6-foot-6 righthander, Tur's arsenal is predicated on power. His fastball jumped about 1.5 mph in 2025, now sitting mid 90s and touching 99, and added even more extension, helping the pitch carry through the zone despite a higher release. He introduced a low-to-mid-90s cutter that gives him a second above-average secondary alongside a mid-80s splitter, which is his best swing-and-miss offering. He'll also work in a solid mid-80s slider. Tur is a fringy strike-thrower who is prone to bouts of wildness. The A's twice promoted Tur with the idea of shortening his outings in relief only for him to work his way back into the rotation.
THE FUTURE: Tur's improvement in 2025 has left the door ajar for him to remain in the rotation, though a shift to the bullpen is more likely—and might help his already powerful arsenal play up, perhaps one day in high-leverage situations.

Year	Age	Club (League)	Level	W	L	ERA	G	GS	IP	H	HR	BB	SO	BB%	SO%	WHIP	AVG
2025	25	Lansing (MWL)	A+	1	3	2.98	9	9	45	40	2	20	43	10.2	21.9	1.32	.234
2025	25	Midland (TL)	AA	3	5	2.93	16	14	68	47	4	34	74	12.1	26.3	1.20	.197
2025	25	Las Vegas (PCL)	AAA	0	1	6.39	5	3	13	11	1	6	13	11.1	24.1	1.34	.234
		Minor League Totals		8	17	4.26	78	37	253	237	22	119	275	10.7	24.7	1.41	.246

22 RYAN LASKO, OF
HIT: 30. **POW:** 45. **RUN:** 60. **FLD:** 60. **ARM:** 60. **BA Grade:** 40. **Risk:** Average. **Adj:** 30.

Born: June 24, 2002. **B-T:** R-R. **HT:** 6-0. **WT:** 202. **Drafted:** Rutgers, 2023 (2nd round). **Signed by:** Ron Vaughn.
TRACK RECORD: Injuries and inconsistency have slowed Lasko's rise since the A's signed him for $1.7 million as the 41st pick in 2023. The 23-year-old missed the first month of 2025 with a soft-tissue leg injury, then played 72 games with High-A Lansing, hitting .241/.359/.339 with five homers before a late-season cameo with Triple-A Las Vegas during the Aviators' playoff run.
SCOUTING REPORT: Lasko's athleticism and high-energy, frenetic play style show up on both sides of the ball. He's a plus runner and thrower in center field who gets to balls through sheer will and occasional disregard for his body as he crashes into the outfield wall or makes diving catches. That aggressiveness can sometimes get him into trouble, and he's still ironing out his routes in center, but he projects as a plus defender at all three spots. Offensively, Lasko lags behind his defense despite solid strike-zone discipline and bat speed. He has below-average bat-to-ball skills and his contact rate has hovered near 70% in consecutive seasons. He struggles to handle premium velocity up in the zone or capitalize on hittable pitches over the plate.
THE FUTURE: While Lasko's defensive tools provide the floor of a fourth outfielder, it's hard to see much more unless his hit tool makes a big leap.

Year	Age	Club (League)	Level	AVG	G	AB	R	H	2B	3B	HR	RBI	BB	SO	SB	OBP	SLG
2025	23	ACL Athletics	Rk	.250	4	12	3	3	0	1	0	2	1	3	0	.400	.417
2025	23	Lansing (MWL)	A+	.241	72	257	44	62	8	1	5	35	41	73	12	.359	.339
2025	23	Las Vegas (PCL)	AAA	.256	13	43	5	11	1	0	1	5	4	10	2	.313	.349
		Minor League Totals		.234	222	813	125	190	37	3	12	92	128	229	48	.350	.331

23 BREYSON GUEDEZ, OF
HIT: 60. **POW:** 40. **RUN:** 45. **FLD:** 45. **ARM:** 45. **BA Grade:** 50. **Risk:** Extreme. **Adj:** 30.

Born: September 28, 2007. **B-T:** L-R. **HT:** 5-11. **WT:** 170. **Signed:** Venezuela, 2025. **Signed by:** Jose Barradas.
TRACK RECORD: Guedez was one of three A's international signees to command around $1.5 million in 2025, joining Shotaro Morii and Ayden Johnson. The Venezuelan had an impressive amateur hitting track record, representing his country in both the U-15 and U-18 World Cups, and that carried over into his pro debut in the Dominican Summer League. The 17-year-old ranked fifth among qualified hitters with a .359 average and added two home runs.
SCOUTING REPORT: The 5-foot-11, 170-pound lefthanded-hitting outfielder has a smooth swing, excellent barrel control and impressive hand-eye coordination that allowed him to make plenty of contact both inside and outside the strike zone. The A's were impressed with his discipline to use all fields and DSL

pitchers rarely beat him in the zone. Guedez can get overeager and will need to tighten his swing decisions after chasing 38% of the time. He doesn't have a ton of power or strength projection, so there will be pressure on his bat as he climbs the system, especially if he ends up in left field. Guedez is an average runner who spent all of his time in left field or right field in 2025.
THE FUTURE: Guedez is expected to make his stateside debut in the Arizona Complex League in 2026. He has the look of a contact-oriented outfielder who could hit for high averages one day with modest power if he can tighten his swing decisions.

Year	Age	Club (League)	Level	AVG	G	AB	R	H	2B	3B	HR	RBI	BB	SO	SB	OBP	SLG
2025	17	DSL Athletics	Rk	.359	53	192	38	69	15	2	2	46	14	20	5	.395	.490
		Minor League Totals		.359	53	192	38	69	15	2	2	46	14	20	5	.395	.490

24 COREY AVANT, RHP
FB: 60. **CB:** 45. **SL:** 55. **CH:** 45. **CTL:** 40. **BA Grade:** 40. **Risk:** Average. **Adj:** 30.

Born: November 6, 2001. **B-T:** R-R. **HT:** 6-3. **WT:** 212. **Drafted:** Wingate, 2023 (9th round). **Signed by:** Neil Avent.
TRACK RECORD: Avant arrived at Division II Wingate University as a two-way player and teammate of future Nationals first-rounder Seaver King. After moving full-time to the mound, he mostly worked in relief before the A's selected him in the ninth round of the 2023 draft. His first full pro season in 2024 was rocky (7.39 ERA), but he took a clear step forward in 2025, forcing his way into the High-A Lansing and posting a 3.65 ERA over 106 innings before finishing the year in Double-A.
SCOUTING REPORT: Avant's stuff jumped in 2025. His firmer mid-90s fastball touched 99 with better shape, carry and impressive spin rates from an above-average extension. He also added roughly 3 mph to a mid-80s slider that flashes above-average shape and two-plane break, and his low-80s curveball got nearly as many misses, though he struggled to throw it for strikes. Avant had much better feel for landing his firm low-90s changeup in the zone. While he's fairly athletic, Avant's operation has some effort and he was a below-average strike-thrower even after cutting his 10.5% walk rate down from 13.5% in 2024.
THE FUTURE: While he improved his chances of sticking as a starter, Avant's impressive fastball and limited control may ultimately work best—and play up—in a multi-inning or late-inning role in the upper minors and beyond.

Year	Age	Club (League)	Level	W	L	ERA	G	GS	IP	H	HR	BB	SO	BB%	SO%	WHIP	AVG
2025	23	Lansing (MWL)	A+	6	6	3.65	29	21	106	93	3	48	101	10.7	22.4	1.33	.239
2025	23	Midland (TL)	AA	0	0	17.36	2	1	5	10	3	2	3	8.3	12.5	2.57	.455
		Minor League Totals		9	13	5.49	68	28	185	203	13	103	187	12.1	22.0	1.65	.281

25 CLARK ELLIOTT, OF
HIT: 50. **POW:** 50. **RUN:** 50. **FLD:** 40. **ARM:** 45. **BA Grade:** 40. **Risk:** Average. **Adj:** 30.

Born: September 29, 2000. **B-T:** L-R. **HT:** 5-11. **WT:** 197. **Drafted:** Michigan, 2022 (2nd round supp.).
Signed by: Rich Sparks.
TRACK RECORD: Elliott parlayed a productive Cape Cod League summer into a strong junior season at Michigan, hitting .337 with 16 home runs in 2022. The A's selected him in the second round that year, but his first two pro seasons were marred by injuries and diminished production. He rebounded in 2025, his age-24 season, batting .251/.395/.422 with 12 home runs and a 16.8% walk rate against a 20.1% strikeout rate across 117 games between High-A Lansing and Double-A Midland.
SCOUTING REPORT: Though not overly physical at 5-foot-11, 197 pounds, Elliott has long geared his swing to maximize pulled contact. Early in his career, that approach led to too many rollovers as he tried to ambush pitchers early in counts. Elliott made adjustments entering 2025, including lowering his hands and setting the bat more vertically pre-pitch, and saw his in-zone contact improve while maintaining excellent swing decisions. As a result, he was particularly effective on pitches on the inner third, especially fastballs, though there are still some holes, particularly on the outer third. Elliott is a good baserunner but has fringy secondary skills and is likely a corner outfielder, so there's pressure on his improvements at the plate to stick.
THE FUTURE: Elliott reestablished himself as a viable upper-minors depth piece for 2026 and has a chance to grow into a reserve outfielder if his approach and contact gains hold.

Year	Age	Club (League)	Level	AVG	G	AB	R	H	2B	3B	HR	RBI	BB	SO	SB	OBP	SLG
2025	24	Lansing (MWL)	A+	.236	42	127	24	30	7	2	4	21	33	30	7	.413	.417
2025	24	Midland (TL)	AA	.259	75	259	41	67	13	3	8	32	48	67	9	.386	.425
		Minor League Totals		.250	270	895	160	224	39	10	20	118	169	223	36	.386	.383

ATHLETICS

26 KENYA HUGGINS, RHP
FB: 55. **SL:** 60. **CH:** 45. **CTL:** 40. **BA Grade:** 45. **Risk:** High. **Adj:** 30.

Born: December 12, 2002. **B-T:** R-R. **HT:** 6-3. **WT:** 247. **Drafted:** Chipola (FL) JC, 2022 (4th round). **Signed by:** Sean Buckley (Reds).

TRACK RECORD: The Reds drafted Huggins in the fourth round in 2022 out of Chipola (Fla.) JC, but Tommy John surgery in 2023 limited him to just 43.2 innings entering 2025. He returned to Low-A Daytona for a third stint and posted a 3.69 ERA over 63.1 innings before the A's acquired him at the trade deadline in the Miguel Andujar deal and assigned him to High-A Lansing.
SCOUTING REPORT: Huggins has long shown premium arm strength. His fastball averaged 93 mph in 2025, sat 95-96 at times in Lansing and touched 97. He pairs the velocity with plus extension and a high release that creates unusual angles. His upper-80s slider flashes plus and was his most effective offering in 2025. Huggins emerged from rehab in better shape and reintroduced an upper-80s changeup. The pitch is less refined but intriguing, generating whiffs nearly half the time, and the A's believe it has room to grow. They may also look to add another breaking ball. Huggins walked 10.1% of hitters and his fairly rigid delivery and arm stroke inhibited his strike-throwing.
THE FUTURE: Huggins entered the offseason Rule 5-eligible but has yet to reach the upper minors. His 2025 progress and unusual release traits give him a chance to remain on a starter track for at least another season, though his fastball-slider combination could play up in relief.

Year	Age	Club (League)	Level	W	L	ERA	G	GS	IP	H	HR	BB	SO	BB%	SO%	WHIP	AVG
2025	22	Daytona (FSL)	A	2	2	3.69	18	15	63	44	3	26	57	10.2	22.4	1.11	.196
2025	22	Lansing (MWL)	A+	0	1	4.30	6	6	15	15	2	6	15	9.5	23.8	1.43	.263
		Minor League Totals		3	6	4.04	39	28	114	99	7	54	118	11.1	24.3	1.35	.232

27 KYLE ROBINSON, RHP
FB: 50. **CB:** 50. **SL:** 40. **CH:** 55. **SP:** 60. **CTL:** 40. **BA Grade:** 40. **Risk:** Average. **Adj:** 30.

Born: July 17, 2003. **B-T:** R-R. **HT:** 6-6. **WT:** 210. **Drafted:** Texas Tech, 2024 (11th round). **Signed by:** Fletcher Byrd.

TRACK RECORD: Robinson was a three-year contributor at Texas Tech and ranked No. 101 in the 2024 draft class, yet fell to the A's in the 11th round. The 21-year-old opened 2025 with High-A Lansing and fared well, pitching to a 3.99 ERA in 70 innings, then went 1-6, 5.29 in 51 innings with Double-A Midland, where his walk rate spiked to 13.5% before he was sent back to Lansing.
SCOUTING REPORT: A 6-foot-6 righthander, Robinson's 93-96 mph fastball seemingly descends out of the clouds from a vertical arm slot not all that dissimilar from Blue Jays righty Trey Yesavage. His best secondary is a borderline plus, low-80s kick changeup with sub-900 rpm spin that dives straight down, and he also throws a more traditional changeup. A solid upper-70s curveball with 15-plus inches of downward break and a mid-80s gyro slider round out a distinctly north-south arsenal. However, the absence of a reliable gloveside weapon was exposed in Double-A, especially against righthanded hitters, and he was just a fringy strike-thrower who works with some crossfire action in his delivery.
THE FUTURE: Robinson's unusual downhill angle helps his fastball-changeup combination, but to stick in a rotation he'll need to go back to the drawing board to sharpen his breaking stuff. He should get another crack at Double-A Midland in 2026.

Year	Age	Club (League)	Level	W	L	ERA	G	GS	IP	H	HR	BB	SO	BB%	SO%	WHIP	AVG
2025	21	Lansing (MWL)	A+	5	6	3.99	14	10	70	72	6	22	50	7.5	17.0	1.34	.268
2025	21	Midland (TL)	AA	1	6	5.29	11	10	51	56	4	31	37	13.5	16.1	1.71	.286
		Minor League Totals		6	12	4.71	28	22	128	137	11	56	96	10.0	17.2	1.51	.277

28 COLE MILLER, RHP
FB: 45. **SL:** 55. **CH:** 55. **CTL:** 60. **BA Grade:** 45. **Risk:** High. **Adj:** 30.

Born: October 19, 2002. **B-T:** R-R. **HT:** 6-6. **WT:** 225. **Drafted:** HS—Thousand Oaks, CA, 2023 (4th round). **Signed by:** Dillon Tung.

TRACK RECORD: The A's gave Miller $1 million out of high school in the fourth round of the 2023 draft, but Tommy John surgery delayed his pro debut until 2025. The 20-year-old showed impressive guile with Low-A Stockton, pitching to a 1.56 ERA in 40.1 innings even though his stuff hasn't returned to pre-injury levels. His older brother, Jake, is a reliever in the Guardians system.
SCOUTING REPORT: Miller's sinking fastball sat 90-92 mph and touched 95 prior to elbow surgery. In 2025, his heater hovered around 90 mph in Stockton, maxing out at 92 with considerable armside run, yet he still managed to strike out 21.4% of hitters. He didn't nibble, either, walking just 5.2% of hitters while landing all three of his pitches for strikes roughly 65% of the time. Miller was quite comfortable

leaning on his pitchability, as well as his low-to-mid-80s changeup and slider to get swings and misses. Miller has a big 6-foot-6 frame and the A's are hopeful another year removed from surgery coupled with some biomechanical tweaks to help regain some rhythm and power in his delivery will help his velocity tick back up in 2026.
THE FUTURE: If his stuff returns, Miller has back-of-the-rotation upside as a groundball-oriented right-hander who can lean on a polished three-pitch mix. He should reach High-A Lansing by the end of 2026.

Year	Age	Club (League)	Level	W	L	ERA	G	GS	IP	H	HR	BB	SO	BB%	SO%	WHIP	AVG
2025	20	ACL Athletics	Rk	0	2	3.09	4	3	12	12	0	3	9	6.1	18.4	1.29	.261
2025	20	Stockton (CAL)	A	1	2	1.56	11	9	40	33	1	8	36	5.0	22.4	1.02	.221
		Minor League Totals		1	4	1.90	15	12	52	45	1	11	45	5.2	21.4	1.08	.231

DARWING OZUNA, OF

HIT: 40. **POW:** 70. **RUN:** 40. **FLD:** 50. **ARM:** 70. **BA Grade:** 50. **Risk:** Extreme. **Adj:** 30.

Born: March 24, 2008. **B-T:** R-R. **HT:** 6-3. **WT:** 190. **Signed:** Dominican Republic, 2025.
Signed by: Juan Carlos De La Cruz/Fernando Encarnacion.
TRACK RECORD: Ozuna was one of four big-money signings in the Athletics' 2025 international class, inking a $1 million bonus out of the Dominican Republic. The 17-year-old made his pro debut that summer. A nagging hamate injury limited him to 35 games and a .211/.301/.311 line with two homers.
SCOUTING REPORT: Ozuna's surface-level production in his pro debut belies his power potential. At 6-foot-3, 190 pounds with a high-waisted frame, Ozuna oozes physicality and has a chance to grow into plus-plus raw power. The teenager is already producing some of the louder exit velocities of any hitter in the system thanks to his strength and bat speed. He's likely a power-over-hit profile in the long run thanks to his longer levers, raw approach and willingness to expand the zone. Ozuna has a second plus tool on his card: an easy plus throwing arm that should fit comfortably in a corner outfield position as he matures and slows down.
THE FUTURE: His hit tool needs plenty of maturation, but Ozuna has the look of a classic corner masher with an impressive combination of size, power and impact potential. The A's were tempted to bring him stateside in 2025. Instead, they'll hope he takes an Edgar Montero-like step forward in his second go-around in rookie ball in 2026.

Year	Age	Club (League)	Level	AVG	G	AB	R	H	2B	3B	HR	RBI	BB	SO	SB	OBP	SLG
2025	17	DSL Athletics	Rk	.211	35	90	12	19	3	0	2	11	9	25	2	.301	.311
		Minor League Totals		.211	35	90	12	19	3	0	2	11	9	25	2	.301	.311

CHEN ZHONG-AO ZHUANG, RHP

FB: 45. **CB:** 45. **SL:** 45. **CH:** 55. **CTL:** 60. **BA Grade:** 35. **Risk:** Mild. **Adj:** 30.

Born: August 25, 2000. **B-T:** R-R. **HT:** 6-1. **WT:** 200. **Signed:** Taiwan, 2021. **Signed by:** Adam Hislop.
TRACK RECORD: Zhuang signed at 21 years old out of Taiwan in 2021 and logged just 42 professional innings prior to 2024 because of a finger injury and elbow surgery. He put himself on the Athletics' radar by spanning three levels that season, then returned to Double-A Midland in 2025, where he went 6-11, 4.08 with a 23.5% strikeout rate to 5.7% walk rate over 145.2 innings, the eighth-most of any minor leaguer. The A's added Zhuang to their 40-man roster in November.
SCOUTING REPORT: Zhuang can generate impressive spin rates and has a penchant for filling up the strike zone with a deep arsenal. His four-seam fastball fluctuates anywhere from 88-96 mph and averaged around 92 in 2025. He commands it well, although it doesn't have a ton of life. His best swing-and-miss offering is a low-80s changeup that flashes plus with over 17 inches of armside fade. Zhuang also has two distinct secondaries: a low-80s slider and a mid-70s curveball that averaged nearly 2,900 rpm. He'll also dabble with a separate splitter. Zhuang is a precise strike-thrower, but evaluators have concerns that he's homer-prone and his stuff won't consistently miss bats in the big leagues.
THE FUTURE: Holding up over a full season was a big step for Zhuang, who has the command and pitch mix to profile as an up-down starter.

Year	Age	Club (League)	Level	W	L	ERA	G	GS	IP	H	HR	BB	SO	BB%	SO%	WHIP	AVG
2025	24	Midland (TL)	AA	6	11	4.08	28	26	146	151	22	35	145	5.7	23.5	1.28	.262
		Minor League Totals		12	17	3.55	59	49	274	261	36	56	272	4.9	23.9	1.16	.245

Drake Baldwin

Atlanta Braves

BY CARLOS COLLAZO

The 2025 season will be one to forget for the Braves.

For the first time since 2017, and for the first time under the direction of eighth-year president of baseball operations Alex Anthopoulos, the Braves had a losing record at 76-86 and finished fourth in an increasingly competitive National League East.

Manager Brian Snitker moved into an advisory role with the team after the season, and Walt Weiss, Snitker's bench coach, was named manager for the 2026 season.

Atlanta's nucleus of young hitters under team control isn't quite so young anymore, and continued durability questions surrounding superstars Ronald Acuña Jr. and Spencer Strider have put additional pressure on the rest of the roster to fill the gaps.

To that end, the emergence of rookie catcher and former top prospect Drake Baldwin was perhaps the most exciting development from the farm system in 2025. The 2022 third-round pick won NL Rookie of the Year after hitting .274/.341/.469 with 10 home runs, a 125 wRC+ and more than three wins above replacement, no matter the source.

In addition to the value Baldwin will continue to add as a hitter and catcher on the major league team, his ROY win netted the Braves their first-ever Prospect Promotion Incentive pick. It will fall at No. 26 overall, immediately after the first round of the 2026 draft.

The 2026 draft is shaping up to be pivotal for the organization. The Braves didn't find much luck in the draft lottery, but their ninth overall pick will represent the highest the team has drafted since 2019, when they selected Baylor catcher Shea Langeliers ninth overall.

Ronit Shah, who was promoted to VP of amateur scouting in January 2025, will lead the team's scouting efforts for the third year with more pick

PROJECTED 2029 LINEUP

Catcher	Drake Baldwin	28
First Base	Matt Olson	35
Second Base	John Gil	23
Third Base	Austin Riley	32
Shortstop	Alex Lodise	25
Left Field	Conor Essenburg	22
Center Field	Michael Harris II	28
Right Field	Diego Tornes	20
Designated Hitter	Ronald Acuña Jr.	31
No. 1 Starter	Spencer Strider	30
No. 2 Starter	Spencer Schwellenbach	29
No. 3 Starter	AJ Smith-Shawver	26
No. 4 Starter	Cam Caminiti	22
No. 5 Starter	JR Ritchie	26
Closer	Hurston Waldrep	26

capital than he has ever had. Atlanta attacked hitters at the top of the 2025 draft in a way that has been uncommon for the organization over the last decade.

The Braves opened the 2025 draft with three consecutive shortstops in prep Tate Southisene and collegians Alex Lodise and Cody Miller across the first three rounds.

Despite that, Atlanta's farm system remains light on hitting talent. Its full-season minor league hitters ranked dead last among all clubs in hits, home runs and OPS (.633).

Pitching is a different story. All five of the Braves' top prospects are pitchers, led by electric lefthander Cam Caminiti.

The Braves have been one of the most productive pitching factories in the sport for years, driven both by a high-volume pitcher acquisition strategy and by the development work overseen by former director of pitching Paul Davis. The Braves moved on from Davis after the season, so monitoring how effective the organization remains on the pitching side will be something to watch.

For years, the Braves have had little to show from the international market, but 2025 Cuban signee Diego Tornes cracks the top 10 and boasts some of the most exciting and explosive physical tools of any hitter in the system—though he's years away from impacting the major league team. ∎

DEPTH CHART

ATLANTA BRAVES

TOP 2026 ROOKIES — RANK
1. JR Ritchie, RHP — 2
2. Didier Fuentes, RHP — 3
3. Lucas Braun, RHP — 7

BREAKOUT PROSPECTS — RANK
1. Conor Essenburg, OF — 15
2. Eric Hartman, OF — 24
3. Owen Carey, OF — 29

SOURCE OF TOP 30 TALENT

Homegrown	28	Acquired	2
College	11	Trade	1
Junior college	1	Rule 5 draft	1
High school	10	Independent league	0
Undrafted free agent	1	Free agent/waivers	0
International	5		

LF
Owen Carey (29)
Logan Braunschweig
Ethan Workinger

CF
Eric Hartman (24)
Isaiah Drake (25)
Patrick Clohisy (28)
Luis Guanipa

RF
Diego Tornes (10)
Conor Essenburg (15)
Douglas Glod

3B
Cody Miller (19)
EJ Exposito

SS
Alex Lodise (6)
John Gil (12)
Tate Southisene (13)
Jim Jarvis (26)
Jose Perdomo

2B
Dixon Williams (23)
Luke Waddell
Ambioris Tavarez

1B
David McCabe (20)
Juan Espinal
Drew Compton

C
Adam Zebrowski
Tyler Tolve
Nick Montgomery

LHP

LHSP
Cam Caminiti (1)
Briggs McKenzie (5)
Herick Hernandez (11)
Landon Beidelschies (20)
Riley Frey

LHRP
Hayden Harris (16)
Carter Holton
Jacob Kroeger

RHP

RHSP
JR Ritchie (2)
Didier Fuentes (3)
Owen Murphy (4)
Lucas Braun (7)
Garrett Baumann (8)
Luke Sinnard (9)
Cedric De Grandpre (21)
Brett Sears (30)
Drue Hackenberg
Zach Royce
Jacob Shafer
Dayner Matos
Aiven Cabral
Rayven Antonio

RHRP
Blake Burkhalter (14)
Rolddy Muñoz (17)
Jhancarlos Lara (22)
Blane Abeyta (28)
Cory Wall
Landon Harper
Raudy Reyes
LJ Mcdonough
Trent Buchanan

ATLANTA BRAVES

1 CAM CAMINITI, LHP

Born: August 8, 2006. **B-T:** L-L. **HT:** 6-2. **WT:** 195.
Drafted: HS—Scottsdale, AZ, 2024 (1st round).
Signed by: Anthony Flora.

TRACK RECORD: Caminiti was the top-ranked high school pitcher in the 2024 class and signed with the Braves for $3,553,800 as the organization's first pick at No. 24 overall. A former two-way player with impressive raw power in high school, Caminiti is now a full-time pitcher and turned in an electric 2025 campaign, primarily with Low-A Augusta. He missed two months of the season with forearm tendinitis. He got on the mound in May, threw a handful of tuneup games in the Florida Complex League, then posted a 2.08 ERA and 31.9% strikeout rate in 56.1 innings and 13 starts with Augusta. Among minor league pitchers who were 18 or younger with at least 50 innings, Caminiti ranked third with 90 strikeouts and fourth in strikeout rate. He's a cousin of the late Ken Caminiti.

BA GRADE
60 Risk: High
Adjusted grade: **45**

SCOUTING GRADES
FB: 60. SL: 55.
CH: 55. CTL: 55.
Projected future grades on 20-80 scouting scale

SCOUTING REPORT: Caminiti has a lean and athletic frame at 6-foot-2, 195 pounds. He creates a tough angle for hitters by working from the first base side of the rubber and throwing across his body with a low release height. Caminiti lowered his arm slot in 2025 and simultaneously added a bit of extension, which helped his four-seam fastball play better at the top of the zone. He went from a two-seam grip in high school to a four-seam grip with the Braves, and in 2025 averaged 93-94 mph and touched 97. The flat nature of the pitch combined with its power should allow it to be at least a plus offering, and he did an excellent job using it to attack the strike zone and get ahead in counts. While the fastball is the centerpiece of Caminiti's arsenal, he has flashed exciting secondaries as well. He got plenty of whiffs on both his slider and changeup against Low-A hitters in 2025. He throws a low-80s, sweeping slider as his go-to secondary pitch. It grades well analytically and can be a nightmare for lefthanded hitters, but it needs more consistency. The Braves are hoping he can add a harder and shorter breaking ball, such as a gyro slider, in the future. Caminiti started throwing a kick changeup in 2025. The pitch sits in the 85-88 mph range with solid armside life and occasional splitter-like depth at its best. It was a reliable miss and chase offering at the lower levels, but it remains a work in progress that Caminiti will need to locate more consistently after he threw it for strikes less than half the time in 2025.

THE FUTURE: Caminiti is the highest-upside arm in Atlanta's system and has the stuff to become a solid No. 3-type starter who pitches a shade better than that on his best days. Those most excited about Caminiti's future could envision a Chris Sale-esque low-slot lefty who dominates with a fastball and slider. While his upside is tantalizing, Caminiti still has a long way to go. After dominating Low-A, he should be ready to start the 2026 season with High-A Rome, where adding command and consistency to his secondaries and potentially deepening his arsenal will be developmental keys.

BEST TOOLS

BATTING
Best Hitter	Diego Tornes
Best Power Hitter	Conor Essenburg
Best Strike-Zone Discipline	John Gil
Fastest Baserunner	Isaiah Drake
Best Athlete	Diego Tornes

PITCHING
Best Fastball	Owen Murphy
Best Curveball	Briggs McKenzie
Best Slider	Jhancarlos Lara
Best Changeup	Briggs McKenzie
Best Control	Lucas Braun

FIELDING
Best Defensive Catcher	Tyler Tolve
Best Defensive Infielder	Alex Lodise
Best Infield Arm	Alex Lodise
Best Defensive Outfielder	Eric Hartman
Best Outfield Arm	Diego Tornes

Year	Age	Club (League)	Level	W	L	ERA	G	GS	IP	H	HR	BB	SO	BB%	SO%	WHIP	AVG
2025	18	FCL Braves	Rk	0	1	7.24	4	4	14	17	4	2	15	3.3	25.0	1.39	.298
2025	18	Augusta (CAR)	A	2	3	2.08	13	13	56	43	1	26	75	11.1	31.9	1.22	.210
		Minor League Totals		2	5	3.08	18	18	73	63	5	28	94	9.1	30.6	1.25	.230

ATLANTA BRAVES

2 JR RITCHIE, RHP
FB: 50. **CB:** 50. **SL:** 55. **CH:** 50. **CT:** 50. **SW:** 50. **CTL:** 50. **BA Grade:** 55. **Risk:** Average. **Adj:** 45.

Born: June 26, 2003. **B-T:** R-R. **HT:** 6-2. **WT:** 185.
Drafted: HS—Bainbridge Island, WA, 2022 (1st round supp.). **Signed by:** Cody Martin.
TRACK RECORD: Ritchie signed with the Braves for $2.4 million as the 35th overall pick in the 2022 draft as a cerebral three-pitch righty with polish beyond his years. He dealt with Tommy John surgery and recovery in 2023 and 2024 but had a strong 2025 season. Ritchie threw 140 innings—a top 15 mark among minor league pitchers—across three levels and posted a 2.64 ERA and 24.8% strikeout rate. He started the Futures Game at Truist Park and was the Braves' 2025 minor league player of the year.
SCOUTING REPORT: Ritchie continues to stand out for his advanced feel to pitch, but his arsenal today looks nothing like it did when he was drafted. Previously a fastball/slider/changeup pitcher, Ritchie now throws seven unique pitches and has an uncanny ability to separate them and manipulate his arsenal seemingly overnight. Ritchie averaged 93.5 mph with his four-seam fastball and touched 96-97. He also throws a two-seam fastball with similar power, an upper-80s changeup, a low-80s curveball, a mid-80s gyro slider, a sweeper that's a tick or two softer and a cutter around 90 mph that pushes 92. Ritchie is comfortable landing his entire mix. While that could be enough to keep hitters off-balance, he lacks a true wipeout offering. In the past, his gyro slider was a swing-and-miss pitch, but it backed up in 2025 to the point where Ritchie threw it less in the second half of the season. Rediscovering that breaking ball or adding more velocity—perhaps by doing a better job sitting into his back leg in his delivery—could help him find another gear.
THE FUTURE: Ritchie is nearing his big league debut and has the tools to be a solid No. 4 starter. He could get an MLB opportunity in 2026.

Year	Age	Club (League)	Level	W	L	ERA	G	GS	IP	H	HR	BB	SO	BB%	SO%	WHIP	AVG
2025	22	Rome (SAL)	A+	4	1	1.30	7	7	42	23	3	10	38	6.4	24.2	0.79	.161
2025	22	Columbus (SL)	AA	1	3	3.49	8	8	39	26	4	17	41	10.4	25.0	1.11	.181
2025	22	Gwinnett (IL)	AAA	3	2	3.02	11	11	60	38	5	27	61	11.1	25.1	1.09	.181
		Minor League Totals		9	11	2.78	45	44	207	136	17	77	227	9.2	27.2	1.03	.184

3 DIDIER FUENTES, RHP
FB: 60. **CB:** 45. **SL:** 50. **CH:** 40. **CTL:** 55. **BA Grade:** 50. **Risk:** Average. **Adj:** 40.

Born: June 17, 2005. **B-T:** R-R. **HT:** 6-0. **WT:** 170.
Signed: Colombia, 2022. **Signed by:** Orlando Covo.
TRACK RECORD: Fuentes signed with the Braves out of Colombia in 2022 without much fanfare, but he elevated his stock as a pro thanks to a strong combination of strikes and fastball life. He pitched effectively at three minor league levels in his age-20 season in 2025, but struggled with fastball location and home runs in his first four major league starts in June and July.
SCOUTING REPORT: Fuentes has a solid frame with more physicality than his official 6-foot, 170-pound frame indicates. He attacks hitters from a low release point and does a nice job getting off the rubber with above-average extension—which helps him throw one of the flattest fastballs in the game. Fuentes added nearly a tick and a half to his fastball velocity and averaged 94.7 mph while touching 98-99. The pitch has both power and life that makes it a swing-and-miss heater at its best, but its shape is reliant on him pounding the upper third of the strike zone and above. Fuentes' brief major league stint showed what could happen to his fastball when he put it in the heart of the zone too often—namely, an .886 opponent slugging percentage and six home runs allowed in just 13 innings. Sharpening his fastball command will be important, as will developing secondaries to keep hitters from sitting on his fastball. Fuentes has toyed with both a sweeper and gyro slider, as well as an 80-83 mph curveball with more depth and an upper-80s splitter. He has a strong track record as an above-average strike-thrower, though his command is not yet at that level.
THE FUTURE: In 2026, Fuentes will pitch as a 21-year-old who has outlier fastball traits and a solid control foundation. His future role will depend on his secondary development and fastball command.

Year	Age	Club (League)	Level	W	L	ERA	G	GS	IP	H	HR	BB	SO	BB%	SO%	WHIP	AVG
2025	20	Rome (SAL)	A+	0	1	5.54	3	3	13	8	0	5	18	9.4	34.0	1.00	.186
2025	20	Columbus (SL)	AA	0	5	4.98	5	5	22	21	1	7	24	7.3	25.0	1.29	.250
2025	20	Gwinnett (IL)	AAA	1	1	3.63	5	5	22	20	3	4	29	4.5	32.6	1.07	.238
2025	20	Atlanta (NL)	MLB	0	3	13.85	4	4	13	23	6	6	12	8.7	17.4	2.23	.383
		Minor League Totals		5	18	3.73	52	48	203	172	20	59	246	7.1	29.6	1.14	.230
		Major League Totals		0	3	13.85	4	4	13	23	6	6	12	8.7	17.4	2.23	.383

ATLANTA BRAVES

4 OWEN MURPHY, RHP

FB: 60. **CB:** 45. **SL:** 55. **CTL:** 50. **BA Grade:** 55. **Risk:** High. **Adj:** 40.

Born: September 27, 2003. **B-T:** R-R. **HT:** 6-1. **WT:** 190.
Drafted: HS—Riverside, IL, 2022 (1st round). **Signed by:** Jeremy Gordon.
TRACK RECORD: Murphy starred as a two-way player at his suburban Chicago high school as a shortstop/righthander. He signed for $2,556,900 as Atlanta's first-round pick in 2022 and has pitched well whenever he's been on the mound. A Tommy John surgery cut short a potential breakout season in 2024, but Murphy returned to the mound in late July 2025 and continued posting. He had a 1.19 ERA in 30.1 innings between Rookie ball and Low-A with a 25.5 K-BB% that was second-best in the Braves' system among pitchers with at least 30 innings.
SCOUTING REPORT: Murphy is a 6-foot-1, 190-pound righthander who works with a clean delivery and three-quarters slot. He primarily works with a three-pitch mix led by a 90-92 mph fastball. His four-seam fastball was down about a half tick of velocity in 2025, and he averaged just under 91 mph while touching 94. The pitch is light on power but has always played up thanks to tremendous riding life and a flat approach angle. The shape of Murphy's fastball could allow it to be effective in the majors even with below-average power, though adding more velocity remains a crucial goal. Murphy throws a mid-80s slider that lacks depth but has solid gloveside action, as well as a downer curveball in the mid 70s. The Braves were happy with his slider progress, and he threw the pitch more frequently compared to 2024. Murphy is also experimenting with a kick changeup, but he's yet to fully break the pitch out in games. He's an above-average athlete and an average strike-thrower who has always done a nice job attacking the top of the zone with his fastball.
THE FUTURE: Murphy's post-surgery 2025 season was a success. Now he needs to find a way to add more power to his mix and show he can miss bats in the upper minors. He has back-end starter upside.

Year	Age	Club (League)	Level	W	L	ERA	G	GS	IP	H	HR	BB	SO	BB%	SO%	WHIP	AVG
2025	21	FCL Braves	Rk	0	0	0.00	1	1	3	0	0	0	5	0.0	55.6	0.00	.000
2025	21	Rome (SAL)	A+	3	0	1.32	6	6	27	15	1	6	29	5.9	28.7	0.77	.161
		Minor League Totals		13	7	3.33	40	40	173	123	12	56	224	8.0	32.2	1.03	.197

5 BRIGGS McKENZIE, LHP

FB: 50. **CB:** 60. **CH:** 55. **CTL:** 50. **BA Grade:** 55. **Risk:** High. **Adj:** 40.

Born: October 11, 2006. **B-T:** L-L. **HT:** 6-2. **WT:** 190.
Drafted: HS—Wendell, NC, 2025 (4th round). **Signed by:** Al Skorupa.
TRACK RECORD: McKenzie ranked as the No. 46 prospect in the 2025 draft and signed an over-slot deal with the Braves for $2,997,500 in the fourth round—the largest bonus in Atlanta's class. McKenzie was an up-arrow prospect early in the spring with his Corinth Holders High team in North Carolina. He showed improved fastball velocity and a refined changeup, but his velocity was inconsistent closer to the draft. He threw at instructional league but not in official games after signing.
SCOUTING REPORT: McKenzie is a lanky 6-foot-2, 190-pound lefthander with a smooth delivery that features a lengthy arm action and a cross-body finish. He's been up to 95 mph with his fastball—and touched 94 mph in instructs—but his average velocity comes and goes and can sit in the low 90s or upper 80s depending on the start. He has great aptitude to spin a breaking pitch with huge spin rates. McKenzie's curveball sits 75-79 mph and routinely gets into the 3,000 rpm range with great depth and biting action at its best. It would be unsurprising if he developed that breaking ball into more of a classic sweeper slider as he adds more strength and power. The development of his mid-80s changeup this spring was key in pushing him up draft boards, and was a pitch Braves officials were enamored of after signing him. He uses a circle change grip that he holds deep in his hand and generates hellacious depth at its best. It has high-end bat-missing potential as he learns to land it with more consistency. McKenzie has been a solid strike-thrower, but the length of his arm action could inhibit his command.
THE FUTURE: McKenzie is slated to pitch at Low-A Augusta in 2026. He has the tools to become a solid No. 3 or 4 starter but has a long way to go. His workmanlike makeup and coachable mindset are assets along the way.

Year	Age	Club (League)	Level	W	L	ERA	G	GS	IP	H	HR	BB	SO	BB%	SO%	WHIP	AVG
2025	18	Did not play															

ATLANTA BRAVES

6 ALEX LODISE, SS

HIT: 40. **POW:** 55. **RUN:** 50. **FLD:** 50. **ARM:** 60. **BA Grade:** 55. **Risk:** High. **Adj:** 40.

Born: March 10, 2004. **B-T:** R-R. **HT:** 6-1. **WT:** 190.
Drafted: Florida State, 2025 (2nd round). **Signed by:** Jon Bunnell.
TRACK RECORD: Lodise was one of the best players in college baseball in 2025, when he was the Atlantic Coast Conference player of the year after hitting .394/.462/.705 with 17 home runs and 18 doubles for Florida State. He ranked as the No. 26 prospect in the class but fell to the second round, where the Braves signed him to a $1,297,500 bonus. Lodise played 25 games with High-A Rome after signing and hit .252/.294/.398 with a 38.5% strikeout rate and 4.6% walk rate.
SCOUTING REPORT: Listed at 6-foot-1, 190 pounds, Lodise is a strong and physical athlete who packs a punch at the plate and likes to swing the bat—a lot. He's an aggressive hitter who swung 53% of the time in his three-year college career and then 54% of the time in his pro debut. That aggression leads to lots of chases as well. Lodise will need to become more selective, and the Braves are also hoping a few mechanical tweaks will help him make contact more in different parts of the zone. Without improving in this area, Lodise could be a streaky hitter who doesn't walk much—he had a sub-10% walk rate in college—and is reliant on how often he can turn on the ball for extra-base damage. He's a solid runner and potentially underrated defender at shortstop. He has better lateral range than his speed might indicate and has a plus arm that helps him make difficult plays from deep positions in the hole. He also has solid arm versatility and is comfortable throwing on the run and from different slots.
THE FUTURE: Lodise has everyday upside as a pull-side power hitter with the defensive chops to stick at shortstop. Whether he gets to that upside depends heavily on the progress he can make with his approach and contact.

Year	Age	Club (League)	Level	AVG	G	AB	R	H	2B	3B	HR	RBI	BB	SO	SB	OBP	SLG
2025	21	Rome (SAL)	A+	.252	25	103	11	26	10	1	1	9	5	42	2	.294	.398
		Minor League Totals		.252	25	103	11	26	10	1	1	9	5	42	2	.294	.398

7 LUCAS BRAUN, RHP

FB: 45. **CB:** 45. **SL:** 50. **CH:** 45. **CT:** 50. **CTL:** 55. **BA Grade:** 45. **Risk:** Mild. **Adj:** 40.

Born: August 26, 2001. **B-T:** R-R. **HT:** 6-0. **WT:** 185.
Drafted: Cal State Northridge, 2023 (6th round). **Signed by:** Kevin Martin.
TRACK RECORD: Braun has been a reliable starter and strike-thrower for the Braves since he signed as a sixth-rounder out of Cal State Northridge for $347,500 in 2023. In each of the last two seasons he eclipsed the 140-inning mark, and in 2025 he posted a 3.67 ERA in 26 starts and 149.2 innings between Double-A Columbus and Triple-A Gwinnett. Braun's 145 strikeouts were the most in Atlanta's system.
SCOUTING REPORT: Braun is a 6-foot, 185-pound righthander who works out of the stretch and sets up on the third base side of the rubber. He continued to add pitches to his arsenal in 2025 and now has six distinct offerings. Braun's four-seam fastball sits 92-93 mph and touches 95, but he also worked in a two-seam fastball much more frequently compared to the 2024 season. His go-to pitch at this point is a mid-80s sweeping slider, which gets heavy usage and is his most consistent swing-and-miss offering. Braun has also worked to implement an 87-91 mph cutter and continues to throw a softer, downer curveball at 78-82 mph and an upper-80s changeup with increased usage versus lefties. Nothing Braun throws is plus. Instead, he relies on his advanced control and command—the best in the system—and an ability to mix and match. Braun's fastball command has always been a strength, and his career 6.7% walk rate points to above-average control.
THE FUTURE: The Braves are hoping there's a bit more velocity to be found with Braun that could unlock a bit more upside. An optimistic outlook could be a Chris Bassitt-like pitcher who finds success with below-average velocity by throwing the kitchen sink with good control. Braun should be ready to help the major league team in 2026, which will be his 40-man roster evaluation season.

Year	Age	Club (League)	Level	W	L	ERA	G	GS	IP	H	HR	BB	SO	BB%	SO%	WHIP	AVG
2025	23	Columbus (SL)	AA	5	5	3.99	24	23	131	110	19	35	134	6.6	25.1	1.11	.225
2025	23	Gwinnett (IL)	AAA	2	1	1.42	3	3	19	9	0	4	11	6.3	17.2	0.68	.150
		Minor League Totals		11	10	3.73	45	43	241	204	27	60	252	6.2	25.9	1.10	.227

ATLANTA BRAVES

8 GARRETT BAUMANN, RHP
FB: 55. **CB:** 40. **SL:** 45. **CH:** 45. **CTL:** 55. **BA Grade:** 50. **Risk:** Average. **Adj:** 40.

Born: August 15, 2004. **B-T:** L-R. **HT:** 6-8. **WT:** 245.
Drafted: HS—Oviedo, FL, 2023 (4th round). **Signed by:** Jon Bunnell.
TRACK RECORD: Baumann signed an over-slot $747,500 deal as a fourth-round pick in 2023 and has been an imposing workhorse since. After a rock-solid first full season with Low-A Augusta in 2024, Baumann replicated his efforts in 2025 with High-A Rome. He posted a 3.40 ERA over 23 starts and 113.2 innings with a 22.5% strikeout rate and 6.4% walk rate.
SCOUTING REPORT: Baumann has been a monstrous, physical presence since his prep days. He stands 6-foot-8, 245 pounds and attacks hitters from a high release point with a delivery that is surprisingly coordinated and synced up for a 20-year-old pitcher of his size. He added more than a tick of velocity to his fastball this year and now averages 95 mph and will touch 99. His four-seam is a steep offering that doesn't generate a ton of whiffs. As a remedy, he began incorporating a two-seamer that would play off his release height and potentially be a weapon at the bottom of the zone. Baumann's ability to throw his fastball for strikes has been an asset for multiple years now—he's thrown it for strikes more than 70% of the time in 2024 and 2025—but there are questions about his secondary pitches. He throws a mid-80s slider with some sweep, a low-80s curveball with more depth and an 86-90 mph splitter. All his secondaries earn fringy reviews and leave him without a reliable swing-and-miss pitch to put hitters away. The splitter could be his best bet, though Baumann might also try to add a harder, tighter gyro slider or a cutter in 2026.
THE FUTURE: Baumann's fastball velocity and command remain strengths, but his secondaries could limit him to a back-end starter or reliever role without improvement. He should begin to face upper-minors competition in 2026.

Year	Age	Club (League)	Level	W	L	ERA	G	GS	IP	H	HR	BB	SO	BB%	SO%	WHIP	AVG
2025	20	Rome (SAL)	A+	6	9	3.40	23	23	114	110	10	31	108	6.4	22.5	1.24	.251
		Minor League Totals		13	14	3.31	44	43	215	200	13	56	198	6.2	22.1	1.19	.244

9 LUKE SINNARD, RHP
FB: 50. **CB:** 45. **SL:** 55. **CH:** 55. **CTL:** 50. **BA Grade:** 50. **Risk:** Average. **Adj:** 40.

Born: August 21, 2002. **B-T:** R-R. **HT:** 6-8. **WT:** 250.
Drafted: Indiana, 2024 (3rd round). **Signed by:** Jeremy Gordon.
TRACK RECORD: The Braves took a shot on Sinnard's upside with a $735,300 deal in the third round out of Indiana even after he missed his 2024 draft year with Tommy John surgery. He then dealt with a nerve issue after his surgery but made his pro debut in 2025. Sinnard split time between Low-A Augusta and High-A Rome, posting a 2.86 ERA over 16 starts and 72.1 innings with a 28.3% strikeout rate. He pitched in the Arizona Fall League after the season.
SCOUTING REPORT: Sinnard has an extra-large frame at 6-foot-8, 250 pounds with plenty of strength and broad, coat-hanger shoulders. He primarily works with a three-pitch mix that includes a fastball, slider and splitter. Sinnard's fastball averaged 93-94 mph and touched 97. It's a steep pitch that comes from a higher slot, with solid riding life, but because of his steep approach and release height the Braves worked with him to add a two-seam variant. Both Sinnard's slider and splitter were effective swing-and-miss pitches against Class A hitters. Sinnard's slider is an upper-80s breaking ball with short, biting action. His splitter is an 80-85 mph pitch with spin rates around 800-900 rpm with solid depth. He uses the slider at a heavy clip versus righties and breaks out the splitter more often against lefties. He also has a rarely used low-80s curveball. The Braves were impressed with the control and command Sinnard showed throughout the season. He tends to attack the zone more than the team would like him to in pitcher's counts, and he might have more strikeout potential if he gets more aggressive and uses his secondaries with the intent to be chase pitches below the zone.
THE FUTURE: Sinnard now needs to show he can miss bats at more age-appropriate levels. He has back-end rotation upside and enough pure stuff to carve out a reliever role if necessary.

Year	Age	Club (League)	Level	W	L	ERA	G	GS	IP	H	HR	BB	SO	BB%	SO%	WHIP	AVG
2025	22	Augusta (CAR)	A	0	2	0.92	7	7	29	22	1	12	41	9.8	33.3	1.16	.202
2025	22	Rome (SAL)	A+	2	4	4.19	9	9	43	36	2	15	45	8.3	24.9	1.19	.221
		Minor League Totals		2	6	2.86	16	16	72	58	3	27	86	8.9	28.3	1.18	.213

ATLANTA BRAVES

10 DIEGO TORNES, OF
HIT: 50. **POW:** 55. **RUN:** 55. **FLD:** 55. **ARM:** 60. **BA Grade:** 55. **Risk:** Extreme.

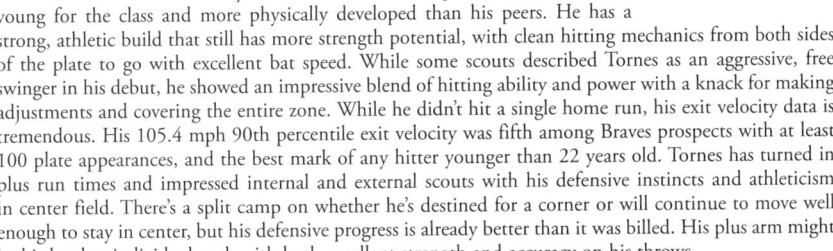

Born: July 3, 2008. **B-T:** B-R. **HT:** 6-2. **WT:** 178.
Signed: Cuba, 2025. **Signed by:** Reymond Nuñez.
TRACK RECORD: The Braves have not received great returns from the international market in years, but Tornes, the team's $2.5 million Cuban headliner from the 2025 class, has the potential to change that. The physical switch-hitter was lauded for his offensive prowess before signing and then ranked as the No. 4 prospect in the Dominican Summer League in 2025.
SCOUTING REPORT: Officially listed at 6-foot-2, 178 pounds, Tornes is both young for the class and more physically developed than his peers. He has a strong, athletic build that still has more strength potential, with clean hitting mechanics from both sides of the plate to go with excellent bat speed. While some scouts described Tornes as an aggressive, free swinger in his debut, he showed an impressive blend of hitting ability and power with a knack for making adjustments and covering the entire zone. While he didn't hit a single home run, his exit velocity data is tremendous. His 105.4 mph 90th percentile exit velocity was fifth among Braves prospects with at least 100 plate appearances, and the best mark of any hitter younger than 22 years old. Tornes has turned in plus run times and impressed internal and external scouts with his defensive instincts and athleticism in center field. There's a split camp on whether he's destined for a corner or will continue to move well enough to stay in center, but his defensive progress is already better than it was billed. His plus arm might be his loudest individual tool, with both excellent strength and accuracy on his throws.
THE FUTURE: Tornes' collection of physical tools gives him more upside than any hitter in the system, but he's years away from the majors with plenty of refinement still needed. He should make his stateside debut in 2026 in what will be his age-17 season.

Year	Age	Club (League)	Level	AVG	G	AB	R	H	2B	3B	HR	RBI	BB	SO	SB	OBP	SLG
2025	16	DSL Braves	Rk	.279	32	122	20	34	5	5	0	13	23	32	24	.395	.402
		Minor League Totals		.279	32	122	20	34	5	5	0	13	23	32	24	.395	.402

11 HERICK HERNANDEZ, LHP
FB: 55. **CB:** 45. **SL:** 60. **CH:** 45. **CTL:** 35. **BA Grade:** 50. **Risk:** High. **Adj:** 35.

Born: August 11, 2003. **B-T:** L-L. **HT:** 5-10. **WT:** 205. **Drafted:** Miami, 2024 (4th round). **Signed by:** Lou Sanchez.
TRACK RECORD: Hernandez pitched two seasons with Miami Dade JC, then upped his draft stock in 2024 with a season at Miami. The Braves signed him in the fourth round for $472,500 after an electric fastball-slider in his brief pro debut. Hernandez missed bats in his first full pro season at High-A Rome—where he posted a 3.57 ERA in 21 starts and 103.1 innings—but also struggled to throw strikes.
SCOUTING REPORT: Hernandez is close to physically maxed out with a 5-foot-10, 205-pound frame. He attacks hitters from a higher, three-quarters slot and primarily works off a strong fastball/slider combination. He throws a four-seam fastball that sits around 93 mph and touches 97 with around 19 inches of induced vertical break—some of the best riding life of any fastball in Atlanta's system. His slider is a high-spin breaking ball in the mid 80s with gyro shape and the power, movement and steep approach angle to be an effective swing-and-miss pitch versus righties and lefties. The fastball and slider accounted for about 67% of his pitch mix in 2025, but he will also mix in a mid-80s splitter and curveball in the upper 70s. Both pitches flash solid and could become legitimate secondaries, but he needs to throw them both for strikes far more frequently. The Braves tried to lower his slot and improve his timing to help him throw more strikes and improve his fastball quality.
THE FUTURE: Hernandez's fastball and slider give him a real path to a big league reliever role. To reach more than that, he needs to improve his command and third and fourth pitches.

Year	Age	Club (League)	Level	W	L	ERA	G	GS	IP	H	HR	BB	SO	BB%	SO%	WHIP	AVG
2025	21	Rome (SAL)	A+	3	6	3.57	22	21	103	70	14	68	127	15.3	28.7	1.34	.193
		Minor League Totals		3	6	3.52	24	23	110	74	14	68	139	14.6	29.8	1.29	.192

ATLANTA BRAVES

12 JOHN GIL, SS
HIT: 50. **POW:** 35. **RUN:** 70. **FLD:** 50. **ARM:** 50. **BA Grade:** 45. **Risk:** Average. **Adj:** 35.

Born: May 14, 2006. **B-T:** R-R. **HT:** 6-1. **WT:** 175. **Signed:** Dominican Republic, 2023. **Signed by:** Miguel Prestol.
TRACK RECORD: Gil signed out of the Dominican Republic in 2023 and used a breakout 2024 season in the low levels of the minors to become one of Atlanta's top position player prospects. He spent the majority of his time with Low-A Augusta in his age-19 season in 2025 and continued to show strong plate skills, hitting .258/.352/.378 in 100 games.
SCOUTING REPORT: Gil has a lean frame at 6-foot-1, 175 pounds with a straightforward operation and some of the best contact and plate skills in Atlanta's system. He has a good understanding of the zone and doesn't expand it much, with above-average contact skills that have allowed him to minimize his strikeouts and walk at a strong clip. Gil is a pull-oriented hitter who hits the ball on the ground a lot, and didn't make significant strides with his 90th percentile exit velocities year over year. He does have respectable top-end exit velocities and some physical projection to dream on, but has now managed isolated slugging numbers under .115 in back-to-back seasons and might always be more of a singles and doubles hitter. He's a great runner who should steal plenty of bases, but needs to refine his baserunning instincts and efficiency. Gil has the hands, actions and arm strength to be a solid shortstop defender, though he will struggle at times on more challenging plays in the hole.
THE FUTURE: Gil's upside is limited because of his power, but he has carrying tools that could push him to major league value with his hit tool, speed and defense.

Year	Age	Club (League)	Level	AVG	G	AB	R	H	2B	3B	HR	RBI	BB	SO	SB	OBP	SLG
2025	19	FCL Braves	Rk	.000	1	2	1	0	0	0	0	0	2	0	0	.500	.000
2025	19	Augusta (CAR)	A	.258	100	399	73	103	25	1	7	48	57	64	50	.352	.378
2025	19	Columbus (SL)	AA	.174	6	23	2	4	0	0	0	1	2	7	4	.240	.174
		Minor League Totals		.267	206	757	151	202	43	3	11	97	122	139	100	.374	.375

13 TATE SOUTHISENE, SS
HIT: 40. **POW:** 50. **RUN:** 60. **FLD:** 55. **ARM:** 60. **BA Grade:** 55. **Risk:** Extreme. **Adj:** 35.

Born: October 6, 2006. **B-T:** R-R. **HT:** 5-11. **WT:** 180. **Drafted:** HS—Henderson, NV, 2025 (1st round). **Signed by:** Alan Hull.
TRACK RECORD: Southisene comes from an athletic baseball family. His older brother Ty was a fourth-round pick of the Cubs in 2024, and his younger brother Troy is a talented prospect in the 2026 class. Tate ranked as the No. 43 prospect in the 2025 draft and signed an under-slot $2,622,500 deal as Atlanta's first-round pick. He struggled mightily in 15 games with Low-A Augusta with a .219/.242/.297 line and 40.9% strikeout rate.
SCOUTING REPORT: Southisene is a 5-foot-11, 180-pound shortstop and righthanded hitter with impressive stretch, torque and bat speed in a swing that features some moving parts. He has a low handset and a big leg kick, which worked fine in high school, where he showed solid barrel feel and strike-zone awareness, but that didn't translate to his brief pro debut. While Southisene reportedly put together solid at-bats in unofficial games, he looked overmatched with Augusta. He swung far too frequently (53% swing rate), missed far too frequently (40% miss rate) and expanded the zone far too frequently (37% chase rate). The silver lining for Southisene was that when he did make contact, he hit the ball quite hard—particularly for his age—but even then his loudest contact was on the ground. Southisene was viewed as an above-average runner pre-draft, but Atlanta was surprised to see him turn in a few 70-grade run times after signing. He has experience at shortstop, center field and second base, and could wind up at any of the three up-the-middle positions. His initial defensive reps should come at shortstop, where he has a strong arm.
THE FUTURE: Southisene's pro debut adds more uncertainty to his offensive profile, but if he can show that was just a blip on the radar he has an enticing power/speed combo and up-the-middle defensive profile.

Year	Age	Club (League)	Level	AVG	G	AB	R	H	2B	3B	HR	RBI	BB	SO	SB	OBP	SLG
2025	18	Augusta (CAR)	A	.219	15	64	10	14	3	1	0	6	1	27	3	.242	.297
		Minor League Totals		.219	15	64	10	14	3	1	0	6	1	27	3	.242	.297

14 BLAKE BURKHALTER, RHP
FB: 55. **CB:** 50. **SL:** 40. **SP:** 50. **CT:** 55. **SW:** 30. **CTL:** 50. **BA Grade:** 40. **Risk:** Mild. **Adj:** 35.

Born: September 19, 2000. **B-T:** R-R. **HT:** 6-0. **WT:** 204. **Drafted:** Auburn, 2022 (2nd round). **Signed by:** Travis Coleman.
TRACK RECORD: Burkhalter was a reliable reliever for Auburn who converted to a starting role in pro ball after the Braves signed him for $650,000 in the second round of the 2022 draft. He pitched as a starter for a season and a half, but moved back to a reliever role in the second half of the 2025 season.

ATLANTA BRAVES

SCOUTING REPORT: Burkhalter is a stocky righty with a 6-foot, 204-pound frame and a delivery that is more in line with a bullpen arm than a starter with some effort and recoil in his finish. He has a deep mix of pitch types, but his cut-ride four-seam fastball and true cutter have long been his best pitches. Burkhalter throws the fastball in the 93-95 mph range and will occasionally hit a 97 or 98, though his velocity didn't make a significant jump after moving back to the bullpen. His 88-92 mph cutter is an above-average pitch and consistent in-zone offering. Because his fastball and cutter have similar shapes, the Braves have attempted to create some different looks with his secondaries, but nothing has clicked so far. Burkhalter has experimented with both a gyro slider in the mid 80s and a sweeper slider in the low 80s. Neither was great and he might have better odds with a low-80s curveball with 12-to-6 shape or a mid-80s kick changeup that looks and plays like a splitter.
THE FUTURE: A reliever only, Burkhalter will need to find a way to miss more bats against upper-level hitters.

Year	Age	Club (League)	Level	W	L	ERA	G	GS	IP	H	HR	BB	SO	BB%	SO%	WHIP	AVG
2025	24	Columbus (SL)	AA	2	5	3.13	14	14	72	63	1	29	65	9.5	21.2	1.28	.237
2025	24	Gwinnett (IL)	AAA	2	2	3.77	18	2	31	28	3	16	23	12.2	17.6	1.42	.248
		Minor League Totals		8	11	3.21	51	33	180	164	7	64	164	8.6	21.9	1.27	.246

15 CONOR ESSENBURG, OF

HIT: 45. **POW:** 55. **RUN:** 40. **FLD:** 50. **ARM:** 60. **BA Grade:** 55. **Risk:** Extreme. **Adj:** 35.

Born: September 18, 2006. **B-T:** R-L. **HT:** 6-2. **WT:** 200. **Drafted:** HS—New Lenox, IL, 2025 (5th round). **Signed by:** Ryan Edges.
TRACK RECORD: Essenburg was a high-level two-way player out of Lincoln-Way West High in New Lenox, Ill. He made waves in the scouting industry after he homered against a 99 mph fastball from lefty flamethrower Jack Bauer in a big-time prep matchup. The Braves lured him away from a Kentucky commitment when they drafted him—as an outfielder—in the fifth round for $1.2 million.
SCOUTING REPORT: At 6-foot-2, 200 pounds and with tremendous bat speed and raw power, Essenburg immediately becomes one of the more exciting sluggers in Atlanta's system. He's a "backwards profile" righthanded hitter and lefthanded thrower who can put a charge into the baseball with an uphill path and high-intent swing. Essenburg's pure hitting ability is a question mark and largely unproven. His high school track record was more limited than most of his peers drafted in the first five rounds, and he didn't play official games after signing. Still, he wowed Braves officials in a bridge league matchup with the Rays when he launched a mid-90s fastball to center. Essenburg is a below-average runner who should be limited to a corner, though he does have a plus throwing arm—he threw 94 mph on the mound—that profiles in right.
THE FUTURE: Amateur scouts were torn on whether Essenburg's upside was greater as a hitter or pitcher, but the Braves seem to view him as a bat-only prospect now. He'll get his first taste of pro ball at the lower levels in 2026 when Atlanta, and everyone else, will get a better feel for the sort of pure hitter he is.

Year	Age	Club (League)	Level	AVG	G	AB	R	H	2B	3B	HR	RBI	BB	SO	SB	OBP	SLG
2025	18	Did not play															

16 HAYDEN HARRIS, LHP

FB: 55. **SW:** 55. **SP:** 45. **CTL:** 50. **BA Grade:** 40. **Risk:** Mild. **Adj:** 35.

Born: March 2, 1999. **B-T:** L-L. **HT:** 6-0. **WT:** 186. **Signed:** Georgia Southern, 2022 (UDFA). **Signed by:** Alan Butts.
TRACK RECORD: Harris signed as an undrafted free agent out of Georgia Southern in 2022. He's been a full-time reliever since entering pro ball, and made his big league debut with three solid relief appearances in September. Harris spent most of his time with Double-A and Triple-A, where he posted a 0.69 ERA over 52 innings. His 30.6 K-BB% was the best mark of any Braves minor leaguer with at least 50 innings.
SCOUTING REPORT: Harris is a sidearming lefthander with a 6-foot, 186-pound frame and one of the lowest release points of any minor league pitcher. That allows him to rely heavily on a 92 mph fastball that touches 95, but plays up from that velocity. It's an extremely flat pitch that he lands in the zone at an above-average clip and misses plenty of barrels at the top of the zone. The 32% miss rate Harris drove with his fastball was one of the best in Atlanta's system. Harris pairs the fastball with a low-80s sweeper slider and a mid-80s splitter. He's more comfortable with the fastball than his secondaries, which was clear in his big league stint when he threw the heater more than 80% of the time. The sweeper could be a weapon for him, but he'll need to continue making strides with his splitter to keep righties off-balance.
THE FUTURE: Harris is a ready-made reliever whose low slot, release point and fastball shape will carry him. His margin for error will be small unless he can add more velocity or take his secondaries to another level.

ATLANTA BRAVES

Year	Age	Club (League)	Level	W	L	ERA	G	GS	IP	H	HR	BB	SO	BB%	SO%	WHIP	AVG
2025	26	Columbus (SL)	AA	4	0	0.79	18	0	23	11	0	7	37	8.2	43.5	0.79	.147
2025	26	Gwinnett (IL)	AAA	2	0	0.31	25	0	29	9	1	12	42	10.8	37.8	0.72	.097
2025	26	Atlanta (NL)	MLB	0	0	3.38	3	0	3	3	0	2	0	16.7	0.0	1.88	.300
		Minor League Totals		15	8	3.06	130	0	159	113	12	74	245	11.3	37.3	1.18	.200
		Major League Totals		0	0	3.38	3	0	3	3	0	2	0	16.7	0.0	1.88	.300

17 ROLDDY MUÑOZ, RHP

FB: 60. **SL:** 70. **CTL:** 30. **BA Grade:** 45. **Risk:** Average. **Adj:** 35.

Born: April 14, 2000. **B-T:** R-R. **HT:** 6-2. **WT:** 183. **Signed:** Dominican Republic, 2019. **Signed by:** Carlos Sequera.
TRACK RECORD: Muñoz signed with the Braves in 2019 out of the Dominican Republic. Since then he's slowly worked his way up the minor league ladder, culminating in a major league debut with three relief appearances in September—where he struggled to throw strikes. The 2025 season was his first pitching exclusively in the upper minors, and between Double-A and Triple-A he posted a 2.85 ERA over 60 innings with a 23% strikeout rate, the lowest of his career.
SCOUTING REPORT: Muñoz is a 6-foot-2, 183-pound righthanded reliever and slider monster whose breaking ball will drive his big league career. The 90-93 mph gyro slider has become his primary pitch and is one of the better breaking balls in the system. It has high spin rates in the 2,500 rpm range and great swing-and-miss potential against righties and lefties. He drove a 41% miss rate with the pitch in the minors and had miss rates north of 40% against batters of either side. The slider is also the pitch Muñoz most reliably throws for strikes. He has less feel for two fastballs, but plenty of velocity. He throws both his four-seam and two-seam fastballs in the 97-100 mph range, with the two-seam variant the one that should help him avoid more big league barrels. Muñoz has thrown a firm, 90 mph changeup but it's not a real factor in his arsenal. He's generally been a well below-average strike-thrower.
THE FUTURE: Muñoz has the slider and velocity to carve out a role in a big league bullpen, but his command could prevent him from working in high-leverage situations.

Year	Age	Club (League)	Level	W	L	ERA	G	GS	IP	H	HR	BB	SO	BB%	SO%	WHIP	AVG
2025	25	Columbus (SL)	AA	2	2	2.11	25	1	38	28	4	23	34	13.9	20.5	1.33	.206
2025	25	Gwinnett (IL)	AAA	1	1	4.15	16	2	22	17	2	10	25	11.1	27.8	1.25	.215
2025	25	Atlanta (NL)	MLB	0	0	12.27	3	0	4	4	1	5	5	23.8	23.8	2.45	.286
		Minor League Totals		15	13	4.07	155	15	272	243	21	135	330	11.2	27.3	1.39	.235
		Major League Totals		0	0	12.27	3	0	4	4	1	5	5	23.8	23.8	2.45	.286

18 LANDON BEIDELSCHIES, LHP

FB: 55. **SL:** 55. **CH:** 40. **CTL:** 50. **BA Grade:** 45. **Risk:** Average. **Adj:** 35.

Born: March 28, 2004. **B-T:** L-L. **HT:** 6-3. **WT:** 230. **Drafted:** Arkansas, 2025 (7th round). **Signed by:** JD French.
TRACK RECORD: Beidelschies started his career as a reliever for Ohio State, but transferred to Arkansas in 2025 where he pitched as a full-time starter in one of the best pitching staffs in college baseball. He ranked as the No. 72 prospect in the draft, but fell to the seventh round, where he signed for $297,500 with the Braves. He made two starts with Low-A Augusta after signing.
SCOUTING REPORT: Beidelschies is a large, well-developed lefthander with a 6-foot-3, 230-pound frame and a strong two-pitch mix that leads his arsenal. He throws a fastball in the 90-94 mph range but will run the pitch up to 98 mph with solid riding life. It's an above-average pitch, though his below-average extension will be a trait to monitor now that he's facing pro hitters. Beidelschies has a second pitch with above-average potential in his mid-80s slider. It's a high-usage breaking ball that he used nearly half the time against same-side hitters with Arkansas. The Braves have already worked on new grips with the slider to help sharpen it even more. Developing a reliable third offering to help him navigate lineups and attack righties will be key. He does have a mid-80s changeup, but it was a distinct third pitch for him in college. Beidelschies was an average strike-thrower in college.
THE FUTURE: Beidelschies should be developed as a starter, though his stuff is loud enough to profile nicely in the pen if needed in the future.

Year	Age	Club (League)	Level	W	L	ERA	G	GS	IP	H	HR	BB	SO	BB%	SO%	WHIP	AVG
2025	21	Augusta (CAR)	A	0	1	7.11	2	2	6	11	2	2	8	6.5	25.8	2.05	.393
		Minor League Totals		0	1	7.11	2	2	6	11	2	2	8	6.5	25.8	2.05	.393

ATLANTA BRAVES

19 CODY MILLER, SS
HIT: 45. **POW:** 40. **RUN:** 60. **FLD:** 50. **ARM:** 50. **BA Grade:** 45. **Risk:** Average. **Adj:** 35.

Born: July 1, 2004. **B-T:** R-R. **HT:** 5-11. **WT:** 189. **Drafted:** East Tennessee State, 2025 (3rd round). **Signed by:** Will Rich.
TRACK RECORD: Miller was a surprise pick on draft day, and one of just two players taken inside the first three rounds not ranked on the BA 500. He signed an under-slot deal for $297,500 after a career year with East Tennessee State. He became the fourth-highest draftee in the program's history, then hit .327/.381/.449 between Low-A Augusta and High-A Rome in 26 games.
SCOUTING REPORT: Miller is a 5-foot-11, 189-pound righthanded hitter with compact strength on his frame and an offensive profile geared around contact. He was a career .330 hitter in three seasons in college, and during the 2025 season he ran a 92% in-zone contact rate. After hitting just four home runs in his first two college seasons combined, Miller hit 18 home runs as a junior. Whether that power translates to pro ball is a question, as most of Miller's power goes to the pull side and his wood bat exit velocities are modest for his age. While Miller does have solid contact skills, he has a tendency to expand the strike zone and likes to swing—a trait shared by many of Atlanta's 2025 draftees. He's a plus runner who went 56-for-62 (90%) on the bases in college and in his pro debut went 10-for-13 (76.9%). Miller has solid defensive tools and could stick at shortstop, but he got innings at third base and second base as well in his pro debut.
THE FUTURE: Miller has a utility infield toolset with a modest offensive ceiling, though his contact skills, speed and defensive versatility could still push him to the majors.

Year	Age	Club (League)	Level	AVG	G	AB	R	H	2B	3B	HR	RBI	BB	SO	SB	OBP	SLG
2025	20	Augusta (CAR)	A	.372	10	43	8	16	2	0	1	11	3	10	4	.417	.488
2025	20	Rome (SAL)	A+	.297	16	64	7	19	3	1	1	6	5	22	6	.357	.422
		Minor League Totals		.327	26	107	15	35	5	1	2	17	8	32	10	.381	.449

20 DAVID McCABE, 1B/3B
HIT: 45. **POW:** 50. **RUN:** 30. **FLD:** 40. **ARM:** 50. **BA Grade:** 40. **Risk:** Mild. **Adj:** 35.

Born: March 25, 2000. **B-T:** B-R. **HT:** 6-3. **WT:** 230. **Drafted:** Charlotte, 2022 (4th round). **Signed by:** Billy Best.
TRACK RECORD: McCabe has been on a roller coaster over the last few seasons. He ranked alongside Drake Baldwin as a top 10 prospect in Atlanta's system after a tremendous 2023 season, then regressed significantly in 2024 and missed time with Tommy John surgery. The 2022 fourth-round pick and $476,400 signee bounced back with a solid 2025 campaign in the upper minors, where his 42 extra-base hits were tied for tops in Atlanta's system.
SCOUTING REPORT: McCabe is a big, sturdy and physical switch-hitter with a 6-foot-3, 230-pound frame and a long track record of strong on-base skills. He's a much more productive hitter from the left side—where he gets to most of his power—but understands the zone and has always posted strong walk rates, even in his down seasons. He owns a career 14.3% walk rate in the minors and has never walked less than the 11.6% clip he posted in Triple-A in 2025. McCabe's pure contact ability and zone coverage are what could hold him back as a hitter. His outer-third plate coverage is questionable and has been exposed more as he's climbed the minor league ladder, and he also has a history of struggling against elite velocity—though he improved in this area in 2025 compared to 2024. McCabe is a 30-grade runner who doesn't have the actions for third base in the majors, and got time at first base and DH only in his Triple-A stint.
THE FUTURE: McCabe's on-base skills and raw power could allow him to provide value as a big league bench bat or reserve. He's largely a finished product entering his age-26 season.

Year	Age	Club (League)	Level	AVG	G	AB	R	H	2B	3B	HR	RBI	BB	SO	SB	OBP	SLG
2025	25	Columbus (SL)	AA	.286	105	371	54	106	23	1	10	52	58	89	2	.379	.434
2025	25	Gwinnett (IL)	AAA	.235	28	98	8	23	4	0	4	19	13	32	1	.321	.398
		Minor League Totals		.258	319	1130	152	292	59	2	34	178	191	303	15	.363	.404

21 CEDRIC DE GRANDPRE, RHP
FB: 55. **CB:** 45. **SL:** 60. **CH:** 50. **CTL:** 45. **BA Grade:** 45. **Risk:** High. **Adj:** 30.

Born: January 25, 2002. **B-T:** R-R. **HT:** 6-2. **WT:** 210. **Drafted:** Chipola (FL) JC, 2022 (13th round). **Signed by:** Jon Bunnell.
TRACK RECORD: De Grandpre is a Canadian native who pitched with Chipola (Fla.) JC and signed with the Braves as a 13th-rounder for $237,500 in 2022. He pitched well in his first full pro season in 2023, but lost the 2024 season entirely with Tommy John surgery. Post-surgery in 2025, De Grandpre made 15 starts and showed much louder stuff than previously, albeit with less control.
SCOUTING REPORT: De Grandpre is a thick and physical righthander with a 6-foot-2, 210-pound frame and big, broad shoulders. He has a mix of five pitches that includes a four-seam fastball, two-seam fastball,

ATLANTA BRAVES

slider, curveball and kick changeup. Both his fastball variants check in at 93-96 mph and the four-seam has touched 98, though he showed much better ability to throw the two-seam for strikes in 2025. His 86-89 mph gyro slider is a hard, biting pitch that earns plus grades. He'll also mix in a sweeping, 82-85 mph curveball and an 85-87 mph kick changeup—both of which see increased usage against lefties. The changeup grades out well metrically and plays like a splitter when he throws a good one, though his feel for the pitch is currently lagging. Improving control in general will be key for De Grandpre, as his 16.1% walk rate was far and away the worst of his career.

THE FUTURE: If De Grandpre can get closer to his previous strike-throwing ability as he gets further away from surgery, he has back-end starting potential. If not, he still might have the pure stuff to pitch in a big league bullpen.

Year	Age	Club (League)	Level	W	L	ERA	G	GS	IP	H	HR	BB	SO	BB%	SO%	WHIP	AVG
2025	23	FCL Braves	Rk	0	0	0.00	2	2	7	6	0	2	13	6.3	40.6	1.09	.214
2025	23	Rome (SAL)	A+	3	4	3.74	13	13	53	35	1	41	66	17.4	28.1	1.43	.188
		Minor League Totals		6	11	3.93	39	34	156	137	6	69	179	10.2	26.6	1.32	.234

22 JHANCARLOS LARA, RHP

FB: 65. **SL:** 70. **CTL:** 20. **BA Grade:** 50. **Risk:** Extreme. **Adj:** 30.

Born: January 15, 2003. **B-T:** R-R. **HT:** 6-3. **WT:** 190. **Signed:** Dominican Republic, 2021.
Signed by: Carlos Sequera/Luis Santos.

TRACK RECORD: Lara signed out of the Dominican Republic in 2021 and for a few years pitched like he might become a hard-throwing starter. Since a breakout 2023 season, however, his strikes have regressed significantly and in 2025 he pitched as a reliever for the majority of his games for the first time in his career. His 31.8% strikeout rate was among the best in Atlanta's system, but his 19.9% walk rate was the worst of his career, the worst in the system and a bottom 10 figure for any minor league pitcher with 50 innings.

SCOUTING REPORT: On the right day, Lara can be unhittable. Those days are far too infrequent because Lara simply cannot reliably attack the zone. The 6-foot-3, 190-pound righty has great arm speed and has continued to trend up with his fastball velocity. He added about two ticks in 2025, sat 98-99 mph and touched 102.6. While the fastball has elite velocity, its life is modest and his feel to command it is poor. Lara pairs the fastball with a wipeout slider in the 86-94 mph range that has hard, biting action with gyro shape at its best but also flashes more of a cutter look at times. He now throws the slider more than his fastball. The pitch is a 70-grade offering and drove a 46% miss rate in 2025. It's one of the best in the system and among the best in the minors according to some analytical models.

THE FUTURE: Despite his nine starts in Triple-A, Lara is a reliever-only, two-pitch righty who has more than enough pure stuff to be a valuable reliever. He'll need to improve his 20-grade control to actualize that arm talent in the majors.

Year	Age	Club (League)	Level	W	L	ERA	G	GS	IP	H	HR	BB	SO	BB%	SO%	WHIP	AVG
2025	22	Columbus (SL)	AA	0	4	11.21	6	5	18	23	5	19	26	19.8	27.1	2.38	.319
2025	22	Gwinnett (IL)	AAA	0	5	6.53	28	9	51	30	4	46	78	19.9	33.8	1.49	.169
		Minor League Totals		7	22	4.72	84	57	263	203	18	193	350	16.4	29.7	1.51	.213

23 DIXON WILLIAMS, 2B

HIT: 45. **POW:** 45. **RUN:** 55. **FLD:** 50. **ARM:** 50. **BA Grade:** 40. **Risk:** Average. **Adj:** 30.

Born: December 19, 2003. **B-T:** L-R. **HT:** 6-2. **WT:** 210. **Drafted:** East Carolina, 2025 (4th round). **Signed by:** Al Skorupa.

TRACK RECORD: Williams was a multi-sport athlete in high school who also played football, and then became a key offensive contributor as a middle infielder with East Carolina. His three-year career culminated in a 14-homer season as a junior in 2025, and he signed for $497,500 in the fourth round with the Braves after ranking as the No. 197 prospect in the draft. Williams played well in a 28-game stint with Low-A Augusta after signing.

SCOUTING REPORT: Williams is a lean, lefthanded hitter with a 6-foot-2, 210-pound frame that could still add a bit more weight in the future. He has a slightly crouched stance and reasonably direct lefthanded swing with a blend of patience and power. His raw power is more solid-average than plus, but he progressively hit for more impact season after season with ECU and does have a track record of getting the ball in the air frequently to take advantage of the power he does have. That continued into his pro debut with a wood bat, where Williams managed fair exit velocities but a great airpull rate. His pure contact skills might always leave him exposed to higher strikeout totals, though that should also come with decent walk rates. Williams is a fine second baseman who was stretched at shortstop in college. He's an above-average runner.

THE FUTURE: Williams has a solid blend of power, patience and speed that could give him second-division upside. Making more contact will be necessary to unlock more.

Year	Age	Club (League)	Level	AVG	G	AB	R	H	2B	3B	HR	RBI	BB	SO	SB	OBP	SLG
2025	21	Augusta (CAR)	A	.269	28	93	14	25	6	3	2	13	16	35	6	.395	.462
		Minor League Totals		.269	28	93	14	25	6	3	2	13	16	35	6	.395	.462

24 ERIC HARTMAN, OF

HIT: 40. **POW:** 40. **RUN:** 55. **FLD:** 60. **ARM:** 50. **BA Grade:** 45. **Risk:** High. **Adj:** 30.

Born: June 16, 2006. **B-T:** L-R. **HT:** 6-1. **WT:** 185. **Drafted:** HS—Okotoks, AB, 2024 (20th round).
Signed by: Cody Martin.
TRACK RECORD: Hartman is a Canadian product who signed for the largest day three bonus the Braves handed out in 2024—a $337,500 deal in the 20th round. He wasn't a big name on pre-draft radars, but earned positive feedback from Braves officials after signing. Hartman missed a month of his first pro season with a hamstring injury but flashed tools on both sides of the ball in the low minors.
SCOUTING REPORT: Hartman is a 6-foot-1, 185-pound outfielder and lefthanded hitter with a solid blend of strength, twitch and athleticism. Among teenagers in the Braves system his blend of exit velocity, contact ability and swing decisions stood out. Hartman is an extremely pull-happy hitter. His 55.2% pull rate was the most in Atlanta's system among hitters with at least 300 plate appearances. All five of his home runs were yanked to the pull side. While Hartman's pull-happy tendencies might get exposed at higher levels, he showed an impressive ability to time up, impact and connect with high-end velocity. He's still learning to recognize and make contact with pro secondaries. Hartman is an above-average runner and strong defender who can handle all three outfield positions. He also played 18 games at second base, but looks more natural in the outfield where he's one of the best defenders in the system.
THE FUTURE: Hartman has a well-rounded toolset and could become a second-division sort of hitter, though he still has a long way to go.

Year	Age	Club (League)	Level	AVG	G	AB	R	H	2B	3B	HR	RBI	BB	SO	SB	OBP	SLG
2025	19	FCL Braves	Rk	.100	6	20	4	2	0	0	0	1	5	7	4	.296	.100
2025	19	Augusta (CAR)	A	.248	83	318	56	79	17	4	5	41	37	85	44	.344	.374
		Minor League Totals		.240	89	338	60	81	17	4	5	42	42	92	48	.341	.358

25 ISAIAH DRAKE, OF

HIT: 30. **POW:** 40. **RUN:** 70. **FLD:** 55. **ARM:** 55. **BA Grade:** 40. **Risk:** Average. **Adj:** 30.

Born: July 15, 2005. **B-T:** L-R. **HT:** 6-0. **WT:** 180. **Drafted:** HS—Atlanta, 2023 (5th round). **Signed by:** Alan Butts.
TRACK RECORD: The Braves took a shot on Drake's tools and athleticism in the 2023 draft and paid him an over-slot $747,500 bonus in the fifth round. His first full season in 2024 was a challenge, but Drake made strides as a hitter in 2025 and progressed to High-A Rome.
SCOUTING REPORT: Drake is a 6-foot, 180-pound outfielder and lefthanded hitter with some of the best secondary tools in Atlanta's system. He's a near top-of-the-scale runner who explodes out of the batter's box and covers huge swaths of ground defensively. He's a high-volume basestealer who went 46-for-59 (78%) on the bases in 2025. Drake entered pro ball as a raw defender, and there are still lapses at times, but he progressed with his routes and instincts and also showed an above-average arm. His most encouraging development came in the contact department. Drake cut his strikeout rate significantly in his second full pro season—35.4% to 21.3%—with the most obvious improvement coming against fastballs. He looked overwhelmed by pro velocity in 2024, but his swing was more direct with better pre-pitch life and rhythm in his hands in 2025. Now he'll need to improve his swing decisions and learn how to elevate the ball a bit more frequently.
THE FUTURE: Drake will enter his age-20 season in 2026. With continued offensive improvement and all-around polish he could profile as a solid backup with upside as a defender and runner.

Year	Age	Club (League)	Level	AVG	G	AB	R	H	2B	3B	HR	RBI	BB	SO	SB	OBP	SLG
2025	19	Augusta (CAR)	A	.260	84	319	41	83	6	6	5	47	39	82	35	.341	.364
2025	19	Rome (SAL)	A+	.303	32	122	11	37	1	0	1	12	8	23	11	.346	.336
		Minor League Totals		.229	208	767	90	176	15	12	8	78	94	241	78	.314	.312

ATLANTA BRAVES

26 JIM JARVIS, SS/2B
HIT: 40. **POW:** 30. **RUN:** 50. **FLD:** 55. **ARM:** 55. **BA Grade:** 35. **Risk:** Mild. **Adj:** 30.

Born: November 6, 2000. **B-T:** L-R. **HT:** 5-10. **WT:** 190. **Drafted:** Alabama, 2023 (11th round). **Signed by:** Mike Smith (Tigers).
TRACK RECORD: Jarvis hails from an athletic family that includes two brothers, Luke and Mike, who played pro baseball and a father, Chip, who played football at San Diego. Jarvis was a reliable shortstop defender for four years at Alabama, was drafted by the Tigers in the 11th round in 2023 and then traded to the Braves in 2025 in a deal that sent righthander Rafael Montero to Detroit.
SCOUTING REPORT: Jarvis is a 5-foot-10, 190-pound shortstop and lefthanded hitter whose contact skills and glove could get him to the majors. He's been a light-hitting, bat-to-ball artist for years going back to his college days, and almost never misses a fastball—with solid production against 93+ mph velocity as well. His offensive value will be driven almost entirely by his contact skills. He has well below-average power, owns a career .340 slugging percentage and has never posted an isolated slugging percentage north of .100. The most homers he's managed in a season were the six he hit in 64 games with a metal bat for Alabama as a senior in 2023. Jarvis is a rock-solid shortstop defender and has been for years. He's more reliable than flashy, but the game doesn't speed up on him and he has solid arm strength that allows him to make tough plays in the hole and throw without his feet set.
THE FUTURE: While a lack of power caps Jarvis' upside, he offers a system light on proven shortstops much-needed upper-level organizational depth at the position. He could have value in a utility infield role.

Year	Age	Club (League)	Level	AVG	G	AB	R	H	2B	3B	HR	RBI	BB	SO	SB	OBP	SLG
2025	24	Erie (EL)	AA	.242	77	277	37	67	14	3	2	29	26	31	8	.316	.336
2025	24	Columbus (SL)	AA	.265	21	83	20	22	8	0	0	8	7	21	6	.344	.361
2025	24	Gwinnett (IL)	AAA	.333	3	9	2	3	2	0	0	2	0	2	0	.400	.556
		Minor League Totals		.245	246	887	144	217	49	6	8	104	99	140	45	.330	.340

27 PATRICK CLOHISY, OF
HIT: 40. **POW:** 40. **RUN:** 55. **FLD:** 55. **ARM:** 50. **BA Grade:** 40. **Risk:** Average. **Adj:** 30.

Born: December 6, 2001. **B-T:** L-L. **HT:** 5-10. **WT:** 190. **Drafted:** Saint Louis, 2024 (11th round). **Signed by:** JD French.
TRACK RECORD: Clohisy ranked as a back-end BA 500 prospect as a senior coming out of Saint Louis, and signed with the Braves as an 11th-round pick for $150,000 in the 2024 draft. He spent the 2025 season with High-A Rome and Double-A Columbus, where he played all three outfield positions and had a slightly above-average wRC+ in both leagues. Clohisy then had a solid tour in the Arizona Fall League where he hit .284/.389/.383 with 22 stolen bases.
SCOUTING REPORT: Clohisy is a 5-foot-10, 190-pound lefthanded hitter who brings some contact ability, speed and center field defense to the table. He has modest raw power and is unlikely to grow into more, but at his best he makes a lot of contact within the zone and can drive the ball on a line to both gaps. Scouts who saw him in the AFL in particular were impressed with his contact ability. He doesn't miss fastballs often, but he also has clear holes to address at the top of the zone and struggles to do much damage against high-end velocity and secondaries in general. Clohisy is an above-average runner who plays hard and can handle center field or be an above-average defender in an outfield corner.
THE FUTURE: Clohisy does enough to be a solid outfield depth option. He'll need to improve as a hitter to find a ceiling beyond that.

Year	Age	Club (League)	Level	AVG	G	AB	R	H	2B	3B	HR	RBI	BB	SO	SB	OBP	SLG
2025	23	Rome (SAL)	A+	.247	92	352	50	87	16	2	3	27	45	76	60	.338	.330
2025	23	Columbus (SL)	AA	.270	39	159	22	43	4	1	4	16	11	29	19	.328	.384
		Minor League Totals		.255	153	589	79	150	27	3	7	51	65	122	82	.334	.346

28 BLANE ABEYTA, RHP
FB: 50. **SL:** 55. **CT:** 55. **CTL:** 50. **BA Grade:** 35. **Risk:** Mild. **Adj:** 30.

Born: September 4, 1998. **B-T:** R-R. **HT:** 6-3. **WT:** 220. **Signed:** Nevada, 2020 (UDFA). **Signed by:** Tyler Robertson (Yankees).
TRACK RECORD: Abeyta pitched two seasons with Modesto (Calif.) JC before he transferred to Nevada for the 2020 season, where he assumed the team's closer role before the season ended because of the Covid pandemic. The Yankees signed him as an undrafted free agent, and four years later the Braves selected him in the minor league phase of the Rule 5 draft. Abeyta struggled with control early in his pro career, but has made great strides in that department. In 2025 he posted a 2.29 ERA with a 32.9% strikeout rate in 51 innings with Double-A Columbus.
SCOUTING REPORT: Abeyta is a 6-foot-3, 220-pound righthander who gets down the mound well with

ATLANTA BRAVES

above-average extension and attacks hitters with a three-pitch mix. He throws a four-seam fastball around 94 mph and will reach back for 96, but the two carrying pitches in his arsenal are a high-usage cutter and sweeper slider. The cutter sits around 88 mph and will touch 92. It's both a pitch that misses bats and his most reliable strike offering. The slider is a true sweeper in the 82-85 mph range that averages 14-15 inches of gloveside movement with above-average potential. He's now been a solid strike-thrower for three seasons.

THE FUTURE: Adding a bit more fastball velocity is next on the to-do list for Abeyta, who now looks like a solid low-leverage pen piece. His background as a starter could allow for some bulk relief outings as well.

Year	Age	Club (League)	Level	W	L	ERA	G	GS	IP	H	HR	BB	SO	BB%	SO%	WHIP	AVG
2025	26	Columbus (SL)	AA	3	1	2.29	43	0	51	34	6	20	68	9.7	32.9	1.06	.187
		Minor League Totals		24	26	5.07	121	66	405	394	50	175	406	9.8	22.6	1.41	.252

29 OWEN CAREY, OF

HIT: 40. **POW:** 50. **RUN:** 50. **FLD:** 50. **ARM:** 50. **BA Grade:** 45. **Risk:** High. **Adj:** 30.

Born: July 22, 2006. **B-T:** L-L. **HT:** 6-0. **WT:** 185. **Drafted:** HS—Londonderry, NH, 2024 (15th round).
Signed by: Brian Sankey.

TRACK RECORD: Carey was an under-the-radar high school prospect out of a Londonderry High program in New Hampshire that's had just two players drafted—righthander Brian Wilson in 2000, and then Carey in 2024. He signed for $150,000 in the 15th round with the Braves instead of heading to Rutgers, and in his first pro season with Low-A Augusta hit .258/.330/.345 in 117 games.
SCOUTING REPORT: Carey is a 6-foot, 185-pound lefthanded outfielder with a solid blend of bat speed, athleticism (he also played hockey in high school) and contact skills. While Carey's offensive line is modest, he acquitted himself nicely in a tough league for hitters—particularly 18-year-old hitters with a multi-sport background from a cold weather state. Carey's exit velocity data was some of the most impressive of any teenager in Atlanta's system, and he also made a lot of contact with a fastball-hunting approach and just a 15.6% strikeout rate. His approach needs refinement. Carey is overly aggressive and is quite pull happy, but in general scouts were impressed with how confident he seemed in the box against older competition. He can play all three outfield positions well, but is more of a solid runner who likely profiles best in a corner because of that.
THE FUTURE: Carey needs a lot more reps and development time, but it's not hard to envision a second-division regular outcome given his tools and athleticism.

Year	Age	Club (League)	Level	AVG	G	AB	R	H	2B	3B	HR	RBI	BB	SO	SB	OBP	SLG
2025	18	Augusta (CAR)	A	.258	117	469	63	121	25	2	4	63	38	82	17	.330	.345
		Minor League Totals		.258	117	469	63	121	25	2	4	63	38	82	17	.330	.345

30 BRETT SEARS, RHP

FB: 40. **CB:** 30. **SL:** 45. **CH:** 40. **CTL:** 55. **BA Grade:** 35. **Risk:** Mild. **Adj:** 30.

Born: May 2, 2000. **B-T:** R-R. **HT:** 6-0. **WT:** 205. **Drafted:** Nebraska, 2024 (7th round). **Signed by:** JD French.

TRACK RECORD: Sears signed for just $12,500 in the seventh round of the 2024 draft with the Braves after an All-America season with Nebraska the prior spring. He was old for the class, but stood out for his advanced control and command, as well as a deep pitch mix. In his first pro season, Sears pitched at four levels. He topped out in Triple-A—where he got hit around in two starts—and posted a 3.65 ERA in 120.2 innings overall.
SCOUTING REPORT: Sears is a 6-foot, 205-pound righthander with a funky delivery that features a deep extended arm action, a low slot and a heavy crossfire landing. From that unusual look he attacks hitters with a diverse mix of five different pitch shapes, led by a fastball and slider. His fastball is a 90-91 mph four-seamer that will top out at 94 mph and help set up the rest of his arsenal. His slider is a mid-80s breaking ball with modest life and more tight, sweeping shape than tilt. The slider is his best secondary, but it's far from a wipeout offering. He also throws a harder cutter in the upper 80s, a fading changeup at 82-86 mph and a slow sweeping curveball in the upper 70s.
THE FUTURE: Sears is a solid upper-minors org starter with good command and a deep mix of pitches, but he will need to add more pure stuff to be a reliable pitcher of any capacity in the majors.

Year	Age	Club (League)	Level	W	L	ERA	G	GS	IP	H	HR	BB	SO	BB%	SO%	WHIP	AVG
2025	25	Augusta (CAR)	A	2	1	1.93	5	2	19	15	1	4	31	5.1	39.7	1.02	.211
2025	25	Rome (SAL)	A+	2		2.00	3	3	18	10	2	2	17	2.9	24.3	0.67	.149
2025	25	Columbus (SL)	AA	6		3.63	15	14	74	56	6	23	74	7.5	24.1	1.06	.204
2025	25	Gwinnett (IL)	AAA	0	2	10.24	2	2	10	11	7	2	6	4.7	14.0	1.34	.297
		Minor League Totals		10	11	3.65	25	21	121	92	16	31	128	6.2	25.7	1.02	.205

Gunnar Henderson

Baltimore Orioles

BY JON MEOLI

A combination of injuries and some early-season underperformance put the 2025 Orioles in a hole they couldn't dig out of, and they were still unpacking the consequences of such a disappointing season.

Brandon Hyde, the manager who led them through a difficult rebuilding period, was fired in mid May with the team floundering at 15-28, and while performance stabilized some, Baltimore ended up trading Cedric Mullins, Ramon Laureano, Ryan O'Hearn and a trio of relievers at the deadline and finishing 75-87.

Mike Elias, who early in 2025 was promoted to president of baseball operations, has the unique challenge of continuing to progress the organization he successfully rebuilt through scouting and player development to win in a completely new landscape. The ownership group led by David Rubenstein and Michael Arougheti adds financial heft to the operation.

Given many of the homegrown players already in place, the Orioles used their financial resources to enhance the roster through trades and free agency. First, Elias swapped Grayson Rodriguez to the Angels for one year of Taylor Ward. Then he signed closer hopeful Ryan Helsley for two years and $28 million and Mets all-star first baseman Pete Alonso for five years and $155 million.

But the reality is, any Orioles success the rest of the decade will be driven mostly by what they already have in-house. Elias chose Craig Albernaz, previously Cleveland's associate manager, as the club's new skipper, with an eye toward getting the most out of the massive group of graduated prospects that through their 2023 and 2024 playoff runs was the source of so much promise.

Baltimore's homegrown lineup regressed in 2025. Injuries limited Adley Rutschman, Jordan Westburg and Colton Cowser, while former top prospects Gunnar Henderson and Jackson Holliday didn't meet the high expectations they set

PROJECTED 2029 LINEUP

Catcher	Adley Rutschman	31
First Base	Pete Alonso	34
Second Base	Jackson Holliday	25
Third Base	Jordan Westburg	30
Shortstop	Gunnar Henderson	28
Left Field	Dylan Beavers	27
Center Field	Enrique Bradfield Jr.	27
Right Field	Colton Cowser	29
Designated Hitter	Samuel Basallo	24
No. 1 Starter	Kyle Bradish	32
No. 2 Starter	Trevor Rogers	31
No. 3 Starter	Tyler Wells	34
No. 4 Starter	Trey Gibson	27
No. 5 Starter	Luis De Leon	26
Closer	Félix Bautista	34

for themselves. The entire group, however, makes for as promising a core as there is in baseball.

The Orioles' rotation, with Kyle Bradish and Tyler Wells returning from elbow surgery in the second half of 2025 and Trevor Rogers revitalizing his career, ended the season far better than it began. And a combination of their deadline trades and a top-heavy draft with four of the top 40 picks, plus a wave of starting pitching prospects nearing the majors, has improved the outlook on the farm.

It's certainly a deeper group than it has been in the past, even if the first-day hitters from Elias' early drafts have accounted for much of the major league success and promise so far.

This front office had to restart the club's Latin American operation from scratch, and top prospect Samuel Basallo, who debuted in the majors in August, was the first product of that group to reach Baltimore. Shortly thereafter, he became their first homegrown prospect to sign a long-term extension.

Every avenue of talent acquisition, from international scouting to the draft to big-ticket free agency, is now open for the Orioles. They already have plenty to be bullish about in-house. But 2025 showed that, much like player development itself, contention is not linear.

There's a lot for the Orioles to be hopeful about in 2026 and beyond, but there's plenty of work to be done to make good on it. ∎

DEPTH CHART

BALTIMORE ORIOLES

TOP 2026 ROOKIES — RANK
1. Samuel Basallo, C — 1
2. Dylan Beavers, OF — 2
3. Anthony Nunez, RHP — 24

BREAKOUT PROSPECTS — Rank
1. Aron Estrada, 2B/OF — 13
2. Joseph Dzierwa, LHP — 21
3. Jordan Sanchez, OF — 23

SOURCE OF TOP 30 TALENT

Homegrown	25	Acquired	5
College	13	Trade	5
Junior college	1	Rule 5 draft	0
High school	2	Independent league	0
Undrafted free agent	1	Free agent/waivers	0
International	8		

LF
Dylan Beavers (2)
Elis Cuevas
Reed Trimble

CF
Nate George (4)
Enrique Bradfield Jr (9)
Slater de Brun (12)
Austin Overn (17)
Vance Honeycutt (30)
Braylin Tavera

RF
Ike Irish (6)
Thomas Sosa (20)
Jordan Sanchez (23)
Stiven Martinez (28)

3B
Joshua Liranzo (29)
Anderson De Los Santos
Luis Almeyda
José Mejia

SS
Wehiwa Aloy (10)
Wilfri De La Cruz (22)
Griff O'Ferrall
Brandon Butterworth
Leandro Arias
Elvin Garcia
Jemone Nuel

2B
Aron Estrada (13)
RJ Austin

1B
TT Bowens
Victor Figueroa

C
Samuel Basallo (1)
Ike Irish (6)
Caden Bodine (16)
Ethan Anderson (27)
Silas Ardoin
Creed Willems
Ryan Stafford
Yasmil Bucce
Andrew Tess

LHP

LHSP
Luis De Leon (5)
Boston Bateman (14)
Joseph Dzierwa (21)
Sebastian Gongora
Carson Dorsey

LHRP
Micah Ashman
Andy Fabian

RHP

RHSP
Trey Gibson (3)
Esteban Mejia (7)
Michael Forret (8)
Braxton Bragg (11)
Nestor German (15)
Levi Wells (18)
Juaron Watts-Brown (19)
JT Quinn (25)
Wellington Aracena (26)
Blake Money
Zach Fruit
Yeiber Cartaya
Keeler Morfe

RHRP
Anthony Nunez (24)
Cameron Foster
Tyson Neighbors
Chayce McDermott
Cameron Weston

BALTIMORE ORIOLES

1. SAMUEL BASALLO, C

Born: August 13, 2004. **B-T:** L-R. **HT:** 6-4. **WT:** 250.
Signed: Dominican Republic, 2021.
Signed by: Michael Cruz/Geraldo Cabrera.

TRACK RECORD: Basallo was connected to the Yankees as a top international signee before New York lost part of its bonus pool for signing free agent Gerrit Cole. The Orioles were emerging from a period of limited participation in the international market and were scaling up their operation at the time, so they had the bonus capacity to add a top talent in Basallo for $1.3 million in January 2021. Their first major international signing turned out to be a boon. Basallo started 2023 at Low-A Delmarva and was the Carolina League MVP before earning two promotions and ending that year at Double-A Bowie, hitting 20 home runs with a .953 OPS in his age-18 season. He spent most of 2024 at Double-A and then produced elite numbers as a 20-year-old at Triple-A Norfolk in 2025 before earning his first callup in August. He hit 23 home runs with a .270 average and .966 OPS in 76 games at Triple-A. Shortly after he debuted, Basallo signed an eight-year, $67 million extension that can keep him in Baltimore through 2034 and escalate to $88.5 million. Basallo had some big moments at the plate for Baltimore but ended up with a .559 OPS in 31 games.

SCOUTING REPORT: Basallo boasts elite bat speed and generates significant power to all fields thanks to his advanced bat-to-ball skills. As he continues to mature and gain experience at the plate against higher-level pitching, he is improving at swinging at pitches he can drive rather than ones his contact ability will allow him to get to. Typically, when power is a player's calling card, it comes with questionable ability to make contact. That's not the case with Basallo. He has plus-plus power and could be one of the game's prolific sluggers, and his contact ability will only help him maximize his significant raw skills. He had a 57.4% hard-hit rate in the minors, and his 90th percentile exit velocity at Triple-A was 108.2 mph, up from 106.5 mph in 2024. That profile will be much more valuable offensively if Basallo can stay behind the plate, and he's constantly improving and working toward that goal. His arm strength, with pop times on throws to second base routinely under 2.0 seconds, isn't an issue. His flexibility and mobility are good for a catcher of his 6-foot-4, 250-pound dimensions. Basallo's progress toward mastering the mental and game-calling side of the position, and his consistency in his receiving, will determine his viability at the position.

BA GRADE: 65 Risk: Average
SCOUTING GRADES: Hit: 55. Power: 70. Run: 40. Field: 45. Arm: 70.
Adjusted grade: 55
Projected future grades on 20-80 scouting scale

BEST TOOLS

BATTING
Best Hitter	Nate George
Best Power Hitter	Samuel Basallo
Best Strike-Zone Discipline	Dylan Beavers
Fastest Baserunner	Enrique Bradfield Jr.
Best Athlete	Nate George

PITCHING
Best Fastball	Esteban Mejia
Best Curveball	Trey Gibson
Best Slider	Trey Gibson
Best Changeup	Nestor German
Best Control	Michael Forret

FIELDING
Best Defensive Catcher	Caden Bodine
Best Defensive Infielder	Griff O'Ferrall
Best Infield Arm	Joshua Liranzo
Best Defensive Outfielder	Enrique Bradfield Jr.
Best Outfield Arm	Jud Fabian

THE FUTURE: Basallo has the potential to be a middle-of-the-order thumper and an all-star regardless of his position, though he would be more valuable to the Orioles behind the plate. His precocious talent and the experience of competing against older players can accelerate his development in the majors and make Basallo an impact regular for the Orioles in 2026 and beyond.

Year	Age	Club (League)	Level	AVG	G	AB	R	H	2B	3B	HR	RBI	BB	SO	SB	OBP	SLG
2025	20	Norfolk (IL)	AAA	.270	76	270	49	73	17	0	23	67	44	76	0	.377	.589
2025	20	Baltimore (AL)	MLB	.165	31	109	10	18	6	0	4	15	6	30	0	.229	.330
		Minor League Totals		.283	401	1460	232	413	81	7	73	269	185	351	24	.366	.498
		Major League Totals		.165	31	109	10	18	6	0	4	15	6	30	0	.229	.330

BALTIMORE ORIOLES

2 DYLAN BEAVERS, OF
HIT: 55. **POW:** 50. **RUN:** 70. **FLD:** 50. **ARM:** 60. **BA Grade:** 55. **Risk:** Mild. **Adj:** 50.

Born: August 11, 2001. **B-T:** L-R. **HT:** 6-4. **WT:** 205.
Drafted: California, 2022 (1st round supp.). **Signed by:** Scott Walter.
TRACK RECORD: Beavers told teams at the 2022 MLB Draft Combine that he knew his swing needed a lot of work. He ended up with a perfect team for that when the Orioles signed him for $2.2 million as the 33rd pick and began the long process of helping him maximize his long levers and elite eye. That took hold in 2025 when he eliminated a sway backward in his swing, which allowed him to be on time with fastballs. That helped his production soar at Triple-A Norfolk. He was the International League MVP thanks to a .304 average, 18 home runs and a .934 OPS, all of which earned him a major league callup in August.
SCOUTING REPORT: Beavers being able to handle fastballs—he hit .305 with a .461 slugging percentage against the pitch at Triple-A—allowed him to stay back on secondaries and take advantage of an elite approach, raising his overall offensive profile in the process. He doesn't whiff or chase often, allowing him to get the best of an above-average hit tool and average power. The swing work Beavers and the Orioles have done have maximized his athleticism and plate discipline, which allows him to be adjustable and generate power naturally without expanding the strike zone or over-swinging in pursuit of slug. Above-average athleticism also shows up in Beavers' plus speed and solid-average outfield defense in the corners—despite some early lapses as he adjusted to major league ballparks.
THE FUTURE: Beavers had one of the best MLB debuts of any recent Orioles prospect for the same reason he can be successful going forward—his approach, contact ability, and newfound adjustability. He could be a solid-average everyday major leaguer and could be in the Rookie of the Year mix in 2026.

Year	Age	Club (League)	Level	AVG	G	AB	R	H	2B	3B	HR	RBI	BB	SO	SB	OBP	SLG
2025	23	Norfolk (IL)	AAA	.304	94	342	78	104	14	2	18	51	68	76	23	.420	.515
2025	23	Baltimore (AL)	MLB	.227	35	110	16	25	5	1	4	14	26	36	2	.375	.400
		Minor League Totals		.278	361	1325	237	369	77	15	44	180	222	335	87	.383	.459
		Major League Totals		.227	35	110	16	25	5	1	4	14	26	36	2	.375	.400

3 TREY GIBSON, RHP
FB: 55. **CB:** 60. **SL:** 60. **CH:** 40. **SW:** 55. **CTL:** 50. **BA Grade:** 55. **Risk:** Average. **Adj:** 45.

Born: May 18, 2002. **B-T:** R-R. **HT:** 6-5. **WT:** 240.
Signed: Liberty, 2023 (UDFA). **Signed by:** Quincy Boyd/Donovan O'Dowd.
TRACK RECORD: Gibson was on the Orioles' radar as a Virginia prep ahead of the five-round 2020 draft, and after he didn't pitch his junior year at Liberty, they rediscovered him in the Cape Cod League in 2023 and signed him as an undrafted free agent. Gibson impressed in the low minors in 2024 before breaking out in 2025 by striking out 40.4% of batters in High-A and then 32.5% in Double-A before finishing at Triple-A Norfolk. Over three levels, Gibson struck out 166 batters with a 1.21 WHIP, 4.26 ERA, and 3.34 FIP in 120.1 innings and earned organizational pitcher of the year honors. Of the 195 pitchers with at least 200 innings in the minors over the last two seasons, Gibson is third among them with a 31.5% strikeout rate.
SCOUTING REPORT: After adding a sinker with unique angles in 2025, Gibson now has a pair of mid-90s fastballs. Righties either hit the new pitch into the ground or took it for strikes. However, Gibson gets his upside from his secondary mix. This year, he added a "death ball" slider, with tight downward break in the mid 80s, to a mix that also includes a plus, mid-80s sweeper, a hard slider and a plus, low-80s curveball. The assortment gives Gibson multiple breaking pitches. He didn't use his changeup much in 2025 but could reintroduce it going forward. He mixed in a cutter in September to help combat righties. His command took significant steps forward and can be average in the future, especially because it applied across his entire arsenal. The additions and improvements, plus his developing knowledge of how to use his growing arsenal, helped Gibson strike out batters at an elite level.
THE FUTURE: Gibson has the potential to be a midrotation starter thanks to his pitch mix and aptitude. He'll return to Triple-A Norfolk in 2026 but could be on the cusp of a major league debut.

Year	Age	Club (League)	Level	W	L	ERA	G	GS	IP	H	HR	BB	SO	BB%	SO%	WHIP	AVG
2025	23	Aberdeen (SAL)	A+	1	2	5.12	9	8	39	32	7	14	67	8.4	40.4	1.19	.216
2025	23	Chesapeake (EL)	AA	3	2	1.55	10	10	52	29	1	18	68	8.6	32.5	0.90	.157
2025	23	Norfolk (IL)	AAA	1	4	7.98	7	7	29	41	5	12	31	8.6	22.3	1.81	.333
		Minor League Totals		9	17	3.99	52	41	214	177	16	84	286	9.2	31.4	1.22	.220

BALTIMORE ORIOLES

4 NATE GEORGE, OF

HIT: 55. **POW:** 45. **RUN:** 70. **FLD:** 70. **ARM:** 50. **BA Grade:** 55. **Risk:** Average.

Born: June 4, 2006. **B-T:** R-R. **HT:** 6-0. **WT:** 200.
Drafted: HS—Minooka, IL, 2024 (16th round). **Signed by:** Ryan Carlson.
TRACK RECORD: George came from the Chicago suburbs to break out at the 2023 WWBA World Championship in Jupiter, Fla., putting himself on scouts' radars by making the all-tournament team. The Orioles stayed on him in 2024, drafted him in the 16th round and used a $455,000 bonus to keep him from Northwest Florida State JC. George proved more than worth it, dominating the Florida Complex League and Carolina League with Low-A Delmarva before ending well at High-A Aberdeen. In all, he produced a .337 average and .896 OPS over three levels. He stole 50 bases in 87 games but was also thrown out 33% of the time.
SCOUTING REPORT: George's contact ability proved advanced in his pro debut. The righthanded batter used a line-drive swing and knack for putting the ball in play to put together one of the best seasons a teenager had anywhere in the minors. George projects to be an above-average hitter with fringe-average power, but he is so dynamic out of the batter's box—with run times of sub-4.0 seconds from home to first base—that he routinely stretches balls into the gaps for extra bases. His double-plus speed helps him in the outfield, where he has the makings of an elite center fielder with more experience. He's still learning to best deploy his speed on the bases, where he racked up 50 steals but was thrown out 25 times. That's all part of the appeal for George. He plays the game at a breakneck pace and is a good bet to continue to improve at the plate and get the most of his skill set.
THE FUTURE: George's combination of contact ability, speed and athleticism creates a high floor for him, and with physical maturation and some more seasoning at the plate, he could be an impact everyday center fielder with a chance for all-star appearances.

Year	Age	Club (League)	Level	AVG	G	AB	R	H	2B	3B	HR	RBI	BB	SO	SB	OBP	SLG
2025	19	FCL Orioles	Rk	.383	23	81	20	31	1	2	3	14	9	14	13	.451	.556
2025	19	Delmarva (CAR)	A	.337	43	163	31	55	8	7	1	21	18	29	25	.410	.491
2025	19	Aberdeen (SAL)	A+	.291	21	79	15	23	5	0	1	7	11	19	12	.380	.392
		Minor League Totals		.337	87	323	66	109	14	9	5	42	38	62	50	.413	.483

5 LUIS DE LEON, LHP

FB: 70. **SL:** 60. **CH:** 60. **SP:** 55. **CTL:** 45. **BA Grade:** 60. **Risk:** High. **Adj:** 45.

Born: April 14, 2003. **B-T:** L-L. **HT:** 6-3. **WT:** 168.
Signed: Dominican Republic, 2021. **Signed by:** Michael Cruz/Gerardo Cabrera.
TRACK RECORD: De Leon signed for just $30,000 as an 18-year-old from the Dominican Republic late in the 2021 signing period. From that unheralded start, he has grown to become one of the Orioles' most promising and successful international finds in years. De Leon overpowered lower-level hitters when he came to the U.S. in 2023 but stumbled with command and execution in the second half of 2024 at High-A Aberdeen. De Leon missed time with an elbow issue early but rebounded there in 2025 and finished well, carrying a 1.80 ERA with 65 strikeouts in 45 innings over his last nine starts between Aberdeen and Double-A Chesapeake.
SCOUTING REPORT: De Leon's raw stuff has always been among the best in the Orioles' system. He boasts a four-seam fastball and two-seamer in the 95-98 mph range that yields a ton of weak, grounded contact. He throws a plus gyro slider in the mid 80s, an emerging mid-80s splitter and a plus changeup that's a touch harder. De Leon's secondaries have always impressed, but emphasizing fastball location to righthanded batters elevated his entire arsenal in the second half of 2025 as the rest of his stuff played up. De Leon's command has always been inconsistent, but he has good zone rates with his fastball, suggesting it's a trait that can continue to improve. Even in the zone, De Leon is hard to square up. He didn't allow a home run in 87.1 innings in 2025, and he is regularly among the minor league leaders in groundball rate. In 2025, his 56.9% groundball rate ranked 12th among pitchers with at least 10 starts.
THE FUTURE: De Leon's maturation and improved execution elevated his performance to a level that in many ways matches the frontline stuff he boasts. A midrotation starter's role feels realistic now, and he could climb quickly toward that from his likely 2026 starting point at Double-A Chesapeake.

Year	Age	Club (League)	Level	W	L	ERA	G	GS	IP	H	HR	BB	SO	BB%	SO%	WHIP	AVG
2025	22	Delmarva (CAR)	A	0	0	4.09	4	4	11	6	0	8	14	16.3	28.6	1.27	.158
2025	22	Aberdeen (SAL)	A+	4	3	3.58	13	11	60	46	0	26	69	10.1	26.7	1.19	.207
2025	22	Chesapeake (EL)	AA	1	0	1.69	3	3	16	13	0	7	24	10.3	35.3	1.25	.217
		Minor League Totals		17	13	3.68	71	52	257	211	5	133	325	11.8	28.9	1.34	.220

BALTIMORE ORIOLES

6 IKE IRISH, OF/C

HIT: 55. **POW:** 55. **RUN:** 45. **FLD:** 45. **ARM:** 65. **BA Grade:** 55. **Risk:** Average. **Adj:** 45.

Born: November 26, 2003. **B-T:** L-R. **HT:** 6-1. **WT:** 200.
Drafted: Auburn, 2025 (1st round). **Signed by:** David Jennings.
TRACK RECORD: Irish was a decorated hitter at Auburn who slugged 39 home runs with a career 1.060 OPS over three seasons with the Tigers. He improved his on-base ability and power as the years went on. As a junior in 2025, Irish made the All-America first team as an outfielder. He led the Southeastern Conference with a .364 average, including a .408 mark in SEC play. Irish signed for a slot bonus of $4.42 million as the 19th overall pick in 2025. As one of the best college hitters in his draft class, he was a good match for an Orioles organization that covets big-conference standouts. Irish made his pro debut at Low-A Delmarva and put the ball on the ground too often, resulting in a .594 OPS in 20 games.
SCOUTING REPORT: At his best, Irish has the well-rounded offensive skill set that the Orioles prize. He controls the strike zone well, has good bat speed and feel for the barrel and rips line drives to all fields when he's at his best. He uses his whole body and keeps the bat in the zone well. That profile makes him a potentially above-average hitter with above-average power, but his overall value will be determined by his defensive role. He caught just 12 games as an Auburn junior, spending most of his time in right field. The Orioles plan to have him catch while rotating in at first base and right—where his plus arm shines—but he'll need to improve his blocking and framing as he develops in pro ball to have a future at the position. He'd be playable in any other spot defensively, but it would put a lot of pressure on his bat.
THE FUTURE: Irish has everyday potential thanks to his ability at the plate alone, and given the Orioles' catching depth, simply being serviceable behind the plate could make him a valuable roster piece who moves around the diamond but is a steady offensive presence. He'll begin 2026 at High-A Frederick.

Year	Age	Club (League)	Level	AVG	G	AB	R	H	2B	3B	HR	RBI	BB	SO	SB	OBP	SLG
2025	21	Delmarva (CAR)	A	.230	20	74	9	17	2	0	1	12	6	19	3	.296	.297
		Minor League Totals		.230	20	74	9	17	2	0	1	12	6	19	3	.296	.297

7 ESTEBAN MEJIA, RHP

FB: 70. **SL:** 60. **CH:** 40. **CTL:** 45. **BA Grade:** 65. **Risk:** Extreme. **Adj:** 45.

Born: March 7, 2007. **B-T:** R-R. **HT:** 6-3. **WT:** 175.
Signed: Dominican Republic, 2024. **Signed by:** Rafael Belen/Gerardo Cabrera.
TRACK RECORD: The Orioles signed Mejia for $150,000 out of the Dominican Republic in the 2024 international class. He received one of the largest bonuses for a pitcher under Baltimore's current front office. He was already up to 91 mph with his fastball and showed the quick arm, frame and physical projection they believed could turn into something more. That happened quickly, with Mejia adding fastball velocity and exploding onto the scene stateside in 2025 thanks to a fastball that regularly hit 100 mph. He ended up striking out nearly 30% of batters with a 1.29 WHIP and 2.94 ERA in 52 innings between the Florida Complex League and Low-A Delmarva.
SCOUTING REPORT: Working with four-seam and two-seam fastballs, Mejia overpowered lower-level hitters with his electric stuff. His heaters sat in the mid-90s and averaged 98.4 mph—and there's still some physical projection left to add to those marks. Mejia is working to be able to consistently get above barrels with his four-seamer, which from a low three-quarters slot gives him the ability to do more consistently than he does, and he generally commands the ball well for his age. Mejia complements his fastballs with a hard gyro slider that has the early makings of a plus pitch, and his changeup lags behind the rest of the group, though it has good shape at its best. Mejia worked to blend his release point for all the pitches as the 2025 season went on, and is athletic enough to repeat his delivery.
THE FUTURE: Mejia is one of the most exciting and high-ceiling pitchers the Orioles have, but there's a lot of work to be done to have him reach his No. 2 starter potential, from physical maturation to secondary pitch refinement. He'll begin his second full pro season at Low-A Delmarva in 2026 in pursuit of those traits.

Year	Age	Club (League)	Level	W	L	ERA	G	GS	IP	H	HR	BB	SO	BB%	SO%	WHIP	AVG
2025	18	FCL Orioles	Rk	1	2	2.45	11	11	40	28	0	25	53	14.2	30.1	1.31	.190
2025	18	Delmarva (CAR)	A	0	2	4.63	3	3	12	8	0	6	14	11.8	27.5	1.20	.195
		Minor League Totals		1	7	3.05	24	24	80	54	0	46	111	13.2	31.9	1.26	.188

BALTIMORE ORIOLES

8 MICHAEL FORRET, RHP

FB: 55. **CB:** 60. **SL:** 50. **CH:** 50. **SW:** 60. **CTL:** 50. **BA Grade:** 55. **Risk:** High. **Adj:** 40.

Born: April 6, 2004. **B-T:** L-R. **HT:** 6-3. **WT:** 190.
Drafted: State JC of Florida, 2023 (14th round). **Signed by:** Brandon Verley.
TRACK RECORD: The Orioles did well to identify Forret early in his first season at the State College of Florida, which competes at the junior college level and used to be known as Manatee JC. Forret's combination of control, makeup and advanced pitch mix prompted Baltimore to sign him to an above-slot $450,000 in the 14th round in 2023. In his full-season debut in 2024, Forret struck out 29% of batters and produced a 1.29 WHIP in the low minors. He missed a month with a back issue in 2025 but was arguably better in his age-21 season, which began at High-A Aberdeen and ended at Double-A Chesapeake. Forret struck out 32% of batters and finished with a 1.58 ERA and 0.82 WHIP in 74 innings.
SCOUTING REPORT: Forret came to the Orioles committed to developing a full starter's arsenal, and he's done that, with one of the broadest and most impressive mixes in the system. He works off low-90s four-seam and sinking fastballs that he's able to locate, with his four-seamer a particular weapon against righties. His "death ball" curveball highlights the rest of his arsenal as a potential plus pitch that generated a high rate of swinging strikes in 2025. Forret has a plus sweeper as well, and while he didn't have feel for his kick changeup—Forret's best pitch in 2024—both that and his traditional changeup are at least above-average pitches as well. Forret has a starter's frame and repeats his delivery, and he took a step forward with his command in 2025, particularly once he got to Double-A.
THE FUTURE: Forret has an attractive combination of precocious command and ability to go with physical projection, which makes him a candidate to become a No. 3 or 4 starter should he continue on the course he charted in 2025. He'll return to Double-A Chesapeake for the start of 2026.

Year	Age	Club (League)	Level	W	L	ERA	G	GS	IP	H	HR	BB	SO	BB%	SO%	WHIP	AVG
2025	21	Aberdeen (SAL)	A+	1	2	1.51	16	15	60	31	3	17	76	7.5	33.5	0.80	.152
2025	21	Chesapeake (EL)	AA	1	0	1.88	3	3	14	9	0	4	15	7.3	27.3	0.91	.180
		Minor League Totals		8	10	2.90	45	35	174	125	11	65	215	9.1	30.2	1.09	.201

9 ENRIQUE BRADFIELD JR., OF

HIT: 50. **POW:** 30. **RUN:** 80. **FLD:** 80. **ARM:** 45. **BA Grade:** 50. **Risk:** Average. **Adj:** 40.

Born: December 2, 2001. **B-T:** L-L. **HT:** 6-1. **WT:** 170.
Drafted: Vanderbilt, 2023 (1st round). **Signed by:** Trent Friedrich.
TRACK RECORD: Bradfield made a serious impact over three years at Vanderbilt thanks to his combination of elite speed and defense, and the Orioles signed him for $4.17 million as the 17th pick in 2023 to help him maximize his unique skill set at the plate. He won a minor league Gold Glove award in 2024, a season in which he hit .272 with a .729 OPS and 72 stolen bases between High-A Aberdeen and Double-A Bowie. A pair of hamstring issues limited him in 2025, but he still had a .779 OPS and 138 wRC+ in 50 Double-A games and ended the year at Triple-A Norfolk before getting more at-bats in the Arizona Fall League.
SCOUTING REPORT: Bradfield continues to make progress at fine-tuning his unique offensive style to best suit his game. He makes a high volume of contact, rarely whiffs, and maximizes those skills by focusing on pitches he can drive and hitting the ball over the infield. He cut his groundball rate from 50.2% in 2024 to 43.4% in 2025, and he uses his elite speed to turn balls in the gap into extra bases. He's improving his quality of contact as he matures and doesn't need to be a slugger in the big leagues. Instead, he can be a table-setter who can get on base by laying down a bunt or lining a ball to the outfield. Then he can impact games by stealing bases and playing elite center field defense. Still, a player with such an offensive profile will need to prove his viability at every level, including the majors, and Bradfield was challenged late in 2025 in Triple-A.
THE FUTURE: There's little doubt that Bradfield can help a major league team as an everyday outfielder thanks to his speed and defense, and his current offensive trajectory points toward that kind of floor. He'll be back at Triple-A Norfolk to start 2026 and could make his major league debut over the summer.

Year	Age	Club (League)	Level	AVG	G	AB	R	H	2B	3B	HR	RBI	BB	SO	SB	OBP	SLG
2025	23	FCL Orioles	Rk	.333	3	9	1	3	0	0	0	0	2	0	0	.455	.333
2025	23	Aberdeen (SAL)	A+	.179	8	28	7	5	2	0	0	0	3	10	4	.258	.250
2025	23	Chesapeake (EL)	AA	.269	50	171	32	46	12	1	2	14	32	37	26	.393	.386
2025	23	Norfolk (IL)	AAA	.179	15	56	9	10	1	1	1	5	4	19	6	.226	.286
		Minor League Totals		.264	209	747	159	197	36	7	7	60	117	154	135	.369	.359

BALTIMORE ORIOLES

10 WEHIWA ALOY, SS

HIT: 45. **POW:** 55. **RUN:** 50. **FLD:** 50. **ARM:** 50. **BA Grade:** 55. **Risk:** High. **Adj:** 40.

Born: February 4, 2004. **B-T:** R-R. **HT:** 6-2. **WT:** 200.
Drafted: Arkansas, 2025 (1st round supp.). **Signed by:** Michael Choice.
TRACK RECORD: Aloy was recruited out of Hawaii to Sacramento State, where he starred as a freshman before he transferred to Arkansas. The jump didn't faze him. He was the Razorbacks' everyday shortstop and hit 14 home runs as a sophomore. Aloy added 20 more homers and finished with a 1.107 OPS in 2025. The Orioles drafted him 31st overall, signed him for a slot bonus of $3.043 million and were impressed with the hard contact ability he showed in his pro debut, when he had an .856 OPS in 20 games at Low-A Delmarva.
SCOUTING REPORT: Aloy's bat speed and ability to generate raw power drive an attractive overall offensive profile, with natural loft to his swing that gives him above-average power potential with a knack for driving the ball to all fields. The utility of that power could be mitigated by a hit tool that is less refined. Aloy can be susceptible to spin and has some swing-and-miss in his game, though the Orioles believe that's more a matter of better identifying pitches he can drive rather than a fundamental skill issue. It's worth noting he's demonstrated the ability to improve his contact rates as he has adjusted to higher-level pitching in college and could do the same in pro ball. Aloy has meaningfully improved his arm strength since signing, and is lean and athletic with the body control and actions to stay at shortstop, though he could handle any position on the infield.
THE FUTURE: The Orioles love the challenge of maximizing players' hit tools in cases where there are other attractive raw traits, and Aloy has that kind of untapped upside. He has the potential to be an impact everyday player if he makes enough contact, given his ability to play a premium defensive position. He'll start at High-A Frederick for his first full season in 2026.

Year	Age	Club (League)	Level	AVG	G	AB	R	H	2B	3B	HR	RBI	BB	SO	SB	OBP	SLG
2025	21	Delmarva (CAR)	A	.288	20	80	14	23	9	1	2	14	8	25	6	.356	.500
		Minor League Totals		.288	20	80	14	23	9	1	2	14	8	25	6	.356	.500

11 BRAXTON BRAGG, RHP

FB: 55. **CT:** 55. **SW:** 55. **CH:** 55. **CTL:** 60. **BA Grade:** 55. **Risk:** High. **Adj:** 40.

Born: October 28, 2000. **B-T:** R-R. **HT:** 6-2. **WT:** 210. **Drafted:** Dallas Baptist, 2023 (8th round). **Signed by:** Ken Guthrie.
TRACK RECORD: Bragg transferred to Dallas Baptist to be a starter after three years in a relief role at Nebraska, and was a below-slot senior sign for $100,000 who spent his entire first full season in 2024 at Low-A Delmarva. There was no such stagnation in 2025. Bragg added a couple ticks of fastball velocity and a new changeup and was promoted out of High-A Aberdeen to Double-A Chesapeake after just three dominant starts. He ended up with a 1.68 ERA and 11.75 strikeouts per nine with a 1.000 WHIP in 59 minor league innings before requiring Tommy John surgery.
SCOUTING REPORT: Bragg has always filled up the zone and missed bats with a diverse arsenal, and with a 93.3 mph average on his fastball in 2024, he wasn't exactly a soft-tosser. But an impactful offseason strength program meant his fastballs were routinely in the 93-96 mph range in 2025 and pushed up into the high 90s. He gets unique ride and run from his lower arm slot on his four-seamer, and emphasized a two-seamer more to get outs on the ground. Bragg's kick-changeup, a new addition in 2025, is at least above-average and flashes plus. That's another bat-misser added to a mix that also includes an above-average sweeper and cutter. His plus control makes the whole package play up.
THE FUTURE: Bragg's injury means his path to being a midrotation starter is delayed by at least a year. He may return at the end of the 2026 season.

Year	Age	Club (League)	Level	W	L	ERA	G	GS	IP	H	HR	BB	SO	BB%	SO%	WHIP	AVG
2025	24	Aberdeen (SAL)	A+	2	0	0.00	3	3	16	6	0	5	18	8.3	30.0	0.67	.109
2025	24	Chesapeake (EL)	AA	2	2	2.32	9	8	43	36	3	12	59	6.9	33.7	1.13	.225
		Minor League Totals		10	8	2.89	40	31	162	140	13	42	205	6.3	30.6	1.12	.228

BALTIMORE ORIOLES

12 SLATER DE BRUN, OF
HIT: 55. **POW:** 40. **RUN:** 70. **FLD:** 60. **ARM:** 55. **BA Grade:** 55. **Risk:** High. **Adj:** 40.

Born: June 8, 2007. **B-T:** L-L. **HT:** 5-10. **WT:** 190. **Drafted:** HS—Bend, OR, 2025 (1st round supp.).
Signed by: David Blume.
TRACK RECORD: De Brun was a standout on the 2024 showcase circuit, building buzz about his draft candidacy as the top prep outfielder in the 2025 class. The Orioles signed him for an above-slot $4 million, the largest bonus outside the first round, to buy him out of Vanderbilt commitment—where de Brun could have also advanced his fledgling music career. Instead, he signed to give the Orioles another high-ceiling prep prospect, an area the club has been successful in recently.
SCOUTING REPORT: The combination of de Brun's youth, athleticism, and contact ability at the plate drives de Brun's upside. He's short to the ball and demonstrates above-average contact ability, which the Orioles feel is supplemented by advanced plate discipline for his age. Despite being strong for his size, de Brun has a hit-over-power profile. He will need to improve his movements to get to fringe-average power. De Brun is also a plus-plus runner who gets the most of his quickness both out of the box and on the basepaths, where he's always a threat to steal and probably will enjoy the Orioles' aggressive approach on the bases in the minors. That speed also helps in center field, where he has good instincts and range along with a strong arm.
THE FUTURE: De Brun has long tried to model his game after Corbin Carroll's, given their regional connection and physical similarities. Coming anywhere close to that would make him a first-division regular who impacts the game in all phases. He could start his pursuit of that goal at Low-A Delmarva in 2026.

Year	Age	Club (League)	Level	AVG	G	AB	R	H	2B	3B	HR	RBI	BB	SO	SB	OBP	SLG
2025	18	Did not play															

13 ARON ESTRADA, 2B/OF
HIT: 50. **POW:** 45. **RUN:** 55. **FLD:** 50. **ARM:** 50. **BA Grade:** 50. **Risk:** Average. **Adj:** 40.

Born: January 13, 2005. **B-T:** B-R. **HT:** 5-8. **WT:** 140. **Signed:** Venezuela, 2022. **Signed by:** Adel Granadillo.
TRACK RECORD: The Orioles had plenty of infielders already committed to their 2022 international class but couldn't pass up Estrada, a $150,000 signee who has outperformed his peers at every level. He was a Dominican Summer League All Star in 2022, a Carolina League postseason all star in 2024 after a strong full-season debut at Low-A Delmarva, and earned that same honor in 2025 in the South Atlantic League for High-A Aberdeen. Estrada eventually reached Double-A Chesapeake with an .813 OPS and 34 steals between the two levels.
SCOUTING REPORT: Estrada has a contact-first profile and doesn't strike out much, which drives much of his offensive upside. He's growing into some power, but at times his overall quality of contact can be hindered by his aggressive approach at the plate, which Estrada is working to improve. He can be an average hitter with fringe-average power, and will need to maximize his offensive profile. Despite some time at shortstop and in the corner outfield, Estrada is best suited for second base and may not end up more than an average defender there. Still, he's an above-average runner who plays the game hard and maximizes his skills on the field.
THE FUTURE: Reaching Double-A and holding his own at age 20 puts Estrada on a good path towards the big leagues, where he can be a bat-first everyday second baseman at his peak. He'll likely be back at Double-A Chesapeake to start 2026.

Year	Age	Club (League)	Level	AVG	G	AB	R	H	2B	3B	HR	RBI	BB	SO	SB	OBP	SLG
2025	20	Aberdeen (SAL)	A+	.284	81	289	41	82	13	7	5	40	35	58	30	.369	.429
2025	20	Chesapeake (EL)	AA	.300	27	100	11	30	3	1	5	13	9	17	4	.355	.500
		Minor League Totals		.293	293	1021	162	299	50	18	23	142	128	187	82	.380	.445

14 BOSTON BATEMAN, LHP
FB: 55. **CB:** 60. **SL:** 60. **CH:** 50. **CTL:** 45. **BA Grade:** 55. **Risk:** High. **Adj:** 40.

Born: September 20, 2005. **B-T:** R-L. **HT:** 6-8. **WT:** 240. **Drafted:** HS—Camarillo, CA, 2024 (2nd round).
Signed by: Spencer Babcock (Padres).
TRACK RECORD: The son of an NFL offensive lineman, Bateman looks like he could have stayed in the family business but instead dominated the California high school circuit and signed for an above-slot $2.5 million with the Padres as the 52nd overall pick in 2024. He was pitching well at Low-A Lake Elsinore when the Orioles acquired him as the top player in an eight-player swap that sent Ramon Laureano and Ryan O'Hearn to San Diego. Bateman ended his first full season at High-A Aberdeen, with a 4.14 ERA and 1.45 WHIP with 9.7 strikeouts per nine in the low minors.

BALTIMORE ORIOLES

SCOUTING REPORT: Bateman was able to use his mid-90s fastball from a high slot to get through his pro debut. He has touched 98 and his fastball leads what's currently a four-pitch mix. He can spin a good curveball in the low 80s and has a mid-to-high-80s slider that both flash plus, while his changeup is also on the harder side and can be average with refinement. Bateman has the makeup and work ethic to attack his developmental needs and make his pitches more consistent both in terms of shape and command, and the Orioles may expand his arsenal to include a cutter and sweeper as well.
THE FUTURE: The raw ingredients and makeup Bateman brings to the table don't come around often, and the Orioles' pitching program could help him reach his ceiling as a solid major league starter. He may take some time to develop, though, and will be back at High-A Aberdeen to start 2026.

Year	Age	Club (League)	Level	W	L	ERA	G	GS	IP	H	HR	BB	SO	BB%	SO%	WHIP	AVG
2025	19	Lake Elsinore (CAL)	A	5	5	4.08	15	15	68	65	1	25	75	8.6	25.8	1.32	.249
2025	19	Delmarva (CAR)	A	0	0	2.45	2	2	7	11	0	2	6	6.1	18.2	1.77	.379
2025	19	Aberdeen (SAL)	A+	0	0	5.56	3	3	11	12	1	11	13	19.6	23.2	2.03	.279
		Minor League Totals		5	5	4.14	20	20	87	88	2	38	94	10.0	24.7	1.45	.264

15 NESTOR GERMAN, RHP

FB: 55. **CB:** 55. **SL:** 55. **SP:** 60. **CT:** 40. **CTL:** 50. **BA Grade:** 50. **Risk:** Average. **Adj:** 40.

Born: February 26, 2002. **B-T:** R-R. **HT:** 6-3. **WT:** 225. **Drafted:** Seattle, 2023 (11th round). **Signed by:** David Blume.
TRACK RECORD: The Orioles thought German had more in the tank in terms of both velocity and pitch mix than his 6.37 ERA at Seattle suggested, and were proven right almost immediately upon German pitching in pro ball. He had a 1.59 ERA with 11 strikeouts per nine in 73.2 innings in the low minors in his full-season debut in 2024, and pitched across three levels to reach Triple-A Norfolk in 2025 with a 3.93 ERA, 10.41 strikeouts per nine and a 1.18 WHIP.
SCOUTING REPORT: German took steps forward in several areas in 2025, pitching deeper into games and getting plenty of weak contact to complement his ability to miss bats. He has a unique, over-the-top delivery and commands the ball well with an ability to work his mid-90s four-seamer up in the zone to get above barrels. He works down in the zone with a hard, high-80s slider that's above-average and boasts an above-average curveball. His plus splitter was one of the best swing-and-miss weapons in the entire system that gives him a way to combat lefties. He experimented with a cutter at the end of the year in Triple-A that could become a bigger part of his arsenal in 2026.
THE FUTURE: German has a sturdy frame and the potential to be a No. 4 starter, with a relief floor given his ability to miss bats. German will be in the Triple-A rotation pushing for his MLB debut.

Year	Age	Club (League)	Level	W	L	ERA	G	GS	IP	H	HR	BB	SO	BB%	SO%	WHIP	AVG
2025	23	Aberdeen (SAL)	A+	0	1	3.60	6	6	25	23	2	10	37	9.5	35.2	1.32	.242
2025	23	Chesapeake (EL)	AA	6	6	3.76	18	17	91	68	8	32	96	8.7	26.0	1.10	.207
2025	23	Norfolk (IL)	AAA	0	0	7.04	2	2	8	9	3	4	10	11.1	27.8	1.70	.281
		Minor League Totals		7	10	3.24	40	37	172	131	13	60	200	8.6	28.6	1.11	.209

16 CADEN BODINE, C

HIT: 60. **POW:** 40. **RUN:** 40. **FLD:** 60. **ARM:** 45. **BA Grade:** 50. **Risk:** Average. **Adj:** 40.

Born: December 2, 2003. **B-T:** B-R. **HT:** 5-10. **WT:** 200. **Drafted:** Coastal Carolina, 2025 (1st round supp.).
Signed by: Quincy Boyd.
TRACK RECORD: Bodine built a reputation as one of the best catchers in all of college baseball over three seasons with Coastal Carolina, helping guide one of the nation's best pitching staffs in 2024 and earning the Buster Posey Award as the NCAA's best backstop. In appreciation of that and Bodine's ability to control the strike zone and make a lot of good contact, the Orioles selected him 30th overall and signed him for a slot bonus of $3.11 million. He fared well in his pro debut at Low-A Delmarva before a bruised hand ended his season a week early.
SCOUTING REPORT: The Orioles were attracted to what they believe is a reliable skill set that Bodine brings, both at and behind the plate. He's an advanced receiver who passes the eye test and screens well analytically, too, with advanced actions and feel for the position. His arm strength might be light, but he makes up for that with a quick and smooth exchange. At the plate, Bodine is a contact-oriented hitter with a knack for finding the barrel and limited in-zone miss, giving him the potential to be a plus hitter, albeit with below-average power. His switch-hitting ability and control of the strike zone still gives him plenty of offensive value, especially given his position.
THE FUTURE: Bodine's potential to stick behind the plate and be a table-setter at it gives him a future as a solid-average major league regular should his skills scale through the minors. He could start 2026 at High-A Frederick.

BALTIMORE ORIOLES

Year	Age	Club (League)	Level	AVG	G	AB	R	H	2B	3B	HR	RBI	BB	SO	SB	OBP	SLG
2025	21	Delmarva (CAR)	A	.326	11	43	6	14	1	0	0	4	5	8	0	.408	.349
		Minor League Totals		.326	11	43	6	14	1	0	0	4	5	8	0	.408	.349

17 AUSTIN OVERN, OF
HIT: 45 **POW:** 45. **RUN:** 70. **FLD:** 70. **ARM:** 50. **BA Grade:** 45. **Risk:** Average. **Adj:** 35.

Born: May 10, 2003. **B-T:** L-R. **HT:** 6-0. **WT:** 175. **Drafted:** Southern California, 2024 (3rd round). **Signed by:** Scott Walter.
TRACK RECORD: Overn played football as well as baseball as a freshman at Southern California, and after focusing solely on baseball as a draft-eligible sophomore, signed for $850,000 as the 97th pick in 2024. He had a .754 OPS at both High-A Aberdeen and Double-A Chesapeake in 2025, hitting 13 home runs with 64 steals in his first full pro season.
SCOUTING REPORT: Overn's dual-sport background means he's still refining his game on the baseball field, but he still has the potential to impact the game in several ways. Overn is a dynamic player who uses his speed and quick-twitch athleticism to impact the game defensively in center field, where he's a great defender, as well as on the bases—and he's already adept at bunting his way on as well. Overn takes good at-bats and gets on base—he walked 13% of the time in 2025—and can hit the ball hard, but some timing deficiencies meant he struggled against velocity in his first full season. He may max out as a fringe-average hitter with fringe-average power, but improving against heaters would raise his overall offensive profile significantly.
THE FUTURE: Overn can be an everyday big leaguer with some improvement in that department, given his ability to play a true center field and the traits to play a corner as well. He'll attack that challenge back at Double-A Chesapeake to start the 2026 season.

Year	Age	Club (League)	Level	AVG	G	AB	R	H	2B	3B	HR	RBI	BB	SO	SB	OBP	SLG
2025	22	Aberdeen (SAL)	A+	.242	84	277	51	67	8	4	8	30	53	96	43	.367	.386
2025	22	Chesapeake (EL)	AA	.266	30	124	23	33	5	0	5	13	9	34	21	.326	.427
		Minor League Totals		.254	135	476	90	121	18	7	14	50	77	155	80	.362	.410

18 LEVI WELLS, RHP
FB: 60. **CB:** 55. **SL:** 55. **CT:** 55. **CH:** 40. **CTL:** 40. **BA Grade:** 50. **Risk:** High. **Adj:** 40.

Born: September 21, 2001. **B-T:** R-R. **HT:** 6-2. **WT:** 215. **Drafted:** Texas State, 2023 (4th round). **Signed by:** Dan Drullinger.
TRACK RECORD: Wells began his college career in Texas Tech's bullpen before spending two seasons at Texas State, where they used his high-octane arm in the rotation. Wells' resume there, plus some impressive stints on Cape Cod, helped him climb the Orioles' draft board, and they signed him for slightly below slot at $500,000 as the 118th pick in 2023. Wells' stuff was far better than the results in his first full season, but he fared well in the high minors in 2025, ending at Triple-A Norfolk.
SCOUTING REPORT: Wells is a fiery competitor whose success on the mound has correlated to improvements in how he controls that, though the same doesn't need to be said about his arsenal, which he fills up the zone with. Wells has both a four-seam and two-seam fastball and sits around 96 mph, though he can touch 100. The Orioles throttled back his velocity to get him deeper into games later in the season. His 90-94 mph cutter, mid-80s sweeper and low-80s curveball are all above-average pitches. Wells has a firm changeup but almost entirely scrapped the pitch in 2025 and it's a distant fifth offering. Wells doesn't miss bats as much as he should given the quality of his stuff but generates plenty of weak contact with it.
THE FUTURE: Wells' stuff is tantalizing to dream on as a back-end starter but he may be more effective in a bullpen role. He'll return to Norfolk, likely as a starter, to push for a major league debut in 2026.

Year	Age	Club (League)	Level	W	L	ERA	G	GS	IP	H	HR	BB	SO	BB%	SO%	WHIP	AVG
2025	23	Chesapeake (EL)	AA	1	6	3.12	20	16	75	70	4	26	80	8.0	24.5	1.28	.238
2025	23	Norfolk (IL)	AAA	1	0	4.79	5	5	21	17	3	13	16	14.4	17.8	1.45	.233
		Minor League Totals		2	6	3.48	25	21	96	87	7	39	96	9.4	23.0	1.32	.237

19 JUARON WATTS-BROWN, RHP
FB: 50. **CB:** 50. **SL:** 60. **CH:** 50. **CTL:** 50. **BA Grade:** 50. **Risk:** High. **Adj:** 35.

Born: February 23, 2002. **B-T:** R-R. **HT:** 6-3. **WT:** 190. **Drafted:** Oklahoma State, 2023 (3rd round).
Signed by: Max Semier (Blue Jays).
TRACK RECORD: Watts-Brown pitched well enough as a redshirt freshman at Long Beach State and then in the Cape Cod League to transfer to Oklahoma State. Toronto then selected him with the 67th pick and signed him for an overslot $1 million in 2023. He was in the midst of a breakout season in the Blue Jays system and was at Double-A New Hampshire when the Orioles acquired him for reliever Seranthony

BALTIMORE ORIOLES

Dominguez at the 2025 deadline. Watts-Brown had a 3.62 ERA with 11.44 strikeouts per nine between High-A and Double-A.

SCOUTING REPORT: Watts-Brown got most of his strikeouts with a mid-80s gyro slider that's at least plus, a pitch with late break that Watts-Brown can both land for strikes early and bury for chase late as it comes off the same line as his fastball. His 92-95 mph four-seamer, though, is quite hittable, and Watts-Brown and the Orioles are searching for solutions there, be it a two-seamer or cutter. He flashes an average low-80s curveball and took a step forward with his kick-change as 2025 progressed. Watts-Brown has an athletic, repeatable delivery and can have average control, though he'll need better fastball command than that.

THE FUTURE: Watts-Brown can pitch in the big leagues in some capacity simply because of his slider, but a starter's role depends on improving his fastball, be it a different shape or adding velocity, to help him get deep into games at the highest level. He'll be back at Double-A Chesapeake in 2026 for his first full season in the Orioles organization.

Year	Age	Club (League)	Level	W	L	ERA	G	GS	IP	H	HR	BB	SO	BB%	SO%	WHIP	AVG
2025	23	Vancouver (NWL)	A+	0	3	3.62	8	8	37	32	2	12	62	7.7	39.7	1.18	.232
2025	23	New Hampshire (EL)	AA	2	2	3.48	11	11	52	38	4	26	53	11.8	24.0	1.24	.201
2025	23	Chesapeake (EL)	AA	1	3	3.82	7	7	35	20	10	12	43	8.7	31.2	0.91	.159
		Minor League Totals		7	19	4.12	47	47	227	177	30	110	289	11.4	29.9	1.26	.211

20 THOMAS SOSA, OF

HIT: 40. **POW:** 55. **RUN:** 50. **FLD:** 45. **ARM:** 60. **BA Grade:** 45. **Risk:** Average. **Adj:** 35.

Born: January 18, 2005. **B-T:** L-L. **HT:** 6-1. **WT:** 180. **Signed:** Dominican Republic, 2022.
Signed by: Rafael Belen/Gerardo Cabrera.

TRACK RECORD: Sosa's power potential and athleticism warranted a $400,000 signing bonus as part of the Orioles' 2022 signing class, and few players in the organization have been challenged more aggressively with their minor league assignments than him. After ending 2024 at High-A Aberdeen, Sosa's 2025 was delayed by a knee issue, and he ultimately played just 47 games with a .716 OPS there before ending his age-20 season at Double-A Chesapeake.

SCOUTING REPORT: Sosa has the makings of a prototypical slugging corner outfielder thanks to his hard contact ability. His 90th percentile exit velocity of 106.7 mph was among the organization's leaders, and he had a 41.3% hard-hit rate. His swing decisions and the swing-and-miss in his game will influence how much of his plus raw power Sosa can get to in a game, and he may end up a below-average hitter as a result. Defensively, Sosa has played some center field but profiles more as a right fielder thanks to average speed and a plus arm. He's a physical athlete whose speed doesn't always fully translate to the field, and his knee injury also cut his stolen base totals in 2025 after stealing 30 in 2024.

THE FUTURE: Sosa's potential to polish his approach and contact skills, as well as his age-advanced assignments, put him on a path to a major league role of some kind, even if it's just providing some thump off the bench against righties. He'll be back in Double-A to start 2026.

Year	Age	Club (League)	Level	AVG	G	AB	R	H	2B	3B	HR	RBI	BB	SO	SB	OBP	SLG
2025	20	Delmarva (CAR)	A	.237	10	38	3	9	0	0	1	5	4	12	1	.326	.316
2025	20	Aberdeen (SAL)	A+	.222	47	167	24	37	9	2	6	31	18	46	3	.309	.407
2025	20	Chesapeake (EL)	AA	.158	11	38	2	6	1	0	2	6	2	11	0	.220	.342
		Minor League Totals		.234	226	777	114	182	40	7	20	102	88	228	31	.322	.381

21 JOSEPH DZIERWA, LHP

FB: 50. **SL:** 45. **CH:** 60. **CTL:** 60. **BA Grade:** 45. **Risk:** Average. **Adj:** 35.

Born: April 21, 2004. **B-T:** R-L. **HT:** 6-8. **WT:** 200. **Drafted:** Michigan State, 2025 (2nd round). **Signed by:** Trent Friedrich.

TRACK RECORD: Dzierwa was a three-sport star and all-state quarterback as a high schooler at Otsego High in Ohio. He thrived on the mound for Michigan State and was the Big Ten pitcher of the year in 2025, when he made 18 starts with a 1.42 ERA with 137 strikeouts and a 0.834 WHIP in 118.2 innings. The Orioles took him 58th overall—the highest they've taken a pitcher since Mike Elias took over in 2018—and signed him for a slightly below slot $1.5 million.

SCOUTING REPORT: Dzierwa threw one of the better changeups in the college class to drive a lot of his success in college, and has a mix that should scale well in pro ball as well. His fastball lives in the low-90s and reaches 95 mph, with run and ride, and he commands the pitch well in and around the zone. Dzierwa's changeup is a platoon-neutral weapon that produced 39% whiff and 44% chase rates in 2025, and his slider is a significant development point. Dzierwa's advanced command profile is also an asset and he could have plus control.

BALTIMORE ORIOLES

THE FUTURE: Dzierwa can climb quickly thanks to his command and plus changeup. Attention to his breaking ball and increased velocity could allow him to fit neatly in the back half of a major league rotation. He could begin his pro career in 2026 at Low-A Delmarva.

Year	Age	Club (League)	Level	W	L	ERA	G	GS	IP	H	HR	BB	SO	BB%	SO%	WHIP	AVG
2025	21	Did not play															

22 WILFRI DE LA CRUZ, SS
HIT: 50. **POW:** 55. **RUN:** 55. **FLD:** 50. **ARM:** 60. **BA Grade:** 55. **Risk:** Extreme. **Adj:** 35.

Born: September 15, 2007. **B-T:** B-R. **HT:** 6-2. **WT:** 170. **Signed:** Dominican Republic, 2025.
Signed by: Alejandro Peña/Gian Guzman/Alex Suarez (Cubs).
TRACK RECORD: De La Cruz's $2.3 million signing bonus was the largest the Cubs gave out in their 2025 international class, and the eighth-largest for a Latin American player in the class league-wide. He was off to a good start for their Dominican Summer League club when Chicago dealt him to the Orioles for reliever Andrew Kittredge in July.
SCOUTING REPORT: De La Cruz has an attractive offensive profile for several reasons: his swing decisions—he had an 11% chase rate after the trade—and lack of whiffs with elevated contact from both sides of the plate give him a chance for an average hit tool moving forward. He also has plenty of power to dream on as he physically matures, given his broad shoulders and projectable 6-foot-2 frame. Above-average power is a possibility. De La Cruz is also an above-average runner who can be an average defender at shortstop but would fit fine at third base if he outgrows short, given his plus arm.
THE FUTURE: The Orioles are excited to bring De La Cruz stateside and see how his skills scale. He can be an everyday shortstop in the big leagues, and will be in the Florida Complex League to start 2026.

Year	Age	Club (League)	Level	AVG	G	AB	R	H	2B	3B	HR	RBI	BB	SO	SB	OBP	SLG
2025	17	DSL Cubs Red	Rk	.267	28	86	18	23	9	2	0	10	26	24	9	.443	.419
2025	17	DSL Orioles Orange	Rk	.235	12	34	8	8	2	1	0	8	20	12	6	.509	.353
		Minor League Totals		.258	40	120	26	31	11	3	0	18	46	36	15	.465	.400

23 JORDAN SANCHEZ, OF
HIT: 45. **POW:** 55. **RUN:** 50. **FLD:** 50. **ARM:** 50. **BA Grade:** 50. **Risk:** High. **Adj:** 35.

Born: October 9, 2005. **B-T:** L-L. **HT:** 6-1. **WT:** 176. **Signed:** Cuba, 2023. **Signed by:** Luis Noel/Gerardo Cabrera.
TRACK RECORD: When Sanchez left Cuba in 2023, competition for his services was hot, and the Orioles' tactic of holding back some bonus money for such situations paid off. He signed for $450,000 and hasn't stopped hitting since. After dominating the Dominican Summer League in 2024, Sanchez was the Florida Complex League MVP in his age-19 season, homering five times with a .950 OPS. He also went deep twice in four games to end the season at Low-A Delmarva.
SCOUTING REPORT: That power production, as well as some on-base ability, define Sanchez's profile at this stage of his career. He makes good swing decisions, walking 14.8% of the time in 2025, but also has an extreme amount of swing-and-miss tendencies that led to a 29.5% strikeout rate in the low minors. His quality of contact when he connects, however, is high. He shows potential above-average power and the ability to pull the ball in the air frequently, and he'll have to slug given he's probably limited to a corner outfield spot and might not ever be more than average there.
THE FUTURE: Sanchez has been old for his levels but even so shows the potential to be an everyday slugging corner outfielder in the majors. He'll start back at Delmarva in 2026.

Year	Age	Club (League)	Level	AVG	G	AB	R	H	2B	3B	HR	RBI	BB	SO	SB	OBP	SLG
2025	19	FCL Orioles	Rk	.293	54	157	32	46	16	3	5	45	31	57	3	.421	.529
2025	19	Delmarva (CAR)	A	.267	4	15	2	4	0	0	2	4	0	5	0	.267	.667
		Minor League Totals		.309	96	301	67	93	29	5	13	86	54	93	8	.419	.568

24 ANTHONY NUNEZ, RHP
FB: 50. **CT:** 60. **SW:** 60. **CH:** 60. **CTL:** 40. **BA Grade:** 50. **Risk:** High. **Adj:** 35.

Born: July 10, 2001. **B-T:** B-R. **HT:** 6-1. **WT:** 230. **Signed:** Tampa, 2024 (UDFA). **Signed by:** Brett Campbell (Mets).
TRACK RECORD: Nunez signed with the Padres of high school as an infielder in the 29th round in 2019, but when he was released in 2021 he was granted eligibility to play at Division II Tampa. He hit there for three years before trying his hand at pitching late in 2024 for Tampa's D-II national championship team. He signed with the Mets as an undrafted free agent that year, dominated pro ball and was part of the Orioles' return for Cedric Mullins at the 2025 trade deadline. After the season, Nunez would have been

BALTIMORE ORIOLES

a minor league free agent but was added to the Orioles' 40-man roster instead.

SCOUTING REPORT: Nunez's pitch mix is the type one would draw up when designing a modern pitcher, which makes sense considering he only just got on the mound. His four-seamer gets weak contact at the top of the zone in the 95-97 mph range, while hitters pound his two-seamer into the ground. What truly separates Nunez is his natural feel for spin and for commanding his changeup. He throws an 89-92 mph cutter as his primary pitch to set the stage for a plus mid-80s sweeper he uses to expand the zone against righthanded hitters and an outstanding kick-changeup that he deploys against lefties. His control is good enough for a high-leverage role—he closed games at Double-A and Triple-A—but he needs to dial in the strike zone in 2026 to ensure that is the case.

THE FUTURE: The Orioles have produced plenty of unheralded bullpen stars this decade. Nunez could be the next that they put into a high-leverage role in relief, and he could compete for a job in the big leagues in spring training.

Year	Age	Club (League)	Level	W	L	ERA	G	GS	IP	H	HR	BB	SO	BB%	SO%	WHIP	AVG
2025	23	Brooklyn (SAL)	A+	1	1	0.63	10	0	14	3	0	5	24	9.6	46.2	0.56	.068
2025	23	Binghamton (EL)	AA	1	0	2.10	22	0	26	12	0	12	36	12.2	36.7	0.94	.146
2025	23	Chesapeake (EL)	AA	0	0	0.00	1	0	1	0	0	0	2	0.0	40.0	0.00	.000
2025	23	Norfolk (IL)	AAA	1	4	3.45	16	0	16	7	2	7	21	10.8	32.3	0.89	.135
		Minor League Totals		3	5	1.99	51	1	59	22	2	24	85	10.6	37.6	0.78	.117

25 JT QUINN, RHP
FB: 60. **SL:** 55. **CH:** 45. **CTL:** 40. **BA Grade:** 50. **Risk:** High. **Adj:** 35.

Born: April 22, 2004. **B-T:** R-R. **HT:** 6-6. **WT:** 210. **Drafted:** Georgia, 2025 (2nd round supp.). **Signed by:** Eric Robinson.

TRACK RECORD: Quinn spent two years at Ole Miss before transferring to Georgia, where he found his command and improved form as a swingman. He made a lower half adjustment in the Cape Cod League that helped him command the ball as well as he ever has, and signed for a slightly below-slot $1.15 million bonus as the 69th pick in the 2025 draft.

SCOUTING REPORT: Quinn has a unique over-the-top delivery that, considering he's 6-foot-6, creates an uncommon release point and adds some deception that helps power his entire arsenal. He has a low-efficiency two-seam and cut four-seam combo in the fastball space, with average velocities in the mid 90s and a peak of 98.2 mph for the Bulldogs. He can miss bats with a mid-80s above-average, depthy slider and mixes in a high-spin curveball in the high 70s. He also has a promising movement profile on his developing kick-change, which at times has negative vertical break. Despite his improvement, Quinn has always been a scattered strike-thrower.

THE FUTURE: If the control improvements Quinn demonstrated in the Cape are durable, his stuff is such that he can develop into a back-half starter, though a reliever role is far more likely. He could start his pro career at Low-A Delmarva to begin 2026.

Year	Age	Club (League)	Level	W	L	ERA	G	GS	IP	H	HR	BB	SO	BB%	SO%	WHIP	AVG
2025	21	Did not play															

26 WELLINGTON ARACENA, RHP
FB: 70. **CT:** 50. **SL:** 50. **CH:** 40. **CTL:** 30. **BA Grade:** 45. **Risk:** High. **Adj:** 30.

Born: December 27, 2004. **B-T:** R-R. **HT:** 6-3. **WT:** 180. **Signed:** Dominican Republic, 2022. **Signed by:** Oliver Dominguez (Mets).

TRACK RECORD: Aracena, signed by the Mets for $70,000 in 2022, came stateside in 2024 but really took a step forward in 2025. He locked in his command as the season progressed at Low-A St. Lucie before being part of the Orioles' return for Gregory Soto. His season finished at High-A Aberdeen.

SCOUTING REPORT: Aracena boasts a hard, high-90s four-seam fastball that topped out at 101 mph, as well as a two-seamer that he doesn't use often. Instead, he complements his four-seamer with a low-90s cutter and a high-80s slider that can both be average. He rounds out his arsenal with a changeup and curveball. Aracena can miss bats with the fastball, cutter and slider, and he dominates when he's able to locate those pitches, but needs to throw more strikes and be more efficient to maximize his power arm.

THE FUTURE: Aracena's arm speed and high-octane arsenal could find a comfortable home in the bullpen if he doesn't fulfill his back-end starter ceiling. His ability to command the ball and round out his arsenal will determine that. He'll return to Aberdeen to start 2026.

Year	Age	Club (League)	Level	W	L	ERA	G	GS	IP	H	HR	BB	SO	BB%	SO%	WHIP	AVG
2025	20	St. Lucie (FSL)	A	1	1	2.38	17	8	64	38	0	35	84	13.2	31.7	1.13	.166
2025	20	Delmarva (CAR)	A	0	0	0.00	1	1	5	1	0	1	6	5.9	35.3	0.43	.063
2025	20	Aberdeen (SAL)	A+	1	1	2.35	5	5	23	10	0	15	24	16.0	25.5	1.09	.130
		Minor League Totals		7	13	3.80	57	38	187	134	5	123	224	15.0	27.3	1.37	.195

BALTIMORE ORIOLES

27 ETHAN ANDERSON, C
HIT: 50. **POW:** 45. **RUN:** 45. **FLD:** 50. **ARM:** 45. **BA Grade:** 45. **Risk:** High. **Adj:** 30.

Born: September 21, 2003. **B-T:** B-R. **HT:** 6-2. **WT:** 215. **Drafted:** Virginia, 2024 (2nd round). **Signed by:** Donovan O'Dowd.

TRACK RECORD: Anderson's bat kept him in the lineup for three years at Virginia, and he finally got to catch some as a junior in 2024 after Kyle Teel was drafted. He was a productive hitter throughout and signed for a below-slot $1.17 million as the 62nd pick in 2024, and had a roller-coaster pro debut. He started hot at High-A Aberdeen, faded badly, then recovered to earn a promotion to Double-A Chesapeake in mid-August. Anderson finished his year with a nice Arizona Fall League stint.

SCOUTING REPORT: Anderson has the potential to be an average hitter thanks to his combination of plate discipline and contact skills, though he fared better from the left side than the right in his first full pro season. He's still growing into his ability to impact the ball in-game, which might ultimately limit his offensive upside and keep him from having more than fringe-average game power. That profile will mean he'll have to continue what was meaningful improvement behind the plate, where Anderson is a good receiver, given the bat may be challenged at first base or in a corner outfield spot.

THE FUTURE: Anderson can be a useful major league catcher thanks to his switch hitting and contact skills, provided the defense holds up. He'll be back at Chesapeake to start 2026.

Year	Age	Club (League)	Level	AVG	G	AB	R	H	2B	3B	HR	RBI	BB	SO	SB	OBP	SLG
2025	21	Aberdeen (SAL)	A+	.257	70	245	26	63	13	1	3	42	31	51	15	.338	.355
2025	21	Chesapeake (EL)	AA	.215	20	65	9	14	1	0	1	3	12	13	0	.338	.277
		Minor League Totals		.256	109	383	44	98	18	3	5	57	52	79	21	.342	.358

28 STIVEN MARTINEZ, OF
HIT: 30. **POW:** 50. **RUN:** 40. **FLD:** 45. **ARM:** 60. **BA Grade:** 50. **Risk:** Extreme. **Adj:** 30.

Born: July 8, 2007. **B-T:** R-R. **HT:** 6-4. **WT:** 198. **Signed:** Dominican Republic, 2024.
Signed by: Francisco Rosario/Gerardo Cabrera.

TRACK RECORD: Martinez signed for $950,000 as one of the headliners in the Orioles' 2024 international class and has been among the youngest at every level he's played at since. He made a good showing that year in the Dominican Summer League and in 2025 had a .733 OPS in the Florida Complex League at age-17 before struggling at Low-A Delmarva in the last month of the season.

SCOUTING REPORT: Martinez has a good all-fields approach and hits the ball hard at good angles, with a 47.2% hard-hit rate and a 90th percentile exit velocity of 104.5 mph at this early stage of his career. He could have above-average power but will need to cut down on the swing-and-miss dramatically and limit his strikeouts to get to it. Martinez can work a walk—he did so at a 16.1% clip in 2025—but a combination of taking strikes and swinging through them with poor bat-to-ball skills limited his offensive impact, particularly at Low-A. While he might only be a fringe-average defender in a corner spot, he's young enough to grow into his skills and find a home that suits his power potential.

THE FUTURE: Martinez will still be one of the youngest players in Low-A when he returns there to start 2026, and his power is exciting, but his hit tool needs to progress significantly.

Year	Age	Club (League)	Level	AVG	G	AB	R	H	2B	3B	HR	RBI	BB	SO	SB	OBP	SLG
2025	17	FCL Orioles	Rk	.217	49	152	29	33	7	3	3	20	33	54	2	.368	.362
2025	17	Delmarva (CAR)	A	.125	25	80	5	10	3	1	0	2	13	46	3	.263	.188
		Minor League Totals		.219	115	365	61	80	15	8	7	55	74	151	7	.364	.362

29 JOSHUA LIRANZO, SS/3B
HIT: 45. **POW:** 55. **RUN:** 45. **FLD:** 50. **ARM:** 60. **BA Grade:** 45. **Risk:** High. **Adj:** 30.

Born: August 25, 2006. **B-T:** R-R. **HT:** 6-3. **WT:** 180. **Signed:** Dominican Republic, 2023.
Signed by: Luis Noel/Gerardo Cabrera.

TRACK RECORD: Liranzo signed for just under $500,000 as part of the Orioles' 2023 international class, following his older brother Thayron—who signed with the Dodgers before being traded to the Tigers—into pro ball. A knee injury cut short Liranzo's Florida Complex League campaign in 2024, meaning he returned to the level in 2025 and fared well there before a challenging second half at Low-A Delmarva.

SCOUTING REPORT: Despite the challenges in full-season ball, there's plenty of upside to Liranzo's game. He hits the ball hard and gets on base, at times being a little too passive and getting himself out of counts, but can have above-average power with fringe-average hitting ability should he refine his approach. Liranzo is a tick below-average as a runner and can hold his own at shortstop but can be at least average at third base, where he might profile best, and boasts a plus arm that shines at the position.

THE FUTURE: Liranzo's adjustment period in Low-A doesn't dim the hopes that he can be an everyday, bat-first third baseman in the big leagues though he will need plenty of development before he gets there. He'll likely return to Delmarva to start 2026.

Year	Age	Club (League)	Level	AVG	G	AB	R	H	2B	3B	HR	RBI	BB	SO	SB	OBP	SLG
2025	18	FCL Orioles	Rk	.292	24	72	13	21	2	2	1	10	18	19	3	.452	.417
2025	18	Delmarva (CAR)	A	.181	54	182	25	33	8	2	1	13	27	65	13	.304	.264
		Minor League Totals		.224	159	505	80	113	20	6	7	51	94	162	27	.363	.329

30 VANCE HONEYCUTT, OF

HIT: 30. **POW:** 50. **RUN:** 65. **FLD:** 70. **ARM:** 60. **BA Grade:** 50. **Risk:** Extreme. **Adj:** 30.

Born: May 17, 2003. **B-T:** R-R. **HT:** 6-3. **WT:** 205. **Drafted:** North Carolina, 2024 (1st round). **Signed by:** Quincy Boyd.
TRACK RECORD: Honeycutt, a two-time Atlantic Coast Conference defensive player of the year and the first high-major player to top 60 home runs and 70 steals for his career, signed for an above-slot $4 million at No. 22 in the 2024 draft and was available to the Orioles there despite his pedigree because of concerns over his contact rates. Those concerns were validated in his pro debut as Honeycutt struck out 40.8% of the time with a 32% in-zone miss rate at High-A Aberdeen.
SCOUTING REPORT: While Honeycutt's contact issues were striking, so were the rest of his tools. He's a plus runner and double-plus center fielder with a plus arm. He also has plus raw power, which is yet to translate to games. But a combination of pitch recognition issues, timing, and a long, steep swing meant Honeycutt was rarely able to make good contact. Significant work will be required for him to generate any value at the plate.
THE FUTURE: Honeycutt could contribute in the big leagues thanks to his speed and defense alone, but will need to make much more contact to be an everyday player. He's a candidate to repeat High-A in 2026.

Year	Age	Club (League)	Level	AVG	G	AB	R	H	2B	3B	HR	RBI	BB	SO	SB	OBP	SLG
2025	22	Aberdeen (SAL)	A+	.171	101	374	48	64	12	6	5	24	56	178	32	.284	.275
		Minor League Totals		.172	114	425	51	73	13	6	5	29	60	202	36	.280	.266

Boston Red Sox

BY ALEX SPEIER

While the Red Sox believe the 2025 season represented the opening of a window of contention fueled by their farm system, the nature of that talent pipeline looks very different from anything seen in the organization in recent years.

The Red Sox entered 2025 with the best positional prospect group in baseball, with Kristian Campbell opening the season in the team's everyday lineup, Marcelo Mayer getting to the big leagues in May, and Roman Anthony following in spectacular fashion in June. None ended the season on the team's active playoff roster.

Campbell, who signed an eight-year, $60 million deal just after Opening Day, struggled in the big leagues and spent the second half of the year at Triple-A. Mayer's season ended early once again, this time with a wrist injury. Even Anthony, whose standout campaign included an eight-year, $130 million extension and netted a third-place finish for American League Rookie of the Year, suffered a season-ending oblique injury, rendering him unavailable for the team's first postseason appearance since 2021.

Instead, Boston's Wild Card Series against the Yankees featured homegrown lefthanded pitchers Payton Tolle and Connelly Early. Tolle, who worked out of the bullpen in the playoffs, reached the big leagues in his first full professional season, while Early, who made a postseason start, entered the Red Sox rotation in his second full pro season.

Their arrivals pointed to a transformation of Boston's prospect group. For the first time in more than a decade, the Red Sox have what appears to be a vital, renewable pitching pipeline capable of graduating arms to the big leagues.

Indeed, Tolle and Early were far from alone, because farm graduates such as Richard Fitts and Hunter Dobbins also provided rotation depth at different points in 2025, with other candidates

PROJECTED 2029 LINEUP

Catcher	Carlos Narvaez	30
First Base	Justin Gonzales	22
Second Base	Marcelo Mayer	26
Third Base	Dorian Soto	21
Shortstop	Franklin Arias	23
Left Field	Roman Anthony	25
Center Field	Ceddanne Rafaela	28
Right Field	Wilyer Abreu	30
Designated Hitter	Kristian Campbell	27
No. 1 Starter	Garrett Crochet	30
No. 2 Starter	Payton Tolle	26
No. 3 Starter	Connelly Early	27
No. 4 Starter	Kyson Witherspoon	24
No. 5 Starter	Brayan Bello	30
Closer	Juan Valera	23

to do so on the horizon. With the team having shifted its draft efforts heavily to pitchers in the last two years under chief baseball officer Craig Breslow, and with the team's pitcher development infrastructure having undergone a significant overhaul, Boston's inventory of young pitchers with big league stuff looks drastically different than it had in prior years.

The result is a Red Sox top prospect list that is almost unrecognizable. The majority of the players in the top 10 are pitchers. Tolle became the first pitcher to rank No. 1 in the system since Jay Groome in 2018.

Meanwhile, the back half of the top 10 is filled primarily by players who were teenagers in the lower levels in 2025, pointing to a system with a great deal of uncertainty and volatility. A number of top prospects, including the Anthony-Campbell-Mayer group that will have significant sway on the team's competitive arc over the rest of the decade, have graduated to the big leagues, while others, such as Kyle Teel, Braden Montgomery and Jhostynxon Garcia, have been traded.

Those trades highlight another shift in how the Red Sox are conducting business. After years in which Boston had hoarded prospects, it has now shifted its focus towards the present, with an openness to deal-making that will continue to result in a system that changes shape frequently. ■

DEPTH CHART

BOSTON RED SOX

TOP 2026 ROOKIES
	RANK
1. Payton Tolle, LHP	1
2. Connelly Early, LHP	3
3. Jake Bennett, LHP	6

BREAKOUT PROSPECTS
	Rank
1. Enddy Azocar, OF	13
2. Harold Rivas, OF	21
3. Hector Ramos, SS	24

SOURCE OF TOP 30 TALENT

Homegrown	25	Acquired	5
College	11	Trade	5
Junior college	0	Rule 5 draft	0
High school	1	Independent league	0
Undrafted free agent	0	Free agent/waivers	0
International	13		

LF
Yophery Rodriguez

CF
Enddy Azocar (13)
Miguel Bleis (18)
Harold Rivas (21)
Nelly Taylor
Anderson Fermin
Isaiah Jackson

RF
Allan Castro (27)

3B
Mikey Romero (19)
Starlyn Nuñez

SS
Franklin Arias (2)
Dorian Soto (9)
Hector Ramos (24)
Jhorman Bravo
Marvin Alcantara

2B
Henry Godbout (11)
Yoeilin Cespedes (20)
Mason White

1B
Justin Gonzales (7)
Josue Brito
Jostin Ogando

C
Gerardo Rodriguez (26)
Johanfran Garcia (29)
Luke Heyman (30)
Franklin Primera
Jorge Rodriguez
Brooks Brannon
Adonys Guzman

LHP

LHSP
Payton Tolle (1)
Connelly Early (3)
Jake Bennett (6)

LHRP
Shane Drohan (16)
Tyler Samaniego (22)
Hayden Mullins (23)
Eduardo Rivera
Dalton Rogers
Jojo Ingrassia

RHP

RHSP
Kyson Witherspoon (4)
Juan Valera (5)
Yhoiker Fajardo (8)
Marcus Phillips (10)
Anthony Eyanson (14)
Sadbiel Delzine (25)

RHRP
Luis Perales (5)
David Sandlin (12)
John Holobetz (15)
Tyler Uberstine (17)
Blake Aita (28)
Ryan Watson
Yordanny Monegro
Conrad Cason
Christian Foutch
Matt McShane
Jacob Mayers

BOSTON RED SOX

1 PAYTON TOLLE, LHP

Born: November 1, 2002. **B-T:** L-L. **HT:** 6-6. **WT:** 250.
Drafted: TCU, 2024 (2nd round).
Signed by: Chris Reilly.

BA GRADE
60 Risk: Mild
Adjusted grade: 55

SCOUTING GRADES
FB: 70. SL: 50. CH: 45.
CT: 50. CTL: 50.
Projected future grades on 20-80 scouting scale

TRACK RECORD: After two years at Wichita State as a power-hitting first baseman and lefthander, Tolle transferred to TCU in 2024 and focused increasingly on the mound. A strong junior season at TCU—he went 7-4 with a 3.21 ERA and 37% strikeout rate—and evident aptitude to develop in a new program convinced the Red Sox to draft Tolle in the second round. He signed for a slightly overslot $2 million and was Boston's highest selection of a pitcher since 2017. Tolle combines distinct mound traits—a mountainous build and a funktastic delivery with incredible extension—and in his 2025 pro unveiling, he made huge gains in his velocity and pitch shapes. He overwhelmed minor league hitters with a 36.5% strikeout rate, which was fourth-highest among minor league pitchers with at least 80 innings, while zooming from High-A through the upper levels. Tolle emerged as the best Red Sox pitching prospect in years, and in late August, he made his MLB debut little more than a year after signing.

SCOUTING REPORT: Tolle leverages his immense 6-foot-6, 250-pound frame to propel himself down the mound and punch hitters in the face while averaging seven and a half feet of extension on his fastball. That elite attribute from a low three-quarters arm slot was hard on hitters when he sat at 91 mph at TCU, and the basis of dominance when he jumped to an average of 95 in the minors. He then averaged 96.6 mph in his big league cameo and hit triple digits for the first time in his life on a pitch that averaged 16.7 inches of ride and 6.7 inches of armside run. Tolle reshaped his secondary mix throughout the season, most notably with the introduction of an 88-90 mph cutter in August that immediately surpassed his gyro slider, kick changeup and curveball in usage. In the minors, he proved capable of missing bats in the zone with that entire mix, and his pitches graded as average or better across the board. In the big leagues, he lacked command of his secondaries and struggled while leaning hard on a fastball he threw 64% of the time, too often down the middle. If Tolle can harness his secondaries—likely with a more balanced fastball/cutter/slider combination with occasional changeups and curveballs to righthanded hitters—in a way comparable to what he showed in the minors, he has the makings of a rotation workhorse.

THE FUTURE: While Tolle wore a jet pack in his 2025 ascent, he'll likely open 2026 in the Triple-A rotation to better define and refine his secondary mix. His double-plus fastball gives him an obvious late-innings floor, but the immense developmental strides he made in 2025 suggest a midrotation—or better—ceiling. "This is hard for me to say, but this guy, he's a Jonny Lester-type guy to me—can't-miss, dominant, big leaguer," Double-A Portland manager Chad Epperson said. "This guy's going to be really, really special."

BEST TOOLS

BATTING
Best Hitter	Franklin Arias
Best Power Hitter	Justin Gonzales
Best Strike-Zone Discipline	Justin Gonzales
Fastest Baserunner	Miguel Bleis
Best Athlete	Nelly Taylor

PITCHING
Best Fastball	Payton Tolle
Best Curveball	Connelly Early
Best Slider	Yhoiker Fajardo
Best Changeup	Connelly Early
Best Control	Juan Valera

FIELDING
Best Defensive Catcher	Franklin Primera
Best Defensive Infielder	Marvin Alcantara
Best Infield Arm	Ahbram Liendo
Best Defensive Outfielder	Nelly Taylor
Best Outfield Arm	Justin Gonzales

Year	Age	Club (League)	Level	W	L	ERA	G	GS	IP	H	HR	BB	SO	BB%	SO%	WHIP	AVG
2025	22	Greenville (SAL)	A+	1	3	3.62	11	10	50	44	6	14	79	6.8	38.3	1.17	.234
2025	22	Portland (EL)	AA	1	1	1.67	6	5	27	13	2	7	37	7.1	37.4	0.74	.144
2025	22	Worcester (IL)	AAA	1	1	3.60	3	3	15	11	2	2	17	3.4	28.8	0.87	.193
2025	22	Boston (AL)	MLB	0	1	6.06	7	3	16	18	5	8	19	10.8	25.7	1.59	.277
		Minor League Totals		3	5	3.04	20	18	92	68	10	23	133	6.3	36.5	0.99	.203
		Major League Totals		0	1	6.06	7	3	16	18	5	8	19	10.8	25.7	1.59	.277

BOSTON RED SOX

2 FRANKLIN ARIAS, SS
HIT: 60. **POW:** 40. **RUN:** 40. **FLD:** 60. **ARM:** 55. **BA Grade:** 55. **Risk:** Average. **Adj:** 45.

Born: November 19, 2005. **B-T:** R-R. **HT:** 5-11. **WT:** 170.
Signed: Venezuela, 2023. **Signed by:** Rollie Pino.
TRACK RECORD: Arias featured natural shortstop actions and unusual feel to shoot liners all over the field as an amateur in Venezuela. That pairing of skills, along with startling maturity, led the Red Sox to sign him for $525,000 in 2023. In 2024, he was named MVP of the Florida Complex League in a season he finished with 36 games for Low-A Salem. Arias returned to the Carolina League to open 2025 and advanced to Double-A Portland as a 19-year-old, becoming one of eight teenage position players at the level.
SCOUTING REPORT: Arias' clock, feel and adaptability on both sides of the ball are atypical for his age. Despite an excellent 2024 season, there were concerns that Arias' attack angle was too steep, rendering him vulnerable to pitches at the top of the zone. He made posture adjustments to flatten his bat path in 2025, resulting in a jump in his in-zone contact rate from 82% in 2024 to 94% in 2025. He struck out just 10% of the time. That approach came with some compromises to his quality of contact, particularly when expanding the zone. Arias' groundball rate rose from 38% in 2024 to 46%. He's also an all-fields hitter, resulting in a clear hit-over-power profile, but with exit velocities topping out around 110 mph, he does have sneaky pop and the chance to add more if he gets stronger. Defensively, Arias has tremendous instincts and sound mechanics that permit him to reliably turn balls in play into outs, profiling as a plus shortstop despite a lack of burst.
THE FUTURE: Arias has the balanced two-way impact to profile as an everyday shortstop—with a chance to push his ceiling if he can grow into more power. He'll open 2026 back in Double-A, with a strong chance to reach Triple-A by midseason.

Year	Age	Club (League)	Level	AVG	G	AB	R	H	2B	3B	HR	RBI	BB	SO	SB	OBP	SLG
2025	19	Salem (CAR)	A	.346	19	78	15	27	4	0	0	9	6	12	4	.407	.397
2025	19	Greenville (SAL)	A+	.265	87	355	43	94	21	1	6	49	32	35	7	.329	.380
2025	19	Portland (EL)	AA	.261	10	46	4	12	2	0	2	8	0	6	1	.250	.435
		Minor League Totals		.299	240	930	153	278	61	4	18	135	107	132	50	.377	.431

3 CONNELLY EARLY, LHP
FB: 50. **CB:** 50. **SL:** 40. **CH:** 60. **SW:** 55. **CTL:** 50. **BA Grade:** 50. **Risk:** Mild. **Adj:** 45.

Born: April 3, 2002. **B-T:** L-L. **HT:** 6-3. **WT:** 200.
Drafted: Virginia, 2023 (5th round). **Signed by:** Wallace Rios.
TRACK RECORD: Even as a soft-throwing junior at Virginia following two years at Army, Early impressed the Red Sox with his pitchability and secondary weapons. Boston placed a fifth-round wager on Early, believing he could make major gains in his stuff in a professional training environment. That's exactly what happened over his first two full professional seasons. In 2025, Early combined a 32% strikeout rate in the upper levels with minimal hard contact, then impressed in his big league unveiling, including an 11-strikeout effort against the Athletics on Sept. 9 that tied a Red Sox franchise record for a pitcher making his debut.
SCOUTING REPORT: Early's fastball, which averaged 90 mph as a college junior, now sits at 93-94 and tops out at 97. Though the offering, which features 15 inches of induced vertical break, garners pedestrian stuff grades, Early creates the kind of deception that allowed him to attack the zone and get whiffs in his debut. He paired the fastball with an excellent mid-80s changeup with sink and fade to his arm side as well as a slider and curveball against righties, while crushing lefties by mixing his four- and two-seamer with a low-80s sweeper that produced a 100% whiff rate—not a typo—on 10 regular-season swings. Early repeats an athletic delivery that permits him to command his arsenal to all parts of the zone. He has struggled at times to maintain stuff after his first time through the order.
THE FUTURE: Early's mix and command are those of a starter, and he'll be in the big league rotation mix to open 2026. He has the ceiling of a No. 3 starter. Likelier, he projects as a No. 4, so long as he can add strength to achieve a starter's durability.

Year	Age	Club (League)	Level	W	L	ERA	G	GS	IP	H	HR	BB	SO	BB%	SO%	WHIP	AVG
2025	23	Portland (EL)	AA	7	2	2.51	15	12	72	52	3	29	96	9.8	32.3	1.13	.202
2025	23	Worcester (IL)	AAA	3	1	2.83	6	6	29	19	2	11	36	9.4	30.8	1.05	.184
2025	23	Boston (AL)	MLB	1	2	2.33	4	4	19	17	0	4	29	5.1	36.7	1.09	.230
		Minor League Totals		13	12	3.32	45	42	206	156	13	79	274	9.1	31.5	1.14	.205
		Major League Totals		1	2	2.33	4	4	19	17	0	4	29	5.1	36.7	1.09	.230

BOSTON RED SOX

4 KYSON WITHERSPOON, RHP
FB: 60. **CB:** 45. **SL:** 55. **CH:** 45. **CT:** 60. **CTL:** 50. **BA Grade:** 55. **Risk:** Average. **Adj:** 45.

Born: August 12, 2004. **B-T:** R-R. **HT:** 6-2. **WT:** 206.
Drafted: Oklahoma, 2025 (1st round). **Signed by:** Fred Petersen.
TRACK RECORD: After mostly playing shortstop in high school, Witherspoon became a two-way player at Northwest Florida State JC. Both Witherspoon and his twin brother Malachi showed live arms that resulted in the pair transferring to Oklahoma for the 2024 season. After a solid sophomore season, Witherspoon tightened his delivery and added strength entering 2025. He dominated for the Sooners by going 10-4 with a 2.65 ERA and 32% strikeout rate to emerge as the best college righthander in the draft. Witherspoon projected as a possible top 10 pick, but when he remained available at No. 15, the Red Sox pounced. They made him their highest pick ever for a college righthander and signed him for $5 million.
SCOUTING REPORT: Witherspoon is a natural tinkerer with grips and pitch shapes, something that flows out of his catch play with his twin brother, a second-round pick by the Tigers. Hearkening to his days as a shortstop, Witherspoon shoots the ball out of his ear, a raptor-like delivery that creates deception. He built a five-pitch arsenal around a fastball that averaged 96 mph and topped out at 99. He bumped up his usage of a swing-and-miss low-90s cutter that proved to be an in-zone weapon, while also setting up a gyro slider for chases. He also showed the ability to shape and change speeds with a high-70s curveball and flashed a changeup that showed potential, though he seldom needed it in college. He repeats his delivery well, resulting in a low walk rate and the ability to get pitches to all quadrants.
THE FUTURE: Witherspoon shows No. 3 starter potential. He'll open 2026 in High-A or perhaps even Double-A and could move quickly. If he pounds the strike zone and finds the right breaking pitch shapes, he could be fast-tracked to the big leagues by early 2027 or even late 2026.

Year	Age	Club (League)	Level	W	L	ERA	G	GS	IP	H	HR	BB	SO	BB%	SO%	WHIP	AVG
2025	20	Did not play															

5 JUAN VALERA, RHP
FB: 60. **SL:** 45. **CH:** 40. **SW:** 50. **CTL:** 55. **BA Grade:** 50. **Risk:** Average. **Adj:** 40.

Born: May 18, 2006. **B-T:** R-R. **HT:** 6-3. **WT:** 205. **Signed:** Dominican Republic, 2023.
Signed by: Juan Carlos Calderon/Todd Claus/Eddie Romero.
TRACK RECORD: Valera's $45,000 signing out of the Dominican Republic in 2023 garnered little notice. Since then, strength and stuff gains in professional baseball made him a head-turner as an 18-year-old in the United States in 2024, when he forged a 1.99 ERA while holding hitters to a .125 average in a season he finished in the Low-A Carolina League. That performance resulted in an aggressive assignment to High-A Greenville as a 19-year-old in 2025. Valera's 5.45 ERA belied an ability to work in the zone (6% walk rate) and miss bats while doing so (28% strikeout rate). He missed three months of 2025 with elbow soreness but returned to games by the end of the season.
SCOUTING REPORT: Valera has a powerful 6-foot-3 starter's build and backs it with a high-octane four-seam fastball that averaged 96.7 mph and topped out just over 100 in 2025. The pitch—which he keeps in the zone—has more cut than ride, a trait that limits whiffs but still leaves batters taking defensive hacks. He started to incorporate a two-seamer late in 2025 to spread the zone with power stuff. Valera also shows the ability to land spin in the zone at a high rate, using a sweeper against righthanded hitters and a shorter gyro slider against lefties. He'll need to improve the feel for his changeup—the least consistent of his secondaries—to get whiffs against lefties.
THE FUTURE: Between his youth, power stuff and ability to work in the strike zone, Valera is young enough to dream on his midrotation potential. Still, there's also a potential fast track into a big league bullpen. He will open 2026 either back in High-A or in Double-A; if the former, he'll probably be a quick mover to the upper levels.

Year	Age	Club (League)	Level	W	L	ERA	G	GS	IP	H	HR	BB	SO	BB%	SO%	WHIP	AVG
2025	19	Greenville (SAL)	A+	1	2	5.45	10	10	38	43	6	10	46	6.0	27.5	1.39	.281
		Minor League Totals		5	5	4.17	36	20	106	87	6	44	117	9.7	25.7	1.24	.222

BOSTON RED SOX

6 JAKE BENNETT, LHP

FB: 55. **CB:** 45. **SL:** 50. **CH:** 60. **CTL:** 60. **BA Grade:** 50. **Risk:** Average. **Adj:** 40.

Born: December 2, 2000. **B-T:** L-L. **HT:** 6-6. **WT:** 230.
Drafted: Oklahoma, 2022 (2nd round). **Signed by:** Cody Staab (Nationals).
TRACK RECORD: The Nationals drafted Bennett out of Oklahoma in the second round in 2022. He got into 15 games in 2023 before missing most of July and September and having Tommy John surgery after the season. Bennett missed all of 2024 and returned to the mound in May 2025, ultimately making 19 appearances spanning 75.1 innings. Most of the innings were compiled for Double-A Harrisburg, and he added 20 more in the Arizona Fall League. In December, the Nationals traded Bennett to the Red Sox for 22-year-old righthander Luis Perales.
SCOUTING REPORT: Bennett is a 6-foot-6 lefthander with a wide assortment of pitches that play up because he gets down the mound with plus extension. While he doesn't blow batters away with raw velocity, Bennett is around the zone with six different pitches he can use to attack both sides of the plate. His four-seam fastball velocity was a tick higher in 2025 than it had been during his pro debut and averaged 92-93 mph and topped out near 96. His low three-quarters arm slot adds deception. He mixes in sinkers and occasional cutters to vary his fastball looks. Bennett's carrying secondary pitch is his mid-80s changeup that fades to his arm side and flummoxes minor league righthanded batters, who hit .210 with no home runs against him in 2025. He has good touch on an average low-to-mid-80s slider and high-70s curveball, both of which he can spot for strikes and elicit some chases. He throws breaking pitches only about 20% of the time, opting for more of a fastball/changeup attack. Bennett has plus control of his entire arsenal.
THE FUTURE: Given his wide repertoire of quality stuff, lefthandedness and feel for the strike zone, Bennett is a no-doubt starter with a good chance to settle in as a No. 4 type in a rotation.

Year	Age	Club (League)	Level	W	L	ERA	G	GS	IP	H	HR	BB	SO	BB%	SO%	WHIP	AVG
2025	24	Fredericksburg (CAR)	A	0	1	1.50	2	2	6	5	0	0	7	0.0	31.8	0.83	.227
2025	24	Wilmington (SAL)	A+	1	2	1.90	7	7	24	17	1	8	24	8.8	26.4	1.06	.205
2025	24	Harrisburg (EL)	AA	1	2	2.56	10	9	46	40	2	11	33	6.0	17.9	1.12	.234
		Minor League Totals		3	11	2.67	34	33	138	122	7	35	137	6.3	24.7	1.13	.238

7 JUSTIN GONZALES, OF/1B

HIT: 50. **POW:** 55. **RUN:** 45. **FLD:** 45. **ARM:** 60. **BA Grade:** 55. **Risk:** High. **Adj:** 40.

Born: December 31, 2006. **B-T:** R-R. **HT:** 6-4. **WT:** 220. **Signed:** Dominican Republic, 2024.
Signed by: Juan Carlos Calderon/Todd Claus/Eddie Romero.
TRACK RECORD: Gonzales is wonderfully perplexing. Though he towered over other amateur showcase participants, the industry ignored him at ages 14 and 15 when he lacked strength and featured below-average tools. But Gonzales improved through game play, and despite an ugly swing, showed big exit velocities while uncorking 98 mph throws from the outfield as a 17-year-old at a scouting event in Colombia. The Red Sox signed him for $250,000 in 2024, unsure whether he would end up on the mound or in the batter's box. Instead, Gonzales displayed uncanny bat-to-ball skills during an outstanding Dominican Summer League season, and the Red Sox pushed him to Low-A Salem as an 18-year-old in 2025 before a season-ending promotion to High-A Greenville.
SCOUTING REPORT: In the box, Gonzales looks almost apologetic for his 6-foot-4 size, hunching in his open stance. As he unfolds, he generates rockets to all fields, with a 90th percentile exit velocity of 107 mph and a top end at 113 mph. He's comfortable catching pitches deep and lining the ball to right field, suggesting true all-fields power potential, and he swings at strikes. The caveat: Gonzales' flat path produces plenty of contact but also a poor 57% groundball rate. If he can adjust his bat path to hit the ball in the air more frequently—sacrificing contact to tap into some of the 70-grade raw power that now plays below-average—he could be a monster. After Gonzales spent 2024 playing first base, the Red Sox tried him in the outfield in 2025. He moves well for his size and has the arm for either corner but will need to improve his jumps and routes to profile anywhere but at first.
THE FUTURE: Gonzales has a wide range of outcomes, from an all-star corner outfielder to a high-contact, low-power first baseman who struggles to be more than a fringy roster member.

Year	Age	Club (League)	Level	AVG	G	AB	R	H	2B	3B	HR	RBI	BB	SO	SB	OBP	SLG
2025	18	FCL Red Sox	Rk	.000	1	4	0	0	0	0	0	1	0	2	0	.000	.000
2025	18	Salem (CAR)	A	.298	81	312	45	93	23	2	4	27	35	52	11	.381	.423
2025	18	Greenville (SAL)	A+	.186	11	43	5	8	0	0	0	4	4	11	1	.265	.186
		Minor League Totals		.294	140	531	79	156	34	6	9	61	58	85	20	.372	.431

BOSTON RED SOX

8 YHOIKER FAJARDO, RHP

FB: 50. **SL:** 55. **CH:** 55. **CTL:** 55. **BA Grade:** 50. **Risk:** Average. **Adj:** 40.

Born: October 3, 2006. **B-T:** R-R. **HT:** 6-3. **WT:** 180.
Signed: Venezuela, 2024. **Signed by:** Ruddy Moreta (White Sox).
TRACK RECORD: Fajardo signed with the White Sox for $400,000 out of Venezuela in 2024. He pounded the strike zone with a low-90s sinker and gyro slider in his 2024 pro debut in the Dominican Summer League, finishing the year with a 3.91 ERA, 30% strikeout rate and 4% walk rate that was one of the lowest in the league. The Red Sox acquired Fajardo from Chicago for reliever Cam Booser in December 2024, and Fajardo made a jump while splitting 2025 between the Florida Complex League and Low-A Salem. He posted a 2.25 ERA and 29% strikeout rate between the levels and was one of four minor league pitchers to throw at least 70 innings without yielding a home run.
SCOUTING REPORT: Fajardo has a repeatable, athletic delivery without a lot of deception, but he throws strikes and avoids barrels by using different pitches to get to different areas of the strike zone. After his fastball sat 92 mph with the White Sox in 2024, he typically pitched at 94 with both a four-seamer and sinker in 2025 while topping out at 96. Fajardo has room to add muscle to his 6-foot-3 frame and turn that top-end velocity into a baseline. He actually threw his high-80s slider slightly more than his fastball in 2025, and he also liberally employed his changeup against lefthanded hitters. Fajardo's control allows him to spread the zone. For now, he lacks a plus offering, but he's young enough to believe he could develop one.
THE FUTURE: Fajardo should compete for a spot in the High-A Greenville rotation as a 19-year-old in 2026. He lacks the ceiling of other pitchers in the top system but has a clearer path to being a back-end starter than most, with a big league ETA of 2027 or 2028.

Year	Age	Club (League)	Level	W	L	ERA	G	GS	IP	H	HR	BB	SO	BB%	SO%	WHIP	AVG
2025	18	Salem (CAR)	A	1	3	2.98	13	13	51	43	0	20	59	9.4	27.8	1.23	.229
		Minor League Totals		2	7	3.44	26	26	102	95	2	28	123	6.6	29.0	1.21	.245

9 DORIAN SOTO, SS

HIT: 50. **POW:** 55. **RUN:** 40. **FLD:** 45. **ARM:** 55. **BA Grade:** 55. **Risk:** High. **Adj:** 40.

Born: February 14, 2008. **B-T:** B-R. **HT:** 6-2. **WT:** 195.
Signed: Dominican Republic, 2025. **Signed by:** Eddie Romero.
TRACK RECORD: As an amateur, Soto produced explosive contact with feel to play shortstop, a combination that led the Red Sox to sign him for $1.4 million, their highest bonus of the 2025 international signing period. His performance in the Dominican Summer League in 2025 did nothing to dampen excitement. Though a wrist injury limited the switch-hitter's ability to bat righthanded in stretches, Soto still showed loud tools to emerge as one of the better prospects coming out of the league.
SCOUTING REPORT: Soto has added significant size and strength since signing with the Red Sox, creating formidable offensive potential. He generates plenty of bat speed with a whippy—and sometimes long—swing, resulting in a 90th percentile exit velocity of 102 mph. He's aggressive on pitches in the zone but has strong bat-to-ball traits, helping to hold his strikeout rate to 16%. He's more advanced as a lefthanded hitter (.311/.372/.432) than when hitting righthanded (.294/.324/.412) but exhibits good baseline traits from both sides and the aptitude to hone his swings and improve. For now, Soto shows a shortstop's natural movements, but he may outgrow the position and land at third base, where his arm and power would play. The Red Sox gave him some exposure to both second and third base in 2025. His speed is currently fringy but could move in either direction depending on the kind of size and strength he adds to a 6-foot-2 frame that is continuing to fill out.
THE FUTURE: Soto will play in the United States in 2026 and has the kind of skill set to make his stay in the Rookie-level Florida Complex League either brief or non-existent before he reaches full-season ball at Low-A Salem.

Year	Age	Club (League)	Level	AVG	G	AB	R	H	2B	3B	HR	RBI	BB	SO	SB	OBP	SLG
2025	17	DSL Red Sox Blue	Rk	.222	3	9	0	2	1	0	0	0	1	2	0	.300	.333
2025	17	DSL Red Sox Red	Rk	.312	44	157	27	49	9	2	2	18	15	26	1	.366	.433
		Minor League Totals		.307	47	166	27	51	10	2	2	18	16	28	1	.362	.428

BOSTON RED SOX

10 MARCUS PHILLIPS, RHP

FB: 60. **SL:** 55. **CH:** 45. **CTL:** 50. **BA Grade:** 55. **Risk:** High. **Adj:** 40.

Born: July 6, 2004. **B-T:** R-R. **HT:** 6-4. **WT:** 245.
Drafted: Tennessee, 2025 (1st round supp.). **Signed by:** Kirk Fredriksson.
TRACK RECORD: Phillips initially enrolled at Iowa Western JC, but his arm hardly garnered notice until he transferred to Tennessee for his sophomore year. He showed a big fastball out of the bullpen in 2024, then made impressive strides as a full-year starter in 2025, posting a 3.90 ERA with a 27% strikeout rate and 9% walk rate. The Red Sox used the No. 33 pick, a supplemental pick they received from the Brewers in a trade, to take Phillips that summer. A South Dakota native, Phillips' father Steve spent several years as a minor league player and manager.
SCOUTING REPORT: Phillips is a formidable presence at 6-foot-4, 245 pounds and possesses size, power and athleticism. He also has evident aptitude, as seen in his significant improvement in a short period of time at Tennessee. His delivery is jerky, with a long backswing and a low-slot release. He typically sat at 95-97 mph and topped out at 100.5 mph with his four-seamer. Despite its power, the pitch lacked hop, resulting in modest whiff rates. His high-spin, mid-to-upper-80s slider was his true swing-and-miss pitch in college. He also showed a promising but underdeveloped changeup. The Red Sox may add a sinker and/or cutter to diversify his repertoire. If he can work consistently in the zone, even without great command, he has the power stuff and unique release traits—big extension and a low release height—to suggest a midrotation ceiling.
THE FUTURE: While Phillips could open 2026 at either Low-A or High-A, his stuff seems capable of overpowering lower-level hitters and he could reach Double-A by the end of the year. Phillips' control will dictate whether he becomes a power bullpen arm or starter.

Year	Age	Club (League)	Level	W	L	ERA	G	GS	IP	H	HR	BB	SO	BB%	SO%	WHIP	AVG
2025	20	Did not play															

11 HENRY GODBOUT, 2B

HIT: 55. **POW:** 40. **RUN:** 40. **FLD:** 45. **ARM:** 50. **BA Grade:** 50. **Risk:** Average. **Adj:** 40.

Born: November 6, 2003. **B-T:** R-R. **HT:** 6-2. **WT:** 190. **Drafted:** Virginia, 2025 (2nd round supp.). **Signed by:** Wallace Rios.
TRACK RECORD: After a standout sophomore season where he slashed .372/.472/.645, Godbout's numbers ticked back as a junior and he hit .309/.397/.497. Still, he continued to show elite strike-zone judgment and rare bat-to-ball abilities with an 8% strikeout rate. The Red Sox believed Godbout could tap into more power, and took him in the second round before signing him for just over $1.09 million. Godbout was one of Boston's few draftees to make his pro debut in 2025, impressing in a 13-game stint with High-A Greenville sandwiched around a hamstring injury.
SCOUTING REPORT: Godbout attacks pitches in the zone with a compact, direct swing whose efficiency allows him to swing at strikes and handle fastballs. In his brief pro sample, he paired a chase rate under 17% with an 88% in-zone contact rate. His exit velocities in college were below major league average, but the Red Sox believe Godbout will respond well to strength and bat speed training that may turn his natural ability to pull the ball in the air into extra bases and homers, especially at Fenway. Godbout played some shortstop in 2025, but he's most likely a second baseman or perhaps third baseman whose primary value will be his bat.
THE FUTURE: Godbout's advanced approach could make him a candidate to open 2026 in Double-A. If he makes strength gains to improve his pull-side power, his best-case scenario would be as an everyday infielder whose in-game power surpasses his raw power.

Year	Age	Club (League)	Level	AVG	G	AB	R	H	2B	3B	HR	RBI	BB	SO	SB	OBP	SLG
2025	21	Greenville (SAL)	A+	.341	13	44	6	15	6	0	0	5	9	6	1	.473	.477
		Minor League Totals		.341	13	44	6	15	6	0	0	5	9	6	1	.473	.477

12 DAVID SANDLIN, RHP
FB: 45. **CB:** 55. **SL:** 60. **SW:** 50. **CH:** 45. **CT:** 45. **CTL:** 50. **BA Grade:** 50. **Risk:** Average. **Adj:** 40.

Born: February 21, 2001. **B-T:** R-R. **HT:** 6-4. **WT:** 215. **Drafted:** Oklahoma, 2022 (11th round).
Signed by: Bobby Shore (Royals).
TRACK RECORD: Acquired from the Royals prior to the 2024 season, Sandlin has shown tantalizing stuff without the results to match. The 2025 season was his healthiest as a professional but featured up-and-down results. A slow start in Double-A gave way to his most consistent run as a starter, in which he pitched to a 2.63 ERA over 10 starts, and a promotion to Triple-A. But an audition for a big league bullpen role went poorly, and Sandlin never got called up. He was added to the 40-man roster in the offseason.
SCOUTING REPORT: Though Sandlin sits at 96-97 mph and can touch 100, his modest extension and high three-quarters slot afford hitters a clean look, making his fastball play below its velocity. Thus, he added a cutter and sinker in 2025 with promising results in Double-A that didn't carry over to Triple-A. He creates numerous breaking ball shapes and speeds, with a sweeper and slider showing wipeout potential against righties. His changeup flashes potential but remains inconsistent as an armside offering for lefties. He throws enough strikes with his diverse repertoire to keep the door open to starting.
THE FUTURE: Sandlin has a No. 4 starter's ceiling but a likelier path to being a leverage bullpen arm. He'll likely open 2026 in the Triple-A rotation with both directions open, but may gain definition about his future role in the coming year.

Year	Age	Club (League)	Level	W	L	ERA	G	GS	IP	H	HR	BB	SO	BB%	SO%	WHIP	AVG
2025	24	Portland (EL)	AA	5	4	3.61	17	13	82	70	7	27	86	8.0	25.4	1.18	.227
2025	24	Worcester (IL)	AAA	4	2	7.61	15	1	24	35	3	13	21	10.9	17.6	2.03	.337
		Minor League Totals		13	10	4.23	57	39	206	200	26	69	247	7.9	28.4	1.30	.253

13 ENDDY AZOCAR, OF
HIT: 45. **POW:** 55. **RUN:** 50. **FLD:** 50. **ARM:** 50. **BA Grade:** 55. **Risk:** High. **Adj:** 40.

Born: February 24, 2007. **B-T:** R-R. **HT:** 6-2. **WT:** 200. **Signed:** Venezuela, 2024.
Signed by: Eddie Romero/Alberto Mejia/Alex Requena.
TRACK RECORD: As an amateur infielder, Azocar intrigued Red Sox evaluators with his contact skills and the projection in his tall, gangly frame. He mustered just three extra-base hits while moving to the outfield in the Dominican Summer League in 2024, but Azocar added 25 pounds of muscle in the offseason and made huge gains in his quality of contact in 2025. He dominated in the Florida Complex League to earn a rapid promotion, then struggled in Low-A.
SCOUTING REPORT: Azocar stands balanced and upright, remaining quiet through his load before creating considerable whip with his well-synced hips and hands to make loud contact. His 90th percentile exit velocities jumped from 98 mph in 2024 to 105 mph in 2025, maxing out at 110.6 mph, suggesting above-average or plus power potential if he can cut down his 44% groundball rate. Doing so could come with risk to his hit tool. He showed excellent bat-to-ball skills on pitches in the zone with an 84% contact rate, but whiffed about half the time when he chased, a combination that creates a lot of variance in his eventual hit tool. Evaluators were divided on his defense. Some saw him as a quality corner and others believed he can be at least above-average in center or right field thanks to strong jumps, above-average speed and routes.
THE FUTURE: After putting himself on the prospect map with promising five-tool indicators in 2025, Azocar's 2026 campaign will be closely watched. If he builds on his gains from last year, he could push for a 2028 big league arrival.

Year	Age	Club (League)	Level	AVG	G	AB	R	H	2B	3B	HR	RBI	BB	SO	SB	OBP	SLG
2025	18	FCL Red Sox	Rk	.385	14	52	6	20	7	1	0	5	6	11	4	.448	.558
2025	18	Salem (CAR)	A	.202	71	258	34	52	9	1	6	26	21	67	11	.273	.314
		Minor League Totals		.240	116	404	57	97	18	3	6	42	45	93	17	.326	.344

14 ANTHONY EYANSON, RHP
FB: 50. **CB:** 55. **SL:** 60. **CH:** 45. **CTL:** 55. **BA Grade:** 50. **Risk:** Average. **Adj:** 40.

Born: October 9, 2004. **B-T:** R-R. **HT:** 6-2. **WT:** 210. **Drafted:** LSU, 2025 (3rd round). **Signed by:** Lee Bryant.
TRACK RECORD: Eyanson spent two years at UC San Diego, including a stint with the USA Collegiate National Team after his freshman year, before transferring to LSU as a junior. There, he emerged as the No. 2 starter behind Kade Anderson and one of the top performers in the country. Eyanson went 12-2 with a 3.00 ERA, 34% strikeout rate and 8% walk rate, creating expectations that he'd go off the board in the first two rounds. Instead, the Red Sox plucked him in the middle of the third round and signed

BOSTON RED SOX

him to an over-slot $1.75 million bonus. He didn't pitch after being drafted.
SCOUTING REPORT: Eyanson experienced an uptick in velocity at LSU, with his fastball sitting at 93 mph and topping out at 96-98. The Red Sox hope he can hold mid-90s velocities, but even in the low 90s, hitters appeared puzzled by the offering, which has almost no horizontal movement and low spin that results in some natural sink. However, he may end up leaning primarily on his two-plane, mid-to-upper-80s slider, a pitch that produced a 52% whiff rate at LSU. He also has a slower strike-stealing curveball. Eyanson exhibited strong command that could help him carve the zone as a starter if he can develop a consistent armside offering for lefties.
THE FUTURE: Eyanson likely will open the year in High-A Greenville, but could move quickly to the upper levels. If his fastball ticks up, he has solid back-of-the-rotation projection. If not, his slider alone would be a bullpen weapon.

Year	Age	Club (League)	Level	W	L	ERA	G	GS	IP	H	HR	BB	SO	BB%	SO%	WHIP	AVG
2025	20	Did not play															

15 JOHN HOLOBETZ, RHP
FB: 55. **SL:** 40. **CH:** 40. **CT:** 40. **CTL:** 60. **BA Grade:** 50. **Risk:** Average. **Adj:** 40.

Born: July 31, 2002. **B-T:** R-R. **HT:** 6-3. **WT:** 190. **Drafted:** Old Dominion, 2024 (5th round).
Signed by: James Fisher (Brewers).
TRACK RECORD: Though he mostly relieved at Radford and Old Dominion, Holobetz appealed to the Brewers for his fastball traits and starter's command. Milwaukee drafted him in the fifth round in 2024 and signed him to a below-slot $322,500 deal, then traded him to the Red Sox in the 2025 Quinn Priester deal. He proved to be an excellent performer across two organizations and three levels, forging a 3.03 ERA and 4% walk rate that ranked third-lowest among minor leaguers who threw at least 100 innings.
SCOUTING REPORT: Holobetz is an exceptional strike-thrower thanks to a repeatable, linear delivery. After joining the Red Sox, he saw a late-season velocity bump, sitting 93-94 mph and topping out at 97 with his four-seamer. His heater's deception is more interesting than its power. A low 5.3-foot release height paired with 6.5 feet of extension creates 17 inches of induced vertical break and excellent command, allowing the fastball to play at the top of the zone. Additional velocity could turn it into a bat-misser at the top of the zone. His slider, cutter and changeup all graded as below-average. The slider has the best chance of becoming average, but Holobetz will need to locate at least one other consistently to remain a starter.
THE FUTURE: A fixture of Boston's offseason training program, Holobetz will start 2026 in Double-A Portland's rotation. His upcoming season should offer clarity about whether he'll stay on a back-end starter track or have a likelier future in the middle innings.

Year	Age	Club (League)	Level	W	L	ERA	G	GS	IP	H	HR	BB	SO	BB%	SO%	WHIP	AVG
2025	22	Carolina (CAR)	A	3	0	3.00	5	3	24	16	1	5	31	5.1	31.3	0.88	.180
2025	22	Greenville (SAL)	A+	4	2	3.43	12	11	63	69	8	10	62	3.8	23.7	1.25	.276
2025	22	Portland (EL)	AA	1	2	2.39	6	5	38	27	1	5	27	3.6	19.6	0.85	.205
		Minor League Totals		8	4	3.03	23	19	125	112	10	20	120	4.0	24.0	1.06	.238

16 SHANE DROHAN, LHP
FB: 45. **CB:** 50. **SL:** 50. **CH:** 55. **CT:** 40. **CTL:** 45. **BA Grade:** 50. **Risk:** Average. **Adj:** 40.

Born: January 7, 1999. **B-T:** L-L. **HT:** 6-3. **WT:** 195. **Drafted:** Florida State, 2020 (5th round). **Signed by:** Dante Ricciardi.
TRACK RECORD: Drohan took a strange, circuitous road back to prospect status. Drafted by the Red Sox as a projectable lefty in 2020, he added power to his repertoire and emerged as a promising starting pitching prospect in 2023. But he struggled after reaching Triple-A and the White Sox plucked him in the Rule 5 Draft. In the spring of 2024, however, he underwent nerve decompression surgery to resolve a longstanding shoulder issue, and was returned to the Red Sox where he rehabbed. Finally healthy, his velocity spiked in 2025 and Drohan dominated in Triple-A. He likely would have reached the big leagues but for forearm irritation that sidelined him for three months.
SCOUTING REPORT: Despite a conventional three-quarters slot, Drohan creates deception while pitching exclusively out of the stretch, hiding the ball well, then unleashing pitches from a compact arm swing. That combination generated a 38% whiff rate in Triple-A in 2025 that registered in the 98th percentile at the level. At points, he sat at 94 mph and touched 97, but his velocity ticked down after the forearm injury. Still, he posted a 38% whiff rate on his four-seamer, with whiff rates above 40% on his newly-added slider, curveball, and changeup. Drohan added a cutter in 2023 but the pitch has been hit hard. Still, it could help him against righties if he can hone its command.
THE FUTURE: Drohan has starter stuff with durability questions after throwing 70 innings in the last two

years. He's on the 40-man roster and will open 2026 in the Triple-A rotation, but could emerge as an early-season bullpen option with a likely long-term role as a multi-inning reliever.

Year	Age	Club (League)	Level	W	L	ERA	G	GS	IP	H	HR	BB	SO	BB%	SO%	WHIP	AVG
2025	26	Greenville (SAL)	A+	0	1	8.53	3	3	6	8	1	5	10	15.2	30.3	2.05	.320
2025	26	Worcester (IL)	AAA	5	1	2.27	12	11	48	32	4	16	67	8.4	35.3	1.01	.185
		Minor League Totals		31	21	4.29	104	89	412	373	49	205	472	11.4	26.3	1.40	.239

17 TYLER UBERSTINE, RHP

FB: 55. **SW:** 45. **CH:** 45. **CT:** 40. **CTL:** 50. **BA Grade:** 40. **Risk:** Low. **Adj:** 40.

Born: June 1, 1999. **B-T:** R-R. **HT:** 6-1. **WT:** 200. **Drafted:** Northwestern, 2021 (19th round). **Signed by:** Todd Gold.
TRACK RECORD: Uberstine is a true underdog story. He was so undersized in high school that he barely pitched and received no college offers. After a late growth spurt, Uberstine tried to walk on at USC but was a late cut, then transferred to Northwestern where he found a pandemic-truncated opportunity in 2020-21 and put himself on the map. He then showed enough in the MLB Draft League to get selected with the Red Sox's penultimate pick of 2021. After a solid first full pro season in 2022, he blew out in the spring of 2023 and missed all of that year and much of 2024. Healthy in 2025, Uberstine finally broke through in the upper minors to earn a 40-man roster spot after the season.
SCOUTING REPORT: Uberstine's operation is built on funk and angle. He works from a compact, low three-quarters arm slot with a release height of just over 5 feet and generates 11 inches of armside run on a 93 mph fastball that tops out at 96. That combination allowed him to produce a hearty 38% whiff rate on the pitch in Triple-A. Beyond that, he features an array of shapes to work to different parts of the zone, leaning mostly on a changeup and slider while also mixing in cutters, sinkers and occasional sweepers. Nothing is overpowering, but Uberstine's ability to mix suggests a multi-inning middle reliever.
THE FUTURE: Uberstine likely will open 2026 in the Triple-A rotation, but should be on speed dial as an optionable source of bullpen innings.

Year	Age	Club (League)	Level	W	L	ERA	G	GS	IP	H	HR	BB	SO	BB%	SO%	WHIP	AVG
2025	26	Portland (EL)	AA	0	1	3.64	6	6	30	27	2	4	35	3.3	29.2	1.04	.241
2025	26	Worcester (IL)	AAA	6	4	3.56	19	15	91	84	16	37	102	9.5	26.2	1.33	.245
		Minor League Totals		11	12	3.57	54	40	225	201	25	78	252	8.2	26.6	1.24	.236

18 MIGUEL BLEIS, OF

HIT: 30. **POW:** 50. **RUN:** 55. **FLD:** 50. **ARM:** 55. **BA Grade:** 50. **Risk:** High. **Adj:** 35.

Born: March 1, 2004. **B-T:** R-R. **HT:** 6-2. **WT:** 200. **Signed:** Dominican Republic, 2021.
Signed by: Eddie Romero/Manny Nanita.
TRACK RECORD: Bleis once had seemingly limitless upside. He signed for $1.5 million in 2021 and dazzled in the Dominican Summer League and Florida Complex League, but a subluxing shoulder that required season-ending surgery in 2023 altered his career arc. The resounding, frequent contact that characterized him at the lowest levels gave way to frequent mis-hits. He'll still flash tools possessed by few others as a reminder of tantalizing upside, but after posting a combined .222/.298/.364 line over the last three years, he looks more like a lottery ticket.
SCOUTING REPORT: Bleis used to sledgehammer pitches in the zone. Since surgery, his swing has been less consistent, leading to frequent infield pop-ups and groundballs. Given that he has the strength and bat speed to produce all-fields power, he may be a case study in the excesses of a pull-happy approach, as his 62% pull rate led the minors. Still, he posted a respectable 11% barrel rate on batted balls and flashes atypical raw power combined with solid defensive ability in center and right. At the least, his defense and speed suggest a future big league role. There still may be a path where he tightens his swing decisions to bump up his hit tool to merely below average, in which case he could still become a regular. But that upside dream recedes with each year of struggle.
THE FUTURE: Left unprotected ahead of the Rule 5 draft after the 2025 season, Bleis should open the year back in Double-A. Now entering his sixth minor league season, he's nearing a crossroads.

Year	Age	Club (League)	Level	AVG	G	AB	R	H	2B	3B	HR	RBI	BB	SO	SB	OBP	SLG
2025	21	Greenville (SAL)	A+	.226	77	287	48	65	15	1	13	41	35	75	20	.314	.422
2025	21	Portland (EL)	AA	.209	30	110	10	23	6	0	1	10	6	31	7	.263	.291
		Minor League Totals		.236	309	1176	177	277	60	10	35	158	112	306	101	.309	.393

BOSTON RED SOX

19 MIKEY ROMERO, 3B
HIT: 40. **POW:** 50. **RUN:** 40. **FLD:** 45. **ARM:** 50. **BA Grade:** 45. **Risk:** Average. **Adj:** 35.

Born: January 12, 2004. **B-T:** L-R. **HT:** 5-11. **WT:** 195. **Drafted:** HS—Orange, CA, 2022 (1st round). **Signed by:** J.J. Altobelli.
TRACK RECORD: Romero was a well-known amateur who played for USA Baseball's 12U and 15U National Teams and then excelled at Orange Lutheran High in Southern California. The Red Sox believed he could stay up the middle and develop more power when they made him a surprise first-round pick in 2022, signing Romero to a below-slot $2.3 million bonus. A series of back injuries, including a stress fracture, derailed his 2023 season and slowed him at the start of 2024. Once healthy, he has shown surprising pop, amassing 98 extra-base hits in 189 games over the last two years.
SCOUTING REPORT: Romero has flipped from a hit-over-power amateur to a power-over-hit pro. He has grooved his swing to drive the ball in the air from gap-to-gap. That approach has produced quality contact, including a 14% barrel rate in Triple-A, but also a lack of discernment, as he chased 33% of the time and posted a 30% strikeout rate at that level. He reliably converts outs when he gets to balls, but his range has diminished in pro ball. As a result, Romero has mostly shifted to third base and risks moving further down the defensive spectrum. He's a below-average runner.
THE FUTURE: Romero is still young with limited game reps. If he tightens his swing decisions, he could elevate his hit tool and have a shot at becoming a regular. If not, he's probably a corner reserve.

Year	Age	Club (League)	Level	AVG	G	AB	R	H	2B	3B	HR	RBI	BB	SO	SB	OBP	SLG
2025	21	Portland (EL)	AA	.254	66	268	40	68	18	4	8	40	23	74	4	.315	.440
2025	21	Worcester (IL)	AAA	.232	45	177	21	41	15	0	9	36	11	58	1	.276	.469
		Minor League Totals		.255	242	986	141	251	69	13	34	159	74	256	10	.309	.454

20 YOEILIN CESPEDES, 2B
HIT: 40. **POW:** 50. **RUN:** 40. **FLD:** 45. **ARM:** 50. **BA Grade:** 50. **Risk:** High. **Adj:** 35.

Born: September 8, 2005. **B-T:** R-R. **HT:** 5-10. **WT:** 180. **Signed:** Dominican Republic, 2023.
Signed by: Eddie Romero/Manny Nanita.
TRACK RECORD: Cespedes showed signs of an impact bat as an amateur when the Red Sox signed him for $1.4 million. He excelled in the Dominican Summer League in 2023, then again in the Florida Complex League in 2024, but a broken hamate prevented him from reaching full-season ball that same year in his stateside debut. He never found his offensive footing when he reached Low-A Salem in 2025, slashing .227/.292/.376 with 10 homers and 101 strikeouts in 110 games.
SCOUTING REPORT: Cespedes is a bowling ball in the box who delivers compact fury in his swing. He attacks pitches in the zone with a flat attack angle that allows him to drive the ball to left and center. As a 19-year-old in 2025, however, his tendency to chase diminished the impact of his strong bat-to-ball skills, and some evaluators thought he'd bulked up in a way that compromised the adjustability of his swing. This has also played into lower-body, soft-tissue injuries during his pro career. Still, he's capable of making contact and tapping into thunder, and he proved capable enough at second base to keep alive the possibility that he'll stay in the middle infield rather than move to third.
THE FUTURE: An assignment to High-A Greenville, which rewards righthanded pull power, could allow Cespedes to re-establish his prospect credentials as a 20-year-old in 2026.

Year	Age	Club (League)	Level	AVG	G	AB	R	H	2B	3B	HR	RBI	BB	SO	SB	OBP	SLG
2025	19	Salem (CAR)	A	.227	110	428	56	97	24	5	10	54	41	101	11	.292	.376
		Minor League Totals		.270	181	710	113	192	49	10	21	116	67	144	15	.333	.456

21 HAROLD RIVAS, OF
HIT: 45. **POW:** 40. **RUN:** 60. **FLD:** 70. **ARM:** 60. **BA Grade:** 50. **Risk:** High. **Adj:** 35.

Born: May 10, 2008. **B-T:** R-R. **HT:** 6-1. **WT:** 175. **Signed:** Venezuela, 2025. **Signed by:** Eddie Romero/Rollie Pino.
TRACK RECORD: The Red Sox signed Rivas out of Venezuela for $950,000 in 2025 based on his spectacular athleticism, speed, defensive ability and well-coordinated swing. In his Dominican Summer League pro debut that summer, he looked like an elite defensive center fielder with a well-rounded game and slashed .258/.393/.384 with as many walks (35) as strikeouts.
SCOUTING REPORT: At 6-foot-1, 175 pounds, Rivas is lean with plenty of room to fill out, and he moves in both the batter's box and in the field with a loose, rhythmic grace. For now, his flat bat path helped generate an above-average 90th percentile exit velocity, chase rate and in-zone whiff rate for his level in 2025. Most of his contact, however, resulted in groundballs and liners. That said, it's not hard to envision added strength and experience allowing Rivas to tap into at least modest power. Defensively, he looks elite, with one evaluator suggesting gold glove potential based on his jumps and plus speed, and he ran

6.5-second 60-yard dashes as an amateur.
THE FUTURE: Rivas's defense and speed permit an unusually high floor for a player who has yet to make his stateside debut. He could grow into power and emerge as a standout everyday type outfielder in his early 20s.

Year	Age	Club (League)	Level	AVG	G	AB	R	H	2B	3B	HR	RBI	BB	SO	SB	OBP	SLG
2025	17	DSL Red Sox Blue	Rk	.258	46	159	41	41	6	4	2	20	35	35	18	.393	.384
		Minor League Totals		.258	46	159	41	41	6	4	2	20	35	35	18	.393	.384

22 TYLER SAMANIEGO, LHP

FB: 50. **SL:** 50. **CH:** 45. **CTL:** 55. **BA Grade:** 45. **Risk:** Average. **Adj:** 35.

Born: January 30, 1999. **B-T:** R-L. **HT:** 6-4. **WT:** 205. **Drafted:** South Alabama, 2021 (15th round).
Signed by: Darren Mazeroski (Pirates).
TRACK RECORD: Drafted as a pure reliever, Samaniego raced to Double-A by May of his first full season in the midst of a 14-appearance hitless run, tied for the longest streak in the minors in 2022. But he never advanced past Double-A in three subsequent years with the Pirates, in no small part due to elbow injuries that sidelined him from July 2024 into May 2025. But once healthy, he largely overpowered hitters in Double-A in 2025. The Pirates added him to their 40-man roster, then traded him to the Red Sox in the five-player Johan Oviedo deal.
SCOUTING REPORT: Samaniego powers his way down the mound with above-average extension from a low release height, mixing mid-90s four-seamers and sinkers, which he managed to consistently locate in the zone despite considerable armside run. He generated a swing-and-miss rate of roughly 30% on his fastballs. He also has a solid low-to-mid-80s slider and infrequently turns to a fringy changeup. Samaniego gave lefties fits, holding them to a .151/.224/.245 line in 2025. His repertoire spreads the strike zone even as he does an impressive job of working within it.
THE FUTURE: Assuming he remains healthy, Samaniego's above-average control of two solid offerings gives him a good chance to contribute in the big leagues as optionable bullpen depth in 2026.

Year	Age	Club (League)	Level	W	L	ERA	G	GS	IP	H	HR	BB	SO	BB%	SO%	WHIP	AVG
2025	26	FCL Pirates	Rk	0	1	3.86	2	1	2	2	1		5	9.1	45.5	1.29	.222
2025	26	Bradenton (FSL)	A	1	1	13.50	2	0	1	3	0	1	3	7.7	23.1	2.63	.500
2025	26	Greensboro (SAL)	A+	1	0	3.86	6	0	7	3	0	3	6	10.7	21.4	0.86	.130
2025	26	Altoona (EL)	AA	1	1	3.08	20	0	26	18	1	6	30	5.7	28.3	0.91	.189
		Minor League Totals		10	8	3.82	127	2	158	119	9	63	182	9.6	27.7	1.15	.208

23 HAYDEN MULLINS, LHP

FB: 55. **SW:** 55. **SL:** 45. **CH:** 45. **CTL:** 40. **BA Grade:** 45. **Risk:** Average. **Adj:** 35.

Born: September 14, 2000. **B-T:** L-L. **HT:** 6-0. **WT:** 194. **Drafted:** Auburn, 2022 (12th round). **Signed by:** Danny Watkins.
TRACK RECORD: Mullins was a highly recruited prep arm who spent two years in Auburn's bullpen before moving to the rotation in 2022 until Tommy John surgery ended his junior season. The Red Sox still took him in the 12th round that year while rehabbing. Once on the mound, Mullins emerged as one of the better performers in the Red Sox system. In 2025, he posted a combined 2.21 ERA between High-A and Double-A while holding hitters to a .175 average, which was sixth-lowest among minor leaguers with 100 innings, along with a 30% strikeout rate.
SCOUTING REPORT: Mullins combines a low release height from his three-quarters arm slot with a spin-efficient 17 inches of carry on his 93-94 mph fastball, which touches 96. That combination vexes hitters when he works at the top of the zone and above. His slider, sweeper and changeup can all miss bats but are inconsistent, and he introduced a cutter late in 2025. Mullins struggles to work in the strike zone and walked 12% of batters in 2025. That likely limits his path forward to middle relief, although if his control or power ticks up, his effectiveness against righties and lefties could allow him to work as a swingman or back-end starter.
THE FUTURE: Left unprotected ahead of the Rule 5 draft, Boston plans to keep Mullins in the rotation in the minors, but he could reach the majors at some point as a reliever in 2026.

Year	Age	Club (League)	Level	W	L	ERA	G	GS	IP	H	HR	BB	SO	BB%	SO%	WHIP	AVG
2025	24	Greenville (SAL)	A+	1	0	1.06	4	3	17	11	1	3	27	4.8	42.9	0.82	.186
2025	24	Portland (EL)	AA	7	2	2.44	18	18	85	51	6	48	96	13.8	27.7	1.17	.175
		Minor League Totals		12	9	3.11	48	42	197	136	17	98	256	11.9	31.0	1.19	.195

BOSTON RED SOX

24 HECTOR RAMOS, SS

HIT: 50. **POW:** 50. **RUN:** 45. **FLD:** 50. **ARM:** 55. **BA Grade:** 50. **Risk:** Extreme. **Adj:** 30.

Born: September 19, 2007. **B-T:** B-R. **HT:** 6-1. **WT:** 168. **Signed:** Dominican Republic, 2025.
Signed by: Eddie Romero/Manny Nanita.
TRACK RECORD: When the Red Sox signed Ramos to a $500,000 bonus in 2025 out of the Dominican Republic as part of a loaded international class, he showed glimpses of a shortstop's actions with power as an amateur. That unusual offensive potential for a middle infielder surfaced in his Dominican Summer League debut that year when he hit .254/.384/.443 with four homers over 36 games.
SCOUTING REPORT: Ramos attacks the ball with an aggressive yet smooth stride, which allows him to swing hard and still maintain an atypically advanced feel for the strike zone, as well as the pitches he can attack. In 2025, he produced high in-zone contact rates, attacked the ball at good angles and had a top-end exit velocity of 107.7 mph, which is an impressive figure for a 17-year-old with remaining physical projection. In a small sample, early platoon splits surfaced. The switch-hitter struck out seven times compared with zero walks in 21 plate appearances against lefties, compared to 23 walks and 26 strikeouts against righties. He didn't appear out of his element at shortstop, but it's possible he'll eventually be better suited for second base, particularly as he adds size.
THE FUTURE: Ramos has a chance to emerge as a two-way impact player in the middle infield by 2029.

Year	Age	Club (League)	Level	AVG	G	AB	R	H	2B	3B	HR	RBI	BB	SO	SB	OBP	SLG
2025	17	DSL Red Sox Blue	Rk	.254	36	122	33	31	7	2	4	25	23	32	1	.384	.443
		Minor League Totals		.254	36	122	33	31	7	2	4	25	23	32	1	.384	.443

25 SADBIEL DELZINE, RHP

FB: 60. **CB:** 45. **SL:** 50. **CH:** 50. **CTL:** 50. **BA Grade:** 50. **Risk:** Extreme. **Adj:** 30.

Born: January 9, 2008. **B-T:** R-R. **HT:** 6-5. **WT:** 220. **Signed:** Venezuela, 2025. **Signed by:** Eddie Romero/Ramon Mora.
TRACK RECORD: The Red Sox signed Delzine for $500,000 in 2025, impressed by not only his size and power but also his feel for a changeup and ability to spin the ball. He logged just 9.1 innings in his Dominican Summer League debut, a product of both some flexor tightness and the organization's desire that he focus more on strengthening his shoulder and arm than pitching as a reduced version of himself.
SCOUTING REPORT: At 6-foot-5, 220 pounds, Delzine looked like a fortress by the time he signed with size rarely seen for a 17-year-old pitcher. He already sits 94-96 mph and touches 98, with a chance for more power as he matures. From the windup, he has a deliberate tempo before his arm whips to the plate from a high three-quarters slot—a sound foundation for a vertical attack that features a curveball with depth, a hard gyro slider that tunnels well off his fastball and a changeup that dives to the arm side. As an amateur, he showed atypically strong control.
THE FUTURE: If healthy, Delzine is a strong candidate to begin 2026 in the Florida Complex League and graduate to Low-A Salem. He has the raw ingredients of a midrotation starter, though with fewer than 10 pro innings and likely 3-4 years before he reaches the big leagues, it's tough to draw meaningful conclusions.

Year	Age	Club (League)	Level	W	L	ERA	G	GS	IP	H	HR	BB	SO	BB%	SO%	WHIP	AVG
2025	17	DSL Red Sox Blue	Rk	0	0	4.82	3	3	9	11	0	1	9	2.6	23.1	1.29	.297
		Minor League Totals		0	0	4.82	3	3	9	11	0	1	9	2.6	23.1	1.29	.297

26 GERARDO RODRIGUEZ, C

HIT: 50. **POW:** 40. **RUN:** 45. **FLD:** 50. **ARM:** 45. **BA Grade:** 45. **Risk:** High. **Adj:** 30.

Born: December 8, 2005. **B-T:** R-R. **HT:** 5-10. **WT:** 180. **Signed:** Venezuela, 2023. **Signed by:** Rollie Pino/Cesar Morillo.
TRACK RECORD: After signing for just $50,000 in 2023, Rodriguez posted a .404 on-base percentage over his first two pro seasons in the complex leagues, but he didn't impact the ball and repeated the Florida Complex League in 2025. The 19-year-old significantly improved his swing metrics and finished the year in Low-A, where he produced an .872 OPS in 22 games.
SCOUTING REPORT: Rodriguez emerged as something of a data darling in 2025. He's squat and stocky, yet moves in surprisingly quick bursts on both sides of the ball after making sizable bat speed gains with his level swing. Though he chases breaking balls off the plate, his 19% whiff rate and 14% in-zone whiff rate were both well above-average for his level and yielded solid contact. He generated a 102.6 mph 90th percentile exit velocity and 110.8 mph max. Rodriguez improved his ball flight in 2025, trading grounders for more liners and flyballs, which suggests an atypically solid hit tool for a catcher with fringy power. Defensively, his strong framing and blocking data suggest average potential behind the plate.
THE FUTURE: Rodriguez showed traits in 2025 to suggest a potential backup big league catcher, but the gains in his underlying metrics suggest a player who can develop in ways to push his ceiling.

BOSTON RED SOX

Year	Age	Club (League)	Level	AVG	G	AB	R	H	2B	3B	HR	RBI	BB	SO	SB	OBP	SLG
2025	19	FCL Red Sox	Rk	.279	47	154	17	43	16	0	0	32	10	23	7	.329	.383
2025	19	Salem (CAR)	A	.297	22	74	9	22	4	1	3	11	9	13	1	.372	.500
		Minor League Totals		.305	138	430	69	131	30	1	7	76	44	61	15	.372	.428

27 ALLAN CASTRO, OF

HIT: 45. **POW:** 40. **RUN:** 50. **FLD:** 50. **ARM:** 50. **BA Grade:** 40. **Risk:** Average. **Adj:** 30.

Born: May 24, 2003. **B-T:** B-R. **HT:** 6-0. **WT:** 170. **Signed:** Dominican Republic, 2019.
Signed by: Manny Nanita/Eddie Romero.
TRACK RECORD: Castro signed out of the Dominican as a middle infielder in 2019 before shifting to the outfield early in his pro career. He has been a steady, if unspectacular, performer over the last three seasons. After struggling in his first Double-A stint in 2024, he tightened his approach in 2025, re-establishing his strike-zone feel with an 11% walk rate and 20% strikeout rate.
SCOUTING REPORT: While Castro's athleticism and strength command attention, his performance has been more solid than exceptional as a professional. He made a more concerted effort to drive the ball in 2024 and he hit a career-high 15 homers but his .229 average sagged. In 2025, he seemingly found more comfort with a line-drive approach that played particularly well as a lefthanded hitter. All seven of his homers came as a lefty, with most of his damage coming on secondary stuff down in the zone. He does contribute defensive value, with fringe-average defense in center and average ability in the corners, and he's also a solid runner.
THE FUTURE: Castro should open 2026 in Triple-A, and could provide the Red Sox with big league depth if any of their lefthanded-hitting outfielders go down with injury. It's not a sexy profile, but he does enough things well to forge a future platoon or reserve role.

Year	Age	Club (League)	Level	AVG	G	AB	R	H	2B	3B	HR	RBI	BB	SO	SB	OBP	SLG
2025	22	Portland (EL)	AA	.268	92	340	43	91	20	2	7	37	44	79	15	.353	.400
		Minor League Totals		.250	422	1520	235	380	87	23	35	180	226	379	62	.352	.407

28 BLAKE AITA, RHP

FB: 45. **CB:** 50. **SW:** 55. **CH:** 40. **CTL:** 50. **BA Grade:** 45. **Risk:** High. **Adj:** 30.

Born: June 11, 2003. **B-T:** R-R. **HT:** 6-4. **WT:** 215. **Drafted:** Kennesaw State, 2024 (6th round).
Signed by: Kirk Fredriksson.
TRACK RECORD: Aita pitched to relatively pedestrian numbers and substandard velocities over two years at Kennesaw State, but his ability to spin the ball and deceptive delivery led the Red Sox to take the draft-eligible sophomore in the sixth round in 2024 for a below-slot $300,000 bonus. In 2025, he made strength and stuff gains that allowed him to improve steadily during a solid pro debut.
SCOUTING REPORT: With a herky-jerky delivery that hitters find off-putting, Aita then creates even more deception by hiding the ball well before releasing it from his ear. That deception as well as carry to his fastball allowed his 93-94 mph fastball, which tops out at 95, to play up. Aita also spins the ball exceptionally well. His low-80s sweeper can at times exceed 3,200 rpm, a mark reached by fewer than 50 big leaguers in 2025, and drove a whiff rate north of 40%. He also works in a curveball. Though he works in the strike zone, his changeup will need to develop for him to remain a starter.
THE FUTURE: Aita will continue to get opportunities to prove he can start, but his sweeper could also give him a path to a bullpen role. He should reach the upper levels in 2026, giving him a potential big league ETA of 2027.

Year	Age	Club (League)	Level	W	L	ERA	G	GS	IP	H	HR	BB	SO	BB%	SO%	WHIP	AVG
2025	22	Salem (CAR)	A	2	3	4.24	10	9	51	46	4	9	45	4.4	22.0	1.08	.240
2025	22	Greenville (SAL)	A+	3	4	3.78	13	10	64	45	9	21	54	8.1	20.9	1.03	.194
		Minor League Totals		5	7	3.98	23	19	115	91	13	30	99	6.5	21.4	1.05	.215

29 JOHANFRAN GARCIA, C
HIT: 40. **POW:** 55. **RUN:** 30. **FLD:** 45. **ARM:** 50. **BA Grade:** 40. **Risk:** Average. **Adj:** 30.

Born: December 8, 2004. **B-T:** R-R. **HT:** 5-11. **WT:** 245. **Signed:** Venezuela, 2022. **Signed by:** Rollie Pino/Eddie Romero.
TRACK RECORD: The younger brother of fellow Red Sox signee Jhostynxon Garcia, Johanfran showed rare power potential as an amateur catcher when Boston signed him for $850,000 in 2022. He looked like an emerging top prospect in 2023 and 2024, but ruptured his ACL with Low-A Salem in 2024 and required surgery that sidelined him for nearly 13 months. Once back in 2025, he advanced to High-A Greenville and showed flashes of his pre-injury promise.
SCOUTING REPORT: Garcia seems driven to launch pull-side moon shots. His explosive swing unabashedly works uphill through the zone and he accepts the entwinement of whiffs and barrels. It's a power-over-hit profile and he struck out 31% of the time in High-A. Defensively, he has the strong hands and arm to stick behind the plate, provided he maintains his body and agility. His weight and conditioning became a pronounced concern during his recovery from surgery. Garcia's inability to do cardio led to a sizable weight gain, though he was down to 245 pounds by the end of the season. He will need to remain diligent about his conditioning and nutrition to absorb the pounding of catching.
THE FUTURE: Garcia has clear strengths—power, receiving, arm strength—that could translate to a career as a No. 2 catcher. With a healthy offseason and the upper minors beckoning, 2026 will be a pivotal year for his future.

Year	Age	Club (League)	Level	AVG	G	AB	R	H	2B	3B	HR	RBI	BB	SO	SB	OBP	SLG
2025	20	FCL Red Sox	Rk	.316	12	38	10	12	3	0	3	13	1	8	0	.333	.632
2025	20	Greenville (SAL)	A+	.249	46	173	27	43	4	0	9	28	18	60	1	.327	.428
		Minor League Totals		.272	188	676	106	184	37	3	22	116	82	186	7	.363	.433

30 LUKE HEYMAN, C
HIT: 40. **POW:** 55. **RUN:** 30. **FLD:** 45. **ARM:** 55. **BA Grade:** 45. **Risk:** High. **Adj:** 30.

Born: July 9, 2003. **B-T:** R-R. **HT:** 6-4. **WT:** 220. **Drafted:** Florida, 2025 (14th round). **Signed by:** Rob Mummau (Mariners).
TRACK RECORD: Heyman was a well-known high schooler and seemed close to cementing his status as a prominent draft prospect by earning all-SEC freshman team honors in 2023. But he had a down year as a draft-eligible sophomore in 2024 and his 24% strikeout rate raised hit tool questions. He bounced back with a strong 2025 campaign, hitting .301/.397/.578 with 13 homers, and the Mariners took him in the 14th round and signed him for $230,000, on par with eighth-round money. The Red Sox acquired him in a November trade for reliever Alex Hoppe.
SCOUTING REPORT: Heyman made strides in his junior spring by slashing his strikeout rate to 19% while improving his receiving and strike-stealing defensively. At the plate, Heyman crouches in his batting stance, then unfolds and unloads on pitches, particularly down in the zone. He demonstrated above-average pullside power that could translate to Fenway. In 2025, his swing was more adjustable and he did a better job using the whole field, especially with two strikes. He has always had a strong arm with pop times under two seconds, but in 2025, he showed progress as a receiver, with scouts seeing an average defender, while data measured an above-average strike-stealer.
THE FUTURE: Heyman has the components to be a platoon catcher, with a chance for more if he builds upon his 2025 offensive and defensive progress.

Year	Age	Club (League)	Level	AVG	G	AB	R	H	2B	3B	HR	RBI	BB	SO	SB	OBP	SLG
2025	21	Did not play															

Pete Crow-Armstrong

Chicago Cubs

BY GEOFF PONTES

Before the 2025 season had even begun, the Cubs' front office set a clear direction for the year ahead.

On Dec. 13, 2024, Chicago shipped first-round pick Cam Smith alongside third baseman Isaac Paredes and righthander Hayden Wesneski to the Astros for star outfielder Kyle Tucker. The move sent a message: the Cubs were all-in on 2025.

Tucker, a pending free agent after the season, produced a solid season, but the Cubs were overwhelmed by the Brewers in the National League Central as Milwaukee cruised to 97 wins.

Despite the defeat in the division, the Cubs won 92 games, their most since 2018, and broke up a six-year stretch of mediocrity. The team clinched a wild card berth with weeks remaining in the season. They eliminated the Padres in the Wild Card Series before falling to the Brewers in the Division Series.

The Cubs enjoyed a few breakouts by young major league players. Top pitching prospect Cade Horton emerged as one of the top rookie pitchers in baseball and went 11-4 over 22 starts and pitched to a 2.67 ERA to finish among the top five rookie pitchers by WAR. Daniel Palencia, no longer a rookie, established himself as a premier reliever racking up 22 saves and striking out 28.4% of batters he faced.

Most importantly, the young core of upper-minors position talent ascended to the majors. Top two prospects Moises Ballesteros and Owen Caissie made their major league debuts and look like they could be key pieces of the Cubs' future. Each saw more action over the final months of the season and showed flashes of what has made them highly rated prospects in recent years.

The Cubs entered the season with arguably the most talented group of Triple-A talent. Five players in the organization's top 12 prospects entering the season opened the year on Iowa's roster. How the Cubs navigate that group of top players will

PROJECTED 2029 LINEUP

Catcher	Miguel Amaya	30
First Base	Michael Busch	31
Second Base	Jefferson Rojas	24
Third Base	Matt Shaw	27
Shortstop	Dansby Swanson	35
Left Field	Owen Caissie	26
Center Field	Pete Crow-Armstrong	27
Right Field	Ethan Conrad	24
Designated Hitter	Moises Ballesteros	25
No. 1 Starter	Cade Horton	28
No. 2 Starter	Jaxon Wiggins	27
No. 3 Starter	Brandon Birdsell	29
No. 4 Starter	Will Sanders	27
No. 5 Starter	Jostin Florentino	24
Closer	Daniel Palencia	29

be telling. After plenty of upper-minors experience between Ballesteros, Caissie, Kevin Alcantara, James Triantos and Jonathon Long, there's potential for the fruit to begin rotting on the vine.

The 2026 season is one to take inventory for the Cubs as they make decisions on which players are part of their future core and which are expendable in trades. How the team navigates this period could have major implications on the direction of the club in the years ahead.

The 2025 draft yielded a potentially dynamic class, led by Wake Forest outfielder Ethan Conrad. The athletic lefthanded hitter's 2025 season was cut short by injury, but he was active in the Arizona backfields in the fall and impressed scouts in limited looks.

In similar fashion, second-rounder Kane Kepley had one of the strongest professional debuts of any 2025 draftee. Assigned to Low-A after the draft, he hit .299/.481/.433 over 28 games with Myrtle Beach. Kepley looks like an ascending talent who could help stabilize the top of the Cubs' system with multiple impending graduations.

The 2026 season looks like a potential bridge year to the Cubs' future, but questions remain. Will they go all-in again in 2026, using their cache of upper minors prospects to acquire talent? Or will they move forward with their potential young core? ∎

DEPTH CHART

CHICAGO CUBS

TOP 2026 ROOKIES — RANK
1. Moises Ballesteros, C — 1
2. Owen Caissie, OF — 2
3. Jaxon Wiggins, RHP — 3

BREAKOUT PROSPECTS — RANK
1. Josiah Hartshorn, OF — 12
2. Dominick Reid, RHP — 13
3. Owen Ayers, C — 18

SOURCE OF TOP 30 TALENT

Homegrown	28	Acquired	2
College	14	Trade	2
Junior college	0	Rule 5 draft	0
High school	6	Independent league	0
Undrafted free agent	0	Free agent/waivers	0
International	8		

LF
Josiah Hartshorn (12)
Kade Snell

CF
Ethan Conrad (5)
Kane Kepley (6)
Kevin Alcantara (7)
Brett Bateman

RF
Owen Caissie (2)
Eli Lovich

3B
Cole Mathis (9)
Juan Cabada (19)
Drew Bowser

SS
Jefferson Rojas (4)
Cristian Hernandez (16)
Angel Cepeda (20)
Juan Tomas (24)
Yahil Melendez

2B
Pedro Ramirez (10)
James Triantos (11)
Ty Southisene (22)
Alexis Hernandez

1B
Jonathon Long (8)
BJ Murray Jr.
Matt Halbach

C
Moises Ballesteros (1)
Owen Ayers (18)
Ariel Armas (29)

LHP

LHSP
Pierce Coppola (26)
Evan Aschenbeck
Drew Gray
Colton Book

LHRP
Riley Martin (21)
Grayson Moore

RHP

RHSP
Jaxon Wiggins (3)
Dominick Reid (13)
Brandon Birdsell (14)
Jostin Florentino (15)
Kaleb Wing (17)
Will Sanders (23)
Erian Rodriguez (25)
Tyler Schlaffer (27)
Brody McCullough (28)
Nick Dean (30)
Grant Kipp
Nazier Mulé
JP Wheat
Yenrri Rojas
Kohl Franklin
Jake Knapp

RHRP
Jack Neely
Zac Leigh
Luis Martinez-Gomez
Adam Stone

CHICAGO CUBS

1. MOISES BALLESTEROS, C

Born: November 8, 2003. **B-T:** L-R. **HT:** 5-10. **WT:** 225.
Signed: Venezuela, 2021.
Signed by: Louie Eljaua/Julio Figueroa/Hector Ortega.

TRACK RECORD: Ballesteros stood out as a youth player with the Venezuelan national team at the 2015 12U World Cup in Taiwan. He maintained his hitting prowess throughout his amateur career and signed with the Cubs for $1.5 million in January 2021. He made his professional debut in the Dominican Summer League in 2021 before he came stateside in 2022. He split his domestic debut between the Arizona Complex League and Low-A. Ballesteros broke out in 2023 by hitting .285/.374/.449 with 14 home runs across three levels. He won the Cubs' minor league player of the year award in 2023 and again in 2024, when he hit .289/.354/.471 with 19 homers between Double-A and Triple-A. Ballesteros spent a majority of the 2025 season with Triple-A Iowa and made his MLB debut on May 13, appearing in 20 games as well as two playoff games.

SCOUTING REPORT: One of the most advanced hitters in the minor leagues, Ballesteros is a lefthanded-hitting, bat-first catcher with major questions around his viability behind the plate. His plus bat-to-ball ability allows him to minimize misses inside the zone and hit a variety of pitch types with very few struggles. Ballesteros is a true contact hitter and is at times overly aggressive and willing to expand the zone. He uses primarily an all-fields approach and a linear swing path and looks to hit the ball gap to gap. His style of hitting is geared toward splattering line drives around the yard, but his underlying power hints at potential for more home runs in time. Ballesteros has plus raw power, backed by plus top end exit velocities to match. A 90th percentile exit velocity of 105.1 mph and a max EV of 112.3 rank in the top 10% of hitters his age. Ballesteros' flatter batted-ball angles lead to fewer home runs than his EVs suggest. Ballesteros rarely strikes out, walks at an average rate and makes lots of hard contact. His long-term defensive home is where things get tricky. Despite an average throwing arm behind the plate, Ballesteros was run on liberally at Triple-A in 2025 and allowed 92 stolen bases on 106 attempts. Ballesteros is a below-average blocker and framer, though he has improved in both areas in recent years. While a majority of Ballesteros' games at Triple-A came behind the plate, he might see more action at first base or DH early in his MLB career. He projects as a below-average defensive catcher but could see consistent action there as part of a platoon. While catching is still up in the air, there's little doubt that Ballesteros will be a successful major league hitter.

THE FUTURE: Ballesteros should compete for batting titles in the coming years as he settles into a catcher/first base/DH role.

BA GRADE: 55 Risk: Mild
Adjusted grade: 50
SCOUTING GRADES: Hit: 60. Power: 55. Run: 30. Field: 40. Arm: 50.
Projected future grades on 20-80 scouting scale

BEST TOOLS

BATTING
Best Hitter	Moises Ballesteros
Best Power Hitter	Owen Caissie
Best Strike-Zone Discipline	Kane Kepley
Fastest Baserunner	Alexey Lumpuy
Best Athlete	Kevin Alcantara

PITCHING
Best Fastball	Jaxon Wiggins
Best Curveball	Riley Martin
Best Slider	Jaxon Wiggins
Best Changeup	Nick Dean
Best Control	Connor Noland

FIELDING
Best Defensive Catcher	Ariel Armas
Best Defensive Infielder	Juan Tomas
Best Infield Arm	Juan Tomas
Best Defensive Outfielder	Brett Bateman
Best Outfield Arm	Kevin Alcantara

Year	Age	Club (League)	Level	AVG	G	AB	R	H	2B	3B	HR	RBI	BB	SO	SB	OBP	SLG
2025	21	Iowa (IL)	AAA	.316	114	446	62	141	29	1	13	76	49	67	5	.385	.473
2025	21	Chicago (NL)	MLB	.298	20	57	12	17	2	1	2	11	9	12	0	.394	.474
		Minor League Totals		.289	466	1681	234	486	102	2	59	276	219	309	19	.371	.457
		Major League Totals		.298	20	57	12	17	2	1	2	11	9	12	0	.394	.474

CHICAGO CUBS

2 OWEN CAISSIE, OF
HIT: 50. **POW:** 65. **RUN:** 45. **FLD:** 45. **ARM:** 60. **BA Grade:** 55. **Risk:** Mild. **Adj:** 50.

Born: July 8, 2002. **B-T:** L-R. **HT:** 6-3. **WT:** 190.
Drafted: HS—Burlington, ON, 2020 (2nd round). **Signed by:** Chris Kemlo (Padres)
TRACK RECORD: A touted Canadian prep hitter, Caissie signed with the Padres for $1.2 million in the second round in 2020. Before he ever played a game for the organization, Caissie was traded to the Cubs in the Yu Darvish deal. Caissie has climbed each rung of the minor league ladder and made his MLB debut on August 14, 2025, in his hometown of Toronto. He appeared in 12 games for the Cubs over the final two months, missing time with a concussion.
SCOUTING REPORT: The early years of Caissie's career were defined by his Thre-True-Outcomes approach. Over the past two seasons, he has improved his contact rates and chase rates. The improvements have pushed Caissie comfortably into the average contact category, while his strikeout rate has dropped in consecutive seasons. Caissie does a good job of staying inside the zone and being aggressive. This plays directly into his strength: quality of contact. Caissie has plus-plus underlying power with 60-grade game power. His batted-ball angles have improved over the last two seasons, and he more consistently shows the ability to hit his best struck drives in the air. He also saw a jump in pull-side air contact in 2025, portending a higher home run ceiling. Caissie is a fringe-average runner who has slowed down over the last few seasons. In turn, this has limited him a bit in right field. He has lost range and is uncoordinated at times on extra-effort plays. He's fringe-average in the corner outfield. Despite good instincts and a plus arm, he is dragged down by below-average hands and range.
THE FUTURE: Caissie is a major league-ready slugging corner outfielder with the prerequisite plate skills to project as an above-average regular.

Year	Age	Club (League)	Level	AVG	G	AB	R	H	2B	3B	HR	RBI	BB	SO	SB	OBP	SLG
2025	22	Iowa (IL)	AAA	.286	99	370	74	106	28	2	22	55	57	121	5	.386	.551
2025	22	Chicago (NL)	MLB	.192	12	26	4	5	1	0	1	4	1	11	0	.222	.346
		Minor League Totals		.280	505	1841	312	515	120	9	81	301	296	632	35	.384	.487
		Major League Totals		.192	12	26	4	5	1	0	1	4	1	11	0	.222	.346

3 JAXON WIGGINS, RHP
FB: 70. **CB:** 45. **SL:** 60. **CH:** 50. **CTL:** 50. **BA Grade:** 60. **Risk:** High. **Adj:** 45.

Born: October 3, 2001. **B-T:** R-R. **HT:** 6-6. **WT:** 225.
Drafted: Arkansas, 2023 (2nd round supp.). **Signed by:** Ty Nichols.
TRACK RECORD: Wiggins struggled for two seasons at Arkansas before having Tommy John surgery prior to his junior season. Despite the injury, the Cubs bet on Wiggins' upside by drafting him 68th overall in 2023 and signing him for $1.4 million. He debuted with the Cubs the following May and enjoyed a strong professional debut. Wiggins climbed three levels to Triple-A in 2025, dominating at each stop. He dealt with arm fatigue during the middle of the season and missed most of July and August. The Cubs played the injury close to the vest, but Wiggins returned in late August.
SCOUTING REPORT: Standing 6-foot-6 with an athletic build, Wiggins looks the part of an innings-eating starting pitcher. His high-powered arsenal and solid combination of pitch characteristics hints at some of the highest upside among pitching prospects who had not yet debuted in MLB. Staying healthy and handling a larger workload has held Wiggins back, hinting at some relief risk. When healthy, his upper-90s fastball is one of the best thrown by a starting pitching prospect. The pitch sits 96-98 mph and touches 100. Wiggins generates a combination of plus ride and armside run, while boasting 6.5 feet of extension. His best secondary pitch is an upper-80s cut-slider that generates whiffs at a well above-average rate. Wiggins pairs his fastball and slider with an upper-80s changeup that plays well off his fastball. His curveball is rarely thrown but sits in the low 80s with a heavy two-plane break. He shows average command of his fastball, slider and changeup and is in the zone with all of his pitches at a high rate.
THE FUTURE: While Wiggins has as much upside as any player in the Cubs' system, his checkered injury history likely limits him to a midrotation role.

Year	Age	Club (League)	Level	W	L	ERA	G	GS	IP	H	HR	BB	SO	BB%	SO%	WHIP	AVG
2025	23	South Bend (MWL)	A+	1	2	1.71	6	5	26	13	1	13	31	12.4	29.5	0.99	.143
2025	23	Knoxville (SL)	AA	2	0	1.93	10	10	42	22	1	17	52	10.4	31.7	0.93	.152
2025	23	Iowa (IL)	AAA	0	2	4.66	3	3	10	9	2	6	14	13.6	31.8	1.55	.243
		Minor League Totals		3	9	2.72	29	28	106	60	6	53	130	12.3	30.2	1.07	.161

CHICAGO CUBS

4 JEFFERSON ROJAS, SS
HIT: 55. **POW:** 45. **RUN:** 55. **FLD:** 50. **ARM:** 60. **BA Grade:** 55. **Risk:** Average. **Adj:** 45.

Born: April 25, 2005. **B-T:** R-R. **HT:** 5-11. **WT:** 150.
Signed: Dominican Republic, 2022. **Signed by:** Glan Guzman/Miguel Diaz.
TRACK RECORD: Signed in January 2022 for $1 million out of the Dominican Republic, Rojas has quickly proved to be a precocious shortstop prospect with advanced skills. He impressed as an 18-year-old for Low-A Myrtle Beach by hitting .268/.345/.404 in 2023. He spent all of 2024 with High-A South Bend and returned to the Midwest League in 2025 before a second-half promotion to Double-A, where he struggled for the final two months.
SCOUTING REPORT: An advanced contact hitter, Rojas' above-average hitting ability is the nucleus of his profile. The righthanded hitter showed no platoon issues during his time in High-A. Rojas shows plus bat-to-ball ability with average swing decisions, leading to lots of quality at-bats. His game power improved in 2025 as he more consistently found the barrel and began to optimize his swing for more pulled contact in the air. Rojas projects for mid-teens home run production but has enough power to find the gaps. He's an above-average runner but isn't an aggressive baserunner, picking his spots and stealing at a high percentage. In the field, Rojas is an average shortstop defender. His footwork and hands leave something to be desired and he's prone to poorly timed dives on extra-effort plays. His arm is plus, and he shows an excellent internal clock on his throws. Rojas is adept at throwing on the run and is very good around the bag, turning double plays consistently. He could slide over to second base or third base, but improvements to his hands and footwork could see him stick at shortstop.
THE FUTURE: Rojas is an advanced hitter who's been three to four years younger than the average player at each level. He has the tools to be an above-average hitting infielder with the ability to play multiple positions.

Year	Age	Club (League)	Level	AVG	G	AB	R	H	2B	3B	HR	RBI	BB	SO	SB	OBP	SLG
2025	20	South Bend (MWL)	A+	.278	67	252	50	70	13	4	11	44	38	47	14	.379	.492
2025	20	Knoxville (SL)	AA	.164	39	146	17	24	6	0	0	15	20	34	5	.279	.205
		Minor League Totals		.254	318	1190	189	302	49	11	25	156	132	225	68	.338	.376

5 ETHAN CONRAD, OF
HIT: 55. **POW:** 55. **RUN:** 55. **FLD:** 55. **ARM:** 50. **BA Grade:** 55. **Risk:** Average. **Adj:** 45.

Born: July 5, 2004. **B-T:** L-L. **HT:** 6-3. **WT:** 220.
Drafted: Wake Forest, 2025 (1st round). **Signed by:** Billy Swoope.
TRACK RECORD: After a standout sophomore campaign at Marist and a strong summer in the Cape Cod League, Conrad transferred to Wake Forest for 2025. There, he played just 21 games before a left shoulder injury required surgery. He hit .372/.495/.744 with seven home runs, 18 walks and 14 strikeouts. The Cubs drafted Conrad 17th overall and signed him for an under-slot $3,563,100. He participated in fall instructional league after signing.
SCOUTING REPORT: One of the top college hitters available in the 2025 draft, Conrad is a taller outfielder with an athletic build that still has some projection remaining. His bat-to-ball skills are advanced. He ran a 92% zone-contact rate in 2025 with Wake Forest and didn't swing and miss against a single pitch thrown in the zone by a lefthanded pitcher. He shows strong contact skills and production across all pitch types. In his first two collegiate seasons, Conrad's approach was more aggressive, but during his truncated season at Wake he showed vastly improved swing decisions that now grade as above-average. Conrad's power is above-average with exit velocity data above the NCAA norm and good hard-hit launch angles. A majority of the pitches Conrad barrels are shot to the opposite field, and finding more consistent pull-side power will likely be a point of emphasis in his development. Conrad is an above-average runner with an average arm who plays an average center field. He has good range and is likely to be above-average in an outfield corner. As Conrad works his way back in 2026, it's likely he sees some time at first base, a position he played at Marist as an underclassman.
THE FUTURE: Conrad has the type of quality all-around tools to rise up prospect ranks in 2026, though his profile carries some risk because of his shoulder injury and shorter track record beyond Marist.

Year	Age	Club (League)	Level	AVG	G	AB	R	H	2B	3B	HR	RBI	BB	SO	SB	OBP	SLG
2025	20	Did not play															

CHICAGO CUBS

6 KANE KEPLEY, OF
HIT: 60. **POW:** 40. **RUN:** 60. **FLD:** 70. **ARM:** 45. **BA Grade:** 50. **Risk:** Average. **Adj:** 40.

Born: February 14, 2004. **B-T:** L-L. **HT:** 5-8. **WT:** 180.
Drafted: North Carolina, 2025 (2nd round). **Signed by:** Billy Swoope.
TRACK RECORD: Kepley spent two seasons at Liberty before transferring to North Carolina. In his single season with the Tar Heels, he hit .291/.451/.444 with three home runs and 45 stolen bases. The Cubs drafted Kepley in the second round in 2025 and signed him for $1.4 million. Kepley had one of the most impressive debuts of any draftee, hitting .299/.481/.433 with two homers and 16 steals in 28 games for Low-A Myrtle Beach.
SCOUTING REPORT: A throwback-style player, Kepley has an undersized, hit tool-driven profile with plus-plus defense in center field. He stands just 5-foot-8 and has limited power, but his hit tool is likely advanced enough to make him a productive big league hitter. Kepley rarely swings and misses, running elite contact rates in 2025 at North Carolina and in his pro debut. He rarely expands the zone while showing aggressive tendencies on strikes. His approach and bat-to-ball skills are consistently good across all pitch types. While Kepley may lack over-the-fence power, he makes consistently hard contact. Kepley lacks impressive top-end exit velocities, but he finds the barrel, and his average exit velocity is in line with major league average. Kepley hits the ball flush at good angles and shows the ability to pull the ball in the air. Kepley is a plus runner and dangerous basestealer who will consistently draw the attention of opposing batteries. He's a plus-plus defender in center, where his plus speed and strong instincts help him cover large swaths of grass.
THE FUTURE: Kepley has an advanced hit tool, more power than one would expect from his frame and a no-doubt center field defensive profile. He looks like a classic table-setter and outstanding everyday center fielder.

Year	Age	Club (League)	Level	AVG	G	AB	R	H	2B	3B	HR	RBI	BB	SO	SB	OBP	SLG
2025	21	Myrtle Beach (CAR)	A	.299	28	97	28	29	1	3	2	15	25	15	16	.481	.433
		Minor League Totals		.299	28	97	28	29	1	3	2	15	25	15	16	.481	.433

7 KEVIN ALCANTARA, OF
HIT: 40. **POW:** 60. **RUN:** 60. **FLD:** 60. **ARM:** 60. **BA Grade:** 50. **Risk:** Average. **Adj:** 40.

Born: July 12, 2002. **B-T:** R-R. **HT:** 6-6. **WT:** 218.
Signed: Dominican Republic, 2018. **Signed by:** Edgar Mateo/Juan Piron (Yankees).
TRACK RECORD: Signed by the Yankees in 2018 for $1 million out of the Dominican Republic, Alcantara was traded to the Cubs three years later in the deal that sent Anthony Rizzo to New York. Over parts of five seasons in the Cubs' system, Alcantara has been a productive but inconsistent performer. He made his MLB debut in late September 2024 but did not return to the major leagues until nearly a year later. He spent a majority of 2025 with Triple-A Iowa and had surgery to repair a sports hernia after the season.
SCOUTING REPORT: Alcantara is an outstanding athlete with loud tools and a wiry 6-foot-6 frame. His batting contributions have been dragged down by poor plate discipline and pitch recognition. Despite a consistent issue with expanding the zone, Alcantara shows average bat-to-ball skills and runs a better than average in-zone contact rate. A righthanded hitter, he has a track record against lefthanders, hitting .320/.396/.588 against southpaws in 2025. Alcantara has plus-plus raw power with a 90th percentile exit velocity that ranks within the 90th percentile. He did a good job of adding more loft to his swing in 2025 and, in turn, found more barrels. He still has a fair amount of groundball contact and a straightaway to opposite-field power swing that will limit his home run totals. An improved approach could also allow Alcantara to capitalize on more of his raw power. While Alcantara is a plus runner, he is only an average basestealer. His running ability translates to the outfield, where he's a plus center fielder with a plus arm.
THE FUTURE: Despite being eight years into his career, Alcantara still has a high variance of outcomes. He has all the tools of an everyday center fielder but is dragged down by hit tool questions.

Year	Age	Club (League)	Level	AVG	G	AB	R	H	2B	3B	HR	RBI	BB	SO	SB	OBP	SLG
2025	22	Iowa (IL)	AAA	.266	102	379	55	101	26	0	17	69	48	128	10	.349	.470
2025	22	Chicago (NL)	MLB	.364	10	11	2	4	0	0	0	1	1	4	1	.417	.364
		Minor League Totals		.278	502	1899	321	528	104	17	65	329	211	551	63	.353	.453
		Major League Totals		.238	13	21	3	5	0	0	0	1	1	5	1	.273	.238

CHICAGO CUBS

8 JONATHON LONG, 1B
HIT: 55. **POW:** 55. **RUN:** 40. **FLD:** 45. **ARM:** 45. **BA Grade:** 45. **Risk:** Mild. **Adj:** 40.

Born: January 20, 2002. **B-T:** R-R. **HT:** 5-11. **WT:** 210.
Drafted: Long Beach State, 2023 (9th round). **Signed by:** Evan Kauffman.
TRACK RECORD: After a strong three-year career at Long Beach State, Long was drafted by the Cubs in the ninth round in 2023. Assigned to High-A South Bend in 2024, he hit his way to Double-A Tennessee in the second half, where he caught fire by hitting .340/.455/.528 over the final 46 games of the season. Long spent all of 2025 with Triple-A Iowa and hit .305/.404/.479 with 20 home runs, production that was 31% better than International League competition. He led the IL with 157 hits and was recognized as the league's all-star first baseman.
SCOUTING REPORT: While not blessed with plus athleticism or size, Long has continued to outperform his pedigree because of a nice blend of contact and power. His bat-to-ball skills are above-average and he limits whiffs with a passive approach. His lack of aggressiveness leads to lots of walks, but he's prone to taking hittable pitches for called strikes too often. Long shows a good blend of on-base skills and contact hitting and should project to hit for higher batting averages with good walk rates. His underlying power is plus and he's shown an ability to get to it in games consistently. Flatter launch angles have led to a higher groundball rate. Long's struggles to pull the ball in the air likely cap his home run output. His exit velocity data and angles are likely enough to produce 18-24 home runs over a full season. If he's able to add loft to his swing in the coming years, it's possible he gets into the mid 20s for home runs. Long is a below-average runner and is likely a primary first baseman. He's a fringe-average defender at first base and can fill in at third base on occasion.
THE FUTURE: Long might have the prerequisite contact and power combination to carve out a niche as a second-division regular.

Year	Age	Club (League)	Level	AVG	G	AB	R	H	2B	3B	HR	RBI	BB	SO	SB	OBP	SLG
2025	23	Iowa (IL)	AAA	.305	140	514	86	157	23	3	20	91	79	116	2	.404	.479
		Minor League Totals		.294	280	1004	185	295	48	3	44	175	162	235	4	.398	.479

9 COLE MATHIS, 3B
HIT: 50. **POW:** 55. **RUN:** 40. **FLD:** 40. **ARM:** 50. **BA Grade:** 50. **Risk:** High. **Adj:** 35.

Born: July 25, 2003. **B-T:** R-R. **HT:** 6-1. **WT:** 195.
Drafted: College of Charleston, 2024 (2nd round). **Signed by:** M'Lynn Dease.
TRACK RECORD: Mathis turned in an outstanding sophomore season at the College of Charleston as a two-way player in 2023. He followed by hitting 11 home runs in the Cape Cod League and making nine appearances on the mound. Mathis didn't pitch at all during his junior season and started slow at the plate before catching fire over the final months of the season. A few weeks after the Cubs drafted Mathis in the second round in 2024, he announced on Instagram that he had Tommy John surgery. He began the 2025 season with Low-A Myrtle Beach, playing in 28 games before he was shut down in mid-May due to a right elbow sprain.
SCOUTING REPORT: Mathis features plus raw power with the ability to impact a game with his bat. He shows average bat-to-ball skills against all pitch types, giving him a stronger contact foundation than most power hitters. Mathis has grown as a hitter over the last two seasons as his approach at the plate has matured. He rarely expands the zone and does a good job of staying fairly aggressive on pitches in the strike zone. Mathis showed plus exit velocities in college and on the Cape but appeared to be affected by his elbow injury with exit velocities that were closer to average. Many are confident that Mathis' power will return when he is fully healthy. He shows an efficient bat path and is adept at launching well-struck drives to his pull side. Due to the injury, Mathis played in the field very little in 2025. Prior to his Tommy John surgery, he was a below-average defender at third base with a plus arm. In the short term, he is likely to see the majority of his time at first base.
THE FUTURE: Mathis' defensive home is up in the air following Tommy John surgery. His average hit tool and above-average game power might be enough to carry his profile to second-division regular status.

Year	Age	Club (League)	Level	AVG	G	AB	R	H	2B	3B	HR	RBI	BB	SO	SB	OBP	SLG
2025	21	Myrtle Beach (CAR)	A	.215	29	107	16	23	9	1	3	14	17	29	0	.336	.402
		Minor League Totals		.215	29	107	16	23	9	1	3	14	17	29	0	.336	.402

CHICAGO CUBS

10 PEDRO RAMIREZ, 2B/3B

HIT: 55. **POW:** 40. **RUN:** 55. **FLD:** 55. **ARM:** 55. **BA Grade:** 45. **Risk:** Average. **Adj:** 35.

Born: April 1, 2004. **B-T:** B-R. **HT:** 5-8. **WT:** 165. **Signed:** Venezuela, 2021.
Signed by: Julio Figueroa/Carlos Figueroa/Cirilo Cumberbatch.
TRACK RECORD: Ramirez signed for $75,000 out of Venezuela in January 2021 and has been a quick study as a professional. He hit .359/.417/.503 in his U.S. debut in 2022 and reached full-season ball by age 18. After two seasons across both levels of Class A, Ramirez spent all of 2025 at Double-A Knoxville, hitting .280/.346/.386 in 129 games. Ramirez was selected as the Southern League player of the month in July and a league all-star.
SCOUTING REPORT: An undersized switch-hitting infielder with the ability to play both second base and third base every day, Ramirez has a hit-over-power offensive profile. What he lacks in terms of impact, he makes up for with plus bat-to-ball skills and a discerning eye at the plate. Ramirez is more comfortable with his lefthanded swing, which translates to better production against righthanders. Ramirez has strong bat-to-ball skills as a righthanded hitter but has a more aggressive approach. His power is below-average with fringy exit velocity data and lots of groundball contact. Ramirez's swings from each side of the plate are geared toward line-drive contact and putting the ball in play. He could find more power in the coming years by adding loft to his swing. An above-average runner, Ramirez is aggressive on the bases. His speed translates to the field, where he shows good range at multiple infield positions. Ramirez is an above-average defender at second and third base who is adept at making plays on the run. He's athletic in the field in terms of making plays on dives, jumps and slides. Ramirez's arm is above-average, with good power and accuracy. It's not uncommon to see him make a nice barehanded play.
THE FUTURE: Ramirez fits a high-end utility profile perfectly. He can play multiple positions competently, while switch-hitting and bringing above-average speed.

Year	Age	Club (League)	Level	AVG	G	AB	R	H	2B	3B	HR	RBI	BB	SO	SB	OBP	SLG
2025	21	Knoxville (SL)	AA	.280	129	500	70	140	21	4	8	73	46	85	28	.346	.386
		Minor League Totals		.294	336	1236	193	363	60	19	21	172	127	208	69	.367	.424

11 JAMES TRIANTOS 2B/OF

HIT: 55. **POW:** 30. **RUN:** 55. **FLD:** 40. **ARM:** 55. **BA Grade:** 45. **Risk:** Average. **Adj:** 35.

Born: January 29, 2003. **B-T:** R-R. **HT:** 5-11. **WT:** 195. **Drafted:** HS—Vienna, VA, 2021 (2nd round).
Signed by: Billy Swoope.
TRACK RECORD: A standout Virginia high school player, Triantos starred as a two-way player and won a 6A state championship in his final game. The Cubs drafted him a few months later in the second round in 2021 and signed him for $2.1 million. Triantos tore his meniscus in spring of 2023 and missed the first few months of that season. After a breakout 2024 in which Triantos reached Triple-A, he returned to the level to begin 2025. He struggled throughout 2025, dealing with leg soreness. He hit just .258/.315/.369 over 102 games with Triple-A Iowa. Triantos was added to the Cubs' 40-man roster after the season.
SCOUTING REPORT: Triantos is an undersized, righthanded-hitting second baseman with plus bat-to-ball skills and advanced basestealing acumen. He uses a simple upright setup in the box with quiet hands. Triantos is a plus contact hitter who rarely swings and misses, and he has run elite zone rates throughout his career. In 2025, Triantos' approach backed up. He chased at a higher rate than at any point in his career and was unusually passive in the strike zone. Triantos has never shown much game power, but his exit velocity data and power production backed up further in 2025. With below-average raw power and flatter launch angles, there's little power projection for Triantos. He is an above-average runner and a plus basestealer who stole 78 bases in 2024 and 2025 combined. Triantos is a below-average second baseman, but due to his speed the Cubs tried him in center field, too. The combination of running ability and his above-average arm make it a natural fit, but he's still raw tracking balls off the bat.
THE FUTURE: Triantos looks like a second-division regular at second base.

Year	Age	Club (League)	Level	AVG	G	AB	R	H	2B	3B	HR	RBI	BB	SO	SB	OBP	SLG
2025	22	South Bend (MWL)	A+	.273	8	33	4	9	4	0	0	4	2	5	3	.306	.394
2025	22	Iowa (IL)	AAA	.258	102	407	65	105	20	2	7	43	31	67	28	.315	.369
		Minor League Totals		.282	446	1757	290	495	88	18	31	216	141	264	117	.341	.405

CHICAGO CUBS

12 JOSIAH HARTSHORN, OF
HIT: 50. **POW:** 55. **RUN:** 45. **FLD:** 50. **ARM:** 55. **BA Grade:** 55. **Risk:** Extreme. **Adj:** 35.

Born: February 2, 2007. **B-T:** B-L. **HT:** 6-2. **WT:** 220. **Drafted:** HS—Orange, CA, 2025 (6th round).
Signed by: Evan Kauffman.
TRACK RECORD: Hartshorn is the latest player drafted out of Southern California high school baseball powerhouse Orange Lutheran. He is a switch-hitter who dealt with a variety of injuries throughout his high school career. Injuries to his elbow, back and oblique would limit him to exclusively lefthanded or righthanded swings for long stretches. The Cubs drafted Hartshorn in the sixth round in 2025 and signed him for a well above-slot bonus of $2 million. He did not debut following the draft.
SCOUTING REPORT: Hartshorn is a physical switch-hitting slugger with average height, present strength and physicality, leaving little room for projection. His lefthanded swing is long, starting with a high leg lift trigger that gets deep into his back leg. It's possible his swing was out of sync due to the injuries he dealt with as a prep. His lefty swing makes use of a scissor kick in his lower half. Hartshorn shows average bat-to-ball skills with an advanced—and at times passive—plate approach. He shows good bat speed from both sides of the plate with present strength. He'll need to add some more loft to his swings in order to get to more consistent game power as a professional. Hartshorn will need to maintain his body as he gets older to maintain his average athleticism. He's an average runner who likely is more of a fringe-average runner at peak. Hartshorn is likely destined for the corner outfield, where his above-average arm will play.
THE FUTURE: Hartshorn is a higher-upside switch-hitter with above-average everyday regular upside but lots of risk.

Year	Age	Club (League)	Level	AVG	G	AB	R	H	2B	3B	HR	RBI	BB	SO	SB	OBP	SLG
2025	18	Did not play															

13 DOMINICK REID, RHP
FB: 50. **CB:** 40. **SL:** 40. **CH:** 60. **CTL:** 50. **BA Grade:** 45. **Risk:** Average. **Adj:** 35.

Born: November 28, 2003. **B-T:** R-R. **HT:** 6-3. **WT:** 201. **Drafted:** Abilene Christian, 2025 (3rd round).
Signed by: Todd George.
TRACK RECORD: Reid spent two seasons at Oklahoma State, pitching a total of 19.1 innings, before transferring to Abilene Christian as a junior in 2025. He made 15 starts and pitched to a 3.26 ERA while striking out 112 batters to 27 walks over 88.1 innings. He made the all-Western Athletic Conference first team. The Cubs drafted Reid in the third round in 2025 and signed him for $649,125.
SCOUTING REPORT: Reid is a prototypical righthanded starter with size and a fully mature physical build. He is a good mover on the mound who gets downhill and creates seven feet of extension on average. His longer arm action gives way to a three-quarters arm slot with slight crossfire delivery. Reid mixes four pitches in a four-seam fastball, changeup, slider and curveball. His four-seam fastball sits 92-94 mph and touches 96 with below-average ride and plane to the plate. His best secondary and best pitch overall is his changeup. It sits 82-84 mph with good vertical separation off his fastball. He kills lift on the pitch while driving armside run. The fastball and changeup dominate Reid's pitch usage, but he also shows a pair of breaking ball shapes: a mini-sweeper slider at 81-82 mph and a two-plane curveball sitting 79-80 mph with more depth than his slider. Reid shows average command of his pitch mix.
THE FUTURE: Reid is a changeup-first righthanded starter with a chance to develop into a No. 5 starter with added fastball velocity or an improved breaking pitch.

Year	Age	Club (League)	Level	W	L	ERA	G	GS	IP	H	HR	BB	SO	BB%	SO%	WHIP	AVG
2025	21	Did not play															

14 BRANDON BIRDSELL, RHP
FB: 50. **CB:** 40. **CH:** 40. **CT:** 50. **CTL:** 55. **BA Grade:** 45. **Risk:** Average. **Adj:** 35.

Born: March 23, 2000. **B-T:** R-R. **HT:** 6-2. **WT:** 240. **Drafted:** Texas Tech, 2022 (5th round). **Signed by:** Todd George.
TRACK RECORD: Birdsell is the rare player who has been drafted three times, first by the Astros out of high school in 2018, then twice at Texas Tech, first in the 11th round by the Twins and then by the Cubs in the fifth round in 2022. He reached Double-A in his first season and then reached Triple-A in 2024. Birdsell returned to Triple-A in 2025 and looked like he was on the verge of his major league debut.. Instead he dealt with persistent elbow pain and missed the first two months. He returned following the all-star break, only to be shut down after four starts. Birdsell had elbow surgery in September and is expected to miss all of 2026.
SCOUTING REPORT: Birdsell is a stocky righthander with average height and a thick lower half. He pitches entirely from the stretch and uses a short arm action and three-quarters arm slot. He mixes four pitches in a four-seam fastball, cutter, curveball and changeup. Birdsell's four-seam fastball sits 93-94 mph and

CHICAGO CUBS

touches 96 with cut-fastball shape, not dissimilar to fellow Cubs hurler Cade Horton. Birdsell show fringy command, but he misses more bats than expected based on his velocity. His upper-80s-to-low-90s cutter is his primary secondary. It sits 88-90 mph with ride and around four inches of horizontal break. Birdsell's curveball has slurvy shape, not too far off from the currently en vogue "deathball" variety. Birdsell's firm upper-80s changeup is used sparingly and is the only pitch in his arsenal with armside break. None of Birdsell's secondaries missed bats in 2025. Previously, his cutter had been an above-average bat-missing pitch. He shows above-average command of his arsenal.

THE FUTURE: Birdsell will return in 2027 and should be ready to fill the role of back-end starter.

Year	Age	Club (League)	Level	W	L	ERA	G	GS	IP	H	HR	BB	SO	BB%	SO%	WHIP	AVG
2025	25	South Bend (MWL)	A+	1	0	3.00	2	2	9	7	1	3	8	7.9	21.1	1.11	.206
2025	25	Iowa (IL)	AAA	1	1	3.38	4	4	19	16	4	8	18	10.0	22.5	1.29	.229
		Minor League Totals		14	18	3.39	57	56	271	256	28	74	257	6.5	22.7	1.22	.248

15 JOSTIN FLORENTINO, RHP

FB: 50. **CH:** 30. **CT:** 45. **SW:** 50. **CTL:** 55. **BA Grade:** 50. **Risk:** High. **Adj:** 35.

Born: December 1, 2004. **B-T:** R-R. **HT:** 6-0. **WT:** 175. **Signed:** Dominican Republic, 2023.
Signed by: Valerio Heredia/Miguel Diaz.

TRACK RECORD: The Cubs signed Florentino out of the Dominican Republic in January 2023 for $395,000. He spent two seasons in the Dominican Summer League before coming stateside to begin 2025. Florentino made his U.S. debut in the Arizona Complex League, making five appearances before seeing a promotion to Low-A Myrtle Beach on June 7. Over 11 appearances in the Carolina League, Florentino pitched to a 1.96 ERA with 67 strikeouts to 20 walks across 59.2 innings.

SCOUTING REPORT: An undersized righthander at 6 feet, 175 pounds, Florentino's pitch mix consists of fastball, sweeper, changeup and cutter. A majority of his usage is split between his fastball and sweeper. Florentino's fastball sits 89-91 mph and touches 92 with around 12 inches of induced vertical break and 11 inches of armside run. On its face, the shape of the pitch is below-average, but his above-average extension and his height drop his release to a staggeringly low 4-foot-8. This unique release characteristic allows the pitch to set up the rest of his repertoire. Florentino's sweeper is an upper-70s breaking ball with an average of 17-18 inches of sweep. It's a higher-spin offering that averages 2,700-2,800 rpm and has a deceptive approach angle. Hitters struggled mightily to identify the pitch. His changeup sits 84-85 mph with solid vertical separation off his fastball, but Florentino struggles to command the pitch. He also throws a mid-80s cutter that's an effective bridge pitch between his fastball and sweeper. Strike-throwing is a primary part of Florentino's success.

THE FUTURE: Florentino shows back-of-the-rotation upside but will need to add power across his pitch mix.

Year	Age	Club (League)	Level	W	L	ERA	G	GS	IP	H	HR	BB	SO	BB%	SO%	WHIP	AVG
2025	20	ACL Cubs	Rk	1	2	3.74	5	4	22	20	2	5	34	5.5	37.4	1.15	.238
2025	20	Myrtle Beach (CAR)	A	4	3	1.96	11	10	60	42	1	20	67	8.0	26.9	1.04	.187
		Minor League Totals		10	8	2.61	39	21	152	116	5	45	176	7.3	28.4	1.06	.206

16 CRISTIAN HERNANDEZ, SS

HIT: 40. **POW:** 50. **RUN:** 60. **FLD:** 55. **ARM:** 55. **BA Grade:** 45. **Risk:** Average. **Adj:** 35.

Born: December 13, 2003. **B-T:** R-R. **HT:** 6-2. **WT:** 175. **Signed:** Dominican Republic, 2021.
Signed by: Gian Guzman/Louie Eljaua/Alex Suarez.

TRACK RECORD: When Hernandez signed with the Cubs for a franchise record international free agent bonus of $3 million in January 2021, many scouts viewed the shortstop as the best player in the class. After a strong debut in the Dominican Summer League after signing, Hernandez struggled in his first two seasons stateside. Repeating Low-A in 2024, he had his best season and reached High-A for the final month. Hernandez returned to High-A for 2025 and spent the entire season in the Midwest League, hitting .252/.329/.365.

SCOUTING REPORT: Hernandez has shown tantalizing tools at times but seems incapable of putting it all together. Despite running the best strikeout rate of his career in 2025, he shows below-average bat-to-ball skills. Hernandez ran a 14.7% swinging-strike rate, his highest since his Low-A debut. His swing decisions are above-average. He balances his aggression in terms avoiding chase while also attacking pitches in the zone at a high rate. Hernandez shows plus underlying power with a 90th percentile exit velocity of 106 mph in 2025, but his shallow launch angles lead to more groundball contact than is ideal. The challenge for Hernandez will be adding loft to his swing without bottoming out his plate skills. He is a plus runner who stole 52 bases on 61 attempts in 2025. Hernandez is an above-average defender at shortstop

CHICAGO CUBS

with an above-average arm. He shows a quick first step, good internal clock and clean hands and actions. Hernandez has plus arm strength but fringy accuracy on his throws.
THE FUTURE: Hernandez looks like a potential second-division regular whose value comes from his glove, baserunning and raw power.

Year	Age	Club (League)	Level	AVG	G	AB	R	H	2B	3B	HR	RBI	BB	SO	SB	OBP	SLG
2025	21	South Bend (MWL)	A+	.252	115	444	54	112	25	2	7	53	53	105	52	.329	.365
		Minor League Totals		.252	430	1577	226	397	73	12	24	195	210	429	150	.342	.359

17 KALEB WING, RHP
FB: 50. **CB:** 40. **SL:** 45. **CH:** 55. **CTL:** 45. **BA Grade:** 50. **Risk:** High. **Adj:** 35.

Born: January 12, 2007. **B-T:** R-R. **HT:** 6-2. **WT:** 180. **Drafted:** HS—Scotts Valley, CA, 2025 (4th round).
Signed by: Gabe Zappin.
TRACK RECORD: The son of White Sox 2001 second-round pick Ryan Wing, Kaleb experienced a great deal of helium his senior year at Scotts Valley High in California as he saw a jump in velocity. Following his senior season, he participated in the collegiate West Coast League with Corvallis. The Cubs drafted him in the fourth round, and he signed for $1.5 million. He did not debut following the draft.
SCOUTING REPORT: Wing is a 6-foot-2, slender righthander with some remaining projection in his high-waisted frame. He uses a semi-windup and a high leg lift that contracts into his body before he drives toward the plate. He closes off his front side and uncorks toward the plate with a short stride and longer arm action, delivering the ball from a high three-quarters arm slot. Wing throws four pitches in a four-seam fastball, curveball, slider and changeup. His four-seam fastball sits 90-92 mph and touches 94 with above-average ride and heavy armside run from a six-foot release height. His primary secondary is a changeup that sits upper 70s with good vertical separation off his fastball. Wing mixes a pair of breaking balls in a curveball and a slider. The slider sits 82-83 mph with cutter-like shape. It looks like a potential bridge pitch between his curveball and fastball. His curveball is a mid-70s pitch with heavy two-plane break and on average 20 inches of drop. Wing shows fringe-average command of his pitch mix.
THE FUTURE: Wing is a projectable righthander with back-end starter upside.

Year	Age	Club (League)	Level	W	L	ERA	G	GS	IP	H	HR	BB	SO	BB%	SO%	WHIP	AVG
2025	18	Did not play															

18 OWEN AYERS, C
HIT: 45. **POW:** 50. **RUN:** 40. **FLD:** 45. **ARM:** 70. **BA Grade:** 45. **Risk:** Average. **Adj:** 35.

Born: June 7, 2001. **B-T:** B-R. **HT:** 6-2. **WT:** 185. **Drafted:** Marshall, 2024 (19th round). **Signed by:** Nate Metzger.
TRACK RECORD: Ayers was not highly recruited out of Sarasota High in Florida and committed to the State JC of Florida. He spent two seasons there before transferring to Marshall, where he spent two additional seasons. He set the Thundering Herd's single-season record for doubles in consecutive seasons. The Cubs drafted Ayers in the 19th round in 2024, signing him for $50,000. He debuted in Low-A in 2025 and spent the entire season with Myrtle Beach. Ayers broke his hand in late July and missed the final month. Following the season, Ayers participated in the Arizona Fall League and was selected as an all-star.
SCOUTING REPORT: Ayers entered pro ball as a light-hitting outfielder who had caught a little in college but played a majority of his time as an outfielder. He added strength heading into 2025 and saw a modest increase in game power. The switch-hitting Ayers is a far better hitter from the left side than the right, struggling to do much damage against lefties while showing a passive approach. Against righthanded pitchers, he's an average hitter with fringy bat-to-ball skills and excellent swing decisions. Ayers' hit tool is heavily boosted by his plus swing decisions. His strength gains heading into the season led to improved exit velocities and game power. He lacks the ability to elevate the ball to his pull side, but his steepest angles come on his hardest-hit balls. Behind the plate, Ayers has a plus-plus arm he uses to control the running game. He's newer to catching and is still improving as a receiver and blocker.
THE FUTURE: Ayers looks like he could carve out a long career as a backup catcher.

Year	Age	Club (League)	Level	AVG	G	AB	R	H	2B	3B	HR	RBI	BB	SO	SB	OBP	SLG
2025	24	Myrtle Beach (CAR)	A	.238	65	231	30	55	14	5	6	47	31	63	7	.341	.420
		Minor League Totals		.228	83	294	36	67	18	5	7	52	37	77	8	.327	.395

CHICAGO CUBS

19 JUAN CABADA, 2B/3B
HIT: 55. **POW:** 45. **RUN:** 55. **FLD:** 45. **ARM:** 45. **BA Grade:** 45. **Risk:** High. **Adj:** 30.

Born: April 30, 2008. **B-T:** L-R. **HT:** 5-10. **WT:** 165. **Signed:** Dominican Republic, 2025.
Signed by: Miguel Diaz/Gian Guzman.
TRACK RECORD: Cabada was a part of an expensive international class for the Cubs in 2025 as they handed out bonuses of $1 million or more to three players. Cabada signed for $1.5 million and debuted in the Dominican Summer League in 2025. Over 42 games, he hit .287/.429/.426 with three home runs and 20 stolen bases. He should make the jump stateside in 2026 in the Arizona Complex League.
SCOUTING REPORT: Cabada is an undersized infielder with a clean lefthanded swing and strong bat-to-ball skills. In his professional debut, he ran a 15.3% zone-whiff rate with strong contact skills on display against all pitch types. Cabada is prone to expanding the zone but it's not at a rate that sinks his approach. He showed some passivity in the zone and his ability to discern balls and strikes will need to improve in the coming years for him to have success. Cabada's swing is flatter and is not conducive for big power. He shows average underlying power and exit velocities, posting a 90th percentile EV of 102.9 mph in 2025. The 17-year-old struggled to get the ball in the air consistently to his pull side in his debut, but he has time to adjust. Cabada is an above-average runner and strong basestealer who was successful on 20 of 23 attempts in 2025. He has limited arm strength, and he split his time between second and third base. Cabada is a fringe-average defender.
THE FUTURE: Cabada looks like a bat-first second baseman with a second-division regular ceiling.

Year	Age	Club (League)	Level	AVG	G	AB	R	H	2B	3B	HR	RBI	BB	SO	SB	OBP	SLG
2025	17	DSL Cubs Red	Rk	.287	42	136	22	39	10	0	3	29	20	31	20	.429	.426
		Minor League Totals		.287	42	136	22	39	10	0	3	29	20	31	20	.429	.426

20 ANGEL CEPEDA, SS/3B
HIT: 40. **POW:** 50. **RUN:** 40. **FLD:** 45. **ARM:** 55. **BA Grade:** 45. **Risk:** High. **Adj:** 30.

Born: October 29, 2005. **B-T:** R-R. **HT:** 6-1. **WT:** 170. **Signed:** Dominican Republic, 2023.
Signed by: Alejandro Pena/Miguel Diaz/Gian Guzman.
TRACK RECORD: A native of New Jersey, Cepeda moved to the Dominican Republic before signing with the Cubs for $1 million in January 2023. He debuted in the Dominican Summer League in 2023 and came stateside the following season, spending the entire year with the Cubs' Arizona Complex League affiliate. Cepeda made his full-season debut in 2025 with Low-A Myrtle Beach, hitting .249/.339/.375 over 100 games.
SCOUTING REPORT: Cepeda is a righthanded-hitting infielder with an average-sized frame and some remaining projection. He sets up at the plate slightly open with his front foot resting on his toe. Cepeda uses a moderate leg lift trigger, followed by a clean, balanced swing path with natural loft. He shows below-average bat-to-ball skills, with lots of swing-and-miss against soft stuff and most of his damage coming against fastballs. Cepeda shows a balanced approach at the plate with at least average swing decisions. He has average power for his age, with the ability to find the barrel on his best contact. He struggles to elevate the ball to his pull side, with a majority of his best contact going to the opposite gap. Cepeda previously was a plus runner but slowed down and now runs below-average home-to-first times. He's a solid baserunner despite the drop in speed. Cepeda's range at shortstop took a hit in 2025, and he looks most likely to move to third base. He should be average at third with an above-average arm.
THE FUTURE: Cepeda should develop into a second-division regular at third base with average power.

Year	Age	Club (League)	Level	AVG	G	AB	R	H	2B	3B	HR	RBI	BB	SO	SB	OBP	SLG
2025	19	Myrtle Beach (CAR)	A	.249	100	381	47	95	14	5	8	49	40	136	27	.339	.375
		Minor League Totals		.269	186	680	106	183	26	13	12	88	85	223	53	.366	.399

21 RILEY MARTIN, LHP
FB: 55. **CB:** 60. **SL:** 50. **CH:** 30. **CTL:** 40. **BA Grade:** 40. **Risk:** Average. **Adj:** 30.

Born: March 19, 1998. **B-T:** L-L. **HT:** 6-1. **WT:** 215. **Drafted:** Quincy (IL), 2021 (6th round). **Signed by:** John Pedrotty.
TRACK RECORD: The Cubs drafted Martin in the sixth round in 2021 out of Division II Quincy in Illinois. He signed for just $1,000 and debuted in Low-A shortly after the draft. After slowly climbing each rung of the minor league ladder, Martin has spent consecutive seasons at Triple-A. After improving across the board in 2025, the Cubs added him to their 40-man roster.
SCOUTING REPORT: Martin is an undersized lefthander with a stocky build. He's a pure relief prospect, but he's capable of going multiple innings. Martin mixes four pitches in a four-seam fastball, curveball, slider and changeup. His bread-and-butter is his fastball and curveball mix, which accounts for 95% of his

CHICAGO CUBS

usage. Martin's four-seam fastball sits 93-95 mph with average ride from his release height. His curveball is his best pitch and sits 85-86 mph with high spin rates and heavy downward break. It's a true plus curveball and one of the better blends of power and movement. Martin also throws an upper-80s slider with cutter break and a rarely used changeup.

THE FUTURE: Martin is a major league-ready middle reliever.

Year	Age	Club (League)	Level	W	L	ERA	G	GS	IP	H	HR	BB	SO	BB%	SO%	WHIP	AVG
2025	27	Iowa (IL)	AAA	6	2	2.69	47	1	64	41	4	35	80	13.4	30.7	1.19	.186
		Minor League Totals		24	13	3.77	173	2	280	212	23	176	407	14.4	33.3	1.39	.209

22 TY SOUTHISENE, 2B
HIT: 55. **POW:** 30. **RUN:** 60. **FLD:** 50. **ARM:** 40. **BA Grade:** 45. **Risk:** High. **Adj:** 30.

Born: July 8, 2005. **B-T:** R-R. **HT:** 5-9. **WT:** 170. **Drafted:** HS—Henderson, NV, 2024 (4th round). **Signed by:** Steve McFarland.

TRACK RECORD: Southisene comes from a baseball family. His twin brother Ty is a two-way player at Southern California, younger brother Tate was a first-round pick of the Braves in 2025 and another younger brother, Troy, is a 2026 shortstop committed to Oregon State. Ty was drafted by the Cubs in the fourth round in 2024 and made his debut in the Arizona Complex League in 2025. The Cubs promoted him to Low-A Myrtle Beach after one game in the ACL.

SCOUTING REPORT: Southisene is a hit-over-power middle infielder with plus speed and baserunning abilities. At the plate, his game is predicated on working deep counts, getting on base and putting hittable pitches in play. His approach is fairly passive. Southisene rarely chases but runs a very low swing rate. He has a poor power profile, with downward launch angles that led to a nearly 60% groundball rate in 2025. Baserunning is the strongest part of his game, and alongside his contact skills, it's his carrying tool. Southisene saw nearly all of his time in the field at second base in 2025 and should be average there. He has a below-average arm, so he likely won't see much time going forward on the left side of the diamond.

THE FUTURE: Southisene looks like a bench bat with speed who could be used situationally.

Year	Age	Club (League)	Level	AVG	G	AB	R	H	2B	3B	HR	RBI	BB	SO	SB	OBP	SLG
2025	19	ACL Cubs	Rk	.333	1	3	0	1	0	0	0	0	1	1	0	.500	.333
2025	19	Myrtle Beach (CAR)	A	.244	90	315	69	77	6	2	0	36	62	58	41	.387	.276
		Minor League Totals		.245	91	318	69	78	6	2	0	36	63	59	41	.388	.277

23 WILL SANDERS, RHP
FB: 45. **CB:** 45. **SL:** 45. **SP:** 50. **CTL:** 55. **BA Grade:** 40. **Risk:** Average. **Adj:** 30.

Born: March 30, 2002. **B-T:** L-R. **HT:** 6-6. **WT:** 230. **Drafted:** South Carolina, 2023 (4th round). **Signed by:** M'Lynn Dease.

TRACK RECORD: Sanders entered his junior season at South Carolina in 2023 with first-round buzz. Instead a knee injury threw his season out of whack, and he had the worst year of his collegiate career. The Cubs drafted him the fourth round in 2023 and signed him for $600,000. After a solid debut season in 2024, Sanders spent 2025 split between Double-A and Triple-A.

SCOUTING REPORT: Sanders is a 6-foot-6 righthander with fringy extension and power across his mix. He throws four pitches in a four-seam fastball, slider, curveball and splitter. His four-seam fastball sits 92-94 mph and touches 97 with well below-average vertical break from his 6-foot-5 release height. Sanders' splitter is his most thrown secondary, sitting 85-87 mph with true splitter shape. The pitch was his most effective bat-misser and chase pitch throughout 2025. Sanders throws his slider more than his curveball. His slider sits in the mid 80s with gyro shape. He shows excellent feel for his slider, running high zone and strike rates. His curveball is his least-thrown pitch but is still deployed regularly throughout starts. It sits in the low 80s with moderate two-plane break. Sanders shows above-average command, which helps amplify his arsenal of fringe-average to average pitches.

THE FUTURE: Sanders has a future as a back-of-the-rotation depth starter.

Year	Age	Club (League)	Level	W	L	ERA	G	GS	IP	H	HR	BB	SO	BB%	SO%	WHIP	AVG
2025	23	Knoxville (SL)	AA	3	2	2.64	9	9	44	38	1	8	44	4.6	25.1	1.04	.233
2025	23	Iowa (IL)	AAA	7	4	6.38	17	14	79	87	14	33	79	9.3	22.2	1.52	.278
		Minor League Totals		12	14	4.87	50	46	220	221	28	85	232	8.8	23.9	1.39	.258

CHICAGO CUBS

24 JUAN TOMAS, SS
HIT: 40. **POW:** 40. **RUN:** 60. **FLD:** 60. **ARM:** 55. **BA Grade:** 45. **Risk:** High. **Adj:** 30.

Born: November 28, 2007. **B-T:** B-R. **HT:** 6-2. **WT:** 177. **Signed:** Dominican Republic, 2025.
Signed by: Alejandro Peña/Miguel Diaz/Gian Guzman/Alex Suarez.

TRACK RECORD: Tomas signed for $1.1 million out of the Dominican Republic in January 2025. Alongside Juan Cabada and Wilfri De La Cruz, Tomas was considered a standout at the time of signing. He debuted in the Dominican Summer League and hit just .186/.352/.301 but impressed with his speed and defensive prowess.

SCOUTING REPORT: An athletic switch-hitter with a tooled-up profile, Tomas fell flat on his face in his pro debut, despite many scouts viewing him as the best player the Cubs signed in 2025. A speedy switch-hitter, Tomas struggled from both sides of the plate, showing a better approach as a righthanded hitter and more power from the left side. He showed below-average bat-to-ball skills in his debut, running a 31% whiff rate on the season. He deploys an incredibly passive approach and ran a low 14.7% chase rate but also took many called strikes. Tomas' on-base skills were strong, perhaps at the expense of more balls in play. He has below-average raw power but has shown loft in his swing that, with added strength, could get to fringe-average game power. Tomas is a plus runner, but his speed didn't play that way on the bases. Where he's truly a standout is in the field. Tomas is the best infield defender in the organization. He receives plus grades at shortstop and shows an above-average arm capable of making the necessary throws.

THE FUTURE: Tomas is a high-variance prospect who could develop into a second-division regular or might never hit enough to reach Triple-A.

Year	Age	Club (League)	Level	AVG	G	AB	R	H	2B	3B	HR	RBI	BB	SO	SB	OBP	SLG
2025	17	DSL Cubs Blue	Rk	.186	36	113	19	21	6	2	1	18	30	42	9	.352	.301
		Minor League Totals		.186	36	113	19	21	6	2	1	18	30	42	9	.352	.301

25 ERIAN RODRIGUEZ, RHP
FB: 50. **SL:** 50. **CH:** 50. **CTL:** 40. **BA Grade:** 45. **Risk:** High. **Adj:** 30.

Born: November 23, 2001. **B-T:** R-R. **HT:** 6-3. **WT:** 190. **Drafted:** HS—Statesboro, GA, 2021 (13th round).
Signed by: Greg Gerard.

TRACK RECORD: A native of Panama, Rodriguez went to high school in the United States. He attended the same Georgia Premier Academy that produced Jonah Tong and Daniel Espino. The Cubs drafted Rodriguez in the 13th round in 2021. After spending full seasons in the Arizona Complex League and Low-A, Rodriguez reached High-A in mid-2024 and impressed. His 2025 season was delayed by injury, but he pitched well upon his return by reaching Double-A during the final four weeks of the season.

SCOUTING REPORT: Rodriguez is an athletic righthander who works exclusively from the stretch. His high leg kick adds deception and the tilt in his left shoulder creates a unique angle on his fastball. Rodriguez mixes three pitches in a four-seam fastball, slider and changeup. His fastball sits 93-95 mph and touches 96 and moves like a two-seamer with a four-seam fastball plane. His most-used secondary is a mid-80s gyro slider that he tunnels well off his fastball to drive whiffs and chases. Rodriguez's go-to secondary against lefthanded hitters is an upper-80s changeup. He shows great feel for the pitch despite little separation off his fastball. Rodriguez has below-average control.

THE FUTURE: Rodriguez has seen success as a starter, but his future lies in the bullpen.

Year	Age	Club (League)	Level	W	L	ERA	G	GS	IP	H	HR	BB	SO	BB%	SO%	WHIP	AVG
2025	23	ACL Cubs	Rk	0	1	6.00	2	2	6	7	1	3	3	12.0	12.0	1.67	.318
2025	23	South Bend (MWL)	A+	6	4	2.81	12	12	64	52	2	22	58	8.3	21.8	1.16	.223
2025	23	Knoxville (SL)	AA	2	1	3.54	4	4	20	21	2	10	15	11.6	17.4	1.52	.288
		Minor League Totals		19	19	4.53	79	35	258	240	14	127	241	11.3	21.4	1.42	.249

26 PIERCE COPPOLA, LHP

FB: 50. **SL:** 50. **SP:** 45. **CTL:** 45. **BA Grade:** 50. **Risk:** Extreme. **Adj:** 30.

Born: December 17, 2002. **B-T:** L-L. **HT:** 6-8. **WT:** 245. **Drafted:** Florida, 2025 (7th round). **Signed by:** Ike Ballou.
TRACK RECORD: Coppola was highly recruited out of the New Jersey prep ranks but had two major injuries during his time with Florida. First was a back injury suffered in his collegiate debut in 2022 when he was named the Gators' Sunday starter. He missed the remainder of that season. The following fall he was cleared to return, but he saw a significant velocity drop due to a shoulder injury that held him out for all of 2023. Coppola returned in 2024 and 2025 but made 15 total starts over the two seasons. The Cubs took a shot on Coppola in the seventh round of the 2025 draft. He made three appearances for Low-A Myrtle Beach.
SCOUTING REPORT: Few pitchers in the Cubs system have the upside of Coppola, but none have as many question marks. He has struggled to stay on the mound, and the inefficiencies in his mechanics likely have led to some wear and tear. The good news is that it gives the Cubs an area where Coppola can make substantial gains. He throws three pitches in a four-seam fastball, slider and splitter. His usage is dominated by his fastball/slider combination, and he didn't throw his splitter in his pro debut. Coppola's fastball sits in the low 90s with below-average ride but heavy armside run. Despite its lack of velocity or ride, he creates a weird angle that helps the pitch play up. His slider sits 78-81 mph with sweeper-like shape. It was an effective bat-misser in college but didn't play that way in his pro debut. Coppola throws a splitter in the mid 80s that projects as a fringe-average pitch. He shows below-average command at present, but it could improve to fringe-average.
THE FUTURE: Coppola is a high-variance prospect who could develop into a dominant reliever or could develop into a back-end starter with improved mechanics.

Year	Age	Club (League)	Level	W	L	ERA	G	GS	IP	H	HR	BB	SO	BB%	SO%	WHIP	AVG
2025	22	Myrtle Beach (CAR)	A	0	0	2.25	3	2	8	5	0	9	14	23.7	36.8	1.75	.179
		Minor League Totals		0	0	2.25	3	2	8	5	0	9	14	23.7	36.8	1.75	.179

27 TYLER SCHLAFFER, RHP

FB: 45. **CB:** 45. **SL:** 45. **CH:** 45. **CTL:** 45. **BA Grade:** 40. **Risk:** Average. **Adj:** 30.

Born: May 24, 2001. **B-T:** R-R. **HT:** 6-1. **WT:** 180. **Drafted:** HS—Flossmoor, IL, 2019 (9th round). **Signed by:** John Pedrotty.
TRACK RECORD: Drafted by the Cubs in the ninth round in 2019, Schlaffer's career has been a slow burn. After spending all of 2023 and 2024 split between both Class A levels, he finally made the jump to Double-A in 2025. He impressed during the season as he saw improvements to his command and ability to drive swings and misses. He was left unprotected for the Rule 5 draft.
SCOUTING REPORT: Schlaffer is an undersized righthander with an uptempo operation and a moderate arm stroke and low three-quarters release. He moves well on the mound and gets plus extension for his height by dropping his release to an outlier 5-foot-3. Schlaffer mixes five pitches in a four-seam fastball, sinker, slider, changeup and curveball. His four-seam fastball sits 92-94 mph and touches 96 with average ride for his release height and a flatter plane of approach to the plate. Schlaffer mixes his trio of secondaries nearly equally, with a mid-80s slider with slurvy shape leading the way. His changeup is his primary secondary against lefthanded hitters and shows moderate separation off his fastball. Schlaffer's curveball sits 82-84 mph with downer shape. Schlaffer shows fringe-average command of his pitch mix.
THE FUTURE: Schlaffer is likely a back-end starter but could potentially move to the bullpen due to the deceptive traits on his four-seam fastball.

Year	Age	Club (League)	Level	W	L	ERA	G	GS	IP	H	HR	BB	SO	BB%	SO%	WHIP	AVG
2025	24	South Bend (MWL)	A+	3	1	4.10	12	12	59	41	7	28	60	11.6	24.8	1.16	.195
2025	24	Knoxville (SL)	AA	4	2	2.78	9	9	45	38	2	18	42	9.6	22.5	1.24	.233
		Minor League Totals		18	15	4.20	76	67	324	282	34	142	315	10.3	22.8	1.31	.235

28 BRODY McCULLOUGH, RHP

FB: 55. **SL:** 50. **CH:** 50. **CTL:** 50. **BA Grade:** 50. **Risk:** Extreme. **Adj:** 30.

Born: June 30, 2000. **B-T:** R-R. **HT:** 6-4. **WT:** 205. **Drafted:** Wingate (NC), 2022 (10th round). **Signed by:** Billy Swoope.
TRACK RECORD: McCullough stood out at Division II Wingate, then caught the attention of big league clubs with a strong pre-draft showing in the Cape Cod League in 2022. The Cubs drafted him in the 10th round that year and signed him for $125,000. His 2024 season was limited to just 14.2 innings after off-season knee surgery delayed his start, then a lat injury suffered in his first start with Double-A Tennessee on May 10 ended it. He injured his forearm in 2025 and had surgery, ending his season before it began.

SCOUTING REPORT: McCullough has missed the majority of the last two seasons with a laundry list of injuries. He generates above-average extension with a fluid operation that gets downhill. He's a good mover with a fast arm and a higher three-quarters arm slot. McCullough mixes three pitches in a four-seam fastball, slider and changeup. His four-seam fastball sits 92-94 mph and touches 95 with true cut-ride shape. McCullough's slider averages 81-83 mph with slurvy shape. It gets some drop and moderate sweep. His mid-80s changeup has good vertical separation off his fastball. Prior to his injury, McCullough showed average command.
THE FUTURE: McCullough has No. 5 starter upside, but he'll need to stay healthy.

Year	Age	Club (League)	Level	W	L	ERA	G	GS	IP	H	HR	BB	SO	BB%	SO%	WHIP	AVG
2025	25	Did not play—Injured															
		Minor League Totals		7	6	3.08	30	24	108	75	7	38	135	8.8	31.2	1.05	.194

29 ARIEL ARMAS, C
HIT: 40. **POW:** 30. **RUN:** 40. **FLD:** 60. **ARM:** 60. **BA Grade:** 40. **Risk:** Average. **Adj:** 30.

Born: November 29, 2002. **B-T:** R-R. **HT:** 5-10. **WT:** 185. **Drafted:** San Diego, 2024 (5th round). **Signed by:** Evan Kauffman.
TRACK RECORD: A native of California, Armas played three seasons at San Diego, winning the West Coast Conference defensive player of the year award in 2024. The Cubs were enamored with Armas' defense and drafted him in the fifth round in 2024.. He signed for $375,000 and was assigned directly to High-A South Bend. He returned to High-A to begin 2025 and spent the entire season there.
SCOUTING REPORT: Armas is a glove-first catcher with outstanding skills behind the plate. He is physically maxed out but is an athletic mover. He's a below-average hitter but shows above-average bat-to-ball skills. His approach has a fair amount of chase, and he's often too passive on pitches in the zone. Armas' power is below-average because of lower exit velocities and poor launch angles. He's adept at putting the ball in play, but his lack of impact limits his results. He's a below-average runner who is unlikely to steal many bases. Behind the plate, he's a plus defender whose receiving, blocking and throwing all grades plus.
THE FUTURE: Armas is a prototype glove-first backup catcher with little offensive impact.

Year	Age	Club (League)	Level	AVG	G	AB	R	H	2B	3B	HR	RBI	BB	SO	SB	OBP	SLG
2025	22	South Bend (MWL)	A+	.234	92	334	28	78	21	1	5	47	38	70	11	.325	.347
		Minor League Totals		.234	92	334	28	78	21	1	5	47	38	70	11	.325	.347

30 NICK DEAN, RHP
FB: 40. **CB:** 40. **SL:** 40. **CH:** 60. **CTL:** 50. **BA Grade:** 30. **Risk:** Low. **Adj:** 30.

Born: December 26, 2000. **B-T:** R-R. **HT:** 6-3. **WT:** 180. **Drafted:** Maryland, 2023 (19th round). **Signed by:** Billy Swoope.
TRACK RECORD: Dean spent four years in the Maryland rotation before the Cubs drafted him in the 19th round in 2023. After a strong professional debut in 2024 across both levels of Class A, Dean returned to High-A to begin the 2025 season. After seven starts, he was promoted to Double-A Knoxville. He struggled mightily in the Southern League and was moved on and off the development list.
SCOUTING REPORT: Dean is an athletic mover on the mound who creates decent extension but lacks power across his arsenal. He mixes four pitches in a four-seam fastball, changeup, slider and curveball. Dean's fastball sits 89-91 mph and touches 94 with 17-19 inches of vertical break on average. His high three-quarters release isn't heavily deceptive, which downplays the above-average ride he gets on his fastball due to his higher release point. Dean's plus changeup is his bread-and-butter and the best in the system. It's a Bugs Bunny-style changeup that moves like a fastball but sits 79-81 mph with good vertical separation off his fastball. Dean mixes a low-80s gyro slider and a mid-70s two-plane curveball. Because Dean is a pronator—which helps amplify his changeup—his breaking pitches both play as below-average. He shows average command of his arsenal.
THE FUTURE: Dean profiles as a depth starter and will likely see limited opportunities in the majors.

Year	Age	Club (League)	Level	W	L	ERA	G	GS	IP	H	HR	BB	SO	BB%	SO%	WHIP	AVG
2025	24	South Bend (MWL)	A+	0	3	4.68	7	7	33	35	3	9	39	6.6	28.5	1.35	.273
2025	24	Knoxville (SL)	AA	1	4	6.19	8	8	32	34	4	10	36	7.3	26.3	1.38	.270
		Minor League Totals		3	7	4.52	22	18	92	86	7	28	111	7.4	29.3	1.24	.246

Chicago White Sox

BY BILL MITCHELL

The White Sox went 60-102 in 2025 for their third consecutive 100-loss season. While that might not sound positive, the club took a meaningful step forward under first-year manager Will Venable.

Chicago improved by 19 wins from the previous season, and its once-maligned farm system graduated a significant number of players. A total of 10 ranked prospects either made the big league club out of spring training or debuted during the season.

Edgar Quero handled the bulk of the work behind the plate before fellow catcher Kyle Teel joined him midway through the year. Chase Meidroth emerged as the club's regular shortstop—until fellow debut Colson Montgomery supplanted him when called up on July 4.

After a midyear reset at the organization's Arizona complex to rework his swing and approach, Montgomery hit .239/.311/.520 with 21 home runs in 71 games.

On the pitching side, Rule 5 pick Shane Smith was an immediate success. He won a rotation job out of spring training and made the all-star team. He was arguably the club's best starter across 29 outings. After battling injuries during his minor league career, Sean Burke started 22 games as a rookie. Grant Taylor, Mike Vasil and Wikelman Gonzalez became valuable bullpen pieces.

Unlike 2024, the White Sox didn't infuse their system via significant trades. Instead, their most valuable trade chip, outfielder Luis Robert Jr., battled injuries and subpar performance.

Down on the farm, Double-A Birmingham, managed by former big league catcher Guillermo Quiroz, won its second straight Southern League championship with the support of many of the organization's Top 30 Prospects, most notably pitchers Noah Schultz, Hagen Smith and Tanner McDougal, second baseman Sam Antonacci and outfielder Braden Montgomery.

Other success stories included Low-A Kannapolis shortstop Caleb Bonemer, who earned Carolina League MVP honors in his first professional season, and the significant improvement of McDougal and lefthander Christian Oppor.

Injuries affected key players in the system, with Schultz and Smith both struggling with control issues and nagging injuries, while pitchers Drew Thorpe, Ky Bush and Mason Adams all missed the season after having Tommy John surgery. Righthander Aldrin Batista pitched just 14 innings due to a stress fracture to his elbow.

Chicago also added intriguing draft talent, headlined by 10th overall pick Billy Carlson, a defensive wizard at shortstop whom the White Sox will try to unlock offensively.

The White Sox continued an early run on high school players with the selections of outfielder Jaden Fauske in the second round, catcher Landon Hodge in the fourth and shortstop Matthew Boughton in the 11th. They took college players with the rest of their picks, with just six of those joining an affiliate after the draft.

The ownership of the White Sox remains somewhat unsettled, with Justin Ishbia reaching an agreement with current owner Jerry Reinsdorf that may give him control of the franchise as soon as 2029. ∎

PROJECTED 2029 LINEUP

Catcher	Kyle Teel	27
First Base	Miguel Vargas	29
Second Base	Chase Meidroth	28
Third Base	Colson Montgomery	27
Shortstop	Billy Carlson	23
Left Field	Caleb Bonemer	23
Center Field	Braden Montgomery	26
Right Field	Jaden Fauske	22
Designated Hitter	Edgar Quero	26
No. 1 Starter	Noah Schultz	26
No. 2 Starter	Grant Taylor	27
No. 3 Starter	Sean Burke	29
No. 4 Starter	Shane Smith	29
No. 5 Starter	Tanner McDougal	26
Closer	Hagen Smith	25

DEPTH CHART

CHICAGO WHITE SOX

TOP 2026 ROOKIES — RANK
1. Hagen Smith, LHP — 2
2. Tanner McDougal, RHP — 6
3. Ky Bush, LHP — 13

BREAKOUT PROSPECTS — RANK
1. Aldrin Batista, RHP — 18
2. Blake Larson, LHP — 22
3. Matthew Boughton, 2B/SS — 30

SOURCE OF TOP 30 TALENT

Homegrown	21	Acquired	9
College	6	Trade	7
Junior college	3	Rule 5 draft	2
High school	9	Independent league	0
Undrafted free agent	0	Free agent/waivers	0
International	3		

LF
Christian Gonzalez
DJ Gladney
Wilfred Veras
Caden Connor
Kaleb Freeman

CF
Samuel Zavala
Nick McLain
Marcelo Alcala
Frank Mieses
Ely Brown

RF
Braden Montgomery (3)
Jaden Fauske (7)
George Wolkow (15)
Casey Saucke
T.J. McCants
Abraham Nunez Jr.

3B
Caleb Bonemer (2)
Alexander Albertus
Alejandro Cruz
Eduardo Herrera
Anthony DePino

SS
Billy Carlson (5)
Kyle Lodise (10)
Javier Mogollon (16)
Jacob Gonzalez (25)
Tanner Murray
Colby Shelton

2B
Sam Antonacci (9)
William Bergolla (12)
Jeral Perez (17)
Matthew Boughton (30)
Rikuu Nishida

1B
Ryan Galanie

C
Landon Hodge (24)
Jose Mendoza
Calvin Harris
Grant Magill
Stiven Flores
Michael Turner

LHP

LHSP
Noah Schultz (1)
Hagen Smith (4)
Christian Oppor (8)
Ky Bush (13)
Blake Larson (22)
Shane Murphy (28)
Tyler Schweitzer
Lucas Gordon

LHRP
Garrett Schoenle
Andrew Sentlinger

RHP

RHSP
Tanner McDougal (6)
Mathias LaCombe (11)
Mason Adams (14)
Aldrin Batista (18)
Jedixson Paez (19)
Gage Ziehl (21)
Luis Reyes (26)
Gabe Davis (27)
Yobal Rodriguez (29)
Maximo Martinez
Duncan Davitt
Blaine Wynk
Diego Perez
Drew McDaniel

RHRP
Alexander Alberto (20)
Jairo Iriarte (23)
Juan Carela
Eric Adler
Pierce George
Dan Wright
Max Banks
Jackson Kelley

CHICAGO WHITE SOX

1 NOAH SCHULTZ, LHP

Born: August 5, 2003. **B-T:** L-L. **HT:** 6-10. **WT:** 240.
Drafted: HS—Oswego, IL, 2022 (1st round).
Signed by: JJ Lally.

TRACK RECORD: Schultz has been one of the most celebrated pitching prospects in the game since the White Sox drafted the Chicago-area prep 26th overall in 2022. Despite flashing big-time stuff on the showcase circuit, he dropped to the late first round after missing part of his senior season with mononucleosis before getting pre-draft exposure in the Prospect League. The lanky, 6-foot-10 Schultz pitched in just a handful of instructional league games after joining the organization and was limited to 10 starts in 2023 due to a flexor strain. Continuing to be handled cautiously by the White Sox, he took the mound for 23 starts in 2024, averaging nearly four innings per outing. That season, his fastball velocity surged forward and helped the pitch become double-plus. The 2025 season proved to be a more challenging year for Schultz. The velocity of both of his four-seam fastball and slider dropped slightly, while his walk rate spiked from 6.7% to 13.8%. These issues were attributed to patellar tendinitis in his right knee that flared up periodically. Schultz's 2025 season ended prematurely in late August and he was also pulled from a planned Arizona Fall League assignment.

SCOUTING REPORT: Schultz's sinker had become even more effective with the increased velocity in 2024, but in 2025 his money pitch had dipped to averaging 94.5 mph and touching 98, a drop of a tick or two. Despite the velo drop, he got more whiffs on the pitch in 2025. When it's right, it becomes even more difficult for hitters because of the extreme deception provided by Schultz's low three-quarters arm slot and the way he hides the ball. He explodes on hitters with run and sink to help get whiffs up in the zone. Schultz's double-plus slider also was down, averaging 81 mph, with the same late, hard movement and a high spin rate. He recorded fewer whiffs with the pitch, which saw its miss rate drop from 42% in 2024 to 34%. Schultz's changeup sits 86-89 mph and is a potentially above-average pitch with late movement and downer action. He used it to keep righthanded hitters from sitting on his slider. He also works in an average 88-91 mph cutter that touches 93 with late action. Using a modified windup, Schultz starts from what looks like a stretch position before going into a small side-rocker step, which helps keep his long levers in sync. Poor control and command were his biggest issues in 2025, when he struggled to land his pitches consistently in the zone, attributable in part to his recurring soreness in his right knee.

THE FUTURE: The White Sox have been patient with Schultz's development. Due to the knee issue, they will have to wait a bit longer until he can contribute in Chicago, but perhaps not too much longer if he reverts to his 2024 form.

BA GRADE
65 Risk: High
Adjusted grade: 50

SCOUTING GRADES
FB: 65. **SL:** 70. **CH:** 55. **CT:** 50. **CTL:** 50.
Projected future grades on 20-80 scouting scale

BEST TOOLS

BATTING
Best Hitter	Sam Antonacci
Best Power Hitter	George Wolkow
Best Strike-Zone Discipline	Sam Antonacci
Fastest Baserunner	Rikuu Nishida
Best Athlete	Braden Montgomery

PITCHING
Best Fastball	Tanner McDougal
Best Curveball	Tanner McDougal
Best Slider	Noah Schultz
Best Changeup	Christian Oppor
Best Control	Mason Adams

FIELDING
Best Defensive Catcher	Grant Magill
Best Defensive Infielder	Billy Carlson
Best Infield Arm	Billy Carlson
Best Defensive Outfielder	Samuel Zavala
Best Outfield Arm	Braden Montgomery

Year	Age	Club (League)	Level	W	L	ERA	G	GS	IP	H	HR	BB	SO	BB%	SO%	WHIP	AVG
2025	21	Birmingham (SL)	AA	4	3	3.34	12	12	57	54	3	36	58	14.4	23.2	1.59	.261
2025	21	Charlotte (IL)	AAA	0	2	9.37	5	5	16	23	3	9	18	11.7	23.4	1.96	.359
		Minor League Totals		5	11	3.06	50	50	188	157	12	75	229	9.5	29.0	1.23	.228

CHICAGO WHITE SOX

2 CALEB BONEMER, SS/3B

HIT: 55. **POW:** 60. **RUN:** 45. **FLD:** 50. **ARM:** 50. **BA Grade:** 60. **Risk:** Average. **Adj:** 50.

Born: October 5, 2005. **B-T:** R-R. **HT:** 6-1. **WT:** 195.
Drafted: HS—Okemos, MI, 2024 (2nd round). **Signed by:** JD Heilmann.
TRACK RECORD: Bonemer was a showcase star in the summer before his senior year at Okemos High in Michigan, and the White Sox drafted him in the second round in 2024. He broke camp with Low-A Kannapolis in 2025 and exceeded even the highest expectations. He batted .281/.400/.458 with 10 home runs and 27 stolen bases in 96 games to earn Carolina League player of the year honors before finishing the year with 11 games for High-A Winston-Salem.
SCOUTING REPORT: Bonemer has an advanced approach at the plate, especially impressive for a teenager. He's made swing adjustments since turning pro, flattening his plane and improving his rhythm, which has helped him make better contact. Bonemer connects on pitches in the zone and has a knack for finding the barrel with above-average bat speed. He should get to plus power at his peak. At times, Bonemer has inconsistent separation in his load but has shown the aptitude for continuous improvement. Questions remain as to his ultimate position. He likely will not stay at shortstop, especially with 2025 first-round pick Billy Carlson coming up behind him. Bonemer can be an average defender at third base, where he spent some time late in the season. He makes the routine plays, and his average arm will be enough for the position, but some observers believe he eventually could wind up in the outfield. An average runner, Bonemer stole 29 bases in 37 attempts, but he may slow down to fringe-average as he matures physically.
THE FUTURE: While Bonemer faces questions as to his ultimate position on the field, his bat is real and profiles him as a potential above-average regular. He'll return to High-A Winston-Salem in 2026 and has a chance to reach the upper minors later in the season.

Year	Age	Club (League)	Level	AVG	G	AB	R	H	2B	3B	HR	RBI	BB	SO	SB	OBP	SLG
2025	19	Kannapolis (CAR)	A	.281	96	349	69	98	26	3	10	58	68	91	27	.400	.458
2025	19	Winston-Salem (SAL)	A+	.278	11	36	8	10	4	1	2	6	7	10	2	.409	.611
		Minor League Totals		.281	107	385	77	108	30	4	12	64	75	101	29	.401	.473

3 BRADEN MONTGOMERY, OF

HIT: 50. **POW:** 60. **RUN:** 50. **FLD:** 50. **ARM:** 70. **BA Grade:** 55. **Risk:** Avg. **Adj:** 45.

Born: April 16, 2003. **B-T:** B-R. **HT:** 6-3. **WT:** 220.
Drafted: Texas A&M, 2024 (1st round). **Signed by:** Lee Bryant (Red Sox).
TRACK RECORD: Montgomery spent two seasons at Stanford, playing both ways as a right fielder and righthanded reliever. He transferred to Texas A&M for his junior 2024 season, which ended when he fractured his right ankle on a slide in the opening super regional game against Oregon. The Red Sox drafted him 12th overall, but he never suited up for a Boston affiliate. The White Sox acquired Montgomery and three other prospects when they traded Garrett Crochet to the Red Sox after the 2024 season. Montgomery played at three levels in 2025 before suffering a season-ending right foot fracture in early September. He made up for lost time in the AFL.
SCOUTING REPORT: The only things slowing Montgomery to date have been injuries to his lower extremities. A switch-hitter, Montgomery has a smooth swing path from an open stance, with quick hands that allow his bat to explode to the baseball. He's aggressive in the box with what has been called "violence in his swing," contributing to a 25% strikeout rate in his pro debut. Montgomery profiles as an average hitter with plus power and solid-average plate discipline. His place in the outfield will perhaps be determined by team needs. He's an average defender and average runner, with a springy, athletic body. He can handle center field, but his plus-plus arm is more than enough for right field. However, some observers see him as more comfortable in left field. He takes a few steps to get rolling out of the batter's box but is fine underway and on the basepaths, with a two-base mentality on balls hit to the outfield.
THE FUTURE: One of the safer bets in the White Sox's system to have a major league career, Montgomery likely will occupy one of the three outfield positions within the next couple of years. He spent 34 games at Double-A in his first pro season and is poised to make his MLB debut in 2026.

Year	Age	Club (League)	Level	AVG	G	AB	R	H	2B	3B	HR	RBI	BB	SO	SB	OBP	SLG
2025	22	Kannapolis (CAR)	A	.304	18	69	14	21	4	0	3	19	10	19	6	.393	.493
2025	22	Winston-Salem (SAL)	A+	.260	69	254	36	66	17	3	8	38	32	70	5	.348	.445
2025	22	Birmingham (SL)	AA	.272	34	125	14	34	13	1	1	11	15	41	3	.364	.416
		Minor League Totals		.270	121	448	64	121	34	4	12	68	57	130	14	.360	.444

CHICAGO WHITE SOX

HAGEN SMITH, LHP
FB: 60. **SL:** 60. **CH:** 45. **CTL:** 40. **BA Grade:** 60. **Risk:** High. **Adj:** 45.

Born: August 19, 2003. **B-T:** L-L. **HT:** 6-3. **WT:** 235.
Drafted: Arkansas, 2024 (1st round). **Signed by:** Dan Budreika.
TRACK RECORD: The White Sox drafted Smith fifth overall in 2024 following his Southeastern Conference pitcher of the year season at Arkansas. He jumped to Double-A Birmingham for his first full season in 2025. Smith missed part of May and most of June due to elbow soreness and time off at the White Sox's complex in Arizona to tweak his mechanics. He returned to Birmingham for the remainder of the year, finishing with a season total of 20 starts with a 3.57 ERA and an outstanding 33.9% strikeout rate but a less than impressive 17.6% walk rate. Smith finished the year with an assignment to the Arizona Fall League, where he walked 10.5%.
SCOUTING REPORT: By the end of 2025, Smith's four-seam fastball velocity was back to the 95 mph average that he displayed in his draft year. Because of his extension, low three-quarters arm slot, flat approach and pure velocity, his fastball is tough for hitters to handle when he locates it, but he didn't throw enough strikes with it in 2025. His fastball tends to draw whiffs and generate ground balls. Smith's 81 mph slurvy slider with good depth is another plus pitch that he can backdoor for strikes or use to expand for chases. The quandary for Smith is whether he can develop a third pitch to go with his two plus offerings. He's still working on a split-grip changeup that averages 86 mph and reaches the low 90s with some sink. It played as below-average in 2025 but would enhance his repertoire if he improves it to fringe-average. The midsummer work on his mechanics helped his delivery, with his rhythm through his windup and leg lift being smoother and his front side and arm path more online.
THE FUTURE: Smith draws divergent opinions from scouts. So much depends on whether he reins in his walk rate and develops a third pitch. He can become a midrotation or better starter or perhaps a dominant closer, with multiple sources evoking the name of Josh Hader in the latter role.

Year	Age	Club (League)	Level	W	L	ERA	G	GS	IP	H	HR	BB	SO	BB%	SO%	WHIP	AVG
2025	21	Birmingham (SL)	AA	3	3	3.57	20	20	76	42	5	56	108	17.6	33.9	1.30	.166
		Minor League Totals		3	3	3.57	20	20	76	42	5	56	108	17.6	33.9	1.30	.166

BILLY CARLSON, SS
HIT: 50. **POW:** 45. **RUN:** 50. **FLD:** 70. **ARM:** 70. **BA Grade:** 60. **Risk:** High. **Adj:** 45.

Born: July 29, 2006. **B-T:** R-R. **HT:** 6-1. **WT:** 185.
Drafted: HS—Corona, CA, 2025 (1st round). **Signed by:** Mike Baker.
TRACK RECORD: In 2025, Corona High had one of the most talented rosters that SoCal scouts had ever seen. Carlson and righthander Seth Hernandez (Pirates) were first-round picks, and third baseman Brady Ebel (Brewers) was drafted just shortly thereafter. Drafted 10th overall by the White Sox, Carlson signed for a full slot bonus of $6,235,900 and played in unofficial bridge league games rather than going to an affiliate.
SCOUTING REPORT: At 6-foot-1, 185 pounds, Carlson is a lean, athletic shortstop who stands out for his glovework and was regarded as one of the very best defenders in the 2025 draft class. While Carlson's defense could already be considered big league-ready, he still has development ahead with his swing and approach at the plate. He already shows MLB average bat speed and hits the ball hard, but he needs an overhaul of his swing to shorten up and become more adjustable. Carlson will make better contact with an early load plus an early land preparation for pitches, allowing him to get the ball to his pull side more often. Carlson was a legitimate two-way player in high school. If he weren't such an outstanding defensive shortstop, he could have been drafted as a pitcher on the merits of a plus fastball that ticked up to 97 mph and a high-spin, hammer curveball. He's already a double-plus defender at shortstop with a double-plus arm. He shows tremendous actions, footwork and instincts on the field. He's an average runner with his feel for the game likely allowing that speed to play up. His makeup is highly regarded, and he interacts well with teammates and coaches.
THE FUTURE: Carlson appears to be the shortstop of the future for the White Sox. He could team up with 2024 second-rounder Caleb Bonemer on the left side of the Chicago infield one day.

Year	Age	Club (League)	Level	AVG	G	AB	R	H	2B	3B	HR	RBI	BB	SO	SB	OBP	SLG
2025	18	Did not play															

CHICAGO WHITE SOX

6 TANNER McDOUGAL, RHP
FB: 65. **CB:** 60. **SL:** 50. **CH:** 45. **CTL:** 40. **BA Grade:** 50. **Risk:** Avg. **Adj:** 40.

Born: April 9, 2003. **B-T:** R-R. **HT:** 6-5. **WT:** 240.
Drafted: HS—Las Vegas, NV, 2021 (5th round). **Signed by:** Mike Baker.
TRACK RECORD: The White Sox drafted McDougal out of high school in Las Vegas in the fifth round in 2021, signing him for $850,000 to pull him away from an Oregon commitment. Tommy John surgery wiped out his 2022 season, while 2023 and 2024 were marked by inconsistent performances and high walk rates. McDougal took a huge step forward in 2025 by improving his command and control. He took the ball for 28 starts between High-A Winston-Salem and Double-A Birmingham, pitching to a 3.26 ERA and showing his durability three years after surgery.
SCOUTING REPORT: McDougal dominates with a plus four-seam fastball that sits in the mid-to-high 90s and touches triple digits, and he holds that velocity deep into games. The pitch is relatively straight and could be a double-plus heater with improved shape. McDougal's high-spin curveball, delivered in the high 70s to low 80s, has depth and sharp break. He complements it with an average slider with tilt that sits 87-90 mph. Rounding out his repertoire is a fringy, hard changeup with tailing action at 88-91 mph. He throws it infrequently. Improved control was key to McDougal's big season. He reduced his walk rate from 13.6% to 10.2%, restoring faith in earlier projections that he would be able to stay in the rotation. Even more impressive was the reduction in walk rate to 7.5% in his 15 starts for Double-A Birmingham in the second half. McDougal has worked hard since joining the organization, including adding more than 40 pounds of strength.
THE FUTURE: McDougal could pitch in a big league rotation one day but still has development ahead. If he continues reducing his walk rate and gets better shape on his fastball, he could project as a midrotation starter. Based on the strength of his fastball and curveball, he also could become a leverage reliever.

Year	Age	Club (League)	Level	W	L	ERA	G	GS	IP	H	HR	BB	SO	BB%	SO%	WHIP	AVG
2025	22	Winston-Salem (SAL)	A+	0	3	3.28	13	13	58	53	4	32	73	12.6	28.7	1.47	.242
2025	22	Birmingham (SL)	AA	3	2	3.23	15	15	56	49	3	17	63	7.5	27.8	1.19	.240
		Minor League Totals		4	21	4.58	77	75	285	255	27	155	349	12.4	28.0	1.44	.240

7 JADEN FAUSKE, OF
HIT: 50. **POW:** 55. **RUN:** 50. **FLD:** 50. **ARM:** 55. **BA Grade:** 55. **Risk:** Extreme. **Adj:** 35.

Born: November 21, 2006. **B-T:** L-R. **HT:** 6-3. **WT:** 200.
Drafted: HS—La Grange Park, IL, 2025 (2nd round). **Signed by:** JJ Lally.
TRACK RECORD: Fauske grew up in suburban Chicago as a White Sox fan, so it was fitting when his hometown team drafted him out of Nazareth Academy in the second round in 2025. He signed for just under $3 million, the highest bonus for any player drafted after the supplemental first round in 2025. Fauske played in unofficial bridge league games at the Arizona complex after signing and impressed observers with his potentially average hit tool and strength at the plate. He was still showing his high school football body but will gain flexibility in a professional strength and fitness regimen.
SCOUTING REPORT: Fauske has a smooth, rhythmic lefthanded swing with good balance, impressive plate coverage and a high contact rate. He has a hit-over-power profile now, but those grades could flip as he develops added strength and flexibility thanks to plenty of barrel accuracy. He draws his fair share of walks because of his knowledge of the strike zone. The 6-foot-3 Fauske played all over the field in high school, including extensive time at catcher as an underclassman. Some scouts believe that he could stay behind the plate if he worked at it, but he primarily played in the outfield during the summer showcase season and as a prep senior so that he could focus on hitting. The White Sox will give Fauske time at all three outfield spots and are especially interested to see if his average speed will play in center field. A corner outfield position is more likely, and his above-average arm will be sufficient for right field.
THE FUTURE: Fauske has a chance to develop into a middle-of-the-order hitter with high on-base percentages. He will get his first chance at full-season ball in 2026, when he will open the season as a 19-year-old for Low-A Kannapolis.

Year	Age	Club (League)	Level	AVG	G	AB	R	H	2B	3B	HR	RBI	BB	SO	SB	OBP	SLG
2025	18	Did not play															

CHICAGO WHITE SOX

8 CHRISTIAN OPPOR, LHP
FB: 60. **SL:** 55. **CH:** 55. **CTL:** 45. **BA Grade:** 50. **Risk:** High. **Adj:** 35.

Born: July 23, 2004. **B-T:** L-L. **HT:** 6-2. **WT:** 190.
Drafted: Gulf Coast State (FL) JC, 2023 (5th round). **Signed by:** Warren Hughes.
TRACK RECORD: Oppor took a leap forward in his development in 2025, his third pro season after being drafted in the fifth round out of Gulf Coast State College, a junior college program. The Wisconsin native spent two seasons in the Arizona Complex League before excelling in his first trip to full-season ball in 2025, which he split between Low-A Kannapolis and High-A Winston-Salem. His strikeout rate increased from 27.1% in 2024 to 31.7% in 2025, while his walk rate dropped from 16.5% to 11.5%.
SCOUTING REPORT: Oppor's stuff has been referred to as "electric." He increased his fastball velocity by a few ticks in 2025, flashed an improved slider and is now credited as having the best changeup in the White Sox's system. Oppor's four-seam fastball averages 95 mph and touches 100, playing up as he combines velocity with life and extension. His 80 mph, sweepier slider with good horizontal shape flashes above-average when he lands it. Batters swing and miss when he gets it in the zone, but he needs to improve the 32% in-zone percentage. Oppor's 80 mph changeup, which he uses more often than his slider, took a jump forward in 2025 with better vertical separation from his fastball. He gets swings and misses with that pitch, landing it in the zone more than 50% of the time. A key factor in Oppor's step forward was gaining better control, with more potential for improvement still ahead. His low three-quarters arm slot provides deception, but he needs to get better at repeating it.
THE FUTURE: Oppor projects as a potential midrotation starter with further improvements to his control and added strength to his lean frame. After a successful growth season at both Class A levels, he should be ready for an assignment to Double-A Birmingham in 2026.

Year	Age	Club (League)	Level	W	L	ERA	G	GS	IP	H	HR	BB	SO	BB%	SO%	WHIP	AVG
2025	20	Kannapolis (CAR)	A	2	2	2.42	5	5	22	12	0	7	34	8.1	39.5	0.85	.160
2025	20	Winston-Salem (SAL)	A+	2	6	3.31	17	17	65	50	6	35	82	12.5	29.3	1.30	.212
		Minor League Totals		6	12	3.58	39	32	133	106	7	72	171	12.7	30.2	1.34	.223

9 SAM ANTONACCI, 2B
HIT: 55. **POW:** 40. **RUN:** 45. **FLD:** 50. **ARM:** 50. **BA Grade:** 45. **Risk:** Avg. **Adj:** 35.

Born: February 6, 2003. **B-T:** L-R. **HT:** 6-0. **WT:** 200.
Drafted: Coastal Carolina, 2024 (5th round). **Signed by:** Kevin Burrell.
TRACK RECORD: The White Sox drafted Antonacci in the fifth round in 2024, signing the Coastal Carolina product for $572,500. He demonstrated his impressive on-base skills in a 2025 season he split between High-A Winston-Salem and Double-A Birmingham, registering a .429 OBP that ranked fourth-best in the minor leagues. Antonacci missed three weeks to injury in May but was a steady performer otherwise, including after a jump to Double-A in mid-July and then in the Arizona Fall League after the season. He led the AFL with 28 hits and 24 runs while posting a .505 OBP.
SCOUTING REPORT: Antonacci possesses solid bat-to-ball skill. He whiffed on just 11.4% pitches in the zone, and his plus swing decisions result in lots of contact. He consistently posts high walk rates, including a 13.3% clip in 2025, while striking out at about the same rate. Antonacci will need to continue to provide value by getting on base until he finds a way to get to more power. While he hit just five home runs in 2025, his 90th percentile exit velocity jumped to 103.1 mph, with a max of 110 mph. He's an average defender at both second base and third base, with his average arm enough for the hot corner. Observers believe he is a better fit at second, his primary position in 2025, though he played all four infield positions and would be an adequate defender on the left side in a utility role. A fringe-average runner, Antonacci used his advanced instincts to steal 48 bases, by far a higher rate than in college or his first pro season.
THE FUTURE: Few doubt that Antonacci will hit, but the rest of his game will need to continue to improve to become a major league contributor. The increase in his exit velocities and his performance in the AFL—1.046 OPS in 19 games—are positive signs that he can fill a big league role.

Year	Age	Club (League)	Level	AVG	G	AB	R	H	2B	3B	HR	RBI	BB	SO	SB	OBP	SLG
2025	22	ACL White Sox	Rk	.500	3	12	3	6	3	0	0	3	2	4	0	.571	.750
2025	22	Winston-Salem (SAL)	A+	.279	64	226	48	63	10	4	4	29	39	37	27	.425	.412
2025	22	Birmingham (SL)	AA	.292	49	168	27	49	8	2	1	25	28	32	21	.435	.381
		Minor League Totals		.298	139	487	100	145	27	7	5	71	86	86	55	.439	.413

CHICAGO WHITE SOX

10 KYLE LODISE, SS

HIT: 50. **POW:** 45. **RUN:** 55. **FLD:** 50. **ARM:** 45. **BA Grade:** 45. **Risk:** Avg. **Adj:** 35.

Born: October 17, 2003. **B-T:** R-R. **HT:** 5-11. **WT:** 180.
Drafted: Georgia Tech, 2025 (3rd round). **Signed by:** Kevin Burrell.
TRACK RECORD: Lodise spent two years at Division II Augusta in Georgia, where he established a track record as a high-contact hitter, before transferring to Georgia Tech in 2025. Lodise hit for much more power with the Yellow Jackets than scouts expected, finishing with a .327/.427/.664 batting line and 16 home runs, a 17.6% strikeout rate and 12.7% walk rate. He was one of the better hitters in the Atlantic Coast Conference, along with his cousin Alex Lodise, a shortstop for Florida State and now a Braves prospect. The White Sox drafted Kyle Lodise in the third round, signing him for $922,500. After a very brief time in unofficial bridge league games in Arizona, Lodise was sent directly to High-A Winston-Salem, one of just six White Sox draft picks sent to an affiliate and the only player to go to High-A.
SCOUTING REPORT: Lodise is the type of player who will continually play above his abilities. His average hit tool is part of a well-rounded game, which also includes good bat-to-ball skills and patience at the plate. He showed more pop than expected during his time at Winston-Salem, with a max exit velocity of 108.5 mph, and he now projects to have at least fringy power. He's an average shortstop defender with good instincts to compensate for a fringy arm. He is perhaps better suited to play second base but can cover the left side of the infield in a utility role. He has above-average speed with a high rate of successful stolen base attempts.
THE FUTURE: While Lodise won't likely generate a lot of prospect buzz, he's the kind of player who will find ways to help his team win games. He may profile best as a valuable utility infielder and is likely to move quickly through the system.

Year	Age	Club (League)	Level	AVG	G	AB	R	H	2B	3B	HR	RBI	BB	SO	SB	OBP	SLG
2025	21	Winston-Salem (SAL)	A+	.185	28	92	14	17	3	1	4	10	15	21	7	.319	.370
		Minor League Totals		.185	28	92	14	17	3	1	4	10	15	21	7	.319	.370

11 MATHIAS LaCOMBE, RHP

FB: 55. **SW:** 55. **CH:** 45. **CTL:** 50. **BA Grade:** 50. **Risk:** High. **Adj:** 35.

Born: June 12, 2002. **B-T:** R-R. **HT:** 6-2. **WT:** 185. **Drafted:** Cochise (AZ) JC, 2023 (12th round). **Signed by:** John Kazanas.
TRACK RECORD: Tucked in southern Arizona, Cochise (Ariz.) JC sits just 20 miles north of the Mexico border and within roughly the same distance of the Wild Wild West town of Tombstone. It's not a typical landing spot for French amateur talent to show up to play junior college baseball, but that's where LaCombe surfaced and first drew meaningful scouting attention in 2023. The White Sox drafted him in the 12th round that year and signed him to an over-slot $450,000 bonus, though a shoulder impingement and subsequent lat strain delayed his pro debut until May 2025. After seven games in the Arizona Complex League, LaCombe moved on to Low-A Kannapolis for 12 appearances, posting a 2.52 ERA with an impressive 32.6% strikeout rate and a 10.7% walk rate.
SCOUTING REPORT: After sitting in the low 90s as an amateur, LaCombe returned in 2025 with an above-average mid-90s sinker that touched 98. He also learned a low-80s sweeper during 2024 instructional league games. It's already an average pitch with great horizontal break from a low release height that gets whiffs and has above-average potential. His 83 mph split-changeup has a chance to get better with more experience. More velocity could be on the way as he better learns how to utilize his lower half in his delivery, and LaCombe has room on his 185-pound frame to add more strength.
THE FUTURE: While there's plenty of development ahead, LaCombe has No. 4 starter upside. He'll likely begin 2026 with High-A Winston-Salem.

Year	Age	Club (League)	Level	W	L	ERA	G	GS	IP	H	HR	BB	SO	BB%	SO%	WHIP	AVG
2025	23	ACL White Sox	Rk	0	1	2.52	12	9	36	23	3	11	50	7.5	34.0	0.95	.184
2025	23	Kannapolis (CAR)	A	0	0	4.08	7	5	18	12	0	13	23	16.9	29.9	1.42	.197
		Minor League Totals		0	1	3.04	19	14	53	35	3	24	73	10.7	32.6	1.11	.188

CHICAGO WHITE SOX

12 WILLIAM BERGOLLA JR., 2B/SS
HIT: 55. **POW:** 20. **RUN:** 60. **FLD:** 55. **ARM:** 55. **BA Grade:** 45. **Risk:** Average. **Adj:** 35.

Born: October 20, 2004. **B-T:** L-R. **HT:** 5-9. **WT:** 175. **Signed:** Venezuela, 2022.
Signed by: Rafael Alvarez/William Mota (Phillies).
TRACK RECORD: Bergolla has baseball bloodlines. His father William appeared in 17 games for the Reds in 2005. The White Sox acquired the younger Bergolla from the Phillies in a 2024 trade deadline deal for lefthanded pitcher Tanner Banks. He spent his first full season in Chicago's system with Double-A Birmingham, where he slashed .286/.342/.333 with 40 steals. His 6.6% miss rate led all minor league hitters with at least 300 plate appearances.
SCOUTING REPORT: Bergolla has plus-plus bat-to-ball skills and his 94% contact rate was among the best in the minors. He has a compact, technically sound swing. The trade-off is that it comes with very little power and a 49.3% groundball rate in 2025. Bergolla is capable of using the whole field, though his approach is geared toward the opposite field, and he has hit just two homers in four minor league seasons. He's an above-average defender at second base, though observers noted his torso can get a touch stiff. Still, he should be able to handle shortstop in a pinch. Bergolla is a plus runner who has made stealing bases more a part of his game the last two seasons. He also has an elite baseball IQ and plus makeup both on and off the field.
THE FUTURE: Bergolla has the floor of a utility middle infielder who gets on base and steals bases, though there's a chance he could become a second-division second baseman if he can add strength to his swing.

Year	Age	Club (League)	Level	AVG	G	AB	R	H	2B	3B	HR	RBI	BB	SO	SB	OBP	SLG
2025	20	Birmingham (SL)	AA	.286	125	486	70	139	19	2	0	36	37	26	40	.342	.333
		Minor League Totals		.291	293	1059	159	308	36	9	1	110	107	84	71	.358	.345

13 KY BUSH, LHP
FB: 45. **SL:** 55. **CH:** 50. **CTL:** 45. **BA Grade:** 45. **Risk:** Average. **Adj:** 35.

Born: November 12, 1999. **B-T:** L-L. **HT:** 6-6. **WT:** 250. **Drafted:** Saint Mary's, 2021 (2nd round).
Signed by: Scott Richardson (Angels).
TRACK RECORD: Bush pitched for three college programs in as many years before the Angels made him their second-round selection in 2021 out of Saint Mary's and signed him to an over-slot $1,747,500 bonus. The White Sox acquired him at the 2023 trade deadline and he made his major league debut just over a year later in August 2024, starting four games before returning to Triple-A Charlotte. Tommy John surgery sidelined the burly lefty for all of 2025.
SCOUTING REPORT: When healthy, Bush deployed a four-pitch mix with above-average extension. His four-seam fastball averaged 93 mph and touched 97 in the minors in 2024, delivered from a high three-quarters arm slot with a wrist wrap in the back. Big league hitters pounded it in his four-outing cameo. Bush's best pitch is an 83-86 mph slider that bores in on righthanded batters. His 72-77 mph curveball also flashes above-average potential. Bush also sells his firm 86 mph changeup well. Bush's control and consistency can wax and wane, and his walk rate hovered between 10-11% in the upper minors in 2023 and 2024. He finds more success when he can expand the plate and needs to get better at putting hitters away with two strikes.
THE FUTURE: Bush's solid pure stuff gives him the profile of a back-of-the-rotation innings-eater. Already on the 40-man roster, he should compete for a spot in the White Sox's rotation once he returns, which shouldn't be too long after spring training.

Year	Age	Club (League)	Level	W	L	ERA	G	GS	IP	H	HR	BB	SO	BB%	SO%	WHIP	AVG
2025	25	Did not play—Injured															
		Minor League Totals		18	18	4.36	63	61	293	266	39	117	299	9.5	24.2	1.31	.241
		Major League Totals		0	3	5.60	4	4	18	20	2	16	11	18.4	12.6	2.04	.290

14 MASON ADAMS, RHP
FB: 45. **CB:** 55. **SL:** 50. **CH:** 50. **CTL:** 60. **BA Grade:** 45. **Risk:** High. **Adj:** 35.

Born: February 23, 2000. **B-T:** R-R. **HT:** 6-1. **WT:** 190. **Drafted:** Jacksonville, 2022 (13th round). **Signed by:** Steffan Segui.
TRACK RECORD: A 13th-round senior sign out of Jacksonville in 2022, Adams ranked 13th in the White Sox system entering 2025 on the strength of his pitchability and strike-throwing after ending the previous season with Triple-A Charlotte. He even had a chance to reach the majors at some point that season. Instead, Adams was one of a handful of White Sox hurlers who needed Tommy John surgery prior to the beginning of the season and he missed all of 2025.
SCOUTING REPORT: Adams commands the zone with five pitches and two fastballs, relying more on his

two-seamer than his four-seamer. Both pitches average 92 mph and touch 94. They play up because of their movement and Adams' ability to locate both pitches. His best secondary pitch is an above-average 81 mph curveball that touches 84. It's his best swing-and-miss pitch and its movement compensates for its lower spin rate. Adams also throws an average 84 mph slider and 88 mph changeup, with the latter having more depth and run than his two-seamer. Adams is quite comfortable pitching to contact and often works backward, pitching to a 24.6% strikeout rate to just a 4.6% walk rate in 17 Double-A starts in 2024. His competitiveness and pitchability have helped him outperform expectations.

THE FUTURE: Adams is expected to return a few months after spring training and should settle into Triple-A Charlotte's rotation once healthy. He's an effective strike-thrower who can round out a rotation.

Year	Age	Club (League)	Level	W	L	ERA	G	GS	IP	H	HR	BB	SO	BB%	SO%	WHIP	AVG
2025	25	Did not play—Injured															
		Minor League Totals		13	10	3.09	49	35	233	217	18	58	239	6.0	24.7	1.18	.245

15 GEORGE WOLKOW, OF

HIT: 30. **POW:** 60. **RUN:** 45. **FLD:** 50. **ARM:** 60. **BA Grade:** 50. **Risk:** High. **Adj:** 35.

Born: January 11, 2006. **B-T:** L-R. **HT:** 6-7. **WT:** 250. **Drafted:** HS—Downers Grove, IL, 2023 (7th round). **Signed by:** JJ Lally.
TRACK RECORD: The White Sox bought Wolkow out of a South Carolina commitment with a $1 million bonus in the seventh round of the 2023 draft. Three years into his pro career, he remains a difficult prospect to project. He has always been younger than his competition since he reclassified from the 2024 high school class and the 19-year-old returned to Low-A in 2025 and he cut his strikeout rate from 40.6% to 29.6% and hit as many homers (13) as the previous season. His reduced miss rate also led to less impact and more ground balls.
SCOUTING REPORT: At 6-foot-7 and with long levers, Wolkow has plus-plus raw power and generates some of the loudest exit velocities in the White Sox system thanks to his plus bat speed. His game will always have plenty of swing-and-miss, although he cut his miss rate from 46% in 2024 to 35% in 2025. He also has plus makeup and is very receptive to coaching. He will need to get better at controlling his swing as well as the strike zone as he tries to identify the right long-term approach. An average outfield defender with a plus arm, Wolkow is best suited for right field as his fringe-average speed slows down with age.
THE FUTURE: The jury remains out on whether Wolkow will make enough contact to be a viable big leaguer. He'll be an interesting follow when he makes his move to High-A Winston-Salem in 2026.

Year	Age	Club (League)	Level	AVG	G	AB	R	H	2B	3B	HR	RBI	BB	SO	SB	OBP	SLG
2025	19	Kannapolis (CAR)	A	.223	116	426	58	95	16	2	13	69	54	147	33	.317	.362
		Minor League Totals		.235	144	523	77	123	24	2	16	76	71	190	38	.336	.380

16 JAVIER MOGOLLON, SS/2B

HIT: 40. **POW:** 50. **RUN:** 60. **FLD:** 50. **ARM:** 55. **BA Grade:** 45. **Risk:** Average. **Adj:** 35.

Born: November 1, 2005. **B-T:** R-R. **HT:** 5-8. **WT:** 170. **Signed:** Venezuela, 2023.
Signed by: Reydel Hernandez/Amador Arias/Ruddy Moreta.
TRACK RECORD: Signed for $75,000 in the 2023 international signing period, Mogollon quickly jumped to the top of that year's White Sox international class. The diminutive middle infielder from Venezuela hit eight homers and posted a 132 wRC+ in the 2024 Arizona Complex League, but his 38.3% strikeout rate raised concerns. He began 2025 with Low-A Kannapolis and produced an .848 OPS through the first month of the season before recurring knee issues ended his year after 51 games. He did, however, cut his strikeout rate to 25%.
SCOUTING REPORT: Mogollon is a quick-twitch athlete with a short, muscular 5-foot-8 build. He takes big swings and, despite his size, has above-average raw power with a max exit velocity of 109.7 mph in his abbreviated 2025 season. Mogollon's contact rate also jumped from 56% in the complex in 2024 to 70% in 2025. Improved swing decisions helped generate more consistent impact, though he still swings and misses plenty. He also takes his fair share of walks. Mogollon has soft hands and enough arm to play shortstop. He can get a bit out of control in the field, so he may be better suited for second base. He's a plus runner with double-digit steals each of his last three seasons.
THE FUTURE: A healthy Mogollon profiles best as a super utility option who is a sum of his parts player. He'll be 20 years old for all of 2026, so the White Sox have no reason to rush him.

Year	Age	Club (League)	Level	AVG	G	AB	R	H	2B	3B	HR	RBI	BB	SO	SB	OBP	SLG
2025	19	Kannapolis (CAR)	A	.220	51	186	36	41	10	3	5	19	30	56	15	.347	.387
		Minor League Totals		.263	144	494	108	130	34	5	23	90	90	153	42	.388	.492

CHICAGO WHITE SOX

17 JERAL PEREZ, 2B

HIT: 45. **POW:** 50. **RUN:** 40. **FLD:** 40. **ARM:** 50. **BA Grade:** 45. **Risk:** Average. **Adj:** 35.

Born: November 6, 2004. **B-T:** R-R. **HT:** 6-0. **WT:** 195. **Signed:** Dominican Republic, 2022.
Signed by: Domingo Toribio (Dodgers).
TRACK RECORD: Perez signed with the Dodgers out of the Dominican Republic in 2022 and was acquired by the White Sox at the 2024 trade deadline as part of a three-team deal. He spent his first full season in Chicago's system in 2025 at High-A Winston-Salem, where he hit .244/.315/.448 and led the South Atlantic League with 22 home runs, a total that also ranked second among White Sox minor leaguers.
SCOUTING REPORT: Perez stands close to the plate with efficient and quick hands, making hard contact with a swing that creates backspin and pulls the ball in the air with power. His optimized ball flights helped make up for just average exit velocities. He controls the zone reasonably well, although he walked just 8.2% of the time, and he can handle velocity. Perez primarily played second base in 2025 with occasional reps at shortstop. He's not a particularly good defender at either spot, and his below-average range raises questions about his long-term defensive home. Perez has added strength and filled out considerably. He doesn't have much physical projection remaining and he has slowed down as he matured.
THE FUTURE: Perez's High-A profile—low averages paired with power and decent on-base skills—captures what kind of hitter he can be. Most of his value is tied to his bat, so his jump to Double-A in 2026 will be a good test of whether his approach can hold up against more advanced pitching.

Year	Age	Club (League)	Level	AVG	G	AB	R	H	2B	3B	HR	RBI	BB	SO	SB	OBP	SLG
2025	20	Winston-Salem (SAL)	A+	.244	125	480	65	117	24	4	22	70	44	112	10	.315	.448
		Minor League Totals		.256	337	1260	206	323	71	9	53	193	171	313	28	.354	.453

18 ALDRIN BATISTA, RHP

FB: 50. **SW:** 45. **CH:** 60. **CTL:** 50. **BA Grade:** 45. **Risk:** High. **Adj:** 30.

Born: May 4, 2003. **B-T:** R-R. **HT:** 6-2. **WT:** 185. **Signed:** Dominican Republic, 2022. **Signed by:** Laiky Uribe (Dodgers).
TRACK RECORD: The White Sox acquired Batista from the Dodgers in August 2023 in a deal involving international slot money that Los Angeles used to sign South Korean pitcher Hyun-Seok Jang. After a strong 2024 season split between Low-A Kannapolis and High-A Winston-Salem, Batista positioned himself as a potential breakout arm entering 2025. He appeared in just one game in his return to Winston-Salem before a stress fracture in his right elbow sidelined him. Batista did not incur ligament damage and returned to action in August to pitch in six more games.
SCOUTING REPORT: Batista leans heavily on a 92-95 mph two-seam fastball that plays up because of plus sink and extension from a low release height. The pitch has 16 inches of horizontal break and bores in on righthanded batters. Batista infrequently uses a 92-96 mph four-seamer that is less effective because of his low release point. His plus, darting 84-87 mph changeup is even nastier than his sinker and tunnels well off the pitch. His 81-83 mph sweeper is still a work in progress but could get to average. Batista is a plus athlete with good body control who operates from a low, rock-step delivery that borders on sidearm. He has room to add strength to his thin, narrow frame.
THE FUTURE: Fully healthy again, Batista enters 2026 as a "pick to click" in the White Sox system. He could develop into a back-of-the-rotation arm if he adds more strength to his frame with a fallback as a mid- to high-leverage reliever who relies on his sinker/changeup combination.

Year	Age	Club (League)	Level	W	L	ERA	G	GS	IP	H	HR	BB	SO	BB%	SO%	WHIP	AVG
2025	22	Winston-Salem (SAL)	A+	2	0	5.79	7	2	14	13	0	7	17	10.6	25.8	1.43	.245
		Minor League Totals		16	7	2.92	57	47	228	179	10	91	246	9.5	25.7	1.18	.216

19 JEDIXSON PAEZ, RHP

FB: 45. **CB:** 45. **SL:** 50. **CH:** 55. **SW:** 45. **CTL:** 70. **BA Grade:** 45. **Risk:** High. **Adj:** 30.

Born: January 17, 2004. **B-T:** R-R. **HT:** 6-1. **WT:** 198. **Signed:** Venezuela, 2021.
Signed by: Alberto Mejia/Eddie Romero (Red Sox).
TRACK RECORD: Paez exhibited unusual control and feel for a three-pitch arsenal as an amateur—suggesting starter potential if he could add strength and power—when the Red Sox signed him for $450,000 in 2021. While his strength gains have been modest, he has consistently carved minor league hitters with an array of pitch shapes and speeds in the zone. In 2025, Boston shortened his outings in hopes he'd feel comfortable reaching for top-end velocity. Instead, a persistent calf injury sidelined Paez for over three months and prevented an anticipated move to Double-A. Boston left him off its 40-man roster and the White Sox selected him second overall in the Rule 5 draft in December.
SCOUTING REPORT: Paez pounds the zone with a full array of pitches, forging a 25% strikeout rate and

4% career walk rate. Despite excellent command, his 91-92 mph fastball touches 94 and is vulnerable to hard contact. Added power has been a career-long focus, but so far the gains have been incremental. Still, he only needs a small bump in fastball velocity to allow the rest of his dancing repertoire, which lights up models, to sing. His mid-80s changeup with armside fade is particularly effective, and his slider, curveball and sweeper all have distinct shapes, allowing him to dissect the zone with his secondaries in a way that could flummox even advanced hitters.

THE FUTURE: Paez now faces the daunting task of sticking on a big league roster without any previous upper minors experience. He could eventually settle into a bulk-innings type role.

Year	Age	Club (League)	Level	W	L	ERA	G	GS	IP	H	HR	BB	SO	BB%	SO%	WHIP	AVG
2025	21	Greenville (SAL)	A+	0	3	2.79	7	7	19	18	4	3	23	3.6	27.7	1.09	.228
		Minor League Totals		17	15	3.22	73	58	308	282	29	49	307	3.9	24.6	1.08	.240

20 ALEXANDER ALBERTO, RHP
FB: 65. **SL:** 50. **CTL:** 45. **BA Grade:** 45. **Risk:** High. **Adj:** 30.

Born: November 2, 2001. **B-T:** R-R. **Ht.:** 6-8. **Wt.:** 203. **Signed:** Dominican Republic, 2019.
Signed by: Danny Santana (Rays).
TRACK RECORD: Alberto signed with the Rays in November 2019, but he waited four years to make his full-season debut because of the Coronavirus pandemic and then a troubling stretch of control issues in the Florida Complex League. His development has sped up since then at the Class A levels, but it now takes a massive leap after the White Sox selected him as a major league Rule 5 pick in December.
SCOUTING REPORT: Pitchers without upper-minors experience rarely stick as MLB Rule 5 picks, but Alberto's combination of exceptional extension—registering just under 7 feet thanks to his long limbs—and nasty fastball gives him a chance. His 97-98 mph cut-fastball touches 101. While it doesn't miss a ton of bats, it moves enough to generate weak contact and righthanders rarely ever pull it. Alberto's hard, sweepy 85-88 mph slider is an average pitch and complements his fastball. Just as hitters worry about his fastball cutting in on them, the slider arrives to run away from their bats. Alberto's control has made big strides, but it will be challenging jumping from A-ball to the big leagues.
THE FUTURE: Alberto's upside makes his addition a worthwhile gamble for the White Sox. The speed of the MLB game could be too fast for him in spring training, but if he handles the jump, he could carve out a role as a future high-leverage reliever with subtle hints of an Emmanuel Clase-type arsenal if everything clicks, even if those chances are slim.

Year	Age	Club (League)	Level	W	L	ERA	G	GS	IP	H	HR	BB	SO	BB%	SO%	WHIP	AVG
2025	23	Charleston (CAR)	A	0	0	1.98	11	0	14	6	0	4	19	7.4	35.2	0.73	.130
2025	23	Bowling Green (SAL)	A+	2	2	2.83	31	0	35	30	1	17	45	11.0	29.0	1.34	.224
		Minor League Totals		6	10	4.18	104	15	172	134	2	104	194	13.6	25.4	1.38	.213

21 GAGE ZIEHL, RHP
FB: 40. **SW:** 55. **CB:** 45. **CT:** 50. **CH:** 45. **CTL:** 55. **BA Grade:** 40. **Risk:** Average. **Adj:** 30.

Born: May 15, 2003. **B-T:** R-R. **HT:** 6-0. **WT:** 223. **Drafted:** Miami, 2024 (4th round). **Signed by:** Ronnie Merrill (Yankees).
TRACK RECORD: Ziehl spent three seasons at Miami, working the last two as a starter, before the Yankees drafted him in the fourth round in 2024 and signed him for $637,000. He made his pro debut in 2025 with 16 starts, mostly for Low-A Tampa. The White Sox acquired him at the trade deadline in exchange for outfielder Austin Slater. Ziehl finished the season with six starts for High-A Winston-Salem, where he posted a 4.01 ERA and a 20-to-5 strikeout-to-walk ratio in 24.1 innings.
SCOUTING REPORT: Even though he commands his fastball well and tweaked it to generate a bit more cut in 2025, Ziehl used his below-average 92 mph four-seamer just 13% of the time. His maxed out 223-pound frame suggests it's unlikely more velocity is on the way. Instead, Ziehl relies on his mid-80s sweeper and 89 mph cutter, throwing those two pitches nearly 70% of the time with near-even distribution. His sweeper has above-average spin rates and is his best swing-and-miss offering. He rounds out his arsenal with a fringy upper-80s changeup that needs more separation from his fastball and a downer 80 mph curveball that he throws the least but generated his highest miss rate in 2025. Ziehl is a consistent strike-thrower.
THE FUTURE: Ziehl's unspectacular repertoire doesn't portend more than an up-down starter or long-relief type role, but his pitchability and command should ensure he reaches the big leagues in some capacity. He will likely begin 2026 with Double-A Birmingham.

CHICAGO WHITE SOX

Year	Age	Club (League)	Level	W	L	ERA	G	GS	IP	H	HR	BB	SO	BB%	SO%	WHIP	AVG
2025	22	Tampa (FSL)	A	4	4	4.00	14	14	74	76	6	14	63	4.5	20.2	1.21	.262
2025	22	Hudson Valley (SAL)	A+	1	0	2.25	1	0	4	3	0	0	3	0.0	21.4	0.75	.231
2025	22	Somerset (EL)	AA	0	0	9.00	1	1	4	9	1	0	4	0.0	19.0	2.25	.429
2025	22	Winston-Salem (SAL)	A+	2	2	4.01	6	6	25	28	0	5	20	4.6	18.5	1.34	.283
		Minor League Totals		7	6	4.12	22	21	107	116	7	19	90	4.2	19.8	1.26	.274

22 BLAKE LARSON, LHP

FB: 60. **SW:** 55. **CH:** 45. **CTL:** 40. **BA Grade:** 50. **Risk:** Extreme. **Adj:** 30.

Born: February 17, 2006. **B-T:** L-L. **HT:** 6-2. **WT:** 180. **Drafted:** HS—Bradenton, FL, 2024 (2nd round supp.).
Signed by: Alan Marr.
TRACK RECORD: The White Sox received a supplemental second-round pick from the Mariners in the 2024 trade for righthander Gregory Santos and used it to select Larson out of IMG Academy, signing him for $1.397 million to buy out a Texas Christian commitment. Larson didn't debut after the draft, instead pitching in instructional league games, then returned to the White Sox complex for a January 2025 minicamp with the goal of adding more strength to his lean frame. Instead, he blew out his elbow and needed season-ending Tommy John surgery in February.
SCOUTING REPORT: Larson fit the preferred White Sox profile as a lanky southpaw with a lower arm slot, and prior to surgery his two-seam fastball sat 93-94 mph and touched 95. He'll likely add a bit more velocity as he packs on more strength. Larson's main secondary is a low-80s sweepy slider that gets swings and misses because of its high spin rate. It has been a chase pitch to lefties and a breaking ball he can backfoot to righties. He seldom used a high-80s changeup in high school, and developing that pitch will be a goal when he gets back on the mound. He'll also need to improve his below-average control and command.
THE FUTURE: Larson is unlikely to get back into games and make his pro debut until after spring training. Depending on his rehab, there's a chance he could reach Low-A Kannapolis by the end of 2026.

Year	Age	Club (League)	Level	W	L	ERA	G	GS	IP	H	HR	BB	SO	BB%	SO%	WHIP	AVG
2025	19	Did not play—Injured															

23 JAIRO IRIARTE, RHP

FB: 50. **SL:** 55. **CH:** 55. **CTL:** 40. **BA Grade:** 45. **Risk:** High. **Adj:** 30.

Born: December 15, 2001. **B-T:** R-R. **HT:** 6-4. **WT:** 240. **Signed:** Venezuela, 2018.
Signed by: Trevor Schumm/Luis Prieto (Padres).
TRACK RECORD: Iriarte was one of the key pieces the White Sox received in the Dylan Cease trade prior to 2024, and he ranked ninth in the White Sox system when he opened 2025 in Triple-A Charlotte's rotation, but his fastball velocity dipped to just 90 mph and he walked 14 batters in as many innings. Chicago sent Iriarte to its Arizona complex for a month of biomechanical work and he resurfaced in Charlotte in early June, pitching to inconsistent results out of the bullpen the rest of the season.
SCOUTING REPORT: In addition to diminished fastball velocity from earlier in his career, Iriarte isn't generating the same spin rates compared to his time with the Padres, either. His 94 mph four-seamer lost vertical ride and movement in 2025. His two secondaries, once above-average offerings, also took a step back, with his 83 mph late-breaking slider lacking the same movement while he struggled to command his 87 mph changeup. Iriarte's strike-throwing backed up at the tail end of the season as well, and evaluators have noted his body has thickened up.
THE FUTURE: Iriarte now looks more like a reliever, and he has some work to do to recapture his previous form, which would allow for a future role near the back end of a bullpen.

Year	Age	Club (League)	Level	W	L	ERA	G	GS	IP	H	HR	BB	SO	BB%	SO%	WHIP	AVG
2025	23	ACL White Sox	Rk	1	0	4.50	2	0	2	2	0	0	2	0.0	25.0	1.00	.286
2025	23	Charlotte (IL)	AAA	2	3	7.24	35	5	46	53	9	37	48	16.7	21.6	1.96	.299
		Minor League Totals		16	28	4.87	132	77	421	391	43	208	464	11.2	24.9	1.42	.247
		Major League Totals		0	1	1.50	6	0	6	3	0	8	6	26.7	20.0	1.83	.143

24 LANDON HODGE, C

HIT: 45. **POW:** 40. **RUN:** 50. **FLD:** 55. **ARM:** 55. **BA Grade:** 50. **Risk:** Extreme. **Adj:** 30.

Born: February 18, 2007. **B-T:** L-R. **HT:** 6-1. **WT:** 175. **Drafted:** HS—Encino, CA, 2025 (4th round). **Signed by:** Carlos Muniz.
TRACK RECORD: Hodge was a bit of a pop-up prospect on the southern California high school circuit. While he appeared at the Area Code Games and PG National the summer before his senior year, he

wasn't heavily scouted until he delivered a strong senior spring in 2025. The White Sox grabbed him in the fourth round and lured him away from his LSU commitment with an over-slot $1,097,500 bonus. He got into a handful of bridge league games after signing.

SCOUTING REPORT: Hodge is a lean lefthanded hitter with impressive athleticism behind the plate who is presently more tools over skills. He has a quick bat and an aggressive approach, though at times he showed more discipline on the high school showcase circuit. He should be able to handle premium velocity with a line-drive swing geared to go gap-to-gap, but he'll need to make some adjustments to tap into his raw power. Like any high school catcher, he'll need plenty of refinement behind the plate, but he has the foundation of an agile, athletic defender with at least above-average potential. He sticks the ball nicely when he receives and can block effectively to go along with an above-average throwing arm.

THE FUTURE: Hodge has a big learning curve ahead of him and should move slowly, meaning he may not see full-season ball until late in 2026 or early 2027.

Year	Age	Club (League)	Level	AVG	G	AB	R	H	2B	3B	HR	RBI	BB	SO	SB	OBP	SLG
2025	18	Did not play															

25 JACOB GONZALEZ, SS
HIT: 40. **POW:** 40. **RUN:** 40. **FLD:** 50. **ARM:** 55. **BA Grade:** 35. **Risk:** Mild. **Adj:** 30.

Born: May 30, 2002. **B-T:** L-R. **HT:** 6-2. **WT:** 205. **Drafted:** Mississippi, 2023 (1st round). **Signed by:** Warren Hughes.

TRACK RECORD: Gonzalez has yet to live up to his draft pedigree since the White Sox selected him 15th overall in 2023 following a three-year career at Ole Miss. After he produced a 100 wRC+ over 89 games with Double-A Birmingham, Gonzalez spent 45 games with Triple-A Charlotte, where he slashed .204/.310/.293 and saw his strikeout percentage and miss rates spike.

SCOUTING REPORT: Coming out of college, Gonzalez faced questions about how his swing could handle higher velocities and more premium stuff. So far, his offensive abilities haven't taken a step forward. He uses a more upright stance now and has good barrel awareness, but doesn't consistently hit for impact or control the zone. He was also not a sure thing to stick at shortstop and has since lost lateral quickness, struggling to alter his routes to the ball once on the move. He saw more time at both second base and third base, which puts more pressure on his bat to develop. Gonzalez has above-average arm strength but struggles with accuracy on throws when moving to his right. He's a below-average runner who steals bases with solid instincts. Gonzalez is well-regarded as a teammate who does the little things to impact winning.

THE FUTURE: Gonzalez will return to Triple-A in 2026 and projects as a backup infielder with versatility to handle multiple spots.

Year	Age	Club (League)	Level	AVG	G	AB	R	H	2B	3B	HR	RBI	BB	SO	SB	OBP	SLG
2025	23	Birmingham (SL)	AA	.244	89	328	41	80	19	2	6	47	28	52	12	.305	.369
2025	23	Charlotte (IL)	AAA	.204	45	147	15	30	7	0	2	14	20	34	5	.310	.293
		Minor League Totals		.232	298	1106	132	257	56	3	17	135	118	185	35	.310	.335

26 LUIS REYES, RHP
FB: 50. **SL:** 55. **CH:** 45. **CTL:** 45. **BA Grade:** 45. **Risk:** High. **Adj:** 30.

Born: October 13, 2005. **B-T:** R-R. **HT:** 6-2. **WT:** 200. **Signed:** Dominican Republic, 2023. **Signed by:** Marco Paddy.

TRACK RECORD: Reyes signed for $700,000 in 2023 and endured both highs and lows in his full-season debut with Low-A Kannapolis two years later. Reyes pitched to a 6.98 ERA over the first two months of the season. He fared much better in June, holding hitters to a .153 average and .424 OPS. He ultimately finished the season with a 4.34 ERA over 87 innings and 23 starts in his age-19 season with a 22.9% strikeout rate compared to a career-best 9.6% walk rate.

SCOUTING REPORT: Reyes throws a pair of 92-95 mph fastballs, but leans mostly on his lively sinker. His above-average 84-88 mph slider is his most trusted pitch, and he used it more than 50% of the time because of its plus shape. Reyes' slider is his best swing-and-miss offering and he also landed it for strikes most frequently of his four offerings. He turns to his firmer 86-90 mph changeup far less often. Reyes uses a high-effort, three-quarters delivery with a simple, small windup and a deliberate tempo in the buildup, falling off to the first base side.

THE FUTURE: Reyes has the size and strength to take on a starter's workload, but he'll need to develop his changeup and clean up his delivery to stay in a rotation. He's ready for High-A Winston-Salem in 2026.

Year	Age	Club (League)	Level	W	L	ERA	G	GS	IP	H	HR	BB	SO	BB%	SO%	WHIP	AVG
2025	19	Kannapolis (CAR)	A	4	9	4.34	23	23	87	85	6	37	88	9.6	22.9	1.40	.251
		Minor League Totals		8	19	5.34	51	42	167	174	14	88	188	11.5	24.6	1.57	.266

CHICAGO WHITE SOX

27 GABE DAVIS, RHP
FB: 60. **SL:** 60. **CH:** 40. **CB:** 40. **CTL:** 40. **BA Grade:** 45. **Risk:** High. **Adj:** 30.

Born: October 21, 2003. **B-T:** R-R. **HT:** 6-9. **WT:** 235. **Drafted:** Oklahoma State, 2025 (5th round). **Signed by:** Dan Budreika.
TRACK RECORD: Davis was the first pitcher the White Sox selected in 2025 when they took him in the fifth round out of Oklahoma State. He had the look of a Day 1 pick entering his draft year before shoulder issues limited him to just 24.1 relief innings. Chicago felt comfortable rolling the dice that it could get him healthy and signed him to a $587,500 bonus. Like every pitcher they drafted, Davis did not make his pro debut or appear in bridge league games.
SCOUTING REPORT: Davis' enormous 6-foot-9, 235-pound frame stands out, as does his plus, high-spin heater that sits in the mid 90s and touches 100. It has a chance to play up even more because of his well above-average extension, though it presently plays down because he struggles with command. Davis' strike-throwing is erratic across the board and he never walked less than 11.8% of hitters in college. Davis' hard mid-80s slider has plus potential, and he'll also mix in a mid-80s changeup and the occasional 80 mph curveball.
THE FUTURE: While the White Sox might try him as a starter, Davis likely fits better in a bullpen where he can air out his plus fastball-slider combination. He'll need to first prove he can withstand a full year of pro ball after never pitching more than 50 innings in college.

Year	Age	Club (League)	Level	W	L	ERA	G	GS	IP	H	HR	BB	SO	BB%	SO%	WHIP	AVG
2025	21	Did not play															

28 SHANE MURPHY, LHP
FB: 35. **CB:** 50. **SL:** 45. **CT:** 45. **SW:** 45. **CH:** 45. **CTL:** 60. **BA Grade:** 35. **Risk:** Mild. **Adj:** 30.

Born: January 19, 2001. **B-T:** L-L. **HT:** 6-5. **WT:** 210. **Drafted:** Chandler Gilbert (AZ) JC, 2022 (14th round). **Signed by:** John Kazanas.
TRACK RECORD: While it's easy to write off Murphy's vanilla velocity, he has been very productive since the White Sox drafted him in the 14th round in 2022 while he was recovering from Tommy John surgery. Murphy broke out in 2025 across three levels, going 10-5, 1.66 over 135.1 innings, mostly with Double-A Birmingham. His 0.89 WHIP led all minor league pitchers who reached full-season ball and his ERA ranked second.
SCOUTING REPORT: A self-described technician, Murphy's four-seamer worked in the 87-92 mph range with plenty of vertical break, though he reportedly touched 95 in college prior to elbow surgery. Murphy's entire arsenal plays up because he's an extreme strike-thrower with an array of options to keep hitters guessing. He has two other fastball shapes, an 86-87 mph cutter and a sinker, and he also works in a 83 mph slider, 79 mph curveball, 75 mph sweeper and an 84 mph changeup. The curveball has the best potential of the bunch, and is the only one of his offspeeds that projects to be average. Murphy benefits from a deceptive high three-quarters delivery and is comfortable quickening his delivery tempo to mess with hitters' timing.
THE FUTURE: Murphy needs to prove he can survive at higher levels, but his 2025 results are a favorable sign. He has the look of an up-down starter who gets by more on guile than stuff.

Year	Age	Club (League)	Level	W	L	ERA	G	GS	IP	H	HR	BB	SO	BB%	SO%	WHIP	AVG
2025	24	Winston-Salem (SAL)	A+	1	0	3.60	3	2	10	7	2	3	12	7.5	30.0	1.00	.189
2025	24	Birmingham (SL)	AA	9	4	1.38	20	18	111	77	8	15	82	3.7	20.1	0.83	.198
2025	24	Charlotte (IL)	AAA	0	1	2.45	3	3	15	11	2	7	10	11.9	16.9	1.23	.216
		Minor League Totals		15	13	3.17	75	62	341	275	41	74	291	5.5	21.8	1.02	.221

CHICAGO WHITE SOX

YOBAL RODRIGUEZ, RHP
FB: 55. **SL:** 45. **CH:** 60. **CTL:** 55. **BA Grade:** 50. **Risk:** Extreme. **Adj:** 30.

Born: February 9, 2008. **B-T:** R-R. **HT:** 6-2. **WT:** 155. **Signed:** Cuba, 2025. **Signed by:** David Keller.
TRACK RECORD: Rodriguez left Cuba in 2022 and was playing for the MVP Baseball Academy in Florida prior to signing with the White Sox in 2025 for $230,000. The 17-year-old had an auspicious start to his pro career in the Dominican Summer League, throwing 18.2 scoreless innings while yielding just four hits. He finished his first pro season with a 2.97 ERA and 33 strikeouts to 13 walks over 30.1 innings, even earning DSL Pitcher of the Month honors in June.
SCOUTING REPORT: At 6-foot-2, 155 pounds, Rodriguez is still very lean, so while his 87-91 mph four-seamer touches 92 now with armside run, the White Sox believe he'll add significant velocity as he gets older, giving his fastball above-average potential. His best secondary is a fading 80 mph changeup that projects as a plus swing-and-miss offering and should have significant separation from his fastball. Rodriguez shows feel to spin an 81 mph slider, though it's still a work in progress. He locates all his pitches well, but his longer, twisting action in his three-quarters delivery may inhibit its repeatability.
THE FUTURE: Rodriguez has a high ceiling as a starting pitcher if he can add strength to his slender frame as he matures. He'll likely spend all of 2026 in the Arizona Complex League.

Year	Age	Club (League)	Level	W	L	ERA	G	GS	IP	H	HR	BB	SO	BB%	SO%	WHIP	AVG
2025	17	DSL White Sox	Rk	0	3	2.97	13	10	30	18	0	13	33	10.0	25.4	1.02	.161
		Minor League Totals		0	3	2.97	13	10	30	18	0	13	33	10.0	25.4	1.02	.161

MATTHEW BOUGHTON, 2B/SS
HIT: 50. **POW:** 45. **RUN:** 60. **FLD:** 55. **ARM:** 55. **BA Grade:** 50. **Risk:** Extreme. **Adj:** 30.

Born: September 10, 2005. **B-T:** R-R. **HT:** 6-2. **WT:** 175. **Drafted:** HS—Colleyville, TX, 2025 (11th round).
Signed by: Alex Glenn.
TRACK RECORD: Boughton was one of the older high schoolers in the 2025 class and turned 20 just two months after the draft. He was not a highly rated draft prospect, but the White Sox regarded the Texas native as a sleeper and signed him to an over-slot $197,500 bonus in the 11th round to keep him from a Texas A&M commitment. His father Michael was a minor league shortstop, coached in the Dodgers system and more recently was his high school coach. Boughton took a regular turn at second base in bridge league games after signing.
SCOUTING REPORT: A multi-sport athlete in high school, Boughton's athleticism and speed immediately stand out. At the plate, he has a chance to be an average hitter with fringe-average power. His fast hands get the barrel through the zone quickly, but he will need to add strength and improve his bat path. Boughton projects as more of a glove-over-bat type and is an above-average defender at both middle infield positions with an above-average arm. He's a plus runner, and his athletic tools and overall instincts for the game could give him a chance to play center field.
THE FUTURE: Boughton turns 21 in September, so he could move relatively quickly if he handles his first taste of full-season ball. His likely ceiling is a super utility role in the big leagues.

Year	Age	Club (League)	Level	AVG	G	AB	R	H	2B	3B	HR	RBI	BB	SO	SB	OBP	SLG
2025	19	Did not play															

Hunter Greene

Cincinnati Reds

BY J.J. COOPER

After dipping below .500 in 2024, the Reds made the playoffs in 2025 for the first time since 2020. They were quickly trounced in two games by the Dodgers in the Wild Card Series. Los Angeles then went on to win it all, but still the season marked a small step forward for the Reds.

The question now is whether there is another gear to reach. The Reds have winning records in four of their last six seasons—but just barely. Their 83 wins in 2025 is their highest total since the Dusty Baker-led team in 2013 won 90 times.

While the current Reds are on an upswing—they closed the 2010s with six consecutive losing seasons—they have fallen short of expectations. Cincinnati has not won a playoff series this century.

Heading into 2026, the Reds continue to straddle the demarcation line between success and failure. With good health and a bit of good fortune, a team with this pitching staff and a star like Elly De La Cruz could make a deeper playoff run.

But with limited position player depth and a modest payroll, injuries and a touch of bad luck can quickly send this team out of playoff contention, as 2024 showed.

In a league in which the Reds are unlikely to spend for top-tier starters, their homegrown rotation is worthy of admiration. Draftees Hunter Greene, Nick Lodolo, Andrew Abbott, Chase Burns and trade acquisition Brady Singer ensure that the Reds are returning a full five-man rotation that mixes top-tier talent and some veteran savvy.

The return from injuries of Rhett Lowder, Julian Aguiar and Brandon Williamson, along with prospects Chase Petty and Jose Franco, could give the club a full rotation of back-up plans as well.

That pitching depth may need to be used to bulk up the lineup. De La Cruz played through a quad injury that derailed his season, but when healthy, he's one of the best shortstops in baseball. De La Cruz hit .284/.359/.495 with 18 home runs and 25 steals in the first half. He hit .236/.303/.363 with four homers and 12 steals in the second.

But he doesn't have enough help. Center fielder T.J. Friedl is a solid complementary player, and the Reds have to hope that Noelvi Marte can take another step forward in right field. First baseman Sal Stewart should provide solid production as well.

But for a team playing in a hitter's haven, the Reds have few power sources. They head into 2026 seemingly one or two bats short of a full lineup.

Stewart is ready to graduate and should immediately hit in the middle of the lineup. That's a big boost for a team that got bottom-five production from first base in 2025.

Other than him, the best Reds big league-ready prospects are largely pitchers or role players. Outfielder Hector Rodriguez, shortstop Edwin Arroyo and utility man Tyler Callihan may play in Cincinnati in 2026, but in more modest roles.

Finding a productive outfielder to play in a corner would do wonders for the offense. The last time the Reds' outfield combined to produce positive bWAR was 2016, when Adam Duvall, Billy Hamilton and Jay Bruce were still Reds.

The hard part has been done. Cincinnati has built a deep homegrown rotation. They have developed a star in De La Cruz.

Now to go deeper in the playoffs, Cincinnati has have to figure out how to get better hitters around De La Cruz. ∎

PROJECTED 2029 LINEUP

Catcher	Alfredo Duno	23
First Base	Sal Stewart	25
Second Base	Matt McLain	30
Third Base	Edwin Arroyo	25
Shortstop	Elly De La Cruz	27
Left Field	Tyson Lewis	23
Center Field	Steele Hall	22
Right Field	Noelvi Marte	27
Designated Hitter	Cam Collier	24
No. 1 Starter	Hunter Greene	29
No. 2 Starter	Chase Burns	26
No. 3 Starter	Rhett Lowder	27
No. 4 Starter	Andrew Abbott	30
No. 5 Starter	Chase Petty	26
Closer	Luis Mey	28

DEPTH CHART

CINCINNATI REDS

TOP 2025 CONTRIBUTORS — RANK
1. Sal Stewart, 1B — 1
2. Rhett Lowder, RHP — 3
3. Jose Franco, RHP — 13

BREAKOUT PROSPECTS — RANK
1. Adolfo Sanchez, OF — 14
2. Mason Morris, RHP — 20
3. Eli Pitts, OF — 23

SOURCE OF TOP 30 TALENT

Homegrown	25	Acquired	5
College	6	Trade	4
Junior college	2	Rule 5 draft	0
High school	6	Independent league	1
Undrafted free agent	0	Free agent/waivers	0
International	11		

LF
Hector Rodriguez (9)
Adolfo Sanchez (14)
Tyler Callihan (18)
Arnaldo Lantigua (25)
Ariel Almonte
Anthony Stephan
Malvin Valdez

CF
Eli Pitts (23)
Carlos Jorge (29)
Ethan O'Donnell
Kyle Henley
Jay Allen II

RF
Mason Neville (17)
Yerlin Confidan

3B
Tyson Lewis (4)
Carlos Sanchez (26)
Ricky Cabrera
Angel Salio
Alfredo Alcantara

SS
Steele Hall (5)
Edwin Arroyo (7)
Liberts Aponte (22)
Naibel Mariano
Rafhlmil Torres

2B
Leo Balcazar (16)
Peyton Stovall

1B
Sal Stewart (1)
Cam Collier (8)

C
Alfredo Duno (2)
Jirvin Morillo (21)
Connor Burns (30)
Will Banfield
Cade Hunter

LHP

LHSP
Kevin Abel
Iker Redona

LHRP
Hunter Hollan
Bryce Hubbart

RHP

RHSP
Rhett Lowder (3)
Chase Petty (6)
Stharlin Torres (10)
Aaron Watson (11)
Julian Aguiar (12)
Sheng-En Lin (15)
Luke Holman (24)
Edgar Colon (27)
José Acuña
Javi Rivera
Ty Floyd
Cole Schoenwetter
Braden Osbolt
Justin Henschel

RHRP
Jose Franco (13)
Zach Maxwell (19)
Mason Morris (20)
Trevor Kuncl (28)
Ovis Portes
Bryce Archie
Hunter Parks
Carson Latimer

CINCINNATI REDS

1 SAL STEWART, 1B

Born: December 7, 2003. **B-T:** R-R. **HT:** 6-1. **WT:** 224.
Drafted: HS—Palmetto Bay, FL, 2022 (1st round supp.).
Signed by: Andrew Fabian.

TRACK RECORD: A product of South Florida powerhouse Westminster Christian, Stewart has been one of the Reds' best hitting prospects since they drafted him 32nd overall in 2022. He has trained with and learned from Manny Machado for years, and when Stewart made it to the major leagues Machado gave him a Rolex as a congratulatory gift. In 2025, Stewart evolved into a more complete player by starting to learn how to pull the ball more consistently to get to his long-untapped power potential. Stewart's 25 home runs between the minors and majors more than doubled his previous career high. By the postseason, he was batting cleanup for the Reds. He drove in nearly half of the Reds' runs in the playoffs. More surprisingly, he also had the team's only stolen base in its Wild Card Series loss to the Dodgers.

SCOUTING REPORT: Stewart's hitting ability has always been his standout tool. He knows the strike zone, and he has a repeatable, consistent swing that helps him avoid long slumps. Stewart begins his swing with a significant timing step, but he's generally on time, with above-average bat speed and barrel control. He posted a sub-.800 OPS in only one month during 2024 and 2025 combined. Midway through the 2025 season at Double-A Chattanooga, Stewart began to get more aggressive and looked to pull balls for power when he was ahead in counts. From June onward, he pulled 14 homers to left and left-center field. He has the rare ability to be a plus hitter with above-average power. Those skills are going to be important, because Stewart's value to a big league club will largely come at the plate. He has a thick and squatty build that limits his range. Stewart's hands work well on the infield, and he's adept at diving to make a play. While he makes plays on what he can reach, he lacks range at second or third base. His well below-average arm is a much bigger issue. Stewart's strongest tracked throw in Triple-A and the majors was 78 mph, which was 7 mph lower than the average arm strength for an MLB third baseman. At first base, that won't be an issue, but he needs more reps to get comfortable with the footwork the position requires. Stewart makes good decisions on the basepaths, and he'll even swipe a bag if pitchers ignore him, but he's a below-average runner now, and is likely to get slower considering he's only 22.

BA GRADE: 55 **Risk:** Mild
Adjusted grade: 50

SCOUTING GRADES: Hit: 65. Power: 55. Run: 40. Field: 45. Arm: 30.
Projected future grades on 20-80 scouting scale

BEST TOOLS

BATTING
Best Hitter — Hector Rodriguez
Best Power Hitter — Tyson Lewis
Best Strike-Zone Discipline — Alfredo Duno
Fastest Baserunner — Steele Hall
Best Athlete — Steele Hall

PITCHING
Best Fastball — Zach Maxwell
Best Curveball — Sheng-En Lin
Best Slider — Rhett Lowder
Best Changeup — Jose Acuña
Best Control — Rhett Lowder

FIELDING
Best Defensive Catcher — Connor Burns
Best Defensive Infielder — Edwin Arroyo
Best Infield Arm — Ricardo Cabrera
Best Defensive Outfielder — Jay Allen
Best Outfield Arm — Malvin Valdez

THE FUTURE: Stewart's bat is MLB ready. With the Reds needing improved production at the infield corners, he will fill a clear team hole if he can be an everyday first baseman who can play second or third base sporadically. Stewart's bat should be heavily relied on in 2026 and beyond, and he could fix what has been a hole at first base since Joey Votto retired.

Year	Age	Club (League)	Level	AVG	G	AB	R	H	2B	3B	HR	RBI	BB	SO	SB	OBP	SLG
2025	21	Chattanooga (SL)	AA	.306	80	294	51	90	19	0	10	44	27	51	13	.377	.473
2025	21	Louisville (IL)	AAA	.315	38	143	27	45	15	0	10	36	19	26	4	.394	.629
2025	21	Cincinnati (NL)	MLB	.255	18	55	11	14	1	0	5	8	3	15	0	.293	.545
		Minor League Totals		.289	323	1167	208	337	85	1	40	202	184	216	42	.390	.466
		Major League Totals		.255	18	55	11	14	1	0	5	8	3	15	0	.293	.545

CINCINNATI REDS

2 ALFREDO DUNO, C
HIT: 40. **POW:** 60. **RUN:** 40. **FLD:** 45. **ARM:** 60. **BA Grade:** 60. **Risk:** High. **Adj:** 45.

Born: January 7, 2006. **B-T:** R-R. **HT:** 6-3. **WT:** 248.
Signed: Venezuela, 2023. **Signed by:** Reds international scouting department.
TRACK RECORD: The key signing in the Reds' 2023 international class, Duno had been limited to DH in 2023 because of a sore arm, and he barely played in 2024 because of a rib injury. Fully healthy in 2025, Duno was the star of the Low-A Florida State League. He finished second in the league with a .287 batting average and first in home runs (18), doubles (32), on-base percentage (.430) and slugging (.518). He then played in the Arizona Fall League.
SCOUTING REPORT: Few young hitters come close to Duno's advanced understanding of the strike zone. His career .425 OBP ranks fourth among active minor league hitters with at least 750 plate appearances. He will not swing at pitches out of the zone, which made him many Low-A pitchers' kryptonite. That approach will be more tested at higher levels, and Duno will have to make adjustments. He has a pull-heavy approach and struggles to cover the outer third of the plate. He was especially vulnerable to velocity away, with a 52% swing-and-miss rate on fastballs on the outer third of the strike zone. Duno's long levers and modest bat-to-ball skills mean that he is unlikely to hit for average against better pitchers, but he could make up for it by drawing walks, and his exceptional power could get him to 25 home runs regularly. Duno moves well for his 6-foot-3, 248-pound size. He's a below-average runner but not a base clogger. Defensively, he's a fringe-average receiver and pitch-framer. He has a plus arm and posts plus pop times at his best, but he sometimes struggles with slow exchanges as he unfurls his body.
THE FUTURE: Duno can likely stay behind the plate at his size, but not if he gets much bigger. Just 10 catchers in MLB history have caught at least 500 games while weighing 245 pounds or more, though AJ Pierzynski and Salvador Perez show it can be done.

Year	Age	Club (League)	Level	AVG	G	AB	R	H	2B	3B	HR	RBI	BB	SO	SB	OBP	SLG
2025	19	Daytona (FSL)	A	.287	113	390	78	112	32	2	18	81	95	91	6	.430	.518
		Minor League Totals		.287	190	658	132	189	48	4	27	138	151	172	14	.425	.495

3 RHETT LOWDER, RHP
FB: 50. **SL:** 65. **CH:** 55. **CTL:** 60. **BA Grade:** 55. **Risk:** Average. **Adj:** 45.

Born: March 8, 2002. **B-T:** R-R. **HT:** 6-2. **WT:** 205.
Drafted: Wake Forest, 2023 (1st round). **Signed by:** Charlie Aliano.
TRACK RECORD: Drafted seventh overall in 2023, Lowder made his MLB debut at the end of August 2024 and was expected to pitch in the Reds' rotation in 2025. Instead, he was sidelined by a cascade of injuries. It was the first time he had ever missed significant time with injury, going back to high school. Lowder had a forearm strain in spring training and then made four minor league appearances in May before injuring his oblique and missing the rest of the season, save for one September rehab start. He threw just 9.1 total innings but showed he was healthy with a stint in the Arizona Fall League.
SCOUTING REPORT: When he returned from his injuries, Lowder did so with a slightly modified delivery. He removed a modest hand pump he used before bringing his hands back down to his waist prior to hand break. He's also more direct to the plate. Before the change, Lowder had a tendency to land drifting toward first base with his lower half as he got down the mound. His stuff showed no degradation in the AFL. He pitched at 93-96 mph with his pair of fastballs and a 65-grade high-80s slider that he can manipulate into different shapes. Lowder will need to separate his two- and four-seam fastballs more effectively in the majors. His four-seamer is most effective as a chase pitch above the zone, which changes eye levels and keeps hitters from sitting on his two-seamer and slider. His changeup will flash above-average, but he doesn't use it enough. Everything plays up because of Lowder's plus control and command.
THE FUTURE: Lowder has the control and stuff to be a solid midrotation arm. He was ready to handle that role in 2025 and, healthy again, should be ready to step into the MLB rotation in 2026. His return should help give the Reds enviable depth in the rotation, where he could team with fellow homegrown pitchers Hunter Greene, Andrew Abbott, Nick Lodolo and Chase Burns.

Year	Age	Club (League)	Level	W	L	ERA	G	GS	IP	H	HR	BB	SO	BB%	SO%	WHIP	AVG
2025	23	ACL Reds	Rk	0	1	6.00	1	1	3	4	1	0	5	0.0	38.5	1.33	.308
2025	23	Dayton (MWL)	A+	0	1	12.00	1	1	3	5	0	1	5	5.9	29.4	2.00	.333
2025	23	Louisville (IL)	AAA	0	1	13.50	3	3	3	6	1	2	3	10.5	15.8	2.40	.375
		Minor League Totals		6	7	4.19	27	27	118	116	11	27	126	5.4	25.4	1.21	.253
		Major League Totals		2	2	1.17	6	6	31	25	0	14	22	10.9	17.2	1.27	.219

CINCINNATI REDS

4 TYSON LEWIS, SS

HIT: 40. **POW:** 65. **RUN:** 55. **FLD:** 45. **ARM:** 60. **BA Grade:** 55. **Risk:** High. **Adj:** 40.

Born: January 10, 2006. **B-T:** L-R. **HT:** 6-2. **WT:** 195.
Drafted: HS—Omaha, NE, 2024 (2nd round). **Signed by:** Mike Keenan.
TRACK RECORD: After leading Omaha's Millard West High to a Nebraska state title, Lewis became the highest-drafted prep hitter in state history when the Reds selected him with the 51st pick of the 2024 draft. He was one of the most productive hitters in the Arizona Complex League in 2025, and he was one of the better hitters in the Low-A Florida State League over the second half of the season.
SCOUTING REPORT: As productive as Lewis was in his pro debut, the Reds are excited about what he might yet become. He is a long, lean, lefthanded hitter with plenty of room to fill out further, but he already hits the ball exceptionally hard. He had the highest 90th percentile exit velocity of all minor league teenagers with at least 100 plate appearances in 2025. His swing has a high finish that leads to majestic lofted home runs at his best, but he often lets the ball get deep on him, limiting him to driving the ball to left field. He began to show more pull-side power late in the 2025 season. Defensively, Lewis' footwork limits him at shortstop, but his plus arm makes up for some of his other limitations. He's an above-average runner underway, but he needs time to get to speed and doesn't have a quick first step. His tool set would fit at third base or in center field if he eventually slides off shortstop.
THE FUTURE: The Reds had Lewis play some third base in instructional league. They aren't ruling out him staying at shortstop, but his bat should fit at multiple positions. Even scouts who aren't as enamored of Lewis believe he's a big leaguer. Some see an impact regular, especially if he gets bigger and stronger, as expected. Lewis should spend the majority of 2026 at High-A Dayton. He had the kind of power potential the Reds have lacked in recent years.

Year	Age	Club (League)	Level	AVG	G	AB	R	H	2B	3B	HR	RBI	BB	SO	SB	OBP	SLG
2025	19	ACL Reds	Rk	.340	46	188	44	64	8	5	6	35	15	51	19	.396	.532
2025	19	Daytona (FSL)	A	.268	35	127	21	34	8	1	3	19	14	51	8	.347	.417
		Minor League Totals		.311	81	315	65	98	16	6	9	54	29	102	27	.376	.486

5 STEELE HALL, SS

HIT: 45. **POW:** 50. **RUN:** 80. **FLD:** 55. **ARM:** 55. **BA Grade:** 55. **Risk:** High. **Adj:** 40.

Born: July 24, 2007. **B-T:** R-R. **HT:** 6-0. **WT:** 180.
Drafted: HS—Trussville, AL, 2025 (1st round). **Signed by:** JR Reynolds.
TRACK RECORD: Hall was supposed to be one of the top high school prospects in the loaded 2026 draft class, but he opted to reclassify to be eligible a year earlier. It paid off. He impressed the Reds when he matched college hitters swing for swing in a pre-draft workout, and Cincinnati responded by drafting Hall ninth overall in 2025. He was the first shortstop the Reds have selected with a top 10 pick since Barry Larkin in 1985. Like most Reds draftees, Hall did not get into an official game after the draft, but he showed elite speed and some power in the unofficial bridge league.
SCOUTING REPORT: The day he signed, Hall became the best athlete in the Reds' minor league system, and the best in the organization other than Elly De La Cruz. Hall is a top-of-the-scale runner. A twitchy athlete, he gets out of the box extremely quickly and can embarrass inattentive outfielders by turning singles into doubles. Defensively, Hall has the first step, solid hands and above-average arm to make all routine plays at shortstop and produce highlight plays at his best. The Reds believe in his power potential. He has a quick bat, with plenty of hand speed and athleticism. But there is some length in his setup and load that could affect his timing at the plate. He struggled with spin at times in the bridge league, but he should be able to develop into a fringe-average to average hitter with average power.
THE FUTURE: The Reds are more conservative than many organizations with how quickly they move their prospects. The club sent prep shortstops Sammy Stafura and Tyson Lewis to the Rookie-level Arizona Complex League the year after they were drafted. Hall could follow that path, but he was drafted much higher than Stafura or Lewis and is more polished. If Hall develops, he could be a top-of-the-order hitter who plays above-average defense at shortstop.

Year	Age	Club (League)	Level	AVG	G	AB	R	H	2B	3B	HR	RBI	BB	SO	SB	OBP	SLG
2025	18	Did not play															

CINCINNATI REDS

6 CHASE PETTY, RHP

FB: 55. **SL:** 50. **CH:** 45. **SW:** 45. **CTL:** 45. **BA Grade:** 50. **Risk:** Average. **Adj:** 40.

Born: April 4, 2003. **B-T:** R-R. **HT:** 6-1. **WT:** 190.
Drafted: HS—Linwood, NJ, 2021 (1st round). **Signed by:** John Wilson (Twins).
TRACK RECORD: Petty has learned how to pitch with different arsenals since the Twins drafted him in the first round in 2021 and then traded him to the Reds in the March 2022 Sonny Gray trade. Petty threw 100 mph in high school, but with an all-arms-and-elbows delivery that was hard to maintain. He smoothed out his delivery and geared down to become a low-90s sinkerballer. After improving his control, his velocity eventually returned. Petty made his MLB debut in 2025, but otherwise it was a year to forget. His 6.39 ERA in the Triple-A International League was second worst among pitchers with at least 100 innings, and he was rocked in three MLB outings.
SCOUTING REPORT: As bad as Petty was in 2025, he has the stuff to be an MLB starter if his command and control improve. His pitch movement has proven to be his enemy. Everything he throws has more armside run than is typical. That makes him a bit unusual—which is good—but no pitch is a true bat-misser. Even after adding a fringe-average mid-80s sweeper, he struggles to consistently force righthanded hitters to defend the outer third of the zone. In 2025, he struggled to locate his four-seam fastball to his glove side. Petty's strike rate dropped from 65% in 2023 to 63% in 2024 to 61% in 2025. He also has a hard, cutterish gyro slider in the low 90s and a hard, high-80s changeup. None of Petty's pitches grades as plus. His four-seam fastball has above-average velocity, but it's a groundball pitch.
THE FUTURE: Petty will pitch as a 23-year-old in 2026, so the Reds have every reason to be patient. He has to improve his ability to locate within the strike zone, and he now projects as a durable back-end starter—or possible leverage reliever—more than a midrotation arm.

Year	Age	Club (League)	Level	W	L	ERA	G	GS	IP	H	HR	BB	SO	BB%	SO%	WHIP	AVG
2025	22	Louisville (IL)	AAA	6	13	6.39	26	26	113	123	17	58	102	11.2	19.6	1.61	.271
2025	22	Cincinnati (NL)	MLB	0	3	19.50	3	2	6	14	3	8	7	20.0	17.5	3.67	.452
		Minor League Totals		8	21	4.16	73	67	294	284	24	108	277	8.6	22.0	1.33	.252
		Major League Totals		0	3	19.50	3	2	6	14	3	8	7	20.0	17.5	3.67	.452

7 EDWIN ARROYO, SS

HIT: 50. **POW:** 30. **RUN:** 55. **FLD:** 55. **ARM:** 55. **BA Grade:** 45. **Risk:** Mild. **Adj:** 40.

Born: August 25, 2003. **B-T:** B-R. **HT:** 6-0. **WT:** 173.
Drafted: HS—Kissimmee, FL, 2021 (2nd round). **Signed by:** Rob Mummau (Mariners).
TRACK RECORD: One of the youngest players in the 2021 draft class, Arroyo made a strong initial impression with the Mariners, his drafting organization. That led to the Reds acquiring him along with Noelvi Marte in the 2022 trade that sent Luis Castillo to Seattle. Arroyo made steady progress until 2024, when he injured his left labrum diving into first base in a spring training game. He had surgery and didn't return to action until the Arizona Fall League. After a slow start at Double-A Chattanooga in 2025, he hit a team-best .296/.357/.403 from July 1 onward.
SCOUTING REPORT: Arroyo produced 49 extra-base hits in 2022 in Class A as an 18-year-old. At that point, the hope was that his power would continue to develop, making him a plus shortstop defender who could also hit in the middle of the lineup. Arroyo's power has flat-lined since then, and it's more likely he will be a bottom-of-the-order bat. The switch-hitter's swings start with an extremely open stance, and he uses a very wide setup. He has excellent plate coverage, and an aggressive approach, but everything he does is geared toward contact rather than generating power. Arroyo rarely stings the ball, but he loves to use the opposite field and is a potentially average hitter. He's truly ambidextrous and pitched as a lefthander as a kid. Arroyo is an above-average, reliable shortstop with quick hands and a good internal clock. He has the body control to make acrobatic and accurate spinning throws on balls up the middle, though his above-average arm isn't as adept at plays deep in the hole. He is an above-average runner.
THE FUTURE: Arroyo was added to the 40-man roster this offseason to protect him from the Rule 5 draft. He's ready to head to Triple-A Louisville, where he should add second and third base versatility and be the on-call option if the Reds need an extra infielder.

Year	Age	Club (League)	Level	AVG	G	AB	R	H	2B	3B	HR	RBI	BB	SO	SB	OBP	SLG
2025	21	Chattanooga (SL)	AA	.284	120	464	63	132	23	4	3	44	40	88	12	.345	.371
		Minor League Totals		.273	380	1494	246	408	78	25	32	198	145	355	72	.344	.423

CINCINNATI REDS

8 CAM COLLIER, 1B/3B

HIT: 55. **POW:** 55. **RUN:** 30. **FLD:** 40. **ARM:** 55. **BA Grade:** 50. **Risk:** Average. **Adj:** 40.

Born: November 20, 2004. **B-T:** L-R. **HT:** 6-2. **WT:** 235.
Drafted: Chipola (FL) JC, 2022 (1st round). **Signed by:** Sean Buckley.
TRACK RECORD: Collier's season started inauspiciously when he injured his left thumb in spring training and required surgery. He didn't get back to Double-A Chattanooga until mid-June. He struggled to shake off rust and his power never made it fully back, though he batted .337/.425/.452 in his final 27 games. Collier hit four home runs in 2025 after hitting 20 in 2024. He went to the Arizona Fall League to make up for some of the lost time. He is the son of former MLB infielder Lou Collier.
SCOUTING REPORT: Even in his fourth pro season, Collier showed that he has a massive gulf between what he is and what he could be. At his best, Collier can be a game-changing hitter, but he has long stretches where he seems lost at the plate. When he keeps his lower half in sync, he can drive 110 mph home runs that turn outfielders into onlookers. When he's struggling, his swing becomes way too rotational, leaving his legs disconnected. He gets out front, relying entirely on his hands to do all the work in his swing. That produces stretches of rolled-over ground balls. He's generally been ineffective against lefthanders, with a sub-.600 OPS in 2024 and 2025. Defensively, Collier was in better shape post-injury, which helped his flexibility, but he remains a below-average fielder at third base with questionable hands. He can make easy plays look difficult. Collier played more first base than third in 2025, a trend that is likely to continue. He has an above-average arm.
THE FUTURE: The 2025 season was somewhat of a lost one for Collier, and Sal Stewart's big step forward means that Collier's path to Cincinnati has gotten more complicated. To make his case for the Reds' first base job, Collier has to become a more consistent hitter.

Year	Age	Club (League)	Level	AVG	G	AB	R	H	2B	3B	HR	RBI	BB	SO	SB	OBP	SLG
2025	20	ACL Reds	Rk	.394	10	33	3	13	3	1	1	6	9	8	1	.524	.636
2025	20	Dayton (MWL)	A+	.293	11	41	6	12	2	0	1	4	5	10	0	.370	.415
2025	20	Chattanooga (SL)	AA	.263	74	259	39	68	16	0	2	38	45	86	0	.377	.347
		Minor League Totals		.259	334	1177	167	305	64	4	32	194	189	343	8	.367	.402

9 HECTOR RODRIGUEZ, OF

HIT: 55. **POW:** 45. **RUN:** 55. **FLD:** 45. **ARM:** 50. **BA Grade:** 45. **Risk:** Mild. **Adj:** 40.

Born: March 11, 2004. **B-T:** L-R. **HT:** 5-10. **WT:** 200.
Signed: Dominican Republic, 2021.
Signed by: Moises De La Mota/Oliver Dominguez (Mets).
TRACK RECORD: A signee of the Mets out of the Dominican Republic in 2021, Rodriguez was quickly traded to the Reds in July 2022 in the trade that sent Tyler Naquin and Phillip Diehl to the Mets. Rodriguez began his career as a speedy second baseman, but he quickly slowed down while also getting stronger. He now is a full-time corner outfielder and has been one of the Reds' most consistent minor league hitters. He has never hit below .280 in a pro season.
SCOUTING REPORT: Rodriguez has long been one of the most swing-happy hitters in the minors, but he's also always had the barrel control and hand-eye coordination to avoid the worst drawbacks of his hyper-aggressive approach. It's hard to beat Rodriguez in the strike zone, and he handles fastballs, breaking balls and changeups alike. His aggressiveness means he posts modest on-base percentages. Rodriguez shows less power, but otherwise stands in well against lefthanders. He has fringe-average power, largely to his pull side, but considering he was only 21, there could be more power as he continues to mature. In the outfield, Rodriguez is a fringe-average defender at best. He can snare a sinking liner from time to time, but is extremely cautious when going back to the wall. His average arm is accurate and he hits the cutoff man. His above-average speed is better used on the basepaths, though he's not an aggressive basestealer.
THE FUTURE: Rodriguez's combination of contact skills and fringe-average power puts him on the border between being a potential regular and a possible platoon outfielder. His defensive limitations hurt him, but as a lefthanded hitter who makes plenty of contact, he could make it to Cincinnati in 2026. The Reds added him to the 40-man roster this offseason to protect him from the Rule 5 draft.

Year	Age	Club (League)	Level	AVG	G	AB	R	H	2B	3B	HR	RBI	BB	SO	SB	OBP	SLG
2025	21	Chattanooga (SL)	AA	.298	82	312	58	93	15	3	12	45	28	48	6	.357	.481
2025	21	Louisville (IL)	AAA	.260	53	215	34	56	8	1	7	20	12	38	9	.304	.405
		Minor League Totals		.289	466	1801	299	521	92	31	53	228	119	289	67	.337	.463

CINCINNATI REDS

10 STHARLIN TORRES, RHP
FB: 55. **CB:** 45. **SL:** 50. **CH:** 55. **CTL:** 60. **BA Grade:** 55. **Risk:** High. **Adj:** 40.

Born: June 19, 2006. **B-T:** R-R. **HT:** 6-0. **WT:** 182.
Signed: Dominican Republic, 2024.
Signed by: Jenfry Del Rosario/Jose Diaz/Enmanuel Cartagena.
TRACK RECORD: As a kid growing up in the Dominican Republic, Torres lived to play baseball and imagined himself as a big league shortstop. By the time he was a teenager, he had realized that his future was on the mound. Signed by the Reds in January 2024, Torres has toyed with hitters in his first two pro seasons. He threw four innings of a combined seven-inning no-hitter in the Dominican Summer League in 2024. He held hitters to sub-.550 OPS in each of his first two pro seasons, and his 4.9% walk rate in 2025 was one of the best in the Arizona Complex League.
SCOUTING REPORT: Torres' combination of present stuff and advanced control and command jumped out, especially in the context of the ACL, where few pitchers fill the zone. Torres sits at 93-94 mph but should get to 95-97 on a consistent basis in a few years. His sinker generates weak contact because of his ability to dot the zone with it, and his four-seam fastball gets swings and misses up in the zone thanks to above-average life to go with a flat plane. He's also shown advanced aptitude for his age. Torres quickly refined and made his slider harder to go with a bigger, slower curveball, and he's showing feel for an above-average changeup with late fade. He shows the ability to manipulate his change, spotting it in the zone for strikes and then burying it out of the zone to induce chases.
THE FUTURE: There are not many teenagers with Torres' advanced ability to spot multiple pitches all around the strike zone. He has the savvy and stuff to be one of the best pitchers in the Low-A Florida State League in 2026, and there is a chance that he could force a promotion to Dayton if he dominates. He projects as a potential midrotation starter, though he will only be 20 in 2026 and has plenty of development ahead.

Year	Age	Club (League)	Level	W	L	ERA	G	GS	IP	H	HR	BB	SO	BB%	SO%	WHIP	AVG
2025	19	ACL Reds	Rk	0	1	1.88	10	6	38	26	2	7	44	4.9	30.6	0.86	.193
		Minor League Totals		2	2	1.81	24	16	95	61	2	20	95	5.7	27.1	0.86	.189

11 AARON WATSON, RHP
FB: 55. **SL:** 55. **CB:** 45. **CH:** 50. **CTL:** 50. **BA Grade:** 55. **Risk:** High. **Adj:** 40.

Born: January 5, 2007. **B-T:** R-R. **HT:** 6-5. **WT:** 205. **Drafted:** HS—Jacksonville, FL, 2025 (2nd round).
Signed by: Andrew Amaro.
TRACK RECORD: Pro teams love to see how amateur players handle pressure in the lead-up to the draft. Watson consistently aced those tests. The Florida signee struck out 10 in a seven-inning complete game at the National High School Invitational. He then threw a perfect game in the Florida regional finals, and then followed it with a one-hit shutout in the state semifinals to get his team to the state finals. The Reds picked him 51st overall, signing him for $2,747,500.
SCOUTING REPORT: Teams looking for a flame-thrower to beat hitters at the top of the zone with a four-seamer weren't going to be enamored by Watson. He's best working down with a hard (93-95 mph) power sinker that already touches 97 and will likely add velocity as he further fills out. He also has shown feel for two distinct breaking balls. His mid-80s above-average slider misses bats and is a pitch he can rely on in almost every outing. His feel for his bigger, slower 77-81 mph curve isn't as consistent, but when it's on it's an effective pitch as well. Like many teenage pitchers, his hard mid-80s changeup needs more development. Watson's delivery is clean and he already has a pro starter's frame with the shoulders and lower half to add another 20-30 pounds. He projects to have average or better control with no significant delivery flaws that need to be cleaned up.
THE FUTURE: Like many high school pitching prospects, Watson is embarking on what will likely be a lengthy adjustment to pro ball. He has the athleticism, body control and sinker-slider pairing to become a durable mid-rotation starter if everything comes together as the Reds and Watson hope.

Year	Age	Club (League)	Level	W	L	ERA	G	GS	IP	H	HR	BB	SO	BB%	SO%	WHIP	AVG
2025	18	Did not play															

CINCINNATI REDS

12 JULIAN AGUIAR, RHP
FB: 55. **SL:** 55. **CB:** 40. **CH:** 45. **CTL:** 60. **BA Grade:** 50. **Risk:** High. **Adj:** 35.

Born: June 4, 2001. **B-T:** L-R. **HT:** 6-0. **WT:** 196. **Drafted:** Cypress (CA) JC, 2021 (12th round). **Signed by:** Mike Misuraca.
TRACK RECORD: Aguiar was one of the best pitchers in junior college in 2020-21, but the Reds thought there was more to come. He rewarded that faith by quickly adding velocity as a pro. He made it to the majors in 2024 for seven starts with the Reds, but his elbow blew out and he had Tommy John surgery in October 2024, which sidelined him for all of 2025. Aguiar has made the most of his time off, bulking up physically with plenty of weight room work.
SCOUTING REPORT: Before his injury, Aguiar was a lower-slot sinker/slider righthander with enough confidence in his changeup to make it a viable third pitch as well. His above-average fastball sits 94-95 mph, but he has touched 97-98 at times. He does mix in a four-seamer as well, but his sinker is his more effective fastball. His 80-81 mph above-average slider is a slower and bigger breaking pitch than most modern sliders. It's not an overpowering pitch, but he has excellent command of it, sweeping it out of the zone for chases, but also dotting the edges in the zone. His low-80s changeup is a pitch he struggles to locate, but it does keep lefties honest, and he'll drop in a bigger and slightly slower high-70s, below-average curveball as a surprise pitch.
THE FUTURE: Aguiar was throwing off the mound before the end of the 2025 season. He should be at full speed for spring training. The Reds do not have an opening in their rotation if everyone is healthy, so Aguiar should get to shake off the rust in Triple-A Louisville. As a talented pitcher already on the 40-man roster, he should be up at some point in 2026 as a starter or reliever if the need arises.

Year	Age	Club (League)	Level	W	L	ERA	G	GS	IP	H	HR	BB	SO	BB%	SO%	WHIP	AVG
2025	24	Did not play—Injured															
		Minor League Totals		23	17	3.38	77	64	346	312	35	93	360	6.4	24.9	1.17	.238
		Major League Totals		2	1	6.25	7	7	32	30	8	12	19	8.6	13.6	1.33	.244

13 JOSE FRANCO, RHP
FB: 55. **SL:** 50. **CH:** 45. **CTL:** 50. **BA Grade:** 45. **Risk:** Mild. **Adj:** 40.

Born: November 25, 2000. **B-T:** R-R. **HT:** 6-2. **WT:** 257. **Signed:** Venezuela, 2018. **Signed by:** Richard Castro/Bob Engle.
TRACK RECORD: It's been a long climb for Franco, who signed out of Venezuela in October 2018. After impressing in the Dominican Summer League in 2019, Franco struggled in his first exposure to full-season ball in 2021 and blew out his elbow in 2022. He missed all of 2023 recovering from Tommy John surgery and returned showing improved control but modest stuff in 2024. His stuff took a step forward in 2025 as he dominated at Double-A Chattanooga and impressed after a promotion to Triple-A.
SCOUTING REPORT: As he's added weight and put his elbow surgery behind him, Franco has gone from being a crafty 91-94 mph righthander to a clever righty who can touch 97 mph regularly and sits 95-96. That added velocity has helped his mid-80s slider as well. He fills the zone with it when he's behind or even in counts, but with two strikes, he consistently hits his target glove side and down just out of the zone. He uses his fringe-average high-80s changeup almost exclusively against lefties. Franco still doesn't blow hitters away, but he battles hitters with MLB average stuff.
THE FUTURE: Franco has largely been used as a starter, but he could make the Reds' 2026 roster as a swingman in the Nick Martinez role, providing spot starts and multi-inning relief appearances.

Year	Age	Club (League)	Level	W	L	ERA	G	GS	IP	H	HR	BB	SO	BB%	SO%	WHIP	AVG
2025	24	Chattanooga (SL)	AA	7	2	2.76	14	12	59	42	4	26	66	10.5	26.7	1.16	.194
2025	24	Louisville (IL)	AAA	3	2	3.51	17	14	51	43	10	28	52	12.7	23.5	1.38	.228
		Minor League Totals		18	19	3.88	106	86	380	323	47	175	448	10.8	27.7	1.31	.228

14 ADOLFO SANCHEZ, OF
HIT: 50. **POW:** 50. **RUN:** 50. **FLD:** 50. **ARM:** 55. **BA Grade:** 50. **Risk:** High. **Adj:** 35.

Born: September 16, 2006. **B-T:** L-L. **HT:** 6-1. **WT:** 185. **Signed:** Dominican Republic, 2024.
Signed by: Reds international scouting department.
TRACK RECORD: The Reds signed Sanchez for $2.7 million in January 2024, but in his first taste of pro ball, he was overmatched by Dominican Summer League pitchers. Sanchez struck out 33.8% of the time in 2024, but in a return to the DSL, he showed massive improvements, hitting .339/.474/.505 with a 13.6% strikeout rate. A minor knee injury ended his season early.
SCOUTING REPORT: Pro ball quickly taught Sanchez that some of his pre-swing movements had to be cleaned up. In his first season, he laid his bat on his shoulder to start his setup, and then brought his hands down with an extended waggle. He cleaned that up for 2025, beginning with a much simpler setup and

more conventional load with quieter hands. That allowed him to be more direct and quicker to the ball. The results were dramatic. While he hasn't shown in-game power, he has well above-average exit velocities, but now he marries that with above-average contact skills as well. Sanchez now looks much more like the polished hitter the Reds scouted as an amateur. Defensively, he splits his time between center and right. His above-average arm plays in either spot.

THE FUTURE: It used to be that repeating the Dominican Summer League was a near kiss of death for a hitter, but with strict roster limits and no short-season leagues, it's becoming more common for hitters to figure out issues before coming to the States. Sanchez will make his U.S. debut in 2026. He projects as a well-rounded, productive outfielder.

Year	Age	Club (League)	Level	AVG	G	AB	R	H	2B	3B	HR	RBI	BB	SO	SB	OBP	SLG
2025	18	DSL Reds	Rk	.339	36	121	36	41	8	3	2	27	24	21	10	.474	.504
		Minor League Totals		.273	81	260	59	71	14	6	4	45	54	81	21	.411	.419

15 SHENG-EN LIN, RHP

FB: 50. **CB:** 55. **CH:** 50. **SW:** 45. **CTL:** 55. **BA Grade:** 50. **Risk:** High. **Adj:** 35.

Born: September 1, 2005. **B-T:** L-R. **HT:** 6-0. **WT:** 202. **Signed:** Taiwan, 2023. **Signed by:** Jamey Storvick/Trey Hendricks.

TRACK RECORD: The Reds have tried to develop Lin as both a position player and a pitcher after signing him out of Taiwan in 2022 for $1.2 million. He was a productive hitter in 2024 as a shortstop/third baseman in the Arizona Complex League before pitching in unofficial bridge and instructional league games. In 2025, Lin began focusing almost entirely on pitching with the exception of some DH appearances. He had two four-inning hitless outings in a five-start stint to end the year in the Low-A Florida State League.

SCOUTING REPORT: Lin's development path shows the challenges of trying to develop a true two-way player. He's touched 97-98 mph in the past, but by the end of the 2025 season, he was topping out at 92-93 in the FSL. At the upper ends of his velocity range, Lin has flashed an above-average fastball with excellent movement characteristics, but it's a fringe-average pitch if he's sitting 92-93. His high-70s knuckle curve is an above-average pitch with depth, and he shows feel for an average changeup. His sweeper is in the same velocity range as his knuckle curve which gives him a useful additional pitch that runs away from righthanded hitters. Lin's delivery makes it hard for hitters to pick up the ball, and he shows plenty of savvy for someone who hasn't been focused purely on pitching.

THE FUTURE: Lin's results in 2025 showed that he already has a solid understanding of how to pitch, but his development is dependent on getting back to the mid 90s and better velocity he's shown in the past. There's every reason to think that he can, as he's just starting to focus on pitching. He should pair with Stharlin Torres in a loaded rotation in the FSL.

Year	Age	Club (League)	Level	W	L	ERA	G	GS	IP	H	HR	BB	SO	BB%	SO%	WHIP	AVG
2025		ACL Reds	Rk	0	1	2.67	10	7	30	19	3	10	40	8.1	32.5	0.96	.174
2025		Daytona (FSL)	A	0	1	3.78	5	5	17	10	1	5	21	7.2	30.4	0.90	.159
		Minor League Totals		0	2	3.06	15	12	47	29	4	15	61	7.8	31.8	0.94	.169

16 LEO BALCAZAR, 2B/SS

HIT: 45. **POW:** 40. **RUN:** 55. **FLD:** 50. **ARM:** 50. **BA Grade:** 45. **Risk:** Average. **Adj:** 35.

Born: June 17, 2004. **B-T:** R-R. **Ht.:** 5-11. **Wt.:** 211. **Signed:** Venezuela, 2021.
Signed by: Aguido Gonzalez/Ricardo Quintero/Richard Castro.

TRACK RECORD: It's been a journey for Balcazar. He looked to be developing into a top prospect in 2023 with Low-A Daytona, but tore his ACL. It took him a year to return, and it's taken him even longer to get back to being an approximation of the live-bodied athlete he was pre-injury. In 2025, he started showing more glimpses of that athleticism as he thinned out his lower half. After splitting time between second base and shortstop during the regular season, he played plenty of third base during the Arizona Fall League.

SCOUTING REPORT: Balcazar doesn't have any overwhelming tools, but he has above-average barrel control with a short stroke. He will collapse his back side too often and shows some vulnerabilities against sliders. He's a fringe-average hitter with below-average power, but he will produce plenty of doubles. Defensively, he's a fringe-average defender at second base and potentially average at third base. He's a below-average shortstop who is unlikely to play the position in the majors. He has an average arm. He still has above-average speed, but he doesn't steal bases.

THE FUTURE: Balcazar is not as twitchy as he used to be, but he has demonstrated that he could be a valuable multi-position backup who can handle three infield spots. The Reds added him to the 40-man roster during the offseason. His versatility is likely his path to a big league role, most likely in 2027.

CINCINNATI REDS

Year	Age	Club (League)	Level	AVG	G	AB	R	H	2B	3B	HR	RBI	BB	SO	SB	OBP	SLG
2025	21	Dayton (MWL)	A+	.262	75	305	40	80	17	1	9	37	29	51	4	.333	.413
2025	21	Chattanooga (SL)	AA	.263	51	186	29	49	3	0	3	20	23	24	4	.349	.328
		Minor League Totals		.273	317	1204	164	329	49	10	29	156	110	268	40	.341	.403

17 MASON NEVILLE, OF

HIT: 45. **POW:** 55. **RUN:** 55. **FLD:** 50. **ARM:** 55. **BA Grade:** 50. **Risk:** High. **Adj:** 35.

Born: January 13, 2004. **B-T:** L-L. **HT:** 6-3. **WT:** 210. **Drafted:** Oregon, 2025 (4th round). **Signed by:** Alec Benavides.
TRACK RECORD: It took them an extra three years, but the Reds finally landed Neville. Cincinnati really liked him in high school and selected him as an 18th-round pick in 2022, even though the Reds knew he was highly unlikely to sign. Neville went to Arkansas, struggled in his lone year there and then blossomed at Oregon, where he hit .290/.429/.724 with a Division I-best 26 home runs as a junior.
SCOUTING REPORT: Neville has big power and above-average speed, but he has struggled to make contact. He struck out 33.5% of the time as a sophomore, and while he cut his strikeout rate in his draft year, he never hit .300 in a college season. His pro debut raised further contact concerns as he struck out 34.4% of the time at Low-A Dayton. Neville has a bat wrap that will need to be cleaned up, but he does generate excellent power and leverage. Neville will start out as a center fielder, but he likely will end up as an above-average defender in a corner.
THE FUTURE: Neville's power and above-average speed make him an intriguing outfielder, although he has plenty of work in the batting cage ahead of him to try to make his swing a little more direct.

Year	Age	Club (League)	Level	AVG	G	AB	R	H	2B	3B	HR	RBI	BB	SO	SB	OBP	SLG
2025	21	Daytona (FSL)	A	.247	23	77	8	19	8	2	1	9	9	31	2	.333	.442
		Minor League Totals		.247	23	77	8	19	8	2	1	9	9	31	2	.333	.442

18 TYLER CALLIHAN, 2B/OF

HIT: 45. **POW:** 50. **RUN:** 50. **FLD:** 45. **ARM:** 50. **BA Grade:** 45. **Risk:** Average. **Adj:** 35

Born: June 22, 2000. **B-T:** L-R. **HT:** 6-0. **WT:** 208. **Drafted:** HS—Jacksonville, FL, 2019 (3rd round).
Signed by: Sean Buckley.
TRACK RECORD: Callihan made his long-awaited MLB debut on April 30, 2025, playing in both halves of a doubleheader. Two games later, his season was over, as he suffered a nasty broken forearm caused when he hit the outfield wall at full speed while attempting a catch in left field. Callihan described his injury to The Athletic as sounding like "two bats snapping in half." Those were his radius and ulna, both of which had to be surgically repaired with plates and screws. There was a lone bright spot in his stomach-churning injury: it meant he was able to spend much of June with his wife as they welcomed their first-born.
SCOUTING REPORT: The forearm injury was just Callihan's latest calamity. He needed Tommy John surgery in 2021. In spring training in 2022, he was involved in a car accident that injured his thumb. He then broke a finger bunting in 2024. He's hit whenever he's healthy, but he's played 100 games in a season only once in his career. Callihan projects as a multi-position lefthanded hitting backup. He has average power, with the barrel control that allows him to get to it without selling out. He's a fringe-average defender at second base and in left field.
THE FUTURE: Callihan should be able to make a full recovery from what was a gruesome injury, but that won't be fully apparent until spring training. His versatility is reminiscent of Spencer Steer, as a hit-first multi-position infielder/outfielder.

Year	Age	Club (League)	Level	AVG	G	AB	R	H	2B	3B	HR	RBI	BB	SO	SB	OBP	SLG
2025	25	Louisville (IL)	AAA	.303	24	89	19	27	4	2	4	12	16	29	6	.410	.528
2025	25	Cincinnati (NL)	MLB	.167	4	6	0	1	0	0	0	1	0	1	0	.167	.167
		Minor League Totals		.262	339	1251	165	328	71	12	31	140	134	328	77	.338	.412
		Major League Totals		.167	4	6	0	1	0	0	0	1	0	1	0	.167	.167

19 ZACH MAXWELL, RHP

FB: 70. **SL:** 60. **CT:** 55. **CTL:** 30. **BA Grade:** 45. **Risk:** Average. **Adj:** 35.

Born: January 26, 2001. **B-T:** R-R. **HT:** 6-6. **WT:** 293. **Drafted:** Georgia Tech, 2022 (6th round). **Signed by:** Jerel Johnson.
TRACK RECORD: Everything with Maxwell is big. His stuff is big—he can throw 102 mph. His walk rate has been even bigger—he had more walks than innings in three years at Georgia Tech. And his nickname is Big Sugar for a reason. Maxwell's official weight at MLB is listed at 275 pounds. That undersells him, as the Reds' media guide lists him at 293 pounds, which made him one of the heaviest players in MLB history when he made his MLB debut with 1.1 scoreless innings against the Cardinals on Aug. 23, 2025.

CINCINNATI REDS

SCOUTING REPORT: There's nothing subtle about Maxwell's approach. He rears back and tries to blow hitters away with a 98-102 mph, plus-plus fastball and an 87-90 mph plus slider. He has added a mid-90s above-average cutter that is a useful bridge pitch. Before hitters could get a pretty easy read as his fastball had carry and arm-side run while his slider has above-average sweep that makes it hard for Maxwell to throw it for strikes. That made the slider an easy take decision and less effective pitch. The cutter gives hitters something that splits the difference and makes his slider a tougher pitch to recognize and take. Maxwell has great stuff, but he doesn't throw any pitch for strikes consistently enough. The cutter did help, as he throws it for strikes 58% of the time compared to his 48% strike rate with his slider. He's a catcher's nightmare, as many of his misses are by several feet.
THE FUTURE: Maxwell's arm is exceptional, but he needs to improve to at least below-average control to be trustworthy in higher-leverage situations. As a pitcher with overwhelming stuff and two options remaining, he should spend at least part of 2026 in Cincinnati.

Year	Age	Club (League)	Level	W	L	ERA	G	GS	IP	H	HR	BB	SO	BB%	SO%	WHIP	AVG
2025	24	Louisville (IL)	AAA	1	3	4.17	51	0	50	42	6	32	59	14.5	26.8	1.49	.225
2025	24	Cincinnati (NL)	MLB	0	0	4.50	8	0	10	10	3	4	13	9.3	30.2	1.40	.256
		Minor League Totals		14	9	3.86	143	0	172	135	10	116	250	15.2	32.8	1.46	.213
		Major League Totals		0	0	4.50	8	0	10	10	3	4	13	9.3	30.2	1.40	.256

20 MASON MORRIS, RHP
FB: 55. **SL:** 55. **CT:** 55. **CTL:** 50. **BA Grade:** 50. **Risk:** High. **Adj:** 35.

Born: August 21, 2003. **B-T:** R-R. **HT:** 6-4. **WT:** 225. **Drafted:** Ole Miss, 2025 (3rd round). **Signed by:** JR Reynolds.
TRACK RECORD: Morris emerged as Ole Miss's fireman out of the bullpen in 2025 after two middling seasons in the Rebels' bullpen. While he was a reliever, he wasn't a closer—he averaged nearly three innings an outing. He generally worked one lengthy relief outing per weekend, including an eight-strikeout, five scoreless inning relief outing against Tennessee. The Reds watched him get better and better as the season progressed, and made him one of the few college relievers in recent years to be taken with a top-100 pick.
SCOUTING REPORT: Morris is now a full-time pitcher, but there's a little more tread on his tires than there is for most power pitchers because he arrived in college as a first baseman/third baseman who also pitched. At his best, he shows feel for two swing-and-miss secondaries to go with a powerful 96-98 mph above-average fastball, a mid-90s cutter and a high-80s slider. His fastball sets the other two pitches up, because it is a bit true. He's used a fringy changeup in the past. Morris had struggled to throw strikes in the past, but showed average control in 2025.
THE FUTURE: The Reds expect to see if Morris can transition to a starting role in pro ball. It shouldn't be a dramatic adjustment, as he was already throwing up to 75 pitches in relief outings. With his power stuff and recent improvements, he could emerge as a third-round steal.

Year	Age	Club (League)	Level	W	L	ERA	G	GS	IP	H	HR	BB	SO	BB%	SO%	WHIP	AVG
2025	21	Daytona (FSL)	A	0	0	9.00	2	2	4	3	1	1	7	6.3	43.8	1.00	.200
		Minor League Totals		0	0	9.00	2	2	4	3	1	1	7	6.3	43.8	1.00	.200

21 JIRVIN MORILLO, C
HIT: 45. **POW:** 50. **RUN:** 40. **FLD:** 45. **ARM:** 55. **BA Grade:** 50. **Risk:** High. **Adj:** 35.

Born: Jan. 10, 2007. **B-T:** B-R. **HT:** 5-11. **WT:** 177. **Signed:** Venezuela, 2024. **Signed by:** Herman Albornoz.
TRACK RECORD: Morillo was one of the second-tier targets of the Reds in a deep 2024 international class. As an amateur, Morillo impressed as a switch-hitting catcher with power potential. The Reds have kept him in the Dominican Summer League for two seasons, and he's shown a blend of power and plate discipline.
SCOUTING REPORT: As a hitter, Morillo was ready to move to the States a year ago. He hasn't shown a ton of in-game power yet, but he stings the ball and should eventually have average power. And he's not a free-swinging hacker, as he shows he knows how to work counts and get pitches to drive. Defensively, Morillo needed a lot more work, which is why he spent two years in the DSL. He is going to have to make significant improvements to stay behind the plate. He improved his footwork and blocking, but they will need to keep progressing. He's shown the desire and willingness to put in the effort. Morillo worked with Corky Miller during instructional league to add polish to his receiving, and the Reds are committed to continuing to develop him as a catcher. He does have an above-average arm, and he threw out 37% of basestealers in the DSL in 2025.
THE FUTURE: Much like Adolfo Sanchez, the Reds have taken it slow with Morillo, giving him two years in the Dominican Summer League before bringing him to the U.S. for the first time during instructs. He is ready for the Arizona Complex League.

CINCINNATI REDS

Year	Age	Club (League)	Level	AVG	G	AB	R	H	2B	3B	HR	RBI	BB	SO	SB	OBP	SLG
2025	18	DSL Reds	Rk	.259	33	116	20	30	8	0	4	27	23	25	6	.381	.431
		Minor League Totals		.257	72	230	51	59	22	1	6	50	63	46	9	.414	.439

22 LIBERTS APONTE, SS

HIT: 40. **POW:** 35. **RUN:** 60. **FLD:** 60. **ARM:** 50. **BA Grade:** 45. **Risk:** High. **Adj:** 30.

Born: November 8, 2007. **B-T:** R-R. **HT:** 6-0. **WT:** 160. **Signed:** Venezuela, 2025. **Signed by:** Victor Serrano/Hernan Albornoz.
TRACK RECORD: Aponte was viewed as one of the best defensive shortstops in the 2025 international market and the Reds' top target. He signed for $1.9 million. In his pro debut, he also showed he's not lost at the plate, demonstrating better than expected bat control thanks to his excellent hand-eye coordination. His seven home runs outpaced the rest of his DSL Rojos team combined.
SCOUTING REPORT: Aponte has buttery smooth hands and fluid, athletic actions. He's what scouts look for defensively, as the game seems to slow down for him when he's making plays at shortstop. He made plenty of errors, but that's to be expected for a rangy shortstop in the DSL. He's a future plus defender with an average arm. Offensively, there's much more work to be done. While Aponte showed solid plate awareness and contact skills in the DSL, his swing has plenty of length, starting with a noisy setup where he cocks the bat over his shoulder. His power in the DSL was surprising as he doesn't hit the ball hard yet, but he did maximize the modest power he has.
THE FUTURE: Aponte had an excellent debut, and his offensive improvements are encouraging, but he has much work left to do at the plate.

Year	Age	Club (League)	Level	AVG	G	AB	R	H	2B	3B	HR	RBI	BB	SO	SB	OBP	SLG
2025	17	DSL Rojos	Rk	.247	45	154	34	38	6	3	7	36	29	35	9	.368	.461
		Minor League Totals		.247	45	154	34	38	6	3	7	36	29	35	9	.368	.461

23 ELI PITTS, OF

HIT: 45. **POW:** 50. **RUN:** 70. **FLD:** 55. **ARM:** 50. **BA Grade:** 50. **Risk:** Extreme. **Adj:** 30

Born: November 22, 2006. **B-T:** R-R. **HT:** 6-1. **WT:** 185. **Drafted:** HS—Atlanta, GA, 2025 (5th round). **Signed by:** Jerel Johnson.
TRACK RECORD: Pitts was long viewed as a player to watch in the 2025 class—he was receiving scholarship offers before he entered high school. But in his draft year, he battled a hamstring injury that largely kept him from being at his best. The South Florida signee signed with the Reds for $572,500.
SCOUTING REPORT: Pitts may not have gotten many chances to show his plus-plus speed in the lead-up to the draft, but it's a key part of his game as it makes him a potentially above-average defender in center and a threat on the basepaths. But Pitts is not just a speedster. His swing is straightforward, with a short stroke that still generates plenty of bat speed and power potential. In some ways, his hamstring injury allowed the Reds to bear down on the other aspects of his game, as he has power and hitting ability in addition to his speed.
THE FUTURE: The Reds often take it slow with high school draftees, and it wouldn't be a surprise to see Pitts head to the Arizona Complex League to make his debut. He has a much higher ceiling than most fifth round picks as a power-speed center fielder.

Year	Age	Club (League)	Level	AVG	G	AB	R	H	2B	3B	HR	RBI	BB	SO	SB	OBP	SLG
2025	18	Did not play															

24 LUKE HOLMAN, RHP

FB: 50. **SL:** 55. **CB:** 45. **CH:** 45. **CTL:** 50. **BA Grade:** 50. **Risk:** Extreme. **Adj:** 30.

Born: January 6, 2003. **B-T:** R-R. **HT:** 6-4. **WT:** 201. **Drafted:** LSU, 2024 (2nd round supp.). **Signed by:** Mike Partida.
TRACK RECORD: The Reds loved drafting productive SEC pitchers. So far the SEC has not loved the Reds back. The Reds' drafted Ty Floyd (LSU) and Hunter Hollan (Arkansas) with top-100 picks in 2023, and both have barely pitched and are expected to miss much of 2026 rehabbing injuries. Holman dominated in LSU's rotation in 2024. The Reds picked him with a supplemental second round pick. He made two starts in 2025 before going down with an elbow injury. He had Tommy John surgery and is expected to be sidelined until mid to late 2026.
SCOUTING REPORT: Holman was one of the better pitchers in the SEC in 2024 despite relatively modest stuff. He sat 91-93 mph in college, and was a tick below that in his brief pro debut. But he gets results because of the above-average riding life of his average fastball. He has mixed in an above-average slider and fringe-average changeup and curveball. He showed average control pre-injury.
THE FUTURE: Holman has to get healthy, but when he does, he then needs to also show he can sharpen

some aspect of his repertoire. While no one doubts his ability to pitch, he will need to develop some sort of true weapon to continue to have success in the strike zone against better pro hitters. Holman is expected to be ready to pitch in games in the second half of the 2026 season.

Year	Age	Club (League)	Level	W	L	ERA	G	GS	IP	H	HR	BB	SO	BB%	SO%	WHIP	AVG
2025	22	Daytona (FSL)	A	0	0	1.00	2	2	9	2	0	4	10	12.1	30.3	0.67	.071
		Minor League Totals		0	0	1.00	2	2	9	2	0	4	10	12.1	30.3	0.67	.071

25 ARNALDO LANTIGUA, OF

HIT: 30. **POW:** 60. **RUN:** 45. **FLD:** 45. **ARM:** 55. **BA Grade:** 50. **Risk:** Extreme. **Adj:** 30.

Born: December 19, 2005. **B-T:** R-R. **HT:** 6-2. **WT:** 200. **Signed:** Dominican Republic, 2023. **Signed by:** Moises Alou Jr.
TRACK RECORD: The Reds played a very small part in the pursuit of Roki Sasaki. While they were never a contender to sign Sasaki, they did send $1.5 million in international bonus pool allotment to the Dodgers in exchange for Lantigua, who was a part of the Dodgers' 2023 international class. Lantigua led the Arizona Complex League with 10 home runs and 25 extra-base hits in his Reds' debut, and then went on to hit two more in 32 games with Low-A Daytona.
SCOUTING REPORT: Lantigua has excellent power, now the question is whether he will hit enough to get to that power. With broad shoulders and muscular legs, he is an embodiment of what teams look for physically in a corner outfielder. Lantigua starts his swing with a significant waggle and sets his hands with a significant load. It makes him vulnerable to pitchers who can mess with his timing, but when he gets timed up and uses his legs in his swing, he can make a baseball disappear. He hits too many weak ground balls, which explains a modest 88 mph average exit velocity, but his 90th percentile EV (104) is well above-average for 19-year-olds. As a hitter, Lantigua's development will depend on pitch recognition and timing. He makes plenty of weak contact when he's fooled, which keeps him from striking out, but could be improved with better pitch selection. He's a fringe-average runner who stays anchored to first base when he reaches. Defensively, he's a left/right fielder with fringe-average defense and an above-average arm.
THE FUTURE: Lantigua has some of the best power potential in the Reds' system, but he's an over-aggressive hitter who will need to adapt as he faces craftier pitchers in full-season ball.

Year	Age	Club (League)	Level	AVG	G	AB	R	H	2B	3B	HR	RBI	BB	SO	SB	OBP	SLG
2025	19	ACL Reds	Rk	.268	49	183	34	49	14	1	10	40	18	44	1	.345	.519
2025	19	Daytona (FSL)	A	.261	32	119	16	31	12	2	2	16	9	34	1	.318	.445
		Minor League Totals		.267	159	554	110	148	37	4	30	122	78	138	12	.365	.511

26 CARLOS SANCHEZ, 3B/OF

HIT: 40. **POW:** 45. **RUN:** 55. **FLD:** 55. **ARM:** 60. **BA Grade:** 40. **Risk:** Average. **Adj:** 30.

Born: January 12, 2005. **B-T:** L-R. **HT:** 6-2. **WT:** 205. **Signed:** Dominican Republic, 2022.
Signed by: Jose Diaz/Enmanuel Cartagena.
TRACK RECORD: When the Reds signed Sanchez in 2022, he was not one of the most prominent signings in an international class that included Ricky Cabrera. But to Sanchez's credit, he's turned himself into a prospect worth paying attention to with a steady, heady approach at the plate and versatility in the field. Sanchez didn't hit in 2024, but he was one of the Florida State League's best hitters in the first half of the season in 2025 and he held his own after a promotion to High-A Dayton.
SCOUTING REPORT: Sanchez has developed into a versatile multi-position infielder/outfielder. He's not going to be an MLB starting shortstop, but he's playable for a day out there, and he's above-average at third. His plus arm helped him make difficult plays on balls to his right. He also took to center field quickly, showing a feel for routes and reads. Offensively, he knows his limitations. He has a short swing geared for gappers to left and left center field. He is a very productive hitter against righthanders (.295/.391/.453) but helpless against lefties (.209/.333/.256).
THE FUTURE: Sanchez is another candidate to be a multi-position backup for the Reds. His ability to hit righthanders as well as he does gives him a solid path to playing time, especially now that he's shown he can also play in the outfield.

Year	Age	Club (League)	Level	AVG	G	AB	R	H	2B	3B	HR	RBI	BB	SO	SB	OBP	SLG
2025	20	Daytona (FSL)	A	.308	60	214	36	66	10	4	4	33	45	67	13	.429	.449
2025	20	Dayton (MWL)	A+	.244	56	201	26	49	10	2	4	29	22	54	7	.320	.373
		Minor League Totals		.270	280	943	182	255	45	10	12	144	209	298	53	.405	.378

CINCINNATI REDS

27 EDGAR COLON, RHP
FB: 55. **SL:** 55. **CH:** 45. **CTL:** 30. **BA Grade:** 50. **Risk:** Extreme. **Adj:** 30.

Born: March 13, 2006. **B-T:** R-R. **HT:** 6-3. **WT:** 180. **Drafted:** HS—Miami, FL, 2024 (11th round). **Signed by:** Nick Rodriguez.
TRACK RECORD: A Puerto Rican native who came to Miami to pitch in high school, Colon was a $247,500 signing as an 11th-round pick in 2024. He made his pro debut in 2025. Statistically, he was quite ineffective, struggling with control issues. But his stuff impressed some scouts and offered encouraging hints for the future.
SCOUTING REPORT: Colon is a four-pitch righthander with a stout frame and a thick lower half. He was kept on tight pitch limits all season, never topping 70 pitches, but within those pitch limits, he flashed dominant stuff. He sat at 94-95 mph and touched 97 with an above-average four-seamer that has above-average carry on a flatter than normal plane. He has a 92-94 sinker with plenty of arm-side run. His 82-86 mph slider also flashes above-average, and he's shown some feel for a mid-80s changeup. Colon's stuff will all play up much better if he can get more consistent with his delivery. He struggles to be on time in syncing up his arms and legs, leading to spiked fastballs in one inning and sailing others well above the zone.
THE FUTURE: Colon's well below-average control is a real concern, but his stuff plays in the zone if he can just find it more regularly. Patience will be required, but if he smooths out his delivery, he has starter stuff.

Year	Age	Club (League)	Level	W	L	ERA	G	GS	IP	H	HR	BB	SO	BB%	SO%	WHIP	AVG
2025	19	ACL Reds	Rk	0	0	3.00	1	1	3	2	0	3	5	25.0	41.7	1.67	.222
2025	19	Daytona (FSL)	A	0	5	5.23	15	12	43	44	5	30	30	15.3	15.3	1.72	.277
		Minor League Totals		0	5	5.09	16	13	46	46	5	33	35	15.9	16.8	1.72	.274

28 TREVOR KUNCL, RHP
FB: 50. **CH:** 40. **SW:** 45. **CT:** 55. **CTL:** 45. **BA Grade:** 40. **Risk:** Average. **Adj:** 30.

Born: February 28, 1999. **B-T:** R-R. **HT:** 6-0. **WT:** 200. **Signed:** Frontier League, 2025. **Signed by:** Eddie Lehr/Joey Jockety.
TRACK RECORD: Stubbornness is a useful quality in a reliever. Kuncl is quite stubborn, persevering when many pitchers would have given up. A shortstop/third baseman who moved to the mound at George Washington, Kuncl went undrafted. So he signed with the Frontier League's Lake Erie Crushers. He spent two years in the Crushers' bullpen in 2022 and 2023 before the Rangers signed him. He was released in spring training, so he returned to Lake Erie to have an all-star season in 2024. He then signed with the Reds, who sent him to Double-A Chattanooga in 2025. He saved 20 games and then dominated the Arizona Fall League, striking out 42% of batters he faced.
SCOUTING REPORT: Normally a player with Kuncl's nomadic track record would be expected to be a crafty soft-tosser. Kuncl has plenty of velocity. He sits 94-96 mph with his four-seamer and can touch 98. He cuts it regularly, although it's not always intentionally. His 86-89 mph cutter is an above-average pitch and he now mixes in a mid-80s sweeper that gives hitters a bigger-breaking pitch to worry about. He has fringe-average control. He has a more varied arsenal than many one-inning relievers, with a below-average change he will spot to lefties as well.
THE FUTURE: Kuncl's Double-A success was an impressive starting point, but it also hinted to the possibility that he could have a big league career. With what Kuncl has already done to get here, he can be counted on to do everything possible to reach that goal.

Year	Age	Club (League)	Level	W	L	ERA	G	GS	IP	H	HR	BB	SO	BB%	SO%	WHIP	AVG
2025	26	Chattanooga (SL)	AA	4	0	2.34	47	0	50	37	3	17	51	8.5	25.6	1.08	.206
		Minor League Totals		4	0	2.71	67	0	70	50	4	28	82	9.9	29.1	1.12	.200

CARLOS JORGE, OF
HIT: 45. **POW:** 35. **RUN:** 60. **FLD:** 60. **ARM:** 55. **BA Grade:** 40. **Risk:** Average. **Adj:** 30.

Born: September 22, 2003. **B-T:** L-R. **Ht.:** 5-10. **Wt.:** 183. **Signed:** Dominican Republic, 2021.
Signed by: Edgard Melo/Enmanuel Cartagena/Richard Jimenez.
TRACK RECORD: Part of a deep Reds' 2021 international class, Jorge blitzed the lower levels of the minors. He consistently ranked among the offensive leaders in the Dominican Summer, Arizona Complex and Florida State Leagues, but his offensive impact slowed as he climbed to High-A. He stole 40 bases in a solid second full season in the Midwest League in 2025.
SCOUTING REPORT: Jorge has grown three inches since he signed, but he remains an undersized line-drive hitter. He showed up slimmer in 2025, which cost him a bit of power, but he also put together better at-bats. Almost all of his below-average power is pull-side, but he is adept at spraying line drives to left field when pitchers stay away from him. He has a solid understanding of the strike zone and made improvements in his contact rate. In rookie ball, he ranked among league OBP leaders, but more

CINCINNATI REDS

advanced pitchers find little reason to give in to a hitter who hit six home runs in 2025. Jorge is an adept basestealer who uses his plus speed well. Jorge's prospect status relies heavily on his defense nowadays. The former shortstop has developed into a plus defender in center field. He ranges far into the gaps. Jorge's past history as an infielder shows with his arm. He knows where the ball needs to go, and has an accurate, above-average arm with a quick release.
THE FUTURE: Jorge's ceiling is a pretty modest one. He projects as a lefthanded hitter who could be a solid fourth outfielder with bat-to-ball skills and plus defense in all three outfield spots. He'll move up to Double-A Chattanooga in 2026.

Year	Age	Club (League)	Level	AVG	G	AB	R	H	2B	3B	HR	RBI	BB	SO	SB	OBP	SLG
2025	21	Dayton (MWL)	A+	.251	110	406	66	102	16	4	6	37	52	87	40	.342	.355
		Minor League Totals		.263	403	1425	264	375	65	29	40	184	184	385	154	.355	.434

30 CONNOR BURNS, C

HIT: 20. **POW:** 30. **RUN:** 30. **FLD:** 70. **ARM:** 60. **BA Grade:** 40. **Risk:** Average. **Adj:** 30.

Born: December 25, 2001. **B-T:** R-R. **Ht.:** 6-1. **Wt.:** 208. **Drafted:** Long Beach State, 2023 (5th round).
Signed by: Mike Misuraca.
TRACK RECORD: When scouts watched Burns at Long Beach State, some viewed him as the best defensive catcher they had ever scouted as an amateur. After two years of producing nothing at the plate, he hit .289/.356/.573 with 14 home runs as a junior, raising hopes he could be a bottom-of-the-order bat. Pro ball has reinforced his futility at the plate. He has hit .184 or lower in each of his three pro seasons.
SCOUTING REPORT: Burns is helpless at the plate, which means while he helps pitchers and saves runs behind the plate, he gives them back by being a total out-maker as a hitter. He missed on 38% of pitches he swung at in the strike zone, a rate of contact futility that was among the worst in the minors. He has some modest power when he does connect, but not enough to overcome a 40% strikeout rate. But Burns is likely to have a lengthy pro career because it's hard to find catchers who are better at the craft behind the plate. From his first year in pro ball, MLB pitchers liked throwing to him in the bullpen because of his receiving. His left hand smoothly and quickly can snag a 99 mph fastball just below the zone and catch it in a way that makes it look like it easily caught the bottom of the zone. He also blocks well, handles pitchers like a vet and has a plus arm. He's a plus-plus defender at catcher, which is why he plays regularly as one of the minors' worst hitters.
THE FUTURE: The hope is that through sheer repetition, Burns will become a better hitter, and then he could carve out a Martin Maldonado-esque career as a glove-only catcher. Burns' defense will keep him around a long time as a Triple-A on-call catcher, and if he can add a bit more power or contact, he could become a big league backup purely because of his defense.

Year	Age	Club (League)	Level	AVG	G	AB	R	H	2B	3B	HR	RBI	BB	SO	SB	OBP	SLG
2025	23	Dayton (MWL)	A+	.192	58	198	27	38	9	0	9	30	18	86	0	.271	.374
2025	23	Chattanooga (SL)	AA	.120	26	75	6	9	2	0	2	4	16	40	0	.275	.227
		Minor League Totals		.182	175	589	76	107	26	3	22	82	82	263	0	.285	.348

Chase DeLauter

Cleveland Guardians

BY CARLOS COLLAZO

The Guardians continue to operate as one of the league's most consistent high-performing, low-payroll teams.

In 2025, Cleveland stalked division rival Detroit and went 21-7 in September and 88-74 overall to win the American League Central for the third time in four years. It was a nail-biting race to the postseason, and one the Guardians had to run without pitchers Emmanuel Clase and Luis Ortiz.

The two were put on nondisciplinary paid leave in July and are facing federal charges related to an illegal sports gambling operation, in which Clase and Ortiz allegedly took bribes related to their pitches.

Fortunately for Cleveland, the Guardians have been a wellspring of homegrown pitching talent. Gavin Williams, Tanner Bibee and Logan Allen remain a solid core in their rotation, while 2020 undrafted free agent Cade Smith continues to look like one of the best relievers in the game.

Next up in the pitching pipeline is No. 5 prospect Parker Messick, who played a crucial role down the stretch of the regular season, making seven starts and posting a 2.72 ERA with excellent control of a deep pitch mix.

Pitching isn't a question for the Guardians. What back-to-back AL Manager of the Year Stephen Vogt needs is more reinforcements behind perennial MVP challenger Jose Ramirez and leadoff hitter Steven Kwan. And the farm seems poised to help.

Cleveland's system is one of the deepest in the league and brimming with hitters up and down the minor league ladder. It's not just slappy, contact-oriented plate-discipline savants, either.

The Guardians have selected more power hitters in recent years of the draft than is usual for them. Their 2025 draft class featured two of the best college sluggers: Jace LaViolette and Nolan Schubart.

PROJECTED 2029 LINEUP

Catcher	Bo Naylor	29
First Base	Ralphy Velazquez	24
Second Base	Travis Bazzana	26
Third Base	Dean Curley	25
Shortstop	Angel Genao	25
Left Field	Steven Kwan	31
Center Field	Jace LaViolette	25
Right Field	Jaison Chourio	24
Designated Hitter	Chase DeLauter	27
No. 1 Starter	Tanner Bibee	30
No. 2 Starter	Gavin Williams	29
No. 3 Starter	Parker Messick	28
No. 4 Starter	Braylon Doughty	24
No. 5 Starter	Khal Stephen	26
Closer	Cade Smith	30

That adds much-needed impact potential and a variety of offensive profiles to a system that remains led by 2024 first overall pick Travis Bazzana, who still looks like a strong pure hitter and well-rounded player, and outfielder Chase DeLauter, who made his big league debut in the postseason and possesses one of the best hit/power/approach combinations in the minors—when healthy.

Health is another question for many of the players in Cleveland's system. DeLauter has dealt with injuries for the entirety of his pro career, but a number of other players had their seasons shortened with injuries of their own including Bazzana (oblique), Angel Genao (shoulder), Khal Stephen (shoulder), Jaison Chourio (shoulder), Juan Brito (thumb, hamstring) and Welbyn Francisca (shoulder).

It wasn't all bad news on the injury front. The biggest wild card in Cleveland's system is 2019 first-round righthander Daniel Espino. After seeing his career halted for three seasons with multiple surgeries, Espino finally returned to the mound late in 2025 and was showing hints of the all-world stuff he showed at his peak.

Espino could impact the club in the short term, and Cleveland's international group has more players to watch in the long term with Venezuelan outfielder Juneiker Caceres leading a strong 2024 international class. ∎

DEPTH CHART

CLEVELAND GUARDIANS

TOP 2026 ROOKIES — RANK
1. Travis Bazzana, 2B — 1
2. Chase DeLauter, OF — 2
3. Parker Messick, LHP — 5

BREAKOUT PROSPECTS — RANK
1. Juneiker Caceres, OF — 11
2. Joey Oakie, RHP — 12
3. Yorman Gómez, RHP — 20

SOURCE OF TOP 30 TALENT

Homegrown	27	Acquired	3
College	12	Trade	3
Junior college	0	Rule 5 draft	0
High school	7	Independent league	0
Undrafted free agent	0	Free agent/waivers	0
International	8		

LF
Juneiker Caceres (11)
Nolan Schubart (21)
Nick Mitchell

CF
Jace LaViolette (7)
Kahlil Watson (19)
Aaron Walton (22)
Petey Halpin (23)
Robert Arias

RF
Chase DeLauter (2)
Jaison Chourio (9)
Alfonsin Rosario (24)

3B
Dean Curley (13)
Juan Brito (15)
Dauri Fernandez (26)
Luke Hill

SS
Angel Genao (4)
Gabriel Rodriguez (27)
Anthony Silva
Jose Devers

2B
Travis Bazzana (1)
Welbyn Francisca (16)

1B
Ralphy Velazquez (3)
Anthony Martinez
Riley Nelson

C
Cooper Ingle (10)
Jacob Cozart (14)
Cannon Peebles

LHP

LHSP
Parker Messick (5)
Josh Hartle (25)
Ryan Webb
Caden Favors
Jackson Humphries
Matt Wilkinson
Michael Kennedy
Ryan Prager

LHRP
Doug Nikhazy (28)
Rafe Schlesinger (29)
Nelson Keljo
Harrison Bodendorf
Ryan DeSanto

RHP

RHSP
Braylon Doughty (6)
Khal Stephen (8)
Joey Oakie (12)
Daniel Espino (17)
Yorman Gómez (20)
Will Hynes (30)
Jogly Garcia
Austin Peterson
Trenton Denholm

RHRP
Andrew Walters (18)
Peyton Pallette
Franco Aleman
Carlos Hernandez
Jake Miller
Tanner Burns
Matt Jachec
Zane Morehouse
Will McCausland

CLEVELAND GUARDIANS

1 TRAVIS BAZZANA, 2B

Born: August 28, 2002. **B-T:** L-R. **HT:** 6-0. **WT:** 199.
Drafted: Oregon State, 2024 (1st round).
Signed by: Conor Glassey.

TRACK RECORD: The Guardians won the No. 1 overall pick in the 2024 draft via the second-ever draft lottery. Cleveland used the pick to take Oregon State second baseman Bazzana and sign him for $8.95 million. He was the face of a massive Guardians draft class that featured more than $19 million in bonus money. An Australia native, Bazzana brought a tremendous track record of high-level hitting ability, but his first full pro season was tarnished by a recurring oblique injury that limited him to 84 games. Splitting time between Double-A and Triple-A, with a few post-injury tuneup games in the complex, Bazzana hit .244/.389/.424 with nine home runs and 17 doubles.

SCOUTING REPORT: Listed at 6 feet and just under 200 pounds, Bazzana is a physically maxed-out lefthanded hitter with impressive physicality and strength in both his lower and upper halves that he uses to power his swing. He can drive the ball to both gaps with authority, but he's at his best when he's pulling the ball in the air—something he did at an excellent clip in college. Bazzana's oblique injury impacted his hitting mechanics at times in 2025, though the Guardians were happy with the strides he made in the second half of the season to improve the direction of his lower half, which leaked out more frequently than is typical for Bazzana. While his plus bat-to-ball skills and solid understanding of the strike zone give him the potential for on-base value and a chance for a plus hit tool, he is still refining his approach. He can get passive versus lefthanders and against secondaries from southpaws in particular. Being more aggressive and swinging with more intent in those scenarios was a developmental focus. Bazzana remains a plus runner when healthy, but his oblique injuries limited him a bit more than is typical on the bases. He was still an efficient runner and went 12-for-14 on stolen bases and is a good enough runner that the idea of him playing center field remains interesting. For now, that idea is purely theoretical, because all of Bazzana's defensive innings have come at second base. Despite his plus speed, Bazzana shows just fringy range at second base, and that might be his biggest shortcoming. Scouts were impressed with his reliability at the position and believe he can be a fine defender who makes all the routine plays. Bazzana continues to throw from a low slot much of the time, though he

BA GRADE	SCOUTING GRADES
55 Risk: Mild	**Hit:** 60. **Power:** 55. **Run:** 60. **Field:** 50. **Arm:** 45.
Adjusted grade: **50**	Projected future grades on 20-80 scouting scale

BEST TOOLS

BATTING
Best Hitter	Travis Bazzana
Best Power Hitter	Ralphy Velazquez
Best Strike-Zone Discipline	Chase DeLauter
Fastest Baserunner	Petey Halpin
Best Athlete	Jace LaViolette

PITCHING
Best Fastball	Andrew Walters
Best Curveball	Braylon Doughty
Best Slider	Joey Oakie
Best Changeup	Parker Messick
Best Control	Braylon Doughty

FIELDING
Best Defensive Catcher	Jacob Cozart
Best Defensive Infielder	Jose Devers
Best Infield Arm	Angel Genao
Best Defensive Outfielder	Petey Halpin
Best Outfield Arm	Alfonsin Rosario

has improved his slot versatility and ranges from a fringy to average arm.

THE FUTURE: Bazzana's profile hasn't changed significantly since draft day, and his combination of hitting prowess and usable power gives him occasional all-star upside. He's expected to play for Australia in the 2026 World Baseball Classic. After that, he shouldn't need much more minor league time before assuming Cleveland's everyday second base job and adding more length to their lineup. ■

Year	Age	Club (League)	Level	AVG	G	AB	R	H	2B	3B	HR	RBI	BB	SO	SB	OBP	SLG
2025	22	ACL Guardians	Rk	.222	7	18	7	4	2	0	0	2	8	4	1	.462	.333
2025	22	Akron (EL)	AA	.256	51	195	43	50	12	3	5	23	29	55	9	.364	.426
2025	22	Columbus (IL)	AAA	.225	26	89	21	20	3	2	4	14	29	32	2	.420	.438
		Minor League Totals		.243	111	403	91	98	24	5	12	51	83	122	17	.384	.417

CLEVELAND GUARDIANS

2 CHASE DeLAUTER, OF
HIT: 55. **POW:** 60. **RUN:** 55. **FLD:** 50. **ARM:** 60. **BA Grade:** 60. **Risk:** Average. **Adj:** 50.

Born: October 8, 2001. **B-T:** L-L. **HT:** 6-3. **WT:** 235.
Drafted: James Madison, 2022 (1st round). **Signed by:** Kyle Bamberger.
TRACK RECORD: DeLauter fell to the middle of the first round in the 2022 draft because of injury questions, and the Guardians pounced on his upside with the 16th overall pick. DeLauter has been every bit the player advertised when on the field, but he's continued to battle injuries that have held him to just 138 games in three years as a professional. Foot injuries have plagued him for years, and in 2025 he had bilateral core surgery and right wrist surgery that added to his lengthy medical history. Even with the injuries, DeLauter became the sixth player in MLB history to make his MLB debut in the postseason when he logged two games in the Wild Card Series.
SCOUTING REPORT: At 6-foot-3, 235 pounds, DeLauter has a special blend of contact skills, impact and strike-zone awareness. He's a selective hitter with a compact swing and has produced at every level he's been at, with some of the best batted-ball data in the Guardians' system. DeLauter's pure hitting ability and power give him a chance to be a real middle-of-the-order bat who can hit for average with 30-plus home runs. Aside from injuries, DeLauter's biggest question now is where he fits defensively. He runs enough to play center field, but his game speed is more solid-average or a tick above compared to his 60-grade straight-line speed underway. He's a fringy center field defender but is above-average in a corner, which is where a majority of his playing time has come in the minors—partially as a response to his durability questions. In Cleveland, DeLauter's future defensive home might depend as much on team construction—where Steven Kwan is an elite defensive left fielder—as his own skill and ability.
THE FUTURE: DeLauter will go as far as his durability takes him, but if he's on the field he looks like an impactful, above-average regular who can play all three outfield positions and help power a lineup.

Year	Age	Club (League)	Level	AVG	G	AB	R	H	2B	3B	HR	RBI	BB	SO	SB	OBP	SLG
2025	23	ACL Guardians	Rk	.182	8	22	3	4	0	0	2	3	6	5	1	.357	.455
2025	23	Columbus (IL)	AAA	.278	34	126	25	35	8	1	5	21	22	23	0	.383	.476
		Minor League Totals		.302	138	504	88	152	40	1	20	87	70	80	8	.384	.504

3 RALPHY VELAZQUEZ, 1B
HIT: 55. **POW:** 60. **RUN:** 30. **FLD:** 45. **ARM:** 60. **BA Grade:** 55. **Risk:** Average. **Adj:** 45.

Born: May 28, 2005. **B-T:** L-R. **HT:** 6-3. **WT:** 240.
Drafted: HS—Huntington Beach, 2023 (1st round). **Signed by:** Chirag Nanavati.
TRACK RECORD: Coming out of high school in Southern California, Velazquez was a bat-first catcher with a strong hitting track record. After signing with the Guardians for $2.5 million as the 23rd overall pick in 2023, he quickly moved to first base. His 2024 season was solid but not loud, and in 2025 he progressed to the upper minors while hitting .265/.342/.497 between High-A and Double-A. Velazquez was one of eight minor league hitters with 20 or more homers at age 20 or younger.
SCOUTING REPORT: At 6-foot-3, 240 pounds, Velazquez is one of the most physical players in Cleveland's system, and he has done a nice job taking advantage of the Guardians' strength and conditioning resources to tighten his body composition. He has a powerful lefthanded swing that comes from a wide and crouched setup in the box. He has tremendous raw power that has led to exit velocities upward of 114 mph. While Velazquez is an aggressive hitter in terms of the frequency of his swings, he pairs that with a solid understanding of the strike zone and bat-to-ball skills that have always led to sustainable strikeout numbers. Velazquez has improved his batted-ball angles, which has helped him tap into his raw power more frequently and could also allow him to run higher BABIP numbers than anticipated given his well below-average speed. Velazquez continues to get some opportunities in left field, but he's best positioned at—and overwhelmingly plays—first base, where he could become a solid defender with a plus arm. His mobility would make him a below-average defender in an outfield corner.
THE FUTURE: Velazquez's pure offensive upside stacks up with Chase DeLauter in Cleveland's system. He could become a plus hit, plus power everyday first baseman and middle-of-the-order masher. He should get a full season in the upper minors in 2026.

Year	Age	Club (League)	Level	AVG	G	AB	R	H	2B	3B	HR	RBI	BB	SO	SB	OBP	SLG
2025	20	Lake County (MWL)	A+	.245	94	371	59	91	20	6	17	63	40	85	1	.323	.469
2025	20	Akron (EL)	AA	.330	28	112	18	37	8	3	5	22	12	19	0	.405	.589
		Minor League Totals		.253	229	883	145	223	54	10	35	154	121	204	10	.345	.455

CLEVELAND GUARDIANS

4 ANGEL GENAO, SS

HIT: 55. **POW:** 45. **RUN:** 50. **FLD:** 50. **ARM:** 60. **BA Grade:** 55. **Risk:** Average. **Adj:** 45.

Born: May 19, 2004. **B-T:** B-R. **HT:** 6-1. **WT:** 185.
Signed: Dominican Republic, 2021. **Signed by:** Anthony Roa.
TRACK RECORD: Genao signed as the headliner of Cleveland's 2021 international class and put together a breakout 2024 season that has been sandwiched between two injury-plagued campaigns in 2023 and 2025. Genao had a right shoulder sprain in spring training in 2025 and didn't get into official games until late May. After a tuneup in the Arizona Complex League, he spent the rest of the season with Double-A Akron, and then made up for lost time in the Dominican Winter League after the season.
SCOUTING REPORT: Genao is a 6-foot-1, 185-pound switch-hitter who features plenty of moving parts with his swing from both sides of the plate, but he's always shown excellent bat-to-ball skills that allow him to keep his strikeouts in check. While his 2025 performance was subdued, Genao still looks like a contact-oriented hitter who can drive the ball to the gaps and handle both velocity and secondary pitches. He added more strength to his frame in 2025, though his home run power will depend on whether he's able to elevate the ball more consistently. Genao has been a groundball and low line-drive hitter for multiple years, and that low launch profile is more extreme from the right side of the plate. His best contact might always be middle-of-the-field line drives, and even with above-average raw power he might never hit more than 18-20 home runs a season. Genao is a solid runner with enough range for shortstop and a plus arm that will be an asset on the left side of the infield. His tools for the position are better now than his skills, and he may simply need more refinement to become an average defender at the position.
THE FUTURE: Genao has the contact ability and tools to be a solid regular, though his ultimate upside will depend on how his batted-ball profile evolves. He is close to a big league opportunity.

Year	Age	Club (League)	Level	AVG	G	AB	R	H	2B	3B	HR	RBI	BB	SO	SB	OBP	SLG
2025	21	ACL Guardians	Rk	.308	8	26	10	8	0	0	3	5	6	4	0	.438	.654
2025	21	Akron (EL)	AA	.259	77	309	39	80	17	4	2	37	29	54	6	.323	.359
		Minor League Totals		.289	359	1390	226	402	86	14	22	180	166	258	59	.366	.419

5 PARKER MESSICK, LHP

FB: 50. **CB:** 45. **SL:** 50. **CH:** 60. **CTL:** 55. **BA Grade:** 50. **Risk:** Mild. **Adj:** 45.

Born: October 26, 2000. **B-T:** L-L. **HT:** 6-0. **WT:** 225.
Drafted: Florida State, 2022 (2nd round). **Signed by:** Matt Linder.
TRACK RECORD: Messick signed with the Guardians for $1.3 million in the second round of the 2022 draft after a strong career as a starter at Florida State. He logged at least 100 innings in each of his full pro seasons and made his major league debut in 2025. Messick was crucial to Cleveland's run to the postseason, posting a 2.72 ERA in seven starts in August and September.
SCOUTING REPORT: Messick is a 6-foot, 225-pound southpaw with command and deception who largely resembles the pitcher he was expected to be on draft day, though with a few refinements in the right direction. He throws a four-seam fastball in the 92-93 mph range that touches 95-96 from a low release point and with a flat approach that helps the pitch play up. His mid-80s changeup has long been viewed as a plus offering and his best pitch. That remains the case. It's a weapon versus righties and helped him generate a 45% miss rate in the minors and a 31% miss rate in his MLB stint. Messick improved both his breaking pitches in 2025, though the improvement of his slider is the most obvious. He added three ticks of velocity to it, and the pitch now sits in the 85-87 mph range. His slider is at least an average pitch that gives him a reliable weapon versus lefties. Messick has also incorporated a two-seam fastball that is thrown more frequently versus lefties. He rounds out his arsenal with an upper-70s curveball that missed far more bats in 2025. While Messick might not have the elite command he showed in his major league run, he's consistently been an above-average strike-thrower of multiple pitch types.
THE FUTURE: Other pitchers in Cleveland's system have more upside, but Messick is a ready-made and reliable No. 4 or 5 starter. He continues to earn rave reviews for his makeup and work ethic and quickly became a clubhouse favorite on the big league club.

Year	Age	Club (League)	Level	W	L	ERA	G	GS	IP	H	HR	BB	SO	BB%	SO%	WHIP	AVG
2025	24	Columbus (IL)	AAA	5	6	3.47	20	20	99	78	9	42	119	10.3	29.1	1.22	.216
2025	24	Cleveland (AL)	MLB	3	1	2.72	7	7	40	46	4	6	38	3.6	23.0	1.31	.289
		Minor League Totals		19	18	3.33	73	70	354	297	30	125	420	8.5	28.5	1.19	.225
		Major League Totals		3	1	2.72	7	7	40	46	4	6	38	3.6	23.0	1.31	.289

CLEVELAND GUARDIANS

BRAYLON DOUGHTY, RHP
FB: 55. **CB:** 65. **CH:** 50. **CTL:** 60. **BA Grade:** 55. **Risk:** Average. **Adj:** 45.

Born: December 7, 2005. **B-T:** R-R. **HT:** 6-1. **WT:** 196.
Drafted: HS—Temecula, CA, 2024 (1st round supp.). **Signed by:** Chirag Nanavati.
TRACK RECORD: Doughty was a top-two-rounds talent in the 2024 draft coming out of Chaparral High in California and signed with the Guardians for $2.57 million as the 36th overall pick. He lived up to his billing in his first pro season with Low-A Lynchburg, where he posted a 3.48 ERA across 85.1 innings with a 27.3% strikeout rate and 6.4% walk rate.
SCOUTING REPORT: Doughty is a 6-foot-1, 196-pound righthander who repeats his delivery well with great natural athleticism, a quick arm and a three-quarters slot. He was lauded for his strike-throwing ability as an amateur and backed up that reputation in his first extended look at pro ball. Doughty does an excellent job attacking the zone with a 93 mph four-seam fastball that touches 96-97 and has solid riding life. While the four-seam variant is his primary fastball, Doughty also has a two-seamer that's a tick lighter on average and could be a useful piece at the bottom of the zone. He threw both fastballs for strikes more than 70% of the time in 2025. Doughty's curveball is his primary swing-and-miss offering. It was always viewed as a potential wipeout offering and it looks even better in pro ball than it did as an amateur. Doughty now throws the pitch harder, in the low 80s, with the same snappy, hard-biting action that leads to plenty of buckled knees and chases below the zone. His ability to land his curveball in the zone consistently speaks to his advanced command. Doughty has a mid-80s changeup and has thrown a harder slider in the past—both of which could become bigger pieces of his arsenal in the future. He picks up pitch shapes quickly, and that could be a developmental lever that gets pulled down the line.
THE FUTURE: Doughty is a high-probability starter with midrotation upside who is ready for High-A competition in 2026. He's a few years away but is one of the most exciting arms in Cleveland's system.

Year	Age	Club (League)	Level	W	L	ERA	G	GS	IP	H	HR	BB	SO	BB%	SO%	WHIP	AVG
2025	19	Lynchburg (CAR)	A	0	7	3.48	22	22	85	84	4	23	99	6.4	27.3	1.25	.254
		Minor League Totals		0	7	3.48	22	22	85	84	4	23	99	6.4	27.3	1.25	.254

JACE LaVIOLETTE, OF
HIT: 45. **POW:** 60. **RUN:** 60. **FLD:** 55. **ARM:** 55. **BA Grade:** 55. **Risk:** High. **Adj:** 40.

Born: December 4, 2003. **B-T:** L-L. **HT:** 6-6. **WT:** 230.
Drafted: Texas A&M, 2025 (1st round). **Signed by:** Brett Stevenson.
TRACK RECORD: LaViolette entered the 2025 draft cycle as one of the favorites to be selected first overall thanks to his outlier combination of size, speed, power and SEC performance. A down draft year in addition to bat-to-ball questions caused him to slip to the back of the first round, where the Guardians signed him to a $4 million deal as the 27th overall pick. He broke his left hand in college postseason play and didn't debut in official pro games after signing.
SCOUTING REPORT: LaViolette is a towering, physical presence in the lefthanded batter's box and is listed at 6-foot-6, 230 pounds. That size and strength leads to thunderous, 70-grade raw power that allowed him to boast some of the best overall power in his draft class. LaViolette got to his power often in the SEC and is the all-time home run leader at Texas A&M with 68 in three seasons. He is also the school's all-time walks leader with 169 and managed a career 19.3% walk rate with strong strike-zone recognition and swing decisions. His contact rate, however, could cap his offensive impact. LaViolette hit just .285 in his college career with a 25.3% strikeout rate and a 71% overall contact rate. He'll need to find the barrel more frequently against pro pitching—and changeups, sliders and left-on-left spin in particular—and adding a bit more life to his hands in what is currently a stiff operation could help. Despite his size, LaViolette is a real plus runner who moves exceptionally well and pairs his speed with good defensive instincts and routes. He should get every opportunity to stick in center field and would be a plus defender in a corner with an above-average arm if he does need to move.
THE FUTURE: LaViolette's upside and impact potential is undeniable with a scouting card littered with above-average or better tools. His contact ability will determine the sort of player he becomes.

Year	Age	Club (League)	Level	AVG	G	AB	R	H	2B	3B	HR	RBI	BB	SO	SB	OBP	SLG
2025	21	Did not play															

CLEVELAND GUARDIANS

8 KHAL STEPHEN, RHP
FB: 55. **CB:** 40. **SL:** 50. **CT:** 50. **SP:** 50. **CTL:** 55. **BA Grade:** 50. **Risk:** Average. **Adj:** 40.

Born: December 21, 2002. **B-T:** R-R. **HT:** 6-4. **WT:** 215.
Drafted: Mississippi State, 2024 (2nd round). **Signed by:** Don Norris (Blue Jays).
TRACK RECORD: Stephen was a well-rounded pitching prospect coming out of Mississippi State and signed with the Blue Jays for $1.12 million in the second round of the 2024 draft. The Guardians acquired him in a 2025 deadline trade that sent Shane Bieber to the Blue Jays. Stephen pitched well across three levels in his pro debut season and topped out at Double-A. In total, he posted a 2.53 ERA in 21 starts and 103 innings with a 27.1% strikeout rate and 4.9% walk rate. He missed a few weeks with a right shoulder impingement in the middle of the summer.
SCOUTING REPORT: Stephen has a prototype starter's frame at 6-foot-4, 215 pounds and fills up the zone with a deep mix of pitches that includes a four-seam fastball, slider, splitter, curveball and cutter. Stephen sits around 93 mph with his fastball and will reach back for 96, but the pitch is amplified by his excellent spin efficiency, riding life and above-average extension. The performance of his fastball backed up a bit after he returned from his shoulder injury, but at its best it is a swing-and-miss pitch that he can use to miss barrels and execute for strikes at a high level. Developing a secondary with above-average potential to complement his fastball will unlock more upside, and he has a number of candidates. He throws a mid-80s slider, a mid-80s splitter, an 88-91 mph cutter and an upper-70s curveball. The slider, splitter and cutter are all solid-average pitches—and he generated a 37% miss rate with both the slider and cutter in 2025—but none is a no-doubt above-average offering.
THE FUTURE: Stephen has likely back-end starter potential as an athletic strike-thrower with above-average control and a deep pitch mix. With a strong offseason and continued performance, he could be in line to make his major league debut in the second half of 2026.

Year	Age	Club (League)	Level	W	L	ERA	G	GS	IP	H	HR	BB	SO	BB%	SO%	WHIP	AVG
2025	22	Dunedin (FSL)	A	3	0	2.06	8	7	39	29	1	7	48	4.6	31.4	0.92	.200
2025	22	Vancouver (NWL)	A+	6	1	1.49	9	9	48	31	2	10	49	5.4	26.6	0.85	.182
2025	22	Akron (EL)	AA	0	1	6.35	4	4	11	17	0	2	11	3.9	21.6	1.68	.347
2025	22	New Hampshire (EL)	AA	0	0	9.00	1	1	4	5	2	1	2	5.6	11.1	1.50	.313
		Minor League Totals		9	2	2.53	22	21	103	82	5	20	110	4.9	27.1	0.99	.216

9 JAISON CHOURIO, OF
HIT: 55. **POW:** 40. **RUN:** 60. **FLD:** 50. **ARM:** 55. **BA Grade:** 55. **Risk:** High. **Adj:** 40.

Born: May 19, 2005. **B-T:** B-R. **HT:** 6-0. **WT:** 188.
Signed: Venezuela, 2022. **Signed by:** Jose Stela.
TRACK RECORD: Chourio signed for $1.2 million out of Venezuela as the Guardians' top international prospect in 2022 and is the younger brother of the Brewers' Jackson Chourio. Jaison put together a tremendous 2024 season as a 19-year-old in Low-A but regressed in 2025 with High-A Lake County, where he failed to hit for much power and also dealt with a shoulder injury that limited him to just 87 games. He played in the Venezuelan League after the season.
SCOUTING REPORT: Despite Chourio's down year, there's still plenty to like with the savvy-eyed switch-hitting outfielder. He still possesses one of the better batting eyes in a Cleveland system filled with high-OBP hitters. Chourio owns a .414 on-base percentage and 19.7% walk rate in a four-year career. While his proponents might point to a strong 18% chase rate, his detractors might say that he's often too passive, and simply lets hittable pitches go by. Chourio is still looking to find a happy balance with his approach, and both his bat speed and 90th percentile exit velocity regressed in 2025. His shoulder injury definitely played a role, but the questions about his power upside from a year ago are only amplified. Chourio is a plus runner with the speed for center, but his missed playing time hampered his defensive development. His reads and route-running didn't improve, and, barring a significant step forward in this department, he is more likely to profile as an average defender in an outfield corner than a regular center fielder. He has a strong arm that could fit in right.
THE FUTURE: Chourio is looking for a fully healthy, bounceback season in 2026 and will need to answer questions about his power and defense to create confidence that he's a future regular. If that doesn't happen, his pure hitting ability and on-base skills could still carry him to a more limited big league role.

Year	Age	Club (League)	Level	AVG	G	AB	R	H	2B	3B	HR	RBI	BB	SO	SB	OBP	SLG
2025	20	ACL Guardians	Rk	.261	8	23	6	6	1	0	0	2	4	10	1	.370	.304
2025	20	Lake County (MWL)	A+	.235	79	285	37	67	6	1	2	24	66	77	9	.380	.284
		Minor League Totals		.270	273	958	191	259	51	7	9	140	240	230	88	.414	.366

CLEVELAND GUARDIANS

10 COOPER INGLE, C
HIT: 55. **POW:** 30. **RUN:** 50. **FLD:** 45. **ARM:** 45. **BA Grade:** 45. **Risk:** Mild. **Adj:** 40.

Born: February 23, 2002. **B-T:** L-R. **HT:** 5-8. **WT:** 190.
Drafted: Clemson, 2023 (4th round). **Signed by:** Michael Cuva.
TRACK RECORD: Ingle signed with the Guardians for $400,000 as a fourth-rounder in the 2023 draft after showing impressive plate and contact skills at Clemson. Those skills have translated to pro ball, and among minor league catchers with at least 600 plate appearances since 2023, Ingle's .407 on-base percentage trails only the Reds' Alfredo Duno at .425.
SCOUTING REPORT: At 5-foot-8, 190 pounds, Ingle is an undersized catcher and lefthanded hitter who will drive his value through on-base skills and contact. He has a low-maintenance swing that's direct to the ball with a level path that leads to lots of line drives to his pull side. In a system deep with hitters who understand the strike zone and make plenty of contact, Ingle's chase rate (18.1%) and miss rate (18.8%) are among the best. He's a selective hitter who doesn't expand the zone frequently, though he can border on too passive at times. Ingle's upside is dependent on the strength and power he's able to gain, which has been a question mark that he has not answered for multiple years. His max exit velocities are below-average for his age, and the limited power that he does tap into in games comes exclusively to his pull side. Cleveland is still hopeful that he can push his frame closer to 200 pounds, which might translate to a bit more pop and better durability behind the plate. Ingle regressed as a defender in 2025 and was a more skittish blocker. He's a fringy but playable defender, with below-average pure arm strength that plays up because he gets rid of the ball quickly with solid accuracy.
THE FUTURE: Entering his age-24 season, Ingle is running out of time to dream of more power coming, but his lengthy track record as a high-on-base hitter still gives him big league value as a workable defensive catcher.

Year	Age	Club (League)	Level	AVG	G	AB	R	H	2B	3B	HR	RBI	BB	SO	SB	OBP	SLG
2025	23	Akron (EL)	AA	.273	92	333	55	91	29	0	9	49	65	70	0	.391	.441
2025	23	Columbus (IL)	AAA	.207	28	82	13	17	7	0	1	6	21	15	0	.383	.329
		Minor League Totals		.281	230	808	130	227	65	1	21	132	168	149	9	.407	.442

11 JUNEIKER CACERES, OF
HIT: 55. **POW:** 50. **RUN:** 45. **FLD:** 50. **ARM:** 50. **BA Grade:** 50. **Risk:** Average. **Adj:** 40.

Born: August 15, 2007. **B-T:** L-L. **HT:** 5-10. **WT:** 168. **Signed:** Venezuela, 2024. **Signed by:** Jesus Morillo.
TRACK RECORD: Caceres signed for $300,000 out of Venezuela in 2024 and immediately looked like one of the best prospects in the Dominican Summer League. He moved stateside in 2025 and continued to stand out against his peers, slashing .270/.379/.410 over 70 games between the Arizona Complex League and Low-A Lynchburg.
SCOUTING REPORT: Caceres is a bat-first outfielder and lefthanded hitter with a solid frame—which is bigger than his listed 5-foot-10, 168 pounds—and enough strength to give him plus raw power. He has a mature offensive approach for his age with the contact ability, power and plate skills to envision a 50-50 offensive profile in the hit and power departments. He doesn't expand the zone frequently and does a nice job hitting the ball out in front, with power that should begin to translate more into games as he elevates the ball more consistently. In 2025, much of his hardest contact came on the ground, which led to 18 doubles and just four home runs. Caceres spent time in all three outfield positions, though his average speed makes it more likely he settles into a corner. He accelerates well enough to provide decent range, but he needs to improve both his first step and routes to become more than an average defender. His arm is fine, but not a real plus tool that is typical of most right fielders.
THE FUTURE: Caceres profiles as a solid regular whose skills continue to impress for his age. He'll only be in his age-18 season in 2026 when he should get more time in Low-A Lynchburg.

Year	Age	Club (League)	Level	AVG	G	AB	R	H	2B	3B	HR	RBI	BB	SO	SB	OBP	SLG
2025	17	ACL Guardians	Rk	.289	40	128	25	37	10	2	3	20	27	18	5	.419	.469
2025	17	Lynchburg (CAR)	A	.250	30	116	15	29	8	0	1	7	9	17	2	.331	.345
		Minor League Totals		.296	110	385	68	114	29	8	4	60	55	53	16	.396	.444

CLEVELAND GUARDIANS

12 JOEY OAKIE, RHP
FB: 65. **SL:** 60. **CH:** 50. **CTL:** 45. **BA Grade:** 60. **Risk:** Extreme. **Adj:** 40.

Born: May 9, 2006. **B-T:** R-R. **HT:** 6-3. **WT:** 200. **Drafted:** HS—Ankeny, IA, 2024 (3rd round). **Signed by:** Alex Botts.
TRACK RECORD: Oakie was a top 50 prospect in the 2024 draft class and signed with the Guardians for $2 million in the third round. In his pro debut in 2025, Oakie made 15 starts between the Arizona Complex League and Low-A Lynchburg. He posted a 5.31 ERA in 59.1 innings with a 28.8% strikeout rate and 14.0% walk rate.
SCOUTING REPORT: Oakie is a stuff-over-polish righthander with a great foundation of physicality and athleticism with his 6-foot-3, 200-pound frame. He has some depth in his arm stroke, and throws from a lower slot. Oakie gets great extension and has a well below-average release height, though he struggles to repeat that release—which impacts his control and command. He throws a heavy, boring four-seam fastball that averaged 95.2 mph and has already been up to 100. The pitch has great life and is a weapon in and out of the zone, and he actually improved its velocity in the second half of the season. Oakie's slider is a plus offering in the 86-90 mph range that has great power, spin and movement. His changeup is his third-best pitch now, and one he hasn't thrown with much frequency, but it's a high-spin offering with plenty of arm-side fade. Oakie has the stuff to overwhelm hitters, but he'll need to improve his pitch making and repeat his mechanics more consistently. He has the athleticism to make those adjustments.
THE FUTURE: Oakie has midrotation upside, but he'll need plenty of development time before he gets there. He should continue pitching in the low minors in 2026 where he'll focus on his delivery and pitch execution.

Year	Age	Club (League)	Level	W	L	ERA	G	GS	IP	H	HR	BB	SO	BB%	SO%	WHIP	AVG
2025	19	ACL Guardians	Rk	2	3	7.46	12	9	35	36	1	23	47	13.5	27.6	1.69	.267
2025	19	Lynchburg (CAR)	A	1	1	2.22	6	6	24	17	3	15	31	14.9	30.7	1.32	.202
		Minor League Totals		3	4	5.31	18	15	59	53	4	38	78	14.0	28.8	1.53	.242

13 DEAN CURLEY, 3B
HIT: 50. **POW:** 50. **RUN:** 50. **FLD:** 50. **ARM:** 55. **BA Grade:** 50. **Risk:** Average. **Adj:** 40.

Born: April 15, 2004. **B-T:** R-R. **HT:** 6-3. **WT:** 218. **Drafted:** Tennessee, 2025 (2nd round). **Signed by:** Jonathan Martin.
TRACK RECORD: Curley established himself as an offensive force in the heart of Tennessee's lineup from day one as a freshman, and entered his draft-eligible sophomore season as one of the more well-rounded hitters in the 2025 class. He didn't take the step forward scouts were hoping for and also had some defensive struggles that caused him to fall into the second round, where the Guardians signed him to a $1.7 million bonus.
SCOUTING REPORT: At 6-foot-3, 218 pounds, Curley has a big league body now with a strong blend of hitting traits that should allow him to be a well-rounded offensive presence. He has a crouched stance and starts his swing with a toe tap before firing quick hands to the ball with few extraneous movements. He's a patient hitter—who might lean into being a bit passive in the heart of the zone at times—who IDs pitches well, doesn't expand the zone and makes contact versus a variety of pitch types and top-tier velocity. Curley has the sort of blended offensive profile that should lead to solid average, on-base ability and 19-25 home run power potential. There are more questions on the defensive side. He struggled at shortstop early in the year and also had a number of throwing errors in the second half of the season as a second baseman. Curley does have plus arm strength, but he lacks the actions and quickness for the middle infield and his arm slot versatility (or lack thereof) is likely best suited for the hot corner.
THE FUTURE: Curley has everyday upside and might be best served playing third base full-time and focusing on his hitting.

Year	Age	Club (League)	Level	AVG	G	AB	R	H	2B	3B	HR	RBI	BB	SO	SB	OBP	SLG
2025	21	Lynchburg (CAR)	A	.242	9	33	4	8	1	0	0	2	2	11	1	.286	.273
		Minor League Totals		.242	9	33	4	8	1	0	0	2	2	11	1	.286	.273

14 JACOB COZART, C
HIT: 35. **POW:** 45. **RUN:** 30. **FLD:** 65. **ARM:** 60. **BA Grade:** 45. **Risk:** Average. **Adj:** 35.

Born: January 9, 2003. **B-T:** L-R. **HT:** 6-3. **WT:** 214. **Drafted:** NC State, 2024 (2nd round). **Signed by:** Michael Cuva.
TRACK RECORD: Cozart was one of the top catchers in the 2024 draft class coming out of NC State, and signed with the Guardians for $2.05 million as a second-rounder. His 13-game pro debut in 2024 is illustrative of not overreacting to small debut samples, as Cozart looked much more like himself in a complete 2025 season where he hit .235/.341/.371 with 15 homers at High-A and Double-A.
SCOUTING REPORT: Cozart is a physical, lefthanded hitting catcher with a 6-foot-3, 214-pound frame

CLEVELAND GUARDIANS

and a tremendous work ethic and mindset behind the plate. He was viewed as a strong defender coming out of the draft, and has only improved in this area of his game in 2025, with glowing reviews across the board. Cozart is dedicated to his craft and is a strong receiver in any location, with advanced blocking skills to go with plus arm strength. He threw out 24% of baserunners across both levels in 2025, but also excels at all the soft skills that separate good catchers from great ones, like game prep and pitcher management. Cozart had a slow start offensively, but flipped a switch in June and managed an OPS of .800 or better from then on. His steep swing and swing-and-miss tendencies might cap his offensive upside, but he does have plus raw power—that will play more fringy in games—and strong on-base skills.
THE FUTURE: Cozart's defensive ability and OBP gives him second-division value at the least, and there's more ceiling if he can find a way to access his power more frequently.

Year	Age	Club (League)	Level	AVG	G	AB	R	H	2B	3B	HR	RBI	BB	SO	SB	OBP	SLG
2025	22	Lake County (MWL)	A+	.229	72	258	35	59	12	1	7	38	41	65	0	.344	.364
2025	22	Akron (EL)	AA	.256	21	82	13	21	3	1	2	11	8	24	0	.330	.390
		Minor League Totals		.223	106	382	50	85	16	2	9	49	56	107	0	.330	.346

15 JUAN BRITO, 2B
HIT: 50. **POW:** 45. **RUN:** 45. **FLD:** 45. **ARM:** 50. **BA Grade:** 45. **Risk:** Average. **Adj:** 35.

Born: September 24, 2001. **B-T:** B-R. **HT:** 6-0. **WT:** 202. **Signed:** Dominican Republic, 2018.
Signed by: Rolando Fernandez/Frank Roa (Rockies).
TRACK RECORD: Brito has been a reliable minor league hitter for years, and after a strong full-season in Triple-A in 2024 was a popular breakout pick who had a chance to impact Cleveland's major league team. Brito struggled in spring training, then played just 31 games because of a string of injuries including thumb and hamstring injuries that both required surgery.
SCOUTING REPORT: Brito is a 6-foot, 202-pound switch-hitter who, when at his best, shows a solid blend of contact, patience and pop. Without elite bat speed, Brito needs to be dialed into his swing decisions and timing, and when he was on the field in 2025 he regressed in both those areas—causing some regression across the board in his batted-ball inputs. His aggressiveness was perhaps the most striking difference in 2025, and Brito both swung more frequently and expanded the zone more frequently against a variety of pitch types. There's an expectation that he'll get back to his typical self with a healthy 2026 season. Brito is a primary second baseman, and that's his best spot defensively. He's a fringy runner with solid hands and average arm strength. It's likely that he gets more exposure to other positions including outfield, first base and third base to create more opportunities for him to contribute in the lineup.
THE FUTURE: The 2025 season was essentially a lost one for Brito. He missed his opportunity to claim the team's second base job, and now top prospect Travis Bazzana is in a position to claim it for himself. Playing off the keystone puts more pressure on Brito's bat, and that could make him more of a backup or platoon type for the Guardians.

Year	Age	Club (League)	Level	AVG	G	AB	R	H	2B	3B	HR	RBI	BB	SO	SB	OBP	SLG
2025	23	ACL Guardians	Rk	.190	7	21	2	4	0	0	1	2	3	8	0	.346	.333
2025	23	Columbus (IL)	AAA	.256	24	82	15	21	6	1	3	15	13	21	4	.357	.463
		Minor League Totals		.273	471	1721	317	470	113	11	56	285	291	329	58	.382	.449

16 WELBYN FRANCISCA, SS
HIT: 50. **POW:** 30. **RUN:** 55. **FLD:** 50. **ARM:** 50. **BA Grade:** 45. **Risk:** Average. **Adj:** 35.

Born: May 17, 2006. **B-T:** B-R. **HT:** 5-11. **WT:** 178. **Signed:** Dominican Republic, 2023. **Signed by:** Gustavo Benzan.
TRACK RECORD: Francisca was the headliner of Cleveland's 2023 international class, then became a top 10 prospect in the system with a strong 2024 stateside debut. He took a step back in 2025 at Low-A Lynchburg, where his bat speed and defense regressed and he also missed time with a shoulder injury.
SCOUTING REPORT: Francisca is a smaller switch-hitter and middle infielder with a 5-foot-11, 178-pound frame. He has a noisy swing that includes a big hand hitch and leg lift from both sides, and without a jump in bat speed that could leave him exposed to high-level velocity. Francisca's intent and swing are better from the right side, though his bat speed and exit velocities regressed on both sides of the plate in 2025. That could be tied to his injury, though he also seemed to fall into phases where he swung more for contact than impact. Francisca does have strong contact skills, but might always be more of a singles hitter who puts the ball on the ground a lot and manages his strikeouts. Francisca has the tools to defend at shortstop, but he made a number of errors—both throwing and mental—and might now project like more of a fringy shortstop and average defensive second baseman. He's a high-energy player who plays the game hard and earns strong reviews for his baserunning.
THE FUTURE: Francisca's 2025 was a step back, and he now profiles like a backup or second-division

CLEVELAND GUARDIANS

regular, though he's still young and could bounce back in 2026 when he faces High-A competition for the first time.

Year	Age	Club (League)	Level	AVG	G	AB	R	H	2B	3B	HR	RBI	BB	SO	SB	OBP	SLG
2025	19	Lynchburg (CAR)	A	.229	98	371	54	85	14	2	3	45	51	73	45	.320	.302
		Minor League Totals		.280	212	814	155	228	39	10	13	112	114	160	75	.371	.400

17 DANIEL ESPINO, RHP
FB: 70. **CB:** 45. **SL:** 60. **CH:** 45. **CTL:** 50. **BA Grade:** 55. **Risk:** Extreme. **Adj:** 35.

Born: January 5, 2001. **B-T:** R-R. **HT:** 6-2. **WT:** 225. **Drafted:** HS—Statesboro, GA, 2019 (1st round). **Signed by:** Ethan Purser.
TRACK RECORD: Espino was one of the highest-upside arms in the 2019 draft class and signed with Cleveland for $2.5 million in the first round. He quickly became one of the most exciting pitching prospects in baseball, but knee injuries and multiple shoulder surgeries derailed his career for three seasons. He finally returned to the mound late in 2025, with one Triple-A appearance and four starts in the Arizona Fall League.
SCOUTING REPORT: Espino is a powerfully-built righthander with a strapping, 6-foot-2, 225-pound frame. At his best before his many injuries, Espino showed some of the most electric stuff in baseball with an 80-grade fastball and a slider that earned 70-grade reviews. It's too early to tell just yet if he's fully back to those levels, but in his abbreviated outings he sat 97-98 mph with his fastball and reached back for triple digits. The hard, upper-80s slider still looks like his best secondary, but it is more of a plus pitch at the moment with a bit more inconsistency and less power than the 2021 version. Espino also throws a slower curveball in the upper 70s and will sparingly mix in a firm changeup. In the past, Espino has shown more than enough control to profile as a starter, but he'll need more innings to rediscover his touch and feel.
THE FUTURE: Espino has endured significant adversity over the last three years. He also dealt with the loss of his father while rehabbing. He's shown remarkable resilience and has earned top-of-the-scale reviews for his makeup and work ethic dating back to his high school days. His future role is a significant question, but with a strong and healthy spring in 2026 he could find himself in the majors quickly.

Year	Age	Club (League)	Level	W	L	ERA	G	GS	IP	H	HR	BB	SO	BB%	SO%	WHIP	AVG
2025	24	Columbus (IL)	AAA	0	1	40.50	1	1	1	3	0	0	1	0.0	20.0	4.50	.600
		Minor League Totals		4	10	3.55	31	31	124	83	14	48	204	9.6	40.7	1.05	.185

18 ANDREW WALTERS, RHP
FB: 70. **SL:** 60. **CTL:** 50. **BA Grade:** 50. **Risk:** High. **Adj:** 35.

Born: December 8, 2000. **B-T:** R-R. **HT:** 6-4. **WT:** 222. **Drafted:** Miami, 2023 (2nd round). **Signed by:** Gustavo Benzan.
TRACK RECORD: Walters signed as a second-rounder for $955,275 in 2023 after a dominant career as a reliever with Miami. He blitzed to the majors just a year later, but has only thrown 10 total big league innings after an injury-plagued 2025 season. Walters dealt with right shoulder stiffness and left a May 31 game with a lat injury that required season-ending surgery.
SCOUTING REPORT: Walters is a classic reliever profile with a loud fastball/slider combo and a large 6-foot-4, 222-pound frame. The fastball has long been his calling card and remains a double-plus offering with a slew of traits that make it difficult to connect with or barrel. He sits around 96-97 mph and will push the pitch up to 100 with excellent carry from a below-average release height and a tremendously flat approach angle. The pitch dominates the strike zone and is a consistent swing-and-miss weapon and chase pitch above the zone. Since getting into pro ball, Walters has added more power to his slider, which is now an 85-89 mph breaking ball with tight movement and plus potential. It's also a plus pitch, but he does need to tighten up the command and consistency. In the past Walters has thrown a changeup, but he's mostly a two-pitch pitcher these days.
THE FUTURE: Walters' shoulder injury adds more risk to his profile, but Cleveland does expect him to be back and healthy to start the 2026 season. If that's the case he's a reliable, plug-and-play bullpen piece.

Year	Age	Club (League)	Level	W	L	ERA	G	GS	IP	H	HR	BB	SO	BB%	SO%	WHIP	AVG
2025	24	Columbus (IL)	AAA	0	0	1.50	12	0	12	5	0	9	23	18.0	46.0	1.17	.125
2025	24	Cleveland (AL)	MLB	0	0	13.50	2	0	1	2	1	0	2	0.0	33.3	1.50	.333
		Minor League Totals		3	0	1.41	29	0	32	18	1	17	61	12.9	46.2	1.09	.161
		Major League Totals		1	0	1.80	11	1	10	3	1	5	8	13.2	21.1	0.80	.094

CLEVELAND GUARDIANS

19 KAHLIL WATSON, OF
HIT: 40. **POW:** 50. **RUN:** 60. **FLD:** 50. **ARM:** 55. **BA Grade:** 45. **Risk:** Average. **Adj:** 35.

Born: April 16, 2003. **B-T:** L-R. **HT:** 5-9. **WT:** 178. **Drafted:** HS—Wake Forest, NC, 2021 (1st round).
Signed by: Blake Newsome (Marlins).
TRACK RECORD: Watson has had a winding pro career since being viewed as one of the elite prep talents of the 2021 draft class, but his 2025 season was perhaps his best yet—both on and off the field. The former Marlins first-round shortstop played outfield exclusively for the first time in his career and tallied more than 15 homers, doubles and steals in the upper minors.
SCOUTING REPORT: Watson is a 5-foot-9, 178-pound lefthanded hitter with great bat speed, foot speed and plus raw power. He's an aggressive hitter with an inconsistent offensive approach and a wide range of opinions on the true quality of his hit tool, but his swing creates natural loft and allows him to drive the ball with authority to the pull side. Watson will be challenged by elite velocity, and he still has his struggles vs. spin, which could either lead to him being a streaky hitter or one who might not be able to realize his power potential in the majors. Watson was drafted as a shortstop, but he's now a full-time outfielder who logged innings in all three spots, though a majority of his time came in center field. He's improved to at least an average defender in center and could be above-average in the corners with explosive, plus-plus top-end speed and an above-average arm. Watson's speed often plays down out of the box, due to a long finish to his swing and inconsistent effort levels.
THE FUTURE: Watson looks like a second-division regular and could be more than that with a bit more contact. The Guardians added him to the 40-man roster in November.

Year	Age	Club (League)	Level	AVG	G	AB	R	H	2B	3B	HR	RBI	BB	SO	SB	OBP	SLG
2025	22	Akron (EL)	AA	.247	59	219	30	54	13	5	8	36	26	72	7	.337	.461
2025	22	Columbus (IL)	AAA	.255	43	149	23	38	7	1	8	25	22	47	10	.358	.477
		Minor League Totals		.234	378	1386	219	325	69	15	56	194	173	476	77	.327	.427

20 YORMAN GÓMEZ, RHP
FB: 55. **CB:** 40. **SW:** 55. **CH:** 40. **CT:** 55. **CTL:** 45. **BA Grade:** 50. **Risk:** High. **Adj:** 35.

Born: November 10, 2002. **B-T:** R-R. **HT:** 5-11. **WT:** 200. **Signed:** Venezuela, 2019. **Signed by:** Jesus Morillo.
TRACK RECORD: Gómez signed as an international league free agent out of Venezuela in 2019, then spent the next four years inching his way up in the minors before a breakout 2025 season. He split time as a starter and reliever with High-A Lake County and Double-A Akron, posting a 2.96 ERA in 121.2 innings to go with a 27.6% strikeout rate.
SCOUTING REPORT: Gómez is a stocky, broad-shouldered righty with a 5-foot-11, 200-pound frame. He throws a deep mix of pitches that includes a four-seam fastball, sweeper, cutter, curveball and changeup. Gómez made a jump with his velocity and now sits around 95 mph and has run the fastball up to 97. In addition to adding more velocity, he improved both his low-80s sweeper and upper-80s cutter, with the sweeper driving a 43.4% miss rate. His best three pitches are the fastball, sweeper and cutter, which makes attacking righties easier for him than lefties. To profile as a starter, he'll need to improve both his upper-70s curveball and mid-80s changeup and get better working deep into games. To that end, adding more strength over the offseason will be key for Gómez, who the Guardians view as one of the better workers in the system.
THE FUTURE: Gómez has No. 4 starter upside, but also carries some reliever risk that could lead to a full-time bullpen role.

Year	Age	Club (League)	Level	W	L	ERA	G	GS	IP	H	HR	BB	SO	BB%	SO%	WHIP	AVG
2025	22	Lake County (MWL)	A+	8	0	2.84	17	6	76	55	3	29	83	9.5	27.3	1.11	.201
2025	22	Akron (EL)	AA	4	2	3.15	10	9	46	38	1	19	56	9.5	28.0	1.25	.215
		Minor League Totals		31	20	3.73	100	82	435	376	27	169	445	9.1	23.9	1.25	.228

21 NOLAN SCHUBART, OF
HIT: 40. **POW:** 60. **RUN:** 30. **FLD:** 40. **ARM:** 50. **BA Grade:** 50. **Risk:** High. **Adj:** 35.

Born: May 10, 2004. **B-T:** L-R. **HT:** 6-5. **WT:** 233. **Drafted:** Oklahoma State, 2025 (3rd round). **Signed by:** Ken Jarrett.
TRACK RECORD: Schubart has exuded power potential since his high school days, then became one of the best sluggers in Oklahoma State history with 59 home runs in three seasons. He boasted some of the most impressive raw power in the 2025 draft class, and after a 19-homer season signed for $730,000 as a third-round pick with the Guardians.
SCOUTING REPORT: Schubart has a hulking, 6-foot-5, 233-pound frame with the sort of strength, size and bat speed you would expect of a player with easy 70-grade raw power. He hits titanic blasts to all

parts of the park with great leverage and plate coverage because of his long limbs. His power comes with impressive patience and strike-zone selectivity that has led to consistently impressive walk rates. Schubart's college walk rate was 18.9% and he posted a 22.7% walk rate in his pro debut. That trade-off is lots of swing-and-miss questions. Schubart's contact skills are well below-average and he might never be more than a 40-grade hitter because of it. He's a plodding runner with below-average speed who will need to improve his defense to be reliable in a corner, and he might be best suited at first base.
THE FUTURE: Schubart has game-changing power that could drive a lineup, but his hit tool carries risk and his defensive abilities will put plenty of pressure on his game power continuing to surface against better pitching.

Year	Age	Club (League)	Level	AVG	G	AB	R	H	2B	3B	HR	RBI	BB	SO	SB	OBP	SLG
2025	21	Lynchburg (CAR)	A	.255	15	51	10	13	2	0	3	7	15	24	1	.424	.471
		Minor League Totals		.255	15	51	10	13	2	0	3	7	15	24	1	.424	.471

22 AARON WALTON, OF
HIT: 45. **POW:** 50. **RUN:** 60. **FLD:** 55. **ARM:** 45. **BA Grade:** 45. **Risk:** Average. **Adj:** 35.

Born: May 14, 2004. **B-T:** R-R. **HT:** 6-3. **WT:** 219. **Drafted:** Arizona, 2025 (2nd round supp.). **Signed by:** Caleigh Tennyson.
TRACK RECORD: Walton was a multi-sport athlete in high school and had a number of Division I offers to play football. He played two seasons with Samford, then transferred to Arizona for the 2025 season where he had a career-best offensive season with a .320 average and 14 home runs. Walton signed for $1.1 million as a supplemental second rounder with the Guardians and played 16 games with Low-A Lynchburg after signing.
SCOUTING REPORT: Walton is a 6-foot-3, 219-pound hitter with a lean frame, an upright stance and a sizable leg kick that gets his swing started. He has a solid amount of strength that leads to solid pull-side power, and as a junior Walton showed an improved ability to get the ball in the air to his pull side to take advantage of that power. He cut his strikeout rate each year in college and showed solid plate skills as a junior, though the moving parts to his swing could make him more of a fringy hitter. He's a plus runner who accelerates quickly and runs the bases well, and the Guardians are bullish on his defensive aptitude in center field—though amateur scouts wondered if his routes would force him to a corner.
THE FUTURE: Walton has a solid all-around toolset and athleticism that could lead to a second-division starter role.

Year	Age	Club (League)	Level	AVG	G	AB	R	H	2B	3B	HR	RBI	BB	SO	SB	OBP	SLG
2025	21	Lynchburg (CAR)	A	.238	16	63	9	15	5	1	1	9	7	21	6	.324	.397
		Minor League Totals		.238	16	63	9	15	5	1	1	9	7	21	6	.324	.397

23 PETEY HALPIN, OF
HIT: 40. **POW:** 30. **RUN:** 70. **FLD:** 60. **ARM:** 50. **BA Grade:** 40. **Risk:** Mild. **Adj:** 35.

Born: May 26, 2002. **B-T:** L-R. **HT:** 5-11. **WT:** 200. **Drafted:** HS—Mountain View, CA, 2020 (3rd round). **Signed by:** Carlos Muniz.
TRACK RECORD: Halpin signed for $1.5 million as a third-rounder and top 100 prospect from the 2020 draft class and made his major league debut five years later. Halpin played in just six major league games in September where he was used as a late-game defensive replacement, but he also made the team's AL Wild Card roster against the Tigers.
SCOUTING REPORT: Halpin is a 5-foot-11, 200-pound outfielder and lefthanded hitter who has been one of Cleveland's most advanced defenders for several years. He's a great runner who covers plenty of ground, and his 29.4 ft/sec Triple-A sprint speed number would place him in the 95th percentile of big leaguers. In addition to just being fast and covering plenty of ground, Halpin is a crisp route-runner who takes a good first step and generally has above-average defensive instincts. He can handle all three outfield positions, but an average arm makes him a better fit for center or left. Halpin is also one of the better baserunners in the system and has gone 66-for-94 (70.2%) in steals in his minor league career. Halpin's offensive package is light. He's a hit-over-power, line-drive oriented hitter who has below-average power and an aggressive approach that limits his on-base value.
THE FUTURE: Halpin is a solid fifth outfield-type who will bring value with his glove and baserunning, though his hit-power combo might prevent him from being a regular contributor in a lineup.

Year	Age	Club (League)	Level	AVG	G	AB	R	H	2B	3B	HR	RBI	BB	SO	SB	OBP	SLG
2025	23	Columbus (IL)	AAA	.249	126	493	86	123	29	5	14	44	51	156	15	.321	.414
2025	23	Cleveland (AL)	MLB	.333	6	6	5	2	0	0	0	0	2	2	0	.500	.333
		Minor League Totals		.253	488	1904	297	481	102	23	42	181	207	519	66	.328	.397
		Major League Totals		.333	6	6	5	2	0	0	0	0	2	2	0	.500	.333

CLEVELAND GUARDIANS

24 ALFONSIN ROSARIO, OF

HIT: 30. **POW:** 50. **RUN:** 50. **FLD:** 50. **ARM:** 70. **BA Grade:** 50. **Risk:** High. **Adj:** 35.

Born: June 21, 2004. **B-T:** R-R. **HT:** 6-2. **WT:** 222. **Drafted:** HS—Lexington, SC, 2023 (6th round).
Signed by: M'Lynn Dease (Cubs).
TRACK RECORD: Rosario was a high-upside toolshed who came out of a strong P27 Academy program in Lexington, S.C., that has produced five draft prospects since 2022. He signed for $325,600 as a sixth-rounder with the Cubs, then was traded to the Guardians in a 2024 deal that sent RHP Eli Morgan to Chicago. Rosario split time between High-A and Double-A in 2025 and hit 21 home runs with a 27.5% strikeout rate.
SCOUTING REPORT: Rosario is powerfully built with a 6-foot-2, 222-pound frame packed with plenty of strength and fast, twitchy hands that lead to eye-popping home runs to the pull side. He has easy plus raw power—and has since his prep days—with a 107.2 mph 90th percentile exit velocity mark among the very best in Cleveland's system. While Rosario's damage on contact is exceptional, he simply swings and misses too frequently. He cut his overall miss rate significantly in 2025, but still managed just a 36% miss rate (one of the worst marks in the system) and a strikeout rate that eclipsed the 30% mark in Double-A. Rosario is a pull-happy hitter who will get the ball in the air, but he has significant contact questions against both velocity and secondaries. He's played center and right field but profiles best in right where his 70-grade arm fits nicely.
THE FUTURE: Rosario's power is tantalizing, but he needs to make significant hit tool progress before he profiles as an everyday regular.

Year	Age	Club (League)	Level	AVG	G	AB	R	H	2B	3B	HR	RBI	BB	SO	SB	OBP	SLG
2025	21	Lake County (MWL)	A+	.268	82	306	49	82	16	2	16	47	37	89	12	.362	.490
2025	21	Akron (EL)	AA	.211	33	128	20	27	6	1	5	17	15	48	2	.303	.391
		Minor League Totals		.241	233	845	133	204	41	7	37	138	112	292	38	.345	.438

25 JOSH HARTLE, LHP

FB: 40. **SL:** 50. **CH:** 50. **CT:** 50. **CTL:** 60. **BA Grade:** 45. **Risk:** Average. **Adj:** 35.

Born: March 24, 2003. **B-T:** L-L. **HT:** 6-6. **WT:** 207. **Drafted:** Wake Forest, 2024 (3rd round).
Signed by: Eric Gatewood (Pirates).
TRACK RECORD: Hartle signed with the Pirates for $850,000 as a third-rounder in the 2024 draft, and was then acquired by the Guardians—along with LHP Michael Kennedy—in a trade that sent Spencer Horwitz to the Pirates. In his first pro season, Hartle largely performed as expected, with a 2.54 ERA in 113.1 innings and 24 starts with modest strikeouts and solid control.
SCOUTING REPORT: Listed at 6-foot-6, 207 pounds, Hartle has a long and lean pitcher's frame and throws from a low three-quarters slot with a bit of a crossfire landing that he repeats well. He attacks hitters with a deep arsenal of pitches—all of which he has advanced feel to land for strikes. Hartle throws a four-seam and two-seam fastball, slider, cutter and changeup. All his pitches are solid, but he lacks a true wipeout offering or reliable swing-and-miss pitch. Hartle sits in the 90-94 mph range with both his fastballs. His mid-80s slider is a slurvy pitch with decent sweeping action that gets heavy usage vs. lefties, while his 88-89 mph cutter serves as a bridge pitch between the fastballs and slider. He has solid feel to land a mid-80s slider that's used more against righties. Hartle's above-average command ties his mix together.
THE FUTURE: Hartle has back-end starting potential, but will have a narrow margin for error against upper-level hitters without adding more power or bite to his secondaries.

Year	Age	Club (League)	Level	W	L	ERA	G	GS	IP	H	HR	BB	SO	BB%	SO%	WHIP	AVG
2025	22	Lake County (MWL)	A+	10	2	2.35	22	22	103	72	2	37	100	8.9	24.0	1.05	.195
2025	22	Akron (EL)	AA	0	1	4.50	2	2	10	13	0	2	7	4.7	16.3	1.50	.325
		Minor League Totals		10	3	2.74	25	24	115	90	2	40	109	8.5	23.2	1.13	.215

26 GABRIEL RODRIGUEZ, SS

HIT: 50. **POW:** 30. **RUN:** 50. **FLD:** 55. **ARM:** 50. **BA Grade:** 50. **Risk:** High. **Adj:** 35.

Born: May 3, 2007. **B-T:** L-R. **HT:** 6-0. **WT:** 161. **Signed:** Venezuela, 2024. **Signed by:** Jesus Morillo.
TRACK RECORD: Rodriguez was a prominent member of Cleveland's 2024 international class. He signed for $500,000 and showed strong plate discipline and baseball instincts in the Dominican Summer League after signing. He played just 28 games in the Arizona Complex League because of a hamstring injury, but in that time hit .294/.393/.402.
SCOUTING REPORT: Rodriguez is a lean, wiry lefthanded hitter with a 6-foot, 160-pound frame that

doesn't portend huge strength gains in the future and a defense-first profile. Rodriguez was one of the better defenders in the ACL, and while he got innings at shortstop, second base and third base, he's likely to stick at shortstop in the long run. Scouts praise his actions, instincts, glove work and quick release. While his arm strength might just be average, it should play up because he's able to get rid of the ball so quickly. Overall he looks like an above-average shortstop defender. At the plate Rodriguez has a light bat with some contact skills, but very little power and an approach that often sees him slapping the ball around early in counts without much authority. To drive offensive value, he'll need to minimize his strikeouts and continue to maintain his solid plate skills.

THE FUTURE: Rodriguez has modest upside, but his defensive ability, instincts and bat-to-ball skills could allow him to carve out a contributing big league role.

Year	Age	Club (League)	Level	AVG	G	AB	R	H	2B	3B	HR	RBI	BB	SO	SB	OBP	SLG
2025	18	ACL Guardians	Rk	.294	28	102	21	30	4	2	1	15	15	23	11	.393	.402
		Minor League Totals		.281	65	210	48	59	10	3	3	39	54	50	20	.458	.400

27 DAURI FERNANDEZ, SS

HIT: 40. **POW:** 50. **RUN:** 60. **FLD:** 50. **ARM:** 60. **BA Grade:** 55. **Risk:** Extreme. **Adj:** 35.

Born: March 7, 2007. **B-T:** B-R. **HT:** 5-9. **WT:** 155. **Signed:** Dominican Republic, 2024. **Signed by:** Anthony Roa.

TRACK RECORD: Fernandez signed for $215,000 with the Guardians as a member of what's looking like a rock solid 2024 international class. While Fernandez wasn't the most high-profile name on signing day, he's increasingly impressed scouts with his physicality and toolset. In 2025 he hit .333/.398/.558 with six home runs as one of the most interesting players in the Arizona Complex League, then earned a promotion to Low-A Lynchburg in August.

SCOUTING REPORT: Fernandez is a switch-hitter and infielder with solid physicality right now and a frame that suggests more strength gains on the way. Fernandez has a solid swing from both sides of the plate with twitchy bat speed and a level path that leads to plenty of doubles now, but the upside for above-average power in the future. While Fernandez has some feel for the barrel, he's one of the most aggressive hitters in Cleveland's system. That leads to early-count swings against pitches he can't drive and a muted walk rate. Scouts also think he'll need to clean up some holes on the inner third of the plate. Fernandez is a bursty, plus runner who has a chance to stick at shortstop with more than enough arm strength, but an erratic defensive game that needs refinement.

THE FUTURE: Fernandez needs more polish on both sides of the ball, but his toolset and physical upside give him everyday upside if he can make the requisite adjustments.

Year	Age	Club (League)	Level	AVG	G	AB	R	H	2B	3B	HR	RBI	BB	SO	SB	OBP	SLG
2025	18	ACL Guardians	Rk	.333	43	156	33	52	9	4	6	27	16	22	16	.398	.558
2025	18	Lynchburg (CAR)	A	.273	7	22	9	6	1	0	0	3	0	3	2	.250	.318
		Minor League Totals		.307	95	345	70	106	19	8	7	60	33	44	26	.375	.470

28 DOUG NIKHAZY, LHP

FB: 45. **CB:** 45. **SL:** 55. **CH:** 45. **SW:** 45. **CTL:** 45. **BA Grade:** 40. **Risk:** Mild. **Adj:** 35.

Born: August 11, 1999. **B-T:** L-L. **HT:** 6-0. **WT:** 210. **Drafted:** Ole Miss, 2021 (2nd round). **Signed by:** CT Bradford.

TRACK RECORD: Nikhazy pitched as a reliable starter for Ole Miss, signed for $1.2 million as a second rounder with the Guardians in the 2021 draft, then made his major league debut with a spot start in April four years later. Nikhazy spent a majority of his time in Triple-A Columbus where he posted a 5.02 ERA over 86 innings and 19 starts with a 21.7% strikeout rate.

SCOUTING REPORT: Nikhazy is a 6-foot, 210-pound lefthander who repeats his delivery, throws from a three-quarters slot and gets a great extension. He added to his pitch mix in 2025 and now throws a five-pitch blend that features a 90-94 mph fastball, slider, curveball, sweeper and changeup. The sweeper was the new look to his mix, and while it was his least used pitch overall, it gave him another shape for lefties and averaged more than 15 inches of glove-side movement. Nikhazy still prefers his harder 85-89 mph slider in all situations, though his 78-82 mph curveball and mid-80s changeup generated the most misses against minor league hitters. Nothing Nikhazy throws is plus, which means his control needs to be locked in, and historically he's been just a fringy strike-thrower.

THE FUTURE: Barring more velocity or better command, Nikhazy looks like a swingman.

Year	Age	Club (League)	Level	W	L	ERA	G	GS	IP	H	HR	BB	SO	BB%	SO%	WHIP	AVG
2025	25	Columbus (IL)	AAA	5	7	5.02	21	19	86	89	15	43	87	11.1	22.5	1.53	.262
2025	25	Cleveland (AL)	MLB	0	1	13.50	2	1	4	5	0	6	5	26.1	21.7	2.75	.294
		Minor League Totals		20	25	4.13	96	89	414	336	49	248	467	13.8	25.9	1.41	.221
		Major League Totals		0	1	13.50	2	1	4	5	0	6	5	26.1	21.7	2.75	.294

29 RAFE SCHLESINGER, LHP

FB: 55. **SL:** 55. **CH:** 50. **CTL:** 45. **BA Grade:** 45. **Risk:** Average. **Adj:** 35.

Born: January 22, 2003. **B-T:** L-L. **HT:** 6-3. **WT:** 200. **Drafted:** Miami, 2024 (4th round). **Signed by:** Gustavo Benzan.
TRACK RECORD: Schlesinger pitched as a reliever for two years with Miami before transitioning to a starter during his 2024 draft season. The Guardians drafted him in the 4th round, signed him for $466,900 and then had him pitch mostly as a starter in his first full season. He posted a 3.56 ERA in 103.2 innings and 19 starts between Low-A Lynchburg and High-A Lake County.
SCOUTING REPORT: Schlesinger is a lean, sidearming lefthander with a 6-foot-3, 200-pound frame who creates uncomfortable at-bats for lefties. He throws a three-pitch mix that includes a fastball, slider and changeup. His fastball sits in the 92-93 mph range and will touch 96 with lots of arm-side life from his extremely low release point. Schlesinger's mid-80s slider is his go-to breaking ball and the pitch he has had the best feel for dating back to his college days. It has modest shape and occasional sweeping depth at its best, though his lower slot often means he gets around the ball and sees it back up to his arm side. The changeup is a mid-80s offering with splitter-like tumble at times and real swing-and-miss potential, but it's his least-used pitch and the one he has the worst command of presently.
THE FUTURE: Schlesinger's arm speed and angles give him tools to work with, though his command might ultimately be too light for a long-term starting role. His stuff could play up in a reliever role, especially vs. lefties.

Year	Age	Club (League)	Level	W	L	ERA	G	GS	IP	H	HR	BB	SO	BB%	SO%	WHIP	AVG
2025	22	Lynchburg (CAR)	A	4	6	3.33	20	16	84	76	2	34	88	9.5	24.6	1.31	.241
2025	22	Lake County (MWL)	A+	1	2	4.50	5	3	20	21	1	9	24	10.5	27.9	1.50	.276
		Minor League Totals		5	10	3.65	28	22	111	103	4	46	123	9.7	25.9	1.34	.247

30 WILL HYNES, RHP

FB: 50. **SL:** 60. **CH:** 50. **CTL:** 55. **BA Grade:** 55. **Risk:** Extreme. **Adj:** 35.

Born: July 7, 2007. **B-T:** R-R. **HT:** 6-2. **WT:** 180. **Drafted:** HS—Mississauga, ON, 2025 (2nd round). **Signed by:** Matt Lindner.
TRACK RECORD: Hynes ranked as the best available Canadian pitching prospect in the 2025 draft class and signed with the Guardians for $950,000 at the 70th overall pick to bypass a commitment to Wake Forest. He was young for the class and only turned 18 a few days before the draft, with a starter-looking package and developing velocity during the spring.
SCOUTING REPORT: Hynes has a lean and still-projectable pitcher's frame at 6-foot-2, 180 pounds. He throws with whippy arm speed from a low three-quarters slot and overall has a clean and athletic operation that bodes well for his strikes. Hynes added power during the spring. After topping out around 90 mph in 2024, he was consistently throwing his fastball in the 90-94 mph range in the spring and also added more bite to his breaking ball. His low-80s slider was the best breaking ball in Cleveland's 2025 draft class. It's a high-spin bender that gets into the 2,900 rpm range and shows excellent lateral bite. As he develops he has the spin capacity to turn the pitch into either a true sweeper or a harder, tighter breaking ball with cutter-like power and break—or both. His mid-80s changeup needs work, but could become a solid third pitch.
THE FUTURE: Hynes is young and far away, but he has some of the traits that Cleveland hit on with righthander Braylon Doughty. He has a classic projection starter package.

Year	Age	Club (League)	Level	W	L	ERA	G	GS	IP	H	HR	BB	SO	BB%	SO%	WHIP	AVG
2025	17	Did not play															

Ezequiel Tovar

Colorado Rockies

BY JESÚS CANO

The Rockies lost 119 games in 2025, which would have received a lot more attention had the White Sox not lost 121 the year before. But Colorado's futility extends beyond the boundaries of one season—no team has lost more games during the 2020s.

The compounding evidence finally forced the organization to confront its direction. The result was a sweeping shake-up at every level of leadership. On the field, the Rockies fired manager Bud Black at the beginning of the season, ending his nine-year tenure. In the front office, general manager Bill Schmidt, who had served in the role since 2021, stepped down at season's end.

For the Rockies, there is nowhere to go but up.

Now, that will be the responsibility—and challenge—facing Paul DePodesta, the newly-hired president of baseball operations. He is tasked with steering the Rockies toward sustained success, which may be the toughest job in baseball.

As history shows, it won't be an easy route. Since their inception in 1993, the Rockies have reached the postseason five times, all via wild card. One of those runs culminated in a magical trip to the 2007 World Series.

That improbable fall surge remains a reminder of what's possible in Colorado with homegrown talent. Back then, the Rockies relied on homegrown stars. Leading that pack was Hall of Famer Todd Helton, who shared the field with a young Troy Tulowitzki and an established Matt Holliday. Each one of them was drafted, signed and developed by Colorado.

And fittingly, as the franchise turns the page to a new era, a familiar name sits at the forefront of their next wave of talent: Ethan Holliday. He is Matt's son and a promising young prospect around whom Colorado aims to build its future.

PROJECTED 2029 LINEUP

Catcher	Hunter Goodman	30
First Base	Charlie Condon	26
Second Base	Roldy Brito	22
Third Base	Ethan Holliday	22
Shortstop	Ezequiel Tovar	28
Left Field	Jared Thomas	26
Center Field	Cole Carrigg	27
Right Field	Max Belyeu	25
Designated Hitter	Kyle Karros	27
No. 1 Starter	Chase Dollander	27
No. 2 Starter	Brody Brecht	27
No. 3 Starter	Jackson Cox	28
No. 4 Starter	JB Middleton	26
No. 5 Starter	Griffin Herring	26
Closer	Welinton Herrera	25

Holliday was drafted fourth overall in 2025 and is still years away, but baseball runs deep in his blood. There is help on the way sooner than later. Charlie Condon, drafted No. 4 overall in 2024, and Jared Thomas have the chance to contribute to the big league team at some point in 2026.

Also promising are players already on the roster who have yet to fully tap into their potential. Adael Amador and Yanquiel Fernandez have been heralded as rising stars within the system, but they have yet to establish themselves.

Chase Dollander, drafted ninth overall in 2023 and the team's No. 1 prospect in 2025, has shown flashes of dominance away from Coors Field. Now, the challenge is to put it all together consistently.

On the international front, Dominican second baseman/outfielder Roldy Brito soared from relative obscurity to one of the organization's best prospects after climbing to Low-A as an 18-year-old.

Holliday, Condon, Thomas, Brito and other Rockies prospects could shape the future of the franchise. Just as Helton, Tulowitzki and Holliday led the charge to the 2007 World Series, and just as homegrown stars Nolan Arenado, Trevor Story, Charlie Blackmon and Kyle Freeland keyed back-to-back Rockies playoff appearances in 2017 and 2018. ∎

DEPTH CHART

COLORADO ROCKIES

TOP 2026 ROOKIES	RANK
1. Carson Palmquist, LHP	17
2. Zac Veen, OF	18
3. McCade Brown, RHP	24

BREAKOUT PROSPECTS	RANK
1. JB Middleton, RHP	11
2. Wilder Dalis, 3B	14
3. Yujanyer Herrera, RHP	29

SOURCE OF TOP 30 TALENT

Homegrown	26	Acquired	4
College	15	Trade	3
Junior college	0	Rule 5 draft	1
High school	3	Independent league	0
Undrafted free agent	0	Free agent/waivers	0
International	8		

LF
Jared Thomas (3)
Sterlin Thompson (21)
Derek Bernard (27)

CF
Cole Carrigg (6)
Robert Calaz (9)
Cristian Arguelles (20)
Yeiker Reyes

RF
Max Belyeu (7)
Zac Veen (18)
Benny Montgomery

3B
Ethan Hedges (13)
Wilder Dalis (14)
Roynier Hernandez

SS
Ethan Holliday (1)
Ashly Andujar (19)
Braylen Wimmer
Kelvin Hidalgo
Andy Perez
Sebastian Blanco

2B
Roldy Brito (5)
Roc Riggio (15)
Dyan Jorge

1B
Charlie Condon (2)
Tanner Thach (28)

C
Cole Messina (23)
Braxton Fulford
Matt Klein
Jimmy Obertop

LHP

LHSP
Luichi Casilla
Konner Eaton
Michael Prosecky
Ben Shields
Bryson Hammer

LHRP
Welinton Herrera (10)
Griffin Herring (12)
Sean Sullivan (16)
Carson Palmquist (17)
Antoine Jean

RHP

RHSP
Brody Brecht (5)
Jackson Cox (8)
JB Middleton (11)
Gabriel Hughes (22)
McCade Brown (24)
Riley Kelly (25)
Sandy Ozuna (30)
Gregory Sanchez
Kevin Martinez

RHRP
RJ Petit (26)
Yujanyer Herrera (29)
Fisher Jameson
Lebarron Johnson Jr.
Eiberson Castellano

COLORADO ROCKIES

1 ETHAN HOLLIDAY, SS

Born: February 23, 2007. **B-T:** L-R. **HT:** 6-4. **WT:** 210.
Drafted: HS—Stillwater, OK, 2025 (1st round).
Signed by: Jesse Retzlaff.

TRACK RECORD: Holliday was viewed as a potential No. 1 pick through much of the lead-up to the 2025 draft. But when the first three teams passed, he wound up coming home, in a sense, to the Rockies. Colorado drafted Ethan's father Matt Holliday back in 1998, while his younger brother Jackson Holliday was the No. 1 overall pick in 2022 and is currently the Orioles' second baseman. With those bloodlines, Ethan has long been on the radar of scouts, first drawing attention as a freshman at Stillwater High in Oklahoma. While his last name commands attention, Ethan's talent stands on its own and he was recognized as BA's 2025 High School Player of the Year. The Rockies signed him for $9 million, a bonus record for a high school player. After a brief two-week stint in the Arizona bridge league, Holliday began his pro career with Low-A Fresno, where he hit .239 with two home runs and a concerning 39% strikeout rate. That was the third-worst strikeout rate by a first-round pick in his draft year in the past decade—minimum 50 plate appearances—bettering only Elijah Green and Vance Honeycutt.

SCOUTING REPORT: Physically, Holliday resembles his father more than his older brother Jackson. He is a well-built lefthanded hitter with the 6-foot-4, 195-pound frame to be a powerful slugger. At the plate, he utilizes a fluid and powerful swing with natural rhythm and balance. He's particularly advanced at pitch recognition, showing the ability to lay off borderline pitches and work deep into counts. Holliday is comfortable taking walks when pitchers refuse to challenge him. He sprays the ball to all fields and doesn't need to over-swing to tap into his raw power—with some scouts projecting legitimate 30-homer upside. But in his pro debut, he was too easy to beat in the strike zone. He swung and missed nearly 43% of the time in 2025, which was among the worst rates in the minors. Holliday will need to shorten his stroke, because he can be beat by quality stuff too often. He should have the strength to do so without sacrificing much power. Scouts said that his bat speed and feel for the zone suggest he could make those adjustments with time and experience. Defensively, Holliday has solid hands and enough arm to handle shortstop for now, but as his frame continues to fill out, a move to third base, a corner outfield spot, or possibly first base appears likely. He's made noticeable strides in his footwork and defensive consistency. He's a below-average runner

BA GRADE
60 Risk: High
Adjusted grade: 45

SCOUTING GRADES
Hit: 45. Power: 65. Run: 40.
Field: 50. Arm: 55.
Projected future grades on 20-80 scouting scale

BEST TOOLS

BATTING
Best Hitter	Roldy Brito
Best Power Hitter	Charlie Condon
Best Strike-Zone Discipline	Wilder Dalis
Fastest Baserunner	Roldy Brito
Best Athlete	Roldy Brito

PITCHING
Best Fastball	Welinton Herrera
Best Curveball	Jackson Cox
Best Slider	Brody Brecht
Best Changeup	Sean Sullivan
Best Control	Sean Sullivan

FIELDING
Best Defensive Catcher	Cole Messina
Best Defensive Infielder	Ashly Andujar
Best Infield Arm	Ethan Hedges
Best Defensive Outfielder	Cole Carrigg
Best Outfield Arm	Cole Carrigg

but has solid instincts on the basepaths.

THE FUTURE: Despite his initial struggles in his pro debut, Holliday has the building blocks to be a cornerstone player for the Rockies. His blend of power, plate discipline and defensive flexibility provides a solid foundation to develop into a dependable everyday player. If he makes more consistent contact, the rest of his game could make him an impact hitter.

Year	Age	Club (League)	Level	AVG	G	AB	R	H	2B	3B	HR	RBI	BB	SO	SB	OBP	SLG
2025	18	Fresno (CAL)	A	.239	18	71	14	17	4	0	2	6	12	33	0	.357	.380
		Minor League Totals		.239	18	71	14	17	4	0	2	6	12	33	0	.357	.380

COLORADO ROCKIES

2 CHARLIE CONDON, 1B
HIT: 45. **POW:** 60. **RUN:** 40. **FLD:** 45. **ARM:** 55. **BA Grade:** 55. **Risk:** Average. **Adj:** 45.

Born: April 14, 2003. **B-T:** R-R. **HT:** 6-6. **WT:** 216.
Drafted: Georgia, 2024 (1st round). **Signed by:** Sean Gamble.
TRACK RECORD: Condon quickly emerged as one of the premier hitters in the 2024 draft class, showcasing elite power at Georgia. He led the nation in batting average and slugging while setting a BBCOR record with 37 home runs and winning College Player of the Year. The Rockies drafted Condon third overall and signed him for $9.25 million, tying the record for the largest draft bonus ever. His pro debut was cut short by a hand injury. Then he broke his wrist diving to catch a ball during spring training in 2025, which delayed his start at High-A Spokane until May 21. Condon advanced to Double-A Hartford in July and hit 14 homers between the two stops.
SCOUTING REPORT: Standing 6-foot-6 with long levers and a well-proportioned, athletic frame, Condon presents an intimidating figure in the batter's box. His swing is low-maintenance and mechanically sound. He uses a controlled toe-tap and compact load to get on plane efficiently and generate consistent lift. While his high-end raw power is undeniable, Condon has struggled against breaking balls and changeups in pro ball, with elevated whiff rates pointing to issues with recognition and timing. There were encouraging signs of progress in 2025. His chase rate declined, indicating improved plate discipline, and he continued to produce top-tier exit velocities. However, he posted an overall whiff rate near 30% and an in-zone whiff rate of 22%. Condon played third base and outfield in college but has focused mostly at first base as a pro. He is playable there with below-average speed and an above-average arm.
THE FUTURE: One of the biggest projects for the new Rockies front office is to help Condon maximize his power and improve his contact rate. He has a chance to be a middle-of-the-lineup cornerstone, but his 2025 struggles raised questions about his ability to reach that ceiling.

Year	Age	Club (League)	Level	AVG	G	AB	R	H	2B	3B	HR	RBI	BB	SO	SB	OBP	SLG
2025	22	ACL Rockies	Rk	.296	9	27	2	8	3	0	0	3	1	10	1	.345	.407
2025	22	Spokane (NWL)	A+	.312	35	138	30	43	6	0	3	17	26	35	0	.431	.420
2025	22	Hartford (EL)	AA	.235	55	200	27	47	7	3	11	38	25	67	1	.342	.465
		Minor League Totals		.249	124	465	65	116	20	4	15	69	56	146	6	.351	.406

3 JARED THOMAS, OF
HIT: 50. **POW:** 50. **RUN:** 55. **FLD:** 50. **ARM:** 50. **BA Grade:** 50. **Risk:** Average. **Adj:** 40.

Born: July 1, 2003. **B-T:** L-L. **HT:** 6-2. **WT:** 190.
Drafted: Texas, 2024 (2nd round). **Signed by:** Garrick Chaffee.
TRACK RECORD: Thomas emerged in his draft year at Texas, hitting .349/.434/.635 with 16 home runs and 18 stolen bases in 60 games as an eligible sophomore. The Rockies drafted him in the second round in 2024 and signed him for $2 million. Thomas shined at High-A Spokane in the first half of 2025, posting a .922 OPS in 73 games, before scuffling in 45 games for Double-A Hartford as his strikeout rate spiked to nearly 35%. He led the Rockies' system in both walks (70) and strikeouts (145).
SCOUTING REPORT: The 6-foot-2, 190-pound Thomas is an average athlete who moves well for his size. He began his pro career playing primarily center field, but when he moved to Hartford, he slid to left field, which is a better long-term fit. Thomas' move to Double-A also exposed the key area of concern: swing-and-miss issues, particularly against better sequencing and breaking stuff. Still, when he makes contact, it is often loud contact—supported by consistently high exit velocities and quality barrel rates. While Thomas' approach leans toward aggression, he generally recognizes pitches well enough to do damage in the zone. His power surge at Texas carried over to Spokane, suggesting that he might one day produce at least average power. Encouragingly, his groundball rate remains low, indicating a swing geared for lift and power. Originally a first baseman in college, Thomas is now a full-time outfielder. He lacks the speed for center but is serviceable on the corners with above-average speed and an average arm.
THE FUTURE: Given the learning curve Thomas experienced at Double-A, he should start in Hartford again. Since he is largely limited to the outfield corners and first base, developing his power will be crucial to determining whether he can be an everyday regular or a useful lefthanded-hitting role player with average or better tools across the board.

Year	Age	Club (League)	Level	AVG	G	AB	R	H	2B	3B	HR	RBI	BB	SO	SB	OBP	SLG
2025	21	Spokane (NWL)	A+	.330	73	291	64	96	13	1	11	45	45	79	22	.427	.495
2025	21	Hartford (EL)	AA	.245	45	163	28	40	10	1	3	15	25	66	11	.347	.374
		Minor League Totals		.302	126	487	97	147	24	2	16	64	73	152	34	.398	.458

COLORADO ROCKIES

4 BRODY BRECHT, RHP
FB: 60. **CB:** 40. **SL:** 60. **CH:** 40. **CTL:** 45. **BA Grade:** 50. **Risk:** High. **Adj:** 35.

Born: September 27, 2002. **B-T:** R-R. **HT:** 6-4. **WT:** 235.
Drafted: Iowa, 2024 (1st round supp.). **Signed by:** Brett Baldwin.
TRACK RECORD: A two-sport athlete when he got to campus at Iowa, Brecht was a wide receiver in football and righthanded pitcher on the diamond. On the football field, he redshirted as a freshman and then caught nine passes for 87 yards in 2022. He then shelved football to focus on pitching and became the Hawkeyes' ace in 2023 and 2024. The transition cemented him as one of the better arms in the college class, though his wildness was a concern, which pushed him outside the top 30 picks. The Rockies drafted Brecht 38th overall in 2024. He impressed in his pro debut for Low-A Fresno in 2025, though he missed a month and a half with a back injury.
SCOUTING REPORT: Scouts are enamored of Brecht's four-seam fastball. He touched triple-digits in college and sat 95 mph and peaked at 98 in 2025. The pitch lacks consistent ride or heavy armside run and does not project as a pitch that will generate exceptional swing-and-miss at the top of the zone. He made significant strides in pro ball by consistently attacking the zone, addressing some of the control concerns that lingered from college. He posted a strong 36.1% strikeout rate and allowed just two home runs over 55.1 innings. Brecht's arsenal is headlined by his upper-80s cut-slider, which serves as both a reliable strike-getter and a swing-and-miss weapon. His fastball remains a work in progress in terms of movement, but its velocity makes it a potentially plus offering. He also mixes in a below-average split-grip changeup in the low 90s and a below-average mid-80s curveball that offers more depth than his slider.
THE FUTURE: Brecht should start the 2026 season at High-A Spokane. His athleticism and two-sport background provide hope that there's more to come. He has a shot of developing into a midrotation starter, with a fallback option of being a power reliever who can throw 100 mph in short stints.

Year	Age	Club (League)	Level	W	L	ERA	G	GS	IP	H	HR	BB	SO	BB%	SO%	WHIP	AVG
2025	22	ACL Rockies	Rk	0	1	1.59	4	4	6	6	0	3	8	11.5	30.8	1.59	.261
2025	22	Fresno (CAL)	A	1	4	2.60	16	16	55	42	2	32	87	13.5	36.7	1.34	.210
		Minor League Totals		1	5	2.51	20	20	61	48	2	35	95	13.3	36.1	1.36	.215

5 ROLDY BRITO, OF/2B
HIT: 55. **POW:** 50. **RUN:** 70. **FLD:** 55. **ARM:** 50. **BA Grade:** 50. **Risk:** High. **Adj:** 35.

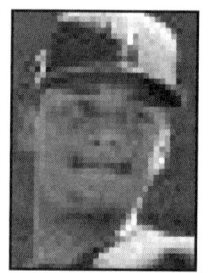

Born: April 8, 2007. **B-T:** B-R. **HT:** 5-11. **WT:** 186.
Signed: Dominican Republic, 2024. **Signed by:** Rolando Fernandez/Omar Frias.
TRACK RECORD: When the Rockies signed Brito for $420,000 out of the Dominican Republic in 2024, they believed he was the best pure hitter in their international class. He has quickly lived up to that projection. Brito led the Arizona Complex League with a .368 batting average in 2025, and he posted the league's second-best on-base percentage at .445 and third-best slugging percentage at .555. That earned him a promotion to Low-A Fresno, and he had the second-best batting average (.375) in the California League over the final month and a half of the season.
SCOUTING REPORT: Brito can flat-out hit, and that's just the tip of the iceberg. He was one of the standout performers in the ACL, impressing scouts with his plate discipline, a mature approach and an ability to work deep counts. A switch-hitter with developing pull-side power from both sides, Brito could grow into more over-the-fence pop as he fills out his athletic 5-foot-11 frame. His double-plus speed is a weapon. He stole 34 bases between the ACL and Low-A Fresno, though he was also caught 14 times, showing that he will need to refine his reads and instincts. In the field, Brito is versatile and twitchy. A shortstop when he signed, he now splits his time between second base and center field. His wheels fit in center but he remains a capable second baseman. Additional infield reps there could boost his value, and versatility always makes a prospect more attractive to his parent club. With a dynamic skill set and high-energy game, Brito has the tools to become an everyday player.
THE FUTURE: Some scouts say Brito's swing and switch-hitting ability is reminiscent of Diamondbacks shortstop Geraldo Perdomo. Brito will be 19 in 2026 and likely will start at Low-A Fresno.

Year	Age	Club (League)	Level	AVG	G	AB	R	H	2B	3B	HR	RBI	BB	SO	SB	OBP	SLG
2025	18	ACL Rockies	Rk	.368	51	182	46	67	13	6	3	21	22	42	22	.445	.555
2025	18	Fresno (CAL)	A	.375	33	136	26	51	7	1	1	17	14	27	13	.442	.463
		Minor League Totals		.328	138	503	99	165	29	8	4	64	63	110	59	.412	.441

COLORADO ROCKIES

6 COLE CARRIGG, OF
HIT: 45. **POW:** 50. **RUN:** 60. **FLD:** 60. **ARM:** 70. **BA Grade:** 45. **Risk:** Average. **Adj:** 35.

Born: May 8, 2002. **B-T:** B-R. **HT:** 6-3. **WT:** 200.
Drafted: San Diego State, 2023 (2nd round supp.). **Signed by:** Matt Hattabaugh.
TRACK RECORD: Few players have pulled off the trifecta of capably playing catcher, shortstop and center field, but Carrigg did exactly that. He played every position other than first base and right field at San Diego State, and then he caught, in addition to playing shortstop and center field, in his pro debut in 2023 after the Rockies drafted him. Carrigg hung up the chest protector in 2024, and he gave up shortstop in 2025 to focus on center field.
SCOUTING REPORT: Carrigg is a tall, athletic switch-hitter with a well-rounded skill set and the versatility to impact the game in multiple ways. His disappointing 2025 campaign at Double-A Hartford can be at least partially attributed to over-aggressiveness. Carrigg features a long-levered swing typical of many Rockies prospects, which contributes to elevated chase and miss rates. This approach has made him especially vulnerable to spin and offspeed pitches. He is comfortable serving the ball to right field or yanking it to left field, but he almost never drives the ball to center. Carrigg hit 11 of his 15 homers in 2025 against fastballs. If he makes enough contact, he could produce average power. He has the plus speed to steal bases efficiently. Carrigg is the Rockies' best minor league center fielder, with the range to cover the massive center field of Coors Field. Scouts have noted he uses his speed to take good routes, and his plus-plus arm is a weapon.
THE FUTURE: While 2025 marked the toughest season of his career, Carrigg's tools remain intact, and with adjustments to his approach, he still has a chance to have a role as an everyday player. His defense, athleticism and speed make him a useful player if he hits enough to make an impact, but, like a number of Rockies prospects, he has to make better swing decisions to make it all work.

Year	Age	Club (League)	Level	AVG	G	AB	R	H	2B	3B	HR	RBI	BB	SO	SB	OBP	SLG
2025	23	Hartford (EL)	AA	.237	123	477	81	113	18	6	15	64	45	145	46	.316	.394
		Minor League Totals		.271	274	1073	200	291	44	25	37	158	109	278	112	.347	.462

7 MAX BELYEU, OF
HIT: 50. **POW:** 55. **RUN:** 50. **FLD:** 50. **ARM:** 60. **BA Grade:** 50. **Risk:** High. **Adj:** 35.

Born: December 15, 2003. **B-T:** L-R. **HT:** 6-2. **WT:** 215.
Drafted: Texas, 2025 (2nd round supp.). **Signed by:** Garrick Chaffee.
TRACK RECORD: Belyeu was named Big 12 Conference player of the year at Texas in 2024. He followed up that campaign with a summer stint on USA Baseball's Collegiate National Team and got off to a strong start in 2025 before a thumb injury sidelined him for about a month. Over three seasons with the Longhorns, Belyeu hit .318/.414/.616 with 27 home runs, a 25% strikeout rate and an 11.5% walk rate. The Rockies drafted him with the final pick of the second supplemental round in 2025 and inked him for $1.1 million. His pro debut was a struggle. Belyeu struck out 35.5% of the time while hitting .150 in 21 games for High-A Spokane, though he did homer four times.
SCOUTING REPORT: Belyeu is a strong, physically developed 6-foot-2, 215-pound lefthanded hitter with a compact swing and quick hands. He has an aggressive approach at the plate and is prone to chasing pitches. Belyeu's plate discipline showed steady improvement throughout his college career, but it regressed dramatically in his brief pro debut. He possesses above-average raw power and projects to hit 20-25 home runs with further refinement. On the bases, Belyeu isn't a burner, but he's a hustling runner who moves well once underway and grades out as average in terms of speed. He is an average defender in right field, where his plus arm could be an asset.
THE FUTURE: Like many Rockies hitting prospects, Belyeu needs to hit to profile as a big leaguer, because he is a corner outfielder without a lot of defensive potential. His struggles in Spokane gave him a solid understanding of how he needs to work to recognize pitches better and focus on making more consistent contact. He should head back to the Northwest League to begin 2026.

Year	Age	Club (League)	Level	AVG	G	AB	R	H	2B	3B	HR	RBI	BB	SO	SB	OBP	SLG
2025	21	Spokane (NWL)	A+	.150	21	80	13	12	0	0	4	9	9	32	3	.244	.300
		Minor League Totals		.150	21	80	13	12	0	0	4	9	9	32	3	.244	.300

COLORADO ROCKIES

8 JACKSON COX, RHP

FB: 55. **CB:** 60. **SW:** 50. **CH:** 40. **CT:** 45. **CTL:** 55. **BA Grade:** 50. **Risk:** High. **Adj:** 35.

Born: September 25, 2003. **B-T:** R-R. **HT:** 6-0. **WT:** 185.
Drafted: HS—Toutle, WA, 2022 (2nd round). **Signed by:** Matt Pignataro.
TRACK RECORD: Cox entered the 2022 draft as one of the most intriguing high school arms available, thanks to his exceptional high-spin curveball. The Rockies selected him in the second round and signed him for $1.85 million, banking on his combination of spin, athleticism and upside. His pro career had barely gotten going when he had Tommy John surgery in July 2023. Cox made his return in 2024 at instructional league, where he showed encouraging signs of regaining the bite and feel on his breaking pitches. Assigned to Low-A Fresno in 2025, he ran up a 15.43 ERA in his first four starts but pitched to a 2.31 ERA in his remaining 19 starts.
SCOUTING REPORT: Cox's combination of present stuff and a deep arsenal stands out in an organization thin on starting pitching prospects. He attacks hitters with a five-pitch mix that includes a four-seam fastball, curveball, slider, changeup and cutter. His fastball sits in the 93-94 mph range and can touch 98, showing late hop and life through the zone. His best pitch remains his plus curveball, a high-spin, two-plane breaker that consistently measures between 2,800–3,000 rpm and serves as a legitimate out pitch. Cox rounds out his arsenal with an average mid-80s sweeper, a firm below-average upper-80s changeup, and a developing low-90s fringe-average cutter. He has no issues throwing his fastball for strikes, but he needs to figure out how to land his curveball and sweeper in the zone at a higher clip.
THE FUTURE: Cox's combination of velocity, spin and his ability to develop different pitches gives him a chance to develop into a solid midrotation starter in an organization that has struggled recently to develop starting pitchers. He should head to High-A Spokane to start 2026.

Year	Age	Club (League)	Level	W	L	ERA	G	GS	IP	H	HR	BB	SO	BB%	SO%	WHIP	AVG
2025	21	Fresno (CAL)	A	4	6	3.39	23	23	85	70	12	25	92	7.3	27.0	1.12	.225
		Minor League Totals		5	6	4.42	33	32	116	109	14	45	124	9.2	25.3	1.33	.249

9 ROBERT CALAZ, OF

HIT: 40. **POW:** 55. **RUN:** 40. **FLD:** 45. **ARM:** 55. **BA Grade:** 50. **Risk:** Extreme. **Adj:** 30.

Born: November 11, 2005. **B-T:** R-R. **HT:** 6-2. **WT:** 202.
Signed: Dominican Republic, 2023. **Signed by:** Orlando Covo.
TRACK RECORD: Calaz signed with the Rockies for $1.7 million in 2023, touted as a polished power hitter with a physically mature frame. That promise quickly showed in the 2023 Dominican Summer League and carried over into an eye-catching U.S. debut in 2024. He began the year in the Arizona Complex League, where he hit .349/.462/.651 with 10 home runs before earning a promotion to Low-A Fresno. Calaz's progress stalled in 2025, when his plate discipline regressed significantly. He batted .259 with 110 strikeouts against just 37 walks in 99 games.
SCOUTING REPORT: Calaz stands 6-foot-2 with room to add more strength to an already-mature frame. He brings explosive raw power to the plate, though his game remains a bit unrefined. Swing-and-miss concerns have followed him since signing—a common caveat with young, power-first hitters—but they've become more pronounced. Calaz's swing starts with an extremely high hand-set, and he sometimes rests the bat on his shoulder before using a waggle to start his trigger. That means he has plenty of length to his swing, which generates big power, but also makes him vulnerable to elevated fastballs and pitchers who can disrupt his timing. Despite the swing-and-miss issues, Calaz's upside remains enticing. He consistently produces some of the highest exit velocities in the Rockies' system, and given his age, there's still physical projection remaining. Defensively, he's a below-average runner who is a fringe-average corner outfielder. He has an above-average arm that adds value in right field.
THE FUTURE: Calaz struggled for the first time as a pro in 2025. He'll jump to High-A Spokane in 2026, looking to bounce back. He has the power potential to be a solid big league regular, but only if he refines his approach and cleans up his swing.

Year	Age	Club (League)	Level	AVG	G	AB	R	H	2B	3B	HR	RBI	BB	SO	SB	OBP	SLG
2025	19	Fresno (CAL)	A	.259	99	371	50	96	16	3	10	55	37	110	7	.338	.399
		Minor League Totals		.298	204	749	144	223	42	12	29	140	96	216	28	.389	.502

10 WELINTON HERRERA, LHP
FB: 60. **SL:** 60. **CH:** 40. **CTL:** 50. **BA Grade:** 45. **Risk:** High. **Adj:** 30.

Born: April 3, 2004. **B-T:** L-L. **HT:** 6-0. **WT:** 166.
Signed: Dominican Republic, 2021. **Signed by:** Rolando Fernandez.
TRACK RECORD: The Rockies signed Herrera out of the Dominican Republic in 2021, and he spent two years in the Dominican Summer League and one in the Arizona Complex League, working almost exclusively as a reliever in all three seasons. He advanced to full-season ball in 2024, making a pair of Class A stops. Herrera began to pick up steam in 2025, when he dominated the High-A Northwest League, represented the Rockies at the Futures Game and earned a mid-May promotion to Double-A Hartford. He ranked fourth in the minors with 17 saves and pitched in the Arizona Fall League after the season.
SCOUTING REPORT: Herrera's combination of low three-quarters arm slot and above-average carry makes his 95-99 mph fastball one of the better heaters in the minors. The lefthander's fastball is almost impossible to lift. Hitters managed just .197/.287/.236 against Herrera's fastball in 2025, and the two home runs he allowed both came against his slider. Though undersized at 6 feet and 166 pounds, he compensates with a polished three-pitch arsenal and a delivery that adds a layer of deception. He pairs his fastball with a hard, low-to-mid-80s gyro slider that serves as his most-used secondary pitch, generating consistent whiffs and chases. Herrera worked on adding a below-average, mid-80s changeup to better handle righthanded hitters, but in a one-inning relief role, a third pitch won't be necessary.
THE FUTURE: Herrera is ready for Triple-A Albuquerque, a hitter's paradise, just like Coors Field. His groundball tendencies are tailor-made for limiting damage. He is expected to be added to the 40-man roster this offseason and could pitch his way to Colorado at some point in 2026. He has the stuff to be a middle reliever.

Year	Age	Club (League)	Level	W	L	ERA	G	GS	IP	H	HR	BB	SO	BB%	SO%	WHIP	AVG
2025	21	Spokane (NWL)	A+	1	0	0.49	15	0	18	8	0	6	29	8.8	42.6	0.76	.129
2025	21	Hartford (EL)	AA	4	5	3.50	37	0	46	41	2	19	70	9.3	34.3	1.29	.232
		Minor League Totals		25	10	3.27	157	1	215	166	5	88	309	9.7	34.2	1.18	.211

11 JB MIDDLETON, RHP
FB: 55. **SL:** 55. **CH:** 55. **CTL:** 50. **BA Grade:** 45. **Risk:** High. **Adj:** 30.

Born: November 24, 2003. **B-T:** R-R. **HT:** 6-0. **WT:** 178. **Drafted:** Southern Mississippi, 2025 (2nd round).
Signed by: Zack Zulli.
TRACK RECORD: Middleton primarily pitched out of Southern Mississippi's bullpen for two seasons before stepping into a starting role in 2025. He immediately broke out with a 2.31 ERA across 16 starts and 105.1 innings, pitching to a 29.4% strikeout rate compared to a 6% walk rate. His control took a big step forward and he ranked second among Division I pitchers with a 0.85 WHIP. Middleton became the highest-drafted pitcher in school history when the Rockies selected him 45th overall. He did not make his pro debut, instead remaining at the team's complex in Scottsdale.
SCOUTING REPORT: Middleton once struggled to crack the upper 80s as a high schooler. Now, the compact righthander works from a high three-quarters slot with lightning-quick arm speed, producing a 93-95 mph fastball that can touch 97. Despite his size, he maintains his velocity deep into outings. Against righthanders, Middleton primarily leans on his fastball-slider combination, while his upper-80s changeup becomes a key weapon against lefties. The slider features tight, upper-80s spin with a gyro-like rotation, occasionally resembling a cutter when it touches 90 mph, and grades as an above-average pitch. Middleton's changeup, with roughly 10 inches of vertical drop relative to his fastball, is a true swing-and-miss pitch, generating a 54% whiff rate in 2025.
THE FUTURE: Middleton's polish and repertoire point toward a solid back-of-the-rotation starter. He should begin 2026 with High-A Spokane.

Year	Age	Club (League)	Level	W	L	ERA	G	GS	IP	H	HR	BB	SO	BB%	SO%	WHIP	AVG
2025	21	Did not play															

COLORADO ROCKIES

12 GRIFFIN HERRING, LHP
FB: 50. **CB:** 45. **SL:** 55. **CH:** 50. **CTL:** 55. **BA Grade:** 45. **Risk:** High. **Adj:** 30.

Born: May 7, 2003. **B-T:** R-L. **HT:** 6-2. **WT:** 200. **Drafted:** LSU, 2024 (6th round).
Signed by: Mike Leuzinger (Yankees).
TRACK RECORD: Herring carved out a prominent role in LSU's bullpen, appearing in 39 games over two seasons and establishing himself as one of the Tigers' most trusted arms. His 2024 performance earned him Baseball America second-team All-American honors. The Yankees selected him in the sixth round that year and signed him to an above-slot $797,500 bonus, but his tenure with New York was brief, as they traded him to Colorado in 2025 as part of the Ryan McMahon deal. Herring made a strong first impression by striking out 40.5% of batters he faced over 30 innings and seven starts with High-A Spokane.
SCOUTING REPORT: Herring has been developed as a starter, which might seem strange for a player with a fastball that averaged a tick under 90 mph in 2025, but his nearly seven feet of extension and slight pause in his delivery create an impressive angle of attack, plenty of deception and a whippy finish. He has found the most success so far with a mid-80s slider that generates plenty of whiffs within the strike zone. Herring also employed a mid-80s changeup with lower spin rates, but it's not a crisp pitch and there's some concern that higher elevations might dilute its effectiveness.
THE FUTURE: If Herring wants to remain a starter, he'll need to add more zip to his fastball, perhaps by packing on some muscle over the offseason. His profile and wipeout slider could fit better in a bullpen. He should begin 2026 in Double-A.

Year	Age	Club (League)	Level	W	L	ERA	G	GS	IP	H	HR	BB	SO	BB%	SO%	WHIP	AVG
2025	22	Tampa (FSL)	A	4	1	1.21	8	8	45	24	2	16	58	9.2	33.3	0.90	.155
2025	22	Hudson Valley (SAL)	A+	3	2	2.22	8	8	45	32	1	20	44	10.9	23.9	1.16	.201
2025	22	Spokane (NWL)	A+	1	1	2.40	7	7	30	14	1	13	47	11.2	40.5	0.90	.141
		Minor League Totals		8	4	1.89	23	23	119	70	4	49	149	10.3	31.4	1.00	.169

13 ETHAN HEDGES, 3B
HIT: 45. **POW:** 50. **RUN:** 50. **FLD:** 50. **ARM:** 65. **BA Grade:** 45. **Risk:** High. **Adj:** 30.

Born: April 19, 2004. **B-T:** R-R. **HT:** 6-1. **WT:** 185. **Drafted:** Southern California, 2025 (3rd round).
Signed by: Tim McDonnell.
TRACK RECORD: Hedges hit over his first two years at Southern California, then pitched in relief as well in 2025. Still, the consensus was that his clearer path to a pro career was with the bat. He backed that up by slashing .346/.462/.619 with 14 home runs, 11 doubles, five triples and 10 stolen bases as a junior. The Rockies drafted him in the third round in 2025 and sent him right to High-A Spokane, where he had a .537 OPS over his first 20 professional games.
SCOUTING REPORT: Hedges showed keen plate discipline in college with a 17.4% strikeout rate compared to a 15.3% walk rate in his junior spring. He profiles as a gap-to-gap hitter with solid bat speed and power to all fields, giving him the baseline tools to impact the game offensively. His body is already filled out, so it's unclear whether much more power is on the way. Hedges' first stint in affiliated ball with Spokane also revealed significant swing-and-miss issues against spin, and he'll need to tighten his pitch recognition and adjust his swing decisions to better handle quality breaking balls. Hedges could develop into a steady defender at third base with good instincts and reliable actions. Unsurprisingly, Hedges' plus arm is an asset on the dirt. He was up to 93 mph on the mound and complemented his fastball with a slider and changeup.
THE FUTURE: A return to High-A in 2026 is in order for Hedges as he embarks on his first full pro season.

Year	Age	Club (League)	Level	AVG	G	AB	R	H	2B	3B	HR	RBI	BB	SO	SB	OBP	SLG
2025	21	Spokane (NWL)	A+	.195	20	77	8	15	3	0	0	3	10	17	2	.303	.234
		Minor League Totals		.195	20	77	8	15	3	0	0	3	10	17	2	.303	.234

14 WILDER DALIS, 3B
HIT: 55. **POW:** 50. **RUN:** 55. **FLD:** 50. **ARM:** 50. **BA Grade:** 45. **Risk:** High. **Adj:** 30.

Born: July 30, 2006. **B-T:** B-R. **HT:** 6-0. **WT:** 170. **Signed:** Venezuela, 2023.
Signed by: Rolando Fernandez/Orlando Medina/Joel Diaz.
TRACK RECORD: Dalis was a bit of a late-bloomer who flew under the radar when the Rockies signed him out of Venezuela in 2023, and he turned in an inauspicious pro debut that year with a .616 OPS in 27 Dominican Summer League games. He made up for it by being one of the best hitters on the 2024 Rockies DSL team and carried that momentum into his stateside debut in 2025, hitting .352 in the

Arizona Complex League before finishing the season in Low-A Fresno.
SCOUTING REPORT: Dalis strikes a notable presence when he steps into the batter's box with a strong, well-built lower half and room on his frame to keep adding physicality as he matures. That provides a solid foundation for future power development. Dalis also has advanced feel for the barrel for his age. He posted above-average overall contact rates and borderline plus in-zone contact rates in 2025 to go along with solid exit velocities for his age. There's some length to his swing that might get exposed against better breaking balls, and some of those struggles surfaced in his time in Fresno. Defensively, he looks most natural at third base and has the arm strength to stick there, but he also mixed in at shortstop and second base.
THE FUTURE: Dalis will head back to Low-A Fresno to begin 2026, where he'll need to prove he can read spin better.

Year	Age	Club (League)	Level	AVG	G	AB	R	H	2B	3B	HR	RBI	BB	SO	SB	OBP	SLG
2025	18	ACL Rockies	Rk	.352	56	179	37	63	12	5	3	42	29	44	10	.440	.525
2025	18	Fresno (CAL)	A	.241	31	116	17	28	7	0	3	22	16	26	6	.333	.379
		Minor League Totals		.305	170	591	114	180	34	7	9	121	99	125	48	.406	.431

15 ROC RIGGIO, 2B

HIT: 45. **POW:** 50. **RUN:** 40. **FLD:** 45. **ARM:** 45. **BA Grade:** 40. **Risk:** Average. **Adj:** 30.

Born: June 11, 2002. **B-T:** L-R. **HT:** 5-9. **WT:** 190. **Drafted:** Oklahoma State, 2023 (4th round).
Signed by: Matt Ranson (Yankees).
TRACK RECORD: Riggio caught scouts' attention while at Thousand Oaks High in greater Los Angeles, where he was teammates with the Athletics' duo of Jacob Wilson and Max Muncy. Instead he honored his commitment to Oklahoma State, where he owned a 1.040 OPS and 29 homers over two college seasons. The Yankees drafted him in the fourth round in 2023 and went well over slot to sign him for $693,000. They dealt Riggio two years later to the Rockies in a package for Jake Bird, and the 23-year-old slashed .256/.346/.389 with two home runs and 14 RBIs in 26 games with Double-A Hartford.
SCOUTING REPORT: Despite a shorter 5-foot-9 frame, Riggio has always produced surprising thump, and he launched 20 homers across 88 minor league games in 2025. He also made some encouraging refinements to his approach, chasing less and making more in-zone contact. Still, scouts have concerns that he tends to leak to his pull side and can struggle against secondaries. His offensive profile also comes with clear platoon concerns. Against lefties, he hit just .181 and struck out 32% of the time, though he homered seven times. Defensively, scouts describe him as a limited second baseman, who doesn't have the projection to play elsewhere along the infield.
THE FUTURE: Riggio's lack of defensive versatility limits him to a likely platoon role at second base, where he could provide meaningful value against righthanders or as a late-game pinch-hitter with some power.

Year	Age	Club (League)	Level	AVG	G	AB	R	H	2B	3B	HR	RBI	BB	SO	SB	OBP	SLG
2025	23	FCL Yankees	Rk	.333	2	6	2	2	0	0	1	2	0	1	0	.333	.833
2025	23	Hudson Valley (SAL)	A+	.264	20	72	20	19	4	1	6	15	20	22	2	.436	.597
2025	23	Somerset (EL)	AA	.261	40	153	25	40	10	0	11	28	13	37	7	.335	.542
2025	23	Hartford (EL)	AA	.256	26	90	13	23	6	0	2	14	14	23	8	.346	.389
		Minor League Totals		.249	110	394	73	98	22	1	20	68	69	107	20	.369	.462

16 SEAN SULLIVAN, LHP

FB: 45. **SL:** 50. **CH:** 60. **CTL:** 60. **BA Grade:** 45. **Risk:** High. **Adj:** 30.

Born: July 22, 2002. **B-T:** R-L. **HT:** 6-5. **WT:** 190. **Drafted:** Wake Forest, 2023 (2nd round). **Signed by:** Jordan Czarniecki.
TRACK RECORD: The Rockies gave Sullivan $1.7 million as the 46th overall pick in 2023 out of Wake Forest. Hip surgery delayed the start of his 2025 season, but he settled into Double-A Hartford's rotation, pitching to a 3.14 ERA with a 24.2% strikeout rate to 6.1% walk rate over 18 starts and 97.1 innings.
SCOUTING REPORT: Few pitchers succeed in the big leagues with an upper-80s fastball, but the Rockies believe Sullivan can do it. The 6-foot-5 lefthander averaged just 87 mph and touched 90 mph in 2025, yet he found success thanks to an unconventional delivery. He starts on the far third-base side of the rubber and releases the ball from a low, funky sidearm slot and nearly 7.5 feet of extension. His elite length and closed setup create serious deception, often hiding the ball from hitters until it has left his hand. He primarily attacks the top of the strike zone, especially on the inner half against lefthanded hitters. Sullivan filled up the zone with a 67% strike percentage in 2025, including a 70% strike rate on his fastball, and he gets plenty of swings and misses across his entire arsenal, which includes both a plus changeup and average slider that range from upper 70s to low 80s.
THE FUTURE: Evaluators have a tough time settling on a future role for Sullivan because of his unique plan of attack, but many see him as a future bulk reliever who can make the occasional spot start. For now, the Rockies plan on keeping him in the rotation.

COLORADO ROCKIES

Year	Age	Club (League)	Level	W	L	ERA	G	GS	IP	H	HR	BB	SO	BB%	SO%	WHIP	AVG
2025	22	ACL Rockies	Rk	0	0	0.00	1	1	3	0	0	1	7	8.3	58.3	0.38	.000
2025	22	Fresno (CAL)	A	0	0	0.00	1	1	4	3	0	0	2	0.0	14.3	0.75	.214
2025	22	Hartford (EL)	AA	9	6	3.14	18	18	97	82	7	24	95	6.1	24.2	1.09	.227
		Minor League Totals		17	8	2.54	37	34	191	147	14	34	215	4.5	28.6	0.95	.208

17 CARSON PALMQUIST, LHP

FB: 45. **CT:** 50. **CH:** 50. **SW:** 45. **CTL:** 50. **BA Grade:** 40. **Risk:** Average. **Adj:** 30.

Born: October 17, 2000. **B-T:** L-L. **HT:** 6-3. **WT:** 185. **Drafted:** Miami, 2022 (3rd round). **Signed by:** Rafael Reyes.

TRACK RECORD: The Rockies selected Palmquist in the third round of the 2022 draft and signed the lefthander for $775,000. He reached the big leagues in May 2025, ultimately going 0-4, 8.91 across 34.1 innings and nine outings. Palmquist otherwise pitched with Triple-A Albuquerque where he posted a 4.64 ERA with 94 strikeouts to 42 walks in 77.2 innings in his age-24 season.

SCOUTING REPORT: Palmquist makes up for a lack of overpowering velocity with plenty of deception. Working from the third base side of the rubber with a compact motion, he briefly reveals the ball before releasing from a low slot paired with 7.4 feet of extension, which ranked in the 97th percentile among major league pitchers. That combination has helped Palmquist's 90-92 mph fastball, which touches 94, play above its velocity in the minors. Still, MLB hitters slugged .719 against it in a small sample. He also works with a mid-70s sweeper, low-80s changeup and low-80s cutter, though he mostly relies on the fastball-sweeper combo. While the sweeper generates strong whiff rates, scouts were skeptical it would hold up against big league hitters. His walk rates have also steadily climbed as a professional. With improved control, evaluators still view him as a viable back-end starter or a low-leverage relief option.

THE FUTURE: Palmquist's major league struggles were jarring, but he remains in the mix for a spot either at the back of their rotation or in the bullpen in 2026.

Year	Age	Club (League)	Level	W	L	ERA	G	GS	IP	H	HR	BB	SO	BB%	SO%	WHIP	AVG
2025	24	Albuquerque (PCL)	AAA	4	5	4.64	26	10	78	62	7	42	94	12.4	27.8	1.34	.219
2025	24	Colorado (NL)	MLB	0	4	8.91	9	7	34	45	10	25	27	14.3	15.4	2.04	.321
		Minor League Totals		18	17	4.12	73	56	289	239	35	141	373	11.5	30.3	1.32	.227
		Major League Totals		0	4	8.91	9	7	34	45	10	25	27	14.3	15.4	2.04	.321

18 ZAC VEEN, OF

HIT: 45. **POW:** 45. **RUN:** 55. **FLD:** 55. **ARM:** 50. **BA Grade:** 40. **Risk:** Average. **Adj:** 30.

Born: December 12, 2001. **B-T:** L-R. **HT:** 6-3. **WT:** 215. **Drafted:** HS—Spruce Creek, FL, 2020 (1st round). **Signed by:** John Cedarburg.

TRACK RECORD: The Rockies drafted Veen ninth overall in 2020 and he moved quickly through the lower levels, reaching Double-A Hartford in 2022. But injuries have since slowed his ascent. A left wrist tendon issue that cost him most of 2023, while back and thumb injuries limited him again during his third stint in Hartford in 2024 before he arrived in Triple-A at the end of the season. Veen finally reached the majors in 2025, debuting on April 8, but was optioned back to Triple-A after hitting .118 over 12 games and spent the rest of the year in Albuquerque.

SCOUTING REPORT: While injuries have slowed his progress, Veen has an intriguing power-speed blend when he's healthy. He has historically shown solid plate discipline and pitch recognition, knowing when to pull the trigger on pitches in the zone, though his approach got a bit more overzealous in 2025. His long, low-ball swing also disrupts his timing and leads to elevated strikeout rates with below-average contact. Pitchers attack his hands and then finish him with breaking balls once he compensates for velocity. While he can drive mistakes when fully extended, fringe-average exit velocities and subpar batted-ball angles limit his game power. An instinctive basestealer with above-average speed, he adds value on the bases and in the corner outfield, though inconsistent reads prevent him from profiling in center field.

THE FUTURE: Veen has continued the trend of Rockies first-rounders who have yet to pan out. He should begin 2026 back in Triple-A.

Year	Age	Club (League)	Level	AVG	G	AB	R	H	2B	3B	HR	RBI	BB	SO	SB	OBP	SLG
2025	23	ACL Rockies	Rk	.286	3	7	2	2	0	0	0	1	4	2	0	.545	.286
2025	23	Albuquerque (PCL)	AAA	.289	90	370	57	107	23	5	11	59	35	84	15	.354	.468
2025	23	Colorado (NL)	MLB	.118	12	34	1	4	1	0	1	2	2	14	1	.189	.235
		Minor League Totals		.267	436	1647	284	439	90	16	51	261	220	454	149	.356	.434
		Major League Totals		.118	12	34	1	4	1	0	1	2	2	14	1	.189	.235

COLORADO ROCKIES

19 ASHLY ANDUJAR, SS/2B
HIT: 50. **POW:** 30. **RUN:** 50. **FLD:** 50. **ARM:** 50. **BA Grade:** 40. **Risk:** Average. **Adj:** 30.

Born: July 29, 2007. **B-T:** B-R. **HT:** 6-1. **WT:** 163. **Signed:** Dominican Republic, 2024.
Signed by: Rolando Fernandez/Frank Roa.
TRACK RECORD: The Rockies have long prioritized shortstops in their international classes and did so again when they signed Andujar for $1.4 million in 2024, the biggest bonus in their international class. Andujar delivered a solid Dominican Summer League debut that year, then followed by hitting .319 over 53 Arizona Complex League games in 2025. He remained at the complex after the season, earning extra reps alongside several members of the Rockies' 2025 draft class.
SCOUTING REPORT: Andujar's game is rooted in excellent contact ability. The switch-hitter whiffed on pitches just 20% of the time in 2025 and rarely misses them within the strike zone. The tradeoff is virtually no impact. He has yet to homer in 104 professional games, and while he only turned 18 in July, his below-average exit velocities and limited power projection suggest there isn't a ton of impact on the way. He's a twitchy athlete with a strong feel for in-game adjustments. Andujar knows how to compensate for slower bat speed by finding the barrel and choking up on the bat in key situations. Defensively, Andujar was one of the ACL's better middle infielders with a fluid lower half and quick release. He's a bit of an awkward baserunner who is slow to get going because of his lanky frame, and he stole 10 fewer bases than in 2024, but scouts believe his running will improve as he becomes more coordinated.
THE FUTURE: Andujar should start in Low-A to begin the year, where his contact skills will be challenged against better pitching.

Year	Age	Club (League)	Level	AVG	G	AB	R	H	2B	3B	HR	RBI	BB	SO	SB	OBP	SLG
2025	17	ACL Rockies	Rk	.319	53	191	32	61	7	0	0	23	15	31	7	.370	.356
		Minor League Totals		.305	104	390	68	119	15	2	0	47	37	62	24	.373	.354

20 CRISTIAN ARGUELLES, OF
HIT: 55. **POW:** 45. **RUN:** 50. **FLD:** 50. **ARM:** 45. **BA Grade:** 50. **Risk:** Extreme. **Adj:** 30.

Born: June 30, 2007. **B-T:** L-L. **HT:** 6-0. **WT:** 177. **Signed:** Venezuela, 2024.
Signed by: Rolando Fernandez/Orlando Medina.
TRACK RECORD: Arguelles was the Rockies' top Venezuelan signee in the 2024 international class for $700,000. He showed early promise in his Dominican Summer League debut, batting .267/.352/.302 with 25 RBIs over 50 games. Although the Rockies were encouraged by his performance, they opted to keep him in the DSL for 2025 to allow him more time to add strength and physically mature. The decision paid off. Arguelles dominated the league in his second stint, earning DSL MVP honors after leading in batting average (.422), slugging (.652), OPS (1.180), hits (79) and total bases (122).
SCOUTING REPORT: Arguelles is a pure hitter with a sound lefthanded swing. He produced excellent contact rates in the DSL in 2025, making contact in the zone at a 91.6% rate and missing just 16.5% of the time. While he repeated the level, his 14.4% walk rate also suggests a solid feel for the strike zone. Arguelles can get a bit aggressive chasing pitches and also hasn't hit for much power, though his impact could tick up if he can pack on more muscle. He's an average runner with a fringy arm who might end up fitting best in a corner outfield spot.
THE FUTURE: Arguelles should start 2026 in the Arizona Complex League and could end in Low-A.

Year	Age	Club (League)	Level	AVG	G	AB	R	H	2B	3B	HR	RBI	BB	SO	SB	OBP	SLG
2025	18	DSL Rockies	Rk	.422	52	187	56	79	16	6	5	55	34	25	6	.528	.652
		Minor League Totals		.348	102	359	85	125	22	6	5	80	52	37	17	.447	.485

21 STERLIN THOMPSON, OF
HIT: 45. **POW:** 45. **RUN:** 45. **FLD:** 40. **ARM:** 55. **BA Grade:** 40. **Risk:** Average. **Adj:** 30.

Born: June 26, 2001. **B-T:** L-R. **HT:** 6-4. **WT:** 195. **Drafted:** Florida, 2022 (1st round supp.). **Signed by:** John Cedarburg.
TRACK RECORD: The Rockies drafted Thompson 31st overall in 2022, but he lost a large chunk of his first full pro season in 2023 to an elbow injury. Thompson spent all of 2024 with Double-A Hartford, where he produced just a .704 OPS but made clear strides in the second half of the year with his timing and quality of contact. Those gains held up in a productive 2025 with Triple-A Albuquerque and the Rockies added Thompson to their 40-man roster after the season to shield him from the Rule 5 draft.
SCOUTING REPORT: Thompson has long been a reliable contact hitter, and that strength held steady in 2025. He generated above-average contact and chase rates, all while producing an above-average 105.1 mph 90th percentile exit velocity. Thompson's lefthanded swing is smooth and efficient. He thrives on hitting pitches in the lower part of the zone, though he's vulnerable to quality spin on the outer edge. He

COLORADO ROCKIES

has fared better against righthanded pitchers in each of the past two seasons, with 15 of his 18 homers coming against righties in 2025. Defensive concerns have followed him throughout his career, and scouts still project him as a below-average corner outfielder.

THE FUTURE: Thompson is likely to open 2026 back in Triple-A, but he could hit his way into the strong side of an outfield platoon in the big leagues.

Year	Age	Club (League)	Level	AVG	G	AB	R	H	2B	3B	HR	RBI	BB	SO	SB	OBP	SLG
2025	24	Albuquerque (PCL)	AAA	.296	120	439	82	130	28	8	18	66	53	107	12	.392	.519
		Minor League Totals		.279	359	1357	218	378	78	13	47	189	139	331	44	.360	.459

22 GABRIEL HUGHES, RHP
FB: 45. **CB:** 45. **SL:** 50. **SP:** 40. **CT:** 50. **CTL:** 50. **BA Grade:** 40. **Risk:** Average. **Adj:** 30.

Born: August 22, 2001. **B-T:** R-R. **HT:** 6-4. **WT:** 220. **Drafted:** Gonzaga, 2022 (1st round). **Signed by:** Matt Pignataro.

TRACK RECORD: Hughes transitioned to full-time pitching as a junior at Gonzaga, where a breakout campaign earned him second-team All-America honors and propelled him to the Rockies, who selected him 10th overall in 2022 and signed him for $4 million. He reached Double-A Hartford the following summer until a torn ulnar collateral ligament ended his season in July and required Tommy John surgery. Hughes returned for 2024 Arizona Fall League action and resumed full-season action in 2025, ending the year in Triple-A. The Rockies added the 24-year-old to their 40-man roster after the season.

SCOUTING REPORT: Nothing Hughes throws is straight. His low-90s cutter touches 94 and jumps on hitters thanks to its 12-13 inches of induced vertical break and nearly seven feet of extension. He also incorporated a low-90s sinker and supported his two fastball shapes with a deep, versatile secondary mix that includes a tight mid-80s slider, a bigger upper-70s curveball that was more of a swing-and-miss option in 2025 and a developing 86 mph splitter. Hughes added more deception and extension after surgery by holding the ball longer in his delivery, though he doesn't miss a ton of bats and his strikeout rate dropped to 17.5% in Triple-A.

THE FUTURE: Hughes has back-of-the-rotation upside. He should begin 2026 in Triple-A and has a chance to make his big league debut later in the season with a strong performance.

Year	Age	Club (League)	Level	W	L	ERA	G	GS	IP	H	HR	BB	SO	BB%	SO%	WHIP	AVG
2025	23	ACL Rockies	Rk	0	0	0.00	1	1	3	1	0	1	5	9.1	45.5	0.75	.100
2025	23	Hartford (EL)	AA	1	3	3.07	9	9	41	27	4	8	35	5.1	22.3	0.85	.184
2025	23	Albuquerque (PCL)	AAA	4	3	5.11	14	14	62	67	9	29	48	10.6	17.5	1.56	.277
		Minor League Totals		11	11	4.89	39	39	175	160	25	65	172	8.7	23.1	1.29	.238

23 COLE MESSINA, C
HIT: 40. **POW:** 50. **RUN:** 50. **FLD:** 55. **ARM:** 55. **BA Grade:** 40. **Risk:** Average. **Adj:** 30.

Born: May 14, 2003. **B-T:** R-R. **HT:** 6-0. **WT:** 230. **Drafted:** South Carolina, 2024 (3rd round). **Signed by:** Jordan Czarniecki.

TRACK RECORD: Messina played three years at South Carolina, emerging as the Gamecocks' everyday catcher in his sophomore and junior seasons. He put together a standout 2024 campaign, hitting .326/.465/.701 with 21 home runs to earn second-team All-American honors. The Rockies drafted him in the third round and signed him for slightly over $1 million. His 2024 pro debut with High-A Spokane got off to a slow start, but he fared better in his return in 2025, hitting .259/.358/.382 in 107 games.

SCOUTING REPORT: Messina is a physical, well-built catcher who combines his sturdy frame with above-average athleticism. In his first professional season, he displayed some of the offensive tools that made him a standout at South Carolina, making tons of contact in the strike zone while striking out just 16.4% of the time. He has yet to get to his solid raw power consistently in games. Messina also had significant reverse platoon splits, hitting .275 with six of his seven homers against righties compared to just .172 against lefties. Defensively, scouts noted Messina made strides with his framing and he threw out 40% of runners from behind the plate.

THE FUTURE: Messina's combination of skills point toward a part-time catcher in the big leagues one day. He should begin 2026 in Double-A.

Year	Age	Club (League)	Level	AVG	G	AB	R	H	2B	3B	HR	RBI	BB	SO	SB	OBP	SLG
2025	22	Spokane (NWL)	A+	.259	107	374	48	97	23	1	7	42	51	72	14	.358	.382
2025	22	Hartford (EL)	AA	.200	3	10	1	2	0	0	0	0	1	0	0	.200	.200
		Minor League Totals		.258	110	384	49	99	23	1	7	42	51	73	14	.354	.378

COLORADO ROCKIES

24 McCADE BROWN, RHP
FB: 50. **CB:** 45. **SL:** 55. **CH:** 45. **CTL:** 40. **BA Grade:** 40. **Risk:** Average. **Adj:** 30.

Born: August 15, 2000. **B-T:** R-R. **HT:** 6-6. **WT:** 225. **Drafted:** Indiana, 2021 (3rd round). **Signed by:** Scott Corman.

TRACK RECORD: After an electric albeit erratic college career, Brown's strike-throwing took a step forward in pro ball in 2022 only to see that progress halted by Tommy John surgery in 2023. Following a lengthy recovery, Brown looked revitalized in his first full season back in 2025, striking out minor league hitters 34.3% of the time while maintaining a 9.8% walk rate. His performance fast-tracked his ascent to the majors. He skipped Triple-A and made his big league debut on Aug. 24. He went 0-5 with a 7.36 ERA in seven starts.

SCOUTING REPORT: Brown's jump in effectiveness stems in part from a move to the third-base side of the rubber, a subtle adjustment that better syncs with his mechanics. The new setup enhances his natural deception, allowing him to hide the ball behind his head before delivering from a three-quarters arm slot with a cross-bodied stride. He relies heavily on a 94-95 mph fastball that can reach 98, attacking hitters at the top of the zone with confidence. His best secondary pitch is a mid-80s slider that he locates consistently and is a genuine bat-misser, generating a 36.5% whiff rate against big leaguers. He's still learning to fully employ his curveball and changeup.

THE FUTURE: Brown emerged as a welcome surprise in the Rockies' system. His ceiling likely fits toward the back of a rotation and he should compete for a spot in Colorado's rotation out of spring training.

Year	Age	Club (League)	Level	W	L	ERA	G	GS	IP	H	HR	BB	SO	BB%	SO%	WHIP	AVG
2025	24	Spokane (NWL)	A+	0	0	1.60	9	9	34	21	2	15	48	11.0	35.3	1.07	.178
2025	24	Hartford (EL)	AA	4	2	3.14	11	11	43	31	4	15	57	8.8	33.5	1.07	.203
2025	24	Colorado (NL)	MLB	0	5	7.36	7	7	26	30	6	17	23	13.5	18.3	1.83	.291
		Minor League Totals		9	9	4.41	54	51	198	172	23	73	267	8.7	31.9	1.24	.231
		Major League Totals		0	5	7.36	7	7	26	30	6	17	23	13.5	18.3	1.83	.291

25 RILEY KELLY, RHP
FB: 60. **CB:** 60. **CH:** 50. **CTL:** 40. **BA Grade:** 45. **Risk:** High. **Adj:** 30.

Born: April 21, 2004. **B-T:** R-R. **HT:** 6-5. **WT:** 240. **Drafted:** UC Irvine, 2025 (4th round). **Signed by:** Matt Hattabaugh.

TRACK RECORD: Kelly was a prominent draft prospect in high school out of California but instead reached UC Irvine, where a back injury impacted him in 2024. He returned healthy in 2025 and pitched to a 3.78 ERA with 70 strikeouts across 66.2 innings and 12 starts. The Rockies selected him in the fourth round and signed him for $700,000. He did not make his pro debut, and instead pitched in bridge and instructional leagues.

SCOUTING REPORT: Kelly is an athletic 6-foot-5, 240-pound righthander with a workhorse frame and a north-south pitching style. He relies heavily on a fastball that he threw nearly 65% of the time in his junior spring, sitting 91-93 mph and touching 96. His heater has above-average ride through the zone. His standout secondary is a high-70s hammer curveball that consistently spins above 3,000 rpm and ranked among the best breaking balls in his class. He complements this with a firm, fading 83 mph changeup that generated a 52% whiff rate and 35% chase rate in 2025. Some scouts believe he could benefit from adding a gloveside breaking pitch to better balance his arsenal. While his command and control remain inconsistent—partly due to prior injury—both have improved.

THE FUTURE: With the potential for two plus pitches, Kelly has intriguing starter upside but also considerable reliever risk if he can't improve his command.

Year	Age	Club (League)	Level	W	L	ERA	G	GS	IP	H	HR	BB	SO	BB%	SO%	WHIP	AVG
2025	21	Did not play															

26 RJ PETIT, RHP
FB: 50. **SL:** 55. **CH:** 45. **CTL:** 50. **BA Grade:** 35. **Risk:** Mild. **Adj:** 30.

Born: September 23, 1999. **B-T:** R-R. **HT:** 6-8. **WT:** 300. **Drafted:** Charleston Southern, 2021 (14th round). **Signed by:** Bryson Barber (Tigers).

TRACK RECORD: The Tigers drafted Petit in the 14th round in 2021, and he slowly worked through their system in a relief role. He spent his 2025 season split between Double-A and Triple-A, where he went 10-2, 2.44 over 47 outings and 66.1 innings along with a 29.5% strikeout rate and 8.2% walk rate. Detroit left him off its 40-man roster, and the Rockies scooped him up with the first pick in the 2025 Rule 5 draft.

SCOUTING REPORT: Petit has a massive 6-foot-8, 300-pound frame and checks a lot of boxes from a performance standpoint. He strikes out batters, shows at least average command and has flashed the ability to generate ground balls at above-average rates. His stuff matches his performance. Petit goes after hitters

COLORADO ROCKIES

with a 95-97 mph four-seam fastball that touches 98 with nearly a foot of armside run from six and a half feet of extension. Petit also has a separate 93-95 mph sinker. His best bat-missing pitch is a mid-80s slider that resembles a "deathball" curveball—a pitch with power and pronounced vertical drop—and he uses his 88 mph changeup nearly as frequently as his slider. It has good vertical separation off his fastball.
THE FUTURE: With a variety of ways to get hitters out and plenty of runway, Petit has a strong chance to stick in the Rockies' bullpen in 2026.

Year	Age	Club (League)	Level	W	L	ERA	G	GS	IP	H	HR	BB	SO	BB%	SO%	WHIP	AVG
2025	25	Erie (EL)	AA	6	1	2.28	27	1	43	29	2	12	46	7.0	26.7	0.95	.187
2025	25	Toledo (IL)	AAA	4	1	2.74	20	1	23	19	2	10	33	10.4	34.4	1.26	.224
		Minor League Totals		15	8	3.31	144	4	185	165	17	61	205	7.7	26.0	1.22	.234

27 DEREK BERNARD, OF

HIT: 40. **POW:** 55. **RUN:** 45. **FLD:** 40. **ARM:** 50. **BA Grade:** 45. **Risk:** High. **Adj:** 30.

Born: August 9, 2005. **B-T:** L-R. **HT:** 5-11. **WT:** 190. **Signed:** Dominican Republic, 2022. **Signed by:** Rolando Fernandez.
TRACK RECORD: Bernard grew up playing in New York City before he signed out of the Dominican for $185,000 in the Rockies' 2022 international class. He debuted that year in the Dominican Summer League and returned in 2023 due to tax implications tied to his split signing bonus. Bernard moved stateside in 2024 with a strong showing in the Arizona Complex League, then advanced to Low-A Fresno in 2025, where he slashed .302/.385/.448 with six home runs.
SCOUTING REPORT: Bernard has hit for high averages at every stop and already flashes promising impact potential as well, with plus raw power and above-average in-game exit velocities in 2025 at just 19 years old. There's a chance he accesses even more power as his frame matures. But his biggest obstacle is his aggressive approach. Bernard missed on pitches roughly a third of the time in 2025 and frequently expanded the strike zone, leading to a 24.1% strikeout rate in Low-A. Bernard is particularly vulnerable against both premium velocity and quality breaking balls. Bernard has also faced defensive concerns early in his career and settled into a corner outfield profile. While he has an average arm, he's a fringe-average runner and is unlikely to provide a lot of defensive value.
THE FUTURE: Bernard has notable power upside, but he'll need to tighten his approach as he climbs the ladder. He's expected to open 2026 at High-A Spokane.

Year	Age	Club (League)	Level	AVG	G	AB	R	H	2B	3B	HR	RBI	BB	SO	SB	OBP	SLG
2025	19	ACL Rockies	Rk	.345	9	29	4	10	4	0	0	2	1	8	2	.367	.483
2025	19	Fresno (CAL)	A	.302	72	252	46	76	17	1	6	33	32	70	13	.385	.448
		Minor League Totals		.306	227	805	156	246	54	11	18	125	95	232	52	.383	.467

28 TANNER THACH, 1B

HIT: 40. **POW:** 55. **RUN:** 30. **FLD:** 45. **ARM:** 50. **BA Grade:** 45. **Risk:** High. **Adj:** 30.

Born: March 11, 2004. **B-T:** L-L. **HT:** 6-4. **WT:** 225. **Drafted:** UNC Wilmington, 2025 (8th round).
Signed by: Jordan Czarniecki.
TRACK RECORD: Thach was the Coastal Athletic Association's Player of the Year in 2024 after hitting .324/.406/.700 with 27 home runs, setting UNC Wilmington's career home run record along the way. His production cooled in 2025—particularly his power output—but he still delivered a strong .325/.409/.538 line with 12 homers, and the Rockies selected him in the eighth round. He received his first taste of pro ball with 18 games at Low-A Fresno to close the year.
SCOUTING REPORT: Thach is a physical 6-foot-4, 225-pound lefthanded masher built around plus bat speed and big raw power to all fields. He creates easy lift through natural strength and torque, though a pronounced barrel tip can lengthen his swing. Small adjustments to his handset could help him stay shorter to the ball and improve timing. His contact skills are solid and his strike-zone awareness trended upward in college, but his 42.6% chase rate in his pro debut was concerning. Thach is a well below-average runner, but he moves well enough around first base, where he looks like a serviceable defender.
THE FUTURE: First base-only profiles are inherently tricky, but Thach's strength, bat speed and raw power gives him a path to the big leagues. Reducing his chase rate will be essential for him to reach his offensive ceiling.

Year	Age	Club (League)	Level	AVG	G	AB	R	H	2B	3B	HR	RBI	BB	SO	SB	OBP	SLG
2025	21	Fresno (CAL)	A	.279	18	68	7	19	2	0	2	15	8	19	1	.375	.397
		Minor League Totals		.279	18	68	7	19	2	0	2	15	8	19	1	.375	.397

29 YUJANYER HERRERA, RHP

FB: 55. **CB:** 50. **SL:** 60. **CH:** 55. **CTL:** 55. **BA Grade:** 50. **Risk:** Extreme. **Adj:** 30.

Born: August 17, 2003. **B-T:** R-R. **HT:** 6-3. **WT:** 175. **Signed:** Venezuela, 2019. **Signed by:** Javier Meza (Brewers).
TRACK RECORD: Herrera signed with the Brewers in 2019 and his production took a significant step forward during the first half of 2024 while with High-A Wisconsin, where he posted a 3.18 ERA with 50 strikeouts and 17 walks over 51 innings. Milwaukee traded him that July to the Rockies in a deal for Nick Mears. Herrera made six starts for High-A Spokane before an elbow injury sidelined him in September and required Tommy John surgery after the season. He missed all of 2025 but returned to pitch during the Rockies' instructional league to promising results.
SCOUTING REPORT: When Herrera returned to the mound in early September, both his fastball and sinker sat comfortably in the 94-96 mph range. He steadily increased his workload throughout the fall, often throwing multiple innings per outing as he rebuilds toward full pre-injury form. Herrera leans primarily on a fastball-slider combination but also mixes in a curveball and an above-average changeup, rounding out a four-pitch arsenal. His go-to secondary, a mid-80s gyro slider with tight, bullet-like spin, generated an elite 26.1% swinging-strike rate in 2024. Herrera's diverse pitch mix keeps hitters off balance. Next up is for Herrera is refining his command, pitch sequencing and overall execution.
THE FUTURE: Herrera has the ingredients to develop into a back-end starter with a fallback as a high-leverage reliever. Assuming he's fully healthy, he should begin 2026 with High-A Spokane.

Year	Age	Club (League)	Level	W	L	ERA	G	GS	IP	H	HR	BB	SO	BB%	SO%	WHIP	AVG
2025	21	Did not play															
		Minor League Totals		20	12	4.84	70	40	273	276	15	132	267	10.9	22.0	1.49	.265

30 SANDY OZUNA, RHP

FB: 55. **SL:** 55. **CH:** 40. **CTL:** 55. **BA Grade:** 50. **Risk:** Extreme. **Adj:** 30.

Born: May 24, 2006. **B-T:** R-R. **HT:** 6-3. **WT:** 177. **Signed:** Dominican Republic, 2023. **Signed by:** Rolando Fernandez.
TRACK RECORD: Ozuna signed for just $45,000 late in the 2023 international period just before the Dominican Summer League season. He debuted three days later and logged 32.1 innings over 14 outings in his pro debut. Ozuna came stateside in 2024 and was one of the most promising pitchers on the Arizona Complex League Rockies roster, but injuries limited him to just six innings in his return to the level in 2025.
SCOUTING REPORT: Ozuna is a projectable righthander with a long, lean frame and the athleticism to add meaningful strength. At 6-foot-3, he repeats a smooth, well-sequenced delivery and effectively hides the ball despite a longer arm action, creating late whip from a high three-quarters slot. When healthy, his 93-96 mph four-seamer can touch 97 with mild cut and fringy ride, and his spin profile suggests he could add a sinker one day. Ozuna's best secondary is a low-to-mid-80s gyro slider that could be a legitimate bat-missing weapon. He has above-average command of both pitches. He also throws a firm, upper-80s changeup that remains a work in progress. Evaluators who saw Ozuna healthy in 2025 still view him as a high-upside arm with significant room for growth.
THE FUTURE: Ozuna has the upside of a No. 4 starter if he can develop a consistent third offering to go with his fastball-slider combination. He should return to the ACL in 2026.

Year	Age	Club (League)	Level	W	L	ERA	G	GS	IP	H	HR	BB	SO	BB%	SO%	WHIP	AVG
2025	19	ACL Rockies	Rk	1	0	1.50	2	1	6	6	0	1	6	4.0	24.0	1.17	.250
		Minor League Totals		6	1	4.18	26	11	75	71	4	32	83	9.9	25.8	1.37	.252

Riley Greene

Detroit Tigers

BY J.J. COOPER

In 2024, the Tigers enjoyed a wonderfully unexpected finish that turned a disappointing first half into one of the organization's best seasons in years.

Detroit looked out of the playoff race in July and early August, but a furious late-season run got them to 86 wins and a playoff appearance. The Tigers then beat the Astros before losing to the Guardians in the American League Division Series.

In 2025, the Tigers enjoyed a wonderfully expected start to the season that made them look like World Series contenders. Paced by ace Tarik Skubal and surprising contributions from players like Javier Baez, Detroit led the AL Central by 14 games in mid July and 11.5 in late August.

Then they collapsed. The Tigers wheezed to a 7-17 record in September that cost them the division crown, which they ceded to the Guardians. But come playoff time, Detroit won its Wild Card Series and lost in the ALDS.

Two seasons that felt incredibly different ended up in almost exactly the same place: 86 or 87 wins and a Division Series exit.

Now, the Tigers have to decide whether to try to take a further step forward or to regroup. Back-to-back Cy Young Award winner Tarik Skubal is entering his final year before free agency. The Tigers could trade him to try to restock for future years, but they would do so knowing that such a move would likely hinder their chances in 2026.

They could also look at the wave of hitters getting ready to join the big league roster and decide if the arrival of top prospect Kevin McGonigle, plus potentially Max Clark and/or Josue Briceño, could give the team another gear to play deeper into October.

These are the kind of problems the Tigers hoped to have when they hired Scott Harris as general manager in 2022. The Tigers went nine years without a playoff appearance. Deciding whether the 2026 roster is positioned to make a World Series

PROJECTED 2029 LINEUP

Catcher	Dillon Dingler	30
First Base	Colt Keith	28
Second Base	Kevin McGonigle	24
Third Base	Bryce Rainer	23
Shortstop	Jordan Yost	22
Left Field	Riley Greene	28
Center Field	Parker Meadows	29
Right Field	Max Clark	24
Designated Hitter	Josue Briceño	24
No. 1 Starter	Jackson Jobe	26
No. 2 Starter	Reese Olson	29
No. 3 Starter	Troy Melton	28
No. 4 Starter	Keider Montero	28
No. 5 Starter	Andrew Sears	26
Closer	Kelvis Salcedo	23

run is a much better problem.

If the Tigers continue this run of success in 2027 and beyond, it will be because they have become an organization that does a great job identifying and developing hitters.

For decades, the Tigers were one of the worst teams in baseball at developing position players, but that flipped in the 2020s. In the five-round 2020 draft, the Tigers selected all hitters. Spencer Torkelson, Dillon Dingler and Colt Keith are MLB regulars.

The 2023 draft looks to be another bumper crop, led by Detroit's top three picks of Clark, McGonigle and second baseman Max Anderson.

Now, the Tigers need to make moves to restock their pitching depth. The arm-heavy 2024 draft class, which saw four pitches selected in the top four rounds, has had significant injury issues. That didn't deter Detroit from spending more than $450,000 on six more pitchers in the 2025 draft class.

Most of those players are years away, so success in 2026 will largely depend on getting production from on-hand pitchers such as Casey Mize, Reese Olson and Jackson Jobe, who is coming off Tommy John surgery.

The Tigers still have holes to fill, but it's hard not to view the current roster as the best the organization has built in years. ■

DEPTH CHART

DETROIT TIGERS

TOP 2026 ROOKIES — RANK
1. Kevin McGonigle, 2B/SS — 1
2. Hao-Yu Lee, 2B/3B — 6
3. Dylan Smith, RHP — 20

BREAKOUT PROSPECTS — RANK
1. Kelvis Salcedo, RHP — 11
2. Jack Penney, 2B — 21
3. Angel De Los Santos, SS — 24

SOURCE OF TOP 30 TALENT

Homegrown	28	Acquired	2
College	13	Trade	2
Junior college	0	Rule 5 draft	0
High school	9	Independent league	0
Undrafted free agent	0	Free agent/waivers	0
International	6		

LF
Seth Stephenson
Brett Callahan
Jesus Pinto

CF
Max Clark (2)
Jackson Strong (29)
Roberto Campos
Samuell Sanchez *

RF
Cris Rodriguez (8)
Nick Dumesnil (23)
Patrick Lee

3B
Bryce Rainer (3)
Izaac Pacheco
Nestor Miranda
Woody Hadeen
Carson Rucker
Gage Workman
Jude Warwick

SS
Jordan Yost (5)
Franyerber Montilla (9)
John Peck (15)
Trei Cruz (17)
Angel De Los Santos (24)
Samuel Gil
Abel Bastidas

2B
Kevin McGonigle (1)
Hao-Yu Lee (6)
Max Anderson (7)
Jack Penney (21)
Jack Goodman

1B
Josue Briceño (4)
Eduardo Valencia (28)

C
Michael Oliveto (10)
Thayron Liranzo (19)

LHP

LHSP
Andrew Sears (14)
Ben Jacobs (18)
Paul Wilson (27)
Grayson Grinsell (30)
Ethan Schiefelbein

LHRP
Jake Miller (22)
Caleb Leys
Ericksson De Los Santos

RHP

RHSP
Kelvis Salcedo (11)
Malachi Witherspoon (12)
Owen Hall (13)
Ryan Hall (16)
Ty Madden (25)
River Hamilton (26)
Lucas Elissalt
Austin Bergner

RHRP
Dylan Smith (20)
Jaden Hamm
Michael Massey
Matt Seelinger
Cale Wetwiska
Antonio Florido
Bryce Alewine

DETROIT TIGERS

1 KEVIN McGONIGLE, SS

Born: August 18, 2004. **B-T:** L-R. **HT:** 5-10. **WT:** 187.
Drafted: HS—Drexel Hill, PA, 2023 (1st round supp.).
Signed by: Jim Bretz.

BA GRADE	SCOUTING GRADES
70 Risk: Mild	Hit: 80. Power: 60. Run: 55. Fielding: 55. Arm: 45.
Adjusted grade: **65**	Projected future grades on 20-80 scouting scale

TRACK RECORD: Coming out of the Covid-canceled 2020 season, word began circulating around the Northeast that there was a special sophomore at Monsignor Bonner High, outside Philadelphia. McGonigle hit nearly .500 in high school and was even more impressive in summer showcases and with Team USA. The Tigers drafted him with a supplemental first-round pick in 2023 after selecting Max Clark in the first round. Three seasons later, it appears that draft could chart the path of the Tigers in the second half of the 2020s and beyond. McGonigle has hit over .300 in each of his first three pro seasons. After wowing with his hitting ability in 2024 in a season slowed by a hamstring injury and broken hamate, he showed improved power in 2025. He missed the first month of the season with an ankle injury, but he propelled High-A West Michigan and then Double-A Erie to playoff appearances. He finished his season by earning MVP honors in the Arizona Fall League, where he also started to learn how to play third base.

SCOUTING REPORT: Even though he will play much of the 2026 season as a 21-year-old, McGonigle is already a savvier hitter than many big leaguers. Velocity? He doesn't blink at seeing top-tier fastballs, as he demonstrated with a monstrous home run on a 100 mph Jarlin Susana heater. Spin? He handled breaking balls with aplomb. Plate coverage? He has no clear holes with his swing. Expand the zone? He has the rare ability to be aggressive on pitches in the strike zone while rarely swinging at bad pitches. Platoon issues? He had a higher OPS against lefties. McGonigle could sometimes be fooled by changeups, but even that is a blemish more than a glaring flaw. He is a perfect example of how having a short but powerful frame can be an advantage for a hitter. At 5-foot-10, he has shorter levers than most, which leads to excellent bat control. His timing and savvy stand out, and he has a quick trigger with plus power when he gets a pitch to pull. He had 52 extra-base hits with just 46 strikeouts in 2025. Defensively, McGonigle is stretched at shortstop. He could play there, but he projects as fringy at best because of limited range and arm strength that is stretched on plays to his right. He is above-average at second base and could even end up being a plus defender there. He could get to playable at third, but his arm will be a limiting factor there as well.

BEST TOOLS

BATTING
Best Hitter	Kevin McGonigle
Best Power Hitter	Josue Briceño
Best Strike-Zone Discipline	Max Clark
Fastest Baserunner	Patrick Lee
Best Athlete	Max Clark

PITCHING
Best Fastball	Moises Rodriguez
Best Curveball	Yosber Sanchez
Best Slider	Kelvis Salcedo
Best Changeup	Kelvis Salcedo
Best Control	Garrett Burhenn

FIELDING
Best Defensive Catcher	Bennett Lee
Best Defensive Infielder	Franyerber Montilla
Best Infield Arm	Franyerber Montilla
Best Defensive Outfielder	Max Clark
Best Outfield Arm	Patrick Lee

He's more reliable than rangy wherever he plays.

THE FUTURE: McGonigle has the ingredients to be a star as a dynamic hitter with defensive value at second base. Second baseman Gleyber Torres' return to Detroit on a one-year qualifying offer blocks the clearest path to McGonigle making the Tigers' Opening Day roster, but his bat is too good to remain in the minors for much longer. He should be the best homegrown Tigers hitter in decades.

Year	Age	Club (League)	Level	AVG	G	AB	R	H	2B	3B	HR	RBI	BB	SO	SB	OBP	SLG
2025	20	Lakeland (FSL)	A	.235	6	17	1	4	2	0	0	0	3	1	0	.350	.353
2025	20	West Michigan (MWL)	A+	.372	36	145	37	54	19	0	7	39	23	19	3	.462	.648
2025	20	Erie (EL)	AA	.254	46	169	30	43	10	2	12	41	33	26	7	.369	.550
		Minor League Totals		.308	183	676	135	208	51	6	25	130	123	84	40	.410	.512

DETROIT TIGERS

2 MAX CLARK, OF
HIT: 60. **POW:** 50. **RUN:** 65. **FLD:** 60. **ARM:** 60. **BA Grade:** 65. **Risk:** Avg. **Adj:** 55

Born: December 21, 2004. **B-T:** L-L. **HT:** 6-1. **WT:** 205.
Drafted: HS—Franklin, IN, 2023 (1st round). **Signed by:** Harold Zonder.
TRACK RECORD: In what was viewed as a five-player top tier of the 2023 draft, the Tigers picked Clark third overall, ahead of Wyatt Langford and Walker Jenkins, and then selected Kevin McGonigle in the supplemental first round. At various stops, Clark and McGonigle have been teammates and winners. They spent the first half of 2025 playing for Midwest League-champion High-A West Michigan and the second with Eastern League runner-up Double-A Erie.
SCOUTING REPORT: Clark's skill set at the plate shares a lot of similarities with McGonigle, but with some rougher edges. He's a wonderfully pesky hitter who uses the whole field with a slashing swing that leads to plenty of hard line drives to left and center field. He rarely swings and misses, and he seldom chases pitches. Clark doesn't handle velocity as well as McGonigle, and while he battles lefties, his power largely disappears against them. Clark's groundball tendencies limit his power. His exit velocities are among the best in the Tigers' system, but they often are scorched grounders. He's working to try to more regularly catch the ball out front to fix this issue. Clark was slowed by shin splints early in the 2025 season, but he shook them off to return to turning in 65-grade run times in the second half. Defensively, Clark is an aggressive center fielder who leaves dents in the outfield wall and divots in the grass. His reads could improve, but his speed helps make him a plus defender, and he has a plus arm.
THE FUTURE: Scouts notice Clark's attention to detail before and during games, and that approach carries over to off-the-field work. He has to be dragged out of the batting cage and he has worked to pack as much muscle as his frame can hold. Clark's plate discipline, swing decisions and well-rounded game should fit in Detroit at some point in 2026—and for many years to come.

Year	Age	Club (League)	Level	AVG	G	AB	R	H	2B	3B	HR	RBI	BB	SO	SB	OBP	SLG
2025	20	West Michigan (MWL)	A+	.285	68	260	49	74	12	2	7	47	65	56	12	.430	.427
2025	20	Erie (EL)	AA	.251	43	171	36	43	5	3	7	20	29	34	7	.360	.439
		Minor League Totals		.270	241	936	178	253	43	12	25	161	176	209	53	.388	.422

3 BRYCE RAINER, SS
HIT: 55. **POW:** 55. **RUN:** 55. **FLD:** 55. **ARM:** 70. **BA Grade:** 65. **Risk:** High. **Adj:** 50

Born: July 3, 2005. **B-T:** L-R. **HT:** 6-3. **WT:** 195.
Drafted: HS—Los Angeles, CA, 2024 (1st round). **Signed by:** Tim McWilliam.
TRACK RECORD: Heading into the 2024 draft, there was a healthy debate as to whether Rainer or Konnor Griffin was the top high school shortstop in the class. Griffin was drafted ninth overall, two picks ahead of Rainer, and emerged in 2025 as the best prospect in the game. Rainer was having an impressive pro debut at Low-A Lakeland until he dislocated his right shoulder sliding back into first base on a pickoff attempt. It was an injury similar to the one that sidelined Brewers catching prospect Jeferson Quero in 2024.
SCOUTING REPORT: Rainer was a two-way player in high school who was a legitimate pro prospect on the mound, but his plus power and a rocket of an arm made him even more promising as a position player. His brief pre-injury pro stint reinforced that notion. His 90th percentile exit velocity of 108 mph was best among Tigers minor leaguers and ranked among the best for a teenager in pro ball. Rainer's swing is best when he's driving the ball to the opposite field or center, and he'll need to develop his pull power, but his opposite-field aptitude should serve him well. He showed solid plate awareness. As a shortstop, Rainer wasn't as rangy, and he didn't have the flashy actions of teammate Franyerber Montilla, but his arm stands out. Rainer's range is solid but unspectacular, but his plus-plus arm creates the ability to make plays other shortstops can't make. He can sling the ball from multiple arm angles, but he is more comfortable throwing on the run than when he sets his feet.
THE FUTURE: Rainer is expected to be healthy for spring training. While he will have to make up for lost development time, his brief time on the field reinforced his status as a well-rounded shortstop prospect. He embraced using his rehab time to work on conditioning and strength training as much as was possible while allowing his shoulder to heal.

Year	Age	Club (League)	Level	AVG	G	AB	R	H	2B	3B	HR	RBI	BB	SO	SB	OBP	SLG
2025	19	Lakeland (FSL)	A	.288	35	125	19	36	5	0	5	22	20	33	9	.383	.448
		Minor League Totals		.288	35	125	19	36	5	0	5	22	20	33	9	.383	.448

DETROIT TIGERS

4 JOSUE BRICEÑO, C/1B

HIT: 45. **POW:** 65. **RUN:** 30. **FLD:** 40. **ARM:** 55. **BA Grade:** 60. **Risk:** High. **Adj:** 45.

Born: September 23, 2004. **B-T:** L-R. **HT:** 6-4. **WT:** 200.
Signed: Venezuela, 2022. **Signed by:** Jesus Mendoza/Delvis Pacheco/Jose Zambrano.
TRACK RECORD: A top target of the Tigers in the 2022 international class, Briceño has been one of the system's most impressive minor league hitters ever since. He starred in the Florida Complex League in 2023, bounced back from a knee injury to win the first-ever Arizona Fall League triple crown in 2024 and hit 20 home runs in 2025. On a Double-A Erie team that also included Thayron Liranzo, Briceño caught every one of the team's postseason games.
SCOUTING REPORT: Briceño is a smart and savvy slugger with big power, but he's also a hitter with several limitations. He has a lengthy swing and average bat speed, and generates his power through leverage, strength and excellent trunk rotation. That means that he can be beaten by quality velocity, but he also punishes breaking and offspeed pitches. He has excellent pitch recognition and strike-zone awareness, and also some adjustability to his swing. He comfortably gets the ball in the air to his pull side, maximizing his power. Despite plenty of work, Briceño remains well below-average at catcher. He struggles with his left hand. He boxes balls around the zone, and he turns borderline pitches into wild pitches. Despite the flaws, he's an adequate pitch-framer who can fluidly bring pitches back into the zone. As long as he can keep balls inside his frame, he's an adept blocker, but he struggles when he relies on his mitt. At first base, his more likely long-term position, he's a big target, but he has limited range and hard hands.
THE FUTURE: Because of his defensive limitations, Briceño has a wider array of possible outcomes than most successful sluggers with Double-A experience. He's a slow-twitch slugger with real defensive questions. If Briceño's bat is as good as expected, he can be a middle-of-the-lineup force, but if his bat is just a grade less than expected, he could end up being an up-and-down Triple-A slugger.

Year	Age	Club (League)	Level	AVG	G	AB	R	H	2B	3B	HR	RBI	BB	SO	SB	OBP	SLG
2025	20	West Michigan (MWL)	A+	.296	55	196	40	58	13	1	15	57	41	40	1	.422	.602
2025	20	Erie (EL)	AA	.232	45	168	20	39	6	2	5	19	25	47	0	.335	.381
		Minor League Totals		.276	239	870	144	240	51	7	33	152	131	186	6	.374	.464

5 JORDAN YOST, SS

HIT: 55. **POW:** 30. **RUN:** 65. **FLD:** 55. **ARM:** 55. **BA Grade:** 55. **Risk:** High. **Adj:** 40.

Born: December 21, 2006. **B-T:** L-R. **HT:** 6-0. **WT:** 175.
Drafted: HS—Tampa, FL, 2025 (1st round). **Signed by:** RJ Burgess.
TRACK RECORD: No team loves a shortstop who can bat lefthanded more than the Tigers. With Zach McKinstry, Trey Sweeney, Kevin McGonigle, Bryce Rainer and switch-hitters Trei Cruz and Franyerber Montilla, the Tigers are stuffed with shortstops who have the platoon advantage with a righthander on the mound. Yost is yet another to add to that group. He was a fast riser in the 2025 draft class who impressed with his quick-developing bat and improving strength. The Tigers picked him 24th overall, making him the third prep shortstop the team has selected in the top 50 picks in the past three drafts, following McGonigle in 2023 and Rainer in 2024.
SCOUTING REPORT: Yost is an athletic shortstop with a clean swing that helps him generate plenty of contact. That's a great starting point for a potential future regular, but to reach that ceiling Yost will have to keep getting stronger. He's always been slight. He weighed just 125 pounds as a ninth grader at Tampa's Sickles High and was a skinny 5-foot-11, 155 pounds as a rising junior. He's still skinny, but at 175 pounds, he's adding enough muscle to provide hope that he can go from being someone with bottom-of-the-scale power to being a line-drive hitter who hits plenty of doubles. Yost is a smooth, twitchy defender. He has an above-average arm with a quick first step and the "baseball rat" makeup that teams love to see at shortstop. With his instincts and tools, he should provide above-average defense at shortstop, though his near plus-plus speed would also fit well in center field.
THE FUTURE: The Tigers hope they've landed a player whose best is yet to come. Yost's lack of present physicality makes him riskier than some of the other shortstops picked in the 2025 draft, but he has the skills to develop into a well-rounded prospect with hitting ability and an above-average glove.

Year	Age	Club (League)	Level	AVG	G	AB	R	H	2B	3B	HR	RBI	BB	SO	SB	OBP	SLG
2025	18	Did not play															

DETROIT TIGERS

6 HAO-YU LEE, 2B/3B
HIT: 50. **POW:** 50. **RUN:** 50. **FLD:** 45. **ARM:** 45. **BA Grade:** 45. **Risk:** Mild. **Adj:** 40.

Born: February 3, 2003. **B-T:** R-R. **HT:** 5-6. **WT:** 210.
Signed: Taiwan, 2021. **Signed by:** Youngster Wang (Phillies).
TRACK RECORD: The Phillies signed Lee out of Taiwan for $570,000 in 2021, and he was on track to potentially become the Phillies' first Asian amateur signee to reach the majors. That goal of reaching MLB seems more likely than ever, but it won't be with the Phillies. Detroit acquired him in the July 2023 trade that sent Michael Lorenzen to Philadelphia. After playing shortstop early in his career, Lee now splits his time equally between second and third base. The Tigers added him to the 40-man roster in November.
SCOUTING REPORT: Lee has developed into a well-rounded, if utterly unflashy, infielder. He offers no plus tool on his scouting report, but he strings together professional at-bats with a solid awareness of how pitchers try to attack him. Lee's best attributes as a hitter are his timing and bat-to-ball skills. He can be induced to chase pitches above the zone, but he makes hard contact on pitches left over the plate. He hits the ball quite hard, though his struggles to pull the ball in the air limit his home run potential. Lee has a stocky build, but he moves relatively fluidly. While he's more serviceable than flashy as a defender, he is capable of playing average defense at second base or fringe-average at third base. His hands work well, but his reaction times are strained at third. He's an instinctual baserunner who can swipe bases despite average speed.
THE FUTURE: Lee has many of the same strengths and weaknesses as Jace Jung and Max Anderson, which leads to a bit of a logjam at Triple-A. Lee's defense is better than either Jung or Anderson, however, and he has some defensive versatility. On a Tigers team whose lineup is getting more and more lefthanded, Lee's ability to produce quality at-bats against lefties could help him carve out a platoon role.

Year	Age	Club (League)	Level	AVG	G	AB	R	H	2B	3B	HR	RBI	BB	SO	SB	OBP	SLG
2025	22	Toledo (IL)	AAA	.243	126	497	81	121	23	8	14	61	65	121	22	.342	.406
		Minor League Totals		.272	376	1446	231	394	73	19	42	207	177	327	68	.361	.436

7 MAX ANDERSON, 2B
HIT: 50. **POW:** 45. **RUN:** 30. **FLD:** 40. **ARM:** 40. **BA Grade:** 45. **Risk:** Avg. **Adj:** 35.

Born: February 28, 2002. **B-T:** R-R. **HT:** 6-0. **WT:** 215.
Drafted: Nebraska, 2023 (2nd round). **Signed by:** Ryan Johnson.
TRACK RECORD: Anderson was a star at Nebraska who hit .414/.461/.771 with 21 home runs as a junior in 2023. Drafted by the Tigers in the second round that year, his first full season didn't show the same impact, and he hit a light .270 in the Midwest League in 2024. Anderson worked on improving his agility over the offseason, largely to help his defense, but it also paid off at the plate. He showed improved power as one of the best hitters in the Double-A Eastern League and earned a late promotion to Triple-A Toledo. To cap it off, he hit .447/.609/.809 in the Arizona Fall League.
SCOUTING REPORT: Anderson's work to improve his range and agility helped significantly. He's still a below-average defender at second base, but that's an improvement from the previous year, when scouts often described him as unplayable. He worked at third base in the AFL, but his below-average arm and slow first step are less of a fit at the position. Offensively, Anderson's approach is unique. He's a front-foot hitter who relies on his excellent hands to stay back and flick balls when he's caught out front. It means he's virtually incapable of pulling quality fastballs in the air, but he has enough bat speed and strength to drive balls out to right and center field, and he can pull offspeed pitches. His excellent contact skills allow his aggressive approach to work. It's hard to see him getting to more than fringe-average power in the big leagues without swing tweaks. He excels against lefthanders and hit .341/.391/.626 against them in 2025.
THE FUTURE: Anderson's 2025 season showed improvement in almost every way possible, but he's still facing a tricky path to a regular big league role. He's a below-average second baseman who doesn't run well enough to move to the outfield. He makes lefthanders pay as a platoon bat, but there aren't many regular jobs for second basemen who are on the roster to hit lefties.

Year	Age	Club (League)	Level	AVG	G	AB	R	H	2B	3B	HR	RBI	BB	SO	SB	OBP	SLG
2025	23	Erie (EL)	AA	.306	90	369	54	113	25	2	14	65	28	59	2	.358	.499
2025	23	Toledo (IL)	AAA	.267	32	135	24	36	6	0	5	23	8	28	1	.327	.422
		Minor League Totals		.282	280	1139	160	321	65	6	32	185	83	190	6	.334	.434

DETROIT TIGERS

8 CRIS RODRIGUEZ, OF
HIT: 40. **POW:** 60. **RUN:** 55. **FLD:** 50. **ARM:** 60. **BA Grade:** 55. **Risk:** Extreme. **Adj:** 35.

Born: January 28, 2008. **B-T:** R-R. **HT:** 6-3. **WT:** 203.
Signed: Dominican Republic, 2025. **Signed by:** Rodolfo Penalo.
TRACK RECORD: Dominican Summer League stats often don't tell the whole story, because pitching and hitting quality in the league vary dramatically from inning to inning. In Rodriguez's case, his 10 home runs, second best in the league, were an accurate testament to some of the best power in the DSL in recent years. Rodriguez's analytical numbers were even more impressive than his homer totals. His 90th percentile exit velocity of 108 mph was best among all 17-year-olds in 2025, and it has been equaled only once in the past three years, by the Rays' Brailer Guerrero in 2023.
SCOUTING REPORT: Rodriguez is already a well-built outfielder, but despite his present strength, he's also a sneaky-agile athlete who gobbles up yards in the outfield with powerful long strides. He has plus-plus bat speed that helps him generate his massive raw power. He will likely slow down as he ages, but he's solid in center field for now and should be an average right fielder down the road with a plus arm. Offensively, Rodriguez's swing has no glaring flaws that should prevent him from making enough contact, but he needs plenty of at-bats to add some of the more subtle skills at the plate. He will swing out of his shoes on breaking pitches down and away. The Tigers are impressed with how hard he works to get better.
THE FUTURE: The Tigers have plenty of reasons to be patient with Rodriguez. While his tools are exceptionally loud, he needs to develop his approach at the plate to get consistently to his top-tier power. The struggles of Guerrero, a prospect with similar strengths and weaknesses, offer an example of the risks inherent in pushing Rodriguez too quickly.

Year	Age	Club (League)	Level	AVG	G	AB	R	H	2B	3B	HR	RBI	BB	SO	SB	OBP	SLG
2025	17	DSL Tigers 2	Rk	.308	50	172	38	53	12	1	10	39	11	42	10	.340	.564
		Minor League Totals		.308	50	172	38	53	12	1	10	39	11	42	10	.340	.564

9 FRANYERBER MONTILLA, SS
HIT: 30. **POW:** 40. **RUN:** 60. **FLD:** 65. **ARM:** 70. **BA Grade:** 55. **Risk:** Extreme. **Adj:** 35.

Born: April 15, 2005. **B-T:** B-R. **HT:** 6-0. **WT:** 160.
Signed: Venezuela, 2022. **Signed by:** Jesus Mendoza/Oscar Garcia.
TRACK RECORD: It was a rough year for Low-A Lakeland shortstops. When the 2025 season began, Bryce Rainer and Montilla shared the job, giving Lakeland two of the most dynamic players at the position in Low-A. A shoulder injury ended Rainer's season on June 3, but Montilla didn't get to settle into his new role for long. His season ended on July 21 when he tore the anterior cruciate ligament in his knee, requiring season-ending surgery.
SCOUTING REPORT: See Montilla on the right day and he looks like a star. Defensively, he makes exceptional plays look easy. He can glide to a ball deep in the shortstop hole and then uncork a laser with his plus-plus arm to nab a hitter on a seemingly surefire infield single. His quick hands erase bad hops, and he goes to the ground and pops back up to throw far easier than most shortstops. Montilla is a near plus-plus defender with a double-plus arm. Offensively, Montilla has a lot of work to do, though he has the building blocks of a solid hitter. After leading the Florida Complex League Tigers to a league title in 2024, he was overmatched in a brief stint in the Florida State League in 2024 but showed significant improvements in 2025. Still, he remains prone to chasing pitches, and he can also be beaten by quality stuff in the zone. He shows occasional home run power, but his line-drive approach is more suited to doubles than homers.
THE FUTURE: ACL repairs usually take between nine to 12 months to heal, so Montilla's recovery will likely stretch into the early part of the 2026 season. Assuming he makes a full recovery, he remains one of the Tigers' most intriguing prospects. He will have to add plenty of polish to become more than a defensive-minded big leaguer, but the Tigers have few position players with more impressive tools. A 2022 signee, Montilla enters his fifth pro season in 2026 and hasn't advanced past Low-A.

Year	Age	Club (League)	Level	AVG	G	AB	R	H	2B	3B	HR	RBI	BB	SO	SB	OBP	SLG
2025	20	Lakeland (FSL)	A	.271	67	258	43	70	16	2	4	29	38	74	27	.368	.395
		Minor League Totals		.245	220	776	138	190	44	7	16	97	143	223	79	.370	.381

DETROIT TIGERS

10 MICHAEL OLIVETO, C

HIT: 50. **POW:** 55. **RUN:** 40. **FLD:** 40. **ARM:** 55. **BA Grade:** 55. **Risk:** Extreme. **Adj:** 35

Born: February 3, 2007. **B-T:** L-R. **HT:** 6-3. **WT:** 185.
Drafted: HS—Hauppauge, NY, 2025 (1st round supp.). **Signed by:** Jim Bretz.
TRACK RECORD: Every now and then, a player will pop at the World Wood Bat Championships, the October Perfect Game event in Jupiter, Fla., which heralds the completion of the showcase circuit. A Long Island prep, Oliveto had barely been seen on the showcase circuit until that 2024 event. By the end of the week, he was a name to know. He hit .615 with two doubles and two home runs in five games, which rocketed him up draft lists. The Tigers scouted Oliveto heavily through the spring, and they were impressed with how he handled velocity in workouts. The Tigers drafted the Yale commit 34th overall in the supplemental first round.
SCOUTING REPORT: The Tigers love to draft pure hitters. Despite facing modest competition for much of his amateur career, Oliveto has the foundational skills to be a solid hitter, thanks to a smooth lefthanded swing that sprays line drives to all fields. He has above-average power potential and more projection remaining than most high school hitters. Defensively, Oliveto is going to need a lot of work and time. The tools are there for him to be a solid defender behind the plate. He has an above-average arm, and he moves well with solid athleticism to go with present strength. But he's far behind his contemporaries in catching experience. He didn't handle much velocity while catching on Long Island, and he'd largely been self-taught until he entered pro ball. He didn't seem awed by catching quality fastballs in unofficial bridge league games and is quite coachable, but there's plenty of projection and development to go.
THE FUTURE: Oliveto is a high-risk, high-reward draftee who could blossom into a steal, but there's also the risk that he will get blown away early in his career by more experienced pros. The combination of a fluid swing, lefty power and positional value at catcher makes him a long-term development priority.

Year	Age	Club (League)	Level	AVG	G	AB	R	H	2B	3B	HR	RBI	BB	SO	SB	OBP	SLG
2025	18	Did not play															

11 KELVIS SALCEDO, RHP

FB: 55. **SL:** 55. **SP:** 55. **CTL:** 50. **BA Grade:** 55. **Risk:** Extreme. **Adj:** 35.

Born: January 23, 2006. **B-T:** R-R. **HT:** 6-0. **WT:** 255. **Signed:** Venezuela, 2023.
Signed by: Jesus Mendoza/Jhohan Acevedo.
TRACK RECORD: A low-cost signing in 2023 out of Venezuela, Salcedo hasn't needed much time to establish himself as one of the Tigers' best pitching prospects. He impressed in the Dominican Summer League in 2024, combined on a seven-inning no-hitter in the Florida Complex League in June 2025 and pitched Low-A Lakeland to a Florida State League title later in the summer.
SCOUTING REPORT: Salcedo has some of the best stuff in the Tigers' organization, with a 93-98 mph shot put of a sinker and two excellent secondaries. His 86-88 mph two-plane slider and 84-86 mph split changeup both grade as future above-average pitches. Salcedo throws his fastball and slider consistently in the zone and frustrates aggressive hitters with split changeups below the zone for chases, generating miss rates above 50% in the lower minors. Salcedo is already thick in the middle with tree trunk-esque legs. His delivery is a bit unorthodox, which leads to concerns that he won't be able to maintain both his present stuff and average control long-term in a starting role. He is a bit stiff, but he repeats his delivery consistently and throws strikes.
THE FUTURE: There are worries about Salcedo's ability to keep doing what he's doing year after year, but he's shown he can generate weak contact and throw strikes. If he holds up, he could be a midrotation starter, with a solid fallback option as a high-leverage reliever.

Year	Age	Club (League)	Level	W	L	ERA	G	GS	IP	H	HR	BB	SO	BB%	SO%	WHIP	AVG
2025	19	FCL Tigers	Rk	4	0	1.99	12	8	45	22	1	19	53	11.0	30.8	0.90	.147
2025	19	Lakeland (FSL)	A	0	0	1.54	6	2	23	8	2	6	32	7.3	39.0	0.60	.107
		Minor League Totals		8	2	3.32	44	23	144	103	6	55	178	9.5	30.6	1.10	.200

DETROIT TIGERS

12 MALACHI WITHERSPOON, RHP

FB: 60. **SL:** 60. **CB:** 55. **CT:** 50. **CH:** 30. **CTL:** 40. **BA Grade:** 50. **Risk:** High. **Adj:** 35

Born: August 12, 2004. **B-T:** R-R. **HT:** 6-3. **WT:** 211. **Drafted:** Oklahoma, 2025 (2nd round). **Signed by:** Steve Taylor.
TRACK RECORD: Witherspoon and his twin brother Kyson developed side-by-side for years. Kyson blossomed into Oklahoma's ace and a first-round pick of the Red Sox in 2025. As the Sooners' Saturday starter, Malachi didn't have the same success. He had an ERA above 5.00 in his two years at Oklahoma and had a 9.87 ERA and 2.13 WHIP at Northwest Florida State JC as a freshman. The Tigers drafted him in the second round in 2025, making the Witherspoons the highest-drafted twins in the same year.
SCOUTING REPORT: Witherspoon's stuff was some of the best in the 2025 draft class. His fastball sits 95-96 mph and touches 100 along with a high-80s slider and a low-80s curve. He also has a barely usable changeup. Witherspoon's slider has power, cut and could develop into a weapon if he develops command of it, and he also throws an 88-90 mph cutter. Witherspoon, however, has never thrown enough strikes. His slider is nasty, but he spins it out of the zone so frequently that he struggles to induce chases. He falls behind hitters too often, which allows them to attack rather than defend. There's not a clear and glaring flaw with his delivery, so the Tigers hope they can help him learn to live in the strike zone.
THE FUTURE: Witherspoon's stuff is just as good as it was when he was a top high school prospect. However, his long history of command struggles leads to plenty of concerns about whether it's fixable. The Tigers have helped improve pitching projects in the past, and Witherspoon is a high-upside talent who will likely need more time in the lower minors than most college draftees.

Year	Age	Club (League)	Level	W	L	ERA	G	GS	IP	H	HR	BB	SO	BB%	SO%	WHIP	AVG
2025	20	Did not play															

13 OWEN HALL, RHP

FB: 60. **SL:** 60. **SP:** 60. **CTL:** 40. **BA Grade:** 50. **Risk:** High. **Adj:** 35.

Born: November 14, 2005. **B-T:** R-R. **HT:** 6-3. **WT:** 185. **Drafted:** HS—Edmond, OK, 2024 (2nd round). **Signed by:** Steve Taylor.
TRACK RECORD: Hall steadily improved as a high schooler, going from an impressive low-90s sophomore righthander to a high-90s senior fireballer. A Vanderbilt signee, Hall instead landed a $1.797 million bonus in 2024 as the Tigers' second-round pick. He didn't make his official debut until April 10 and he was shut down after three innings on May 1. He missed the rest of the season with a stress reaction in his shoulder.
SCOUTING REPORT: Hall only pitched from spring training through the first day of May, but that brief exposure impressed scouts, even as he walked nine batters in nine innings. Hall showed a loose, live arm that mixed 95-96 mph fastballs with mid-80s plus sliders and a high-80s split changeup. All three could eventually become plus pitches, but he has a long road ahead. Hall showed bottom-of-the-scale control during his brief pro debut, but he was better than that in spring training, and strike-throwing generally hasn't historically been an issue for him. He's athletic with an easy delivery.
THE FUTURE: Hall has midrotation starter upside, but his pro resumé can currently be written on a business card. He should head back to Low-A Lakeland for a second try at getting settled into pro ball.

Year	Age	Club (League)	Level	W	L	ERA	G	GS	IP	H	HR	BB	SO	BB%	SO%	WHIP	AVG
2025	19	Lakeland (FSL)	A	0	0	7.00	4	4	9	7	1	9	9	23.1	23.1	1.78	.241
		Minor League Totals		0	0	7.00	4	4	9	7	1	9	9	23.1	23.1	1.78	.241

14 ANDREW SEARS, LHP

FB: 50. **SL:** 55. **CH:** 45. **CTL:** 55. **BA Grade:** 45. **Risk:** Average. **Adj:** 35.

Born: August 30, 2002. **B-T:** L-L. **HT:** 6-3. **WT:** 210. **Drafted:** Connecticut, 2023 (10th round). **Signed by:** Jim Bretz.
TRACK RECORD: Sears spent two years at Division III Rhode Island College before transferring into Connecticut's weekend rotation. The Tigers' scouting department liked his stuff despite his 6.24 ERA, and he was the team's 10th-round selection in 2023. Sears had an impressive debut in 2024, but he got into better shape and was even stronger in 2025 as he reached Double-A to end the season. He helped pitch Erie to the Eastern League Championship Series with two solid starts.
SCOUTING REPORT: Sears moved across the rubber from the first base side to the third base side in the middle of 2024 and unlocked much-improved control. His walk rate slid from 17.5% to 7.6% after the change, and he maintained that improved rate in 2025. From the first base side, he created great angles, but he struggled to find the plate. From the third base side, his low three-quarters release point was much more direct to the plate. Sears attacks with an average 93-94 mph fastball that touches 97, an 82-84 mph, above-average slider and an 86-88 mph, below-average changeup. His delivery and low arm slot create

deception, and Sears now shows above-average control.
THE FUTURE: Sears has long looked like a lefty reliever, but his improved conditioning and ability to work to four quadrants of the zone give him a chance to start. He will be a fixture in Double-A Erie's rotation.

Year	Age	Club (League)	Level	W	L	ERA	G	GS	IP	H	HR	BB	SO	BB%	SO%	WHIP	AVG
2025	22	West Michigan (MWL)	A+	7	4	2.95	20	16	82	64	8	29	94	8.4	27.2	1.13	.208
2025	22	Erie (EL)	AA	1	2	5.02	6	6	29	32	3	7	29	5.7	23.8	1.36	.278
		Minor League Totals		8	6	3.46	27	22	112	96	11	38	124	8.1	26.3	1.20	.226

15 JOHN PECK, SS

HIT: 40. **POW:** 40. **RUN:** 60 **FLD:** 60. **ARM:** 55. **BA Grade:** 45. **Risk:** Average. **Adj:** 35.

Born: July 18, 2002. **B-T:** R-R. **HT:** 6-0. **WT:** 184. **Drafted:** Pepperdine, 2023 (7th round). **Signed by:** Tim McWilliam.
TRACK RECORD: A three-year starter at Pepperdine, Peck broke out with a .361/.417/.578 line as a sophomore. But just as scouts started to bear down, he backed up. He struggled in the Cape Cod League in 2022 and in his draft year, when he hit .272/.353/.441. The Tigers loved his glove, and he has rewarded their belief by developing at the plate.
SCOUTING REPORT: Peck is a spray hitter with a straightforward, simple swing. He can be beaten by velocity, and he's vulnerable to pitchers who can change speeds, but he's developed into an excellent mistake hitter. If a pitcher hangs a slider, Peck will punish him. So far, he's seen plenty of mistakes in Class A. Despite his production, there are some underlying concerns. He can get too aggressive, and he can be beaten in the zone by quality stuff. Defensively, Peck does everything scouts want to see from an infielder. He has a quick first step, quick actions, fast hands and a blazing release that makes his above-average arm play up. His defense should get him to the majors, and he's capable of playing second, third and shortstop at an above-average level. He's a plus runner as well.
THE FUTURE: Peck is not expected to remain a .300 hitter, but he fits the Tigers' upcoming needs quite well. On a team filled with lefthanded-hitting infielders, Peck's righthanded bat, speed and versatile glove could fit as a Zach McKinstry type of multi-position player.

Year	Age	Club (League)	Level	AVG	G	AB	R	H	2B	3B	HR	RBI	BB	SO	SB	OBP	SLG
2025	22	West Michigan (MWL)	A+	.307	93	374	78	115	22	1	10	59	32	104	17	.364	.452
2025	22	Erie (EL)	AA	.274	25	95	10	26	5	0	1	10	9	21	2	.340	.358
		Minor League Totals		.288	208	782	136	225	41	6	14	95	82	212	60	.362	.409

16 RYAN HALL, RHP

FB: 55. **SL:** 55. **CH:** 40. **CTL:** 45. **BA Grade:** 50. **Risk:** High. **Adj:** 35.

Born: April 5, 2007. **B-T:** R-R. **HT:** 6-1. **WT:** 175. **Drafted:** HS—Suwanee, GA, 2025 (5th round).
Signed by: George Schaefer.
TRACK RECORD: A multi-sport athlete at Suwanee's North Gwinnett High, Hall threw for nearly 2,000 yards and 32 touchdowns in his senior season and split his time between both sports. So while he has an excellent arm, he hasn't added much polish yet, and he has work to do to turn a football body into a pitcher's frame. The Georgia Tech signee landed a $997,500 bonus from the Tigers. Like most of the Tigers' prep draftees, he did not get into an official game after the 2025 draft.
SCOUTING REPORT: Hall was all promise but very little pure stuff in the summer before his senior year. On the showcase circuit, he sat in the upper 80s and touched 92. He found another gear the following spring. He was sitting in the low 90s as a senior and touched 95 while also showing more strength and delivery consistency. He shows feel for a potentially above-average slider and a developing, below-average changeup. Hall's control needs to improve, but evaluators believe it will because he's an athletic mover without much experience on the mound.
THE FUTURE: Hall's two-sport background points to plenty of athleticism and upside, but he will need more development than most Georgia high school pitchers. The Tigers are doubling down on athletic prep arms who will require patience, and Hall fits that description perfectly.

Year	Age	Club (League)	Level	W	L	ERA	G	GS	IP	H	HR	BB	SO	BB%	SO%	WHIP	AVG
2025	18	Did not play															

DETROIT TIGERS

17 TREI CRUZ, SS

HIT: 40. **POW:** 40. **RUN:** 55. **FLD:** 55. **ARM:** 55. **BA Grade:** 40. **Risk:** Mild. **Adj:** 35.

Born: July 5, 1998. **B-T:** B-R. **HT:** 6-2. **WT:** 203. **Drafted:** Rice, 2020 (3rd round). **Signed by:** Bryce Mosier.
TRACK RECORD: Cruz is the son of big league outfielder Jose Cruz Jr. and the grandson of Astros great Jose Cruz. The Tigers made him their third-round pick in the club's excellent 2020 draft, which has seen four of the six picks make the majors. Cruz didn't hit for average or power in his first three pro seasons, but he improved in a return to Double-A Erie in 2024 and 2025 was his best pro season.
SCOUTING REPORT: Cruz has long had tools, but his approach and skills have started to catch up to his potential. Cruz is a true shortstop who has become a more reliable defender after being prone to mental mistakes earlier in his pro career. He's an above-average defender with quick hands and an above-average arm who can make plays in the hole. He played all three outfield spots and has dabbled with second and third base as well. He is capable of playing almost anywhere on the diamond in a pinch. He's an above-average runner. As a hitter, he showed better pitch recognition in 2025, and now projects as a below-average hitter with below-average power.
THE FUTURE: Cruz will likely become the fifth player from the Tigers' 2020 draft to reach the majors. He was added to the 40-man roster in the offseason. Cruz will return to Triple-A Toledo, but if injuries strike, he could be up at any moment in 2026. He's a utility infielder who can handle shortstop.

Year	Age	Club (League)	Level	AVG	G	AB	R	H	2B	3B	HR	RBI	BB	SO	SB	OBP	SLG
2025	26	Erie (EL)	AA	.275	69	262	56	72	22	2	7	35	54	66	9	.402	.454
2025	26	Toledo (IL)	AAA	.284	58	190	39	54	11	2	6	31	48	55	8	.423	.458
		Minor League Totals		.237	529	1905	325	451	108	15	46	234	368	548	63	.360	.382

18 BEN JACOBS, LHP

FB: 50. **SL:** 50. **CB:** 45. **CH:** 55. **CTL:** 45. **BA Grade:** 45. **Risk:** Average. **Adj:** 35.

Born: June 11, 2004. **B-T:** L-L. **HT:** 6-1. **WT:** 195. **Drafted:** Arizona State, 2025 (3rd round). **Signed by:** Joey Lothrop.
TRACK RECORD: Huntington Beach High has had a long string of future pros, but it's Jacobs who set the school record for single-season strikeouts (99). As a freshman, Jacobs went to UCLA as a freshman and barely pitched, but he immediately earned a spot in the weekend rotation at Arizona State in 2024. He also pitched for USA Baseball's College National Team that summer. He went 4-4, 4.95 but with a 32% strikeout rate as a junior.
SCOUTING REPORT: Jacobs is a polished four-pitch lefthander who can get his fastball up to 95 mph but generally sat at 92-93 mph in college. The pitch has solid riding life that helps it play up. He has some feel to manipulate a low-80s slider. He can tighten it up to play more like a harder cutter when he needs to throw it for a strike. He also drops in a mid-70s curve, and his low-80s changeup could end up as his best pitch in pro ball, but he'll need to use it regularly against righthanded hitters. Jacobs needs better feel to locate his breaking balls and changeup, but the Tigers believe he has room to develop.
THE FUTURE: Jacobs is a potential back-of-the-rotation starter who should be able to move through the lower minors quicker than much of the Tigers' recent pitching draftees. While he has polish, he likely needs to either add a bit more stuff or improve his control to get ready for High-A and above.

Year	Age	Club (League)	Level	W	L	ERA	G	GS	IP	H	HR	BB	SO	BB%	SO%	WHIP	AVG
2025	21	Did not play															

19 THAYRON LIRANZO, C

HIT: 30. **POW:** 50. **RUN:** 30. **FLD:** 45. **ARM:** 60. **BA Grade:** 45. **Risk:** Average. **Adj:** 35.

Born: July 5, 2003. **B-T:** B-R. **HT:** 6-3. **WT:** 195. **Signed:** Dominican Republic, 2021. **Signed by:** Domingo Toribio (Dodgers).
TRACK RECORD: Just before the Tigers embarked on their late-season run to a playoff spot in 2024, they were sellers at the trade deadline. They received Liranzo and Trey Sweeney as the return on the deal that sent Jack Flaherty (temporarily) to the Dodgers. Liranzo hit 24 home runs as a 19-year-old switch-hitting catcher in Low-A in 2023. He hit for the Tigers' post-trade in 2024, but he found Double-A much tougher, as his strikeout rate soared to 31.7% in 2025.
SCOUTING REPORT: In general, because of the heavy workload required to learn a pitching staff, catchers take longer to develop. Similarly, switch-hitters often struggle early in their pro careers because of the demands of working on two swings. Liranzo checks both boxes. He still hit the ball exceptionally hard when he connected, but he was far too beatable in the strike zone. His swings are so steep and uphill that if his timing is just fractionally off, he's not going to make solid contact, and his timing in 2025 was often significantly off. Defensively, he showed improvements in spring training working with MLB pitchers, but he still has work to do behind the plate.

THE FUTURE: Even after he struggled, the Tigers added Liranzo to the 40-man roster to protect him from the Rule 5 draft. Liranzo still has the talent to be a big leaguer if he improves his swing path and continues to improve defensively, but the expectations have been lowered by his Double-A struggles.

Year	Age	Club (League)	Level	AVG	G	AB	R	H	2B	3B	HR	RBI	BB	SO	SB	OBP	SLG
2025	21	Erie (EL)	AA	.206	88	339	49	70	16	0	11	45	47	125	0	.308	.351
		Minor League Totals		.235	318	1164	199	274	70	3	51	184	201	381	6	.353	.432

20 DYLAN SMITH, RHP

FB: 55. **CB:** 40. **SP:** 55. **SW:** 45. **CTL:** 50. **BA Grade:** 40. **Risk:** Mild. **Adj:** 35.

Born: May 28, 2000. **B-T:** R-R. **HT:** 6-2. **WT:** 185. **Drafted:** Alabama, 2021 (3rd round). **Signed by:** Mike Smith.
TRACK RECORD: For years, evaluators wondered what Smith could accomplish if he could string together an extended run of healthy outings. In 2025, the Tigers finally found out. Not coincidentally, Smith made his MLB debut. He missed a month with a shoulder injury, but otherwise was a picture of durability when compared with the rest of his career.
SCOUTING REPORT: Smith's move to the bullpen in 2025 helped unlock a clearer path to the majors, as he's struggled to stay healthy when starting. But the desire to keep him healthy also meant he never pitched in consecutive days prior to his MLB debut. When working in the minors, Smith threw every three days, a routine that isn't plausible in the major leagues. Smith's stuff fits in an MLB bullpen. His 94-96 mph fastball can touch 98 with less armside run than most four-seamers. His slider has morphed into an average mid-80s sweeper that gives him a pitch with horizontal movement to pair with his above-average, high-80s splitter. He didn't throw his bigger, slower 78-80 mph curve in the majors, but it's a useful early-count surprise pitch that he almost always throws in 0-0 or 1-0 counts.
THE FUTURE: Smith is an optionable reliever who can ride the Toledo-Detroit shuttle. He's going to have to demonstrate he can handle back-to-back outings to stick in Detroit, but he's ready to be a middle-inning, one-inning reliever.

Year	Age	Club (League)	Level	W	L	ERA	G	GS	IP	H	HR	BB	SO	BB%	SO%	WHIP	AVG
2025	25	Lakeland (FSL)	A	0	0	0.00	1	1	1	0	0	1	1	25.0	25.0	1.00	.000
2025	25	West Michigan (MWL)	A+	2	0	1.42	5	0	6	5	0	2	7	8.3	29.2	1.11	.227
2025	25	Erie (EL)	AA	1	1	1.80	12	0	20	9	0	7	27	9.6	37.0	0.80	.136
2025	25	Toledo (IL)	AAA	1	0	3.65	12	0	12	8	1	7	22	14.0	44.0	1.22	.190
2025	25	Detroit (AL)	MLB	1	0	1.38	7	0	13	6	0	5	4	10.4	8.3	0.85	.150
		Minor League Totals		13	14	3.92	78	46	223	208	17	82	243	8.7	25.7	1.30	.245
		Major League Totals		1	0	1.38	7	0	13	6	0	5	4	10.4	8.3	0.85	.150

21 JACK PENNEY, 2B/SS

HIT: 45. **POW:** 45. **RUN:** 50. **FLD:** 45. **ARM:** 50. **BA Grade:** 45. **Risk:** Average. **Adj:** 35.

Born: August 19, 2002. **B-T:** L-R. **HT:** 6-1. **WT:** 190. **Drafted:** Notre Dame, 2024 (5th round). **Signed by:** Matt Zmuda.
TRACK RECORD: Penney was a modestly productive infielder at Notre Dame, getting on base and showing some power, but he also was a career .261 hitter who never hit .300 in any of three seasons. But he hit better than that with a wood bat in the Cape Cod League, which caught scouts' eyes. Penney missed a month in 2025 with a left shoulder separation, but returned with no further issues and had a solid season at High-A West Michigan.
SCOUTING REPORT: The Tigers believed Penney was a better hitter than he showed at Notre Dame, and so far they have been rewarded. Penney's 91 mph average exit velocity is above-average, although he hasn't pulled the ball in the air enough for that to turn into much productive power. He also has above-average contact skills and solid plate discipline. He draws enough walks to post excellent on-base percentages. Penney is a fringe-average defender at second who is stretched at shortstop. With an average arm, he's also playable at third.
THE FUTURE: Penney projects as a bat-first utility infielder who could be an everyday second baseman if he keeps improving. While his surface-level stats have never been flashy, his well-rounded offensive profile gives him a shot to become a useful lefthanded-hitting infielder who can play multiple positions.

Year	Age	Club (League)	Level	AVG	G	AB	R	H	2B	3B	HR	RBI	BB	SO	SB	OBP	SLG
2025	22	FCL Tigers	Rk	.000	1	3	0	0	0	0	0	0	1	0	.000	.000
2025	22	Lakeland (FSL)	A	.121	11	33	5	4	0	0	1	7	13	0	.326	.121
2025	22	West Michigan (MWL)	A+	.262	71	252	34	66	11	1	5	44	46	62	6	.382	.373
		Minor League Totals		.243	83	288	39	70	11	1	5	45	53	76	6	.372	.340

DETROIT TIGERS

22 JAKE MILLER, LHP
FB: 50. **SL:** 50. **CH:** 50. **CTL:** 60. **BA Grade:** 45. **Risk:** Average. **Adj:** 35.

Born: June 27, 2001. **B-T:** L-L **HT:** 6-2. **WT:** 185. **Drafted:** Valparaiso, 2022 (8th round). **Signed by:** Austin Cousino.
TRACK RECORD: Miller enters 2026 knocking on the door of the majors, and it's hard to think of few less-likely paths. After redshirting in 2020 at Valparaiso, Miller posted a 13.50 ERA in 2021 and a 5.58 ERA in his draft year. After the Tigers drafted him, he posted a 8.59 ERA in 2022 and a 7.13 ERA in 2023. Over four seasons, he hadn't posted a sub-7.00 ERA. Since then, he's 9-3, 1.85 across three levels while transitioning from relieving to starting. And he's done so without a major leap in stuff, as he's only added 1-2 mph of velocity.
SCOUTING REPORT: Miller missed much of the 2025 season with back and hip injuries that required surgery on both hip labrums. The Tigers shut him down at the end of April, but he returned for two starts at the end of the year. He lacks a dominant pitch, but his 91-93 mph four-seam fastball plays as average because of its well above-average life. He mixes in a 78-80 mph slider and mid-80s changeup that both also flash average. Miller's plus control and command is vital to his success. He doesn't have the stuff to blow hitters away, but he does avoid barrels.
THE FUTURE: Miller should be part of the Tigers' MLB plans at some point in 2026 as a swingman who can start or relieve in fill-in roles. His offseason addition to the 40-man roster and three remaining options should help speed that ascent. If he does get the call, he will become Valparaiso's second big leaguer in the past half century, joining Lloyd McClendon.

Year	Age	Club (League)	Level	W	L	ERA	G	GS	IP	H	HR	BB	SO	BB%	SO%	WHIP	AVG
2025	24	Lakeland (FSL)	A	0	0	0.00	2	2	3	6	0	0	5	0.0	31.3	2.00	.375
2025	24	Erie (EL)	AA	0	0	2.12	4	4	17	14	1	4	16	6.0	23.9	1.06	.222
		Minor League Totals		9	6	3.54	42	23	137	123	14	39	168	6.8	29.4	1.18	.236

23 NICK DUMESNIL, OF
HIT: 40. **POW:** 50. **RUN:** 60. **FLD:** 55. **ARM:** 45. **BA Grade:** 45. **Risk:** Average. **Adj:** 35.

Born: March 27, 2004. **B-T:** R-R. **HT:** 6-2. **WT:** 210. **Drafted:** Cal Baptist, 2025 (8th round). **Signed by:** Tim McWilliam.
TRACK RECORD: Dumesnil didn't need time to settle into college baseball. He hit .333 as a freshman at Cal Baptist, then hit .311 in the West Coast League. He was even better in 2024, hitting .362 with 19 home runs. He upped his game again that summer with a wood bat by hitting .311/.377/.489 for Brewster in the Cape Cod League. Dumesnil had a solid 2025 season at Cal Baptist, hitting .360/.442/.498, but evaluators worried about his contact ability and diminished power. His brief pro debut showed solid contact and contact rates, even if his surface-level numbers were poor.
SCOUTING REPORT: Dumesnil seemed to struggle to get comfortable at the plate for parts of his junior season, but he made minor adjustments late in the year. His swing has some flexibility, and there's more power than he showed in 2025 as well. Dumesnil likes to be aggressive early in counts, but he prides himself on his two-strike approach. He is an excellent athlete with strength and plus speed. He could be an average defender in center field and plus on the corners, although he has a fringe-average arm.
THE FUTURE: Unlike most eighth-round picks, Dumesnil has MLB starter potential if he manages to reach the top of his ability level. He has a clearer route to being a multi-position backup.

Year	Age	Club (League)	Level	AVG	G	AB	R	H	2B	3B	HR	RBI	BB	SO	SB	OBP	SLG
2025	21	Lakeland (FSL)	A	.203	16	59	12	12	5	0	0	5	17	14	9	.390	.288
		Minor League Totals		.203	16	59	12	12	5	0	0	5	17	14	9	.390	.288

24 ANGEL DE LOS SANTOS, SS
HIT: 45. **POW:** 45. **RUN:** 50. **FLD:** 50. **ARM:** 55. **BA Grade:** 50. **Risk:** Extreme. **Adj:** 30.

Born: March 3, 2008. **B-T:** R-R. **HT:** 6-1. **WT:** 161. **Signed:** Dominican Republic, 2025. **Signed by:** Rodolfo Pena.
TRACK RECORD: A $387,500 signee in January 2025 out of the Dominican Republic, De Los Santos was considered one of the better defenders in the Tigers' international class. That proved true in his first stint in the Dominican Summer League, and he showed an advanced hitting approach as well. De Los Santos missed nearly a month at the start of the season with a quad injury, but he was the DSL Tigers 1's best hitter from the day he returned.
SCOUTING REPORT: De Los Santos shows plenty of promise as a hitter. He coils at the plate, crowding the pitcher from a closed setup. He sets up with his front foot grounded in the box by just the tips of his toes before he goes into a toe tap, keeping all of his weight back until he explodes into his swing. It's a tad unconventional, but he has good barrel control and the rotational speed to generate solid power for his age. De Los Santos has a whippy bat with quick hands that also are apparent in the field. Defensively,

he has to become more consistent, but he has athletic footwork and an above-average arm up the middle.
THE FUTURE: De Los Santos has all the foundational tools to be a well-rounded middle infielder. His bat and arm give him a number of potential landing spots, but nothing he's shown so far rules out him sticking at shortstop for the long-term.

Year	Age	Club (League)	Level	AVG	G	AB	R	H	2B	3B	HR	RBI	BB	SO	SB	OBP	SLG
2025	17	DSL Tigers 1	Rk	.370	29	81	20	30	9	1	1	16	11	17	7	.465	.543
		Minor League Totals		.370	29	81	20	30	9	1	1	16	11	17	7	.465	.543

25 TY MADDEN, RHP
FB: 45. **CB:** 45. **SL:** 45. **CH:** 45. **CT:** 45. **CTL:** 45. **BA Grade:** 40. **Risk:** Average. **Adj:** 30.

Born: February 21, 2000. **B-T:** R-R. **HT:** 6-4. **WT:** 215. **Drafted:** Texas, 2021 (1st round supp.). **Signed by:** George Schaefer.
TRACK RECORD: A durable and successful starter at Texas, Madden has toyed with his release point and pitch mix to try to figure out the best way to work around a relatively dead-zone fastball. He had some success in Detroit as a bulk reliever in 2024, but his 2025 season was a washout as he rehabbed from a shoulder injury.
SCOUTING REPORT: The Tigers like to help their pitchers develop varied arsenals. That's been the path for Madden, who throws five fringe-average pitches. His fastball touches 97-98 mph at its best, but it's never played to that velocity, and he doesn't carry that velo through his starts. At 92-94, his fastball is quite hittable. His fringe-average curve, slider, changeup and cutter are all adequate, but none of the four is a bat-misser unless Madden stays a step ahead in the rock-paper-scissors game that is the batter-pitcher battle. Madden is around the zone, but his command isn't sharp enough to always hit his spots in the zone.
THE FUTURE: The Tigers announced in November that Madden was medically cleared for a normal offseason. He is expected to be at full speed for spring training, when he will compete for a job in the Tigers' rotation or bullpen. Unless his stuff picks up, he fits best as a multi-inning reliever or spot-starter.

Year	Age	Club (League)	Level	W	L	ERA	G	GS	IP	H	HR	BB	SO	BB%	SO%	WHIP	AVG
2025	25	Did not play—Injured															
		Minor League Totals		14	15	4.30	74	73	337	309	50	131	403	9.2	28.2	1.30	.241
		Major League Totals		1	1	4.30	6	1	23	25	2	8	17	7.9	16.8	1.44	.275

26 RIVER HAMILTON, RHP
FB: 55. **SL:** 50. **CB:** 50. **CH:** 45. **CTL:** 45. **BA Grade:** 50. **Risk:** Extreme. **Adj:** 30.

Born: October 4, 2006. **B-T:** R-R. **HT:** 6-3. **WT:** 195. **Drafted:** HS—Gresham, OR, 2025 (11th round). **Signed by:** Cal Towey.
TRACK RECORD: Oregon has become a bit of a prep pitching factory in recent years, with prospects like Noble Meyer, Mick Abel, Kruz Schoolcraft and fellow Tigers pitching prospect Paul Wilson. Hamilton, the Tigers' 11th-round pick in 2025, is another example. He is extremely projectable, with more velocity likely to come. He missed much of the 2025 spring with an elbow injury. The Tigers still made a big investment, signing him for a well above-slot $497,500. Hamilton's elbow injury did not improve with rest and rehab, and he eventually had Tommy John surgery.
SCOUTING REPORT: Hamilton has shown both above-average velocity potential and the ability to spin a breaking ball. It's an excellent foundation for a starting pitcher, although Hamilton was likely headed toward a slower development path even before elbow surgery. Hamilton's fastball shape isn't exceptional, but considering his frame, it won't be surprising if he goes from sitting in the low 90s now and touching 95 to sitting 94-95 mph and touching the upper 90s in a few years. He has shown the ability to spin a pair of breaking balls, with a two-plane slider and a mid-70s downer curve. He will need to develop the feel for his changeup, which flashes fringe-average potential. His control is fringe-average and his delivery isn't effortless.
THE FUTURE: Hamilton is expected to be back on the mound by late summer, but it will likely 2027 before he settles into a pro routine. He has starter traits with plenty of projection and present stuff.

Year	Age	Club (League)	Level	W	L	ERA	G	GS	IP	H	HR	BB	SO	BB%	SO%	WHIP	AVG
2025	18	Did not play															

DETROIT TIGERS

27 PAUL WILSON, LHP
FB: 60. **SL:** 60. **CB:** 55. **CH:** 40. **CTL:** 40. **BA Grade:** 50. **Risk:** Extreme. **Adj:** 30.

Born: December 11, 2004. **B-T:** R-L. **HT:** 6-3. **WT:** 210. **Drafted:** HS—Lake Oswego, OR, 2023 (3rd round). **Signed by:** Cal Towey.

TRACK RECORD: The son of Giants pitcher Trevor Wilson, Paul's velocity spiked in his senior year of high school, catapulting him to a $1,697,500 bonus. Wilson's first year of pro ball in 2024 was a brutal introduction. He lost his stuff and control, as he walked a batter an inning while sitting 90-92 mph. Wilson seemed poised for a turnaround in 2025. He showed much crisper stuff, but his elbow blew out in his fourth start and he missed the rest of the season after having Tommy John surgery.

SCOUTING REPORT: Wilson was not expected to move quickly, but his stuff prior to injury in 2025 was closer to the best version of himself from high school and offers encouragement for what he can be once healthy. He sat 94-95 mph and touched 97 in his brief 2025 action. Wilson's delivery has some stiffness, and he will sail and spike pitches too often because of his below-average control, but he has well above-average stuff for a lefthanded starter. With improved arm speed, his plus slider played better as well. He has flashed an above-average curve, and he did throw it once in his four 2025 starts for a nasty swing-and-miss. Developing his below-average changeup needs to be a post-surgery focus.

THE FUTURE: While elbow surgery slowed Wilson's rocky path through pro ball, few 21-year-old pitchers have his level of arm talent, especially if he can find the strike zone more consistently.

Year	Age	Club (League)	Level	W	L	ERA	G	GS	IP	H	HR	BB	SO	BB%	SO%	WHIP	AVG
2025	20	Lakeland (FSL)	A	0	1	4.26	3	2	6	7	0	6	11	18.8	34.4	2.05	.280
		Minor League Totals		1	3	6.26	14	10	42	51	4	42	45	19.7	21.1	2.23	.305

28 EDUARDO VALENCIA, C/1B
HIT: 40. **POW:** 45. **RUN:** 30. **FLD:** 30. **ARM:** 45. **BA Grade:** 45. **Risk:** High. **Adj:** 30

Born: January 25, 2000. **B-T:** R-R. **HT:** 6-2. **WT:** 233. **Signed:** Venezuela, 2018. **Signed by:** Aldo Perez/Carlos Santana.

TRACK RECORD: A 2018 international signing, Valencia has looked more like organizational depth for most of his pro career. A backup catcher and first baseman, he didn't make it to full-season ball for good until 2022. In 2025, he forced himself into regular playing time with a breakout season. His 24 home runs were twice as many as his total in his first five combined seasons and he was one of Toledo's best hitters.

SCOUTING REPORT: Valencia is a limited player, but he makes the most of his tools and skills. He will look lost on one swing, then hit a ball 400 feet on the next pitch. He improved his swing decisions, contact rate and ability to hit the ball in the air in 2025, which is an almost impossible trifecta. As good as he was in 2025, he still has a narrow path to a big league role. He's a well below-average catcher who struggles with blocking, but he posts fringe-average pop times. He's below-average at first base as well and fits best as a DH.

THE FUTURE: The Tigers added Valencia to the 40-man roster, so he will head to spring training looking to show he's MLB-ready. Finding a defensive fit will be their biggest challenge. He could be a third catcher or backup first baseman/DH, but that likely means he will be on call at Triple-A.

Year	Age	Club (League)	Level	AVG	G	AB	R	H	2B	3B	HR	RBI	BB	SO	SB	OBP	SLG
2025	25	Erie (EL)	AA	.304	53	194	29	59	5	0	11	40	16	45	0	.359	.500
2025	25	Toledo (IL)	AAA	.319	50	185	35	59	13	2	13	55	27	41	0	.405	.622
		Minor League Totals		.275	363	1255	190	345	67	3	36	213	132	237	10	.349	.419

29 JACKSON STRONG, OF

HIT: 40. **POW:** 40. **RUN:** 60. **FLD:** 60. **ARM:** 45. **BA Grade:** 40. **Risk:** Average. **Adj:** 30.

Born: August 26, 2003. **B-T:** L-L. **HT:** 6-1. **WT:** 185. **Drafted:** Canisius, 2024 (7th round). **Signed by:** Jim Bretz.

TRACK RECORD: Strong was a two-time first-team honoree in the Metro Atlantic Athletic Conference, where he ranked within the top 10 in batting average, slugging and home runs in 2024 and 2025. He was a right fielder in college at Canisius, but his plus speed has led the Tigers to make him primarily a center fielder in pro ball.

SCOUTING REPORT: Strong is a well-rounded outfielder with no overwhelming tools, but enough skills to be an MLB backup. He posts below-average exit velocities, but he pulls the ball in the air consistently enough to get to below-average power. Strong's swing is a bit grooved at times but he has solid timing to make it work. He struggled after his promotion to High-A West Michigan, and he'll have to show he has the contact skills to handle better pitching.

THE FUTURE: Strong is highly unlikely to be a big league regular, but he could be a center fielder who can play defense, run and hit for just enough power to carve out a big league role.

DETROIT TIGERS

Year	Age	Club (League)	Level	AVG	G	AB	R	H	2B	3B	HR	RBI	BB	SO	SB	OBP	SLG
2025	21	Lakeland (FSL)	A	.277	73	267	38	74	16	6	5	42	39	87	18	.382	.438
2025	21	West Michigan (MWL)	A+	.222	23	81	16	18	4	0	4	6	13	32	2	.330	.420
		Minor League Totals		.268	105	380	56	102	23	6	9	53	54	127	23	.369	.432

30 GRAYSON GRINSELL, LHP

FB: 30. **CB:** 40. **CH:** 60. **CTL:** 55. **BA Grade:** 40. **Risk:** Average. **Adj:** 30.

Born: February 2, 2004. **B-T:** L-L. **HT:** 6-1. **WT:** 195. **Drafted:** Oregon, 2025 (6th round). **Signed by:** Cal Towey.

TRACK RECORD: Grinsell arrived at Oregon thinking he would be the Ducks' next center fielder. But injuries struck the pitching staff and he instead cemented himself as a pitcher. MLB teams have found success in recent years drafting pitchers with modest velocity and excellent command, then helping those pitchers develop pro-quality velocity. Grinsell had a dominat 9-3, 3.01 season at Oregon, but he did so with a well below-average fastball.
SCOUTING REPORT: Grinsell sat at 87-89 mph at Oregon and touched 91-92. The Tigers will need to get him to the upper ends of his velocity range for him to succeed in pro ball, and his above-average riding life would help it play effectively if he can get to the low 90s regularly. His plus changeup is as important to him as his fastball because it keeps hitters off-balance. His mid-70s curveball will need to get tighter and harder to succeed, which goes back to him developing more arm speed. He has above-average command, but his control might suffer in pro ball if he has to nibble to avoid hard contact.
THE FUTURE: Grinsell is a capable organization arm if he doesn't improve his stuff, but his changeup, feel and command all would be excellent if he added three or four ticks of velocity.

Year	Age	Club (League)	Level	AVG	G	AB	R	H	2B	3B	HR	RBI	BB	SO	SB	OBP	SLG
2025	21	Did not play															

Hunter Brown

Houston Astros

BY GEOFF PONTES

For the first time since 2016, the Astros missed the playoffs in 2025.

The organization continued its run of 11 consecutive winning seasons but finished second in the American League West and lost a tiebreaker to the Tigers for the final wild card spot. Despite this, the Astros saw some positive developments with homegrown talent.

Shortstop Jeremy Peña produced the best season of his career, despite dealing with injuries. Off-season trade acquisition Cam Smith broke camp with the team and established himself as the team's everyday right fielder, flashing power and on-base skills.

Former top prospects Zach Dezenzo and Shay Whitcomb graduated from rookie status in 2025, featuring primarily as bench players. Jacob Melton and Brice Matthews each made their major league debuts and are likely to be big parts of the Astros' lineup in the coming years.

As has become customary with the Astros, they had multiple pitchers outproduce their pedigree in the major leagues in 2025. Ryan Gusto, the team's No. 14 prospect entering the season, performed well in the Houston rotation before he was dealt to the Marlins in the Jesus Sanchez trade.

Righthander AJ Blubaugh retains his rookie status entering 2026 and could be an underrated pick for the Rookie of the Year award. He pitched to a 1.69 ERA in 32 innings, pitching mostly in long relief. Blubaugh could be the next Astros draftee to plant himself into the team's longterm rotation plans. Lefthander Colton Gordon provided emergency starter depth when injuries forced the team to look for options internally. While Gordon's production was subpar, his 86 innings had value for a team dealing with a rotation brutalized by injury.

Of the 33 pitchers the Astros used in 2025, 19 of them call Houston their original signing organization.

PROJECTED 2029 LINEUP

Catcher	Walker Janek	26
First Base	Ethan Frey	25
Second Base	Brice Matthews	27
Third Base	Xavier Neyens	22
Shortstop	Jeremy Peña	31
Left Field	Zach Cole	28
Center Field	Jacob Melton	28
Right Field	Cam Smith	26
Designated Hitter	Jose Altuve	39
No. 1 Starter	Hunter Brown	30
No. 2 Starter	Spencer Arrighetti	29
No. 3 Starter	Ronel Blanco	35
No. 4 Starter	Anderson Brito	24
No. 5 Starter	AJ Blubaugh	28
Closer	Miguel Ullola	27

Among these homegrown pitchers, former Astros No. 1 prospect Hunter Brown produced the best season of his career and established himself as one of the best righthanded starters in the game. Brown earned his first all-star nod with a 2.43 ERA and 206 strikeouts across 185.1 innings. Brown is another shining example of the Astros' ability to identify players in the draft and develop them to reach their higher-end outcomes.

Houston's 2025 draft class promises to be one of its strongest in recent memory, particularly on the position player side. The team took one of the top high school hitters available in Washington high school shortstop Xavier Neyens. Known for his plus raw power, he is one of the highest-profile amateurs the Astros have landed in years. He boasts true top 50 prospect in the game upside.

Third-round pick Ethan Frey out of LSU made a quick transition to pro ball. The outfielder hit .330/.434/.470 with three home runs over 26 games with Low-A Fayetteville and was one of the top performers among 2025 draftees. He and Neyens could potentially lead the Astros' prospect rankings a year from now and provide the team upside sorely missing in recent years.

The Astros may have fallen from their perch atop the AL West in 2025, but it looks like more of a blip than a trend. ■

DEPTH CHART

HOUSTON ASTROS

TOP 2026 ROOKIES — RANK
1. Jacob Melton, OF — 1
2. Brice Matthews, 2B — 5
3. AJ Blubaugh, RHP — 6

BREAKOUT PROSPECTS — RANK
1. Lucas Spence, OF — 13
2. Anthony Huezo, OF — 16
3. Nick Potter, RHP — 26

SOURCE OF TOP 30 TALENT

Homegrown	30	Acquired	0
College	17	Trade	0
Junior college	0	Rule 5 draft	0
High school	3	Independent league	0
Undrafted free agent	3	Free agent/waivers	0
International	7		

LF
Joseph Sullivan (15)
Anthony Huezo (16)
Yensi De La Cruz

CF
Jacob Melton (1)
Kevin Alvarez (7)
Lucas Spence (13)
Zach Cole (14)
Anthony Millan
Elijah Fareley

RF
Ethan Frey (4)
Luis Baez
Nehomar Ochoa

3B
Pascanel Ferreras
Hector Salas
Sami Manzueta

SS
Xavier Neyens (2)
German Ramirez (22)
Landon Arroyos
Caden Powell

2B
Brice Matthews (5)
Nick Monistere (24)

1B
Will Bush (20)
Wes Clarke
Zach Daudet

C
Walker Janek (9)
Jase Mitchell (18)
Jancel Villarroel (21)
Collin Price

LHP

LHSP
Trey Dombroski

LHRP
Colby Langford

RHP

RHSP
Anderson Brito (3)
AJ Blubaugh (6)
Ethan Pecko (8)
Bryce Mayer (10)
Ryan Forcucci (11)
Jackson Nezuh (17)
James Hicks (22)
Jose Fleury (23)
Alonzo Tredwell (25)
Cole Hertzler (28)
Joey Mancini
Juan Bello
Andrew Taylor

RHRP
Miguel Ullola (12)
Parker Smith (19)
Nick Potter (26)
Hudson Leach (27)
Alimber Santa (30)
Michael Knorr
Alex Santos II

HOUSTON ASTROS

1 JACOB MELTON, OF

Born: September 7, 2000. **B-T:** L-L. **HT:** 6-3. **WT:** 208.
Drafted: Oregon State, 2022 (2nd round).
Signed by: Tim Costic.

TRACK RECORD: Melton wasn't heavily recruited out of his Oregon high school, so he attended Linn-Benton (Ore.) JC and earned all-conference honors in his single season there. He transferred to Oregon State as a sophomore, but his season was cut short by the pandemic. Melton enjoyed a breakout campaign in 2021 by hitting .404/.466/.697 in 32 games before a shoulder injury ended his season. He went undrafted in 2021 and returned to OSU for a third year in 2022, when he hit .360/.424/.671 to earn first-team All-America honors and won the Pacific-12 Conference player of the year award. The Astros selected Melton in the second round of the 2022 draft and signed him for an under-slot $1 million. Over Melton's first three full seasons, he climbed two levels a year, reaching Triple-A in the second half of 2024. Melton began 2025 back with Triple-A Sugar Land, missing a little over a month over the first six weeks of the season with upper-back discomfort. He returned in mid May and earned his first MLB callup on June 1. Melton sprained his right ankle on June 13 and was placed on the injured list. He returned in late July but was optioned back to Triple-A on Aug. 1. Melton was recalled two more times before the end of the season.

SCOUTING REPORT: Melton is a toolsy outfielder who has found success despite a very unusual swing and bat path. Throughout his minor league career, he has shown above-average contact skills, particularly in-zone with strong swing decisions. That was not the case in his scattered MLB time. Melton struggled against offspeed pitches on the outer half of the plate and breaking balls down and in. Elevated fastballs also gave him fits. It took some time for Melton to adjust to each level, and it's possible the stop-and-start nature of his season messed with his timing. Melton still projects as an average hitter and shows plus raw power. He has produced eye-popping high-end exit velocities and has gotten to more of his power with improved batted-ball angles in recent seasons. Melton's 90th percentile exit velocity of 107.7 mph hints at more game power to come. He showed more power in Triple-A 2025 than at any point in his career. Melton is a plus runner who has been a successful basestealer. He's capable of stealing 20 or more bases a year, with the ability to leg out extra bases. His speed translates to the outfield, where he's above-average at all three spots but is best in center field, where he's adept at making plays against the wall. He shows good range and takes good routes to the ball. Melton has an average arm.

THE FUTURE: Melton looks ready to join the Astros full-time in 2026 and should quickly provide average everyday value in center field.

BA GRADE: 50 **Risk:** Mild
SCOUTING GRADES: Hit: 45. Power: 55. Run: 60. Field: 55. Arm: 50.
Adjusted grade: 45
Projected future grades on 20-80 scouting scale

BEST TOOLS

BATTING
Best Hitter	Kevin Alvarez
Best Power Hitter	Xavier Neyens
Best Strike-Zone Discipline	Jacob Melton
Fastest Baserunner	Joseph Sullivan
Best Athlete	Zach Cole

PITCHING
Best Fastball	Anderson Brito
Best Curveball	Anderson Brito
Best Slider	AJ Blubaugh
Best Changeup	Jackson Nezuh
Best Control	James Hicks

FIELDING
Best Defensive Catcher	Walker Janek
Best Defensive Infielder	Brice Matthews
Best Infield Arm	Xavier Neyens
Best Defensive Outfielder	Jacob Melton
Best Outfield Arm	Luis Baez

Year	Age	Club (League)	Level	AVG	G	AB	R	H	2B	3B	HR	RBI	BB	SO	SB	OBP	SLG
2025	24	Sugar Land (PCL)	AAA	.286	35	126	26	36	16	0	6	17	22	30	12	.389	.556
2025	24	Houston (AL)	MLB	.157	32	70	7	11	0	1	0	7	6	29	7	.234	.186
		Minor League Totals		.255	262	1009	179	257	59	3	48	139	116	259	93	.334	.462
		Major League Totals		.157	32	70	7	11	0	1	0	7	6	29	7	.234	.186

HOUSTON ASTROS

2 XAVIER NEYENS, SS
HIT: 45. **POW:** 65. **RUN:** 45. **FLD:** 50. **ARM:** 60. **BA Grade:** 60. **Risk:** High. **Adj:** 45.

Born: October 29, 2006. **B-T:** L-R. **HT:** 6-4. **WT:** 205.
Drafted: HS—Mount Vernon, WA, 2025 (1st round). **Signed by:** Tim Costic.
TRACK RECORD: Neyens ranked as the No. 19 prospect for the 2025 draft and stood out among high school position players. He was regarded as having the best strike-zone judgment among preps and more power than anybody on the high school side but Ethan Holliday. Early in the draft scouting process, Neyens had a chance to go in the top half of the first round. Concerns around his hit tool dropped him to the Astros at pick No. 21, and he signed for $4,120,000. Neyens did not debut following the draft, but the touted slugger should begin 2026 at Low-A Fayetteville.
SCOUTING REPORT: A physical power hitter who should grow into more strength as his body matures, Neyens is an average athlete who is unlikely to stick at shortstop. His physicality could make him a slugging third baseman. Neyens is a lefthanded batter who sets up with a wider base and his hands set by the back of his head. He employs a large leg kick that contracts into his body, leading into a long stride. It's a powerful swing that generates lots of clean backspin, and he peppers hard-struck fly balls to all parts of the yard. There's some swing-and-miss in Neyens' game. Offspeed and breaking pitches at times can give him fits. Those highest on Neyens think he can iron out his issues and rely on strong swing decisions early; others worry he'll always run high whiff rates. More than likely, his strikeout rates will be higher during his early seasons in pro ball. Neyens is an average runner but will slow down to fringe-average at peak. A shortstop as an amateur, Neyens is likely to move to third base eventually. He has the requisite plus arm and skilled enough hands and actions to be average there.
THE FUTURE: Neyens is one of the highest upside players from the 2025 draft class. If he can prove his hit tool is average, he could blossom into a 30-home run slugger at third base.

Year	Age	Club (League)	Level	AVG	G	AB	R	H	2B	3B	HR	RBI	BB	SO	SB	OBP	SLG
2025	18	Did not play															

3 ANDERSON BRITO, RHP
FB: 60. **CB:** 60. **CH:** 55. **CT:** 45. **SW:** 50. **CTL:** 50. **BA Grade:** 60. **Risk:** High. **Adj:** 45.

Born: July 7, 2004. **B-T:** R-R. **HT:** 5-11. **WT:** 200.
Signed: Venezuela, 2023. **Signed by:** Jose Palacios/Daniel Gamboa.
TRACK RECORD: Signed out of Venezuela in November 2023 for just $10,000, Brito has blossomed into one of the best prospects in the Astros' system. In 2024, he showed up to spring sitting in the mid 90s and touching 99 mph. Brito was assigned to the Dominican Summer League but climbed three levels to reach Low-A Fayetteville. He made 12 starts for High-A Asheville in 2025 before going down with a stress reaction in his shoulder that cost him the final two months of the season. Brito participated in the Arizona Fall League following the season.
SCOUTING REPORT: An undersized power righthander, Brito does a good job getting down the mound and creating above-average extension. This allows his fastball to play up with a high three-quarters arm slot due to the combination of extension and his 5-foot-11 height. Brito mixes a four-seam fastball, cutter, curveball, sweeper and changeup. His four-seamer is a plus pitch that sits 95-97 mph and touches 100 mph with plus ride and cut from a flat approach. The pitch has all the elements of a plus fastball. He uses his low-90s cutter as a bridge between his fastball and his breaking stuff. Brito's mid-80s curveball is his best secondary pitch. It's a plus, two-plane banger that drives whiffs in bunches. His sweeper is a little firmer and flatter and drives solid results. His changeup is thrown exclusively to lefties and, in tandem with his curveball, gives him two weapons in off-hand matchups. His changeup features good vertical separation off his fastball with 10 mph between the two pitches. He has the potential for three above-average to plus pitches with average control.
THE FUTURE: Brito has the upside of a midrotation starter, but his smaller frame could push him to high-leverage relief.

Year	Age	Club (League)	Level	W	L	ERA	G	GS	IP	H	HR	BB	SO	BB%	SO%	WHIP	AVG
2025	20	Asheville (SAL)	A+	0	1	3.28	12	12	49	36	1	28	65	13.4	31.1	1.30	.202
		Minor League Totals		4	3	2.36	27	21	103	64	5	49	147	11.7	35.0	1.10	.177

HOUSTON ASTROS

4 ETHAN FREY, OF

HIT: 50. **POW:** 60. **RUN:** 50. **FLD:** 50. **ARM:** 45. **BA Grade:** 50. **Risk:** Average. **Adj:** 40.

Born: March 15, 2004. **B-T:** R-R. **HT:** 6-5. **WT:** 220.
Drafted: LSU, 2025 (3rd round). **Signed by:** Landon Townsley.
TRACK RECORD: Frey made the back of the BA 500 draft ranking out of high school in 2022 as a power-oriented catcher who was already 6-foot-4. He helped lead his Rosepine High team to a pair of Louisiana state titles, then was a part of an LSU team that won national championships in 2023 and 2025. He was a centerpiece of the LSU lineup in 2025, when he hit .331/.420/.641 with 13 home runs and 15 doubles in 62 games. The Astros drafted Frey in the third round in 2025, signing him for $997,500. He debuted after the draft with Low-A Fayetteville and impressed. Over 26 games with the Woodpeckers, he hit .330/.434/.470 with three home runs and nine stolen bases.
SCOUTING REPORT: Frey is a tall, athletic righthanded hitter who moves well in the box and in the outfield. He sets up deep into his back leg and uses a toe-tap timing mechanism. He likes to get extended in his swing and shows the ability to adjust to a variety of locations and pitch heights. Frey shows above-average bat-to-ball skills, with a patient approach that can border on passive. He looks to get on base and should run higher walk rates, but he could take more looking strikes than is ideal. Frey has plus raw power and has shown the ability to get into it in games with LSU and post-draft. He produces plus exit velocity data, with a 90th percentile exit velocity of 108.3 mph and a max of 113.8 mph. Frey is an average runner whom the Astros believe can stick in the outfield. He has played some center field but is likely best suited for a corner. His fringe-average arm could be a concern.
THE FUTURE: During his outstanding pro debut, Frey showed average hitting ability and the potential for above-average power. He is a future everyday regular in the corner outfield.

Year	Age	Club (League)	Level	AVG	G	AB	R	H	2B	3B	HR	RBI	BB	SO	SB	OBP	SLG
2025	21	Fayetteville (CAR)	A	.330	26	100	20	33	5	0	3	17	20	25	9	.434	.470
		Minor League Totals		.330	26	100	20	33	5	0	3	17	20	25	9	.434	.470

5 BRICE MATTHEWS, 2B

HIT: 30. **POW:** 55. **RUN:** 60. **FLD:** 50. **ARM:** 45. **BA Grade:** 50. **Risk:** Average. **Adj:** 40.

Born: March 16, 2002. **B-T:** R-R. **HT:** 5-11. **WT:** 190.
Drafted: Nebraska, 2023 (1st round). **Signed by:** Drew Pearson.
TRACK RECORD: As a junior in 2023, Matthews produced Nebraska's first 20-homer, 20-steal season. The Astros drafted him 28th overall that year and signed him for $2,478,200. Matthews was assigned to High-A Asheville to begin his first full pro season. After just 21 games, he was promoted to Double-A and eventually reached Triple-A Sugar Land. Matthews returned to Triple-A to begin 2025 and was called up to Houston on July 11.
SCOUTING REPORT: Matthews is a toolsy infielder with a nice combination of power and speed—but also major contact questions. He has an average-sized build with quick-twitch actions and explosive athleticism. The one tool he lacks, however, is the hit tool. Matthews' bat-to-ball skills are below-average, and he's prone to swinging and missing in the zone. He is a passive hitter by nature, but he's made strides in this regard, balancing aggression and patience well at Triple-A in 2025. This approach led to a jump in swinging strikes but a boost in contact quality. Matthews shows above-average raw power with lofty launch angles that help him optimize his hardest contact. The uphill nature of his swing leads to lots of flyball contact, maximizing his raw power but also introducing some whiffs. Matthews' power isn't his only explosive skill. He's also a plus runner and a basestealing threat who could one day steal 30-plus bases per season. His speed translates to the field, where he has good range and actions at second base. Matthews can fill in at shortstop, third base or in center field, though he is limited on the left side of the infield by his fringy throwing arm.
THE FUTURE: Matthews is an MLB-ready utility player with some hit tool questions.

Year	Age	Club (League)	Level	AVG	G	AB	R	H	2B	3B	HR	RBI	BB	SO	SB	OBP	SLG
2025	23	Sugar Land (PCL)	AAA	.260	112	419	70	109	18	7	17	64	70	139	41	.371	.458
2025	23	Houston (AL)	MLB	.167	13	42	6	7	0	0	4	9	2	20	1	.222	.452
		Minor League Totals		.254	226	831	144	211	39	8	36	119	141	288	91	.375	.450
		Major League Totals		.167	13	42	6	7	0	0	4	9	2	20	1	.222	.452

HOUSTON ASTROS

6 AJ BLUBAUGH, RHP
FB: 55. **CB:** 45. **CH:** 50. **CT:** 45. **SW:** 55. **CTL:** 50. **BA Grade:** 45. **Risk:** Mild. **Adj:** 40.

Born: July 4, 2000. **B-T:** R-R. **HT:** 6-2. **WT:** 180.
Drafted: Wisconsin-Milwaukee, 2022 (7th round). **Signed by:** Drew Pearson.
TRACK RECORD: In 2023, Blubaugh's first full professional season, he exceeded 100 innings and reached Double-A. After returning to the level in 2024, he was promoted to Triple-A after one start. Blubaugh returned to Triple-A in 2025 but quickly got called up to Houston on April 30. He had three different stints with the Astros and amassed 32 innings.
SCOUTING REPORT: A lanky but athletic 6-foot-2 righthander, Blubaugh is a strong mover on the mound and does a good job getting downhill and creating above-average extension. He can struggle to repeat his mechanics and will lose his release point. Blubaugh mixes a four-seam fastball, curveball, sweeper, cutter and changeup. His four-seam fastball sits 93-94 mph and touches 98 with average ride and above-average armside run. The sweeper is Blubaugh's best breaking pitch and sits 82-83 mph with 14 or more inches of sweep on average. His changeup is his go-to pitch against lefties and he shows average command of the pitch with good velocity and vertical separation off his fastball. His changeup is more of a weak-contact pitch than a swing-and-miss offering. Blubaugh uses his cutter as a bridge pitch between his four-seam fastball and sweeper. Blubaugh also throws a curveball as a change-of-pace pitch with two-plane break, but it's a below-average offering. He has average control and his strike-throwing has improved. He struggled to adjust to the ABS challenge system at Triple-A and the tighter strike zone. Blubaugh could find more strikes with greater consistency in his mechanics.
THE FUTURE: Blubaugh could find his way into a rotation spot in 2026 but offers the Astros a bulk reliever immediately.

Year	Age	Club (League)	Level	W	L	ERA	G	GS	IP	H	HR	BB	SO	BB%	SO%	WHIP	AVG
2025	24	Sugar Land (PCL)	AAA	5	8	5.27	22	19	99	97	10	58	101	12.8	22.3	1.57	.252
2025	24	Houston (AL)	MLB	3	1	1.69	11	3	32	17	6	11	35	8.9	28.2	0.88	.152
		Minor League Totals		25	16	4.39	82	59	346	319	35	160	370	10.7	24.8	1.38	.244
		Major League Totals		3	1	1.69	11	3	32	17	6	11	35	8.9	28.2	0.88	.152

7 KEVIN ALVAREZ, OF
HIT: 55. **POW:** 55. **RUN:** 50. **FLD:** 50. **ARM:** 55. **BA Grade:** 55. **Risk:** High. **Adj:** 40.

Born: January 13, 2008. **B-T:** L-L. **HT:** 6-4. **WT:** 184.
Signed: Cuba, 2025. **Signed by:** Charlie Gonzalez.
TRACK RECORD: Alvarez left Cuba along with his father in December 2021 and settled in the Dominican Republic. He blossomed into one of the top players in the 2025 international class and signed with the Astros for $2 million in January. Assigned to the Dominican Summer League, Alvarez hit .301/.419/.455 with two home runs, 11 stolen bases and more walks than strikeouts. He made the DSL all-star team and ranked as the league's No. 6 prospect.
SCOUTING REPORT: Alvarez is an explosive athlete who shows refined baseball skills to go with his 6-foot-4 size and explosiveness. He has a smooth lefthanded swing with a bigger leg-kick trigger mechanism and a smooth, quick swing with a flatter bat path on contact. Alvarez had little trouble against DSL pitchers and ran an 89.2% zone-contact rate while showing a nice balance of patience and aggressiveness at the plate. While his size and bat speed may give him the look of a pure power hitter, Alvarez's polish at the plate and his ability to avoid whiffs are rare among teenage players with longer levers. He shows potential for plus game power, though his swing is geared more toward hard line-drive contact. Alvarez hit a ball 110 mph in the DSL in 2025 for a preview of what may be to come. If he can add more consistent loft to his swing, he has the underlying strength to hit 25-plus home runs annually. He's an above-average runner but expected to slow down as he matures and likely will settle in as an average runner. He shows good routes in center field and an above-average arm but will likely fit best in a corner outfield spot long term.
THE FUTURE: Alvarez has a strong combination of hittability and power. He could blossom into an above-average regular one day.

Year	Age	Club (League)	Level	AVG	G	AB	R	H	2B	3B	HR	RBI	BB	SO	SB	OBP	SLG
2025	17	DSL Astros Blue	Rk	.301	47	156	31	47	12	3	2	33	23	19	11	.419	.455
		Minor League Totals		.301	47	156	31	47	12	3	2	33	23	19	11	.419	.455

HOUSTON ASTROS

8 ETHAN PECKO, RHP

FB: 55. **CB:** 45. **CH:** 45. **CT:** 55. **SW:** 50. **CTL:** 50. **BA Grade:** 50. **Risk:** Average. **Adj:** 40.

Born: August 25, 2002. **B-T:** R-R. **HT:** 6-2. **WT:** 195.
Drafted: Towson, 2023 (6th round). **Signed by:** Bobby St. Pierre.
TRACK RECORD: Pecko spent two seasons with Towson after spending his freshman season as an injury redshirt at La Salle. He pitched to a 3.21 ERA his junior season and the Astros drafted him in the sixth round in 2023. Pecko climbed three levels in his first full professional season, reaching Double-A Corpus Christi. His 2025 campaign got off to a late start with a forearm injury, and he missed the first two months before joining Corpus Christi on June 1. Over 11 appearances in Double-A, Pecko pitched to a 4.40 ERA and struck out 45 in 43 innings. He earned a promotion to Triple-A on Aug. 1 and made eight starts for Sugar Land.
SCOUTING REPORT: Pecko is a pitchability righthander with a simple operation, deceptive release traits and a kitchen-sink approach to pitching. He generates pedestrian extension, but his lower three-quarters arm slot creates a low release height that amplifies his arsenal. Mixing four-seam fastball, curveball, cutter, sweeper and changeup, Pecko does a good job of moving the ball around the zone and keeping hitters off-balance. His four-seamer sits 93-94 mph and touches 98. He generates an average amount of ride from his release height, but his ability to land the pitch at the top of the zone allows the flatter plane to play up. Pecko's breaking balls are used interchangeably, with his hard upper-80s cutter the best of the bunch. His low-80s curveball is a two-plane breaking ball that he uses to steal strikes and get weak contact. While his low-to-mid-80s sweeper is the best bat-missing pitch of the bunch, it plays much better in same-side matchups. Pecko's changeup is splitter-like in the mid-80s, but he struggles to command the pitch. He shows average control across his arsenal.
THE FUTURE: Pecko fits perfectly into the No. 5 starter bucket and could be up in 2026.

Year	Age	Club (League)	Level	W	L	ERA	G	GS	IP	H	HR	BB	SO	BB%	SO%	WHIP	AVG
2025	22	FCL Astros	Rk	0	0	4.50	1	1	2	2	0	0	2	0.0	25.0	1.00	.250
2025	22	Corpus Christi (TL)	AA	2	6	4.40	11	10	43	37	4	15	45	8.7	26.2	1.21	.239
2025	22	Sugar Land (PCL)	AAA	1	4	3.09	8	7	35	34	2	12	48	7.9	31.8	1.31	.248
		Minor League Totals		5	16	4.11	45	34	164	151	13	64	209	9.1	29.7	1.31	.240

9 WALKER JANEK, C

HIT: 40. **POW:** 50. **RUN:** 45. **FLD:** 60. **ARM:** 70. **BA Grade:** 50. **Risk:** Average. **Adj:** 40.

Born: September 24, 2003. **B-T:** R-R. **HT:** 6-0. **WT:** 190.
Drafted: Sam Houston, 2024 (1st round). **Signed by:** Brian Sheffler.
TRACK RECORD: Janek spent three seasons at Sam Houston State and won the Buster Posey Award as the best college catcher in 2024. The Astros drafted him with the No. 28 pick that year and signed him for just under $3.2 million. Janek debuted following the draft with High-A Asheville and returned to the level to begin 2025. He would spend the entire season in the South Atlantic League, hitting .263/.333/.433 with 12 home runs in 98 games. Janek participated in the Arizona Fall League following the season.
SCOUTING REPORT: Janek is a glove-first catcher with a lighter bat. Physically, he's already maxed out with no remaining projection. He's average in size and athleticism but moves and throws well behind the plate. As a hitter, Janek has a stiff righthanded swing with a grooved bat path. He shows little ability to adjust to pitches inside or on in the upper quadrants of the strike zone. Poor swing decisions hardly do Janek any favors, and he is prone to expanding the zone while being too passive in the zone at other times. He shows average power with average exit velocity data and good launch angles. Janek shows the ability to find loft on his best-struck drives, but his inability to consistently find the barrel is a problem. A fringe-average runner, Janek moves well behind the plate. His defensive chops at catcher in terms of receiving and throwing are his carrying tools. He's a fluid and easy mover, with silky smooth hands as a receiver. Janek does an exemplary job of keeping the ball in front of him and controlling his blocks. His plus-plus arm keeps baserunners honest, and he regularly flashes pop times under 1.90 seconds.
THE FUTURE: Janek is a plus defensive catcher with a limited offensive profile. With slight improvements to his hit tool, he could develop into an everyday catcher.

Year	Age	Club (League)	Level	AVG	G	AB	R	H	2B	3B	HR	RBI	BB	SO	SB	OBP	SLG
2025	22	Asheville (SAL)	A+	.263	92	358	58	94	21	2	12	46	30	106	30	.333	.433
		Minor League Totals		.244	117	455	68	111	27	3	13	57	34	136	30	.309	.402

HOUSTON ASTROS

10 BRYCE MAYER, RHP

FB: 55. CB: 55. CH: 40. CT: 40. SW: 55. CTL: 50. BA Grade: 55. Risk: High. Adj: 40.

Born: February 11, 2002. **B-T:** R-R. **HT:** 6-3. **WT:** 210.
Drafted: Missouri, 2024 (16th round). **Signed by:** Freddy Perez.
TRACK RECORD: Mayer spent two seasons with St. Charles (Mo.) JC before transferring to Missouri for his junior season. He missed all of 2023 with injuries. He returned to Missouri for a fourth season and made 17 appearances for the Tigers. The Astros drafted Mayer in the 16th round in 2024. Mayer debuted with Low-A Fayetteville following the draft and returned there to begin 2025. After five appearances he was promoted to High-A Asheville. Mayer reached Double-A Corpus Christi by July. He was transferred to the development list in late August.
SCOUTING REPORT: A physically mature righthander, Mayer is an athletic mover on the mound who generates above-average extension. His low release height and high spin efficiency allow him to create a deceptively flat vertical approach angle on his fastball, which allows him to generate whiffs at high rates. Mayer mixes five pitches: a four-seam fastball, cutter, curveball, sweeper and changeup. He sits 92-93 mph and touches 95 on his fastball, but the pitch plays up due to its unique traits. Mayer's curveball is his most-thrown offspeed pitch and sits in the high 70s with heavy two-plane break. His sweeper is thrown nearly 1-for-1 to his curveball, with ride and heavy sweep. Mayer's upper-80s cutter is a bridge pitch that sets up his pair of bigger breaking pitches. Mayer uses his mid-80s changeup, which has good vertical and velocity separation, exclusively to lefthanded hitters. He shows average command and the ability to land all of his pitches for strikes. Mayer is still stretching out as a starter, and the Astros were cautious with his innings, adding a bit of relief risk to Mayer's profile.
THE FUTURE: Mayer has a starter's arsenal and unique traits. He'll look to build up his innings, but he has No. 4 starter upside.

Year	Age	Club (League)	Level	W	L	ERA	G	GS	IP	H	HR	BB	SO	BB%	SO%	WHIP	AVG
2025	23	Fayetteville (CAR)	A	0	0	4.08	5	3	18	17	1	6	30	7.8	39.0	1.30	.254
2025	23	Asheville (SAL)	A+	3	2	2.85	9	9	41	29	4	9	45	5.6	28.1	0.93	.192
2025	23	Corpus Christi (TL)	AA	1	4	5.90	7	4	29	30	3	12	37	9.0	27.6	1.45	.256
		Minor League Totals		4	6	4.11	21	16	88	76	8	27	112	7.3	30.2	1.17	.227

11 RYAN FORCUCCI, RHP

FB: 60. CB: 45. SL: 55. CH: 50. CTL: 55. BA Grade: 55. Risk: High. Adj: 40.

Born: December 2, 2002. **B-T:** R-R. **HT:** 6-3. **WT:** 205. **Drafted:** UC San Diego, 2024 (2nd round). **Signed by:** Eli Tupuola.
TRACK RECORD: Astros fans have yet to see Forcucci pitch, as the 2024 second round pick had Tommy John surgery just weeks prior to the draft. Over three seasons at UC San Diego the California native was a key part of the Tritons rotation. His performance improved in each season, as Forcucci was enjoying a career season in 2025 when he went down after five starts. At the time of his injury Forcucci had pitched to a 2.16 ERA with 37 strikeouts to six walks across 25 innings. Forcucci missed all of the 2025 season but is expected to be fully healthy heading into spring training.
SCOUTING REPORT: It's hard to know what changes have been made or how Forcucci's stuff has returned since his surgery. Prior to his injury, Forcucci relied heavily on a fastball and slider heavy approach. His four-seam fastball sat 93-94 mph and touched 97 with plus ride from a lower release height. Despite below-average extension, Forcucci creates a flat approach angle due to his lower three-quarters slot and high spin efficiency. His slider sits in the mid-80s with gyro-cut shape. Forcucci matches his slider release point well with his fastball and also throws it for strikes. In 2024 Forcucci was mixing in an upper-70s downer curveball more, but it's a change-of-pace pitch more than a swing-and-miss offering. Forcucci's firm upper-80s changeup flashed average potential with good vertical separation off of his heater. Forcucci shows above-average command of his arsenal with pitchability.
THE FUTURE: Forcucci has low end No. 3 starter upside.

Year	Age	Club (League)	Level	W	L	ERA	G	GS	IP	H	HR	BB	SO	BB%	SO%	WHIP	AVG
2025	22	Did not play—Injured															

HOUSTON ASTROS

12 MIGUEL ULLOLA, RHP
FB: 55. **CB:** 45. **SL:** 40. **CH:** 45. **CT:** 55. **CTL:** 30. **BA Grade:** 50. **Risk:** Average. **Adj:** 40.

Born: June 19, 2002. **B-T:** R-R. **HT:** 6-1. **WT:** 205. **Signed:** Dominican Republic, 2021.
Signed by: Alfredo Ulloa/Hassan Wessin.
TRACK RECORD: Signed for just $75,000 out of the Dominican Republica in January 2021, Ullola has steadily progressed throughout the Astros organization and now is on the cusp of the major leagues. Ullola spent all of 2025 with Triple-A Sugar Land after a late season appearance there to end 2024. Ullola made 28 appearances—including 23 starts—with the Space Cowboys pitching to a 3.88 ERA with 131 strikeouts to 78 walks. Following the season, Ullola was added to the Astros 40-man roster.
SCOUTING REPORT: Despite not being a hard thrower, Ullola fits into the good stuff with bad command bucket. Ullola is physically maxed out with a strong, muscular frame. Ullola has a simple and easy operation, doing an excellent job of getting downhill, generating nearly seven feet of extension on average. Ullola throws five pitches in a four-seam fastball, cutter, curveball, slider and changeup. The fastball sits 92-94 mph with plus ride, heavy cut and a flatter approach angle. The pitch is a true swing and miss offering in the zone. Despite strong results Ullola shows poor command of the pitch. Ullola's upper-80s cutter is his main secondary but is more of a bad contact driver than swing-and-miss offering. Ullola's curveball has bat-missing potential but is rarely thrown for a strike, and his changeup shows fringy separation off of his fastball but has been his most effective swing-and-miss pitch to date.
THE FUTURE: Ullola likely lacks the command to start and instead will be a multi-inning weapon capable of dominating when he's locating.

Year	Age	Club (League)	Level	W	L	ERA	G	GS	IP	H	HR	BB	SO	BB%	SO%	WHIP	AVG
2025	23	Sugar Land (PCL)	AAA	7	6	3.88	28	23	114	75	7	78	131	15.9	26.6	1.35	.186
Minor League Totals				18	27	4.32	113	76	431	287	35	294	576	15.6	30.7	1.35	.187

13 LUCAS SPENCE, OF
HIT: 50. **POW:** 50. **RUN:** 60. **FLD:** 55. **ARM:** 60. **BA Grade:** 50. **Risk:** Average. **Adj:** 40.

Born: January 27, 2003. **B-T:** L-L. **HT:** 6-1. **WT:** 195. **Signed:** Southern Illinois-Edwardsville, 2024 (UDFA).
Signed by: Freddy Perez.
TRACK RECORD: Spence spent two seasons at Black Hawk (Ill.) JC as a two-way player, earning NJCAA all-region honors. He transferred to Southern Illinois-Edwardsville for his junior season and hit .385/.473/.552 over 56 games while making 14 appearances on the mound. Spence went unselected in the 2024 draft but signed with the Astros shortly after. He jumped three levels in his first full season hitting .244/.368/.403 and reaching Double-A by early August.
SCOUTING REPORT: Spence is a plus athlete with little remaining projection. He shows average bat-to-ball ability with plus swing decisions, showing the ability to get on-base while limiting swing and miss due to his selectivity. Spence struggles to hit lefthanded pitching and does his damage against righties. Spence shows a tick better than average raw power but it plays more like gap power in games. A flatter swing path leads to lots of line drives and hard, top-spun groundballs. Spence did add more lift as the season progressed, slashing his groundball rate as he climbed to Double-A. With solid exit velocity data there's a chance that improved angles lead to average power. Spence is a plus runner bordering on plus-plus. He flies out the box and pushes outfielders to hustle on balls to the gaps. Spence's speed translates to the field where he's an above-average outfielder capable of playing all three outfield positions. He also has a plus arm and uncorks beautiful on-line throws.
THE FUTURE: Spence is a future strong-side platoon bat who should move all around the outfield.

Year	Age	Club (League)	Level	AVG	G	AB	R	H	2B	3B	HR	RBI	BB	SO	SB	OBP	SLG
2025		Fayetteville (CAR)	A	.286	23	77	16	22	5	1	0	4	18	18	11	.450	.377
2025		Asheville (SAL)	A+	.239	63	234	38	56	18	2	6	34	30	70	10	.337	.410
2025		Corpus Christi (TL)	AA	.225	30	111	22	25	8	0	4	17	25	34	6	.370	.405
Minor League Totals				.237	140	502	86	119	31	5	11	59	88	144	31	.365	.384

14 ZACH COLE, OF
HIT: 30. **POW:** 60. **RUN:** 60. **FLD:** 55. **ARM:** 70. **BA Grade:** 50. **Risk:** High. **Adj:** 35.

Born: August 4, 2000. **B-T:** L-R. **HT:** 6-2. **WT:** 190. **Drafted:** Ball State, 2022 (10th round). **Signed by:** Scott Oberhelman.
TRACK RECORD: Cole hit .361/.449/.727 with 13 home runs as a junior at Ball State, earning all-MAC first-team and all-defensive team honors. The Astros selected Cole in the 10th round of the 2022 draft and signed him for $97,500. After two solid seasons to begin his career, Cole went nuclear in 2025, hitting .279/.377/.539 with 19 home runs across Double-A and Triple-A, earning a callup on Sept. 12.

HOUSTON ASTROS

SCOUTING REPORT: An outlier athlete, Cole is rotationally explosive with a tooled-up profile. Where he ultimately lands as a hitter is a larger question mark. Cole's approach to hitting is quintessentially three true outcomes. He swings and misses at a high rate, but limits some of the exposure of his natural swing and miss tendencies thanks to advanced, but at times passive, swing decisions. He is an above-average hitter vs. righthanded pitching but struggles heavily against lefties, leaving him a strongside platoon bat long term. Cole's power and contact quality is his carrying tool at the plate. His 109.9 mph 90th percentile exit velocity in 2025 is in the 99th percentile. He has a knack for finding the barrel and creating excellent quality of contact. Cole is a plus runner and his speed translates to the outfield, where he's an above-average defender. Cole is capable of playing all three outfield spots with a plus-plus arm that keeps runners honest.
THE FUTURE: Cole is a platoon outfielder with plus defense.

Year	Age	Club (League)	Level	AVG	G	AB	R	H	2B	3B	HR	RBI	BB	SO	SB	OBP	SLG
2025	24	Corpus Christi (TL)	AA	.267	82	307	54	82	19	6	14	49	42	129	15	.363	.505
2025	24	Sugar Land (PCL)	AAA	.353	15	51	9	18	3	1	5	16	10	17	3	.459	.745
2025	24	Houston (AL)	MLB	.255	15	47	9	12	2	0	4	11	5	20	3	.327	.553
		Minor League Totals		.249	317	1160	188	289	66	18	51	180	161	459	87	.357	.469
		Major League Totals		.255	15	47	9	12	2	0	4	11	5	20	3	.327	.553

15 JOSEPH SULLIVAN, OF
HIT: 50. **POW:** 45. **RUN:** 55. **FLD:** 50. **ARM:** 55. **BA Grade:** 45. **Risk:** Average. **Adj:** 35.

Born: July 1, 2002. **B-T:** L-L. **HT:** 6-0. **WT:** 200. **Drafted:** South Alabama, 2024 (7th round). **Signed by:** Landon Townsley.
TRACK RECORD: Sullivan dealt with injuries and struggled in 2024 with South Alabama, dropping to the Astros in the seventh round. Sullivan signed for $239,400 and a year later looks like a potential steal. Assigned to High-A to begin the season, Sullivan reached Double-A by late July, hitting for a .798 OPS in his professional debut with 17 home runs and 42 stolen bases. Sullivan comes from an athletic family—his grandfather Pat Sullivan won the 1971 Heisman Trophy at Auburn and his father played college football at Auburn and TCU.
SCOUTING REPORT: Sullivan has an unusual swing and uncanny setup at the plate, starting with an open stance before a leg kick gives way to a quick, flat swing. Despite a swing more typical of a contact hitter, Sullivan shows fringy bat-to-ball skills with strong swing decisions and an elite ability to get on base. Sullivan does a majority of his damage against righthanded pitching and struggles in left-on-left matchups. While Sullivan does show above-average raw power, his flatter swing leads to lots of top spin and ball flight that underperforms his exit velocity data. Improved angles could see Sullivan get to above-average game power, but it's fringy at present. Sullivan is an above-average runner with excellent instincts on the bases and aggressive tendencies. He's average in center field but his routes are inconsistent, leading to defensive lapses. He will make some nice plays coming in and has the speed and above-average arm to be above-average in either corner outfield spot.
THE FUTURE: Sullivan is a future fourth outfielder with strong-side platoon splits.

Year	Age	Club (League)	Level	AVG	G	AB	R	H	2B	3B	HR	RBI	BB	SO	SB	OBP	SLG
2025	22	Asheville (SAL)	A+	.233	75	262	51	61	11	2	15	35	65	91	34	.411	.462
2025	22	Corpus Christi (TL)	AA	.191	31	110	17	21	2	0	2	14	23	42	8	.357	.264
		Minor League Totals		.220	106	372	68	82	13	2	17	49	88	133	42	.395	.403

16 ANTHONY HUEZO, OF
HIT: 30. **POW:** 60. **RUN:** 50. **FLD:** 50. **ARM:** 50. **BA Grade:** 55. **Risk:** Extreme. **Adj:** 35.

Born: November 2, 2005. **B-T:** L-R. **HT:** 6-2. **WT:** 185. **Drafted:** HS—Rancho Cucamonga, CA, 2023 (12th round).
Signed by: Eli Tupuola.
TRACK RECORD: Huezo was just 17 years old when the Astros picked him in the 12th round in 2023 and paid him $397,500. He spent parts of three seasons with the Astros' Florida Complex League affiliate. After breaking out in his third go round of the FCL, Huezo earned a promotion to Low-A Fayetteville, where he impressed hitting .301/.363/.410 over 22 games. Huezo filled in for two games with Triple-A Sugar Land when the team had a roster emergency in mid-June.
SCOUTING REPORT: Huezo is an above-average athlete with impressive strength and rotational explosiveness. Huezo has a well-balanced and fluid lefthanded swing that's geared for loft and hard struck fly balls. Huezo is a passive hitter with below-average on-base skills and his more selective approach mitigates some of the natural swing and miss in his profile. He is an excellent fastball hitter, handling velocity well, but struggles against offspeed and spin. Huezo has a nose for the barrel and despite a below-average hit tool he seems to rarely make anything but hard contact. Huezo in 2025 posted a 90th percentile exit velocity of 106.7 mph, an elite number for his age. Huezo projects for plus power, at the risk of his hit tool backing up against more advanced competition. An average runner, Huezo has a little more speed once underway,

HOUSTON ASTROS

allowing him to be average in center field and potentially above-average in a corner.
THE FUTURE: Huezo could develop into an everyday power-hitting corner outfielder but he'll need to continue to refine his hit tool.

Year	Age	Club (League)	Level	AVG	G	AB	R	H	2B	3B	HR	RBI	BB	SO	SB	OBP	SLG
2025	19	FCL Astros	Rk	.231	43	130	28	30	9	3	6	26	19	51	12	.371	.485
2025	19	Fayetteville (CAR)	A	.301	22	83	14	25	1	1	2	12	8	24	6	.363	.410
2025	19	Sugar Land (PCL)	AAA	1.000	2	1	0	1	0	0	0	0	0	0	0	1.000	1.000
		Minor League Totals		.214	127	402	70	86	16	5	14	57	56	156	27	.332	.383

17 JACKSON NEZUH, RHP
FB: 55. **CB:** 40. **SP:** 55. **CT:** 50. **SW:** 40. **CTL:** 50. **BA Grade:** 45. **Risk:** Average. **Adj:** 35.

Born: February 11, 2002. **B-T:** R-R. **HT:** 6-1. **WT:** 190. **Drafted:** Louisiana-Lafayette, 2023 (14th round).
Signed by: Landon Townsley.
TRACK RECORD: Nezuh never fulfilled his recruiting hype at Florida State or Louisiana-Lafayette and fell to the Astros in the 14th round of the 2023 draft. In his first two professional seasons Nezuh has found a level of success that escaped him in college. He made 18 appearances—16 starts—for Double-A Corpus Christi. He missed six weeks with a right elbow strain in late May and returned in early July.
SCOUTING REPORT: Nezuh is an undersized righthander who does a good job getting downhill and generates above-average extension. Nezuh has a simple operation with a semi-windup, short, compact arm action and high three-quarters slot. He does a good job repeating his operation leading to above-average fastball control. Nezuh throws five pitches: a four-seam fastball, slider, sweeper, curveball and changeup. His fastball sits 93-94 mph and touches 96 with above-average ride and cut, and he lands it for strikes consistently. Nezuh's splitter was his most thrown secondary and it's a true chase pitch, as it was rarely thrown in-zone in 2025. The splitter is Nezuh's best swing-and-miss pitch but improved command would make it a potential plus pitch. Nezuh mixes a trio of breaking ball shapes in a mid-80s cutter, high-70s-to-low-80s sweeper and an upper-70s curveball. The cutter has true cutter shape with ride and heavy cut and Nezuh shows advanced command for the pitch. His sweeper is a work in progress and his curveball is rarely used. Despite plus fastball control, Nezuh shows fringe-average command of his secondaries.
THE FUTURE: Nezuh is a future depth starter who could move between spot-starter and long reliever.

Year	Age	Club (League)	Level	W	L	ERA	G	GS	IP	H	HR	BB	SO	BB%	SO%	WHIP	AVG
2025	23	FCL Astros	Rk	0	0	2.08	2	1	4	2	1	3	5	18.8	31.3	1.15	.154
2025	23	Corpus Christi (TL)	AA	3	9	4.48	18	16	72	69	9	25	71	8.1	23.0	1.30	.248
		Minor League Totals		11	15	4.07	47	33	197	166	20	76	227	9.2	27.4	1.23	.226

18 JASE MITCHELL, C
HIT: 40. **POW:** 55. **RUN:** 40. **FLD:** 45. **ARM:** 60. **BA Grade:** 50. **Risk:** Extreme. **Adj:** 30.

Born: September 30, 2006. **B-T:** L-R. **HT:** 6-3. **WT:** 195. **Drafted:** HS—Lewes, DE, 2025 (7th round).
Signed by: Mike Picollo.
TRACK RECORD: A native of Delaware, Mitchell played for the same Cape Henlopen program that produced big leaguer Zack Gelof. Like Gelof, Mitchell won the state's Gatorade player of the year award. Mitchell spurned his Kentucky commitment after the Astros selected him in the seventh round of the 2025 draft. He signed for an over-slot bonus of $797,500 but did not debut following the draft.
SCOUTING REPORT: Mitchell is a tall, physical teenager with a frame that portends coming strength and power. He deploys a toe tap timing mechanism and longer stride, tapping into his lower half in his swing. Despite longer levers Mitchell shows the ability to stay compact and handle pitches on the inner half. He shows nice adjustability in his hands, with the ability to keep the barrel behind the ball even when fooled by spin. Mitchell is likely to show more swing and miss in his professional debut than he did as an amateur, particularly against spin and premium velocity. Mitchell is physical with the strength to drive the ball to all parts of the yard and his power will likely improve with age as he gets stronger. His swing has natural loft allowing him to get to his power. Mitchell is athletic behind the plate, moving well in and out of a one knee stance with fringe-average blocking and receiving. Mitchell shows a plus arm and clean transfers on his throws.
THE FUTURE: Mitchell is a risk/reward profile as a high school catcher with power.

Year	Age	Club (League)	Level	AVG	G	AB	R	H	2B	3B	HR	RBI	BB	SO	SB	OBP	SLG
2025	18	Did not play															

HOUSTON ASTROS

19 PARKER SMITH, RHP
FB: 50. **SL:** 45. **CH:** 45. **SW:** 50. **CTL:** 45. **BA Grade:** 40. **Risk:** Average. **Adj:** 30.

Born: March 5, 2002. **B-T:** R-R. **HT:** 6-4. **WT:** 230. **Drafted:** Rice, 2024 (4th round). **Signed by:** Brian Sheffler.
TRACK RECORD: Smith earned all-Conference USA honors and an invite to the USA collegiate national team. The Astros, undeterred, selected Smith in the fourth round of the 2024 draft and signed him for $447,500. Smith missed the first two months of the 2025 season with a back injury and made his debut in the Florida Complex League. After three rehab starts he was promoted to Low-A Fayetteville. There Smith made 12 starts and pitched to a 3.32 ERA.
SCOUTING REPORT: A tall righthanded sinkerballer, Smith has a high-effort operation with a near-side-arm slot. His ability to get down the mound coupled with his low arm slot combine to create an unusual look, producing a steep sinker from a low release height. Those traits enhance Smith's sinker, which sits at 92-93 mph and touches 95 mph, as the primary offering in his four-pitch mix. He peppers the zone with the pitch and drives weak groundball contact. While the sinker is his primary fastball, he also mixes in a four-seam that generates whiffs at the top of the zone. Smith throws two breaking balls in a low-80s sweeper and a mid-80s gyro slider. The two pitches have nearly even usage and results. Smith's changeup shows bat-missing potential, as he kills lift on the pitch while generating over 16 inches of armside run on average, but he has 20-grade command of it.
THE FUTURE: Smith will continue to get opportunities to start but he likely fits best as a one-inning, groundball-driving reliever with a unique look.

Year	Age	Club (League)	Level	W	L	ERA	G	GS	IP	H	HR	BB	SO	BB%	SO%	WHIP	AVG
2025	22	FCL Astros	Rk	0	0	2.08	3	2	9	5	0	5	8	13.9	22.2	1.15	.172
2025	22	Fayetteville (CAR)	A	5	3	3.32	15	12	60	58	0	25	55	9.8	21.6	1.39	.258
		Minor League Totals		5	3	3.16	18	14	68	63	0	30	63	10.3	21.6	1.36	.248

20 WILL BUSH, C/1B
HIT: 30. **POW:** 55. **RUN:** 30. **FLD:** 40. **ARM:** 60. **BA Grade:** 40. **Risk:** Average. **Adj:** 30.

Born: March 3, 2004. **B-T:** L-R. **HT:** 6-4. **WT:** 235. **Drafted:** Tyler (Texas) JC, 2023 (16th round). **Signed by:** Brian Sheffler.
TRACK RECORD: Bush was not heavily recruited out of Birdland High in North Richland, Texas. He attended Tyler (Texas) JC for one season hitting .357/.510/.615 in 2023 and catching the attention of the Astros. They selected Bush in the 16th round of the 2023 draft, signing him for $150,000. After a brief debut in the complex in 2023, and an unimpressive full season debut in 2024, Bush broke out in 2025. Beginning the season at High-A Asheville, Bush hit .247/.370/.441 with 12 home runs over 73 games, earning a promotion to Double-A in August.
SCOUTING REPORT: Bush is tall and physical, with a maxed out 6-foot-4, broad-shouldered frame. It's a bat-first profile heavily driven by his lumberjack strength and plus raw power. Bush is a below-average contact hitter who struggles against elevated fastballs and sliders in. His strikeout risk is mitigated by above-average swing decisions that lead to high walk rates. Bush is a three-true-outcomes style hitter with plus raw power to match his high walk and strikeout totals. His large frame produces a longer, lofty swing perfectly made to do damage. Bush matches above-average exit velocity data with good angles and produces a high rate of barrel contact. If Bush can make enough contact he has 20-plus home run upside. Behind the plate Bush is fairly stiff and limited as a receiver. His plus arm might be enough to earn him continued play behind the plate.
THE FUTURE: If Bush can make enough contact he could be a part-time, power-hitting catcher and bat off the bench.

Year	Age	Club (League)	Level	AVG	G	AB	R	H	2B	3B	HR	RBI	BB	SO	SB	OBP	SLG
2025	21	Asheville (SAL)	A+	.247	73	247	45	61	12	0	12	36	44	84	7	.370	.441
2025	21	Corpus Christi (TL)	AA	.175	24	80	8	14	4	0	3	11	14	21	3	.333	.338
		Minor League Totals		.228	197	632	97	144	30	1	24	99	106	204	15	.354	.392

21 JANCEL VILLARROEL, C
HIT: 50. **POW:** 45. **RUN:** 45. **FLD:** 40. **ARM:** 50. **BA Grade:** 45. **Risk:** High. **Adj:** 30.

Born: January 17, 2005. **B-T:** R-R. **HT:** 5-8. **WT:** 176. **Signed:** Venezuela, 2022. **Signed by:** Jose Palacios/Daniel Gamboa.
TRACK RECORD: Villarroel was an under-the-radar signing by the Astros. They landed the catcher for $10,000 out of Venezuela in August 2022. He briefly debuted in the Dominican Summer League after signing and returned there for a full season in 2023. Villarroel came stateside in 2024 and reached Low-A by mid-June. Villarroel returned to Low-A in 2025, hitting .258/.360/.385 and earning a late-season callup to High-A.

HOUSTON ASTROS

SCOUTING REPORT: Villarroel is an undersized, bat-first catcher who showed improved bat-to-ball skills in 2025. With a tweak to his setup and posture Villarroel was able to unlock more contact and cleaner barrels with greater regularity. His approach remains aggressive as he's prone to expanding the zone. There's still some swing and miss against soft stuff, but much of that is approach-based. Villarroel's swing is conducive for generating hard contact but its flatter bat path creates lots of top spin and little loft. Much of Villarroel's power will come in the form of doubles to the gaps and low double-digit home run totals. Behind the plate Villarroel's blocking is good, but he struggles to control rebounds and ricochets. His hands are a bit lumbering, but his framing has come along in the last few seasons. Villarroel shows plus arm strength but his throwing accuracy leaves much to be desired.
THE FUTURE: Villarroel looks like a backup catcher long term with a bat-driven profile.

Year	Age	Club (League)	Level	AVG	G	AB	R	H	2B	3B	HR	RBI	BB	SO	SB	OBP	SLG
2025	20	Fayetteville (CAR)	A	.258	85	314	45	81	16	3	6	45	42	64	20	.360	.385
2025	20	Asheville (SAL)	A+	.263	15	57	8	15	2	0	2	9	3	13	0	.295	.404
		Minor League Totals		.269	233	815	150	219	45	7	18	127	113	185	39	.378	.407

22 JAMES HICKS, RHP

FB: 45. **CB:** 40. **SL:** 45. **CH:** 50. **SW:** 50. **CTL:** 55. **BA Grade:** 40. **Risk:** Average. **Adj:** 30.

Born: May 9, 2001. **B-T:** R-R. **HT:** 6-2. **WT:** 190. **Drafted:** South Carolina, 2023 (13th round). **Signed by:** Andrew Johnson.
TRACK RECORD: Hicks made two starts for South Carolina in 2022 before he had Tommy John surgery. Following a successful return from surgery, the Astros selected Hicks in the 13th round in 2023 and signed him for $150,000. After a strong first full professional season in 2024, Hicks began 2025 with Double-A Corpus Christi. In his fourth start he was hit by a comebacker and fractured his right forearm. He missed all of May through July and returned for the final seven weeks of the season. Hicks made up time in the Arizona Fall League after the season, winning AFL pitcher of the year.
SCOUTING REPORT: Hicks is an average-sized righthander with a deep pitch mix, above-average control and a deceptive low three-quarters slot. Hicks is a short strider and generates little extension. He does repeat his operation well and finds success due to his ability to command the ball. Hicks mixes two fastball shapes in a low-90s four-seam and a low-90s sinker. Hicks throws three breaking ball shapes in an upper-70s sweeper, a mid-80s cut-slider and an upper-70s two-plane curveball. The sweeper is the best of the group, followed by the slider, which works as a bridge pitch. Hicks' changeup is his most-used secondary and is an effective chase pitch as well as a groundball generator.
THE FUTURE: Hicks' season was cut short but he continues to show advanced command and pitchability that should work as a swingman.

Year	Age	Club (League)	Level	AVG	G	AB	R	H	2B	3B	HR	RBI	BB	SO	SB	OBP	SLG
2025	24	Corpus Christi (TL)	AA	1	5	5.59	11	10	47	57	7	14	46	6.8	22.3	1.52	.306
		Minor League Totals		7	9	4.26	39	24	158	177	20	45	167	6.5	24.2	1.40	.281

23 JOSE FLEURY, RHP

FB: 40. **CB:** 40. **CH:** 60. **CT:** 45. **SW:** 40. **CTL:** 55. **BA Grade:** 40. **Risk:** Average. **Adj:** 30.

Born: March 8, 2002. **B-T:** R-R. **HT:** 6-0. **WT:** 185. **Signed:** Dominican Republic, 2021.
Signed by: Roman Ocumarez/Alfredo Ulloa/Jose Torres.
TRACK RECORD: Fleury signed weeks before the end of 2021 international signing window for $10,000. An older, under-the-radar signing, Fleury flourished as a professional. After a breakout 2024 at Double-A, Fleury returned to the level to begin 2025. After 10 dominant starts Fleury was promoted to Triple-A on July 1. With Sugar Land he struggled mightily over his first six appearances, allowing 21 earned runs over 12 innings. Fleury found his stride over his final 33.1 innings, pitching to a 3.78 ERA.
SCOUTING REPORT: Fleury is an undersized righthander with little remaining projection. Fleury throws from a high three-quarters slot with a clean arm action. He gets down the mound well and creates plus extension for his height. His four-seam fastball sits 89-92 mph with above-average ride and armside run. Fleury commands the pitch well, consistently landing it in the zone setting up his changeup and trio of breaking balls. He throws his changeup nearly one-for-one with his fastball. It sits in the upper-70s with dramatic sink and armside run and good separation off his fastball. His command of his changeup is plus-plus with one of the highest offspeed zone rates in the minors. Fleury throws a trio of breaking balls in a cutter at 82-85 mph, an upper-70s sweeper and a mid-70s curveball.
THE FUTURE: Fleury is a classic depth starter with a plus changeup that drives his success.

HOUSTON ASTROS

Year	Age	Club (League)	Level	W	L	ERA	G	GS	IP	H	HR	BB	SO	BB%	SO%	WHIP	AVG
2025	23	Corpus Christi (TL)	AA	3	1	1.82	10	10	40	26	2	9	37	6.1	25.0	0.88	.188
2025	23	Sugar Land (PCL)	AAA	2	1	6.95	13	9	45	48	11	26	41	12.9	20.4	1.63	.276
		Minor League Totals		12	9	3.62	78	48	293	219	31	113	354	9.5	29.7	1.13	.206

24 NICK MONISTERE, 2B/3B

HIT: 45. **POW:** 45. **RUN:** 55. **FLD:** 45. **ARM:** 55. **BA Grade:** 40. **Risk:** Average. **Adj:** 30.

Born: January 27, 2004. **B-T:** R-R. **HT:** 6-0. **WT:** 192. **Drafted:** Southern Mississippi, 2025 (4th round). **Signed by:** Landon Townsley.

TRACK RECORD: Monistere began his career as a two-way player at Southern Mississippi but dropped pitching as a sophomore in 2024. In 2025 Monistere broke out, hitting .323/.410/.623 with 21 home runs to earn third-team All-America honors. The Astros drafted Monistere in the fourth round of the 2025 draft and signed him for $397,500. Monistere debuted after the draft with 26 games at Low-A Fayetteville.

SCOUTING REPORT: Monistere added strength that translated to power in 2025. Monistere deploys an aggressive swing with a lot of pre-pitch hand movement in his setup. He takes big swings at the ball looking to do damage. He showed average contact skills in college and his professional debut. Where he gets into trouble is his aggressive and, at times, overzealous approach. Pitchers who attack Monistere with spin away tend to elicit chases and whiffs. The power improved in 2025 but it's still fringe-average due to a lack of loft. Monistere is an above-average runner but not an aggressive base stealer. After playing primarily second base during his time with Southern Miss, Monistere saw time at every infield position in pro ball. His positional versatility is his greatest asset defensively. He's fringe-average at second but his above-average arm might be best suited for third base.

THE FUTURE: Monistere could develop into a utility infielder with the ability to play every position but catcher.

Year	Age	Club (League)	Level	AVG	G	AB	R	H	2B	3B	HR	RBI	BB	SO	SB	OBP	SLG
2025	21	Fayetteville (CAR)	A	.168	26	101	10	17	2	0	2	16	9	28	5	.254	.248
		Minor League Totals		.168	26	101	10	17	2	0	2	16	9	28	5	.254	.248

25 ALONZO TREDWELL, RHP

FB: 45. **CB:** 55. **SL:** 45. **CH:** 45. **CTL:** 50. **BA Grade:** 45. **Risk:** High. **Adj:** 30.

Born: May 8, 2002. **B-T:** L-R. **HT:** 6-8. **WT:** 230. **Drafted:** UCLA, 2023 (2nd round). **Signed by:** Tim Costic.

TRACK RECORD: Tredwell was a highly-touted prep pitcher who missed time with Tommy John surgery his junior year of high school. He spent two seasons at UCLA and missed the second half of his sophomore season with a back injury. Tredwell was hurt again in his professional debut in 2024, as a shoulder strain on July 14th ended his season prematurely. The 2025 season proved to be Tredwell's healthiest since his freshman year at UCLA. Tredwell threw 100 innings across three levels and reached Double-A in early August.

SCOUTING REPORT: Standing 6-foot-8, Tredwell strikes an imposing figure on the mound, and he uses his length to get downhill and create difficult angles for hitters. Tredwell hides the ball well with a longer arm action and throws from a high three-quarters slot. He mixes four pitches in a four-seam fastball, slider, curveball and splitter. Tredwell's fastball velocity was down a tick from his final season at UCLA, sitting 91-93 mph. He has added more cut and now generates seven feet of extension on average. Tredwell's primary breaking ball is his low-to-mid-80s slider with short slider shape. His downer curveball in the mid-to-high-70s is his best bat-missing pitch and was effective in Double-A. Tredwell scrapped his previous changeup for a mid-80s splitter in 2025 that showed potential.

THE FUTURE: Tredwell shows average command of four-pitch mix and enough deception to project as a depth starter or long reliever.

Year	Age	Club (League)	Level	W	L	ERA	G	GS	IP	H	HR	BB	SO	BB%	SO%	WHIP	AVG
2025	23	Fayetteville (CAR)	A	2	1	3.94	12	8	48	36	6	21	52	10.8	26.7	1.19	.213
2025	23	Asheville (SAL)	A+	1	1	3.68	7	4	29	27	1	12	30	9.4	23.4	1.33	.250
2025	23	Corpus Christi (TL)	AA	2	1	3.18	7	4	23	22	2	12	40	11.5	38.5	1.50	.244
		Minor League Totals		6	9	4.30	43	30	157	138	12	83	189	12.1	27.6	1.41	.236

26 NICK POTTER, RHP
FB: 60. **SL:** 50. **CTL:** 40. **BA Grade:** 40. **Risk:** Average. **Adj:** 30.

Born: February 11, 2004. **B-T:** R-R. **HT:** 6-4. **WT:** 195. **Drafted:** Wichita State, 2025 (5th round). **Signed by:** Jim Stevenson.
TRACK RECORD: Potter spent two seasons at Crowder (MO) JC before transferring to Wichita State prior to 2025. Potter was used exclusively as a reliever, made 23 appearances and pitched to a 3.34 ERA with 33 strikeouts to 17 walks across 29.2 innings. The Astros selected Potter in the fifth round and signed him for $336,600. He did not debut following the draft.
SCOUTING REPORT: Potter is a tall, athletic righthander with an up-tempo operation and a ton of arm speed. He throws exclusively from the stretch but is able to generate lots of power from his lower half due to a high leg lift and ability to get downhill. Potter's longer arm action gives way to a true three-quarters slot with a crossfire delivery. The tempo and explosiveness of Potter's operation create lots of deception. By the same token it's difficult to repeat, leading to inconsistency with his release points. Potter throws two pitches in a four-seam fastball and slider. His fastball sits 95-97 mph and touches 100 with plus ride and heavy cut. Potter's slider sits 83-85 mph with baby sweeper shape, getting around seven inches of sweep and around an inch of drop. Potter looks like a relief-only prospect with two pitches and below-average command.
THE FUTURE: Potter has the mix of a power, high-leverage relief arm and will likely end up in the pen.

Year	Age	Club (League)	Level	W	L	ERA	G	GS	IP	H	HR	BB	SO	BB%	SO%	WHIP	AVG
2025	21	Did not play															

27 HUDSON LEACH, RHP
FB: 55. **CB:** 60. **CT:** 50. **CTL:** 40. **BA Grade:** 40. **Risk:** Average. **Adj:** 30.

Born: June 16, 2002. **B-T:** R-R. **HT:** 6-3. **WT:** 211. **Signed:** Miami (Ohio), 2023 (UDFA). **Signed by:** Scott Oberhelman.
TRACK RECORD: Leach spent two seasons with Creighton pitching a total of 22.2 innings across 13 appearances before he transferred to Miami (Ohio). In his one season with the Redhawks, Leach struck out 51 batters over 31.1 innings. Leach signed with the Astros as an undrafted free agent in 2023. He made his professional debut in 2024, pitching in the Rookie-level Florida Complex League and both Class A levels. He returned to High-A to begin the 2025 season and pitched his way to Triple-A.
SCOUTING REPORT: Leach is a tall, physical righthander with a mature physique and present strength. Leach is a three-pitch relief-only prospect with a power mix and swing-and-miss stuff. From a three-quarters slot, Leach delivers an above-average mid-to-high-90s fastball with above-average ride and plane. It's a good bat-missing pitch but was hit hard in Triple-A at the end of the 2025 season. His high-80s cutter sat 88-90 mph with less ride and more sweep than most cutters. Leach's plus curveball is his best pitch sitting 82-85 mph with heavy two-plane break and spin rates in the 2,800-3,000 rpm range. Leach shows better command of his curveball than his cutter or fastball.
THE FUTURE: Leach is a future middle reliever with three power pitches that miss bats. He has just enough control to be effectively wild.

Year	Age	Club (League)	Level	W	L	ERA	G	GS	IP	H	HR	BB	SO	BB%	SO%	WHIP	AVG
2025	23	FCL Astros	Rk	1	0	8.10	3	0	3	1	0	5	6	33.3	40.0	1.80	.100
2025	23	Asheville (SAL)	A+	1	1	3.98	17	0	20	16	1	10	35	11.5	40.2	1.28	.222
2025	23	Corpus Christi (TL)	AA	0	0	3.72	9	0	10	7	1	5	14	12.2	34.1	1.24	.206
2025	23	Sugar Land (PCL)	AAA	0	1	12.71	5	0	6	9	1	4	8	13.8	27.6	2.29	.360
		Minor League Totals		3	5	4.71	58	1	73	56	6	50	104	15.7	32.6	1.46	.217

28 COLE HERTZLER, RHP
FB: 50. **CB:** 45. **SL:** 55. **CH:** 40. **CTL:** 45. **BA Grade:** 45. **Risk:** High. **Adj:** 30.

Born: June 21, 2003. **B-T:** R-R. **HT:** 6-4. **WT:** 235. **Drafted:** Liberty, 2024 (5th round). **Signed by:** Andrew Johnson.
TRACK RECORD: Hertzler got to campus at Liberty as a two-way player, and he saw a majority of his action his first two seasons as a position player. Prior to his junior year, Hertzler committed to pitching and it paid off as he earned second team all-Conference USA honors in 2024. The Astros selected Hertzler in the fifth round of the 2024 draft, signing him for $393,700. Hertzler pitched with Low-A Fayetteville in 2025, but a forearm sprain in his fourth start of the season put him on the shelf for most of the season.
SCOUTING REPORT: A premium athlete for his size and body type, Hertzler has the ability to mix four pitches with more potential power to come. Hertzler throws four pitches in a four-seam fastball, slider, changeup and curveball. His fastball sits 92-93 mph and touches 96 with average ride and some cut. Hertzler's best secondary is a mid-80s gyro slider that's thrown from a similar release to his fastball and kept A-ball hitters off-balance in 2025. His low-to-mid-80s changeup had good results but is a below-average pitch without much separation from the fastball. His low-80s curveball is a deathball-style break-

ing ball that shows potential as a swing-and-miss and chase pitch. Hertzler shows fringe-average command of his stuff but could get to average control.

THE FUTURE: Hertzler will likely move to the bullpen, where his fastball and multiple breaking ball shapes will play up.

Year	Age	Club (League)	Level	W	L	ERA	G	GS	IP	H	HR	BB	SO	BB%	SO%	WHIP	AVG
2025	22	Fayetteville (CAR)	A	0	0	1.13	4	4	16	12	0	6	22	9.4	34.4	1.13	.211
		Minor League Totals		0	0	1.29	6	4	21	17	1	9	28	10.6	32.9	1.24	.227

29 GERMAN RAMIREZ, SS

HIT: 40. **POW:** 45. **RUN:** 55. **FLD:** 50. **ARM:** 60. **BA Grade:** 45. **Risk:** High. **Adj:** 30.

Born: July 28, 2006. **B-T:** R-R. **HT:** 6-0. **WT:** 179. **Signed:** Dominican Republic, 2023.
Signed by: Raymon Sanchez/Alfredo Ulloa/Alfred Ramirez.
TRACK RECORD: Ramirez was one of the Astros top signings from the 2023 international signing class, signing for $1.2 million. He debuted in the Dominican Summer League at 16 years old, nearly two years younger than the average DSL player. Ramirez came stateside in 2024 and has spent most of the last two seasons in the Florida Complex League. After hitting .245/.340/.417 in the FCL, Ramirez was promoted to Low-A Fayetteville.
SCOUTING REPORT: Ramirez is an averaged-sized right-right middle infielder with twitchy actions and quick hands. He sets up slightly closed, before he explodes with a violent leg kick and a hand pump in his load. He takes big, aggressive hacks looking to do damage but can be made to look foolish at times against spin. Ramirez shows below-average bat-to-ball skills and over-aggressive swing decisions. He does show above-average power for his age with a 103.6 mph 90th percentile exit velocity in 2025. He'll need to add loft to his swing to hit for more power, but the ingredients are there for fringe-average game power. Ramirez is an above-average runner out of the box but not much of a stolen base threat. Ramirez is an average defender at multiple spots in the infield with a plus arm to handle all throws at shortstop or third base.
THE FUTURE: Ramirez has the skills and makeup of a future utility infielder.

Year	Age	Club (League)	Level	AVG	G	AB	R	H	2B	3B	HR	RBI	BB	SO	SB	OBP	SLG
2025	18	FCL Astros	Rk	.245	48	163	26	40	11	4	3	29	20	41	4	.340	.417
2025	18	Fayetteville (CAR)	A	.143	21	70	7	10	1	0	0	8	5	28	2	.208	.157
		Minor League Totals		.228	168	589	77	134	22	7	5	76	59	162	19	.307	.314

30 ALIMBER SANTA, RHP

FB: 55. **CB:** 30. **SL:** 60. **CH:** 45. **SW:** 55. **CTL:** 40. **BA Grade:** 40. **Risk:** Average. **Adj:** 30.

Born: May 3, 2003. **B-T:** R-R. **HT:** 5-10. **WT:** 228. **Signed:** Dominican Republic, 2020.
Signed by: Alfredo Ulloa/Hassan Wessin.
TRACK RECORD: The Astros signed Santa in February 2020 for $75,000 out of the Dominican Republic. After showing flashes of plus stuff over the early portion of his career, he put together a strong season in 2025. Over 46 appearances spanning 70 innings, he pitched to a 2.31 ERA with a 55.2% groundball rate and a 27.9% strikeout rate.
SCOUTING REPORT: Santa has below-average command and struggled with walks during his short stint in Triple-A. However, he shows a good blend of out-generating stuff and the ability to induce both ground balls and whiffs. He mixes a mid-to-high-80s slider with heavy cut, a mid-90s fastball with four-seam and sinker variations, as well as a sweeper, curveball and changeup. It's a deep pitch mix with feel for spin and the ability to move the ball around the zone with a variety of different shapes. A plus 86-89 mph slider with late break is his primary pitch and was an excellent bat-misser. His sinker saw more and more action over the last year and has helped transform him into a groundball-driving reliever. Santa's sweeper is his naughtiest pitch, running high whiff rates and a fair amount of chases. He showed improving control but is still a below-average strike thrower.
THE FUTURE: Santa is a future one-inning reliever capable of driving groundballs at elite rates.

Year	Age	Club (League)	Level	W	L	ERA	G	GS	IP	H	HR	BB	SO	BB%	SO%	WHIP	AVG
2025	22	Corpus Christi (TL)	AA	3	1	1.26	31	0	57	35	2	23	63	10.2	27.9	1.02	.176
2025	22	Sugar Land (PCL)	AAA	0	1	6.92	15	0	13	11	0	16	19	23.5	27.9	2.08	.220
		Minor League Totals		7	15	4.73	103	23	221	196	15	146	276	14.7	27.8	1.55	.237

Kansas City Royals

BY BILL MITCHELL

The Royals' 2025 season requires some perspective.

Two years ago, projecting an 80-82 record would've been seen as optimistic. But after jumping from 56 wins in 2023 to 86 wins and an American League Division Series appearance in 2024, Kansas City didn't take another step forward in 2025, in part because of pitching injuries and substandard outfield play.

None of the Royals' outfielders who played more than 50 games reached a .700 OPS. Their offseason acquisition of Jonathan India as a table-setter didn't work out. Key starting pitchers Cole Ragans and Kris Bubic combined for just 33 starts due to injuries. The best pitching news was rookie lefthander Noah Cameron, who posted a 2.99 ERA and 3.8 bWAR over 24 starts.

Face of the franchise Bobby Witt Jr. had another outstanding season, while first baseman Vinnie Pasquantino put up a solid year with 32 home runs and 113 RBIs. Third baseman Maikel Garcia trended upward with an .800 OPS, and 35-year-old catcher Salvador Perez continued beating back Father Time, clubbing 30 home runs with 100 RBIs.

Because of hitting woes in Kansas City, assistant hitting coaches Joe Dillon and Keoni DeRenne were replaced by Connor Dawson and Marcus Thames. Drew Saylor was removed as minor league director of hitting performance. Assistant pitching coach Zach Bove departed to become the White Sox's pitching coach.

Royals minor league player of the year Carter Jensen had a breakout season split between Double-A and Triple-A before the lefthanded-hitting catcher got the call to Kansas City in September.

Jac Caglianone, the sixth pick in the 2024 draft, hit 20 homers in 66 minor league games in his first full pro season and forced his way to the majors,

PROJECTED 2029 LINEUP

Catcher	Blake Mitchell	24
First Base	Jac Caglianone	26
Second Base	Josh Hammond	22
Third Base	Maikel Garcia	29
Shortstop	Bobby Witt Jr.	29
Left Field	Carter Jensen	26
Center Field	Carson Roccaforte	27
Right Field	Sean Gamble	23
Designated Hitter	Vinnie Pasquantino	31
No. 1 Starter	Cole Ragans	31
No. 2 Starter	Noah Cameron	30
No. 3 Starter	Kendry Chourio	21
No. 4 Starter	David Shields	22
No. 5 Starter	Drew Beam	26
Closer	Lucas Erceg	34

though he struggled mightily after his callup.

Deeper down the system, 18-year-old lefthander David Shields earned Carolina League pitcher of the year honors in his first professional season. Another major win for Royals international scouting and player development was the rise of 17-year-old Venezuelan righty Kendry Chourio, part of a strong 2025 international class. Signed in January, he climbed from the Dominican Summer League to the Arizona Complex League and the Carolina League before his 18th birthday. Shields and Chourio now rank as two of the three best prospects in the organization.

High-A Quad Cities posted the best record among Royals affiliates at 74-58, but Low-A Columbia went on the deepest postseason run, pushing to within one win of a Carolina League title after a 64-65 regular season.

In their second draft with Brian Bridges as director, the Royals targeted athleticism and versatility with their 21 selections. They used their top two choices on high school athletes, taking outfielder/second baseman Sean Gamble 23rd overall and shortstop Josh Hammond 28th overall.

The Royals used their Prospect Promotion Incentive draft pick, which they earned for Witt's runner-up finish for 2024 AL MVP, to select Hammond. ∎

DEPTH CHART

KANSAS CITY ROYALS

TOP 2026 ROOKIES — RANK
1. Carter Jensen, C — 1
2. Luinder Avila, RHP — 9

BREAKOUT PROSPECTS — RANK
1. Steven Zobac, RHP — 14
2. Dennis Colleran Jr., RHP — 27
3. Freddy Conteras, RHP — 29

SOURCE OF TOP 30 TALENT

Homegrown	29	Acquired	1
College	9	Trade	1
Junior college	0	Rule 5 draft	0
High school	11	Independent league	0
Undrafted free agent	0	Free agent/waivers	0
International	9		

LF
Luke Nowak
Spencer Nivens

CF
Carson Roccaforte (13)
Asbel Gonzalez (16)
Nolan Sailors

RF
Gavin Cross (17)
Daniel Lopez
Henry Ramos
Roni Cabrera

3B
Jhonayker Ugarte
Jose Cerice

SS
Josh Hammond (5)
Yandel Ricardo (10)
Warren Calcaño (19)
Ramcell Medina (20)
Daniel Vazquez
Austin Charles
Tyriq Kemp

2B
Sean Gamble (6)
Darison Garcia
Javi Vaz
Tyson Moran

1B
JC Vanek
Derlin Figueroa
Brett Squires

C
Carter Jensen (1)
Blake Mitchell (4)
Ramon Ramirez (7)
Moises Marchán
Brooks Bryan
Hyungchan Um

LHP

LHSP
David Shields (3)
Justin Lamkin (18)
Frank Mozzicato (28)
Hunter Owen
Tyson Guerrero
Jordan Woods

LHRP
Mason Miller
Chazz Martinez
Nate Ackenhausen

RHP

RHSP
Kendry Chourio (2)
Drew Beam (8)
Felix Arronde (11)
Ben Kudrna (12)
Steven Zobac (14)
Michael Lombardi (15)
Grayson Boles (21)
Blake Wolters (22)
Mason Black (23)
Cameron Millar (25)
Freddy Contreras (29)
Henry Williams (30)
Hiro Wyatt
Josh Hansell
Tanner Jones
Bryson Dudley
Coleman Picard
Emmanuel Reyes
Shane Van Dam
Kyle DeGroat

RHRP
Luinder Avila (9)
Shane Panzini (26)
Dennis Colleran Jr. (27)
A.J. Causey
Yeri Perez
Eric Cerantola
LP Langevin
Max Martin
Ethan Bosacker
Aiden Jimenez
Hunter Alberini
Matthew Hoskins
Kamden Edge

KANSAS CITY ROYALS

1 CARTER JENSEN, C

Born: July 3, 2003. **B-T:** L-R. **HT:** 6-1. **WT:** 210.
Drafted: HS—Kansas City, MO, 2021 (3rd round).
Signed by: Matt Price.

BA GRADE: 60 Risk: Mild
Adjusted grade: 55
SCOUTING GRADES: Hit: 55. Power: 60. Run: 40. Field: 50. Arm: 65.
Projected future grades on 20-80 scouting scale

TRACK RECORD: A Kansas City native who grew up attending Royals games and played on the organization's scout team, Jensen fulfilled a lifelong dream when he debuted for his hometown team in September 2025. The Royals drafted the lefthanded-hitting catcher in the third round in 2021 and signed him away from an LSU commitment—where he planned to room with fellow Royals farmhand Ben Kudrna—for $1,097,500. Instead, they wound up sharing digs at the Royals' complex in Surprise, Ariz. Jensen has slowly ascended the Royals system and broke out in 2025, slashing a combined .290/.377/.501 with 20 home runs between Double-A and Triple-A. Once he reached the majors, he shared catching duties with his boyhood idol Salvador Perez and hit .300 with three homers over 20 games. He played winter ball in the Dominican Republic after the season.

SCOUTING REPORT: Jensen's offensive game is built on a well-rounded skill set. He has elite feel for the barrel, quick hands and a compact swing. His natural understanding of the strike zone has always allowed him to make excellent swing decisions. That foundation of patience and quality contact has helped carry him through the Royals' system. Early on, he generally paired low batting averages with higher on-base percentages. Jensen began tapping into his plus raw power more consistently in 2024, then took another leap forward in 2025, when he rarely expanded and mostly punished pitches inside the strike zone at well-struck angles. Jensen upped his hard-hit launch angle and overall exit velocities, plus he far more consistently used the whole field. He increased his average exit velocity by 4.6 mph, and his in-zone contact rate leveled up to nearly 87% in Triple-A. As such, Jensen's outlook remained optimistic even early in the year at Double-A Northwest Arkansas, when an inordinate amount of hard-hit outs suppressed his surface-level production. Jensen really turned it up a notch once he reached Triple-A Omaha, improving his splits so that he's no longer a liability against lefthanders. Jensen was productive against all pitch types in his limited big league sample, too. While not a finished product defensively, Jensen has made strides. Evaluators noted he improved his framing, blocking and receiving. At 6-foot-1, 210 pounds, he has a strong frame for a catcher, good hands and a nearly double-plus arm. He's expected to slow down to a below-average runner over time, but his impressive instincts allowed him to swipe 10 bags in the minors in 2025.

THE FUTURE: Jensen projects as an everyday big league catcher who has enough natural athleticism to handle a corner outfield position if needed. With longtime Royals backup catcher Freddy Fermin gone, Jensen is expected to break camp with the Royals and continue to benefit from playing alongside Perez's savvy veteran leadership.

BEST TOOLS

BATTING
Best Hitter	Carter Jensen
Best Power Hitter	Carter Jensen
Best Strike-Zone Discipline	Blake Mitchell
Fastest Baserunner	Asbel Gonzalez
Best Athlete	Sean Gamble

PITCHING
Best Fastball	Dennis Colleran Jr.
Best Curveball	Luinder Avila
Best Slider	Steven Zobac
Best Changeup	Kendry Chourio
Best Control	David Shields

FIELDING
Best Defensive Catcher	Blake Mitchell
Best Defensive Infielder	Josh Hammond
Best Infield Arm	Josh Hammond
Best Defensive Outfielder	Carson Roccaforte
Best Outfield Arm	Henry Ramos

Year	Age	Club (League)	Level	AVG	G	AB	R	H	2B	3B	HR	RBI	BB	SO	SB	OBP	SLG
2025	21	NW Arkansas (TL)	AA	.292	68	274	40	80	9	4	6	37	30	70	7	.360	.420
2025	21	Omaha (IL)	AAA	.288	43	153	32	44	11	1	14	39	30	52	3	.404	.647
2025	21	Kansas City (AL)	MLB	.300	20	60	12	18	6	0	3	13	9	12	0	.391	.550
		Minor League Totals		.249	484	1736	275	432	88	18	61	245	317	493	50	.364	.426
		Major League Totals		.300	20	60	12	18	6	0	3	13	9	12	0	.391	.550

KANSAS CITY ROYALS

2 KENDRY CHOURIO, RHP
FB: 60. **CB:** 55. **CH:** 60. **CTL:** 60. **BA Grade:** 60. **Risk:** High. **Adj:** 45.

Born: October 1, 2007. **B-T:** R-R. **HT:** 6-0. **WT:** 160.
Signed: Venezuela, 2025. **Signed by:** Jose Gualdron/Daniel Guerrero.
TRACK RECORD: Chourio was unquestionably the biggest surprise in the Royals' system in 2025 after the club signed him out of Venezuela for $247,500 in January. International signings rarely reach the U.S. the same year they sign, but Chourio not only crossed over from the Dominican Summer League—he then advanced past the Arizona Complex League after three starts. He finished his whirlwind season with Low-A Columbia, where he took regular rotation turns for the Carolina League champions. The 17-year-old Chourio showed pinpoint control and preternatural composure at all three levels, walking just five in 51.1 innings.
SCOUTING REPORT: Chourio's four-seam fastball averaged 95 mph and touched 98 with riding life, which is especially impressive considering his smaller 6-foot, 160-pound stature. He uses his lean strength and athleticism to consistently throw strikes, and he pounded the zone with his heater in 2025. While Chourio can run his fastball into the upper 90s with ease, the Royals preferred to see him sit in the mid 90s. He pairs the fastball with a sharp 78 mph curveball that has high spin rates and downward movement. It's a potentially above-average offering. Chourio rounds out his arsenal with an effective 87 mph fading changeup that has plus potential. Scouts lauded Chourio's advanced pitchability for his age. He repeats his three-quarters arm slot well and should have little issue maintaining his mechanics as he adds strength because of his body control.
THE FUTURE: After Chourio moved more quickly than expected, the Royals could pump the brakes on his ascension through the Class A levels. Even so, his early-career success and polish could help him reach Double-A before he turns 19. He has the upside of a No. 2 or 3 starter.

Year	Age	Club (League)	Level	W	L	ERA	G	GS	IP	H	HR	BB	SO	BB%	SO%	WHIP	AVG
2025	17	ACL Royals	Rk	0	0	2.45	3	3	11	12	0	0	17	0.0	35.4	1.09	.261
2025	17	DSL Royals Ventura	Rk	1	0	2.04	5	4	18	12	0	1	22	1.5	32.8	0.74	.185
2025	17	Columbia (CAR)	A	1	3	5.16	6	6	23	20	2	4	24	4.2	25.0	1.06	.227
		Minor League Totals		2	3	3.51	14	13	51	44	2	5	63	2.4	29.9	0.95	.221

3 DAVID SHIELDS, LHP
FB: 45. **CB:** 55. **SL:** 55. **CH:** 50. **CTL:** 60. **BA Grade:** 55. **Risk:** Average. **Adj:** 45.

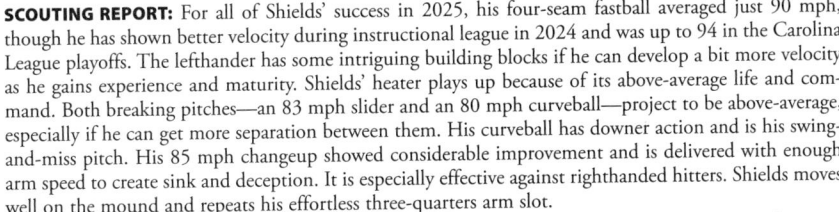

Born: September 9, 2006. **B-T:** L-L. **HT:** 6-2. **WT:** 215.
Drafted: HS—Pittsburgh, 2024 (2nd round). **Signed by:** Tim Bittner.
TRACK RECORD: Shields was one of the younger players in the 2024 draft after reclassifying just prior to his senior year at Pittsburgh's Mount Lebanon High. He didn't turn 18 until nearly two months after the draft and was expected to spend most of his first full pro season in the Arizona Complex League in 2025. Instead, the Royals promoted Shields to Low-A Columbia after only one ACL start. He thrived in his first season with a full-season affiliate, helping the Fireflies reach the Carolina League championship series. He was named the league's pitcher of the year and finished his season with a 2.38 ERA and 86 strikeouts to just 15 walks in 75.2 innings.
SCOUTING REPORT: For all of Shields' success in 2025, his four-seam fastball averaged just 90 mph, though he has shown better velocity during instructional league in 2024 and was up to 94 in the Carolina League playoffs. The lefthander has some intriguing building blocks if he can develop a bit more velocity as he gains experience and maturity. Shields' heater plays up because of its above-average life and command. Both breaking pitches—an 83 mph slider and an 80 mph curveball—project to be above-average, especially if he can get more separation between them. His curveball has downer action and is his swing-and-miss pitch. His 85 mph changeup showed considerable improvement and is delivered with enough arm speed to create sink and deception. It is especially effective against righthanded hitters. Shields moves well on the mound and repeats his effortless three-quarters arm slot.
THE FUTURE: While he lacks a plus pitch, Shields commands his arsenal well and has room for more development. He profiles as a midrotation starter. He'll still be a teenager for most of the 2026 season but should be able to handle the jump to High-A.

Year	Age	Club (League)	Level	W	L	ERA	G	GS	IP	H	HR	BB	SO	BB%	SO%	WHIP	AVG
2025	18	ACL Royals	Rk	0	1	9.00	1	1	4	4	1	0	5	0.0	31.3	1.00	.267
2025	18	Columbia (CAR)	A	3	1	2.01	18	18	72	58	3	15	81	5.2	28.3	1.02	.218
		Minor League Totals		3	2	2.38	19	19	76	62	4	15	86	5.0	28.5	1.02	.221

KANSAS CITY ROYALS

4 BLAKE MITCHELL, C
HIT: 30. **POW:** 55. **RUN:** 30. **FLD:** 55. **ARM:** 70. **BA Grade:** 55. **Risk:** High. **Adj:** 40.

Born: August 3, 2004. **B-T:** L-R. **HT:** 6-1. **WT:** 215.
Drafted: HS—Sinton, TX, 2023 (1st round). **Signed by:** Josh Hallgren.
TRACK RECORD: A two-time Texas Gatorade Player of the Year, Mitchell was the top available catching prospect in the 2023 draft when the Royals drafted the LSU commit eighth overall and signed him for an under-slot $4,897,500. After a solid season at Low-A in 2024, Mitchell's 2025 season was derailed by injuries. He suffered a hand injury in spring training that required right hamate surgery and, after being given a four-to-six week timeline to return, didn't reach the Arizona Complex League until early May. Hand soreness sidelined him after just four games and kept him off the field for another month. Mitchell reached High-A Quad Cities in early July, but lingering hand issues likely contributed to a subpar slash line of .207/.373/.296 and two home runs in 49 games.
SCOUTING REPORT: Mitchell has plus raw power that comes with significant swing-and-miss issues that have limited him to a .223 minor league batting average over 184 games. In 2024, he benefited from implementing a narrower stance that created a more efficient swing and allowed him to better use the whole field. Holes still remain in Mitchell's swing, though, and his recurring strikeout issues contributed to his struggles in 2025, especially on pitches inside the zone. He has always countered those high strikeout rates with high walk rates and he rarely expands the zone. Mitchell's defensive work was fine upon his return. His strong hands help him receive well and his plus-plus throwing arm allowed him to throw out 31% of basestealers during his 30 games behind the plate in Quad Cities.
THE FUTURE: Mitchell deserves a mulligan for his injury-marred 2025 season and still has everyday catcher upside. Assuming his strength and timing return in 2026 following a healthy offseason, he should be ready for a second crack at High-A.

Year	Age	Club (League)	Level	AVG	G	AB	R	H	2B	3B	HR	RBI	BB	SO	SB	OBP	SLG
2025	20	ACL Royals	Rk	.286	11	28	5	8	2	0	1	7	8	10	3	.487	.464
2025	20	Quad Cities (MWL)	A+	.207	49	169	23	35	7	1	2	12	45	71	9	.372	.296
		Minor League Totals		.223	184	627	102	140	26	4	21	73	150	244	39	.379	.378

5 JOSH HAMMOND, SS/3B
HIT: 50. **POW:** 55. **RUN:** 50. **FLD:** 55. **ARM:** 60. **BA Grade:** 55. **Risk:** High. **Adj:** 40.

Born: September 21, 2006. **B-T:** R-R. **HT:** 6-1. **WT:** 210.
Drafted: HS—High Point, NC, 2025 (1st round supp.). **Signed by:** Blake Newsome.
TRACK RECORD: Hammond entered his senior spring at Wesleyan Christian Academy in 2025 regarded as a potential top 100 draft pick on the mound, where he was up to 99 mph. But the two-way North Carolina prep and Wake Forest commit switched up and instead preferred to advance as a position player so he could take the field every day. The risk paid off when the Royals drafted Hammond 28th overall and signed him for $3,197,500. Kansas City earned the Prospect Promotion Incentive draft pick via Bobby Witt Jr.'s 2024 runner-up American League MVP finish. Hammond spent the rest of the summer playing in unofficial bridge league games—he homered in his first at-bat—and then instructional league alongside fellow first-rounder Sean Gamble.
SCOUTING REPORT: Hammond hits with a rotational swing featuring a long, flat, sweepy bat path and solid bat speed. He uses his plus raw power to drive the ball with authority to both gaps, and he's already flashing the ability to backspin balls to his pull side. Hammond fights a tendency to leak out early on his front side versus secondary pitches. It looks like a power-over-hit profile in the long run, but he has enough feel for contact to project as an average hitter with more reps. Hammond spent time at both shortstop and third base upon arriving at the Royals' complex. His actions, range and solid hands likely fit best at third base, where he could be an above-average defender with a plus arm. The son of a longtime college coach, Hammond is an intense competitor with an elite feel for the game.
THE FUTURE: All that time spent around the game could help Hammond move relatively quickly, perhaps on a similar development track as Gamble. He'll head to Low-A Columbia for 2026 and could one day be an above-average big league third baseman.

Year	Age	Club (League)	Level	AVG	G	AB	R	H	2B	3B	HR	RBI	BB	SO	SB	OBP	SLG
2025	18	Did not play															

KANSAS CITY ROYALS

6 SEAN GAMBLE, 2B/OF

HIT: 50. **POW:** 50. **RUN:** 60. **FLD:** 50. **ARM:** 55. **BA Grade:** 55. **Risk:** High. **Adj:** 40.

Born: July 6, 2006. **B-T:** L-R. **HT:** 6-1. **WT:** 188.
Drafted: HS—Bradenton, FL, 2025 (1st round). **Signed by:** Vance Vizcaino.
TRACK RECORD: Gamble and fellow top pick Josh Hammond epitomize the Royals' emphasis on athleticism in their 2025 draft class. Kansas City drafted Gamble 23rd overall and bought him out of a Vanderbilt commitment for $3,997,500. He primarily played second base at IMG Academy, his final high school stop, but saw more time in the outfield during the 2024 summer showcase season. Gamble spent the remainder of his draft summer playing in unofficial bridge league games and then instructional league at the Royals' complex in Arizona.
SCOUTING REPORT: A lefthanded hitter with an intriguing mix of high-end tools, Gamble's bat speed and athleticism grab evaluators' attention. As an underclassman, he'd swing with intent and explosion that led to plenty of impact—but also plenty of whiffs. Gamble's plan of attack evolved as he matured, and he showed a much more polished swing on the 2024 summer showcase circuit. It's now much more compact, efficient and direct, with average bat speed and a quiet rhythm. Gamble's approach was much more passive in his initial exposure at the Royals' complex after the draft. He's an easy plus runner who gets out of the box quickly and should be a consistent basestealing threat. Gamble spent time at both second base and outfield during his time at the complex. His plus speed and above-average arm are a better fit for center field, though the Royals haven't made a decision on his long-term defensive home. Gamble has advanced baseball instincts and acumen, and he earns high marks for his competitive nature.
THE FUTURE: Gamble turned 19 just before the draft, so he's age-appropriate for a full-season debut in 2026. He's ticketed to make his debut with Low-A Columbia alongside Hammond. While there's still plenty of development ahead, Gamble's tools and athleticism give him a head start.

Year	Age	Club (League)	Level	AVG	G	AB	R	H	2B	3B	HR	RBI	BB	SO	SB	OBP	SLG
2025	18	Did not play															

7 RAMON RAMIREZ, C

HIT: 50. **POW:** 55. **RUN:** 40. **FLD:** 45. **ARM:** 55. **BA Grade:** 50. **Risk:** High. **Adj:** 35.

Born: June 15, 2005. **B-T:** R-R. **HT:** 6-0. **WT:** 180.
Signed: Venezuela, 2023. **Signed by:** Juan Feliciano/Daniel Guerrero/Roberto Aquino.
TRACK RECORD: Ramirez signed out of Venezuela in 2023 and immediately jumped onto the scene when he arrived in the U.S. for the Royals' fall instructional league, showing feel to hit and big power. After a strong Arizona Complex League season in 2024, Ramirez made his full-season debut with Low-A Columbia in 2025 and slashed .244/.339/.442 with 11 homers and a .198 isolated slugging percentage in 77 games. He was off to a solid start before missing nearly two months of the Carolina League season with left hand inflammation. His numbers dipped significantly after his return, with his Carolina League OPS dropping from .838 to .775.
SCOUTING REPORT: Ramirez has an appealing combination of offensive tools at his disposal. He's a fluid mover in the box with an efficient swing and an early leg lift. He has also already demonstrated the ability to make adjustments. For those reasons, he projects to hit for both average and power. He has the bat speed to handle velocity, but he sells out at times and needs to get deeper into counts. Ramirez is adept at using all fields, with more than 50% of balls going middle to opposite field. An outfielder before signing with the Royals, Ramirez is still a work in progress behind the plate, with the missed time in 2025 further delaying his defensive development. He has plus arm strength but needs to improve his blocking and receiving. His body looked firmer in 2025, increasing his chances of staying behind the plate. A below-average runner, Ramirez doesn't clog the bases and can steal the occasional bag, but speed will not be part of his game.
THE FUTURE: Ramirez has plenty of development ahead, but if he continues improving his defense he projects as a bat-over-glove catcher. He should be ready to move to High-A Quad Cities to begin 2026.

Year	Age	Club (League)	Level	AVG	G	AB	R	H	2B	3B	HR	RBI	BB	SO	SB	OBP	SLG
2025	20	ACL Royals	Rk	.304	7	23	3	7	1	0	1	5	0	3	1	.292	.478
2025	20	Columbia (CAR)	A	.244	70	258	48	63	12	3	11	56	36	65	6	.339	.442
		Minor League Totals		.274	167	573	105	157	32	4	27	121	83	128	14	.371	.485

KANSAS CITY ROYALS

8 DREW BEAM, RHP

FB: 55. **CB:** 50. **CH:** 50. **CT:** 45. **CTL:** 60. **BA Grade:** 45. **Risk:** Average. **Adj:** 35.

Born: February 14, 2003. **B-T:** R-R. **HT:** 6-4. **WT:** 208.
Drafted: Tennessee, 2024 (3rd round). **Signed by:** Nick Hamilton.
TRACK RECORD: Beam was always part of star-studded staffs during his three years in the rotation at Tennessee, pitching alongside top 100 draft picks Chase Dollander, Blade Tidwell and Ben Joyce. Beam ranked as the No. 41 prospect in the 2024 draft, and the Royals managed to land him in the third round at No. 76 overall and sign him for $1,097,500. He made his pro debut in 2025, making 26 starts with High-A Quad Cities. There, he pitched to a 3.83 ERA with a 20.5% strikeout rate and 5.6% walk rate in 131.2 innings.
SCOUTING REPORT: A pitch-to-contact type of hurler, Beam is a reliable strike-thrower who has made year-over-year improvements to his walk rate dating back to his freshman year of college. His best pitch is an above-average 93-96 mph four-seam fastball that can touch 97 with good movement. He lands it for strikes roughly 70% of the time, and he mixes in the occasional sinker that is a beat slower. Beam lacks a clear plus offering, instead relying on different shapes and speeds to keep hitters off-balance as he consistently fills up the zone. His average 80 mph curveball has good depth and is his best secondary weapon, though it could be better with a touch more velocity. His fringy 90 mph cutter is sometimes classified as a slider. He delivers an average 87 mph changeup with fade and sink that he lands for strikes with an easy arm action. Beam's delivery requires some maintenance. He has a big leg kick and a high arm swing that can be inconsistent but adds deception.
THE FUTURE: Beam profiles as a reliable back-of-the-rotation starter who eats innings and might see a jump in velocity and the performance of his secondaries if he moved to shorter outings in a relief role. He will head to Double-A to start the 2026 season.

Year	Age	Club (League)	Level	W	L	ERA	G	GS	IP	H	HR	BB	SO	BB%	SO%	WHIP	AVG
2025	22	Quad Cities (MWL)	A+	7	10	3.83	26	26	132	127	8	30	110	5.6	20.5	1.19	.256
		Minor League Totals		7	10	3.83	26	26	132	127	8	30	110	5.6	20.5	1.19	.256

9 LUINDER AVILA, RHP

FB: 55. **CB:** 60. **CH:** 45. **CTL:** 45. **BA Grade:** 40. **Risk:** Mild. **Adj:** 35.

Born: August 21, 2001. **B-T:** R-R. **HT:** 6-3. **WT:** 195.
Signed: Venezuela, 2018. **Signed by:** Jose Figuera/Joelvis Gonzalez.
TRACK RECORD: Avila has embarked on a slow, measured trek through the Royals' system since signing out of Venezuela in 2018. The righthander finally reached the big leagues in 2025 and performed well in 13 relief appearances, posting a 1.29 ERA with 16 strikeouts in 14 innings. Used mostly as a starter in the minors, Avila has missed time with injuries each of the last two seasons. A right shoulder impingement cost him two months in 2025 and delayed his major league debut until Aug. 13, and a rib cage injury sidelined him for seven weeks in 2024. Avila otherwise spent the bulk of 2025 with Triple-A Omaha, pitching to a 5.23 ERA with 61 strikeouts in 53.1 innings and 14 outings, including nine starts.
SCOUTING REPORT: Avila goes after hitters with a pair of mid-90s fastballs that can touch 98 mph: a four-seamer with heavy sinking action and a separate sinker. Both could be above-average offerings in the future with a bit better shape. Avila's 82 mph curveball was his most frequently used offering both in the minors and in his stint in the Royals' bullpen. It's a potential plus pitch that has tight, downer action that misses barrels and was his best swing-and-miss offering in 2025. Avila's sparingly used, fringy 88 mph changeup has good depth and is deployed primarily as a swing-and-miss pitch to lefties. Avila repeats his high three-quarters arm slot, has a cool demeanor on the mound and has been noted as a tough competitor.
THE FUTURE: While he's been developed as a starter throughout his minor league career, Avila profiles best as a multi-inning reliever whose stuff tightens up in shorter stints. He's big league-ready and could work his way into more leveraged relief throughout the season.

Year	Age	Club (League)	Level	W	L	ERA	G	GS	IP	H	HR	BB	SO	BB%	SO%	WHIP	AVG
2025	23	Quad Cities (MWL)	A+	0	0	3.00	3	3	6	4	0	3	10	13.0	43.5	1.17	.200
2025	23	Omaha (IL)	AAA	2	3	5.23	14	9	53	48	7	23	61	10.0	26.4	1.33	.236
2025	23	Kansas City (AL)	MLB	1	1	1.29	13	0	14	7	0	6	16	10.7	28.6	0.93	.143
		Minor League Totals		23	35	4.54	120	92	477	420	28	210	448	10.2	21.7	1.32	.236
		Major League Totals		1	1	1.29	13	0	14	7	0	6	16	10.7	28.6	0.93	.143

KANSAS CITY ROYALS

10 YANDEL RICARDO, SS
HIT: 40. **POW:** 40. **RUN:** 50. **FLD:** 55. **ARM:** 60. **BA Grade:** 50. **Risk:** High. **Adj:** 35.

Born: October 6, 2006. **B-T:** B-R. **HT:** 6-2. **WT:** 180.
Signed: Cuba, 2024. **Signed by:** Nicolas Bautista/Roberto Aquino/Daniel Guerrero.
TRACK RECORD: Ricardo was the top prospect from Cuba in 2024 when he signed for $2.4 million, one of the international class' 10 biggest bonuses. He debuted in the Dominican Summer League that year, then came stateside in 2025 and performed well in the Arizona Complex League, slashing .342/.438/.533 with 17 steals in 33 games before a promotion to Low-A Columbia in late June. Ricardo's .212/.279/.268 line in 50 Carolina League games was not nearly as impressive, though that's not uncommon for an 18-year-old in a brutal hitting environment.
SCOUTING REPORT: While Ricardo has a chance for above-average defense, his development will hinge on the maturation of his offensive game. The switch-hitter has shown a smooth, repeatable swing and impact potential from both sides. He has good bat speed and a penchant for finding the barrel, but will need to tighten his aggressive swing decisions to improve his contact ability and get more balls in the air. He offered at pitches nearly 55% of the time in 2025 and chased plenty, which contributed to a higher percentage of ground balls and infield popups once he arrived at Low-A. Scouts were impressed with Ricardo's defense at shortstop, where he has above-average potential. He has solid actions, quick feet and a plus arm. He's capable of making the routine plays, though he can get a bit flashy at times, and should stick at shortstop provided he doesn't outgrow the position and lose twitchiness. Ricardo is an average runner now who could slow down with age.
THE FUTURE: Ricardo should return to Low-A Columbia for a second chance to build on his momentum from the ACL. He has a ways to go, but he could develop into a glove-over-bat second-division regular at shortstop.

Year	Age	Club (League)	Level	AVG	G	AB	R	H	2B	3B	HR	RBI	BB	SO	SB	OBP	SLG
2025	18	ACL Royals	Rk	.342	33	120	26	41	7	5	2	21	18	35	17	.438	.533
2025	18	Columbia (CAR)	A	.212	50	179	24	38	6	2	0	14	13	41	14	.279	.268
		Minor League Totals		.246	128	463	77	114	20	13	4	58	56	110	45	.340	.371

11 FELIX ARRONDE, RHP
FB: 55. **SL:** 55. **CH:** 55. **CTL:** 50. **BA Grade:** 45. **Risk:** Average. **Adj:** 35.

Born: April 25, 2003. **B-T:** R-R. **HT:** 6-3. **WT:** 185. **Signed:** Cuba, 2021. **Signed by:** Elias Despradel.
TRACK RECORD: The Royals signed Arronde for $100,000 in 2021 and he spent most of the next three seasons in short-season ball, but his performance in 2024 and 2025 at the Class A levels put the Cuba native on the map. Arronde pitched to a sub-3.00 ERA in two consecutive seasons and was one of High-A Quad Cities' best starters in 2025, posting a 2.80 ERA and holding opposing batters to a .207 average.
SCOUTING REPORT: Arronde's improvement in 2025 was keyed by adding strength to his tall, projectable frame. His arsenal leans heavily on his above-average 94 mph four-seamer that touches 97. He threw it 60% of the time and commands his fastball well. Arronde also tightened up his mid-80s slider and it became a more usable pitch for him in 2025. He's still working on a split changeup that averages 85 mph with late movement. It's an average pitch that generated a whiff rate over 41% in 2025 and has above-average potential, but he doesn't use it very often. Arronde delivers his three-pitch mix from a clean and easy high three-quarters slot.
THE FUTURE: Arronde's next test awaits when he moves to Double-A in 2026. He needs to continue to develop his secondaries and add strength to remain a starter. He has a chance for three above-average pitches, though some observers think he'd thrive in a bullpen role where his velocity would likely tick up.

Year	Age	Club (League)	Level	W	L	ERA	G	GS	IP	H	HR	BB	SO	BB%	SO%	WHIP	AVG
2025	22	Quad Cities (MWL)	A+	5	7	2.80	26	24	129	97	9	42	101	8.1	19.5	1.08	.210
		Minor League Totals		14	28	3.35	85	66	347	280	28	122	336	8.5	23.5	1.16	.219

KANSAS CITY ROYALS

12 BEN KUDRNA, RHP
FB: 40. **SL:** 55. **CB:** 40. **CH:** 60. **CTL:** 50. **BA Grade:** 45. **Risk:** Average. **Adj:** 35.

Born: January 30, 2003. **B-T:** R-R. **HT:** 6-3. **WT:** 220. **Drafted:** HS—Overland Park, KS, 2021 (2nd round). **Signed by:** Matt Price.
TRACK RECORD: The Royals have made a habit of signing Kansas City-area high school products, which includes Kudrna, who signed an over-slot $3 million bonus as a second-round pick in 2021. Given his age, his fourth professional season featured some expected growing pains, especially after reaching Triple-A at just 22 years old in 2025. He spent most of the year with Double-A Northwest Arkansas, striking out 96 batters over 94 innings and 20 starts while posting a 4.21 ERA, which included a 1.47 ERA in four July starts. The Royals added him to their 40-man roster after the season.
SCOUTING REPORT: Kudrna leans primarily on a below-average 93 mph fastball that touches 97 but lacks deception and hasn't taken a velocity jump in pro ball. He has also tinkered with a sinker. Instead, Kudrna's best offering is a mid-to-upper-80s circle changeup with plenty of bottom, registering 15 inches of fade and seven inches of vertical drop. He complements the changeup with an above-average mid-80s bullet slider. He experimented with a 78 mph curveball, but barely used it in games because it negatively affected the performance of his other offerings. He pitches from a high three-quarters arm slot, but his effortful delivery impacts the consistency of his strike-throwing.
THE FUTURE: The Royals plan to continue developing Kudrna as a starter, and he profiles as a back-of-the-rotation arm. Some observers wondered whether he'd benefit from a shift to the bullpen, where he'd have a better chance of holding his fastball velocity and could simplify his secondary mix.

Year	Age	Club (League)	Level	W	L	ERA	G	GS	IP	H	HR	BB	SO	BB%	SO%	WHIP	AVG
2025	22	NW Arkansas (TL)	AA	2	7	4.21	20	19	94	88	7	33	96	8.3	24.0	1.29	.244
2025	22	Omaha (IL)	AAA	0	1	14.29	4	3	11	14	3	17	10	27.0	15.9	2.74	.326
		Minor League Totals		15	28	4.37	86	82	402	393	42	180	390	10.4	22.5	1.43	.258

13 CARSON ROCCAFORTE, OF
HIT: 45. **POW:** 55. **RUN:** 55. **FLD:** 60. **ARM:** 55. **BA Grade:** 45. **Risk:** Average. **Adj:** 35.

Born: March 29, 2002. **B-T:** L-L. **HT:** 6-1. **WT:** 200. **Drafted:** Louisiana-Lafayette, 2023 (2nd round supp.). **Signed by:** Cody Clark.
TRACK RECORD: The Royals used their 2023 supplemental second-round pick on Roccaforte, who closed the 2024 season with a strong second half for High-A Quad Cities. He returned there in 2025 and kept on hitting for power while walking more. Roccaforte put up even better numbers once he reached Double-A Northwest Arkansas, slashing .290/.387/.475, and hit 18 homers across the two levels. He then put together a solid showing in the Arizona Fall League.
SCOUTING REPORT: Roccaforte has steadily transformed into a power-first approach in pro ball. His upright, narrow stance is even taller now, with his hands now hanging out over the plate to begin an at-bat. Roccaforte's power growth was noticeable in 2025: his combined .212 isolated slugging percentage far exceeded his output from either of his first two pro seasons. It has come at the expense of contact. His strikeout rate jumped to 29.4%, though he also walked 14.9% of the time, and his approach is geared heavily toward elevating balls to his pull side. Roccaforte is a plus outfield defender with an above-average arm. He's a no-doubt center fielder who can handle all three outfield spots, and he used his above-average speed to steal 43 bases in 55 attempts.
THE FUTURE: For a team that desperately needs outfield help, Roccaforte's emergence could have him contributing to the big league team in the not-too-distant future. He has the floor of a powerful, speedy fourth outfielder, with a chance to become a second-division regular if he can make more contact.

Year	Age	Club (League)	Level	AVG	G	AB	R	H	2B	3B	HR	RBI	BB	SO	SB	OBP	SLG
2025	23	Quad Cities (MWL)	A+	.237	82	279	49	66	15	5	13	45	55	101	33	.364	.466
2025	23	NW Arkansas (TL)	AA	.290	45	183	32	53	15	2	5	29	27	61	10	.387	.475
		Minor League Totals		.239	280	1049	162	251	60	14	28	151	157	335	93	.340	.403

14 STEVEN ZOBAC, RHP
FB: 55. **SL:** 60. **SP:** 45. **CTL:** 60. **BA Grade:** 45. **Risk:** Average. **Adj:** 35.

Born: October 14, 2000. **B-T:** R-R. **HT:** 6-2. **WT:** 205. **Drafted:** California, 2022 (4th round). **Signed by:** Buddy Gouldsmith.
TRACK RECORD: Originally a two-way player at Cal, Zobac turned to pitching full-time as a junior and saw his stuff jump. The Royals took notice and made him their fourth-round pick in 2022. A knee injury stymied his 2025 season and limited him to just 44.2 innings and 14 starts. While his 21.1% strikeout rate and 8% walk rate were solid, the 24-year-old was battered by opposing hitters to a .346 average and

KANSAS CITY ROYALS

a 7.68 ERA in 36.1 innings with Double-A Northwest Arkansas.
SCOUTING REPORT: Zobac attacks hitters with two above-average or better pitches. His 93 mph four-seam fastball touches 96 with good life and above-average ride. In a small sample in 2025, Zobac threw his plus slider 1.5 mph harder than in 2024, and it averaged nearly 88 mph and touched 91, albeit with a lower spin rate. He shelved his changeup in exchange for an 86-87 mph splitter, but he plans to reintroduce the changeup in 2026, which should give him an offering with more separation from his fastball and slider. Zobac delivers his pitches with a simple, repeatable delivery and fields his position well. His left knee issues affected how he landed in his delivery and impacted his command in 2025.
THE FUTURE: If healthy in 2026, Zobac could move quickly. He could get to the big leagues as a leverage reliever sooner rather than later if his changeup takes a step forward.

Year	Age	Club (League)	Level	W	L	ERA	G	GS	IP	H	HR	BB	SO	BB%	SO%	WHIP	AVG
2025	24	ACL Royals	Rk	0	1	5.40	3	3	8	9	2	2	8	5.6	22.2	1.32	.290
2025	24	NW Arkansas (TL)	AA	0	3	7.68	11	11	36	55	8	14	37	8.0	21.1	1.90	.357
		Minor League Totals		13	18	4.20	61	55	261	263	22	69	266	6.3	24.1	1.27	.261

15 MICHAEL LOMBARDI, RHP

FB: 60. **CB:** 60. **SL:** 40. **CH:** 45. **CTL:** 45. **BA Grade:** 50. **Risk:** High. **Adj:** 35.

Born: September 20, 2003. **B-T:** R-R. **HT:** 6-3. **WT:** 201. **Drafted:** Tulane, 2025 (2nd round). **Signed by:** Cody Clark.
TRACK RECORD: Lombardi was a two-way player at Tulane, but his draft outlook was much better on the mound, where he struck out 73 batters over 42 innings in his final college season. The Royals selected him in the second round in 2025 and signed him for $1,297,500. Lombardi stayed at the Royals' Arizona complex after signing and pitched in fall instructional league games.
SCOUTING REPORT: A plus athlete with good raw stuff, Lombardi added more than three ticks to his fastball in his junior spring. The pitch sat 92-95 mph and touched 97 with good swing-and-miss shape. Lombardi's best secondary is a 77-81 mph curveball that has plus depth and gives him another plus offering. Lombardi's cutterish 83-89 mph slider still needs some development, as does his fringy 83-85 mph changeup. He was a below-average strike-thrower in college and particularly struggled to land his secondaries. Lombardi's delivery requires a moderate amount of effort, although he gets down the mound well with a shallow, short arm path and an over-the-top release to finish with extreme release height and approach to the plate. The Royals were impressed with his makeup.
THE FUTURE: Given his two-way status and relatively short track record of starting, Lombardi needs more polish than the average college arm, but he has a midrotation ceiling if he can throw more consistent strikes and find a better third offering. He'll likely begin 2026 with Low-A Columbia with a chance to get to High-A Quad Cities quickly.

Year	Age	Club (League)	Level	W	L	ERA	G	GS	IP	H	HR	BB	SO	BB%	SO%	WHIP	AVG
2025	21	Did not play															

16 ASBEL GONZALEZ, OF

HIT: 50. **POW:** 40. **RUN:** 60. **FLD:** 60. **ARM:** 55. **BA Grade:** 50. **Risk:** High. **Adj:** 35

Born: January 2, 2006. **B-T:** R-R. **HT:** 6-2. **WT:** 170. **Signed:** Venezuela, 2023.
Signed by: Alberto Garcia/Jose Gualdron/Joelvis Gonzalez.
TRACK RECORD: Gonzalez signed for just $157,000 in 2023 out of Venezuela. Two years later, he was one of the Royals' most intriguing breakout prospects in his full-season debut. A prototypical leadoff hitter, Gonzalez stole 30 bases in 36 attempts in April alone, and slashed .353/.469/.380 through the middle of May. But his production dipped significantly from there and he finished the year with a .239/.365/.289 line and a Carolina League-leading 78 steals.
SCOUTING REPORT: Gonzalez has an efficient swing with a bat path geared for consistent contact, but his meager slugging numbers define his biggest need for improvement after producing well below-average exit velocities and barrel rates in 2025. He ran a 50% groundball rate, though his plus speed allowed him to beat out plenty of infield grounders. With a lean, lanky frame, Gonzalez needs to add more strength to better impact the baseball. Defensively, he's a plus outfielder who moves gracefully across the grass and gets good reads in center field. His above-average arm is plenty for the position. Gonzalez is the fastest runner in the Royals' system and he's aggressive on the bases, but he'll need to clean up his efficiency after getting caught stealing 25% of the time.
THE FUTURE: There's plenty of time for Gonzalez to mature into his body as he enters his age-20 season in 2026. His speed and defense will carry him for now, but the development of his bat will determine whether he lives up to his leadoff hitter profile.

KANSAS CITY ROYALS

Year	Age	Club (League)	Level	AVG	G	AB	R	H	2B	3B	HR	RBI	BB	SO	SB	OBP	SLG
2025	19	Columbia (CAR)	A	.239	115	415	82	99	12	3	1	21	54	86	78	.365	.289
		Minor League Totals		.249	203	715	147	178	33	7	2	59	95	150	118	.370	.323

17 GAVIN CROSS, OF

HIT: 40. **POW:** 50. **RUN:** 50. **FLD:** 50. **ARM:** 50. **BA Grade:** 45. **Risk:** Avg. **Adj:** 35.

Born: September 13, 2001. **B-T:** L-L. **HT:** 6-3. **WT:** 210. **Drafted:** Virginia Tech, 2022 (1st round). **Signed by:** Tim Bittner.
TRACK RECORD: When the Royals drafted Cross ninth overall in 2022, they hoped he'd move quickly and grab hold of a starting outfield job. That hasn't happened. Injuries and illness have sapped the Virginia Tech product's athleticism. He returned to Double-A Northwest Arkansas in 2025 and slashed .186/.230/.326 through June, then missed a couple weeks with a back injury. He turned his season around after returning and boosted his final line to .241/.291/.413 in his age-24 season.
SCOUTING REPORT: Coming out of college, Cross was billed as a consistent, powerful lefthanded hitter. He still has a power-over-hit profile at the plate, but he's been stiffer with a slower bat in pro ball. Cross is even more pull-oriented now, and over 50% of his batted balls went to right field in 2025. Cross' strikeout rate jumped from 24.1% to 26.4% while his walk rate dipped from 10.3% to 6.5%. While he hit a career-high 17 homers, he hits fewer line drives now. An average defender who gets good jumps, Cross is better suited for right field, where his average arm will play. An average runner who will slow down with age, he is successful on the basepaths thanks to good instincts.
THE FUTURE: The Royals didn't add Cross to their 40-man roster, leaving him exposed in the Rule 5 draft. He'll need to rediscover his amateur hitting track record to avoid becoming much more than a fourth outfielder or an up-down option.

Year	Age	Club (League)	Level	AVG	G	AB	R	H	2B	3B	HR	RBI	BB	SO	SB	OBP	SLG
2025	24	NW Arkansas (TL)	AA	.241	114	465	75	112	23	3	17	64	33	134	23	.291	.413
		Minor League Totals		.242	340	1317	202	319	70	8	52	206	145	387	80	.321	.426

18 JUSTIN LAMKIN, LHP

FB: 50. **SL:** 55. **CB:** 45. **CH:** 45. **CTL:** 55. **BA Grade:** 45. **Risk:** High. **Adj:** 30.

Born: June 1, 2004. **B-T:** R-L. **HT:** 6-4. **WT:** 210. **Drafted:** Texas A&M, 2025 (2nd round supp.). **Signed by:** Josh Hallgren.
TRACK RECORD: Lamkin was a top 300 draft prospect out of high school in 2022. Instead, he reached campus at Texas A&M and became a reliable three-year workhorse who improved his control each year. Lamkin turned in a career season in 2025, which finished with a 3.42 ERA over 15 starts and 84.1 innings with a 28% strikeout rate and 5.4% walk rate. The Royals used their supplemental second-round pick to select him 71st overall in 2025 and signed him for $1,161,200. Instead of going out to an affiliate, Lamkin stayed behind to pitch in the fall instructional league program.
SCOUTING REPORT: Lamkin takes the mound with a solid if unspectacular four-pitch mix. He lands his average 91-94 mph fastball for strikes with some carry and gloveside action. His only above-average pitch is an 83-85 mph gyro slider that he delivers with turn and occasional tilt. Lamkin started working with a 78-81 mph curveball with wider break after arriving at the Royals' complex. He rounds out his toolkit with an 83-86 mph changeup that has mild tumble and depth. He throws it with deception and it's a weapon against righthanded batters. Lamkin has above-average control and walked just 19 batters in his final college season. He has a compact delivery with deception through his back side and short, soft finish out front through his release.
THE FUTURE: Lamkin profiles as a durable back-end starter with a chance for more if he develops a true putaway pitch and expands his repertoire, perhaps with an improved curveball or changeup.

Year	Age	Club (League)	Level	W	L	ERA	G	GS	IP	H	HR	BB	SO	BB%	SO%	WHIP	AVG
2025	21	Did not play															

19 WARREN CALCAÑO, SS

HIT: 50. **POW:** 40. **RUN:** 55. **FLD:** 60. **ARM:** 55. **BA Grade:** 50. **Risk:** Extreme. **Adj:** 30.

Born: October 17, 2007. **B-T:** B-R. **HT:** 6-2. **WT:** 165. **Signed:** Cuba, 2025.
Signed by: Nicolas Bautista/Roberto Aquino/Daniel Guerrero/Rene Francisco.
TRACK RECORD: For the second straight year, the Royals' top international bonus went to a Cuban shortstop when they signed Calcaño for $1,847,500 in 2025. He was originally supposed to sign for $2.5 million until a physical revealed a shoulder issue. While his pro debut in the Dominican Summer League was cut short after nine games to a season-ending shoulder injury, he impressed observers by batting .346/.514/.538.

KANSAS CITY ROYALS

SCOUTING REPORT: As an amateur, Calcaño stood out for his defensive actions, instincts and arm strength. He's a twitchy athlete with a quick bat and good bat-to-ball skills from both sides of the plate. He stays through the middle of the field with a line-drive approach and the bat control to develop into a hitter with high on-base percentages and doubles power, and he'll likely add more power with room to pack strength onto his frame. Even with his impressive performance at the plate in a small DSL sample, Calcaño's plus defense and above-average arm suggest he'll be more of a glove-over-bat type who can stick at shortstop. He's light on his feet and moves around with good body control, soft hands and a nose for the ball, possessing good defensive instincts. An above-average runner, he stole seven bases in his nine-game DSL stint.
THE FUTURE: If his shoulder is healthy, Calcaño should make his stateside debut in the Arizona Complex League in 2026. There's a long way to go, but he has everyday shortstop upside.

Year	Age	Club (League)	Level	AVG	G	AB	R	H	2B	3B	HR	RBI	BB	SO	SB	OBP	SLG
2025	17	DSL Royals Fortuna	Rk	.346	9	26	7	9	2	0	1	2	8	10	7	.514	.538
		Minor League Totals		.346	9	26	7	9	2	0	1	2	8	10	7	.514	.538

20 RAMCELL MEDINA, SS

HIT: 50. **POW:** 50. **RUN:** 45. **FLD:** 55. **ARM:** 50. **BA Grade:** 50. **Risk:** Extreme. **Adj:** 30.

Born: November 13, 2007. **B-T:** R-R. **HT:** 6-1. **WT:** 155. **Signed:** Dominican Republic, 2025.
Signed by: Michael Acevedo/Roberto Aquino/Daniel Guerrero/Rene Francisco.
TRACK RECORD: Medina received the Royals' second-highest bonus in the 2025 international class when he signed out of the Dominican Republic for $947,500. He launched his career in the Dominican Summer League, batting .260/.398/.404 and appearing in the DSL all-star game. He posted impressive numbers in his pro debut, with a 16.7% walk rate, 14% strikeout rate and just a 19.5% miss rate. He was the only DSL player the Royals brought to the states for the fall instructional league program.
SCOUTING REPORT: Medina has significant developmental work ahead, but shows the raw ingredients of a physical corner infielder. His swing is long with a pronounced hip roll and big turn, entering the zone steeply and often with effort. Medina's defensive work in the DSL graded as plus, but he was more error-prone during instructs and would occasionally airmail throws to first base. At 6-foot-1, Medina already has broad, square shoulders and a dense, muscular lower half. So while he's a shortstop now, he might fit best at third as he continues to add strength. He's a fringe-average runner who will likely slow down even more as he adds bulk, and speed is not expected to be a big part of his game.
THE FUTURE: While his development will require plenty of patience and reps, Medina is expected to spend most, if not all, of 2026 in the Arizona Complex League, where he'll be 18 the entire season.

Year	Age	Club (League)	Level	AVG	G	AB	R	H	2B	3B	HR	RBI	BB	SO	SB	OBP	SLG
2025	17	DSL Royals Ventura	Rk	.260	44	146	32	38	7	4	2	25	31	26	7	.398	.404
		Minor League Totals		.260	44	146	32	38	7	4	2	25	31	26	7	.398	.404

21 GRAYSON BOLES, RHP

FB: 55. **CB:** 40. **SL:** 55. **CH:** 50. **CTL:** 45. **BA Grade:** 50. **Risk:** Extreme. **Adj:** 30.

Born: September 18, 2006. **B-T:** R-R. **HT:** 6-5. **WT:** 215. **Drafted:** HS—San Diego, CA, 2025 (18th round).
Signed by: Rich Morales.
TRACK RECORD: The Royals rolled the dice that they could sign Boles when they selected the San Diego prep product in the 18th round of the 2025 draft and lured him away from a Texas commitment with a $500,000 bonus. In doing so, he became the first draft pick from San Diego's St. Augustine High School since Giants 1970 first-rounder John D'Acquisto. Boles remained at the Royals' Arizona complex after the draft and got into a few September instructional league games.
SCOUTING REPORT: Boles is a tall 6-foot-5 righthander with a strong lower half who should get even stronger once he matures. He mostly leaned on a two-pitch mix in instructs. Both his two-seam fastball and slider have above-average potential. His heater sat 92-94 mph in fall games with firm, diving sink. His 81-84 mph slider showed tight turn and good shape, with good tilt and finish through the plate. In high school, Boles flashed feel for a mid-80s changeup that could become an average and reliable third offering, and he also occasionally used a mid-70s curveball. He's a below-average strike-thrower from a delivery that stops and starts with effort and a crossbody finish. Boles is competitive on the mound.
THE FUTURE: There's plenty of development ahead, but Boles projects as a big-bodied midrotation starter. He'll be 19 next season and will likely spend the bulk of the year in the Arizona Complex League.

Year	Age	Club (League)	Level	AVG	G	AB	R	H	2B	3B	HR	RBI	BB	SO	SB	OBP	SLG
2025	18	Did not play															

KANSAS CITY ROYALS

22 BLAKE WOLTERS, RHP
FB: 45. **SL:** 50. **CH:** 50. **CTL:** 40. **BA Grade:** 45. **Risk:** High. **Adj:** 30.

Born: October 25, 2004. **B-T:** R-R. **HT:** 6-4. **WT:** 210. **Drafted:** HS—Mahomet, IL, 2023 (2nd round). **Signed by:** Scott Melvin.
TRACK RECORD: Wolters signed an above-slot $2.8 million bonus when the Royals drafted the Arizona commit 44th overall in 2023. He quickly piqued evaluators' interest by running his fastball up to 99 mph and spinning a wipeout slider at times over 2,600 rpm. He went out to Low-A Columbia in 2024 and was shut down after 14 starts once he reached his innings limit. Wolters returned to the level in 2025, but he was limited to just 47.1 innings and 12 starts in part because of a shoulder impingement, and also because he walked too many batters, posting identical 19.3% walk and strikeout rates.
SCOUTING REPORT: Wolters' fastball averaged 93 mph in 2025 with subpar shape, though the Royals believe it can rebound with some restored power. His short-breaking 85 mph slider also had lower spin rates than previous years. He'll need to restore some velocity to both offerings for them to become above-average pitches again. Wolters leaned on his 86-87 mph changeup more frequently as a whiff-getter in 2025, but it could use more separation from his fastball. He's expected to experiment with a curveball in 2026. When healthy, Wolters can repeat his three-quarters delivery, but his command is inconsistent.
THE FUTURE: If Wolters can regain his previous form and velocity, he has the upside of a starter who pitches toward the back of a rotation.

Year	Age	Club (League)	Level	W	L	ERA	G	GS	IP	H	HR	BB	SO	BB%	SO%	WHIP	AVG
2025	20	Columbia (CAR)	A	2	2	3.99	12	12	47	34	3	40	40	19.3	19.3	1.56	.209
		Minor League Totals		4	5	4.11	26	26	103	91	7	65	86	14.3	18.9	1.51	.239

23 MASON BLACK, RHP
FB: 45. **SW:** 50. **CT:** 50. **SP:** 40. **CTL:** 40. **BA Grade:** 40. **Risk:** Average. **Adj:** 30.

Born: December 10, 1999. **B-T:** R-R. **HT:** 6-3. **WT:** 230. **Drafted:** Lehigh, 2021 (3rd round). **Signed by:** John DiCarlo (Giants).
TRACK RECORD: Black ranked eighth in the Giants' system entering 2025 and has spent parts of his previous two seasons in the big leagues. But he struggled to get on track in either Triple-A or the majors during that stretch and his Triple-A strikeout rate dropped from 30.3% in 2023 to 21.5% in 2025. Needing to clear a 40-man roster spot, San Francisco designated Black for assignment and traded him to the Royals for pitcher Logan Martin after the season.
SCOUTING REPORT: The root of Black's woes is a drop in fastball velocity. Black has sat in the mid 90s in the past and threw two fastball variations—a four-seamer and a sinker—in 2025 that both averaged under 93 mph. Black's once-plus sweeper has also regressed and averaged 82 mph in 2025. Black's loss of power is mechanical, as he leaks power in his delivery because of his lead leg block. He tends to open up too early and swing his leg past his ideal landing area. In addition to his fastball-sweeper combination, Black also works in a 90 mph cutter and a fading 87 mph splitter.
THE FUTURE: An obvious change-of-scenery candidate, Black could fill a spot at the back of the Royals' rotation or as a multi-inning reliever if the velocity comes back. He's on their 40-man roster with a good chance of breaking camp with the major league team.

Year	Age	Club (League)	Level	W	L	ERA	G	GS	IP	H	HR	BB	SO	BB%	SO%	WHIP	AVG
2025	25	Sacramento (PCL)	AAA	3	10	5.81	30	24	119	114	17	62	114	11.7	21.5	1.47	.250
2025	25	San Francisco (NL)	MLB	0	0	6.75	1	0	4	5	2	0	5	0.0	26.3	1.25	.263
		Minor League Totals		18	29	4.32	103	97	439	385	57	189	492	10.1	26.3	1.31	.235
		Major League Totals		1	5	6.47	10	8	40	51	9	15	36	8.0	19.1	1.64	.304

24 HUNTER PATTESON, LHP
FB: 55. **SL:** 50. **CH:** 60. **CTL:** 50. **BA Grade:** 40. **Risk:** Avg. **Adj:** 30.

Born: April 4, 2000. **B-T:** L-L. **HT:** 6-4. **WT:** 190. **Drafted:** Central Florida, 2022 (5th round). **Signed by:** Daniel Guerrero.
TRACK RECORD: Patteson was in the midst of a breakout season at Central Florida in 2022 when Tommy John surgery ended his season early. The Royals still selected him in the fifth round that year. He made eight rehab outings in 2023, then spent all of 2024 split between both Class A levels. Back at High-A Quad Cities in 2025, Patteson was outstanding over 13 starts, pitching to a 1.99 ERA and a 63-to-23 strikeout-to-walk ratio. The Royals promoted him to Double-A Northwest Arkansas, where he yielded 10 homers in 49 innings.
SCOUTING REPORT: Patteson's four-seamer averaged 92 mph but his velocity spiked to nearly 97 mph after reaching Double-A, returning to pre-surgery levels. He will need to learn how to work with that extra

fastball velocity. His primary breaking ball is an 81-87 mph slider, and he also has a mid-80s changeup with plus potential, though both secondaries are works in progress. Patteson maximizes his arsenal by consistently moving the ball around the strike zone and leveraging his advanced pitchability. He works from a three-quarters slot with a rotational delivery, closed landing and compact, on-line finish.
THE FUTURE: Though he's already 25 with less than half a season of Double-A experience, Patteson could get a chance to one day carve out a role at the back of a rotation if his stuff takes another step forward in 2026.

Year	Age	Club (League)	Level	W	L	ERA	G	GS	IP	H	HR	BB	SO	BB%	SO%	WHIP	AVG
2025	25	Quad Cities (MWL)	A+	5	1	1.99	13	13	72	52	3	23	63	8.0	22.0	1.04	.199
2025	25	NW Arkansas (TL)	AA	4	0	4.41	11	8	49	47	10	16	44	7.7	21.3	1.29	.250
		Minor League Totals		12	5	3.19	43	38	195	163	18	50	186	6.4	23.6	1.09	.225

25 CAMERON MILLAR, RHP
FB: 55. **SL:** 50. **CH:** 50. **CTL:** 50. **BA Grade:** 50. **Risk:** Extreme. **Adj:** 30.

Born: May 5, 2007. **B-T:** R-R. **HT:** 6-2. **WT:** 200. **Drafted:** HS—Martinez, CA, 2025 (3rd round).
Signed by: Buddy Gouldsmith.
TRACK RECORD: Millar generated buzz during his senior spring when his velocity spiked to 97 mph, his lean frame looked stronger and he streamlined his delivery. The Royals selected the Northern California righthander in the third round in 2025 and signed him to an overslot $1,497,500 deal to keep him from his Arizona commitment. He didn't make his pro debut, but he got into September game action during the fall instructional league program.
SCOUTING REPORT: Millar's four-seamer sat 90-95 mph in instructs, and was delivered with a simple, quiet delivery that has deep tilt as he gathers energy down the mound. He gets average lift on his fastball. Millar's 83-85 mph slider is currently a fringe-average offering with shape and depth, though he could get it to at least average with more reps. His third offering is an 80-83 mph changeup with big tumble and fade through the zone. Millar has a clean delivery from a three-quarters slot, but he needs to tighten up the consistency of his release point. He's a strong competitor on the mound.
THE FUTURE: Millar has the ingredients of at least a No. 4 starter, though it's far too early in his career to place limits on his upside. His development will be a slow burn, and he'll likely spend his first season in the Arizona Complex League in 2026.

Year	Age	Club (League)	Level	W	L	ERA	G	GS	IP	H	HR	BB	SO	BB%	SO%	WHIP	AVG
2025	18	Did not play															

26 SHANE PANZINI, RHP
FB: 60. **CB:** 55. **SL:** 45. **CH:** 40. **CTL:** 45. **BA Grade:** 40. **Risk:** Avg. **Adj:** 30.

Born: October 30, 2001. **B-T:** R-R. **HT:** 6-3. **WT:** 220. **Drafted:** HS—Red Bank, NJ, 2021 (4th round).
Signed by: Casey Fahy.
TRACK RECORD: It took until midway through his fourth pro season for Panzini to reach the upper minors, finally advancing to Double-A Northwest Arkansas in 2025 after posting a 2.76 ERA with 36 strikeouts in 29.1 innings at High-A Quad Cities. He was even more impressive in Double-A, with a 27% strikeout rate and .240 opponents average, before ending the year with five starts for Triple-A Omaha.
SCOUTING REPORT: Healthy once again in 2025, Panzini's velocity ticked up and he pitched as both a starter and multi-inning reliever. He sat 91-93 mph as a starter early in the season, and his velocity jumped to 95-99 mph from the bullpen. He maintained that velocity increase and his 18.4 inches of vertical break later in the year when he mostly worked as a starter. Of his secondaries, Panzini most frequently turned to an above-average 79 mph curveball that has 11-to-5 movement and 12 inches of depth. It could be an above-average pitch in time. His 87 mph slider has some sweep, and his below-average 85-89 mph changeup is still a work-in-progress without much depth.
THE FUTURE: Panzini's optimal future role might be as a swingman, though his increased velocity and fastball/curveball combination could be even more effective in shorter spurts out of the bullpen.

Year	Age	Club (League)	Level	W	L	ERA	G	GS	IP	H	HR	BB	SO	BB%	SO%	WHIP	AVG
2025	23	Quad Cities (MWL)	A+	1	2	2.76	8	2	29	25	0	11	36	9.1	29.8	1.23	.229
2025	23	NW Arkansas (TL)	AA	5	0	3.16	13	10	57	52	7	21	65	8.7	27.0	1.28	.240
2025	23	Omaha (IL)	AAA	2	1	4.76	5	5	23	25	7	15	13	13.8	11.9	1.76	.269
		Minor League Totals		14	21	4.58	81	63	320	324	42	167	333	11.9	23.7	1.53	.268

KANSAS CITY ROYALS

27 DENNIS COLLERAN JR., RHP
FB: 70. **SW:** 50. **CT:** 60. **CTL:** 30. **BA Grade:** 45. **Risk:** High. **Adj:** 30.

Born: August 20, 2003. **B-T:** R-R. **HT:** 6-3. **WT:** 215. **Drafted:** Northeastern, 2024 (7th round). **Signed by:** Joe Barbera.
TRACK RECORD: Despite a subpar season at Northeastern, the Royals were intrigued enough by Colleran's triple-digit velocity to select the Massachusetts native in the seventh round in 2024. He debuted in 2025 with 22 appearances in relief for Low-A Columbia, then climbed to High-A Quad Cities and later Double-A Northwest Arkansas. Colleran yielded just one run over his last 17 innings and then performed well in the Arizona Fall League.
SCOUTING REPORT: Colleran's best weapon is a blazing upper-90s four-seam fastball that touched 101 mph with heavy armside sink. It's a plus-plus pitch and the best heater in the system. Early in the season, lower-level hitters geared up for the velocity better than expected, but his overall effectiveness improved once he created more separation between his fastball and secondaries. His sweeper, once 87-88 mph early in the season, now works at 85-87 with more movement and projects as an average weapon against right-handed hitters. He complements it with a plus 92 mph cutter that looks like a slider with more depth that he leans on against lefties. He rarely throws his well below-average changeup, and he also walked 12.8% of batters.
THE FUTURE: Colleran's high-octane velocity is intriguing. He'll need to refine his secondaries and cut his walk rates, but he has late-inning upside if he can throw more strikes.

Year	Age	Club (League)	Level	W	L	ERA	G	GS	IP	H	HR	BB	SO	BB%	SO%	WHIP	AVG
2025	21	Columbia (CAR)	A	4	0	4.06	22	0	31	22	1	19	39	14.5	29.8	1.32	.198
2025	21	Quad Cities (MWL)	A+	5	0	1.83	21	0	34	14	3	14	33	10.6	25.0	0.82	.126
2025	21	NW Arkansas (TL)	AA	0	0	0.00	1	0	1	0	0	1	0	33.3	0.0	1.00	.000
		Minor League Totals		9	0	2.85	44	0	66	36	4	34	72	12.8	27.1	1.06	.161

28 FRANK MOZZICATO, LHP
FB: 40. **CB:** 60. **CH:** 45. **CTL:** 30. **BA Grade:** 40. **Risk:** Average. **Adj:** 30.

Born: June 19, 2003. **B-T:** L-L. **HT:** 6-3. **WT:** 175. **Drafted:** HS—Manchester, CT, 2021 (1st round). **Signed by:** Casey Fahy.
TRACK RECORD: Inconsistent results have plagued Mozzicato ever since the Royals surprised many by drafting him seventh overall in 2021. His velocity ticked up coming out of spring training in 2025, and he was outstanding over seven starts with High-A Quad Cities, pitching to a 1.24 ERA and a 25.3% strikeout rate to earn a Futures Game selection. Mozzicato's subsequent promotion to Double-A proved far more challenging. His walk rate ballooned to 19.4% and opponents hit .278 against the lefthander.
SCOUTING REPORT: Mozzicato's four-seamer was up to 94 mph in the spring, but he didn't hold that velocity, and his heater averaged just over 90 mph in the regular season with 18 inches of induced vertical break. Mozzicato's plus 80 mph curveball with more than 2,600 rpm of spin has never left his side. He uses a fringy mid-80s circle changeup to keep hitters off his fastball. Ongoing delivery issues continue to haunt the slender southpaw. His long arm stroke and slow tempo make it difficult to sync up his delivery. The Royals worked with Mozzicato to speed up his delivery in the hopes of finding more repeatable mechanics.
THE FUTURE: The Royals left Mozzicato unprotected ahead of the Rule 5 draft. While they have no plans to move him to the bullpen, external evaluators wonder if he's best suited for a role as a lefty specialist.

Year	Age	Club (League)	Level	W	L	ERA	G	GS	IP	H	HR	BB	SO	BB%	SO%	WHIP	AVG
2025	22	Quad Cities (MWL)	A+	1	0	1.24	7	7	36	15	2	22	37	15.1	25.3	1.02	.124
2025	22	NW Arkansas (TL)	AA	2	5	7.46	17	13	57	58	10	53	48	19.4	17.6	1.96	.278
		Minor League Totals		7	20	4.69	64	60	255	198	30	193	304	17.0	26.7	1.53	.215

29 FREDDY CONTRERAS, RHP
FB: 60. **CB:** 55. **CH:** 50. **CTL:** 45. **BA Grade:** 50. **Risk:** Extreme. **Adj:** 30.

Born: August 10, 2008. **B-T:** B-R. **HT:** 5-11. **WT:** 178. **Signed:** Dominican Republic, 2025.
Signed by: Eddy Abad/Roberto Aquino/Daniel Guerrero.
TRACK RECORD: While fellow pitcher Kendry Chourio's sensational breakout headlined the Royals' 2025 international signing class, Contreras may not be as far behind his Dominican Summer League teammate as some expected. Contreras, who didn't turn 17 until the final week of the DSL season, signed for $147,500 and then pitched to a 3.30 ERA with 37 strikeouts to 13 walks in 30 innings, earning a DSL all-star nod.
SCOUTING REPORT: Contreras is a lean righthander with a four-seamer that was in the low 90s early in the season, but averaged 95 mph and touched 98 by the end of the year. He commands it well and it

projects as a plus offering. His 79 mph curveball has above-average potential with good spin and movement, and Contreras also has feel for an 87 mph changeup. Both secondaries generated plenty of whiffs in the DSL. Contreras is highly competitive and confident on the mound.

THE FUTURE: Given his youth, a return to the DSL would make sense for Contreras. However, the Royals haven't shied away from aggressive assignments for teenage arms, so he very well could open 2026 in the Arizona Complex League with a solid fastball-curveball combination that gives him a high floor for his age.

Year	Age	Club (League)	Level	W	L	ERA	G	GS	IP	H	HR	BB	SO	BB%	SO%	WHIP	AVG
2025	16	DSL Royals Ventura	Rk	1	1	3.30	10	9	30	22	0	13	37	10.4	29.6	1.17	.202
		Minor League Totals		1	1	3.30	10	9	30	22	0	13	37	10.4	29.6	1.17	.202

30 HENRY WILLIAMS, RHP

FB: 45. **CB:** 55. **SL:** 50. **CH:** 50. **CTL:** 55. **BA Grade:** 40. **Risk:** Average. **Adj:** 30.

Born: September 18, 2001. **B-T:** R-R. **HT:** 6-5. **WT:** 228. **Drafted:** Duke, 2022 (3rd round).
Signed by: Jake Koenig (Padres).
TRACK RECORD: Williams pitched just 37 innings in his first two seasons at Duke, then had Tommy John surgery before his junior season, but that didn't dissuade the Padres from taking the big righthander in the third round of the 2022 draft. The Royals acquired him at the 2023 trade deadline in a deal for Scott Barlow, and Williams has slowly traversed Kansas City's system since then. He spent the bulk of his age-23 season with Double-A Northwest Arkansas, where he posted a serviceable 21.6% strikeout rate and a career-best 7.8% walk rate.
SCOUTING REPORT: Williams is an effective strike-thrower with a solid four-pitch arsenal and above-average command. His 92 mph four-seamer touches 95 with life and his command helps the fringe-average pitch play up. His best pitch is a big 78-80 mph curveball which he consistently lands for strikes. He throws a short, tight mid-80s gyro slider that complements the curveball. He rounds out his arsenal with feel for an average 86-89 mph changeup. With a simple, repeatable three-quarters delivery, Williams gets plus extension that helped generate above-average chase rates across his arsenal in 2025.
THE FUTURE: His profile isn't sexy, but Williams has the look of a dependable back-of-the-rotation option with a high probability of reaching that floor because he commands all four of his pitches.

Year	Age	Club (League)	Level	W	L	ERA	G	GS	IP	H	HR	BB	SO	BB%	SO%	WHIP	AVG
2025	23	NW Arkansas (TL)	AA	5	6	4.24	21	19	108	112	11	36	100	7.8	21.6	1.37	.270
2025	23	Omaha (IL)	AAA	0	2	10.13	2	2	8	9	1	8	6	18.6	14.0	2.13	.281
		Minor League Totals		13	18	4.35	62	59	285	264	29	117	261	9.7	21.6	1.34	.249

Nolan Schanuel

Los Angeles Angels

BY TAYLOR BLAKE WARD

Following a 90-loss campaign in 2025, the Angels have not had a winning season in a decade.

The club's 10th consecutive losing record and 11th straight year without a playoff appearance—both the longest active streaks in the majors—reinforced an identity of middling results and instability, while the organization remains hopeful its budding young core can finally turn the page on a decade of frustration.

If there's stability anywhere in the organization, it's in the front office. Perry Minasian enters his sixth season as general manager, the longest tenure for an Angels GM since Bill Stoneman stepped down after 2007.

The managerial seat, however, has seen unprecedented turnover. Kurt Suzuki became the sixth full-time manager over a nine-year span when he signed an unconventional one-year deal in October. He'll bring a new coaching staff that will include recent development coaches Andy Schatzley (infield) and Keith Johnson (third base), plus respected pitching coach Mike Maddux.

The Angels' young core saw growth in 2025. Zach Neto delivered his second straight 20-20 season with five or more bWAR. Nolan Schanuel recorded a 107 OPS+, Jo Adell launched 37 home runs and Jose Soriano logged a career-high 169 innings. Reid Detmers had a 3.12 FIP as a reliever, while recent top prospects Christian Moore and Caden Dana held their heads above water.

However, the Angels missed opportunities to replenish their talent by failing to move impending free agents at the trade deadline, headlined by Kenley Jansen. Within the industry, that decision was widely attributed to owner Arte Moreno. It was not all that dissimilar from the club holding onto Shohei Ohtani in 2023.

Minasian has tried to cultivate a burgeoning young core via an aggressive draft-and-develop approach, carving out a reputation alongside ama-

PROJECTED 2029 LINEUP

Catcher	Logan O'Hoppe	29
First Base	Nolan Schanuel	27
Second Base	Christian Moore	26
Third Base	Denzer Guzman	25
Shortstop	Zach Neto	28
Left Field	Matthew Lugo	28
Center Field	Nelson Rada	23
Right Field	Jo Adell	30
Designated Hitter	Mike Trout	37
No. 1 Starter	Grayson Rodriguez	29
No. 2 Starter	Tyler Bremner	25
No. 3 Starter	Jose Soriano	30
No. 4 Starter	Reid Detmers	29
No. 5 Starter	Caden Dana	25
Closer	Ben Joyce	28

teur scouting director Tim McIlvaine for emphasizing polished, near-MLB ready players in the early rounds of the draft. So far, that has netted modest returns. The Angels have had the first player from each draft reach the majors from 2021-24: Chase Silseth, Neto, Schanuel and Ryan Johnson.

That trend continued in 2025 when the Angels surprised some by drafting Tyler Bremner, an advanced college strike-thrower, at No. 2 overall, then followed suit by drafting potential quick-moving arms Chase Shores and Nate Snead in rounds two and three.

But the 2025 draft also signaled a bit of a philosophical shift after the club signed seven prep pitchers. McIlvaine noted it was the club's first real opportunity in years to take multiple long-term development projects. His previous selections of high school arms Trey Gregory-Alford and Dylan Jordan have paired well with high-upside signings made under international director Brian Parker.

That pairing led to success at the lower levels in 2025. The Angels' Arizona Complex League affiliate won a title and Low-A Inland Empire finished as California League runners-up.

The Angels' system has plenty of arm talent but remains mostly high-variance overall, with several pitchers projecting best in relief and limited position-player upside because of players' questionable pure hitting ability. ■

DEPTH CHART

LOS ANGELES ANGELS

TOP 2026 ROOKIES	RANK
1. Ryan Johnson, RHP	2
2. Denzer Guzman, SS	9
3. Nelson Rada, OF	4

BREAKOUT PROSPECTS	RANK
1. Chase Shores, RHP	13
2. Hayden Alvarez, OF	20

SOURCE OF TOP 30 TALENT

Homegrown	27	Acquired	3
College	7	Trade	3
Junior college	0	Rule 5 draft	0
High school	9	Independent league	0
Undrafted free agent	0	Free agent/waivers	0
International	11		

LF
Joe Redfield Jr.
Dario Laverde
Jorge Ruiz
David Calabrese
Rio Foster

CF
Nelson Rada (4)
Hayden Alvarez (20)
Anthony Scull
TJ Ford

RF
Raudi Rodriguez (21)
Yojancel Cabrera
Randy De Jesus

3B
Gabriel Davalillo (5)
Joswa Lugo (6)
Cole Fontenelle

SS
Denzer Guzman (9)
Yilver De Paula (26)
Capri Ortiz

2B
Adrian Placencia
Felix Morrobel
David Mershon
Nick Rodriguez

1B
Anthony Santa Cruz de Oviedo
Ryland Zaborowski
Jake Munroe

C
Juan Flores (17)
Marlon Quintero (25)

LHP

LHSP
Johnny Slawinski (7)
Talon Haley (11)
Sam Aldegheri (15)
Xavier Mitchell (23)
Mitch Farris (29)
Freddy Hernandez

LHRP
Samy Natera Jr.
Alton Davis II
Leonard Garcia

RHP

RHSP
Tyler Bremner (1)
Ryan Johnson (2)
Dylan Jordan (10)
Barrett Kent (14)
Walbert Ureña (16)
Joel Hurtado (22)
Ubaldo Soto (24)
Peyton Olejnik (27)
Austin Gordon (28)
Luke LaCourse (30)
Dioris De La Rosa
Wilner Berroteran
Ryan Costeiu

RHRP
George Klassen (3)
Trey Gregory-Alford (8)
Chris Cortez (12)
Chase Shores (13)
Nate Snead (18)
CJ Gray (19)
Najer Victor
Jared Southard
Victor Mederos
Keythel Key

LOS ANGELES ANGELS

1 TYLER BREMNER, RHP

Born: April 20, 2004. **B-T:** R-R. **HT:** 6-2. **WT:** 190.
Drafted: UC Santa Barbara, 2025 (1st round).
Signed by: Bo Hughes.

TRACK RECORD: Bremner spent his first two years at UC Santa Barbara as a swingman, with strong performances as a sophomore and in the summer with USA Baseball's Collegiate National Team making him one of the top arms available in the 2025 draft class. Bremner started slowly as a junior, allowing five home runs and posting a 4.24 ERA with a 26% strikeout rate through his first seven starts. He quickly turned the corner and posted a 2.91 ERA with a 44% strikeout rate with no home runs allowed over his next seven starts, including six double-digit strikeout games, helping him become the Gauchos' all-time strikeout leader with 295. Bremner pitched the whole season with the declining health of his mother Jennifer on his mind. She tragically died on June 11 after a five-year battle with breast cancer. One month afterward, Los Angeles drafted Bremner second overall and signed him for 75% of slot value at $7,689,525.

SCOUTING REPORT: Bremner is a lean 6-foot-2, 190-pound righthander with an ideal starter's build and foundation for a midrotation future. He works early counts with his lively fastball that sits 94-96 mph and touches 98. His heater can sink to his arm side at the bottom of the zone and ride when elevated, but it was hit hard by amateur hitters who ambushed it early in counts. There are metric qualities—such as 17 inches of induced vertical break—that indicate it should improve with professional pitch design and not see it be purely a velocity-driven plus pitch. Bremner's mid-80s changeup is a double-plus offering that he can get in and out of jams with, whether by weak contact or swing-and-miss to both righties and lefties. The pitch plays well off his fastball, holding a similar plane with late fade. He can locate it well and will throw it in any count. Bremner's mid-to-upper-80s slider occasionally flashed above-average as an underclassman, but the consistency and feel backed up during his junior year. Improved breaking ball consistency is an early development focus. With a low-effort, repeatable delivery and a three-quarters arm slot, Bremner is a plus strike-thrower who can locate his three-pitch mix, giving more faith to his starter projection. Questions about his durability in college have carried into pro ball, where general soreness precluded him from getting post-draft reps in instructional league.

THE FUTURE: Bremner has all the ingredients to become a midrotation starter. Some outside the organization believe he will be a rotation option in 2026. An argument can be made that a lengthier focus on pitch design and remaining physical projection could maximize his upside. Bremner looks like a staple in the Angels' rotation for the next half-decade or more.

BA GRADE
55 Risk: Average
Adjusted grade: 45

SCOUTING GRADES
FB: 60. **SL:** 50. **CH:** 70. **CTL:** 60.
Projected future grades on 20-80 scouting scale

BEST TOOLS

BATTING
Best Hitter for Average	Nelson Rada
Best Power Hitter	Joswa Lugo
Best Strike-Zone Discipline	Nelson Rada
Fastest Baserunner	Capri Ortiz
Best Athlete	Raudi Rodriguez

PITCHING
Best Fastball	Chris Cortez
Best Curveball	George Klassen
Best Slider	Ryan Johnson
Best Changeup	Tyler Bremner
Best Control	Tyler Bremner

FIELDING
Best Defensive Catcher	Juan Flores
Best Defensive Infielder	Denzer Guzman
Best Infield Arm	Denzer Guzman
Best Defensive Outfielder	Nelson Rada
Best Outfield Arm	Randy de Jesus

Year	Age	Club (League)	Level	W	L	ERA	G	GS	IP	H	HR	BB	SO	BB%	SO%	WHIP	AVG
2025	21	Did not play															

LOS ANGELES ANGELS

2 RYAN JOHNSON, RHP
FB: 55. **CB:** 40. **SL:** 60. **CH:** 45. **CT:** 60. **CTL:** 60. **BA Grade:** 50. **Risk:** Mild. **Adj:** 45.

Born: August 5, 2002. **B-T:** B-R. **HT:** 6-6. **WT:** 215.
Drafted: Dallas Baptist, 2024 (2nd round). **Signed by:** K.J. Hendricks.
TRACK RECORD: As a Dallas Baptist junior, Johnson set the school's single-season (151) and career (341) strikeout records. The Angels drafted him in 2024, using the compensatory second-round pick gained from Shohei Ohtani's free agent departure. Johnson broke camp with the Angels in 2025 to become the 24th player in history to make the jump from the draft to MLB without spending a day in the minor leagues. His big league stint ended after 14 relief appearances. He landed at High-A Tri-City, where he was stellar before arm fatigue ended his season in August.
SCOUTING REPORT: Johnson is a 6-foot-6 righthander with a swing-and-miss arsenal and unorthodox mechanics. He starts his delivery with a truncated overhead windup with a sidestep before going into a short, slinging arm action from a low three-quarters slot, finishing with violence. The high effort has not diminished his control and creates deception for his five-pitch arsenal. Johnson works primarily off his plus, low-90s sweeper/cutter. He can manipulate the shape and velocity of the pitch and locate it for strikes in any count. His fastball peaks at 99 mph and sits 93-94 as a starter—and a tick higher in relief—with plus armside run. It tunnels with his slider to give him an east-west profile. Johnson will incorporate an upper-70s curveball and mid-80s split changeup to lefthanders, but both are fringe-average at best. His starter chances hinge on whether he can repeat his herky-jerky mechanics over extended outings.
THE FUTURE: Johnson will continue developing as a starter, with a late-inning relief role serving as a fallback option. Future role questions introduce variance, but there is little doubt that he can become an impact arm in some capacity.

Year	Age	Club (League)	Level	W	L	ERA	G	GS	IP	H	HR	BB	SO	BB%	SO%	WHIP	AVG
2025	22	Tri-City (NWL)	A+	4	3	1.88	12	12	57	41	3	10	65	4.6	29.7	0.89	.196
2025	22	Los Angeles (AL)	MLB	1	1	7.36	14	0	15	24	4	5	16	6.9	22.2	1.98	.364
		Minor League Totals		4	3	1.88	12	12	57	41	3	10	65	4.6	29.7	0.89	.196
		Major League Totals		1	1	7.36	14	0	15	24	4	5	16	6.9	22.2	1.98	.364

3 GEORGE KLASSEN, RHP
FB: 70. **CB:** 55. **SL:** 60. **CH:** 40. **CTL:** 45. **BA Grade:** 55. **Risk:** High. **Adj:** 40.

Born: January 26, 2002. **B-T:** R-R. **HT:** 6-2. **WT:** 195.
Drafted: Minnesota, 2023 (6th round). **Signed by:** Derrick Ross (Phillies).
TRACK RECORD: Klassen missed his freshman year at Minnesota after having Tommy John surgery and pitched sparingly until cracking the Golden Gophers' rotation as a junior in 2023. He struggled to throw strikes, but the Phillies took a flier on his alluring arsenal in the sixth round and helped him make colossal strike-throwing improvements in 2024, when he had a 1.97 ERA and 38% strikeout rate across two Class A stops before being dealt to the Angels at the trade deadline with Sam Aldegheri for Carlos Estevez. Klassen was hit around with Double-A Rocket City in 2025 and missed time after being hit in the head by a comebacker but continued his strike-throwing progression and ended the year with a solid outing for Triple-A Salt Lake.
SCOUTING REPORT: Klassen is a lean, athletic 6-foot-2 righthander with an electric arsenal and midrotation upside after making substantial strides with his mechanics and control. With elite arm speed, Klassen's four-seam and two-seam fastballs sit 97-98 mph and peak at 101 with solid late life. He added a knockout upper-80s slider to his arsenal to contrast the velocity of his mid-80s power curveball. Both breaking pitches have similar depth and sweep, but he commands and relies on his slider more heavily, and can manipulate its break into a cutter-esque shape. Klassen has a well below-average upper-80s changeup he rarely uses. The Phillies helped simplify his delivery to create more stability, eliminate some crossfire and clean up his arm path, which improved his control substantially. The Angels continued to improve his control by lessening the effort in his delivery, though his command is still below-average.
THE FUTURE: Klassen will have a chance to crack the Angels' rotation out of spring training. To do so, he must improve his command. His trio of plus offerings gives him a fallback option of high-leverage relief.

Year	Age	Club (League)	Level	W	L	ERA	G	GS	IP	H	HR	BB	SO	BB%	SO%	WHIP	AVG
2025	23	Rocket City (SL)	AA	4	12	5.35	24	24	103	106	8	46	126	10.0	27.4	1.48	.264
2025	23	Salt Lake (PCL)	AAA	0	0	3.00	1	1	6	6	0	1	8	4.2	33.3	1.17	.261
		Minor League Totals		10	17	4.24	47	47	202	176	13	93	269	10.7	31.0	1.33	.233

LOS ANGELES ANGELS

4 NELSON RADA, OF

HIT: 60. **POW:** 30. **RUN:** 60. **FLD:** 60. **ARM:** 50. **BA Grade:** 50. **Risk:** Average. **Adj:** 40.

Born: August 24, 2005. **B-T:** L-L. **HT:** 5-9. **WT:** 185.
Signed: Venezuela, 2022. **Signed by:** Marlon Urdaneta/Joel Chicarelli.
TRACK RECORD: Rada signed with the Angels for $1.85 million in 2022 and has been fast-tracked through the system. After Rada's stellar performance with Low-A Inland Empire as the youngest player on any full-season Opening Day roster in 2023, the Angels skipped him over High-A and direct to Double-A Rocket City in 2024 as an 18-year-old. He was predictably overmatched by older competition. After returning to Rocket City in 2025, Rada found his footing offensively and earned a promotion to Triple-A Salt Lake prior to his 20th birthday in August. He posted an identical 122 wRC+ at both Double-A and Triple-A.
SCOUTING REPORT: Rada is a high-contact, lefthanded outfielder with everyday, table-setting upside. His innate bat-to-ball skills allow him to make contact to all fields with a tendency for going the other way. A highly selective hitter who controls the zone with plus swing decisions, Rada rarely swings and misses but can be beat on the inner half, something that improved over the past year as he was more connected and athletic in the box. Still maturing physically, his stocky 5-foot-9 frame creates a split camp on how much over-the-fence power projection remains. Most of his slugging results from hard hits to the gaps and down the lines. Even his strongest supporters project only fringe-average power. With above-average speed, Rada's instinctual baserunning gives him a plus run tool and makes him a basestealing nuisance. In center field, he makes advanced reads with a smooth glove, making him a future impact defender at a premium position.
THE FUTURE: Rada is on track to see the big leagues as a 20-year-old in 2026. His speed, contact and defense give him everyday potential, though his lack of power limits his overall upside.

Year	Age	Club (League)	Level	AVG	G	AB	R	H	2B	3B	HR	RBI	BB	SO	SB	OBP	SLG
2025	19	Rocket City (SL)	AA	.277	93	328	48	91	13	1	1	22	45	82	34	.380	.332
2025	19	Salt Lake (PCL)	AAA	.323	42	161	33	52	6	3	1	17	30	35	20	.433	.416
		Minor League Totals		.273	423	1520	278	415	56	13	6	144	231	358	171	.384	.339

5 GABRIEL DAVALILLO, C/3B

HIT: 50. **POW:** 55. **RUN:** 30. **FLD:** 40. **ARM:** 50. **BA Grade:** 50. **Risk:** High. **Adj:** 35.

Born: November 6, 2007. **B-T:** R-R. **HT:** 5-11. **WT:** 210.
Signed: Venezuela, 2025. **Signed by:** Marlon Urdaneta/Joel Chicarelli.
TRACK RECORD: Davalillo is a member of a multi-generational Venezuelan baseball family. He and his older brother David, a Rangers pitching prospect, are the sons of David Davalillo Sr., a former professional infielder and long-time coach in the Mets organization. Their grandfather is Vic Davalillo, a 16-year big league outfielder who played in the 1960s and '70s. Arguably the top catcher available in the 2025 international signing period, Gabriel signed with the Angels for $2 million. During his pro debut in the Dominican Summer League, he slashed .314/.415/.554 with seven home runs and more walks (19) than strikeouts (14) in 41 games.
SCOUTING REPORT: Davalillo is a bat-first catcher with immense power projection. He has a mature body at 5-foot-11, 210 pounds and has gained concerning weight since signing. With the frame comes strength that produces all-fields home run power from the right side. With his natural strength and damage-minded swing, Davalillo can turn even mis-hits into home runs. His swing can get erratic at times, but that has not diminished his ability to make contact. His approach has yet to be tested by advanced pitchers, but his ability to stay in the zone and limit swing-and-miss give him a well-rounded offensive profile. Behind the plate, Davalillo needs plenty of work on blocking and receiving. He has plus arm strength, but the length in his transfer makes his arm fringy at best. Despite his weight gains, he remains a fair athlete who tried third base during instructional league and showed good footwork and promising initial returns. He will split time between catching and third base in 2026.
THE FUTURE: Davalillo has immense batting upside but will have to control his conditioning and improve behind the plate. He will make his stateside debut in 2026.

Year	Age	Club (League)	Level	AVG	G	AB	R	H	2B	3B	HR	RBI	BB	SO	SB	OBP	SLG
2025	17	DSL Angels	Rk	.302	41	139	28	42	7	1	7	31	23	21	3	.408	.518
		Minor League Totals		.302	41	139	28	42	7	1	7	31	23	21	3	.408	.518

LOS ANGELES ANGELS

6 JOSWA LUGO, SS
HIT: 45. **POW:** 55. **RUN:** 50. **FLD:** 50. **ARM:** 55. **BA Grade:** 55. **Risk:** Extreme. **Adj:** 35.

Born: January 24, 2007. **B-T:** R-R. **HT:** 6-3. **WT:** 187.
Signed: Dominican Republic, 2024. **Signed by:** Frank Tejeda.
TRACK RECORD: The younger brother of Dawel Lugo, who played parts of three seasons with the Tigers from 2018 to 2020, Joswa signed with the Angels for $2.3 million as the headliner of their 2024 international class. It's the second-highest bonus in club history for an international amateur player, trailing only Roberto Baldoquin's $8 million in 2014. Lugo showed his offensive upside in his 2024 pro debut in the Dominican Summer League, hitting .301 with an .836 OPS and helping lead his club to the DSL championship. In his 2025 stateside debut, he produced a .271/.375/.372 slash line in 35 games before his season was halted with a back strain.
SCOUTING REPORT: Lugo is a physical, righthanded-hitting infielder with exceptional power upside. Balanced and synced through his swing, he handles the barrel well and displays plus raw power and elite exit velocities—north of 112 mph—that portend above-average power because of his high-end bat speed and barrel control. Lugo will have to overhaul his pitch recognition and exercise swing restraint. He too often gets in swing mode, which leads to weak contact and concerning swing-and-miss, particularly on secondaries. If he can refine his aggression, he has a solid all-fields contact and power baseline befitting of a middle-of-the-order hitter. Defensively, Lugo has good body control and instincts with an above-average arm that should keep him on the left side of the infield. Physical gains to his 6-foot-3 frame may slow down his middling speed and athleticism, moving him off shortstop and to third base.
THE FUTURE: Lugo has middle-of-the-order upside but will have to improve his pitch selection to become an impact power hitter. The extent of his physical maturation will dictate his future defensive home. He will get his first taste of playing at a full-season affiliate in 2026.

Year	Age	Club (League)	Level	AVG	G	AB	R	H	2B	3B	HR	RBI	BB	SO	SB	OBP	SLG
2025	18	ACL Angels	Rk	.271	35	129	19	35	7	0	2	23	19	40	1	.375	.372
		Minor League Totals		.289	88	322	50	93	18	3	7	60	36	91	19	.372	.429

7 JOHNNY SLAWINSKI, LHP
FB: 55. **CB:** 45. **SL:** 50. **CH:** 50. **CTL:** 55. **BA Grade:** 50. **Risk:** High. **Adj:** 35.

Born: February 26, 2007. **B-T:** L-L. **HT:** 6-3. **WT:** 180.
Drafted: HS—Johnson City, TX, 2025 (3rd round). **Signed by:** Kevin Ellis.
TRACK RECORD: Slawinski was a four-sport star for small-town Lyndon B. Johnson High in Texas, playing football, basketball, track and field and baseball. Seeing an uptick in velocity, he struck out 177 batters his senior year—second-best in the nation—while allowing four runs in 75 innings. His pitching talents made him one of the better lefthanders in the 2025 draft class, and the Angels took him in the third round, luring him away from a Texas A&M commitment with a bonus of $2,497,500, on par with late first-round slot values.
SCOUTING REPORT: Slawinski is an athletic 6-foot-3 lefthander with rotation upside. As a prep senior, he went from sitting in the upper 80s to now sitting 90-93 mph and touching 95 with solid riding action. He throws a pair of breaking pitches: a low-80s, two-plane slider that gained bite and power his senior year and flashes above-average, and a fringy curveball that is slower and loopier. Slawinski has some feel for a low-80s changeup with notable fading action. His full arsenal—particularly his fastball—plays up due to his ability to mix and locate with ease. As he matures physically, Slawinski should be able to sustain his velocity and gain more mechanical consistency in his drop-and-drive delivery. He has all the ingredients and foundation to dream on a pitchability rotation arm. He is praised for his makeup and competitiveness.
THE FUTURE: Slawinski has a high ceiling by nature of being lefthanded and showing feel to locate a four-pitch arsenal at a young age. The ingredients are ripe for a back-end rotation arm, while improvements to his secondaries could raise his stock to a midrotation future. He'll make his pro debut in 2026 in the low minors.

Year	Age	Club (League)	Level	W	L	ERA	G	GS	IP	H	HR	BB	SO	BB%	SO%	WHIP	AVG
2025	18	Did not play															

LOS ANGELES ANGELS

8 TREY GREGORY-ALFORD, RHP
FB: 65. **CB:** 40. **SL:** 60. **CH:** 30. **CTL:** 45. **BA Grade:** 50. **Risk:** High. **Adj:** 35.

Born: May 4, 2006. **B-T:** R-R. **HT:** 6-5. **WT:** 235.
Drafted: HS—Colorado Springs, CO, 2024 (11th round). **Signed by:** Jayson Durocher.
TRACK RECORD: Gregory-Alford carried a strong summer showcase circuit and performance for USA Baseball's 18U National Team into a solid spring at Coronado High in Colorado Springs in 2024. Then he touched 99.7 mph at the MLB Draft Combine. The Angels monitored his progress, never missing a start, and signed him to a $1,957,500 bonus—a record for an 11th-round pick—to lure him away from Virginia. Gregory-Alford had a stellar pro debut in 2025, pitching to a 2.86 ERA over 78.2 innings between the Arizona Complex League and Low-A California League and helping both teams to their championship series.
SCOUTING REPORT: Gregory-Alford is a physical 6-foot-5 righthander with elite arm strength and arm speed. He works primarily off his fastball that sits 94-98 mph and touches 101. It gets on hitters in a hurry due to solid extension and the angle he creates, though it has limited life and doesn't miss as many bats as expected from that type of velocity. Gregory-Alford complements his heater with a hard, mid-80s slider that can miss bats in and out of the zone and flashes plus. He will use a curveball as change-of-pace offering and sparingly throws a dead-action changeup that sits 89-94 mph, though both lag well behind his slider as fringy or below-average secondaries. Gregory-Alford has a low-effort delivery but can rush his quick-tempo mechanics, leading to erratic strike-throwing. He'll have to find a true third offering and better fastball shape to profile as more than a power reliever, but he has size and velocity with ease rarely seen from a teenager.
THE FUTURE: Gregory-Alford has the kind of velocity typical of big leaguers, but he will need to find a true third pitch and improve his control to tap into his upside and be more than a power-armed reliever.

Year	Age	Club (League)	Level	W	L	ERA	G	GS	IP	H	HR	BB	SO	BB%	SO%	WHIP	AVG
2025	19	ACL Angels	Rk	4	4	3.54	12	10	53	53	2	20	48	8.9	21.4	1.37	.266
2025	19	Inland Empire (CAL)	A	1	0	1.42	6	6	25	16	0	13	20	12.4	19.0	1.14	.180
		Minor League Totals		5	4	2.86	18	16	79	69	2	33	68	10.0	20.7	1.30	.240

9 DENZER GUZMAN, SS/3B
HIT: 40. **POW:** 50. **RUN:** 45. **FLD:** 55. **ARM:** 60. **BA Grade:** 50. **Risk:** High. **Adj:** 35.

Born: February 8, 2004. **B-T:** R-R. **HT:** 6-1. **WT:** 190.
Drafted: Dominican Republic, 2021. **Signed by:** Domingo Garcia.
TRACK RECORD: Guzman signed with the Angels for $2 million out of the Dominican Republic in January 2021 and hit well in Rookie ball before scuffling at full-season affiliates, hitting .232 with a .649 OPS and 27.8% strikeout rate across three levels in 2023 and 2024. Guzman began tapping into his power in 2025 while cutting down his strikeouts, posting a 119 wRC+ with 17 home runs between Double-A Rocket City and Triple-A Salt Lake. The Angels moved him from shortstop to third base to better suit the big league club and called him up on Sept. 13.
SCOUTING REPORT: Guzman is a glove-first shortstop with power projection. His swing is geared for pull-side damage but can get long and grooved uphill, leading to swing-and-miss tendencies. He handles fastballs well, with his biggest hurdles coming on swing decisions and barrel adjustments on offspeeds from righthanders. Discipline on breaking pitches and in-zone contact will dictate how often Guzman can tap into his above-average raw power. He is a fringe-average runner who is better underway than in quick bursts, limiting his ability to steal bases. Because he has maintained his athleticism and agility as he's matured, Guzman is an above-average shortstop defender with the cadence and rhythm for the position. He shows ease on the backhand play and solid range up the middle, supported by a plus arm. He added third base to enhance his versatility and embellish the Angels' depth chart.
THE FUTURE: Guzman has the floor of a utility infielder because of his glove and power, while improvements to his hit tool and discipline could turn him into a bottom-of-the-lineup regular. He will have a chance to break camp as the Angels' starting third baseman out of spring training in 2026.

Year	Age	Club (League)	Level	AVG	G	AB	R	H	2B	3B	HR	RBI	BB	SO	SB	OBP	SLG
2025	21	Rocket City (SL)	AA	.242	93	335	39	81	23	1	11	53	41	92	8	.334	.415
2025	21	Salt Lake (PCL)	AAA	.262	36	130	26	34	7	0	6	21	21	45	6	.366	.454
2025	21	Los Angeles (AL)	MLB	.190	13	42	4	8	1	0	2	3	1	22	0	.209	.357
		Minor League Totals		.241	443	1616	226	389	84	14	36	223	185	464	47	.323	.377
		Major League Totals		.190	13	42	4	8	1	0	2	3	1	22	0	.209	.357

LOS ANGELES ANGELS

10 DYLAN JORDAN, RHP
FB: 60. **CH:** 45. **SW:** 55. **CTL:** 50. **BA Grade:** 45. **Risk:** Average. **Adj:** 35.

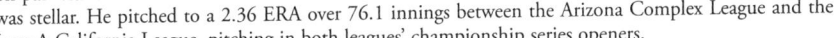

Born: October 15, 2005. **B-T:** R-R. **HT:** 6-3. **WT:** 205.
Drafted: HS—Melbourne, FL, 2024 (5th round). **Signed by:** Luis Raffan.
TRACK RECORD: Jordan was a regular on the summer showcase circuit as a prep and elevated his draft stock during his senior year by boosting his velocity while leading Viera High to a Florida district title. The Angels were bullish on his size and projection and drafted him in the fifth round in 2024. They signed him away from a Florida State commitment with a $1.25 million bonus on par with slot values late in the second round. Jordan's pro debut in 2025 was stellar. He pitched to a 2.36 ERA over 76.1 innings between the Arizona Complex League and the Low-A California League, pitching in both leagues' championship series openers.
SCOUTING REPORT: Jordan is a 6-foot-3, 205-pound righthander with a drop-and-drive delivery and slingy, low three-quarters arm slot. His plus extension down the mound gives him an effective sinker/slider combo. His fastball sits 91-94 mph and touches 96 with more than 16 inches of run when operating as a sinker in the lower quadrants. Jordan's low-80s sweeper flashes above-average and plays well off his fastball, staying on a heater plane before snapping off to his glove side. He has solid command and attacks the zone with both pitches, with most misses being by small margins. Jordan has a rudimentary changeup that projects as a passable third option, with fair fade to his arm side to keep lefthanded hitters honest. Both of Jordan's secondaries flash promise, though both need more consistency. As he continues maturing physically, he should be able to maintain velocity and mechanical consistency throughout workloads and reach his workhorse starter projection. He is praised for his competitive makeup.
THE FUTURE: Jordan needs to fine-tune his secondaries but has the foundation of a back-of-the-rotation sinker/sweeper starter.

Year	Age	Club (League)	Level	W	L	ERA	G	GS	IP	H	HR	BB	SO	BB%	SO%	WHIP	AVG
2025	19	ACL Angels	Rk	2	1	3.21	12	12	48	44	3	21	55	10.0	26.3	1.36	.239
2025	19	Inland Empire (CAL)	A	2	0	0.94	7	7	29	19	0	9	30	8.3	27.5	0.98	.198
		Minor League Totals		4	1	2.36	19	19	76	63	3	30	85	9.4	26.7	1.22	.225

11 TALON HALEY, LHP
FB: 55. **CB:** 60. **SL:** 50. **CH:** 50. **CTL:** 50. **BA Grade:** 55. **Risk:** Extreme. **Adj:** 35.

Born: January 22, 2006. **B-T:** R-L. **HT:** 6-2. **WT:** 200. **Drafted:** HS—Olive Branch, MS, 2025 (12th round).
Signed by: Joel Murrie.
TRACK RECORD: Haley's path to pro baseball has been defined by adversity. He had Tommy John surgery prior to his high school career, then was diagnosed with non-Hodgkin's lymphoma after recovering. He learned to throw righthanded so he could pitch while receiving chemotherapy treatment and was declared cancer-free in August 2022. He tore his left UCL again in 2024 and had internal brace surgery. Fully healthy in 2025, Haley broke out during his senior spring at Lewisburg High in Mississippi. The Angels selected him in the 12th round and signed him for just under $900,000—roughly third-round money—to buy him out of a Vanderbilt commitment.
SCOUTING REPORT: Haley is an athletic, projectable lefthander with an exciting four-pitch mix. His 91-94 mph fastball touches 97 with plus riding life. He can spin a pair of breaking balls led by an upper-70s hammer curve that flashes plus. His low-80s two-plane slider also shows potential, though it can blend with his curve and diminish the effectiveness of both, forcing him to rely more on his fastball. Haley's low-80s changeup is a serviceable kill-spin weapon and may become his best secondary, though he didn't use it much as an amateur. Haley gets down the mound exceptionally well with an athletic delivery and has shown feel for mixing and locating. The Angels hope to help Haley refine the rhythm and tempo of his delivery so it becomes less violent.
THE FUTURE: Haley has one of baseball's best human-interest stories, but his medical history creates extreme variance. He has considerable upside if he can remain healthy.

Year	Age	Club (League)	Level	W	L	ERA	G	GS	IP	H	HR	BB	SO	BB%	SO%	WHIP	AVG
2025	19	Did not play															

LOS ANGELES ANGELS

12 CHRIS CORTEZ, RHP
FB: 70. **SL:** 60. **CH:** 40. **CTL:** 30. **BA Grade:** 45. **Risk:** Average. **Adj:** 35.

Born: October 6, 2002. **B-T:** R-R. **HT:** 6-1. **WT:** 205. **Drafted:** Texas A&M, 2024 (2nd round). **Signed by:** Kevin Ellis.
TRACK RECORD: Cortez split time between the rotation and bullpen over three years at Texas A&M before settling into a multi-inning, high-leverage relief role as a junior. He posted a 2.78 ERA and 36.7% strikeout rate over 62.2 innings, helping the Aggies reach the College World Series final. The Angels selected him 45th overall in 2024 and signed him to an under-slot bonus just shy of $1.6 million. Cortez spent his pro debut in 2025 with High-A Tri-City, logging 113.2 innings across 26 starts with a 4.28 ERA and an alarming 16.4% walk rate.
SCOUTING REPORT: Cortez is a power-armed righthander with an electric sinker-slider combination. His plus-plus sinker averages 98 mph and touches 101 with 17 inches of horizontal break, busting righthanded bats on the inner half and flying away from lefthanded hitters. He counters his sinker with a hard, swing-and-miss slider that he can manipulate from a mid-80s vertical breaker to an 87-91 mph horizontal secondary with more sweep and cutting action. He'll need a more consistent release and feel for his breaker for it to become a plus weapon. Cortez rarely uses his mid-80s changeup. His plus arm speed and low-effort delivery helps him easily access powerful velocity and hold it throughout outings, but he is a below-average strike-thrower likely destined for the bullpen.
THE FUTURE: The Angels will continue developing Cortez as a starter despite below-average control. If he moves to relief, his powerful sinker/slider combination could allow him to move quickly with high-leverage upside.

Year	Age	Club (League)	Level	W	L	ERA	G	GS	IP	H	HR	BB	SO	BB%	SO%	WHIP	AVG
2025	22	Tri-City (NWL)	A+	3	8	4.28	26	26	114	94	5	84	114	16.6	22.2	1.57	.224
		Minor League Totals		3	8	4.28	26	26	114	94	5	84	114	16.6	22.2	1.57	.224

13 CHASE SHORES, RHP
FB: 65. **SL:** 55. **CH:** 45. **CTL:** 40. **BA Grade:** 50. **Risk:** High. **Adj:** 35.

Born: May 21, 2004. **B-T:** R-R. **HT:** 6-8. **WT:** 245. **Drafted:** LSU, 2025 (2nd round). **Signed by:** Kevin Ellis.
TRACK RECORD: Shores was a touted prep arm who made it to campus at LSU and made immediate contributions as a freshman before an elbow injury forced Tommy John surgery in April 2023 and sidelined him through 2024. He returned to the Tigers' rotation to open his junior year, though his most meaningful production came in relief. Shores finished the season with 2.2 scoreless innings to help LSU clinch the College World Series title. The Angels drafted him 47th overall in 2025 and signed him for full slot value at $2,077,200.
SCOUTING REPORT: Shores is a massive 6-foot-8 righthander with a power arsenal. His fastball averages just over 97 mph and can touch 102 with a fair amount of armside run. It's more of a velocity-driven pitch right now that may need better life to induce more swings and misses. His best secondary is a hard, high-spin slider that flashes plus in the upper 80s as a gyro-style breaker that darts under the zone, though he can manipulate its shape and power to become more of an 87-91 mph sweeper. Shores' upper-80s changeup is a distant third offering. A good athlete with some remaining projection, he works from a low three-quarters slot with the mechanical markers to give him a shot as a starter, though his below-average control makes it more likely he ends up in relief.
THE FUTURE: Shores' special arm talent and athleticism will give him every opportunity to develop as a starter. His power arsenal could ultimately work best in high-leverage situations.

Year	Age	Club (League)	Level	W	L	ERA	G	GS	IP	H	HR	BB	SO	BB%	SO%	WHIP	AVG
2025	21	Did not play															

14 BARRETT KENT, RHP
FB: 55. **CB:** 45. **SL:** 55. **CH:** 45. **CTL:** 45. **BA Grade:** 50. **Risk:** High. **Adj:** 35.

Born: September 29, 2004. **B-T:** R-R. **HT:** 6-4. **WT:** 215. **Drafted:** HS—Pottsboro, TX, 2023 (8th round). **Signed by:** K.J. Hendricks.
TRACK RECORD: Kent stood out on the summer showcase circuit, but his velocity and performance wavered during the spring of 2023. The Angels were undeterred, especially after an impressive private workout, and signed him for $997,500 in the eighth round to forgo an Arkansas commitment. He threw 113 innings for Low-A Inland Empire as a 19-year-old in 2024. Nagging elbow injuries limited most of his 2025 campaign and required Tommy John surgery in September.
SCOUTING REPORT: Kent is a projectable 6-foot-4 righthander with starter traits. He works primarily off a 93-96 mph fastball that touches 98 with some carry. Prior to elbow surgery, strength and conditioning

LOS ANGELES ANGELS

gains helped Kent better hold his velocity throughout starts. His mid-80s slider flashes above-average shape and two-plane action, tunneling well with his fastball. Kent has decent feel for a mid-80s changeup, but he'll need to sell it better for it to become at least an average offering. He also mixes in a sparsely-used low-80s downer curveball as a change-of-pace offering. Kent's delivery works downhill and he is generally around the zone, especially to his arm side, but will need to improve his command within the strike zone. So far he has posted fringy walk rates as a professional, though his loose arm and repeatable delivery create optimism that he can make some strides with his control.
THE FUTURE: He'll miss all of 2026 because of elbow surgery, but Kent's athleticism and arsenal provide a midrotation ceiling when he gets back on the mound.

Year	Age	Club (League)	Level	W	L	ERA	G	GS	IP	H	HR	BB	SO	BB%	SO%	WHIP	AVG
2025	20	ACL Angels	Rk	0	0	2.25	4	3	8	8	0	5	9	15.2	27.3	1.63	.286
2025	20	Inland Empire (CAL)	A	1	0	1.98	6	6	27	24	1	16	22	13.3	18.3	1.46	.231
		Minor League Totals		4	14	4.93	39	36	157	148	14	86	166	12.2	23.6	1.49	.247

15 SAM ALDEGHERI, LHP
FB: 50. **CB:** 45. **SL:** 55. **CH:** 50. **CTL:** 45. **BA Grade:** 45. **Risk:** Average. **Adj:** 35.

Born: September 19, 2001. **B-T:** L-L. **HT:** 6-1. **WT:** 210. **Signed:** Italy, 2019. **Signed by:** Claudio Scerrato (Phillies).
TRACK RECORD: Aldegheri signed with the Phillies out of Italy for $210,000 in 2019, but the early years of his pro career were interrupted by the pandemic as well as back and shoulder injuries. He finally broke out in 2024, prompting the Angels to acquire him alongside George Klassen at the trade deadline in a deal for Carlos Estevez. That same summer, he became the first Italian born-and-raised pitcher to appear in the majors, debuting on Aug. 30, 2024. Aldegheri's stuff backed up in 2025. He made four big league appearances, but otherwise spent most of the year at Double-A Rocket City, where he finished strong with a 2.30 ERA over his final nine starts.
SCOUTING REPORT: Aldegheri is a pitchability lefthander with an average arsenal. His velocity dipped at times in 2025, but at its best his four-seamer averages 92 mph and can touch 96. The pitch gets on hitters quickly due to 16-17 inches of induced vertical break, though it generated below-average whiff rates overall. His above-average low-80s slider is his primary swing-and-miss secondary. Aldegheri steals strikes and changes pace with his mid-70s curveball and his low-80s changeup has become effective against righthanded batters. Aldegheri generally locates his four-pitch mix well, though his command backed up in 2025 before rebounding late in the season.
THE FUTURE: Aldegheri's pitchability and floor will give him a chance to crack the Angels' rotation in 2026. To reach his back-end starter ceiling, he'll need to prove his late-season progress wasn't a fluke.

Year	Age	Club (League)	Level	W	L	ERA	G	GS	IP	H	HR	BB	SO	BB%	SO%	WHIP	AVG
2025	23	Rocket City (SL)	AA	8	8	3.72	23	23	128	116	12	58	110	10.5	19.9	1.36	.240
2025	23	Salt Lake (PCL)	AAA	0	0	5.40	1	1	5	5	1	2	3	8.3	12.5	1.40	.250
2025	23	Los Angeles (AL)	MLB	0	2	7.90	4	2	14	20	3	10	12	13.7	16.4	2.20	.345
		Minor League Totals		19	19	3.67	79	69	346	294	25	153	395	10.3	26.6	1.29	.226
		Major League Totals		0	2	7.90	4	2	14	20	3	10	12	13.7	16.4	2.20	.345

16 WALBERT UREÑA, RHP
FB: 60. **SL:** 45. **CH:** 55. **CTL:** 40. **BA Grade:** 50. **Risk:** High. **Adj:** 35.

Born: January 25, 2004. **B-T:** R-R. **HT:** 6-0. **WT:** 210. **Signed:** Dominican Republic, 2021. **Signed by:** Jochy Cabrera.
TRACK RECORD: Ureña signed for $140,000 in 2021 out of the Dominican Republic, but arm issues delayed his pro debut to the following year, where he was up to 100 mph in the Arizona Complex League. He then jumped on a level-per-year trajectory that landed him in Double-A Rocket City in 2025. Ureña logged a 4.39 ERA over 135.1 innings at 21 years old and ended the season with a 10-strikeout cameo at Triple-A. The Angels added him to the 40-man roster in November to protect him from the Rule 5 draft.
SCOUTING REPORT: Ureña is an undersized 6-foot righthander with special arm strength and velocity. His 95-99 mph fastball touches 102 with good sinking action and he has racked up high groundball rates since converting to a two-seam grip late in 2023. Ureña is nearing physical maturation but could likely sit in the triple digits in short stints. He has experimented with multiple breaking ball grips in pursuit of a truer breaker that can better neutralize lefthanded batters on the inner half. He settled on a mid-80s cut-slider in 2025. Ureña's mid- to upper-80s changeup has solid fade, flashes plus and was his most-used secondary in 2025. His simple, repeatable delivery allows him to access his premium velocity with ease, albeit with a scattered release point that causes control issues.
THE FUTURE: Entering his age-22 season, Ureña needs to improve his breaking ball and feel to tap into his high-upside starter ceiling. Otherwise, his power sinker and fringy control is well-suited for an impact relief role.

Year	Age	Club (League)	Level	W	L	ERA	G	GS	IP	H	HR	BB	SO	BB%	SO%	WHIP	AVG
2025	21	Rocket City (SL)	AA	6	9	4.39	27	27	135	115	8	70	115	12.1	19.8	1.37	.231
2025	21	Salt Lake (PCL)	AAA	0	0	3.18	1	1	6	4	0	3	10	12.5	41.7	1.24	.190
		Minor League Totals		15	27	4.62	78	75	354	304	18	219	331	14.0	21.1	1.48	.233

17 JUAN FLORES, C

HIT: 30. **POW:** 45. **RUN:** 30. **FLD:** 60. **ARM:** 70. **BA Grade:** 45. **Risk:** Average. **Adj:** 35.

Born: February 13, 2006. **B-T:** R-R. **HT:** 5-10. **WT:** 215. **Signed:** Venezuela, 2023. **Signed by:** Vicente Lupo.
TRACK RECORD: Flores signed with the Angels for $280,000 as one of the best defensive catchers in the 2023 international class. The Angels promoted him aggressively and he reached High-A Tri-City in 2024 at 18 years old, but his offensive success stalled. Flores returned to Tri-City in 2025 and had a .475 OPS through June before finding an offensive groove with a .780 OPS over his final two months with Tri-City, which he carried over to the Arizona Fall League.
SCOUTING REPORT: A glove-first catcher, Flores has a short, sturdy build. He struggles to sync up his righthanded swing, which can get upper-body dominant and cause him to swing over pitches. He made mechanical adjustments in 2025 to help elevate the ball more consistently, and when he stays on plane his natural strength produces pull-side damage with at least average raw power. Flores handles velocity fine, but his aggressive approach led to concerning chase rates against secondaries and likely caps him as a bottom-of-the-order hitter. His glove is his calling card. Flores has plus arm strength, a quick transfer and regularly posts sub-1.9-second pop times on throws to second base. His athleticism shows up in his solid lateral mobility behind the plate, and he can pick anything in the dirt like an infielder. His receiving and game-calling continue to improve.
THE FUTURE: Flores is a future impact defender, and his glove provides an opportunity for him to become a big league backup. He'll need to hit more to become a second-division regular. He turns 20 in February and is ready for the upper minors.

Year	Age	Club (League)	Level	AVG	G	AB	R	H	2B	3B	HR	RBI	BB	SO	SB	OBP	SLG
2025	19	Tri-City (NWL)	A+	.207	89	305	38	63	11	0	10	40	18	94	0	.283	.341
		Minor League Totals		.233	236	844	119	197	45	1	21	118	57	217	10	.310	.364

18 NATE SNEAD, RHP

FB: 60. **CB:** 55. **SL:** 45. **CH:** 40. **CT:** 50. **CTL:** 45. **BA Grade:** 40. **Risk:** Mild. **Adj:** 35.

Born: March 16, 2004. **B-T:** R-R. **HT:** 6-2. **WT:** 215. **Drafted:** Tennessee, 2025 (3rd round supp.). **Signed by:** Joel Murrie.
TRACK RECORD: Snead transferred to Tennessee in 2024 following a solid freshman campaign at Wichita State and quickly became one of the nation's most reliable relievers. Over his two years in the Vols' bullpen, he pitched to a 3.67 ERA over 75 innings with 11 saves. The Angels selected him with a supplemental third-round pick in 2025, signing him under slot for $597,500.
SCOUTING REPORT: Snead is a 6-foot-2, 215-pound power arm with a five-pitch arsenal. He relies heavily on his 96-97 mph fastball that can touch 101. The pitch has some late sink from his low three-quarter slinging arm slot that helps generate plenty of groundballs. Snead has a tight, mid-80s slider and a low-90s cutter that touches 94. Both flash average but are inconsistent and can blend together. The quality of his slider regressed as he increased the usage of the cutter. Snead's low-80s curveball is his best swing-and-miss secondary, and he rarely uses his hard changeup. Snead was a fringy strike-thrower in college, though some scouts think his athleticism and makeup give him a chance to start.
THE FUTURE: The Angels plan to develop Snead as a starter, but his scattered strikes and big-time fastball make him a prime candidate to move quickly if he moves to the bullpen.

Year	Age	Club (League)	Level	W	L	ERA	G	GS	IP	H	HR	BB	SO	BB%	SO%	WHIP	AVG
2025	21	Did not play															

19 CJ GRAY, RHP

FB: 60. **SL:** 55. **CH:** 50. **CTL:** 40. **BA Grade:** 50. **Risk:** Extreme. **Adj:** 30.

Born: January 25, 2007. **B-T:** R-R. **HT:** 6-2. **WT:** 205. **Drafted:** HS—Kannapolis, NC, 2025 (5th round). **Signed by:** Nick Gorneault.
TRACK RECORD: Gray was a two-sport star at Brown High outside Charlotte who had Division I scholarship offers to play quarterback, but he preferred to be on the mound. He ran his fastball up to 96.5 mph at the MLB Draft Combine, where his arm speed and athleticism caught the Angels' attention. They went well over slot to sign him to a $1.25 million bonus in the fifth round to lure him away from an NC State commitment, and Gray then stood out in the Angels' instructional league.

SCOUTING REPORT: While still raw, Gray is an electric athlete on the mound with immense upside. His elite arm speed allows his fastball to sit 94-96 mph and touch 99 with powerful sink and a movement profile that could make it a no-doubt plus offering one day if he can get a better handle on where it's going. Both his mid-80s slider and mid-80s changeup are projectable pitches in the early stages of their development, and Gray's slider will occasionally flash plus shape. His athletic drop-and-drive delivery allows him to explode down the mound from a low three-quarters arm slot. The Angels began working with Gray to better repeat his delivery so he can throw more strikes and more frequently tap into his raw tools.
THE FUTURE: Gray moves exceptionally well and has some of the highest upside in the Angels' organization, though that comes with extreme variance. He's a long-term development project.

Year	Age	Club (League)	Level	W	L	ERA	G	GS	IP	H	HR	BB	SO	BB%	SO%	WHIP	AVG
2025	18	Did not play															

20 HAYDEN ALVAREZ, OF
HIT: 50. **POW:** 40. **RUN:** 60. **FLD:** 50. **ARM:** 50. **BA Grade:** 45. **Risk:** High. **Adj:** 35.

Born: March 19, 2007. **B-T:** R-R. **HT:** 6-3. **WT:** 190. **Signed:** Dominican Republic, 2024. **Signed by:** Jochy Cabrera.
TRACK RECORD: Alvarez signed the second-largest deal in the Angels' 2024 international class when he inked a $685,000 bonus. He enjoyed a solid pro debut in the Dominican Summer League that year on a team that reached the circuit's league championship, then made his stateside debut in 2025 where he was the catalyst for the Angels' title-winning Arizona Complex League team. Alvarez slashed .335/.427/.429 with 24 stolen bases and was then promoted to Low-A Inland Empire, where he played for his third league championship in a 13-month span and posted an .895 OPS over 76 plate appearances.
SCOUTING REPORT: An athletic outfielder with a great body, Alvarez has enticing tools. He has a simple, efficient and compact righthanded swing with a solid feel for contact, especially in the strike zone. He's quite disciplined with solid plate coverage, rarely chasing in 2025, though more advanced pitching could test his patience. There's plenty of room for Alvarez to fill out his 6-foot-3, 190-pound frame, but his middling bat speed suggests a fringy power ceiling. He's a plus runner and aggressive baserunner who loves to utilize his speed. Scouts were mixed on his center field defense, where he's an average thrower who has some aptitude for the position, but may need to rein in some of his decision-making as he matures.
THE FUTURE: Alvarez has a well-rounded profile and some of the biggest upside among position players in the Angels' system, even if there's plenty of development ahead to reach a ceiling as an everyday outfielder.

Year	Age	Club (League)	Level	AVG	G	AB	R	H	2B	3B	HR	RBI	BB	SO	SB	OBP	SLG
2025	18	ACL Angels	Rk	.335	55	182	38	61	5	3	2	26	31	41	24	.427	.429
2025	18	Inland Empire (CAL)	A	.355	20	62	12	22	5	0	0	18	10	8	9	.459	.435
		Minor League Totals		.302	125	420	93	127	20	6	3	73	72	84	65	.405	.400

21 RAUDI RODRIGUEZ, OF
HIT: 45. **POW:** 45. **RUN:** 60. **FLD:** 50. **ARM:** 50. **BA Grade:** 40. **Risk:** Average. **Adj:** 30.

Born: July 3, 2003. **B-T:** R-R. **HT:** 6-0. **WT:** 190. **Drafted:** HS—Statesboro, GA, 2023 (19th round). **Signed by:** Chris McAlpin.
TRACK RECORD: Rodriguez grew up in the Dominican Republic and moved to the United States as a teenager. The Angels drafted him out of the Georgia Premier Academy as a 19th-rounder in 2023, then signed him for $100,000. He spent two seasons in the Arizona Complex League and entered 2025 ticketed for a reserve role for Low-A Inland Empire. Instead, Rodriguez transformed himself into one of the system's best performers, finishing with 21 doubles, 14 triples and 14 homers to go along with 38 steals. He then produced a 1.164 OPS in the Arizona Fall League and was named the Angels' 2025 minor league player of the year by Baseball America.
SCOUTING REPORT: Rodriguez is an athletic 6-foot outfielder with an intriguing combination of power and speed. His quick, loose righthanded swing produces excellent bat speed and plus exit velocities, though his level bat path doesn't always translate to over-the-fence power. He's likely a fringe-average hitter at best. Scouts noted he tends to step in the bucket, and he missed pitches nearly a third of the time in 2025. He's also susceptible to in-zone fastballs. A plus runner, Rodriguez is aggressive on the bases and in the outfield, where his first step and direct routes helped his transition from right field to center field. He could be an average defender at all three outfield positions.
THE FUTURE: Rodriguez is a late-bloomer who will have to prove his low-level production can translate against better pitching entering his age-22 season. He's a potential fourth outfielder with upside.

Year	Age	Club (League)	Level	AVG	G	AB	R	H	2B	3B	HR	RBI	BB	SO	SB	OBP	SLG
2025	21	Inland Empire (CAL)	A	.281	125	481	90	135	21	14	14	83	63	130	38	.372	.470
		Minor League Totals		.279	166	605	110	169	24	16	15	93	78	163	43	.370	.446

LOS ANGELES ANGELS

22 JOEL HURTADO, RHP
FB: 60. **SL:** 60. **CH:** 30. **CTL:** 45. **BA Grade:** 40. **Risk:** Average. **Adj:** 30.

Born: February 6, 2001. **B-T:** R-R. **HT:** 6-2. **WT:** 180. **Signed:** Dominican Republic, 2022.
Signed by: Jonathan Genao/Russell Cabrera.
TRACK RECORD: The Angels signed Hurtado for just $10,000 at 21 years old late in 2022. He broke out the following year with Low-A Inland Empire and has steadily climbed the ladder since. He spent almost all of 2025 with Double-A Rocket City, pitching to a 2.70 ERA over 18 starts while missing two months of action before one start with Triple-A Salt Lake at the end of the season. The Angels left him unprotected ahead of the Rule 5 draft but he did not get picked.
SCOUTING REPORT: Hurtado is a strong, lean 6-foot-2 righthander with a powerful fastball-slider combination. His sinker averaged nearly 96 mph in 2025 and he even uncorked a 104.4 mph heater that was the hardest pitch thrown in the minors. He has racked up grounders at least 50% of the time in every pro season. Hurtado can hold his velocity deep into outings, but he didn't flirt with his peak velocity as frequently in 2025. Instead, he focused on strike-throwing and his walk rates took a massive step forward, although he also missed fewer bats. His 86 mph gyro slider is his most-used pitch and flashes plus. He scrapped his curveball, instead turning to an 87 mph changeup after tinkering with a splitter grip.
THE FUTURE: Despite solid performance as a starter, Hurtado's fringe-average command and lack of a consistent third offering could push him to a groundball-oriented relief role.

Year	Age	Club (League)	Level	W	L	ERA	G	GS	IP	H	HR	BB	SO	BB%	SO%	WHIP	AVG
2025	24	Rocket City (SL)	AA	5	6	2.70	18	18	87	81	6	27	56	7.5	15.5	1.25	.246
2025	24	Salt Lake (PCL)	AAA	0	0	3.60	1	1	5	3	0	1	3	5.3	15.8	0.80	.176
		Minor League Totals		21	20	4.22	72	59	326	311	19	150	304	10.5	21.3	1.41	.251

23 XAVIER MITCHELL, LHP
FB: 55. **CB:** 55. **CH:** 45. **CTL:** 50. **BA Grade:** 40. **Risk:** Average. **Adj:** 30.

Born: July 13, 2006. **B-T:** L-L. **HT:** 6-3. **WT:** 165. **Drafted:** HS—Plano, TX, 2025 (13th round). **Signed by:** K.J. Hendricks.
TRACK RECORD: Mitchell was a member of USA Baseball's 18U National Team in 2024 and pitched well in glimpses early during his senior season with Dallas-area Prestonwood Christian Academy before missing most of the spring with shoulder fatigue. The Angels signed him for $872,500 in the 13th round—mid–third-round money—to lure him away from a Texas commitment.
SCOUTING REPORT: The Angels were drawn to Mitchell's athletic, projectable 6-foot-3 frame with significant physical upside. His low-90s fastball touches 94 and plays up because of how it comes out of his hand and his ability to ride the upper rail for whiffs. His upper-70s hammer curveball pairs well with his fastball to give him a pair of north-south weapons. It has great spin, depth and regularly flashes plus. He added a nascent low-80s changeup that shows early promise with fair fade. He throws it with good arm speed, but it still has a ways to go. A high-level athlete, Mitchell repeats his high three-quarter crossfire delivery and throws strikes at a high clip. Adding more strength to his slender frame should help his velocity increase and allow Mitchell to better repeat his delivery.
THE FUTURE: Mitchell has the feel to pitch, athleticism and body upside to dream of a midrotation future. He will start his pro career in the lower minors in 2026.

Year	Age	Club (League)	Level	W	L	ERA	G	GS	IP	H	HR	BB	SO	BB%	SO%	WHIP	AVG
2025	18	Did not play															

24 UBALDO SOTO, RHP
FB: 60. **CB:** 45. **SL:** 40. **CH:** 50. **CTL:** 45. **BA Grade:** 45. **Risk:** High. **Adj:** 30.

Born: July 12, 2006. **B-T:** R-R. **HT:** 6-2. **WT:** 185. **Signed:** Dominican Republic, 2023. **Signed by:** Frank Tejeda.
TRACK RECORD: Soto was the Angels' top pitching target when he signed for $250,000 via the Dominican Republic in 2023. He pitched to a 1.44 ERA over 100 innings across two seasons in the Dominican Summer League, and carried that success into his stateside debut. Soto logged 73.2 innings between the Arizona Complex League and Low-A, finishing with a 3.91 ERA. He earned the win in the deciding ACL championship game and later took the loss in the deciding game of the California League title for Low-A Inland Empire.
SCOUTING REPORT: Soto's fastball sat in the upper 80s in 2023. Two years later, the projectable 6-foot-2 righthander sits 92-95 and touched 97 in 2025 with added carry. Soto's fastball gets on hitters quickly thanks to his above-average extension. His low-80s changeup tunnels off the fastball well and flashes above-average potential, giving his north-south attack an option that can generate weak contact. His go-to breaking ball is an upper-70s curveball that needs better shape and power to become less predictable out of

his hand. He may eventually incorporate a shorter low-80s slider in the future. Soto adds some deception with a backside stab in his delivery, but that same move can disrupt his timing and lead to scattered strikes.
THE FUTURE: If Soto can sharpen his mechanics and find a better breaking ball, he has back-of-the-rotation upside.

Year	Age	Club (League)	Level	W	L	ERA	G	GS	IP	H	HR	BB	SO	BB%	SO%	WHIP	AVG
2025	18	ACL Angels	Rk	3	1	5.14	12	6	49	39	5	24	53	11.3	24.9	1.29	.215
2025	18	Inland Empire (CAL)	A	3	0	1.46	6	4	25	12	2	11	30	11.6	31.6	0.93	.146
		Minor League Totals		18	2	2.49	41	28	174	124	8	78	181	11.0	25.4	1.16	.203

25 MARLON QUINTERO, C

HIT: 40. **POW:** 30. **RUN:** 40. **FLD:** 60. **ARM:** 70. **BA Grade:** 40. **Risk:** Average. **Adj:** 30.

Born: November 27, 2006. **B-T:** R-R. **HT:** 5-9. **WT:** 175. **Signed:** Panama, 2024. **Signed by:** Raul Gonzalez.
TRACK RECORD: Quintero signed out of Panama for $25,000 in 2024 as a catch-and-throw backstop. A broken hamate interrupted his Dominican Summer League debut that season, but he rebounded with a breakout 2025 season. He hit .311 as the primary catcher for the Angels' Arizona Complex League championship team and then ended the season with Low-A Inland Empire, batting .258 during their run to the California League finals. He threw out 49% of basestealers across both stops.
SCOUTING REPORT: Quintero is a small, athletic catcher whose value is driven by his defense. He is a well-rounded defender and solid receiver who has shown good lateral mobility behind the plate. He's a double-plus thrower and is quick out of his crouch with quick hands that help him regularly post sub-1.9-second pop times. His throwing accuracy helps him control the running game at a high level. His arm strength and above-average blocking should retain defensive value even as automated balls and strikes become more prevalent. Offensively, Quintero has solid bat-to-ball skills but a hyper-aggressive approach. A righthanded hitter, his hands tend to drift and he has fringy bat speed, limiting his offensive ceiling. He's a below-average runner.
THE FUTURE: Quintero's glove is good enough to carry him to the big leagues in a backup role, but his offense needs to make a leap to carve out a bigger role.

Year	Age	Club (League)	Level	AVG	G	AB	R	H	2B	3B	HR	RBI	BB	SO	SB	OBP	SLG
2025	18	ACL Angels	Rk	.311	45	161	20	50	9	0	1	29	7	32	4	.347	.385
2025	18	Inland Empire (CAL)	A	.258	18	62	8	16	2	0	0	12	2	9	3	.265	.290
		Minor League Totals		.286	79	273	41	78	12	2	1	45	19	45	10	.332	.355

26 YILVER DE PAULA, SS

HIT: 45. **POW:** 30. **RUN:** 60. **FLD:** 55. **ARM:** 55. **BA Grade:** 45. **Risk:** High. **Adj:** 30.

Born: January 15, 2008. **B-T:** B-R. **HT:** 5-11. **WT:** 180. **Signed:** Dominican Republic, 2025. **Signed by:** Cesar Baez.
TRACK RECORD: The Angels signed De Paula out of the Dominican Republic in 2025 for $900,000, the second-largest bonus in their international class behind Gabriel Davalillo. De Paula was off to a stellar start to his pro debut in the Dominican Summer League, reaching base in 21 of his first 40 plate appearances. His season was cut short after 10 games when he injured his left shoulder on a diving play, requiring surgery. De Paula attended but did not participate in stateside instructs at the end of the year.
SCOUTING REPORT: De Paula is an athletic, glove-first shortstop whose defensive actions stand out at an early age. He's a plus runner with quick feet and twitchy athleticism, which gives him excellent range at shortstop. With an above-average arm and a strong internal clock, he could become an above-average defender at the position. At the plate, the switch-hitter finds the barrel from both sides with a line-drive-oriented swing. His approach and swing decisions garnered positive reviews early on, though they remain largely untested. The Angels believe he could develop into a fringe-average hitter. His power is geared toward the gaps and he doesn't project for more than below-average impact.
THE FUTURE: De Paula has the foundational tools of a speedy, versatile bench infielder, though he is years away from being a finished product. He will make his stateside debut in 2026.

Year	Age	Club (League)	Level	AVG	G	AB	R	H	2B	3B	HR	RBI	BB	SO	SB	OBP	SLG
2025	17	DSL Angels	Rk	.387	10	31	10	12	0	0	1	7	7	6	6	.525	.484
		Minor League Totals		.387	10	31	10	12	0	0	1	7	7	6	6	.525	.484

27 PEYTON OLEJNIK, RHP
FB: 50. **SL:** 60. **CH:** 45. **CTL:** 45. **BA Grade:** 40. **Risk:** Average. **Adj:** 30.

Born: December 4, 2002. **B-T:** L-R. **HT:** 6-11. **WT:** 210. **Drafted:** Miami (Ohio), 2024 (6th round). **Signed by:** Dennis Moeller.

TRACK RECORD: The son of former 6-foot-9 Michigan State pitcher Tom Olejnik, Peyton is two inches taller after growing 13 inches from his freshman year of high school to his junior year at Miami (Ohio). He caught the Angels' attention after striking out 37.6% of batters in the MLB Draft League in 2024. They drafted him in the sixth round and signed him for $200,000. In 2025, the 22-year-old led the Low-A California League with 130 strikeouts over 128.2 innings.
SCOUTING REPORT: Olejnik's towering 6-foot-11 frame gives hitters a unique look. He works from a low three-quarter slot, which creates a challenging flat plane, and he leans on his fastball-slider combination. His 91-95 mph fastball plays up because of its riding life and natural extension. Olejnik reshaped his gyro slider into a low-80s sweeper with nearly a foot of horizontal break and 2,700 rpm of spin, though he needs to dial in the shape. His upper-80s changeup also has nearly 18 inches of horizontal break and could be serviceable although he uses it infrequently. Olejnik is a fair strike-thrower who manages to generally keep his extra-long limbs synced up, with room to add more strength to his frame.
THE FUTURE: Given his size and angles, Olejnik's profile could fit well in relief. He will need to sharpen his command and further develop his changeup to stick as a starter.

Year	Age	Club (League)	Level	W	L	ERA	G	GS	IP	H	HR	BB	SO	BB%	SO%	WHIP	AVG
2025	22	Inland Empire (CAL)	A	6	7	4.20	25	25	129	122	7	63	130	11.2	23.1	1.44	.249
		Minor League Totals		6	7	4.20	25	25	129	122	7	63	130	11.2	23.1	1.44	.249

28 AUSTIN GORDON, RHP
FB: 50. **CB:** 50. **SL:** 50. **CH:** 45. **CTL:** 55. **BA Grade:** 40. **Risk:** Avg. **Adj:** 30.

Born: June 14, 2003. **B-T:** R-R. **HT:** 6-5. **WT:** 210. **Drafted:** Clemson, 2024 (4th round). **Signed by:** Chris McAlpin.

TRACK RECORD: Gordon was solid as a sophomore in Clemson's rotation, but a bout with mononucleosis as a junior pushed him back to the Tigers' bullpen, where he became one of the nation's top closers in 2024. That led to the Angels drafting him in the fourth round. The Angels deployed him as a starter in his pro debut in 2025 over 84.1 innings and 21 starts. His 25.3% strikeout rate and 7.2% walk rate painted a rosier picture than his 5.44 ERA.
SCOUTING REPORT: Gordon is a long-limbed, loose-moving 6-foot-5 righthander who can locate his four-pitch arsenal. His 92-93 mph fastball has modest ride and run and can touch 97 in shorter stints. He spins two separate breaking balls: a mid-80s slider and an upper-70s curveball that he can vary in power. His rarely used mid-80s changeup lags behind the rest of his secondaries. Gordon lacks a true putaway pitch, instead relying on sequencing, his above-average control and a deceptively athletic double-pump delivery.
THE FUTURE: Gordon has the size, repertoire and pitchability to fit into the back of a rotation, though his chances of reaching that ceiling would improve if he can find a true swing-and-miss pitch to put batters away. He has a fallback as a low-leverage multi-inning reliever.

Year	Age	Club (League)	Level	W	L	ERA	G	GS	IP	H	HR	BB	SO	BB%	SO%	WHIP	AVG
2025	22	Tri-City (NWL)	A+	4	5	5.44	21	21	84	88	12	27	95	7.2	25.3	1.36	.260
		Minor League Totals		4	5	5.44	21	21	84	88	12	27	95	7.2	25.3	1.36	.260

29 MITCH FARRIS, LHP

FB: 30. **SL:** 50. **CH:** 60. **CTL:** 55. **BA Grade:** 35. **Risk:** Mild. **Adj:** 30.

Born: February 14, 2001. **B-T:** L-L. **HT:** 6-2. **WT:** 195. **Drafted:** Wingate, 2023 (14th round). **Signed by:** Billy Best (Braves).

TRACK RECORD: Farris was a 14th-round pick by the Braves in 2023 after winning a national title with Division II Wingate. He pitched to a 2.96 ERA across four levels in his first two seasons before the Angels acquired him for Davis Daniel during the 2024 offseason. Farris broke out in 2025 with Double-A Rocket City, where he struck out 28% of batters, generated a 15% swinging-strike rate and pitched to a 4.27 ERA. His performance earned him a September callup, during which he made five starts and allowed 19 runs over 24.1 innings.
SCOUTING REPORT: Farris is a soft-tossing 6-foot-2 lefthander who added 3 mph to his fastball in 2025. His heater now hovers round 90 mph, peaks at 93 and plays up because of his deception and command. His upper-70s changeup is his best putaway pitch. It has screwball action and 46 inches of vertical drop, generating a miss rate over 53% in the minors. Farris' short low-80s slider is a serviceable tertiary option. His subdued, low-effort delivery helps him maintain his high release point and throw strikes, though

he has minimal room for mistakes and needs to consistently command his fastball to avoid significant damage.
THE FUTURE: Now on the 40-man roster with all his options remaining, Farris has a low ceiling and should serve as a long-term swingman and spot starter.

Year	Age	Club (League)	Level	W	L	ERA	G	GS	IP	H	HR	BB	SO	BB%	SO%	WHIP	AVG
2025	24	Rocket City (SL)	AA	3	8	4.27	23	22	116	115	10	55	142	10.8	28.0	1.47	.261
2025	24	Los Angeles (AL)	MLB	1	3	6.66	5	5	24	24	4	11	24	10.3	22.4	1.44	.261
		Minor League Totals		4	10	3.92	36	27	158	148	13	79	201	11.5	29.3	1.43	.249
		Major League Totals		1	3	6.66	5	5	24	24	4	11	24	10.3	22.4	1.44	.261

30 LUKE LaCOURSE, RHP

FB: 45. **SL:** 65. **CH:** 45. **CTL:** 50. **BA Grade:** 45. **Risk:** High. **Adj:** 30.

Born: October 17, 2006. **B-T:** R-R. **HT:** 6-3. **WT:** 215. **Drafted:** HS—Auburn, MI, 2025 (6th round).
Signed by: Dennis Moeller.
TRACK RECORD: LaCourse was a standout on the 2024 summer circuit thanks to his exceptional ability to spin a baseball. Despite an inconsistent senior spring, the Angels selected him in the sixth round of the 2025 draft and signed him away from a Michigan State commitment for $512,500.
SCOUTING REPORT: Few pitchers in baseball can spin a breaking ball like LaCourse. The 6-foot-3 righthander has a low-80s slider with unicorn traits and spin rates between 3,300-3,500 rpm that create two-plane break and frisbee-like sweep. It's already a true swing-and-miss weapon with the potential to become a top-of-the-scale breaker. LaCourse has quality spin on an 89-91 mph fastball that touches 94 and spins at 2,600 rpm, which helps it ride through the zone despite modest velocity. His mid-80s changeup shows some depth and could become a serviceable option. With a fairly simple delivery that ends with some recoil, LaCourse can fill the zone and be an efficient strike-thrower. He's nearly maxed out physically, but strength gains would enhance his mechanical consistency and ability to retain velocity over extended outings.
THE FUTURE: LaCourse has starter traits and will get every chance to develop into a rotation option, though his slider alone should give him a long-term floor in a relief role. He'll make his pro debut in 2026.

Year	Age	Club (League)	Level	W	L	ERA	G	GS	IP	H	HR	BB	SO	BB%	SO%	WHIP	AVG
2025	18	Did not play															

Roki Sasaki

Los Angeles Dodgers

BY JOSH NORRIS

When Mookie Betts fielded Alejandro Kirk's grounder, stepped on second base and fired to Freddie Freeman, the Dodgers claimed their second straight World Series championship and became the first team since the 1998, 1999 and 2000 Yankees to win consecutive titles.

The seven-game epic took every piece of the Dodgers' talented roster. From two-way unicorn Shohei Ohtani, ace Yoshinobu Yamamoto and stalwart first baseman Freddie Freeman to rock solid catcher Will Smith and utility infielder Miguel Rojas, the Dodgers received contributions from every corner of the organization.

The team's closer came from an unexpected source. Japanese righthander Roki Sasaki, who was posted over the winter and chose the Dodgers, entered the year as the sport's No. 1 prospect. The beginning to his year was rocky, and he dealt with both injuries and underperformance. Once he returned, his high-90s fastball and lethal splitter gave hitters fits in high-pressure situations.

When Sasaki graduated from prospect consideration, the race to ascend to the top spot was run by four outfielders. Two—Eduardo Quintero and Josue De Paula—came to the organization via the international market. The other two—Zyhir Hope and Mike Sirota—were shrewd trade pickups.

All four have a variety of gifts, but Quintero reached No. 1 thanks to a well-rounded skill set and a chance to stick in center field. The margins among the quartet are thin, though.

In the draft, Los Angeles used picks 40 and 41 to draft a pair of Arkansas products. Lefty Zach Root went first, followed a few minutes later by outfielder Charles Davalan.

Although the top part of the system has plenty of jewels, the group is a little thinner than usual thanks to the graduations of Sasaki and catcher Dalton Rushing, plus injuries to talented prospects such as Kellon Lindsey, Joendry Vargas, River

PROJECTED 2029 LINEUP

Catcher	Will Smith	35
First Base	Dalton Rushing	29
Second Base	Tommy Edman	34
Third Base	Alex Freeland	28
Shortstop	Mookie Betts	37
Left Field	Josue De Paula	25
Center Field	Eduardo Quintero	23
Right Field	Andy Pages	28
Designated Hitter	Shohei Ohtani	36
No. 1 Starter	Yoshinobu Yamamoto	31
No. 2 Starter	Blake Snell	37
No. 3 Starter	Shohei Ohtani	36
No. 4 Starter	Roki Sasaki	27
No. 5 Starter	Emmet Sheehan	29
Closer	Edgardo Henriquez	27

Ryan and Kyle Hurt. Sasaki's signing also cost the Dodgers the bulk of their international signing money, so their teams in the Dominican Summer League weren't as lustrous as they had been in the past few seasons.

The Dodgers added prospects at the trade deadline as well, importing outfielders James Tibbs III and Zach Ehrhard from the Red Sox and lefty Adam Serwinowski from the Reds, who also had shipped them Sirota over the winter. In all, 10 of the team's Top 30 Prospects have entered the organization via trades.

With three World Series titles since 2020, the Dodgers have the look of a juggernaut. Ohtani, Yamamoto and Sasaki should be key pieces of the roster for years, and Smith, Betts and Andy Pages—a surprise defensive star during the Fall Classic—are in for the long haul as well.

The team obviously has the financial firepower and the big-market allure to import any free agent it chooses. Its cluster of high-end prospects and young, controllable big leaguers give it plenty of ammo for the trade market as well.

Combine those factors with a talented, aggressive front office and player development staff, and you have the recipe for an organization primed for success in the coming years.

From stars to prospects to leadership, everything points to more blue Octobers ahead. ∎

DEPTH CHART

LOS ANGELES DODGERS

TOP 2026 ROOKIES — RANK
1. Alex Freeland, SS — 7
2. River Ryan, RHP — 13

BREAKOUT PROSPECTS — RANK
1. Christian Zazueta, RHP — 12
2. Kellon Lindsey, SS — 16
3. Brendan Tunink, OF — 18

SOURCE OF TOP 30 TALENT

Homegrown	20	Acquired	10
College	6	Trade	0
Junior college	1	Rule 5 draft	0
High school	6	Independent league	0
Undrafted free agent	0	Free agent/waivers	0
International	7		

LF
Zyhir Hope (4)
Charles Davalan (6)
Zach Ehrhard (21)

CF
Eduardo Quintero (1)
Mike Sirota (3)
Kendall George (11)
Brendan Tunink (18)
Landyn Vidourek (27)
Jaron Elkins
Chris Newell

RF
Josue De Paula (2)
Ching-Hsien Ko (17)
James Tibbs III (26)

3B
Emil Morales (9)
Chase Harlan (10)

SS
Alex Freeland (7)
Joendry Vargas (15)
Kellon Lindsey (16)
Aidan West (19)
Noah Miller (23)

2B
Reyli Mariano
Sean McLain

1B
Jose Meza
Ryan Ward

C
Gio Cueto
Anson Aroz
Eduardo Rojas

LHP

LHSP
Jackson Ferris (5)
Zach Root (8)
Adam Serwinowski (14)
Sterling Patick (30)
Jakob Wright
Justin Chambers

LHRP
Ronan Kopp (28)
Maddux Bruns
Myles Caba

RHP

RHSP
Christian Zazueta (12)
Marlon Nieves (24)
Cam Leiter (25)
Jose Rodriguez (29)
Hyun-Seok Jang
Aidan Foeller
Payton Martin
Samuel Sanchez
Luis Carias
Brady Smith
Oliver Gonzalez
Samuel Saviñon

RHRP
River Ryan (13)
Patrick Copen (20)
Kyle Hurt (22)
Peter Heubeck
Reynaldo Yean
Ryan Brown
Logan Tabeling
Cam Day
Alex Makarewich
Shai Romero

LOS ANGELES DODGERS

1 EDUARDO QUINTERO, OF

Born: September 16, 2005. **B-T:** R-R. **HT:** 6-1. **WT:** 175.
Signed: Venezuela, 2023.
Signed by: Cristian Guzman/Andres Simancas.

TRACK RECORD: Quintero signed with the Dodgers in 2023 as a catcher but quickly shifted to center field because his speed and athleticism would have been wasted behind the plate. The move paid dividends in short order, and Quintero immediately began signaling that he was one of the system's top talents. His exploits led to championships in the Dominican Summer and Arizona Complex leagues in each of his first two professional seasons, and he ranked as the No. 1 prospect in the ACL in 2024. Quintero's stock continued rising in 2025, when he racked up 19 home runs and 47 stolen bases in a season split between both Class A levels. In a system chock full of talented outfielders, Quintero's well-rounded game and high ceiling have pushed him to the top of the heap.

SCOUTING REPORT: Entering the 2025 season, there was little doubt about Quintero's ability to make contact and get on base, but his flat swing path left his future power potential in question. He and the Dodgers tweaked his swing plane in the off-season and immediately saw results after Quintero returned to Low-A Rancho Cucamonga. He added loft to his cut without sacrificing much in the way of contact and by season's end had more than tripled his career home run total. While Quintero's exit velocities stayed roughly the same, getting the ball in the air more often made a huge difference. He lowered his groundball rate from 43% in 2024 to 35.5% in 2025. The raw ingredients are there. The next steps will revolve around the finer points of becoming a complete hitter before reaching the highest level. Namely, evaluators would like to see Quintero learn the ideal times to deploy his best swings and when the wiser play would be to take what the pitcher gives him and aim for contact over impact. Other scouts would like to see Quintero take a more direct stride to the pitcher in order to allow himself as much plate coverage as possible. The 113 games Quintero played in 2025 were the highest total of his career, and he'll need to pack on a bit more strength to be as fresh as possible during the season's final months. Defensively, Quintero is the likeliest of the system's top-tier outfielders to stick in center field. He uses above-average speed to patrol all sectors of the grass fairly easily, and his above-average arm would still be useful if he had to move to a corner in deference to a better defender up the middle.

BA GRADE
60 Risk: Average
Adjusted grade: 50

SCOUTING GRADES
Hit: 60. **Power:** 55. **Run:** 55.
Field: 55. **Arm:** 55.
Projected future grades on 20-80 scouting scale

BEST TOOLS

BATTING
Best Hitter — Eduardo Quintero
Best Power Hitter — Josue De Paula
Best Strike-Zone Discipline — Josue De Paula
Fastest Baserunner — Kendall George
Best Athlete — Mike Sirota

PITCHING
Best Fastball — Adam Serwinowski
Best Curveball — Peter Heubeck
Best Slider — Patrick Copen
Best Changeup — Ryan Brown
Best Control — Christian Zazueta

FIELDING
Best Defensive Catcher — Gio Cueto
Best Defensive Infielder — Noah Miller
Best Infield Arm — Emil Morales
Best Defensive Outfielder — Eduardo Quintero
Best Outfield Arm — Landyn Vidourek

THE FUTURE: Given the glut of outfielders in the Dodgers' system and the organization's unlimited checkbook, Quintero will have to continue proving himself at every stop if he wants to be part of the club's long-term future. He will likely start back at High-A in 2026 but should get to the upper levels in short order. If everything clicks, he could be an everyday center fielder who provides value on both sides of the ball.

Year	Age	Club (League)	Level	AVG	G	AB	R	H	2B	3B	HR	RBI	BB	SO	SB	OBP	SLG
2025	19	R. Cucamonga (CAL)	A	.306	81	317	73	97	18	6	14	53	65	88	35	.426	.533
2025	19	Great Lakes (MWL)	A+	.259	32	116	28	30	4	1	5	16	23	35	12	.384	.440
		Minor League Totals		.303	245	880	219	267	48	19	27	154	179	224	101	.427	.493

LOS ANGELES DODGERS

2 JOSUE DE PAULA, OF
HIT: 60. POW: 60. RUN: 40. FLD: 45. ARM: 50. BA Grade: 60. Risk: Average. Adj: 50.

Born: May 24, 2005. **B-T:** L-L. **HT:** 6-5. **WT:** 225.
Signed: Dominican Republic, 2022. **Signed by:** Laiky Uribe.
TRACK RECORD: After he was born in New York, De Paula moved with his family to the Dominican Republic during his teenage years. He signed with Los Angeles in 2022 and excelled in the Dominican Summer League in his pro debut, then skipped the Arizona Complex League in favor of a sophomore season split between both Class A levels. Despite a few minor injuries, he reached Double-A in 2025 as a 20-year-old.
SCOUTING REPORT: De Paula is one of the purest hitters in the system and produced a season in 2025 that only scratched the surface of his potential. Using a fairly passive approach overall, the lefthanded hitter did a solid job staying within the strike zone and doing damage on hittable pitches. Scouts were particularly enthused by his ability to adjust within at-bats. A perfect example came during the 2025 Futures Game, when De Paula swung through one slider from White Sox lefthander Noah Schultz only to send one into the seats a few pitches later. Even though De Paula hit just 12 home runs, scouts are confident that he will one day be a plus hitter with plus power. He made strides defensively and gave evaluators reason to believe he could be a fringe-average corner outfielder. He'll get to the balls hit his way, but is unlikely to make many highlight-reel plays. Improvement in the field was a big point of emphasis throughout the 2025 season, and he worked with outfield coordinator Daniel Nava to get himself on a track that would keep him on the grass. De Paula is a below-average runner but his impressive instincts on the basepaths helped him swipe 32 bases in 40 attempts.
THE FUTURE: De Paula will likely return to Double-A to begin 2026. With early, sustained success, he could make his big league debut late in the season and has a chance to settle in as a masher.

Year	Age	Club (League)	Level	AVG	G	AB	R	H	2B	3B	HR	RBI	BB	SO	SB	OBP	SLG
2025	20	Great Lakes (MWL)	A+	.263	98	342	65	90	16	1	12	44	81	86	32	.406	.421
2025	20	Tulsa (TL)	AA	.000	4	18	0	0	0	0	0	0	1	5	0	.053	.000
		Minor League Totals		.279	336	1213	231	338	61	8	29	176	244	278	89	.405	.414

3 MIKE SIROTA, OF

HIT: 55. POW: 50. RUN: 60. FLD: 55. ARM: 55. BA Grade: 55. Risk: Average. Adj: 45.

Born: June 16, 2003. **B-T:** R-R. **HT:** 6-3. **WT:** 190.
Drafted: Northeastern, 2024 (3rd round). **Signed by:** John Ceprini (Reds).
TRACK RECORD: Sirota entered his 2024 draft season at Northeastern as one of the best prospects in the class. A subpar year in which he batted under .300 for the first time tanked his stock and allowed the Reds to pounce on him in the third round. Less than a year later Cincinnati dealt him to Los Angeles—along with a draft pick that was eventually used on Arkansas outfielder Charles Davalan—for Gavin Lux. In his first test as a pro, Sirota was a revelation. He torched the competition at both Class A stops before a knee injury in early July ended his season.
SCOUTING REPORT: After joining the list of players to never play an official game for his original organization, Sirota spent 2025 looking like the player area scouts believed had the talent to go in the first round. Those who saw him for High-A Great Lakes reported a player with a diverse blend of skills. His plus bat speed, strong hands and knack for finding the barrel add up to 60-grade raw power. Sirota's overall approach was fairly passive, and he did an outstanding job at staying within the strike zone. When he did swing, he produced some of the best exit velocities in the system. Those figures included a 90th percentile EV of 107.1 mph, which was higher than any of the organization's top prospects outside of Zyhir Hope. Defensively, Sirota is a smooth, consistent center fielder who grades as potentially above-average at the position thanks to plus speed and an above-average arm that would play in either corner if he had to slide over in deference to a superior defender. Scouts also laud Sirota for his hard-nosed style of play and outstanding makeup.
THE FUTURE: Sirota should be ready for spring training. Once he's back in action, he'll get back on the path to a future as a center fielder with the skills to hit toward the top of a lineup.

Year	Age	Club (League)	Level	AVG	G	AB	R	H	2B	3B	HR	RBI	BB	SO	SB	OBP	SLG
2025	22	R. Cucamonga (CAL)	A	.354	24	99	26	35	8	2	7	24	15	25	1	.443	.687
2025	22	Great Lakes (MWL)	A+	.316	35	117	22	37	8	1	6	30	33	34	4	.458	.556
		Minor League Totals		.333	59	216	48	72	16	3	13	54	48	59	5	.452	.616

LOS ANGELES DODGERS

4 ZYHIR HOPE, OF
HIT: 40. **POW:** 60. **RUN:** 55. **FLD:** 50. **ARM:** 50. **BA Grade:** 55. **Risk:** Average. **Adj:** 45.

Born: January 19, 2005. **B-T:** L-L. **HT:** 6-0. **WT:** 195.
Drafted: HS—Stafford, VA, 2023 (11th round). **Signed by:** Billy Swoope (Cubs).
TRACK RECORD: Hope showed plenty of tools and upside as an amateur, and the Cubs bet their 11th-round pick in 2023—and a $400,000 bonus—that they could add the polish necessary to turn his tools into skills. Before they could apply a second coat, they shipped him and lefty Jackson Ferris to the Dodgers for Michael Busch. In his first two seasons with the Dodgers, Hope has shown flashes of loud tools mixed with some of the same holes indicated during his amateur days.
SCOUTING REPORT: Hope has power and speed in spades. Now, to help those skills show up more often, he'll have to improve his approach and make more contact. The lefthanded batter has plenty of bat speed and boatloads of raw juice, but an uppercut swing makes him exploitable. His overall (33.9%) and zone (26.8%) miss rates were below-average and led to prolonged boom-or-bust stretches at High-A Great Lakes. He makes up for some of his whiff tendencies with a sharp batting eye, but evaluators have pointed out his weaknesses against changeups from righthanders. He also struggles against lefthanders, against whom he hit just .215/.372/.322 in 2025. Hope's chances of cashing in on his value will hinge on whether he can stick in center field. To this point, the odds of that happening seem low. Scouts both inside and outside the organization believe he's likely to wind up as a left fielder, where there will be more pressure on the offensive aspects of his game. He has an average arm and above-average speed, though he needs to improve his first step and make his routes more efficient.
THE FUTURE: Hope ended his season in Double-A and will likely return there to begin 2026. If everything clicks, he could be a corner outfielder with the kind of power-speed profile teams covet. To reach those heights, he'll need to close a few of the holes in his swing.

Year	Age	Club (League)	Level	AVG	G	AB	R	H	2B	3B	HR	RBI	BB	SO	SB	OBP	SLG
2025	20	Great Lakes (MWL)	A+	.264	121	439	67	116	27	3	13	75	78	139	26	.377	.428
2025	20	Tulsa (TL)	AA	.316	6	19	2	6	2	0	0	5	1	4	1	.350	.421
		Minor League Totals		.275	199	714	123	196	45	3	25	125	128	218	39	.391	.451

5 JACKSON FERRIS, LHP
FB: 60. **CB:** 60. **SL:** 55. **CH:** 40. **CT:** 50. **CTL:** 40. **BA Grade:** 55. **Risk:** High. **Adj:** 40.

Born: January 15, 2004. **B-T:** L-L. **HT:** 6-4. **WT:** 205.
Drafted: HS—Bradenton, FL, 2022 (2nd round). **Signed by:** Tom Clark (Cubs).
TRACK RECORD: Ferris split his high school career between North Carolina and IMG Academy in Bradenton, Fla., from which he was drafted by the Cubs in the second round in 2022. He dazzled in his first full season as a pro, leading to his inclusion—with fellow prospect Zyhir Hope—in the deal in which the Dodgers traded Michael Busch to the Cubs. Ferris spent all of 2025 at Double-A Tulsa, where he produced mixed results. His stuff was among the best in the system, but his consistency, control and command often lacked and led to more walks than were ideal. He ranked third in the Texas League with 135 strikeouts.
SCOUTING REPORT: Scouts universally praise Ferris' pitch mix, which is led by two- and four-seam fastballs and a cutter, as well as a slider, a curveball and a changeup. The two-seamer was new in 2025, and Ferris moved to the popular kick-changeup grip to help the pitch gain more depth. His fastball and curveball each grade as potentially plus pitches, and the latter ranks as the best of its type in the system. He backs his signature offerings with a slider and cutter that range from average to slightly above-average, as well as a changeup that lags behind the rest of his mix. To get the most out of his stuff, he'll have to improve the quality and quantity of his strikes. Scouts noticed that Ferris got fatigued early and his stuff waned later in games, so he'll need to add strength to his frame. His longer arm stroke, which includes a hook and a wrap, limits his repeatability and sometimes leads to scattershot outings.
THE FUTURE: If Ferris can improve his stamina and strike-throwing, he has the type of stuff that profiles in the middle of big league rotations. If not, he could make for a useful late-game reliever. The 2026 season will provide further clues as to which path he'll take.

Year	Age	Club (League)	Level	W	L	ERA	G	GS	IP	H	HR	BB	SO	BB%	SO%	WHIP	AVG
2025	21	Tulsa (TL)	AA	10	7	3.86	26	24	126	118	9	66	135	11.8	24.2	1.46	.246
		Minor League Totals		17	17	3.50	71	69	309	246	16	156	357	11.8	27.0	1.30	.217

LOS ANGELES DODGERS

6 CHARLES DAVALAN, OF
HIT: 55. **POW:** 45. **RUN:** 55. **FLD:** 50. **ARM:** 40. **BA Grade:** 50. **Risk:** Average. **Adj:** 40.

Born: December 16, 2003. **B-T:** L-R. **HT:** 5-9. **WT:** 190.
Drafted: Arkansas, 2025 (1st round supp.). **Signed by:** Tim Adkins.
TRACK RECORD: Davalan started his career at Florida Gulf Coast, where he posted a .927 OPS with 10 home runs. He spent that summer with Cotuit of the Cape Cod League—where he was teammates with fellow 2025 Dodgers draftee Logan Lunceford—and then transferred to Arkansas for a season as a draft-eligible sophomore. Davalan quickly adjusted to the Southeastern Conference and posted a .994 OPS with 14 home runs while helping lead Arkansas to within a game of the College World Series finals. The Dodgers swooped up Davalan with the 41st pick in the draft, just minutes after they'd selected fellow Razorback Zach Root with the 40th selection. The Canadian-born Davalan signed for $1,997,500, a shade under the slot value for the pick.
SCOUTING REPORT: Davalan built his reputation on being a pure hitter, and the Dodgers had him valued as one of the best in the class. The strong, compact, lefthanded hitter tweaked his setup heading into his lone year in Fayetteville, and the results were loud. High-quality contact came at an outstanding clip, cementing the Dodgers' confidence in his abilities. Davalan is likely a hit-over-power player at the highest level, which would profile nicely if he's able to stick in center field. He has a chance to do just that thanks to above-average speed, but he's unlikely to be more than fringe-average in center field. If he does move over, his below-average arm likely limits him to left field. Davalan played all three outfield positions in college and also got time at second base, which could be an option as a pro as well.
THE FUTURE: Davalan opened his pro career with eight regular season games with Low-A Rancho Cucamonga. He'll likely begin 2026 at High-A Great Lakes, where he'll work toward a ceiling as a table-setting center fielder.

Year	Age	Club (League)	Level	AVG	G	AB	R	H	2B	3B	HR	RBI	BB	SO	SB	OBP	SLG
2025	21	R. Cucamonga (CAL)	A	.500	8	34	7	17	3	1	1	10	3	5	3	.541	.735
		Minor League Totals		.500	8	34	7	17	3	1	1	10	3	5	3	.541	.735

7 ALEX FREELAND, SS/3B
HIT: 45. **POW:** 45. **RUN:** 45. **FLD:** 50. **ARM:** 50. **BA Grade:** 45. **Risk:** Mild. **Adj:** 40.

Born: August 24, 2001. **B-T:** B-R. **HT:** 6-2. **WT:** 200.
Drafted: Central Florida, 2022 (3rd round). **Signed by:** Wes Sargent.
TRACK RECORD: Freeland was born with a clubfoot that required surgery to fix, but it didn't stop him from thriving on the diamond. The Central Florida alum, whom the Dodgers chose with their third-round pick in 2022, enjoyed a breakout season in 2024 and made his big league debut in 2025. He got into 29 games and hit his first home run against five-time all-star Yu Darvish.
SCOUTING REPORT: Nothing about Freeland's game jumps off the page, but with a few adjustments he has the chops to settle in as a steady player whose versatility helps him carve out regular playing time. He did a solid job in the minor leagues of blending plate discipline with hard contact, but his miss rates jumped in the big leagues once he started seeing a steadier diet of non-fastballs. In both the minors and majors, the switch-hitting Freeland showed a clear platoon split—thanks in part to below-average bat speed from the right side—though he worked Triple-A lefties for a fair amount of walks. Freeland is steady and playable at shortstop but played mostly third base and second base in deference to Mookie Betts. Given the Dodgers' veteran roster, versatility will be Freeland's most likely avenue to regular playing time. His steady hands and average arm should be enough to ably handle third base, but his offensive game might be a little short of the position's typical profile.
THE FUTURE: Freeland got a taste of the big leagues in 2025. To stay there, he'll have to adjust to MLB pitching. Doing so might require more seasoning at Triple-A, but he will have chances to re-emerge in the big leagues in 2026.

Year	Age	Club (League)	Level	AVG	G	AB	R	H	2B	3B	HR	RBI	BB	SO	SB	OBP	SLG
2025	23	Oklahoma City (PCL)	AAA	.263	106	415	77	109	30	0	16	82	73	111	18	.384	.451
2025	23	Los Angeles (NL)	MLB	.190	29	84	10	16	2	1	2	6	11	35	1	.292	.310
		Minor League Totals		.256	356	1346	242	345	80	5	46	219	236	386	82	.374	.426
		Major League Totals		.190	29	84	10	16	2	1	2	6	11	35	1	.292	.310

LOS ANGELES DODGERS

8 ZACH ROOT, LHP
FB: 50. **CB:** 55. **SL:** 50. **CH:** 55. **CTL:** 55. **BA Grade:** 50. **Risk:** Average. **Adj:** 40.

Born: February 6, 2004. **B-T:** L-L. **HT:** 6-2. **WT:** 210.
Drafted: Arkansas, 2025 (1st round). **Signed by:** Tim Adkins.
TRACK RECORD: With the 40th and 41st picks in the 2025 draft, the Dodgers went hog wild, selecting Root and outfielder Charles Davalan consecutively out of Arkansas. Root started his career with two seasons at East Carolina before transferring to Arkansas for his junior year. With the Razorbacks, Root went 9-6 and racked up 126 strikeouts in 99.1 innings while helping lead his team to within a game of the College World Series finals. The Dodgers signed Root for $2,197,500 and shut him down for the rest of the year.
SCOUTING REPORT: Root works with a full four-pitch complement and adds deception thanks to a funky delivery that contains a high leg lift and a three-quarters arm slot. His arsenal is fronted by a sinking fastball in the mid 90s and backed by a potentially above-average curveball and changeup as well as a slider that could be an average pitch. The latter breaking ball features 1-to-7 break and was used against both lefties and righties, and the Dodgers would like to see Root throw his changeup more as a professional than he did in college. The biggest questions about Root revolve around how many bats he'll miss as he moves up the minor league ladder. He was less a bat-misser than a barrel-misser in college, and the Dodgers will consider adding a four-seam fastball to his mix to help him get whiffs up in the zone. Despite all of its moving parts, Root maintains and repeats his delivery well, which gives evaluators confidence that he'll get to above-average control in the big leagues.
THE FUTURE: Root's college pedigree means he'll likely start his pro career at High-A Great Lakes. There, he'll work on shaping his arsenal into that of a big league starter. He has a chance to pitch at the back end of a rotation in a few years.

Year	Age	Club (League)	Level	W	L	ERA	G	GS	IP	H	HR	BB	SO	BB%	SO%	WHIP	AVG
2025	21	Did not play															

9 EMIL MORALES, SS
HIT: 50. **POW:** 60. **RUN:** 50. **FLD:** 45. **ARM:** 55. **BA Grade:** 55. **Risk:** High. **Adj:** 40.

Born: September 22, 2006. **B-T:** R-R. **HT:** 6-3. **WT:** 200.
Signed: Dominican Republic, 2024. **Signed by:** Dawlyn Lantigua/Paul Brazon.
TRACK RECORD: Morales was one of the best prospects available in the 2024 international class and signed with the Dodgers on Jan. 15. He starred in the Dominican Summer League, where he posted an OPS of 1.169. After a slow start stateside in the Arizona Complex League, Morales turned it on in the latter half of the 2025 season and finished with nine home runs. He stayed hot in the Low-A California League, swatting five home runs in 30 games with Rancho Cucamonga.
SCOUTING REPORT: No matter where Morales winds up on the diamond, the bulk of his value will be tied to his offense. He's got plenty of thunder in his bat, but an over-aggressive approach led to slightly below-average miss rates. Scouts noted a particular need to tighten his zone against spin and with two strikes. Once he improved in those areas, his fortunes turned and he began putting his raw strength to good use on pitches he could damage. He was one of just six players 18 or younger who clubbed 14 or more home runs in 2025. Scouts are near universal in their belief that Morales will not stick at shortstop. His above-average arm would play just fine at third base, but if he gets too big for the dirt, his arm would also fit well in right field. He has average speed for now, but even if he slows down a tick, he should be serviceable in the outfield. His offensive package would fit a corner profile. Scouts also raved about Morales' makeup and the strong leadership qualities he showed at such a young age.
THE FUTURE: Morales is likely to split his 2026 season between the Class A levels, with a chance at his Double-A debut late in the season if everything goes well. He has all the tools to mash, but his final defensive home remains a question.

Year	Age	Club (League)	Level	AVG	G	AB	R	H	2B	3B	HR	RBI	BB	SO	SB	OBP	SLG
2025	18	ACL Dodgers	Rk	.300	59	233	55	70	13	3	9	43	31	76	6	.383	.498
2025	18	R. Cucamonga (CAL)	A	.339	30	124	21	42	11	0	5	27	17	33	5	.420	.548
		Minor League Totals		.322	135	509	124	164	35	3	28	116	88	154	23	.423	.568

LOS ANGELES DODGERS

10 CHASE HARLAN, 3B

HIT: 40. **POW:** 55. **RUN:** 50. **FLD:** 50. **ARM:** 55. **BA Grade:** 55. **Risk:** High. **Adj:** 40.

Born: July 9, 2006. **B-T:** R-R. **HT:** 6-3. **WT:** 205.
Drafted: HS—Doylestown, PA, 2024 (3rd round). **Signed by:** Paul Murphy.
TRACK RECORD: The Dodgers chose Harlan with their third-round pick in 2024 and went more than two times over slot to sign him for $1,747,500. A nagging hip injury from his amateur days as a Pennsylvania prep led to surgery after the draft. Harlan made his pro debut in the Arizona Complex League in 2025 and reached full-season ball during the dog days of summer. Combined, Harlan swatted nine home runs, including three in 26 Low-A games.
SCOUTING REPORT: Scouts in the ACL gushed over Harlan's raw gifts, with some tabbing his raw power as a true 80. His top-end exit velocity of 114.7 mph provides a key piece of the evidence behind that assertion. Now, the question will be whether he can refine his hit tool enough to regularly access that kind of thump. Harlan's miss rates were just OK, and scouts noticed particular weaknesses against premium velocity and spin. That was especially true toward the latter part of the season, which the Dodgers attributed to the longer workload, especially in his first full year back from surgery. After tweaks to his setup and mechanics, Harlan's swing is short and simple, with only a moderate hand load required to put charges into baseballs. Harlan mashed lefthanders in a small sample but was only fair against righties. Already 6-foot-3 and 205 pounds, Harlan's chances of sticking at third base will require him to maintain his quickness and athleticism as he matures. His plus arm strength would also fit in right field, where his power would also profile if he has to move in the coming years. Scouts also give him high marks for his work ethic.
THE FUTURE: Harlan will return to Low-A in 2026, when he'll work to improve against offspeed pitches and try to stay deft enough on his feet to remain on the dirt.

Year	Age	Club (League)	Level	AVG	G	AB	R	H	2B	3B	HR	RBI	BB	SO	SB	OBP	SLG
2025	18	ACL Dodgers	Rk	.288	42	156	31	45	13	1	6	38	18	35	1	.356	.500
2025	18	R. Cucamonga (CAL)	A	.240	26	104	12	25	3	0	3	20	18	32	2	.358	.356
		Minor League Totals		.269	68	260	43	70	16	1	9	58	36	67	3	.357	.442

11 KENDALL GEORGE, OF

HIT: 50. **POW:** 30. **RUN:** 80. **FLD:** 55. **ARM:** 40. **BA Grade:** 45. **Risk:** Average. **Adj:** 35.

Born: October 29, 2004. **B-T:** L-L. **HT:** 5-10. **WT:** 170. **Drafted:** HS—Humble, TX, 2023 (1st round).
Signed by: Clint Bowers.
TRACK RECORD: After he got stronger during his senior season of high school, George's stock rose. The Dodgers took him with their first-round selection and used a $1,847,500 bonus to sign him away from a commitment to Arkansas. He swiped 100 bases in 2025, bringing his career total to 153, which stands as the third-most in the minors during that span.
SCOUTING REPORT: Now that Chandler Simpson is in the big leagues, George has a case for the fastest man in the minor leagues. The lefty swinger is adept at turning and burning, which is necessary considering he doesn't hit the ball very hard. His average exit velocity in 2025 was just 81.2 mph, the second-lowest figure in the minor leagues among players with 500 or more plate appearances. His 90th percentile figure of 97.2 mph paints a better picture, and one of the highlights of his season was a long home run off of Reds fireballer Chase Burns when both were in the Midwest League. Still, he doesn't find the barrel very often, and he rarely pulls the ball with any sort of authority. His offensive sweet spot will likely come on line drives and grounders instead of fly balls. George's elite speed helps him cover plenty of ground in the outfield, but he still has plenty of work to do when it comes to first steps and route running. Those areas will need to be sharpened if he is to stick in center field.
THE FUTURE: In 2026, George will move to the upper levels for the first time. There, he'll need to dial in on defense in order to stay in center field. If he can, his path to big league playing time is clear. If not, he's likely no more than a player who can create havoc off the bench.

Year	Age	Club (League)	Level	AVG	G	AB	R	H	2B	3B	HR	RBI	BB	SO	SB	OBP	SLG
2025	20	Great Lakes (MWL)	A+	.295	111	424	93	125	9	7	3	34	84	78	100	.409	.370
		Minor League Totals		.309	139	524	117	162	14	7	3	44	101	98	117	.419	.380

LOS ANGELES DODGERS

12 — CHRISTIAN ZAZUETA, RHP
FB: 60. **SL:** 40. **CH:** 55. **CTL:** 55. **BA Grade:** 50. **Risk:** High. **Adj:** 35.

Born: October 7, 2004. **B-T:** R-R. **HT:** 6-3. **WT:** 180. **Signed:** Mexico, 2022. **Signed by:** Lee Sigman (Yankees).

TRACK RECORD: Zazueta signed with the Yankees in 2022 on the strength of a body with plenty of remaining projection and an athletic background that included a father who played for nearly two decades in Mexico. After two seasons in the Dominican Summer League, New York dealt him to Los Angeles in the deal that netted them reliever Caleb Ferguson. He's made steady progress with the Dodgers and reached High-A for a season-ending cameo.

SCOUTING REPORT: Zazueta has begun to build on the projection teams saw in him as an amateur, having added roughly 17 pounds to his frame since signing. The gains have amplified his mix, which currently includes an excellent fastball and changeup as well as a developing breaking ball. His heater sits around 93 mph and peaked at 98 in 2025 and is effective thanks to a lower release height and excellent extension. His changeup, which comes in around 85 mph, was his most missed and chased pitch and projects to be above-average. Its shape is inconsistent, but at its best it shows strong fade and tail away from lefties. All year, Zazueta worked to find an ideal breaking ball. He went back and forth between a slider and a sweeper—sometimes with both at once until they started blending together—and there's still work to be done in that department. He threw plenty of strikes and should have at least above-average control when he reaches the big leagues.

THE FUTURE: Zazueta will return to High-A in 2026. There, he'll work to find the best breaking ball for his delivery as a way to round out his arsenal.

Year	Age	Club (League)	Level	W	L	ERA	G	GS	IP	H	HR	BB	SO	BB%	SO%	WHIP	AVG
2025	20	R. Cucamonga (CAL)	A	7	2	2.44	16	16	66	53	7	16	80	5.9	29.7	1.04	.215
2025	20	Great Lakes (MWL)	A+	0	0	0.00	1	1	1	0	0	0	1	0.0	25.0	0.00	.000
		Minor League Totals		14	12	4.08	56	48	212	186	26	61	242	6.9	27.4	1.17	.232

13 — RIVER RYAN, RHP
FB: 70. **CB:** 55. **SL:** 60. **CH:** 55. **CT:** 40. **CTL:** 45. **BA Grade:** 55. **Risk:** Extreme. **Adj:** 35.

Born: August 17, 1998. **B-T:** R-R. **HT:** 6-2. **WT:** 195. **Drafted:** UNC Pembroke, 2021 (11th round).
Signed by: Jake Koenig/Nick Brannon (Padres).

TRACK RECORD: Ryan was a two-way player at UNC Pembroke and was initially drafted by the Padres as a hitter. He shifted to the mound during the 2021 instructional league, where—despite homering off of future big leaguer Walter Pennington—it became obvious that his future was as a pitcher. San Diego swapped him to Los Angeles for infielder Matt Beaty in 2022. Ryan reached the big leagues in 2024 but he missed all of 2025 after having Tommy John surgery. When he made his debut, he became just the second big leaguer from his alma mater.

SCOUTING REPORT: Before the injury, Ryan showed an intriguing upside thanks to vicious pure stuff and the kind of athleticism that comes with a position player's background. He has a deep mix, but the gems of his arsenal are a double-plus fastball that reached triple digits and a potentially plus slider with short, sharp break in the mid 80s. He complemented those pitches with a curveball and changeup that each had ceilings of 55-grade offerings, and a below-average cutter. His control was fringy, and he walked nine hitters over 20.1 big league frames. Ryan was throwing live batting practice sessions in the fall and his stuff looked to have returned intact.

THE FUTURE: Even at 27 years old, Ryan's stuff gives him plenty of upside, and he could pitch plenty of MLB innings in 2026. Given that he's pitched just 44 innings in the last two seasons, he'll likely be used as a multi-inning reliever as he builds back toward a fuller workload.

Year	Age	Club (League)	Level	W	L	ERA	G	GS	IP	H	HR	BB	SO	BB%	SO%	WHIP	AVG
2025	25	Did not play—Injured															
		Minor League Totals		3	11	3.22	49	45	176	145	15	75	212	10.1	28.5	1.25	.223
		Major League Totals		1	0	1.33	4	4	20	15	1	9	18	11.1	22.2	1.18	.208

14 — ADAM SERWINOWSKI, LHP
FB: 60. **CB:** 55. **CH:** 40. **CTL:** 45. **BA Grade:** 45. **Risk:** Average. **Adj:** 35.

Born: June 7, 2004. **B-T:** L-L. **HT:** 6-5. **WT:** 204. **Drafted:** HS—Taylor, SC, 2022 (15th round).
Signed by: Charlie Aliano (Reds).

TRACK RECORD: The Reds took Serwinowski in the 15th round of the 2022 draft and used $125,000 to sign him away from a commitment to South Carolina. During his tenure with the Reds, he steadily emerged as one of the system's more intriguing arms, albeit one with considerably more development remaining. He was dealt to the Dodgers from the Rays as part of a three-way deal that sent catching prospect Hunter Feduccia to Tampa Bay.

SCOUTING REPORT: Serwinowski is a highly competitive lefthander whose size and funky delivery accentuate a developing arsenal. His mix is led with one of the best fastballs in the organization, a low-to-mid-90s heater that has plenty of carry through the zone and plays up thanks to a delivery with 6.8 feet of extension. He backs it with a sweepy curveball in the low 80s with above-average potential as well as an inconsistent changeup in the high 80s. At its best, the pitch fades away from lefties, but it needs plenty of work to be an effective piece of his arsenal. The next step—beyond continued sharpening of his entire mix—will be to add a slider with more north-south action as a velocity bridge between his fastball and curve. His command is only fringy, and he'll need to find a way to land his offspeeds in the zone more often.

THE FUTURE: Serwinowski will likely return to Double-A to begin his 2026 season. If he can bring his changeup forward and improve his command, he has a chance to fit in the back of a rotation. If not, his future is likely as a bulk reliever.

Year	Age	Club (League)	Level	W	L	ERA	G	GS	IP	H	HR	BB	SO	BB%	SO%	WHIP	AVG
2025	21	Dayton (MWL)	A+	1	7	4.84	18	17	74	68	9	39	92	11.7	27.7	1.44	.241
2025	21	Great Lakes (MWL)	A+	4	0	1.83	6	6	34	23	3	14	44	9.9	31.0	1.08	.185
2025	21	Tulsa (TL)	AA	0	0	9.00	1	1	3	6	0	2	4	11.8	23.5	2.67	.400
		Minor League Totals		5	7	3.92	37	30	140	111	13	72	184	12.0	30.6	1.31	.217

15 JOENDRY VARGAS, SS

HIT: 40. **POW:** 55. **RUN:** 50. **FLD:** 50. **ARM:** 60. **BA Grade:** 55. **Risk:** Extreme. **Adj:** 35.

Born: November 8, 2005. **B-T:** R-R. **HT:** 6-4. **WT:** 175. **Signed:** Dominican Republic, 2023. **Signed by:** Alant Moncon.

TRACK RECORD: In 2023, Vargas was one of the most sought-after prospects on the international market. He signed with the Dodgers for $2,077,500 and posted strong seasons in the Dominican Summer and Arizona Complex leagues. He won championships at both levels and reached full-season ball for the first time in 2025. His season was mostly lost thanks to a stress fracture in his left wrist that limited him to just 32 games.

SCOUTING REPORT: When he was on the field, Vargas' year was rough. He hit just .226 and struck out at a clip of nearly 31%. His overall and zone-miss rates were poor, and he chased at a clip of 41.3%. All of those marks—especially the chase rate—were higher than he'd posted in the ACL in 2024. He was placed on and activated from the injured list three separate times, which prevented him from getting into any sort of rhythm or making any adjustments. He did find the barrel at a decent rate and put his best-struck drives in the air, marking some of the lone positives in his season. In the field, he showed plenty of bouncy athleticism and managed a few highlight reel plays in his short sample. He has more than enough arm strength for the left side, and he got a handful of starts at third base as well. He is a fringy runner who can get to average underway and showed enough savvy on the basepaths to swipe 17 bags in his limited action.

THE FUTURE: Vargas' 2025 season can be counted as a lost year. In 2026, he'll look to hit the reset button and work toward the goals he'd hoped to achieve. To get to his impact potential, he'll need to drastically cut down on his miss rates and sharpen his pitch recognition.

Year	Age	Club (League)	Level	AVG	G	AB	R	H	2B	3B	HR	RBI	BB	SO	SB	OBP	SLG
2025	19	ACL Dodgers	Rk	.273	3	11	3	3	0	0	1	2	0	4	0	.273	.545
2025	19	R. Cucamonga (CAL)	A	.221	29	122	14	27	3	1	4	22	11	41	17	.285	.361
		Minor League Totals		.290	118	449	104	130	24	5	16	79	62	115	47	.378	.472

16 KELLON LINDSEY, SS

HIT: 50. **POW:** 40. **RUN:** 80. **FLD:** 55. **ARM:** 50. **BA Grade:** 55. **Risk:** Extreme. **Adj:** 35.

Born: September 21, 2005. **B-T:** R-R. **HT:** 6-2. **WT:** 175. **Drafted:** HS—Wauchula, FL, 2024 (1st round). **Signed by:** Wes Sargent.

TRACK RECORD: After starring in two sports at his Florida high school, Lindsey was selected by the Dodgers with the 21st overall pick in 2024. He signed for $3,297,500 and turned pro instead of landing on campus at Florida. He got his first pro experience at instructional league in 2024, but his first year in affiliated ball was limited to just 32 games at Low-A because of an impingement in his right shoulder. His season ended on May 14.

SCOUTING REPORT: The Dodgers knew Lindsey's development would be a little bit of a project, but they believed his 80-grade speed, defense and athleticism would at least give him a solid floor. He spent his first year as a pro working on a swing change that would help him stay behind the ball longer and turn more of his contact into impact. In limited action, Lindsey did a solid job staying within the zone but

LOS ANGELES DODGERS

swung and missed at rates higher than would be ideal. Scouts attributed those whiffs to the transition to his new swing. Defensively, Lindsey is an athletic player whose blazing speed would fit well at shortstop or in center field. Given his injury, it's understandable that his throws were a bit wonky in 2025.
THE FUTURE: In 2026, Lindsey will get a second chance at a first impression. Once his shoulder heals, he will return to Low-A Rancho Cucamonga. In the California League, he'll look to get used to his new swing and make his profile more complete.

Year	Age	Club (League)	Level	AVG	G	AB	R	H	2B	3B	HR	RBI	BB	SO	SB	OBP	SLG
2025	19	ACL Dodgers (ACL)	Rk	.235	4	17	3	4	1	0	1	3	1	6	1	.263	.471
2025	19	R. Cucamonga (CAL)	A	.280	28	118	29	33	7	0	2	19	22	45	10	.394	.390
		Minor League Totals		.274	32	135	32	37	8	0	3	22	23	51	11	.379	.400

17 CHING-HSIEN KO, OF
HIT: 55. **POW:** 50. **RUN:** 50. **FLD:** 50. **ARM:** 50. **BA Grade:** 45. **Risk:** Average. **Adj:** 35.

Born: August 11, 2006. **B-T:** L-R. **HT:** 6-3. **WT:** 215. **Signed:** Taiwan, 2024. **Signed by:** Allen Lin/Jon Deeble.
TRACK RECORD: The Dodgers signed Ko out of Taiwan in June 2024 and let him get his feet wet for nine games in the Dominican Summer League. After an offseason to rest, Ko split his first full season between the Arizona Complex League and Low-A Rancho Cucamonga. He was outstanding in the ACL, including league-best marks with a .445 on-base percentage and 1.026 OPS, but faced a bit more resistance once he reached the California League.
SCOUTING REPORT: Despite the gaudy numbers, Ko's game needed plenty of polish during his time in the ACL. As the summer wore on, he opened his stance, adjusted his bat path and began to use the whole field more often. All of those changes helped accentuate his knowledge of the strike zone and knack for delivering the barrel. His discerning eye stayed intact once he reached full-season ball, but he struggled against both fastballs and changeups at the level. Well-executed offspeed pitches often lead to pitfalls in young players, but the issues against fastballs might stem in part from a dip in bat speed scouts noticed in the season's final months. After playing mostly center field in Arizona, Ko spent the bulk of his time in the Cal League manning left field. His array of average marks for his defense and speed likely puts him there long term.
THE FUTURE: Ko should return to Low-A to begin 2026 for more seasoning against the kind of stuff that troubled him toward the end of the year. He has the look of a second-division regular with a touch more upside.

Year	Age	Club (League)	Level	AVG	G	AB	R	H	2B	3B	HR	RBI	BB	SO	SB	OBP	SLG
2025	18	ACL Dodgers	Rk	.367	53	180	43	66	15	2	4	30	39	40	5	.487	.539
2025	18	R. Cucamonga (CAL)	A	.219	32	114	18	25	3	2	0	4	23	32	1	.355	.281
		Minor League Totals		.303	94	323	69	98	21	4	5	44	73	79	7	.438	.440

18 BRENDAN TUNINK, OF
HIT: 40. **POW:** 55. **RUN:** 60. **FLD:** 50. **ARM:** 50. **BA Grade:** 50. **Risk:** High. **Adj:** 35.

Born: October 2, 2005. **B-T:** L-L. **HT:** 6-0. **WT:** 190. **Drafted:** HS—Sterling, IL, 2024 (8th round).
Signed by: David Pearson.
TRACK RECORD: After starring as a baseball player and a wrestler in high school in Illinois, Tunink intrigued scouts enough to earn selection in the eighth round in 2024. He signed for a well over-slot bonus of $410,000 that kept him from landing on campus for Notre Dame. Tunink got his feet wet during instructional league, then spent his first official season in the Arizona Complex League. He hit .300/.417/.550 at the level but stayed in Glendale after the year for more work at instructs.
SCOUTING REPORT: Tunink is one of the most athletic players in the Dodgers' system, but he has clear holes to fix before he can get the most out of his ability. His swing path is geared to do damage on pitches down and in but leaves him with holes elsewhere. Those vulnerable patches showed up in elevated miss rates overall (34%) and on pitches in the zone (26.8%). Tunink makes plenty of impact when he connects, as shown by a 90th percentile exit velocity of 102.6 mph. Scouts believe Tunink can hold down center field thanks to plus speed, but he'll need to sharpen up his instincts to play even cleaner defense. He has average arm strength.
THE FUTURE: After a year in the desert, Tunink should move to Low-A in 2026 for his full-season debut. He has plenty of upside but needs to add a fair amount of polish to reach his ceiling.

Year	Age	Club (League)	Level	AVG	G	AB	R	H	2B	3B	HR	RBI	BB	SO	SB	OBP	SLG
2025	19	ACL Dodgers	Rk	.300	39	140	35	42	10	5	5	17	27	51	9	.417	.550
		Minor League Totals		.300	39	140	35	42	10	5	5	17	27	51	9	.417	.550

19 AIDAN WEST, SS

HIT: 45. **POW:** 50. **RUN:** 60. **FLD:** 45. **ARM:** 50. **BA Grade:** 50. **Risk:** High. **Adj:** 35.

Born: April 24, 2007. **B-T:** L-R. **HT:** 6-2. **WT:** 205. **Drafted:** HS—Columbia, MD, 2025 (4th round). **Signed by:** Paul Murphy.

TRACK RECORD: In 2024, the Dodgers added toolsy shortstop Kellon Lindsey to their system. A year later, they repeated the feat when they called West's name in the fourth round. They signed him away from a commitment to NC State with a bonus of $1,272,500 and let him get his feet wet in instructional league.

SCOUTING REPORT: West's calling card is his mix of hittability and power, which could be amplified if he adds a bit more strength to his projectable frame. The Dodgers are bullish about that aspect of his game, believing the way his hands work portends plenty of thump in his future. His swing is quick and direct, with a flat plane through the zone designed to spray line drives across the outfield. He showed a bit of vulnerability against secondaries on the 2024 showcase circuit, but they were more blemishes than red flags. He's turned in double-plus run times as an amateur but could settle in around plus once he gains strength. Defensively, he might be stretched at shortstop and could settle in at second or third base in a few years. His average arm strength would play at either spot on the diamond.

THE FUTURE: West will likely get his first official pro action in the Arizona Complex League. He has a chance to be an average third baseman with a well-rounded skill set.

Year	Age	Club (League)	Level	AVG	G	AB	R	H	2B	3B	HR	RBI	BB	SO	SB	OBP	SLG
2025	18	Did not play															

20 PATRICK COPEN, RHP

FB: 60. **CB:** 45. **SW:** 70. **CT:** 60. **CTL:** 30. **BA Grade:** 50. **Risk:** High. **Adj:** 35.

Born: February 15, 2002. **B-T:** R-R. **HT:** 6-6. **WT:** 235. **Drafted:** Marshall, 2023 (7th round). **Signed by:** Marty Lamb.

TRACK RECORD: Copen, a Marshall product, was the Dodgers' seventh-round pick in 2023. He signed for $225,000 on the strength of a pitch package with plenty of opportunities for growth. He was one of the system's breakout arms in 2024 until a line drive back to the mound struck him in the head and left him with injuries that ultimately cost him the vision in his right eye. Undaunted, he returned in 2025 and bullied hitters across two levels and finished with a system-best 152 strikeouts.

SCOUTING REPORT: At its best, Copen's stuff can overwhelm hitters. He works with five pitches, including four-seam and sinking fastballs that live at 92-94 mph and peak at 99, and a cutter that comes in a couple of ticks slower. He supports the fastballs with a sweepy slider in the mid 80s and a downer curveball in the low 80s. Copen's stuff is filthy, and his repertoire produces more swords than all of the Medieval Times restaurants combined. Problem is, he doesn't throw enough strikes. His 87 walks were the most of any Dodgers pitcher, and his overall strike rate was just 57%. His frenetic delivery lends itself to power over precision, and none of his pitches were thrown in the zone more than 58% of the time. Copen is likely to add a changeup in 2026, but the version has not been settled upon.

THE FUTURE: Copen has more than enough stuff to be a force at the back of a bullpen. To reach that ceiling, he'll need to throw a lot more strikes.

Year	Age	Club (League)	Level	W	L	ERA	G	GS	IP	H	HR	BB	SO	BB%	SO%	WHIP	AVG
2025	23	Great Lakes (MWL)	A+	3	1	2.25	10	10	48	22	1	32	77	16.0	38.5	1.13	.135
2025	23	Tulsa (TL)	AA	1	6	4.52	17	17	70	63	1	52	75	16.0	23.1	1.65	.241
		Minor League Totals		12	11	3.52	52	49	215	164	5	141	252	15.0	26.7	1.42	.213

21 ZACH EHRHARD, OF

HIT: 50. **POW:** 45. **RUN:** 55. **FLD:** 50. **ARM:** 50. **BA Grade:** 45. **Risk:** Average. **Adj:** 35.

Born: January 21, 2003. **B-T:** R-R. **HT:** 5-10. **WT:** 190. **Drafted:** Oklahoma State, 2024 (4th round). **Signed by:** Chris Reilly (Red Sox).

TRACK RECORD: The Red Sox were intrigued enough by Ehrhard that they drafted him twice. They called his name in the 13th round in 2021, when he was in high school in Florida. Instead, he spent three seasons at Oklahoma State and one summer in the Cape Cod League, where he was part of a loaded Hyannis squad that also featured Cam Smith, Jamie Arnold and Mike Sirota. Boston drafted him in the fourth round in 2024, then shipped him to Los Angeles in the deal that sent Dustin May to the Red Sox.

SCOUTING REPORT: Ehrhard is the kind of player who does just enough right to carve out a big league career. He knows the strike zone, hits the ball decently hard and puts his best-struck drives in the air more often than not. Added strength and bat speed amplified Ehrhard's power in 2025, though his slugging percentage in the big leagues might be filled with more doubles than home runs. With the Red Sox,

LOS ANGELES DODGERS

Ehrhard played more in left field. After the trade, he shifted to center field. His above-average speed plays at both spots, and his average arm strength fits anywhere in the grass. He moves well to his right and left, but his routes and jumps are shaky on balls hit over his head.
THE FUTURE: Ehrhard's year-over-year gains made him a valuable trade chip. He has a chance to be a second-division regular who earns playing time by doing a little bit of everything.

Year	Age	Club (League)	Level	AVG	G	AB	R	H	2B	3B	HR	RBI	BB	SO	SB	OBP	SLG
2025	22	Greenville (SAL)	A+	.342	31	111	24	38	10	0	1	22	26	27	7	.471	.459
2025	22	Portland (EL)	AA	.227	58	211	29	48	13	1	8	23	20	49	16	.305	.412
2025	22	Tulsa (TL)	AA	.282	34	131	32	37	7	1	5	20	21	21	14	.391	.466
		Minor League Totals		.272	123	453	85	123	30	2	14	65	67	97	37	.374	.439

22 KYLE HURT, RHP
FB: 60. **CB:** 40. **SL:** 40. **CH:** 60. **CTL:** 40. **BA Grade:** 40. **Risk:** Mild. **Adj:** 30.

Born: May 30, 1998. **B-T:** R-R. **HT:** 6-3. **WT:** 240. **Drafted:** Southern California, 2020 (5th round).
Signed by: Tim McDonnell (Marlins).
TRACK RECORD: Hurt was drafted by the Phillies in the 34th round out of high school in 2017 and then again by the Marlins in the fifth and final round of the pandemic-shortened 2020 draft. Miami dealt him and Alex Vesia to the Dodgers in February 2021 in exchange for reliever Dylan Floro. Hurt made his big league debut in 2023 and opened his career with a flourish by retiring all-stars Fernando Tatis Jr., Juan Soto and Manny Machado. He reached MLB again in 2024 but missed most of 2025 while recovering from Tommy John surgery.
SCOUTING REPORT: At his best, Hurt attacks hitters with a fastball and a changeup that each projected as plus pitches before his surgery. He mixed in a slider and a curveball as well, but both of those offerings needed to take steps forward to even get to fringe-average. He rarely threw either breaking ball during his time in the big leagues. His control in Triple-A in 2024 was well below-average. He returned toward the end of the season and was part of the Dodgers' group of pitchers asked to stay ready for the playoffs.
THE FUTURE: With a full offseason to rest, Hurt should enter 2026 hunting for a spot in the Opening Day bullpen. He fits as a middle reliever and could up his stock a bit by bringing the quality of one or both of his breaking balls forward a touch.

Year	Age	Club (League)	Level	W	L	ERA	G	GS	IP	H	HR	BB	SO	BB%	SO%	WHIP	AVG
2025	27	Oklahoma City (PCL)	AAA	1	0	1.93	7	0	9	10	0	5	10	11.9	23.8	1.61	.270
		Minor League Totals		12	13	4.40	83	41	209	162	16	130	329	14.1	35.8	1.40	.210
		Major League Totals		0	1	1.04	4	1	9	8	0	1	6	3.0	18.2	1.04	.250

23 NOAH MILLER, SS
HIT: 40. **POW:** 30. **RUN:** 40. **FLD:** 70. **ARM:** 60. **BA Grade:** 40. **Risk:** Mild. **Adj:** 35.

Born: November 12, 2002. **B-T:** B-R. **HT:** 5-11. **WT:** 190. **Drafted:** HS—Fredonia, WI, 2021 (1st round supp.).
Signed by: Joe Bisensius (Twins)
TRACK RECORD: The younger brother of journeyman infielder Owen Miller, Noah was drafted by the Twins in the supplemental first round of the 2021 draft. He was dealt to the Dodgers in 2024 for Manuel Margot. He missed part of the season while completing his rehab from a torn meniscus in his left knee.
SCOUTING REPORT: Miller is the Dodgers' best infield defender and has the skills to lock down any position on the dirt. He is quick, agile and fearless and has a strong, accurate throwing arm as well. Those skills alone should get him to the big leagues and keep him there for a long time. The switch-hitter is much better from the left side, and all but three of his extra-base hits came from that side of the dish. He does a solid job hitting pitches in the strike zone, but he needs to tone down his chase rate quite a bit. Miller's exit velocities are OK, but he could get more out of his bat by getting the ball in the air more often. He made strides in that regard after moving from Double-A to Triple-A but still has further to go. Miller was most successful against breaking pitches but struggled against velocity, and registered just two extra-base hits against heaters thrown 94 mph or harder.
THE FUTURE: Miller is ready for the big leagues, where he could hit toward the bottom of the order and become a pitcher's best friend on defense.

Year	Age	Club (League)	Level	AVG	G	AB	R	H	2B	3B	HR	RBI	BB	SO	SB	OBP	SLG
2025	22	ACL Dodgers	Rk	.333	8	24	6	8	2	1	0	5	6	1	0	.452	.500
2025	22	Tulsa (TL)	AA	.291	27	103	12	30	3	1	1	11	6	24	0	.336	.369
2025	22	Oklahoma City (PCL)	AAA	.238	59	227	31	54	12	0	4	35	11	44	1	.269	.344
		Minor League Totals		.235	478	1807	260	424	71	12	23	195	221	407	44	.319	.325

LOS ANGELES DODGERS

24 MARLON NIEVES, RHP
FB: 60. **SL:** 40. **CH:** 45. **SW:** 60. **CTL:** 40. **BA Grade:** 45. **Risk:** Average. **Adj:** 35.

Born: June 10, 2005. **B-T:** R-R. **HT:** 6-3. **WT:** 170. **Signed:** Dominican Republic, 2023. **Signed by:** Domingo Toribio.
TRACK RECORD: Nieves signed with the Dodgers in 2023, then spent his first two seasons in the Dominican Summer League. He earned a berth in the league's all-star game in 2024. Nieves moved stateside in 2025 and started percolating during extended spring training. He was one of Los Angeles' more eye-opening arms in the Arizona Complex League and finished the year in Low-A.
SCOUTING REPORT: The Dodgers realized that Nieves' four-seam fastball wasn't going to be an effective pitch, so they used Dustin May as an inspiration and switched to a two-seamer. The pitch sat around 94 mph, maxed at 98 and—in concert with his sweeper—gave him the foundation for an east-west attack plan. Nieves complements his bread-and-butter pitches with a heavy changeup in the high 80s and a harder slider that at times looks like a cutter and is thrown around 88 mph. To make his mix more effective, he'll need to find the zone more often. None of his pitches landed in the zone more than 50% of the time, though scouts noticed that his misses typically weren't by large margins. He controls his long levers well, and there aren't any glaring red flags in his delivery.
THE FUTURE: Nieves should head back to Low-A in 2026. He has the upside of a rotation piece but will need to up his command and control in a big way to reach that ceiling.

Year	Age	Club (League)	Level	W	L	ERA	G	GS	IP	H	HR	BB	SO	BB%	SO%	WHIP	AVG
2025	20	ACL Dodgers	Rk	4	0	3.23	12	8	47	31	1	25	57	12.2	27.8	1.18	.181
2025	20	R. Cucamonga (CAL)	A	1	0	2.21	8	8	37	19	1	19	37	13.1	25.5	1.04	.157
		Minor League Totals		6	3	3.81	42	36	137	102	6	88	149	14.7	24.9	1.39	.209

25 CAM LEITER, RHP
FB: 60. **CB:** 60. **SL:** 55. **CH:** 50. **CTL:** 40. **BA Grade:** 55. **Risk:** Extreme. **Adj:** 35.

Born: January 20, 2004. **B-T:** R-R. **HT:** 6-5. **WT:** 234. **Drafted:** Florida State, 2025 (4th round). **Signed by:** Wes Sargent.
TRACK RECORD: Leiter has plenty of baseball in his bloodline. His father, Kurt, pitched in the Orioles' system, and his uncles Al and Mark and cousins Mark Jr. and Jack have decades of big league experience. After a season at Central Florida, Leiter moved to Florida State for his sophomore season. A shoulder injury ended that year after just 35 innings, and Tommy John surgery kept him out all of 2025. Still, the Dodgers bet on Cam's upside, selected him in the fourth round and signed him for $1,346,600.
SCOUTING REPORT: Leiter has a big, physical frame and knockout stuff at his best. His fastball sat in the mid 90s and reached up to 99 with plenty of life through the zone. Both his curveball and slider have flashed plus, though the latter pitch can look more like a cutter when it reaches the upper part of its velocity. His changeup has average potential but was a clear fourth pitch in his mix. Leiter's strikes were scattered when healthy, and his control will likely be below-average when he reaches the highest level. The Dodgers were considering adding a splitter and sinker to his mix.
THE FUTURE: Leiter was throwing bullpens in Arizona in the fall and is expected to be ready for Opening Day after an offseason of rest and recovery. He has some of the highest upside among Los Angeles' lower-level pitchers.

Year	Age	Club (League)	Level	W	L	ERA	G	GS	IP	H	HR	BB	SO	BB%	SO%	WHIP	AVG
2025	21	Did not play															

26 JAMES TIBBS III, OF
HIT: 50. **POW:** 45. **RUN:** 40. **FLD:** 45. **ARM:** 50. **BA Grade:** 40. **Risk:** Average. **Adj:** 30.

Born: October 1, 2002. **B-T:** L-L. **HT:** 6-0. **WT:** 201. **Drafted:** Florida State, 2024 (1st round). **Signed by:** Jim Gabella (Giants).
TRACK RECORD: After watching his three standout seasons at Florida State, the Giants were impressed enough with Tibbs to draft him with the 13th overall pick. His tenure with San Francisco didn't last long. Eleven months later, Tibbs was dealt to Boston in the trade that brought all-star Rafael Devers to the Giants. Six weeks later, the Red Sox sent him and Zach Ehrhard to the Dodgers for righty Dustin May.
SCOUTING REPORT: During his first two stops, Tibbs' production was underwhelming. When he moved to the Dodgers, the tide turned a little bit. The offense-friendly Texas League certainly played a part, but he also made a slight adjustment to his swing mechanics. With the Giants and Red Sox, he employed a leg kick before getting into two-strike counts. With the Dodgers, the move became a timing step. He also became more aggressive during his time with Double-A Tulsa, going from 4.1 and 4.2 pitches per plate appearance with the Giants and Red Sox to 3.8 with the Dodgers. He'll need to clean up a bit of noise at the top of his swing to have more success against premium velocity. Tibbs should be just sound enough

LOS ANGELES DODGERS

on defense to play a fringe-average right field, though he's gotten some exposure to first base as well. He is a below-average runner.
THE FUTURE: After three organizations in his first season and a half, Tibbs has shown himself to be a player with a fair amount of skills but without any flashy tools. He should spend 2026 between the upper levels and has the ceiling of a second-division regular corner outfielder.

Year	Age	Club (League)	Level	AVG	G	AB	R	H	2B	3B	HR	RBI	BB	SO	SB	OBP	SLG
2025	22	Eugene (NWL)	A+	.246	57	207	41	51	10	1	12	32	42	45	3	.379	.478
2025	22	Portland (EL)	AA	.207	30	116	16	24	2	1	1	7	19	39	2	.319	.267
2025	22	Tulsa (TL)	AA	.269	36	134	25	36	5	2	7	32	29	36	5	.407	.493
		Minor League Totals		.242	149	565	96	137	22	4	22	77	98	156	10	.359	.412

27 LANDYN VIDOUREK, OF
HIT: 40. **POW:** 60. **RUN:** 60. **FLD:** 50. **ARM:** 70. **BA Grade:** 45. **Risk:** High. **Adj:** 30.

Born: November 6, 2003. **B-T:** L-R. **HT:** 6-1. **WT:** 192. **Drafted:** Cincinnati, 2025 (3rd round). **Signed by:** Marty Lamb.
TRACK RECORD: Vidourek's first two seasons at Cincinnati were strong, but he took things up a notch in his draft season. The 14 home runs he swatted were four more than his total over his first two seasons. The Dodgers called Vidourek's name in the third round and signed him for $552,750. He started his pro career with 16 games at Low-A Rancho Cucamonga.
SCOUTING REPORT: In a brief sample at Low-A, Vidourek showed the strengths and weaknesses of his game. He hit the ball incredibly hard, producing a 90th percentile exit velocity of 110.3 mph. He also swung and missed far too often, punching out in 25 of his 74 plate appearances and posting a miss rate of 35.2%. Velocity up in the zone is a particular weakness he will need to correct. His skill set perfectly fits a corner-outfield profile, especially thanks to a double-plus arm that grades as the best in the system. He spent most of his time at Cincinnati in right field, but the Dodgers moved him around a bit in Rancho and plan to give him some exposure in center field, where his plus speed would be an asset.
THE FUTURE: Vidourek's speed, arm strength and power give him a high upside. If he can cut down on his miss rates, he could shoot up the rankings. His college pedigree could lead to a ticket to High-A Great Lakes to begin the 2026 season.

Year	Age	Club (League)	Level	AVG	G	AB	R	H	2B	3B	HR	RBI	BB	SO	SB	OBP	SLG
2025	21	R. Cucamonga (CAL)	A	.313	16	67	5	21	5	1	1	6	7	25	3	.378	.463
		Minor League Totals		.313	16	67	5	21	5	1	1	6	7	25	3	.378	.463

28 RONAN KOPP, LHP
FB: 60. **SL:** 60. **CTL:** 30. **BA Grade:** 40. **Risk:** Average. **Adj:** 30.

Born: July 28, 2002. **B-T:** L-L. **HT:** 6-8. **WT:** 235. **Drafted:** South Mountain JC, 2021 (12th round). **Signed by:** Brian Compton.
TRACK RECORD: Kopp presented scouts with a bit of a puzzle in 2021. The small sample he produced in the pandemic-shortened season was uneven, and he went unselected in the five-round draft. Instead, he moved to Arizona's South Mountain JC, and the Dodgers called his name in the 12th round. He signed for $125,000 and has spent his entire career pairing standout stuff with well below-average control.
SCOUTING REPORT: Kopp is a pure relief prospect with two pitches: a mid-90s four-seamer that averaged more than 18 inches of induced vertical break and a high-80s slider with varying amounts of depth and sweep. Kopp is big, physical and lefthanded, and his delivery features a frenetic, bow-and-arrow arm action that creates deception and limits his ability to throw strikes. He landed both pitches in the zone at an identical rate of 47.3%, and he finished the year with a 16.6% walk rate. Velocity and movement give both of his offerings the chance to be big league-caliber weapons. Now, he needs to throw them for strikes far more often. Evaluators within the organization believe the improved work ethic he showed in 2025 gives him a chance to make the necessary strides.
THE FUTURE: If he can significantly upgrade his control and command, Kopp has a chance to be a stuff monster in the late innings. The Dodgers believe they can get him there, and they put him on their 40-man roster to shield him from the Rule 5 draft.

Year	Age	Club (League)	Level	W	L	ERA	G	GS	IP	H	HR	BB	SO	BB%	SO%	WHIP	AVG
2025	22	Tulsa (TL)	AA	1	3	2.53	28	0	32	23	0	22	50	15.9	36.2	1.41	.202
2025	22	Oklahoma City (PCL)	AAA	1	1	4.56	21	0	26	23	1	20	41	17.4	35.7	1.68	.242
		Minor League Totals		9	12	3.25	144	32	244	171	14	177	381	16.6	35.6	1.43	.197

LOS ANGELES DODGERS

29 JOSE RODRIGUEZ, RHP
FB: 55. **SL:** 55. **CH:** 70. **CTL:** 40. **BA Grade:** 40. **Risk:** Average. **Adj:** 30.

Born: July 18, 2001. **B-T:** R-R. **HT:** 6-6. **WT:** 210. **Signed:** Mexico, 2019. **Signed by:** Juvenal Soto.
TRACK RECORD: Rodriguez signed with the Dodgers out of Mexico in 2019 but had his debut delayed by the pandemic that wiped out the 2020 minor league season. He spent his first two seasons in the Dominican Summer League, then two more at the Class A levels before splitting his 2025 season between Double-A and Triple-A. His season ended on Sept. 7 with a knee injury that necessitated placement on the 60-day injured list.
SCOUTING REPORT: Rodriguez is big and physical and uses a funky delivery to wipe hitters out with an array of wicked pitches. He gets deception thanks to a hip turn and his pitches play up thanks to between 6.8 and 7.1 feet of extension. His changeup is the gem of his arsenal and grades as the best in the system. It comes in at around 86 mph, has more than a foot of horizontal break and garnered a miss rate of 65%. His four-seam and sinking fastballs each sit in the mid 90s and peak around 99. The sinker is the better of the two variants, but he needs to do a much better job commanding both versions. Rodriguez's slider also gave hitters fits. The mid-80s bender has short, sharp break at its best, but his command of the pitch is also scattershot.
THE FUTURE: In a vacuum, Rodriguez's combination of velocity, movement and deception can bring hitters to their knees. He'll need to drastically improve his command to get the most out of his stuff.

Year	Age	Club (League)	Level	W	L	ERA	G	GS	IP	H	HR	BB	SO	BB%	SO%	WHIP	AVG
2025	23	Tulsa (TL)	AA	1	0	8.25	8	1	12	14	1	8	20	14.3	35.7	1.83	.298
2025	23	Oklahoma City (PCL)	AAA	8	2	4.71	37	1	42	33	7	27	64	14.2	33.7	1.43	.213
		Minor League Totals		24	5	4.72	106	5	151	140	14	64	224	9.6	33.7	1.35	.241

30 STERLING PATICK, LHP
FB: 55. **CB:** 45. **CH:** 40. **CT:** 50. **CTL:** 50. **BA Grade:** 40. **Risk:** Average. **Adj:** 30.

Born: June 9, 2005. **B-T:** L-L. **HT:** 6-1. **WT:** 180. **Drafted:** HS—West Covina, CA, 2023 (18th round). **Signed by:** Brent Mayne.
TRACK RECORD: Patick spent his amateur career at California's South Hills High, which also produced big leaguers Jacob Amaya, Jason Giambi and Aaron Small. The Dodgers selected him in the 18th round in 2023 and signed him to an over-slot bonus of $347,500 to keep him from honoring his commitment to UC Santa Barbara. He split his 2025 season between the Class A levels and struck out 108 hitters in 92.1 innings.
SCOUTING REPORT: Patick's delivery is deceptive and high-energy, featuring a rocker step and a glove tap before throwing from a three-quarters slot. He works primarily with a four-seam fastball, cutter, curveball and changeup, though he started sprinkling in a sweeper by season's end. He tinkered with the grips on his changeup throughout the year. His fastball sits around 93 mph and has peaked at 97 with solid life through the zone. His best breaking pitch is the cutter, which averaged 88 mph and had the best strike and chase rates of any of his offerings. The biggest to-do item on Patick's list will be to throw his other three pitches for strikes more often. None of them was in the zone more than 36% of the time, and only his changeup was a strike at a rate of better than 50%.
THE FUTURE: Patick ended his 2025 season at High-A Great Lakes and will return there to begin 2026. If he can find the zone more often with his entire arsenal, he has a chance to fit as a No. 5 starter or a middle reliever. The progress of his sweeper will be worth monitoring as well.

Year	Age	Club (League)	Level	W	L	ERA	G	GS	IP	H	HR	BB	SO	BB%	SO%	WHIP	AVG
2025	20	R. Cucamonga (CAL)	A	2	5	4.01	23	19	85	78	5	37	100	10.0	27.0	1.35	.240
2025	20	Great Lakes (MWL)	A+	0	0	3.86	2	2	7	8	0	2	8	6.5	25.8	1.43	.276
		Minor League Totals		2	6	4.25	31	26	106	97	5	46	122	10.0	26.5	1.35	.241

Eury Perez

Miami Marlins

BY JACOB RUDNER

PROJECTED 2029 LINEUP

Catcher	Joe Mack	26
First Base	Agustín Ramirez	27
Second Base	Xavier Edwards	29
Third Base	Aiva Arquette	25
Shortstop	Starlyn Caba	23
Left Field	Kyle Stowers	31
Center Field	Cam Cannarella	25
Right Field	Jakob Marsee	28
Designated Hitter	Kemp Alderman	26
No. 1 Starter	Eury Pérez	26
No. 2 Starter	Thomas White	24
No. 3 Starter	Edward Cabrera	31
No. 4 Starter	Robby Snelling	25
No. 5 Starter	Ryan Weathers	29
Closer	Ronny Henriquez	29

The Marlins' 2025 finish at 79-83 is less informative than the structural groundwork beneath it. The organization has undergone a substantive shift: a system once scattered by preferences now communicates with clarity across every rung. Hitters in the big league clubhouse receive the same evaluation pillars as teenagers in the Dominican Summer League, and developmental priorities have become measurable, not theoretical.

This coherence is underpinned by a deliberate emphasis on physical development. Miami has replaced traditional offseason patterns with year-round strength programming focused on durability, movement quality and sustainable skill growth. Improvements are no longer hoped for. They are engineered. Early returns have been unmistakable.

The depth of Miami's lower system is increasingly robust. For the first time in more than a decade, the Marlins are not relying on a single wave of prospects to rescue their roster. They have crafted a layered pipeline built from both draft and international talent pools. The 2025 draft class was entirely composed of college players, a strategic decision favoring developmental predictability. The high-variance high school demographic has effectively shifted into the international sector, where Miami can guide young players from their earliest professional stages in a unified language.

Three of the organization's top four prospects—lefthanders Thomas White and Robby Snelling and catcher Joe Mack—are projected to reach the big leagues in 2026. That level of proximity, combined with true depth beneath them, positions Miami to gradually improve its major league roster from within rather than hoping for improbable bursts of talent.

Sustainable impact, however, requires organizational follow-through. Development alone will not compensate for attrition if the club cannot retain its best players or support them with targeted free agent spending. The system has produced legitimate major league breakouts in the past two seasons; now the objective is repetition. Miami needs a pipeline that generates reliable contributors with enough regularity to raise the competitive floor.

The urgency of this moment is defined by history. Since 2003, the Marlins have delivered just six winning seasons. That stretch has been marked by disconnected philosophies and inconsistent application. The present structure under president of baseball operations Peter Bendix is a departure. It scales cleanly from the DSL to the majors and no longer relies on improvisation or isolated departmental expertise. The club operates from a shared framework that gives players the same expectations, regardless of level.

What happens next will determine whether Miami merely improves its image or genuinely changes its trajectory. The organization now has depth, a coherent developmental system and a philosophy tied to actionable strength principles rather than aspirational slogans. The infrastructure exists. The question is whether Miami can support it with the capital, continuity and roster construction required to sustain competitiveness. The Marlins are positioned to build. Now they must complete that task. ∎

DEPTH CHART

MIAMI MARLINS

TOP 2026 ROOKIES — RANK
1. Thomas White, LHP — 1
2. Robby Snelling, LHP — 2
3. Joe Mack, C — 4

BREAKOUT PROSPECTS — RANK
1. Fenwick Trimble, OF — 11
2. Esmil Valencia, OF — 16
3. Eliazar Dishmey, RHP — 24

SOURCE OF TOP 30 TALENT

Homegrown	22	Acquired	8
College	6	Trade	8
Junior college	0	Rule 5 draft	0
High school	7	Independent league	0
Undrafted free agent	0	Free agent/waivers	0
International	9		

LF
Brandon Compton (8)
PJ Morlando (18)
Max Williams

CF
Cam Cannarella (7)
Fenwick Trimble (11)
Dillon Head (13)
Andrew Salas (14)
Matthew Etzel
Emaarion Boyd

RF
Kemp Alderman (6)
Luis Cova (12)
Esmil Valencia (16)
Jose Castro (29)
Ian Lewis
Andres Valor

3B
Aiva Arquette (3)
Maximo Acosta (28)
Echedry Vargas
Abrahan Ramirez

SS
Starlyn Caba (10)
Luis Arana (15)
Chase Jaworsky
Carter Johnson
Payton Green

2B
Jared Serna (27)
Jacob Berry
Drew Faurot

1B
Deyvison De Los Santos (30)
Chris Arroyo

C
Joe Mack (4)
Ryan Ignoffo
Garret Forrester

LHP

LHSP
Thomas White (1)
Robby Snelling (2)
Keyner Benitez (17)
Nate Payne (23)
Joey Volini

LHRP
Kifraidy Encarnacion (26)
Dax Fulton
Kaiden Wilson

RHP

RHSP
Kevin Defrank (5)
Karson Milbrandt (9)
Noble Meyer (19)
Liomar Martinez (20)
Grant Shepardson (21)
Eliazar Dishmey (24)
Pedro Montero
Jose Paulino
Eiver Mosquera
Adrian Peña
Adriano Marrero

RHRP
Jose White (22)
William Kempner (25)
Nigel Belgrave
Josh Ekness

MIAMI MARLINS

1 THOMAS WHITE, LHP

Born: September 29, 2004. **B-T:** L-L. **HT:** 6-5. **WT:** 240.
Drafted: HS—Andover, MA, 2023 (1st round supp.).
Signed by: Alex Smith.

TRACK RECORD: The top high school lefthander in the 2023 draft class, White signed with the Marlins for a well over-slot $4.1 million as the 35th overall pick. He wasted no time making an impact in his first full pro season, striking out nearly 30% of hitters with a 2.81 ERA across two Class A levels in 2024. He remained on his meteoric trajectory in 2025 with a 2.31 ERA and dominant 38.6% strikeout rate while advancing from High-A Beloit to Triple-A Jacksonville. Control remains White's lone blemish. His walk rate climbed from 9.2% in 2024 to 13.6% in 2025, and he has said he plans to overhaul his delivery ahead of his fourth professional season.

SCOUTING REPORT: White has begun to grow into his long-levered 6-foot-5, 240-pound frame. He's added roughly 10 pounds since 2024, with even more physicality likely to come. The added strength has only sharpened his already electric arsenal. Working from a compact arm stroke that stays hidden until the last instant, he fires from a high three-quarters arm slot and unleashes a fastball that sits 94-96 mph, touches 99 and carries late life through the zone. The pitch rides up on hitters with both vertical carry and subtle armside run—a combination that produced a 34% miss rate and swing-and-miss utility against both righthanded and lefthanded bats. His best weapon is a sweeping low-to-mid-80s slider that tunnels perfectly off his heater. It misses bats at a premium clip—50% miss rate, 31% chase rate in 2025—and can both back-foot righties and dart away from lefties. His mid-80s changeup took a leap forward in 2025, showing fade and late tumble, and it was particularly effective against righthanders, who struggle to pick it up before it dives below the barrel. White ranked third among minor leaguers with at least 80 innings in strikeout rate in 2025, and all three of his pitches are legitimate putaway options. The question, as it often is with young power arms, is control. White is unlikely to ever be a precise, paint-the-black type. For now, his focus is simply filling the zone consistently. His walk rate climbed in 2025, a sign of either chasing whiffs off the plate or losing rhythm in his delivery. That inconsistency can lead to inefficiency, which was frequently evident, as he pitched into the sixth inning just twice in 2025. Yet, even when laboring, White competes and tends to tighten his execution when traffic builds.

BA GRADE: 70 Risk: High
Adjusted grade: 55

SCOUTING GRADES
FB: 60. **SL:** 70. **CH:** 65. **CTL:** 45.
Projected future grades on 20-80 scouting scale

BEST TOOLS

BATTING
Best Hitter	Cam Cannarella
Best Power Hitter	Kemp Alderman
Best Strike-Zone Discipline	Fenwick Trimble
Fastest Baserunner	Dillon Head
Best Athlete	Ian Lewis

PITCHING
Best Fastball	Kevin Defrank
Best Curveball	Josh White
Best Slider	Thomas White
Best Changeup	Thomas White
Best Control	Robby Snelling

FIELDING
Best Defensive Catcher	Joe Mack
Best Defensive Infielder	Starlyn Caba
Best Infield Arm	Maximo Acosta
Best Defensive Outfielder	Andrew Pintar
Best Outfield Arm	Esmil Valencia

THE FUTURE: White's raw stuff is already among the most advanced in the minors and is only getting better, giving him all the ingredients of a frontline starter. If he can refine his delivery and strike-throwing, he has the makings of a potential ace. White reached Triple-A as a 20-year-old in 2025 and should reach the majors in 2026.

Year	Age	Club (League)	Level	W	L	ERA	G	GS	IP	H	HR	BB	SO	BB%	SO%	WHIP	AVG
2025	20	Beloit (MWL)	A+	2	2	2.83	9	9	35	22	0	17	53	11.7	36.6	1.11	.176
2025	20	Pensacola (SL)	AA	2	1	1.59	10	10	45	30	2	24	75	12.6	39.3	1.19	.183
2025	20	Jacksonville (IL)	AAA	0	0	3.86	2	2	9	3	0	10	17	25.0	42.5	1.39	.111
		Minor League Totals		10	8	2.65	45	44	190	146	8	95	272	11.7	33.5	1.27	.209

MIAMI MARLINS

2 ROBBY SNELLING, LHP
FB: 60. **CB:** 60. **SL:** 55. **CH:** 55. **CTL:** 50. **BA Grade:** 60. **Risk:** Average. **Adj:** 50.

Born: December 19, 2003. **B-T:** R-L. **HT:** 6-2. **WT:** 227.
Drafted: HS—Reno, NV, 2022 (1st round supp.). **Signed by:** Tim Reynolds (Padres).
TRACK RECORD: A standout two-sport athlete in high school, Snelling chose baseball over football after signing with the Padres for $3 million—$1 million over slot—as a supplemental first-round pick. He dominated his first full season in 2023 with a 1.82 ERA, rising to Double-A and earning Minor League Pitcher of the Year honors. But a rocky 2024 followed. Snelling's command and sharpness faded en route to a 6.01 ERA in 16 starts before he was traded to the Marlins. He rebounded in 2025, ranking fourth in the minors with 166 strikeouts, fifth with a 2.51 ERA and excelling at Triple-A Jacksonville with a 1.27 ERA and 81 strikeouts to 17 walks over 63.2 innings.
SCOUTING REPORT: Snelling's 2024 struggles stemmed from erratic command, a passive approach and a velocity dip that left him sitting 91-93 mph and topping out at 95. His 2025 rebound began with regained power and subtle tweaks to his delivery, which is now more upright and repeatable and helped restore his reputation as an advanced strike-thrower. From a high three-quarters slot, he averaged 94.5 mph and touched 99 with a relatively flat approach angle to produce a 30% miss rate and 31% chase rate on fastballs—including 37% and 40%, respectively, at Triple-A. He also leaned more on a sharp, two-plane low-80s curveball now viewed as plus, reshaped his slider into a tighter gyro look and turned his firm, high-80s changeup into a reliable chase weapon against righthanded hitters. The improved mechanics yielded a career-best 7.1% walk rate alongside a 30.3% strikeout rate.
THE FUTURE: After quelling many of the doubts raised by his uneven 2024, Snelling now straddles the line between a No. 2 and No. 3 starter who could break camp with the Marlins in 2026. If he begins in Triple-A, his major league debut shouldn't be too far down the road.

Year	Age	Club (League)	Level	W	L	ERA	G	GS	IP	H	HR	BB	SO	BB%	SO%	WHIP	AVG
2025	21	Pensacola (SL)	AA	3	5	3.61	14	14	72	66	6	22	85	7.3	28.2	1.22	.238
2025	21	Jacksonville (IL)	AAA	6	2	1.27	11	11	64	46	4	17	81	6.9	32.9	0.99	.203
		Minor League Totals		24	20	3.17	71	71	355	324	31	118	399	8.0	27.1	1.25	.242

3 AIVA ARQUETTE, SS
HIT: 50. **POW:** 60. **RUN:** 45. **FLD:** 50. **ARM:** 60. **BA Grade:** 60. **Risk:** Average. **Adj:** 50.

Born: October 17, 2003. **B-T:** R-R. **HT:** 6-5. **WT:** 220.
Drafted: Oregon State, 2025 (1st round). **Signed by:** Scott Fairbanks.
TRACK RECORD: Arquette broke out in 2024 at Washington, where he hit .325/.384/.574 with 12 home runs. He then transferred to Oregon State in 2025, shifted from second base to shortstop and elevated his game further by slashing .354/.461/.654 with 19 home runs. The Marlins drafted him seventh overall and signed him for a slot value bonus of $7,149,900.
SCOUTING REPORT: At 6-foot-5 and 220 pounds, Arquette looks the part of a modern slugger. His free and easy righthanded swing generates above-average bat speed and plus raw power, allowing him to drive the ball to all fields while punishing mistakes to his pull side. Though swing-and-miss and chase tendencies have accompanied that pop, he refined his approach in 2025, showing improved plate discipline and producing a thunderous 93.5 mph average exit velocity with a 59% hard-hit rate. At times, he over-corrected—his 60% zone-swing rate reflected a bit of hesitation—but the overall approach was more measured and mature. Arquette moves well for his size, grading as an average runner once underway. He's never been a true basestealing threat, yet he matched his college high with seven steals in 27 games at High-A Beloit to align with the Marlins' emphasis on basepath aggression. Defensively, he's shown enough fluidity and arm strength to stick at shortstop, with above-average instincts, reliable hands and a plus, accurate arm from a lower slot. His physicality and offensive profile could ultimately fit at third base if a move becomes necessary.
THE FUTURE: Arquette's combination of body control and powerful frame made him one of few sure-thing middle infielders in a 2025 draft class thin on them. He has the bat, arm strength and internal clock to remain at a premium position and should at least reach the upper minors in 2026.

Year	Age	Club (League)	Level	AVG	G	AB	R	H	2B	3B	HR	RBI	BB	SO	SB	OBP	SLG
2025	21	Beloit (MWL)	A+	.242	27	99	11	24	5	0	1	10	17	27	7	.350	.323
		Minor League Totals		.242	27	99	11	24	5	0	1	10	17	27	7	.350	.323

MIAMI MARLINS

4. JOE MACK, C

HIT: 40. **POW:** 55. **RUN:** 40. **FLD:** 60. **ARM:** 65. **BA Grade:** 55. **Risk:** Average. **Adj:** 45.

Born: December 27, 2002. **B-T:** L-R. **HT:** 6-0. **WT:** 210.
Drafted: HS—East Amherst, NY, 2021 (1st round supp.). **Signed by:** Alex Smith.
TRACK RECORD: After an injury-shortened first full pro season in 2022 and a relatively poor 2023 campaign, Mack finally broke through in 2024, launching 24 home runs and lighting up the Midwest League on his way to Double-A Pensacola and Top 100 Prospects status. His ascent continued in 2025. It took just 13 strong games in Double-A to earn a promotion to Triple-A Jacksonville, where he hit .250/.320/.459 with 18 home runs, 18 doubles and a 90 mph average exit velocity over 99 games.
SCOUTING REPORT: Mack features a distinctive look in the box. The lefthanded batter stands tall with a high handset and compact load. Earlier in his career, he used a leg kick for timing and rhythm, but he pared it down in 2025. His quick bat and strong forearms help him generate above-average raw power that plays in games despite a modest hit tool. Mack's pitch recognition and discipline are roughly average—he swung and missed in the zone 25% of the time and chased 28%—but when he connects, the contact is loud, producing high-end exit velocities to his pull side. A below-average runner overall, he moves fluidly for his size and position with a smooth gait and better-than-expected agility. Behind the plate, he's an above-average receiver who presents pitches quietly and earns strikes on the edges, aided by near plus mobility and soft hands. His plus arm controls the run game. He threw out 32% of basestealers in 2025.
THE FUTURE: Mack's blend of defense, power and a refined approach makes him one of the top catching prospects in the upper minors. The Marlins added Mack to the 40-man roster this offseason, shielding him from the Rule 5 draft. He will likely begin 2026 at Triple-A as the Marlins find playing time for him along with big league catchers Agustin Ramirez and Liam Hicks.

Year	Age	Club (League)	Level	AVG	G	AB	R	H	2B	3B	HR	RBI	BB	SO	SB	OBP	SLG
2025	22	Pensacola (SL)	AA	.318	13	44	12	14	4	0	3	5	10	12	1	.464	.614
2025	22	Jacksonville (IL)	AAA	.250	99	364	58	91	18	2	18	53	35	115	8	.320	.459
		Minor League Totals		.239	420	1530	215	365	70	3	57	189	197	447	12	.332	.400

5. KEVIN DEFRANK, RHP

FB: 70. **SW:** 55. **CH:** 60. **CTL:** 45. **BA Grade:** 60. **Risk:** Extreme. **Adj:** 40.

Born: August 11, 2008. **B-T:** R-R. **HT:** 6-5. **WT:** 235.
Signed: Dominican Republic, 2025. **Signed by:** Sahir Fersobe.
TRACK RECORD: The Marlins were enamored of Defrank's blend of raw stuff and athleticism when they signed him out of the Dominican Republic in 2025. They signed him for $560,000, handing him the fourth-largest bonus given to a pitcher in that international signing class. He quickly validated the investment, posting a 3.19 ERA with 34 strikeouts to 10 walks over 31 innings in the Dominican Summer League. He was 16 years old for most of the season.
SCOUTING REPORT: Defrank stands out before even taking the mound. He boasts a listed 6-foot-5, 235-pound frame that's unusually thick and muscular for a teenager. The Marlins were first drawn to his exceptional arm speed and athleticism, traits that allowed him to reach the mid 90s at signing and sit in the upper 90s now while occasionally touching triple digits. His fastball features both run and ride. It's still a bit raw in shape but already overpowering for his age. He complements it with a plus changeup showing heavy sink and fade, along with a sweeping slider that many evaluators project as a future plus pitch. Defrank uses a high leg kick and a fluid three-quarters release that accentuates his arm speed. His physicality is an asset, but maintaining it will be crucial, because avoiding bad weight as he matures will be key to preserving his velocity and smooth delivery. Right now, he shows a standout combination of flexibility and power that allows him to get his body into ideal positions as he moves down the mound.
THE FUTURE: Having turned 17 in August, Defrank could return to the DSL in 2026, with a U.S. debut later in the year well within reach. If he can maintain his athleticism and continue refining his delivery, he has the ingredients of a future frontline starter—though he remains several developmental steps away from realizing that potential.

Year	Age	Club (League)	Level	W	L	ERA	G	GS	IP	H	HR	BB	SO	BB%	SO%	WHIP	AVG
2025	16	DSL Miami	Rk	0	1	3.19	10	10	31	30	1	10	34	7.1	24.1	1.29	.250
		Minor League Totals		0	1	3.19	10	10	31	30	1	10	34	7.1	24.1	1.29	.250

MIAMI MARLINS

6 KEMP ALDERMAN, OF
HIT: 45. **POW:** 60. **RUN:** 45. **FLD:** 45. **ARM:** 60. **BA Grade:** 50. **Risk:** Average. **Adj:** 40.

Born: August 20, 2002. **B-T:** R-R. **HT:** 6-2. **WT:** 235.
Drafted: Mississippi, 2023 (2nd round). **Signed by:** Davis Knapp.
TRACK RECORD: Alderman was one of the most visible successes under the Marlins' revamped player development efforts, which emphasized simplified communication to help hitters focus on three key pillars: swing decisions, contact rate and quality of contact. After hitting eight home runs with a .242 average in 2024, Alderman broke out in 2025, slugging 22 homers with 22 steals and a .285/.338/.482 line across 110 games at Double-A Pensacola and 20 at Triple-A Jacksonville. The performance marked not just a surge in output, but proof of concept for Miami's developmental overhaul.
SCOUTING REPORT: Alderman is a stocky righthanded hitter with massive power—a defining trait that's endured even after trimming 20 pounds since being drafted. He's worked diligently to streamline his swing, quieting his mechanics and maintaining a tighter path than most hitters with his power profile. Despite that progress, chase tendencies remain. He swung at pitches out of the zone 30% of the time in 2025, showing improved restraint against high velocity but continued vulnerability to spin. Even so, Alderman's overall approach improved markedly, as he attacked strikes aggressively and limited mistakes. Whether his bat-to-ball skills hold up against major league pitching will be his key test. Defensively, Alderman projects as a corner outfielder with a plus arm that once produced mid-90s velocity off the mound in his amateur days. He's a solid runner underway, though he's still refining his timing on the bases.
THE FUTURE: Alderman's power surge in 2025 vaulted him into near-big league readiness and solidified his status as a bat-first corner outfielder with a power-over-hit profile. His defense has improved, but his impact will come at the plate. A strong spring could earn him a spot on the Opening Day roster.

Year	Age	Club (League)	Level	AVG	G	AB	R	H	2B	3B	HR	RBI	BB	SO	SB	OBP	SLG
2025	22	Pensacola (SL)	AA	.282	110	412	56	116	13	5	15	53	34	102	20	.337	.447
2025	22	Jacksonville (IL)	AAA	.303	20	76	13	23	7	0	7	17	5	22	2	.341	.671
		Minor League Totals		.261	241	894	115	233	43	8	31	131	73	241	31	.321	.431

7 CAM CANNARELLA, OF
HIT: 55. **POW:** 30. **RUN:** 60. **FLD:** 70. **ARM:** 30. **BA Grade:** 50. **Risk:** Average. **Adj:** 40.

Born: September 6, 2003. **B-T:** L-R. **HT:** 6-0. **WT:** 185.
Drafted: Clemson, 2025 (1st round supp.). **Signed by:** Brett Bittiger.
TRACK RECORD: Cannarella burst onto the scene as the 2023 ACC freshman of the year after hitting .388 with 24 stolen bases at Clemson. He followed with another standout campaign in 2024, increasing his home run total from seven to 11 despite playing through a shoulder injury that limited his running game and ability to throw. After having labrum surgery before the 2025 season, Cannarella returned to form as a junior. He cemented his offensive reputation as a career .360/.453/.551 hitter, and the Marlins drafted him 43rd overall and signed him for a slightly over-slot bonus of $2,277,425. He batted .284/.337/.375 with six doubles in 22 games during his pro debut with High-A Beloit.
SCOUTING REPORT: A wiry 6-foot center fielder, Cannarella stands out for his exceptional athleticism, defense and pure hitting ability. The lefthanded batter hits from an open stance with a somewhat busy hand load, but he consistently makes quality swing decisions and above-average contact to produce sharp line drives to all fields. Offensively, he's a clear hit-over-power player—he hit just three home runs as a junior and is unlikely to exceed double digits in pro ball—but his advanced barrel control and feel for the zone give him a realistic chance to remain a .300 hitter. Cannarella's calling card is his defense. His plus speed and outstanding instincts make him a natural in center field, where he routinely tracks down balls in the gaps and makes highlight-reel plays. His arm strength remains a concern. It was below-average even before his labrum injury and has since regressed further.
THE FUTURE: Cannarella's near-elite center field defense and above-average hit tool make him worth the gamble even if his arm strength never fully returns. He's expected to open 2026 back at High-A Beloit.

Year	Age	Club (League)	Level	AVG	G	AB	R	H	2B	3B	HR	RBI	BB	SO	SB	OBP	SLG
2025	21	Beloit (MWL)	A+	.284	22	88	11	25	6	1	0	6	7	18	1	.337	.375
		Minor League Totals		.284	22	88	11	25	6	1	0	6	7	18	1	.337	.375

MIAMI MARLINS

8 BRANDON COMPTON, OF

HIT: 40. **POW:** 60. **RUN:** 50. **FLD:** 45. **ARM:** 45. **BA Grade:** 50. **Risk:** Average. **Adj:** 40.

Born: October 27, 2003. **B-T:** L-L. **HT:** 6-1. **WT:** 225.
Drafted: Arizona State, 2025 (2nd round). **Signed by:** Scott Stanley.
TRACK RECORD: Compton made an immediate splash as a freshman at Arizona State in 2024, hitting .355/.427/.661 with 14 home runs and 16 doubles to earn Pac-12 freshman of the year honors. He carried that momentum into a strong summer with Cotuit in the Cape Cod League and entered his 2025 draft-eligible season with high expectations. Though he regressed slightly, Compton still produced a solid .278/.383/.498 line with nine home runs and 19 doubles while upping his walk rate from 10.8% to 15.3%. The Marlins drafted him in the second round and signed him for $2 million, which was slightly under slot value. Compton hit .217/.354/.359 with two home runs, a 32.7% strikeout rate and 16.8% walk rate in his first taste of pro ball with High-A Beloit.
SCOUTING REPORT: Compton packs considerable strength and power into his barrel-chested 6-foot-1, 225-pound frame. He generates easy plus raw power with a short, compact lefthanded swing that produces 90th percentile exit velocities around 110 mph. While power is his calling card, his approach remains volatile. After a strong start to 2025, his discipline regressed, as he expanded the zone too often and swung through quality velocity. He hit just .139 against fastballs at 93 mph or higher. He'll need to refine his pitch recognition and contact skills, particularly against spin. Compton does show some on-base ability with a 13.2% career walk rate as an amateur, but there's pressure on his bat given his likely future in left field, where he profiles as an average runner and a fringy thrower and defender.
THE FUTURE: The Marlins bet on Compton's power when they selected him in the second round. For him to meet those expectations, continued refinement of his approach will be key. He's expected to begin that process back at High-A Beloit in 2026.

Year	Age	Club (League)	Level	AVG	G	AB	R	H	2B	3B	HR	RBI	BB	SO	SB	OBP	SLG
2025	21	Beloit (MWL)	A+	.217	27	92	9	20	3	2	2	17	19	37	8	.354	.359
		Minor League Totals		.217	27	92	9	20	3	2	2	17	19	37	8	.354	.359

9 KARSON MILBRANDT, RHP

FB: 55. **CB:** 55. **SL:** 50. **CH:** 45. **CT:** 60. **CTL:** 40. **BA Grade:** 50. **Risk:** Average. **Adj:** 40.

Born: April 21, 2004. **B-T:** R-R. **HT:** 6-2. **WT:** 190.
Drafted: HS—Liberty, MO, 2022 (3rd round). **Signed by:** Ryan Cisterna.
TRACK RECORD: A two-sport star at Liberty High and Missouri's 2022 Gatorade player of the year, Milbrandt was drafted by the Marlins in the third round in 2022 and signed for an over-slot $1.5 million. After posting a 5.09 ERA with 94 strikeouts over 97.1 innings between Low-A Jupiter and High-A Beloit in 2023, he took a step forward with a 4.33 ERA and 91 strikeouts in 97.2 innings the following year. His 2025 campaign was his best yet: a 3.00 ERA with 113 strikeouts, 48 walks over 90 innings and a late-season promotion to Double-A Pensacola.
SCOUTING REPORT: At 6-foot-2 and 190 pounds, Milbrandt boasts an athletic frame, low-effort delivery and plus arm speed. Prior to the 2025 season, he added roughly 20 pounds of healthy weight to better harness his mechanics and address control issues that plagued his first two pro seasons. Working from a mid three-quarters arm slot, he sits 94-96 mph with his fastball, touches 98 and is most effective when elevating it for swings and misses. He leaned more heavily on his slider in 2025—up to about 30% usage—and the mid-to-high-80s pitch produced a 33% miss rate and 43% chase rate with sharp two-plane break. He also mixes in a tight low-80s curveball with strong vertical depth that misses bats at a 46% clip and elicits chases 36% of the time, while also showing a high-80s cutter that evaluators believe could become a plus pitch after it generated a 40% whiff rate in 2025.
THE FUTURE: The Marlins get one more season to evaluate Milbrandt for the 40-man roster. That provides time to continue developing him deliberately while refining his mechanics and tightening his command. He has the pure stuff to project as a back-end starter, but improved strike-throwing will be essential to keep him from shifting to the bullpen.

Year	Age	Club (League)	Level	W	L	ERA	G	GS	IP	H	HR	BB	SO	BB%	SO%	WHIP	AVG
2025	21	Jupiter (FSL)	A	0	0	0.00	1	1	2	0	0	1	2	12.5	25.0	0.50	.000
2025	21	Beloit (MWL)	A+	2	5	3.26	19	19	77	59	3	43	101	12.8	30.1	1.32	.208
2025	21	Pensacola (SL)	AA	1	0	1.69	2	2	11	8	0	4	10	8.9	22.2	1.13	.200
		Minor League Totals		7	19	4.17	68	68	285	255	13	156	298	12.4	23.6	1.44	.237

MIAMI MARLINS

10 STARLYN CABA, SS
HIT: 50. **POW:** 35. **RUN:** 60. **FLD:** 70. **ARM:** 55. **BA Grade:** 50. **Risk:** High. **Adj:** 35.

Born: December 6, 2005. **B-T:** B-R. **HT:** 5-9. **WT:** 160.
Signed: Dominican Republic, 2023. **Signed by:** Luis Garcia (Phillies).
TRACK RECORD: Caba signed with the Phillies for the top bonus in their 2023 international class and impressed in his debut, which was cut short by a left elbow injury. He returned in 2024 with no lingering effects, earning the No. 1 spot on the Florida Complex League prospects ranking before a late-season promotion to Low-A Clearwater, where he played 26 games. The Marlins acquired Caba from Philadelphia in a December 2024 trade for Jesús Luzardo. In 2025, he appeared in 51 games for Low-A Jupiter, hitting .222/.335/.278 with one home run. He missed two months after spraining his left thumb while sliding into second base.
SCOUTING REPORT: Caba hasn't yet replicated the offensive success of his 2024 stateside debut in the FCL. He has struggled to find consistent impact in Class A with two organizations. He hits from both sides of the plate with a flat, contact-oriented swing and lacks the strength to produce more than modest exit velocities. Though his batting line hasn't reflected it, Caba shows patience and rarely chases. Evaluators believe that even modest offensive improvement could carry him through the system because of his elite defense. A fluid, instinctive shortstop with an above-average arm, Caba's twitch and body control allow him to make rangy plays to either side look routine. A plus runner, he stole 50 bases in 79 games in 2024 but just 14 in 51 games in 2025. He capped his season in the Arizona Fall League.
THE FUTURE: Caba will be just 20 years old entering his fourth professional season. The athletic middle infielder will need to show real offensive progress to unlock his full potential. If his bat develops, he projects as a top-of-the-order catalyst with Gold Glove-caliber defense at a premium position. If it doesn't, his glove alone may not be enough to lift him beyond a replacement-level profile.

Year	Age	Club (League)	Level	AVG	G	AB	R	H	2B	3B	HR	RBI	BB	SO	SB	OBP	SLG
2025	19	Jupiter (FSL)	A	.222	51	194	28	43	6	1	1	21	34	34	14	.335	.278
		Minor League Totals		.254	141	500	101	127	14	4	3	55	113	84	67	.392	.316

11 FENWICK TRIMBLE, OF
HIT: 55. **POW:** 45. **RUN:** 60. **FLD:** 50. **ARM:** 45. **BA Grade:** 50. **Risk:** High. **Adj:** 35.

Born: August 29, 2002. **B-T:** R-R. **HT:** 6-3. **WT:** 200. **Drafted:** James Madison, 2024 (4th round).
Signed by: Blake Newsome.
TRACK RECORD: Trimble turned a strong sophomore season at James Madison in 2024 into a fourth-round pick by Miami and signed for $550,000. He held his own at Low-A Jupiter after the draft, then opened 2025 at High-A Beloit before reaching Double-A Pensacola. Across the two stops he hit .253/.372/.402 with seven home runs, 19 doubles and 31 steals in 35 tries while posting an 18.8% strikeout rate and 13.8% walk rate.
SCOUTING REPORT: Trimble owns a short, efficient swing with above-average bat speed driven by strong wrists, which helped him to produce better underlying data than his surface stats might suggest in his first full professional season. Trimble recorded 88 mph average and 104 mph 90th percentile exit velocities. He rarely expanded the zone in 2025, chasing just 21% of the time, which he paired with an 18% in-zone whiff rate. The next step is generating more loft to access his strength. His contact rate and on-base ability play up because he's a consistently impactful baserunner who improved his reads and jumps. He's an above-average athlete whose speed and routes fit center field, though his arm grades as fringe-average and may push him to left field.
THE FUTURE: Trimble's plate discipline, contact skills, power potential and chance to play center field give him a path to value. If he adds launch angle and maintains his efficiency on the bases, he projects as a regular with on-base skill and secondary value. He should return to Double-A to open 2026, with a realistic chance to reach Triple-A by midseason.

Year	Age	Club (League)	Level	AVG	G	AB	R	H	2B	3B	HR	RBI	BB	SO	SB	OBP	SLG
2025	22	FCL Marlins	Rk	.250	1	4	0	1	0	0	0	0	1	0	.250	.250
2025	22	Beloit (MWL)	A+	.284	29	102	16	29	7	2	2	14	20	23	15	.407	.422
2025	22	Pensacola (SL)	AA	.237	54	190	23	45	12	0	6	27	29	43	16	.355	.395
		Minor League Totals		.255	113	416	49	106	23	4	7	53	54	88	42	.351	.380

MIAMI MARLINS

12 LUIS COVA, OF
HIT: 50. **POW:** 55. **RUN:** 65. **FLD:** 55. **ARM:** 50. **BA Grade:** 55. **Risk:** Extreme. **Adj:** 35.

Born: February 1, 2007. **B-T:** R-R. **HT:** 6-1. **WT:** 160. **Signed:** Venezuela, 2024.
Signed by: Adrian Lorenzo/Roman Ocumarez/Manny Padron/Nestor Moreno.
TRACK RECORD: Cova signed for $1.4 million as the centerpiece of Miami's 2024 international class and reported to the Dominican Summer League that year. He showed modest results in his debut, hitting .239/.376/.348 with three home runs, nine doubles and 36 stolen bases in 55 games. He repeated the level in 2025 and produced a significant uptick in performance, batting .299/.422/.537 with nine homers, 11 doubles and 35 steals in 50 games.
SCOUTING REPORT: Cova entered Miami's system with promising baseline traits: strike-zone awareness, near double-plus speed, at least average contact ability and average strength that produced mostly ground-ball contact. Miami reworked his righthanded swing to create more loft and access additional power, resulting in a jump in 90th percentile exit velocity from 98.8 to 101.7 mph and a better hard-hit launch angle in 2025. His flyball and line-drive rates rose by about 10% as well. The added intent brought corresponding increases in miss and strikeout rates, though both remained manageable. Cova's speed translates to high-end baserunning value and, paired with an average arm, could help to keep him in center field.
THE FUTURE: Repeating the DSL is not ideal, but Cova's year-over-year progress was tangible and supported by meaningful data gains. Entering his age-19 season, he remains a long-term development project but is a strong candidate to move stateside to start 2026. He has the upside of an everyday outfielder.

Year	Age	Club (League)	Level	AVG	G	AB	R	H	2B	3B	HR	RBI	BB	SO	SB	OBP	SLG
2025	18	DSL Marlins	Rk	.299	50	177	49	53	11	2	9	35	34	40	35	.422	.537
		Minor League Totals		.269	105	361	93	97	20	3	12	61	69	63	71	.398	.440

13 DILLON HEAD, OF
HIT: 45. **POW:** 40. **RUN:** 70. **FLD:** 60. **ARM:** 50. **BA Grade:** 50. **Risk:** High. **Adj:** 35.

Born: October 11, 2004. **B-T:** L-L. **HT:** 6-0. **WT:** 185. **Drafted:** HS—Flossmoor, IL, 2023 (1st round).
Signed by: Troy Hoerner (Padres).
TRACK RECORD: Head was a favorite of Padres GM A.J. Preller in the 2023 draft and became San Diego's first-round pick. However, his stay with San Diego was short-lived. He played 48 games before being traded to Miami for Luis Arraez a month into the 2024 season. Shortly after the deal, Head injured his left hip and required season-ending surgery. Healthy again in 2025, he returned to Low-A Jupiter and hit .223/.334/.318 with four home runs, four doubles, nine triples—fourth most in the Florida State League—and 36 stolen bases.
SCOUTING REPORT: Head's amateur profile was built on an advanced hit tool, strong plate discipline and double-plus speed, but his pro production hasn't matched that foundation. He remains disciplined and ran a 13.8% walk rate and 13% in-zone whiff rate in 2025, yet his lefthanded swing produced below-average contact quality. His 85.2 mph average exit velocity was paired with a low 8.8% barrel rate and poor expected results. His groundball rate climbed from his limited 2024 sample into 2025, and though he posted more line drives, the overall batted-ball impact remained light. Head's speed and defense continue to provide the most reliable value. Even after surgery, he grades as a double-plus runner, with some evaluators placing him at the top of the scale. He handles center field with cleaner routes, improved jumps and a slightly above-average arm, giving him a legitimate chance to stay at the position.
THE FUTURE: Head must generate more authoritative line-drive contact to project beyond a speed-and-defense profile, but those tools give him a strong baseline. He's likely to return to High-A Beloit to begin 2026 after playing only one game there in 2025.

Year	Age	Club (League)	Level	AVG	G	AB	R	H	2B	3B	HR	RBI	BB	SO	SB	OBP	SLG
2025	20	Jupiter (FSL)	A	.223	96	359	60	80	4	9	4	39	58	81	36	.334	.318
2025	20	Beloit (MWL)	A+	.333	1	3	0	1	0	0	0	0	1	1	1	.500	.333
		Minor League Totals		.235	150	578	95	136	14	15	7	61	84	131	46	.337	.348

14 ANDREW SALAS, OF/SS
HIT: 55. **POW:** 35. **RUN:** 60. **FLD:** 60. **ARM:** 55. **BA Grade:** 55. **Risk:** Extreme. **Adj:** 35.

Born: March 4, 2008. **B-T:** B-R. **HT:** 6-2. **WT:** 180. **Signed:** Venezuela, 2025. **Signed by:** Adrian Lorenzo/Manny Padron.
TRACK RECORD: Salas signed with Miami for $3.7 million in 2025, the highest bonus for a Venezuelan international free agent in his class. The Marlins pushed the 6-foot-2 switch-hitter aggressively to Low-A Jupiter in 2025, where he was the youngest player in the Florida State League. He hit .186/.319/.245 with three home runs, nine doubles and 39 steals, striking out 110 times with 72 walks across 104 games. Salas'

brothers Ethan and Jose Jr. also play professionally, with the former ranking as the Padres' top prospect.
SCOUTING REPORT: Salas entered pro ball with advanced feel and game awareness, which showed in a 15.9% walk rate that ranked fifth in the FSL and third among league teenagers, but he swung at only about 38% of pitches—a passive approach. His quiet load and short, direct swing create a line-drive profile, yet he was overmatched, batting under .150 against offspeed pitches and producing an 80.8 mph average exit velocity, the fifth lowest in the minors among players with at least 250 plate appearances. His contact quality was light across the board, and though his launch characteristics were sound when he did connect, he did not hit the ball hard enough to benefit from them. Signed as a shortstop, he spent most of 2025 in center field, where his athleticism, range and strong arm translated cleanly.
THE FUTURE: At 17, Salas needs physical development and improved performance against secondary pitches. His instincts, discipline and defensive versatility give him upside as a hit-first center fielder or shortstop if the bat progresses. He should return to Jupiter in 2026.

Year	Age	Club (League)	Level	AVG	G	AB	R	H	2B	3B	HR	RBI	BB	SO	SB	OBP	SLG
2025	17	Jupiter (FSL)	A	.186	104	371	56	69	9	2	3	21	72	110	39	.319	.245
		Minor League Totals		.186	104	371	56	69	9	2	3	21	72	110	39	.319	.245

15 LUIS ARANA, SS/3B
HIT: 60. **POW:** 35. **RUN:** 55. **FLD:** 55. **ARM:** 60. **BA Grade:** 55. **Risk:** Extreme. **Adj:** 35.

Born: March 19, 2008. **B-T:** B-R. **HT:** 5-10. **WT:** 154. **Signed:** Venezuela, 2025. **Signed by:** Néstor Moreno.
TRACK RECORD: Arana signed with Miami out of Venezuela for $30,000, a modest figure that made him an under-the-radar addition to the club's 2025 international class. Assigned to the Dominican Summer League, he performed well as a 17-year-old, hitting .297/.419/.476 with five home runs, 10 doubles, 28 steals and a strong 30-to-18 walk-to-strikeout ratio over 50 games.
SCOUTING REPORT: Arana produces surprising impact relative to his 5-foot-10, 154-pound frame. A switch-hitter, he owns a clean, on-plane swing from both sides with above-average bat speed and strong feel for contact. He is extremely selective—bordering on passive—but showed advanced bat-to-ball skills with just a 9% in-zone whiff rate. His present power lags. His 83.7 mph average exit velocity and 98.3 mph 90th percentile are both quite light, but there is still room for strength gains remaining. Defensively, Arana grew up in center field but moved to shortstop before signing and split time almost evenly between short and third in the DSL, where he showed plus arm strength and sound footwork. With added physicality, he profiles on the left side. Without it, he could shift to second base or return to the outfield. He is a plus runner whose basestealing efficiency varied due to timing inconsistencies, though he showed above-average overall potential on the bases.
THE FUTURE: Arana's trajectory depends on physical maturation, which the organization expects as he approaches his 18th birthday. His zone feel, switch-hit contact skills and defensive versatility give him developmental runway. He could repeat the DSL, but a stateside debut in 2026 remains possible.

Year	Age	Club (League)	Level	AVG	G	AB	R	H	2B	3B	HR	RBI	BB	SO	SB	OBP	SLG
2025	17	DSL Miami	Rk	.297	52	185	47	55	10	4	5	35	30	18	28	.419	.476
		Minor League Totals		.297	52	185	47	55	10	4	5	35	30	18	28	.419	.476

16 ESMIL VALENCIA, OF
HIT: 50. **POW:** 45. **RUN:** 65. **FLD:** 55. **ARM:** 65. **BA Grade:** 50. **Risk:** High. **Adj:** 35.

Born: October 9, 2005. **B-T:** R-R. **HT:** 5-10. **WT:** 182. **Signed:** Dominican Republic, 2023.
Signed by: Raymon Sanchez/Alfredo Ulloa/Hassan Wessin (Astros).
TRACK RECORD: Valencia signed with the Astros out of the Dominican Republic in 2023 and made his stateside debut in the Florida Complex League in 2024. He spent most of 2025 at Low-A Fayetteville before being traded to Miami for Jesús Sánchez at the deadline. Post-trade, he excelled at Low-A Jupiter, hitting .327/.367/.510 with three home runs, five doubles and 14 steals in 24 games.
SCOUTING REPORT: Valencia is a 5-foot-10, 182-pound righthanded hitter with an upright, closed stance and a medium-high handset. His aggressive style permeates every part of his game, which cuts both ways. He posted a 33% whiff rate and near-40% chase rate, yet he produced frequent quality contact, especially late in 2025 when he logged multiple 100-plus mph batted balls, including three in his Jupiter debut. He is a savvy runner rather than a pure burner, using reads and anticipation to steal bases and take extra bases, though a 77% stolen base success rate reflects occasional poor decisions. Defensively, he handles center field and has shown the athleticism to stay there, and evaluators consider his arm one of the best in Miami's system. Continued improvement to his routes and reads will determine whether he remains up the middle or shifts to a corner.
THE FUTURE: Valencia's late-season jump in contact quality gives evaluators optimism, though he still

MIAMI MARLINS

needs to sharpen his swing decisions and continue adding strength. His speed-driven game and emerging power support the projection of at least a useful platoon outfielder. He should open 2026 in High-A Beloit.

Year	Age	Club (League)	Level	AVG	G	AB	R	H	2B	3B	HR	RBI	BB	SO	SB	OBP	SLG
2025	19	Fayetteville (CAR)	A	.263	83	300	42	79	9	2	5	36	22	82	50	.325	.357
2025	19	Jupiter (FSL)	A	.327	24	98	13	32	5	2	3	21	8	17	14	.367	.510
		Minor League Totals		.277	194	730	111	202	26	10	12	99	54	158	91	.337	.389

17 KEYNER BENITEZ, LHP
FB: 50. **SL:** 50. **CH:** 60. **SW:** 45. **CTL:** 40. **BA Grade:** 55. **Risk:** Extreme. **Adj:** 35.

Born: May 23, 2006. **B-T:** L-L. **HT:** 6-1. **WT:** 165. **Signed:** Dominican Republic, 2023.
Signed by: Adrian Lorenzo/Roman Ocumarez/Angel Izquierdo.
TRACK RECORD: Benitez signed with Miami for $225,000 out of the Dominican Republic in 2023, reached the States at 18, and excelled across time in the Florida Complex League and at Low-A Jupiter. He returned to Jupiter in 2025 and posted a 3.89 ERA with 33 strikeouts and 24 walks in 37 innings before being sent back to the FCL for a month due in part to on-field immaturity.
SCOUTING REPORT: Benitez is a slender 6-foot-1 lefthander with a drop-and-drive delivery and a three-quarters slot that generates above-average extension, helping his fastball variants play above their 92-94 mph velocity. His four-seamer has limited carry but above-average armside run, while his sinker creates even more horizontal action. Benitez's best pitch is a mid-80s changeup with nearly 10 inches of vertical separation from his four-seamer and significant fade. Evaluators think it could evolve into a double-plus pitch. He also mixes a tight, low-to-mid-80s slider and a high-70s sweeper; neither spins particularly well and both project as average. Benitez's shapes and improving velocity give him a strong foundation, but strike-throwing remains his chief obstacle. His 13% walk rate in 2025 was a step back from 9.9% in 2024, reflecting inconsistency in repeating his delivery.
THE FUTURE: With youth and physical projection, Benitez has the ingredients for a midrotation starter if he can significantly improve consistency and strike-throwing. For now, control issues limit his reliability. He should open 2026 in High-A Beloit.

Year	Age	Club (League)	Level	W	L	ERA	G	GS	IP	H	HR	BB	SO	BB%	SO%	WHIP	AVG
2025	19	FCL Marlins	Rk	1	0	1.59	4	3	17	9	0	7	18	10.3	26.5	0.94	.155
2025	19	Jupiter (FSL)	A	1	1	3.89	11	10	37	41	1	24	33	14.0	19.3	1.76	.289
		Minor League Totals		4	7	3.14	42	37	169	128	7	85	172	12.0	24.3	1.26	.212

18 PJ MORLANDO, OF
HIT: 40. **POW:** 50. **RUN:** 55. **FLD:** 50. **ARM:** 45. **BA Grade:** 45. **Risk:** Average. **Adj:** 35.

Born: May 16, 2005. **B-T:** L-R. **HT:** 6-3. **WT:** 198. **Drafted:** HS—Summerville, SC, 2024 (1st round).
Signed by: Blake Newsome.
TRACK RECORD: The Marlins drafted Morlando 16th overall in 2024 despite a down senior spring and signed him for $3.4 million—$1.3 million under slot. His pro debut ended almost immediately due to a lumbar stress reaction. He returned in 2025 and played 58 games, including 52 with Low-A Jupiter, where he batted .226/.361/.353 with five home runs, seven doubles, six steals, a 27.4% strikeout rate and a 17.8% walk rate.
SCOUTING REPORT: Morlando's plus raw power was showcased clearly when he won the 2024 MLB High School All-American Derby, but questions about its game utility persisted. In 2025, that gap was reflected in batted-ball data: a below-average 84.8 mph average exit velocity versus a slightly above-average 102.2 mph 90th percentile EV. Miami opened Morlando's stance and raised his handset to improve his position to hit, but he struggled to make consistent contact, posting a 30.7% overall miss rate and 22.1% in-zone miss rate. He showed solid strike-zone feel with a 20.9% chase rate. Morlando generates limited loft and does not pull the ball in the air often, reducing his ability to access his raw strength. Defensively, he played mostly left field in 2025 and projects to stay there with an average arm and questions about his athleticism.
THE FUTURE: Morlando must make substantially more in-zone contact and lift the ball more frequently to access his underlying power. Without that, his path to professional value becomes unclear, and he currently projects as a platoon corner outfielder. He is likely to return to Low-A to open 2026.

Year	Age	Club (League)	Level	AVG	G	AB	R	H	2B	3B	HR	RBI	BB	SO	SB	OBP	SLG
2025	20	FCL Marlins	Rk	.067	6	15	5	1	0	0	0	0	10	9	2	.462	.067
2025	20	Jupiter (FSL)	A	.226	52	190	33	43	7	1	5	30	36	62	6	.361	.353
		Minor League Totals		.214	59	206	38	44	7	1	5	30	46	71	8	.369	.330

MIAMI MARLINS

19 JOSH WHITE, RHP
FB: 50. **CB:** 65. **SL:** 60. **CTL:** 45. **BA Grade:** 45. **Risk:** Average. **Adj:** 35.

Born: November 24, 2000. **B-T:** R-R. **HT:** 6-1. **WT:** 205. **Drafted:** California, 2022 (5th round). **Signed by:** Scott Fairbanks.

TRACK RECORD: White was drafted out of California in the fifth round in 2022 and has developed into one of Miami's most productive relief prospects. He dominated in 2025, posting a 1.86 ERA with 107 strikeouts and 23 walks across 67.2 innings, including a 2.23 ERA at Triple-A Jacksonville, which won the Triple-A national championship with White in its bullpen.

SCOUTING REPORT: A pure reliever, White attacks from a uniquely vertical, high-effort slot with plus intensity. His fastball sits 92-95 mph, touches 97, and plays at the top of the zone with carry and above-average extension, which helped it produce a roughly 30% chase rate in 2025. He backs it up with a mid-80s curveball that evaluators rated the best in Miami's system. It generated a 59% miss rate last season. His upper-80s slider features plus depth, and he locates it competently. As a fourth-year pro, White executed his full mix with fringe-average command and consistently won on pitch quality.

THE FUTURE: Added to Miami's 40-man roster in November, White is positioned to make his big league debut, possibly after a stint back at Triple-A. He projects as a reliable middle reliever with the potential to handle leverage if his 2025 performance level holds.

Year	Age	Club (League)	Level	W	L	ERA	G	GS	IP	H	HR	BB	SO	BB%	SO%	WHIP	AVG
2025	24	Pensacola (SL)	AA	6	0	1.27	18	0	28	12	0	12	50	11.1	46.3	0.85	.126
2025	24	Jacksonville (IL)	AAA	4	1	2.29	27	2	39	27	2	11	57	7.1	37.0	0.97	.193
		Minor League Totals		14	9	2.84	121	14	199	144	12	87	262	10.5	31.8	1.16	.201

20 NOBLE MEYER, RHP
FB: 45. **CB:** 50. **SL:** 50. **CH:** 50. **SW:** 55. **CTL:** 35. **BA Grade:** 50. **Risk:** High. **Adj:** 35.

Born: January 10, 2005. **B-T:** R-R. **HT:** 6-5. **WT:** 185. **Drafted:** HS—Beaverton, OR, 2023 (1st round). **Signed by:** Scott Fairbanks.

TRACK RECORD: Meyer was one of the marquee prep arms in the 2023 draft thanks to premium velocity and pitch shapes, going No. 10 overall as the first high school pitcher taken and signing for $4.5 million, about $1 million under slot. He logged 11 innings between the Florida Complex League and Low-A Jupiter in his debut, excelled briefly in Low-A in 2024, then struggled with High-A Beloit. Returning to Beloit in 2025, Meyer posted a 4.41 ERA with 72 strikeouts and 38 walks in 65.1 innings.

SCOUTING REPORT: Meyer still flashes the traits that made him a first-rounder: a long, slingy, three-quarters slot, a flat vertical approach angle on his fastball, excellent extension, a sweeper that spins north of 2,700 rpm with more than 14 inches of horizontal break and a changeup that shows significant fade and tumble. The premium velocity has vanished, though. Meyer averaged 91.6 mph in 2025 and reached 97 only a handful of times. His strike-throwing is well below-average, too, evidenced by a 12.8% walk rate, and hitters punished mistakes. He leaned more on his hard, upper-80s slider and sweeper in 2025, likely in search of feel, but still struggled to avoid barrels and walks. He did not pitch more than five innings in any of his 19 outings.

THE FUTURE: Meyer once projected as a potential No. 2 starter, but his developmental outlook is now uncertain. A bullpen future becomes increasingly likely unless his velocity returns and he makes significant gains in command. He could reach Double-A with improvement in 2026, but a return to Beloit is plausible after his 2025 struggles.

Year	Age	Club (League)	Level	W	L	ERA	G	GS	IP	H	HR	BB	SO	BB%	SO%	WHIP	AVG
2025	20	Beloit (MWL)	A+	1	7	4.41	19	19	65	53	4	38	72	12.8	24.3	1.39	.218
		Minor League Totals		3	15	4.19	43	42	150	106	12	100	172	15.0	25.8	1.37	.196

21 LIOMAR MARTINEZ, RHP
FB: 50. **SL:** 60. **CB:** 60. **CH:** 40. **SW:** 60. **SP:** 45 **CTL:** 45. **BA Grade:** 45. **Risk:** Average. **Adj:** 35.

Born: June 25, 2005. **B-T:** R-R. **HT:** 6-2. **WT:** 165. **Signed:** Dominican Republic, 2022. **Signed by:** Angel Izquierdo.

TRACK RECORD: Martinez signed with Miami for $80,000 out of the Dominican Republic in 2022 and posted a 4.13 ERA in the Dominican Summer League. His 2023 stateside debut was rocky, producing a 9.53 ERA with 22 strikeouts and 14 walks in 28.1 innings. He made steady progress in 2024 across the Florida Complex League and Low-A Jupiter, posting a 4.88 ERA with 52 strikeouts and 39 walks in 51.2 innings. Returning to Jupiter in 2025, Martinez delivered his best season yet, recording a 3.30 ERA with 119 strikeouts and 41 walks over 101 innings.

SCOUTING REPORT: Martinez has a lean, 6-foot-2, 165-pound, highly projectable frame with a loose, low-effort delivery and solid arm speed. His best pitch is a high-70s, top-down curveball that earned a

MIAMI MARLINS

47% miss rate despite 35% usage. He pairs it with a 92-94 mph fastball with carry up and sink down. The pitch had a flat approach angle that plays at the top of the zone. He also mixes a low-80s sweeper with strong horizontal action and a two-plane breaking slider. A mid-80s changeup and splitter trail behind as developmental pieces. His whippy, three-quarters release helps all of his offerings play up and gives him avenues to access further velocity as he gains strength.

THE FUTURE: Martinez showed the ingredients of a six-pitch starter with movement, deception and projection. Continued strike-throwing gains will determine whether he reaches his ceiling as a back-end starter. He should open 2026 at High-A Beloit with a path to Double-A if he carries forward last season's improvements.

Year	Age	Club (League)	Level	W	L	ERA	G	GS	IP	H	HR	BB	SO	BB%	SO%	WHIP	AVG
2025	20	Jupiter (FSL)	A	5	5	3.30	22	20	101	72	9	41	119	9.7	28.1	1.12	.197
		Minor League Totals		9	17	4.65	57	44	205	178	24	102	207	11.2	22.7	1.37	.230

22 GRANT SHEPARDSON, RHP

FB: 45. **CH:** 45. **CT:** 50. **SW:** 55 **CTL:** 45. **BA Grade:** 45. **Risk:** Average. **Adj:** 35.

Born: October 10, 2005. **B-T:** R-R. **HT:** 6-1. **WT:** 195. **Drafted:** HS—Highlands Ranch, CO, 2024 (5th round).
Signed by: Scott Stanley.

TRACK RECORD: Shepardson rose late in the 2024 draft cycle and was selected by Miami in the fifth round, signing well over slot to bypass his commitment to San Francisco. He debuted in 2025 and excelled in the Florida Complex League, posting a 3.67 ERA with 47 strikeouts and 18 walks in 41.2 innings. Promoted to Low-A Jupiter late in the year, he struggled in six relief outings, walking more than a batter per inning.

SCOUTING REPORT: A well-built 6-foot-1 righthander, Shepardson uses a deep arm stroke in a drop-and-drive delivery with a three-quarters release and slight crossfire. He moves well on the mound and shows solid arm speed across a three-pitch core: a low-to-mid-90s fastball, a high-spin sweeper and a mid-80s cutter with excellent spin. His upper-80s changeup shows tumble and fade and offers useful separation off his fastball, though he rarely uses it. His heater has some carry at the top of the zone and a flat approach angle that pairs well with the changeup. Shepardson showed reasonably steady strike-throwing in the FCL, but his control backed up in Jupiter, with walks becoming an issue late in the season.

THE FUTURE: If Shepardson sharpens his control and continues to develop both the velocity and shape of his fastball, he has the ingredients for a midrotation starter, though his frame is somewhat undersized for that outcome. A back-end starter or multi-inning bullpen profile is more likely. He should return to Low-A Jupiter to open 2026.

Year	Age	Club (League)	Level	W	L	ERA	G	GS	IP	H	HR	BB	SO	BB%	SO%	WHIP	AVG
2025	19	FCL Marlins	Rk	2	3	3.67	11	10	42	36	3	18	47	10.1	26.4	1.30	.238
2025	19	Jupiter (FSL)	A	2	2	5.93	6	0	14	10	0	15	12	21.7	17.4	1.83	.204
		Minor League Totals		4	5	4.23	17	10	55	46	3	33	59	13.4	23.9	1.43	.230

23 NATE PAYNE, LHP

FB: 50. **CB:** 60. **SL:** 50. **CH:** 55. **CTL:** 40. **BA Grade:** 45. **Risk:** Average. **Adj:** 35.

Born: August 19, 2005. **B-T:** L-L. **HT:** 6-3. **WT:** 200. **Drafted:** HS—Harrisburg, PA, 2024 (18th round).
SIGNED BY: Alex Smith.

TRACK RECORD: The Marlins drafted Payne out of the Pennsylvania prep ranks in the 18th round in 2024, signing him for $235,000. Then viewed as a softer-throwing lefty with feel, he debuted in 2025 and quickly stood out, leading the Florida Complex League with 55 strikeouts in 39.2 innings before earning a promotion to Low-A Jupiter. He remained effective there and finished his first pro season with a 3.20 ERA and 73 strikeouts to 37 walks in 56.1 innings.

SCOUTING REPORT: Based on his 2025 performance, Payne looked like a late-round steal. He worked off a fastball that reached the mid 90s while mixing a slider, curveball and kick-changeup. His high-70s curveball was widely viewed as a plus pitch, featuring strong depth and spin, and some evaluators projected his changeup—average now—to become a future plus offering. He throws from a three-quarters slot with easy velocity and gets ride up in the zone, though his fastball is most effective with run and sink at the knees. His pitch mix gives him multiple avenues to miss bats, though strike-throwing remains inconsistent.

THE FUTURE: Payne has sufficient size, physicality and pitch quality to project as a potential back-of-the-rotation starter if he improves his ability to repeat his delivery and find the zone more consistently. If starter command never fully arrives, the strength and diversity of his secondaries could make him a valuable lefthanded bullpen option.

MIAMI MARLINS

Year	Age	Club (League)	Level	W	L	ERA	G	GS	IP	H	HR	BB	SO	BB%	SO%	WHIP	AVG
2025	19	FCL Marlins	Rk	2	5	3.18	11	11	40	26	1	23	55	14.1	33.7	1.24	.197
2025	19	Jupiter (FSL)	A	0	1	3.24	6	6	17	6	1	14	18	21.5	27.7	1.20	.120
		Minor League Totals		2	6	3.20	17	17	56	32	2	37	73	16.2	32.0	1.22	.176

24 ELIAZAR DISHMEY, RHP

FB: 50. **CB:** 50. **SL:** 55. **CH:** 55. **CTL:** 45. **BA Grade:** 50. **Risk:** High. **Adj:** 35.

Born: October 25, 2004. **B-T:** R-R. **HT:** 6-1. **WT:** 175. **Signed:** Dominican Republic, 2022. **Signed by:** Angel Izquierdo.

TRACK RECORD: Dishmey signed out of the Dominican Republic for $50,000 in 2022. After an uneven performance at Low-A Jupiter in 2024, he returned there to open 2025 and posted a 3.13 ERA with 76 strikeouts and 42 walks in 74.2 innings. Promoted to High-A Beloit as a 20-year-old, he excelled, recording a 2.19 ERA with 32 strikeouts and just six walks in 24.2 innings to close out 2025.
SCOUTING REPORT: Dishmey showed the depth of his arsenal in 2025, working a five-pitch mix from a low-effort delivery and low three-quarters slot with above-average extension. His two- and four-seam fastballs sit 91-94 mph, touch 97, and play with run and sink at the knees and run-ride up in the zone. He spins the ball well and throws a borderline-plus, low-80s slider with sweep. He also mixes a high-70s two-plane curveball and a low-to-mid-80s changeup with significant fade and good separation off his fastball. Control was inconsistent early—reflected in 42 walks at Low-A—but sharpened notably after promotion, a promising sign for his long-term outlook.
THE FUTURE: Dishmey's outcome range is wide. Added strength, improved consistency and possible velocity gains could elevate him toward a No. 3 starter ceiling, while a back-end rotational or bullpen role remain a realistic alternative if his strike-throwing stalls. He will return to High-A Beloit in 2026 to continue refining mechanics and command after a highly encouraging 2025.

Year	Age	Club (League)	Level	W	L	ERA	G	GS	IP	H	HR	BB	SO	BB%	SO%	WHIP	AVG
2025	20	Jupiter (FSL)	A	3	5	3.13	17	15	75	48	2	42	76	13.5	24.4	1.21	.191
2025	20	Beloit (MWL)	A+	2	0	2.19	5	5	25	16	1	6	32	6.5	34.4	0.89	.184
		Minor League Totals		10	14	4.09	55	41	207	163	13	96	235	10.9	26.8	1.25	.216

25 WILLIAM KEMPNER, RHP

FB: 65. **SW:** 60. **CH:** 35. **CTL:** 35. **BA Grade:** 40. **Risk:** Mild. **Adj:** 35.

Born: June 18, 2001. **B-T:** R-R. **HT:** 6-0. **WT:** 222. **Drafted:** Gonzaga, 2023 (3rd round). **Signed by:** Larry Casian (Giants).

TRACK RECORD: The Giants drafted Kempner in the third round out of Gonzaga in 2023 and traded him to Miami for bonus pool space prior to 2025. He broke out in his first year with the organization, posting a 2.26 ERA with 95 strikeouts and 40 walks over 67.2 innings across three levels. He closed the season at Triple-A Jacksonville, recording a 2.65 ERA with 25 strikeouts and 15 walks in 17 innings.
SCOUTING REPORT: Kempner gives hitters an atypical look with a low-slot, crossfire delivery and a fastball that sat 94-96 mph, touched 99 and played with an unusually flat attack angle. The pitch averaged roughly 17 inches of run and consistently fooled hitters when located near the zone. His feel for spin is evident in a 3,000 rpm mid-80s sweeper with well above-average horizontal break. He nominally offers a mid-80s split-changeup, but he threw it about 1% of the time in 2025 and it is not currently a meaningful part of his mix. His stuff is loud and unique, though his command can waver.
THE FUTURE: Kempner is a reliever through and through, and his fastball/sweeper combination has the potential to play in leverage situations. Miami added him to its 40-man roster and expects him to contribute in the majors at some point in 2026.

Year	Age	Club (League)	Level	W	L	ERA	G	GS	IP	H	HR	BB	SO	BB%	SO%	WHIP	AVG
2025	24	Beloit (MWL)	A+	1	2	3.04	19	0	27	19	0	10	39	9.0	35.1	1.09	.196
2025	24	Pensacola (SL)	AA	1	1	1.13	16	0	24	11	0	15	31	15.6	32.3	1.08	.139
2025	24	Jacksonville (IL)	AAA	3	0	2.65	13	0	17	8	2	15	25	19.7	32.9	1.35	.138
		Minor League Totals		12	8	3.10	91	7	139	100	8	76	184	12.6	30.5	1.26	.199

26 KIFRAIDY ENCARNACION, LHP

FB: 70. **SL:** 55. **CH:** 45. **CTL:** 30. **BA Grade:** 55. **Risk:** Extreme. **Adj:** 35.

Born: October 26, 2005. **B-T:** L-L. **HT:** 6-4. **WT:** 187. **Signed:** Dominican Republic, 2024. **Signed by:** Angel Izquierdo.

TRACK RECORD: Miami signed Encarnacion out of the Dominican Republic for $165,000 in 2024 and briefly saw why before Tommy John surgery shut him down. He returned in 2025 and again teased significant upside, striking out six and allowing just three hits across five games, while also walking 16 hitters in three official innings. The box scores read like modern art, but the raw ingredients remain undeniable.

MIAMI MARLINS

SCOUTING REPORT: Encarnacion is a 6-foot-4 lefty with an upper-90s fastball that reached 101 mph in 2025 and a slider that flashes plus. His changeup shows real fade and sits around average at present. His long, athletic delivery is as promising as any individual pitch, though he struggles mightily to repeat it. His fastball plays like a heat-seeking missile that hasn't quite been told what the target is, and his best bullets in 2025 were nowhere near the zone. His precision is more sawed-off shotgun than scalpel, but the physical ingredients are tantalizing.
THE FUTURE: Encarnacion's outcome range is enormous. With cleaner mechanics and significantly improved strike-throwing, he has the raw stuff of at least a midrotation starter. Without improvement, the command is too scattered to justify even a bullpen projection. Miami will almost certainly keep him in the DSL or move him to the Florida Complex League in 2026 while they try to figure out what to make of their most volatile, occasionally awe-inspiring, pitching prospect.

Year	Age	Club (League)	Level	W	L	ERA	G	GS	IP	H	HR	BB	SO	BB%	SO%	WHIP	AVG
2025	19	DSL Miami	Rk	0	2	39.00	5	2	3	3	0	16	6	55.2	20.7	6.33	.250
		Minor League Totals		0	2	12.66	7	4	11	5	0	21	16	35.0	26.7	2.44	.135

27 JARED SERNA, SS/2B

HIT: 45. **POW:** 40. **RUN:** 55. **FLD:** 50. **ARM:** 45. **BA Grade:** 40. **Risk:** Mild. **Adj:** 35.

Born: June 1, 2002. **B-T:** R-R. **HT:** 5-7. **WT:** 174. **Signed:** Mexico, 2019. **Signed by:** Lee Sigman (Yankees).
TRACK RECORD: Serna signed with the Yankees for $10,000 out of Mexico in 2019 and consistently exceeded expectations, which helped prompt Miami to acquire him in the Jazz Chisholm Jr. deal in 2024. He went straight to Double-A Pensacola and briefly reached Triple-A before returning to Pensacola for most of 2025, when he hit .223/.305/.277 with three home runs, eight doubles and 15 steals in 25 attempts. He closed the year with 10 games at Triple-A.
SCOUTING REPORT: Serna is undersized but twitchy with real bat speed and aggression, traits that allowed him to hit 19 and 15 home runs in 2023 and 2024. In 2025, however, his underlying contact quality collapsed. His average launch angle dropped to 6.6 degrees, and even when he hit the ball hard, he lacked lift and intent. He still produced an 88 mph average exit velocity and 102 mph 90th percentile while showing strong zone control and limited whiffs, but the batted-ball profile muted his production. Defensively, Serna retains above-average shortstop ability and plays with fearless intent, though his arm grades closer to fringe-average. His athleticism and instincts make him playable around the infield.
THE FUTURE: Serna needs to rediscover loft to access his power and avoid a replacement-level, utility-only trajectory. If he lifts the ball again while maintaining his zone control, he has a path to more regular at-bats. He will return to Triple-A to open 2026 and is on Miami's 40-man roster, positioning him to debut at some point in the season.

Year	Age	Club (League)	Level	AVG	G	AB	R	H	2B	3B	HR	RBI	BB	SO	SB	OBP	SLG
2025	23	Pensacola (SL)	AA	.223	101	386	51	86	8	2	3	28	42	69	15	.305	.277
2025	23	Jacksonville (IL)	AAA	.235	10	34	7	8	2	0	0	2	7	6	5	.366	.294
		Minor League Totals		.255	465	1761	300	449	97	8	46	237	216	332	105	.347	.398

28 MAXIMO ACOSTA, 3B/SS

HIT: 45. **POW:** 40. **RUN:** 50. **FLD:** 50. **ARM:** 60. **BA Grade:** 40. **Risk:** Mild. **Adj:** 35.

Born: October 29, 2002. **B-T:** R-R. **HT:** 5-11. **WT:** 187. **Signed:** Venezuela, 2019.
Signed by: Rafic Saab/Jhonny Gomez (Rangers).
TRACK RECORD: Acosta signed with Texas for $1.65 million as a headliner in the 2019 international class, but his developmental arc was delayed by the pandemic and further interrupted by injury in 2021. He climbed to Double-A over the next three years and produced his best season in 2024 before being traded to Miami. In 2025, he spent most of the season with Triple-A Jacksonville, hitting .224/.314/.366 with 13 home runs, 13 doubles and 33 steals in 42 attempts. He earned a late-season callup to Miami and hit .204/.295/.389 with three home runs in 19 major league games.
SCOUTING REPORT: The strides Acosta made late in his Rangers tenure—most notably cutting his strikeout rate—did not stick in 2025. His punchouts nearly doubled at Triple-A, and his contact quality trended downward. He chased and whiffed at a 27% clip and rarely pulled the ball in the air, limiting his impact largely to line-drive contact. He does have the strength to generate firm contact on occasion, but too often it arrives without ideal lift or intent. Defensively, Acosta is playable across the infield except at first base. He has a plus arm and good footwork. The versatility has value, though it aligns more with a bench utility projection than an everyday profile.
THE FUTURE: Having debuted, Acosta's next step is determining whether he can meaningfully improve his strikeout outcomes and produce more authoritative air contact. If that shift materializes, he could

carve out more regular playing time. Absent that, he fits best as a righthanded utility piece with decent speed, defensive flexibility and sporadic impact.

Year	Age	Club (League)	Level	AVG	G	AB	R	H	2B	3B	HR	RBI	BB	SO	SB	OBP	SLG
2025	22	Jacksonville (IL)	AAA	.224	115	410	56	92	13	3	13	50	50	123	33	.314	.366
2025	22	Miami (NL)	MLB	.204	19	54	7	11	1	0	3	5	6	17	1	.295	.389
		Minor League Totals		.258	453	1692	255	436	85	10	37	208	160	383	136	.328	.385
		Major League Totals		.204	19	54	7	11	1	0	3	5	6	17	1	.295	.389

29 JOSE CASTRO, OF

HIT: 40. **POW:** 55. **RUN:** 45. **FLD:** 50. **ARM:** 50. **BA Grade:** 50. **Risk:** Extreme. **Adj:** 30.

Born: October 31, 2006. **B-T:** R-R. **HT:** 6-3. **WT:** 180. **Signed:** Dominican Republic, 2024. **Signed by:** Sahir Fersobe.
TRACK RECORD: Castro signed with Miami for $450,000 out of the Dominican Republic in 2024 and debuted in the Dominican Summer League, showing standout raw strength but little contact feel, hitting .148 across 52 games. Returning to the DSL in 2025, he made a substantial leap, posting a DSL-record 16 home runs with 14 doubles and a .264/.399/.585 line, supported by much improved swing decisions.
SCOUTING REPORT: Castro arrived in far better launch positions in 2025 after reworking his swing and tightening his approach. He produced excellent exit velocities for the level and ranked among minor league leaders with a 37% air-pull rate, a strong indicator of usable game power. He still missed too frequently, and the question now becomes whether his bat-to-ball ability will scale against more advanced pitching. His raw power is confidently plus, but the hit tool remains uncertain. Defensively, Castro is an average athlete with an above-average arm, profiling naturally in a corner-outfield role.
THE FUTURE: If Castro makes enough contact to consistently access his plus raw power, he has a chance to develop into a middle-of-the-order corner bat. If the swing-and-miss issues persist against full-season pitching, his ceiling drops to a lower-impact bench role. He is likely bound for the States in 2026, at which point his ability to hit more advanced pitching will determine whether he can turn his elite DSL power output into sustainable production.

Year	Age	Club (League)	Level	AVG	G	AB	R	H	2B	3B	HR	RBI	BB	SO	SB	OBP	SLG
2025	18	DSL Miami	Rk	.264	52	193	46	51	14	0	16	51	34	62	8	.399	.585
		Minor League Totals		.210	104	362	80	76	17	0	21	73	78	135	16	.368	.431

30 DEYVISON DE LOS SANTOS, 1B

HIT: 30. **POW:** 60. **RUN:** 35. **FLD:** 35. **ARM:** 45. **BA Grade:** 45. **Risk:** High. **Adj:** 30.

Born: June 21, 2003. **B-T:** R-R. **HT:** 6-1. **WT:** 215. **Signed:** Dominican Republic, 2019.
Signed by: Cesar Geronimo Jr./Wil Tejada (Diamondbacks).
TRACK RECORD: De Los Santos signed with the Diamondbacks out of the Dominican Republic in 2019 on the strength of immense raw power. Cleveland selected him in the 2024 Rule 5 draft but returned him the following spring training. Arizona then dealt him to Miami for A.J. Puk during the season. He finished 2024 with a staggering 40 minor league home runs, but regressed sharply in 2025, hitting .240/.313/.359 with 12 homers, 11 doubles and 103 strikeouts.
SCOUTING REPORT: De Los Santos has near-elite raw power, and is capable of generating towering impact from a long, violent righthanded swing. That component has never been in doubt. The problem remains swing decisions. He expands the zone far too often and does not make enough contact to consistently reach that power. Chasing at elevated rates severely limits the utility of his strength, and his 2025 regression highlighted the risks of his approach. He must hit a large volume of home runs to make his offensive profile viable. Defensively, he grades below-average at first base, with limited mobility and little positional flexibility.
THE FUTURE: The calculus is simple but unforgiving: De Los Santos has to hit enough to access his power. If he does not, he will struggle to hold down a regular big league role. Miami expects him to reach the majors in 2026, and his ability to rein in his approach will dictate whether he becomes more than a one-dimensional slugger.

Year	Age	Club (League)	Level	AVG	G	AB	R	H	2B	3B	HR	RBI	BB	SO	SB	OBP	SLG
2025	22	Jupiter (FSL)	A	.333	2	6	2	2	0	0	0	2	1	0	.500	.333
2025	22	Jacksonville (IL)	AAA	.241	106	399	54	96	11	1	12	54	36	99	16	.311	.363
		Minor League Totals		.279	546	2135	335	595	97	9	102	378	157	583	29	.332	.476

Jackson Chourio

Milwaukee Brewers

BY BEN BADLER

The Brewers had the best regular season record in baseball in 2025, won their third straight National League Central title and reached the playoffs for the seventh time in the last eight years.

Their ability to build a perennial playoff team in a smaller market has made their baseball operations department one of the most admired in the industry, reflected in the Brewers winning the 2025 Organization of the Year award.

While the Brewers went deeper into the playoffs than they had since 2018, the season still ended on a sour note when they were swept by the Dodgers in the NL Championship Series.

The Brewers haven't been to a World Series since 1982, but the talent on the major league team and throughout their farm system, combined with the team's impressive scouting and player development departments, should continue to position Milwaukee to be a consistent playoff team going forward.

One of the strengths of the farm system is its homegrown international prospects. Even after the graduation of Jackson Chourio in 2024, four of the Brewers' top seven prospects are players signed out of Latin America. That includes their top two prospects, middle infielders Jesús Made and Luis Peña, who both signed out of the Dominican Republic in 2024.

Made reached Double-A as an 18-year-old at the end of the 2025 season and has become one of the top 10 prospects in baseball as a switch-hitter with an elite combination of hitting ability, strike-zone judgment, bat speed and athleticism. Peña is another standout hitter with outstanding bat-to-ball skills, power that spiked in 2025 and excellent speed.

In the draft, the Brewers have top 10 prospects they drafted from high school (shortstop Cooper Pratt), college (catcher Marco Dinges and third baseman Andrew Fischer) and the junior college

PROJECTED 2029 LINEUP

Catcher	Jeferson Quero	26
First Base	Andrew Fischer	25
Second Base	Brice Turang	29
Third Base	Jesús Made	22
Shortstop	Cooper Pratt	24
Left Field	Jackson Chourio	25
Center Field	Luis Lara	24
Right Field	Sal Frelick	29
Designated Hitter	Luis Peña	22
No. 1 Starter	Jacob Misiorowski	27
No. 2 Starter	Quinn Priester	28
No. 3 Starter	Logan Henderson	27
No. 4 Starter	Bishop Letson	24
No. 5 Starter	Tyson Hardin	27
Closer	Abner Uribe	29

ranks with righthander Logan Henderson. They have shown a particular knack for signing under-scouted, unheralded high school prospects in the later rounds of the draft. That group includes two of their top 10 prospects—righthander Bishop Letson and second baseman Josh Adamczewski—as well as first baseman Luke Adams and right-hander Ethan Dorchies, among others.

Milwaukee's top three prospects—Made, Peña and Pratt—probably won't factor in the MLB picture in 2026. But Henderson, catcher Jeferson Quero and lefthander Robert Gasser should all get opportunities in Milwaukee. Luis Lara has a sneaky chance to do so as well as an elite defensive center fielder with a high-contact bat likely to open the year in Triple-A Nashville.

Overall, the Brewers have one of the game's best farm systems. Made and Peña provide two premium prospects at the top, while the talent throughout their Top 30 Prospects is among the deepest in the game. The organization's ability to sign quality international prospects and draft high school prospects with breakout potential continues to keep the talent flowing at the lower levels.

Few organizations can match Milwaukee's regular season success over the last decade—or their outlook to continue winning over the next half-decade. Now it's time for the Brewers to turn that consistent contention into a championship run. ∎

DEPTH CHART

MILWAUKEE BREWERS

TOP 2026 ROOKIES — RANK
1. Logan Henderson, RHP — 4
2. Jeferson Quero, C — 7
3. Robert Gasser, LHP — 14

BREAKOUT PROSPECTS — RANK
1. Brady Ebel, SS — 13
2. Ethan Dorchies, RHP — 15
3. Frank Cairone, LHP — 22

SOURCE OF TOP 30 TALENT

Homegrown	28	Acquired	2
College	9	Trade	2
Junior college	1	Rule 5 draft	0
High school	12	Independent league	0
Undrafted free agent	0	Free agent/waivers	0
International	6		

LF
Tyler Black (24)
Jadyn Fielder
Gerlyn Payano

CF
Luis Lara (6)
Braylon Payne (17)
Brailyn Antunez
Josiah Ragsdale
Kenny Fenelon

RF
Handelfry Encarnacion (27)
Jose Anderson
Pedro Ibarguen
Alexander Frias

3B
Luis Peña (2)
Andrew Fischer (10)
Brock Wilken (18)
Juan Baez

SS
Jesús Made (1)
Cooper Pratt (3)
Brady Ebel (13)
CJ Hughes
Cristopher Acosta

2B
Josh Adamczewski (9)
Daniel Dickinson (29)
Juan Ortuño
Dylan O'Rae

1B
Luke Adams (12)
Blake Burke (16)
Eric Bitonti (20)
Mike Boeve

C
Jeferson Quero (7)
Marco Dinges (8)
Kevin Garcia
Matthew Wood

LHP

LHSP
Robert Gasser (14)
J.D. Thompson (19)
Frank Cairone (22)
Tate Kuehner

LHRP
Wande Torres
Anthony Flores

RHP

RHSP
Logan Henderson (4)
Bishop Letson (5)
Tyson Hardin (11)
Ethan Dorchies (15)
Bryce Meccage (23)
Josh Knoth (25)
Jayden Dubanewicz (26)
Manuel Rodriguez (28)
Coleman Crow (30)
Jacob Morrison
Jaron DeBerry
Tyler Renz
Enniel Cortez
Joshua Flores

RHRP
Craig Yoho (21)
Brett Wichrowski
K.C. Hunt
Tyler Bryant
Will Childers
Yerlin Rodriguez

MILWAUKEE BREWERS

1 JESÚS MADE, SS

Born: May 8, 2007. **B-T:** B-R. **HT:** 6-1. **WT:** 194.
Signed: Dominican Republic, 2024.
Signed by: Julio De La Cruz.

BA GRADE
70 Risk: Average
Adjusted grade: 60

SCOUTING GRADES
Hit: 70. **Power:** 60. **Run:** 60.
Field: 50. **Arm:** 60.
Projected future grades on 20-80 scouting scale

TRACK RECORD: The 2024 international signing class will have a major impact on the Brewers for years to come. The biggest bonus the Brewers paid that year went to Venezuelan shortstop Jorge Quintana, who signed for $1.7 million, then was traded to the Padres in 2025. Their next two highest bonuses went to a pair of Dominican shortstops, Jesus Made ($950,000) and Luis Peña ($800,000), both of whom have become two of the best teenage prospects in the game. Made in particular has the look of a future star. After debuting in the Dominican Summer League in 2024, Made became the organization's No. 1 prospect and the organization's co-minor league player of the year. In 2025, he skipped the Rookie-level Arizona Complex League and opened in Low-A Carolina. He earned an August promotion to High-A Wisconsin and was even better there before finishing the season in Double-A Biloxi as an 18-year-old, repeating as the Brewers' minor league player of the year.

SCOUTING REPORT: Made is a well-rounded offensive threat with a mix of polished hitting ability and power for his age. He has a compact, smooth and whippy swing with good balance, rhythm and timing from both sides of the plate. Made tracks and identifies pitches well, showing the ability to let pitches travel deep into the hitting zone and use the whole field. His hand-eye coordination and the adjustability in his swing enable him to square up both fastballs and offspeed stuff at a high clip. His swing decisions are advanced for his age, and he consistently puts together quality at-bats. Made can barrel elite velocity and has the bat speed to already flash plus raw power. His flatter swing path doesn't generate a ton of loft, but with the power he has now and strength projection to grow into more, there's potential for 25-plus home run juice in his prime. Made is athletic and a plus runner who stole 47 bases in 2025, so the upside is there for a 30-30 season. Made has the raw tools for shortstop, but the defensive component of his game will need the most work. He has the quick-twitch athleticism, plus arm and range to stick in the dirt. He's not as instinctual in the field as he is at the plate, but he could develop into a solid defensive shortstop if he can improve his reliability and internal clock. With Cooper Pratt a better fielder also in the organization, Made ultimately might end up at third base—where he could be an above-average defender—or possibly second base.

BEST TOOLS

BATTING
Best Hitter	Jesús Made
Best Power Hitter	Eric Bitonti
Best Strike-Zone Discipline	Tyler Black
Fastest Baserunner	Braylon Payne
Best Athlete	Braylon Payne

PITCHING
Best Fastball	Bishop Letson
Best Curveball	Josh Knoth
Best Slider	Bishop Letson
Best Changeup	Craig Yoho
Best Control	Manuel Rodriguez

FIELDING
Best Defensive Catcher	Jeferson Quero
Best Defensive Infielder	Cooper Pratt
Best Infield Arm	Brady Ebel
Best Defensive Outfielder	Luis Lara
Best Outfield Arm	Jose Anderson

THE FUTURE: Made could follow in the footsteps of Jackson Chourio as a Brewers international signing who reaches the major leagues as a 20-year-old and develops into a franchise cornerstone. Wherever he ends up in the infield, Made could be a perennial all-star. He should start 2026 in Double-A Biloxi.

Year	Age	Club (League)	Level	AVG	G	AB	R	H	2B	3B	HR	RBI	BB	SO	SB	OBP	SLG
2025	18	Carolina (CAR)	A	.267	83	322	55	86	21	3	4	46	53	78	40	.373	.388
2025	18	Wisconsin (MWL)	A+	.343	27	108	20	37	7	2	2	12	13	22	5	.415	.500
2025	18	Biloxi (SL)	AA	.261	5	23	6	6	0	1	0	3	1	8	2	.292	.348
		Minor League Totals		.298	166	628	144	187	37	12	12	89	106	136	75	.402	.452

MILWAUKEE BREWERS

2 LUIS PEÑA, SS/2B
HIT: 55. **POW:** 50. **RUN:** 70. **FLD:** 40. **ARM:** 60. **BA Grade:** 60. **Risk:** High. **Adj:** 45.

Born: November 13, 2006. **B-T:** R-R. **HT:** 5-11. **WT:** 185.
Signed: Dominican Republic, 2024. **Signed by:** Julio De La Cruz.
TRACK RECORD: The Brewers signed Peña for $800,000 in 2024, making him one of their three big international signings of the year along with fellow Dominican shortstop Jesus Made and Venezuelan shortstop Jorge Quintana. After a stellar pro debut that year in the Dominican Summer League, Peña skipped the Rookie-level Arizona Complex League and had an outstanding season with Low-A Carolina as an 18-year-old in 2025. He earned a promotion to High-A Wisconsin in August.
SCOUTING REPORT: Peña combines impressive athleticism and hand-eye coordination as an offensive-oriented infielder. He has an aggressive approach but with a balanced, controlled swing that stays behind the ball well with excellent barrel accuracy, leading to minimal swing-and-miss in his game. Peña showed significantly improved power in 2025, getting stronger and doing a better job of pulling the ball in the air. It's now average raw power with exit velocities up to 113 mph, though his swing path is geared more for line drives than loft. Peña showed a better approach in 2025, but he needs to continue to become a more selective hitter, with chase tendencies that got him into trouble once he got promoted to High-A. Peña is a good athlete and a plus-plus runner with a plus arm, but his defense is still shaky. Shortstop is a long shot, and while he could fit at second or third base, his hands, internal clock and defensive instincts will need to improve. His speed would be an asset if he were to move to the outfield.
THE FUTURE: Peña isn't quite as well-rounded or advanced in swing decisions compared to Jesus Made, but he is one of the most talented teenage prospects in the minor leagues. He's likely to return to Wisconsin to begin 2026 and could reach the big leagues before his 21st birthday.

Year	Age	Club (League)	Level	AVG	G	AB	R	H	2B	3B	HR	RBI	BB	SO	SB	OBP	SLG
2025	18	Carolina (CAR)	A	.308	71	273	59	84	14	6	6	52	28	41	41	.375	.469
2025	18	Wisconsin (MWL)	A+	.168	25	101	10	17	4	0	3	12	6	27	3	.220	.297
		Minor League Totals		.307	140	537	112	165	34	12	10	100	49	83	83	.372	.471

3 COOPER PRATT, SS
HIT: 50. **POW:** 45. **RUN:** 60. **FLD:** 55. **ARM:** 60. **BA Grade:** 55. **Risk:** Average. **Adj:** 45.

Born: August 18, 2004. **B-T:** R-R. **HT:** 6-3. **WT:** 206.
Drafted: HS—Senatobia, MS, 2023 (6th round). **Signed by:** Scott Nichols.
TRACK RECORD: Pratt signed with the Brewers for $1.35 million on an above-slot deal as a sixth-round pick out of high school in 2023. He became one of the organization's top prospects in 2024, when he finished the year with 23 games in High-A Wisconsin, then drew an aggressive assignment in 2025 to spend all year in Double-A Biloxi as a 20-year-old. Pratt's .238/.343/.348 slash line wasn't particularly inspiring, though it was still an OPS above the Southern League average.
SCOUTING REPORT: Pratt's high baseball IQ is apparent in all facets of the game. His swing is simple, balanced and stays short to the ball for a 6-foot-3 hitter. Pratt will expand the strike zone a touch more often than he should, particularly against sliders down and away, but he has a good sense of timing with the hand-eye coordination that leads to a low swing-and-miss rate. Pratt's biggest offensive question is how much power he will develop. While he has the size to project more power to come, he doesn't have big bat speed and his top-end exit velocities are below-average, so he doesn't project to be a big home run threat. Pratt moves well for his size with plus speed underway. He doesn't have typical quick-twitch explosiveness that a lot of teams prefer at shortstop, but he compensates for it with his instincts and internal clock to project to stick at the position. While he doesn't have the range to make some of the more acrobatic, high-light-reel plays, his hands and feet work well, he has good body control and a quick release to a plus arm.
THE FUTURE: While fellow shortstop Jesús Made is a potential star in Milwaukee's farm system, Pratt's edge on defense gives him the inside track to become the Brewers' shortstop of the future. He should open 2026 in Triple-A and should make his major league debut either by the end of the year or in 2027.

Year	Age	Club (League)	Level	AVG	G	AB	R	H	2B	3B	HR	RBI	BB	SO	SB	OBP	SLG
2025	20	Biloxi (SL)	AA	.238	120	437	71	104	22	1	8	62	67	80	31	.343	.348
		Minor League Totals		.261	228	829	136	216	39	5	16	115	114	172	62	.355	.378

MILWAUKEE BREWERS

4 LOGAN HENDERSON, RHP
FB: 50. **CT:** 45. **SL:** 40. **CH:** 60. **CTL:** 60. **BA Grade:** 50. **Risk:** Mild. **Adj:** 45.

Born: March 2, 2002. **B-T:** R-R. **HT:** 6-0. **WT:** 209.
Drafted: McLennan (TX) JC (4th round). **Signed by:** K.J. Hendrick.
TRACK RECORD: Henderson was the NJCAA Division I pitcher of the year as a freshman in 2021 when he won a national championship with McLennan (Texas) JC, then signed with the Brewers as a fourth-round pick. An avulsion fracture in his right elbow in spring training required surgery, wiping out nearly all of his 2022 season. He pitched well in 2023 and 2024 and kept it going in 2025, when he made his major league debut in April and pitched well between Milwaukee and Triple-A. His season ended after his Aug. 3 outing due to a flexor strain in his right elbow.
SCOUTING REPORT: Pitching from a compact, efficient delivery, Henderson has success by filling the strike zone and keeping hitters off-balance with his changeup. His fastball sits at 91-95 mph and tickles 96. That's slightly below-average velocity for a starter, but a low release height helps the pitch play up. He's a prolific strike-thrower with both his fastball and his plus changeup. It's an unusually high-spin changeup that averages 19 inches of fade and 10 mph off his fastball while maintaining his arm speed and repeating his release point to disguise the pitch well. Henderson leans heavily on those two pitches, with his changeup a major reason why he has similar results against lefties as righties. Henderson has found success at every level despite the lack of a great breaking ball. His low-to-mid 80s slider is a below-average pitch with short break, and he introduced a mid-to-upper 80s cutter to give hitters another wrinkle.
THE FUTURE: Henderson should immediately factor into Milwaukee's big league pitching staff and likely in their rotation in 2026. He's had multiple elbow injuries since signing, and there is some concern about his ability to log a typical starter's workload, but if he can do that, he has the stuff to stick in the rotation.

Year	Age	Club (League)	Level	W	L	ERA	G	GS	IP	H	HR	BB	SO	BB%	SO%	WHIP	AVG
2025	23	Nashville (IL)	AAA	10	4	3.59	16	15	78	62	9	24	87	7.7	27.9	1.11	.218
2025	23	Milwaukee (NL)	MLB	3	0	1.78	5	5	25	17	3	8	33	8.1	33.3	0.99	.187
		Minor League Totals		21	14	3.26	60	59	251	186	30	71	320	7.1	32.2	1.02	.205
		Major League Totals		3	0	1.78	5	5	25	17	3	8	33	8.1	33.3	0.99	.187

5 BISHOP LETSON, RHP
FB: 55. **SL:** 60. **CH:** 45. **CTL:** 55. **BA Grade:** 55. **Risk:** High. **Adj:** 40.

Born: September 15, 2004. **B-T:** R-R. **HT:** 6-4. **WT:** 170.
Drafted: HS—Floyd Knobs, IN, 2023 (11th round). **Signed by:** Ginger Poulson.
TRACK RECORD: Lightly recruited at his Indiana high school before committing to Purdue, Letson saw his velocity tick up as the draft neared. That development, along with his physical projection, athleticism and upside drew the Brewers to sign him for $482,600 as an 11th-round pick in 2023. Letson had a promising debut in 2024, though his season ended due to elbow soreness. In 2025 he pitched well but was again limited to fewer than 50 innings after missing a little more than three months in the middle of the season due to right shoulder impingement.
SCOUTING REPORT: Letson has the most upside of any pitcher in the Brewers' farm system. He's a long-limbed righthander with a fast, whippy arm and is an excellent mover down the mound, generating 7.5 feet of extension that would rank among the highest in the majors. That extension and his lower release height help his stuff play up, starting with a four-seam fastball that sits at 92-95 mph and touches 98, and a lively two-seamer with above-average armside run. Letson still has more space left to fill out, so there could be another uptick in velocity coming. His low-80s slider flashes plus, spinning at 2,300-2,500 rpm with wide lateral break and two-plane depth at its best. Letson rarely throws his mid-80s changeup, and when he does, it's typically a below-average pitch that doesn't miss many bats. Letson is athletic and a good strike-thrower for his age, particularly for a long-levered, 6-foot-4 pitcher, though he's still learning to repeat his release point on his secondaries to match his fastball.
THE FUTURE: Durability continues to be a question for Letson, but he has the stuff and control to pitch in the middle of the rotation, with the upside for more if his velocity takes another jump. He should start 2026 with Double-A Biloxi.

Year	Age	Club (League)	Level	W	L	ERA	G	GS	IP	H	HR	BB	SO	BB%	SO%	WHIP	AVG
2025	20	Wisconsin (MWL)	A+	2	2	1.69	10	8	37	28	1	9	43	6.3	30.3	0.99	.214
2025	20	Biloxi (SL)	AA	0	0	9.00	1	1	4	3	1	3	6	17.6	35.3	1.50	.214
		Minor League Totals		3	6	2.84	27	23	105	74	8	39	106	9.4	25.5	1.08	.202

MILWAUKEE BREWERS

6 LUIS LARA, OF
HIT: 50. **POW:** 30. **RUN:** 70. **FLD:** 70. **ARM:** 60. **BA Grade:** 50. **Risk:** Average. **Adj:** 40.

Born: November 17, 2004. **B-T:** B-R. **HT:** 5-8. **WT:** 167.
Signed: Venezuela, 2022. **Signed by:** Jose Rodriguez.
TRACK RECORD: Lara was a smaller, skinny player as an amateur in Venezuela, but he developed into an explosive athlete with skills that translated on both sides of the ball when the Brewers signed him for $1.1 million in 2022. As a 20-year-old with Double-A Biloxi in 2025, Lara led the Southern League in walks, ranked second in stolen bases and, despite hitting just .257/.369/.343, posted an OPS above the league average.
SCOUTING REPORT: Lara is just 5-foot-8, but he has a promising blend of quick-twitch athleticism and refined game skills, particularly in center field, where he has become an elite defender. His speed ticked up in 2025 to become a plus-plus runner, he gets great reads off the bat, accelerates quickly and takes crisp routes with excellent range, turning in highlight-reel catches. He has a plus arm and an efficient release, giving him the tools and instincts to potentially win a Gold Glove. That will only happen if Lara hits enough to be an everyday big leaguer. Lara has outstanding hand-eye coordination, producing one of the best contact rates in the organization. He uses his small strike zone to his advantage and doesn't chase often. What Lara lacks is power. He has never hit more than four home runs in a season, and there isn't much physical projection remaining. However, his exit velocities ticked up in 2025, even reaching 110 mph, so there's more present power he could unlock if he can add loft.
THE FUTURE: Lara's elite defense at a premium position and bat-to-ball skills give him a chance to be an average regular along the lines of Nationals center fielder Jacob Young or Cardinals center fielder Victor Scott II. There's risk he could end up more of a fourth outfielder, but there's also greater, sneaky upside if he's able to tap into more game power.

Year	Age	Club (League)	Level	AVG	G	AB	R	H	2B	3B	HR	RBI	BB	SO	SB	OBP	SLG
2025	20	Biloxi (SL)	AA	.257	136	513	79	132	32	3	2	40	86	99	44	.369	.343
		Minor League Totals		.261	391	1481	251	386	75	12	10	131	192	265	126	.356	.348

7 JEFERSON QUERO, C
HIT: 50. **POW:** 50. **RUN:** 30. **FLD:** 55. **ARM:** 45. **BA Grade:** 50. **Risk:** Average. **Adj:** 40.

Born: October 8, 2002. **B-T:** R-R. **HT:** 5-11. **WT:** 205.
Signed: Venezuela, 2019. **Signed by:** Reinaldo Hidalgo.
TRACK RECORD: Quero signed out of Venezuela for $200,000 in 2019 and reached Double-A as a 20-year-old in 2023. Since then, injuries have slowed his progress and taken a toll on his tools. In his first game of 2024, Quero tore the labrum in his right shoulder diving back to first base, then had season-ending surgery. In 2025, a hamstring strain prevented him from rejoining Triple-A Nashville until June. Quero hit just .259/.333/.362 in 30 games in June and July, then batted .250/.339/.470 over 28 games in August and September.
SCOUTING REPORT: By the end of the season, Quero mostly looked like the same hitter he was before the shoulder injury. He sets up with an open stance, keeps his hands quiet and makes contact at a high clip. Quero is a good fastball hitter, but his aggressive approach gets him into trouble, so he will need to improve his plate discipline. He has average raw power that gives him a chance to be a 20-plus home run threat. A well below-average runner, Quero was once one of the best defensive catching prospects in the game, but the regression of his arm strength is a major concern. Prior to his injury, Quero had a plus-plus arm that stacked up among the best in the minors. In 2025, he showed significantly diminished power on his throws with fringe-average arm strength, recording pop times of 1.95 seconds on his best throws but typically above 2.0 seconds as he threw out just 17% of basestealers. He remains a skilled receiver, blocker and earns high marks for his intangibles behind the plate.
THE FUTURE: If Quero's arm strength improves to become above-average—if not the elite tool it once was—the upside is there for him to be an above-average regular. If it doesn't, his path to a starting role becomes clouded.

Year	Age	Club (League)	Level	AVG	G	AB	R	H	2B	3B	HR	RBI	BB	SO	SB	OBP	SLG
2025	22	ACL Brewers	Rk	.371	11	35	10	13	3	0	5	13	7	5	0	.500	.886
2025	22	Nashville (IL)	AAA	.255	58	216	32	55	14	1	6	44	25	35	2	.336	.412
		Minor League Totals		.276	278	1022	158	282	56	4	39	171	113	194	21	.353	.453

MILWAUKEE BREWERS

8 MARCO DINGES, C

HIT: 45. **POW:** 60. **RUN:** 40. **FLD:** 40. **ARM:** 60. **BA Grade:** 50. **Risk:** Average. **Adj:** 40.

Born: September 5, 2003. **B-T:** R-R. **HT:** 5-11. **WT:** 190.
Drafted: Florida State, 2024 (4th round). **Signed by:** Ketchum Marsh.
TRACK RECORD: Dinges transferred from Tallahassee Community College to Florida State for the 2024 season. While almost exclusively serving as a DH for the Seminoles, Dinges hit .323/.415/.583 with 15 home runs that season and signed with the Brewers for $500,000 as a fourth-round pick. He was one of the bigger up-arrow prospects in the lower minors in 2025, hitting a combined .300/.416/.514 with 13 homers in 77 games between Low-A Carolina and High-A Wisconsin.
SCOUTING REPORT: Dinges has become one of the top power-hitting catchers in the minors. He has plus-plus raw power with big bat speed and an approach looking to do damage. Dinges takes a high-throttle swing with some length and effort to it, with the look of a hitter who should have holes, but so far through the lower levels, he has been a strong performer while keeping his strikeout rate in check at 19.2% in 2025. Dinges' stock will climb if he proves he can stick behind the plate. A below-average runner, Dinges is a solid athlete for a catcher and has a plus arm. He consistently gets pop times under 2.0 seconds on throws to second base and under 1.9 on his best throws. He didn't spend much time behind the plate in college, which is evident in his blocking, release and throwing accuracy. The progress Dinges made defensively in 2025 has him trending toward becoming a playable defender at catcher, but there's still risk he could end up in left field.
THE FUTURE: If everything clicks, Dinges could become a power-hitting catcher who hits 25-plus home runs. If he can't stick at catcher, the offensive upside is still there for a big league role in an outfield corner, though with less likelihood of being an everyday player.

Year	Age	Club (League)	Level	AVG	G	AB	R	H	2B	3B	HR	RBI	BB	SO	SB	OBP	SLG
2025	21	Carolina (CAR)	A	.353	26	85	13	30	8	1	3	27	21	14	4	.500	.576
2025	21	Wisconsin (MWL)	A+	.273	51	172	29	47	4	1	10	35	28	47	1	.371	.483
		Minor League Totals		.300	77	257	42	77	12	2	13	62	49	61	5	.416	.514

9 JOSH ADAMCZEWSKI, 2B

HIT: 55. **POW:** 50. **RUN:** 45. **FLD:** 30. **ARM:** 40. **BA Grade:** 50. **Risk:** Average. **Adj:** 40.

Born: May 10, 2005. **B-T:** L-R. **HT:** 5-11. **WT:** 190.
Drafted: HS—St. John, IN, 2023 (15th round). **Signed by:** Ginger Poulson.
TRACK RECORD: Colleges weren't heavily recruiting Adamczewski when he committed to Ball State, but he never made it to campus after he signed with the Brewers for $252,500 as a 15th-round pick in 2023. He hit well in the Rookie-level Arizona Complex League in 2024, then emerged as one of the better hitting prospects in the organization in 2025, mostly with Low-A Carolina before a mid-August bump to High-A Wisconsin. A back injury limited him to 71 games.
SCOUTING REPORT: Adamczewski has a hitterish look in the batter's box. He has a calm, balanced swing and takes a tight turn of the barrel in a compact, adjustable lefthanded stroke. His bat gets on plane early and stays there a long time with great plate coverage and an all-fields approach. He tracks pitches well, has a good sense of the strike zone and average raw power. That hasn't translated to big home run totals yet, but he's capable of going deep to any part of the park when he gets off his best swing. There's a lot to like with Adamczewski at the plate, but his defense remains well below-average at second base. His hands, footwork and internal clock will need improvement to stick. A fringe-average runner with a below-average arm, Adamczewski should still primarily be a second baseman in 2026, but he got exposure to left field late in Wisconsin and in the Arizona Fall League.
THE FUTURE: An up-arrow prospect heading into 2026, Adamczewski will likely return to Wisconsin to open the year but should finish in the upper levels. Improving his defense to stick as an offensive-oriented second baseman would enhance his value, but his offensive upside is good enough to handle a role in left field if needed.

Year	Age	Club (League)	Level	AVG	G	AB	R	H	2B	3B	HR	RBI	BB	SO	SB	OBP	SLG
2025	20	ACL Brewers	Rk	.333	9	30	12	10	3	1	0	2	6	5	0	.432	.500
2025	20	Carolina (CAR)	A	.359	46	167	36	60	12	4	5	38	29	37	4	.459	.569
2025	20	Wisconsin (MWL)	A+	.196	16	56	7	11	3	0	0	6	8	11	3	.292	.250
		Minor League Totals		.315	115	406	97	128	33	5	8	73	77	92	15	.430	.480

MILWAUKEE BREWERS

10 ANDREW FISCHER, 3B

HIT: 50. **POW:** 60. **RUN:** 40. **FLD:** 40. **ARM:** 55. **BA Grade:** 50. **Risk:** Average. **Adj:** 40.

Born: May 25, 2004. **B-T:** L-R. **HT:** 6-1. **WT:** 210.
Drafted: Tennessee, 2025 (1st round). **Signed by:** Ketchum Marsh.
TRACK RECORD: Fischer played at Duke as a freshman, Ole Miss as a sophomore and then transferred to Tennessee in 2025. He showed power at every stop and had his best season with the Volunteers, hitting .341/.497/.760 with 25 home runs in 65 games before the Brewers drafted him in the first round at No. 20 overall and signed him for $3.5 million. Fischer made his pro debut with High-A Wisconsin and he performed well, though he played through a wrist injury that hampered his exit velocities.
SCOUTING REPORT: Fischer's plus power is his calling card. Hitting from a crouched stance, Fischer has good bat speed in a steep swing geared to hit the ball in the air. He's a patient hitter who will draw his walks and has a knack for hitting the ball out front with loft to his pull side with a chance to be a 25-plus home run threat. He could end up a power-over-hit player with a swing path that looks like it could leave some holes, but some scouts think he's a more complete hitter than he gets credit for thanks to good plate coverage and zone control. A below-average runner, Fischer played exclusively first base at Tennessee, but in his pro debut the Brewers played him at third base, a position he had played earlier in his college career. The initial returns were encouraging. Fischer will need to get better coming in on balls, but he has the lateral agility, hands and above-average arm that give him a chance to be a serviceable defender at third base.
THE FUTURE: Fischer was one of the more complete offensive threats available in the 2025 draft. He could be up in Milwaukee by 2027, either at third base or first base, with the upside to hit in the middle of their lineup.

Year	Age	Club (League)	Level	AVG	G	AB	R	H	2B	3B	HR	RBI	BB	SO	SB	OBP	SLG
2025	21	Wisconsin (MWL)	A+	.311	19	74	8	23	5	1	1	10	11	22	8	.402	.446
		Minor League Totals		.311	19	74	8	23	5	1	1	10	11	22	8	.402	.446

11 TYSON HARDIN, RHP

FB: 55. **SL:** 55. **CT:** 50. **CH:** 40. **CTL:** 55. **BA Grade:** 50. **Risk:** Average. **Adj:** 40.

Born: November 19, 2001. **B-T:** R-R. **HT:** 6-2. **WT:** 188. **Drafted:** Mississippi State, 2024 (12th round).
Signed by: Scott Nichols.
TRACK RECORD: After two seasons at Daytona State (Fla.) JC, Hardin transferred to Mississippi State, where he had a 12.81 ERA in 19.2 innings of relief in 2023. He was better in 2024 with a 3.22 ERA in 36.1 innings—though he still struggled with control—but the Brewers were intrigued by the way he moved on the mound and his pitch traits to draft him in the 12th round and sign him for $147,500. Hardin took a huge leap forward in 2025. Moved to a starting role, Hardin threw more strikes, finished the year in Double-A Biloxi—though he missed six weeks in July and August with arm fatigue—and won the organization's pitcher of the year award.
SCOUTING REPORT: Hardin's stuff in pro ball in 2025 was similar to what it was in college, but his pitch usage and control changed. He threw 65% fastballs at Mississippi State, but he dropped that to 45% in 2025 and ramped up the frequency of his slider and cutter. He throws a mix of four-seam and two-seam fastballs, sitting at 92-95 mph and touching 97, and it's a pitch that plays up from his lower release height with good extension. His sweeping slider is an above-average pitch that spins at 2,400-2,500 rpm with 12 inches of lateral break to miss bats. His upper-80s cutter is an average pitch that gives him another wrinkle that he can use against righties or lefties, especially since his firm changeup is a below-average pitch he doesn't use often. Hardin walked 13.9% of batters his draft year in college, but in 2025 he posted a 4.3% walk rate, pounding the zone especially with his fastball and cutter.
THE FUTURE: Hardin looks like a late-round gem for the Brewers. If he can repeat his 2025 success and prove his durability in a starter role, he has a chance to develop into a No. 3 or 4 starter with the possibility of making his major league debut by the end of 2026.

Year	Age	Club (League)	Level	W	L	ERA	G	GS	IP	H	HR	BB	SO	BB%	SO%	WHIP	AVG
2025	23	Wisconsin (MWL)	A+	4	3	2.34	11	11	58	57	0	9	62	3.9	26.7	1.14	.258
2025	23	Biloxi (SL)	AA	2	2	3.29	10	10	38	39	3	8	34	5.1	21.8	1.23	.267
		Minor League Totals		7	5	2.80	23	22	100	100	3	19	98	4.7	24.2	1.19	.262

12 LUKE ADAMS, 1B/3B

HIT: 45. **POW:** 55. **RUN:** 40. **FLD:** 40. **ARM:** 50. **BA Grade:** 50. **Risk:** Average. **Adj:** 40.

Born: April 24, 2004. **B-T:** R-R. **HT:** 6-4. **WT:** 240. **Drafted:** HS—Hinsdale, IL, 2022 (12th round).
Signed by: Ginger Poulson.
TRACK RECORD: Adams was a Michigan State commit before the Brewers drafted him in the 12th round in 2022 and signed him for $282,500. Adams has done it with an unconventional style, but he has been an on-base machine with a career .423 OBP despite hitting just .236. His on-base prowess continued in 2025 with Double-A Biloxi, though a shoulder injury limited him to 72 games.
SCOUTING REPORT: Adams is a polarizing prospect with an unorthodox swing. With a pull-heavy approach, he loads with a big leg kick, strides closed and often cuts himself off, creating a high pop-up rate that hurts his batting average. Despite his funky swing, Adams doesn't swing and miss much and he has plus raw power. He walks a lot because he's extremely patient to the point of being passive—his 33% swing rate was the lowest among Brewers full-season minor leaguers—and he's a magnet for hit by pitches. Drafted as a third baseman, Adams still spent some time at third in 2025 but got most of his playing time at first base. He's slowed to a below-average runner as he's filled out, and while his average arm is fine for the left side of the infield, his footwork, actions and range have him trending more toward first base.
THE FUTURE: Adams' believers point to the fact that his results have continued now at the upper levels, but he still has skeptics because of his swing and positional limits. He should be ready for Triple-A in 2026 and could make his major league debut by the end of the year.

Year	Age	Club (League)	Level	AVG	G	AB	R	H	2B	3B	HR	RBI	BB	SO	SB	OBP	SLG
2025	21	Wisconsin (MWL)	A+	.217	8	23	8	5	2	0	0	4	9	4	0	.472	.304
2025	21	Biloxi (SL)	AA	.232	64	211	50	49	13	0	11	38	43	60	10	.409	.450
		Minor League Totals		.240	182	605	141	145	36	3	23	103	135	171	49	.412	.423

13 BRADY EBEL, SS

HIT: 55. **POW:** 50. **RUN:** 40. **FLD:** 50. **ARM:** 70. **BA Grade:** 55. **Risk:** High. **Adj:** 40.

Born: July 25, 2007. **B-T:** L-R. **HT:** 6-3. **WT:** 195. **Drafted:** HS—Corona, CA, 2025 (1st round supp).
Signed by: Hashim Cole.
TRACK RECORD: Ebel grew up around big leaguers. His father Dino is the third base coach for the Dodgers, and Brady has the mechanics and instincts of someone raised by a major league coach. After playing for a Corona (Calif.) High team that had two players selected ahead of him in the first round of the 2025 draft, Ebel went No. 32 overall to the Brewers and signed for $2.75 million.
SCOUTING REPORT: At 17, Ebel was one of the youngest players drafted in 2025. His baseball IQ is advanced beyond his years, evident in how he manages his at-bats and controls the strike zone. He has a calm, balanced swing with quiet hands, taking a compact turn into the hitting zone with an approach geared for line drives. Ebel doesn't have big bat speed, but he's young with a lot of physical upside left in his 6-foot-3 frame and could grow into bigger power once he fills out. Ebel played third base in high school in 2025 because he was teammates with White Sox first-round shortstop Billy Carlson, but he otherwise has been a shortstop. He's a below-average runner whose first-step quickness and range might be better suited at third base, where he could be an above-average defender. The Brewers will start Ebel's development at shortstop, where his instincts, internal clock and plus-plus arm stand out.
THE FUTURE: After debuting in Low-A in 2025, Ebel should return to the level in 2026. He has the upside to be a high on-base threat somewhere on the left side of the infield.

Year	Age	Club (League)	Level	AVG	G	AB	R	H	2B	3B	HR	RBI	BB	SO	SB	OBP	SLG
2025	17	Carolina (CAR)	A	.241	16	58	6	14	1	0	0	4	6	17	0	.333	.259
		Minor League Totals		.241	16	58	6	14	1	0	0	4	6	17	0	.333	.259

14 ROBERT GASSER, LHP

FB: 50. **SL:** 55. **CT:** 50. **CH:** 45. **CTL:** 50. **BA Grade:** 45. **Risk:** Average. **Adj:** 35.

Born: May 31, 1999. **B-T:** L-L. **HT:** 6-0. **WT:** 192. **Drafted:** Houston, 2021 (2nd round). **Signed by:** Kevin Ham (Padres).
TRACK RECORD: The Brewers acquired Gasser from the Padres in the 2022 trade deadline deal for Josh Hader. Gasser led Triple-A pitchers in strikeouts in 2023, made his major league debut in 2024, but in June that year had Tommy John surgery. He returned to minor league games in June 2025, made a pair of starts in the major leagues in September, then pitched in two relief outings for the Brewers in the postseason.
SCOUTING REPORT: Gasser gets down the mound well to generate good extension from a low release height. He has good control of a fastball that sits at 91-94 mph and touched 95 mph in 2025, mixing

a four-seamer with a two-seamer that has above-average armside run. He throws those pitches around 50% of the time and leans heavily on his secondary stuff, the best of which is a low-80s slider that's an above-average pitch with 14 inches of sweep. His upper-80s cutter is an average pitch that he mainly uses against righties. His changeup has good shape and fade, but it's a firm, upper-80s pitch that's just five mph off his fastball.
THE FUTURE: Entering his age-27 season, Gasser has the stuff to pitch in the back of a rotation. He should get that opportunity in 2026, though he could end up in a multi-inning relief role or shuttling back and forth between Milwaukee and Triple-A.

Year	Age	Club (League)	Level	W	L	ERA	G	GS	IP	H	HR	BB	SO	BB%	SO%	WHIP	AVG
2025	26	ACL Brewers	Rk	0	0	0.00	1	1	1	1	0	0	0	0.0	0.0	1.00	.333
2025	26	Wisconsin (MWL)	A+	0	0	3.60	3	3	5	3	0	1	5	5.9	29.4	0.80	.200
2025	26	Nashville (IL)	AAA	3	2	2.25	10	6	32	25	1	10	36	7.7	27.7	1.09	.214
2025	26	Milwaukee (NL)	MLB	0	2	3.18	2	2	6	5	1	4	5	13.8	17.2	1.59	.217
		Minor League Totals		19	16	3.63	76	71	337	301	29	121	410	8.5	28.8	1.25	.238
		Major League Totals		2	2	2.67	7	7	34	33	3	5	21	3.5	14.7	1.13	.256

15 ETHAN DORCHIES, RHP
FB: 50. **SL:** 55. **SP:** 55. **CT:** 45. **CTL:** 55. **BA Grade:** 55. **Risk:** High. **Adj:** 40.

Born: October 22, 2006. **B-T:** R-R. **HT:** 6-6. **WT:** 227. **Drafted:** HS—Cary, IL, 2024 (10th round). **Signed by:** Ginger Poulson.
TRACK RECORD: Dorchies was lightly recruited when he committed to Illinois-Chicago. Extremely young for his 2024 class—he turned 18 in October after his draft year—Dorchies signed with the Brewers as a 10th-round pick for $162,500, which could prove an incredible bargain. Dorchies' stuff ticked up in 2025 during an impressive debut in the Rookie-level Arizona Complex League, then continued to pitch well after a promotion to Low-A Carolina.
SCOUTING REPORT: Dorchies has a lot of projection arrows pointing up. He's a young, 6-foot-6 right-hander who gets great extension into a relatively lower release height for a pitcher his size. His raw stuff isn't overpowering, but it has already trended up with the projection for more. After touching the low 90s in high school, Dorchies in 2025 was sitting in the low 90s and touched 96 mph with a mix of four- and two-seam fastballs and could have another gear in the tank. It's a diverse arsenal with nothing plus now but feel for everything, including a low-80s slider with tight rotation, good sweep and two-plane depth at times. He throws a spin-killing splitter—less than 700 rpm—with heavy tumble that can be a bat-missing pitch to both lefties and righties. His upper-80s cutter gives hitters another look with shorter break off his slider that he uses to hitters from both sides. Dorchies has a longer arm action but has better body control than most long-limbed teenage pitchers, so he throws a lot of strikes with his fastball, though his walk rate did tick up once he got to Low-A.
THE FUTURE: Dorchies has starter traits with the look of a pitcher who is just scratching the surface of his potential, making him a breakout candidate heading into 2026.

Year	Age	Club (League)	Level	W	L	ERA	G	GS	IP	H	HR	BB	SO	BB%	SO%	WHIP	AVG
2025	18	ACL Brewers	Rk	0	0	1.67	6	3	27	15	0	8	32	7.6	30.5	0.85	.158
2025	18	Carolina (CAR)	A	0	3	3.27	13	8	55	36	4	27	57	11.8	25.0	1.15	.183
		Minor League Totals		0	3	2.74	19	11	82	51	4	35	89	10.5	26.7	1.05	.175

16 BLAKE BURKE, 1B
HIT: 40. **POW:** 60. **RUN:** 30. **FLD:** 45. **ARM:** 40. **BA Grade:** 45. **Risk:** Average. **Adj:** 35.

Born: June 11, 2003. **B-T:** L-L. **HT:** 6-3. **WT:** 236. **Drafted:** Tennessee, 2024 (1st round supp.). **Signed by:** Jeff Simpson.
TRACK RECORD: After hitting in the middle of the lineup for Tennessee during its national championship run in 2024, Burke signed with the Brewers for $2.1 million as a supplemental first-round pick at No. 34 overall. In 2025, Burke was solid in High-A Wisconsin, then flourished upon an August promotion to Double-A Biloxi, where he hit .300/.377/.579 with 11 home runs in 37 games after hitting five homers in 95 games previously.
SCOUTING REPORT: Power is the calling card for Burke. He's big, strong and has 70-grade raw power with top-end exit velocities that stack up among the best in the system, including a max of 117 mph. Getting to that power in games was something Burke struggled with early in the season. Part of that is swing decisions that he still has to improve because he's an aggressive hitter who will expand the zone. But Burke also made a swing and approach change at the end of the season to generate more loft and catch the ball out front more. The result was his groundball rate dropped from 54% in High-A to 44% in Double-A with better ability to pull balls in the air and higher overall production. He will need to get better against lefties after hitting .265/.351/.347 against them in 2025. A well below-average runner, Burke's is a fringe-average defender with a below-average arm whose value will come from what he does in the batter's box.

MILWAUKEE BREWERS

THE FUTURE: If Burke's swing change continues to yield the same improvements he showed late in 2025, he could develop into a 30-plus home run hitter, though he will still need to tighten his strike-zone discipline. A platoon first baseman could be another outcome.

Year	Age	Club (League)	Level	AVG	G	AB	R	H	2B	3B	HR	RBI	BB	SO	SB	OBP	SLG
2025	22	Wisconsin (MWL)	A+	.289	95	350	43	101	21	2	5	48	49	94	12	.380	.403
2025	22	Biloxi (SL)	AA	.300	37	140	21	42	6	0	11	34	16	41	3	.377	.579
		Minor League Totals		.291	137	506	64	147	27	2	16	82	67	139	15	.378	.447

17 BRAYLON PAYNE, OF

HIT: 30. **POW:** 50. **RUN:** 70. **FLD:** 45. **ARM:** 50. **BA Grade:** 50. **Risk:** High. **Adj:** 35.

Born: August 14, 2006. **B-T:** L-L. **HT:** 6-2. **WT:** 186. **Drafted:** HS—Missouri City, TX, 2024 (1st round). **Signed by:** Craig Smajstrla.
TRACK RECORD: Drafted as a 17-year-old, Payne was young for his class and stood out for his speed and athleticism when the Brewers signed him for $3.44 million as a first-round pick at No. 17 overall in 2024. In pro ball, Payne has shown a different profile than expected, showing surprising strength and raw power, though with more swing-and-miss tendencies.
SCOUTING REPORT: Payne is a quick-twitch athlete with plus-plus speed. His strength and bat speed help him produce plus raw power, giving him one of the better power-speed combinations in Milwaukee's farm system. However, there's still a lot for Payne to clean up to get the most out of those tools. He uses an unorthodox swing where his hips open early, his upper and lower halves get disconnected costing him balance and he has trouble recognizing spin. That led to a 30% strikeout rate and a lot of ground balls, with a swing path that prevents him from tapping into his raw power. Payne's speed and average arm give him the tools for center field, but his reads and routes need improvement to stick there.
THE FUTURE: There's a wide range of outcomes for Payne, who could have a breakout if he's able to make the right adjustments, but the crudeness to his game is still a long-term project. High-A Wisconsin should be up next.

Year	Age	Club (League)	Level	AVG	G	AB	R	H	2B	3B	HR	RBI	BB	SO	SB	OBP	SLG
2025	18	Carolina (CAR)	A	.240	77	288	55	69	9	4	8	30	52	103	31	.354	.382
		Minor League Totals		.250	81	304	58	76	10	5	8	35	55	106	35	.363	.395

18 BROCK WILKEN, 3B

HIT: 40. **POW:** 60. **RUN:** 20. **FLD:** 40. **ARM:** 60. **BA Grade:** 45. **Risk:** Average. **Adj:** 35.

Born: June 17, 2002. **B-T:** R-R. **HT:** 6-4. **WT:** 225. **Drafted:** Wake Forest, 2023 (1st round). **Signed by:** Taylor Frederick.
TRACK RECORD: Wilken hit 31 home runs and drew 69 walks—both single-season records for Wake Forest—during his draft year in 2023 before the Brewers drafted him that year in the first round. His 2024 season was a disaster. He got hit in the face by a fastball in April, causing multiple fractures, and he struggled the rest of the season. In 2025 with Double-A Biloxi, Wilken was showing the patience and power that drew the Brewers to him in college, though a freak knee injury in a clubhouse celebration in June kept him out for two months before he returned in late August.
SCOUTING REPORT: Wilken is a slugger who combines power and patience. He's a strong, 6-foot-4 righthanded hitter whose swing can get steep and stiff at times with a pull-heavy approach geared to catch the ball out front. That leaves him vulnerable to swinging and missing, especially against sliders, but he hammers fastballs and has the discipline to rack up walks to help offset some of the strikeouts that come with his power. He has minimal speed. Wilken has a plus arm at third base, but his quickness, lateral range and footwork leave him as a below-average defender at best at the position and will likely end up shifting him over to first base.
THE FUTURE: There's a chance Wilken develops into an everyday player at first or third base, though a platoon righthanded-hitting first baseman is a more likely outcome. He should start 2026 in Triple-A Nashville with a chance to make his major league debut by the end of the year.

Year	Age	Club (League)	Level	AVG	G	AB	R	H	2B	3B	HR	RBI	BB	SO	SB	OBP	SLG
2025	23	Biloxi (SL)	AA	.226	79	270	46	61	17	0	18	46	69	93	2	.387	.489
		Minor League Totals		.225	235	840	131	189	41	4	40	126	165	273	7	.358	.426

MILWAUKEE BREWERS

19 J.D. THOMPSON, LHP
FB: 55. **CB:** 50. **SL:** 50. **CH:** 50. **CTL:** 50. **BA Grade:** 50. **Risk:** High. **Adj:** 35.

Born: September 28, 2003. **B-T:** R-L. **HT:** 6-0. **WT:** 200. **Drafted:** Vanderbilt, 2025 (2nd round).
Signed by: Ketchum Marsh.
TRACK RECORD: Thompson was a two-year member of Vanderbilt's rotation and was the team's most effective pitcher in 2025. The Brewers drafted him that year in the second round with the 59th overall pick and signed him for $1,560,200.
SCOUTING REPORT: Thompson is a 6-foot lefthander with a strong, compact build. There's no one wipe-out pitch in his arsenal, but he's a strike-thrower who mixes four pitches effectively. He has good control of a fastball that cruises in the low 90s and touches 96 mph. His velocity sat higher than normal toward the end of the 2025 college season, and it's a fastball that plays up because of its riding life to miss bats at the top of the zone. His upper-70s curveball is a lower-spin breaking ball, but it's an average pitch that's effective and plays well off his fastball. His average changeup was his best swing-and-miss pitch in college. It has good separation off his heater, peeling 10 mph off his fastball with good fade and late tumble. His mid-80s slider with late tilt is another average offering that gives him another shape to attack hitters and he added a harder cutter after signing.
THE FUTURE: Thompson has the stuff and control that could fit in the back of a rotation. He should be ready for High-A Wisconsin in 2026.

Year	Age	Club (League)	Level	W	L	ERA	G	GS	IP	H	HR	BB	SO	BB%	SO%	WHIP	AVG
2025	21	Did not play															

20 ERIC BITONTI, 1B
HIT: 30. **POW:** 70. **RUN:** 40. **FLD:** 50. **ARM:** 60. **BA Grade:** 50. **Risk:** High. **Adj:** 35.

Born: November 17, 2005. **B-T:** L-R. **HT:** 6-5. **WT:** 236. **Drafted:** HS—San Bernardino, CA, 2023 (3rd round).
Signed by: Daniel Cho.
TRACK RECORD: Despite being one of the youngest players in the 2023 high school class, Bitonti long stood out for his massive 6-foot-5 frame and power. The Brewers drafted Bitonti in the third round in 2023 and signed him for a well above-slot bonus of $1.75 million. Bitonti still has gigantic power, but strikeouts limited his production in 2025 with Low-A Carolina.
SCOUTING REPORT: Bitonti's strengths and weaknesses as a hitter are obvious. He can blast deep, majestic home runs from the middle of the field over to his pull side with plus-plus raw power. There's plenty of strength and leverage behind Bitonti's swing, but it also leaves him with holes. He steps in the bucket, so he can crush balls middle-in, but he has trouble handling stuff on the outer third, while the extreme steepness of his swing led to a lot of swing-and-miss against elevated fastballs. Overall, Bitonti struck out at a 33% clip, a rate he has to cut down to succeed at higher levels. He did walk 13% of the time, something that will be important to help alleviate strikeouts that will always be part of his game. A shortstop in high school, Bitonti played mostly third base in 2024 but moved full-time to first base in 2025. He still takes ground balls regularly at third base, where he has surprising body control for his size and a plus arm, but he seems likely to remain a first baseman.
THE FUTURE: Bitonti flashes the 30-home run, impact slugger look that the Brewers were hoping for when they drafted him, but he will have to find a way to make more contact to get to a major league role. High-A Wisconsin is up next.

Year	Age	Club (League)	Level	AVG	G	AB	R	H	2B	3B	HR	RBI	BB	SO	SB	OBP	SLG
2025	19	Carolina (CAR)	A	.238	118	428	58	102	21	0	19	77	66	169	17	.341	.421
		Minor League Totals		.258	181	648	108	167	39	4	29	128	118	245	26	.372	.465

21 CRAIG YOHO, RHP
FB: 45. **SL:** 50. **CH:** 70. **CTL:** 50. **BA Grade:** 40. **Risk:** Mild. **Adj:** 35.

Born: October 23, 1999. **B-T:** R-R. **HT:** 6-2. **WT:** 235. **Drafted:** Indiana, 2023 (8th round). **Signed by:** Ginger Poulson.
TRACK RECORD: A position player at Houston for two years before transferring to Indiana, Yoho had Tommy John surgery twice in college and a knee surgery. Despite Yoho's limited time on the mound, the Brewers drafted him in the eighth round in 2023 and signed him for $10,000. Yoho reached Triple-A in 2024 and made his major league debut in April 2025. He came up intermittently later in the season, but he spent most of the season in Triple-A Nashville, posting a minor league ERA of 0.94 for the second straight season.
SCOUTING REPORT: A reliever entering his age-26 season, Yoho is older for a prospect despite having just two seasons in pro ball. He pitches from a lower release height into a low three-quarters slot with above-

MILWAUKEE BREWERS

average extension on a fastball that sits 92-94 mph and touches 96 with lively armside run. The separator for Yoho is his plus-plus changeup, a filthy pitch that he throws more than his fastball. Yoho sells his changeup well by maintaining his arm speed but having it peel 15 mph off his fastball with heavy tumble and outstanding fade, making it a swing-and-miss weapon against both lefties and righties. Yoho's average slider has tight rotation and it does miss bats, but he doesn't throw it often, mainly using it against righties early in counts. He throws an occasional fringe-average cutter as well. Yoho walked too many hitters in the big leagues, but he showed average control in the minors.

THE FUTURE: Yoho has the stuff to pitch as a middle reliever and could jump into that role in Milwaukee in 2026. His changeup is good enough to give him high-leverage upside despite lacking a power fastball.

Year	Age	Club (League)	Level	W	L	ERA	G	GS	IP	H	HR	BB	SO	BB%	SO%	WHIP	AVG
2025	25	Nashville (IL)	AAA	6	1	0.94	43	0	48	26	0	20	60	10.5	31.4	0.97	.157
2025	25	Milwaukee (NL)	MLB	0	0	7.27	8	0	9	8	1	9	7	22.0	17.1	1.96	.276
		Minor League Totals		10	3	1.17	94	0	108	63	1	44	164	9.9	36.9	0.99	.164
		Major League Totals		0	0	7.27	8	0	9	8	1	9	7	22.0	17.1	1.96	.276

22 FRANK CAIRONE, LHP

FB: 55. **SL:** 60. **CH:** 45. **CT:** 50. **CTL:** 45. **BA Grade:** 50. **Risk:** High. **Adj:** 35.

Born: September 14, 2007. **B-T:** R-L. **HT:** 6-2. **WT:** 200. **Drafted:** HS—Franklinville, NJ, 2025 (2nd round supp). **Signed by:** Steve DiTrolio.

TRACK RECORD: As an underclassman in high school, Cairone wasn't heavily recruited before he committed to Coastal Carolina. Young for the 2025 class—he was still 17 on draft day—Cairone was mostly pitching the mid-to-upper 80s the summer before his draft year, then in 2025 jumped into the low 90s. That velocity spike—along with his slider and other traits—propelled him up draft boards, with the Brewers selecting him in the supplemental second round (68th overall) and signing him for $1,097,500.

SCOUTING REPORT: Cairone has an array of promising projection indicators. He will pitch all of 2026 as an 18-year-old, and while he has a thicker build with some physical maturity, there could be another velocity increase still to come. Cairone pitches in the low 90s and touches 94 mph. He comes at hitters from a low release height out of a low three-quarters slot with above-average extension, release traits that help his fastball play up. His low-80s slider has wide sweep across the zone with tight rotation, often spinning above 2,800 rpm, to get a high dose of swing-and-miss to project as a plus pitch. Cairone mixes in an occasional mid-80s cutter and didn't throw his changeup much in high school, leading some scouts to project a below-average changeup, but the Brewers internally see signs of that pitch beating those projections. It's mostly a sound delivery, but there is some effort to his operation and he will need to tighten his command.

THE FUTURE: Cairone is one of the best breakout candidates in the lower levels of the Brewers' system entering 2026. He's young enough that it wouldn't be a surprise for him to open in the Rookie-level Arizona Complex League, but he should see Low-A Wilson at some point in 2026.

Year	Age	Club (League)	Level	W	L	ERA	G	GS	IP	H	HR	BB	SO	BB%	SO%	WHIP	AVG
2025	17	Did not play															

23 BRYCE MECCAGE, RHP

FB: 50. **CB:** 50. **SL:** 55. **CH:** 40. **CTL:** 50. **BA Grade:** 50. **Risk:** High. **Adj:** 35.

Born: March 21, 2006. **B-T:** R-R. **HT:** 6-4. **WT:** 210. **Drafted:** HS—Pennington, NJ, 2024 (2nd round). **Signed by:** Steve DiTrolio.

TRACK RECORD: Meccage grew up around pitching minds. His father Jeremy was a pitching coach for Princeton for 10 years. His uncle Justin was the Brewers' Triple-A pitching coach in 2025 and is now the Giants' pitching coach. The Brewers drafted Meccage out of high school in 2024 with their second-round pick and signed him for $2.5 million. He didn't dominate, but he had a solid pro debut with Low-A Carolina in 2025.

SCOUTING REPORT: Meccage has a strong, physically mature 6-foot-4 frame and gets down the mound well to generate above-average extension. He pitches off a fastball that sits at 92-96 mph, touches 98 mph and has solid ride, mostly throwing it to the middle or top of the zone. Meccage shows aptitude to spin multiple breaking balls. The one that gets the most swinging strikes is an 82-86 mph slider that flashes above-average with short, late tilt. The other is a high-spin curveball that he's still learning to land in the zone more often but could be an average or better pitch. His changeup is a below-average pitch that he rarely uses. Meccage is a solid strike-thrower for his age who could end up with average control but is still tightening his command.

THE FUTURE: If Meccage can refine at least one of his secondary pitches into a true plus pitch to miss more bats, he has the potential to fit into the back of a rotation. He's ready for High-A Wisconsin in 2026.

Year	Age	Club (League)	Level	W	L	ERA	G	GS	IP	H	HR	BB	SO	BB%	SO%	WHIP	AVG
2025	19	Carolina (CAR)	A	1	4	4.35	19	19	70	61	4	26	69	8.9	23.6	1.24	.238
		Minor League Totals		1	4	4.35	19	19	70	61	4	26	69	8.9	23.6	1.24	.238

24 TYLER BLACK, OF/1B
HIT: 50. **POW:** 45. **RUN:** 60. **FLD:** 45. **ARM:** 40. **BA Grade:** 40. **Risk:** Mild. **Adj:** 35.

Born: July 26, 2000. **B-T:** L-R. **HT:** 6-1. **WT:** 200. **Drafted:** Wright State, 2021 (1st round supp.). **Signed by:** Pete Vuckovich Jr.
TRACK RECORD: Drafted 33rd overall in 2021, Black reached the major leagues in 2024 with three quick stints in Milwaukee, but he spent most of the season in Triple-A Nashville. He struggled at the end of the season and those offensive issues carried over into 2025. A broken hamate bone in his left hand in spring training that required surgery didn't help Black, who made a couple of brief cameos in the major leagues but spent most of the season back in Triple-A.
SCOUTING REPORT: One of Black's greatest strengths has always been his strike-zone discipline. Despite his struggles, that was still evident throughout 2025. Black picks up spin, tracks pitches well and doesn't often expand the strike zone, traits that consistently enable him to walk at a high clip. However, his Triple-A strikeout rate jumped a tick to 26.5% and his overall miss rates spiked, particularly against fastballs. While the injury might have had lingering effects, his lack of home run power continues to be a question, especially now that he's playing left field and first base. Black is a good athlete and a plus runner, but his arm is below-average and defense doesn't come naturally to him when he is in the infield.
THE FUTURE: As a 25-year-old, Black is now on the older end for a prospect. If the injury was what led to his struggles in 2025, he's a rebound candidate. However, with questions about his offensive profile at the positions he now plays, a path to playing time in Milwaukee is difficult, making him a potential change-of-scenery candidate.

Year	Age	Club (League)	Level	AVG	G	AB	R	H	2B	3B	HR	RBI	BB	SO	SB	OBP	SLG
2025	24	ACL Brewers	Rk	.387	10	31	7	12	2	1	1	5	8	3	0	.513	.613
2025	24	Nashville (IL)	AAA	.243	61	222	33	54	10	2	4	34	43	71	22	.369	.360
2025	24	Milwaukee (NL)	MLB	.250	5	8	1	2	1	0	0	1	5	1	0	.538	.375
		Minor League Totals		.270	386	1408	266	380	68	24	42	222	271	336	115	.399	.442
		Major League Totals		.211	23	57	5	12	3	0	0	3	12	18	3	.357	.263

25 JOSH KNOTH, RHP
FB: 55. **CB:** 60. **SL:** 60. **CH:** 40. **CTL:** 50. **BA Grade:** 50. **Risk:** High. **Adj:** 35.

Born: August 10, 2005. **B-T:** R-R. **HT:** 6-1. **WT:** 190. **Drafted:** HS—Medford, NY, 2023 (1st round supp.).
Signed by: Steve DiTrolio.
TRACK RECORD: One of the youngest players in the 2023 class, Knoth was 17 when the Brewers drafted him with the No. 33 overall pick that year and signed him for $2 million. Knoth had a solid pro debut in 2024 with Low-A Carolina, though he missed the tail end of the season with elbow soreness. The news turned worse entering the 2025 season when Knoth had Tommy John surgery, keeping him out for the year.
SCOUTING REPORT: Knoth is an athletic righthander with a compact delivery and good arm action. He pitches off a fastball that sits at 92-95 mph and touches 96 with ride and cut. The standout trait for Knoth is his ability to spin his breaking stuff at more than 3,000 rpm. His 78-81 mph curveball is a plus pitch with good depth that he relied on as his main putaway pitch when he was in high school, but in pro ball he used it more as a pitch to get called strikes. He instead used his slider as his main out pitch in pro ball. It's a plus slider at 82-88 mph that Knoth manipulates to get wider sweep at the lower end and shorter, late break when he throws it with more power. Knoth's 88-90 mph changeup has solid fade but it's firm off his fastball and didn't get much usage. Knoth is a solid strike-thrower for his age, but there are times when he loses his direction to the plate and his command wavers.
THE FUTURE: Knoth showed midrotation starter potential prior to getting hurt, though the injury and his size will raise more questions about his durability. He's set to return in 2026 and should pitch with High-A Wisconsin.

Year	Age	Club (League)	Level	W	L	ERA	G	GS	IP	H	HR	BB	SO	BB%	SO%	WHIP	AVG
2025	19	Did not play—Injured															
		Minor League Totals		4	6	4.48	21	21	84	78	7	40	96	11.1	26.6	1.40	.248

MILWAUKEE BREWERS

26 JAYDEN DUBANEWICZ, RHP
FB: 50. **SL:** 50. **CH:** 50. **CTL:** 60. **BA Grade:** 45. **Risk:** High. **Adj:** 30.

Born: March 23, 2006. **B-T:** R-R. **HT:** 6-3. **WT:** 170. **Drafted:** HS—Parkland, FL, 2024 (16th round).
Signed by: Joseph Rivera.
TRACK RECORD: Since the draft dropped to 20 rounds in 2021, the Brewers have been the most aggressive team in baseball signing high school players in rounds 11-20. One potential success story from that group is Dubanewicz, who passed on a Florida commitment to sign with the Brewers for $665,000 as a 16th-round pick in 2024. He filled the strike zone in a solid pro debut in 2025, first in the Rookie-level Arizona Complex League before a June promotion to Low-A Carolina.
SCOUTING REPORT: Dubanewicz is a lanky, long-limbed pitcher who gets above-average extension on a fastball that parks at 90-93 mph and reaches 95. There's still a ton of space on his frame to pack on more weight, which could allow him to add more velocity. Dubanewicz doesn't miss many bats with his fastball, but he's a high-level strike-thrower with both his fastball and slider, walking just 5.6% of hitters in his first season. He throws a low-80s slider that's relatively lower spin with late, short tilt and plays up because of his ability to execute it consistently down and for chases. His mid-80s changeup comes in a little firm off his fastball and he has a tendency to drop his release point with it, but it's a pitch that has good fade and could become an average pitch.
THE FUTURE: Dubanewicz has appealing traits that are more about projection than present stuff. He's a candidate to take a leap forward in the next couple years if he's able to get stronger and add more power behind his arsenal to help him miss more bats.

Year	Age	Club (League)	Level	W	L	ERA	G	GS	IP	H	HR	BB	SO	BB%	SO%	WHIP	AVG
2025	19	ACL Brewers	Rk	3	0	2.66	5	4	24	20	0	8	23	8.0	23.0	1.18	.217
2025	19	Carolina (CAR)	A	5	4	2.30	14	7	59	53	4	11	41	4.6	17.2	1.09	.242
		Minor League Totals		8	4	2.40	19	11	82	73	4	19	64	5.6	18.9	1.12	.235

27 HANDELFRY ENCARNACION, OF
HIT: 50. **POW:** 50. **RUN:** 45. **FLD:** 45. **ARM:** 50. **BA Grade:** 45. **Risk:** High. **Adj:** 30.

Born: June 8, 2007. **B-T:** L-L. **HT:** 5-11. **WT:** 175. **Signed:** Dominican Republic, 2024. **Signed by:** Jose Morales.
TRACK RECORD: Despite being a small player early in the amateur scouting process, Encarnacion impressed the Brewers with his advanced lefthanded hitting ability when they signed him as a 16-year-old out of the Dominican Republic for $400,000 on Jan. 15, 2024. After a modest pro debut in the Dominican Summer League in 2024, Encarnacion showed more power and better performance in 2025 when he jumped to the Rookie-level Arizona Complex League, though his numbers tailed once he got to Low-A Carolina.
SCOUTING REPORT: Encarnacion's bat is his calling card. He sets up with an open stance, loads with a leg kick and takes a hard front side move to the ball that opens him up early, but his hands work compact to the ball with good barrel control. Encarnacion tracks pitches well, makes good swing decisions and doesn't have much swing-and-miss to his game. The uptick in power he showed in 2025 was a pleasant surprise. His 90th percentile exit velocity increased more than 3 mph to where he's now showing flashes of average raw power. While Encarnacion isn't that big, with his youth and a frame that's still physically immature, there's potential for him to continue adding power. That will be key for Encarnacion, who plays all three outfield positions but is a fringe-average runner who fits best in a corner.
THE FUTURE: Encarnacion should open 2026 back in Low-A, where he will be one of the organization's most intriguing lower-level hitting prospects to watch.

Year	Age	Club (League)	Level	AVG	G	AB	R	H	2B	3B	HR	RBI	BB	SO	SB	OBP	SLG
2025	18	ACL Brewers	Rk	.289	48	190	40	55	18	0	5	37	19	33	6	.369	.463
2025	18	Carolina (CAR)	A	.155	28	103	8	16	4	1	0	11	10	22	0	.237	.214
		Minor League Totals		.234	107	393	66	92	28	1	7	67	52	76	10	.338	.364

28 MANUEL RODRIGUEZ, RHP
FB: 40. **SL:** 55. **CT:** 50. **CH:** 40. **CTL:** 70. **BA Grade:** 45. **Risk:** High. **Adj:** 30.

Born: August 8, 2005. **B-T:** R-R. **HT:** 6-2. **WT:** 180. **Signed:** Mexico, 2022. **Signed by:** Mario Mendoza.
TRACK RECORD: Signed out of Mexico when he was 16 for $40,000 in 2022, Rodriguez has breezed through the system thanks to outstanding control and pitchability. He flourished all season in 2025 at High-A Wisconsin as a 19-year-old before getting a September bump to Double-A Biloxi.
SCOUTING REPORT: With a simple delivery and good arm action, Rodriguez has outstanding control. He walked just 2.7% of hitters in 2025 and has an uncanny ability to repeat his release point, enabling him

to pound the strike zone with potential plus-plus control. Why isn't he ranked higher? His fastball sits at 87-89 mph and tickles 91. It's a cutting, high-spin fastball north of 2,600 rpm that plays up because of his control and deception in the way he hides the ball behind his body, but Rodriguez will likely need to figure out a way to throw harder to continue his success against major league hitters. Rodriguez mixes his stuff liberally—he throws his fastball less than one third of the time—and has advanced feel to spin and consistently execute a mid-to-upper-70s slider with good sweep. It's a potential above-average pitch and he works in a shorter cutter in the low 80s that he will use in any count. His changeup has been effective against lower-level hitters but it's typically a below-average pitch that's only 4 mph off his fastball.
THE FUTURE: If Rodriguez can squeeze out more velocity, he could fit into the back of a rotation. He should be one of the youngest pitchers in Double-A to open 2026.

Year	Age	Club (League)	Level	W	L	ERA	G	GS	IP	H	HR	BB	SO	BB%	SO%	WHIP	AVG
2025	19	Wisconsin (MWL)	A+	3	5	3.01	18	18	84	68	12	15	84	4.6	25.6	0.99	.220
2025	19	Biloxi (SL)	AA	0	0	3.00	1	1	6	4	1	0	4	0.0	16.7	0.67	.174
		Minor League Totals		8	12	3.67	41	29	167	149	24	34	146	5.0	21.5	1.10	.235

29 DANIEL DICKINSON, 2B

HIT: 50. **POW:** 40. **RUN:** 50. **FLD:** 45. **ARM:** 50. **BA Grade:** 45. **Risk:** High. **Adj:** 30.

Born: December 5, 2003. **B-T:** R-R. **HT:** 6-0. **WT:** 190. **Drafted:** LSU, 2025 (6th round). **Signed by:** Scott Nichols.
TRACK RECORD: Dickinson raked for two years at Utah Valley before transferring to LSU for his junior season. He hit .315/.458/.525 with nearly as many walks (40) as strikeouts (42) for the Tigers in 2025 as their primary three-hole hitter en route to a national championship. Dickinson was a top 100 draft prospect, so the Brewers were pleasantly surprised when they were able to draft him in the sixth round and sign him for $325,000.
SCOUTING REPORT: Dickinson doesn't jump out for his raw tools, but he has a good offensive approach and a knack for being on time at the plate. It's a simple righthanded swing that he starts with a small turn of the heel and takes a short, direct path to the ball. It's a quick stroke that helps him catch up to good velocity, he has good plate coverage and has a good sense of the strike zone. His power is below-average, and even that power vanished during his 2024 summer in the Cape Cod League, creating more questions about how his production will translate with wood bats. He's an average runner with an average arm who isn't a standout defender at second base but should provide serviceable defense at the position.
THE FUTURE: Dickinson fits the typical Brewers hitting prospect archetype as a hitter with good bat-to-ball skills and swing decisions. He should make his pro debut at one of their Class A affiliates.

Year	Age	Club (League)	Level	AVG	G	AB	R	H	2B	3B	HR	RBI	BB	SO	SB	OBP	SLG
2025	21	Did not play															

30 COLEMAN CROW, RHP

FB: 40. **CB:** 55. **SL:** 50. **CH:** 40. **CTL:** 55. **BA Grade:** 40. **Risk:** Average. **Adj:** 30.

Born: December 30, 2000. **B-T:** R-R. **HT:** 6-0. **WT:** 180. **Drafted:** HS—Zebulon, GA, 2019 (28th round). **Signed by:** Todd Hogan (Angels).
TRACK RECORD: The Angels drafted Crow out of high school in 2019 but he has had a slow ascension in part due to injuries. In 2023, Crow made four starts before needing Tommy John surgery and also switched teams twice, first going to the Mets in a June trade, then after the season moving to the Brewers in a deal for outfielder Tyrone Taylor. He missed the 2024 season. Crow returned in 2025, was effective for Double-A Biloxi and made two Triple-A starts in July before missing the rest of the season due to a flexor strain in his right elbow. The Brewers added Crow to the 40-man roster in November 2025 to prevent him from becoming a minor league free agent.
SCOUTING REPORT: Crow is a 6-foot righthander who has above-average control—he walked just 6% of hitters in 2025—and is able to throw both his fastball and breaking stuff for strikes at a high rate. It's a light fastball, sitting in the low 90s and touching 94 mph, without projection to throw harder. Where Crow has success is with his ability to spin the ball. His mid-to-upper-70s curveball is an above-average pitch with outstanding rotation, averaging 3,000 rpm with sharp bite to get a high dose of empty swings. His hard slider at 85-88 mph is a short, cutter-like pitch. Crow has a below-average changeup but rarely throws it.
THE FUTURE: With his durability questions and lack of a changeup, Crow is likely to end up in the bullpen as a low-leverage reliever or swingman. He should return to Triple-A Nashville to open 2026.

Year	Age	Club (League)	Level	W	L	ERA	G	GS	IP	H	HR	BB	SO	BB%	SO%	WHIP	AVG
2025	24	Biloxi (SL)	AA	4	0	2.51	10	10	43	31	2	8	52	4.8	31.1	0.91	.199
2025	24	Nashville (IL)	AAA	0	1	7.71	2	2	7	9	1	4	12	12.1	36.4	1.86	.321
		Minor League Totals		19	7	4.12	53	49	264	250	33	82	285	7.3	25.3	1.26	.246

Byron Buxton

Minnesota Twins

BY IAN CUNDALL

The Twins found themselves at a crossroads heading into the 2025 trade deadline. The American League Central, which for years had been the worst division in baseball, was improving around them, and they were stuck in no man's land after entering the season with playoff aspirations.

With the prospect of another losing season on the horizon, financial questions lingering in the background ever since they lost their regional sports network and the team still for sale, the Twins chose a lane and engaged in a sizable summer selloff.

In total they made nine trades, exporting 11 players and importing 13. The trades weren't limited to moving veterans or rentals either. They moved Carlos Correa, who was signed for at least three more seasons, to save $70 million and also dealt all of their high-leverage bullpen arms who had multiple years of team control.

The Twins now find themselves in the midst of a "retooling" as president of baseball operations Derek Falvey said after the deadline. They were unable to get over the hump in the playoffs when they were willing to spend, and now it's unclear what payroll limitations they will be operating under for the foreseeable future after the Pohlad family announced they were no longer looking to sell the team in August.

As a result, the Twins' best path to returning to contention likely now runs through talent identification and player development.

Fortunately, the Twins have a strong track record in both areas on the pitching side. The majority of contributing pitchers in recent years were either acquired via trade and then developed or later-round college draftees who exceeded expectations.

The Twins targeted three arms who fit that mold at the deadline: Taj Bradley, Mick Abel and Kendry Rojas. Adding that group to the upper-level arms already in the system, including Connor Prielipp,

PROJECTED 2029 LINEUP

Position	Player	Age
Catcher	Eduardo Tait	22
First Base	Royce Lewis	30
Second Base	Luke Keaschall	26
Third Base	Kaelen Culpepper	26
Shortstop	Marek Houston	24
Left Field	Gabriel Gonzalez	24
Center Field	Walker Jenkins	23
Right Field	Emmanuel Rodriguez	25
Designated Hitter	Byron Buxton	35
No. 1 Starter	Zebby Matthews	28
No. 2 Starter	Connor Prielipp	27
No. 3 Starter	Mick Abel	27
No. 4 Starter	Dasan Hill	23
No. 5 Starter	Simeon Woods Richardson	28
Closer	Charlee Soto	23

gives the Twins a solid group to potentially rebuild their pitching staff in short order.

Looking even further down the system, the arms are arguably even more exciting. Dasan Hill and Charlee Soto have considerable upside, and their 2025 draft class features three higher-ceiling arms in Riley Quick, James Ellwanger and Matt Barr.

The Twins' track record of developing hitting prospects over the last few years is more mixed. They have had a lot of early-round draftees make the big leagues, but most haven't lived up to their potential. Second baseman Luke Keaschall, drafted in the second round in 2023, could be the start of a turnaround after his impressive debut. There's also a strong case to be made that Walker Jenkins is the most important player in the organization. He looks like their best bet at a franchise cornerstone.

For the Twins to get back into contention soon, they need to start hitting on bats and continue to add them—potentially via the third overall pick in the 2026 draft, which they won in the draft lottery.

With free agency likely off the table, the quickest path to contention is going to come from within. Hitting on the young major leaguers they acquired at the deadline and the group of prospects they have in the high minors is a start.

However, it could still take some time for them to get back to the level of competitiveness their fans have come to expect. ∎

DEPTH CHART

MINNESOTA TWINS

TOP 2026 ROOKIES — RANK
1. Walker Jenkins, OF — 1
2. Emmanuel Rodriguez, OF — 2
3. Connor Prielipp, LHP — 4

BREAKOUT PROSPECTS — RANK
1. Riley Quick, RHP — 11
2. Santiago Castellanos, RHP — 17
3. Matt Barr, RHP — 19

SOURCE OF TOP 30 TALENT

Homegrown	23	Acquired	7
College	8	Trade	7
Junior college	1	Rule 5 draft	0
High school	7	Independent league	0
Undrafted free agent	1	Free agent/waivers	0
International	6		

LF
Gabriel Gonzalez (10)
Teilon Serrano (27)
Kala'i Rosario (30)
Kyler Fedko
Ricardo Olivar
Dameury Pena

CF
Walker Jenkins (1)
Maddux Houghton

RF
Emmanuel Rodriguez (2)
Brandon Winokur (15)
Eduardo Beltre
Yasser Mercedes

3B
Kaelen Culpepper (3)
Quentin Young (12)
Billy Amick

SS
Marek Houston (9)
Tanner Schobel
Danny De Andrade
Bruin Agbayani

2B
Haritzon Castillo (25)
Kyle DeBarge (28)
Ramiro Dominguez

1B
Hendry Mendez (14)
Enrique Jimenez (29)
Joyner Perez

C
Eduardo Tait (5)
Khadim Diaw (24)
Noah Cardenas

LHP

LHSP
Connor Prielipp (4)
Dasan Hill (6)
Kendry Rojas (8)

LHRP
Yordi Jose
Michael Carpenter
Kade Bragg
Garrett Horn

RHP

RHSP
Charlee Soto (7)
Riley Quick (11)
Andrew Morris (13)
Adrian Bohorquez (16)
Santiago Castellanos (17)
James Ellwanger (18)
Matt Barr (19)
Geremy Villoria (26)

RHRP
Jose Olivares (20)
Marco Raya (21)
Ryan Gallagher (22)
John Klein (23)
C.J. Culpepper
Jason Reitz
Yoel Roque
Trent Baker
Hunter Hoopes
Cole Peschl

MINNESOTA TWINS

1 WALKER JENKINS, OF

Born: February 19, 2005. **B-T:** L-R. **HT:** 6-3. **WT:** 224.
Drafted: HS—Southport, NC, 2023 (1st round).
Signed by: Ty Dawson.

BA GRADE
65 Risk: Average
Adjusted grade: 55

SCOUTING GRADES
Hit: 70. Power: 50. Run: 55.
Field: 60. Arm: 55.
Projected future grades on 20-80 scouting scale

TRACK RECORD: Jenkins was seen as one of the top talents in the 2023 draft when the Twins selected him fifth overall and was a well-known amateur, having played for the USA Baseball 18U National Team as an underclassman in 2021. He also made the team in 2022 but was unable to play because of a hamate injury. That was his second noteworthy injury as an amateur. He also missed his freshman season recovering from hip impingement surgery. In pro ball, Jenkins has performed when healthy. He got off to a slow start in 2024 due to a quad injury and then missed six weeks with a hamstring injury. He came back strong and ended the year at Double-A Wichita. In 2025, he suffered a left ankle sprain in spring training but tried to play through it. He was the third-youngest player in the Texas League on Opening Day, but after two games was shut down due to lingering soreness. He returned to Wichita in June and ended up hitting .309/.426/.487. He was promoted to Triple-A St. Paul in late August and after going 1-for-20 in his first series, he hit .296/.351/.479 the rest of the season.

SCOUTING REPORT: Jenkins is a potential five-tool player who stands out physically and is an elite athlete. There is little wasted movement in his lefthanded swing, and it evokes visual comparisons to Hall of Famer and former Twins all-star Joe Mauer. Jenkins starts in an open stance with his hands high and employs a slight leg lift, before finishing high with two hands on the bat. He has a solid approach and above-average bat-to-ball skills, though his contact rate decreased slightly in 2025 as a tradeoff intended to create more impact. Jenkins is adept at hitting fastballs of all velocities and comfortable hitting secondaries. His average exit velocity has increased each year, and he produces above-average EVs for his age with a max of 110.1 mph. He has one of the highest barrel rates in the Twins' system but needs to refine his batted-ball angles to reach his power ceiling. His power is primarily to his pull side, and there is a difference in his exit velocities to his pull side compared to the opposite field. The lefthanded hitter has never hit a home run against a lefthander as a professional, but that isn't seen as a long-term concern. Jenkins is a potential plus defender in all outfield positions. He has strong instincts and plenty of range for center field, but due to his track record of lower body injuries, might fit best in a corner, where his above-average arm would comfortably play. Jenkins is also an above-average runner but could see that decline as he ages.

THE FUTURE: Jenkins has the best chance to become a franchise cornerstone of any Twins prospect. His balanced skill set gives him a high floor, and his upside will be determined by how his power develops. He should start at Triple-A in 2026 and could reach the big leagues in short order.

BEST TOOLS

BATTING
Best Hitter	Walker Jenkins
Best Power Hitter	Emmanuel Rodriguez
Best Strike-Zone Discipline	Emmanuel Rodriguez
Fastest Baserunner	Kyle DeBarge
Best Athlete	Walker Jenkins

PITCHING
Best Fastball	Charlee Soto
Best Curveball	Marco Raya
Best Slider	Connor Prielipp
Best Changeup	Connor Prielipp
Best Control	Andrew Morris

FIELDING
Best Defensive Catcher	Noah Cardenas
Best Defensive Infielder	Marek Houston
Best Infield Arm	Quentin Young
Best Defensive Outfielder	Maddux Houghton
Best Outfield Arm	Brandon Winokur

Year	Age	Club (League)	Level	AVG	G	AB	R	H	2B	3B	HR	RBI	BB	SO	SB	OBP	SLG
2025	20	FCL Twins	Rk	.000	1	1	1	0	0	0	0	2	0	0	.667	.000
2025	20	Fort Myers (FSL)	A	.280	8	25	4	7	0	0	1	2	5	6	2	.419	.400
2025	20	Wichita (TL)	AA	.309	52	191	38	59	11	1	7	24	34	44	11	.426	.487
2025	20	St. Paul (IL)	AAA	.242	23	91	13	22	6	1	2	8	9	26	4	.324	.396
		Minor League Totals		.295	192	718	123	212	44	10	19	114	115	137	40	.399	.464

MINNESOTA TWINS

2 EMMANUEL RODRIGUEZ, OF
HIT: 40. **POW:** 60. **RUN:** 55. **FLD:** 55. **ARM:** 60. **BA Grade:** 60. **Risk:** High. **Adj:** 45.

Born: February 28, 2003. **B-T:** L-L. **HT:** 6-0. **WT:** 215.
Signed: Dominican Republic, 2019. **Signed by:** Manuel Luciano.
TRACK RECORD: Rodriguez signed for $2.5 million out of the Dominican Republic in 2019 and has performed when on the field, but he has yet to play 100 games in a season. He missed four months in 2022 with a left knee sprain and another month in 2023 with an abdominal injury. In 2024, he missed time with a thumb injury that required offseason surgery. In 2025, he was slowed by a thumb sprain in spring training, and an abdominal injury in May kept him out until early July. In his fourth game back, he strained his oblique and was out until September. Overall, he played 65 games and 20% of those were rehab assignments.
SCOUTING REPORT: Rodriguez is a stocky outfielder with a strong lower half and supreme knowledge of the strike zone. There is significant variance in his profile because of questions with his hit tool. His chase rate is one of the lowest in the system, and he has a career walk rate above 20%. Rodriguez can get overly passive and likes to let the ball get deep. His career strikeout rate is over 30% and he ranks near the bottom of the system in contact rate. When he makes contact, he hits the ball extremely hard. His 90th percentile exit velocity of 109.2 mph was the highest in the system, but to reach his power potential he needs to elevate the ball to his pull side more consistently. He is an aggressive baserunner with above-average speed. Defensively, he has a plus arm and could play center field but likely profiles better in a corner to limit defensive wear and tear.
THE FUTURE: Rodriguez will head back to Triple-A to start 2026 and should make his major league debut during the season. If he stays healthy and can make enough contact, he has all-star upside, but there's a lot of risk in his profile and a path where he doesn't make enough contact against MLB pitchers.

Year	Age	Club (League)	Level	AVG	G	AB	R	H	2B	3B	HR	RBI	BB	SO	SB	OBP	SLG
2025	22	FCL Twins	Rk	.294	5	17	4	5	1	0	0	1	2	6	0	.368	.353
2025	22	Fort Myers (FSL)	A	.321	8	28	4	9	1	0	0	3	8	12	1	.472	.357
2025	22	St. Paul (IL)	AAA	.258	52	163	35	42	7	1	6	27	45	67	9	.429	.423
		Minor League Totals		.254	295	981	243	249	46	17	50	161	278	389	59	.424	.488

3 KAELEN CULPEPPER, SS
HIT: 50. **POW:** 45. **RUN:** 50. **FLD:** 50. **ARM:** 60. **BA Grade:** 55. **Risk:** Average. **Adj:** 45.

Born: December 29, 2002. **B-T:** R-R. **HT:** 6-0. **WT:** 185.
Drafted: Kansas State, 2024 (1st round). **Signed by:** J.R. DiMercurio.
TRACK RECORD: Culpepper was a standout player at Kansas State, where he was a three-time All-Big 12 Conference selection and played for USA Baseball's Collegiate National Team one summer. The Twins drafted him 21st overall in 2024, and he played 26 games after signing, making it to High-A Cedar Rapids. In 2025 he returned to Cedar Rapids and excelled, earning a promotion to Double-A Wichita in mid-June. Culpepper got off to a quick start there but saw his performance tail off at the end of his first full season. He was selected to the Futures Game in July and named the Twins' minor league player of the year after hitting .289/.375/.469 with 20 home runs.
SCOUTING REPORT: Culpepper is an athletic infielder with minimal remaining projection. He has a balanced profile with no standout tool and no glaring weaknesses either. He has solid bat speed and clears his hips freely, allowing him to whip the bat through the zone. He's comfortable hitting velocity and was one of two hitters in the Twins' system with an OPS above .700 against both changeups and breaking balls in 2025. He rarely misses pitches in the zone, but his approach needs refinement. He is prone to chase, especially changeups down and out of the zone. He has average raw power that plays primarily to his pull side. His power plays below that in games, and he needs to elevate the ball more consistently. Culpepper has a plus arm but is not a lock to stick at shortstop due to his lack of range. He projects as fringe-average there but profiles better at second or third base, where he could be average or better.
THE FUTURE: Whether Culpepper starts at Double-A or Triple-A in 2026, he will continue to develop as a shortstop. He has regular potential even if he moves off the position, but his value would be maximized if he can stay up the middle.

Year	Age	Club (League)	Level	AVG	G	AB	R	H	2B	3B	HR	RBI	BB	SO	SB	OBP	SLG
2025	22	Cedar Rapids (MWL)	A+	.293	54	215	38	63	9	2	9	34	26	40	15	.385	.479
2025	22	Wichita (TL)	AA	.285	59	239	39	68	7	1	11	30	24	50	10	.367	.460
		Minor League Totals		.280	139	553	94	155	20	4	23	76	61	105	29	.367	.456

MINNESOTA TWINS

4 CONNOR PRIELIPP, LHP
FB: 60. **SL:** 60. **CH:** 60. **CTL:** 55. **BA Grade:** 55. **Risk:** Average. **Adj:** 45.

Born: January 10, 2001. **B-T:** L-L. **HT:** 6-2. **WT:** 210.
Drafted: Alabama, 2022 (2nd round). **Signed by:** Matt Williams.
TRACK RECORD: Prielipp had an impressive freshman season at Alabama but missed most of the next two years after having Tommy John surgery. He slid to the second round of the 2022 draft and didn't pitch after signing. In his first professional start of 2023, his elbow flared up. He tried rest and rehab, but the issue remained, so he had internal brace surgery in July 2023. He returned a year later and impressed in nine short outings. In 2025, the Twins built his workload up slowly. He stayed healthy and threw 82.2 innings between Double-A Wichita and Triple-A St. Paul. The total was more than the previous five seasons combined. In his final start, he threw a career-high six innings and 84 pitches. After the season he was named the Twins' minor league pitcher of the year.
SCOUTING REPORT: Prielipp is a maxed-out lefthander with an advanced three-pitch mix and deceptive delivery. His arm action is short, and he hides the ball well. Prielipp's fastball sits 94-96 mph and touches 98. He has solid command of the offering, and it shows bat-missing ability up in the zone. He started mixing in a sinker in St. Paul and will look to incorporate it more in 2026. Prielipp's mid-80s slider is his most-used secondary and a potential plus offering. It has the highest spin rate in the system and premium bat-missing ability. If hitters do make contact, they primarily strike weak grounders. His high-80s changeup also shows plus potential. It plays more due to feel and command than shape. He can locate it on the edges of the plate at will and bury it down when looking for a whiff.
THE FUTURE: Durability is the main thing holding Prielipp back. He has the most polished arsenal in the Twins' system but could look to round it out by adding a second breaking ball. He projects as a midrotation starter and should make his major league debut at some point in 2026.

Year	Age	Club (League)	Level	W	L	ERA	G	GS	IP	H	HR	BB	SO	BB%	SO%	WHIP	AVG
2025	24	Wichita (TL)	AA	0	6	3.65	19	19	62	74	5	18	73	6.7	27.0	1.49	.307
2025	24	St. Paul (IL)	AAA	1	3	5.14	5	4	21	20	2	13	25	14.0	26.9	1.57	.253
		Minor League Totals		1	9	4.14	27	26	91	103	7	35	108	8.7	26.9	1.51	.292

5 EDUARDO TAIT, C
HIT: 40. **POW:** 60. **RUN:** 30. **FLD:** 45. **ARM:** 60. **BA Grade:** 60. **Risk:** High. **Adj:** 45.

Born: August 27, 2006. **B-T:** L-R. **HT:** 6-0. **WT:** 239.
Signed: Panama, 2022. **Signed by:** Abdiel Ramos (Phillies).
TRACK RECORD: Tait originally signed with the Phillies out of Panama for $90,000 in January 2023. In his debut, he was named a Dominican Summer League all-star as one of the youngest players in the league. He came stateside in 2024 and hit 11 home runs in 80 games between the Florida Complex League and Low-A Clearwater. He went back to Clearwater to start 2025 and was named to the Futures Game in July. He was promoted to High-A a few days after playing in it. Just over a week later, the Phillies dealt him to the Twins in the Jhoan Duran trade. He was assigned to High-A Cedar Rapids and hit in the middle of the order during their playoff run.
SCOUTING REPORT: Tait's frame is close to maxed out, even though he is just 19. His bat speed and contact skills are impressive but mask a raw approach. He makes poor swing decisions and his chase rate is the highest in the system. He also struggles against good velocity. Improving in those areas is key for his offensive development. He gets more leeway with his hit tool because of his ability to impact the baseball. He produces exit velocities that are impressive for an established major leaguer, let alone a teenager, and his batted-ball angles are good. He elevates the ball to his pull side with ease and has power to the opposite field as well. Defensively, it's uncertain whether Tait can stay at catcher. He lacks athleticism and struggles blocking balls in the dirt, especially when he has to move laterally. His receiving is improving, and his arm is plus, consistently producing pop times around 1.9 seconds on throws to second base.
THE FUTURE: Tait's upside is as a middle-of-the-order bat, but there is risk due to questions with his hit tool and defense. He'll likely start 2026 in Cedar Rapids, where he will again be one of the youngest players in the Midwest League.

Year	Age	Club (League)	Level	AVG	G	AB	R	H	2B	3B	HR	RBI	BB	SO	SB	OBP	SLG
2025	18	Clearwater (FSL)	A	.251	75	291	41	73	19	1	11	51	30	64	0	.322	.436
2025	18	Jersey Shore (SAL)	A+	.296	7	27	2	8	3	0	0	6	0	1	0	.286	.407
2025	18	Cedar Rapids (MWL)	A+	.250	30	120	11	30	10	0	3	14	6	34	0	.286	.408
		Minor League Totals		.285	207	769	111	219	57	5	23	156	61	161	9	.344	.462

MINNESOTA TWINS

6 DASAN HILL, LHP

FB: 55. **CB:** 50. **SW:** 60. **CH:** 60. **CTL:** 45. **BA Grade:** 60. **Risk:** High. **Adj:** 45.

Born: December 25, 2005. **B-T:** R-L. **HT:** 6-5. **WT:** 185.
Drafted: HS—Grapevine, TX, 2024 (2nd round supp). **Signed by:** Trevor Brown.
TRACK RECORD: The Twins signed Hill away from Dallas Baptist with an over-slot bonus of $2 million as the 69th overall pick in 2024. He didn't pitch after signing and showed up to spring training noticeably stronger in 2025. He made the Low-A Fort Myers Opening Day roster as the third-youngest pitcher in the league, but the Twins were cautious, and he didn't top 60 pitches until June. He was promoted in mid-August to High-A Cedar Rapids, where he made three regular season and one playoff start, during which he completed five innings for the first time in his career.
SCOUTING REPORT: Hill has gained around 20 pounds since he was drafted and started to fill out his 6-foot-5 frame, though he will always be on the lanky side. Hill throws from a three-quarters arm slot with a high release height. His 94-96 mph fastball comes in on a steep plane but plays below its velocity. He now tops out at 98 mph, a considerable increase from where he was as an amateur. Hill's fastball command is below-average and he's more comfortable throwing strikes with his secondaries. His best secondary is his 83-85 mph changeup which has substantial separation from his fastball and flashes plus potential. It misses bats at an above-average rate and has the highest zone rate of any of his pitches. His 81-84 mph sweeper flashes similar plus potential. He is comfortable landing it in the zone, and it misses bats at a slightly higher rate than his changeup. He rounds out his arsenal with a high-70s curveball that is primarily a chase pitch but also misses bats at a high rate.
THE FUTURE: Hill is just scratching the surface of his potential, and all his pitches have the chance to improve. His midrotation upside is littered with reliever risk. He will return to Cedar Rapids to start 2026, with the eye toward making it to Double-A in his age-20 season.

Year	Age	Club (League)	Level	W	L	ERA	G	GS	IP	H	HR	BB	SO	BB%	SO%	WHIP	AVG
2025	19	Fort Myers (FSL)	A	0	2	2.77	16	16	52	35	2	33	68	14.9	30.6	1.31	.190
2025	19	Cedar Rapids (MWL)	A+	0	2	5.40	3	3	10	9	0	7	15	15.6	33.3	1.60	.243
		Minor League Totals		0	4	3.19	19	19	62	44	2	40	83	15.0	31.1	1.35	.199

7 CHARLEE SOTO, RHP

FB: 60. **SL:** 50. **CH:** 60. **CTL:** 50. **BA Grade:** 55. **Risk:** High. **Adj:** 40.

Born: August 31, 2005. **B-T:** B-R. **HT:** 6-3. **WT:** 210.
Drafted: HS—Kissimmee, FL, 2023 (1st round supp). **Signed by:** Brett Dowdy.
TRACK RECORD: Soto was just 17 years old when the Twins drafted him 34th overall in 2023. He was assigned in 2024 to Low-A Fort Myers, where he was the youngest pitcher in the league. The Twins were cautious with his workload, so he threw just 74 innings in an up-and-down season. Soto made the jump to High-A Cedar Rapids to start 2025 and was again the youngest pitcher in his league. After three starts he felt minor triceps discomfort and went on the injured list. He tried rest and rehab, but discomfort remained so he had minor elbow surgery in August to remove a bone spur.
SCOUTING REPORT: Soto is close to maxed-out physically, with a sturdy build. He throws both a four-seam fastball and a sinker with distinct shapes. His four-seamer sits 96-98 mph and tops out at 100 with above-average ride and generates whiffs at an above-average rate. Compared to 2024, his average four-seam velocity was up almost 2 mph and had just under three more inches of induced vertical break. His sinker sits a tick lower with heavy armside run. It doesn't miss many bats but is adept at generating weak contact. Soto's best secondary pitch is his potentially plus high-80s changeup. It has just over 17 inches of horizontal break and misses bats at an elite rate. Soto also throws an 85-89 mph gyro slider. It doesn't miss many bats right now, but he can throw it for strikes. Soto's strike-throwing improved across the board in 2025, but the sample is so small that it is hard to read too much into it.
THE FUTURE: Soto is expected to be ready to go in spring training in 2026. He should head back to Cedar Rapids with an eye toward a promotion to Double-A over the summer. He has midrotation upside, but his range of outcomes is wide and he has considerable reliever risk.

Year	Age	Club (League)	Level	W	L	ERA	G	GS	IP	H	HR	BB	SO	BB%	SO%	WHIP	AVG
2025	19	Cedar Rapids (MWL)	A+	0	1	1.38	3	3	13	9	0	4	15	7.5	28.3	1.00	.196
		Minor League Totals		1	8	4.66	24	23	87	87	6	37	102	9.7	26.6	1.43	.260

MINNESOTA TWINS

8 KENDRY ROJAS, LHP
FB: 55. **SL:** 50. **SP:** 50. **CTL:** 55. **BA Grade:** 50. **Risk:** Average. **Adj:** 40.

Born: November 26, 2002. **B-T:** L-L. **HT:** 6-2. **WT:** 190.
Signed: Cuba, 2020. **Signed by:** Erick Ramirez/Luis Natera (Blue Jays).
TRACK RECORD: The Blue Jays signed Rojas for $215,000 out of Cuba in October 2020. He spent four seasons in the low minors and missed substantial time due to injury in 2022 (lat) and 2024 (shoulder). After a strong end to 2024, Rojas missed the first two months of 2025 with an abdominal injury suffered in spring training. He was assigned to Double-A on July 1 after a month-long rehab assignment. He made four starts there before being promoted to Triple-A Buffalo, where he made his debut on July 30. The next day, he was traded to the Twins with Alan Roden for Louis Varland and Ty France. He was assigned to Triple-A St. Paul but struggled as he got acclimated to a new organization and the different Triple-A baseball.
SCOUTING REPORT: Rojas is a medium-framed lefthander with solid pitchability. He's maxed out physically and an average athlete. He throws from a three-quarters arm slot with above-average extension and higher release height. He has a balanced arsenal with all his pitches projecting as at least average. His fastball sits 92-95 mph and maxes out at 98 with ride. He will also cut it on occasion and use it to generate soft contact. His slider is his most-used secondary pitch against lefthanded hitters, but he will throw it to righthanders also. It sits 85-88 mph with short tilt and shows both strike-stealing and bat-missing ability. His splitter is his primary out pitch against righthanded hitters. It sits 86-89 mph, but he struggles to consistently land it in the zone. It shows similar bat-missing potential as his slider.
THE FUTURE: Rojas was added to the 40-man roster and should open the season in St. Paul. He projects as a No. 5 starter with multi-inning relief as a fallback and could contribute in the major leagues in 2026.

Year	Age	Club (League)	Level	W	L	ERA	G	GS	IP	H	HR	BB	SO	BB%	SO%	WHIP	AVG
2025	22	FCL Blue Jays	Rk	0	0	3.60	2	2	5	5	0	2	8	9.5	38.1	1.40	.263
2025	22	Dunedin (FSL)	A	1	0	0.00	4	3	13	5	0	3	18	6.5	39.1	0.62	.122
2025	22	New Hampshire (EL)	AA	0	2	3.86	4	4	19	18	2	2	30	2.7	40.0	1.07	.247
2025	22	Buffalo (IL)	AAA	0	1	10.80	1	1	5	10	2	2	6	8.0	24.0	2.40	.435
2025	22	St. Paul (IL)	AAA	1	2	6.59	8	8	27	37	3	23	28	15.9	19.3	2.20	.314
		Minor League Totals		11	16	3.63	73	60	280	252	21	103	326	8.7	27.6	1.27	.237

9 MAREK HOUSTON, SS
HIT: 50. **POW:** 40. **RUN:** 55. **FLD:** 70. **ARM:** 60. **BA Grade:** 50. **Risk:** Average. **Adj:** 40.

Born: April 14, 2004. **B-T:** R-R. **HT:** 6-3. **WT:** 205.
Drafted: Wake Forest, 2025 (1st round). **Signed by:** Ty Dawson.
TRACK RECORD: Houston was seen as one of the best defensive shortstops in the 2025 draft after starting at Wake Forest for three years. He improved considerably at the plate each year. His OPS went from .635 in 2023 to 1.055 in 2025, and he nearly doubled his home run total each year. The Twins drafted him 16th overall in 2025 and signed him for a slightly under-slot bonus of $4.5 million. He went straight to Low-A Fort Myers, where he hit .370 in 12 games and was quickly promoted to High-A Cedar Rapids. There, he hit .152 in 12 games, but he was a key contributor in the Kernels' Midwest League division series victory against Beloit by hitting .417 with three runs.
SCOUTING REPORT: Houston added noticeable strength heading into his draft year but retained his athleticism. His swing is short and direct to the ball, and he has above-average bat-to-ball skills. He rarely swung and missed during his pro debut and controls the strike zone well but can be overly passive at times. Even though he is listed at 6-foot-3, 205 pounds, Houston has below-average power and his exit velocities in pro ball were lower than at Wake Forest. Slight improvements with his bat speed and quality of contact would go a long way toward rounding out his offensive profile. Houston is also an above-average runner with solid instincts. Defensively, he's a no-doubt shortstop. He has soft hands and fluid actions and is comfortable ranging in any direction, using his length to cover ground effortlessly. He has a quick release, a plus arm and throws off-balance with ease.
THE FUTURE: Houston will likely start 2026 in Cedar Rapids with the eye toward a quick promotion to Double-A Wichita. His defense gives him a high floor, and his offensive development will determine whether he profiles as a role player or an everyday regular.

Year	Age	Club (League)	Level	AVG	G	AB	R	H	2B	3B	HR	RBI	BB	SO	SB	OBP	SLG
2025	21	Fort Myers (FSL)	A	.370	12	54	10	20	4	0	0	9	5	13	6	.424	.444
2025	21	Cedar Rapids (MWL)	A+	.152	12	46	4	7	1	0	1	2	3	8	1	.220	.239
		Minor League Totals		.270	24	100	14	27	5	0	1	11	8	21	7	.330	.350

MINNESOTA TWINS

10 GABRIEL GONZALEZ, OF

HIT: 55. **POW:** 50. **RUN:** 40. **FLD:** 40. **ARM:** 50. **BA Grade:** 50. **Risk:** Average. **Adj:** 40.

Born: January 4, 2004. **B-T:** R-R. **HT:** 5-10. **WT:** 239.
Signed: Venezuela, 2021. **Signed by:** Luis Martinez (Mariners).
TRACK RECORD: The Mariners signed Gonzalez for $1.3 million out of Venezuela in February 2021. He spent three years in the organization, reaching High-A Everett in 2023. He was traded to the Twins in January 2024 as part of the return for second baseman Jorge Polanco. Gonzalez was limited by a back injury for most of 2024 and hit just .255/.326/.381 with four home runs. He was healthy in 2025 and showed the offensive upside the Twins expected when they acquired him. He hit over .300 at three different levels and finished the season in Triple-A St. Paul, where he hit more home runs in 34 games than he did in all of 2024.
SCOUTING REPORT: Heading into 2025, Gonzalez worked hard to improve his conditioning and add muscle to his stocky frame. His offensive profile is unique because he is extremely aggressive but also has an advanced feel for contact. Gonzalez sees among the fewest pitches in the system and chases too often, but rarely misses pitches in the zone. His walk rate improved in 2025 and his exit velocities against right-handers also improved. This is notable given his past platoon splits. Gonzalez's swing isn't designed for power, and his fairly poor batted-ball angles mean his game power plays below his above-average raw. He crushes lefthanders, and that alone might be enough to carry him to the big leagues even with the volatility in his hit tool. Defensively, Gonzalez doesn't project to add much value. His arm strength is average at best and though his defense is improving, it still projects as below-average.
THE FUTURE: Gonzalez was added to the 40-man roster and shouldn't require much more time in Triple-A in 2026. He profiles as a hit-over-power fringe regular and could carve out a role because of his ability to hit lefthanders. His upside is limited by his lack of defensive value and speed.

Year	Age	Club (League)	Level	AVG	G	AB	R	H	2B	3B	HR	RBI	BB	SO	SB	OBP	SLG
2025	21	Cedar Rapids (MWL)	A+	.319	34	138	22	44	12	1	5	28	13	22	1	.378	.529
2025	21	Wichita (TL)	AA	.344	55	212	39	73	19	2	4	15	26	30	5	.429	.509
2025	21	St. Paul (IL)	AAA	.316	34	133	14	42	7	0	6	23	9	28	2	.358	.504
		Minor League Totals		.311	365	1420	245	441	90	12	48	222	127	247	36	.382	.492

11 RILEY QUICK, RHP

FB: 60. **SL:** 50. **CH:** 55. **CT:** 55. **CTL:** 45. **BA Grade:** 55. **Risk:** High. **Adj:** 40.

Born: April 29, 2004. **B-T:** R-R. **HT:** 6-6. **WT:** 255. **Drafted:** Alabama, 2025 (1st round supp.).
Signed by: Hal Hughes.
TRACK RECORD: It wasn't a certainty Quick would even play baseball in college as he received SEC offers as an offensive lineman in high school and his brother Pierce played college football for Alabama and Georgia Tech. He ultimately decided to focus solely on baseball and spent three years at Alabama, where he only threw 87 innings and missed a year with Tommy John surgery. The Twins drafted him 36th overall in 2025 and signed him for a slot-value bonus of $2.69 million.
SCOUTING REPORT: Quick brings unique size and athleticism to the mound at 6-foot-6, 255 pounds. He throws from a low three-quarters arm slot with a crossfire delivery. His fastball sits 96-98 mph and tops out at 99, but plays below its velocity. He throws both a sinker and four-seamer equally, but their usage will likely be tweaked in pro ball. There are differing opinions over what Quick's best secondary pitch is. He uses his 84-88 mph slider the most but it is inconsistent and his changeup and cutter show more potential. His changeup shows the most bat-missing ability with a combination of deceptive arm speed and late fade and he really took to his low-90s cutter, which he started throwing in 2025. His strike-throwing improved in 2025 and will be a key area for his development going forward.
THE FUTURE: Quick brings a fascinating skill set that the Twins now have the chance to mold. He has midrotation upside, but that projection is fluid given his limited experience as a full-time pitcher. He'll start 2026 at a full-season affiliate, with High-A Cedar Rapids not out of the question given his pitch quality.

Year	Age	Club (League)	Level	W	L	ERA	G	GS	IP	H	HR	BB	SO	BB%	SO%	WHIP	AVG
2025	21	Did not play															

MINNESOTA TWINS

12 QUENTIN YOUNG, 3B/SS
HIT: 40. **POW:** 60. **RUN:** 55. **FLD:** 50. **ARM:** 70. **BA Grade:** 60. **Risk:** Extreme. **Adj:** 40.

Born: March 2, 2007. **B-T:** R-R. **HT:** 6-6. **WT:** 225. **Drafted:** HS—Westlake Village, CA, 2025 (2nd round). **Signed by:** Dylan Tashjian.

TRACK RECORD: Young comes from a family of athletes. His uncles Dmitiri and Delmon both played in the major leagues and his aunt DeAnn played college softball. Quentin has a lengthy amateur track record including time with USA Baseball's 18U National Team in 2024 and finished his SoCal high school career by setting an Oaks Christian School record for home runs. He reclassified from the 2026 class in 2023 and was committed to LSU. The Twins drafted him 54th overall in 2025, and he made his pro debut in September, playing five games for Low-A Fort Myers.

SCOUTING REPORT: Young is a physical specimen, listed at 6-foot-6, 225 pounds, with surprising athleticism for his size. His swing is long, with a pronounced hitch, and there are major questions about his ability to make contact. His swing decisions also need work and he needs to do a better job controlling the strike zone. Hit tool development is everything for him as his power potential is massive. He has easy plus-plus raw power, but its utility in game will depend on his contact ability. Young has above-average speed and his defensive skill set is advanced for his age. His plus-plus arm will play anywhere and he has a good chance to stick at third base where he shows solid instincts and average hands and range.

THE FUTURE: Young's combination of tools give him one of the highest ceilings in the system, but there is substantial risk. His development will be slow and his range of outcomes is wide. He will likely start 2026 in Fort Myers where he will be one of the youngest players in the league.

Year	Age	Club (League)	Level	AVG	G	AB	R	H	2B	3B	HR	RBI	BB	SO	SB	OBP	SLG
2025	18	Fort Myers (FSL)	A	.118	5	17	3	2	0	0	0	3	2	9	0	.227	.118
		Minor League Totals		.118	5	17	3	2	0	0	0	3	2	9	0	.227	.118

13 ANDREW MORRIS, RHP
FB: 50. **CB:** 45. **SW:** 45. **SL:** 55. **CH:** 45. **CT:** 50. **CTL:** 55. **BA Grade:** 45. **Risk:** Mild. **Adj:** 40.

Born: September 1, 2001. **B-T:** R-R. **HT:** 6-0. **WT:** 195. **Drafted:** Texas Tech, 2022 (4th round). **Signed by:** Trevor Brown.

TRACK RECORD: Morris started 2025 with Triple-A St. Paul and looked poised to make his major league debut before a right forearm strain kept him out for seven weeks. That was the second arm injury of his pro career as he missed six weeks in 2023 with biceps tendinitis. He returned in August and his performance was markedly better than prior to his injury. He threw 94.2 innings overall which was the second most of his career. In November, he was added to the 40-man roster.

SCOUTING REPORT: Morris is an undersized righthander with solid pitchability. He lacks a plus pitch, but has a plethora of fringe-average offerings and above-average control. He throws from a high three-quarters arm slot with a high release height. His fastball sits in the mid 90s and touches 99, but it plays below its velocity. He also throws a two-seam that grades out similarly. Morris' best secondary is his above-average mid-to-high-80s slider. It has more depth than tilt and is his most consistent bat-missing offering. He also throws a solid-average low-90s cutter that is consistently around the zone. Morris rounds out his arsenal with a trio of fringe-average secondaries in his sweeper, curveball and changeup. His sweeper is the most intriguing as it adds an east-west element to his primarily north-south arsenal. Continued refinement of it will be a key going forward to stick as a starter.

THE FUTURE: Morris enters 2026 as a major league depth option. He projects as a swingman capable of filling in as a back-end starter, with short relief as fallback where his stuff could play up.

Year	Age	Club (League)	Level	W	L	ERA	G	GS	IP	H	HR	BB	SO	BB%	SO%	WHIP	AVG
2025	23	St. Paul (IL)	AAA	4	6	4.09	21	19	95	98	11	28	89	7.0	22.4	1.33	.272
		Minor League Totals		22	13	3.02	66	60	313	295	21	79	302	6.1	23.2	1.19	.246

14 HENDRY MENDEZ, OF
HIT: 60. **POW:** 45. **RUN:** 40. **FLD:** 30. **ARM:** 40. **BA Grade:** 50. **Risk:** Average. **Adj:** 40.

Born: November 7, 2003. **B-T:** L-L. **HT:** 6-3. **WT:** 175. **Signed:** Dominican Republic, 2021. **Signed by:** Gary Peralta (Brewers).

TRACK RECORD: Mendez originally signed with the Brewers in 2021 and was traded to the Phillies after the 2023 season. He got off to a strong start in 2025 as a 21-year-old in Double-A, before the Twins acquired him at the deadline in the Harrison Bader trade. He was assigned to Double-A Wichita where he was even better, hitting .324/.461/.450. Overall he hit 11 home runs, one shy of his career total.

SCOUTING REPORT: Mendez has a short, direct swing and elite contact ability. His 85% contact rate was among the highest in the system and his approach is advanced. He has a potential plus hit tool and consistently makes hard contact. He has above-average raw power, but it doesn't translate in game due to his flat bat path. His batted-ball angles are poor and he struggles to elevate the ball, especially to his pull side. He did show some progress in that area in 2025 as his 54% groundball rate was the lowest of his career. Mendez needs to hit because his speed is below-average and he lacks defensive value. His arm is also below-average, his range and routes are poor, even for a left fielder. He started working at first base late in the season but didn't appear in any games there.

THE FUTURE: Mendez was added to the 40-man, but could find himself back in Wichita to start 2026. His value is solely tied up in his bat and if he continues to hit and is able to tap into his raw power, he has fringe-regular upside. That lane is narrow, however, due to his lack of secondary skills.

Year	Age	Club (League)	Level	AVG	G	AB	R	H	2B	3B	HR	RBI	BB	SO	SB	OBP	SLG
2025	21	Reading (EL)	AA	.290	85	297	44	86	13	3	8	46	40	44	6	.374	.434
2025	21	Wichita (TL)	AA	.324	33	111	24	36	3	1	3	16	27	21	4	.461	.450
		Minor League Totals		.276	419	1467	214	405	66	13	23	191	221	239	23	.374	.386

15 BRANDON WINOKUR, 3B/SS/OF

HIT: 30. **POW:** 60. **RUN:** 60. **FLD:** 50. **ARM:** 70. **BA Grade:** 55. **Risk:** Extreme. **Adj:** 35.

Born: December 16, 2004. **B-T:** R-R. **HT:** 6-6. **WT:** 210. **Drafted:** HS—Huntington Beach, CA, 2023 (3rd round).
Signed by: John Leavitt.
TRACK RECORD: Winokur got off to a slow start with High-A Cedar Rapids in 2025 as a 20-year-old from Southern California experiencing spring in the Midwest for the first time. As the weather warmed, so did Winokur. His OPS increased each month through July, and even though he struggled in August, he still set new career highs with 17 home runs and 26 steals.
SCOUTING REPORT: Winokur remains one of the best athletes in the system and though his triple slash regressed, his strikeout rate dropped and his underlying contact metrics improved slightly. They still remain well below-average, so there's still a lot of development needed with his hit tool. When Winokur does make contact he can really impact the baseball. His raw power is plus-to-better and he punishes mistakes. His plus-plus arm profiles anywhere and he will continue to develop as a shortstop, while also rotating in at third base and in the outfield. If he stays on the dirt it will likely be at third base, but scouts are intrigued by what he would look like in right field where he could be an above-average defender.
THE FUTURE: Even though Winokur should return to Cedar Rapids in 2026, that's not a concern. His development will be a slow burn and is unlikely to be linear. His tools are loud, but his biggest weakness is the one that is most likely to determine his future. There remains high-variance in his profile, but if he can make enough contact to tap into his power and allow his secondary tools to shine, he has all-star potential.

Year	Age	Club (League)	Level	AVG	G	AB	R	H	2B	3B	HR	RBI	BB	SO	SB	OBP	SLG
2025	20	Cedar Rapids (MWL)	A+	.226	122	474	65	107	20	3	17	68	44	131	26	.304	.388
		Minor League Totals		.233	139	540	79	126	25	3	21	85	48	154	26	.308	.407

16 ADRIAN BOHORQUEZ, RHP

FB: 60. **CB:** 50. **SL:** 55. **CH:** 40. **CTL:** 40. **BA Grade:** 50. **Risk:** High. **Adj:** 35.

Born: March 3, 2005. **B-T:** R-R. **HT:** 6-1. **WT:** 210. **Signed:** Venezuela, 2023. **Signed by:** Oswaldo Troconis.
TRACK RECORD: Bohorquez got off to a slow start with Low-A Fort Myers in 2025 but worked hard to improve his conditioning over the course of the season. He was at his best after a late-season promotion to High-A Cedar Rapids, where he reached 70 pitches in five of six appearances. In Fort Myers, he only reached that total twice in 14 appearances. His 6.1% walk rate in Cedar Rapids was a career best.
SCOUTING REPORT: Bohorquez is a late bloomer who has gotten better each year. His strike-throwing is trending upward and his velocity has also improved. He now sits 94-96 and tops out at 98 with good shape and a high spin rate. Bohorquez's feel for spin is advanced and he has a pair of breaking balls that have at least average potential. His high-80s hard slider improved as the season went on and is now seen as the slightly better pitch. It has cut-slider shape and he has better control of it than his 78-81 mph curveball. His curveball is also an intriguing pitch with vertical depth and one of the highest spin rates in the system at over 2,900 rpm. He rounds out his arsenal with a hard changeup that is a work in progress.
THE FUTURE: Bohorquez is trending more toward a starter than ever before, but still has reliever risk. He likely would move quicker in relief, but given the quality of his stuff, he should continue to develop as a starter back in Cedar Rapids in 2026.

Year	Age	Club (League)	Level	W	L	ERA	G	GS	IP	H	HR	BB	SO	BB%	SO%	WHIP	AVG
2025	20	Fort Myers (FSL)	A	2	3	4.66	14	10	48	34	6	25	57	11.7	26.6	1.22	.192
2025	20	Cedar Rapids (MWL)	A+	1	1	3.52	5	4	23	19	1	6	28	6.1	28.6	1.09	.224
		Minor League Totals		5	11	4.30	37	27	132	97	9	66	156	11.5	27.2	1.23	.200

MINNESOTA TWINS

17 SANTIAGO CASTELLANOS, RHP
FB: 55. **SW:** 60. **CH:** 60. **CT:** 40. **CTL:** 45. **BA Grade:** 55. **Risk:** Extreme. **Adj:** 35.

Born: July 17, 2008. **B-T:** R-R. **HT:** 5-10. **WT:** 150. **Signed:** Venezuela, 2025. **Signed by:** Edgar Guerra.
TRACK RECORD: Castellanos signed with the Twins in January 2025 for $247,500. He was one of the youngest pitchers in the class and didn't turn 17 until July, over a month into his pro career. He quickly emerged as one of the top pitchers in the Dominican Summer League, striking out 36 while only walking nine in 29 innings. He ranked seventh in the Top 35 DSL Prospects list after the 2025 season.
SCOUTING REPORT: The main knock on Castellanos is his size, as he is only 5-foot-10 with a medium frame and minimal projection. He is twitchy and athletic, with a very quick arm. The ball comes easy out of his hand and his fastball sits 92-94 mph and touches 96. It has rise and run and he throws it for strikes. Castellanos has two secondaries that will flash plus in his sweeper and changeup. His sweeper averaged over 15 inches of horizontal break and missed bats at an elite rate in the DSL. His changeup didn't miss as many bats, but some evaluators think it has more long-term potential. His feel for pitching is also so advanced that the Twins had him experiment with both a slider and cutter, but the former didn't yield results.
THE FUTURE: Castellanos will come stateside in 2026. He doesn't have the typical physical projection of a 17-year-old, but he is advanced for his age and has feel for secondaries that should allow him to acclimate quickly to more advanced competition. Given his age and size, the error bars are high, but he has the early makings of a potential midrotation starter.

Year	Age	Club (League)	Level	W	L	ERA	G	GS	IP	H	HR	BB	SO	BB%	SO%	WHIP	AVG
2025	16	DSL Twins	Rk	1	2	2.79	9	8	29	23	0	9	36	7.4	29.8	1.10	.215
		Minor League Totals		1	2	2.79	9	8	29	23	0	9	36	7.4	29.8	1.10	.215

18 JAMES ELLWANGER, RHP
FB: 60. **CB:** 55. **SL:** 50. **CH:** 30. **CT:** 45. **CTL:** 40. **BA Grade:** 55. **Risk:** Extreme. **Adj:** 35.

Born: May 15, 2004. **B-T:** R-R. **HT:** 6-4. **WT:** 205. **Drafted:** Dallas Baptist, 2025 (3rd round). **Signed by:** Trevor Brown.
TRACK RECORD: The Twins selected Ellwanger in the third round and signed him for an over-slot bonus of $1 million after his sophomore year at Dallas Baptist. He was a three-sport athlete in high school, but ended up going to college after signability concerns pushed him to the 19th round of the 2023 draft. Ellwanger was limited to 17.2 innings in 2024 due to a flexor strain, but impressed in the Cape Cod League that summer, before a breakout 2025 season where he struck out 95 in 63.1 innings.
SCOUTING REPORT: Ellwanger is an athletic 6-foot-4 righthander with projection remaining. He throws from a high three-quarters slot with a high release height. His arm is quick and his fastball sits 95-98 mph and touches 100. He throws it on a downhill plane, but it has average shape and his command and control are inconsistent. Ellwanger's best secondary is his 81-85 mph curveball which flashes above-average to plus potential. It's a true 12-6 breaker with a high spin rate and vertical depth. He also throws a high-80s slider and low-90s cutter which function primarily as pitches to get ahead rather than put hitters away. He uses his changeup sparingly and that could be deemphasized further in pro ball.
THE FUTURE: Ellwanger will make his pro debut in 2026, likely with Low-A Fort Myers. He has reliever risk due to his limited track record of throwing strikes, but with his combination of size, arm speed and stuff, it makes sense to develop him as a starter initially. If things click he has considerable upside in that role.

Year	Age	Club (League)	Level	W	L	ERA	G	GS	IP	H	HR	BB	SO	BB%	SO%	WHIP	AVG
2025	21	Did not play															

19 MATT BARR, RHP
FB: 55. **CB:** 55. **SL:** 60. **CTL:** 40. **BA Grade:** 55. **Risk:** Extreme. **Adj:** 35.

Born: January 16, 2006. **B-T:** R-R. **HT:** 6-6. **WT:** 195. **Drafted:** SUNY Niagara (NY) JC, 2025 (5th round). **Signed by:** Nick Venuto.
TRACK RECORD: Barr was one of the top junior college prospects in the 2025 draft after a dominant freshmen season at SUNY Niagara, where he was named Division III juco pitcher of the year. He was committed to Tennessee and impressed at the MLB Draft Combine where he had the second-highest spin rate on his curveball and slider of all pitchers who threw bullpens. The Twins selected him in the fifth round and signed him for a well over-slot bonus of $762,500.
SCOUTING REPORT: Barr has a ways to go to fill out his 6-foot-6, 195 pound frame. His fastball sits 92-94 mph and tops out at 97 mph. He projects to add velocity as he matures and needs to continue to refine his control which is inconsistent right now. Barr's outlier ability to spin the ball is a potential carrying trait. He throws both a mid-to-high-80s slider and low-80s curveball that have spin rates around

3,000 rpm. They are high quality breaking balls with a lot of movement and his feel for them is advanced. Both have premium bat-missing potential, but his slider is more advanced right now and projects as a potential plus offering, while his curveball projects as above-average. Barr didn't use a changeup as an amateur, but could look to add one in pro ball.
THE FUTURE: Barr should make his pro debut in 2026 with Low-A Fort Myers. His development will likely be slow and he is not a lock to stick as a starter. His combination of physical projection and outlier feel for spin make him an intriguing pitching prospect that could move quickly up this list with a strong debut.

Year	Age	Club (League)	Level	W	L	ERA	G	GS	IP	H	HR	BB	SO	BB%	SO%	WHIP	AVG
2025	19	Did not play															

20 JOSE OLIVARES, RHP
FB: 60. **CB:** 45. **SL:** 55. **CH:** 55. **CTL:** 30. **BA Grade:** 50. **Risk:** High. **Adj:** 35.

Born: January 18, 2003. **B-T:** R-R. **HT:** 6-1. **WT:** 199. **Signed:** Venezuela, 2021. **Signed by:** Luis Lajara.
TRACK RECORD: Olivares signed for $100,000 out of Venezuela in January 2021. He spent two years in Low-A, before moving up to High-A Cedar Rapids in 2025. His performance there was inconsistent, but he saved the best for last, throwing six innings and allowing only one hit, one unearned run and two walks, while striking out 10, in his final regular season start.
SCOUTING REPORT: Olivares is an average-framed righthander with a quick arm. His fastball sits in the mid 90s and tops out at 99 with 20 inches of induced vertical break. His control is inconsistent and improving this area will be the key for him to have a chance to start. Olivares controls his secondaries better than his fastball. He uses his high-80s slider with short vertical break frequently and it has the highest whiff rate of all his pitches. It has above-average potential as does his changeup which he throws in the same velocity band. His changeup plays well off the vertical shape of his fastball as it's thrown with similar arm speed and has armside fade. He also will show a fringe-average curveball that he primarily uses to get ahead.
THE FUTURE: Olivares will likely return to Cedar Rapids to start 2026, though a move to Double-A isn't out of the question. He has No. 4 starter upside, but his control is so volatile that he is likely best suited for a bullpen role. His range of outcomes there vary from an up-and-down reliever to a potential high-leverage arm.

Year	Age	Club (League)	Level	W	L	ERA	G	GS	IP	H	HR	BB	SO	BB%	SO%	WHIP	AVG
2025	22	Cedar Rapids (MWL)	A+	6	6	4.38	22	21	90	66	4	57	107	14.7	27.6	1.36	.202
		Minor League Totals		16	17	4.88	78	62	275	241	25	149	296	12.4	24.6	1.42	.232

21 MARCO RAYA, RHP
FB: 50. **CB:** 60. **SW:** 55. **CH:** 45. **CT:** 55. **CTL:** 40. **BA Grade:** 45. **Risk:** Average. **Adj:** 35.

Born: August 7, 2002. **B-T:** R-R. **HT:** 6-1. **WT:** 170. **Drafted:** HS—Laredo, TX, 2020 (4th round). **Signed by:** Trevor Brown.
TRACK RECORD: Despite being added to the 40-man roster after the 2024 season and staying healthy all of 2025, Raya spent the entire season in Triple-A St. Paul. He worked as a starter until mid-August, but struggled and transitioned to the bullpen. He made nine appearances in relief with mixed results.
SCOUTING REPORT: Raya is undersized but shows premium stuff when he's on. In 2025, he relied more on his cutter, sweeper and curveball and deemphasized his four-seamer, sinker and changeup. His fastball sits 94-96 mph, but he struggles to control it and it plays below its velocity. As a result, he will pitch off his 89-92 mph cutter which plays above-average due to his ability to locate it. When looking for whiffs Raya goes to his sweeper and curveball. His curveball is a plus offering with depth and premium bat-missing ability. He can land it in the zone or bury it when looking for whiffs, primarily against lefties. He uses his sweeper similarly, just mostly against righties.
THE FUTURE: Raya enters 2026 as a reliever for the first time with a chance to make the major league team out of camp. He will likely pare down his arsenal in relief, which could allow the pitches he focuses on to play up. He has leverage upside, but there's a risk that his lack of fastball quality and inconsistent strike-throwing will limit him to more of an up-and-down depth profile.

Year	Age	Club (League)	Level	W	L	ERA	G	GS	IP	H	HR	BB	SO	BB%	SO%	WHIP	AVG
2025	22	St. Paul (IL)	AAA	2	8	6.02	30	20	99	103	16	57	102	12.6	22.6	1.62	.269
		Minor League Totals		5	14	4.51	72	60	231	200	30	102	247	10.3	24.9	1.31	.231

22 RYAN GALLAGHER, RHP

FB: 50. **CB:** 40. **SL:** 55. **CH:** 55. **CTL:** 50. **BA Grade:** 45. **Risk:** Average. **Adj:** 35.

Born: January 19, 2003. **B-T:** L-R. **HT:** 6-3. **WT:** 195. **Drafted:** UC Santa Barbara, 2024 (6th round). **Signed by:** Jim Woodward (Cubs).

TRACK RECORD: The Cubs selected Gallagher in the sixth round of the 2024 draft out of UC Santa Barbara. He earned Big West Conference freshman of the year honors in 2022, but missed his sophomore season with Tommy John surgery. He returned as a junior and earned All-American honors. He didn't pitch after signing and made his pro debut in 2025 in High-A. He was promoted to Double-A in mid-July and after two impressive starts was traded to the Twins as part of the Willi Castro trade. He had some trouble with home runs after being assigned to Double-A Wichita, allowing seven in 37.2 innings.
SCOUTING REPORT: Gallagher is a throwback north-south righthander who throws from a vertical slot. His pitches grade well in models due to their unique shapes. His fastball sits in the low 90s, but plays above that due to more than 20 inches of induced vertical break. He has good command of it and it jumps on hitters. Gallagher's 82-85 mph slider has more depth than tilt and the highest whiff rate of all his pitches. It grades as above-average, as does his 76-79 mph changeup, which has elite separation and a combination of drop and fade. Gallagher will also mix in a strike-stealing curveball early in counts.
THE FUTURE: Gallagher will likely head back to Wichita in 2026. He projects as a multi-inning reliever, but if his fastball velocity takes a step forward, he could develop into a back-end starter.

Year	Age	Club (League)	Level	W	L	ERA	G	GS	IP	H	HR	BB	SO	BB%	SO%	WHIP	AVG
2025	22	South Bend (MWL)	A+	4	6	3.72	14	14	73	65	9	16	85	5.4	28.6	1.11	.232
2025	22	Knoxville (SL)	AA	0	0	1.59	2	2	11	5	1	4	11	9.3	25.6	0.79	.132
2025	22	Wichita (TL)	AA	4	1	5.50	8	8	38	47	7	10	37	5.9	21.9	1.51	.301
		Minor League Totals		8	7	4.07	24	24	122	117	17	30	133	5.9	26.1	1.21	.247

23 JOHN KLEIN, RHP

FB: 55. **CB:** 50. **SP:** 45. **CT:** 45. **CTL:** 50. **BA Grade:** 40. **Risk:** Mild. **Adj:** 35.

Born: April 22, 2002. **B-T:** R-R. **HT:** 6-5. **WT:** 225. **Signed:** Iowa Central JC, 2022 (UDFA). **Signed by:** Joe Bisenius.

TRACK RECORD: Klein is a Minnesota native who has progressed steadily since signing as an undrafted free agent after the 2022 draft. He had a nondescript first two years, but gained 20 pounds of muscle heading into the 2025 season. He started in Double-A Wichita and impressed, earning a late-season promotion to Triple-A St. Paul. After the season, he was added to the 40-man to protect him from the Rule 5 draft.
SCOUTING REPORT: Klein is a tall righthander with a pitchability-over-stuff profile. His fastball is his best pitch and sits 93-95 mph and tops out at 97. That's almost two ticks higher than 2024, and there's a chance it could continue to increase. Klein relies on his fastball to protect his trio of secondaries. His average 78-82 mph curveball has solid depth and misses the most bats. He can land his fringe-average 85-87 mph splitter for strikes and get chase on it, but it doesn't miss many bats. Klein also has a fringe-average cutter that generates weak contact more than whiffs.
THE FUTURE: Klein is a high-probability major leaguer, but his upside is limited by the lack of an above-average secondary pitch. He has a stable floor of an up-and-down depth arm. If his stuff continues to improve, he could develop into a multi-inning reliever with a small chance to start. He will start in St. Paul and look to make his major league debut in 2026.

Year	Age	Club (League)	Level	W	L	ERA	G	GS	IP	H	HR	BB	SO	BB%	SO%	WHIP	AVG
2025	23	Wichita (TL)	AA	7	5	3.12	24	11	81	70	6	24	95	6.9	27.4	1.17	.225
2025	23	St. Paul (IL)	AAA	0	5	6.66	7	4	26	26	1	13	33	11.1	28.2	1.52	.260
		Minor League Totals		17	17	4.21	68	48	267	252	20	99	281	8.5	24.0	1.31	.244

24 KHADIM DIAW, C

HIT: 50. **POW:** 40. **RUN:** 45. **FLD:** 45. **ARM:** 50. **BA Grade:** 45. **Risk:** Average. **Adj:** 35.

Born: August 23, 2003. **B-T:** R-R. **HT:** 6-1. **WT:** 215. **Drafted:** Loyola Marymount, 2024 (3rd round). **Signed by:** Brian Tripp.

TRACK RECORD: Diaw became the first player of Senegalese descent to be drafted when the Twins took him in the third round in 2024. He went to High-A Cedar Rapids to start 2025 but only played 42 games due to a pair of injuries—a fractured wrist on a hit by pitch and a pulled hamstring.
SCOUTING REPORT: Diaw is an athletic righthanded hitter with a medium frame. He has solid bat speed and above-average contact skills and is adept at working counts. His swing is on the long side and more designed for line drives than flyballs. Diaw is willing to use all fields but needs to elevate the ball more to his pull side. His hard-hit rate and exit velocities are below-average and his raw power is fringe-average at

best. Finding more impact at the plate will be key for him going forward. Diaw is agile for a catcher and already improving as a receiver and game-caller. His arm plays as average. He is still on the raw side given his limited experience, but he works hard and has a chance to stay behind the plate. He has outfield as a fallback option, where he also continues to get reps.
THE FUTURE: Diaw will likely head back to Cedar Rapids to start 2026. He's still developing behind the plate, so his progress could be slow, but his upside will be maximized if he can stick there.

Year	Age	Club (League)	Level	AVG	G	AB	R	H	2B	3B	HR	RBI	BB	SO	SB	OBP	SLG
2025	21	Fort Myers (FSL)	A	.333	3	9	1	3	1	0	1	4	1	3	0	.500	.778
2025	21	Cedar Rapids (MWL)	A+	.294	39	119	24	35	4	1	3	20	19	27	4	.446	.420
		Minor League Totals		.286	66	213	40	61	8	1	5	30	31	44	8	.422	.404

25 HARITZON CASTILLO, SS/2B
HIT: 50. **POW:** 40. **RUN:** 50. **FLD:** 50. **ARM:** 50. **BA Grade:** 50. **Risk:** Extreme. **Adj:** 30.

Born: March 23, 2008. **B-T:** B-R. **HT:** 5-10. **WT:** 175. **Signed:** Venezuela, 2025. **Signed by:** Marlon Nava.
TRACK RECORD: The Twins signed Castillo in January 2025 for $947,500, which was the third-highest bonus in their international class. He started the Dominican Summer League season strong, hitting .333/.453/.490 in 128 plate appearances, but only hit .139/.205/.250 in his final 39 plate appearances. He was the Twins' lone representative in the DSL all-star game, where he walked and scored the tying run.
SCOUTING REPORT: The switch-hitting Castillo isn't the most projectable player, but he's instinctual and works hard. His swing is fluid and he has advanced feel for contact. His 95% zone-contact rate in 2025 was the highest in the system. Castillo lacks strength and his angles are poor, which limits his power. He doesn't barrel the ball consistently or pull it in the air and produces below-average exit velocities. He will show sneaky power but doesn't project for more than fringe-average raw. Castillo is an average runner and has solid baserunning instincts. Defensively, he is capable of playing all infield spots except for first base, but profiles best at second base where he projects as average. He is confident and instinctual in the field, but doesn't have the range for shortstop and his arm plays as average.
THE FUTURE: Castillo isn't the toolsiest player, but brings a well-rounded skill set. He'll come stateside in 2026 where he'll look to continue to develop his approach and get stronger so he can impact the baseball more.

Year	Age	Club (League)	Level	AVG	G	AB	R	H	2B	3B	HR	RBI	BB	SO	SB	OBP	SLG
2025	17	DSL Twins	Rk	.283	39	138	32	39	8	3	2	31	24	22	12	.395	.428
		Minor League Totals		.283	39	138	32	39	8	3	2	31	24	22	12	.395	.428

26 GEREMY VILLORIA, RHP
FB: 50. **SL:** 55. **CH:** 50. **CTL:** 45. **BA Grade:** 50. **Risk:** Extreme. **Adj:** 30.

Born: August 14, 2008. **B-T:** R-R. **HT:** 6-3. **WT:** 180. **Signed:** Venezuela, 2025. **Signed by:** Jonatan Hernandez (Phillies).
TRACK RECORD: Villoria signed with the Phillies for $425,000 in January 2025. He was one of the youngest pitchers in the Dominican Summer League, only turning 17 just before his final start. The Twins acquired him at the trade deadline along with Hendry Mendez for Harrison Bader.
SCOUTING REPORT: Villoria has a medium frame at 6-foot-3, 180 pounds with some remaining projection. He throws from a three-quarters arm slot and is a short strider for his height. His body is in sync in his delivery and he repeats it well. His fastball sits in the low 90s and tops out at 94 mph with rise and run. He's consistently around the zone, but it doesn't miss many bats. He's also toyed with a two-seam fastball to deepen his arsenal. Villoria's best pitch is his high-70s slider which flashes above-average potential. It has a plus spin rate and shows late bite. He needs to land it more consistently, but it already misses bats at a high rate. His changeup has good shape and misses bats at a similarly high rate, but it lacks separation and he rarely throws it competitively. He gets whiffs on it off chase which isn't certain to translate against better competition.
THE FUTURE: Villoria has the early makings of a potential back-end starter, but he has a long way to go developmentally. He'll come stateside in 2026 where he'll look to improve his velocity and continue to refine his secondaries.

Year	Age	Club (League)	Level	W	L	ERA	G	GS	IP	H	HR	BB	SO	BB%	SO%	WHIP	AVG
2025	16	DSL Phillies Red	Rk	0	1	4.50	5	5	14	11	0	4	19	7.0	33.3	1.07	.212
2025	16	DSL Twins	Rk	0	0	2.25	3	3	8	9	0	3	5	8.1	13.5	1.50	.273
		Minor League Totals		0	1	3.68	8	8	22	20	0	7	24	7.4	25.5	1.23	.235

27 TEILON SERRANO, OF

HIT: 40. **POW:** 60. **RUN:** 60. **FLD:** 45. **ARM:** 50. **BA Grade:** 50. **Risk:** Extreme. **Adj:** 30.

Born: May 22, 2008. **B-T:** L-R. **HT:** 5-11. **WT:** 200. **Signed:** Dominican Republic, 2025. **Signed by:** Roman Barinas.
TRACK RECORD: The Twins signed Serrano for $847,500 in January 2025 after his expected deal with the Dodgers fell through when they won the Roki Sasaki sweepstakes. He made his debut in the Dominican Summer League and hit .258/.386/.426 with five home runs and 21 steals, but saw his performance decline in the latter part of the season while playing through an injury.
SCOUTING REPORT: Serrano is strong, athletic and already close to maxed-out physically. His contact rate is below-average but he will take a walk. He is comfortable hitting fastballs, but struggles to identify secondary pitches. What makes Serrano so intriguing is his ability to impact the baseball. His 90th percentile exit velocity of 103.8 mph ranks just outside the top 10 of all prospects 18 or younger in 2025. His batted-ball angles are good and he already can elevate to the pull side. Serrano is an aggressive baserunner with plus speed. He plays all three outfield positions right now, but likely profiles best in left field long-term due to his only average arm. If he can stick in center his value would rise.
THE FUTURE: Serrano will bring his intriguing combination of power and speed stateside in 2026. He has the early makings of a potential regular, but he's got significant development remaining. How quickly he moves and his ultimate value will be determined by how his hit tool progresses.

Year	Age	Club (League)	Level	AVG	G	AB	R	H	2B	3B	HR	RBI	BB	SO	SB	OBP	SLG
2025	17	DSL Twins	Rk	.258	41	155	47	40	7	2	5	21	28	48	21	.386	.426
		Minor League Totals		.258	41	155	47	40	7	2	5	21	28	48	21	.386	.426

28 KYLE DeBARGE, 2B/SS/OF

HIT: 40. **POW:** 40. **RUN:** 65. **FLD:** 55. **ARM:** 45. **BA Grade:** 40. **Risk:** Average. **Adj:** 30.

Born: July 15, 2003. **B-T:** R-R. **HT:** 5-9. **WT:** 175. **Drafted:** Louisiana-Lafayette, 2024 (1st round supp.).
Signed by: Kyle Van Hook.
TRACK RECORD: After being drafted 33rd overall in 2024, DeBarge spent his first full season in 2025 with High-A Cedar Rapids. With Kaelen Culpepper also on the roster, he played mostly second base for the first time in his career. After the season, he was named a Rawlings Minor League Gold Glove winner for his performance there. He also wreaked havoc on the bases with his 66 stolen bases, leading the Twins organization by 28 and ranking seventh overall in the minors.
SCOUTING REPORT: DeBarge is an undersized righthanded hitter with minimal projection. He's a dead-pull hitter who makes a fair amount of contact but is overly passive at the plate. He sees a lot of pitches, sometimes to his detriment, as he will take hittable pitches early in counts. He's more comfortable hitting fastballs than secondaries and his swing can get long, leading to a lot of pop-ups. DeBarge's power is below-average and unlikely to be a major part of his game. He is an excellent baserunner with plus-to-better speed. DeBarge acclimated well to second base in 2025 and projects as a plus defender there. He also plays shortstop and center field, but at those spots he projects as more fringe-average. His fringe-average arm profiles best at second.
THE FUTURE: DeBarge should make the jump to Double-A Wichita in 2026. His upside is limited, but his combination of speed and defensive versatility are intriguing for a potential utility role.

Year	Age	Club (League)	Level	AVG	G	AB	R	H	2B	3B	HR	RBI	BB	SO	SB	OBP	SLG
2025	21	Cedar Rapids (MWL)	A+	.237	121	459	77	109	23	5	8	65	70	121	66	.347	.362
		Minor League Totals		.237	147	561	91	133	25	8	9	86	82	149	81	.342	.358

29 ENRIQUE JIMENEZ, C/1B

HIT: 40. **POW:** 50. **RUN:** 30. **FLD:** 40. **ARM:** 50. **BA Grade:** 45. **Risk:** High. **Adj:** 30.

Born: November 3, 2005. **B-T:** B-R. **HT:** 5-9. **WT:** 223. **Signed:** Venezuela, 2023.
Signed by: Alejandro Rodriguez/Jesus Mendoza/Raul Leiva (Tigers).
TRACK RECORD: Jimenez originally signed with the Tigers for $1.25 million in 2023. He repeated the Florida Complex League to start 2025 before the Twins acquired him at the deadline for Chris Paddack and Randy Dobnak and assigned him to Low-A Fort Myers. He impressed there, equaling his FCL home run total in half the number of games.
SCOUTING REPORT: The switch-hitting Jimenez has a short, stocky frame with no projection. He has a patient approach for his age and solid contact skills and batted-ball angles. His lefthanded swing is more polished and he has more thump from that side. Velocity gives him trouble, but he hits the ball hard consistently and most of his contact is line drives or fly balls. His power projects as average, but is trending in the right direction. His 90th percentile exit velocity increased after the Twins acquired him and he

showed more over-the-fence power. Defensively, Jimenez isn't a lock to stay at catcher but will see his value increase substantially if he can. His blocking and receiving needs work, but he works hard and wants to get better. He has a quick release and his arm plays average.
THE FUTURE: Jimenez will return to Fort Myers in 2026 with an eye toward a midseason promotion to High-A. His bat is trending in the right direction, but his upside will be determined by whether or not he can stick behind the plate.

Year	Age	Club (League)	Level	AVG	G	AB	R	H	2B	3B	HR	RBI	BB	SO	SB	OBP	SLG
2025	19	FCL Tigers	Rk	.250	48	168	27	42	10	2	6	32	23	42	4	.339	.440
2025	19	Fort Myers (FSL)	A	.269	23	78	15	21	2	1	6	18	23	24	1	.431	.551
		Minor League Totals		.257	160	536	88	138	32	7	16	86	98	140	13	.374	.433

30 KALA'I ROSARIO, OF

HIT: 40. **POW:** 55. **RUN:** 45. **FLD:** 45. **ARM:** 50. **BA Grade:** 40. **Risk:** Average. **Adj:** 30.

Born: July 2, 2002. **B-T:** R-R. **HT:** 6-0. **WT:** 205. **Drafted:** HS—Hilo, HI, 2020 (5th round). **Signed by:** John Lewis.
TRACK RECORD: Rosario repeated Double-A Wichita in 2025 and had the best statistical season of his career. He stayed healthy all year and set career highs in most offensive categories. He made the biggest jump on the bases where his 32 steals doubled his total from the previous four seasons combined. Even with his improved performance, Rosario was left unprotected in the Rule 5 draft for the second time.
SCOUTING REPORT: Rosario is maxed-out physically with a strong, sturdy frame. He has a power-over-hit profile and a patient approach, though he does chase at a slightly elevated rate. His overall contact skills are below-average, but they play much better against lefthanders than righthanders. His strikeout rate was 7% lower against lefthanders in 2025 and he has had platoon splits throughout his career. When Rosario connects, he can really impact the ball. He's got plus raw power and his hard-hit rate and exit velocities were among the best in the system. Though Rosario has a fringe-average speed at best, he is an aggressive baserunner with solid instincts. Defensively, he is limited to the corner outfield, where his average arm profiles better in left than right.
THE FUTURE: Rosario will enter 2026 on the bubble of Double-A and Triple-A due to the Twins' high-minors outfield depth. If he can make enough contact, he still could carve out a role as reserve outfielder due to his ability to hit lefthanders, but that's a narrow lane to travel.

Year	Age	Club (League)	Level	AVG	G	AB	R	H	2B	3B	HR	RBI	BB	SO	SB	OBP	SLG
2025	22	Wichita (TL)	AA	.256	130	497	92	127	30	5	25	83	73	159	32	.358	.487
		Minor League Totals		.251	477	1772	286	444	107	16	73	300	236	609	48	.346	.453

Francisco Alvarez

New York Mets

BY MATT EDDY

The Mets had the best record in MLB on June 12 at 45-24.

It was all downhill from there.

New York went 38-54 after that point, with three separate losing streaks of at least seven games apiece. After ceding the National League East division lead to the Phillies in late June, the Mets stayed in the wild card hunt until the final day of the season, a 4-0 loss to the Marlins.

An 83-79 record was obviously not how president of baseball operations David Stearns drew things up when the Mets opened the year with an MLB-high $323 million payroll.

Signing Juan Soto to a record $765 million deal worked as planned. The 26-year-old set career highs with 43 home runs and 38 stolen bases and finished third in NL MVP voting. Shortstop Francisco Lindor and first baseman Pete Alonso rounded out a lineup core that propelled the Mets to fifth in baseball with 224 homers and a 112 wRC+.

Run prevention was another matter. The Mets' defense was below-average by any measure, while the club's starting pitchers threw the fourth-fewest innings in MLB. The rotation's overall ERA (4.13) ranked 18th but ballooned to 5.27 after June 12. Mets relievers buckled under the workload and produced mediocre overall results.

While Stearns' rotation signings Frankie Montas, Clay Holmes, Sean Manaea and Griffin Canning yielded mixed results, the fruits of the organization's minor league pitching development, headed by director Eric Jagers, nearly saved the season.

No. 1 prospect Nolan McLean debuted on Aug. 16 and pitched effectively in the majority of his eight starts. The 24-year-old finished 5-1, 2.06 with 57 strikeouts in 48 innings and remains a leading Rookie of the Year candidate in 2026.

Jonah Tong, the Minor League Pitcher of the Year, and Brandon Sproat followed McLean to the rotation and produced mixed results. More significantly for the future, this trio is just the tip of

PROJECTED 2029 LINEUP

Catcher	Francisco Alvarez	27
First Base	Ryan Clifford	25
Second Base	Jett Williams	25
Third Base	Brett Baty	29
Shortstop	Francisco Lindor	35
Left Field	Carson Benge	26
Center Field	AJ Ewing	24
Right Field	Juan Soto	30
Designated Hitter	Jacob Reimer	25
No. 1 Starter	Nolan McLean	27
No. 2 Starter	Jonah Tong	26
No. 3 Starter	Brandon Sproat	28
No. 4 Starter	Jack Wenninger	27
No. 5 Starter	Jonathan Santucci	26
Closer	Christian Scott	30

the iceberg for the organization's pitching outlook.

Collectively, Mets full-season minor league pitchers led all 30 organizations with a 3.64 ERA, .219 opponent average and 26.9% strikeout rate. Low-A St. Lucie and Double-A Binghamton led their leagues in ERA. High-A Brooklyn ranked second. All three teams reached the playoffs, with Binghamton and Brooklyn capturing league titles.

The Mets had not had three full-season playoff teams in one year since 2014. As an organization, the Mets had the fifth-best overall minor league winning percentage after finishing near the bottom in 2023 and 2024.

A number of the organization's top position prospects—outfielder Carson Benge, shortstop Jett Williams and first baseman Ryan Clifford—finished 2025 at Triple-A.

The Mets had the second-lowest draft bonus pool in 2025 and used their top two picks on athletic college infielders Mitch Voit and Antonio Jimenez. The club deviated from its recent draft strategy by going over slot to sign a pair of prep righthanders, fourth-rounder Peter Kussow and eighth-rounder Camden Lohman. Tong is the only other prep arm ranked in the top 30 prospects.

With one of the top farm systems in baseball and the capacity to add payroll, the Mets are positioned to rebound from a disastrous 2025 season. ∎

DEPTH CHART

NEW YORK METS

TOP 2026 ROOKIES — RANK
1. Nolan McLean, RHP — 1
2. Carson Benge, OF — 2
3. Jonah Tong, RHP — 3

BREAKOUT PROSPECTS — RANK
1. Eli Serrano III, OF — 17
2. Randy Guzman, OF/1B — 21
3. Franklin Gomez, LHP — 22

SOURCE OF TOP 30 TALENT

Homegrown	26	Acquired	4
College	13	Trade	3
Junior college	0	Rule 5 draft	0
High school	8	Independent league	1
Undrafted free agent	0	Free agent/waivers	0
International	5		

LF
John Bay
Edward Lantigua

CF
Carson Benge (2)
AJ Ewing (6)
Nick Morabito (13)
Wyatt Vincent

RF
Eli Serrano III (17)

3B
Jacob Reimer (8)
Elian Peña (12)
Trey Snyder (26)

SS
Jett Williams (4)
Marco Vargas (18)
Boston Baro (19)
Antonio Jimenez (20)
Anthony Frobose

2B
Mitch Voit (11)
Jeremy Rodriguez (28)
Colin Houck

1B
Ryan Clifford (7)
Randy Guzman (21)

C
Chris Suero (14)
Daiverson Gutierrez (25)
Kevin Parada
Ronald Hernandez
Yovanny Rodriguez
Josmir Reyes

LHP

LHSP
Jonathan Santucci (10)
Zach Thornton (15)
Franklin Gomez (22)

LHRP
Felipe De La Cruz

RHP

RHSP
Nolan McLean (1)
Jonah Tong (3)
Brandon Sproat (5)
Jack Wenninger (9)
Will Watson (16)
RJ Gordon (24)
Peter Kussow (29)
Cam Tilly (30)
Camden Lohman
Jace Hampson
Nate Hall
Dillon Stiltner

RHRP
Jonathan Pintaro (23)
Dylan Ross (27)
Ryan Lambert
Saul Garcia
Calvin Ziegler
Douglas Orellana
Peyton Prescott
Joel Diaz
Brett Banks
Frank Camarillo

NEW YORK METS

1 NOLAN McLEAN, RHP

Born: July 24, 2001. **B-T:** R-R. **HT:** 6-2. **WT:** 214.
Drafted: Oklahoma State, 2023 (3rd round).
Signed by: Scott Thomas.

TRACK RECORD: When the Mets drafted McLean in the third round in 2023, he was primarily a righthanded reliever and power-hitting outfielder for Oklahoma State. He continued as a two-way player in pro ball until the second half of 2024, when he dropped hitting after reaching Double-A Binghamton. Focusing his energy solely on pitching paid dividends in 2025, when McLean raced through Double-A with a 1.37 ERA in five starts, reached Triple-A Syracuse on May 9 and led all minor league pitchers with 38 strikeouts in July. The Mets called McLean up for his MLB debut on Aug. 16, and he fired 5.1 scoreless innings with eight strikeouts against the Mariners. He threw four quality starts in eight tries while pitching to a 2.06 ERA with 57 strikeouts in 48 innings.

SCOUTING REPORT: The Mets knew McLean had an athletic, strong frame and a promising fastball/slider foundation when they drafted him. They quickly learned about his adaptability and strong work ethic. All through his time in the minor leagues, McLean worked to refine his pitch shapes and expand his repertoire to find the right mix to combat batters of both hands. Ultimately, he reached that point in the second half of 2025, as typified by his Aug. 27 start against the Phillies when he pitched eight scoreless innings and generated at least one whiff on six different pitch types. McLean's main weapons are a plus mid-90s two-seam fastball that averages 16 inches of armside run and a double-plus mid-80s sweeper that breaks 16 or more inches to his glove side. This vicious east-west attack delivered from a low three-quarters slot sets up the rest of his arsenal, which against righthanded batters consists mostly of plus low-80s curveballs and above-average mid-90s four-seam fastballs to change eye levels. Against lefthanded batters, McLean emphasizes his breaking pitches along with his low-90s cutter to work inside and his mid-80s changeup to attack armside. He has shown a growing willingness to front-door his two-seamer to lefty hitters and also to back-foot them with his slider. What makes McLean difficult to handle is his quality stuff and unpredictability. He throws each of his six pitch types—ranging from 77 mph curveballs to 98 mph fastballs—to any batter in any count. His control is average and likely to improve with experience,

BA GRADE
65 Risk: Average
Adjusted grade: 55

SCOUTING GRADES
FB: 60. **CB:** 60. **SL:** 60.
CH: 55. **SW:** 70. **CTL:** 50.
Projected future grades on 20-80 scouting scale

BEST TOOLS

BATTING
Best Hitter — AJ Ewing
Best Power Hitter — Ryan Clifford
Best Strike-Zone Discipline — Elian Peña
Fastest Baserunner — Jett Williams
Best Athlete — Nick Morabito

PITCHING
Best Fastball — Jonah Tong
Best Curveball — Nolan McLean
Best Slider — Brandon Sproat
Best Changeup — Jack Wenninger
Best Control — Irving Cota

FIELDING
Best Defensive Catcher — Chris Suero
Best Defensive Infielder — Marco Vargas
Best Infield Arm — Jett Williams
Best Defensive Outfielder — Nick Morabito
Best Outfield Arm — Yohairo Cuevas

because his delivery is simple and repeatable.

THE FUTURE: In the words of one scout, McLean's high-spin breaking stuff and low-spin changeup are "how you draw it up." He showed in his eight-start MLB debut that he is major league ready. He was the Mets' best pitcher down the stretch and is ready to assume a prominent role in the rotation. He has the ingredients to become a prototype No. 2 starter. McLean retains his rookie status for 2026 and will likely add Prospect Promotion Incentive eligibility, giving the Mets a chance to add a draft pick after the first round if he factors for a major award in his first three seasons.

Year	Age	Club (League)	Level	W	L	ERA	G	GS	IP	H	HR	BB	SO	BB%	SO%	WHIP	AVG
2025	23	Binghamton (EL)	AA	3	1	1.37	5	5	26	20	0	12	30	11.1	27.8	1.22	.213
2025	23	Syracuse (IL)	AAA	5	4	2.78	16	13	87	58	8	38	97	10.6	27.0	1.10	.185
2025	23	New York (NL)	MLB	5	1	2.06	8	8	48	34	4	16	57	8.5	30.3	1.04	.200
		Minor League Totals		12	15	3.10	48	44	227	175	18	94	245	10.0	26.0	1.19	.213
		Major League Totals		5	1	2.06	8	8	48	34	4	16	57	8.5	30.3	1.04	.200

NEW YORK METS

2 CARSON BENGE, OF

HIT: 60. **POW:** 55. **RUN:** 50. **FLD:** 55. **ARM:** 65. **BA Grade:** 55. **Risk:** Mild. **Adj:** 50.

Born: January 20, 2003. **B-T:** L-R. **HT:** 6-2. **WT:** 185.
Drafted: Oklahoma State, 2024 (1st round). **Signed by:** Trey Cobb.
TRACK RECORD: Benge played outfield and pitched for two seasons at Oklahoma State, where he was roommates with fellow two-way player and future Mets teammate Nolan McLean. The Mets drafted Benge with the 19th overall pick in 2024. He dropped pitching as a pro and established himself as a Top 100 Prospect in 2025 when he hit .281/.385/.472 with 15 home runs and 22 stolen bases in 116 games across three levels. He reached Triple-A Syracuse in mid August. His 150 wRC+ ranked 19th in the minors among batters with 400 plate appearances.
SCOUTING REPORT: Benge has quality tools across the board, but his top attribute is his ability to drive the ball with authority to the opposite field. High-A Brooklyn hitting coach Bryan Muniz describes it as his "superpower." While most of Benge's batted balls go to left field, he is beginning to hunt pitches he can drive for power, and he hit a vast majority of his 15 homers to right field in 2025. He is a versatile and fairly discerning hitter with a high zone-contact rate against all pitch types. He should hit for average, walk and produce above-average power. Benge hangs in versus lefthanders but has not shown the same level of impact in same-side matchups. He posts average run times to first base but is a bit faster underway. Most rival clubs see Benge as a solid-average defender in center field and above-average in a corner. His plus arm plays in right field. The Mets laud his leadership skills.
THE FUTURE: Benge is an athletic, hard-working, do-everything type of hitter and a future quality regular. The question is whether he will mash enough for a corner or defend well enough for center to become an occasional all-star. He finished 2025 at Triple-A and, given his age, production and progression, could play his way into the Mets' big league plans early in 2026.

Year	Age	Club (League)	Level	AVG	G	AB	R	H	2B	3B	HR	RBI	BB	SO	SB	OBP	SLG
2025	22	Brooklyn (SAL)	A+	.302	60	225	47	68	18	5	4	37	41	50	15	.417	.480
2025	22	Binghamton (EL)	AA	.317	32	126	28	40	6	1	8	23	18	23	4	.407	.571
2025	22	Syracuse (IL)	AAA	.178	24	90	12	16	1	1	3	13	9	19	3	.272	.311
		Minor League Totals		.280	131	496	97	139	28	7	17	81	79	106	25	.389	.468

3 JONAH TONG, RHP

FB: 65. **CB:** 45. **SL:** 40. **CH:** 60. **CTL:** 45. **BA Grade:** 55. **Risk:** Average. **Adj:** 45.

Born: June 19, 2003. **B-T:** R-R. **HT:** 6-1. **WT:** 180.
Drafted: HS—Statesboro, GA, 2022 (7th round). **Signed by:** Marlin McPhail.
TRACK RECORD: Tong burst on the prospect scene in 2024 when he struck out 160 batters in 113 innings. He followed with an epic 2025 season, mostly at Double-A Binghamton, in which he led all minor league pitchers with 179 strikeouts, a 1.43 ERA and a .148 opponent average. He was recognized as the BA Minor League Pitcher of the Year. The Mets called up Tong on Aug. 29.
SCOUTING REPORT: Tong's game revolves around his fastball and the mechanics he uses to achieve its unique characteristics. His delivery was inspired by former Giants ace Tim Lincecum—a fellow smaller-statured, hard-throwing righthanded starter. Tong loads his arm in a similar fashion, with a deep arm plunge as he puts his weight on his back leg. Firing forward, Tong points his lead foot toward the first-base dugout and tilts his torso dramatically to achieve his high overhand arm slot. He gets incredible extension and true backspin on a four-seamer that yields more than 19 inches of vertical ride—one of the highest totals among minor league starters. Tong upped his velocity from 92 mph in 2024 to 94 in 2025 and developed a Vulcan grip for his changeup. The mid-80s pitch produced devastating results against minor league batters but did not have the same success in MLB. He throws occasional high-spin curveballs and sliders that have at least average potential. Tong's effortful mechanics inhibit his command on all pitches, and he has run higher walks rates throughout his career.
THE FUTURE: Tong was 22 when called up following just two Triple-A starts, and his inexperience showed at times. He throws fastballs or changeups about 85% of the time and will need better command of those pitches or better breaking stuff to become a No. 3 starter. He will get another MLB look in 2026.

Year	Age	Club (League)	Level	W	L	ERA	G	GS	IP	H	HR	BB	SO	BB%	SO%	WHIP	AVG
2025	22	Binghamton (EL)	AA	8	5	1.59	20	20	102	50	2	44	162	11.1	40.8	0.92	.143
2025	22	Syracuse (IL)	AAA	2	0	0.00	2	2	12	8	0	3	17	6.7	37.8	0.94	.190
2025	22	New York (NL)	MLB	2	3	7.71	5	5	19	24	3	9	22	10.3	25.3	1.77	.312
		Minor League Totals		16	11	2.54	57	53	248	160	8	116	377	11.5	37.3	1.11	.180
		Major League Totals		2	3	7.71	5	5	19	24	3	9	22	10.3	25.3	1.77	.312

NEW YORK METS

4. JETT WILLIAMS, SS/2B

HIT: 55. **POW:** 45. **RUN:** 65. **FLD:** 50. **ARM:** 60. **BA Grade:** 55. **Risk:** Average. **Adj:** 45.

Born: November 3, 2003. **B-T:** R-R. **HT:** 5-8. **WT:** 175.
Drafted: HS—Heath, TX, 2022 (1st round). **Signed by:** Gary Brown.

TRACK RECORD: Williams drew notice on the amateur circuit as a shorter-stature player with a high energy level and quality tools. The Mets drafted him 14th overall in 2022 and watched him reach Double-A at the tail end of a breakthrough 2023 season. Wrist surgery limited him to 33 games in 2024, but Williams rebounded in 2025 with a strong season spent mostly at Double-A, plus 34 games at Triple-A. He batted .261/.363/.465 with 17 home runs and 34 steals in 130 games. Williams tied for the Mets' minor league lead with 226 total bases and finished ninth in the minor leagues with 58 extra-base hits.

SCOUTING REPORT: Williams does a little of everything well, highlighted by his plus speed and versatility to play shortstop, second base and center field. He stays within his strike zone, consistently draws walks, gets on base and steals bases. He's best when he leans into things he does best—hitting line drives, taking extra bases and occasionally hunting a pitch to drive over the wall with fringe-average power. His swing gets too big at times and costs him with empty flyouts. Dialing in his bat-to-ball skills could also improve his overall contact rate on in-zone pitches, which is ordinary. Williams sees most of his action at shortstop and has improved there since turning pro with a quicker first step and enhanced range. He's average at the position and also fluid. His plus arm plays in the middle infield and surprisingly well in the outfield, where his competitive throws averaged 91.4 mph. He is a capable outfielder with decent routes and jumps and average range.

THE FUTURE: Williams showed off his best self in 96 Double-A games, hitting .281/.390/.477 with 62 walks, 44 extra-base hits and 32 steals in 39 tries. He has a chance to become a table-setting regular, most likely in the middle infield.

Year	Age	Club (League)	Level	AVG	G	AB	R	H	2B	3B	HR	RBI	BB	SO	SB	OBP	SLG
2025	21	Binghamton (EL)	AA	.281	96	352	70	99	29	5	10	37	62	96	32	.390	.477
2025	21	Syracuse (IL)	AAA	.209	34	134	21	28	5	2	7	15	14	35	2	.285	.433
		Minor League Totals		.256	294	1049	201	269	65	17	31	117	206	290	90	.388	.439

5. BRANDON SPROAT, RHP

FB: 50. **CB:** 55. **SL:** 60. **CH:** 60. **SW:** 60. **CTL:** 50. **BA Grade:** 50. **Risk:** Mild. **Adj:** 45.

Born: September 17, 2000. **B-T:** R-R. **HT:** 6-3. **WT:** 215.
Drafted: Florida, 2023 (2nd round). **Signed by:** Brett Campbell.

TRACK RECORD: The Mets drafted Sproat in the third round in 2022 but did not sign him. They picked him again in the second round in 2023 as a Florida senior and signed him for slot value. Sproat breezed through High-A and Double-A in 2024 before hitting a wall at Triple-A Syracuse. He continued to flounder at the level in 2025, and through his first 22 starts for Syracuse, spanning two seasons, Sproat ran up a 6.45 ERA with a 15.7% strikeout rate. He righted the ship in late June 2025, and in 11 appearances afterward he had a 2.44 ERA and 30% strikeout rate. The Mets called up Sproat on Sept. 7, and he made four MLB starts of varying quality.

SCOUTING REPORT: Coming out of college, Sproat was regarded as an athletic righthander with arm speed who emphasized his fastball and changeup. Shaky control introduced reliever risk. As a pro, he's morphed into a pitcher whose control is good enough to start and whose breaking stuff stands out. Sproat threw his mid-80s sweeper and high-70s curveball about a third of the time in his MLB debut and leaned on them as putaway pitches. He also throws a harder slider. Sproat's sinker sits 94-96 mph, but despite that velocity, it operates as a groundball or set-up pitch rather than a whiff pitch. The same goes for his average four-seamer. Lefthanded batters saw Sproat better and were largely responsible for his ballooning Triple-A ERA. He mitigated the effect by throwing more four-seam fastballs, curves and changeups to lefties. His power changeup remains a plus pitch at 89-91 mph with lots of armside life.

THE FUTURE: Sproat throws hard, throws strikes and has a wide repertoire, including strong feel for spin and offspeed. He has all the ingredients to be a No. 4 starter or better, and he's ready to assume that role in 2026.

Year	Age	Club (League)	Level	W	L	ERA	G	GS	IP	H	HR	BB	SO	BB%	SO%	WHIP	AVG
2025	24	Syracuse (IL)	AAA	8	6	4.24	26	25	121	97	9	53	113	10.4	22.1	1.24	.218
2025	24	New York (NL)	MLB	0	2	4.79	4	4	21	18	0	7	17	8.3	20.2	1.21	.243
		Minor League Totals		15	10	3.83	50	48	237	184	23	95	244	9.7	25.0	1.18	.214
		Major League Totals		0	2	4.79	4	4	21	18	0	7	17	8.3	20.2	1.21	.243

NEW YORK METS

6 AJ EWING, OF/2B

HIT: 60. **POW:** 40. **RUN:** 65. **FLD:** 55. **ARM:** 55. **BA Grade:** 55. **Risk:** Average. **Adj:** 45.

Born: August 10, 2004. **B-T:** L-R. **HT:** 6-0. **WT:** 160.
Drafted: HS—Springboro, OH, 2023 (4th round supp.). **Signed by:** Joe Raccuia.

TRACK RECORD: The Mets drafted Ewing near the end of the fourth round in 2023, using the compensatory pick they gained from Jacob deGrom signing with the Rangers. Ewing quickly hit his way out of the Florida Complex League in 2024 and started back at Low-A St. Lucie in 2025. He advanced to High-A Brooklyn at the end of April and moved to Double-A Binghamton in mid August. He batted .315/.400/.429 in 124 games, ranking fifth in the minors with 70 stolen bases, sixth with 10 triples and eighth with 153 hits.

SCOUTING REPORT: Ewing has a well-rounded game centered on strong swing decisions, line-drive contact to all fields and plus speed. He tweaked his swing in 2025 to improve his batted-ball angles and make more contact. Ewing's line-drive rate climbed by more than 10 percentage points, while his swinging-strike rate fell from 12% to about 9% as he moved up the ladder. His instincts and decision-making stand out, as evidenced by a system-best .401 on-base percentage and 70-for-81 showing on the bases. Ewing hits the ball hard enough to run into a few home runs, but his spray approach limits his power to below-average. A high school shortstop, Ewing has primarily played center field in pro ball with occasional starts at second base. He's improved his jumps and max speed in the outfield and should be an above-average option in center and a plus one on the corners with an above-average arm.

THE FUTURE: Ewing does a lot of things that can help a team win, beginning with the potential for plus hitting ability and plus speed. Additionally, he bats lefthanded, gets on base and plays up the middle. The versatility to play outfield and infield only helps his cause. Ewing finished 2025 at Double-A and should reach Triple-A in 2026, putting him on the MLB radar as a 21-year-old.

Year	Age	Club (League)	Level	AVG	G	AB	R	H	2B	3B	HR	RBI	BB	SO	SB	OBP	SLG
2025	20	St. Lucie (FSL)	A	.400	18	65	15	26	3	4	1	20	15	10	14	.506	.615
2025	20	Brooklyn (SAL)	A+	.288	78	299	52	86	16	4	2	26	46	66	44	.387	.388
2025	20	Binghamton (EL)	AA	.339	28	121	20	41	7	2	0	9	7	29	12	.371	.430
		Minor League Totals		.283	221	812	149	230	40	13	13	107	136	220	84	.388	.413

7 RYAN CLIFFORD, 1B/OF

HIT: 40. **POW:** 60. **RUN:** 50. **FLD:** 50. **ARM:** 60. **BA Grade:** 50. **Risk:** Average. **Adj:** 40.

Born: July 20, 2003. **B-T:** L-L. **HT:** 6-3. **WT:** 200.
Drafted: HS—Cary, NC, 2022 (11th round). **Signed by:** Andrew Johnson (Astros).

TRACK RECORD: The Mets acquired Clifford when they dealt Justin Verlander to the Astros at the 2023 trade deadline. He has blossomed into their top power prospect, hitting 19 home runs in 2024—mostly at Double-A—and a career-high 29 homers in 2025 to lead the system and rank sixth in the minors. He also paced Mets minor leaguers with 93 RBIs and 85 walks while tying for the lead with 226 total bases. Clifford spent most of 2025 at Double-A before moving to Triple-A on Aug. 12.

SCOUTING REPORT: Not many prospects batters hit the ball as hard as Clifford, whose 108.6 mph 90th percentile exit velocity was one of the top figures in the minor leagues. He gets the most out of his double-plus raw power by hitting the ball in the air to his pull side. The biggest improvement the lefthanded-hitting Clifford made in 2025 was improving against high fastballs and dramatically improving his overall zone-contact rate. He also upped his aggressiveness to swing at more pitches and put more early-count offerings in play. The strategy reduced his strikeout rate by four percentage points without sacrificing power. He takes his walks, but his flyball profile will translate to low batting averages. Despite his size, Clifford is an average runner who is capable on the outfielder corners. His plus arm plays in right field. He is also a quality defender at first base.

THE FUTURE: The Mets laud Clifford as a hard worker dedicated to improving his craft in the batting cage. His bat will determine how far he advances in MLB. He has the power-and-patience approach that could play if he can clear the high offensive bar at first base. Clifford could hit his way into a big league look in 2026 after returning to Triple-A to open the season.

Year	Age	Club (League)	Level	AVG	G	AB	R	H	2B	3B	HR	RBI	BB	SO	SB	OBP	SLG
2025	21	Binghamton (EL)	AA	.243	105	367	56	89	18	1	24	75	63	113	4	.355	.493
2025	21	Syracuse (IL)	AAA	.219	34	114	15	25	5	0	5	18	22	35	3	.359	.395
		Minor League Totals		.242	408	1416	220	343	75	1	74	252	266	479	18	.370	.453

NEW YORK METS

8 JACOB REIMER, 3B
HIT: 50. **POW:** 60. **RUN:** 40. **FLD:** 45. **ARM:** 55. **BA Grade:** 50. **Risk:** Average. **Adj:** 40.

Born: February 2, 2004. **B-T:** R-R. **HT:** 6-2. **WT:** 205.
Drafted: HS—Yucaipa, CA, 2022 (4th round). **Signed by:** Glenn Walker.
TRACK RECORD: The Mets liked Reimer in high school more than most teams and went over slot to sign him in the fourth round of the 2022 draft. The decision looks good after Reimer hit 17 home runs with a 157 wRC+ in 2025, the latter of which ranked fourth among all minor league batters with at least 400 plate appearances. He announced a breakout season with a three-homer game for High-A Brooklyn on April 30. Promoted to Double-A in late June, Reimer struggled with strikeouts initially before finishing with a .627 slugging percentage in his final 30 games.
SCOUTING REPORT: Player development is seldom linear, and Reimer is a perfect example. In his first full pro season in 2023, he got on base at a high clip but showed limited power. Then he missed all but 25 games in 2024 with a hamstring injury. Heading into 2025, Reimer made key adjustments to improve his bat speed and range of motion to put himself in a better position to stay behind the ball and rotate through the hitting zone. The result was one of the best 90th percentile exit velocities in the system and a swing optimized to pull the ball in the air. Reimer has a good zone-contact rate for a young hitter with plus power, and he does a good job swinging at strikes, so he should maintain an average hit tool. He is an average runner who will slow down but has good baserunning instincts. Reimer has the above-average arm to play third base, but he needs to tighten up his ball security and throwing accuracy after making 16 errors in 2025.
THE FUTURE: Reimer started 15 games at first base in 2025 and might see more time there. Such a move would up the pressure on his bat, but he has shown the ability to adapt to challenges in the batter's box. Reimer will be ready for Triple-A early in 2026 and could enter the MLB picture late in the season.

Year	Age	Club (League)	Level	AVG	G	AB	R	H	2B	3B	HR	RBI	BB	SO	SB	OBP	SLG
2025	21	Brooklyn (SAL)	A+	.284	61	229	52	65	18	4	8	39	32	52	11	.384	.502
2025	21	Binghamton (EL)	AA	.279	61	215	36	60	14	1	9	38	26	60	4	.374	.479
		Minor League Totals		.269	256	881	163	237	50	6	26	140	141	213	18	.386	.428

9 JACK WENNINGER, RHP
FB: 55. **CB:** 45. **SL:** 55. **SP:** 70. **CTL:** 50. **BA Grade:** 50. **Risk:** Average. **Adj:** 40.

Born: March 14, 2002. **B-T:** L-R. **HT:** 6-4. **WT:** 210.
Drafted: Illinois, 2023 (6th round). **Signed by:** Chris Heidt.
TRACK RECORD: The Mets chose Wenninger out of Illinois in the sixth round of the same 2023 draft class that yielded Nolan McLean and Brandon Sproat. Coming out of college, Wenninger was a tall strike-thrower with a nasty splitter—a combination he used to dominate Class A hitters in 2024 with 140 strikeouts in 115 innings. He proved it was no fluke with a breakthrough 2025 at Double-A that included a 2.92 ERA and 147 strikeouts in a system-best 135.2 innings. Wenninger pitched the clinching win for Binghamton in both rounds of the Eastern League playoffs, striking out 20 in 11 innings and allowing two runs on four hits.
SCOUTING REPORT: Wenninger is a strong athlete and, in player development parlance, a great worker. In 2025, he proved he was much more than that by holding higher velocity, expanding his repertoire and leaning into his double-plus splitter. Wenninger improved his average four-seam fastball velocity to 94.5 mph and topped out near 98. The pitch gets above-average ride from his high arm slot. He incorporated a mid-90s sinker to help him work armside to righthanded hitters. Wenninger merged his slider and cutter into a tight mid-80s slider he threw dramatically more often. His mid-80s splitter remains his bread-and-butter pitch. He can throw it in the zone for whiffs or in the dirt for chases to batters on either side of the plate. Late in the season, he began incorporating a spike-grip curveball in the low 80s for a different look. Wenninger throws strikes with all his pitches and is a competitor with strong mound presence.
THE FUTURE: Wenninger has all the ingredients to be a No. 4 starter. He could be more than that if his splitter plays as successfully in the majors as it does against minor league hitters. He is ready for Triple-A and a likely MLB debut in the second half of the season.

Year	Age	Club (League)	Level	W	L	ERA	G	GS	IP	H	HR	BB	SO	BB%	SO%	WHIP	AVG
2025	23	Binghamton (EL)	AA	12	6	2.92	26	26	136	114	13	42	147	7.6	26.4	1.15	.225
		Minor League Totals		15	10	3.69	43	37	210	182	23	67	240	7.6	27.3	1.19	.229

10 JONATHAN SANTUCCI, LHP

FB: 60. **CB:** 50. **SL:** 65. **CH:** 40. **CTL:** 50. **BA Grade:** 55. **Risk:** High. **Adj:** 40.

Born: December 28, 2002. **B-T:** L-L. **HT:** 6-2. **WT:** 195.
Drafted: Duke, 2024 (2nd round). **Signed by:** Daniel Coles.
TRACK RECORD: Like fellow top Mets prospects Nolan McLean and Carson Benge, Santucci has a background as a two-way player. He played both ways as a Duke freshman before committing to the mound and becoming the Mets' second-round pick in 2024. Santucci got off to a rough start at High-A Brooklyn in 2025—8.14 ERA, seven home runs in six starts—before righting the ship and cruising to Double-A Binghamton in July. He pitched to a 1.95 ERA and .186 opponent average with two home runs allowed in his final 20 starts, striking out 30% of batters. He pitched effectively in the Eastern League playoffs.
SCOUTING REPORT: Santucci throws his slider more than his four-seam fastball—an approach that works because he commands his powerful, deceptive slider. It averages 87 mph and maxes out near 93 with a lot of vertical drop. He can locate the pitch for strikes or bury it late in the count. It looks like a fastball out of his hand before falling off the table. Santucci's fastball averages 94 mph and tops out at 97 with enough ride and extension in his delivery to help the pitch play up. He began incorporating a low-80s curveball to give him a change-of-pace pitch. His changeup is in the development stage, and he doesn't throw it often. He walked 14% of batters as a college junior, but he improved his control dramatically in pro ball by focusing on throwing to the middle of the plate and letting the action on his pitches take over.
THE FUTURE: Santucci stands out in a Mets system that has largely been devoid of lefthanders for the past decade outside of David Peterson and Steven Matz. Santucci's platoon-neutral slider, quality velocity and improved strike-throwing give him a real shot to become a No. 3 or 4 big league starter, just like Peterson and Matz. He will be ready for Triple-A in short order.

Year	Age	Club (League)	Level	W	L	ERA	G	GS	IP	H	HR	BB	SO	BB%	SO%	WHIP	AVG
2025	22	Brooklyn (SAL)	A+	5	4	3.46	15	13	68	62	7	23	75	8.1	26.4	1.26	.240
2025	22	Binghamton (EL)	AA	4	0	2.52	10	10	50	33	2	18	63	9.1	32.0	1.02	.189
		Minor League Totals		9	4	3.06	25	23	118	95	9	41	138	8.5	28.7	1.16	.219

11 MITCH VOIT, 2B

HIT: 50. **POW:** 50. **RUN:** 60. **FLD:** 50. **ARM:** 60. **BA Grade:** 50. **Risk:** Average. **Adj:** 40.

Born: September 30, 2004. **B-T:** R-R. **HT:** 6-0. **WT:** 201. **Drafted:** Michigan, 2025 (1st round). **Signed by:** Chad Langley.
TRACK RECORD: In three seasons at Michigan, two of them as a two-way player, Voit finished ninth in program history with 356 total bases. Narrowing the list to just three-year players, he ranked second. Voit dropped pitching as a junior in 2025 following offseason arm surgery to focus on hitting and playing second base. It paid off with a career year in which he hit .346/.471/.668 with 14 home runs and 14 steals in 56 games. The Mets drafted Voit with their first-round pick at No. 38 overall—which was dropped 10 spots as a competitive balance tax threshold penalty—and signed him for $1.75 million.
SCOUTING REPORT: Voit began to generate late first-round buzz as he emerged as a Michigan junior. The selling points were his strong zone-contact rate, sturdy swing decisions and plenty of hard contact at ideal angles. Voit is a 6-foot righthanded batter with a strong build and solid lower half. He uses a simple swing with above-average bat speed and the swing path to be a steady line-drive hitter. He has the muscle to hit the ball out of the park when he catches it out front. Voit is a plus runner and efficient basestealer who went 20-for-21 in a 22-game sample with Low-A St. Lucie in his pro debut. He is a sure thing at second base with sound hands and an accurate, plus arm. He looked playable at shortstop in a few pro appearances.
THE FUTURE: Voit should settle in with average overall offensive potential and strong supporting tools bolstered by positional versatility. He could develop into a regular second baseman or perhaps a potential infield/outfield utility player.

Year	Age	Club (League)	Level	AVG	G	AB	R	H	2B	3B	HR	RBI	BB	SO	SB	OBP	SLG
2025	20	St. Lucie (FSL)	A	.235	22	85	18	20	2	0	1	8	13	24	20	.343	.294
		Minor League Totals		.235	22	85	18	20	2	0	1	8	13	24	20	.343	.294

NEW YORK METS

12 ELIAN PEÑA, SS
HIT: 45. **POW:** 55. **RUN:** 40. **FLD:** 45. **ARM:** 55. **BA Grade:** 55. **Risk:** High. **Adj:** 40.

Born: October 19, 2007. **B-T:** L-R. **HT:** 5-10. **WT:** 180. **Signed:** Dominican Republic, 2025. **Signed by:** Steve Barningham.
TRACK RECORD: The Mets signed Peña for $5 million, handing the Dominican shortstop the largest bonus for a Latin American amateur during the 2025 signing period. It also was the highest bonus for a Mets international amateur, and not far behind Kevin Parada's franchise draft record of $5,019,735. Peña opened his pro debut in the Dominican Summer League and got off to a brutal start. He went 0-for-26 in his first nine games but then got in a rhythm and hit .342 with 23 extra-base hits, including nine home runs, in his final 46 games.
SCOUTING REPORT: Peña pressed in the early stages of 2025 as he felt the weight of expectations. Once he collected his first hit, he seemed to relax and get back to his strengths. Peña is a selective hitter who recognizes spin and whose approach can border on passivity, but he knows what to do when he gets his pitch. He has a compact lefthanded swing and a steep bat path designed to put the ball in the air. He has more of a power-over-hit profile with above-average raw power. Peña has a thicker lower half and is heavy on his feet. Some scouts expressed concern about a lack of twitch and his overall physical maturity as a 17-year-old. He has almost no shot to stick at shortstop because of questionable hands and range, but he has the above-average arm for third base. He stole 21 bases in the DSL but doesn't project to be a basestealing threat.
THE FUTURE: Peña's hitting instincts and pitch identification skill give him a shot to develop into a roughly average major league hitter who likely winds up at third base.

Year	Age	Club (League)	Level	AVG	G	AB	R	H	2B	3B	HR	RBI	BB	SO	SB	OBP	SLG
2025	17	DSL Mets Orange	Rk	.292	55	178	47	52	13	1	9	33	36	36	21	.421	.528
		Minor League Totals		.292	55	178	47	52	13	1	9	33	36	36	21	.421	.528

13 NICK MORABITO, OF
HIT: 50. **POW:** 30. **RUN:** 60. **FLD:** 60. **ARM:** 45. **BA Grade:** 45. **Risk:** Average. **Adj:** 35.

Born: May 7, 2003. **B-T:** R-R. **HT:** 5-11. **WT:** 185. **Drafted:** HS—Washington, DC, 2022 (2nd round supp.).
Signed by: Joe Raccuia.
TRACK RECORD: The Mets drafted Morabito 75th overall in 2022, using the compensatory second-round pick they gained when free agent Noah Syndergaard signed with the Angels. Morabito played primarily shortstop in high school but shifted to center field with the Mets. After a slow start to his pro career, he got on track in 2024 by hitting .312 with 60 walks and 59 stolen bases in 119 games at both Class A levels. Morabito moved up to Double-A Binghamton in 2025 and stole 49 bases in 118 games while improving his power production. He shined in the Arizona Fall League with 25 hits, 16 steals and 10 walks in 17 games.
SCOUTING REPORT: Morabito's plus speed plays in center field and on the bases. He is one of 12 minor leaguers to steal at least 100 bases across 2024 and 2025. His speed helps him outrun mistakes in the outfield as he continues to improve at the position. Morabito is an above-average center fielder with a good chance to grade as plus as he continues to gain reps. His arm is fringy but accurate. Morabito does a lot of things well at the plate but nothing exemplary. He is a spray hitter who tends to swing at strikes and let the ball travel before committing. This results in a lot of groundball contact and not much pulled contact in the air, so his power output will be well below-average. Morabito can compensate for a lack of impact with line-drive contact and by taking extra bases with his legs.
THE FUTURE: The Mets added Morabito to the 40-man roster in November to shield him from the Rule 5 draft. Time at Triple-A is on tap to help him hone his speed and defense, which are potential carrying tools that give him a chance to become an extra outfielder.

Year	Age	Club (League)	Level	AVG	G	AB	R	H	2B	3B	HR	RBI	BB	SO	SB	OBP	SLG
2025	22	Binghamton (EL)	AA	.273	118	436	63	119	27	2	6	59	47	115	49	.348	.385
		Minor League Totals		.291	300	1122	174	327	54	10	12	118	143	276	130	.381	.389

14 CHRIS SUERO, C/OF
HIT: 30. **POW:** 55. **RUN:** 50. **FLD:** 45. **ARM:** 55. **BA Grade:** 50. **Risk:** High. **Adj:** 35.

Born: January 27, 2004. **B-T:** R-R. **HT:** 6-0. **WT:** 205. **Signed:** Dominican Republic, 2022. **Signed by:** Wilson Peralta.
TRACK RECORD: Suero signed out of the Dominican Republic in 2022, but he grew up in the U.S. and played high school ball in the Bronx for one year in 2019 before moving. He converted from outfielder to catcher just before turning pro and has made steady progress behind the plate. Suero began to distinguish himself at High-A Brooklyn in 2024 with his athleticism and plate approach. He tuned up his power in

NEW YORK METS

2025 as he reached Double-A Binghamton, while his 140 wRC+ ranked 33rd among all minor league hitters—and fifth among catchers—with at least 400 plate appearances.

SCOUTING REPORT: Suero is a natural, high-energy leader who is bilingual and adept at building relationships with his pitchers. He caught a career-high 73 games in 2025—plus five more in the playoffs and eight in the Arizona Fall League—and helped guide the Brooklyn and Binghamton pitching staffs to dominant seasons. Suero has an above-average arm and fringy blocking ability. The Mets challenged him to improve his framing in 2025, and he made enough progress to stake his future at the position. Suero is a power-oriented hitter with a good eye for the strike zone who will take his "A" swing almost exclusively. The approach led to a career-high 16 homers in 2025 but also a 29% strikeout rate fueled by a 25% zone-miss rate. His bat speed and exit velocity markers authenticate his above-average power. He runs well and stole 35 bases in 2025.

THE FUTURE: Suero still plays left field and first base on occasion but is looking more like a potential backup catcher who brings power and versatility to a roster.

Year	Age	Club (League)	Level	AVG	G	AB	R	H	2B	3B	HR	RBI	BB	SO	SB	OBP	SLG
2025	21	Brooklyn (SAL)	A+	.240	74	242	53	58	11	1	13	51	41	86	25	.382	.455
2025	21	Binghamton (EL)	AA	.221	41	136	25	30	5	0	3	17	29	53	10	.374	.324
		Minor League Totals		.234	287	917	176	215	41	5	29	149	171	287	62	.376	.385

15 ZACH THORNTON, LHP

FB: 55. **CB:** 45. **SL:** 55. **CH:** 45. **CT:** 60. **CTL:** 60. **BA Grade:** 50. **Risk:** High. **Adj:** 35.

Born: January 17, 2002. **B-T:** L-L. **HT:** 6-3. **WT:** 170. **Drafted:** Grand Canyon, 2023 (5th round). **Signed by:** Brian Reid.

TRACK RECORD: Thornton played high school ball in Lawrence, Kan., and pitched for two seasons at Barton JC in his home state. He transferred to Grand Canyon as a junior and quickly emerged as the Antelopes' Friday night starter and one of the top rising prospects for the 2023 draft. The Mets drafted Thornton in the fifth round and signed him for a slightly below-slot $350,000. He pitched at the Class A levels in 2024 as a hybrid starter-reliever before taking a leap forward in 2025, when he pitched to a 1.98 ERA and 0.81 WHIP in 72.2 innings, mostly for Double-A Binghamton. His season ended in late June after 14 starts with an oblique injury.

SCOUTING REPORT: Thornton is a 6-foot-3 lefthander with a projectable build who has already added 15-20 pounds of good weight as a professional. He upped the velocity across his arsenal while improving his plan of attack in 2025, year three of his development. He improved his strikeout rate to 28.5%, nearly 10 percentage points higher than in 2024, while walking just 4% of batters, the lowest rate among Mets minor league pitchers with at least 10 starts. In fact, Thornton's control of his solid-average arsenal is his greatest asset. In 2025 he registered strike rates north of 70% on three pitch types: a low-90s four-seam fastball that tops out near 96 mph with good ride, a high-80s cutter and mid-80s slider. He locates his hard stuff well to his glove side to get inside on righthanded hitters. Thornton has a full arsenal that also includes a sinker, a mid-70s curveball to disrupt timing and a low-80s changeup he is developing to give him an armside weapon.

THE FUTURE: Thornton's plus control of solid stuff as well as his overall poise and fearlessness make him a strong rotation candidate, probably more toward the back end, unless he adds more velocity.

Year	Age	Club (League)	Level	W	L	ERA	G	GS	IP	H	HR	BB	SO	BB%	SO%	WHIP	AVG
2025	23	Brooklyn (SAL)	A+	3	0	0.44	4	4	21	12	1	2	25	2.6	32.1	0.68	.162
2025	23	Binghamton (EL)	AA	3	2	2.60	10	10	52	36	4	9	53	4.6	27.0	0.87	.197
		Minor League Totals		11	6	3.01	34	26	141	125	9	29	132	5.1	23.2	1.09	.239

16 WILL WATSON, RHP

FB: 60. **SL:** 50. **CH:** 55. **CTL:** 45. **BA Grade:** 45. **Risk:** Average. **Adj:** 35.

Born: November 7, 2002. **B-T:** R-R. **HT:** 6-1. **WT:** 180. **Drafted:** Southern California, 2024 (7th round). **Signed by:** Rusty McNamara.

TRACK RECORD: Watson played high school ball in Burlington, Wash., about halfway between Seattle and Vancouver. He attended three California-based colleges in three years, beginning at Division III Cal Lutheran followed by San Joaquin Delta JC and, finally, Southern California. The Mets drafted him out of USC in the seventh round in 2024, and Watson climbed three levels to Double-A Binghamton in his first full season, ranking among the Mets minor league leaders with 142 strikeouts, 121.1 innings and a 2.60 ERA. Watson finished the year in the rotation for the Eastern League champions.

SCOUTING REPORT: The Mets were drawn to Watson's fastball characteristics in the draft. The 6-foot-1 righthander gets down the mound with plus extension and a low release height on his mid-90s fastball that tops near 98 mph. He throws a lot of strikes with the pitch and used it to generate a 19% whiff rate in 2025. He throws his four-seamer nearly half the time, and the pitch could add velocity as he furthers his development. Watson's most reliable secondary pitch is his 87 mph changeup with strong armside life. He mixes in an upper-80s gyro slider (or cutter) to compete in the zone and a sweepier mid-80s slider to expand for chases. Watson ran an 11.6% walk rate and typically worked five innings or fewer in his 2025 starts.

THE FUTURE: Watson's pro workload is trending in the right direction after he moved from the USC bullpen to rotation as a junior. His stuff would play up in a bullpen role or serve him as a back-end starter or swingman.

Year	Age	Club (League)	Level	W	L	ERA	G	GS	IP	H	HR	BB	SO	BB%	SO%	WHIP	AVG
2025	22	St. Lucie (FSL)	A	0	4	3.66	10	8	39	30	3	21	43	12.7	25.9	1.30	.211
2025	22	Brooklyn (SAL)	A+	1	3	1.70	14	13	64	45	3	28	77	10.8	29.7	1.15	.199
2025	22	Binghamton (EL)	AA	2	2	3.44	4	2	18	13	2	9	22	12.2	29.7	1.20	.200
		Minor League Totals		4	9	2.61	30	23	124	90	9	58	145	11.4	28.5	1.19	.203

17 ELI SERRANO III, OF

HIT: 40. **POW:** 50. **RUN:** 55. **FLD:** 55. **ARM:** 50. **BA Grade:** 50. **Risk:** High. **Adj:** 35.

Born: May 1, 2003. **B-T:** L-L. **HT:** 6-6. **WT:** 200. **Drafted:** NC State, 2024 (4th round). **Signed by:** Daniel Coles.
TRACK RECORD: Serrano is the son of former Stetson catcher and Giants 1998 second-round pick Sammy Serrano. Eli spent two years at NC State before the Mets drafted him in the fourth round in 2024. He turned heads in his first full season in 2025, serving as leadoff hitter and versatile outfielder for a dynamic High-A Brooklyn lineup that dominated the South Atlantic League in the first half and hung on to win the league title.
SCOUTING REPORT: Serrano is a 6-foot-6 lefthanded hitter with a well-rounded batting profile. In 2025, he batted .243/.366/.441 through May 23 while playing half his games in a brutal Brooklyn home park. He rolled his ankle at the end of May and had just a .604 OPS the rest of the way. Serrano does a good job staying within the strike zone and limiting in-zone whiff rate (17%) for such a long-levered hitter. He hits the ball hard and keeps it off the ground. If he can improve his ability to sync his swing and pull the ball in the air, he could reach 20-plus home runs. Serrano is an above-average runner who has above-average range in center field and an average arm that plays at all three outfield spots. Despite his speed, he hasn't shown a knack for stealing bases in college or pro ball.
THE FUTURE: Serrano is a sum-of-his-parts player with no major flaw and no single outstanding attribute. As he continues to develop, he could emerge as a contributor to a big league outfield mix, most likely as a platoon option versus righthanders.

Year	Age	Club (League)	Level	AVG	G	AB	R	H	2B	3B	HR	RBI	BB	SO	SB	OBP	SLG
2025	22	Brooklyn (SAL)	A+	.222	88	324	51	72	21	1	7	46	50	77	9	.332	.358
		Minor League Totals		.222	88	324	51	72	21	1	7	46	50	77	9	.332	.358

18 MARCO VARGAS, SS/2B

HIT: 45. **POW:** 30. **RUN:** 55. **FLD:** 65. **ARM:** 60. **BA Grade:** 45. **Risk:** Average. **Adj:** 35.

Born: May 14, 2005. **B-T:** L-R. **HT:** 5-11. **WT:** 179. **Signed:** Mexico, 2022. **Signed by:** Andres Guzman/Adrian Puig (Marlins).
TRACK RECORD: Signed by the Marlins out of Mexico in 2022, Vargas joined the Mets organization a year later in the trade that sent closer David Robertson to Miami. Vargas missed most of his first full year with the club in 2024 after suffering a wrist injury. Back at it in 2025, he ripped through Low-A St. Lucie to earn a quick promotion to High-A Brooklyn. His surface production was tepid, but he maintained a high walk rate and stole 38 bases in 95 games.
SCOUTING REPORT: Vargas is known for his strong bat-to-ball skills and his outstanding glove. He now stands as the best defensive infielder in the Mets' minor league system, with outstanding range, sure hands and a strong arm to handle both shortstop and second base at a plus level. Vargas does a good job swinging at strikes and making contact, but he didn't have much to show for it in 2025, with a .258/.352/.323 batting line. Adding bat speed and a better understanding of which pitches he can drive will help, but Vargas will always be a hit-over-power, on-base-oriented hitter. He's an above-average runner and a threat to steal.
THE FUTURE: Vargas' fielding skill buys him time to develop his bat, but for now he's trending toward a backup infielder or utility role.

Year	Age	Club (League)	Level	AVG	G	AB	R	H	2B	3B	HR	RBI	BB	SO	SB	OBP	SLG
2025	20	St. Lucie (FSL)	A	.409	13	44	14	18	3	0	1	5	10	7	2	.527	.545
2025	20	Brooklyn (SAL)	A+	.239	95	355	45	85	9	4	1	42	48	82	38	.328	.296
		Minor League Totals		.267	252	904	166	241	43	8	6	120	180	197	80	.387	.352

19 BOSTON BARO, SS/3B
HIT: 50. **POW:** 30. **RUN:** 55. **FLD:** 50. **ARM:** 55. **BA Grade:** 45. **Risk:** Average. **Adj:** 40.

Born: August 23, 2004. **B-T:** L-R. **HT:** 6-2. **WT:** 185. **Drafted:** HS—Mission Viejo, CA, 2023 (8th round).
Signed by: Glenn Walker.
TRACK RECORD: The Mets went over slot to sign Baro out of a UCLA commitment in the eighth round in 2023. He had a productive first full season in 2024, mostly at Low-A St. Lucie, in which he hit for average, drew walks and played three infield positions. Baro's 2025 season started on a strong note when he hit an opposite-field home run against Nationals lefthander Alex Clemmey in the teams' Spring Breakout exhibition, but his season at High-A Brooklyn was a struggle from beginning to end.
SCOUTING REPORT: Despite owning a picturesque lefthanded swing and improving his bat speed and high-end exit velocity in 2025, Baro could never seem to get going at Brooklyn. He finished the year with worse surface numbers across the board than he had in 2024. The Mets point to swing decisions as the culprit. His swing rate and chase rate both increased sharply in 2025 as he hunted outside the zone to do damage. The lean, 6-foot-2 Baro will need to continue adding strength to his frame to access even 10-home run power. He makes enough contact at good angles to become an average hitter. Baro is a natural shortstop who has branched out to third base, where his above-average arm plays, and second base, where his range and hands fit. He doesn't have classic shortstop actions and probably settles into a multi-position role. Baro is an above-average runner and proficient basestealer.
THE FUTURE: Baro does a lot of things well but nothing exemplary, and many scouts see him becoming a lefthanded-hitting super-utility player.

Year	Age	Club (League)	Level	AVG	G	AB	R	H	2B	3B	HR	RBI	BB	SO	SB	OBP	SLG
2025	20	Brooklyn (SAL)	A+	.224	103	393	43	88	16	5	4	38	31	88	28	.282	.321
		Minor League Totals		.252	205	779	100	196	37	10	8	87	82	165	37	.323	.356

20 ANTONIO JIMENEZ, SS
HIT: 40. **POW:** 50. **RUN:** 55. **FLD:** 55. **ARM:** 60. **BA Grade:** 50. **Risk:** High. **Adj:** 35.

Born: June 15, 2004. **B-T:** R-R. **HT:** 6-1. **WT:** 200. **Drafted:** Central Florida, 2025 (3rd round). **Signed by:** Cesar Aranguren.
TRACK RECORD: Jimenez played his freshman year at Miami before transferring to Central Florida in 2025, following a stopover in the Cape Cod League. He blossomed as a hitter with regular play as the Knights' shortstop, batting .329/.407/.575 with 11 home runs in 55 games. The Mets drafted Jimenez in the third round and signed him for an under-slot $564,000. He and first-rounder Mitch Voit formed the double-play duo for Low-A St. Lucie through the Florida State League playoffs.
SCOUTING REPORT: Jimenez is an aggressive righthanded hitter who has made progress in recent years dialing in his strike zone and finding the barrel more often. He is not a finished product by any means but does a good job swinging at strikes and keeping strikeouts in check. Jimenez hit five homers with wood bats in the 2024 Cape Cod League and performed well against velocity in the Big 12 Conference, but he will need to improve his batted-ball angles in pro ball to reduce his groundball rate and get to his average power potential. Jimenez is a sound defensive shortstop with a plus arm. He played the position in 17 of 26 games during his pro debut for Low-A St. Lucie, while also seeing time at third base. Some scouts think he will fit better at third base in the long run. Jimenez is an above-average runner who can steal the occasional base.
THE FUTURE: Jimenez has tools—power, fielding and throwing—that could carry him up the minor league ladder if he develops them. If it comes together, he could become a big league option at shortstop or third base.

Year	Age	Club (League)	Level	AVG	G	AB	R	H	2B	3B	HR	RBI	BB	SO	SB	OBP	SLG
2025	21	St. Lucie (FSL)	A	.263	26	95	12	25	1	0	0	14	12	15	8	.345	.274
		Minor League Totals		.263	26	95	12	25	1	0	0	14	12	15	8	.345	.274

21 RANDY GUZMAN, 1B/OF
HIT: 30. **POW:** 65. **RUN:** 30. **FLD:** 40. **ARM:** 50. **BA Grade:** 50. **Risk:** High. **Adj:** 35.

Born: April 19, 2005. **B-T:** R-R. **HT:** 6-4. **WT:** 215. **Signed:** Dominican Republic, 2022. **Signed by:** Kelvin Dominguez.
TRACK RECORD: Guzman is the younger brother of former Rangers first baseman Ronald Guzman. Randy signed for just $10,000 out of the Dominican Republic in September 2022 and did not make his pro debut until he was 18. Guzman hit just .186 with a .648 OPS in two Dominican Summer League seasons but went on a power binge in 2025 that carried him from the Florida Complex League to Low-A St. Lucie. He hit 10 home runs in 75 total games and slugged .604 in a 26-game sample in the Florida State League to close the season.

SCOUTING REPORT: Guzman is a mature-bodied, 6-foot-4 righthanded hitter with a good blend of contact and impact for a player of his size. What sets him apart are his strong work ethic and high-end bat speed. The Mets say that Guzman already has a mid-70s mph average swing speed, which is where high-end MLB sluggers live. Like many young hitters, Guzman chases too often, but when he swings at strikes, he makes a lot of impactful contact. His zone-contact rate of 82% was good for a young power hitter, while his 90th percentile exit velocity of 108 mph trailed only Ryan Clifford among Mets minor leaguers in 2025. Guzman isn't much of a runner and is limited defensively to first base or possibly an outfield corner if he doesn't lose too much mobility as he ages.
THE FUTURE: Guzman's late power surge as a 20-year-old and his contact/impact hitting profile engender hope that he can take another step forward at his Class A assignments in 2026.

Year	Age	Club (League)	Level	AVG	G	AB	R	H	2B	3B	HR	RBI	BB	SO	SB	OBP	SLG
2025	20	FCL Mets	Rk	.282	49	156	18	44	9	0	7	33	15	33	0	.371	.474
2025	20	St. Lucie (FSL)	A	.333	26	96	15	32	13	2	3	24	6	21	2	.381	.604
		Minor League Totals		.249	142	462	56	115	34	3	15	80	60	138	3	.351	.433

22 FRANKLIN GOMEZ, LHP

FB: 50. **SL:** 60. **CH:** 55. **SW:** 50. **CTL:** 45. **BA Grade:** 50. **Risk:** High. **Adj:** 35.

Born: July 6, 2005. **B-T:** L-L. **HT:** 5-10. **WT:** 220. **Signed:** Venezuela, 2022. **Signed by:** Andres Nuñez.
TRACK RECORD: The Mets signed Gomez out of Venezuela for $10,000 in 2022. When he debuted in the Dominican Summer League that year he was still just 16 years old. He spent another season in Rookie ball and then one in Low-A, working mostly as a starter. When Gomez returned to St. Lucie to open 2025, Mets pitching coordinator Kyle Rogers challenged him to improve his velocity to lock in a rotation spot. Gomez put in the work and his velocity improved sharply as he pitched his way to High-A Brooklyn in August.
SCOUTING REPORT: Gomez is a thicker 5-foot-10 lefthander whose fastball averaged 92-93 mph in 2025, which was up nearly three ticks compared with an average of 90 mph in 2024. His cutter and two-seamer made similar velo jumps. Gomez has advanced feel for a pair of sliders, including a sweepy low-80s slider with depth he can use to back-foot righthanded hitters. He sells a mid-80s changeup that features outstanding fade at its best. Young and still learning to pitch with enhanced stuff, Gomez showed below-average control in 2025. He never exceeded 79 pitches in an appearance and seldom got all the way through the lineup twice, but the growth he showed in 2025 was a positive sign for his development.
THE FUTURE: Gomez impressed the Mets with his work ethic and improved arsenal in 2025. He will be 20 years old when 2026 opens, most likely with him in the Brooklyn rotation. Gomez looks like a future starter, though his strong secondary pitches and handedness give him a fallback as a leverage reliever.

Year	Age	Club (League)	Level	W	L	ERA	G	GS	IP	H	HR	BB	SO	BB%	SO%	WHIP	AVG
2025	19	St. Lucie (FSL)	A	3	1	1.85	14	7	49	30	1	23	42	11.7	21.4	1.09	.178
2025	19	Brooklyn (SAL)	A+	0	2	4.70	6	6	23	31	1	11	26	9.9	23.4	1.83	.330
		Minor League Totals		13	20	3.39	69	47	239	213	9	113	264	10.9	25.4	1.37	.237

23 JONATHAN PINTARO, RHP

FB: 50. **CH:** 40. **CT:** 55. **SW:** 55. **CTL:** 40. **BA Grade:** 40. **Risk:** Mild. **Adj:** 35.

Born: November 7, 1997. **B-T:** R-R. **HT:** 6-2. **WT:** 235. **Signed:** Pioneer League, 2024. **Signed by:** Jaymie Bane.
TRACK RECORD: Pintaro has one of the more remarkable origin stories. He pitched for Division II Shorter in Georgia for five seasons in the span of six years before spending 2023 in the independent Pioneer League. He headed back to the league in 2024, when the Mets signed him on June 3 after three starts. Pintaro quickly pitched his way into the High-A Brooklyn rotation and reached Double-A and then Triple-A for one start. For an encore in 2025, Pintaro made 11 Double-A starts before the Mets called him up to make one relief appearance on June 25. He spent the rest of the season at Triple-A Syracuse, working mostly as a reliever.
SCOUTING REPORT: Pintaro has an east-west pitching profile and a low three-quarters arm slot that makes him deadly in same-side matchups but vulnerable to lefthanded batters. His platoon splits in 2025 paint the picture. Across all levels, he allowed a .189 average and .597 OPS to righthanders; the corresponding figures versus lefties were .305 and .929. Pintaro throws mostly fastballs and sliders, altering his looks by shuffling between mid-90s four-seamers and sinkers and a low-90s cutter, while throwing a low-80s sweeper to expand the zone. His cutter and sweeper are above-average weapons. Working as a starter forced him to throw a below-average changeup that draws whiffs when he's ahead in the count. Pintaro works only from the stretch and sets up on the extreme third base side of the rubber. His control is below-average.

NEW YORK METS

THE FUTURE: Pintaro's future is in the bullpen, where he can be effective when spotted against a string of mostly righthanded batters. He should log big league innings in 2026.

Year	Age	Club (League)	Level	W	L	ERA	G	GS	IP	H	HR	BB	SO	BB%	SO%	WHIP	AVG
2025	27	Binghamton (EL)	AA	0	2	3.40	11	11	42	32	4	15	57	8.8	33.3	1.11	.212
2025	27	Syracuse (IL)	AAA	2	3	5.22	17	5	40	37	5	29	46	15.8	25.0	1.66	.250
2025	27	New York (NL)	MLB	0	0	27.00	1	0	1	2	0	2	1	33.3	16.7	6.00	.500
		Minor League Totals		5	11	3.52	45	31	156	127	12	72	178	10.9	26.8	1.28	.224
		Major League Totals		0	0	27.00	1	0	1	2	0	2	1	33.3	16.7	6.00	.500

24 R.J. GORDON, RHP

FB: 50. **CB:** 45. **SL:** 55. **CH:** 60. **CTL:** 50. **BA Grade:** 45. **Risk:** Average. **Adj:** 35.

Born: October 26, 2001. **B-T:** R-R. **HT:** 6-0. **WT:** 210. **Drafted:** Oregon, 2024 (13th round). **Signed by:** Rich Morales.

TRACK RECORD: Gordon is a SoCal high school product who pitched collegiately for four years at Oregon, missing his junior year after having an internal brace procedure on his elbow. The Mets drafted Gordon in the 13th round in 2024, and he raced to Double-A Binghamton in his pro debut the following year. He finished the year in the rotation for the Eastern League champions on the heels of a season in which his 147 strikeouts trailed only Jonah Tong among Mets minor leaguers.

SCOUTING REPORT: Gordon has added a bit of velocity since signing but is more of a command-and-control starter than a power-oriented one. He took to the Mets' pitching development philosophy of attacking the middle of the zone and letting the action on his pitches do the work. His walk rate dropped from near 11% as an Oregon senior to 8.5% in his pro debut. Gordon pitches at 92-93 mph and can muscle up to 96 but uses his four-seamer mostly to set up his secondary pitches. He kills spin on a low-80s changeup that gets at least 10 mph of separation and shows armside life. Gordon throws his mid-80s slider more than any pitch and commands it for called strikes and chases below the zone, sometimes throwing a sweepier version. He also mixes in an occasional mid-70s curveball.

THE FUTURE: Gordon has succeeded against minor league hitters with command and pitch variety, making him a prospective back-of-the-rotation option or swingman in the big leagues.

Year	Age	Club (League)	Level	W	L	ERA	G	GS	IP	H	HR	BB	SO	BB%	SO%	WHIP	AVG
2025	23	Brooklyn (SAL)	A+	5	2	3.06	15	11	68	60	8	31	76	10.6	26.0	1.34	.233
2025	23	Binghamton (EL)	AA	6	1	3.69	11	10	61	53	7	15	71	6.1	28.7	1.11	.231
		Minor League Totals		11	3	3.36	26	21	129	113	15	46	147	8.5	27.3	1.24	.232

25 DAIVERSON GUTIERREZ, C

HIT: 40. **POW:** 30. **RUN:** 30. **FLD:** 55. **ARM:** 55. **BA Grade:** 45. **Risk:** High. **Adj:** 30.

Born: September 11, 2005. **B-T:** R-R. **HT:** 6-0. **WT:** 225. **Signed:** Venezuela, 2023. **Signed by:** Andres Nuñez.

TRACK RECORD: The Mets made Gutierrez their top target in their 2023 international class, signing the Venezuelan catcher for $1.9 million. He advanced through the Rookie levels in 2023 and 2024, showing advanced on-base skills. Gutierrez earned his first Opening Day full-season assignment in 2025, and the 19-year-old finished his season at Low-A St. Lucie with 86 games caught, more than any other Mets minor league catcher and the highest total by a teenager in the 2020s.

SCOUTING REPORT: Gutierrez has strong bat-to-ball skills and a disciplined approach. His 13.4% walk rate was one of the highest in the Mets' system in 2025. He tends to put too many pitcher's pitches in play, resulting in a lot of contact that lacks authority and preempts his average raw power. Tapping into more power will be a key focus in 2026. Gutierrez has the defensive chops to potentially carry him to an MLB role even if his bat stagnates. He shines as a blocker and pitch framer and has an above-average arm. Working on throwing accuracy is a development goal for him.

THE FUTURE: Gutierrez's journey continues at High-A Brooklyn in 2026 as he builds reps on his long climb up the minor league ladder. His profile at this stage most resembles a future backup catcher.

Year	Age	Club (League)	Level	AVG	G	AB	R	H	2B	3B	HR	RBI	BB	SO	SB	OBP	SLG
2025	19	St. Lucie (FSL)	A	.242	91	327	54	79	10	0	4	41	53	58	6	.362	.309
		Minor League Totals		.229	178	607	95	139	27	0	8	76	91	112	9	.356	.313

NEW YORK METS

26 TREY SNYDER, 2B/3B
HIT: 45. **POW:** 30. **RUN:** 55. **FLD:** 50. **ARM:** 55. **BA Grade:** 45. **Risk:** High. **Adj:** 30.

Born: September 21, 2005. **B-T:** R-R. **HT:** 6-1. **WT:** 197. **Drafted:** HS—Liberty, MO, 2024 (5th round).
Signed by: Trey Cobb.
TRACK RECORD: The Mets made Snyder a focal point of their 2024 draft class, the first under scouting director Kris Gross. The Mets drafted Carson Benge and Jonathan Santucci in the first and second rounds and paid them their top two bonuses. Their third-highest went to Snyder, a Kansas City-area high school shortstop whom they drafted in the fifth round. Snyder spent the entire 2025 season with Low-A St. Lucie, and while he hit just .220 with five home runs in 115 games, he stole 41 bases and drew 72 walks, both of which ranked third in the Mets' system.
SCOUTING REPORT: As Snyder grinded through his first full season in the Florida State League, the Mets were impressed with his work ethic and resiliency in a growth season. As a prep, he had a reputation as a hit-over-power player with more of a line-drive, lower launch-angle attack, which has proved to be accurate in pro ball. For a young hitter, Snyder manages the strike zone well and shows above-average bat-to-ball skills. The Mets will continue to try to coax more exit velocity and pulled-flyball contact out of him, especially because he is not a lock to stick at shortstop. He played more second base and third base for St. Lucie, and his above-average arm and fundamentals give him a chance at average infield defense. He played a handful of games in center field down the stretch and in the FSL playoffs. Snyder is more of an above-average runner but a smart and aggressive basestealer.
THE FUTURE: As Snyder enters his third pro season, the Mets will be looking for the 20-year-old to begin to make adjustments on his own. It will be a crucial season for him to show growth at the plate.

Year	Age	Club (League)	Level	AVG	G	AB	R	H	2B	3B	HR	RBI	BB	SO	SB	OBP	SLG
2025	19	St. Lucie (FSL)	A	.220	115	431	58	95	12	1	5	48	72	96	41	.336	.288
		Minor League Totals		.219	121	453	63	99	12	1	5	51	76	102	42	.335	.283

27 DYLAN ROSS, RHP
FB: 60. **CB:** 40. **SL:** 50. **SP:** 60. **CTL:** 30. **BA Grade:** 40. **Risk:** Average. **Adj:** 30.

Born: September 1, 2000. **B-T:** R-R. **HT:** 6-5. **WT:** 250. **Drafted:** Georgia, 2022 (13th round). **Signed by:** Marlin McPhail.
TRACK RECORD: Ross was high school teammates with Guardians prospect Daniel Espino at Georgia Premier Academy. He pitched briefly at Eastern Kentucky in 2020 before the pandemic wiped out the season and then moved to Northwest Florida State JC in 2021, making 12 starts. Ross transferred to Georgia in 2022 and made two starts before succumbing to Tommy John surgery. The Mets drafted him in the 13th round that year. While rehabbing in 2023, Ross required UCL revision surgery that cost him even more time. He returned in September 2024, making one appearance for Low-A St. Lucie. Healthy in 2025, he marched through three levels, striking out 80 in 54 innings. The Mets called him up on Sept. 27 but did not pitch him in the final two games.
SCOUTING REPORT: Ross is a physical 6-foot-5 righthander who goes after hitters with a 96-98 mph fastball that has touched 101, and he backs it up with a complement of two swing-and-miss secondary pitches. He threw his low-90s splitter more than any pitch in 2025 and commands it for called strikes and chases. His splitter gets up near 95 mph and is effective in part because of its extremely low spin rate in the 800 rpm range. Ross throws a power slider in the high 80s that he uses to expand the zone and elicit chase. He throws a curveball left over from his starter days but doesn't need it much in relief. He walked nearly 15% of batters in 2025 and just wasn't in the zone much with any of his pitches.
THE FUTURE: Ross' control will need to improve to be entrusted with high-leverage relief work, but he made a lot of progress in what was effectively his pro debut in 2025. He will be in play for MLB innings.

Year	Age	Club (League)	Level	W	L	ERA	G	GS	IP	H	HR	BB	SO	BB%	SO%	WHIP	AVG
2025	24	Brooklyn (SAL)	A+	2	0	1.54	10	0	12	8	0	8	23	15.4	44.2	1.37	.182
2025	24	Binghamton (EL)	AA	0	0	4.35	11	0	10	10	3	3	18	6.7	40.0	1.26	.244
2025	24	Syracuse (IL)	AAA	0	0	1.69	28	0	32	11	1	22	39	17.3	30.7	1.03	.107
		Minor League Totals		2	0	2.17	49	0	54	29	4	33	80	14.7	35.7	1.15	.154

28 JEREMY RODRIGUEZ, SS/2B
HIT: 45. **POW:** 30. **RUN:** 50. **FLD:** 50. **ARM:** 50. **BA Grade:** 45. **Risk:** High. **Adj:** 30.

Born: July 4, 2006. **B-T:** L-R. **HT:** 6-0. **WT:** 170. **Signed:** Dominican Republic, 2023.
Signed by: Cesar Geronimo Jr./Peter Wardell/Jose Ortiz (D-backs).
TRACK RECORD: Rodriguez signed with the Diamondbacks for $1.25 million in 2023 and debuted in the Dominican Summer League as a 16-year-old. Arizona traded him to the Mets that summer for Tommy

Pham in a season in which it went on to win the National League pennant. Rodriguez spent the 2025 season as the primary shortstop for Low-A St. Lucie in his first taste of full-season ball. He was 18 years old for the first half of the season, and his youth showed in his .202/.304/.236 batting line.
SCOUTING REPORT: Youth and the best bat-to-ball skills in the system are Rodriguez's biggest selling points. He is a lean, 6-foot lefthanded hitter with a good eye for the strike zone and a swing geared for contact to all fields. He had one of the highest groundball rates and lowest pull rates among Mets minor leaguers with at least 400 plate appearances in 2025. Rodriguez will have to add significant strength and enhance his intent to do damage to reach even below-average power. On the plus side, he upped his high-end exit velocity readings in 2025. Rodriguez is a capable defender at shortstop but better at second base with sound hands and an average arm. He is an average runner.
THE FUTURE: Unless he finds another gear offensively, Rodriguez is trending toward a hit-over-power utility type of profile.

Year	Age	Club (League)	Level	AVG	G	AB	R	H	2B	3B	HR	RBI	BB	SO	SB	OBP	SLG
2025	18	St. Lucie (FSL)	A	.202	112	420	56	85	7	2	1	40	60	94	34	.304	.236
		Minor League Totals		.242	213	782	118	189	27	9	7	93	114	162	70	.340	.326

29 PETER KUSSOW, RHP
FB: 55. **CB:** 40. **SL:** 55. **CH:** 45. **CTL:** 50. **BA Grade:** 50. **Risk:** Extreme. **Adj:** 30.

Born: December 8, 2006. **B-T:** R-R. **HT:** 6-5. **WT:** 205. **Drafted:** HS—Hartland, WI, 2025 (4th round). **Signed by:** Chad Langley.
TRACK RECORD: Kussow emerged as the top high school talent from Wisconsin in the 2025 draft and wound up being the only player from the state selected when the Mets drafted him in the fourth round. New York went more than $340,000 over slot to sign him away from a Louisville commitment for $555,800. Kussow represented a departure from recent draft strategy for the Mets, who had not gone over slot to sign a high school pitcher since committing a combined $4.65 million to sign Josh Wolf and Matt Allan in 2019.
SCOUTING REPORT: Kussow has a lanky 6-foot-5 build and good extension down the mound. He grew into velocity as an Arrowhead Union High senior. After pitching at 89-90 mph on the 2024 showcase circuit, Kussow raised the bar to 93-95 mph with a max of 97 as a senior. His most prized secondary pitch is his high-80s slider, which he can throw early in counts or late for chase. Like most prep righthanders, he is only just beginning to incorporate a changeup. He also has shown a breaking pitch with more of a 12-to-6 curveball shape.
THE FUTURE: It will be years before the Mets know for sure what they have in Kussow, but year three in 2027 will be an important checkpoint in his development. He represents a new challenge for a Mets player development apparatus that hasn't worked with many high school pitchers.

Year	Age	Club (League)	Level	W	L	ERA	G	GS	IP	H	HR	BB	SO	BB%	SO%	WHIP	AVG
2025	18	Did not play															

30 CAM TILLY, RHP
FB: 50. **CB:** 40. **SW:** 60. **SP:** 70. **CTL:** 40. **BA Grade:** 45. **Risk:** High. **Adj:** 30.

Born: June 27, 2004. **B-T:** R-R. **HT:** 6-2. **WT:** 207. **Drafted:** Auburn, 2025 (7th round). **Signed by:** Jet Butler.
TRACK RECORD: Tilly pitched for two seasons at Auburn, where 27 of his 33 appearances came in relief. As a draft-eligible sophomore in 2025 he made six starts among his 19 appearances and struck out 58 in 46 innings. The Mets drafted Tilly in the seventh round and went over slot to sign him for $397,500. They will probably give him a chance to start in pro ball.
SCOUTING REPORT: Tilly's standout pitch is his mid-80s splitter. It features dramatic drop, and he locates it well enough for zone-whiff and chases, making it a true out pitch. The Mets put a big grade on that pitch as well as his sweeper, which features late bite and two-plane break in the low 80s. Tilly pitches at 92-94 mph and touches 97, and the Mets believe they can help him develop his fastball—or perhaps fastballs—to play against batters of both hands. He also throws a mid-70s curveball that would become more prominent in a starting role. Control has been a problem for Tilly dating back to high school in Indiana. Improving it will be another area of focus.
THE FUTURE: The Mets have cultivated college pitchers who were predominantly relievers—ranging from Christian Scott to Nolan McLean to Will Watson—into productive pro starters. Tilly could be one of the next projects in that line.

Year	Age	Club (League)	Level	W	L	ERA	G	GS	IP	H	HR	BB	SO	BB%	SO%	WHIP	AVG
2025	21	Did not play															

Jasson Dominguez

New York Yankees

BY JOSH NORRIS

As has been the case for most of the last 16 seasons since their last championship, the Yankees in 2025 were good . . . just not good enough.

After coming a tiebreaker away from winning the American League East, New York topped Boston in the Wild Card Series but fell in the next round to eventual pennant-winner Toronto.

The team weathered the spring training loss of ace Gerrit Cole to Tommy John surgery and the midseason loss of righty Clarke Schmidt to the same procedure. The push to make the postseason didn't come cheap. GM Brian Cashman unloaded 15 prospects to acquire relievers Camilo Doval and David Bednar, third baseman Ryan McMahon, outfielder Austin Slater and infielders Amed Rosario and Jose Caballero.

As a result, the Yankees' farm system is as shallow as it's been in years. But it's not empty. Shortstop George Lombard Jr. and righthanders Elmer Rodriguez and Carlos Lagrange should contribute in the coming years, and 2025 first-rounder Dax Kilby earned rave reviews in his brief pro debut.

The biggest enigma in the system is Spencer Jones, a hulking lefthanded hitter with light-tower power who went on a smashing spree in the weeks ahead of the trade deadline. Even with that outburst, he struck out a system-worst 179 times. His upside is among the highest in the organization, and it's easy to envision him in the middle of the Yankees' lineup. It's also easy to envision him never making enough contact to escape the minor leagues.

Though they have produced plenty of players who were used in trades to supplement the big league roster, the Yankees signaled their displeasure with the team's international program when they fired director Donny Rowland, who had spent 15 years in the role and more than two decades as a member of the organization.

PROJECTED 2029 LINEUP

Catcher	Austin Wells	29
First Base	Ben Rice	30
Second Base	Dax Kilby	22
Third Base	George Lombard Jr.	24
Shortstop	Anthony Volpe	28
Left Field	Spencer Jones	26
Center Field	Dillon Lewis	28
Right Field	Aaron Judge	37
Designated Hitter	Jasson Dominguez	26
No. 1 Starter	Max Fried	35
No. 2 Starter	Cam Schlittler	28
No. 3 Starter	Elmer Rodriguez	25
No. 4 Starter	Luis Gil	31
No. 5 Starter	Will Warren	30
Closer	Carlos Lagrange	26

The Yankees also fired big league coaches Mike Harkey and Travis Chapman and replaced them with Jake Hirst, who had been the team's minor league hitting coordinator, and Desi Druschel, who spent a season with the Mets after being on the Yankees' staff from 2022 to 2024.

The biggest win from the farm was the emergence of 24-year-old righthander Cam Schlittler, who added velocity and turned in one of the best postseason performances in franchise history when he spun eight shutout innings with 12 strikeouts and no walks in an elimination game against Boston in the Wild Card Series. Top prospect outfielder Jasson Dominguez was a regular part of the lineup for most of the season, but defensive liabilities made him the odd man out down the stretch.

Time and again, the Yankees have come close to securing their 28th World Series championship. They've developed homegrown stars, signed big-money free agents and been aggressive in trades. Since 2009, all that's added up to is frustration.

The next wave of reinforcements is on its way, but the Blue Jays and Red Sox have accumulated enough firepower to make the division a jungle of juggernauts for the foreseeable future.

To get back to the promised land, ownership and the front office will have to be aggressive and creative on all fronts. A little bit more help from the farm would also go a long way. ■

DEPTH CHART

NEW YORK YANKEES

TOP 2026 ROOKIES — RANK
1. Elmer Rodriguez, RHP — 2
2. Carlos Lagrange, RHP — 4

BREAKOUT PROSPECTS — RANK
1. Mac Heuer, RHP — 12
2. Jack Cebert, RHP — 19

SOURCE OF TOP 30 TALENT

Homegrown	27	Acquired	3
College	12	Trade	3
Junior college	1	Rule 5 draft	0
High school	4	Independent league	0
Undrafted free agent	3	Free agent/waivers	0
International	7		

LF
Brando Mayea (27)

CF
Spencer Jones (6)
Dillon Lewis (8)
Brendan Jones (13)

RF
Francisco Vilorio (23)
Jace Avina (25)
Wilson Rodriguez
Estivenzon Montero

3B
Dylan Jasso (26)
Roderick Arias
Richard Matic

SS
George Lombard Jr. (1)
Stiven Marinez (22)
Core Jackson
Bryce Martin-Grudzielanek
Jackson Lovich
Mani Cedeño

2B
Dax Kilby (3)
Kaeden Kent (16)
Enmanuel Tejeda
Juan Matheus
Juan Torres

1B
Engelth Ureña
T.J. Rumfield

C
Ediel Rivera
Queni Pineda
Manuel Palencia

LHP

LHSP	LHRP
Brock Selvidge (14)	Xavier Rivas (24)
Kyle Carr (15)	Allen Facundo (28)
Pico Kohn (17)	Franyer Herrera
Henry Lalane (21)	

RHP

RHSP	RHRP
Elmer Rodriguez (2)	Carlos Lagrange (4)
Ben Hess (5)	Cade Winquest (18)
Bryce Cunningham (7)	Harrison Cohen (20)
Thatcher Hurd (9)	Jose M. Rodriguez (29)
Chase Hampton (10)	Carson Coleman (30)
Cade Smith (11)	Brian Hendry
Mac Heuer (12)	Tony Rossi
Jack Cebert (19)	Kevin Stevens
Wyatt Parliament	Thomas Balboni Jr.
J.T. Etheridge	Eric Reyzelman
Brendan Beck	Sabier Marte
	Jordarlin Mendoza
	Michael Arias

NEW YORK YANKEES

1 GEORGE LOMBARD JR., SS

Born: June 2, 2005. **B-T:** R-R. **HT:** 6-3. **WT:** 205.
Drafted: HS—Pinecrest, FL, 2023 (1st round).
Signed by: Ronnie Merrill.

TRACK RECORD: The son of the former big leaguer and current Tigers bench coach by the same name, Lombard was a multi-sport athlete at Gulliver Prep in the Miami area. He was the Yankees' first-round pick in 2023, joining Anthony Volpe (2019) and Dax Kilby (2024) as prep shortstops New York has selected in the first round in recent years. Lombard split his first full season between both Class A stops in 2024. He was one of the buzziest players in spring training 2025, and he carried that momentum into the first part of his season. After blitzing the South Atlantic League for a .329/.495/.488 line over 24 games, Lombard was promoted to Double-A Somerset for the rest of the season. He struggled against more advanced competition but scouts still believe he has a chance to be a quality big leaguer. Lombard also earned a spot in the 2025 Futures Game.

SCOUTING REPORT: When Lombard was going well, scouts viewed him as a player with a polished all-around game and a skill set accentuated by the kind of makeup that comes with baseball bloodlines. He could hit for average and power in near-equal measure and has the skills to play an average big league shortstop with a bit more polish. Once Lombard reached Double-A, it became clear that the road to that ceiling might be a little longer than anticipated. He has bat-to-ball skills, but scouts who saw him in Double-A noted that he would get too passive at times and get himself into counts pitchers could exploit. His zone-miss rate was slightly elevated, but he did a good job throughout the season of staying disciplined and not chasing. His biggest issue right now is against elevated fastballs. According to data recorded by Synergy Sports, Lombard hit .169/.169/.260 on heaters in the upper third of the zone. Following the 2025 season, his goal was to increase his bat speed and alter his bat path in a way that allows him to handle the entire strike zone. Scouts also would like him to become more consistently direct to the ball instead of pulling off. He hits the ball hard enough—his 90th percentile exit velocity was 103.2 mph—but he rarely pulls it in the air, which will also be a point of focus in the coming years. Defensively, Lombard has the chops to play an average shortstop, but multiple scouts mentioned the possibility of moving to third base, where he could be an above-average defender with enough development time. His arm is average, but he needs to clean up his footwork, which sometimes causes his throws to get offline. Evaluators universally praise Lombard for his instincts and awareness on the diamond.

THE FUTURE: Lombard will likely return to Double-A to begin 2026. If he repeats last year's script, he'll nuke the level early and earn a quick jump to Triple-A. If he can get stronger and become a more complete hitter, he has a chance to be a well-rounded player who fits on the left side of the infield.

BA GRADE: 55 Risk: Average
Adjusted grade: 45
SCOUTING GRADES: Hit: 50. Power: 55. Run: 60. Field: 50. Arm: 50.
Projected future grades on 20-80 scouting scale

BEST TOOLS

BATTING
Best Hitter for Average — Dax Kilby
Best Power Hitter — Spencer Jones
Best Strike-Zone Discipline — George Lombard Jr.
Fastest Baserunner — Dax Kilby
Best Athlete — Dax Kilby

PITCHING
Best Fastball — Carlos Lagrange
Best Curveball — Elmer Rodriguez
Best Slider — Ben Hess
Best Changeup — Carlos Lagrange
Best Control — Elmer Rodriguez

FIELDING
Best Defensive Catcher — Ediel Rivera
Best Defensive Infielder — George Lombard Jr.
Best Infield Arm — Roderick Arias
Best Defensive Outfielder — Dillon Lewis
Best Outfield Arm — Dillon Lewis

Year	Age	Club (League)	Level	AVG	G	AB	R	H	2B	3B	HR	RBI	BB	SO	SB	OBP	SLG
2025	20	Hudson Valley (SAL)	A+	.329	24	82	22	27	8	1	1	13	23	22	11	.495	.488
2025	20	Somerset (EL)	AA	.215	108	391	68	84	24	4	8	36	64	124	24	.337	.358
		Minor League Totals		.236	255	943	155	223	59	7	14	100	161	272	78	.359	.358

NEW YORK YANKEES

2 ELMER RODRIGUEZ, RHP
FB: 60. **CB:** 55. **SL:** 50. **SW:** 55. **CT:** 50. **SP:** 50. **CTL:** 60. **BA Grade:** 55. **Risk:** Average. **Adj:** 45.

Born: August 18, 2003. **B-T:** R-R. **HT:** 6-4. **WT:** 160.
Drafted: HS—Guaynabo, PR, 2021 (4th round). **Signed by:** Edgar Perez (Red Sox)
TRACK RECORD: Rodriguez was initially drafted by the Red Sox in 2021 out of high school in Puerto Rico. The righthander ranked as the No. 10 prospect in the Florida Complex League the next year and steadily improved his stock as he moved up the ladder. He was dealt to the Yankees after the 2024 season in the trade that sent catcher Carlos Narvaez to Boston. After a breakout 2025 season that saw him strike out 176 hitters—the second-most in the minors—Rodriguez vaulted up the rankings and earned a spot on the Yankees' 40-man roster.
SCOUTING REPORT: Rodriguez marries a lanky, broad-shouldered, projectable frame with a diverse arsenal that helps him solve both righties and lefties. He throws a full complement of fastballs that includes four- and two-seamers as well as a cutter, and he backs them with a sweeper and a splitter he uses as his changeup. Both his sinker and four-seamer peaked in the upper 90s, and the cutter gave him an extra option he could use to land in the zone. Rodriguez's mid-70s, downer curve was his most-missed pitch at 45.2% and his changeup was his most-chased pitch at 36.2%. His splitter, sweeper and curveball each garnered miss rates north of 40%. His control improved after he moved from High-A to Double-A and has a chance to be plus once he reaches the big leagues. In addition to his ability to move his pitches around the zone, Rodriguez also earned praise from scouts for his competitive demeanor.
THE FUTURE: Rodriguez began the year in High-A and ended it with a cameo in Triple-A, where he should begin the 2026 season. He has a chance to make his big league debut at some point after midseason and could one day settle in as a midrotation starter with a chance for a little bit more depending on how his body fills out as he matures.

Year	Age	Club (League)	Level	W	L	ERA	G	GS	IP	H	HR	BB	SO	BB%	SO%	WHIP	AVG
2025	21	Hudson Valley (SAL)	A+	6	4	2.26	15	14	84	52	1	37	99	10.9	29.0	1.06	.174
2025	21	Somerset (EL)	AA	5	3	2.64	11	11	61	44	2	20	74	8.2	30.3	1.04	.198
2025	21	Scranton/WB (IL)	AAA	0	1	7.20	1	1	5	8	0	0	3	0.0	13.6	1.60	.381
		Minor League Totals		20	18	2.48	68	63	305	225	8	124	342	9.9	27.4	1.15	.203

3 DAX KILBY, SS
HIT: 60. **POW:** 55. **RUN:** 55. **FLD:** 50. **ARM:** 40. **BA Grade:** 60. **Risk:** High. **Adj:** 45.

Born: November 17, 2006. **B-T:** L-R. **HT:** 6-2. **WT:** 190.
Drafted: HS—Newnan, GA, 2025 (1st round). **Signed by:** Billy Godwin.
TRACK RECORD: Kilby checked in as the No. 75 prospect on BA's final ranking of the 2025 draft class, and the Yankees pounced on him with their first-round pick. They spent $2,797,500 to sign him away from a commitment to Clemson and then watched as he posted one of the best pro debuts of the summer. The lefty swinger hit .353/.457/.441 and finished with more walks (13) than strikeouts (11) in an 18-game pro debut at Low-A Tampa.
SCOUTING REPORT: Throughout the course of his time in the Florida State League, Kilby's play earned the praise of rival evaluators. In particular, scouts were wowed by the shortstop's ability to pair contact, impact and a keen knowledge of the strike zone. Kilby's in-zone miss and chase rates were each below 8%, and his overall miss rate was just 15%. All three marks ranged from above-average to elite. Kilby's swing is short, quick and powerful, and his swing decisions were excellent as well. In addition to his baseball skills, Kilby's athleticism—which he showed off in pre-draft workouts and after the season at the Yankees' fall instructional camp—ranged into outlier territory. That aspect of his game shows up in speed that ranks among the best in the system and a 40-inch vertical leap. Kilby is a shortstop for now but might need to move off the position as he moves up the ladder because of a stiffer arm slot and below-average arm that might push him to second base or the outfield one day.
THE FUTURE: After an outstanding first test in pro ball, Kilby has immediately shot into the upper echelon of the system's prospects and entered the offseason as one of the most up-arrow players to emerge from the 2025 draft class. He should split his 2026 season between the Class A levels and could finish the year as the system's No. 1 prospect.

Year	Age	Club (League)	Level	AVG	G	AB	R	H	2B	3B	HR	RBI	BB	SO	SB	OBP	SLG
2025	18	Tampa (FSL)	A	.353	18	68	19	24	2	2	0	9	13	11	16	.457	.441
		Minor League Totals		.353	18	68	19	24	2	2	0	9	13	11	16	.457	.441

NEW YORK YANKEES

4 CARLOS LAGRANGE, RHP
FB: 60. **SL:** 55. **SW:** 60. **CH:** 40. **CTL:** 45. **BA Grade:** 55. **Risk:** Average. **Adj:** 45.

Born: May 25, 2003. **B-T:** R-R. **HT:** 6-6. **WT:** 230.
Signed: Dominican Republic, 2022. **Signed by:** Luis Brito/Ethan Sander.
TRACK RECORD: Lagrange was one of the stars of the Yankees' 2023 Florida Complex League team thanks to a massive 6-foot-6 frame and a high-octane fastball. A back injury in 2024 limited him to just 21 innings in the regular season before a trip to the Arizona Fall League. Lagrange stayed healthy in 2025 and rung up 168 strikeouts in 120 innings. His strikeout total ranked third overall in the minor leagues behind Jonah Tong and Elmer Rodriguez. He also earned the starting nod against the Orioles in the teams' Spring Breakout meeting in March.
SCOUTING REPORT: Lagrange's game is based around a powerful fastball that averaged 98 mph and peaked at 102. Among pitchers who threw their four-seamers 400 or more times, just five registered the same kind of velocity as Lagrange. The righthander backs his fastball with both a gyro slider and sweeper and throws the latter nearly twice as often as the former. Occasionally the gyro version will lose its shape and appear cutterish. He rounds out his mix with a changeup that is effective because of an 8 mph separation from his fastball rather than standout action. Lagrange is a big-bodied, slow-twitch athlete who needs everything to sync up perfectly to find the zone with regularity. His long limbs also make it hard to repeat his delivery and release point often enough to project average control or command.
THE FUTURE: Lagrange split his season between High-A and Double-A and should spend most of 2026 at Triple-A. There, he will be tested by the automated ball-strike system and its smaller strike zone. He's likely to continue being developed as a starter, but scouts nearly universally believe his home is in the bullpen. In a reliever's role, Lagrange has the kind of stuff that make him a dominant force in the late innings and potentially a high-end closer.

Year	Age	Club (League)	Level	W	L	ERA	G	GS	IP	H	HR	BB	SO	BB%	SO%	WHIP	AVG
2025	22	Hudson Valley (SAL)	A+	4	2	4.10	8	8	42	31	4	12	64	7.1	38.1	1.03	.203
2025	22	Somerset (EL)	AA	7	6	3.22	16	15	78	51	4	50	104	14.9	31.0	1.29	.185
		Minor League Totals		11	9	3.84	51	47	201	130	14	112	282	13.1	32.9	1.20	.181

5 BEN HESS, RHP
FB: 55. **CB:** 50. **SL:** 60. **SW:** 40. **CH:** 50. **CTL:** 55. **BA Grade:** 50. **Risk:** Average. **Adj:** 40.

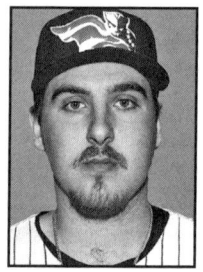

Born: September 3, 2002. **B-T:** R-R. **HT:** 6-4. **WT:** 255.
Drafted: Alabama, 2024 (1st round). **Signed by:** Chuck Bartlett.
TRACK RECORD: Hess was drafted in the first round in 2024 out of Alabama, where he spent the vast majority of his time as a member of the Crimson Tide's rotation. The Yankees were enthused enough by Hess' combination of stuff and reliability that they spent $2,747,500 to add him to their system. He didn't pitch after being drafted and then split his 2025 pro debut between High-A and Double-A. He was mostly healthy but missed about a month in May and June with a non-arm injury. He finished the year with 139 strikeouts in 103.1 innings.
SCOUTING REPORT: Hess' frame and arsenal give him the look of a classic workhorse who eats innings at the back of a rotation. His fastball sits around 93 mph and peaked at 97 and averaged 18.6 inches of induced vertical break, which helped it play as a potentially above-average pitch. His offspeed mix includes both gyro and sweeper sliders as well as a curveball and a changeup. Hess added the sweeper after he returned from injury as a way to give him breaking pitches that played both vertically and horizontally. Hess also worked with the Yankees to change the grip on his changeup to give it a deeper bottom. In concert, his slider is a potentially plus offering, but the rest of his mix mostly hovers between fringy and average. Hess' repertoire gives him avenues to attack lefties and righties in all quadrants of the strike zone. His goal in 2026 will be to continue to develop his sinker and turn his changeup into a pitch that can be effective against both lefties and righties.
THE FUTURE: After a successful first year in pro ball, Hess should split his 2026 sophomore season between the upper levels. With a little more refinement of his offspeed pitches, he could be the same kind of steady rotation presence as he was for three seasons in Tuscaloosa.

Year	Age	Club (League)	Level	W	L	ERA	G	GS	IP	H	HR	BB	SO	BB%	SO%	WHIP	AVG
2025	22	Hudson Valley (SAL)	A+	4	3	3.51	15	15	67	43	2	33	94	11.9	33.9	1.14	.179
2025	22	Somerset (EL)	AA	3	1	2.70	7	7	37	22	1	13	45	9.0	31.3	0.95	.172
		Minor League Totals		7	4	3.22	22	22	103	65	3	46	139	10.9	33.0	1.07	.177

NEW YORK YANKEES

6 SPENCER JONES, OF

HIT: 30. **POW:** 60. **RUN:** 60. **FLD:** 50. **ARM:** 50. **BA Grade:** 60. **Risk:** Extreme. **Adj:** 40.

Born: May 14, 2001. **B-T:** L-L. **HT:** 6-6. **WT:** 240.
Drafted: Vanderbilt, 2022 (1st round). **Signed by:** Chuck Bartlett.
TRACK RECORD: The Yankees drafted Jones in the first round in 2021 out of Vanderbilt, and he's spent his career flashing loud tools in spurts. In 2024, he became the first Yankees minor leaguer ever to strike out 200 times in a season. He added 179 more in a 2025 season split between Double-A and Triple-A, though he paid off the strikeouts with 35 home runs, the second-highest total in the minors. A scorching stretch around the trade deadline made it appear as if Jones had put it all together, but he struggled in August and September.
SCOUTING REPORT: Jones' scouting report is the same as ever: When everything is going well, he has the look of a five-tool player who can take a starring role in the center of a lineup. Most times, however, poor swing decisions and a long-levered 6-foot-6 frame lead to alarming levels of swing-and-miss that included a whiff rate of 42.6% that was tied with the Cubs' Alexey Lumpuy for the highest mark in the minors among players with 400 or more plate appearances. There have been hints of progress under the hood. Jones' miss rate with two strikes was around 30%, compared to roughly 50% in all other counts. He's also shown the ability to flatten his bat path somewhat, but there are plenty of times when he gets too uphill and becomes vulnerable to fastballs at the top of the zone and spin down and away. His swing decisions also need to improve. Jones tinkered with swings and stances throughout the year in an effort to find something that helped him winnow his strike zone without zapping his immense raw power. He is a plus runner who could provide average defense in center field as a young player.
THE FUTURE: Jones' array of outcomes is as wide as any prospect. If he can get to even fringy hittability, he could land on multiple all-star teams.

Year	Age	Club (League)	Level	AVG	G	AB	R	H	2B	3B	HR	RBI	BB	SO	SB	OBP	SLG
2025	24	Somerset (EL)	AA	.274	49	175	42	48	8	0	16	32	32	70	10	.389	.594
2025	24	Scranton/WB (IL)	AAA	.274	67	263	60	72	15	1	19	48	26	109	19	.342	.555
		Minor League Totals		.271	331	1318	225	357	80	11	56	204	140	484	99	.344	.476

7 BRYCE CUNNINGHAM, RHP

FB: 55. **CB:** 50. **SL:** 55. **CH:** 55. **CTL:** 55. **BA Grade:** 55. **Risk:** High. **Adj:** 40.

Born: December 20, 2002. **B-T:** R-R. **HT:** 6-4. **WT:** 235.
Drafted: Vanderbilt, 2024 (2nd round). **Signed by:** Ricky Castle.
TRACK RECORD: Cunningham's amateur career featured three excellent seasons with Vanderbilt and two tours in the Cape Cod League. In his freshman season, he was teammates with current Yankees prospects Spencer Jones and Greysen Carter. Cunningham struck out 96 hitters in 84.2 innings in his junior year with the Commodores, and the Yankees took him in the second round in 2024. He did not pitch after signing and spent his first pro year at High-A Hudson Valley. He missed about two months with a shoulder injury and made up some of those lost innings in the Arizona Fall League.
SCOUTING REPORT: Cunningham's pro debut can be split into halves. Before the injury, he was one of the best pitchers in the system and looked to have a case as its top pitching prospect. Afterward, he lost some of his ability to command his arsenal and got hit hard as a result. In four turns in August, Cunningham went 0-2, 8.22 with eight strikeouts and eight walks over 7.2 innings. He struggled in the AFL as well, allowing 15 earned runs and nine walks in 13 innings. When things were going well for Cunningham, scouts were heartened by a mix that included four pitches that graded between 50 and 55 on the 20-80 scouting scale. Cunningham is in the process of adding a sweeper. He threw the pitch a bit in the AFL but should incorporate it into his mix more often in 2026. Getting the sweeper where it needs to be would give him another avenue of attack against righthanded hitters. For now, he needs a healthy offseason and a chance to return to the form he showed in the first half of the 2025 season.
THE FUTURE: If he can return to full health and prove the last half of his pro debut was little more than a hiccup, Cunningham has a chance to be a midrotation starter.

Year	Age	Club (League)	Level	W	L	ERA	G	GS	IP	H	HR	BB	SO	BB%	SO%	WHIP	AVG
2025	22	Hudson Valley (SAL)	A+	5	3	2.82	12	11	54	42	4	19	55	8.6	25.0	1.12	.213
		Minor League Totals		5	3	2.82	12	11	54	42	4	19	55	8.6	25.0	1.12	.213

NEW YORK YANKEES

8 DILLON LEWIS, OF

HIT: 40. **POW:** 60. **RUN:** 60. **FLD:** 55. **ARM:** 60. **BA Grade:** 55. **Risk:** High. **Adj:** 40.

Born: June 12, 2003. **B-T:** R-R. **HT:** 6-3. **WT:** 220.
Drafted: Queens University of Charlotte, 2024 (13th round). **Signed by:** Ricky Castle.
TRACK RECORD: During his amateur career, Lewis truly was the king of Queens. He spent three seasons at Queens University of Charlotte and a summer with Queen City of the Southern Collegiate Baseball League. In his final season in college, he showed off a blend of power and speed that enticed the Yankees to take a chance on him in the 13th round in 2024. Those traits have translated to pro ball, and he opened eyes during his first full pro season.
SCOUTING REPORT: In a season split between both Class A stops, Lewis blended power and speed into a profile that could help him shoot up the rankings with a bit more polish. His impact potential showed up in a 90th percentile exit velocity of 107.7 mph that placed him in the same range as top prospects like Bryce Eldridge and Konnor Griffin. Lewis faces more questions about his hit tool thanks to mechanics that could leave him vulnerable to better pitching as he prepares to move into the upper levels. The Yankees worked with Lewis to make his actions in the batter's box less stiff and rigid and add some malleability to his bat path. If the changes stick, he will increase his barrel accuracy and allow himself to do damage on a wider variety of pitches and locations. Defensively, Lewis is the best outfielder in the Yankees' system. He uses plus speed and solid jumps and routes to lock down center field, and his strong, accurate arm makes him even more of a defensive asset. He was one of just 12 players in the minor leagues to hit 20 doubles and 20 home runs and steal 20 bases.
THE FUTURE: Lewis will likely return to High-A to begin 2026 but should reach the upper levels by season's end. If properly developed, his tool set gives him the ceiling of an above-average everyday center fielder who can be a dynamic force on both sides of the ball.

Year	Age	Club (League)	Level	AVG	G	AB	R	H	2B	3B	HR	RBI	BB	SO	SB	OBP	SLG
2025	22	Tampa (FSL)	A	.250	46	176	33	44	9	2	9	29	18	55	13	.323	.477
2025	22	Hudson Valley (SAL)	A+	.228	76	289	39	66	12	3	13	50	36	69	13	.320	.426
		Minor League Totals		.238	136	517	82	123	25	5	23	85	58	133	29	.320	.439

9 THATCHER HURD, RHP

FB: 55. **CB:** 55. **SL:** 60. **CTL:** 45. **BA Grade:** 55. **Risk:** Extreme. **Adj:** 35.

Born: December 9, 2002. **B-T:** R-R. **HT:** 6-4. **WT:** 230.
Drafted: LSU, 2024 (3rd round). **Signed by:** Mike Leuzinger.
TRACK RECORD: As an amateur, Hurd spurned pro ball and instead honored his commitment to UCLA. He spent a solid freshman season with the Bruins before hitting the transfer portal and landing with LSU for his next two years. In Baton Rouge, Hurd struggled with control and command but was also the winning pitcher in the final game of the Tigers' College World Series championship in 2023. Hurd was the first of two LSU products New York drafted in 2024, joining since-traded lefty Griffin Herring. The Yankees selected Hurd in the third round in 2024, but his pro debut stalled before it got started when he had Tommy John surgery in April 2025.
SCOUTING REPORT: At his best, Hurd has a mix of three pitches that each grade as potentially above-average or plus. The signature of his repertoire is a powerful sweeper slider in the mid 80s. Its velocity and analytical characteristics gave it a chance to become a true 60-grade weapon on the 20-80 scouting scale. The righthander sandwiches his slider with a mid-90s fastball that has reached 99 mph and a downer curveball in the low 80s. The combination of the three pitches gives Hurd weapons he can use to attack all parts of the strike zone against both lefthanders and righthanders. The next step, once he's healthy again, will be to improve shaky control that saw him rack up a walk rate of 11.2% of hitters in his last year with LSU.
THE FUTURE: Hurd's recovery from Tommy John surgery will likely delay his 2026 debut past minor league Opening Day. Once healthy, he has the pedigree to spend most of the year at High-A with a chance to reach the upper levels by season's end, in much the same way 2024 first-rounder Ben Hess did in 2025. He fits the mold of a back-end starter with upside if he improves his control.

Year	Age	Club (League)	Level	W	L	ERA	G	GS	IP	H	HR	BB	SO	BB%	SO%	WHIP	AVG
2025	22	Did not play—Injured															

NEW YORK YANKEES

10 CHASE HAMPTON, RHP
FB: 60. **CB:** 55. **SL:** 55. **CH:** 45. **CT:** 50. **CTL:** 60. **BA Grade:** 55. **Risk:** Extreme. **Adj:** 35.

Born: August 7, 2001. **B-T:** R-R. **HT:** 6-2. **WT:** 225.
Drafted: Texas Tech, 2022 (6th round). **Signed by:** Brian Rhees.
TRACK RECORD: Hampton was the Yankees' sixth-round pick in 2022 out of Texas Tech. A year later, he burst onto the scene and pitched his way into the upper crust of the organization's pitchers. He lost that momentum in 2024 and 2025 as his development was stunted by injuries. Hampton dealt with elbow and lower-body issues in 2024, and then had Tommy John surgery the following April that wiped out all of his 2025 season. All told, he's pitched just 18.2 innings since his breakthrough 2023. Hampton should return at some point in 2026, though the beginning of his season might be delayed while he completes his rehab process. The Yankees added him to their 40-man roster in November 2025 to shield him from the Rule 5 draft.
SCOUTING REPORT: It's been two full seasons since Hampton has been at his best, but his peak performance leaves room for optimism. In 2023, when he pitched his way to Double-A, the righthander showed off a dazzling four-pitch mix. His fastball peaked in the mid 90s and both of his breaking balls flashed above-average potential. His changeup was fringy and a tick behind the rest of his mix, and it was slated to be an area of focus in 2024 if everything went well. Hampton also will mix in a cutter that showed average potential. He ties it all together with control that looked like it could be plus in the big leagues. The last two seasons of rehab have given him time to work on his mental skills while recovering from his injuries.
THE FUTURE: If Hampton's stuff returns intact, he has a chance to pitch his way to the big leagues. Hampton's limited workload over the last two years will make it trickier for him to build himself into a rotation piece. If he can, the long layoff might be worth the wait.

Year	Age	Club (League)	Level	W	L	ERA	G	GS	IP	H	HR	BB	SO	BB%	SO%	WHIP	AVG
2025	23	Did not play—Injured															
		Minor League Totals		4	4	3.45	27	27	125	96	14	46	161	8.9	31.3	1.13	.208

11 CADE SMITH, RHP
FB: 55. **SL:** 60. **CB:** 45. **SW:** 40. **CTL:** 50. **BA Grade:** 45. **Risk:** Average. **Adj:** 35.

Born: April 9, 2002. **B-T:** R-R. **HT:** 6-1. **WT:** 205. **Drafted:** Mississippi State, 2023 (6th round). **Signed by:** Chuck Bartlett.
TRACK RECORD: After a high school career at Mississippi's DeSoto Central, Smith continued his amateur career in the Magnolia State. He spent his next three seasons at Mississippi State, the last two of which were as a part of the Bulldogs' rotation. The Yankees drafted Smith in the sixth round in 2023 and signed him for $282,900. He's struggled to stay healthy over his first two years but made up for lost time with a stint in the 2025 Arizona Fall League.
SCOUTING REPORT: Despite dealing with a pair of lower-body injuries, Smith was impressive when he got on the mound. Operating with a four-seamer that sat in the low 90s and peaked at 96, a curveball, sweeper and gyro slider, Smith notched 42 strikeouts in 39.2 innings in the regular season, then added 14 more—against just two walks—in the AFL. He uses his combination of four-seamer and slider, which has sharp, deep break, to form an effective north-south attack. Smith's curveball is a fringier pitch, and he had trouble throwing it for strikes at the same rate as his other offerings. The addition of the sweeper, which is in its early stages, helps him attack from side to side as well. He commanded his fastball better in 2025, which made his slider more effective as well. Scouts also saw a kick changeup during spring training, but he did not use the pitch during the regular year. Smith shows average control.
THE FUTURE: After a season stymied by injuries, Smith will look to put together a fuller workload in 2026, when he is likely to reach the upper levels for the first time. Beyond building up his innings total, he'll try to bring one of his sweeper or curveball to the level of his fastball and slider. If he can, he could fit in the back of a rotation.

Year	Age	Club (League)	Level	W	L	ERA	G	GS	IP	H	HR	BB	SO	BB%	SO%	WHIP	AVG
2025	23	FCL Yankees	Rk	0	0	0.00	2	2	4	1	0	2	4	11.8	23.5	0.69	.071
2025	23	Tampa (FSL)	A	0	0	3.38	1	1	3	3	0	0	3	0.0	27.3	1.13	.273
2025	23	Hudson Valley (SAL)	A+	2	1	2.76	8	8	33	20	2	16	35	12.0	26.3	1.10	.172
		Minor League Totals		8	7	3.16	30	28	125	83	7	58	153	11.3	29.7	1.13	.184

NEW YORK YANKEES

12 MAC HEUER, RHP

FB: 60. **CB:** 40. **SL:** 50. **CH:** 50. **CTL:** 50. **BA Grade:** 45. **Risk:** Average. **Adj:** 35.

Born: July 7, 2004. **B-T:** R-R. **HT:** 6-5. **WT:** 265. **Drafted:** Texas Tech, 2025 (8th round). **Signed by:** Brian Rhees.
TRACK RECORD: Heuer was homeschooled but made his way through the showcase circuit and was drafted by Cleveland in the 16th round in 2023. When he wasn't on the mound, Heuer found time to raise an ewe named Oakley who won grand champion at the 2022 Georgia Junior National Livestock Show. Heuer spent the next two seasons at Texas Tech before the Yankees drafted him in the eighth round. He signed for $400,000, nearly double the recommended slot value. He did not pitch after signing.
SCOUTING REPORT: In college, Heuer worked with a full complement of four pitches, led by a fastball that peaked at 97 mph and backed by a changeup and slider in the mid 80s and a curveball in the high 70s. Heuer's heater worked well when located up in the zone, where it has the kind of life and velocity to zoom past bats. His slider alternated between hard, sweeping break and downer action and has the chance to be an average pitch. Heuer's changeup has fade and depth away from lefties and could be an average offering as well. His curveball has downer break, but needs more power behind it before it can be much more than a wrinkle against lefthanders or a strike-stealer. Heuer is big and physical and utilizes a delivery with a short, compact action and crossfire finish.
THE FUTURE: Heuer's first stop as a pro could be at High-A Hudson Valley. He's already cleaned up his body a bit since joining the Yankees and has the makings of a powerful back-end starter.

Year	Age	Club (League)	Level	W	L	ERA	G	GS	IP	H	HR	BB	SO	BB%	SO%	WHIP	AVG
2025	20	Did not play															

13 BRENDAN JONES, OF

HIT: 50. **POW:** 50. **RUN:** 60. **FLD:** 60. **ARM:** 40. **BA Grade:** 45. **Risk:** Average. **Adj:** 35.

Born: April 24, 2002. **B-T:** L-L. **HT:** 5-10. **WT:** 175. **Drafted:** Kansas State, 2024 (12th round). **Signed by:** Matt Ranson.
TRACK RECORD: Jones made steady progress over three seasons at Kansas State. In his final year, he led the Big 12 in walks (55) and stolen bases (40) and became the first player in school history to be a finalist for the Rawlings Gold Glove award. The Yankees drafted him in the 12th round in 2024, and he spent his first two seasons as a pro making a name for himself.
SCOUTING REPORT: Scouts flocked to KSU in 2024 to see eventual Twins first-rounder Kaelen Culpepper. While they were there, Jones popped onto some radars. In a 2025 season split between High-A and Double-A, the lefthanded hitter did a lot of things right. He controlled the zone, hit the ball hard and used plus speed to impact the game in the field and on the basepaths. Scouts see a player who could be an average hitter with fringy power who can turn line drives into extra bases. He spent the majority of his time in center field, though he got his fair share of reps at both corner outfield spots as well. His 40-grade arm is the only below-average tool on his card, and it would likely push him to left field in the event he had to move.
THE FUTURE: If he makes the big leagues, the KSU alum can smile and say he went from Manhattan to the Bronx. He'll likely reach Triple-A in 2026 and his big league debut isn't out of the question. He fits as a hard-nosed center fielder who does a little bit of everything.

Year	Age	Club (League)	Level	AVG	G	AB	R	H	2B	3B	HR	RBI	BB	SO	SB	OBP	SLG
2025	23	Hudson Valley (SAL)	A+	.236	44	174	35	41	6	2	4	23	30	38	23	.349	.362
2025	23	Somerset (EL)	AA	.250	80	284	54	71	14	6	7	46	52	71	28	.365	.415
		Minor League Totals		.248	148	533	105	132	25	8	14	88	111	130	69	.377	.403

14 BROCK SELVIDGE, LHP

FB: 50. **CB:** 40. **SW:** 50. **CH:** 40. **CT:** 55. **CTL:** 45. **BA Grade:** 45. **Risk:** Average. **Adj:** 35.

Born: August 28, 2002. **B-T:** R-L. **HT:** 6-3. **WT:** 215. **Drafted:** HS—Chandler, AZ, 2021 (3rd round). **Signed by:** Troy Afenir.
TRACK RECORD: Selvidge signed with the Yankees for $1.5 million in 2021 as a third-rounder out of high school in Arizona. He moved deliberately through the system until 2024, when a breakout year saw him reach Double-A and earn a spot in the Futures Game. He did not pitch in the annual event, however, because of a pinched nerve in his biceps that required surgery.
SCOUTING REPORT: After he returned, Selvidge made some alterations to his arsenal. He added a curveball to complement his four-seamer and create more of a north-south profile within his mix. Selvidge's repertoire now includes five pitches: the curveball, a four-seamer, sweeper, changeup and cutter. He throws the mid-80s cutter most often. It has plenty of bite, and created the most strikes and chases of any part of his arsenal, though the Yankees would like to make him less reliant on it in 2026. He shows solid ability to manipulate the shape of his sweeper, landing it in the zone armside and also burying it at the

feet of lefties. Selvidge rarely threw his changeup, which sat around 85 mph with decent fading life away from righties. The Yankees worked with Selvidge at instructs to tweak his delivery in order to help him regain some of the velocity he'd lost during the rehab process. His stuff plays down because he has less than 6 feet of extension on all of his pitches.

THE FUTURE: After a healthy offseason, the Yankees hope Selvidge returns in the spring with more zip and cleaner mechanics. If he does, he has a chance to be a No. 4 starter.

Year	Age	Club (League)	Level	W	L	ERA	G	GS	IP	H	HR	BB	SO	BB%	SO%	WHIP	AVG
2025	22	FCL Yankees	Rk	0	0	0.00	1	1	3	3	0	1	2	8.3	16.7	1.50	.273
2025	22	Tampa (FSL)	A	0	1	3.60	2	2	5	2	0	5	5	20.0	20.0	1.40	.100
2025	22	Somerset (EL)	AA	2	6	4.92	16	15	75	69	6	38	61	11.8	18.9	1.43	.251
		Minor League Totals		20	19	3.88	73	68	341	307	19	137	345	9.4	23.6	1.30	.238

15 KYLE CARR, LHP

FB: 45. **SW:** 50. **CH:** 45. **CT:** 40. **CTL:** 50. **BA Grade:** 45. **Risk:** Average. **Adj:** 35.

Born: May 6, 2002. **B-T:** L-L. **HT:** 6-1. **WT:** 185. **Drafted:** Palomar (CA) JC, 2023 (3rd round).
Signed by: Troy Afenir/Scott Lovekamp.

TRACK RECORD: After a season at San Diego, Carr transferred to Palomar (CA) JC, where a successful season led to the Yankees taking him in the third round of the 2023 draft. He spent the 2024 season with High-A Hudson Valley, where his stuff looked down across the board and he got hit hard. Carr bounced back in a return to High-A in 2025, but ran into plenty of resistance upon reaching Double-A.

SCOUTING REPORT: Carr works with four-seam, sinking and cut fastballs, and he backs that trio with a sweeper and a changeup. The cutter is the newest addition, installed midway through 2025 as a way to give him a harder breaking ball than his current mid-70s sweeper. Scouts reported progress during spring training, and he opened his second season by pitching to a 1.96 ERA in the South Atlantic League, which helped him earn the league's pitcher of the year honor. Still, there's plenty of room for improvement. The Yankees worked with Carr to tweak his stride and make him more cross-body. The resulting deception should allow him to get more empty swings. He worked to continue to refine his secondaries and get stronger during instructional league. He throws a fair amount of strikes, but hitters at Double-A showed him that he needs to refine his command.

THE FUTURE: Carr will return to Double-A to begin 2026. There, he'll focus on sharpening his cutter and improving his command. With a bit more power behind his mix, he could be a No. 5 starter.

Year	Age	Club (League)	Level	W	L	ERA	G	GS	IP	H	HR	BB	SO	BB%	SO%	WHIP	AVG
2025	23	Hudson Valley (SAL)	A+	8	6	1.96	22	22	119	81	6	47	104	9.8	21.7	1.07	.190
2025	23	Somerset (EL)	AA	0	1	8.56	3	3	14	14	2	8	13	13.6	22.0	1.61	.275
		Minor League Totals		9	15	3.57	49	49	237	192	13	110	212	11.1	21.4	1.27	.222

16 KAEDEN KENT, SS

HIT: 50. **POW:** 45. **RUN:** 40. **FLD:** 45. **ARM:** 50. **BA Grade:** 45. **Risk:** Average. **Adj:** 35.

Born: August 29, 2003. **B-T:** L-R. **HT:** 6-2. **WT:** 200. **Drafted:** Texas A&M, 2025 (3rd round). **Signed by:** Brian Rhees.

TRACK RECORD: The son of Hall of Fame second baseman Jeff Kent, Kaeden spent three seasons at Texas A&M and played two summers in the Cape Cod League. In 2024 with Brewster, he was teammates with fellow Cooperstown progeny Carsten Sabathia. The Yankees drafted Kent in the third round in 2025 and signed him for $741,900. He got his feet wet with 25 games at High-A Hudson Valley, where he hit .186/.217/.265 with two home runs and 19 strikeouts.

SCOUTING REPORT: With the Aggies, Kent moved around the diamond before settling at shortstop in his draft year. Scouts believe his lack of range might lead to him moving to second base. In college, Kent used a short, quick swing to damage pitches in the zone and did a solid job of not chasing. Once he got to pro ball, things went a bit haywire. He looked jumpy in the box and he was increasingly willing to wave at pitches out of the zone. His chase rate in his pro sample was 36.4%, and his swing decisions and quality of contact plummeted. His bat path also went awry, and the Yankees worked with him in instructional league to smooth it out while trying to add bat speed.

THE FUTURE: Kent will likely return to Hudson Valley in 2026. There, the Yankees hope he will revert to something closer to the form he showed as an amateur. If he does, he's a relatively high-floor player with second-division regular upside.

Year	Age	Club (League)	Level	AVG	G	AB	R	H	2B	3B	HR	RBI	BB	SO	SB	OBP	SLG
2025	21	Hudson Valley (SAL)	A+	.186	25	102	8	19	2	0	2	17	3	19	0	.217	.265
		Minor League Totals		.186	25	102	8	19	2	0	2	17	3	19	0	.217	.265

NEW YORK YANKEES

17 PICO KOHN, LHP

FB: 50. **CB:** 40. **SL:** 55. **CH:** 45. **CTL:** 55. **BA Grade:** 45. **Risk:** Average. **Adj:** 35.

Born: October 2, 2002. **B-T:** L-L. **HT:** 6-4. **WT:** 200. **Drafted:** Mississippi State, 2025 (4th round). **Signed by:** Chuck Bartlett.
TRACK RECORD: Kohn's given name is William, but he called himself Pico as a youngster and the name stuck. Despite Gatorade naming him Alabama player of the year in 2020, he went undrafted and landed at Mississippi State. He missed the 2023 season while rehabbing from Tommy John surgery but got back on the mound in 2024, then pitched a career-high 80 innings for the Bulldogs in 2025. The Yankees drafted him in the fourth round later that summer and signed him for $547,800. He did not pitch after signing.
SCOUTING REPORT: Kohn works with four pitches, led by a potentially average fastball that reaches 95 mph and backed by a slider, curveball and changeup. His delivery is funky, and his three-quarters arm slot adds deception to his mix. The slider is a particularly effective pitch and could be an above-average offering in the big leagues. He threw the low-80s breaker nearly a third of the time, followed by a harder changeup and a slower curveball that worked primarily as an early-count strike-stealer. The Yankees were intrigued by Kohn's combination of velocity, strikes and feel to spin the baseball. Two years after the surgery, Kohn does a good job holding his velocity deep into outings.
THE FUTURE: Kohn's fastball and slider should give him a floor of a multi-inning reliever. Bringing one of his other two pitches up a notch or two would give himself a higher chance of pitching in a rotation. His college pedigree might mean an early ticket to High-A Hudson Valley.

Year	Age	Club (League)	Level	W	L	ERA	G	GS	IP	H	HR	BB	SO	BB%	SO%	WHIP	AVG
2025	22	Did not play															

18 CADE WINQUEST, RHP

FB: 55. **CB:** 55. **CH:** 30. **CT:** 50. **SW:** 45. **CTL:** 50. **BA Grade:** 40. **Risk:** Mild. **Adj:** 35.

Born: April 30, 2000. **B-T:** R-R. **HT:** 6-2. **WT:** 205. **Drafted:** Texas, 2022 (8th round). **Signed by:** Pete Parise (Cardinals).
TRACK RECORD: After four seasons at Texas and a summer in the Cape Cod League, Winquest in 2022 became the Cardinals' eighth-round pick. His work in the minor leagues has predominantly come as a starter, and he split the 2025 season between High-A Peoria and Double-A Springfield, where he threw a career-high 106 innings. After the season, he was selected by the Yankees in the major league phase of the Rule 5 draft, becoming their first MLB Rule 5 pick since 2011, when they took Brad Meyers from the Nationals.
SCOUTING REPORT: Winquest works with a five-pitch arsenal that allows him to miss bats and get grounders, and he throws plenty of strikes as well. His four-seam fastball sits in the mid 90s and touches 98 with a bit of cutting life. He pairs it with a curveball in the upper 70s he can land in the zone or bury for chases. He also throws a true cutter and a sweeper, and will mix in the very occasional changeup as well. Winquest's control is roughly average, and could tick up if he could throw his sweeper and curveball in the zone more often. He gets solid extension across the board, but the 6.7 feet he gets on his fastball is the top mark in his arsenal.
THE FUTURE: Winquest will get a chance in spring training to earn a spot in the Yankees' bullpen. If he can, he fits as a spot starter or a bulk reliever.

Year	Age	Club (League)	Level	W	L	ERA	G	GS	IP	H	HR	BB	SO	BB%	SO%	WHIP	AVG
2025	25	Peoria (MWL)	A+	2	6	4.52	17	15	64	63	4	27	68	9.5	23.9	1.41	.259
2025	25	Springfield (TL)	AA	3	1	3.19	8	8	42	42	3	12	42	6.8	23.9	1.28	.263
		Minor League Totals		8	16	4.19	58	38	213	194	14	92	219	10.0	23.8	1.34	.244

19 JACK CEBERT, RHP

FB: 60. **SL:** 60. **CH:** 45. **CT:** 55. **CTL:** 55. **BA Grade:** 45. **Risk:** Average. **Adj:** 35.

Born: April 1, 2002. **B-T:** R-R. **HT:** 6-3. **WT:** 209. **Drafted:** Texas Tech, 2025 (15th round). **Signed by:** Brian Rhees.
TRACK RECORD: After three seasons at South Florida, Cebert transferred to Texas Tech for his senior season. He pitched out of the bullpen with the Red Raiders, whose pitching staff also included fellow 2025 Yankees draftee Mac Heuer. The Yankees selected Cebert in the 15th round and sent him to High-A Hudson Valley for his pro debut, where he made five relief appearances.
SCOUTING REPORT: Cebert started for South Florida as a sophomore and junior, and the Yankees might return him to that role in 2026. They've been heartened by the velocity he's shown in the early stages of his career. Cebert added a cutter to a mix that also includes a four-seamer, sinker, sweeper and changeup. He threw a curveball in college as well, but it's unlikely to be part of his mix going forward. His complement of fastballs allows him to handle lefties and righties alike, and his sweeper has hard, late break designed

to induce plenty of weak swings. The changeup shows average fade and depth away from lefties. Cebert's delivery is up-tempo with a glove tap that appears a bit more pronounced on fastballs. His arm stroke is compact in the back and long out front, with more than 6.6 feet of extension in pro ball. He threw plenty of strikes both in college and in his short pro sample.
THE FUTURE: If nothing else changes, Cebert could move quickly through the system in a reliever's role. The road could be longer as a starter, but the gamble might be worth the risk. He should reach Double-A in 2026.

Year	Age	Club (League)	Level	W	L	ERA	G	GS	IP	H	HR	BB	SO	BB%	SO%	WHIP	AVG
2025	23	Hudson Valley (SAL)	A+	0	0	2.84	5	0	6	4	2	1	11	4.0	44.0	0.79	.167
		Minor League Totals		0	0	2.84	5	0	6	4	2	1	11	4.0	44.0	0.79	.167

20 HARRISON COHEN, RHP

FB: 50. **CT:** 55. **CH:** 40. **CTL:** 45. **BA Grade:** 40. **Risk:** Mild. **Adj:** 35.

Born: May 28, 1999. **B-T:** R-R. **HT:** 6-1. **WT:** 200. **Signed:** George Washington, 2022 (UDFA). **Signed by:** Matt Hyde.
TRACK RECORD: In 2022, after completing his fourth and final season at George Washington, Cohen headed out for his second tour of the Cape Cod League. That summer, he was part of a loaded Cotuit team that has already produced eight big leaguers. If Cohen reaches MLB, he'd be the first pitcher of the group to do so. The year prior, he was teammates on Cotuit with current New York first baseman Ben Rice. The Yankees signed Cohen as an undrafted free agent, and he split the 2025 season between the upper levels. New York left him off its 40-man roster and unprotected ahead of the Rule 5 draft.
SCOUTING REPORT: Cohen works with a four-seam fastball in the low 90s with roughly 18 inches of induced vertical break, a mid-80s breaking pitch that rides the line between cutter and slider and a changeup in the same velocity band. The cutter and changeup each induced chases at rates of greater than 30% and miss rates between 43-48%. Cohen struggles to land any of his pitches in the zone could cause problems against savvier hitters content to take a walk. His delivery is deceptive and frenetic and features a high leg kick and compact arm action. Toward the end of the year, he also removed a hand break from his mechanics.
THE FUTURE: Cohen is a near-ready big leaguer best suited for a role in middle relief. If he can find the zone more often with his pitches, he could unlock a touch more ceiling.

Year	Age	Club (League)	Level	W	L	ERA	G	GS	IP	H	HR	BB	SO	BB%	SO%	WHIP	AVG
2025	26	Somerset (EL)	AA	1	2	2.01	20	0	22	12	1	13	30	14.0	32.3	1.12	.158
2025	26	Scranton/WB (IL)	AAA	2	0	1.57	29	1	29	14	0	17	29	14.7	25.0	1.08	.146
		Minor League Totals		11	5	2.42	103	2	130	81	7	65	155	12.1	28.8	1.12	.176

21 HENRY LALANE, LHP

FB: 50. **SL:** 45. **CH:** 45. **CTL:** 45. **BA Grade:** 50. **Risk:** Extreme. **Adj:** 30.

Born: May 18, 2004. **B-T:** L-L. **HT:** 6-8. **WT:** 235. **Signed:** Dominican Republic, 2021. **Signed by:** Jose Ravelo.
TRACK RECORD: Lalane signed with New York in 2021, then was a part of a prospect-laden club in the Florida Complex League two years later. He dazzled for two innings in the Yankees' 2024 Spring Breakout game, but the last two years have been filled with injuries and underperformance. He had shoulder surgery over the offseason and had to wait until July 22 to make his first official appearance of 2025.
SCOUTING REPORT: Before the surgery, Lalane was one of the brightest young talents in the system. Afterward, his stuff appeared severely diminished and he looked wholly generic. His fastball, which in previous years had touched 97 mph, averaged 92 mph. His changeup came in 10 mph slower, and his slider was a loose breaker in the mid 70s that, according to data from Synergy Sports, he threw just 10 times in 2025 and not once for a strike. Lalane struggled to find the strike zone in the Florida State League, walking 13 of the 73 (17.8%) hitters he faced. His delivery was out of sync, and he started to rush down the mound before his upper half could catch up. After so few innings over the last two seasons, he needs to get stronger to regain some of the velocity he lost while rehabbing.
THE FUTURE: The last two years of rehab and sporadic pitching have dimmed Lalane's star considerably. He and the Yankees hope a full offseason of rest will help his stuff return to its former glory. For now, the road back to that level of promise is long and daunting.

Year	Age	Club (League)	Level	W	L	ERA	G	GS	IP	H	HR	BB	SO	BB%	SO%	WHIP	AVG
2025	21	FCL Yankees	Rk	0	0	6.00	1	1	3	1	1	1	2	9.1	18.2	0.67	.100
2025	21	Tampa (FSL)	A	0	0	1.65	6	6	16	10	1	13	20	17.8	27.4	1.41	.182
		Minor League Totals		6	8	3.65	44	39	143	114	9	66	160	10.8	26.2	1.26	.219

22 STIVEN MARINEZ, SS
HIT: 45. **POW:** 40. **RUN:** 55. **FLD:** 50. **ARM:** 45. **BA Grade:** 50. **Risk:** Extreme. **Adj:** 30.

Born: August 20, 2007. **B-T:** L-R. **HT:** 5-10. **WT:** 175. **Signed:** Dominican Republic, 2024.
Signed by: Dennis Woody/Lorenzo Piron.
TRACK RECORD: Marinez signed with the Yankees in December 2024 and spent his first professional season in the Dominican Summer League in 2025, where he hit .275 and showed an interesting blend of skills across the board. He was one of just eight players in the DSL who finished the year with more than 40 walks and 20 stolen bases.
SCOUTING REPORT: Marinez is a glove-first shortstop with the chops to stick at the position. His above-average speed and arm strength give him the necessary ingredients to produce the range and throws required for the left side of the infield, and scouts see a potentially average defender in the long run. He's strong-bodied and twitchy, which helps him produce plenty of bat speed. He needs to create more separation in his swing, however, and work on staying direct through the ball. Scouts thought Marinez's bat path could use improvement but he showed strong plate discipline. Those traits showed up under the hood as well, with a chase rate of just 17.5% but below-average overall and zone-miss rates.
THE FUTURE: After a strong DSL debut, Marinez's next step will be a stateside move to the Florida Complex League. There, he'll look to iron out his bat path and continue building toward a future as a true shortstop who hits toward the bottom of a lineup.

Year	Age	Club (League)	Level	AVG	G	AB	R	H	2B	3B	HR	RBI	BB	SO	SB	OBP	SLG
2025	17	DSL NYY Bombers	Rk	.275	47	160	37	44	7	3	1	17	41	46	22	.424	.375
		Minor League Totals		.275	47	160	37	44	7	3	1	17	41	46	22	.424	.375

23 FRANCISCO VILORIO, OF
HIT: 40. **POW:** 60. **RUN:** 55. **FLD:** 50. **ARM:** 70. **BA Grade:** 50. **Risk:** Extreme. **Adj:** 30.

Born: October 31, 2006. **B-T:** R-R. **HT:** 6-4. **WT:** 224. **Signed:** Dominican Republic, 2024.
Signed by: Luis Brito/Dennis Woody.
TRACK RECORD: The crown jewel of the Yankees' 2024 international class, Vilorio signed for $1.75 million and spent his first pro season that year in the Dominican Summer League. He produced a fair amount of power but far too many strikeouts. Vilorio repeated the level in 2025 and made a bit of progress.
SCOUTING REPORT: Vilorio is big, physical and produces big-time impact when he connects. His max exit velocity of 115.3 mph was one of the hardest-hit balls in the system in 2025, besting even Spencer Jones' top-end EV. He improved his miss rates across the board, going from 39.5% in 2024 to 28.2% in 2025. He also improved his zone-miss and chase rates by 9% and 15%, respectively. To get the most out of his raw juice, he'll need to get the ball in the air more often after hitting more grounders in 2025. Scouts who saw him in the DSL believe he's probably stretched in center field and would fit better in right. His powerful bat would profile there just fine thanks to a double-plus throwing arm. He's a plus runner as well, but could slow down with age.
THE FUTURE: After two seasons in the DSL, Vilorio will move stateside in 2026. There, he'll try to keep improving his contact rates without sacrificing any of his power. He fits as a classic thumping right fielder.

Year	Age	Club (League)	Level	AVG	G	AB	R	H	2B	3B	HR	RBI	BB	SO	SB	OBP	SLG
2025	18	DSL NYY Yankees	Rk	.279	49	183	39	51	10	3	0	19	30	54	8	.387	.366
		Minor League Totals		.242	91	331	61	80	18	4	4	38	46	110	16	.346	.356

24 XAVIER RIVAS, LHP
FB: 50. **SL:** 55. **CH:** 50. **CTL:** 45. **BA Grade:** 45. **Risk:** High. **Adj:** 30.

Born: July 11, 2002. **B-T:** L-L. **HT:** 6-3. **WT:** 245. **Drafted:** Mississippi, 2024 (16th round). **Signed by:** Chuck Bartlett.
TRACK RECORD: In high school, Rivas was a three-sport varsity letter winner. He stuck with baseball for college, and after two years at Indianapolis, Rivas transferred to Mississippi. He pitched in 2023 but missed his draft year after having Tommy John surgery in February 2024. The Yankees took a chance on him in the 16th round and he debuted in 2025. Rivas made 10 starts at Low-A Tampa and five more for High-A Hudson Valley.
SCOUTING REPORT: Rivas is a tall, physical lefty who works with a rigid, stretch-only delivery and a three-pitch mix that annihilated lower-level hitters. His fastball peaked at 93 mph but featured an average of 18 inches of induced vertical break and Rivas backs it with a splitter and slider that each sit around 81 mph. Both of his offspeeds drove whiffs at rates of more than 50%, and the splitter was chased 35% of the time. Neither pitch was a strike more than 56% of the time, and he struggled to land either of them in the zone. Given the long layoff, Rivas' lack of finesse was to be expected. Ideally, the Yankees would like

NEW YORK YANKEES

him to fine-tune his command and add a few more ticks of velocity to his fastball. He is a fiery competitor.
THE FUTURE: Rivas should return to High-A to begin 2026 but could reach the upper levels by midseason. With a full offseason to rest, he could emerge as one of the system's breakout arms.

Year	Age	Club (League)	Level	W	L	ERA	G	GS	IP	H	HR	BB	SO	BB%	SO%	WHIP	AVG
2025	22	FCL Yankees	Rk	1	0	1.15	4	3	16	4	0	9	22	14.8	36.1	0.83	.078
2025	22	Tampa (FSL)	A	2	3	5.80	10	10	40	37	5	27	47	14.4	25.1	1.59	.237
2025	22	Hudson Valley (SAL)	A+	3	1	1.23	5	5	29	9	1	14	44	12.4	38.9	0.78	.095
		Minor League Totals		6	4	3.38	19	18	85	50	6	50	113	13.9	31.3	1.17	.166

25 JACE AVINA, OF

HIT: 40. **POW:** 50. **RUN:** 50. **FLD:** 50. **ARM:** 55. **BA Grade:** 40. **Risk:** Average. **Adj:** 30.

Born: June 6, 2003. **B-T:** R-R. **HT:** 6-0. **WT:** 205. **Drafted:** HS—Sparks, NV, 2021 (14th round).
Signed by: Joseph Grisham (Brewers).
TRACK RECORD: The Brewers took Avina out of high school in Nevada in 2021, and he spent the first couple years of his career teasing at his potential. He was traded—along with outfielder Brian Sanchez—to the Yankees in 2023 in the deal that sent Jake Bauers to Milwaukee. He reached Double-A for the first time in 2025.
SCOUTING REPORT: Avina's name dotted Best Tools ballots when he was in the early stages of his career, but the path to turning them into consistent skills hasn't been without plenty of roadblocks. Avina does a decent job managing the strike zone and hits the ball fairly hard when he makes contact, but there are obvious holes in his profile. Right now, the biggest hitch in his giddy-up is his performance against lefthanders. He hit just .173/.292/.333 against them over 96 plate appearances. He was brutalized by changeups as well, hitting just .077 against them according to data from Synergy Sports. Avina is an average defender who moved around all three outfield spots in near-equal measure. His average speed will likely push him to a corner, and his above-average arm strength would fit just fine in right field.
THE FUTURE: Avina is likely to split his 2026 season between the upper levels. He has a chance to be a bench bat who handles righties and can play sound defense in the outfield.

Year	Age	Club (League)	Level	AVG	G	AB	R	H	2B	3B	HR	RBI	BB	SO	SB	OBP	SLG
2025	22	Hudson Valley (SAL)	A+	.295	52	176	37	52	13	0	8	31	30	54	3	.412	.506
2025	22	Somerset (EL)	AA	.224	46	170	18	38	11	0	3	14	19	50	2	.314	.341
		Minor League Totals		.251	353	1244	200	312	82	5	50	198	164	423	23	.360	.445

26 DYLAN JASSO, 3B

HIT: 45. **POW:** 50. **RUN:** 40. **FLD:** 45. **ARM:** 50. **BA Grade:** 40. **Risk:** Average. **Adj:** 30.

Born: November 30, 2002. **B-T:** R-R. **HT:** 6-1. **WT:** 220. **Signed:** New Mexico JC, 2023 (UDFA). **Signed by:** Brian Rhees.
TRACK RECORD: Jasso was born in Mexico and played one season at New Mexico JC, where he hit .453 with 25 home runs. The Yankees took a chance on him and signed him as an undrafted free agent, and he's made steady progress up the minor league ladder. Jasso reached Double-A for the first time in 2025 and clubbed 13 home runs. He also saw time in the Mexican Winter League between 2024 and 2025.
SCOUTING REPORT: Jasso doesn't have a plus tool on his card, but he does just enough to be interesting. He hits the ball plenty hard—his average and 90th percentile exit velocities are 90.8 mph and 103.7 mph, respectively—and doesn't run particularly high miss rates. He could, however, stand to make more contact on pitches in the zone. Jasso bounced around the infield in 2025 and saw time at all three non-shortstop positions. Mostly, he played third base and could stick there as a solid-average defender with just enough arm strength for the position. He's a below-average runner and has attempted to steal just five times as a professional.
THE FUTURE: After a solid season with Somerset, Jasso should advance to Triple-A in 2026. If he can match his Double-A production, he could get a cup of coffee by season's end. He projects as a versatile bench bat who can move around the infield.

Year	Age	Club (League)	Level	AVG	G	AB	R	H	2B	3B	HR	RBI	BB	SO	SB	OBP	SLG
2025	22	Somerset (EL)	AA	.257	127	478	62	123	17	6	13	76	42	130	1	.326	.400
		Minor League Totals		.256	268	994	140	254	55	10	25	164	105	260	3	.336	.406

27 BRANDO MAYEA, OF

HIT: 45. **POW:** 40. **RUN:** 50. **FLD:** 50. **ARM:** 50. **BA Grade:** 45. **Risk:** High. **Adj:** 30.

Born: September 12, 2005. **B-T:** R-R. **HT:** 5-11. **WT:** 180. **Signed:** Dominican Republic, 2023. **Signed by:** Juan Piron.
TRACK RECORD: Mayea moved from Cuba to the Dominican Republic before signing with the Yankees in 2023 for $4.35 million. His career has been waylaid by underperformance and injuries. After starting off hot in a repeat of the Florida Complex League, Mayea hurt his ankle on May 30 and missed the rest of the season.
SCOUTING REPORT: On the surface, Mayea was on his way to a breakout before landing on the injured list. He hit three home runs in 20 games, matching his total from 73 games over the previous two seasons. Under the hood, the picture was less rosy. With two strikes, he did a good job shortening up and hunting contact. Earlier in counts, he hunted home runs, which led to big-time miss rates, including an overall mark of 35.7% and an in-zone rate of 25.8%. The Yankees pushed Mayea to find an approach that melded the best of those two worlds into something more selectively aggressive. Defensively, he played mostly center field in the FCL, but scouts already noticed he had slowed down in 2024, so his future is likely in a corner. He's a fringy runner who gets closer to average underway.
THE FUTURE: Mayea will likely return to the FCL for a third stint in 2026. He needs to refine his approach and make more contact to get to his ceiling, which is as a second-division regular corner outfielder.

Year	Age	Club (League)	Level	AVG	G	AB	R	H	2B	3B	HR	RBI	BB	SO	SB	OBP	SLG
2025	19	FCL Yankees	Rk	.297	20	74	19	22	4	1	3	9	6	19	4	.373	.500
		Minor League Totals		.282	93	354	69	100	13	4	6	36	44	89	45	.376	.393

28 ALLEN FACUNDO, LHP

FB: 70. **SL:** 60. **CH:** 30. **CTL:** 40. **BA Grade:** 45. **Risk:** High. **Adj:** 30.

Born: September 3, 2002. **B-T:** L-L. **HT:** 6-2. **WT:** 222. **Signed:** Dominican Republic, 2021. **Signed by:** Luis Tinoco.
TRACK RECORD: Facundo's road to the prospect radar has taken plenty of twists and turns. He signed in 2021 but he missed all of 2022 and threw no more than 39 innings in each of the following three seasons. Nevertheless, big-time stuff from the left side has put him back on the prospect map.
SCOUTING REPORT: If you throw 100 mph, people are going to notice. If you throw 100 mph with your left hand, people are really going to notice. Facundo does just that, and he used his high-octane heat to bully Florida State League hitters. His fastball got past bats at the top of the zone, and he employed both four-seam and sinking variants. His slider is a mid-80s breaker with plenty of sweep and depth that works running away from lefties or landing at the feet of righties. His changeup is in its nascent stages and doesn't project to be much more than below-average. Facundo's arm stroke is short and compact with only fair extension out front. His strikes were a bit scattered, and his control in the big leagues is likely to be below-average.
THE FUTURE: Facundo's velocity jump and lefthandedness give him a strong foundation upon which to dream. If he can throw more strikes and bring his changeup forward, he could be a leverage reliever.

Year	Age	Club (League)	Level	W	L	ERA	G	GS	IP	H	HR	BB	SO	BB%	SO%	WHIP	AVG
2025	22	FCL Yankees	Rk	0	0	0.00	2	1	5	2	0	3	10	14.3	47.6	0.94	.111
2025	22	Tampa (FSL)	A	1	1	2.14	8	8	34	22	0	14	35	10.6	26.5	1.07	.195
		Minor League Totals		7	5	2.86	43	29	148	96	1	71	207	11.6	33.8	1.13	.184

29 JOSE M. RODRIGUEZ, RHP
FB: 60. **CB:** 55. **SL:** 40. **CH:** 55. **CTL:** 45. **BA Grade:** 45. **Risk:** High. **Adj:** 30.

Born: January 6, 2004. **B-T:** R-R. **HT:** 5-11. **WT:** 170. **Signed:** Dominican Republic, 2023. **Signed by:** Lorenzo Piron.
TRACK RECORD: Rodriguez signed with the Yankees in 2023 and went to the Dominican Summer League for his pro debut. After missing all of 2024 with a shoulder injury, he re-emerged in the Florida Complex and Florida State leagues and showed solid stuff but scattered strikes.
SCOUTING REPORT: Despite standing just 5-foot-11 and weighing in at 170 pounds, Rodriguez can bring the heat. His four-seam fastball averaged around 94 mph and peaked at 97 with fair life through the zone. To make the fastball even better, Rodriguez will need to get it in the zone more often. He backs it with a high-80s curveball, a mid-80s changeup and the occasional slider in the same velocity range. Both the curveball and changeup have the chance to reach above-average with further refinement. Rodriguez's velocity has jumped in recent years thanks to mechanical tweaks that allow him to be more efficient when driving down the mound, and his array of offspeeds took off a bit as well. He's fearless on the mound and showed a willingness to throw any pitch in any count.
THE FUTURE: After getting hit around a bit in Low-A, it's clear Rodriguez has plenty of development remaining. There's little question about the quality of his stuff, but he'll have to be around the zone more often to make the most of his talent. He'll return to Low-A in 2026 and has a chance to be a leverage reliever.

Year	Age	Club (League)	Level	W	L	ERA	G	GS	IP	H	HR	BB	SO	BB%	SO%	WHIP	AVG
2025	21	FCL Yankees	Rk	1	5	2.25	11	8	44	26	0	27	45	14.5	24.2	1.20	.173
2025	21	Tampa (FSL)	A	4	1	5.14	6	5	28	24	3	19	28	15.3	22.6	1.54	.238
		Minor League Totals		5	8	3.81	23	13	78	59	4	56	81	16.1	23.3	1.47	.213

30 CARSON COLEMAN, RHP
FB: 60. **SW:** 55. **CH:** 45. **CTL:** 40. **BA Grade:** 45. **Risk:** High. **Adj:** 30.

Born: April 7, 1998. **B-T:** R-R. **HT:** 6-2. **WT:** 190. **Signed:** Kentucky, 2020 (UDFA). **Signed by:** Mike Gibbons.
TRACK RECORD: Coleman was originally drafted by the Rays in the 33rd round in 2019. He opted to return to Kentucky for his junior season and went unselected in the pandemic-shortened five-round draft. The Yankees signed him as a free agent, and he was in their system through 2023, when the Rangers selected him in the Rule 5 draft. Shoulder and elbow surgeries kept him from ever throwing an official pitch with Texas, and he was returned to New York in 2025. He pitched 17 dominant innings in the minors, peaking at Double-A.
SCOUTING REPORT: Coleman's money pitch is a nasty sinker in the mid 90s with hard, late bite down and away from lefthanders. The pitch helped him get grounders at a rate of 55% during his time in Double-A. He backed the heater mostly with a sweeper slider and the occasional changeup with steep drop and fade. Coleman's delivery is uptempo and violent, and he is a relief-only prospect. He projects to have fringy command when he reaches the big leagues.
THE FUTURE: Finally healthy, Coleman has a chance to make his debut in 2026. He was outrighted off the 40-man roster when he was returned to New York, so he'll have to earn a return to that spot again. He projects as a middle reliever who can overwhelm hitters in big moments.

Year	Age	Club (League)	Level	W	L	ERA	G	GS	IP	H	HR	BB	SO	BB%	SO%	WHIP	AVG
2025	27	FCL Yankees	Rk	0	0	3.00	3	1	3	2	0	0	3	0.0	23.1	0.67	.167
2025	27	Tampa (FSL)	A	0	0	0.00	3	1	3	0	0	0	4	0.0	40.0	0.00	.000
2025	27	Hudson Valley (SAL)	A+	0	0	0.00	4	0	4	1	0	1	3	7.7	23.1	0.50	.083
2025	27	Somerset (EL)	AA	0	0	2.57	7	0	7	5	0	1	5	3.7	18.5	0.86	.200
		Minor League Totals		4	6	3.27	92	2	116	80	5	47	159	9.7	32.7	1.10	.194

Alec Bohm

Philadelphia Phillies

BY JOSH NORRIS

PROJECTED 2029 LINEUP

Catcher	Kehden Hettiger	25
First Base	Bryce Harper	36
Second Base	Aidan Miller	25
Third Base	Alec Bohm	32
Shortstop	Trea Turner	36
Left Field	Justin Crawford	25
Center Field	Dante Nori	24
Right Field	Gabriel Rincones	28
Designated Hitter	Kyle Schwarber	36
No. 1 Starter	Cristopher Sánchez	32
No. 2 Starter	Andrew Painter	26
No. 3 Starter	Jesús Luzardo	31
No. 4 Starter	Aaron Nola	36
No. 5 Starter	Gage Wood	25
Closer	Jhoan Duran	31

The Phillies' season ended in sudden, heartbreaking fashion in the Division Series when reliever Orion Kerkering's throw home in extra innings went awry and allowed the Dodgers to score the series-winning run.

After the shock subsided, they were left to pick up the pieces and begin regrouping for 2026. Part of the plan involved re-upping with slugger Kyle Schwarber, who made it to free agency but landed back with Philadelphia in December on a five-year deal.

Keeping the veteran slugger in Citizens Bank Park is a good start, but the next step will involve fortifying the pitching staff. President of baseball operations Dave Dombrowski, manager Rob Thomson and crew hope righthander Andrew Painter will play a big role.

After a standout showing in the 2024 Arizona Fall League, Painter's 2025 season at Triple-A was uneven. The organization attributed it to rust, as well as a fastball that had lost some of its luster and was hit hard in the International League. If the pitch gains a bit more carry through the zone in 2026, he could be a big help in the team's quest for its first World Series championship since 2008.

Top prospect Aidan Miller might not be far behind. After some early struggles at Double-A, he rounded into form and showed off his tremendous upside. The gains he's made at shortstop as a professional have stuck, and he has the potential to be an offensive force who sticks up the middle. Trea Turner's presence might push him to another infield position in the long run, but his bat has more than enough thump to profile on a corner.

Outfielder Justin Crawford continued to hit for a high average, but a frustratingly high groundball rate polarized evaluators. He should make his MLB debut in 2026 as well.

In the draft, scouting director Brian Barber went with Arkansas righthander Gage Wood in the first round. Wood's stock reached an all-time high during the postseason, when he authored one of the greatest performances in the history of the College World Series by striking out 19 in a no-hitter against Murray State.

The organization's prospect cache took a hit at the deadline when it struck a series of deals at the cost of plenty of young talent. The show-stealer was the move that brought closer Jhoan Duran in from Minnesota for righthander Mick Abel and catcher Eduardo Tait. The two clubs hooked up again when the Phillies added outfielder Harrison Bader for prospects Hendry Mendez and Geremy Villoria.

The Phillies have plenty of star power in their lineup, an aggressive front office and a handful of near-proximity prospects who could provide plenty of impact for years to come. All of those elements should be helpful in an NL East with the similarly situated Mets and a league with the juggernaut Dodgers flexing 3,000 miles away under the California sun.

The pieces are there to contend. To get back to the mountaintop, the Phillies will need their high-priced stars—Bryce Harper, Schwarber, Turner and starting pitchers Zack Wheeler and Aaron Nola—to play to their full potential and their youngest pieces to get up to speed as quickly as possible.

The task won't be easy, but what would the Phillies be without a heavy dose of high hopes? ■

DEPTH CHART

PHILADELPHIA PHILLIES

TOP 2026 ROOKIES	RANK
1. Andrew Painter, RHP	2
2. Justin Crawford, OF	3

BREAKOUT PROSPECTS	RANK
1. Sean Youngerman, RHP	12
2. Ramon Marquez, RHP	13
3. Gabe Craig, RHP	19

SOURCE OF TOP 30 TALENT

Homegrown	26	Acquired	4
College	9	Trade	3
Junior college	0	Rule 5 draft	1
High school	9	Independent league	0
Undrafted free agent	1	Free agent/waivers	0
International	7		

LF
Justin Crawford (3)

CF
Dante Nori (6)
Griffin Burkholder (15)
Dylan Campbell
John Spikerman
TJayy Walton
Victor Cardoza

RF
Gabriel Rincones Jr. (7)
Raylin Heredia

3B
Carson DeMartini (14)

SS
Aidan Miller (1)
Romeli Espinosa (24)
Bryan Rincon (30)
Matthew Ferrara
Logan Dawson

2B
Aroon Escobar (4)
Devin Saltiban (20)
Robert Moore

1B
Keaton Anthony (25)
Austin Murr

C
Alirio Ferrebus (16)
Anderson Araujo (23)
Kehden Hettiger
Caleb Ricketts

LHP

LHSP
Cade Obermueller (10)
Mavis Graves
Angel Liranzo
Juan Amarante

LHRP
James Tallon (29)
Tristan Garnett

RHP

RHSP
Andrew Painter (2)
Gage Wood (5)
Matthew Fisher (8)
Moisés Chace (9)
Cody Bowker (11)
Sean Youngerman (12)
Ramon Marquez (13)
Jean Cabrera (22)
Luke Gabrysh

RHRP
Seth Johnson (17)
Alex McFarlane (18)
Gabe Craig (19)
Zach McCambley (21)
Saul Teran (26)
Yoniel Curet (27)
Casey Steward (28)
Wen-Hui Pan
Daniel Harper
Ryan Degges
Evan Gates

PHILADELPHIA PHILLIES

1 AIDAN MILLER, SS

Born: June 9, 2004. **B-T:** R-R. **HT:** 6-2. **WT:** 205.
Drafted: HS—Dunedin, FL, 2023 (1st round).
Signed by: Bo Way.

TRACK RECORD: Miller's amateur history is long and decorated. He was a part of three of USA Baseball's National Teams, and he hit .423 as a member of the 18U squad. That track record of success led the Phillies to call Miller's name in the first round of the 2023 draft despite a broken left wrist that sidelined him for the bulk of his senior season at Florida's New Port Richey High. So far, the risk has been well worth the reward. Miller has improved in every area and now stands not only as the Phillies' top prospect but also as a premier overall talent. He advanced to Triple-A in his second full season as a professional and was slated for further development in the Arizona Fall League before being pulled before Opening Day.

SCOUTING REPORT: Out of the draft, few believed in Miller's ability to play shortstop. Now, it's hard to find scouts who think he doesn't have the chops to man the position for years in the big leagues. Miller's actions have become more explosive, his footwork has steadied and his arm stroke has improved, leading to more consistent, accurate throws with plenty of zip for shortstop or third base. Now, scouts believe he can handle every type of play a shortstop would be required to make, including slow rollers, grounders deep in the hole and flies to the shallow part of the grass. About the only thing standing in his way is the presence of Phillies megastar Trea Turner. No matter where he winds up, Miller has the offensive chops to profile. He began his 2025 season back at Double-A and struggled early. Evaluators inside and outside the system attributed his slow start to an inordinately high amount of breaking balls thrown his way. Once he adjusted his approach and started letting it rip on fastballs he could handle, his fortunes began to turn. After an excellent May, Miller hit a summer swoon before producing a sweltering August and September that saw him hit .356/.491/.607 with six home runs across 36 games in Double-A and Triple-A. In time, Miller has a chance to be a well-rounded hitter who hits for average, gets on base and produces power in near-equal measure. That prognosis is a departure from his amateur scouting report that predicted power over hitting ability. The improvement stems from an ability to cover the entirety of the plate, handle multiple pitch types and a knack for knowing when to unleash his best swings. Miller is an average runner whose value on the basepaths is boosted by outstanding instincts that allowed him to rack up 59 stolen bases in 2025.

THE FUTURE: Miller was slated to get reps at third base in the AFL, and he will likely get experience there during spring training and the regular season in order to clear a path to the big leagues. Once ready, he has the skills to provide the Phillies with value on both sides of the ball.

BA GRADE
65 Risk: Average
Adjusted grade: 55

SCOUTING GRADES
Hit: 55. Power: 55. Run: 50.
Field: 60. Arm: 60.
Projected future grades on 20-80 scouting scale

BEST TOOLS

BATTING
Best Hitter	Justin Crawford
Best Power Hitter	Gabriel Rincones
Best Strike-Zone Discipline	Aidan Miller
Fastest Baserunner	Justin Crawford
Best Athlete	Matthew Fisher

PITCHING
Best Fastball	Andrew Painter
Best Curveball	Gage Wood
Best Slider	Gabe Craig
Best Changeup	Ramon Marquez
Best Control	Sean Youngerman

FIELDING
Best Defensive Catcher	Kehden Hettiger
Best Defensive Infielder	Bryan Rincon
Best Infield Arm	Bryan Rincon
Best Defensive Outfielder	Dylan Campbell
Best Outfield Arm	Griffin Burkholder

Year	Age	Club (League)	Level	AVG	G	AB	R	H	2B	3B	HR	RBI	BB	SO	SB	OBP	SLG
2025	21	Reading (EL)	AA	.259	108	405	74	105	25	2	13	41	73	116	52	.382	.427
2025	21	Lehigh Valley (IL)	AAA	.333	8	27	8	9	2	0	1	1	9	7	7	.514	.519
		Minor League Totals		.265	238	893	156	237	58	9	25	104	150	238	86	.383	.434

PHILADELPHIA PHILLIES

2 ANDREW PAINTER, RHP
FB: 60. **CB:** 55. **SL:** 60. **SW:** 55. **CH:** 50. **CTL:** 60. **BA Grade:** 65. **Risk:** High. **Adj:** 50.

Born: April 10, 2003. **B-T:** R-R. **HT:** 6-7. **WT:** 215.
Drafted: HS—Fort Lauderdale, FL, 2021 (1st round). **Signed by:** Victor Gomez.
TRACK RECORD: Drafted in the first round in 2021, Painter's 2022 season was one for the record books. He became one of just a handful of high school pitchers to reach Double-A in their first full professional seasons. His elbow started barking during the spring of 2023, and the resulting Tommy John surgery kept him out of action until the 2024 Arizona Fall League. Painter spent his 2025 season at Triple-A Lehigh Valley, where he showed flashes of his upside but also plenty of areas that required further polish.
SCOUTING REPORT: The biggest area of concern during Painter's 2025 season was the downgrade in fastball quality. The pitch retained its premium velocity but began showing more cut than carry and became more hittable as a result. The Phillies attribute some of that backslide to Painter's arm slot dropping as the season wore on. If he can raise his arm slot, the team believes the pitch will return to its previous form. Painter also made several alterations to his arsenal, including the additions of a two-seamer and a sweeper and a move to a split-changeup grip. The sweeper was introduced as another way to combat lefties, and the new changeup worked better with his delivery and produced much more movement. Beyond addressing the downturn in fastball quality, Painter's next step is to turn his control into command and learn which of his pitches play best in different sections of the strike zone and how to properly sequence his mix.
THE FUTURE: Despite Painter's middling year, scouts are still quite bullish and see a future as at least a midrotation starter. How his fastball looks next season and beyond will go a long way toward determining whether those evaluations come true.

Year	Age	Club (League)	Level	W	L	ERA	G	GS	IP	H	HR	BB	SO	BB%	SO%	WHIP	AVG
2025	22	Clearwater (FSL)	A	0	2	3.97	4	4	11	10	2	1	12	2.2	26.7	0.97	.227
2025	22	Lehigh Valley (IL)	AAA	5	6	5.40	22	22	107	119	18	46	111	9.7	23.4	1.55	.281
		Minor League Totals		11	10	3.44	52	52	228	200	25	72	290	7.6	30.8	1.19	.233

3 JUSTIN CRAWFORD, OF
HIT: 55. **POW:** 40. **RUN:** 70. **FLD:** 50. **ARM:** 50. **BA Grade:** 55. **Risk:** Average. **Adj:** 45.

Born: January 13, 2004. **B-T:** L-R. **HT:** 6-3. **WT:** 175.
Drafted: HS—Las Vegas, 2022 (1st round). **Signed by:** Zach Friedman.
TRACK RECORD: The son of four-time all-star outfielder Carl Crawford, Justin has been one of the most productive hitters for average in the minor leagues since the Phillies drafted him 17th overall out of high school in 2022. Crawford spent all of 2025 at Triple-A Lehigh Valley and hit .334 to rank third in the full-season minor leagues. He owns a career .332 average as a pro.
SCOUTING REPORT: There's little doubt about Crawford's ability to make hard contact. Now, the question is whether he'll ever get the ball in the air often enough to turn it into impact. His groundball rate over the last two seasons is 60.2%, fourth-worst in the minors among players with 500 or more at-bats. He's made minor improvements year over year in that department, but he still lets the ball travel too far into the strike zone to put balls over infielders' heads and into gaps, where his double-plus speed would open the door for extra bases. If Crawford's power never materializes, it's imperative that he sticks in center field. Whether he can is the subject of debate. Scouts see a player whose elite speed can help him make up for late jumps and rough routes, while analysts rate him as one of the worst defensive center fielders in the minor leagues. Part of the reason for the disparity is because the Phillies have had Crawford play a more shallow center field in order to amplify his excellent ability to come in on shallow flies. The strategy downgrades his chances of reaching deeper drives, thus dinging his ratings. His game-breaking speed and average arm would make Crawford a plus defender in left field, but a long-term move would require him to unlock more power to fit the offensive profile.
THE FUTURE: Crawford will have an opportunity to make the Phillies' Opening Day roster, but his ultimate value will key on whether he can turn his raw strength into higher-quality contact.

Year	Age	Club (League)	Level	AVG	G	AB	R	H	2B	3B	HR	RBI	BB	SO	SB	OBP	SLG
2025	21	Lehigh Valley (IL)	AAA	.334	112	440	88	147	23	4	7	47	58	91	46	.411	.452
		Minor League Totals		.322	325	1304	246	420	70	17	19	177	129	268	145	.385	.446

PHILADELPHIA PHILLIES

4 AROON ESCOBAR, 2B
HIT: 55. **POW:** 45. **RUN:** 40. **FLD:** 40. **ARM:** 50. **BA Grade:** 50. **Risk:** Average. **Adj:** 40.

Born: January 1, 2005. **B-T:** R-R. **HT:** 5-11. **WT:** 221.
Signed: Venezuela, 2022. **Signed by:** Rafael Alvarez/William Mota.
TRACK RECORD: After a middling first two professional seasons in the Dominican Summer League, Escobar took off in his first stateside season in 2024, batting .338 with a .495 on-base percentage in a Florida Complex League season shortened by shin splints in both legs. He spent most of 2025 with Low-A Clearwater before advancing to High-A in July and finally to Double-A for five games. Escobar finished with 15 home runs and an 18.2% strikeout rate in 120 games.
SCOUTING REPORT: Escobar's game is predicated on plenty of contact with sprinkles of power as well. He pairs a zone-miss rate of just 16% with a 90th percentile exit velocity of 104.7 mph. To get the most out of his strength and bat-to-ball skills, Escobar will have to learn to turn on pitches and pull them with authority, which is a weak point of his game at the moment. Toward the later part of the season, scouts noticed that pitchers were having success pounding him inside with fastballs as well as a little bit more willingness to chase than he'd shown at either Class A stop. It's crucial that Escobar gets to every ounce of his offensive potential, because his defensive value is likely to be fringe-average at best. His body is already softer than one would like, and he'll have to stay on top of his conditioning in order to stick at second base. His footwork gets lazy at times, which leads to a lack of range on grounders and waning accuracy on his throws. Both of those areas need to be sewn up if Escobar is to remain up the middle.
THE FUTURE: Escobar will likely return to Double-A Reading to begin 2026. If he can stay on top of his conditioning and do a better job protecting the inside part of the plate against premium velocity, he has a chance to be an offensive-minded second baseman.

Year	Age	Club (League)	Level	AVG	G	AB	R	H	2B	3B	HR	RBI	BB	SO	SB	OBP	SLG
2025	20	Clearwater (FSL)	A	.285	69	270	52	77	12	0	11	42	32	51	10	.377	.452
2025	20	Jersey Shore (SAL)	A+	.256	46	168	28	43	1	3	4	19	22	41	14	.348	.369
2025	20	Reading (EL)	AA	.182	5	22	2	4	0	1	0	1	2	6	0	.250	.273
		Minor League Totals		.262	225	790	156	207	26	5	22	124	121	147	57	.378	.391

5 GAGE WOOD, RHP
FB: 70. **CB:** 50. **SL:** 60. **CH:** 45. **CTL:** 50 **BA Grade:** 50. **Risk:** Average. **Adj:** 40.

Born: December 15, 2003. **B-T:** R-R. **HT:** 6-0. **WT:** 205.
Drafted: Arkansas, 2025 (1st round). **Signed by:** Tommy Field.
TRACK RECORD: Arkansas ruled the back half of the first round of the 2025 draft. Four Razorbacks were taken in a 16-pick stretch, beginning with Wood by the Phillies at pick No. 26. Wood spent three seasons in Fayetteville that culminated with a 19-strikeout no-hitter against Murray State in the College World Series. A little less than a month later, Wood heard his name called in the draft, and he signed for $3 million. He made his pro debut toward the end of the season with Low-A Clearwater, including an outing in the Florida State League playoffs.
SCOUTING REPORT: There's zero doubt that Wood has the stuff to dominate hitters. The question is: Will he do so as a starter or as a reliever? The righthander's 2025 season was interrupted by a shoulder injury that cost him two months, and his heaviest career workload is 59.1 innings, which came in 2024 and includes a stint in the Cape Cod League. One factor pointing toward a future in a rotation is a full, four-pitch repertoire headed by a dynamite fastball/curveball combination that he leaned on heavily with Arkansas. Beyond its velocity, Wood's fastball earns raves for its analytical properties and the resulting miss rate of 32% in college. The Phillies would like Wood to use his slider—which they believe has at least average potential—and his changeup as he integrates himself into pro ball. The changeup, held with a split-finger grip, was seldom used in college and is a clear fourth pitch at this point. Another part of Wood's professional education will involve learning how to moderate his between-start workload.
THE FUTURE: Wood's college pedigree should allow him to move rapidly through the system. He should reach High-A Jersey Shore early in 2026 with a chance to advance quickly to the upper levels.. He'll get plenty of chances to start, but he has a fallback option as a shutdown reliever as well.

Year	Age	Club (League)	Level	W	L	ERA	G	GS	IP	H	HR	BB	SO	BB%	SO%	WHIP	AVG
2025	21	Clearwater (FSL)	A	0	1	4.50	1	1	2	1	0	2	5	22.2	55.6	1.50	.143
		Minor League Totals		0	1	4.50	1	1	2	1	0	2	5	22.2	55.6	1.50	.143

PHILADELPHIA PHILLIES

6 DANTE NORI, OF
HIT: 50. **POW:** 30. **RUN:** 60. **FLD:** 60. **ARM:** 45. **BA Grade:** 50. **Risk:** High. **Adj:** 35.

Born: October 7, 2004. **B-T:** L-L. **HT:** 5-10. **WT:** 190.
Drafted: HS—Northville, MI, 2024 (1st round). **Signed by:** Derrick Ross.
TRACK RECORD: Nori was one of the older high school players available in the 2024 draft, but the Phillies still felt strongly enough about his profile to select him 27th overall and pay him $2,497,500 to turn pro out of his Michigan high school rather than matriculate to Mississippi State. In his first full season as a pro, Nori raced from Low-A Clearwater to Double-A Reading and ranked among the top five in the organization in hits (127), walks (75) and stolen bases (52).
SCOUTING REPORT: Nori's game is based on contact and speed, and he showed both skills in spades in 2025. His zone-miss rate was just 13.1%, good enough to place him among the best in the system. His at-bats are professional, he knows the strike zone and he has just enough raw thump to occasionally put a charge into a ball. To get to more power, he'll need to add more of a load to his swing and put his lower half to better use, though his body is compact and likely maxed out, so he won't be able to rely on further projection for a power boost. He also could stand to improve his direction to the ball, which scouts say sometimes includes a leak to his pull side. Nori is a solid center fielder who could get to plus by ironing out some of the routes he takes to fly balls, though his plus speed might help him make up for some of the messier paths. His fringe-average arm fits just fine up the middle but would limit him to left field if he had to move off the position.
THE FUTURE: Nori will return to Double-A Reading, where his experience in colder weather will help him survive the early months in the Eastern League. He has a chance to be a table-setter who gets on base and holds down center field, but he'll need plenty of work to reach that ceiling.

Year	Age	Club (League)	Level	AVG	G	AB	R	H	2B	3B	HR	RBI	BB	SO	SB	OBP	SLG
2025	20	Clearwater (FSL)	A	.262	109	423	63	111	16	11	4	43	66	75	37	.363	.381
2025	20	Jersey Shore (SAL)	A+	.279	11	43	8	12	2	0	0	4	8	8	13	.396	.326
2025	20	Reading (EL)	AA	.190	5	21	1	4	0	1	0	0	1	2	2	.227	.286
		Minor League Totals		.261	125	487	72	127	18	12	4	47	75	85	52	.361	.372

7 GABRIEL RINCONES JR., OF
HIT: 40. **POW:** 60. **RUN:** 30. **FLD:** 45. **ARM:** 55. **BA Grade:** 45. **Risk:** Average. **Adj:** 35.

Born: March 3, 2001. **B-T:** L-R. **HT:** 6-4. **WT:** 225.
Drafted: Florida Atlantic, 2022 (3rd round). **Signed by:** Victor Gomez.
TRACK RECORD: Rincones was drafted out of Florida Atlantic in 2022 and has spent most of his pro career showing flashes of his tools in between stints on the injured list. He dealt with a shoulder injury in 2022 and then had surgery on his left thumb in 2024. He made up for lost time in the Arizona Fall League, where he walked more than he struck out and was named to the league's annual Fall Stars Game. The son of a former Mariners minor league pitcher, Rincones was healthy at Triple-A Lehigh Valley for the entire 2025 season and set career highs for games played (119) and home runs (18).
SCOUTING REPORT: Rincones is one of the best ball-strikers in the organization, and his average, 90th percentile and maximum exit velocities all rank among the best in the system. He does a good job of staying within the strike zone, and his chase rate is above-average as well. Both traits showed up in his 80 walks, which were second in the system behind only top prospect Aidan Miller. Rincones' biggest weakness is lefthanded pitchers, who held him to a slash line of just .107/.215/.107 without an extra-base hit over 65 plate appearances in 2025. By contrast, those numbers against righthanders were .261/.392/.480 with all of his 18 home runs. All but one of his 78 games in the field came in right field, where his improved conditioning helped him play fringe-average defense. He has above-average arm strength and threw out five runners on the bases in 2025. Rincones' well below-average speed is masked by excellent instincts on the bases that allowed him to swipe 21 bases in 26 tries with Lehigh Valley.
THE FUTURE: Rincones looks like a strong-side platoon player on a contender or a regular on a non-contender. The 2025 season was his best yet, and he could be in line to make his MLB debut in 2026.

Year	Age	Club (League)	Level	AVG	G	AB	R	H	2B	3B	HR	RBI	BB	SO	SB	OBP	SLG
2025	24	Lehigh Valley (IL)	AAA	.240	119	412	81	99	22	1	18	73	80	114	21	.370	.430
		Minor League Totals		.246	307	1125	203	277	69	5	44	165	175	322	76	.357	.434

PHILADELPHIA PHILLIES

8 MATTHEW FISHER, RHP
FB: 55. **CB:** 50. **SL:** 60. **CH:** 45. **CTL:** 50. **BA Grade:** 50. **Risk:** High. **Adj:** 35.

Born: March 14, 2006. **B-T:** R-R. **HT:** 6-3. **WT:** 200.
Drafted: HS—Evansville, IN, 2025 (7th round). **Signed by:** Derrick Ross.
TRACK RECORD: Fisher was a two-sport athlete in high school and won Gatorade player of the year for the state of Indiana after racking up 42 touchdowns in his senior season at Evansville's Memorial High. Drafted in the seventh round in 2025, Fisher was signed away from a commitment to Indiana with a $1.25 million bonus, the second largest in the Phillies' draft class and the highest seventh-round figure in draft history.
SCOUTING REPORT: Fisher's combination of stuff and athleticism made him an extremely attractive prospect. He starts his four-pitch mix with a low-90s fastball with plenty of cut-ride action from a lower release height. The pitch topped out at 95 mph in his final season of high school. His best offspeed pitch is a potentially plus slider, and he backs it with a slower curveball and a potentially fringe-average changeup. He shows a strong feel for spin throughout his arsenal. Like Dante Nori in 2024, Fisher was 19 when he was drafted and was one of the older prep players on the board. The righthander has an ideal pitcher's frame at 6-foot-3, 200 pounds, though there's still room for strength gains and he showed signs of fatigue down the stretch in high school. Fisher does a good job repeating his delivery and projects for average control, especially if he gets stronger and can maintain his best stuff throughout the course of the longer seasons he's set to encounter in the minor leagues.
THE FUTURE: Fisher did not debut in 2025 and instead headed to fall instructional camp. His combination of stuff, analytical markers and athleticism could add up to a high ceiling, and the Phillies bet big on those variables coalescing into a pitcher who will be well worth the wait over the next few years.

Year	Age	Club (League)	Level	W	L	ERA	G	GS	IP	H	HR	BB	SO	BB%	SO%	WHIP	AVG
2025	19	Did not play															

9 MOISÉS CHACE, RHP
FB: 60. **SL:** 60. **CH:** 50. **SW:** 55. **CTL:** 45. **BA Grade:** 50. **Risk:** High. **Adj:** 35.

Born: June 9, 2003. **B-T:** R-R. **HT:** 6-1. **WT:** 210.
Signed: Venezuela, 2019. **Signed by:** Koby Perez (Orioles).
TRACK RECORD: Chace signed with the Orioles in 2019 but didn't debut until 2021 after the pandemic wiped out the 2020 minor league season. After three nondescript seasons with Baltimore, Chace broke out in 2024 and was included in a trade to the Phillies that sent Gregory Soto to the Orioles. Righthander Seth Johnson also came to the Phillies in the deal. Chace looked poised to raise his profile even higher in 2025—and perhaps finish the year in the big leagues—but he reported to spring training out of shape and with diminished stuff. He eventually required Tommy John surgery, which he had in June.
SCOUTING REPORT: At his best, Chace worked with a mid-90s fastball that peaked at 98 mph and had the analytical characteristics to miss plenty of bats. The pitch's diminished velocity was the first sign of trouble in 2025. He complemented his fastball with a short, hard slider and a sweeper, as well as a changeup. The slider featured sharp break and was effective against hitters from both sides of the plate, while the sweeper was one of his go-to offerings to get hitters to swing and miss. The changeup was Chace's least-refined offspeed pitch, but scouts believed it had a chance to get to average with further development. He was also set this season to work on honing his command and doing a better job of getting ahead of hitters to set up his best strikeout pitches. He made six starts at Double-A Reading before landing on the injured list, and his control still showed the need for sizable improvement. He walked 12 hitters in 16.2 innings.
THE FUTURE: Chace's injury has dimmed his ceiling and delayed his timeline to the big leagues. He should return at some point this summer and could jump on the reliever track once he returns. Before a decision is made, he and the team will have to see if his stuff returns intact.

Year	Age	Club (League)	Level	W	L	ERA	G	GS	IP	H	HR	BB	SO	BB%	SO%	WHIP	AVG
2025	22	Reading (EL)	AA	0	0	3.24	6	6	17	15	3	12	19	16.0	25.3	1.62	.242
		Minor League Totals		12	13	4.39	74	45	227	177	18	152	304	15.0	30.1	1.45	.214

PHILADELPHIA PHILLIES

10 CADE OBERMUELLER, LHP

FB: 50. **SL:** 60. **CH:** 50. **CTL:** 45. **BA Grade:** 50. **Risk:** High. **Adj:** 35.

Born: July 28, 2003. **B-T:** L-L. **HT:** 6-0. **WT:** 170.
Drafted: Iowa, 2025 (2nd round). **Signed by:** Nate Field.

TRACK RECORD: The Rangers drafted Obermueller in the 19th round in 2024, but he chose to return to Iowa for another chance to improve his draft stock. He responded by cutting his walk rate nearly in half while raising his strikeout rate a few ticks as well. The Phillies pounced on him in the second round in 2025 and signed him for $1,197,500. After tossing a career-high 83.1 innings, Obermueller was shut down after signing.

SCOUTING REPORT: The Phillies liked what they'd seen from Obermueller in 2024, when he was teammates with righthander Marcus Morgan, whom the Phillies drafted in the ninth round that summer. They became even more interested in Obermueller when he started throwing strikes at a much higher clip thanks to a much more controlled delivery than he had shown in years past. Couple those gains with a delivery that features a low release height, excellent extension and a low-90s sinker that clipped 97 mph in his draft year, and the upside was enough to make them pull the trigger in the second round. Obermueller backs his fastball with a sweeper that featured 20 inches of break. He also has a firm, seldom-used changeup that scouts believe could be average if he throws it more often. The Phillies also might work with Obermueller to add a shorter breaking ball to his mix to give him another offspeed pitch he can throw in the zone to set up his sweeper to finish hitters.

THE FUTURE: Obermueller's smaller frame and currently limited pitch mix might lead him down a reliever's path. For now, the Phillies will bet that the gains he showed in his draft year will be sticky enough to give him a chance to stick as a back-end starter in a few years. If not, his sinker and slider should be an effective combination in the late innings.

Year	Age	Club (League)	Level	W	L	ERA	G	GS	IP	H	HR	BB	SO	BB%	SO%	WHIP	AVG
2025	21	Did not play															

11 CODY BOWKER, RHP

FB: 60. **SL:** 50. **CH:** 60. **CT:** 40. **CTL:** 50. **BA Grade:** 45. **Risk:** Average. **Adj:** 35.

Born: December 18, 2003. **B-T:** R-R. **HT:** 6-1. **WT:** 212. **Drafted:** Vanderbilt, 2025 (3rd round). **Signed by:** Timi Moni.

TRACK RECORD: In high school, Bowker was a powerful outfielder who earned Maine's Gatorade player of the year honor in 2022. He started his college career at Georgetown, where he was a two-way player as a freshman before transitioning to the mound full-time as a sophomore. He spent the summer before his junior year in the Cape Cod League, then transferred to Vanderbilt. Bowker punched out 99 hitters and walked just 28 over 72 innings with the Commodores, then was taken by the Phillies in the third round. He signed for $700,000 and was shut down afterward. He will make his pro debut in 2026.

SCOUTING REPORT: Bowker's low-slot delivery creates plenty of funk and deception, but by no means is he a smoke-and-mirrors artist. The righty heads a four-pitch mix with a low-90s fastball that plays up because of excellent life through the zone and can appear to rise thanks to a delivery where his back knee is nearly touching the ground upon release. He backs it with a potentially plus changeup in the mid 80s that is sold well thanks to the sustained effort throughout his delivery. His cutter and slider can blend together at times, but the former has slicing, almost Frisbee-like action at its best. Although their shapes are similar, the cutter comes in about 8 mph faster than the slider. Despite his complicated delivery, Bowker projects to have average control.

THE FUTURE: Bowker's college pedigree could earn him a ticket to High-A Jersey Shore to officially begin his pro career. His deep arsenal could help him land a spot in the back of a rotation one day.

Year	Age	Club (League)	Level	W	L	ERA	G	GS	IP	H	HR	BB	SO	BB%	SO%	WHIP	AVG
2025	21	Did not play															

PHILADELPHIA PHILLIES

12 SEAN YOUNGERMAN, RHP
FB: 55. **SL:** 50. **CH:** 50. **CTL:** 55. **BA Grade:** 50. **Risk:** High. **Adj:** 35.

Born: July 9, 2004. **B-T:** R-R. **HT:** 6-3. **WT:** 230. **Drafted:** Oklahoma State, 2025 (4th round). **Signed by:** Tommy Field.
TRACK RECORD: After two seasons at Westmont College and summers in the California Collegiate and Cape Cod leagues, Youngerman transferred to Oklahoma State for his draft season. With the Cowboys, Youngerman punched out 59 against just eight walks over 52 innings. He was used predominantly out of the bullpen but made eight starts. The Phillies took him in the fourth round and shut him down after signing, but he got some work in at the team's minor league complex in Florida.
SCOUTING REPORT: Youngerman leads his mix with a 93-95 mph fastball that gets up to 98. He does an excellent job throwing the heater for strikes, and the pitch has plenty of life through the zone that often helps it play above its velocity. He backs it with a slider-cutter hybrid with horizontal break and a changeup in the mid 80s with heavy sinking action toward the feet of righthanders. The Phillies believe both of Youngerman's offspeed pitches have the potential to be average big league offerings. With his three pitches and excellent strike-throwing ability, Youngerman has the pieces to be developed as a starter. The Phillies plan to take that tack with him once he makes his professional debut in 2026.
THE FUTURE: Youngerman has the qualities needed to project as a back-end starter. Now, he'll need to bring his offspeed offerings forward a few clicks in the Phillies' pitching lab. He has the pedigree to start his career at High-A Jersey Shore.

Year	Age	Club (League)	Level	W	L	ERA	G	GS	IP	H	HR	BB	SO	BB%	SO%	WHIP	AVG
2025	20	Did not play															

13 RAMON MARQUEZ, RHP
FB: 55. **SL:** 40. **CH:** 60. **CTL:** 60. **BA Grade:** 50. **Risk:** High. **Adj:** 35.

Born: September 19, 2005. **B-T:** R-R. **HT:** 6-1. **WT:** 210. **Signed:** Mexico, 2025. **Signed by:** Charlie Gastelum.
TRACK RECORD: Marquez was born in Phoenix but moved to Mexico and signed for $10,000 in January 2025. He began his career in the Florida Complex League and quickly began to percolate as one of the team's top arms in the lower levels. He earned a promotion to Low-A Clearwater in August. After a rocky full-season debut, he allowed just three runs over his final 14 innings. He struck out 18 and walked just two in that span. He finished with a flourish, striking out seven over five one-hit innings.
SCOUTING REPORT: Right now, Marquez's money-makers are a 92-96 mph four-seamer and a changeup, which he complements with a slider that needs plenty of refinement. The fastball has ride-run properties and bores in on righthanded hitters, while the changeup shows sudden drop and produced a miss rate of 62.1%. The slider will occasionally flash fringe average, but the pitch needs a lot more work to consistently reach those heights. His delivery is compact and repeatable, which allowed him to pound the zone at both of his stops. He walked just 17 hitters in 55 innings and projects to have plus control. Beyond refinement of his slider, Marquez needs to get strong enough to hold up to a longer workload, and the Phillies might also add a two-seamer to his mix.
THE FUTURE: After a fantastic debut, Marquez should return to Low-A to begin 2026. He has a chance to fit toward the back of a rotation once he's fully formed.

Year	Age	Club (League)	Level	W	L	ERA	G	GS	IP	H	HR	BB	SO	BB%	SO%	WHIP	AVG
2025	19	FCL Phillies	Rk	1	3	4.50	10	8	38	36	4	12	50	7.1	29.8	1.26	.245
2025	19	Clearwater (FSL)	A	2	0	4.24	4	4	17	16	0	5	22	7.1	31.4	1.24	.258
		Minor League Totals		3	3	4.42	14	12	55	52	4	17	72	7.1	30.3	1.25	.249

14 CARSON DeMARTINI, SS
HIT: 40. **POW:** 50. **RUN:** 45. **FLD:** 55. **ARM:** 55. **BA Grade:** 45. **Risk:** Average. **Adj:** 35.

Born: Dec. 27, 2002. **B-T:** L-R. **HT:** 6-0. **WT:** 194. **Drafted:** Virginia Tech, 2024 (4th round). **Signed by:** Kellan McKeon.
TRACK RECORD: DeMartini spent three years with Virginia Tech and a summer in the Cape Cod League before the Phillies chose him in the fourth round in 2024. After a 24-game post-draft stint with Low-A, DeMartini opened his 2025 season with a strong turn at High-A and a tougher look with Double-A Reading.
SCOUTING REPORT: After an outstanding stint in the South Atlantic League, DeMartini struggled mightily in his first test at Double-A. Righthanders, lefthanders, fastballs and offspeeds vexed him, and he struck out more than 25% of the time and produced just 15 extra-base hits in 292 plate appearances. Scouts saw a player caught in between a pull-happy approach and a more balanced, all-fields plan of attack. His overall and zone-miss rates were high, but the contact he made was loud. DeMartini's 90th percentile exit velocity was 104.2 mph and he maxed out at 111.4 mph. He spent most of his defensive reps at third

base but got a fair amount of time at shortstop as well. Ultimately, his best fit is at third base, where he can be an above-average defender with an above-average arm. DeMartini is a fringe-average runner whose instincts allowed him to swipe 45 bases.
THE FUTURE: After a rough introduction to the upper levels, DeMartini will need to retool his approach to find a way to make more contact. If he can do that, he has the defensive value to handle both positions on the left side of the infield in a utility role with plenty of paths to playing time.

Year	Age	Club (League)	Level	AVG	G	AB	R	H	2B	3B	HR	RBI	BB	SO	SB	OBP	SLG
2025	22	Jersey Shore (SAL)	A+	.284	53	190	34	54	10	1	8	30	31	64	18	.402	.474
2025	22	Reading (EL)	AA	.202	66	257	37	52	10	3	2	22	28	75	27	.291	.288
		Minor League Totals		.250	143	539	89	135	25	6	12	61	68	153	53	.347	.386

15 GRIFFIN BURKHOLDER, OF
HIT: 40. **POW:** 50. **RUN:** 70. **FLD:** 50. **ARM:** 55. **BA Grade:** 50. **Risk:** High. **Adj:** 35.

Born: August 3, 2005. **B-T:** R-R. **HT:** 6-2. **WT:** 195.
Drafted: HS—South Riding, VA, 2024 (2nd round). **Signed by:** Jeff Zona.
TRACK RECORD: The Phillies spread a large chunk of their 2024 bonus pool to their first two choices—Dante Nori and Burkholder, high school outfielders whom they chose in the first and second rounds of the draft. Each player earned an identical bonus of $2,497,500, and Burkholder's was used to keep him from playing at West Virginia. A hamstring injury limited Burkholder to just one game in his pro debut and then just 34 in 2025 with more health issues. He was placed on the 60-day injured list on Aug. 3 and did not return.
SCOUTING REPORT: Despite the lack of action, the Phillies still believe in Burkholder's upside. At his best, he shows the potential to produce both power and speed. The former trait showed up in some of the system's best raw exit velocity numbers, albeit in a short sample and against lower-level competition. His overall and zone-miss rates were higher than ideal as well. When he's healthy, Burkholder has impressed scouts with his big league body, raw power, arm strength and double-plus speed. There's plenty in his approach that needs to tighten up, and his swing decisions are poor as well.
THE FUTURE: Once healthy, Burkholder will get a second chance at a first impression. That opportunity will likely come at the Class A levels. He has a chance to be an everyday outfielder with plenty of tools.

Year	Age	Club (League)	Level	AVG	G	AB	R	H	2B	3B	HR	RBI	BB	SO	SB	OBP	SLG
2025	19	FCL Phillies	Rk	.190	15	58	5	11	4	0	2	8	5	17	1	.266	.362
2025	19	Clearwater (FSL)	A	.203	19	69	11	14	6	1	2	5	7	25	0	.309	.406
		Minor League Totals		.202	35	129	17	26	10	2	4	13	12	42	1	.293	.403

16 ALIRIO FERREBUS, C
HIT: 45. **POW:** 50. **RUN:** 40. **FLD:** 50. **ARM:** 45. **BA Grade:** 50. **Risk:** High. **Adj:** 35.

Born: September 12, 2005. **B-T:** R-R. **HT:** 6-2. **WT:** 214. **Signed:** Venezuela, 2023. **Signed by:** Elvis Garcia.
TRACK RECORD: Ferrebus signed out of Venezuela and spent his first season and a half in the Dominican Summer League before earning a promotion to the Florida Complex League in the middle of the season. He spent the first 25 games of 2025 back in the FCL before moving to Low-A Clearwater. His season was limited to just 60 games by a broken wrist. He made up for some of that lost time with a stint in the Australian Winter League.
SCOUTING REPORT: Ferrebus doesn't have a plus tool on his card, but he has a chance to be fringy to average in every area except speed. He does a good job making contact on pitches within the strike zone but will need to work on his chase rate as he moves up the ladder. There's plenty of raw thump in Ferrebus' bat, and he finished the year with respective 90th percentile and max exit velocities of 104.2 mph and 112 mph, but his yearlong groundball rate of 56.3% kept him from maximizing his damage. Ferrebus is strong-bodied and physical, and he has a chance to be an average defender behind the plate if he can stay limber enough. Scouts believe he has at least average arm strength but will need to iron out his throwing mechanics to become more accurate when trying to cut down attempted base burglars. He's a below-average runner.
THE FUTURE: Ferrebus has the chops to be an average catcher with offensive upside as well, but his power numbers will be worth monitoring after coming back from the wrist injury. He should begin the year back at Low-A.

Year	Age	Club (League)	Level	AVG	G	AB	R	H	2B	3B	HR	RBI	BB	SO	SB	OBP	SLG
2025	19	FCL Phillies	Rk	.267	25	90	15	24	5	1	4	18	11	17	0	.368	.478
2025	19	Clearwater (FSL)	A	.219	44	160	22	35	6	0	1	25	6	28	2	.272	.275
		Minor League Totals		.275	114	389	63	107	21	1	9	71	32	69	8	.357	.404

PHILADELPHIA PHILLIES

17 SETH JOHNSON, RHP

FB: 60. **CB:** 40. **SL:** 50. **SP:** 40. **CTL:** 40. **BA Grade:** 40. **Risk:** Mild. **Adj:** 35.

Born: September 19, 1998. **B-T:** R-R. **HT:** 6-1. **WT:** 204. **Drafted:** Campbell, 2019 (1st round supp.).
Signed by: Joe Hastings (Rays).
TRACK RECORD: Johnson began his amateur career as a position player for Louisburg (N.C.) JC. He transferred to Campbell for his draft season and tried his hand at pitching, to fantastic results. The Rays took him with the 40th overall pick and dealt him to Baltimore in 2022, just before he had Tommy John surgery. The Phillies acquired him—along with righty Moises Chace—in the deal that sent Gregory Soto to the Orioles.
SCOUTING REPORT: By and large, Johnson works with a four-seamer and slider. The heater averaged 97 mph and the slider came in around 88 mph. He utilized a low-90s splitter as his changeup, and sprinkled in a mid-70s curveball with true downer action. All together, Johnson did a solid job getting whiffs and limiting walks, but he needs to improve his command to miss more bats overall. His arm action is a bit rigid, which limits his precision and leads to the kinds of mistakes hitters typically turn into extra bases. That's proved particularly true against big leaguers, who have reached him for four home runs over 15 innings spread across the last two seasons. Johnson's background as a position player has made him one of the best overall athletes in the system.
THE FUTURE: There's no doubt that Johnson has bat-missing pitches. To do so more often, he'll need to sharpen his command. His future is as a middle reliever, and he'll fight for a longer look—and possibly a spot on the Opening Day roster—in spring training. He has one minor league option remaining.

Year	Age	Club (League)	Level	W	L	ERA	G	GS	IP	H	HR	BB	SO	BB%	SO%	WHIP	AVG
2025	26	Lehigh Valley (IL)	AAA	5	5	4.75	39	4	61	58	4	35	67	12.9	24.7	1.53	.253
2025	26	Philadelphia (NL)	MLB	1	1	4.26	10	0	13	11	3	4	17	7.4	31.5	1.18	.220
		Minor League Totals		14	21	3.18	104	62	297	257	25	136	333	10.8	26.4	1.32	.233
		Major League Totals		1	2	9.00	11	1	15	19	4	7	17	9.7	23.6	1.73	.297

18 ALEX McFARLANE, RHP

FB: 60. **SL:** 60. **CTL:** 40. **BA Grade:** 40. **Risk:** Average. **Adj:** 30.

Born: June 9, 2001. **B-T:** R-R. **HT:** 6-3. **WT:** 200. **Drafted:** Miami, 2022 (4th round). **Signed by:** Victor Gomez.
TRACK RECORD: If he makes it, McFarlane would become just the 16th big leaguer born in the Virgin Islands. He pitched collegiately at Miami, where his numbers were middling. The Phillies saw enough ceiling to call his name in the fourth round in 2022 and sign him for $575,000. After a season and change with Low-A Clearwater, McFarlane missed the 2024 season while recovering from Tommy John surgery. He returned in 2025 and showed enough promise to merit addition to the 40-man roster after the season.
SCOUTING REPORT: Before the surgery, McFarlane's upside was as a starter who could use a sinker, slider and splitter to overwhelm hitters at the back of a rotation. Now, his future is trending toward the bullpen and the splitter might be de-emphasized. The Phillies worked with McFarlane this year to clean up the grip on his four-seamer to improve its quality, and they shifted him on the rubber to get better angles on his arsenal. Scouts like McFarlane's raw stuff but foresee issues if he can't better repeat his delivery. In particular, he has trouble locating his sinker in spots that would get him the grounders he seeks. They also believe the slider has taken a step back, though it still projects as a plus pitch.
THE FUTURE: None of McFarlane's four appearances at Double-A came as a starter, and it's increasingly likely that the bullpen will be his permanent home. His debut could come at some point in 2026 and with a little more polish he fits as a middle reliever who thrives on weak contact.

Year	Age	Club (League)	Level	W	L	ERA	G	GS	IP	H	HR	BB	SO	BB%	SO%	WHIP	AVG
2025	24	Jersey Shore (SAL)	A+	2	9	4.72	24	18	74	60	4	40	74	12.5	23.1	1.35	.221
2025	24	Reading (EL)	AA	2	0	6.35	4	0	6	7	0	3	8	12.0	32.0	1.76	.318
		Minor League Totals		4	16	5.40	47	37	138	125	9	84	163	13.7	26.5	1.51	.243

19 GABE CRAIG, RHP

FB: 60. **SL:** 70. **CTL:** 50. **BA Grade:** 40. **Risk:** Average. **Adj:** 30.

Born: July 3, 2001. **B-T:** R-R. **HT:** 6-5. **WT:** 209. **Drafted:** Baylor, 2025 (5th round). **Signed by:** Tommy Field.
TRACK RECORD: Craig's six seasons in college included stops at Tyler (Texas) JC, Texas A&M and three seasons at Baylor. The righthander's final season with the Bears was dominance defined. In 32 innings, he allowed 13 hits and just three walks. He struck out 51 of the 113 hitters he faced, good for a 45.1% clip. The Phillies drafted him in the fifth round in 2025 and signed him to a well below-slot bonus of $197,500. His first pro experience consisted of three one-inning relief appearances at Low-A Clearwater.

SCOUTING REPORT: Given his age and pedigree, Craig has the potential to move through the minors quickly. An outstanding slider should also aid that rise. The pitch has the potential to be a double-plus weapon and already stands among the best in the system. The pitch sits in the mid 80s and features the kind of devastating sweep and depth that turns hitters into pretzels. Currently, he works with a mid-90s four-seam fastball with excellent riding life through the zone. He might add a two-seamer in the coming seasons. Craig has a whippy arm, a low slot and is an athletic mover on the mound. His strike-throwing improved drastically in his final year at Baylor, and he projects to reach average control.
THE FUTURE: Craig has the kind of pitch mix that can help him buzzsaw through the minor leagues. At the very least, he should reach Double-A. If his strike-throwing improvements are sticky, he could be an impact reliever.

Year	Age	Club (League)	Level	W	L	ERA	G	GS	IP	H	HR	BB	SO	BB%	SO%	WHIP	AVG
2025	23	Clearwater (FSL)	A	0	0	0.00	3	0	3	0	0	1	5	10.0	50.0	0.33	.000
		Minor League Totals		0	0	0.00	3	0	3	0	0	1	5	10.0	50.0	0.33	.000

20 DEVIN SALTIBAN, OF/2B

HIT: 40. **POW:** 50. **RUN:** 55. **FLD:** 50. **ARM:** 50. **BA Grade:** 45. **Risk:** High. **Adj:** 30.

Born: February 15, 2005. **B-T:** R-R. **HT:** 5-9. **WT:** 189. **Drafted:** HS—Hilo, HI, 2023 (3rd round).
Signed by: Demerius Pittman.
TRACK RECORD: Saltiban was an outfielder in high school, but a Phillies crosschecker saw him take grounders in warmups and was intrigued. They drafted him in the third round in 2023 on the strength of the kind of skill set that required patience but was dripping with upside. He hinted at that potential during the 2024 season, but his follow-up campaign was stunted by a ruptured testicle. He spent his winter playing in Australia.
SCOUTING REPORT: Saltiban's injury played a big part in the disjointed nature of his season. When he was on the field, however, there were clear weaknesses. While his contact was plenty loud, his miss rates were high. His overall mark was 31.5%, and his in-zone and chase rates were elevated as well. Add those numbers up, and the result is a 31.2% strikeout rate over 66 games at High-A. He split his time in Jersey Shore mainly between second base and center field. Saltiban is quick and athletic and tracks balls well in center field to all sectors. His above-average speed and average arm strength fit there as well. He's a bit stretched at second base, which is understandable considering his lack of experience at the position. Scouts also praised Saltiban for his hard work and overall makeup.
THE FUTURE: Saltiban should begin 2026 back at Jersey Shore, where he will look to put a rough 2025 campaign in the rearview. Above all, he needs to make more contact, but his overall game needs plenty of polish as well. He fits best as a versatile bench player.

Year	Age	Club (League)	Level	AVG	G	AB	R	H	2B	3B	HR	RBI	BB	SO	SB	OBP	SLG
2025	20	FCL Phillies	Rk	.054	10	37	4	2	1	0	1	1	2	10	0	.146	.162
2025	20	Clearwater (FSL)	A	.600	1	5	2	3	0	0	1	3	0	0	0	.600	1.200
2025	20	Jersey Shore (SAL)	A+	.190	66	263	36	50	10	3	5	22	21	92	19	.269	.308
		Minor League Totals		.199	87	347	52	69	13	3	8	33	26	109	24	.275	.323

21 ZACH McCAMBLEY, RHP

FB: 45. **SL:** 55. **CT:** 50. **CH:** 30. **CTL:** 50. **BA Grade:** 40. **Risk:** Average. **Adj:** 30.

Born: May 4, 1999. **B-T:** L-R. **HT:** 6-2. **WT:** 225. **Drafted:** Coastal Carolina, 2020 (3rd round).
Signed by: Blake Newsome (Marlins).
TRACK RECORD: After two full seasons with Coastal Carolina and a summer in the Cape Cod League, McCambley was ready to use his junior season to raise his stock to its peak. Instead, the pandemic happened. Even so, the Marlins saw enough to spend their third-round pick on him and sign him for $775,000. He reached Double-A Pensacola in his first pro season and has spent time at the level in each of the following four seasons. The Phillies selected him in the major league phase of the 2025 Rule 5 draft.
SCOUTING REPORT: McCambley's four-pitch mix is led primarily by a barrage of sliders and cutters. The former pitch sits around 84 mph and gets the most whiffs of any pitch in his arsenal, while the latter checks a few ticks hotter and is thrown for the most strikes. McCambley's four-seamer peaks at 97 with decent life through the zone, and his changeup is well behind the rest of his repertoire. McCambley is strong-bodied and employs the kind of up-tempo delivery best suited for the bullpen, where he's pitched almost without exception since 2023. He throws plenty of strikes and should have average control.
THE FUTURE: McCambley will get a chance in 2026 to crack the Phillies' bullpen. If he doesn't, he should still have a shot at his MLB debut with Miami. He fits as a low-leverage reliever.

PHILADELPHIA PHILLIES

Year	Age	Club (League)	Level	W	L	ERA	G	GS	IP	H	HR	BB	SO	BB%	SO%	WHIP	AVG
2025	26	Pensacola (SL)	AA	1	0	2.11	11	0	21	13	1	7	31	8.5	37.8	0.94	.176
2025	26	Jacksonville (IL)	AAA	1	3	3.32	36	0	41	33	2	15	52	8.9	30.8	1.18	.224
		Minor League Totals		17	22	4.27	134	40	320	273	39	142	383	10.4	28.0	1.30	.231

22 JEAN CABRERA, RHP
FB: 50. **SL:** 45. **CH:** 50. **SW:** 50. **CTL:** 55. **BA Grade:** 40. **Risk:** Average. **Adj:** 30.

Born: October 20, 2001. **B-T:** R-R. **HT:** 6-1. **WT:** 160. **Signed:** Venezuela, 2019. **Signed by:** Rafael Alvarez/William Mota.
TRACK RECORD: Cabrera signed with the Phillies in 2019 but had to wait until 2021 to make his debut thanks to the pandemic that canceled the 2020 minor league season. He debuted in 2021 in the Dominican Summer League and won the organization's pitcher of the year award. He was added to the 40-man roster after the 2024 season and spent his entire 2025 season at Double-A Reading.
SCOUTING REPORT: Cabrera is effective without any flash. He pounds the zone with an arsenal of five pitches that range fringy to average and ties them together with potentially above-average control. He works with four-seam and sinking fastballs, both of which typically arrive around 93 mph with fair life through the zone. He backs them with two slider variants—a sweeper and a gyro. The sweeper is thrown far more often and parks in the low 80s, while the gyro comes in a few ticks hotter. Cabrera rounds out the mix with a potentially average changeup in the mid 80s that drew the most misses and chases in his mix. He throws all of his pitches for strikes at rates between 59%-69% and is unafraid to challenge hitters. He allowed 11 home runs all season, an especially impressive figure while playing at hitter-happy Reading.
THE FUTURE: If Cabrera starts in the big leagues, it's likely to be as a No. 5 on a second-division club. Otherwise, he fits as a swingman who eats innings in low-leverage situations.

Year	Age	Club (League)	Level	W	L	ERA	G	GS	IP	H	HR	BB	SO	BB%	SO%	WHIP	AVG
2025	23	Reading (EL)	AA	6	9	3.81	26	26	137	107	11	61	127	10.6	22.2	1.23	.214
		Minor League Totals		22	27	3.78	90	83	424	399	29	154	435	8.6	24.4	1.30	.250

23 ANDERSON ARAUJO, C
HIT: 45. **POW:** 50. **RUN:** 30. **FLD:** 45. **ARM:** 50. **BA Grade:** 45. **Risk:** High. **Adj:** 30.

Born: April 8, 2008. **B-T:** R-R. **HT:** 5-11. **WT:** 177. **Signed:** Venezuela, 2025. **Signed by:** Franklin Rojas.
TRACK RECORD: Araujo was a low-dollar sign as part of the Phillies' 2025 class but has done a fine job separating himself from the pack. His seven home runs were the most of any player on either of the organization's two teams in the Dominican Summer League and were just two fewer than the White squad's team total.
SCOUTING REPORT: Araujo has plenty of offensive upside, but there's plenty of refinement needed before he reaches his ceiling. Scouts in the Dominican Republic praised him for his strong sense of the strike zone and the way he manages at-bats for someone so young. Despite a fairly aggressive approach, Araujo kept his miss rates in check and did a great job making contact on pitches in the zone. His exit velocities have maxed out at 104 mph, but scouts believe he could get even more out of his bat by improving his barrel accuracy. He also has a bit of a hole on the inside of the plate. His defensive reps were split roughly 60-40 between catcher and first base, and evaluators would like to see his footwork and instincts improve behind the dish.
THE FUTURE: Araujo's next stop will be the Florida Complex League, where he'll look to continue building on a strong professional debut and working to stick behind the plate. He has the ceiling of an offensive-minded backup catcher.

Year	Age	Club (League)	Level	AVG	G	AB	R	H	2B	3B	HR	RBI	BB	SO	SB	OBP	SLG
2025	17	DSL Phillies Red	Rk	.289	45	159	35	46	11	3	7	29	19	37	11	.377	.528
		Minor League Totals		.289	45	159	35	46	11	3	7	29	19	37	11	.377	.528

24 ROMELI ESPINOSA, SS
HIT: 40. **POW:** 50. **RUN:** 60. **FLD:** 55. **ARM:** 60. **BA Grade:** 45. **Risk:** High. **Adj:** 30.

Born: June 6, 2008. **B-T:** R-R. **HT:** 6-4. **WT:** 170. **Signed:** Dominican Republic, 2025. **Signed by:** Luis Garcia.
TRACK RECORD: Espinosa signed with the Phillies in 2025 for $250,000 and posted a strong debut in the Dominican Summer League. His time in the league also included a berth in the all-star game, and he was the only player on his team with more than one home run.
SCOUTING REPORT: Espinosa's game is based around athleticism and projection. He has plenty of room to stack muscle onto his 6-foot-4 frame, and he's got the skills to stick up the middle as well. He's got plenty of bat speed for his age and does a good job staying within the strike zone despite an aggressive

approach that will need to be toned down as he moves up the ladder. He'll show flashes of solid raw power, including max exit velocities up to 109 mph, but he'll need to be more discerning to get the most impact out of his contact. He is a bouncy defender with a plus arm that would work at either shortstop or third base, depending on how his body develops. Espinosa is a plus runner as well and swiped 12 bags in 16 attempts. A great deal of his future rides on his ability to pack on muscle while maintaining his fluid movements.
THE FUTURE: Espinosa's next stop is the Florida Complex League, where he'll work to get stronger and become more selective at the plate. He has the upside of a true shortstop with gifts on both sides of the ball.

Year	Age	Club (League)	Level	AVG	G	AB	R	H	2B	3B	HR	RBI	BB	SO	SB	OBP	SLG
2025	17	DSL Phillies White	Rk	.282	41	149	28	42	6	5	2	12	10	34	12	.363	.430
		Minor League Totals		.282	41	149	28	42	6	5	2	12	10	34	12	.363	.430

25 KEATON ANTHONY, 1B

HIT: 55. **POW:** 40. **RUN:** 30. **FLD:** 50. **ARM:** 50. **BA Grade:** 40. **Risk:** Average. **Adj:** 30.

Born: June 24, 2001. **B-T:** R-R. **HT:** 6-2. **WT:** 230. **Signed:** Iowa, 2023 (UDFA). **Signed by:** Justin Munson.
TRACK RECORD: After three years at Iowa and a summer in the Cape Cod League, Anthony was signed by the Phillies as an undrafted free agent in 2023. From day one, he's quietly hit his way through the minor leagues. He split his 2025 season between Double-A Reading and Triple-A Lehigh Valley but was limited by a hamstring injury to just 82 games.
SCOUTING REPORT: Anthony was an outfielder and occasional pitcher during his time with the Hawkeyes. Since turning pro, he hasn't taken a rep anywhere but first base. His athleticism has made him a fine defender at the position, but his hit-over-power profile makes him a little bit out of place offensively. He does a fine job controlling the zone and making contact—his chase rates are a little bit high—but he hits the ball on the ground too often to maximize his impact. That trend was especially true at Triple-A, where he posted a 48% groundball rate over 33 games. Scouts believe Anthony's swing will need serious tweaking if he is to put more balls over the fence. He is a well below-average runner who has attempted just five stolen bases in three seasons as a professional.
THE FUTURE: Anthony will likely return to Triple-A to begin 2026. There, he'll need to start hitting for the power required from a first baseman. If he can, he could have an Otto Kemp-like run as a bat off the bench.

Year	Age	Club (League)	Level	AVG	G	AB	R	H	2B	3B	HR	RBI	BB	SO	SB	OBP	SLG
2025	24	Reading (EL)	AA	.330	49	182	23	60	21	1	4	29	14	40	0	.380	.522
2025	24	Lehigh Valley (IL)	AAA	.313	33	134	14	42	10	0	2	10	12	33	0	.374	.433
		Minor League Totals		.324	199	738	97	239	52	3	16	115	82	150	4	.402	.467

26 SAUL TERAN, RHP

FB: 60. **SL:** 60. **CT:** 40. **CTL:** 50. **BA Grade:** 40. **Risk:** Average. **Adj:** 30.

Born: March 20, 2002. **B-T:** R-R. **HT:** 6-1. **WT:** 192. **Signed:** Venezuela, 2022. **Signed by:** William Mota.
TRACK RECORD: Teran signed out of Venezuela as part of the same class that landed the Phillies William Bergolla Jr. and Aroon Escobar. He dealt with shoulder inflammation in both 2023 and 2024 before throwing a career-best 48.1 innings in 2025 and ascending from Low-A to Double-A. He's worked out of the bullpen nearly exclusively all his career, having made just one start since his debut season in the Dominican Summer League.
SCOUTING REPORT: Teran complements a trio of four-seam, sinking and cutting fastballs with a nasty, sweepy slider in the mid 80s. Pitching backwards is the norm for Teran, who uses his slider to set up his fastball variants. The pitch produced a .164 average and was the finisher for 45 of Teran's 56 strikeouts. Its 39% miss rate was the highest of any pitch in his mix. Teran used his four-seamer and sinker near-equally and only occasionally sprinkled in the cutter. His most-used fastball variants average about 93 mph, while his cutter checks in around 89 mph on average. Teran sometimes falls off to the first-base side in his delivery, but he manages to throw a fair amount of strikes and should have average control once he reaches the big leagues.
THE FUTURE: Teran will return to Double-A to begin 2026 and has an outside chance of reaching the big leagues by the end of the season. He fits as a middleman who uses an east-west attack to get his outs.

Year	Age	Club (League)	Level	W	L	ERA	G	GS	IP	H	HR	BB	SO	BB%	SO%	WHIP	AVG
2025	23	Clearwater (FSL)	A	2	1	1.00	15	0	18	13	0	3	31	4.3	44.9	0.89	.203
2025	23	Jersey Shore (SAL)	A+	3	0	1.38	22	0	26	16	0	13	23	13.0	23.0	1.12	.184
2025	23	Reading (EL)	AA	0	0	2.08	3	0	4	4	0	0	2	0.0	11.8	0.92	.235
		Minor League Totals		9	6	3.24	97	4	139	115	9	57	158	9.7	27.0	1.24	.225

PHILADELPHIA PHILLIES

27 YONIEL CURET, RHP
FB: 70. **SL:** 50. **CH:** 30. **CTL:** 40. **BA Grade:** 45. **Risk:** High. **Adj:** 30.

Born: November 3, 2002. **B-T:** R-R. **HT:** 6-2. **WT:** 250. **Signed:** Dominican Republic, 2019.
Signed by: Daniel Santana (Rays).
TRACK RECORD: The Rays signed Curet out of the Dominican Republic in 2019 for $150,000, and the investment quickly looked like a bargain. He solved strike-throwing woes early in the 2024 season before a move to Double-A, where he was dominant. His 2025 was scuttled by a shoulder injury, however, and he was dealt to the Phillies in a December deal that netted righthander Tommy McCollum for the Rays. Following the season, Curet pitched for Escogido in the Dominican League.
SCOUTING REPORT: When he's right, Curet can overpower hitters with a mix of four-seam and sinking fastballs, as well as a slider and a changeup. The fastballs each sit in the mid 90s, and his offspeed pitches average around 87 mph. The slider is a short, sharp breaker that looks like a cutter without much depth. Curet's changeup works mostly because of velocity separation and oftentimes looks like a backup slider. It will occasionally flash fade away from lefties. Curet is thick-framed from scalp to toes and utilizes an upper-half heavy delivery with an upright finish that does not leave much room for precision.
THE FUTURE: Curet has the velocity to beat hitters. Now, he needs something softer to mess with their timing and to find the strike zone far more often. If he clears those hurdles, he fits as a middle reliever. He should begin 2026 back at Triple-A Lehigh Valley.

Year	Age	Club (League)	Level	W	L	ERA	G	GS	IP	H	HR	BB	SO	BB%	SO%	WHIP	AVG
2025	22	FCL Rays	Rk	1	0	0.00	3	2	5	2	0	0	8	0.0	38.1	0.38	.111
2025	22	Montgomery (SL)	AA	1	0	1.45	5	5	19	12	0	5	19	6.8	26.0	0.91	.185
2025	22	Durham (IL)	AAA	1	3	6.03	8	7	31	34	2	26	35	17.4	23.5	1.91	.298
		Minor League Totals		24	16	3.10	97	80	371	244	16	219	486	13.8	30.7	1.25	.189

28 CASEY STEWARD, RHP
FB: 60. **SL:** 50. **CH:** 45. **SW:** 55. **CTL:** 40. **BA Grade:** 40. **Risk:** Average. **Adj:** 30.

Born: August 2, 2001. **B-T:** R-R. **HT:** 6-5. **WT:** 260. **Drafted:** Washburn (KS), 2023 (19th round). **Signed by:** Justin Munson.
TRACK RECORD: Steward spent three seasons at Division-II Washburn (Kansas) and a year in the MLB Draft League before the Phillies called his name in the 19th round in 2023. He signed for $150,000 and pitched six innings in his pro debut. He's spent the last two seasons between Low-A and High-A, including a complete 2025 campaign in the South Atlantic League.
SCOUTING REPORT: Steward is one of the hardest-throwers in the Phillies system, and his 101.2 mph sinker was the fastest pitch thrown in the organization all season. He was one of the standout arms in the team's Spring Breakout game, but his regular year was rocky thanks to slipshod control and command. He shifted to the third-base side of the rubber toward the end of the season and saw better results with the way his four-seamer played through the zone. Steward backs his four- and two-seam fastballs with a slider, sweeper and a changeup. None of his pitches outside his fastball grades as plus, and nothing in his arsenal garnered a miss rate of better than 26.1%. He needs to throw more strikes overall, and he did better in that regard after shifting to the bullpen.
THE FUTURE: If he can throw more strikes and be around the zone more often, Steward has a shot to be a middle reliever who can overpower hitters in one-inning bursts. His next stop is Double-A Reading.

Year	Age	Club (League)	Level	W	L	ERA	G	GS	IP	H	HR	BB	SO	BB%	SO%	WHIP	AVG
2025	23	Jersey Shore (SAL)	A+	3	10	5.93	25	19	88	95	9	44	80	10.8	19.7	1.58	.274
		Minor League Totals		11	15	4.53	52	39	197	178	14	105	186	12.0	21.3	1.44	.240

PHILADELPHIA PHILLIES

29 JAMES TALLON, LHP
FB: 55. **SL:** 55. **CH:** 45. **CTL:** 40. **BA Grade:** 40. **Risk:** Average. **Adj:** 30.

Born: September 29, 2003. **B-T:** L-L. **HT:** 6-5. **WT:** 195. **Drafted:** Duke, 2025 (6th round). **Signed by:** Kellan McKeon.
TRACK RECORD: Tallon's three seasons at Duke were spent almost exclusively in the bullpen, making just four starts in his career. The lefty struck out 31% of the hitters he faced in 2025 and was taken by the Phillies in the sixth round thanks to a combination of a deceptive delivery, remaining physical projection and untapped potential across his arsenal. He was shut down after signing and will debut in 2026.
SCOUTING REPORT: Tallon is a tall lefty who attacks hitters from a low slot with a three-pitch mix. He leans hard on his 93-95 mph fastball, which plays up thanks to his vertical approach angle and riding life through the zone. He backs it with a mid-80s slider with cutterish action and the occasional changeup in the mid 80s. The Phillies believe his offspeed pitches have untapped potential that can be mined as he moves through the system. Tallon's arm action, which features a deep plunge, has hindered his ability to throw strikes and will need to be ironed out as a pro.
THE FUTURE: Tallon's most likely path to the big leagues is as a one-inning reliever, but the Phillies might try to stretch him out some and get him into a bulk role. No matter which road his career takes, the key to his success will be sharpening the quality and command of his offspeed pitches.

Year	Age	Club (League)	Level	W	L	ERA	G	GS	IP	H	HR	BB	SO	BB%	SO%	WHIP	AVG
2025	21	Did not play															

30 BRYAN RINCON, SS
HIT: 30. **POW:** 30. **RUN:** 55. **FLD:** 60. **ARM:** 60. **BA Grade:** 40. **Risk:** High. **Adj:** 25.

Born: February 8, 2004. **B-T:** S-R. **HT:** 5-11. **WT:** 189. **Drafted:** HS—Pittsburgh, 2022 (14th round). **Signed by:** Jeff Zona Jr.
TRACK RECORD: The Phillies drafted Rincon out of a Pittsburgh high school in the 14th round in 2022 and have watched him turn into one of the system's most reliable infield defenders. His last two seasons have been waylaid by injuries—a hamstring in 2024 and a broken hamate bone in 2025—and he's never done much at all at the plate. He's played in the Arizona Fall League in each of the last two seasons.
SCOUTING REPORT: Rincon has spent parts of the last three seasons at High-A, but surgeries have cost him significant portions of each of the last two years. When he's been on the field, he's produced little to no impact at the plate. Part of the problem is an extremely passive approach that saw him swing 38.9% of the time. His upper and lower halves are disconnected, leaving him mostly unable to do damage on hittable pitches. Making better swing decisions might make for slight improvements, but his mechanics need plenty of work as well. Rincon's infield defense and arm strength grade as the best in the system, and he's an above-average runner as well. Those traits should lead to plenty of value in the field, but probably not enough to help him profile as a regular.
THE FUTURE: If he can stay healthy, Rincon should make it to the upper levels for the first time in 2026. Without any improvements, he could get a cup of coffee in the big leagues. If he can become more than an automatic out at the plate, he could see regular playing time for a second-division club.

Year	Age	Club (League)	Level	AVG	G	AB	R	H	2B	3B	HR	RBI	BB	SO	SB	OBP	SLG
2025	21	Jersey Shore (SAL)	A+	.181	84	299	58	54	13	2	6	31	50	103	40	.304	.298
		Minor League Totals		.206	197	678	128	140	32	3	16	92	125	188	71	.337	.333

Paul Skenes

Pittsburgh Pirates

BY MARK CHIARELLI

While the Pirates had little to celebrate in the majors in 2025, their decade-long run of futility may finally be nearing a turning point.

That's because Konnor Griffin, the ninth overall pick in 2024, exceeded every expectation in his first pro season, accomplishing feats rarely seen from teenagers. The 19-year-old harnessed his dynamic athleticism and a retooled swing to scale three levels and hit .333 with 21 homers and 65 steals. By the end of the year, Griffin was the top-ranked prospect in baseball and was the Minor League Player of the Year.

For a franchise and fan base starving for competitive baseball, it's difficult to overstate the significance of Griffin's emergence as a potential franchise anchor. The Pirates haven't reached the playoffs since 2015—the last time they finished within 13 games of first place in the National League Central. They are 365-505 since Ben Cherington took over after the 2019 season.

He was faced with the unenviable task of restocking an organization despite significant payroll limitations. But Pittsburgh has also struggled to develop or acquire enough productive big league hitters, with first-rounders Nick Gonzales (2019), Henry Davis (2021) and Termarr Johnson (2022) all falling short of expectations so far. The Pirates finished last in runs per game (3.6) in 2025.

Their hitting woes also underscore a player development imbalance when compared to their success grooming pitchers, especially Paul Skenes, the club's 23-year-old pitching wunderkind who added a Cy Young Award to his resumé after winning NL Rookie of the Year in 2024. The pressure and scrutiny on Cherington and Co. to maximize their window with baseball's best young starter has only intensified entering 2026.

If they can find a way to bridge the gap, it will be hard for the Pirates not to win more games quite soon if the Griffin-Skenes pairing pans out like

PROJECTED 2029 LINEUP

Catcher	Rafael Flores	28
First Base	Spencer Horwitz	31
Second Base	Termarr Johnson	24
Third Base	Jared Triolo	31
Shortstop	Konnor Griffin	23
Left Field	Jhostynxon Garcia	26
Center Field	Oneil Cruz	30
Right Field	Edward Florentino	22
Designated Hitter	Bryan Reynolds	34
No. 1 Starter	Paul Skenes	27
No. 2 Starter	Bubba Chandler	26
No. 3 Starter	Seth Hernandez	22
No. 4 Starter	Jared Jones	27
No. 5 Starter	Braxton Ashcraft	29
Closer	Antwone Kelly	25

most of the baseball industry expects. Nine of baseball's last 12 No. 1 prospects have produced at least one 5 WAR season. Of MLB teams that had two players produce 5 or more WAR in the same season over the last 15 years, 62% reached the postseason. On average, those teams won 90 games.

And while the Pirates can champion Griffin's year as an early draft-and-development win, perhaps most encouraging is that he's not alone. Fellow teenager Edward Florentino emerged from obscurity to piece together one of the most impressive seasons by a teenage slugger in the lower minors, giving Pittsburgh's suddenly resurgent hitting development program another win in 2025.

There's plenty of work to be done considering only Griffin (21 games) has reached Double-A, but it's a step in the right direction. Pittsburgh's pitching pipeline continued to churn out rotation types in 2025, with Bubba Chandler reaching the majors late in the season. Jared Jones is also expected back in 2026, creating quite a fearsome top three alongside Skenes.

Understandably, there's still some skepticism for a fan base that has endured multiple rebuild cycles. Griffin alone cannot cover up all of the organization's flaws. But as he hurtles toward stardom, the club finally has a potential star-level young hitter to build around, and a 2026 debut certainly not out of the question. Finally, better days are ahead. ∎

DEPTH CHART

PITTSBURGH PIRATES

TOP 2026 ROOKIES — RANK
1. Konnor Griffin, SS — 1
2. Bubba Chandler, RHP — 2
3. Jhostynxon Garcia, OF — 5
4. Rafael Flores, C — 6

BREAKOUT PROSPECTS — RANK
1. Darell Morel, SS — 17
2. Duce Gourson, 2B — 21
3. Johan De Los Santos, SS — 30

SOURCE OF TOP 30 TALENT

Homegrown	24	Acquired	6
College	7	Trade	6
Junior college	0	Rule 5 draft	0
High school	7	Independent league	0
Undrafted free agent	0	Free agent/waivers	0
International	10		

LF
Billy Cook
Estuar Suero

CF
Jhostynxon Garcia (5)
Mitch Jebb
Gabriel Rodriguez
Armstrong Muhoozi
Will Taylor
Brian Sanchez
Lonnie White Jr.

RF
Edward Florentino (3)
Esmerlyn Valdez (11)
Edgar Walker
Ivan Brethowr

3B
Murf Gray (27)
Jhonny Severino
Eddie Rynders
Hyung Seung Lee

SS
Konnor Griffin (1)
Wyatt Sanford (12)
Sammy Stafura (14)
Darell Morel (17)
Jack Brannigan (28)
Johan De Los Santos (30)
Javier Rivas
Gustavo Melendez
Yordany De Los Santos
Tsung-Che Cheng
Kendrick Herrera

2B
Termarr Johnson (6)
Nick Yorke (19)
Duce Gourson (21)
Keiner Delgado
Dylan Palmer

1B
Tony Blanco (29)
Callan Moss
Jared Jones
Nick Cimillo

C
Rafael Flores (5)
Omar Alfonzo (13)
Axiel Plaz (20)
Easton Carmichael (26)
Edgleen Perez
Richard Ramirez
Shawn Ross

LHP

LHSP
Hunter Barco (9)
Connor Wietgrefe
Anthony Solometo

LHRP
Reinold Navarro (16)
Keuri Almonte
Jaden Woods

RHP

RHSP
Bubba Chandler (2)
Seth Hernandez (4)
Antwone Kelly (8)
Wilber Dotel (10)
Khristian Curtis (15)
Thomas Harrington (18)
Jesus Travieso (22)
Levi Sterling (23)
Jeter Martinez (24)
Zander Mueth (25)
Carlson Reed
Irwin Ramirez
Sean Sullivan
Jack Anker
Po-Yu Chen

RHRP
Ryan Harbin
David Matoma
Brandan Bidois
Alessandro Ercolani
Gavin Adams

PITTSBURGH PIRATES

1. KONNOR GRIFFIN, SS/OF

Born: April 24, 2006. **B-T:** R-R. **HT:** 6-4. **WT:** 225.
Drafted: HS—Flowood, MS, 2024 (1st round).
Signed by: Darren Mazeroski.

TRACK RECORD: Griffin was the most decorated high school player in the 2024 draft, winning High School Player of the Year after a senior spring in Mississippi in which he hit .559 and stole 85 bases. The Pirates drafted him ninth overall that July and signed him for $6,532,025, but even they couldn't have anticipated how quickly he'd emerge as the No. 1 overall prospect and the 2025 Minor League Player of the Year. The 19-year-old hit .333/.415/.527 with 21 homers and 65 steals across 122 games, beginning the year with Low-A Bradenton and finishing in Double-A Altoona. Griffin became the first-ever drafted teenager to hit at least 20 homers and steal at least 40 bases, joining only Andruw Jones, Ronald Acuña Jr., Jackson Chourio and Alex Escobar.

SCOUTING REPORT: At 6-foot-4, 225 pounds, Griffin's size and speed combination is reminiscent of an NFL strong safety, and he uses his exceptional physical tools to impact every facet of the game. He produces some of the highest exit velocities of any teenager in the sport and does damage to all fields. He's also a plus-plus runner once underway. For all his athleticism, Griffin entered pro ball facing significant concern about whether his swing and feel for contact would hold up against more advanced pitchers. He took a decisive first step in answering those questions in 2025. Griffin retooled his swing over the offseason to clean up his arm bar and add more depth, and he kept his strikeout rate under 22% and contact rate above 75% despite scaling three levels in his first pro season. He also handled premium velocity well. Griffin still has areas to refine—especially against spin—and he's still learning to pull the ball in the air consistently, but there's far more confidence now that he has a shot to develop into at least an above-average hitter. Evaluators are also more bullish that Griffin can stay at shortstop, where his range, instincts and plus-plus arm graded out favorably in 2025 while making just seven errors all season. Griffin cleaned up his footwork as the season progressed and plays with a calm internal clock. He spent the bulk of his defensive time at shortstop, though he also played 15 games in center field. Unsurprisingly given his skills, Griffin's capable of covering large swaths of ground in the outfield, and he's one of the rare players who could conceivably develop into a plus defender at two premium positions. Coaches and evaluators alike also rave about his aptitude and leadership qualities.

THE FUTURE: Griffin's ascension in 2025 is a franchise-altering development for an organization that has struggled to produce quality big league hitters since Andrew McCutchen and needs to find a running mate to pair with Paul Skenes. Even if Griffin's pure hitting ability gets tested, his power, speed and defense give him multiple paths to provide star-level value while having the upside of an MVP-caliber shortstop. A big league debut in 2026 isn't out of the question for Griffin, who doesn't turn 20 until late April.

BA GRADE: 75 / Risk: Average
Adjusted grade: 65
SCOUTING GRADES: Hit: 60. Power: 70. Run: 80. Field: 60. Arm: 70.
Projected future grades on 20-80 scouting scale

BEST TOOLS

BATTING
Best Hitter	Edward Florentino
Best Power Hitter	Tony Blanco Jr.
Best Strike-Zone Discipline	Edgleen Perez
Fastest Baserunner	Konnor Griffin
Best Athlete	Konnor Griffin

PITCHING
Best Fastball	Reinold Navarro
Best Curveball	Seth Hernandez
Best Slider	Ryan Harbin
Best Changeup	Seth Hernandez
Best Control	Connor Wietgrefe

FIELDING
Best Defensive Catcher	Richard Ramirez
Best Defensive Infielder	Jack Brannigan
Best Infield Arm	Konnor Griffin
Best Defensive Outfielder	Konnor Griffin
Best Outfield Arm	Konnor Griffin

Year	Age	Club (League)	Level	AVG	G	AB	R	H	2B	3B	HR	RBI	BB	SO	SB	OBP	SLG
2025	19	Bradenton (FSL)	A	.338	50	207	49	70	10	2	9	36	15	53	26	.396	.536
2025	19	Greensboro (SAL)	A+	.325	51	194	48	63	11	2	7	36	28	46	33	.432	.521
2025	19	Altoona (EL)	AA	.337	21	83	20	28	2	0	5	22	7	23	6	.418	.542
		Minor League Totals		.333	122	484	117	161	23	4	21	94	50	122	65	.415	.527

PITTSBURGH PIRATES

2 BUBBA CHANDLER, RHP
FB: 70. **CB:** 45. **SL:** 55. **CH:** 60. **CTL:** 50. **BA Grade:** 65. **Risk:** Average. **Adj:** 55.

Born: September 14, 2002. **B-T:** B-R. **HT:** 6-3. **WT:** 218.
Drafted: HS—Bogart, GA, 2021 (3rd round). **Signed by:** Cam Murphy.
TRACK RECORD: Chandler entered 2025 on the cusp of the majors after positioning himself as one of baseball's most coveted pitching prospects. He dominated Triple-A early, pitching to a 2.03 ERA with a 35% strikeout rate through May. The Pirates kept Chandler in Indianapolis, however, and he fell into a two-month slump posting a 5.96 ERA amid fluctuating command. Chandler managed to steer out of the skid and on Aug. 16 he reached the big leagues, where he threw far more strikes, with 31 strikeouts to four walks in 31.1 innings.
SCOUTING REPORT: Chandler's plan of attack is built around overpowering hitters with one of baseball's most impressive fastballs. He was up to 102 mph in 2025 and averaged 98.9 once he reached the big leagues. Chandler has no issue holding velocity and throws his fastball with above-average extension and impressive carry at the top of the zone. Everything else layers in around it. His plus low-90s changeup was his best swing-and-miss weapon, while his upper-80s-to-low-90s slider grades solid-average and succeeds because of its pure power. He also mixes in a fringy mid-80s curveball that works as a change of pace with about 14 mph separation off his fastball. Chandler's athleticism allows him to maintain velocity deep into outings, but he remains an imprecise strike-thrower. His struggles in 2025 largely stemmed from lapses in fastball command and difficulty landing his offspeed pitches for strikes, which left him vulnerable when hitters sat on velocity.
THE FUTURE: If Chandler sharpens his command, especially with his secondaries, and keeps hitters from keying on his fastball, he could be a No. 2 starter who settles in behind Paul Skenes in the rotation.

Year	Age	Club (League)	Level	W	L	ERA	G	GS	IP	H	HR	BB	SO	BB%	SO%	WHIP	AVG
2025	22	Indianapolis (IL)	AAA	5	6	4.05	24	24	100	95	8	53	121	12.0	27.4	1.48	.250
2025	22	Pittsburgh (NL)	MLB	4	1	4.02	7	4	31	25	2	4	31	3.2	25.0	0.93	.214
		Minor League Totals		26	18	3.73	89	83	372	308	35	173	457	11.0	29.0	1.29	.224
		Major League Totals		4	1	4.02	7	4	31	25	2	4	31	3.2	25.0	0.93	.214

3 EDWARD FLORENTINO, OF
HIT: 60. **POW:** 60. **RUN:** 40. **FLD:** 45. **ARM:** 55. **BA Grade:** 65. **Risk:** High. **Adj:** 50.

Born: November 11, 2006. **B-T:** L-R. **HT:** 6-4. **WT:** 190.
Signed: Dominican Republic, 2024. **Signed by:** Esteban Alvarez.
TRACK RECORD: If not for Konnor Griffin, Florentino's breakout would've been the biggest win for Pirates player development in 2025. Just a year after signing out of the Dominican Republic for $395,000 and making his pro debut, the 18-year-old emerged as one of the sport's most intriguing teenagers. He blitzed Rookie-level pitching over 29 games in the Florida Complex League, then carried that momentum to Low-A Bradenton. At the two stops he combined to slash .290/.400/.548 with 16 homers and 35 steals across 83 games.
SCOUTING REPORT: Evaluators marveled at Florentino's rare blend of plus raw power, discipline and advanced feel for contact at such a young age. His lefthanded swing has natural loft and impressive bat speed. While some external evaluators wondered if Florentino's swing path may one day leave him vulnerable at the top of the zone, he was quite difficult to beat in the strike zone in 2025, making contact nearly 90% of the time. He rarely chases, and once he lured pitchers into the zone he displayed a penchant for damage. The scary part? The Pirates believe Florentino has plenty of room to pack on more strength to his gangly 6-foot-4 frame. How Florentino's body develops will dictate where he ends up defensively. He's a fringy runner who may slow further as he fills out, but his instincts allow him to steal bases efficiently and take surprisingly sharp routes—especially closing on balls—in center field, where he played most of 2025. Long term, a corner spot may suit him best. The Pirates also raved about his aptitude and knack for making quick adjustments—traits that reminded some of Griffin.
THE FUTURE: Even if he shifts off center field, Florentino's offensive foundation gives him the upside of a middle-of-the-order bat with all-star potential.

Year	Age	Club (League)	Level	AVG	G	AB	R	H	2B	3B	HR	RBI	BB	SO	SB	OBP	SLG
2025	18	FCL Pirates	Rk	.347	29	95	23	33	6	2	6	23	16	22	6	.442	.642
2025	18	Bradenton (FSL)	A	.262	54	195	37	51	17	0	10	36	33	56	29	.380	.503
		Minor League Totals		.280	132	436	100	122	33	4	21	87	87	114	43	.411	.518

PITTSBURGH PIRATES

4 SETH HERNANDEZ, RHP
FB: 65. **CB:** 55. **SL:** 55. **CH:** 70. **CTL:** 55. **BA Grade:** 65. **Risk:** High. **Adj:** 50.

Born: June 28, 2006. **B-T:** R-R. **HT:** 6-4. **WT:** 195.
Drafted: HS—Corona, CA, 2025 (1st round). **Signed by:** Mark Sluys.
TRACK RECORD: The Pirates' pitching development program has excelled at maximizing recent athletic high school pitchers such as Jared Jones, Bubba Chandler and Braxton Ashcraft. None entered pro ball with the pedigree or present skills of Hernandez, whom Pittsburgh drafted sixth in 2025 and signed for $7.25 million. Hernandez headlined a loaded Corona (Calif.) High team that also produced top 35 overall draft picks Billy Carlson and Brady Ebel.
SCOUTING REPORT: At 6-foot-4, 195 pounds, Hernandez presents size, polish and present velocity rarely seen in a teenager. His mid-90s fastball touched triple digits during his senior spring, and he should regularly sit in the upper 90s one day as he adds more strength. Even with his velocity, some amateur evaluators questioned how consistently the pitch would miss bats in pro ball because of its shape. Hernandez complements it with a low-80s changeup and two distinct breaking balls. His double-plus changeup is the jewel of his secondaries. Hernandez throws it with a circle grip and shows advanced feel to use it to both miss bats and land for strikes. He also mixes a mid-to-upper-80s slider and a low-80s curveball, each flashing above-average potential with a bit more power since turning pro. The Pirates were particularly impressed by how he tightened his slider into more of a swing-and-miss pitch. Hernandez throws plenty of strikes, moves well on the mound with an advanced understanding of how to create power in his delivery and even drew some amateur interest as a legitimate two-way prospect.
THE FUTURE: While high school righthanders carry inherent risk, Hernandez has frontline potential and has drawn comparisons to Hunter Greene and Jackson Jobe. With his athleticism, deep repertoire and advanced strike-throwing, he has the ingredients to move quickly and is set to make his pro debut.

Year	Age	Club (League)	Level	W	L	ERA	G	GS	IP	H	HR	BB	SO	BB%	SO%	WHIP	AVG
2025	19	Did not play															

5 JHOSTYNXON GARCIA, OF
HIT: 40. **POW:** 55. **RUN:** 50. **FLD:** 55. **ARM:** 55. **BA Grade:** 45. **Risk:** Mild. **Adj:** 40.

Born: December 11, 2002. **B-T:** R-R. **HT:** 6-0. **WT:** 220. **Signed:** Venezuela, 2019. **Signed by:** Rollie Pino/Eddie Romero (Red Sox).
TRACK RECORD: Garcia stood out in amateur workouts in Venezuela both by the way he glided across the outfield and drove the ball out of the park. Still, his early pro development was deliberate, and he entered 2024 as a fourth outfielder in Low-A. Thanks to major strength and bat speed gains entering that year, he asserted himself as a prospect. He led the Red Sox system with 23 home runs while reaching Double-A in 2024, then again led the system with 21 round-trippers in 2025, a year spent mostly at Triple-A Worcester but that also included his first MLB callup. Boston then dealt him to the Pirates in the offseason for righthander Johan Oviedo.
SCOUTING REPORT: Over years of strength work and bat speed training, Garcia has grown into power. His maximum exit velocity jumped from 105 mph in 2022 to 113 in 2025. His hips explode open on pitches in the bottom half of the zone, resulting in tape-measure shots, though a steep bat path has rendered him vulnerable to whiff on pitches above the belt. He has worked to flatten his swing to counter those pitches, while also training diligently to improve his swing decisions. Still, his 35% chase rate and 34% whiff rate at Triple-A point to a below-average hit tool. Defensively, Garcia plays with skill and flair, delighting in catching fly balls at his hip. His range and arm are above-average in right field and he's at least adequate in center. Though he has average speed, Garcia is a smart player and good baserunner, though not a basestealer.
THE FUTURE: If Garcia keeps building on his swing decision improvements of recent years, he has a chance to become a big league regular with a strong floor as a righthanded-hitting fourth outfielder. He now has a clearer path to big league playing time in Pittsburgh.

Year	Age	Club (League)	Level	AVG	G	AB	R	H	2B	3B	HR	RBI	BB	SO	SB	OBP	SLG
2025	22	Portland (EL)	AA	.256	33	117	19	30	5	1	3	17	18	29	4	.355	.393
2025	22	Worcester (IL)	AAA	.271	81	317	60	86	12	3	18	58	27	102	3	.334	.498
2025	22	Boston (AL)	MLB	.143	5	7	0	1	1	0	0	0	2	5	0	.333	.286
		Minor League Totals		.261	370	1347	257	352	67	21	55	209	166	379	42	.351	.465
		Major League Totals		.143	5	7	0	1	1	0	0	0	2	5	0	.333	.286

PITTSBURGH PIRATES

6 RAFAEL FLORES, C/1B

HIT: 40. **POW:** 60. **RUN:** 30. **FLD:** 45. **ARM:** 40. **BA Grade:** 45. **Risk:** Mild. **Adj:** 40.

Born: November 7, 2000. **B-T:** R-R. **HT:** 6-4. **WT:** 220.
Signed: Rio Hondo (CA) JC, 2022 (UDFA). **Signed by:** Dave Keith (Yankees).
TRACK RECORD: Flores went undrafted in 2022 after stints at two California junior colleges and was playing summer ball in Alaska when the Yankees signed him for just $75,000. Three years later, that decision looks like a remarkable bit of scouting and development. After a swing change early on as a pro, Flores slugged his way to the upper minors, producing 20-plus homers in each of the past two seasons. The Pirates acquired him as the lead piece in the 2025 deadline deal that sent David Bednar to New York. He debuted for Pittsburgh in September.
SCOUTING REPORT: Power is Flores' carrying tool. The sturdily built righthanded hitter employs a big leg kick and above-average bat speed to generate some of the loudest exit velocities in Pittsburgh's system and all-fields power. The tradeoff is considerable swing-and-miss. Flores whiffed nearly a third of the time in the minors in 2025 and remains vulnerable up in the zone and on the inner third. The Pirates believe further swing adjustments—particularly improving rotation efficiency and barrel adjustability—could help him tap into even more consistent pull-side juice. Defensively, Flores is a serviceable receiver with adequate framing and game-calling skills, though his slower transfer and inconsistent throwing accuracy raise questions about his long-term upside behind the plate. He logged most of his minor league innings at catcher but also saw time at first base, where he appeared in six of his seven big league games.
THE FUTURE: Flores' swing-and-miss remains a blemish on his right-on-right profile, but his power and defensive versatility across catcher and first base give him a chance to emerge as an everyday regular. He should compete for a big league role out of spring training in 2026.

Year	Age	Club (League)	Level	AVG	G	AB	R	H	2B	3B	HR	RBI	BB	SO	SB	OBP	SLG
2025	24	Somerset (EL)	AA	.287	87	335	48	96	23	1	15	56	30	94	6	.346	.496
2025	24	Indianapolis (IL)	AAA	.281	36	135	17	38	4	1	6	28	15	41	0	.363	.459
2025	24	Scranton/WB (IL)	AAA	.211	10	38	3	8	0	0	1	4	11	13	0	.388	.289
2025	24	Pittsburgh (NL)	MLB	.200	7	15	0	3	2	0	0	0	2	7	0	.294	.333
		Minor League Totals		.275	364	1338	188	368	74	3	53	203	171	387	17	.361	.454
		Major League Totals		.200	7	15	0	3	2	0	0	0	2	7	0	.294	.333

7 TERMARR JOHNSON, 2B

HIT: 50. **POW:** 50. **RUN:** 45. **FLD:** 45. **ARM:** 45. **BA Grade:** 50. **Risk:** Average. **Adj:** 40.

Born: June 11, 2004. **B-T:** L-R. **HT:** 5-9. **WT:** 190.
Drafted: HS—Atlanta, GA, 2022 (1st round). **Signed by:** Cam Murphy.
TRACK RECORD: The Pirates drafted Johnson fourth overall in 2022 in a class that has produced more first-round misses than hits so far. His development has been a slower burn. The 21-year-old spent all of 2025 with Double-A Altoona, where he was again one of the younger hitters in the league, and slashed .272/.363/.382 with a 119 wRC+ in 119 games. He finished strong by hitting .326 over his final 36 games, though he homered only once after July 1.
SCOUTING REPORT: Considered one of the most polished high school hitters of the last two decades coming out of the draft, Johnson's offensive identity in pro ball remains in flux after three full seasons. His most productive full season came in 2023, when he posted a 139 wRC+ with an approach geared more toward power and patience. His 2025 season landed somewhere in between those two approaches. Johnson continues to show advanced zone control and posted a career-best 75.4% contact rate. He pairs that with above-average bat speed and raw power, especially to his pull side. That power doesn't always translate into games, and his underlying impact numbers were more average. Caveat: his home ballpark in Altoona did him no favors. Johnson has exploitable holes on the outer third, where he struggles to do much damage, and the Pirates worked with him to slowly move his stance closer to the plate. Defensively, Johnson played exclusively at second base in 2025 after splitting time at shortstop earlier in his career. He has solid hands, but fringy range and arm strength, making him a fit only at the keystone.
THE FUTURE: Johnson's limited defensive value means he'll have to hit to become an everyday regular at second base. If Johnson can find a way for all the ingredients to coalesce, a big league debut in the first half of 2026 isn't out of the question.

Year	Age	Club (League)	Level	AVG	G	AB	R	H	2B	3B	HR	RBI	BB	SO	SB	OBP	SLG
2025	21	Altoona (EL)	AA	.272	119	434	67	118	15	3	9	35	59	93	20	.363	.382
		Minor League Totals		.251	357	1241	230	311	50	5	41	146	254	339	56	.384	.398

PITTSBURGH PIRATES

8 ANTWONE KELLY, RHP
FB: 70. **SL:** 50. **CH:** 55. **CT:** 45. **CTL:** 55. **BA Grade:** 50. **Risk:** Average. **Adj:** 40.

Born: September 1, 2003. **B-T:** R-R. **HT:** 6-1. **WT:** 247.
Signed: Aruba, 2021. **Signed by:** Eugene Helder.
TRACK RECORD: The Pirates have a strong track record of developing under-the-radar arms, and Kelly fit that profile with a breakout 2025. Signed out of Aruba in 2021, he made his stateside debut the following year and steadily climbed the ladder. In 2025, he pitched to a 3.02 ERA over 107.1 innings between High-A Greensboro and Double-A Altoona, striking out 27.2% of batters compared to a career-best 7.7% walk rate.
SCOUTING REPORT: Added power across his entire arsenal has unlocked another level for Kelly. Having grown three inches and added more than 60 pounds from his previous weight of 183 pounds, the righthander reshaped his body entering 2025 after an oblique injury hampered him the year before. Those strength gains translated to an additional 3 mph on a fastball that now averages 97, touches 101 and carries well through the zone. He throws it for strikes roughly 70% of the time, showing advanced control, though his delivery isn't particularly deceptive and produced only average whiff rates. He has solid feel for an above-average upper-80s changeup that has significant vertical separation and induced a whiff in nearly 40% of swings. Kelly's upper-80s slider shows above-average potential but remains inconsistent, and he shelved his cutter later in the season to focus on slider development. With above-average command and the ability to hold velocity deep into outings, his path to a rotation role depends on refining his breaking ball into another reliable swing-and-miss option.
THE FUTURE: Kelly's velocity spike raised his ceiling. If his slider takes a similar step forward in 2026, he projects as a midrotation starter with the fallback as a late-inning reliever who can overpower hitters. An MLB debut in 2026 isn't out of the question after he closed 2025 at Double-A Altoona.

Year	Age	Club (League)	Level	W	L	ERA	G	GS	IP	H	HR	BB	SO	BB%	SO%	WHIP	AVG
2025	21	Greensboro (SAL)	A+	1	1	3.03	14	14	59	41	4	17	70	7.4	30.4	0.98	.192
2025	21	Altoona (EL)	AA	2	2	3.00	11	11	48	40	2	16	46	8.2	23.5	1.17	.226
		Minor League Totals		9	7	3.11	61	43	211	174	10	75	237	8.6	27.2	1.18	.223

9 HUNTER BARCO, LHP
FB: 55. **SL:** 50. **SP:** 55. **CT:** 40. **CTL:** 45. **BA Grade:** 45. **Risk:** Mild. **Adj:** 40.

Born: December 15, 2000. **B-T:** L-L. **HT:** 6-4. **WT:** 225.
Drafted: Florida, 2022 (2nd round). **Signed by:** Cam Murphy.
TRACK RECORD: Barco was a well-known amateur who made 29 starts at Florida before Tommy John surgery ended his college career in 2022. The Pirates drafted him 44th overall that year, though his recovery and a 2024 stress fracture in his leg ate into his development. Pittsburgh managed his workload carefully in 2025, but he was healthier aside from a brief shoulder strain in May. He cleared 100 innings for the first time as a pro before debuting in a big league relief role in September.
SCOUTING REPORT: The 6-foot-4, 225-pound lefthander found success as a starter in the upper minors by leaning on a 93 mph fastball that plays more on shape and deception than raw velocity. Thrown from a very low slot, the pitch creates a difficult approach angle, and he filled the zone with it nearly 70% of the time in 2025. Barco had a much tougher time commanding his secondaries, but he generates whiffs with both his average low-80s slider and above-average mid-80s splitter. He added a mid-80s cutter as a developmental offering—especially against lefties—that can steal strikes and enhance how the splitter plays off his breaking pitches. Whether Barco has enough precision to remain a starter is an open question. His intricate delivery requires some maintenance, and his strike-throwing wavers when he isn't squared to the batter at release.
THE FUTURE: Barco has back-of-the-rotation upside if he can throw enough quality strikes to turn over a lineup twice. If not, he has the fallback of a multi-inning reliever. He'll compete for a role in the Pirates' crowded rotation out of spring training.

Year	Age	Club (League)	Level	W	L	ERA	G	GS	IP	H	HR	BB	SO	BB%	SO%	WHIP	AVG
2025	24	Altoona (EL)	AA	1	0	0.00	6	6	26	11	0	7	34	7.4	36.2	0.70	.131
2025	24	Indianapolis (IL)	AAA	3	1	3.79	21	17	74	59	5	42	82	13.0	25.4	1.37	.215
2025	24	Pittsburgh (NL)	MLB	1	0	0.00	2	0	3	3	0	0	3	0.0	25.0	1.00	.250
		Minor League Totals		8	5	3.04	54	47	184	135	10	77	227	10.1	29.8	1.15	.203
		Major League Totals		1	0	0.00	2	0	3	3	0	0	3	0.0	25.0	1.00	.250

PITTSBURGH PIRATES

10 WILBER DOTEL, RHP
FB: 60. **SL:** 55. **SP:** 50. **CTL:** 55. **BA Grade:** 50. **Risk:** Average. **Adj:** 40.

Born: September 25, 2002. **B-T:** R-R. **HT:** 6-3. **WT:** 228.
Signed: Dominican Republic, 2020. **Signed by:** Cristino Valdez.
TRACK RECORD: Dotel was an older sign late in the 2020 scouting cycle as an 18-year-old out of the Dominican Republic. He has since emerged as a dependable workhorse who has logged more than 300 innings since 2023 while jumping on a level-a-year trajectory. He spent all of 2025 with Double-A Altoona, where he posted a 4.15 ERA with 131 strikeouts over 125.2 innings—the most by any Pirates minor leaguer—and a career-best 8% walk rate. He ranked third in the Eastern League in strikeouts for an Altoona team that made the playoffs.
SCOUTING REPORT: The powerful, 6-foot-3, 228-pound righthander has added about 5 mph over the past two seasons to his fastball, which is now averaging 96 and touching 100. He has also worked to better separate his four-seamer and two-seamer while replacing a fringy changeup with a mid-80s splitter in 2025 that he commands more consistently and has emerged as a solid-average swing-and-miss pitch. His upper-80s slider flashes plus. Based on raw traits, it's one of the more impressive offerings in Pittsburgh's system, though he has a tendency to overthrow it in two-strike counts. Dotel is still learning how to sequence his now well-rounded arsenal, and his 24% strikeout rate lagged behind his pure stuff for the second consecutive season. That wasn't due to control issues, however, as he landed each of his pitches in the zone at least 60% of the time.
THE FUTURE: Like fellow power righthander Antwone Kelly, Dotel boasts elite velocity, the chance for at least two plus pitches and enough strikes to remain a starter. Continued refinement of his slider and ability to finish at-bats could push him into the back of a rotation, with a high-leverage relief role as a strong fallback.

Year	Age	Club (League)	Level	W	L	ERA	G	GS	IP	H	HR	BB	SO	BB%	SO%	WHIP	AVG
2025	22	Altoona (EL)	AA	7	9	4.15	27	27	126	111	14	43	131	8.0	24.5	1.23	.234
		Minor League Totals		27	18	4.13	95	81	379	319	41	184	367	11.2	22.4	1.33	.226

11 ESMERLYN VALDEZ, OF/1B
HIT: 40. **POW:** 65. **RUN:** 40. **FLD:** 40. **ARM:** 45. **BA Grade:** 45. **Risk:** Average. **Adj:** 35.

Born: January 27, 2004. **B-T:** R-R. **HT:** 6-2. **WT:** 227. **Signed:** Dominican Republic, 2021. **Signed by:** Victor Santana.
TRACK RECORD: Valdez signed for $130,000 out of the Dominican Republic in 2021 and established himself as one of the minors' more dangerous power bats in 2024, when he slugged 22 homers for Low-A Bradenton. He followed with 26 more in 2025, doing most of his damage at High-A Greensboro before hitting .260/.363/.409 with six homers in 51 games for Double-A Altoona. Valdez made the Futures Game and ranked third among players 21 or younger in homers, trailing only the Mariners' Lazaro Montes (32) and the Mets' Ryan Clifford (29).
SCOUTING REPORT: With an uphill swing geared toward all-fields damage and easy plus raw power, Valdez makes no secret about his intent in most at-bats. He made some adjustments in 2025 to tap into that power more consistently and raised his 90th percentile exit velocity by nearly 3 mph compared to 2024. Earlier in his career, Valdez's steep swing path inhibited him from making consistent contact. After modestly cutting down his attack angle and chase rates, he improved his contact rate to a career-best 72.4% in 2025. Valdez will need to prove his plan of attack can work against more advanced pitching. His miss rate still hovered around 30%, and there are concerns that his swing remains vulnerable to velocity up in the zone and sliders away. He can fly open early on his front side as well. Defensively, Valdez offers limited value. He's a below-average runner with a fringy arm in right field and also saw time at first base, though scouts believe he moves better in the outfield.
THE FUTURE: Valdez's home-road splits and sheer underlying power should allay concerns that his 2025 home run barrage is a Greensboro-aided breakout. Righthanded corner profiles are tough, but his 2025 breakout put him on the Pirates' map and Triple-A Indianapolis awaits early in 2026.

Year	Age	Club (League)	Level	AVG	G	AB	R	H	2B	3B	HR	RBI	BB	SO	SB	OBP	SLG
2025	21	Greensboro (SAL)	A+	.303	72	277	46	84	18	1	20	57	31	77	2	.385	.592
2025	21	Altoona (EL)	AA	.260	51	181	29	47	7	1	6	29	25	53	1	.363	.409
		Minor League Totals		.262	356	1205	202	316	67	5	62	224	166	376	13	.366	.480

PITTSBURGH PIRATES

12 WYATT SANFORD, SS
HIT: 50. **POW:** 40. **RUN:** 55. **FLD:** 55. **ARM:** 55. **BA Grade:** 50. **Risk:** High. **Adj:** 35.

Born: November 24, 2005. **B-T:** L-R. **HT:** 5-11. **WT:** 187. **Drafted:** HS—Frisco, TX, 2024 (2nd round).
Signed by: John Lombardo.
TRACK RECORD: The Pirates drafted Sanford 47th overall in 2024 and signed him for $2,497,500, making him one of two prep picks they landed just outside the first round alongside righthander Levi Sterling. Sanford impressed in his 2025 debut. The 19-year-old produced a 165 wRC+ with as many walks as strikeouts in 20 games in the Florida Complex League before moving to Low-A Bradenton, where he slashed .238/.342/.378 with four homers in 44 games. He combined for 34 stolen bases across both levels before a groin injury ended his season in early August.
SCOUTING REPORT: Sanford doesn't have gaudy tools, but his instincts and competitiveness stand out the longer evaluators watch him. He rarely gives away at-bats or outs. Sanford flashed advanced feel for the barrel and was tough to beat in the strike zone in Bradenton—not to mention a bit unlucky on balls in play. Most of his impact came to the pull side, and while he projects for only fringy power, he made small adjustments—including a heel-up stance and lower handset—late in the year. Defensively, Sanford has a strong feel for shortstop with sure hands and an above-average arm. The Pirates believe he can be a plus defender up the middle, though some evaluators were less convinced early in the season about him sticking at shortstop. His heady nature also helps his above-average speed play up on the bases.
THE FUTURE: Even without a clear carrying tool, Sanford's well-rounded skill set gives him a chance to develop into a second-division regular who sticks at shortstop.

Year	Age	Club (League)	Level	AVG	G	AB	R	H	2B	3B	HR	RBI	BB	SO	SB	OBP	SLG
2025	19	FCL Pirates	Rk	.259	20	54	17	14	1	1	1	6	15	15	13	.487	.370
2025	19	Bradenton (FSL)	A	.238	44	164	29	39	7	2	4	19	19	39	21	.342	.378
		Minor League Totals		.243	64	218	46	53	8	3	5	25	34	54	34	.384	.376

13 OMAR ALFONZO, C
HIT: 40. **POW:** 55. **RUN:** 20. **FLD:** 45. **ARM:** 50. **BA Grade:** 45. **Risk:** Average. **Adj:** 35.

Born: August 3, 2003. **B-T:** L-R. **HT:** 6-1. **WT:** 235. **Signed:** Venezuela, 2019. **Signed by:** Jesus Morelli.
TRACK RECORD: Alfonzo was born in Minnesota while his father, former big leaguer Eliezer Alfonzo, was in the minors. He signed with the Pirates for $150,000 as part of their 2019 international class, though the pandemic delayed his debut until 2021. Now 22, he reached the upper minors for the first time in 2025, hitting .243/.354/.396 with career highs in home runs (14) and strikeouts (137) across High-A Greensboro and Double-A Altoona.
SCOUTING REPORT: Alfonzo wields a thunderous bat. His 108.4 mph 90th percentile exit velocity through mid-September ranked third among minor league catchers with at least 200 plate appearances, and he has steadily added roughly 6 mph to that figure over the past two seasons. Alfonzo also shows patience that sometimes borders on passivity and will work counts. The concern is whether his swing will allow him to make enough consistent contact. His strikeout and miss rates both hovered near 30% in 2025, and he has a tendency to roll over pitches to the pull side. A thickly-built 235 pounds, he offers little value on the bases but should remain behind the plate. He's a solid blocker and framer, with above-average arm strength that plays down at times due to inconsistent footwork and transfers.
THE FUTURE: He's unlikely to hit for high averages, but he has the ceiling of a second-division catcher as a damage threat with solid on-base and defensive skills.

Year	Age	Club (League)	Level	AVG	G	AB	R	H	2B	3B	HR	RBI	BB	SO	SB	OBP	SLG
2025	21	Greensboro (SAL)	A+	.261	67	234	41	61	9	0	11	34	44	79	2	.389	.440
2025	21	Altoona (EL)	AA	.218	49	170	15	37	9	1	3	22	19	58	0	.302	.335
		Minor League Totals		.241	358	1163	166	280	49	4	35	163	212	363	7	.363	.380

14 SAMMY STAFURA, SS
HIT: 40. **POW:** 50. **RUN:** 60. **FLD:** 55. **ARM:** 45. **BA Grade:** 50. **Risk:** High. **Adj:** 35

Born: November 15, 2004. **B-T:** R-R. **HT:** 6-0. **WT:** 188. **Drafted:** HS—Cortlandt Manor, NY, 2023 (2nd round).
Signed by: John Ceprini (Reds).
TRACK RECORD: Stafura has moved slowly since the Reds drafted him 43rd overall out of the New York high school ranks in 2023. He racked up 770 career Low-A plate appearances, mostly in Cincinnati's system, and slashed .258/.382/.396 with 10 homers during that span. The Reds traded Stafura to the Pirates at the 2025 deadline for Ke'Bryan Hayes. After a brief four-game stint in Bradenton, Pittsburgh sent Stafura to High-A Greensboro, where he struggled to a .512 OPS in 26 games.

PITTSBURGH PIRATES

SCOUTING REPORT: Stafura's sturdy frame and quick-twitch athleticism bleeds into several areas of his game. He's a plus runner with 30-plus steals in each of the last two seasons, and he plays an above-average shortstop with range, sure hands and a reliable internal clock, though his throwing accuracy can waver. Offensively, he shows solid-average raw power—especially to the pull side—and his solid strike-zone recognition led to high walk rates that helped buoy his production in Low-A. His future will hinge on the development of his approach and feel for contact. Stafura's swing can look rigid at times, and pitchers found success against him with velocity up and breaking stuff away. He also struggles at times to backspin the ball, limiting how much of his raw power plays in games.
THE FUTURE: Stafura's glove, defensive versatility and speed set the floor of a potential big league utility-man, with the chance for more if he can refine his undercooked approach and unlock more consistent offensive impact.

Year	Age	Club (League)	Level	AVG	G	AB	R	H	2B	3B	HR	RBI	BB	SO	SB	OBP	SLG
2025	20	Daytona (FSL)	A	.261	89	322	48	84	18	9	4	48	63	97	28	.392	.410
2025	20	Bradenton (FSL)	A	.250	4	16	1	4	1	1	0	0	1	6	0	.294	.438
2025	20	Greensboro (SAL)	A+	.160	26	94	11	15	3	0	2	12	10	26	4	.257	.255
		Minor League Totals		.243	223	819	137	199	37	16	15	120	146	256	63	.364	.382

15 KHRISTIAN CURTIS, RHP

FB: 60. **CB:** 50. **SL:** 55. **CT:** 55. **CH:** 55. **CTL:** 45. **BA Grade:** 45. **Risk:** Average. **Adj:** 35.

Born: May 9, 2002. **B-T:** R-R. **HT:** 6-3. **WT:** 213. **Drafted:** Arizona State, 2023 (12th round). **Signed by:** Derrick Van Dusen.
TRACK RECORD: Curtis signed for $497,500 as a 12th-round pick in 2023 after a college career at Texas A&M and Arizona State that included a botched Tommy John surgery and significant nerve damage in his right arm. Now healthy, the 23-year-old spent most of 2025 at High-A Greensboro, where he posted a 3.98 ERA with 116 strikeouts in 108.2 innings, a notable rebound after opening the year with an 11.48 ERA in April.
SCOUTING REPORT: Curtis works with a mid-90s fastball that touches 98 mph with above-average extension and carry and sets the table for a wide mix of secondaries. He's been a fringy strike-thrower, struggling early in 2025 to sync his delivery and arm action, but his command improved as the season progressed. His preferred secondary is a low-90s cutter that produces both strikes and whiffs at an above-average rate. He also owns a promising albeit inconsistent mid-80s changeup with nearly 18 inches of horizontal movement. Scouts like the shape of his upper-70s curveball, and he manipulates his mid-80s slider for added sweep. The cutter, slider and changeup all flash above-average potential and each generated whiff rates of at least 40%.
THE FUTURE: Curtis certainly has the repertoire to remain on a starter track if his strike-throwing continues to improve. Some evaluators, however, believe streamlining his mix could accelerate his path to the majors in a bullpen role. He finished 2025 in Double-A Altoona and should return there to open 2026.

Year	Age	Club (League)	Level	W	L	ERA	G	GS	IP	H	HR	BB	SO	BB%	SO%	WHIP	AVG
2025	23	Greensboro (SAL)	A+	8	5	3.98	26	26	109	91	12	46	116	9.8	24.8	1.26	.222
2025	23	Altoona (EL)	AA	0	0	0.00	1	0	2	0	0	0	3	0.0	50.0	0.00	.000
		Minor League Totals		8	5	3.90	27	26	111	91	12	46	119	9.7	25.1	1.24	.219

16 REINOLD NAVARRO, LHP

FB: 70. **SL:** 60. **CH:** 40. **CTL:** 30. **BA Grade:** 55. **Risk:** Extreme. **Adj:** 35.

Born: October 21, 2006. **B-T:** L-L. **HT:** 5-11. **WT:** 195. **Signed:** Dominican Republic, 2024. **Signed by:** Daurys Nin.
TRACK RECORD: When Navarro was an amateur in the Dominican Republic, he mostly sat in the mid-to-upper 80s. The Pirates signed him for $270,000 in 2024 and quickly saw his velocity spike. By 2025, the 18-year-old was pushing into the upper 90s over 32 innings split between the Florida Complex League and Low-A Bradenton. He struck out 61 hitters but also walked 40.
SCOUTING REPORT: Navarro presents quite an uncomfortable at-bat. Hitters must contend with one of the minors' best pure fastballs without having much of a clue where it will end up. His mid-90s fastball touches 99 mph with 21 inches of induced vertical break and generated whiffs nearly half the time, making it a potential plus-plus pitch. He pairs it with a hard, mid-80s gyro slider that produced similar swing-and-miss rates. He will mix in a nascent changeup, but he mostly tries to overwhelm hitters with his two potentially plus offerings. The problem is throwing them for strikes. Navarro is quite erratic, landing just 44% of his pitches in the zone for 2025, with lightning-fast arm speed that often outruns the rest of his mechanics. Scouts noted his delivery tends to work around his body, though the Pirates believe some late-season tweaks to his direction down the mound could pay off in 2026.
THE FUTURE: Navarro's command and feel for pitching needs to take a gargantuan leap, but he has sig-

PITTSBURGH PIRATES

nificant upside, and his potent two-pitch mix could one day settle into the back of a bullpen if he finds more strikes.

Year	Age	Club (League)	Level	W	L	ERA	G	GS	IP	H	HR	BB	SO	BB%	SO%	WHIP	AVG
2025	18	FCL Pirates	Rk	0	1	2.81	9	8	26	7	0	20	47	19.0	44.8	1.05	.088
2025	18	Bradenton (FSL)	A	0	1	15.63	6	4	6	3	0	20	14	45.5	31.8	3.63	.136
		Minor League Totals		0	2	5.34	15	12	32	10	0	40	61	26.8	40.9	1.56	.098

17 DARELL MOREL, SS

HIT: 40. **POW:** 55. **RUN:** 55. **FLD:** 50. **ARM:** 55. **BA Grade:** 55. **Risk:** Extreme. **Adj:** 35.

Born: September 15, 2007. **B-T:** L-R. **HT:** 6-5. **WT:** 174. **Signed:** Dominican Republic, 2025. **Signed by:** Leudy Castro.
TRACK RECORD: Morel was originally expected to sign with the Dodgers in the 2025 international class, but their pursuit of Roki Sasaki left his deal in limbo. The Pirates swooped in and signed the Dominican native for just under $1.78 million—nearly $1 million more than he was projected to receive from Los Angeles. In his pro debut, Morel slashed .287/.425/.414 with 26 steals and nearly as many walks (37) as strikeouts (45) over 50 Dominican Summer League games.
SCOUTING REPORT: At 6-foot-5 with long levers, Morel's size, athleticism and impact potential stand out immediately. He's a lefthanded hitter with smooth, natural leverage and plus raw power potential, though it didn't always materialize in DSL games. That's because pitchers identified a hole on the inside of his swing, especially against hard stuff, and he struggled to turn on those pitches. He's still learning how to consistently access his best bat speed, and he can get a bit pull happy, and the Pirates are working with him on a more consistent barrel path. For his height, Morel moves with surprising fluidity at shortstop and has above-average arm strength. He's a plus runner underway and has a shot to stick at the position, though he could ultimately move off to either third base or left field as he gets older and fills out.
THE FUTURE: Morel is a projectable long-term project with upside that's easy to fall in love with. He could one day develop into a well-rounded and impactful infielder, though the hit tool remains the biggest variable.

Year	Age	Club (League)	Level	AVG	G	AB	R	H	2B	3B	HR	RBI	BB	SO	SB	OBP	SLG
2025	17	DSL Pirates Gold	Rk	.287	50	157	45	45	9	4	1	25	37	45	26	.425	.414
		Minor League Totals		.287	50	157	45	45	9	4	1	25	37	45	26	.425	.414

18 THOMAS HARRINGTON, RHP

FB: 40. **CB:** 50. **SW:** 55. **CT:** 45. **SP:** 55. **CTL:** 55. **BA Grade:** 40. **Risk:** Mild. **Adj:** 35.

Born: July 12, 2001. **B-T:** R-R. **HT:** 6-2. **WT:** 185. **Drafted:** Campbell, 2022 (1st round supp.). **Signed by:** Mike Bradford.
TRACK RECORD: The Pirates drafted Harrington 36th overall in 2022 and he soon carved out a reputation as a strike-throwing artist. He ranked among Baseball America's Top 100 Prospects entering 2025 but struggled badly in his first taste of the majors. Harrington was hit hard in two April outings and again when recalled in August at Colorado, surrendering 15 runs across 8.2 innings. His return to Triple-A Indianapolis brought little relief. He pitched to a 5.34 ERA and allowed 20 homers in 96 innings, and his season ended early with a groin injury.
SCOUTING REPORT: Harrington has never had overpowering velocity—his fastball sits in the low 90s—but previously masked it with command and pitch variety, flashing up to seven different shapes. That command backed up in 2025. His 8% walk rate at Triple-A nearly doubled his mark across three levels in 2024, and his previously plus command looked closer to average. The Pirates pointed to mechanical issues in his delivery that cropped up in the offseason. That development, coupled with some sequencing experimentation as he looked for the right combination that can get big leaguers out, spelled trouble. Hitters whiffed on his fastball just 15% of the time, but Harrington did generate more swing-and-miss with an above-average mid-80s splitter and a sweeper. He also mixed an upper-80s cutter, low-80s curveball and occasional two-seamer.
THE FUTURE: Harrington's struggles underscored his slim margin for error as he tries to carve out a back-of-the-rotation role. He'll look for a reset in 2026, although the depth chart around him is getting deeper.

Year	Age	Club (League)	Level	W	L	ERA	G	GS	IP	H	HR	BB	SO	BB%	SO%	WHIP	AVG
2025	23	Indianapolis (IL)	AAA	7	9	5.34	21	20	96	93	20	33	90	8.0	21.7	1.31	.251
2025	23	Pittsburgh (NL)	MLB	0	1	15.58	3	1	9	18	3	7	7	14.0	14.0	2.88	.429
		Minor League Totals		21	18	3.73	69	67	341	304	43	93	351	6.6	25.1	1.17	.239
		Major League Totals		0	1	15.58	3	1	9	18	3	7	7	14.0	14.0	2.88	.429

19 NICK YORKE, 2B/OF

HIT: 55. **POW:** 45. **RUN:** 50. **FLD:** 45. **ARM:** 45. **BA Grade:** 40. **Risk:** Mild. **Adj:** 35.

Born: April 2, 2002. **B-T:** R-R. **HT:** 6-0. **WT:** 210. **Drafted:** HS—San Jose, CA, 2020 (1st round).
Signed by: Josh Labandeira (Red Sox).
TRACK RECORD: The Red Sox surprised many when they selected Yorke 17th overall in 2020. Traded to the Pirates in 2024 for righthander Quinn Priester, Yorke debuted in the majors later that year and was expected to solidify a big league role in 2025. Instead, he struggled mightily, spending most of the season with Triple-A Indianapolis, where he posted a 103 wRC+ in 103 games, before hitting .232/.264/.319 over 22 games in another late-season stint with Pittsburgh.
SCOUTING REPORT: Yorke has long stood out for his bat-to-ball skills and ability to damage pitches over the heart of the plate. His approach, however, has fluctuated between a patient, right-center focus and a more aggressive, pull-heavy plan. Yorke reverted to the former in 2024 and leaned into it even more frequently in 2025, perhaps to his detriment, while chasing more often. Yorke possesses above-average raw power and can impact balls on the inner third, but his swing plane limits how much of that power shows in games. He has also always fared better against righthanded pitchers in the minors. Yorke's a solid runner and saw time defensively at every infield spot except shortstop along with right field for Pittsburgh. He's a fringy defender across the board who will have to derive value from his versatility.
THE FUTURE: Yorke enters his age-24 season looking to reestablish his offensive identity and prove his bat can play in the majors. He has a path as a bat-first utility player, though the clock's ticking for him to secure that role.

Year	Age	Club (League)	Level	AVG	G	AB	R	H	2B	3B	HR	RBI	BB	SO	SB	OBP	SLG
2025	23	Indianapolis (IL)	AAA	.287	103	401	55	115	21	3	7	59	36	97	17	.348	.406
2025	23	Pittsburgh (NL)	MLB	.232	22	69	7	16	3	0	1	8	3	15	1	.264	.319
		Minor League Totals		.284	513	2032	332	578	109	14	57	299	232	483	77	.362	.436
		Major League Totals		.226	33	106	11	24	3	0	3	13	7	27	3	.272	.340

20 AXIEL PLAZ, C

HIT: 40. **POW:** 60. **RUN:** 20. **FLD:** 40. **ARM:** 60. **BA Grade:** 50. **Risk:** High. **Adj:** 35.

Born: August 12, 2005. **B-T:** R-R. **HT:** 5-11. **WT:** 243. **Signed:** Venezuela, 2022. **Signed by:** Jesus Morelli.
TRACK RECORD: Plaz signed out of Venezuela in 2022 and reached Low-A Bradenton two years later, where he slugged 15 homers, then returned to the level in 2025, where he hit for similar power and better average with a .262/.348/.450 line and nine homers through 55 games. Injuries have cut into his development and wiped out most of the second half of his 2025 season. Plaz has played just 150 games over the last two seasons, briefly resurfacing with High-A Greensboro at the end of the year.
SCOUTING REPORT: Plaz is a squat 5-foot-11, 243 pounds, and his double-plus raw power rivals only Konnor Griffin among teenagers in Pittsburgh's system. He punishes mistakes—especially fastballs—to all fields when he gets his hands extended. Plaz's overall offensive approach, though, is fairly crude. He was more aggressive in 2025, swinging over half the time, and chased out of the zone at nearly a 36% rate. He also infrequently pulls his best contact from his flatter barrel path. Plaz also has a cannon of an arm behind the plate and the Pirates felt his game-calling took a step early in the season after he hired a tutor in the offseason to improve his English, but his receiving and blocking remain raw.
THE FUTURE: There are a lot of caveats with Plaz's profile on both sides of the ball. Still, teenage catchers rarely have his power potential. He should start 2026 with High-A Greensboro where his power to right-center could produce impressive home run totals if he can stay healthy.

Year	Age	Club (League)	Level	AVG	G	AB	R	H	2B	3B	HR	RBI	BB	SO	SB	OBP	SLG
2025	19	Bradenton (FSL)	A	.262	55	202	27	53	11	0	9	40	21	47	1	.348	.450
2025	19	Greensboro (SAL)	A+	.086	11	35	5	3	1	0	1	6	5	6	0	.214	.200
		Minor League Totals		.225	215	663	104	149	39	2	29	128	96	197	4	.342	.421

21 DUCE GOURSON, 2B

HIT: 55. **POW:** 45. **RUN:** 50. **FLD:** 50. **ARM:** 55. **BA Grade:** 45. **Risk:** Average. **Adj:** 35.

Born: September 20, 2002 **B-T:** L-R. **HT:** 5-11. **WT:** 203. **Drafted:** UCLA, 2024 (9th round). **Signed by:** Brian Tracy.
TRACK RECORD: Ethan "Duce" Gourson was a three-year starter at second base for UCLA and played for USA Baseball's Collegiate National Team in 2023. The Pirates signed him for $187,500 as a ninth-round pick in 2024, and after a quiet debut, he broke through in 2025 by hitting .275/.370/.439 with 10 homers and 31 steals between High-A Greensboro and Double-A Altoona.
SCOUTING REPORT: At just 5-foot-11, 203 pounds, Gourson burnished a reputation in college as a

PITTSBURGH PIRATES

heady, skills-over-tools type who was content to slash baseballs to the opposite field. But he made meaningful offseason adjustments prior to 2025, adding bat speed while refining his swing and approach to generate more impact without sacrificing contact. He pairs strong swing decisions and strike-zone control with above-average exit velocities and a better understanding of how to optimize his contact quality from gap to gap. His short, direct stroke allows him to handle velocity, and he made noticeable gains in damaging offspeed pitches in 2025. Gourson's baseball IQ shows up on the bases and helps his average speed play up. In the field, he's a solid defender at second base who gained experience at third and first base and has an above-average arm.

THE FUTURE: Gourson's a detail-oriented player who knows how to maximize his tools. He put himself on the map in 2025 and has the ceiling of a reliable big league utility infielder.

Year	Age	Club (League)	Level	AVG	G	AB	R	H	2B	3B	HR	RBI	BB	SO	SB	OBP	SLG
2025	22	Greensboro (SAL)	A+	.261	39	138	29	36	9	1	5	18	17	28	21	.368	.449
2025	22	Altoona (EL)	AA	.284	56	197	27	56	12	1	5	20	23	61	10	.372	.431
		Minor League Totals		.262	117	409	69	107	26	2	10	46	55	110	35	.372	.408

22 JESUS TRAVIESO, RHP
FB: 50. **SL:** 55. **CH:** 50. **SW:** 45. **CTL:** 45. **BA Grade:** 50. **Risk:** High. **Adj:** 35.

Born: March 22, 2007. **B-T:** R-R. **HT:** 5-11. **WT:** 160. **Signed:** Venezuela, 2024.
Signed by: Cesar Morillo/Rolando Pino/Alberto Mejia (Red Sox).
TRACK RECORD: Though he weighed roughly 150 pounds and stood just 5-foot-11 as an amateur, Travieso featured a lightning fast arm, athleticism and the ability to spin a breaking ball when the Red Sox started scouting him, and his velocity came quickly after signing. After a solid Dominican Summer League debut in 2024, Travieso held surprisingly big velocities while posting a 32% strikeout rate and 13% walk rate in his 2025 stateside debut. Boston shipped him to the Pirates in December along with Jhostynxon Garcia in the Johan Oviedo trade.
SCOUTING REPORT: Travieso's power stuff belies his stature, with a well-timed kinetic chain that allowed him to sit at 97 mph and top out at 100 in 2025. Even with those high velocities, he threw more gyro sliders and sweepers than fastballs. His breaking balls generated huge whiff rates, while his fastball—due partly to just 5.5 feet of extension—played below its velocity. He also used his changeup about 15% of the time, and the pitch missed lefthanded bats in Low-A. Travieso's size will likely engender skepticism about whether he can sustain velocity, and the effort required to reach the upper 90s comes with control questions. Still, if Travieso can continue to get stronger and harness his high-octane stuff, he has starter upside.
THE FUTURE: Travieso now joins a deep cadre of young lower-level Pirates arms. He could begin 2026 with Low-A Bradenton and get to High-A Greensboro if his velocity gains hold.

Year	Age	Club (League)	Level	W	L	ERA	G	GS	IP	H	HR	BB	SO	BB%	SO%	WHIP	AVG
2025	18	FCL Red Sox	Rk	1	3	2.77	12	10	39	26	1	25	52	15.3	31.9	1.31	.194
2025	18	Salem (CAR)	A	2	0	3.51	7	6	26	31	2	11	38	9.2	31.7	1.64	.287
		Minor League Totals		3	6	3.24	30	27	86	76	3	46	117	12.2	31.1	1.42	.236

23 LEVI STERLING, RHP
FB: 50. **CB:** 55. **SL:** 45. **CH:** 55. **CTL:** 50. **BA Grade:** 50. **Risk:** High. **Adj:** 35.

Born: September 2, 2006. **B-T:** R-R. **HT:** 6-4. **WT:** 214. **Drafted:** HS—Sherman Oaks, CA, 2024 (1st round supp.).
Signed by: Brian Tracy.
TRACK RECORD: Sterling was still 17 when the Pirates selected him 37th overall out of the California prep ranks in 2024. He stood out for his advanced pitchability despite playing shortstop all the way through high school. The righthander struggled more with strikes than expected in his first full season, spending nearly all of 2025 in the Florida Complex League.
SCOUTING REPORT: Sterling has begun to add strength to his projectable 6-foot-4 frame and topped out at 95 mph in 2025. He struggled to hold velocity, with his four-seamer ranging 87-92 mph and showing armside run from a low release height. He shows feel for a four-pitch mix. Sterling's low-80s curveball gained power in 2025 with big shape and surprising depth for his arm slot. His low-to-mid-80s changeup also has above-average potential with more than 18 inches of armside fade, and he rounds it out with a tighter mid-80s slider. Praised for his strike-throwing and easy operation as an amateur, Sterling's delivery fell out of sync at times in 2025 and he struggled to spot his secondaries. Even so, his athleticism, feel and repeatability suggest he can grow into average control as he learns to better maintain his delivery and hold velocity deeper into outings.
THE FUTURE: Sterling has the frame, repertoire and traits to remain a starter with the ceiling of a groundball-oriented back-of-the-rotation arm. He should open 2026 at Low-A Bradenton.

PITTSBURGH PIRATES

Year	Age	Club (League)	Level	W	L	ERA	G	GS	IP	H	HR	BB	SO	BB%	SO%	WHIP	AVG
2025	18	FCL Pirates	Rk	3	2	6.54	11	9	32	35	2	21	30	14.0	20.0	1.77	.282
2025	18	Bradenton (FSL)	A	0	0	0.00	1	0	2	2	0	2	4	16.7	33.3	1.71	.222
		Minor League Totals		3	2	6.09	12	9	34	37	2	23	34	14.2	21.0	1.76	.278

24 JETER MARTINEZ, RHP
FB: 60. **SL:** 55. **CH:** 45. **CTL:** 40. **BA Grade:** 50. **Risk:** High. **Adj:** 35.

Born: February 16, 2006. **B-T:** R-R. **HT:** 6-4. **WT:** 180. **Signed:** Mexico, 2023. **Signed by:** David Velazquez (Mariners).

TRACK RECORD: Martinez didn't focus on pitching until he was 15, then signed with the Mariners out of Mexico for $600,000 in 2023. His raw stuff made him a trendy breakout pick entering 2025, but he struggled in his first taste of full-season ball at Low-A Modesto. At the trade deadline, Seattle dealt him to the Pirates for reliever Caleb Ferguson. Martinez spent nearly a month refining his delivery at Pittsburgh's complex before making two brief appearances in Bradenton to close the year.

SCOUTING REPORT: Martinez hooks evaluators in with his arm strength and present stuff, then leaves them to consider whether he'll have the craftsmanship to refine it. The 6-foot-4 righthander already works in the mid 90s, and the Pirates believe he can better distinguish his four-seam and two-seam fastballs. His best secondary is a mid-80s slider with sharp, two-plane break, while his upper-80s changeup flashes impressive shape but lacks consistent feel. Strikes were an issue in 2025. Martinez walked 13.7% of hitters, struggled with sequencing and often spiraling in big innings. He has a physical delivery and arm stroke, and Pittsburgh used his month of development at Pirate City to work on delivery tweaks that could alleviate stress on his arm and potentially lead to better strikes.

THE FUTURE: Acquired for a rental reliever, Martinez is a classic upside dart throw for an organization known for pitching development. His arm talent is evident, but he'll need significant polish to approach a midrotation ceiling. He's likely to return to Low-A to open 2026.

Year	Age	Club (League)	Level	W	L	ERA	G	GS	IP	H	HR	BB	SO	BB%	SO%	WHIP	AVG
2025	19	Bradenton (FSL)	A	0	1	30.86	2	1	2	7	0	4	6	21.1	31.6	4.71	.500
2025	19	Modesto (CAL)	A	2	6	6.18	16	16	63	63	1	38	60	13.2	20.9	1.61	.264
		Minor League Totals		4	13	4.57	41	36	152	117	3	93	170	13.9	25.4	1.38	.211

25 ZANDER MUETH, RHP
FB: 60. **SL:** 55. **CH:** 50. **CTL:** 35. **BA Grade:** 50. **Risk:** High. **Adj:** 35.

Born: June 22, 2005. **B-T:** R-R. **HT:** 6-5. **WT:** 220. **Drafted:** HS—Belleville, IL, 2023, (2nd round supp.). **Signed by:** Anthony Wycklendt.

TRACK RECORD: Mueth has shown flashes of big stuff and erratic command since the Pirates drafted him 67th overall in 2023 and signed him for just under $1.8 million. After a strong pro debut in 2024, when he logged a 1.58 ERA over 51.1 innings in the Florida Complex League, his progress stalled in 2025. Limited by shoulder and abdominal strains, he threw just 26 innings between the FCL and Low-A Bradenton, posting a 6.58 ERA with nearly as many walks (29) as strikeouts (34).

SCOUTING REPORT: Aesthetically, the 6-foot-5, 220-pound Mueth draws frequent comparisons to Red Sox RHP Tanner Houck. Mueth works from a low arm slot with a sinking mid-90s fastball that touches 98 mph and runs hard to his arm side. Unlike Houck, who leans heavily on a sweeper, Mueth has settled on a more traditionally-shaped mid-80s slider that the Pirates believe gives him the best chance to one day develop consistent feel and command. Mueth also has spotty feel for his seldom-used upper-80s changeup that flashes average potential. His biggest hurdle remains control. Mueth's long arm action and rotational delivery often disrupt timing and release consistency, causing erratic strike-throwing.

THE FUTURE: Mueth's physicality and two potential plus pitches fit a starting profile, but he'll need to harness his stuff to stay on a starter track. He's expected to be healthy entering 2026.

Year	Age	Club (League)	Level	W	L	ERA	G	GS	IP	H	HR	BB	SO	BB%	SO%	WHIP	AVG
2025	20	FCL Pirates	Rk	0	0	2.25	2	2	4	3	0	4	6	21.1	31.6	1.75	.200
2025	20	Bradenton (FSL)	A	0	4	7.36	10	10	22	22	1	25	28	21.6	24.1	2.14	.259
		Minor League Totals		7	8	3.42	32	31	100	72	3	79	113	16.9	24.2	1.51	.199

PITTSBURGH PIRATES

26 EASTON CARMICHAEL, C
HIT: 50. **POW:** 50. **RUN:** 50. **FLD:** 45. **ARM:** 45. **BA Grade:** 45. **Risk:** Average. **Adj:** 35.

Born: November 3, 2003. **B-T:** R-R. **HT:** 6-1. **WT:** 200. **Drafted:** Oklahoma, 2025 (3rd round). **Signed by:** Brandon Rembert.
TRACK RECORD: Carmichael showed steady progress over three seasons at Oklahoma, capped by a breakout junior year in 2025. After posting an .868 OPS with five homers in the Cape Cod League, he hit .329 with 17 home runs and 14 steals as the Sooners' catcher. The Pirates drafted him in the third round and signed him for $977,000. Assigned directly to High-A Greensboro, Carmichael hit just .120 with 11 strikeouts in 14 games while battling a nagging wrist injury.
SCOUTING REPORT: Carmichael has above-average athleticism for a catcher and saw his power take a jump in 2025 after minor swing adjustments. He's naturally strong and shows a compact stroke with feel for the barrel, giving him a chance for average hit and power tools. Most of his college damage came to the pull side, and High-A arms quickly tested his approach against spin on the outer third. Carmichael's athleticism shows up in his mobility behind the plate. He'll need to refine his framing and receiving, and he has fringy arm strength. Carmichael's a solid runner, so his physical tools could allow him to find another home defensively if his catching skills can't catch up.
THE FUTURE: There's work to do on both sides of the ball, but Carmichael has the upside of a second-division regular if he can leverage his tool set consistently in pro ball.

Year	Age	Club (League)	Level	AVG	G	AB	R	H	2B	3B	HR	RBI	BB	SO	SB	OBP	SLG
2025	21	Greensboro (SAL)	A+	.120	14	50	3	6	0	0	1	2	2	11	1	.185	.180
		Minor League Totals		.120	14	50	3	6	0	0	1	2	2	11	1	.185	.180

27 MURF GRAY, 3B

HIT: 50. **POW:** 50. **RUN:** 30. **FLD:** 45. **ARM:** 60. **BA Grade:** 45. **Risk:** Average. **Adj:** 35.

Born: December 30, 2003. **B-T:** R-R. **HT:** 6-4. **WT:** 230. **Drafted:** Fresno State, 2025 (2nd round). **Signed by:** Mike Sansoe.
TRACK RECORD: Gray, whose first name is Triston, isn't the most famous Fresno State baseball alum—that distinction belongs to Aaron Judge—but Gray actually doubled Judge's college home run total (36). Gray was the Bulldogs' most notable draft prospect since Judge when the Pirates selected him 73rd overall in 2025 and signed him for $997,500. Pittsburgh opted to delay his pro debut, instead assigning him to the complex to focus on strength and conditioning after signing.
SCOUTING REPORT: A physical 6-foot-4, 230-pound righthanded hitter, Gray combines impressive raw strength and bat speed with a flatter swing path and feel for the barrel that helped him hit for high averages in college. He'll need to tamp down his aggressive, pull-heavy approach that led to a 6.1% college walk rate, and the Pirates began working to stabilize his lower half to help him reach pitches low and away and use the opposite field more consistently. Gray is a surehanded defender at third base with a plus arm, but his limited lateral mobility and size could eventually push him across the diamond to first base. At times, the game can also speed up on him defensively.
THE FUTURE: The Pirates believe Gray's combination of bat speed, contact ability and raw power can translate to an everyday corner role, though his uncertain defensive future heightens the risk.

Year	Age	Club (League)	Level	AVG	G	AB	R	H	2B	3B	HR	RBI	BB	SO	SB	OBP	SLG
2025	21	Did not play															

28 JACK BRANNIGAN, SS/3B
HIT: 40. **POW:** 55. **RUN:** 50. **FLD:** 55. **ARM:** 60. **BA Grade:** 40. **Risk:** Average. **Adj:** 35.

Born: March 11, 2001. **B-T:** R-R. **HT:** 6-1. **WT:** 210. **Drafted:** Notre Dame, 2022 (3rd round).
Signed by: Anthony Wycklendt.
TRACK RECORD: Since being drafted in the third round in 2022 out of Notre Dame, where he starred as a two-way player, Brannigan has struggled to stay healthy. He's never played more than 87 games in a season, missing time with a quad strain in 2023, left shoulder issues in 2024 and right shoulder labrum surgery in 2025. Before the injury ended his Double-A debut, he hit .225/.329/.358 over 59 games.
SCOUTING REPORT: While another injury and modest surface-level production clouded his season, Brannigan made some subtle under-the-hood improvements. He hit the ball harder in 2025 and chased less despite facing tougher competition. His contact skills are fringy, but his uphill, pull-oriented swing produces above-average power that has offset a 27% career strikeout rate. A former college reliever, Brannigan's plus arm was once his loudest tool, though the surgery adds uncertainty to its recovery. He can make every throw from the left side of the infield, with solid hands and instincts that make up for average range. He began his career more comfortable at third base but has since transitioned to playing above-average shortstop defense.

PITTSBURGH PIRATES

THE FUTURE: Now 25 and freshly added to the 40-man roster, Brannigan faces a pivotal year. If he stays healthy, his defensive flexibility and power give him a chance to carve out a bench role or utility spot at the upper levels.

Year	Age	Club (League)	Level	AVG	G	AB	R	H	2B	3B	HR	RBI	BB	SO	SB	OBP	SLG
2025	24	Altoona (EL)	AA	.225	59	204	29	46	8	2	5	30	25	62	9	.329	.358
		Minor League Totals		.245	251	903	168	221	40	7	45	151	134	293	51	.356	.454

29 TONY BLANCO JR., 1B
HIT: 30. **POW:** 80. **RUN:** 20. **FLD:** 40. **ARM:** 70. **BA Grade:** 50. **Risk:** Extreme. **Adj:** 30.

Born: May 14, 2005. **B-T:** R-R. **HT:** 6-7. **WT:** 283. **Signed:** Dominican Republic, 2022. **Signed by:** Omelbis Corporan.
TRACK RECORD: Evaluators have long marveled at the hulking 6-foot-7, 283-pound Blanco's prodigious power. Yet injuries have limited his chances to show it. Since signing for $900,000 in 2022, he has played just 109 games while growing into his massive frame. A hamstring strain delayed his 2025 debut until July, limiting him to 28 Low-A games during a year marked by tragedy. His father, former big leaguer Tony Blanco, died in April after a nightclub roof collapse in the Dominican Republic.
SCOUTING REPORT: When Blanco makes flush contact, there isn't a ballpark in baseball that can hold him. While recouping at-bats in the Arizona Fall League, he stung a ball 120.4 mph. That would've tied Vladimir Guerrero Jr. for the second-hardest hit ball in the majors last year and only two others, Oneil Cruz and Shohei Ohtani, surpassed 120 mph. How frequently he'll get to that power is another question. His approach and swing decisions need tightening, and he'll have to reduce his swing-and-miss to access his elite power more regularly. He has a plus arm, but his size almost certainly restricts him to first base or DH, evoking comparisons to Miguel Sano or Jesus Aguilar.
THE FUTURE: There aren't many players in baseball with Blanco's blend of size, strength and boom-or-bust nature. If he can stay healthy and refine his approach, he has massive big league impact potential.

Year	Age	Club (League)	Level	AVG	G	AB	R	H	2B	3B	HR	RBI	BB	SO	SB	OBP	SLG
2025	20	FCL Pirates	Rk	.167	2	6	1	1	0	0	1	2	0	4	0	.167	.667
2025	20	Bradenton (FSL)	A	.264	28	106	10	28	3	0	7	21	18	42	0	.368	.491
		Minor League Totals		.260	108	362	43	94	15	1	18	69	47	146	1	.346	.456

30 JOHAN DE LOS SANTOS, SS
HIT: 60. **POW:** 30. **RUN:** 60. **FLD:** 55. **ARM:** 50. **BA Grade:** 50. **Risk:** Extreme. **Adj:** 30.

Born: February 17, 2005. **B-T:** L-R. **HT:** 5-8. **WT:** 171. **Signed:** Dominican Republic, 2025. **Signed by:** Daurys Nin.
TRACK RECORD: The younger brother of Pirates shortstop prospect Yordany De Los Santos, Johan signed for $2.25 million out of the Dominican Republic, the top bonus in Pittsburgh's 2025 international class. He then ranked sixth in the Dominican Summer League with a .353 average along with 34 steals over 44 games and twice as many walks (27) to strikeouts (13) despite being one of the youngest players in his signing class.
SCOUTING REPORT: Pitchers in the DSL simply couldn't beat the diminutive De Los Santos in the strike zone. The lefthanded hitter already has plus bat-to-ball skills and impressive hand-eye coordination, which helps him move the ball from gap to gap. Listed at just 5-foot-8, 171 pounds, De Los Santos produced the second-lightest 90th percentile exit velocity among Pirates minor leaguers with at least 100 plate appearances, and he's not expected to grow into much power. He's a plus runner with great instincts who makes everyone around him better, and the Pirates think he can stick at shortstop because he's a fundamentally-sound defender with a quick first step, though his hands could be tested as he moves up the ladder.
THE FUTURE: After his impressive debut, the Pirates didn't rule out pushing De Los Santos straight to Low-A Bradenton for his age-17 season. His table-setting skills could one day fit near the top or bottom of a big league lineup.

Year	Age	Club (League)	Level	AVG	G	AB	R	H	2B	3B	HR	RBI	BB	SO	SB	OBP	SLG
2025	16	DSL Pirates Black	Rk	.353	44	139	43	49	9	3	0	27	27	13	34	.451	.460
		Minor League Totals		.353	44	139	43	49	9	3	0	27	27	13	34	.451	.460

Masyn Winn

St. Louis Cardinals

BY GEOFF PONTES

Entering 2023, the Cardinals had only one season with a losing record since 2000. Over the last three seasons, St. Louis has posted three sub-.500 records as it navigates a true rebuild for the first time since the mid 1950s.

The Cardinals will continue to evolve in 2026. That's because longtime president of baseball operations John Mozeliak retired, and newly promoted PBO Chaim Bloom is moving the organization in a different direction.

After being one of the most progressive teams in baseball over the first half of the 21st century, the Cardinals have fallen behind other teams in the information age. What was once a sound approach became stale.

The Cardinals hired Bloom following the 2023 season. First he was an advisor focused on upgrading systems with a focus on pitching development. Two years later, the gains made under Bloom's tenure are clear to see. An organization once averse to amateur pitchers with big stuff has embraced higher risk and higher reward profiles in recent seasons. This is evidenced by the Cardinals' 2025 draft class.

Lefthander Liam Doyle and righthander Tanner Franklin, St. Louis' first and third picks, both out of Tennessee, are illuminating examples of this change in approach.

The Cardinals have also been one of the most aggressive rebuilding clubs in the game in the trade market over the last several seasons. They made a series of trades within days of the 2025 trade deadline. St. Louis acquired Jesus Baez, Frank Elissalt and Nate Dohm from the Mets for Ryan Helsley. They added Blaze Jordan from the Red Sox for Steven Matz, and Skylar Hales and Mason Molina from the Rangers for Phil Maton.

The Cardinals then made waves after the season by shipping Sonny Gray to the Red Sox for lefthander Brandon Clarke and righthander Richard Fitts. These trades signify a change in approach for the Cardinals and a clear direction.

PROJECTED 2029 LINEUP

Catcher	Rainiel Rodriguez	22
First Base	Alec Burleson	30
Second Base	Thomas Saggese	27
Third Base	JJ Wetherholt	26
Shortstop	Masyn Winn	27
Left Field	Jordan Walker	27
Center Field	Victor Scott II	28
Right Field	Joshua Baez	26
Designated Hitter	Ivan Herrera	29
No. 1 Starter	Liam Doyle	25
No. 2 Starter	Quinn Mathews	28
No. 3 Starter	Matthew Liberatore	29
No. 4 Starter	Tanner Franklin	25
No. 5 Starter	Ixan Henderson	27
Closer	Matt Svanson	30

The club now heads into 2026 with some decisions on their hands. Despite their struggles in recent years, St. Louis has a predominantly homegrown core of position players, many of whom might be out of contract by the time the team is ready to compete again.

Players such as second baseman Brendan Donovan and outfielder Lars Nootbaar could fetch good value on the trade market. Additionally, trading those veterans creates opportunities for some of the Cardinals' young-and-close talent, headlined by Triple-A shortstop JJ Wetherholt.

The system's No. 1 prospect is possibly the best prospect the Cardinals have had in at least a decade, and he might be their best since the late Oscar Taveras. Wetherholt has the look of a multi-time all-star infielder capable of holding down any spot at the top of the order. He is a true five-tool prospect with one of the most polished hit tools among those who played in the minor leagues in 2025.

Could Wetherholt be the cornerstone of the Cardinals' next sustained run of success? Only time will tell, but after years of half-measures, St. Louis seems headed in a new direction.

The Cardinals' farm system is the most talented it has been in years, and that could stand to improve with more potential trades on the way leading up to Opening Day 2026. ∎

DEPTH CHART

ST. LOUIS CARDINALS

TOP 2026 ROOKIES — RANK
1. JJ Wetherholt, SS — 1
2. Joshua Baez, OF — 4
3. Quinn Mathews, LHP — 5

BREAKOUT PROSPECTS — RANK
1. Ryan Mitchell, SS/OF — 12
2. Deniel Ortiz, 3B — 19
3. Jack Gurevitch, 1B — 22

SOURCE OF TOP 30 TALENT

Homegrown	22	Acquired	8
College	15	Trade	6
Junior college	1	Rule 5 draft	1
High school	3	Independent league	1
Undrafted free agent	0	Free agent/waivers	0
International	3		

LF
Zach Levenson (26)
Travis Honeyman (29)
Miguel Ugueto
Ian Petrutz

CF
Ryan Mitchell (12)
Nathan Church (16)
Chase Davis (27)
Royelny Strop
Kenly Hunter

RF
Joshua Baez (4)
Matt Koperniak
Mike Antico

3B
Jesus Baez (15)
Deniel Ortiz (19)
Cesar Prieto

SS
JJ Wetherholt (1)
Yairo Padilla (11)
Jeremy Rivas
Jalin Flores
Sebastian Dos Santos

2B
Bryan Torres (25)
Jonathan Mejia
Yeferson Portolatin

1B
Jack Gurevitch (22)
Blaze Jordan (30)

C
Rainiel Rodriguez (3)
Jimmy Crooks (9)
Leonardo Bernal (10)
Ryan Campos
Sammy Hernandez
Juan Rujano

LHP

LHSP
Liam Doyle (2)
Quinn Mathews (5)
Brandon Clarke (6)
Ixan Henderson (8)
Cooper Hjerpe (17)
Cade Crossland (18)
Brycen Mautz (20)
Braden Davis (21)
Mason Molina
Pete Hansen
Alex Cornwell
Bernard Mack
Yadiel Batista

LHRP
Michael Watson
Jack Findlay

RHP

RHSP
Tanner Franklin (7)
Tekoah Roby (13)
Nate Dohm (24)
Branneli Franco
Brian Holiday
Sem Robberse
Juan Garcia
Hancel Rincon
Darlin Saladin
Ryan Murphy
Chen-Wei Lin

RHRP
Tink Hence (14)
Frank Elissalt (23)
Matt Pushard (28)
Andre Granillo
Zak Kent

ST. LOUIS CARDINALS

1 JJ WETHERHOLT, SS

Born: September 10, 2002. **B-T:** L-R. **HT:** 5-10. **WT:** 190.
Drafted: West Virginia, 2024 (1st round).
Signed by: TC Calhoun.

TRACK RECORD: Wetherholt played for Andy Bednar at Mars Area High outside Pittsburgh and was teammates with Andy's son Will Bednar, the Giants' 2021 first-round pick, before committing to West Virginia. After hitting .308 as a freshman in 2022, Wetherholt followed it up with an outstanding sophomore season at WVU in which he hit .449/.517/.787 and led the nation in batting average. After an injury-plagued junior season, Wetherholt was drafted by the Cardinals seventh overall and signed for $6.8 million. He was assigned to Double-A Springfield out of camp to begin 2025 and would go on to hit .300/.425/.466 in 62 games. Days before participating in the Futures Game, Wetherholt was promoted to Triple-A Memphis, where he hit .314/.416/.562 in 47 games. His .421 on-base percentage ranked fifth overall in the minors.

BA GRADE
65 Risk: Mild
Adjusted grade: 60

SCOUTING GRADES
Hit: 70. Power: 55. Run: 55.
Fielding: 55. Arm: 55.
Projected future grades on 20-80 scouting scale

SCOUTING REPORT: Wetherholt is an above-average athlete with a strong and physically mature build with little room for additional physical projection. He is a well-rounded player who does everything at an average or better level. Make no mistake: Wetherholt's profile is driven by his advanced hit tool and developed plate skills. He has a simple, low-effort operation at the plate. The lefthanded batter sets up open, with his hands loosely set below his shoulder. He uses a flatter swing path that often connects for his best-struck drives to the opposite field. His loose, adjustable hands and discerning eye at the plate limit his swing and miss, leading to plus contact rates. His ability to identify balls from strikes sets him apart from other top prospects. Wetherholt rarely expands the zone but is aggressive on pitches over the heart of the plate. He has shown average power throughout his career but began to show more over-the-fence thump during his time at Triple-A. Wetherholt makes consistent hard contact at good angles but lacks higher top-end exit velocities synonymous with 30-homer hitters. He'll likely settle within the 18-24 home run range for his prime seasons with lots of doubles and a higher batting average. Wetherholt is an above-average runner who will show plus run times. Speed is an underappreciated aspect of his profile, and he's a strong baserunner who will likely steal 15-20 bases per season in the early years of his career. In the field, Wetherholt is an adept defender who projects to stick on the left side of the infield. His defense at shortstop is good enough to make him an above-average defender over the long haul. If he should move to third base, he projects as a plus defender, where his above-average arm fits.

BEST TOOLS

BATTING
Best Hitter	JJ Wetherholt
Best Power Hitter	Rainiel Rodriguez
Best Strike-Zone Discipline	JJ Wetherholt
Fastest Baserunner	Joshua Baez
Best Athlete	Joshua Baez

PITCHING
Best Fastball	Liam Doyle
Best Curveball	Tekoah Roby
Best Slider	Tanner Franklin
Best Changeup	Braden Davis
Best Control	Tekoah Roby

FIELDING
Best Defensive Catcher	Jimmy Crooks
Best Defensive Infielder	JJ Wetherholt
Best Infield Arm	Yairo Padilla
Best Defensive Outfielder	Nathan Church
Best Outfield Arm	Joshua Baez

THE FUTURE: Wetherholt will likely break camp with the Cardinals to begin 2026 and could be the long-term answer at multiple positions on the infield. He's a star in the making and the best hitter the Cardinals have produced in a decade.

Year	Age	Club (League)	Level	AVG	G	AB	R	H	2B	3B	HR	RBI	BB	SO	SB	OBP	SLG
2025	22	Springfield (TL)	AA	.300	62	223	39	67	14	1	7	34	44	40	14	.425	.466
2025	22	Memphis (IL)	AAA	.314	47	185	43	58	14	1	10	25	28	33	9	.416	.562
		Minor League Totals		.304	138	513	100	156	33	2	19	79	88	88	25	.418	.487

ST. LOUIS CARDINALS

2 LIAM DOYLE, LHP
FB: 70. **CB:** 40. **SL:** 50. **SP:** 55. **CT:** 50. **CTL:** 50. **BA Grade:** 60. **Risk:** Average. **Adj:**

Born: June 3, 2004. **B-T:** R-L. **HT:** 6-2. **WT:** 220.
Drafted: Tennessee, 2025 (1st round). **Signed by:** TC Calhoun.
TRACK RECORD: A New Hampshire prep star, Doyle threw five no-hitters and a perfect game over four seasons at Pinkerton Academy. Few players have leveraged the transfer portal as well as Doyle, who spent one season each at Coastal Carolina, Mississippi and Tennessee. As a junior for the Volunteers in 2025, he pitched to a 10-4 record, 3.20 ERA and 164 strikeouts in 95.2 innings and earned first-team All-America honors. The Cardinals drafted him fifth overall and signed him for $7.25 million. Doyle made two appearances after signing.
SCOUTING REPORT: Doyle is a physical lefthander with average height but a muscular and athletic frame. His higher-effort operation creates a bit of deception with a longer arm action, low three-quarters arm slot and a crossfire finish. Because of this, he faces relief questions despite a track record of success as a starter. Doyle mixes five pitches in his four-seam fastball, cutter, slider, curveball and splitter. During his time at Tennessee, he threw his fastball more than 62% of the time, something likely to tick down in pro ball. Doyle's fastball is a double-plus pitch that generated high swinging-strike rates in the SEC. It sits 95-97 mph and touches 100 with plus vertical ride from a low release height. His secondary pitch usage is divided equally between an above-average, mid-to-high-80s splitter, an average cutter, an average sweeper and a low-80s curveball. The splitter is clearly Doyle's best bat-missing secondary, and development of a dependable breaking ball will be a point of emphasis. He has average control but shows above-average command by landing his pitches to chosen zones with regularity.
THE FUTURE: Doyle is a fast-moving college lefthander who could pitch his way to the middle of the Cardinals' rotation by mid-2026.

Year	Age	Club	Level	W	L	ERA	G	GS	IP	H	HR	BB	SO	HR/9	BB%	SO%	WHIP
2025	21	Palm Beach (FSL)	A	0	0	5.40	1	1	2	1	1	2	3	28.6	42.9	1.80	.200
2025	21	Springfield (TL)	AA	0	0	0.00	1	1	2	2	0	0	3	0.0	37.5	1.00	.250
		Minor League Totals		0	0	2.45	2	2	4	3	1	2	6	13.3	40.0	1.36	.231

3 RAINIEL RODRIGUEZ, C
HIT: 60. **POW:** 65. **RUN:** 30. **FLD:** 45. **ARM:** 60. **BA Grade:** 60. **Risk:** Average. **Adj:** 50.

Born: January 4, 2007. **B-T:** R-R. **HT:** 5-10. **WT:** 197.
Signed: Dominican Republic, 2024. **Signed by:** Darlumis Almonte/Alix Martinez.
TRACK RECORD: Born in the Dominican Republic, Rodriguez's family moved to Philadelphia when he was entering fifth grade. After playing baseball in the U.S. through his freshman year of high school, he moved back to the D.R. at age 16. He signed with the Cardinals in April 2024 for $300,000 and debuted in the Dominican Summer League two months later. After hitting .345/.462/.683 and being named a DSL all-star, Rodriguez came stateside in 2025. He played at three levels, starting in the Florida Complex, reaching Low-A Palm Beach in June and High-A Peoria in September. He hit .276/.399/.555 with 20 home runs in 84 games.
SCOUTING REPORT: Since stepping foot on a professional baseball field, Rodriguez has displayed a blend of advanced plate skills, plus-plus raw power and elite batted-ball angles. His knack for finding the barrel is his defining skill. He shows the ability to consistently drive the ball in the air. Rodriguez's contact skills and swing decisions are above-average for age and level, and he does a good job limiting strikeouts and getting on base. While the plate skills are impressive Rodriguez's plus-plus raw power is his loudest tool. He consistently gets to it in games by running high barrel and pulled-air rates. Rodriguez is an optimized hitter with strong underlying skills, power and launch. Behind the plate, he is more of a work in progress. He has a plus arm and does a good job of controlling the running game but is a below-average blocker and receiver. He has a good chance to stick behind the plate and could make large strides as a receiver and framer in the coming years.
THE FUTURE: Rodriguez is one of the highest upside prospects in the game. If it all clicks, he could be an all-star-level bat with average catcher defense.

Year	Age	Club (League)	Level	AVG	G	AB	R	H	2B	3B	HR	RBI	BB	SO	SB	OBP	SLG
2025	18	FCL Cardinals	Rk	.373	20	59	23	22	6	0	7	16	16	15	1	.513	.831
2025	18	Palm Beach (FSL)	A	.249	60	225	34	56	15	1	13	43	38	48	3	.373	.498
2025	18	Peoria (MWL)	A+	.294	4	17	2	5	1	0	0	4	0	2	0	.294	.353
		Minor League Totals		.298	125	443	94	132	34	4	30	101	84	90	5	.420	.596

ST. LOUIS CARDINALS

4 JOSHUA BAEZ, OF

HIT: 55. **POW:** 65. **RUN:** 60. **FLD:** 50. **ARM:** 60. **BA Grade:** 60. **Risk:** High. **Adj:** 45.

Born: June 28, 2003. **B-T:** R-R. **HT:** 6-3. **WT:** 220.
Drafted: HS—Brookline, MA, 2021 (2nd round). **Signed by:** Jim Negrych.
TRACK RECORD: A standout Boston-area high school player with a physical frame and a tantalizing combination of tools, Baez signed for $2.25 million in the second round of the 2021 draft. He spent his first three full professional seasons struggling with injuries and swing-and-miss issues. After the 2024 season, Baez made adjustments to his swing and found another gear at the plate. He hit .287/.384/.500 with 20 home runs and 54 stolen bases between High-A and Double-A. Most importantly, Baez cut his strikeout rate from 35.5% in 2024 to 20.6% in 2025. It was a true renaissance season for Baez.
SCOUTING REPORT: A physical specimen, Baez looks like a football player in the outfield. He has a muscular frame with quick-twitch athleticism and impressive power output. After years of struggling with poor bat-to-ball skills and middling swing decisions, Baez made a few radical changes that manifested in significantly more contact. He reworked his lower half in the offseason and then made further adjustments over the first month of the 2025 season with High-A Peoria, getting more upright and closing his swing. What resulted was the best production of his career. Baez now projects as an average contact hitter with plus on-base skills. His raw power is 70-grade and he gets to it in games more consistently with the adjustments to his swing. A plus runner, Baez was one of the best basestealers in the minors in 2025 and presents a true plus power and speed combination. He can handle center field but is better in a corner. He has a plus arm that is capable of making every throw on the field.
THE FUTURE: Baez broke out in a major way in 2025 and looks like he could debut for the Cardinals in 2026. He's a potential above-average regular with the potential for 30 home runs and 30 stolen bases.

Year	Age	Club (League)	Level	AVG	G	AB	R	H	2B	3B	HR	RBI	BB	SO	SB	OBP	SLG
2025	22	Peoria (MWL)	A+	.317	38	145	32	46	8	2	4	24	18	36	20	.404	.483
2025	22	Springfield (TL)	AA	.271	79	273	46	74	15	1	16	55	41	67	34	.374	.509
		Minor League Totals		.246	334	1120	192	275	61	9	43	174	158	394	118	.352	.431

5 QUINN MATHEWS, LHP

FB: 50. **CB:** 45. **SL:** 55. **CH:** 60. **CTL:** 50. **BA Grade:** 50. **Risk:** Mild. **Adj:** 45.

Born: October 4, 2000. **B-T:** L-L. **HT:** 6-5. **WT:** 188.
Drafted: Stanford, 2023 (4th round). **Signed by:** Stacey Pettis.
TRACK RECORD: Mathews spent four years in the Stanford rotation. He returned for a fourth season after being drafted by the Rays in the 19th round in 2022. He would go on to win Pacific-12 Conference pitcher of the year honors in 2023 and was selected that July in the fourth round by the Cardinals. An outstanding professional debut in 2024, in which he climbed from Low-A to Triple-A, earned Mathews BA's Minor League Pitcher of the Year award. His 2025 campaign was marred by a left shoulder injury in April that required a six-week stint on the injured list.
SCOUTING REPORT: Mathews is a tall, lean lefthander with little to no remaining projection. A year after making waves with added velocity and strong results to match, he dealt with a mechanical issue in 2025 that manifested in left shoulder soreness. Mathews returned in late May and struggled with command leading up to the all-star break. He returned to form somewhat in the second half but still struggled with strike-throwing. Mathews saw a drop in velocity across his arsenal, only for it to return over the final starts of 2025 for Triple-A Memphis. Mathews throws a four-seam fastball, a newly added two-seam fastball, a mid-80s cut-slider, a low-80s changeup and a curveball. His changeup is his best secondary pitch and a true plus pitch. His slider is above-average and leads to a lot of positive outcomes. His curveball is a fourth pitch but is effective at driving whiffs and bad contact. Mathews dealt with substantial strike-throwing issues in 2025, and it was likely driven by the injury. His previous track record suggests average or better control.
THE FUTURE: The 2025 season is one Mathews would like to forget. Despite the struggles, he looks like a viable long-term No. 4 starter who could reach St. Louis as soon as 2026.

Year	Age	Club (League)	Level	W	L	ERA	G	GS	IP	H	HR	BB	SO	BB%	SO%	WHIP	AVG
2025	24	FCL Cardinals	Rk	0	0	0.00	1	1	2	1	0	0	4	0.0	57.1	0.50	.143
2025	24	Palm Beach (FSL)	A	0	0	0.00	1	1	3	2	0	0	4	0.0	36.4	0.67	.182
2025	24	Memphis (IL)	AAA	4	7	3.93	22	22	94	76	6	74	107	17.5	25.4	1.60	.224
		Minor League Totals		10	11	3.36	41	41	190	135	11	108	247	13.4	30.8	1.28	.200

ST. LOUIS CARDINALS

6 BRANDON CLARKE, LHP
FB: 60. **CB:** 55. **SL:** 70. **SW:** 55. **CTL:** 40. **BA Grade:** 60. **Risk:** Extreme. **Adj:** 40.

Born: April 10, 2003. **B-T:** L-L. **HT:** 6-4. **WT:** 220.
Drafted: State JC of Florida, 2024 (5th round). **Signed by:** Dante Riccardi (Red Sox).
TRACK RECORD: Despite elite raw power across his pitch mix, Clarke dropped in the 2024 draft due to his checkered injury history and control issues. The Red Sox loved Clarke's upside and drafted him in the fifth round. He signed for $400,000 and made waves in the team's preseason Spring Breakout game, touching 101 mph and flashing a plus slider. Clarke was assigned to Low-A Salem out of camp and dominated over three appearances to earn a quick promotion to High-A Greenville. After just four appearances, Clarke was shut down with blister issues. He returned in late June but struggled with command and his season ended on Aug. 8. Following the season, the Red Sox traded Clarke and Richard Fitts to the Cardinals for veteran starter Sonny Gray.
SCOUTING REPORT: Clarke is a hyper-athletic lefthander with power across his pitch mix. He's a strong mover on the mound, generating an elite average of 7-feet, 3-inches of extension. His low three-quarters slot pairs with his extension to create a unique angle. Clarke mixes five pitches in a four-seam fastball, two-seam fastball, slider, curveball and sweeper. Clarke's primary fastball is his two-seamer that sits 96-98 mph and touches 100 with less sink and more running action to his arm side. Clarke's four-seam fastball is similar velocity but the pitch lacks plane or movement. The slider is Clarke's signature pitch. It sits 87-88 mph with 8-10 inches of sweep. He commands his slider better than any pitch in his arsenal and shows above-average feel for it. Clarke's sweeper sits in the low-to-mid 80s with 15-plus inches of horizontal break. It was used far less than his standard slider. He also will show a curveball with similar sweep and downer break. Clarke shows below-average command, but there's some question how much his strike throwing was impeded by the reoccurring blister issue.
THE FUTURE: Clarke has a wide range of outcomes from midrotation starter to potential dominant power reliever.

Year	Age	Club (League)	Level	W	L	ERA	G	GS	IP	H	HR	BB	SO	BB%	SO%	WHIP	AVG
2025	22	Salem (CAR)	A	0	0	0.93	3	3	10	2	0	2	17	5.6	47.2	0.41	.061
2025	22	Greenville (SAL)	A+	0	3	5.08	11	11	28	15	0	25	43	18.1	31.2	1.41	.150
		Minor League Totals		0	3	4.03	14	14	38	17	0	27	60	15.5	34.5	1.16	.128

7 TANNER FRANKLIN, RHP
FB: 70. **SL:** 55. **CH:** 45. **CT:** 50. **CTL:** 45. **BA Grade:** 55. **Risk:** High. **Adj:** 40.

Born: May 25, 2004. **B-T:** R-R. **HT:** 6-5. **WT:** 240.
Drafted: Tennessee, 2025 (2nd round). **Signed by:** TC Calhoun.
TRACK RECORD: After two seasons pitching out of the bullpen for Kennesaw State, Franklin made the jump to Tennessee prior to his junior season in 2025. He made a career-high 27 appearances for the Volunteers, striking out 52 across 38.2 innings. The Cardinals drafted Franklin in the second round in 2025 and signed him for a little over $1.1 million. To begin his professional career, he was deployed as a starter across three appearances at both Class A levels.
SCOUTING REPORT: Franklin is a 6-foot-5, physical righthander who delivers the ball from a three-quarters arm slot with a slight crossfire finish. Entering his junior campaign, Franklin added 3 mph to his four-seam fastball and improved his spin efficiency, which resulted in more ride, armside run and a more deceptive plane of approach to the plate. Franklin's fastball is now a double-plus pitch, with velocity, movement and release traits befitting its 70 grade. His go-to secondary pitch is a cutter in the low 90s. Much like his fastball, his cutter also jumped more than 3 mph. The pitch added ride and lost horizontal break, creating more cut. Franklin's slider is a mid-80s mini-sweeper with shorter break than a traditional sweeper. The slider drives the highest miss rate in his arsenal and projects as an above-average pitch. His changeup was rarely used but showed good vertical separation off his fastball and the potential to become an average pitch. He threw a curveball as a sophomore at Kennesaw State but ditched the pitch when he transferred to Tennessee. Franklin's command is fringe-average and will need to improve for him to make the jump to a starting role.
THE FUTURE: The Cardinals plan to deploy Franklin as a starter in 2026. Equipped with plus stuff and improved command, he could successfully make the jump into the rotation.

Year	Age	Club (League)	Level	W	L	ERA	G	GS	IP	H	HR	BB	SO	BB%	SO%	WHIP	AVG
2025	21	Palm Beach (FSL)	A	0	0	0.00	1	1	2	1	0	1	4	12.5	50.0	1.00	.143
2025	21	Peoria (MWL)	A+	0	0	2.25	2	2	4	3	0	4	5	20.0	25.0	1.75	.214
		Minor League Totals		0	0	1.50	3	3	6	4	0	5	9	17.9	32.1	1.50	.190

ST. LOUIS CARDINALS

8 IXAN HENDERSON, LHP
FB: 50. **CB:** 40. **SL:** 55. **CH:** 50. **CT:** 30. **CTL:** 55. **BA Grade:** 45. **Risk:** Mild. **Adj:** 40.

Born: January 29, 2002. **B-T:** L-L. **HT:** 6-2. **WT:** 200.
Drafted: Fresno State, 2023 (8th round). **Signed by:** Stacey Pettis.
TRACK RECORD: Henderson spent three seasons at Fresno State, his hometown school, earning all-Mountain West Conference honors in 2022 and 2023. The Cardinals drafted Henderson in the eighth round in 2023 and signed him for $230,000. After spending the 2024 season split between Low-A and High-A, Henderson broke camp with Double-A Springfield in 2025. Across 25 starts spanning 132 innings, he pitched to a 2.59 ERA and won the Texas League ERA title. The league's pitcher of the year, Henderson broke out in a big way.
SCOUTING REPORT: Henderson is an average-sized lefthander with a longer arm action and a deceptive three-quarters arm slot. He repeats his mechanics well and shows a deep arsenal of pitches, keeping hitters off-balance despite a lack of velocity. Henderson's fastball sits 92-94 mph and touches 95-96. The pitch has average ride but late armside run that explodes on hitters. He has plus command of his fastball and does a good job of avoiding the heart of the plate. Henderson thrives on his ability to work the top and bottom of the zone effectively. His top secondary pitch is a sweeper sitting in the low 80s with more than a foot of horizontal break on average with some tilt. Henderson's changeup is his best swing-and-miss pitch and shows good vertical separation off his fastball. He will mix in a mid-70s curveball with two-plane break as a change of pace from his sweeper. He threw a few cutters during the 2025 season, but it was used sparingly. Henderson's control is better than his walk rates suggest, and the lefthander does a good job of navigating the shadow zone and avoiding barrels.
THE FUTURE: Henderson looks like a soon-to-the-majors No. 5 starter with limited upside. The 2026 season and his first taste of Triple-A will be a test of his fastball quality.

Year	Age	Club (League)	Level	W	L	ERA	G	GS	IP	H	HR	BB	SO	HR/9	BB%	SO%	WHIP
2025	23	Springfield (TL)	AA	9	7	2.59	25	25	132	99	5	51	134	9.6	25.2	1.14	.210
Minor League Totals				15	9	2.37	45	36	209	151	7	82	218	9.7	25.7	1.12	.201

9 JIMMY CROOKS, C
HIT: 45. **POW:** 50. **RUN:** 30. **FLD:** 55. **ARM:** 55. **BA Grade:** 45. **Risk:** Mild. **Adj:** 40.

Born: July 19, 2001. **B-T:** L-R. **HT:** 6-1. **WT:** 210.
Drafted: Oklahoma, 2022 (4th round). **Signed by:** Pete Parise.
TRACK RECORD: After starting his college career at McLennan Junior College in Texas, Crooks transferred to Oklahoma, where he spent two seasons. The Cardinals drafted him in the fourth round in 2022, and he has moved a level a year since signing. After winning the Texas League MVP in 2024, Crooks spent most of 2025 with Triple-A Memphis. The Cardinals called up Crooks on Aug. 29, and he spent the final month of the season with the team.
SCOUTING REPORT: A year after breaking out at the plate, Crooks took a step back in his first full season at Triple-A. He struggled against spin and consistently whiffed on breaking balls in the zone. This in turn shrunk his contact rates and increased his strikeouts. In addition to the swing-and-miss, Crooks' approach backed up and he chased pitches at a higher rate. He produced similar power numbers in 2025 thanks to improved top-end exit velocities. Crooks' batted-ball angles are inconsistent and worse than they were in 2024. He still has a fairly high barrel rate, despite an inability to pull the ball in the air consistently. Behind the plate, Crooks is an above-average defender who is an excellent blocker. He does a good job of keeping the ball in front of him and controlling bounces on low pitches. His arm is above-average, allowing him to overcome below-average exchanges. Crooks looks like a sure thing to stick behind the plate and could develop into an above-average defender. His step backward as a hitter in 2025 leads to some questions around his viability as a primary catcher.
THE FUTURE: The lefthanded-hitting Crooks ascended to MLB in late 2025 and looks to be a part of the Cardinals' catching platoon headed into 2026.

Year	Age	Club (League)	Level	AVG	G	AB	R	H	2B	3B	HR	RBI	BB	SO	SB	OBP	SLG
2025	23	Memphis (IL)	AAA	.274	98	390	61	107	21	1	14	79	36	114	0	.337	.441
2025	23	St. Louis (NL)	MLB	.133	15	45	3	6	0	1	1	1	0	17	0	.152	.244
Minor League Totals				.285	325	1197	186	341	72	6	40	221	143	315	6	.368	.455
Major League Totals				.133	15	45	3	6	0	1	1	1	0	17	0	.152	.244

ST. LOUIS CARDINALS

10 LEONARDO BERNAL, C

HIT: 50. **POW:** 50. **RUN:** 30. **FLD:** 45. **ARM:** 60. **BA Grade:** 50. **Risk:** Average. **Adj:** 40.

Born: February 13, 2004. **B-T:** B-R. **HT:** 6-0. **WT:** 200.
Signed: Panama, 2021. **Signed by:** Damaso Espino.
TRACK RECORD: Bernal signed out of Panama in 2021 for $680,000. After debuting in the Dominican Summer League, he jumped stateside to begin 2022, skipping the Florida Complex League entirely. After spending all of 2022 and 2023 with Low-A Palm Beach, Bernal made the jump to High-A in 2024. He spent all of 2025 with Double-A Springfield and hit .247/.332/.395 in 107 games, making 87 starts behind the plate.
SCOUTING REPORT: Bernal is a switch-hitting catcher with a maxed-out physical frame and a stout build. His righthanded swing is far more advanced than his lefthanded one. Bernal's approach from the lefthanded side is better—he makes more contact and chases less. However, his righthanded swing generates more power and better angles on contact, leading to better results. Overall he shows average plate skills and average power when balancing his two swings. Bernal does a good job of avoiding whiffs and tends to stay inside of his approach. Adding impact when hitting lefthanded would truly boost his hitting profile to above-average. Bernal is a bigger-bodied catcher and has limited mobility. His blocking suffers due to a lack of athleticism behind the plate. He'll need to control blocked balls better to be an average or better defender. Bernal's arm is plus, and he consistently clocks sub-1.95 pop times on throws to second base. As an above-average framer and plus throwing catcher, Bernal is a sure bet to stick behind the plate, even if his blocking remains subpar.
THE FUTURE: Bernal looks like a rotation catcher who will see most of his starts against lefthanded pitchers. Improvements to his lefthanded swing and blocking ability could push him into everyday catcher territory.

Year	Age	Club (League)	Level	AVG	G	AB	R	H	2B	3B	HR	RBI	BB	SO	SB	OBP	SLG
2025	21	Springfield (TL)	AA	.247	107	396	58	98	19	0	13	70	49	77	13	.332	.394
		Minor League Totals		.251	384	1368	196	344	69	5	39	229	170	288	28	.338	.395

11 YAIRO PADILLA, SS

HIT: 55. **POW:** 50. **RUN:** 60. **FLD:** 55. **ARM:** 60. **BA Grade:** 55. **Risk:** High. **Adj:** 40.

Born: June 28, 2007. **B-T:** B-R. **HT:** 6-2. **WT:** 199. **Signed:** Dominican Republic, 2024.
Signed by: Darluimis Almonte/Alix Martinez.
TRACK RECORD: Padilla signed with the Cardinals out of the Dominican Republic in January 2024 for $760,000. He debuted in the Dominican Summer League a few months later, hitting .287/.391/.404 with 22 stolen bases. Padilla made the jump stateside in 2025 and spent the season in the Florida Complex League. There, the shortstop hit .283/.396/.367 with 18 walks to 21 strikeouts in 38 games.
SCOUTING REPORT: Padilla is a switch-hitting shortstop who is an exciting and projectable athlete. His body has matured in pro ball and he is a couple inches taller and nearly 30 pounds heavier than he was when he signed. Early in his career, Padilla has employed a contact-focused but passive approach at the plate, leading to low strikeout rates and high walk totals. Padilla shows plus bat-to-ball skills and rarely swings outside the zone. He's often far too passive on pitches over the heart of the plate, and that's an area that could likely be exploited by more advanced pitchers. Even though Padilla lacks present power production, evaluators view him as a player who will grow into above-average power in time. His top-end exit velocities support this with a 102.1 mph 90th percentile EV, which is above-average for age and level. Padilla struggles to pull the ball in the air from both sides of the plate, though his power is more pronounced when batting lefthanded. Padilla is a plus runner who should steal 20-plus bases annually at peak. His defense projects to be above-average in time, with good actions and athleticism. His plus arm is among the best in the Cardinals' system.
THE FUTURE: Padilla is a player with a lot of variance. He could be an everyday shortstop, but it's going to take years to gel. He should make his full-season debut in 2026.

Year	Age	Club (League)	Level	AVG	G	AB	R	H	2B	3B	HR	RBI	BB	SO	SB	OBP	SLG
2025	18	FCL Cardinals	Rk	.283	38	120	21	34	4	3	0	10	18	21	24	.396	.367
		Minor League Totals		.285	73	256	54	73	9	7	1	27	35	50	46	.393	.387

ST. LOUIS CARDINALS

12 RYAN MITCHELL, SS/OF
HIT: 55. **POW:** 50. **RUN:** 55. **FLD:** 50. **ARM:** 50. **BA Grade:** 55. **Risk:** High. **Adj:** 40.

Born: January 21, 2007. **B-T:** L-R. **HT:** 6-2. **WT:** 185. **Drafted:** HS—Germantown, TN, 2025 (2nd round).
Signed by: Dirk Kinney.
TRACK RECORD: Mitchell won a gold medal with USA Baseball's 15U National Team in 2022 as one of the linchpins of the American lineup. Throughout his touted prep career outside Memphis, he earned a reputation as an advanced hitter with projectable power. The Cardinals loved what they saw from Mitchell as an amateur and drafted him in the second round in 2025. He signed for a bonus of $2.25 million and did not debut following the draft.
SCOUTING REPORT: Mitchell's hitting prowess earned him a reputation as an amateur as one of the best pure hitters in the country. He stands 6-foot-2, 185 pounds with some remaining projection and average athleticism. A lefthanded hitter, Mitchell sets up wide in the box, with a deep bend in his knees and a high hand set. He has a fairly quiet load and shows the ability to get on plane with pitches. Mitchell uses a toe tap that gives way to a stride that further extends his wide base as he rotates on his front foot. He shows above-average bat-to-ball skills with advanced swing decisions. Mitchell shows above-average raw power and posts impressive exit velocities in games and batting practice. His swing is more geared toward line-drive contact, and added loft could help his power projection jump half a grade. An above-average runner, many scouts believe that Mitchell will move to the outfield, where the Cardinals announced him in the draft after he had played primarily shortstop as an amateur. The team plans to use Mitchell in both the infield and outfield. He looks like an average defender with an average arm.
THE FUTURE: Mitchell has the tools to develop into an above-average everyday regular if it all clicks.

Year	Age	Club (League)	Level	AVG	G	AB	R	H	2B	3B	HR	RBI	BB	SO	SB	OBP	SLG
2025	18	Did not play															

13 TEKOAH ROBY, RHP
FB: 55. **CB:** 60. **SL:** 55. **CH:** 55. **CTL:** 55. **BA Grade:** 60. **Risk:** Extreme. **Adj:** 40.

Born: September 18, 2001. **B-T:** R-R. **HT:** 6-1. **WT:** 210. **Drafted:** HS—Pensacola, FL, 2020 (3rd round).
Signed by: Brian Morrison (Rangers).
TRACK RECORD: Roby's name rose up boards late in the 2020 draft cycle, and the Rangers called his name in the third round of the truncated five-round draft. Traded by Texas to the Cardinals in a 2023 deadline deal, Roby was added to St. Louis' 40-man roster after 2024. He is a talented righthander whose career has been consistently sidetracked by injuries. He missed time in 2021 due to elbow pain, then missed parts of 2023 and 2024 with a shoulder injury. In 2025 things came to a head. After dominating across 10 starts with Double-A Springfield, Roby was promoted to Triple-A, where after six strong starts he went down with an elbow injury. He had Tommy John surgery in July 2025 and is expected to miss all of 2026.
SCOUTING REPORT: Roby is an undersized righthander with a strong build who is maxed out physically. He uses a simple operation with a semi-windup, moderate arm swing and higher three-quarters slot. There's some effort at the point of release, and his timing comes and goes. Roby throws five pitches in a four-seam fastball, sinker, curveball, slider and changeup. His four-seam fastball sits 94-96 mph and touches 98 with average ride and cut from a 5-foot-8 release height. He generates above-average extension, creating a flatter plane on his fastball. His sinker is used sparingly and is slightly softer than his four-seamer. His breaking ball usage is split evenly between a low-80s downer curveball and an upper-80s gyro slider. Both breaking pitches are effective whiff and chase pitches. Roby's changeup sits 83-84 mph with significant vertical separation off his fastball. His changeup was his best bat-missing pitch.
THE FUTURE: Roby has the makings of a potential midrotation starter, but he'll need to maintain health.

Year	Age	Club (League)	Level	W	L	ERA	G	GS	IP	H	HR	BB	SO	BB%	SO%	WHIP	AVG
2025	23	Springfield (TL)	AA	4	2	2.49	10	10	47	34	4	11	57	6.0	31.1	0.96	.200
2025	23	Memphis (IL)	AAA	3	2	4.02	6	6	31	33	4	8	30	6.0	22.6	1.31	.266
		Minor League Totals		16	23	4.33	68	67	302	278	44	91	356	7.2	28.1	1.22	.242

14 TINK HENCE, RHP
FB: 50. **SL:** 50. **CH:** 50. **CTL:** 50. **BA Grade:** 55. **Risk:** High. **Adj:** 40.

Born: August 6, 2002. **B-T:** R-R. **HT:** 6-1. **WT:** 195. **Drafted:** HS—Watson Chapel, AR, 2020 (2nd round supp.).
Signed by: Dirk Kinney.
TRACK RECORD: The Cardinals landed Hence in the supplemental second round of the 2020 draft, signing him for $1.15 million. They methodically limited his innings over his first few seasons before taking off the reins in 2023, when he pitched a career-high 96 innings. After beginning the 2024 with a

ST. LOUIS CARDINALS

dominant stretch at Double-A, Hence was shut down for a month with shoulder and chest tightness. He returned in late July but was limited to just 25 innings over eight starts. In 2025, Hence began the season on the 60-day injured list with a right rib cage strain. He returned to Double-A on June 20 and threw 4.1 innings of a combined no-hitter. Hence made just two more appearances before he was shut down with a shoulder injury and placed on the injured list.

SCOUTING REPORT: Hence is an undersized righthander who has displayed true durability concerns over the last several seasons. He's an athletic mover who repeats his mechanics, and coming into 2025 had always thrown strikes at least an average rate. Injuries derailed his 2025 season, costing him both velocity and control. Hence mixes a four-seam fastball, slider and changeup. Previously, he had thrown a curveball but didn't throw the pitch in 2025. Hence's fastball lost 2 mph in 2025, while he saw drops in vertical break, extension and fastball plane. What used to be a tight gyro slider in the mid 80s got looser and lost velocity in 2025. The changeup, Hence's best pitch, was fairly unaffected by his drop in stuff and remains a plus pitch. Hence previously had above-average command, but it backed up considerably in 2025 as his walk rate doubled.

THE FUTURE: The Cardinals have discussed moving Hence to the bullpen permanently. In that role he would likely find success as a high-leverage option.

Year	Age	Club (League)	Level	W	L	ERA	G	GS	IP	H	HR	BB	SO	BB%	SO%	WHIP	AVG
2025	22	FCL Cardinals	Rk	0	0	0.00	1	1	1	0	0	1	1	20.0	20.0	2.00	.250
2025	22	Palm Beach (FSL)	A	0	0	0.00	3	3	6	4	0	3	8	12.5	33.3	1.17	.200
2025	22	Peoria (MWL)	A+	0	1	4.91	1	1	4	2	0	3	1	20.0	6.7	1.36	.182
2025	22	Springfield (TL)	AA	0	0	4.22	3	3	11	6	1	6	14	14.3	33.3	1.13	.167
		Minor League Totals		8	12	3.25	75	68	257	208	20	91	327	8.7	31.3	1.16	.222

15 JESUS BAEZ, SS/3B

HIT: 50. **POW:** 50. **RUN:** 40. **FLD:** 45. **ARM:** 60. **BA Grade:** 50. **Risk:** Average. **Adj:** 40.

Born: February 26, 2005. **B-T:** R-R. **HT:** 5-10. **WT:** 180. **Signed:** Dominican Republic, 2022.
Signed by: Oliver Dominguez/Moises De La Mota (Mets).

TRACK RECORD: The Mets signed Baez in January 2022 for $275,000 out of the Dominican Republic. Over two seasons in Rookie ball, he underproduced his strong underlying data. That changed in 2024 when Baez tore through the Florida State League over the first half of the season. Unfortunately, eight games after he was promoted to High-A Brooklyn, he tore the meniscus in his right knee, ending his season. Baez spent the majority of his 2025 with High-A Brooklyn, but as the Mets chased a playoff berth, he was traded to the Cardinals alongside Frank Elissalt and Nate Dohm for closer Ryan Helsley.

SCOUTING REPORT: Baez is an undersized righthanded-hitting infielder with a short but stocky build with present strength throughout his frame. He sets up open in the box and takes clean balanced swings that produce primarily line-drive contact. Baez shows above-average bat-to-ball skills with fringe-average swing decisions, often expanding the zone while showing some passivity on strikes. Baez shows a knack for finding the barrel and shows above-average quality of contact on a consistent basis. He projects for average power, but his raw power hints at above-average power upside. His flatter launch angles detract from some of his game power and likely cap his home run upside. Baez is a below-average runner and will likely never make much impact as a baserunner. Baez has split time throughout the infield playing shortstop, third base and second base. Due to his lack of range, his best position long term is third base, where his plus arm will play.

THE FUTURE: Baez is a future third baseman with a good balance of contact hitting and average power.

Year	Age	Club (League)	Level	AVG	G	AB	R	H	2B	3B	HR	RBI	BB	SO	SB	OBP	SLG
2025	20	St. Lucie (FSL)	A	.217	6	23	3	5	0	0	0	0	3	3	0	.308	.217
2025	20	Brooklyn (SAL)	A+	.244	70	254	43	62	11	0	10	42	33	49	7	.337	.406
2025	20	Peoria (MWL)	A+	.243	27	111	14	27	3	0	4	15	10	28	2	.303	.378
		Minor League Totals		.243	269	994	157	242	49	2	34	151	118	205	31	.329	.399

16 NATHAN CHURCH, OF

HIT: 50. **POW:** 40. **RUN:** 60. **FLD:** 60. **ARM:** 70. **BA Grade:** 40. **Risk:** Low. **Adj:** 40.

Born: July 12, 2000. **B-T:** L-L. **HT:** 5-10. **WT:** 180. **Drafted:** UC Irvine, 2022 (11th round). **Signed by:** Chris Rodriguez.

TRACK RECORD: A two-way player for El Toro High outside Los Angeles, Church headed to UC Irvine after winning a D1 sectional title his senior year. He redshirted his freshman campaign in 2019 after he had Tommy John surgery and returned in 2020, only for the season to be cut short. After two strong seasons for the Anteaters, Church was drafted by the Cardinals in the 11th round in 2022. Over three pro seasons, he has moved methodically up the minor league ladder, reaching Triple-A in 2025. Church was called up to the Cardinals on Aug. 17 and made his MLB debut the same day.

ST. LOUIS CARDINALS

SCOUTING REPORT: Church is an athletic, contact-first lefthanded hitter with plus speed and dynamic defensive ability in the outfield. Up until his struggles in his first taste of MLB action, he had compiled nearly even strikeout-to-walk totals, while running some of the lowest swinging-strike rates in the system. Church uses an inside-out swing, looking to hit the ball to the left side of the infield so he can use his legs to put pressure on opposing defenders. He has plus-plus bat-to-ball abilities with below-average swing decisions. That's not uncommon for players of Church's ilk, because his primary approach is putting the ball in play. He has below-average power, but he has enough underlying raw thump to sting harder groundballs and line drives, boosting his potential batting impact. He's unlikely to hit more than 8-10 home runs a season but is not devoid of power. Church is a plus runner but a conservative basestealer. His speed translates to the outfield, where he's a plus defender in center field with a plus-plus arm.
THE FUTURE: Church is a quintessential fourth outfielder at near peak.

Year	Age	Club (League)	Level	AVG	G	AB	R	H	2B	3B	HR	RBI	BB	SO	SB	OBP	SLG
2025	24	Palm Beach (FSL)	A	.154	4	13	3	2	1	0	0	1	1	2	1	.214	.231
2025	24	Springfield (TL)	AA	.336	29	119	21	40	7	1	6	19	8	10	6	.380	.563
2025	24	Memphis (IL)	AAA	.335	53	215	43	72	11	4	7	30	24	25	9	.400	.521
2025	24	St. Louis (NL)	MLB	.179	27	56	9	10	1	0	1	8	3	18	1	.254	.250
		Minor League Totals		.281	359	1379	225	388	66	9	25	164	131	171	64	.353	.397
		Major League Totals		.179	27	56	9	10	1	0	1	8	3	18	1	.254	.250

17 COOPER HJERPE, LHP

FB: 55. **CB:** 45. **CH:** 55. **CT:** 45. **CTL:** 50. **BA Grade:** 50. **Risk:** High. **Adj:** 35.

Born: March 16, 2001. **B-T:** L-L. **HT:** 6-3. **WT:** 200. **Drafted:** Oregon State, 2022 (1st round).
Signed by: Chris Rodriguez/Donnie Marbut.
TRACK RECORD: Hjerpe enjoyed an outstanding junior season with Oregon State in which he led the nation in strikeouts and was selected as first team all-Pacific-12 Conference. The Cardinals drafted him 22nd overall in the first round and signed him for $3.18 million. Hjerpe's time on the mound in pro ball has been limited by persistent elbow problems. He missed time in 2023 after having surgery to remove loose bodies in his elbow. He returned in 2024 and reached Double-A, but he re-injured his elbow in July and was shut down. Hjerpe had Tommy John surgery in the spring of 2025 and missed the entire season. The Cardinals added Hjerpe to the 40-man roster after the season.
SCOUTING REPORT: Hjerpe is a sidearming lefthander with a unique angle that keeps hitters off-balance. He mixes four pitches in a fastball, curveball, cutter and changeup. Hjerpe's low slot creates an outlier plane of approach to the plate on his low-90s fastball. His 4-foot release height on his pitches keeps batters uncomfortable as he generates heavy east-west movement on his pitch mix. Hjerpe's curveball is an upper-70s sweeper with some drop and 16-18 inches of horizontal break. His changeup reverses the movement of his curveball, with true sink and 16-18 inches of armside run. Hjerpe added a mid-80s cutter as a professional. It shows true cutter shape. When healthy, he has shown the ability to miss bats in the zone with all four of his pitches. Prior to his injury he had shown average command.
THE FUTURE: Hjerpe is a deceptive lefthander who still has a chance of developing into a No. 5 starter.

Year	Age	Club (League)	Level	W	L	ERA	G	GS	IP	H	HR	BB	SO	BB%	SO%	WHIP	AVG
2025	24	Did not play—Injured															
		Minor League Totals		4	7	3.38	25	23	93	57	11	53	127	13.7	32.8	1.18	.176

18 CADE CROSSLAND, LHP

FB: 50. **CB:** 45. **SL:** 45. **CH:** 60. **CTL:** 50. **BA Grade:** 45. **Risk:** Average. **Adj:** 35.

Born: February 1, 2004. **B-T:** L-L. **HT:** 6-2. **WT:** 210. **Drafted:** Oklahoma, 2025 (4th round). **Signed by:** Dirk Kinney.
TRACK RECORD: Crossland began his college career at Division II Ouachita Baptist in Arkadelphia, Ark. Following his freshman season he transferred to Weatherford JC in Texas before committing to Oklahoma as a junior. In Crossland's single season with the Sooners, he struggled at times with the jump to SEC competition but finished third on the team in strikeouts and provided a gutsy seven-inning performance against Nebraska in the Chapel Hill Regional. The Cardinals drafted Crossland in the fourth round in 2025 and signed him for $729,500.
SCOUTING REPORT: Crossland is a lefthander with prototype size and power throughout his frame and the ability to repeat his mechanics. He uses a semi-windup with a moderate arm swing and a three-quarters release. He's a short-strider who doesn't get down the mound, which boosts the height of his release. Crossland mixes four pitches in a four-seam fastball, curveball, slider and changeup. His primary two pitches are his fastball and a changeup, which accounted for more than 80% of his usage during his single season at Oklahoma. His fastball sits 92-93 mph and touches 98 with above-average ride and heavy armside run. Crossland's changeup is his best pitch and was his most effective swing-and-miss pitch at

ST. LOUIS CARDINALS

Oklahoma. It has a strong combination of vertical and velocity separation off the fastball. Crossland mixes a curveball and slider in the low 80s but struggles to spin the ball consistently. He shows average control.
THE FUTURE: Crossland has an opportunity to grow into a back-end starter but is more likely rotation depth.

Year	Age	Club (League)	Level	W	L	ERA	G	GS	IP	H	HR	BB	SO	BB%	SO%	WHIP	AVG
2025	21	Did not play															

19 DENIEL ORTIZ, 1B/3B
HIT: 40. **POW:** 55. **RUN:** 55. **FLD:** 40. **ARM:** 55. **BA Grade:** 45. **Risk:** Average. **Adj:** 35.

Born: August 24, 2004. **B-T:** R-R. **HT:** 6-1. **WT:** 230. **Drafted:** Walters State (TN) JC, 2024 (16th round).
Signed by: TC Calhoun.
TRACK RECORD: Ortiz is a native of Puerto Rico who moved to Lynn, Mass., in his youth. He attended St. Mary's High before transferring to Redan High in Georgia for his senior year. He committed to Walters State JC in Tennessee and spent two seasons there, hitting .387/.535/.771 with 34 home runs over 117 games. The Cardinals drafted Ortiz in the 16th round in 2024 and signed him for $200,000. He debuted at Low-A in 2025 and reached High-A over the last month of the season. Ortiz hit .300/.416/.462 with 13 home runs across 107 games in 2025.
SCOUTING REPORT: Ortiz was a notable scouting find by the Cardinals, who landed him in the later rounds of the draft and bet on his upside. His skills came to the surface immediately as a professional. Ortiz showed advanced swing decisions and above-average contact quality right away. Ortiz has below-average bat-to-ball skills and ran higher in-zone whiff rates in his pro debut. Ortiz mitigates some of the risk of his hit tool with above-average swing decisions. He rarely expands the zone and is very aggressive on strikes. Ortiz shows above-average raw power with the ability to get to it in games. He has a lofty swing that allows him to elevate the ball consistently. He elevates the ball to his pull side and consistently finds the barrel. Ortiz is an above-average runner and good basestealer. His defense at third and first base is below-average but he shows an above-average arm.
THE FUTURE: Ortiz is a second-division regular with a quality hit tool and defensive questions.

Year	Age	Club (League)	Level	AVG	G	AB	R	H	2B	3B	HR	RBI	BB	SO	SB	OBP	SLG
2025	20	Palm Beach (FSL)	A	.285	77	260	46	74	10	1	10	36	49	88	31	.406	.446
2025	20	Peoria (MWL)	A+	.336	30	110	15	37	9	0	3	15	18	29	8	.438	.500
		Minor League Totals		.300	107	370	61	111	19	1	13	51	67	117	39	.416	.462

20 BRYCEN MAUTZ, LHP
FB: 50. **CB:** 45. **SL:** 55. **CH:** 40. **CTL:** 50. **BA Grade:** 45. **Risk:** Average. **Adj:** 35.

Born: July 17, 2001. **B-T:** L-L. **HT:** 6-3. **WT:** 190. **Drafted:** San Diego, 2022 (2nd round). **Signed by:** Chris Rodriguez.
TRACK RECORD: The Cardinals drafted Mautz in the second round in 2022 and signed him for $1.1 million. They have been methodical in their development of Mautz, moving him to one level per season throughout his professional career. After a down 2024, he bounced back in a big way in 2025 by pitching to a 2.98 ERA over 114.2 innings with Double-A Springfield and striking out 28.6% of batters. The Cardinals added Mautz to their 40-man roster following the season.
SCOUTING REPORT: Mautz is a low-slot lefthander with a prototypical pitcher's build and a long, slinky arm action. He creates a difficult angle on his pitches and dominates in left-on-left matchups. Mautz throws five pitches in a four-seam fastball, two-seam fastball, slider, curveball and changeup. He mixes his two fastball and breaking ball shapes heavily, with the four-seam and slider seeing most of the usage. Mautz's four-seam fastball sits 92-94 mph and touches 97 with a flat vertical approach angle. His two-seamer features sink and heavy armside run and is a good groundball-driving pitch. The slider is Mautz's bread-and-butter dating back to college. It sits 83-85 mph with cutter shape and a unique angle that allows it to drive whiffs and chases. His curveball is a moderate two-plane breaking ball in the upper 70s. His changeup is used sparingly but has good separation off of his fastball. Mautz shows average command of his pitch mix.
THE FUTURE: Mautz is a potential back-end starter as soon as 2026 but has limited longterm upside.

Year	Age	Club (League)	Level	AVG	G	AB	R	H	2B	3B	HR	RBI	BB	SO	SB	OBP	SLG
2025	23	Springfield (TL)	AA	8	3	2.98	25	25	115	94	13	33	134	7.1	28.6	1.11	.219
		Minor League Totals		15	25	4.07	72	72	340	318	37	125	377	8.5	25.8	1.30	.243

ST. LOUIS CARDINALS

21 BRADEN DAVIS, LHP
FB: 45. **SL:** 45. **CH:** 60. **CT:** 45. **CTL:** 45. **BA Grade:** 45. **Risk:** Average. **Adj:** 35.

Born: April 9, 2003. **B-T:** L-L **HT:** 5-11. **WT:** 180. **Drafted:** Oklahoma, 2024 (5th round). **Signed by:** Dirk Kinney.
TRACK RECORD: Davis spent two years in the bullpen for Sam Houston State before a standout summer in the Cape Cod League propelled him to Oklahoma. After a solid showing in his single season with the Sooners, the Cardinals drafted Davis in the fifth round in 2024. Davis debuted with Low-A Palm Beach to begin 2025, making 17 appearances before he was promoted to High-A Peoria on July 20. Davis finished the season with a 2.85 ERA and a 33.8% strikeout rate.
SCOUTING REPORT: Davis is an undersized lefty with a changeup that mystifies opposing batters. While Davis lacks the projection and size typical of a starting pitcher, he has a good feel for his arsenal and the ability to command the ball and escape catching too much of the plate. Davis walks this tightrope with a low-90s fastball with good ride, run and plane to the plate. His changeup is a plus pitch that has missed bats at every level of competition. He mixes two breaking balls in a mid-80s cutter and a slurvy low-80s slider. Strike-throwing has eluded Davis. He very much pitches to the outer reaches of the zone, a product of not wanting to challenge hitters over the center of the plate.
THE FUTURE: Davis has back-end starter upside but could work as a deceptive lefthander out of the pen.

Year	Age	Club (League)	Level	W	L	ERA	G	GS	IP	H	HR	BB	SO	BB%	SO%	WHIP	AVG
2025	22	Palm Beach (FSL)	A	2	1	3.18	17	14	74	43	4	52	103	17.1	33.9	1.29	.173
2025	22	Peoria (MWL)	A+	3	2	2.21	8	8	37	15	0	23	50	15.4	33.6	1.04	.123
		Minor League Totals		5	3	2.85	25	22	110	58	4	75	153	16.6	33.8	1.21	.156

22 JACK GUREVITCH, 1B
HIT: 55. **POW:** 50. **RUN:** 40. **FLD:** 45. **ARM:** 50. **BA Grade:** 45. **Risk:** Average. **Adj:** 35.

Born: March 9, 2004. **B-T:** L-R **HT:** 6-0. **WT:** 215. **Drafted:** San Diego, 2025 (3rd round). **Signed by:** Chris Rodriguez.
TRACK RECORD: Over three seasons at San Diego, Gurevitch was a consistent performer for the Toreros who earned all-West Coast Conference freshman team honors in 2023. He starred in the Cape Cod League in 2024, earning all-star honors. In 2025, Gurevitch went nuclear at USD, hitting .371/.477/.681 with 17 home runs to earn all-WCC first team honors. The Cardinals drafted Gurevitch in the third round in 2025 and signed him for $879,000. He debuted with Low-A Palm Beach following the draft.
SCOUTING REPORT: Gurevitch is an average-sized, lefthanded-hitting first baseman with a stocky but strong build. He deploys a fairly simple setup at the plate with a deep bend in his knees and a high hand set. Gurevitch uses a simple toe tap and stride before giving way to a level, clean bat path. He shows loose, adjustable hands capable of hitting a variety of pitch types and locations. He didn't see much mid-90s velocity in college, and there are some questions about how he'll adjust to more velocity in pro ball. He shows average bat-to-ball skills with plus swing decisions. He shows average power, as his above-average exit velocity data is limited by flatter launch angles. Gurevitch is a below-average runner and not a basestealing threat. His primary position is first base, but he has seen action at third base. He has an average arm.
THE FUTURE: Gurevitch is a bat-first prospect who profiles as a second-division regular or platoon bat.

Year	Age	Club (League)	Level	AVG	G	AB	R	H	2B	3B	HR	RBI	BB	SO	SB	OBP	SLG
2025	21	Palm Beach (FSL)	A	.181	22	83	10	15	1	1	1	4	13	33	5	.303	.253
		Minor League Totals		.181	22	83	10	15	1	1	1	4	13	33	5	.303	.253

23 FRANK ELISSALT, RHP
FB: 55. **SL:** 50. **SW:** 50. **SP:** 30. **CT:** 40. **CTL:** 40. **BA Grade:** 40. **Risk:** Average. **Adj:** 30.

Born: March 25, 2002. **B-T:** B-R. **HT:** 6-2. **WT:** 210. **Drafted:** Nova Southeastern (FL), 2024 (19th round). **Signed by:** Nelson Mompierre (Mets).
TRACK RECORD: Elissalt was drafted by the Mets in the 19th round in 2024 out of Division II Nova Southeastern in Florida. He made his pro debut following the draft with one appearance for Low-A St. Lucie. He returned to the Florida State League to begin in 2025 and pitched to a 3.02 ERA over 18 appearances. Elissalt was promoted to High-A Brooklyn on July 18 and made two appearances before he was traded to the Cardinals in the Ryan Helsley deal. Elissalt spent the remainder of 2025 with High-A Peoria. He missed two weeks in August with minor biceps tendinitis but returned the final week.
SCOUTING REPORT: Elissalt is an athletic righthander who pitches exclusively from the stretch. He has a high leg lift, followed by a long arm action. He fires the ball from a three-quarters arm slot and gets over his front side as he gets downhill. Elissalt throws five pitches in a four-seam fastball, sweeper, slider, splitter and cutter. Elissalt's four-seam fastball sits 94-96 mph and touches 98 with a flat approach angle and

above-average ride. His two breaking ball shapes—a low-80s sweeper and mid-80s gyro slider—see nearly equal usage. Elissalt infrequently mixed in a splitter and a low-90s cutter, but neither pitch is a primary part of his mix. He tended to go two or three innings per start and is unlikely to be a starter long term.
THE FUTURE: Elissalt is a future multi-inning reliever.

Year	Age	Club (League)	Level	W	L	ERA	G	GS	IP	H	HR	BB	SO	BB%	SO%	WHIP	AVG
2025	23	St. Lucie (FSL)	A	3	4	3.02	18	7	51	30	4	21	57	10.4	28.4	1.01	.172
2025	23	Brooklyn (SAL)	A+	1	1	3.18	2	0	6	5	1	0	8	0.0	38.1	0.88	.250
2025	23	Peoria (MWL)	A+	0	2	5.59	4	3	10	7	0	8	6	19.0	14.3	1.55	.206
		Minor League Totals		4	7	3.39	25	10	66	42	5	29	72	10.9	27.1	1.07	.183

24 NATE DOHM, RHP
FB: 50. **CB:** 40. **SL:** 50. **CH:** 40. **CTL:** 45. **BA Grade:** 40. **Risk:** Average. **Adj:** 30.

Born: January 9, 2003. **B-T:** R-R. **HT:** 6-4. **WT:** 210. **Drafted:** Mississippi State, 2024 (3rd round).
Signed by: Jet Butler (Mets).
TRACK RECORD: An Indiana native, Dohm committed to Ball State out of high school and spent one season with the Cardinals before transferring to Mississippi State prior to 2023. In 2024, Dohm made the jump to the Bulldogs' rotation. He dominated over the first four weeks of the season, a campaign cut short by an arm injury. Dohm was drafted by the Mets in the third round in 2024 and signed for $797,500. He made his professional debut with Low-A St. Lucie in 2025 and earned a promotion to High-A Brooklyn on May 15. He was traded to the Cardinals at the 2025 trade deadline as part of the package for Ryan Helsley.
SCOUTING REPORT: Dohm is a prototypical righthanded starter with an athletic operation and low three-quarters arm slot. He does a good job of getting downhill to create above-average extension that amplifies the angle on his fastball. Dohm throws four pitches in a four-seam fastball, slider, curveball and changeup. His four-seam fastball sits 93-95 mph and touches 97 at peak with above-average riding life. Dohm pairs that with a mid-80s slider with gyro shape that is his best swing-and-miss pitch. His changeup is a firm offering with Bugs Bunny shape that he struggles to command. He throws an upper-70s curveball, but it's rarely used. Dohm shows fringe-average command of his pitch mix.
THE FUTURE: Dohm has a chance to start but will likely move to the bullpen with a two-pitch focus.

Year	Age	Club (League)	Level	W	L	ERA	G	GS	IP	H	HR	BB	SO	BB%	SO%	WHIP	AVG
2025	22	St. Lucie (FSL)	A	2	3	3.18	7	7	28	28	1	10	34	8.2	27.9	1.34	.255
2025	22	Brooklyn (SAL)	A+	1	2	2.62	11	10	34	28	4	13	43	9.0	29.7	1.19	.217
2025	22	Peoria (MWL)	A+	0	2	5.11	5	5	12	11	2	9	13	16.1	23.2	1.62	.239
		Minor League Totals		3	7	3.24	23	22	75	67	7	32	90	9.9	27.9	1.32	.235

25 BRYAN TORRES, 2B/OF
HIT: 55. **POW:** 30. **RUN:** 50. **FLD:** 50. **ARM:** 50. **BA Grade:** 40. **Risk:** Average. **Adj:** 30.

Born: July 2, 1997. **B-T:** L-R. **HT:** 5-7. **WT:** 165. **Signed:** HS—Caguas, PR, 2015 (UDFA).
Signed by: Manolo Hernandez (Brewers).
TRACK RECORD: A native of Puerto Rico, Torres went undrafted out of high school in 2015 and signed with the Brewers as a free agent catcher. He spent three seasons in the Dominican Summer League before coming stateside in 2018. The Giants selected Torres in the minor league phase of the Rule 5 draft in 2020 but released him after one season. After two seasons in the independent American Association, Torres signed with the Cardinals in the fall of 2023. After two strong seasons in the upper minors, he was added to the Cardinals' 40-man roster.
SCOUTING REPORT: In his early years as a professional, Torres felt his best attribute, his speed, was sacrificed due to the rigors of catching and its impact on his legs. In independent ball, Torres moved to the outfield and showed baserunning ability and contact skills. So far with the Cardinals, he has shown the ability to make contact at a plus rate and walk more than he strikes out. He has a well below-average power profile. Torres is unlikely to hit more than a handful of homers in a season, even with full-time playing reps. He's only an average runner, but he's a cerebral player who makes great reads on the bases and reads pitcher tendencies quickly. Torres is a versatile defender capable of filling in at any position across the diamond, but his best positions are corner outfield and second base.
THE FUTURE: Already 28 years old, Torres could earn a spot on the Cardinals' bench out of camp.

Year	Age	Club (League)	Level	AVG	G	AB	R	H	2B	3B	HR	RBI	BB	SO	SB	OBP	SLG
2025	27	Memphis (IL)	AAA	.328	104	332	58	109	16	1	9	51	70	57	26	.441	.464
		Minor League Totals		.311	370	1222	207	380	59	10	12	145	189	186	81	.402	.405

ST. LOUIS CARDINALS

26 ZACH LEVENSON, OF
HIT: 50. **POW:** 45. **RUN:** 45. **FLD:** 45. **ARM:** 45. **BA Grade:** 40. **Risk:** Average. **Adj:** 30.

Born: March 6, 2002. **B-T:** R-R. **HT:** 6-0. **WT:** 211. **Drafted:** Miami, 2023 (5th round). **Signed by:** Josh Lopez.
TRACK RECORD: After one season at Seminole State JC in Florida, Levenson transferred to Miami where he spent two seasons, breaking out as a junior. The Cardinals drafted Levenson in the fifth round in 2025 and signed him for $381,300. Levenson struggled in 2024, hitting .215/.317/.367 before a wrist injury ended his season. He bounced back in 2025, producing a 119 wRC+ over 82 games in his return to High-A. Levenson was promoted to Double-A in mid-August and hit .275/.350/.484 in 26 games.
SCOUTING REPORT: After stalling out in his first full season, Levenson made wholesale changes heading into 2025. He improved his swing decisions, power and launch-angle distribution, and the results followed. An average contact hitter, Levenson previously had been dragged down by below-average swing decisions. That changed in 2025, and he now shows above-average on-base skills. Levenson's raw power saw a jump—his 90th percentile exit velocity jumped 2 mph year over year. After showing extremely steep launch angles in his debut, he flattened out a little and found more consistent barrels without losing loft in his swing altogether. Levenson is a fringe-average runner who's best suited for an outfield corner. His fringe-average arm is accurate but lacks the power to keep runners honest.
THE FUTURE: Levenson is a future fourth outfielder who can provide power and contact hitting.

Year	Age	Club (League)	Level	AVG	G	AB	R	H	2B	3B	HR	RBI	BB	SO	SB	OBP	SLG
2025	23	Peoria (MWL)	A+	.236	82	284	48	67	12	2	8	38	56	63	7	.373	.377
2025	23	Springfield (TL)	AA	.275	26	91	11	25	7	0	4	19	10	22	2	.350	.484
		Minor League Totals		.239	212	749	116	179	37	4	26	109	111	184	18	.345	.403

27 CHASE DAVIS, OF
HIT: 30. **POW:** 50. **RUN:** 50. **FLD:** 50. **ARM:** 60. **BA Grade:** 45. **Risk:** High. **Adj:** 30.

Born: December 5, 2001. **B-T:** L-L. **HT:** 6-1. **WT:** 216. **Drafted:** Arizona, 2023 (1st round). **Signed by:** Scott Cousins.
TRACK RECORD: Davis was once a touted prep recruit who landed on campus at Arizona. He spent three seasons with the Wildcats, earning all Pacific-12 Conference honors his junior season. The Cardinals drafted him 21st overall in 2023, signing him for $3,618,200. In 2024, Davis climbed three levels and reached Double-A by the end of the season. He returned to Double-A to begin 2025 but struggled with contact and hit .242/.358/.353 with 10 home runs.
SCOUTING REPORT: Davis is a power-hitting outfielder with significant hit tool concerns. Over his three years in pro ball, he has flattened out his swing in search of more consistent bat-to-ball ability. Unfortunately, it hasn't worked. Davis has struggled to make contact. He struggles to hit spin and off-speed, running high whiff rates against all breaking ball types, splitters and changeups. He still shows strong on-base skills, with swing decisions mitigating some of the risk. Davis has plus raw power but has gotten to less and less of it in recent years as he's struggled to make contact and his bat path has flattened. He's an average runner who can take the extra base when the opportunity arises. He saw a majority of his time in the field in 2025 in center field, where he's an average defender. He has a plus arm that is capable of making all the necessary throws.
THE FUTURE: Davis has second-division regular upside if he can improve his bat-to-ball skills.

Year	Age	Club (League)	Level	AVG	G	AB	R	H	2B	3B	HR	RBI	BB	SO	SB	OBP	SLG
2025	23	Springfield (TL)	AA	.242	113	414	61	100	16	0	10	48	67	146	9	.358	.353
		Minor League Totals		.243	259	926	132	225	51	1	22	141	148	293	21	.355	.371

28 MATT PUSHARD, RHP
FB: 55. **CB:** 45. **CH:** 30. **CT:** 50. **SW:** 55. **CTL:** 50. **BA Grade:** 40. **Risk:** Average. **Adj:** 30.

Born: October 27, 1997. **B-T:** R-R. **HT:** 6-4. **WT:** 250. **Signed:** Maine, 2022 (UDFA). **Signed by:** Alex Smith (Marlins).
TRACK RECORD: Pushard signed with the Marlins as an undrafted free agent out of Maine in July 2022. He has moved quickly throughout the minor leagues and reached Triple-A in 2024. He returned to the level in 2025 and pitched to a 3.61 ERA with 73 strikeouts across 62.1 innings. After a full season with Jacksonville, he was left unprotected by the Marlins for the Rule 5 draft. He was selected by the Cardinals with the seventh pick.
SCOUTING REPORT: A pure relief prospect, Pushard is a big-bodied righthander who throws exclusively from the stretch. He mixes five pitches in a four-seam fastball, cutter, sweeper, curveball and changeup. A majority of his usage is split between his four-seam fastball, cutter and sweeper. His four-seam fastball sits 94-96 mph and touches 97 with average ride, plane and extension. It was an excellent bat-missing pitch at Triple-A and should be an above-average pitch in the majors. His cutter is his most thrown secondary

ST. LOUIS CARDINALS

pitch at 87-89 mph with cut-slider shape. It's less of a swing-and-miss pitch and more of a bad-contact driver. Pushard's sweeper is a good bat-misser that drove whiffs at a rate of 35% in 2025. His curveball is a change-of-pace pitch that plays well off his two other breaking ball shapes.
THE FUTURE: Pushard will try to stick with the Cardinals as a reliever. If not, he risks being returned to the Marlins.

Year	Age	Club (League)	Level	W	L	ERA	G	GS	IP	H	HR	BB	SO	BB%	SO%	WHIP	AVG
2025	27	Jacksonville (IL)	AAA	4	5	3.61	49	1	62	49	3	23	73	9.0	28.5	1.16	.214
		Minor League Totals		10	12	3.21	134	1	174	126	12	67	199	9.3	27.6	1.11	.197

29 TRAVIS HONEYMAN, OF
HIT: 55. **POW:** 30. **RUN:** 55. **FLD:** 45. **ARM:** 40. **BA Grade:** 40. **Risk:** Average. **Adj:** 30.

Born: October 2, 2001. **B-T:** R-R. **HT:** 6-2. **WT:** 190. **Drafted:** Boston College, 2023 (3rd round). **Signed by:** Jim Negrych.
TRACK RECORD: Honeyman is a Long Island native who traveled a few hours north to play at Boston College out of high school. He spent three seasons with the Eagles but was constantly hurt and played just 94 games in three seasons. It's been much of the same as a professional after St. Louis drafted him in the third round in 2023. In his first three pro seasons, Honeyman saw five separate injured list trips. The 2025 season was Honeyman's healthiest. He played 82 games and hit .287/.411/.367 over both levels of Class A.
SCOUTING REPORT: A series of nagging soft-tissue injuries have seriously hampered Honeyman early in his career. In 2025, he saw more health and reminded scouts why he once had early-round draft buzz. Honeyman is an above-average athlete with good plate skills. He makes lots of contact and shows average swing decisions and on-base skills. His underlying power is well below-average, and his flatter swing leads to more groundball contact than is ideal. He's likely to top out at well below-average power, even with projected strength gains. Honeyman is an above-average runner who picks his spots on the bases, and he is often limited by aches and pains. He played the field for the first time as a professional in 2025 and saw time at all three outfield spots. Honeyman is a fringe-average outfielder with a below-average arm.
THE FUTURE: If Honeyman can stay healthy, he has a chance to make it as a reserve player.

Year	Age	Club (League)	Level	AVG	G	AB	R	H	2B	3B	HR	RBI	BB	SO	SB	OBP	SLG
2025	23	Palm Beach (FSL)	A	.321	29	106	19	34	5	1	2	8	20	19	7	.446	.443
2025	23	Peoria (MWL)	A+	.268	53	183	35	49	5	1	1	20	27	43	3	.390	.322
		Minor League Totals		.298	102	362	71	108	21	2	3	31	55	73	12	.411	.392

30 BLAZE JORDAN, 1B/3B
HIT: 50. **POW:** 45. **RUN:** 30. **FLD:** 45. **ARM:** 60. **BA Grade:** 45. **Risk:** High. **Adj:** 30.

Born: December 19, 2002. **B-T:** R-R. **HT:** 6-0. **WT:** 220. **Drafted:** HS—Southaven, MS, 2020 (3rd round). **Signed by:** Danny Watkins (Red Sox).
TRACK RECORD: Jordan was a touted Mississippi prep at an early age who reclassified from the 2021 high school draft class to be eligible in 2020. The Red Sox selected him in the third round and signed him for a bonus of $1.75 million. Jordan spent parts of three seasons with Double-A Portland as he returned to the level to begin 2025. He was promoted to Triple-A to begin June. The Red Sox traded Jordan to the Cardinals at the 2025 trade deadline for lefthanded reliever Steven Matz.
SCOUTING REPORT: Dating back to his high school days, Jordan's raw power and plus bat speed have always been his calling cards. Despite this reputation, he is more pure contact hitter than slugger. His bat-to-ball skills are plus. He ran a 13.5% in-zone whiff rate across all levels in 2025. A free-swinger, Jordan looks to put the ball in play and is aggressive on the edges of the zone, often hitting pitches he should take. This is a limiting factor for Jordan, who is a plodding corner player. Improving his on-base skills will be imperative for him surviving in the major leagues and will likely help him tap into more game power. Jordan has shown plus raw power with a 90th percentile exit velocity of 106.3 mph, but his flatter, contact-driven swing and aggressive approach lead to lots of poor direction on well-struck balls. Jordan is a below-average runner with limited range, which likely pushes him to first base long term, despite really good hands and actions at third base.
THE FUTURE: If Jordan can tighten his approach, he could develop into a second-division regular.

Year	Age	Club (League)	Level	AVG	G	AB	R	H	2B	3B	HR	RBI	BB	SO	SB	OBP	SLG
2025	22	Portland (EL)	AA	.320	44	150	30	48	11	0	6	37	22	19	3	.415	.513
2025	22	Memphis (IL)	AAA	.198	41	172	21	34	6	1	7	37	10	22	2	.242	.366
2025	22	Worcester (IL)	AAA	.298	44	171	29	51	11	1	6	25	11	19	0	.341	.480
		Minor League Totals		.283	488	1890	261	534	120	8	62	340	157	296	15	.341	.453

Fernando Tatis Jr.

San Diego Padres

BY PETER FLAHERTY

The Padres' 2025 season was similar to what fans have grown accustomed to over the last handful of years.

San Diego jockeyed for position atop the National League West with the eventual World Series-champion Dodgers only to finish in second place. Then the Padres dropped a decisive third game in the Wild Card Series to the Cubs.

As is typical, the season featured a major move from GM A.J. Preller. At the trade deadline, he dealt a trio of Top 10 Prospects—Leo De Vries, Braden Nett and Henry Baez—as part of the package sent to the Athletics to acquire all-star reliever Mason Miller and JP Sears. While that move alone would make for a headline-grabbing deadline, Preller was far from finished.

He then packaged another trio of prospects in Boston Bateman, Cobb Hightower and Tyson Neighbors to send to the Orioles to acquire Ryan O'Hearn and Ramon Laureano. He also traded depth starters Ryan Bergert and Stephen Kolek to the Royals for catcher Freddy Fermin. The last of Preller's major deadline moves involved sending outfielder Brandon Lockridge to the Brewers to acquire veteran stater Nestor Cortes Jr. and current No. 5 prospect Jorge Quintana.

Despite multiple high-profile moves that more or less gutted the farm system, the end result of San Diego's season remained unchanged. Since 2006, the Padres have not won the NL West title and have reached the NL Championship series only once.

As it turns out, the in-season fireworks at the trade deadline proved to be a harbinger for the offseason. Despite being under contract for two more seasons, manager Mike Shildt announced his retirement just days after the team's defeat to the Cubs. He later joined the Orioles as a minor league instructor.

Less than a month later, former Padres reliever Craig Stammen was announced as the club's next manager. Just a week after that, the Seidler family—who has been part of Padres ownership since 2012—said that they would be evaluating their future with the Padres, "including a potential sale of the franchise."

While it was a busy offseason off the field, Padres baseball operations was quiet through the Winter Meetings. That could change with Preller perpetually being in win-now mode and always finding creative ways to accomplish his goals.

While that mentality is admirable and has led San Diego to the postseason in four of the last six seasons, it has come at the expense of the farm system. The Padres' farm looks drastically different than it did last year, and there's very little depth. There's an exciting trio at the top of the system—catcher Ethan Salas and lefthanders Kruz Schoolcraft and Kash Mayfield—though after that it's very much a dealer's choice.

While the Padres have traded away plenty of amateur talent in recent seasons, the level of desirability of said talent is testament not only to San Diego's scouting and evaluation acumen, but it also speaks to the organization's developmental chops. The 2026 season will be a big one for San Diego. While the Dodgers will be viewed by many as the division favorites, the Padres again have the necessary pieces to compete at a high level and make a deep playoff run. ■

PROJECTED 2029 LINEUP

Catcher	Ethan Salas	22
First Base	Jake Cronenworth	35
Second Base	Xander Bogaerts	36
Third Base	Manny Machado	36
Shortstop	Jorge Quintana	22
Left Field	Ryan Wideman	25
Center Field	Jackson Merrill	25
Right Field	Fernando Tatis Jr.	30
Designated Hitter	Kale Fountain	23
No. 1 Starter	Nick Pivetta	36
No. 2 Starter	Kruz Schoolcraft	22
No. 3 Starter	Miguel Mendez	26
No. 4 Starter	Kash Mayfield	24
No. 5 Starter	Humberto Cruz	22
Closer	Mason Miller	30

DEPTH CHART

SAN DIEGO PADRES

TOP 2026 ROOKIES — RANK
1. Bradgley Rodriguez, RHP — 9
2. Garrett Hawkins, RHP — 23
3. Tirso Ornelas, OF — 26

BREAKOUT PROSPECTS — RANK
1. Tucker Musgrove, RHP — 12
2. Braedon Karpathios, OF — 13
3. Deivid Coronil, 3B — 22

SOURCE OF TOP 30 TALENT

Homegrown	29	Acquired	1
College	3	Trade	1
Junior college	3	Rule 5 draft	0
High school	8	Independent league	0
Undrafted free agent	1	Free agent/waivers	0
International	14		

LF
Tirso Ornelas (26)
Kai Murphy
Albert Fabian

CF
Ryan Wideman (8)
Nerwilian Cedeño
Kai Roberts

RF
Braedon Karpathios (13)
Kavares Tears (19)
Jacob Campbell

3B
Deivid Coronil (22)
Rosman Verdugo (29)
Ripken Reyes

SS
Jorge Quintana (5)
Jhoan De La Cruz (21)
Francisco Acuña

2B
Clay Dungan
Anthony Vilar
Marcos Castañon

1B
Kale Fountain (10)
Romeo Sanabria (15)

C
Ethan Salas (1)
Ty Harvey (7)
Lamar King Jr. (14)
Truitt Madonna (17)

LHP

LHSP
Kruz Schoolcraft (2)
Kash Mayfield (3)
Jagger Haynes (11)
Luis Gutierrez (24)
Carlos Alvarez (28)
Jackson Wolf

LHRP
Harry Gustin
Miguel Cienfuegos
Ryan Och
Fernando Sanchez

RHP

RHSP
Miguel Mendez (4)
Humberto Cruz (6)
Tucker Musgrove (12)
Michael Salina (16)
Lan-Hong Su (18)
Kannon Kemp (20)
Bryan Balzer (25)
Victor Lizarraga (30)
Eric Yost
Clark Candiotti
Carson Montgomery
Sean Barnett
Isaiah Lowe

RHRP
Bradgley Rodriguez (9)
Garrett Hawkins (23)
Francis Peña (27)
Josh Mallitz
Manuel Castro

SAN DIEGO PADRES

1 ETHAN SALAS, C

Born: June 1, 2006. **B-T:** L-R. **HT:** 6-1. **WT:** 185.
Signed: Venezuela, 2023.
Signed by: Luis Prieto/Trevor Schumm/Jake Koenig.

TRACK RECORD: The top prospect in the 2023 international signing period, Salas' $5.6 million bonus was the highest in the class. He made his pro debut that same season with Low-A Lake Elsinore, but the Padres got everyone's attention when they promoted the then-17-year-old to High-A Fort Wayne and then Double-A San Antonio. Salas spent the entirety of the 2024 season with Fort Wayne, where he hit .206/.288/.311 with 33 extra-base hits and 10 stolen bases. He proceeded to play in the Arizona Fall League with Peoria and was named an AFL all-star. Salas' 2025 campaign was limited to just 10 games with San Antonio due to a stress fracture in his back.

SCOUTING REPORT: Salas is a defense-first prospect who stands out for his Gold Glove-caliber defense. He has ultra-soft hands, receives the ball well and does an outstanding job of controlling balls in the dirt. Salas' transfers are quick, and he consistently delivers strong, accurate throws to bases. Between his plus arm, receiving skills and ability to handle pitching staffs, he emphatically checks a lot of boxes defensively. Salas' offensive outlook is far more murky. Mechanically, he stands fairly tall in the lefthanded batter's box with a slightly open front side and an ear-high handset. Salas has an under-control operation which includes a slight barrel tip that serves as a timing mechanism and a small stride. It's a simple and easy swing without a whole lot of moving parts. In 2024, Salas made a handful of small adjustments that ended up having a positive impact on his game. His taller stance and raised handset are a byproduct of him wanting to put more of an emphasis on working down and through the ball. Salas' bat-to-ball skills are above-average, and between 2024 and 2025 he's posted an overall in-zone contact rate of 86%. While Salas' power is geared more toward doubles than home runs, he has an all-fields approach and has shown he can drive the ball from gap to gap. Salas has long demonstrated an understanding of the strike zone, and he's decreased his strikeout rate in each of his professional seasons. Between 2023 and 2024 it sank from 25.8% to 20.9%. Salas is a bit susceptible to secondary pitches—especially changeups—which yield the majority of his swings and misses.

THE FUTURE: It's no secret that 2026 is a big year for Salas. After a topsy-turvy 2024 season and an injury-shortened 2025, the 19-year-old backstop has logged just 123 professional games since the conclusion of the 2023 season. His defense serves as a reassuring anchor to his profile, but his eventual offensive profile is up in the air. Salas certainly fits the mold of a hit-over-power player, but there are questions as to how much he's going to hit. He could catch in the big leagues tomorrow, but he will need to prove that he can produce at the plate.

BA GRADE: 55 Risk: Average
Adjusted grade: 45
SCOUTING GRADES: Hit: 45. Power: 45. Run: 45. Field: 70. Arm: 60.
Projected future grades on 20-80 scouting scale

BEST TOOLS

BATTING
Best Hitter	Romeo Sanabria
Best Power Hitter	Kale Fountain
Best Strike-Zone Discipline	Ryan Jackson
Fastest Baserunner	Ryan Wideman
Best Athlete	Ryan Wideman

PITCHING
Best Fastball	Michael Salina
Best Curveball	Harry Gustin
Best Slider	Miguel Mendez
Best Changeup	Bradgley Rodriguez
Best Control	Josh Mallitz

FIELDING
Best Defensive Catcher	Ethan Salas
Best Defensive Infielder	Jorge Quintana
Best Infield Arm	Jorge Quintana
Best Defensive Outfielder	Ryan Wideman
Best Outfield Arm	Ryan Wideman

Year	Age	Club (League)	Level	AVG	G	AB	R	H	2B	3B	HR	RBI	BB	SO	SB	OBP	SLG
2025	19	San Antonio (TL)	AA	.188	10	32	5	6	1	0	0	5	6	5	2	.325	.219
		Minor League Totals		.221	211	792	97	175	47	4	17	120	98	205	21	.309	.355

SAN DIEGO PADRES

2 KRUZ SCHOOLCRAFT, LHP
FB: 60. **SL:** 55. **CH:** 55. **CTL:** 50. **BA Grade:** 55. **Risk:** High. **Adj:** 40.

Born: April 18, 2007. **B-T:** L-L. **HT:** 6-8. **WT:** 229.
Drafted: HS—Portland, OR, 2025 (1st round). **Signed by:** Justin Baughman.
TRACK RECORD: Initially a member of the draft class of 2026, Schoolcraft announced in December 2023 that he was reclassifying to the 2025 class. A two-way player throughout his prep career at Oregon's Sunset High in Beaverton, Schoolcraft boasted thunderous raw power at the plate to go along with good defense at first base and his ability on the mound. Schoolcraft had significant first-round buzz throughout the 2025 draft cycle, and the Padres drafted him 25th overall. He signed to a full-slot signing bonus of $3.61 million. Schoolcraft made one start with Low-A Lake Elsinore after the draft, logging 1.2 innings.
SCOUTING REPORT: A towering 6-foot-8, 229-pound lefthander, Schoolcraft has impressive coordination for a pitcher of his size. He repeats his delivery well and his elite extension figures to enable his entire arsenal to play up. Schoolcraft's fastball sits in the low-to-mid 90s, but it was up to 99 mph in unofficial bridge league action after the draft. He commands his heater well and uses it to set up his secondaries. Schoolcraft's low-to-mid-80s changeup is his best non-fastball, and it routinely flashes above-average. He completes his arsenal with a low-80s slider. His slider's power and movement profile give it a chance to evolve into an above-average offering. Schoolcraft's command is average and he consistently competes in and around the strike zone.
THE FUTURE: Schoolcraft's upside is immense. Not only does he look every bit the part of a starter, but he has front-of-the-rotation upside. Between his "now" stuff and projection remaining, Schoolcraft's ceiling is sky high, and at age 19 in 2026, the Padres have no reason to rush him. He is in line to begin 2026 with Lake Elsinore.

Year	Age	Club (League)	Level	W	L	ERA	G	GS	IP	H	HR	BB	SO	BB%	SO%	WHIP	AVG
2025	18	Lake Elsinore (CAL)	A	0	0	10.80	1	1	2	1	0	3	4	33.3	44.4	2.40	.167
		Minor League Totals		0	0	10.80	1	1	2	1	0	3	4	33.3	44.4	2.40	.167

3 KASH MAYFIELD, LHP
FB: 50. **SL:** 55. **CH:** 60. **CTL:** 60. **BA Grade:** 55. **Risk:** High. **Adj:** 40.

Born: February 8, 2005. **B-T:** L-L. **HT:** 6-4. **WT:** 200.
Drafted: HS—Elk City, OK, 2024 (1st round). **Signed by:** Steve Moritz.
TRACK RECORD: Mayfield established himself as one of the more polished strike-throwers in the 2024 draft class as an underclassman and was eventually selected 25th overall by the Padres. Mayfield signed a full-slot deal worth $3,442,100 and didn't make his professional debut until 2025. Mayfield enjoyed plenty of success with Low-A Lake Elsinore, posting a 2.97 ERA with 88 strikeouts and 28 walks across 60.2 innings in 19 starts.
SCOUTING REPORT: Mayfield has a controlled, low-effort delivery that he repeats well. He has impressive control of his body and attacks hitters from a slightly lowered three-quarters slot. Mayfield's fastball averaged 90.9 mph and was up to 95 with life through the zone. It has a bit of a dead-zone profile—meaning that the vertical and horizontal break numbers are similar—but Mayfield's ability to command the pitch allows him to get the most out of it. He is able to avoid hard contact, and the vast majority of whiffs he generates with his fastball come in the top third of the zone when he locates it above the barrel. Mayfield's bread-and-butter pitch is his changeup. It sits in the low-to-mid 80s, and it's another offering for which he has an advanced feel. Mayfield throws his change with conviction, and it regularly flashes both armside fade and late tumble. It's a plus pitch that in 2025 generated a whopping 55% miss rate. Mayfield rounds out his arsenal with a high-70s-to-low-80s slider. He's shown the ability to manipulate its shape, and it's a particularly difficult look for lefthanded hitters. It flashes two-plane break and garnered a 37% whiff rate in 2025. Mayfield's plus pitchability is a cherry on top.
THE FUTURE: After dominating Low-A in 2025, Mayfield is positioned to begin his 2026 campaign with High-A Fort Wayne. With an appealing blend of strikes and stuff, he projects as a potential No. 3 starter.

Year	Age	Club (League)	Level	W	L	ERA	G	GS	IP	H	HR	BB	SO	BB%	SO%	WHIP	AVG
2025	20	Lake Elsinore (CAL)	A	1	5	2.97	19	19	61	46	2	28	88	10.9	34.1	1.22	.207
		Minor League Totals		1	5	2.97	19	19	61	46	2	28	88	10.9	34.1	1.22	.207

SAN DIEGO PADRES

4 MIGUEL MENDEZ, RHP
FB: 55. **SL:** 60. **CH:** 50. **CTL:** 45. **BA Grade:** 55. **Risk:** High. **Adj:** 40.

Born: July 1, 2002. **B-T:** R-R. **HT:** 6-3. **WT:** 175.
Signed: Dominican Republic, 2021. **Signed by:** Jhonattan Feliz.
TRACK RECORD: Mendez had only been pitching for six months when the Padres signed him out of the Dominican Republic for just $10,000 in 2021. He began to show signs of blossoming in 2024, when he posted a 3.86 ERA with 86 strikeouts in 81.2 innings for Low-A Lake Elsinore. In 2025, he worked a miniscule 1.32 ERA with 70 strikeouts in 61.1 innings for High-A Fort Wayne. Mendez earned an August promotion to Double-A San Antonio, where he didn't quite have the same success but still managed to punch out 30 in 22.1 innings.
SCOUTING REPORT: Listed at 6-foot-3 and 175 pounds, Mendez has a slender, projectable build with some length in his lower half. His athleticism is evident on the mound, and he has a dynamic delivery with a degree of explosiveness. Mendez attacks hitters out of a slightly lowered three-quarters slot with no shortage of arm speed and features a fastball, slider and a changeup. Mendez's heater sits in the mid-to-upper-90s with both run and ride through the zone. It jumps out of his hand and plays especially well in the top half of the strike zone, which is also where it generates the vast majority of its swings and misses. Mendez's tight mid-to-upper-80s slider regularly generates empty swings. It flashes plus with sharp two-plane tilt, though against righthanded hitters it will sometimes have more length than depth. Mendez used his upper-80s-to-low-90s changeup just 8% of the time, but its results were encouraging. It garnered a 37% miss rate while flashing effective tumble and fade. His command is still a work in progress, but he decreased his walk rate from 14.9% to 11% between 2024 and 2025.
THE FUTURE: Mendez has one of the higher ceilings of any pitching prospect in San Diego's system and—assuming his command and control improve—could make his major league debut as soon as 2026.

Year	Age	Club (League)	Level	W	L	ERA	G	GS	IP	H	HR	BB	SO	BB%	SO%	WHIP	AVG
2025	22	Lake Elsinore (CAL)	A	1	0	3.97	3	3	11	11	0	4	18	8.0	36.0	1.32	.256
2025	22	Fort Wayne (MWL)	A+	7	3	1.32	12	12	61	38	3	24	70	9.8	28.6	1.01	.180
2025	22	San Antonio (TL)	AA	0	4	8.06	6	6	22	22	4	17	30	15.9	28.0	1.75	.259
		Minor League Totals		11	13	4.73	67	47	211	174	14	115	243	12.3	26.0	1.37	.221

5 JORGE QUINTANA, SS
HIT: 40. **POW:** 45. **RUN:** 45. **FLD:** 55. **ARM:** 55. **BA Grade:** 50. **Risk:** High. **Adj:** 35.

Born: April 5, 2007. **B-T:** B-R. **HT:** 6-2. **WT:** 185.
Signed: Venezuela, 2024. **Signed by:** Fernando Veracierto (Brewers).
TRACK RECORD: A member of the Brewers' 2024 international class, Quintana received a $1.7 million signing bonus, the largest in the group. Following a mediocre offensive campaign in the Dominican Summer League in 2024, Quintana's production was almost identical through 50 games in the Arizona Complex League in 2025. He and Nestor Cortes Jr. were dealt to the Padres at the 2025 trade deadline for Brandon Lockridge.
SCOUTING REPORT: A 6-foot-2 switch-hitter with projection remaining, Quintana was signed because of his offensive upside. The switch-hitter has an open stance in the batter's box with a high handset and a noticeable leg lift and barrel tip in his load. Quintana has flashed present impact to his pull side and his 90th percentile exit velocity of 104.1 mph ranks ninth among all hitters in the system. His power should only continue to tick up as he matures physically, though there are hit tool questions. Quintana did a nice job of staying within the strike zone and chased at a respectable 25% clip. But there are clear pitch recognition issues, and his contact skills were below-average in 2025. He struggled mightily against secondary pitches. The most encouraging part of Quintana's game continues to be his defense. After making positive strides with Milwaukee, that trend continued in 2025. While not the twitchiest athlete, he has smooth actions, above-average range, a reliable internal clock and an above-average arm. Quintana in 2025 also looked comfortable attacking the baseball and throwing from multiple arm slots.
THE FUTURE: Quintana's upside and up-the-middle profile are the two biggest positives in his profile, but how much he'll hit is still up in the air. After getting his feet wet in the Padres' system in 2025, he projects to spend most—if not all—of the 2026 season with Low-A Lake Elsinore.

Year	Age	Club (League)	Level	AVG	G	AB	R	H	2B	3B	HR	RBI	BB	SO	SB	OBP	SLG
2025	18	ACL Brewers	Rk	.264	50	201	30	53	13	3	3	23	24	50	19	.349	.403
2025	18	Lake Elsinore (CAL)	A	.193	25	83	12	16	3	0	1	5	15	34	7	.317	.265
		Minor League Totals		.246	128	484	79	119	30	6	6	59	72	135	48	.349	.370

SAN DIEGO PADRES

HUMBERTO CRUZ, RHP
FB: 50. **SL:** 55. **CH:** 55. **CTL:** 50. **BA Grade:** 50. **Risk:** High. **Adj:** 35.

Born: December 18, 2006. **B-T:** R-R. **HT:** 6-1. **WT:** 170.
Signed: Mexico, 2024. **Signed by:** Emanuel Rangel.
TRACK RECORD: Cruz headlined the group of international pitchers the Padres signed in 2024. San Diego needed more bonus pool space to get Cruz's deal across the finish line, so the Padres opted to trade 2023 12th-rounder Blake Dickerson to the Tigers to acquire the necessary funds. Cruz ultimately signed for $750,000 out of Mexico. Across 14 starts between the Arizona Complex League and Low-A Lake Elsinore in 2025, Cruz ran up a 7.58 ERA with 35 strikeouts and 17 walks in 38 innings. At the end of the season, Cruz had internal brace surgery on his elbow.
SCOUTING REPORT: Cruz is a slightly undersized righthander who has a high-waisted frame with room to continue to fill out. He has an athletic delivery that features an abbreviated arm stroke, and he attacks hitters out of a three-quarters slot with present arm speed. Cruz's fastball averaged nearly 94 mph and was up to 97, though he'll need to refine its shape. While it's a high-spin pitch, it has a dead-zone profile and is not a bat-misser. Cruz's best offering is his low-to-mid-80s gyro slider. It flashes above-average potential, and the shape of it will vary. At times it takes on a sharp, two-plane look with depth and glove-side life, while at others it looks more like a true gyro slider with far more depth than lateral break. Cruz rounds out his arsenal with a mid-to-upper-80s changeup that profiles as a potentially above-average third pitch. Cruz throws it with conviction, flashing ample armside fade as an effective bat-misser.. His command is average and his ceiling is that of a midrotation starter.
THE FUTURE: There's a chance that Cruz's elbow procedure leaves him on the shelf for the entire 2026 season. There's no reason to rush the young righthander, and when he returns—either in late 2026 or in 2027—expect him to regain his footing in Lake Elsinore.

Year	Age	Club (League)	Level	W	L	ERA	G	GS	IP	H	HR	BB	SO	BB%	SO%	WHIP	AVG
2025	18	ACL Padres	Rk	0	4	8.31	8	8	17	21	3	8	15	10.1	19.0	1.67	.304
2025	18	Lake Elsinore (CAL)	A	0	3	6.97	6	6	21	20	5	9	20	9.8	21.7	1.40	.253
		Minor League Totals		0	7	7.20	16	16	40	42	8	18	37	10.1	20.7	1.50	.271

TY HARVEY, C
HIT: 45. **POW:** 55. **RUN:** 40. **FLD:** 50. **ARM:** 55. **BA Grade:** 45. **Risk:** High. **Adj:** 35.

Born: July 28, 2006. **B-T:** R-R. **HT:** 6-2. **WT:** 215.
Drafted: HS—Bradenton, FL, 2025 (5th round). **Signed by:** John Martin.
TRACK RECORD: A four-year standout at Inspiration Academy in Florida, Harvey posted a video game-like .571/.682/1.044 slash line with 24 extra-base hits in 31 games as a high school senior in 2025. He ranked inside the top 250 draft prospects and was eventually selected by the Padres in the fifth round. Harvey's pro debut consisted of a seven-game stint with Low-A Lake Elsinore in which he went 4-for-23 (.174) with an RBI.
SCOUTING REPORT: Harvey is a 6-foot-2, 215-pound catcher whose combination of power and arm strength carries his profile. He has strength and physicality throughout his impressive frame. Harvey has a simple setup in the box as well as a fairly compact operation with present bat and hand speed. Harvey's bat speed and strength give him exciting power potential, though there are some swing-and-miss concerns which could hinder him from tapping into it consistently in games. While it was across a small sample, Harvey sported an unimpressive overall contact rate of 58%. On a more encouraging note, he displayed sound swing decisions and the ability to get on base. Harvey's hit tool will need a coat of polish, though his ability to impact the ball is exciting. Harvey has the defensive skills to stick behind the dish. His above-average arm is the headliner, but he's also demonstrated solid catch-and-throw skills with consistent strong, accurate throws to bases.
THE FUTURE: A catcher with tools to impact the game on both sides of the ball, Harvey is an intriguing addition to the Padres' organization. As the calendar flips to 2026, he is on track to spend most of the season with Low-A Lake Elsinore. However, an in-season promotion to High-A Fort Wayne is within the realm of possibility.

Year	Age	Club (League)	Level	AVG	G	AB	R	H	2B	3B	HR	RBI	BB	SO	SB	OBP	SLG
2025	18	Lake Elsinore (CAL)	A	.174	7	23	3	4	0	0	0	1	7	12	0	.367	.174
		Minor League Totals		.174	7	23	3	4	0	0	0	1	7	12	0	.367	.174

SAN DIEGO PADRES

RYAN WIDEMAN, OF
HIT: 40. **POW:** 55. **RUN:** 60. **FLD:** 50. **ARM:** 55. **BA Grade:** 50. **Risk:** High. **Adj:** 35.

Born: November 4, 2003. **B-T:** R-R. **HT:** 6-5. **WT:** 204.
Drafted: Western Kentucky, 2025 (3rd round). **Signed by:** Matt Maloney.
TRACK RECORD: Following a stellar two-year stint at Georgia Highlands JC, Wideman didn't miss a beat in his lone season at Western Kentucky in 2025. Across 60 games, he hit .398/.466/.652 with 10 home runs and 45 stolen bases en route to winning both player and newcomer of the year honors for Conference USA. The Padres drafted Wideman in the third round and signed him for an under-slot $650,000. Wideman spent 26 games with Low-A Lake Elsinore.
SCOUTING REPORT: The 6-foot-5, 204-pound Wideman is a tool shed with a wide variety of gifts. He has a high-waisted and athletic frame with strength throughout. Wideman has a bit of a unique look in the batter's box. He deploys a high leg lift and a small stride. He has plenty of bat speed and has flashed particular impact to his pull side. While Wideman's raw power is above-average, he has hit more doubles than home runs to this point. He is a plus runner—as well as an effective basestealer—and he is a nuisance on the basepaths for opposing batteries. Wideman can go get it in center field and routinely flashes plenty of range in all directions with an above-average arm. The biggest question mark with Wideman is undoubtedly his hit tool. He's aggressive by nature and a bit of a free-swinger. Last spring he chased at a 40% clip, and in a brief pro debut he chased at a 35% rate. Picking up spin out of the pitcher's hand has been a particular bugaboo, and Wideman will need to iron out his pitch recognition skills as he develops.
THE FUTURE: Wideman's tools and upside make him an exciting prospect, though whether he's able to make enough contact is yet to be seen. Wideman will likely begin his 2026 campaign back with Lake Elsinore before earning a promotion to High-A Fort Wayne.

Year	Age	Club (League)	Level	AVG	G	AB	R	H	2B	3B	HR	RBI	BB	SO	SB	OBP	SLG
2025	21	Lake Elsinore (CAL)	A	.229	26	96	13	22	2	1	0	12	12	32	11	.330	.271
		Minor League Totals		.229	26	96	13	22	2	1	0	12	12	32	11	.330	.271

BRADGLEY RODRIGUEZ, RHP
FB: 55. **SL:** 50. **CH:** 65. **CTL:** 50. **BA Grade:** 45. **Risk:** Average. **Adj:** 35.

Born: November 16, 2003. **B-T:** R-R. **HT:** 6-0. **WT:** 203.
Signed: Venezuela, 2021. **Signed by:** Luis Prieto.
TRACK RECORD: The Padres signed Rodriguez out of Venezuela in 2021 for $700,000, but elbow issues wiped out his ensuing two seasons. He's been able to make up for lost time in 2024 and 2025, ascending from Low-A Lake Elsinore to the major leagues. In his debut season, Rodriguez allowed one run across 7.2 innings and collected nine strikeouts.
SCOUTING REPORT: Rodriguez is an undersized righthander with some length and physicality in his lower half. He works exclusively out of the stretch and features an explosive operation in which he attacks hitters out of a high three quarters slot. Rodriguez has a deep, stabbing arm stroke, and his delivery is typical for a reliever. He deploys two different fastballs—a four-seam and a sinker—that both sit in the upper 90s and have been up to 100 mph. The former plays well up in the zone thanks to its riding life and Rodriguez's relatively flat vertical approach angle. His sinker is bowling ball-esque with power sink. At times it will get in on the hands of righthanded hitters. Rodriguez's upper-80s-to-low-90s changeup is at least a plus pitch and generated a combined 45% miss rate in 2025. He's comfortable using it against both righthanded and lefthanded hitters, and it consistently flashes big-time fade to his arm side. Rodriguez completes his arsenal with a cut-slider hybrid that's short in shape, but at times will show late and effective gloveside life.
THE FUTURE: A reliever through and through, Rodriguez has a chance to break camp and open the 2026 season on the major league roster. If he is unable to do so, expect him to start the season at Triple-A with the chance to earn a callup to San Diego in relatively short order.

Year	Age	Club (League)	Level	W	L	ERA	G	GS	IP	H	HR	BB	SO	BB%	SO%	WHIP	AVG
2025	21	San Antonio (TL)	AA	4	0	3.22	18	0	22	15	1	5	31	5.6	34.8	0.90	.181
2025	21	El Paso (PCL)	AAA	2	0	3.14	15	0	14	9	0	11	7	18.0	11.5	1.40	.188
2025	21	San Diego (NL)	MLB	1	0	1.17	7	0	8	4	0	3	9	9.7	29.0	0.91	.160
		Minor League Totals		10	1	3.52	88	3	123	83	6	63	140	12.3	27.4	1.19	.190
		Major League Totals		1	0	1.17	7	0	8	4	0	3	9	9.7	29.0	0.91	.160

SAN DIEGO PADRES

10 KALE FOUNTAIN, 1B/3B
HIT: 30. **POW:** 60. **RUN:** 45. **FLD:** 45. **ARM:** 55. **BA Grade:** 50. **Risk:** High. **Adj:** 35.

Born: August 14, 2005. **B-T:** R-R. **HT:** 6-5. **WT:** 225.
Drafted: HS—Firth, NE, 2024 (5th round). **Signed by:** Troy Hoerner.
TRACK RECORD: During a decorated career at Norris High, Fountain shattered multiple Nebraska state records. His 31 home runs, 154 RBIs and 84 stolen bases are all state records, and he set the home run record while still a junior. Fountain parlayed his performance into an eventual fifth-round selection by the Padres in 2024 and signed an over-slot deal worth $1.7 million. He had Tommy John surgery in October 2024, but he still made his professional debut in 2025, appearing in 65 games between the Arizona Complex League and Low-A Lake Elsinore.
SCOUTING REPORT: At 6-foot-5, 225 pounds, Fountain has an extra-large frame with strength and physicality throughout. A power-oriented hitter, he has thunderous bat speed and plus raw power that the Padres hope he will be able to tap into in games on a consistent basis. To do so, he will need to shore up his hit tool and pitch recognition skills. In his 65-game debut, secondary pitch types vexed the physical corner infielder. He posted contact rates of 57% and 71% against sliders and changeups, respectively. One silver lining is that Fountain's swing decisions were solid and he posted a respectable walk rate of 12.5%. Fountain spent the vast majority of his 2025 campaign at first base, but given that he'll be fully recovered from his elbow surgery by the time spring training rolls around in 2026, he is also expected to get reps at third base—where he has an above-average arm—and in left field.
THE FUTURE: Much of Fountain's upside is contingent on how much he is able to hit. He has the most impressive raw power of any Padres minor leaguer, though that doesn't mean much if he's unable to get to it consistently.

Year	Age	Club (League)	Level	AVG	G	AB	R	H	2B	3B	HR	RBI	BB	SO	SB	OBP	SLG
2025	19	ACL Padres	Rk	.262	31	107	24	28	6	1	1	18	18	31	12	.386	.364
2025	19	Lake Elsinore (CAL)	A	.195	34	123	16	24	2	0	2	16	17	34	9	.311	.260
		Minor League Totals		.226	65	230	40	52	8	1	3	34	35	65	21	.346	.309

11 JAGGER HAYNES, LHP
FB: 40. **SL:** 50. **CH:** 50. **CTL:** 45. **BA Grade:** 45. **Risk:** Average. **Adj:** 35.

Born: September 20, 2002. **B-T:** L-L. **HT:** 6-3. **WT:** 196. **Drafted:** HS—Cerro Gordo, NC, 2020 (5th round).
Signed by: Jake Koenig.
TRACK RECORD: Haynes was selected in the fifth round of the shortened 2020 draft and signed for $300,000, but he didn't make his debut until 2023 because of a prolonged recovery from Tommy John surgery. Haynes' results have been positive in his return. After spending 2023 and 2024 with Low-A Lake Elsinore and High-A Fort Wayne, Haynes spent all of 2025 with Double-A San Antonio and pitched to a 4.11 ERA with 101 strikeouts to 62 walks across 103 innings.
SCOUTING REPORT: Haynes has a prototype pitcher's build with a thick lower half. He has a drop-and-drive delivery and attacks out of a high three-quarters slot. Haynes deploys a three-pitch mix that includes a low-90s fastball, a low-to-mid-80s slider and a mid-to-upper-80s changeup. His fastball isn't a true bat-misser and is modest in shape, but Haynes commands it well enough to escape significant damage. His slider and changeup are undoubtedly his bread-and-butter pitches. In 2025 they generated impressive whiff rates of 48% and 43%, respectively. Haynes' confidence in his slider is evident. He's comfortable throwing it in any count and has shown the ability to manipulate its shape. At times it will look like a true gyro slider with more depth than length while also taking on more of a two-plane look. Haynes' changeup is a valuable third pitch against righthanded hitters. It gets solid separation off his fastball and flashes effective tumble with a bit of fade. Haynes' command is fringy, and making some of his misses more competitive would likely yield positive results.
THE FUTURE: Haynes could begin the 2026 season with Triple-A El Paso, though it would not be surprising to see him return to San Antonio prior to earning a promotion. Regardless, he projects as a back-end starter who could make his major league debut in 2027.

Year	Age	Club (League)	Level	W	L	ERA	G	GS	IP	H	HR	BB	SO	BB%	SO%	WHIP	AVG
2025	22	San Antonio (TL)	AA	3	4	4.11	26	25	103	83	12	62	101	14.0	22.8	1.41	.223
		Minor League Totals		5	13	4.33	60	58	239	195	25	140	244	13.6	23.8	1.40	.225

SAN DIEGO PADRES

12 TUCKER MUSGROVE, RHP
FB: 60. **CB:** 45. **SW:** 55. **CTL:** 40. **BA Grade:** 50. **Risk:** High. **Adj:** 35.

Born: February 1, 2002. **B-T:** R-R. **HT:** 6-3. **WT:** 194. **Drafted:** Mobile, 2023 (7th round). **Signed by:** Clint Harrison.
TRACK RECORD: Musgrove was drafted as a pitcher in 2023 after a standout two-way career at NAIA Mobile in Alabama. The Padres signed him for $175,000, and he had Tommy John surgery shortly after signing. He was on the shelf for all of 2024 and made his pro debut in 2025 with Low-A Lake Elsinore. Across 14 appearances and 20.1 innings, Musgrove compiled a 5.40 ERA and collected 26 strikeouts. Musgrove made six appearances in the Arizona Fall League after the season.
SCOUTING REPORT: Musgrove is an athletic righthander who works exclusively out of the stretch and attacks out of a three-quarters arm slot. He moves well on the mound with present arm speed and relies heavily on his fastball/slider combination. If it wasn't for Michael Salina, Musgrove's heater would arguably be the best in the system. It sits in the mid-to-upper 90s and has been up to 100 mph with solid carry in the top half of the zone. His average spin rate on his four-seamer was an impressive 2,486 rpm, and Musgrove's flat vertical approach angle enhances the pitch's riding effect. It consistently gets above the barrel of opposing hitters, and in 2025 it generated a 39% miss rate. Musgrove's mid-to-upper-80s sweeper is inconsistent in shape, but at its best it flashes sharp, lateral life with a bit of late bite. Like his heater, Musgrove's slider also is a consistent generator of whiffs. Musgrove rounds out his arsenal with a seldom-used mid-to-upper-80s curveball that's bigger in shape with downward bite. Musgrove's command is scattershot at the moment but should improve as he continues to add mileage to his arm.
THE FUTURE: Musgrove's athleticism and high-end stuff both serve as exciting building blocks for his development. He will get the chance to prove himself as a starter, but if he eventually moves to the bullpen, he profiles as a dynamic reliever.

Year	Age	Club (League)	Level	W	L	ERA	G	GS	IP	H	HR	BB	SO	BB%	SO%	WHIP	AVG
2025	23	Lake Elsinore (CAL)	A	2	0	5.40	14	7	20	15	2	10	26	11.8	30.6	1.25	.205
		Minor League Totals		2	0	5.40	14	7	20	15	2	10	26	11.8	30.6	1.25	.205

13 BRAEDON KARPATHIOS, OF
HIT: 40. **POW:** 50. **RUN:** 45. **FLD:** 50. **ARM:** 55. **BA Grade:** 45. **Risk:** Average. **Adj:** 35.

Born: June 19, 2003. **B-T:** L-L. **HT:** 5-11. **WT:** 195. **Signed:** Harford (MD) JC, 2022 (UDFA). **Signed by:** Danny Sader.
TRACK RECORD: Karpathios signed as an undrafted free agent for $125,000 following a standout 2022 season at Harford Community College in which he hit .377/.560/.746 with 10 home runs and 49 walks to just 30 strikeouts. After some initial growing pains, Karpathios has come into his own and is fresh off a breakout 2025 season. Between High-A Fort Wayne and Double-A San Antonio, he hit .249/.357/.413 with 22 doubles and a career-best 15 home runs.
SCOUTING REPORT: Karpathios is a strong-bodied athlete who has an appealing blend of tools on both sides of the ball. His batted-ball data can go toe-to-toe with anyone in the Padres' system and—given his blend of advanced swing decisions and impact—is perhaps the best. While there's some swing-and-miss against secondary pitches, it hasn't hindered Karpathios' production. He feasted on fastballs, hitting over .290 with 25 extra-base hits in 2025. Along with his overall chase rate of just 19%, Karpathios posted a strong 90th percentile exit velocity of 105.8 mph. He is capable of generating quality contact to all fields, but his ability to drive the ball with authority to the opposite field is particularly impressive. Karpathios is an above-average athlete who is capable of handling all three outfield positions. He has range in either direction to go along with an average arm. His defensive profile is best suited for right field.
THE FUTURE: Karpathios' year-over-year improvement is an encouraging sign, and he was a bit of a revelation in 2025. If he can ride the momentum he built, there's a chance he could end up at Triple-A before long and make his big league debut in 2027.

Year	Age	Club (League)	Level	AVG	G	AB	R	H	2B	3B	HR	RBI	BB	SO	SB	OBP	SLG
2025	22	Fort Wayne (MWL)	A+	.254	103	366	53	93	19	1	12	55	65	118	9	.370	.410
2025	22	San Antonio (TL)	AA	.225	21	80	10	18	3	2	3	10	8	28	0	.295	.425
		Minor League Totals		.243	211	699	114	170	39	7	16	96	149	244	16	.378	.388

14 LAMAR KING JR., C
HIT: 45. **POW:** 40. **RUN:** 45. **FLD:** 50. **ARM:** 50. **BA Grade:** 45. **Risk:** Average. **Adj:** 35.

Born: December 7, 2003. **B-T:** R-R. **HT:** 6-3. **WT:** 215. **Drafted:** HS—Towson, MD, 2022 (4th round). **Signed by:** Danny Sader.
TRACK RECORD: A highly regarded prepster and the son of a former NFL defensive end of the same name, King was drafted in the fourth round in 2022 and signed a full-slot deal worth $502,800. After two stints in the Arizona Complex League, King had right shoulder surgery in the fall of 2023, which

delayed his full-season debut until well into 2024. In 2025 he batted .274/.353/.384 with 30 doubles, four home runs and 21 stolen bases in 105 games between Low-A Lake Elsinore and High-A Fort Wayne.
SCOUTING REPORT: King has an atypical profile in that he's a hit-over-power catcher. He has an open stance in the box to go along with a fairly simple swing in which there aren't a lot of moving parts. King has present bat speed, and his swing is geared more toward the gaps than home runs. While secondaries—particularly curveballs and changeups—are a little bit of a bugaboo, he has above-average bat-to-ball skills and solid swing decisions. His in-zone contact rate and chase rate of 86% and 26% are both solid marks. King's batted-ball data doesn't jump off the page, but he has enough strength and generates enough impact to drive the ball to the gaps. King is on the larger side for a catcher and his shoulder is still working his way back to 100%, but his arm strength improved to average in 2025. He moves reasonably well for his size. He nabbed just 10% of basestealers in 2025, but that figure should improve as his shoulder returns to full health. King is an effective basestealer who wisely picks his spots to run.
THE FUTURE: King will be 22 in 2026 and figures to start the year with High-A Fort Wayne before earning a promotion to Double-A San Antonio. With a smattering of fringe-average and average tools, he looks the part of backup catcher.

Year	Age	Club (League)	Level	AVG	G	AB	R	H	2B	3B	HR	RBI	BB	SO	SB	OBP	SLG
2025	21	Lake Elsinore (CAL)	A	.286	81	311	50	89	24	1	4	37	38	68	18	.370	.408
2025	21	Fort Wayne (MWL)	A+	.233	24	90	4	21	6	0	0	7	6	25	3	.289	.300
		Minor League Totals		.276	184	649	97	179	40	8	4	72	85	157	29	.374	.381

15 ROMEO SANABRIA, 1B
HIT: 45. **POW:** 45. **RUN:** 30. **FLD:** 45. **ARM:** 50. **BA Grade:** 45. **Risk:** Average. **Adj:** 35.

Born: May 2, 2002. **B-T:** L-R. **HT:** 6-4. **WT:** 248. **Drafted:** Indian River State (FL) JC, 2022 (18th round).
Signed by: Cliff Terracuso.
TRACK RECORD: The Padres drafted Sanabria in the 18th round in 2022 following an outstanding juco season at Indian River in which he hit .400/.471/.578. He proceeded to hit the ground running with an excellent pro debut in 2023 and has followed suit with productive 2024 and 2025 seasons. Sanabria spent all of 2025 with Double-A San Antonio where he hit .257/.309/.376 with a career-high 12 home runs.
SCOUTING REPORT: Sanabria is a first baseman through and through, which places a lot of pressure on his bat. So far, he has been up to the challenge. Sanabria has a solid hit-power combination, and in 2025 flashed above-average bat-to-ball skills to go along with fringe-average power. His in-zone contact rate of 86% and 90th percentile exit velocity of 105.7 mph were both impressive marks within the organization. Sanabria struggles with whiffs and chase tendencies against secondaries but does damage against fastballs. In 2025, Sanabria hit .285/.341/.448 with 18 extra-base hits against all heaters. Sanabria's highest quality of contact comes to his pull side, but he has enough strength in his 6-foot-4, 248-pound frame to drive the ball to the opposite field. He handles himself well at first base and will stick at the position.
THE FUTURE: Sanabria figures to begin the 2026 season back in the Texas League, though he's on track to earn a promotion to Triple-A El Paso. He'll need to continue to hit and projects as an MLB depth piece.

Year	Age	Club (League)	Level	AVG	G	AB	R	H	2B	3B	HR	RBI	BB	SO	SB	OBP	SLG
2025	23	San Antonio (TL)	AA	.257	119	452	54	116	18	0	12	56	38	107	4	.309	.376
		Minor League Totals		.283	332	1194	180	338	76	2	31	194	175	310	11	.370	.428

16 MICHAEL SALINA, RHP
FB: 60. **SL:** 55. **CTL:** 45. **BA Grade:** 50. **Risk:** High. **Adj:** 35.

Born: January 30, 2004. **B-T:** R-R. **HT:** 6-1. **WT:** 215. **Drafted:** St. Bonaventure, 2025 (4th round). **Signed by:** Will Scott.
TRACK RECORD: Salina began his college career at George Mason before transferring to St. Bonaventure ahead of his sophomore season. He came into his own with the Bonnies, and following an impressive 2024 campaign and a loud fall season, he cemented himself as one of the top college arms in the Northeast. Salina's season was limited to just four starts in 2025 due to an arm injury that required Tommy John surgery, but he pitched to a 4.15 ERA with 26 strikeouts in 17.1 innings.
SCOUTING REPORT: Salina is a slightly undersized righthander who works exclusively out of the stretch and features a high-effort delivery in which he has big-time arm speed. His calling card is his mid-to-upper-90s fastball that has reached triple digits. It jumps out of his hand and was overpowering for opposing hitters in 2025. Salina generated whiff and chase rates of 34% and 33% with his heater. He pairs it with a mid-to-upper-80s slider that flashes two-plane break. Both pitches are viable swing-and-miss offerings, but he lacks a true third pitch and his command remains fringy. There's certainly reliever risk and Salina will need to expand his arsenal in order to stick as a starter, but his fastball/slider combination is perhaps the loudest one-two punch in the system.

SAN DIEGO PADRES

THE FUTURE: After having Tommy John surgery in April 2025, Salina's pro debut will likely wait until the middle of the spring or early summer 2026. The Padres will attempt to develop the high-octane righthander as a starter, but there's a chance he ends up as a two-pitch reliever.

Year	Age	Club (League)	Level	W	L	ERA	G	GS	IP	H	HR	BB	SO	BB%	SO%	WHIP	AVG
2025	21	Did not play															

17 TRUITT MADONNA, C
HIT: 30. **POW:** 55. **RUN:** 30. **FLD:** 45. **ARM:** 50. **BA Grade:** 50. **Risk:** High. **Adj:** 35.

Born: March 12, 2007. **B-T:** R-R. **HT:** 6-3. **WT:** 215. **Drafted:** HS—Seattle, WA, 2025 (11th round).
Signed by: Justin Baughman.
TRACK RECORD: Madonna hit over .400 with 16 extra-base hits across 26 games as a high school senior and committed to UCLA. A breakout 12-game stint in the MLB Draft League in which he hit .279/.360/.512 with four doubles and a pair of home runs catapulted him into the 11th round of the 2025 draft and landed him an over-slot deal with the Padres worth $654,000. He made his pro debut with Low-A Lake Elsinore after the draft and hit .185/.267/.278 with three doubles over 14 games.
SCOUTING REPORT: At 6-foot-3, 215 pounds, Madonna is physical with noticeable strength throughout his frame. While his above-average raw power serves as an intriguing building block, he will need to prove he can hit enough to get to it consistently in a game. He has a noticeable hand press in his load and his swing can get long, which contributed to a 53% overall contact rate in his pro debut. Picking up secondaries out of the pitcher's hand proved to be particularly difficult as Madonna posted a chase rate north of 30% against every type of non-fastball. Madonna still managed to flash impressive strength and all-fields power. He will need to work hard to refine his defensive skills to stick behind the plate, where he is larger than the average player at his position. He's a somewhat stiff mover with limited lateral range and an average arm. An eventual move to first base isn't out of the question.
THE FUTURE: Madonna will turn 19 in March 2026 and could return to Low-A to begin the season, though a stint in the Arizona Complex League shouldn't be ruled out.

Year	Age	Club (League)	Level	AVG	G	AB	R	H	2B	3B	HR	RBI	BB	SO	SB	OBP	SLG
2025	18	Lake Elsinore (CAL)	A	.185	14	54	4	10	3	1	0	5	6	23	0	.267	.278
		Minor League Totals		.185	14	54	4	10	3	1	0	5	6	23	0	.267	.278

18 LAN-HONG SU, RHP
FB: 50. **SL:** 55. **CH:** 45. **CTL:** 50. **BA Grade:** 50. **Risk:** High. **Adj:** 35.

Born: March 4, 2007. **B-T:** R-R. **HT:** 6-1. **WT:** 150. **Signed:** Taiwan, 2025. **Signed by:** Chris Kemp.
TRACK RECORD: Even after signing Carlos Alvarez, Deivid Coronil and Jhoan De La Cruz, the Padres had enough pool money left to sign Su in October 2025 for $775,000. A native of Taiwan, Su was excellent in the WBSC U-18 World Cup, where he pitched to a 1.91 ERA with 14 strikeouts across 7.1 innings.
SCOUTING REPORT: Su has a lean, ultra-projectable 6-foot-1 frame with ample room to add physicality. He has a whippy arm stroke with big-time arm speed and has an appealing combination of pitchability and pure stuff. Su's fastball sits in the upper 80s to low 90s with life in the top half of the zone and should experience a velocity jump as he continues to fill out. Su has advanced feel for an above-average slider, which he spins well. It profiles as the most reliable swing-and-miss offering in his arsenal. Su rounds out his three-pitch mix with a changeup that's more of a show pitch at this stage. As Su continues to fill out, expect his entire arsenal to tick up both in terms of velocity and dynamism.
THE FUTURE: Su will make his professional debut in 2026, likely in the Arizona Complex League. As is common with most international signees, there is no need to push the envelope or rush his development. Su is one of the more interesting arms to follow in the system.

Year	Age	Club (League)	Level	W	L	ERA	G	GS	IP	H	HR	BB	SO	BB%	SO%	WHIP	AVG
2025	18	Did not play															

19 KAVARES TEARS, OF
HIT: 30. **POW:** 50. **RUN:** 55. **FLD:** 50. **ARM:** 55. **BA Grade:** 45. **Risk:** Average. **Adj:** 35.

Born: August 25, 2002. **B-T:** L-L. **HT:** 6-0. **WT:** 200. **Drafted:** Tennessee, 2024 (4th round). **Signed by:** Tyler Stubblefield.
TRACK RECORD: Tears was a key cog in Tennessee's national championship lineup in 2024, when he hit .324/.427/.643 with 16 doubles and 20 home runs en route to a fourth-round selection and full-slot signing bonus worth $525,000. Tears made his pro debut in 2025 and spent the entire season with Low-A Lake Elsinore, where he hit .227/.320/.385 with 22 doubles and 13 home runs.

SAN DIEGO PADRES

SCOUTING REPORT: Tears is a strong, physical outfielder with a longstanding reputation as a power-over-hit profile. The impact he's able to generate is impressive—his 90th percentile exit velocity of 106.4 mph was the third-best mark in the system in 2025—but there are questions surrounding his hit tool and whether or not he'll make enough contact for his power to continue to be a valuable in-game tool. Tears made contact at just a 63% clip in 2025 and struggled mightily against spin, showing a tendency to expand the strike zone down and away against sliders and changeups. Until he shows marked improvement in both his hitting ability and pitch-recognition skills, teams will continue to exploit his inefficiencies. Tears has over-the-fence power to all fields, but it won't mean much if he can't put the ball in play on a regular basis. He is an above-average runner once underway, and his legs and above-average arm make his defensive skills most conducive to right field.
THE FUTURE: After logging more than 100 games at Low-A in 2025 and having turned 23 in August, Tears is on track to open 2026 at High-A Fort Wayne. The Midwest League, especially early in the season, is notoriously difficult for hitters. Tears will need to show that his hit tool has taken a step forward.

Year	Age	Club (League)	Level	AVG	G	AB	R	H	2B	3B	HR	RBI	BB	SO	SB	OBP	SLG
2025	22	Lake Elsinore (CAL)	A	.227	107	410	49	93	22	2	13	65	58	138	6	.320	.385
		Minor League Totals		.227	107	410	49	93	22	2	13	65	58	138	6	.320	.385

20 KANNON KEMP, RHP
FB: 50. **SL:** 45. **CH:** 50. **CTL:** 50. **BA Grade:** 50. **Risk:** High. **Adj:** 35.

Born: September 3, 2004. **B-T:** R-R. **HT:** 6-6. **WT:** 250. **Drafted:** HS—Weatherford, TX, 2023 (8th round).
Signed by: Matt Scaffner.
TRACK RECORD: Kemp was a late-bloomer on the mound who was used as a reliever for part of his high school career. The Padres drafted him in the eighth round in 2023 and signed him to an over-slot $625,000 bonus. Kemp didn't make his pro debut until 2025, as he was sidelined for the entire 2024 season while recovering from a shoulder impingement. He pitched to a 5.56 ERA with 64 strikeouts to 32 walks across 77.2 innings between the Arizona Complex League and Low-A Lake Elsinore. He proceeded to have a productive seven-inning stint in the Arizona Fall League during which he allowed only one run.
SCOUTING REPORT: Standing in at 6-foot-6, 250 pounds, Kemp is an imposing presence on the mound. He operates exclusively out of the stretch and attacks from a slightly lowered three-quarters slot with an abbreviated arm stroke. Kemp's fastball sits 93-96 mph and has been up to 98 with natural run and sink. Between his arm slot and steeper approach angle, consistently locating his fastball in the bottom half of the zone would serve him well. Kemp's mid-to-upper-80s gyro slider lacks teeth at present, but he displayed encouraging feel for the offering. He threw his slider for strikes 65% of the time and also showed that he was capable of manipulating its shape. It often looks like a true downer gyro, but on occasion he generates two-plane shape, which is effective when back-footing lefthanded hitters. Kemp threw his upper-80s changeup just 10% of the time, but it looks the part of a viable third pitch to deploy against lefthanded hitters. It routinely flashed late tumble and generated a 43% whiff rate. Kemp's command is still a work in progress, but it projects as average.
THE FUTURE: Although there's some reliever risk, Kemp has appealing upside as a starter. He has a prototypical pitcher's frame to go along with a true three-pitch mix and average command. He is still just 21 years old and figures to begin 2026 with High-A Fort Wayne.

Year	Age	Club (League)	Level	W	L	ERA	G	GS	IP	H	HR	BB	SO	BB%	SO%	WHIP	AVG
2025	20	ACL Padres	Rk	0	2	4.88	5	3	24	22	1	8	16	7.9	15.8	1.25	.244
2025	20	Lake Elsinore (CAL)	A	3	5	5.87	13	7	54	64	3	24	48	9.6	19.3	1.64	.298
		Minor League Totals		3	7	5.56	18	10	78	86	4	32	64	9.1	18.3	1.52	.282

21 JHOAN DE LA CRUZ, SS
HIT: 50. **POW:** 40. **RUN:** 55. **FLD:** 50. **ARM:** 55. **BA Grade:** 50. **Risk:** High. **Adj:** 35.

Born: November 16, 2007. **B-T:** B-R. **HT:** 5-9. **WT:** 165. **Signed:** Dominican Republic, 2025. **Signed by:** Chris Kemp.
TRACK RECORD: De La Cruz signed with the Padres for $1 million in January 2025. He posted a .259/.477/.360 slash line with five doubles, three triples, one home run and more walks (46) than strikeouts (45) in his Dominican Summer League debut season.
SCOUTING REPORT: At 5-foot-9, 165 pounds, De La Cruz has a medium, slightly undersized frame and doesn't have a carrying tool. However, he has solid all-around skills and a chance to stick at shortstop. De La Cruz is a switch-hitter with above-average bat-to-ball skills and a swing that's geared toward line drives to all fields. Even though he was just 17 years old in 2025, it's reasonable to project below-average home run output. He didn't grow much throughout the scouting process and his frame is more of a finished product than projectable. Though walks in the DSL can be easier to come by, De La Cruz controlled

SAN DIEGO PADRES

the strike zone and showed a polished approach. On the dirt, he displays sound actions and good hands with a slightly above-average arm. He's also an above-average runner, which serves him well both on the basepaths and on the infield.
THE FUTURE: De La Cruz is a long-term development project, but he's a promising middle infielder who should stick at a premium position. He projects to make his stateside debut in 2026.

Year	Age	Club (League)	Level	AVG	G	AB	R	H	2B	3B	HR	RBI	BB	SO	SB	OBP	SLG
2025	17	DSL Padres Gold	Rk	.259	51	139	37	36	5	3	1	21	46	45	11	.477	.360
		Minor League Totals		.259	51	139	37	36	5	3	1	21	46	45	11	.477	.360

DEIVID CORONIL, 3B

HIT: 40. **POW:** 50. **RUN:** 60. **FLD:** 50. **ARM:** 55. **BA Grade:** 55. **Risk:** Extreme. **Adj:** 35.

Born: October 4, 2007. **B-T:** B-R. **HT:** 6-3. **WT:** 162. **Signed:** Venezuela, 2025. **Signed by:** Luis Prieto.
TRACK RECORD: Coronil was one of the most exciting Venezuelan prospects in the 2025 international signing period when he signed with the Padres for $900,000. While he flashed upside, his Dominican Summer League debut wasn't without growing pains. He hit just .186/.327/.214 with three extra-base hits—and zero home runs—across 45 games.
SCOUTING REPORT: While Coronil has an exciting combination of raw tools, athleticism and upside, he isn't without a degree of rawness. Listed at 6-foot-3, 162 pounds, he has a lean, lanky build with plenty of room to fill out. Coronil is a switch-hitter whose swing from the left side is loftier than it is from the right. He had nothing to show for it in the DSL, but prior to being signed, he flashed most of his home run power from the left side. Coronil's power upside is exciting to dream on, but there are questions about his hit tool. There's plenty of swing-and-miss in his profile, which might hinder him from ever getting to his power consistently. He is a plus runner with an above-average arm, but he's trending toward growing out of shortstop and moving to third base or possibly center field.
THE FUTURE: There is zero reason to rush Coronil, who is on track to make his Arizona Complex League debut in 2026. His hitting ability will need to take a sizable step forward, but his tools and upside give him a reasonably high ceiling.

Year	Age	Club (League)	Level	AVG	G	AB	R	H	2B	3B	HR	RBI	BB	SO	SB	OBP	SLG
2025	17	DSL Padres Gold	Rk	.186	45	140	23	26	2	1	0	12	21	47	8	.327	.214
		Minor League Totals		.186	45	140	23	26	2	1	0	12	21	47	8	.327	.214

GARRETT HAWKINS, RHP

FB: 55. **SW:** 55. **CTL:** 50. **BA Grade:** 45. **Risk:** Average. **Adj:** 35.

Born: February 10, 2000. **B-T:** R-R. **HT:** 6-5. **WT:** 230. **Drafted:** British Columbia, 2021 (9th round). **Signed by:** Chris Kemlo.
TRACK RECORD: Hawkins was drafted in the ninth round in the 2021 draft following a standout career at the University of British Columbia and an exceptional run in the MLB Draft League. Following a productive pro debut and a strong 2023 season that saw him collect 120 strikeouts across 93 innings, Hawkins missed the entire 2024 season recovering from Tommy John surgery. After primarily using Hawkins as a starter, the Padres opted to move him back to the bullpen in 2025. In his return to the mound, he pitched to a 1.50 ERA with 80 strikeouts across 60 innings between High-A Fort Wayne and Double-A San Antonio.
SCOUTING REPORT: A physical 6-foot-5 righthander, Hawkins relies heavily on his fastball/sweeper combination. His fastball sits in the mid-to-upper 90s and has been up to 98 mph with plus carry in the top half of the zone. It averaged nearly 21 inches of ride in 2025, and Hawkins did well at consistently locating it in the upper regions. Not surprisingly, that's where his heater is at its best and also where it generates the vast majority of swings and misses. It consistently gets over the barrel of opposing hitters and generated miss and chase rates of 33% and 34%, respectively. Hawkins' low-to-mid-80s sweeper averaged almost 15 inches of lateral break and it's a pitch that he uses mostly against righthanded hitters.
THE FUTURE: Hawkins is a surefire reliever who was added to San Diego's 40-man roster in November 2025 ahead of the Rule 5 draft. Hawkins could make his major league debut at some point in 2026 and projects as an effective back-end reliever.

Year	Age	Club (League)	Level	W	L	ERA	G	GS	IP	H	HR	BB	SO	BB%	SO%	WHIP	AVG
2025	25	Fort Wayne (MWL)	A+	8	1	1.43	32	0	44	17	1	13	60	8.0	37.0	0.68	.116
2025	25	San Antonio (TL)	AA	1	0	1.69	13	0	16	11	0	10	20	15.2	30.3	1.31	.196
		Minor League Totals		17	12	3.39	77	25	183	155	19	61	242	8.1	32.0	1.18	.226

SAN DIEGO PADRES

24 LUIS GUTIERREZ, LHP
FB: 45. **SL:** 45. **CH:** 45. **CTL:** 55. **BA Grade:** 45. **Risk:** Average. **Adj:** 35.

Born: July 31, 2003. **B-T:** L-L. **HT:** 6-0. **WT:** 175. **Signed:** Venezuela, 2019. **Signed by:** Trevor Schumm.

TRACK RECORD: Gutierrez was signed out of Venezuela as a teenager in 2019 before making his professional debut in the Dominican Summer League in 2021. Outside of a rocky stint in the Arizona Complex League in 2023, Gutierrez has been a steady performer. The 2025 season was the best of his career. Gutierrez began the year with Low-A Lake Elsinore before finishing with Triple-A El Paso. Across four levels, he pitched to a 3.31 ERA with 115 strikeouts to just 44 walks across 125 innings.

SCOUTING REPORT: An undersized southpaw, Gutierrez has a simple, repeatable operation in which he attacks out of a high three-quarters slot and maintains good direction toward home plate. He has seen steady velocity gains year-over-year, and in 2025 his fastball sat in the 91-94 mph range but was up to 97. It has a dead-zone profile with unremarkable spin characteristics, but Gutierrez's above-average command allows him to optimize its shape and consistently locate it in the top half of the zone, particularly to his arm side. Gutierrez supplements his fastball with a mid-to-upper-80s changeup that flashes effective tumble with a bit of fade, and a mid-80s slider. His slider is shorter in shape, but at times takes on a two-plane look with more length against lefthanded hitters. He's also demonstrated the ability to back-foot it to righties. Gutierrez's two offspeed offerings generated miss rates of 30% and 40%, respectively.

THE FUTURE: Gutierrez profiles as a back-end starter, but his above-average pitchability gives him a reasonably high floor. After traversing four levels in 2025, Gutierrez is on track to begin 2026 with Double-A San Antonio.

Year	Age	Club (League)	Level	W	L	ERA	G	GS	IP	H	HR	BB	SO	BB%	SO%	WHIP	AVG
2025	21	Lake Elsinore (CAL)	A	2	3	2.88	10	6	50	32	3	20	46	9.9	22.7	1.04	.180
2025	21	Fort Wayne (MWL)	A+	2	3	3.74	13	13	65	67	4	22	59	7.7	20.7	1.37	.263
2025	21	San Antonio (TL)	AA	1	0	0.00	1	1	5	2	0	2	4	11.1	22.2	0.80	.125
2025	21	El Paso (PCL)	AAA	0	0	5.40	1	1	5	6	1	0	6	0.0	28.6	1.20	.300
		Minor League Totals		14	15	4.30	77	44	287	285	20	123	263	9.8	21.0	1.42	.260

25 BRYAN BALZER, RHP
FB: 50. **SL:** 55. **CH:** 45. **CTL:** 45. **BA Grade:** 45. **Risk:** High. **Adj:** 30.

Born: October 27, 2004. **B-T:** L-R. **HT:** 6-1. **WT:** 190. **Signed:** Japan, 2023. **Signed by:** Trevor Schumm.

TRACK RECORD: Born and raised in Japan, Balzer signed out of high school outside Tokyo for a modest $10,000 in January 2023. Upon signing, he had Tommy John surgery and did not make his pro debut until 2024. Balzer managed his first fully healthy pro season in 2025 and posted a 7.92 ERA with 49 strikeouts to 28 walks across 50 innings with Low-A Lake Elsinore.

SCOUTING REPORT: Balzer is an athletic 6-foot-1, 190-pound righthander who pitches exclusively out of the stretch and attacks out of a slightly lowered three-quarters slot. He relies heavily on his sinker/slider combination, though he'll also mix in an occasional changeup. Balzer's sinker has been up into the mid 90s, and it flashes plenty of armside run and sink. It darts and dives away from lefthanded hitters and bears in on the hands of righties, though it didn't miss a lot of bats in 2025 and got hit around. His command is spotty, which caused him to leave his heater out over the middle of the plate. Balzer's low-to-mid-80s slider is without a doubt his best pitch. It flashes plus with sharp lateral break and plenty of length, and is especially a weapon against righthanded hitters given its shape and Balzer's arm slot. He rounds out his arsenal with a seldom-used split-changeup that will flash natural fade and a bit of tumble, though it's a distant third pitch. He'll need to work hard to add a viable third offering and show he can get lefthanded hitters out in order to stick as a starter.

THE FUTURE: Balzer is an athletic mover and a low-mileage arm with no shortage of upside, but there are questions about whether he'll reach his ceiling. His scattershot command and lack of arsenal depth could eventually lead him to a bullpen role.

Year	Age	Club (League)	Level	W	L	ERA	G	GS	IP	H	HR	BB	SO	BB%	SO%	WHIP	AVG
2025	20	Lake Elsinore (CAL)	A	1	6	7.92	16	13	50	61	3	28	49	11.6	20.3	1.78	.310
		Minor League Totals		1	6	7.74	22	15	57	69	3	31	56	11.4	20.5	1.75	.308

26 TIRSO ORNELAS, OF
HIT: 45. **POW:** 45. **RUN:** 45. **FLD:** 45. **ARM:** 50. **BA Grade:** 35. **Risk:** Mild. **Adj:** 30.

Born: March 11, 2000. **B-T:** L-R. **HT:** 6-3. **WT:** 200. **Signed:** Mexico, 2016. **Signed by:** Trevor Schumm.

TRACK RECORD: Ornelas signed with the Padres for $1.5 million in 2016 and he's been a steady performer ever since. He made his MLB debut in 2025 before quickly being optioned to Triple-A El Paso. Ornelas missed nearly two months in 2025 due to plantar fasciitis.

SAN DIEGO PADRES

SCOUTING REPORT: Ornelas is largely a finished product from a tools standpoint, but has an appealing hit-and-power blend that's been on display during his career. He saw an uptick in power following the 2022 season, which can partially be attributed to a few setup changes. Most notably, Ornelas raised his handset which helped him work down and through the ball to generate backspin. It's an adjustment that's withstood the test of time, and Ornelas has hit double-digit home runs in each of the last three seasons. He has above-average bat-to-ball skills, and in 2025 he worked an 88% overall in-zone contact rate. The vast majority of Ornelas' home run power comes to his pull side. He is a fringy left fielder with an average arm.
THE FUTURE: Ornelas has been a productive hitter across every minor league level who figures to continue to get opportunities in the major leagues. While he might begin 2026 in El Paso again, Ornelas could be up with the big league club before long. He is a solid fourth outfielder and depth piece with a reasonably high floor.

Year	Age	Club (League)	Level	AVG	G	AB	R	H	2B	3B	HR	RBI	BB	SO	SB	OBP	SLG
2025	25	El Paso (PCL)	AAA	.289	82	318	63	92	21	0	10	57	46	64	7	.384	.450
2025	25	San Diego (NL)	MLB	.071	7	14	0	1	0	0	0	1	2	2	0	.188	.071
		Minor League Totals		.274	965	3576	551	981	210	22	84	511	454	771	56	.358	.416
		Major League Totals		.071	7	14	0	1	0	0	0	1	2	2	0	.188	.071

27 FRANCIS PEÑA, RHP
FB: 50. **SL:** 55. **CTL:** 45. **BA Grade:** 40. **Risk:** Average. **Adj:** 30.

Born: January 25, 2001. **B-T:** R-R. **HT:** 6-1. **WT:** 170. **Signed:** Dominican Republic, 2022. **Signed by:** Alvin Duran.
TRACK RECORD: Unlike most international prospects who sign as teenagers, Peña signed for $10,000 a few days before his 21st birthday out of the Dominican Republic in 2022. He made his stateside debut in 2023 and put together a successful 2024 season that spanned three levels. Peña spent all of 2025 as a reliever with Triple-A El Paso, where he pitched to a modest 4.99 ERA with 47 strikeouts to 34 walks in 52.1 innings across 43 relief appearances.
SCOUTING REPORT: Despite being slightly undersized, Peña is high-waisted with some length in his lower half. He pitches exclusively out of the stretch and has an explosive, drop-and-drive delivery and a short arm stroke. He attacks from a three-quarters slot and a five-and-a-half foot release height. Peña's power sinker/slider combination makes for an effective east-west profile. His sinker sits in the mid-to-upper 90s and has been up to 100 mph with both run and sink, but it plays up thanks to Peña's outstanding extension of more than seven feet. His slider is more effective from a swing-and-miss standpoint and regularly flashes two-plane break. It garnered a miss rate greater than 30% and was most effective against lefthanded hitters. Peña showed the ability to get the pitch in and under their hands with a version of the pitch with shorter shape. Peña walked 14% of batters in 2025 as he contended with hitter-friendly conditions at El Paso and the ABS challenge strike zone.
THE FUTURE: Peña is a two-pitch reliever who has climbed efficiently through San Diego's system and is on his way to making his major league debut in 2026.

Year	Age	Club (League)	Level	W	L	ERA	G	GS	IP	H	HR	BB	SO	BB%	SO%	WHIP	AVG
2025	24	El Paso (PCL)	AAA	4	4	4.99	43	0	52	50	4	34	47	14.3	19.8	1.61	.255
		Minor League Totals		14	15	3.85	125	0	173	161	10	77	170	10.2	22.5	1.38	.243

28 CARLOS ALVAREZ, LHP
FB: 50. **CB:** 45. **CH:** 45. **CTL:** 30. **BA Grade:** 50. **Risk:** Extreme. **Adj:** 30.

Born: November 14, 2007. **B-T:** L-L. **HT:** 6-4. **WT:** 195. **Signed:** Dominican Republic, 2025.
Signed by: Jonathan Feliz/Carlos Tavares.
TRACK RECORD: The Padres signed Alvarez out of the Dominican Republic in January 2025 for $1 million. His signing bonus was the highest in the Padres' 2025 international class. Alvarez's price tag rose close to his signing date as the the Padres were in limbo as a finalist to sign Roki Sasaki, then increased his bonus to keep him from other clubs. Alvarez's Dominican Summer League debut in 2025 was shaky, though he was 17 years old for the entire season. He struck out 23 and walked 31 across 23 innings.
SCOUTING REPORT: While Alvarez lacks polish, he fits the description of an "intriguing ball of clay to mold" to a T. He has a prototype 6-foot-4 pitcher's frame and there's plenty to dream on from a projection standpoint. In his DSL debut, Alvarez deployed a mix of four- and two-seam fastballs that sat in the low 90s and touched 95 mph. Given his long levers and physical upside, it's not too difficult to envision Alvarez's fastball eventually creeping into the upper 90s. He has a low-80s slurvy breaking ball, though his most used—and most effective—secondary pitch in the DSL was a changeup that flashed a healthy amount of armside fade. Alvarez has a tantalizing blend of pure stuff and projection, but his control and general pitchability are both a ways away.

THE FUTURE: There's a high degree of volatility in Alvarez's profile. He could dial in his command and control and blossom into an effective starter, though it could also continue to evade him, which means he'll be destined for the bullpen.

Year	Age	Club (League)	Level	W	L	ERA	G	GS	IP	H	HR	BB	SO	BB%	SO%	WHIP	AVG
2025	17	DSL Padres Brown	Rk	0	0	0.00	1	1	4	1	0	3	4	18.8	25.0	1.00	.083
2025	17	DSL Padres Gold	Rk	0	2	11.84	11	11	19	17	1	28	19	26.4	17.9	2.37	.233
		Minor League Totals		0	2	9.78	12	12	23	18	1	31	23	25.4	18.9	2.13	.212

29 ROSMAN VERDUGO, 2B/3B

HIT: 40. **POW:** 45. **RUN:** 40. **FLD:** 45. **ARM:** 50. **BA Grade:** 40. **Risk:** Average. **Adj:** 30.

Born: February 2, 2005. **B-T:** R-R. **HT:** 5-11. **WT:** 180. **Signed:** Mexico, 2022. **Signed by:** Bill McLaughlin.
TRACK RECORD: Verdugo inked a $700,000 bonus as a 16-year-old out of Mexico in 2022 and made his stateside debut in the Arizona Complex League that year. His production has remained relatively stagnant throughout each of his three professional seasons, though in 2025 with High-A Fort Wayne he hit .205/.339/.354 with 15 doubles and a career-high 13 home runs.
SCOUTING REPORT: While Verdugo has improved his chase rates year-over-year, significant contact questions have remained omnipresent. On top of an overall contact rate of 65%, he posted an in-zone contact rate of just 72% in 2025. Picking up shapes out of the pitcher's hand has proven to be a difficult task for Verdugo, who is especially susceptible to spin anywhere on the outer half of the plate. On top of his deficiencies against secondaries, he struggles against fastballs in the top-third of the zone. While Verdugo's hit tool has a long way to go, some of his underlying batted-ball data is promising. On top of his pull-oriented approach, Verdugo has shown a knack for lifting the ball to his pull side to go along with good launch angle data and ever-improving impact. A below-average runner, Verdugo has an average arm with limited range at second and third base.
THE FUTURE: Verdugo will have just turned 21 by the time spring training begins, but 2026 is an important year for him. He'll need to display an improved hit tool, a task that's become even more imperative given his modest defensive profile.

Year	Age	Club (League)	Level	AVG	G	AB	R	H	2B	3B	HR	RBI	BB	SO	SB	OBP	SLG
2025	20	Fort Wayne (MWL)	A+	.205	117	404	59	83	15	3	13	43	72	158	6	.339	.354
		Minor League Totals		.221	411	1432	202	317	79	13	34	196	211	500	33	.330	.366

30 VICTOR LIZARRAGA, RHP

FB: 40. **CB:** 40. **SL:** 50. **CH:** 40. **CTL:** 50. **BA Grade:** 35. **Risk:** Mild. **Adj:** 30.

Born: November 30, 2003. **B-T:** R-R. **HT:** 6-3. **WT:** 180. **Signed:** Mexico, 2021.
Signed by: Bill McLaughlin/Emanuel Rangel/Trevor Schumm/Chris Kemp.
TRACK RECORD: Lizarraga was Mexico's top pitching prospect in the 2021 international class, and the Padres signed the 17-year-old for $1 million. Lizarraga had been a consistent performer across each of his first three professional seasons, but he took a step back in 2025 and pitched to a 5.77 ERA with an uninspiring strikeout-to-walk ratio of 92-to-60. All but two of his starts came with Double-A San Antonio, where he got particularly roughed up.
SCOUTING REPORT: Lizarraga is a 6-foot-3 righthander who features a whippy arm stroke and attacks out of a slightly lowered three-quarters slot with a release height that's just over 5 feet. He is a "kitchen sink" pitcher who has five distinct offerings. His four-seam fastball sits in the low 90s and has a dead-zone profile, but it plays well up in the top-third of the zone thanks to a flat approach angle. Lizarraga also features two slider shapes—an upper-70s-to-low-80s sweeper and a mid-80s gyro slider—though he uses the former far more than the latter. Lizarraga's sweeper averaged almost 14 inches of lateral break and is an effective weapon against righthanded hitters. Lizarraga's mid-70s curveball flashes solid depth at times, but it lacks bite. He completes his deep arsenal with a mid-80s changeup on which he does a nice job of killing spin. It flashes both tumble and fade at times, but opposing hitters pulverized it in 2025. Lizarraga is an average strike-thrower who has a particular feel for his fastball and slider.
THE FUTURE: Lizarraga's upside starts and stops at No. 5 starter. Both his pitches and command are average, and while he could make his major league debut as soon as 2026, he projects as a back-of-the-rotation fill-in starter.

Year	Age	Club (League)	Level	W	L	ERA	G	GS	IP	H	HR	BB	SO	BB%	SO%	WHIP	AVG
2025	21	San Antonio (TL)	AA	4	10	6.21	25	23	91	97	10	54	87	12.9	20.8	1.65	.271
2025	21	El Paso (PCL)	AAA	1	0	1.80	2	2	10	8	0	6	5	14.0	11.6	1.40	.229
		Minor League Totals		17	24	4.52	79	76	320	302	25	143	300	10.2	21.3	1.39	.248

Heliot Ramos

San Francisco Giants

BY JOSH NORRIS

For the fourth season in a row, the Giants finished with between 79 and 81 wins.

The biggest roadblocks to contention are the back-to-back World Series-champion Dodgers and the go-for-broke Padres occupying the top spots in the National League West. Another roadblock has been a farm system that has not produced impact regulars.

Now, after an excellent year in the minor leagues, the Giants can see a wave of talent approaching the San Francisco Bay.

The first taste came late in the season when top prospect Bryce Eldridge made his big league debut. The hulking lefty swinger took his lumps, but he's young, powerful and should have plenty of opportunities in 2026 to establish himself.

Eldridge retained the top spot in the system, but one of the organization's youngest talents is hot on his heels. Shortstop Josuar Gonzalez signed with the Giants on Jan. 15 and spent his first pro season lighting the Dominican Summer League on fire. Scouts who saw him during instructional league reported the kind of ceiling rarely seen in an 18-year-old.

But wait, there's more.

The Giants had the top prospect in two short-season leagues. Gonzalez got the nod in the DSL, and breakout hitter Jhonny Level earned the honor in the Arizona Complex League, where he was one of the league's best hitters from beginning to end.

He was part of an ACL convoy of up-arrow talent. The group also included upstart pitchers Keyner Martinez, Argenis Cayama and Luis De La Torre, all of whom matriculated to Low-A San Jose and helped the club win the California League.

Outfielder Bo Davidson also put forth a season that vaulted him from undrafted free agent to top 100 prospect.

San Francisco also introduced a heaping helping of Tennessee twang to their organization. During the summer, they imported outfielder Drew Gilbert and righthander Blade Tidwell in a trade with the Mets and drafted Volunteers infielder Gavin Kilen with their first-round selection.

An even bigger shockwave hit when they hired Tennessee head coach Tony Vitello to replace manager Bob Melvin. Vitello was one of college baseball's premier skippers, and he became the first person in history to become a big league manager without a day as a professional coach. The Giants also added Volunteers pitching coach Frank Anderson—the father of former big leaguer Brett Anderson—to their big league staff.

Adding Gilbert and Tidwell from the Mets for reliever Tyler Rogers was just one of the many moves San Francisco made at the deadline to revitalize their farm system. They added four prospects from the Yankees for Camilo Doval and another from the Royals for Mike Yastrzemski.

None of those moves matched the immediate impact of the one they made in June, when they sent Jordan Hicks, two prospects and a lot of cash to the Red Sox for 28-year-old first baseman Rafael Devers. The deal infused the middle of San Francisco's lineup with a proven slugger to team with Willy Adames and Matt Chapman.

The Giants' road back to the playoffs in recent years has been littered with obstacles. A rejuvenated farm system might help the team clear a path forward. ∎

PROJECTED 2029 LINEUP

Catcher	Patrick Bailey	28
First Base	Bryce Eldridge	24
Second Base	Willy Adames	33
Third Base	Matt Chapman	36
Shortstop	Josuar Gonzalez	21
Left Field	Drew Gilbert	28
Center Field	Jung-Hoo Lee	30
Right Field	Heliot Ramos	30
Designated Hitter	Rafael Devers	32
No. 1 Starter	Logan Webb	33
No. 2 Starter	Landen Roupp	30
No. 3 Starter	Jacob Bresnahan	24
No. 4 Starter	Keyner Martinez	24
No. 5 Starter	Carson Whisenhunt	28
Closer	Randy Rodriguez	29

DEPTH CHART

SAN FRANCISCO GIANTS

TOP 2026 ROOKIES	RANK
1. Carson Whisenhunt, LHP	10
2. Trevor McDonald, RHP	14
3. Trent Harris, RHP	20

BREAKOUT PROSPECTS	RANK
1. Carlos Gutierrez, OF	13
2. Luis De La Torre, LHP	17

SOURCE OF TOP 30 TALENT

Homegrown	24	Acquired	6
College	8	Trade	6
Junior college	1	Rule 5 draft	0
High school	3	Independent league	0
Undrafted free agent	2	Free agent/waivers	0
International	10		

LF
Wade Meckler
Scott Bandura
Damian Bravo

CF
Bo Davidson (3)
Dakota Jordan (7)
Trevor Cohen (9)
Carlos Gutierrez (13)
Cam Maldonado (22)
Jonah Cox
Andy Polanco
Djean Macares

RF
Jose Ortiz

3B
Ramon Peralta
Robert Hipwell
Zander Darby

SS
Josuar Gonzalez (2)
Jhonny Level (4)
Lorenzo Meola (20)
Yulian Barreto (29)
Maui Ahuna
Walker Martin

2B
Gavin Kilen (8)
Diego Velasquez (23)
Nate Furman
Dario Reynoso

1B
Bryce Eldridge (1)
Parks Harber (15)

C
Daniel Susac (16)
Jesus Rodriguez (18)
Adrian Sugastey
Daniel Rogers
Luke Shliger

LHP

LHSP	LHRP
Jacob Bresnahan (5)	Luis De La Torre (17)
Carson Whisenhunt (10)	Jack Choate
Joe Whitman (24)	Reggie Crawford
Carlos De La Rosa (25)	Greg Farone
Jordan Gottesman	

RHP

RHSP	RHRP
Keyner Martinez (6)	Trent Harris (21)
Argenis Cayama (11)	Yunior Marte (28)
Blade Tidwell (12)	Gerelmi Maldonado (30)
Trevor McDonald (14)	Drake George
Josh Bostick (19)	Hunter Dryden
Alberto Laroche (26)	Niko Mazza
Reid Worley (27)	Jose T. Perez
Luke Mensik	

SAN FRANCISCO GIANTS

1 BRYCE ELDRIDGE, 1B

Born: October 20, 2004. **B-T:** L-R. **HT:** 6-7. **WT:** 240.
Drafted: HS—Vienna, VA, 2023 (1st round).
Signed by: John DiCarlo.

TRACK RECORD: When he was a two-way player in high school, Eldridge's future appeared to be on the mound. Given that he stands 6-foot-7 and threw 96 mph, that seemed reasonable. Then he started crushing baseballs, and his path to the big leagues shifted to the batter's box. He swatted eight home runs for USA Baseball's 18U National Team, and the Giants drafted him in the first round in 2023. He signed for $3,997,500. In his first full season, Eldridge was electric. The first baseman rocketed from Low-A to Triple-A, hitting 23 home runs along the way. His 2025 season was delayed by a left wrist injury, but he recovered enough to hit 25 home runs between Double-A and Triple-A. He made his big league debut on Sept. 15 and notched a three-run double off Tyler Glasnow for his first MLB hit. Eldridge had surgery in October to remove a bone spur from his left wrist. He's expected to be ready for spring training.

SCOUTING REPORT: Eldridge's calling card is his power, which showed up in spades in the minor leagues. His 90th percentile exit velocity of 107.7 mph was fourth-highest in the system among players with 300 or more plate appearances. He's an equal-opportunity slugger, too, with true pole-to-pole power against a variety of pitch types. Clearly, Eldridge's thump will drive his profile. Now, the question is: How complete of a hitter will he be? His strikeout-to-walk ratio was roughly 3-to-1 in the minor leagues, and he punched out 13 times in 37 big league plate appearances. His overall miss rate of 33.7% was a bit higher than is ideal, and his in-zone (22.5%) and chase (27.3%) rates were a touch on the high side as well. Though he didn't show much of a platoon split, Eldridge had a weakness against left-on-left spin. He had a miss rate of 46% against same-side sliders, not including a 73% mark against sweepers from southpaws. Eldridge's youth—he played the entire season as a 20-year-old—leads evaluators to believe he'll close those holes as he matures and gets more experience against the wiliest of pitchers. Eldridge's explosive bat speed and relatively short swing for someone his size also point to a hitter who should get better as he ages, though he will likely always be a power-over-hit player. Defensively, he still needs plenty of work and might never be better than fringy at first base. Specifically,

BA GRADE
60 Risk: Mild
Adjusted grade: **55**

SCOUTING GRADES
Hit: 40. Power: 70. Run: 30.
Fielding: 40. Arm: 55.
Projected future grades on 20-80 scouting scale

BEST TOOLS

BATTING
Best Hitter for Average — Carlos Gutierrez
Best Power Hitter — Bryce Eldridge
Best Strike-Zone Discipline — Nate Furman
Fastest Baserunner — Josuar Gonzalez
Best Athlete — Dakota Jordan

PITCHING
Best Fastball — Keyner Martinez
Best Curveball — Trent Harris
Best Slider — Keyner Martinez
Best Changeup — Carson Whisenhunt
Best Control — Alberto Laroche

FIELDING
Best Defensive Catcher — Adrian Sugastey
Best Defensive Infielder — Josuar Gonzalez
Best Infield Arm — Jhonny Level
Best Defensive Outfielder — Jonah Cox
Best Outfield Arm — Jose Ortiz

he has an above-average arm, but his accuracy can be spotty. He's not the rangiest defender at the position, either. Eldridge is a well below-average runner.

THE FUTURE: Eldridge will have a chance to win the first base job out of camp, but with Rafael Devers in tow for the foreseeable future, there's no guarantee that Eldridge will make the Opening Day roster. Given that he'll be 21 years old for the entire 2026 season and that he's played the equivalent of less than two full seasons in the minor leagues, there's plenty of time for more seasoning. When he's ready, he has the skills to be a cornerstone player.

Year	Age	Club (League)	Level	AVG	G	AB	R	H	2B	3B	HR	RBI	BB	SO	SB	OBP	SLG
2025	20	ACL Giants	Rk	.333	2	6	1	2	0	0	0	1	1	0	0	.429	.333
2025	20	Richmond (EL)	AA	.280	34	125	14	35	8	0	7	20	13	39	0	.350	.512
2025	20	Sacramento (PCL)	AAA	.249	66	253	31	63	13	0	18	63	28	88	1	.322	.514
2025	20	San Francisco (NL)	MLB	.107	10	28	1	3	2	0	0	4	7	13	0	.297	.179
		Minor League Totals		.279	249	939	137	262	53	2	54	194	121	293	8	.360	.512
		Major League Totals		.107	10	28	1	3	2	0	0	4	7	13	0	.297	.179

SAN FRANCISCO GIANTS

2 JOSUAR GONZALEZ, SS
HIT: 50. **POW:** 45. **RUN:** 70. **FLD:** 70. **ARM:** 60. **BA Grade:** 65. **Risk:** High. **Adj:** 50.

Born: October 16, 2007. **B-T:** B-R. **HT:** 6-0. **WT:** 167.
Signed: Dominican Republic, 2025. **Signed by:** Jonathan Bautista.
TRACK RECORD: Gonzalez was one of the most talented players available in the 2025 international class, and the Giants inked him for $2,997,500 on Jan. 15. Immediately, he set to work proving that the investment was wise. His combination of offensive and defensive skills made him an easy choice for the top prospect in the Dominican Summer League, and he continued wowing evaluators after he moved stateside for instructional league.
SCOUTING REPORT: Gonzalez's toolset is led by sublime defense, which grades as an easy 70. He can make any play required by a big league shortstop thanks to standout range, strong instincts, fluid actions and an arm that easily grades as plus. Gonzalez's offensive numbers don't jump off the page in the way that other DSL wunderkinds' have in years past, but a look under the hood shows a player with an elite sense of the strike zone and more thump than would be expected from a player his size. The switch-hitting Gonzalez shows more power from the left side and a handsier, more contact-oriented swing from the right. His tools give him a tantalizing base and helped him post one of the best seasons from a 17-year-old in the DSL. He's far from a finished product, however. In the coming years, he'll have to prove that his approach holds up against more advanced arms, and he'll need to add strength to his frame in order to withstand the rigors of a full minor league season.
THE FUTURE: After a strong first pro season, Gonzalez is likely to see time in full-season ball in 2026. Whether he jumps there during or after the Arizona Complex League season remains to be seen, but he should reach Low-A at some point. He has a future as a lockdown shortstop who hits toward the top of the lineup and creates havoc on the bases.

Year	Age	Club (League)	Level	AVG	G	AB	R	H	2B	3B	HR	RBI	BB	SO	SB	OBP	SLG
2025	17	DSL Giants Black	Rk	.288	52	191	52	55	10	5	4	24	37	36	33	.404	.455
		Minor League Totals		.288	52	191	52	55	10	5	4	24	37	36	33	.404	.455

3 BO DAVIDSON, OF
HIT: 45. **POW:** 60. **RUN:** 60. **FLD:** 55. **ARM:** 55. **BA Grade:** 55. **Risk:** Average. **Adj:** 45.

Born: July 5, 2002. **B-T:** L-R. **HT:** 6-2. **WT:** 205.
Signed: Caldwell Tech (NC) JC, 2023 (UDFA). **Signed by:** DJ Jauss/Paul Faulk.
TRACK RECORD: Davidson's ascent into the highest realm of the Giants' system stands as a testament to the power of dogged scouting. The toolsy outfielder played at two North Carolina junior colleges before turning evaluators' heads in the summer Coastal Plain League. After flashes of potential over his first two pro seasons, Davidson broke out with a strong turn at High-A Eugene in 2025 that earned him his first upper-level look and a spot on the Top 100 Prospects.
SCOUTING REPORT: Davidson is as tooled-up as they come in the Giants' system, but there's some polish to his game, too. He's a physical player with gifts on both sides of the ball, including power enough to produce 18 home runs and respective 90th percentile and maximum exit velocities of 105.5 and 112.5 mph. He showed improved pitch recognition at High-A, and his strikeout rate jumped just 2 percentage points after moving to Double-A Richmond. He'll likely settle in as a fringe-average hitter with above-average bat speed and plus power, especially after he vastly improved his flyball rate after he joined the Eastern League. His miss rates were roughly average across the board. Davidson has a chance to stick in center field thanks to speed that gets to plus underway and an above-average arm that would be a weapon if he has to move to a corner. Scouts are split on whether he can stick up the middle, and a great deal of that outcome is dependent on how physical he gets as he continues to mature and add strength. If he moves to left or right field, Davidson should be an above-average defender.
THE FUTURE: Davidson will likely return to Double-A to begin 2026 and should reach Triple-A by season's end. If he keeps adding polish to his tool set, he has a chance to impact the game with his power, speed and defense. If he can stick in center field, his value will be significantly amplified.

Year	Age	Club (League)	Level	AVG	G	AB	R	H	2B	3B	HR	RBI	BB	SO	SB	OBP	SLG
2025	22	Eugene (NWL)	A+	.309	72	282	53	87	14	6	10	56	49	74	12	.412	.507
2025	22	Richmond (EL)	AA	.234	42	167	23	39	2	1	8	14	19	45	7	.312	.401
		Minor League Totals		.294	183	687	127	202	32	15	28	117	109	184	25	.395	.507

SAN FRANCISCO GIANTS

4 JHONNY LEVEL, SS
HIT: 55. **POW:** 55. **RUN:** 45. **FLD:** 55. **ARM:** 60. **BA Grade:** 55. **Risk:** Average. **Adj:** 45.

Born: March 29, 2007. **B-T:** B-R. **HT:** 5-10. **WT:** 154.
Signed: Venezuela, 2024. **Signed by:** Juan Marquez.
TRACK RECORD: After signing for $997,500 in 2024 as one of the centerpieces of the Giants' signing class, Level has been outstanding over his first two pro seasons. He was one of the best prospects in the Dominican Summer League during his debut, then ratcheted his game up a couple of notches in 2025 to rank No. 1 in the Arizona Complex League, where his nine home runs and 108 total bases each ranked second. Level finished the year with 31 games at Low-A San Jose.
SCOUTING REPORT: In his first stateside test, Level proved to be a hitting machine. He torched the competition in the ACL thanks to a well-rounded offensive game that includes hitting ability from both sides of the plate and more power than would be expected from a smaller player. Level's frame gives him a bit of a leg up in the box thanks to shorter arms that provide fewer holes for pitchers to attack. His overall and in-zone miss rates are stellar, and he gets the ball in the air often enough to allow his above-average raw juice to translate into doubles and home runs. Some scouts saw a bit of a hole against velocity up in the strike zone. In the field, Level has the above-average range to both sides, soft hands and plus arm to stick at shortstop. His arm strength can sometimes be muted by a longer throwing stroke. If he sticks at shortstop, he should be an average defender. If he moves to second base, he could be above-average and will have plenty of offensive value to profile at the position.
THE FUTURE: The bulk of the Giants' most prized prospects are clustered at the lowest affiliates, and Level is one of the most talented of the bunch. He and Josuar Gonzalez could form key pieces of the team's core, buttressing a young, talented group that could also feature fellow top prospect Bo Davidson in center field.

Year	Age	Club (League)	Level	AVG	G	AB	R	H	2B	3B	HR	RBI	BB	SO	SB	OBP	SLG
2025	18	ACL Giants	Rk	.288	58	219	50	63	10	4	9	38	33	40	17	.375	.493
2025	18	San Jose (CAL)	A	.236	31	127	30	30	2	1	3	12	17	30	4	.333	.339
		Minor League Totals		.271	137	524	124	142	23	6	22	96	80	106	39	.371	.464

5 JACOB BRESNAHAN, LHP
FB: 60. **SL:** 50. **CH:** 60. **CTL:** 55. **BA Grade:** 55. **Risk:** Average. **Adj:** 45.

Born: June 27, 2005. **B-T:** L-L. **HT:** 6-4. **WT:** 195.
Drafted: HS—Sumner, WA, 2023 (13th round). **Signed by:** Conor Glassey (Guardians).
TRACK RECORD: After a strong senior season at high school in Washington—and status as one of the younger players in the 2023 draft class—Bresnahan intrigued the Guardians enough to draft him in the 13th round and sign him for $375,000. Cleveland dealt Bresnahan to the Giants in 2024 for Alex Cobb. He broke out in 2025 by striking out 124 hitters in 93 innings for Low-A San Jose, a feat that earned him pitcher of the year honors in the California League.
SCOUTING REPORT: Bresnahan's combination of physicality, projection and stuff makes him the top arm in San Francisco's system. The lefty works with three pitches: a low-90s fastball with an average of more than 20 inches of induced vertical break, a low-80s slider and a mid-80s changeup. The fastball is the gem of Bresnahan's arsenal, and its velocity—it peaked at 96 mph—combined with its movement profile makes it an easy plus pitch. His changeup is another dynamite offering, but it's actually two pitches in one. Both versions are kick changeups, but by varying the degree to which he kicks out his finger, Bresnahan can alternate between a pitch he can use for called strikes and another that dives out of the zone and induces silly swings. He rounds out his mix with a sharp-breaking slider that might need to tighten up a little bit but has average potential. He's thrown strikes at a clip of 64% in each of the last two seasons and should have above-average control in the big leagues despite a slight wrist wrap in the back of his delivery. The Giants would like Bresnahan to learn how to pitch backward and not lean on his fastball quite as much as he moves up the ladder.
THE FUTURE: Bresnahan will move to High-A Eugene in 2026 and has a chance to be a midrotation starter if he can bring his slider ahead just a touch.

Year	Age	Club (League)	Level	W	L	ERA	G	GS	IP	H	HR	BB	SO	BB%	SO%	WHIP	AVG
2025	20	San Jose (CAL)	A	9	3	2.61	22	22	93	67	2	43	124	11.3	32.5	1.18	.201
		Minor League Totals		10	7	2.76	37	37	147	108	5	63	193	10.4	32.0	1.16	.203

SAN FRANCISCO GIANTS

KEYNER MARTINEZ, RHP
FB: 60. **SW:** 60. **CH:** 45. **CTL:** 55. **BA Grade:** 55. **Risk:** High. **Adj:** 40.

Born: August 16, 2004. **B-T:** R-R. **HT:** 6-1. **WT:** 165.
Signed: Venezuela, 2023. **Signed by:** Edgar Fernandez/Ciro Villalobos/Joe Salermo.
TRACK RECORD: Martinez signed out of Venezuela as an 18-year-old in July 2023 and didn't make his pro debut until the following year in the Arizona Complex League. In his first turn in the desert, Martinez looked like a pitcher with little more than a live arm. A year later, his stuff ticked up, his arsenal widened and he surged up the system's pitching hierarchy. After a dominant run in the ACL, Martinez finished the year in Low-A, where he helped San Jose claim the California League crown.
SCOUTING REPORT: At the very least, Martinez will likely be able to bully hitters with his fastball and slider. The former sits in the mid 90s and peaked at 98 with solid carrying life. He pounded the zone with the pitch, collecting strikes at a 70% clip and misses at a rate of 25.5%. Martinez backs it with a sweeping slider that went through a dramatic transformation from the version he used in 2024. The Giants suggested a grip switch during a bullpen session, and Martinez took to the change immediately. Now, the breaking ball is an out pitch and an easy plus offering. He introduced his changeup in the middle of the 2025 season and scouts universally said that he showed improved feel for the pitch as the year went along. The righthander's strike-throwing dipped a bit after moving to Low-A, so he'll have to work a bit to improve his control against more advanced hitters. Martinez's physicality should help him hold up to a starter's workload, though some scouts believe an upright finish and a lack of extension in his delivery could lead him to the bullpen.
THE FUTURE: Martinez should return to Low-A in 2026. If he can hold up to a longer workload and bring his changeup forward a couple of ticks, he has a ceiling of a midrotation starter.

Year	Age	Club (League)	Level	W	L	ERA	G	GS	IP	H	HR	BB	SO	BB%	SO%	WHIP	AVG
2025	20	ACL Giants	Rk	3	1	1.90	15	8	47	42	1	10	67	5.3	35.6	1.10	.240
2025	20	San Jose (CAL)	A	2	1	2.86	6	3	22	21	2	11	30	11.5	31.3	1.45	.250
		Minor League Totals		6	3	2.47	40	11	102	90	5	37	120	8.7	28.2	1.25	.238

DAKOTA JORDAN, OF
HIT: 40. **POW:** 60. **RUN:** 55. **FLD:** 50. **ARM:** 55. **BA Grade:** 55. **Risk:** Average. **Adj:** 45.

Born: May 9, 2003. **B-T:** R-R. **HT:** 6-0. **WT:** 220.
Drafted: Mississippi State, 2024 (4th round). **Signed by:** Jeff Wood.
TRACK RECORD: The signings of free agents Blake Snell and Matt Chapman cost the Giants their second- and third-round picks in 2024. After selecting James Tibbs III in the first round, they took Jordan—a Mississippi State product with Southeastern Conference pedigree and plenty of upside—in the fourth round. In his first full year in 2025, Jordan showed impact potential—and plenty of warts—while helping Low-A San Jose win the California League championship. He missed the last few weeks of the season with a strained oblique.
SCOUTING REPORT: Despite a hyperaggressive approach that saw him swing more than half the time, Jordan makes a decent amount of contact and struck out at a clip of just 22.6% in a full season at Low-A. When lumber meets leather, the results are usually loud. His 90th percentile exit velocity of 108.4 mph was the highest in the Giants' system, and he racked up 35 extra-base hits in 88 games. Jordan is unlikely to ever be more than a below-average pure hitter, but his brute strength and improved approach and mechanics should allow him to get to a great deal of his raw juice. Defensively, Jordan has a chance to stick in center field, but he'll have to work to make that outcome a reality. His above-average speed allows him to get most flies hit his way, and his experience as a wide receiver and defensive back in high school gives him plenty of experience when it comes to tracking balls in flight. His above-average arm strength would be an asset in right or left field if he had to move to a corner.
THE FUTURE: After a shortened but standout season in Low-A, Jordan's next stop is High-A Eugene. If he can make incremental improvements to his approach without sacrificing his impact potential, he has a chance to be a slugger who hits in the lower third of a lineup.

Year	Age	Club (League)	Level	AVG	G	AB	R	H	2B	3B	HR	RBI	BB	SO	SB	OBP	SLG
2025	22	San Jose (CAL)	A	.311	88	370	71	115	15	6	14	82	37	95	27	.377	.497
		Minor League Totals		.305	90	377	72	115	15	6	14	83	37	97	28	.371	.488

SAN FRANCISCO GIANTS

8. GAVIN KILEN, SS

HIT: 55. POW: 45. RUN: 45. FLD: 50. ARM: 45. BA Grade: 50. Risk: Average. Adj: 40.

Born: March 28, 2004. **B-T:** L-R. **HT:** 5-11. **WT:** 187.
Drafted: Tennessee, 2025 (1st round). **Signed by:** Nick Long.
TRACK RECORD: Kilen was drafted by the Red Sox in the 13th round in 2022 but opted to head to school at Louisville. He stayed there for two seasons before transferring to Tennessee for his draft season in 2025. After a successful year with the Volunteers, Kilen was drafted by the Giants at No. 13 overall and signed for $5,247,500. He played 10 games with Low-A San Jose before a hip bruise landed him on the shelf for the remainder of the year. After the season, San Francisco hired Tennessee head coach Tony Vitello to replace Bob Melvin as manager. Giants draft pick Maui Ahuna and trade acquisitions Drew Gilbert and Blade Tidwell also are former Vols.
SCOUTING REPORT: Kilen's scouting report is littered with solid but not spectacular tools, and he makes his money by putting the bat on the ball with regularity. The lefty swinger rarely missed a pitch in the zone in college, and the same held true during his small professional sample. His chase rate with San Jose was higher than he'd shown during his amateur career. After hitting just nine home runs over two seasons with Louisville—including zero in 46 games as a freshman—Kilen slammed 15 in his lone year in Knoxville thanks to improvements in his approach and swing decisions. Scouts believe he'll likely settle in with fringe-average power as a pro. Kilen is a solid defender at shortstop but limited range and fringy arm strength might push him to second base as he moves up the ladder. That's especially true if he ever shares a roster with a sublime gloveman like Josuar Gonzalez at some point in his career.
THE FUTURE: After an offseason to heal from hamstring and hip injuries, Kilen will look to begin his first full season with a clean bill of health. He has a chance to be an offensive-minded second baseman with contact and on-base skills. His college pedigree could lead to a jump to High-A Eugene.

Year	Age	Club (League)	Level	AVG	G	AB	R	H	2B	3B	HR	RBI	BB	SO	SB	OBP	SLG
2025	21	San Jose (CAL)	A	.205	10	39	5	8	1	1	0	5	3	5	0	.279	.282
		Minor League Totals		.205	10	39	5	8	1	1	0	5	3	5	0	.279	.282

9. TREVOR COHEN, OF

HIT: 55. POW: 40. RUN: 55. FLD: 55. ARM: 60. BA Grade: 55. Risk: High. Adj: 40.

Born: October 29, 2003. **B-T:** L-L. **HT:** 6-1. **WT:** 195.
Drafted: Rutgers, 2025 (3rd round). **Signed by:** Carmen Carcone.
TRACK RECORD: After the Giants surrendered their 2025 second-round pick for signing free agent Willy Adames, they spent their third-round pick on Cohen, an outfielder from Rutgers with a variety of gifts on both sides of the ball. In his draft year with the Scarlet Knights, Cohen hit .387/.460/.523 with 24 doubles, two home runs, 19 stolen bases and just 15 strikeouts in 273 plate appearances. He finished his college career with more walks (80) than strikeouts (62) and did the same over 28 games with Low-A San Jose.
SCOUTING REPORT: With their first two picks in the 2025 draft, the Giants emphasized contact in a major way with first-round pick Gavin Kilen and Cohen, who rarely missed in college or as a pro. In fact, Cohen's zone-miss rate with San Jose was 9.2%. He hits the ball plenty hard but needs to get the ball off the ground to make the most of his tools. If he can do that, he projects for 40-grade power. Cohen filled the void created in center field in San Jose when Dakota Jordan hit the injured list. He manned the position ably, and evaluators believe he has the speed and instincts to stick there. In his pro sample, he showed above-average speed and excellent jumps. He has the chops to man all three outfield spots thanks to plus arm strength, but he'd need to tap into every bit of his power potential in order to profile in either corner. Cohen is an above-average runner with outstanding instincts that allowed him to swipe 39 bases in 45 chances in college and eight more in 10 tries as a pro.
THE FUTURE: Cohen's time at Rutgers should give him the pedigree to matriculate to High-A Eugene, where he'll likely split center field with Dakota Jordan in 2026. His bat-to-ball skills and defense give him a solid floor, but an increase in the power department could help him break out.

Year	Age	Club (League)	Level	AVG	G	AB	R	H	2B	3B	HR	RBI	BB	SO	SB	OBP	SLG
2025	21	San Jose (CAL)	A	.327	28	107	23	35	3	1	1	15	20	15	8	.438	.402
		Minor League Totals		.327	28	107	23	35	3	1	1	15	20	15	8	.438	.402

SAN FRANCISCO GIANTS

10 CARSON WHISENHUNT, LHP
FB: 55. CB: 40. SL: 45. CH: 70. CTL: 55. BA Grade: 45. Risk: Mild. Adj: 40.

Born: October 10, 2000. **B-T:** L-L. **HT:** 6-3. **WT:** 214.
Drafted: East Carolina, 2022 (2nd round). **Signed by:** DJ Jauss.
TRACK RECORD: Even after Whisenhunt was suspended for his draft year at East Carolina, the Giants were undeterred and leaned on their history with him and his work in the Cape Cod League before deciding to select him in the second round in 2022. He reached Triple-A Sacramento in 2024 and returned there in 2025. Whisenhunt showed enough improvement to earn his first big league callup and five starts with San Francisco. Whisenhunt also dealt with a minor shoulder impingement during the season.
SCOUTING REPORT: As ever, Whisenhunt's future is dependent on the state of his breaking ball. Currently, he has both a slider and a curveball, though neither is a standout offering. The former pitch is most effective in the 83-86 mph range with gyro shape, while the latter is best deployed as a strike-stealer early in counts. If either of those offerings took a step forward, Whisenhunt's chances to remain in the rotation would jump in kind. His fastball sits around 92 mph and peaks at 95, but the Giants would like to see him hold the pitch in the higher reaches of that velo band deeper into games. The gem of Whisenhunt's arsenal is his changeup, which sits in the low 80s and can be thrown for called strikes or whiffs in equal measure. In the minor leagues, his changeup was a strike more than 70% of the time and garnered miss and chase rates of 35.3% and 43.5%, respectively.
THE FUTURE: With his MLB debut under his belt, Whisenhunt will get a crack at joining San Francisco's rotation on Opening Day. To do so, he'll need to find a consistent, useful breaking ball and maintain his best stuff deeper into outings.

Year	Age	Club (League)	Level	W	L	ERA	G	GS	IP	H	HR	BB	SO	BB%	SO%	WHIP	AVG
2025	24	Sacramento (PCL)	AAA	9	5	4.43	21	21	108	112	13	35	95	7.7	20.9	1.37	.273
2025	24	San Francisco (NL)	MLB	2	1	5.01	5	5	23	22	6	12	16	11.8	15.7	1.46	.250
		Minor League Totals		13	11	4.19	68	67	284	272	30	115	333	9.5	27.4	1.36	.252
		Major League Totals		2	1	5.01	5	5	23	22	6	12	16	11.8	15.7	1.46	.250

11 ARGENIS CAYAMA, RHP
FB: 60. SL: 55. CH: 50. CTL: 55. BA Grade: 55. Risk: High. Adj: 40.

Born: September 15, 2006. **B-T:** R-R. **HT:** 6-1. **WT:** 186. **Signed:** Venezuela, 2024. **Signed by:** Robert Moron.
TRACK RECORD: Cayama signed with the Giants out of Venezuela in 2024 but was limited by a bout of pneumonia to just 24.1 innings in his pro debut. A year later, after moving stateside, he asserted himself as one of the best pitchers in a wave of young talent percolating in the lowest levels of San Francisco's system. He matriculated to Low-A by season's end, but his stuff waned a bit down the stretch.
SCOUTING REPORT: At his best, Cayama can bully hitters with a powerful four-pitch mix led by a mid-90s fastball with strong riding action through the top of the zone and a sinker in the same velocity range. He complements the fastballs with a gyro slider in the low 80s that he can land in the zone or drop at hitters' feet for swings and misses. He ties the array together with a seldom-thrown mid-80s changeup with plenty of velocity separation and fading life. Scouts praised Cayama's ability to command and control his arsenal at such a young age, and he threw strikes with everything but his changeup at clips of better than 60%. Cayama's delivery is clean, athletic and repeatable, and his entire mix could be amplified if he's able to stack strength onto his 6-foot-1 frame. His fastball is a potential plus pitch, while both of his offspeeds should be at least average.
THE FUTURE: Cayama should return to Low-A to begin 2026, with a chance at High-A Eugene by season's end. If he gets stronger, he has the ceiling of a midrotation starter. If not, his already-potent pitch mix could fit as a leverage reliever.

Year	Age	Club (League)	Level	W	L	ERA	G	GS	IP	H	HR	BB	SO	BB%	SO%	WHIP	AVG
2025	18	ACL Giants	Rk	1	1	2.25	12	12	48	33	0	18	55	9.1	27.8	1.06	.191
2025	18	San Jose (CAL)	A	1	0	8.16	6	3	14	24	2	10	7	13.7	9.6	2.37	.387
		Minor League Totals		2	2	3.32	28	25	87	78	2	37	91	9.8	24.1	1.33	.239

SAN FRANCISCO GIANTS

12 BLADE TIDWELL, RHP
FB: 60. **SL:** 55. **CH:** 45. **SW:** 70. **CT:** 40. **CTL:** 50. **BA Grade:** 45. **Risk:** Mild. **Adj:** 40.

Born: June 8, 2001. **B-T:** R-R. **HT:** 6-4. **WT:** 207. **Drafted:** Tennessee, 2022 (2nd round). **Signed by:** Nathan Beuster (Mets).
TRACK RECORD: With Tony Vitello in the dugout and Drew Gilbert in the outfield, the Giants' roster already has a couple of dollops of Tennessee flavor. If Tidwell makes the cut on Opening Day, San Francisco may well reidentify as Knoxville West. The Mets took the righthander in the second round of the 2022 draft, and he made his big league debut on May 4. Two months later, he was traded to San Francisco as part of the deal that brought Tyler Rogers to Queens.
SCOUTING REPORT: When he was with the Mets, Tidwell's arsenal was led by a mid-90s four-seam fastball and backed up by a mix of sliders, sinkers and sweepers. After moving to the Giants, his usage pattern shifted. The Giants used Tidwell's first months in their organization to take stock of his mix, and with Triple-A Sacramento he became a slider monster of the highest order. In the Pacific Coast League, Tidwell's sweeper and slider were his most-used pitches, with his trio of fastballs coming next and his changeup sprinkled in as well. The sweeper is the gem of his arsenal, grading as a potential double-plus pitch and one of the best of its type in the minor leagues. His four-seamer has plenty of cut-ride action and plays best on the top rail of the strike zone, while his sinker provides a sharp contrast at roughly the same velocity, giving hitters one less way to decipher one from the other. Tidwell has a physical frame, a short action in the back of his arm swing and threw strikes at a 62% clip in the minor leagues before struggling a bit in his big league look.
THE FUTURE: Tidwell's frame and stuff give him a chance to eat innings at the back of a rotation if he can sharpen up his command just a touch. If not, he has the power arsenal to work multiple innings at the end of games. He should see plenty of big league time in 2026.

Year	Age	Club (League)	Level	W	L	ERA	G	GS	IP	H	HR	BB	SO	BB%	SO%	WHIP	AVG
2025	24	Sacramento (PCL)	AAA	0	0	1.50	4	3	18	9	0	5	24	7.4	35.3	0.78	.145
2025	24	Syracuse (IL)	AAA	6	4	4.10	17	14	79	70	8	32	87	9.5	25.7	1.29	.233
2025	24	New York (NL)	MLB	1	1	9.00	4	2	15	23	4	10	10	12.8	12.8	2.20	.348
		Minor League Totals		20	24	4.00	77	69	345	279	40	171	396	11.6	27.0	1.31	.220
		Major League Totals		1	1	9.00	4	2	15	23	4	10	10	12.8	12.8	2.20	.348

13 CARLOS GUTIERREZ, OF
HIT: 60. **POW:** 40. **RUN:** 55. **FLD:** 55. **ARM:** 50. **BA Grade:** 50. **Risk:** High. **Adj:** 35.

Born: August 22, 2004. **B-T:** L-R. **HT:** 5-10. **WT:** 174. **Signed:** Mexico, 2023. **Signed by:** Mark O'Sullivan.
TRACK RECORD: Nobody knew it yet, but two future Giants prospects were in opposing dugouts when the United States squared off against Mexico at the 2022 U-18 World Cup. The U.S. had Bryce Eldridge in their lineup and on the mound, and Mexico had Gutierrez, who went 12-for-29 in the tournament. He signed with San Francisco the following January and has quietly been one of the organization's best bat-to-ball artists ever since. In 60 games at Low-A San Jose, Gutierrez hit .351/.445/.452 before a lower back injury ended his season.
SCOUTING REPORT: The lefthanded-hitting Gutierrez rarely swung and missed, didn't chase and produced fair enough exit velocities to project fringy power at the highest level. His hit tool is based around supreme bat control that allows him to manipulate the barrel to all sectors of the strike zone while rarely offering at pitches outside of it. Just three of his hits were on pitches that would likely have been called balls. He hit .410 on fastballs, according to data measured by Synergy Sports, and backed that up with a .284 mark on all offspeeds. Gutierrez is an above-average runner who can hack it in center field but might defer to a stronger defender at the position. His average arm would fit best in left field, but a move to the corner without the corresponding power jump might leave him as a bit of a profile issue.
THE FUTURE: For now, Gutierrez needs to stay healthy. His entire pro career spans just 85 games, including just 25 over two seasons in the complexes. He'll likely split his 2026 campaign between the Class A levels and has the look of a pest atop a lineup who can make contact and steal bags.

Year	Age	Club (League)	Level	AVG	G	AB	R	H	2B	3B	HR	RBI	BB	SO	SB	OBP	SLG
2025	20	San Jose (CAL)	A	.351	60	248	60	87	11	4	2	30	37	40	26	.445	.452
		Minor League Totals		.352	85	338	79	119	15	6	3	40	49	47	38	.443	.459

14 TREVOR McDONALD, RHP

FB: 60. **CB:** 50. **CH:** 45. **SW:** 60. **CTL:** 50. **BA Grade:** 40. **Risk:** Mild. **Adj:** 35.

Born: February 26, 2001. **B-T:** R-R. **HT:** 6-2. **WT:** 201. **Drafted:** HS—Lucedale, MS, 2019 (11th round).
Signed by: Jeff Wood.

TRACK RECORD: The Giants drafted McDonald in the 11th round in 2019 and used an $800,000 bonus to keep him from landing at South Alabama. The pandemic and injuries threw roadblocks in McDonald's path to the big leagues, but he was added to the 40-man roster after the 2023 season and made his MLB debut on the final day of the 2024 season. He made three more appearances—two starts—with San Francisco in 2025.

SCOUTING REPORT: McDonald works primarily with two pitches—a low-90s sinker and a low-80s sweeper—but he'll mix in a few other offerings as well. The sinker is a particularly nasty offering, showing hard zip away from lefthanders. He commands it well enough to use as an effective option to back-door to righties as well. McDonald re-introduced a four-seam fastball, which sat in the low 90s but had a dead-zone profile. The best of the rest of his mix was an inconsistent mid-80s changeup that at its peak showed fade and drop and was most effective as a way to draw chases from lefthanders. McDonald is a physical righthander with a strong lower half who uses a delivery with a moderately short action in the back, abbreviated extension and a lower release height.

THE FUTURE: McDonald will have a chance to crack San Francisco's pitching staff on Opening Day. If he does, he has a shot as either a fifth starter or a bulk reliever. His future would be amplified if he can bring his changeup forward a touch.

Year	Age	Club (League)	Level	W	L	ERA	G	GS	IP	H	HR	BB	SO	BB%	SO%	WHIP	AVG
2025	24	Sacramento (PCL)	AAA	9	9	5.31	29	24	142	144	22	62	144	9.9	22.9	1.45	.264
2025	24	San Francisco (NL)	MLB	1	0	1.80	3	2	15	13	1	2	14	3.3	23.3	1.00	.228
		Minor League Totals		23	25	3.83	114	84	451	418	39	181	472	9.3	24.2	1.33	.247
		Major League Totals		1	0	1.50	4	2	18	13	1	3	15	4.3	21.4	0.89	.197

15 PARKS HARBER, 3B/OF/1B

HIT: 50. **POW:** 55. **RUN:** 40. **FLD:** 40. **ARM:** 50. **BA Grade:** 45. **Risk:** Average. **Adj:** 35.

Born: September 25, 2001. **B-T:** R-R. **HT:** 6-3. **WT:** 225. **Signed:** North Carolina, 2024 (UDFA).
Signed by: Stewart Smothers (Yankees).

TRACK RECORD: After three seasons at Georgia and one summer with the Cape Cod League, Harber transferred to North Carolina for his final college go-round. With the Tar Heels, Harber produced a 1.073 OPS. He signed with the Yankees as an undrafted free agent and hit his way onto the radar before being included in the package that brought Camilo Doval to New York. He produced at every stop in the minor leagues, then posted a stellar season in the Arizona Fall League.

SCOUTING REPORT: First and foremost, Harber is a hitter. He hits the ball hard and often, producing a 90th percentile exit velocity of 107.9 mph. The figure placed him third in the organization, behind just Dakota Jordan and Marco Luciano. His next test will come in Double-A, where he'll face savvier pitchers than he encountered at the lower levels. There's no questioning Harber's impact. Now, he'll have to learn how to pull velocity. All of his pull-side home runs in 2025 came on hanging breaking balls. All of his home runs against fastballs went to center field or the opposite way. Although he's gotten his body in better shape over the course of the season, virtually all of his value is likely to come from the batter's box. He grades well analytically at third base, but evaluators generally believe first base is his future home.

THE FUTURE: If Harber can produce at Double-A at a level anywhere near what he did at the Class A stops, his prospect stock will gain serious helium. It'll be a bonus if he can stick at third base or hack it in the outfield.

Year	Age	Club (League)	Level	AVG	G	AB	R	H	2B	3B	HR	RBI	BB	SO	SB	OBP	SLG
2025	23	Tampa (FSL)	A	.304	20	69	12	21	4	2	3	13	12	22	4	.422	.551
2025	23	Eugene (NWL)	A+	.333	25	87	20	29	6	0	7	24	16	22	0	.454	.644
2025	23	Hudson Valley (SAL)	A+	.326	34	135	20	44	11	1	3	27	16	35	2	.395	.489
		Minor League Totals		.312	102	369	71	115	28	5	14	83	59	103	10	.413	.528

SAN FRANCISCO GIANTS

16 DANIEL SUSAC, C
HIT: 45. **POW:** 50. **RUN:** 40. **FLD:** 50. **ARM:** 55. **BA Grade:** 45. **Risk:** Average. **Adj:** 35.

Born: May 14, 2001. **B-T:** R-R. **HT:** 6-4. **WT:** 219. **Drafted:** Arizona, 2022 (1st round). **Signed by:** Jeff Urlaub (Athletics).
TRACK RECORD: The Athletics drafted Susac 19th overall in 2022 out of Arizona, where he won Pac-12 freshman of the year in 2021. He spent all of 2025 with Triple-A Las Vegas, slashing .275/.349/.483 with 18 homers, the second-most in the system, over 97 games while missing time with an oblique injury. His brother Andrew spent parts of six seasons in the big leagues as a catcher. Daniel was selected by the Twins in the 2025 Rule 5 draft then quickly traded to San Francisco.
SCOUTING REPORT: Susac's professional career has been a vexing combination of steady surface-level production and inconsistent approach. At times, he shows evaluators the ingredients of an everyday catcher: strong hand-eye coordination and bat-to-ball skills, solid-average raw power and some slight improvements to tap into his pull-side power. But there are other times where his approach breaks down and his aggressiveness, especially chasing below the zone, becomes untenable. Defensively, Susac's 6-foot-4 frame presents both advantages and challenges. His catch-and-throw skills stand out thanks to his arm strength, and he actually has decent mobility for his size. Still, he's sometimes forced to throw from his knees, where his accuracy suffers. His game-calling is still hit-or-miss.
THE FUTURE: Susac's patience and defense have yet to take a meaningful step forward in pro ball, which limits his ceiling to a likely second-division or backup catcher.

Year	Age	Club (League)	Level	AVG	G	AB	R	H	2B	3B	HR	RBI	BB	SO	SB	OBP	SLG
2025	24	Las Vegas (PCL)	AAA	.275	97	360	48	99	19	1	18	68	35	109	7	.349	.483
		Minor League Totals		.280	324	1223	151	343	65	9	39	195	99	332	23	.341	.444

17 LUIS DE LA TORRE, LHP
FB: 60. **CB:** 40. **SL:** 55. **CH:** 40. **CTL:** 45. **BA Grade:** 45. **Risk:** Average. **Adj:** 35.

Born: September 6, 2003. **B-T:** L-L. **HT:** 6-0. **WT:** 188. **Signed:** Dominican Republic, 2023. **Signed by:** Joe Salermo.
TRACK RECORD: De La Torre was born in Phoenix and spent most of his childhood and adolescent years in the United States before moving to the Dominican Republic. The Giants signed him as a 19-year-old in 2023 for $10,000 and then sent him to the Dominican Summer League for his pro debut for the first two seasons of his career. He moved stateside in 2025 and was yet another prospect in the Giants' impressive cachet of lower-level talent.
SCOUTING REPORT: When he tried out for the Giants, De La Torre's fastball fluctuated around 82-85 mph. The team liked the way he commanded the pitch, however, and signed him with the idea that there was much more in the tank. They were right. Now, his heater sits in the mid 90s and reaches 98. He backs it with a slider in the mid 80s that shows two-plane break and gets whiffs against righties and lefties alike. Those two pitches make up the bulk of his mix, but he'll also flip in the occasional low-90s changeup or low-80s curveball. Both pitches work as strike-stealers or bridge pitches between the two gems of his arsenal. De La Torre's frame is strong and his delivery is loose and easy, but his command might only be fringe-average and most of his best stuff plays to his glove side.
THE FUTURE: De La Torre's two excellent pitches give him a floor of a lefty-neutralizing force. If one of his other two pitches takes a step forward, he might fit in the back of the rotation. He'll likely split his 2026 season between the Class A levels.

Year	Age	Club (League)	Level	W	L	ERA	G	GS	IP	H	HR	BB	SO	BB%	SO%	WHIP	AVG
2025	21	ACL Giants	Rk	2	1	3.72	10	7	39	28	2	16	62	9.9	38.3	1.14	.200
2025	21	San Jose (CAL)	A	2	2	1.77	8	8	36	22	0	11	47	7.9	33.6	0.93	.173
		Minor League Totals		10	3	3.22	37	16	112	78	2	45	160	9.7	34.4	1.10	.195

18 JESUS RODRIGUEZ, C
HIT: 50. **POW:** 40. **RUN:** 30. **FLD:** 40. **ARM:** 60. **BA Grade:** 40. **Risk:** Mild. **Adj:** 35.

Born: April 23, 2002. **B-T:** R-R. **HT:** 5-10. **WT:** 208. **Signed:** Venezuela, 2018. **Signed by:** Roney Calderon (Yankees).
TRACK RECORD: After signing out of Venezuela in 2018, Rodriguez moved methodically through the minor leagues before hitting his stride in High-A in 2024. He was added to the Yankees' 40-man roster after the season, then rewarded New York's faith by becoming one of the best hitters at Triple-A Scranton/Wilkes-Barre. He was part of the four-player package San Francisco acquired in the deal that sent reliever Camilo Doval to the Bronx. He played in the Venezuelan Winter League after the season.
SCOUTING REPORT: Rodriguez can make plenty of contact and a fair amount of impact, but his offensive strengths would play up if he could do a better job attacking pitches in the strike zone. The righthanded hitter produced nearly equally against both righties and lefties, which will give him a clearer path to the

SAN FRANCISCO GIANTS

big leagues. A few more roadblocks could be removed if he can sharpen his defensive skills. Rodriguez is already an excellent framer, and he has a strong enough arm and a quick enough transfer to erase 33% of attempted basestealers in 2025. To complete the package, he'll need to do a much better job blocking and receiving. He has a tendency to get lackadaisical behind the plate, and nine of his 11 passed balls in 2025 came on pitches that did not hit the dirt. One was on a pitch that was called a strike. Rodriguez is a below-average runner.

THE FUTURE: Rodriguez has very attractive elements to his game—bat-to-ball skills and a strong arm—but he also has plenty of flaws he'll need to overcome. In particular, he needs to become better at receiving and blocking. If he can, he can be an offensive-minded backup behind Patrick Bailey.

Year	Age	Club (League)	Level	AVG	G	AB	R	H	2B	3B	HR	RBI	BB	SO	SB	OBP	SLG
2025	23	Somerset (EL)	AA	.107	7	28	1	3	0	0	0	2	2	6	1	.167	.107
2025	23	Sacramento (PCL)	AAA	.322	39	152	21	49	6	0	2	16	18	17	4	.399	.401
2025	23	Scranton/WB (IL)	AAA	.317	78	309	54	98	14	3	5	41	46	55	16	.409	.430
		Minor League Totals		.309	406	1493	261	462	84	17	32	226	202	245	70	.395	.453

19 JOSH BOSTICK, RHP

FB: 60. **CB:** 40. **SW:** 50. **CH:** 55. **CTL:** 55. **BA Grade:** 45. **Risk:** Average. **Adj:** 35.

Born: October 20, 2001. **B-T:** R-R. **HT:** 6-4. **WT:** 205. **Drafted:** Grayson (TX) JC, 2023 (8th round).
Signed by: Seth Simmons.
TRACK RECORD: Bostick's collegiate journey took him to three schools, finally stopping at Grayson JC in Texas in 2023. He was a two-way player as an amateur, and the Giants drafted him as a pitcher in the eighth round and signed him for $397,500. He spent all of 2024 in Low-A and all of 2025 at High-A.
SCOUTING REPORT: Bostick's mix and usage patterns went through a refinement period in 2025. Toward the second half of the year he got more comfortable relying on pitches other than his fastball, which has the kind of shape the Giants like their arms to utilize up in the zone. He complemented the heater with a sweeper against righties and a deep-breaking curveball against lefthanders. He rounds out the mix with a split-change that plays against hitters on both sides of the plate. There's a chance the mix winnows in 2026, with the curveball possibly being deemphasized in favor of the changeup as the primary weapon against lefties. Scouts also noticed that Bostick will sometimes slow his arm on his offspeed pitches, which will need to be corrected as he faces savvier hitters.
THE FUTURE: Bostick will face his biggest test yet in 2026, when he heads to Double-A Richmond as part of the team's inaugural season at CarMax Park. If he can get his changeup to its full potential, he could be a back-end starter or bulk reliever.

Year	Age	Club (League)	Level	W	L	ERA	G	GS	IP	H	HR	BB	SO	BB%	SO%	WHIP	AVG
2025	23	Eugene (NWL)	A+	9	6	3.71	24	23	119	97	21	39	139	7.9	28.2	1.14	.218
		Minor League Totals		11	15	4.21	54	48	231	201	32	85	267	8.7	27.3	1.24	.233

20 LORENZO MEOLA, SS

HIT: 45. **POW:** 40. **RUN:** 55. **FLD:** 60. **ARM:** 55. **BA Grade:** 45. **Risk:** Average. **Adj:** 35.

Born: December 17, 2003. **B-T:** R-R. **HT:** 5-11. **WT:** 172. **Drafted:** Stetson, 2025 (4th round). **Signed by:** Jim Gabella.
TRACK RECORD: After three seasons at Stetson and three stints in summer ball—including a stop in the Cape Cod League—Meola was selected by San Francisco in the fourth round in 2025. He signed for $652,000 and got his pro career running with 16 games for California League-champion San Jose.
SCOUTING REPORT: Meola is a glove-first shortstop who might rate as the best at the position in the system were it not for Josuar Gonzalez. He has soft hands, sound footwork and the above-average arm strength necessary to man the position in the long term, though he often deferred to Jhonny Level at San Jose. Meola's defensive skills allowed him to start immediately at Stetson, and gave him the baseline athleticism that set the stage for gains in the coming years. He swatted a career-best 11 home runs in his junior year with the Hatters, then added three more in pro ball. In his pro debut, Meola found the barrel often and hit the ball hard, but he also showed more zone-miss and chase than would be considered ideal. He's an above-average runner as well, though he was not asked to steal bases often in college.
THE FUTURE: Meola has a chance to be a defensive-minded shortstop with a fair amount of power in his bat. Because Level and Gonzalez are likely to begin the year at Low-A and the Arizona Complex League, an assignment to High-A Eugene might be the best way to get Meola a steady shortstop workload.

Year	Age	Club (League)	Level	AVG	G	AB	R	H	2B	3B	HR	RBI	BB	SO	SB	OBP	SLG
2025	21	San Jose (CAL)	A	.273	16	66	7	18	4	0	3	7	4	17	3	.314	.470
		Minor League Totals		.273	16	66	7	18	4	0	3	7	4	17	3	.314	.470

SAN FRANCISCO GIANTS

21 TRENT HARRIS, RHP
FB: 55. **CB:** 55. **SW:** 50. **CH:** 45. **CTL:** 50. **BA Grade:** 40. **Risk:** Mild. **Adj:** 35.

Born: January 22, 1999. **B-T:** R-R. **HT:** 6-2. **WT:** 200. **Signed:** UNC Pembroke, 2023 (UDFA). **Signed by:** Paul Faulk.
TRACK RECORD: Harris was a two-way player at both High Point University and UNC Pembroke. He spent two seasons with Wilson in the Coastal Plain League, where he was teammates with fellow future Giants farmhand Shane Rademacher. He won the CPL's pitcher of the year award in 2023 and then signed with San Francisco as an undrafted free agent. The righthander reached Triple-A in 2025 and made an appearance in the Futures Game.
SCOUTING REPORT: Harris works with a four-pitch mix led by a cut-ride fastball in the mid 90s and backed by a sweeper, curveball and split-change. All four pitches are amplified by a delivery with roughly 6.7 feet of extension. In concert, Harris' mix gives him options against righties and lefties and in all four quadrants of the strike zone. All of his offerings have swing-and-miss potential. Now, he needs to throw more of them for called strikes. He landed his sweeper in the zone 56% of the time, but none of his other offerings got to that threshold. The Giants would also like to see Harris learn how to better execute game plans in an effort to prepare him for what he'll need to do to be successful in the big leagues.
THE FUTURE: Harris will likely return to Triple-A for Opening Day but has a chance to reach MLB at some point in 2026. He has a future as a middle reliever who can be effective against righties and lefties.

Year	Age	Club (League)	Level	W	L	ERA	G	GS	IP	H	HR	BB	SO	BB%	SO%	WHIP	AVG
2025	26	Richmond (EL)	AA	1	1	1.69	13	0	16	11	1	4	25	6.3	39.1	0.94	.183
2025	26	Sacramento (PCL)	AAA	3	1	5.44	30	0	41	43	5	15	40	8.5	22.7	1.40	.269
		Minor League Totals		17	5	2.56	94	0	158	115	12	47	203	7.5	32.5	1.03	.200

22 CAM MALDONADO, OF
HIT: 45. **POW:** 50. **RUN:** 60. **FLD:** 50. **ARM:** 45. **BA Grade:** 45. **Risk:** Average. **Adj:** 35.

Born: November 8, 2003. **B-T:** R-R. **HT:** 6-3. **WT:** 200. **Drafted:** Northeastern, 2025 (7th round). **Signed by:** Carmen Carcone.
TRACK RECORD: In 2025, the Giants spent back-to-back picks on prospects from Northeastern. In the sixth round, they selected lefty Jordan Gottesman. A round later, they took Maldonado, who had just set career highs for doubles (17), home runs (15) and RBIs (59). The outfielder signed for $287,500 and then made his pro debut with California League-champion San Jose.
SCOUTING REPORT: The well-built Maldonado has the potential to produce the coveted power-speed profile while sticking in center field. He showed hints of those traits in his pro debut, when he made plenty of contact with above-average impact as well. He did an especially good job on pitches in the zone, which he contacted at an 85.1% clip. He also swiped six bags without being caught. His operation is stiffer than most, but he has quick enough hands to get the barrel to spots all around the zone and shoot hard-struck drives all over the park. He still has to sharpen his pitch recognition, which showed up as an area for polish both at Northeastern and then again as a pro. Maldonado is a plus runner, which should give him plenty of leeway to stick in center field.
THE FUTURE: Maldonado will likely split his 2026 season between the Class A levels. If he can improve his fortunes against offspeed pitches, he has the ceiling of a center fielder who can hit for power and cause havoc on the bases.

Year	Age	Club (League)	Level	AVG	G	AB	R	H	2B	3B	HR	RBI	BB	SO	SB	OBP	SLG
2025	21	San Jose (CAL)	A	.237	17	59	6	14	6	0	0	10	11	18	5	.352	.339
		Minor League Totals		.237	17	59	6	14	6	0	0	10	11	18	5	.352	.339

23 DIEGO VELASQUEZ, 2B
HIT: 50. **POW:** 40. **RUN:** 55. **FLD:** 50. **ARM:** 55. **BA Grade:** 40. **Risk:** Average. **Adj:** 30.

Born: October 1, 2003. **B-T:** B-R. **HT:** 6-1. **WT:** 191. **Signed:** Venezuela, 2021. **Signed by:** Robert Moron.
TRACK RECORD: The Giants signed Velasquez for $900,000 for his potential to produce a wide array of skills. He's been one of the system's quickest movers and has been among the youngest players at each stop in his career. The same was true in 2025 in the Eastern League, where he played all season as a 21-year-old.
SCOUTING REPORT: Velasquez does a lot of things well, but he's not a standout at any facet of the game. His best quality is his ability to make contact. His miss (14.7%) and chase (20.1%) rates were both excellent, and he was one of five minor leaguers 21 or younger to post a zone-miss rate of less than 10% over the course of 500 or more plate appearances. Now, he needs to put a bit more impact behind that contact. That's especially true after he shifted to second base in 2025. He's not the rangiest defender in the world, but he's surehanded and can be counted upon to make the routine play. He also does well tracking flies

into the outfield grass. Velasquez has above-average arm strength and a strong enough internal clock to know when he needs to add a bit more zip on his throws. He's an above-average runner.
THE FUTURE: Velasquez will likely move up to Triple-A in 2026 and could get a bit of an offensive boost from the friendly parks around the league. He projects as a second-division regular second baseman who can hit toward the bottom of an order.

Year	Age	Club (League)	Level	AVG	G	AB	R	H	2B	3B	HR	RBI	BB	SO	SB	OBP	SLG
2025	21	Richmond (EL)	AA	.256	128	473	60	121	20	1	2	32	70	81	19	.362	.315
		Minor League Totals		.270	460	1679	231	453	81	8	15	177	211	311	72	.360	.354

24. JOE WHITMAN, LHP
FB: 40. **SL:** 60. **CH:** 50. **CT:** 45. **CTL:** 55. **BA Grade:** 45. **Risk:** High. **Adj:** 30.

Born: September 17, 2001. **B-T:** L-L. **HT:** 6-5. **WT:** 200. **Drafted:** Kent State, 2023 (2nd round). **Signed by:** Todd Coryell.
TRACK RECORD: Whitman was the first lefthander off the board in 2023, when the Giants called his name in the second round. He signed for $805,575 and spent his first full year as a pro between the Class A levels. He pitched at Double-A Richmond all of 2025, to middling results.
SCOUTING REPORT: For Whitman to succeed, he's going to have to fix his fastball. The pitch comes in around 92 mph and topped at 95, but it often leaves the bat much faster. Hitters teed off against the four-seamer in 2025, hitting .305/.372/.469 on the pitch at Richmond. All 10 of the home runs Whitman allowed came on fastballs as well. Offspeeds, however, were another story. Hitters managed a line of just .211/.270/.287—including just seven extra-base hits—against Whitman's slider and changeup. Whitman also introduced a cutter in 2025. The pitch sat in the high 80s and was used sparingly, starting in May. Whitman threw three of his four pitches for strikes at clips of better than 62%. His changeup—which checked in at 46%—was mostly used as a finishing flourish for strikeouts against righthanders.
THE FUTURE: The 2026 season will be a fulcrum for Whitman. If he can't find a way to get hitters off his fastball, he likely will not escape the minor leagues. If he does, there could be a path back to a spot in the back of a rotation.

Year	Age	Club (League)	Level	W	L	ERA	G	GS	IP	H	HR	BB	SO	BB%	SO%	WHIP	AVG
2025	23	Richmond (EL)	AA	5	11	5.29	26	26	117	129	10	47	124	9.2	24.2	1.50	.285
		Minor League Totals		7	16	4.82	44	43	177	176	12	76	191	9.9	24.8	1.42	.261

25. CARLOS DE LA ROSA, LHP
FB: 60. **SL:** 55. **CH:** 50. **CTL:** 50. **BA Grade:** 50. **Risk:** Extreme. **Adj:** 30.

Born: November 30, 2007. **B-T:** L-L. **HT:** 5-11. **WT:** 178. **Signed:** Dominican Republic, 2025.
Signed by: Edgar Mateo/Luis Rodriguez (Yankees).
TRACK RECORD: De La Rosa signed with the Yankees out of the Dominican Republic in 2025, then immediately started opening eyes in the Dominican Summer League. His mix of present stuff and poise made him one of the better pitchers in the league, and he earned a spot in the DSL's annual all-star game. Shortly thereafter, he was included in the deal that sent Giants reliever Camilo Doval to New York.
SCOUTING REPORT: Beyond the Giants, De La Rosa drew interest from multiple clubs at the trade deadline. He was coveted for a fastball in the low-to-mid 90s that averaged nearly 20 inches of induced vertical break as well as a pair of secondaries that showed promise. His slider is currently a sweepier pitch, but the Giants would like to remap it with more drop to help it pair better with his fastball. Scouts also noticed that he tended to drop his slot on the pitch. He rounds out the mix with a changeup in the mid 80s that had enough velocity separation from his fastball to project as an average offering. De La Rosa's body is mostly maxed out, so there's little room for any projection. The lefthander was lauded for his highly competitive demeanor as well.
THE FUTURE: De La Rosa's next stop is the Arizona Complex League, where he will join Alberto Laroche and Reid Worley to form a second wave of interesting arms on the backfields across the Phoenix valley. He has the upside of a No. 4 starter.

Year	Age	Club (League)	Level	W	L	ERA	G	GS	IP	H	HR	BB	SO	BB%	SO%	WHIP	AVG
2025	17	DSL NYY Yankees	Rk	0	1	5.32	7	7	22	27	1	5	36	4.9	35.0	1.45	.281
2025	17	DSL Giants Black	Rk	0	0	3.48	3	2	10	10	0	5	15	11.4	34.1	1.45	.256
		Minor League Totals		0	1	4.73	10	9	32	37	1	10	51	6.8	34.7	1.45	.274

SAN FRANCISCO GIANTS

26 ALBERTO LAROCHE, RHP
FB: 55. **SL:** 50. **CH:** 40. **CTL:** 55. **BA Grade:** 50. **Risk:** Extreme. **Adj:** 30.

Born: December 1, 2005. **B-T:** R-R. **HT:** 5-11. **WT:** 171. **Signed:** Dominican Republic, 2024.
Signed by: Joe Salermo/Felix Peguero.
TRACK RECORD: Laroche signed with the Giants in April 2024 but was sidelined due to an administrative issue and limited to just three innings in the Dominican Summer League. He returned to the level in 2025 and was one of San Francisco's brightest stars. He was one of three Giants prospects to earn a spot in the league's annual all-star game and finished the year with 34 strikeouts and just six walks in 38.1 innings.
SCOUTING REPORT: Laroche works with a mix of four-seam and sinking fastballs, and he complements the heaters with a slider and a changeup. The sinker is by far the most frequently thrown version, with the four-seamer used almost as a way to give hitters another option to consider. The four-seamer peaked at 96 mph while the sinker reached 98 mph. The next step in Laroche's development will be to migrate his slider into more of an east-west pitch instead of its current shape. He'll also need to utilize his changeup more often after it was a clear third pitch in his mix during the 2025 season. While his control was among the best in the DSL, he still has some work to do when it comes to command of his arsenal. That's particularly true with his four-seamer, which could become a bigger piece of his mix as Laroche moves through the minors.
THE FUTURE: After a season and change in the DSL, Laroche will come stateside in 2026. He's likely to team up with lefty Carlos De La Rosa and Reid Worley to form one of the more interesting rotations in the Arizona Complex League. He has the upside of a back-end starter.

Year	Age	Club (League)	Level	W	L	ERA	G	GS	IP	H	HR	BB	SO	BB%	SO%	WHIP	AVG
2025	19	DSL Giants Black	Rk	1	3	2.11	10	10	38	30	0	6	34	3.9	22.2	0.94	.213
		Minor League Totals		1	3	1.96	12	11	41	33	0	6	36	3.6	21.8	0.94	.217

27 REID WORLEY, RHP
FB: 50. **SL:** 60. **CH:** 45. **CTL:** 45. **BA Grade:** 45. **Risk:** High. **Adj:** 30.

Born: June 27, 2006. **B-T:** R-R. **HT:** 6-2. **WT:** 175. **Drafted:** HS—Canton, GA, 2025 (9th round). **Signed by:** Nick Long.
TRACK RECORD: Though he was taken in the ninth round, Worley earned the third-highest bonus in San Francisco's 2025 draft class. The $747,500 he received was used to keep him from landing on campus at Kennesaw State. He earned that bonus on the strength of a prototype pitcher's frame, a loose arm action and an elite ability to spin the baseball. He did not pitch in official games but appeared during instructional league.
SCOUTING REPORT: Worley's slider is one of the best in the system. Thrown with an unconventional, spiked grip, it spins at better than 3,000 rpm and shows huge sweep across the zone that can get plenty of silly swings. The next step will be bringing his fastball forward a few notches. Currently, the pitch reaches 93 mph, but the Giants believe that strength gains and an improved delivery will help him add a few more ticks of velocity in the coming years. Specifically, they'd like to see him improve his posture and work down the mound more efficiently. Like most high school pitchers, Worley's changeup is a clear third piece of his arsenal. It will need to take steps forward if he is to become a serious candidate for a spot in a big league rotation.
THE FUTURE: Worley's first pro exposure will likely come in the Rookie-level Arizona Complex League. If he can bring his fastball and changeup forward, he has a chance to be a back-end starter. If not, he could be a spin monster in the pen.

Year	Age	Club (League)	Level	W	L	ERA	G	GS	IP	H	HR	BB	SO	BB%	SO%	WHIP	AVG
2025	19	Did not play															

28 YUNIOR MARTE, RHP
FB: 60. **SL:** 40. **CH:** 50. **CTL:** 40. **BA Grade:** 40. **Risk:** Average. **Adj:** 30.

Born: September 8, 2003. **B-T:** R-R. **HT:** 6-2. **WT:** 180. **Signed:** Dominican Republic, 2022. **Signed by:** Edis Perez (Royals).
TRACK RECORD: The Royals signed Marte out of the Dominican Republic in 2022. He moved a level a year before reaching full-season ball for the first time in 2024. He started his 2025 season back at Low-A Columbia before being dealt from Kansas City to San Francisco in the deal that made outfielder Mike Yastrzemski a Royal.
SCOUTING REPORT: Marte's 2025 season was stymied early by poor conditioning. He lost weight as the season went along and by season's end looked physical and powerful. The righthander works with a three-pitch mix fronted by a lively mid-90s fastball that peaked at 98 mph. He backs it with a downer slider and a changeup that each sit around 86 mph. The changeup is ahead of the slider and garnered a miss

rate of 45%. The pitch behaves like a splitter, with sharp downward bite. Marte's slider is short and sharp but needs to be landed in the strike zone more often in order to be effective as he moves up the minor league ladder. Marte's large frame, long levers and high-effort delivery don't portend much in the way of finesse, though he did a solid job of throwing strikes until the last few weeks of the season, when he was well past his career high for innings pitched.
THE FUTURE: Marte's fastball gives him a plus pitch. If he can bring one of his offspeeds to the same level, he has a chance to be a leverage reliever. In the meantime, he'll continue to get chances to prove himself as a starter.

Year	Age	Club (League)	Level	W	L	ERA	G	GS	IP	H	HR	BB	SO	BB%	SO%	WHIP	AVG
2025	21	Columbia (CAR)	A	3	5	2.74	19	19	82	61	4	20	79	6.3	24.7	0.99	.205
2025	21	San Jose (CAL)	A	0	0	3.60	5	3	20	16	0	9	17	10.8	20.5	1.25	.219
		Minor League Totals		3	12	4.22	56	44	183	182	11	53	167	6.8	21.5	1.28	.256

29 YULIAN BARRETO, SS

HIT: 50. **POW:** 30. **RUN:** 50. **FLD:** 60. **ARM:** 60. **BA Grade:** 50. **Risk:** Extreme. **Adj:** 30.

Born: March 12, 2008. **B-T:** R-R. **HT:** 5-10. **WT:** 185. **Signed:** Venezuela, 2025. **Signed by:** Ciro Villalobos Jr.
TRACK RECORD: Barreto signed with San Francisco out of Venezuela in January 2025 and was the recipient of one of the three seven-figure bonuses the Giants handed out in that year's class. He spent his debut season in the Dominican Summer League, where he was one of San Francisco's representatives in the circuit's all-star game.
SCOUTING REPORT: As an amateur, Barreto showed off a well-rounded skill set led by bat-to-ball ability and the athleticism and arm strength for the left side of the infield. Despite being signed as a shortstop, he slid to second in deference to Josuar Gonzalez. No matter where Barreto winds up defensively, he has smooth hands, solid footwork and a plus arm. At the plate, he did an excellent job of staying within the strike zone and attacking pitches he could handle. He finished the year with a zone-miss rate of just 8.9%. He didn't make much impact on contact, however, and most of his power will likely be limited to doubles on balls to the gaps.
THE FUTURE: The next stop for Barreto will be the Arizona Complex League, where he'll be part of the next wave of young Giants prospects. He figures to be part of a stacked ACL club that also includes Gonzalez and pitchers Carlos De La Rosa, Alberto Laroche and Reid Worley. He projects as a defensive-minded shortstop who hits toward the bottom of a lineup.

Year	Age	Club (League)	Level	AVG	G	AB	R	H	2B	3B	HR	RBI	BB	SO	SB	OBP	SLG
2025	17	DSL Giants Orange	Rk	.322	53	180	43	58	6	2	1	29	36	33	9	.449	.394
		Minor League Totals		.322	53	180	43	58	6	2	1	29	36	33	9	.449	.394

30 GERELMI MALDONADO, RHP

FB: 60. **SL:** 55. **BA Grade:** 40. **Risk:** Average. **Adj:** 30.

Born: December 21, 2003. **B-T:** R-R. **HT:** 6-2. **WT:** 170. **Signed:** Venezuela, 2021. **Signed by:** Robert Moron.
TRACK RECORD: Maldonado signed with the Giants in 2021 and has moved slowly through the minors. He debuted in full-season ball in 2023 but lost his 2024 season to Tommy John surgery. He returned in 2025 to Low-A San Jose, where he was used in multi-inning bursts at the beginning of games. His season high, which came on June 28, was 3.2 innings. He helped San Jose claim the California League championship.
SCOUTING REPORT: For now, Maldonado attacks hitters with two pitches: a four-seam fastball that averaged 98 mph and peaked at 101 and a slider with powerful two-plane break that sat around 84 mph. Beyond simply building his innings total, Maldonado spent the year tinkering with the grips on both pitches in order to increase their effectiveness. He also needs to show better command of the slider. The team has looked into adding a two-seamer or a changeup to Maldonado's mix as well. Maldonado is much heavier than his listed weight of 170 pounds, so he'll need to continue to work to maintain his conditioning as he moves up the ladder. Doing so will help him repeat his delivery and throw enough strikes to reach the big leagues as a flamethrower in the late innings.
THE FUTURE: Maldonado's next step will be High-A Eugene. He's a pure relief prospect with overpowering stuff in need of refinement across the board. The road to his ceiling is winding, but it might be worth the wait.

Year	Age	Club (League)	Level	W	L	ERA	G	GS	IP	H	HR	BB	SO	BB%	SO%	WHIP	AVG
2025	21	San Jose (CAL)	A	0	4	3.97	23	20	59	49	2	44	69	16.2	25.4	1.58	.225
		Minor League Totals		3	8	4.06	69	50	193	158	10	120	239	14.0	27.8	1.44	.223

Julio Rodriguez

Seattle Mariners

BY JESÚS CANO

Cal Raleigh gave Mariners fans one of the best memories in franchise history when he hit a walk-off home run to send the Mariners to the playoffs in 2022, breaking a 20-year drought.

At the time, Raleigh was an ascending homegrown talent with a productive bat and excellent defense. What few could have predicted was just how quickly Raleigh would use that moment as a launching point to elevate his game. In 2023, he asserted himself as a rising bona fide superstar.

Fast forward to 2025, and Raleigh is already making the six-year, $105 million contract he signed entering the season look like a bargain after a historic performance.

Raleigh smashed 60 home runs to set the MLB record for homers in a single season by a primary catcher, the all-time mark for a switch-hitter and the single-season home run record in Mariners franchise history. He finished second in American League MVP voting behind Aaron Judge.

The story of the 2025 Mariners felt destined for a storybook ending—one so rare that only a handful of franchises ever dare to imagine it. That dream fell just short when a loss to the Blue Jays in Game 7 of the AL Championship Series denied Seattle a trip to the World Series for the first time in franchise history.

The disappointment lingered, heavy and unavoidable. Seattle was painfully close. While no words can fully ease that sting, there is reason for optimism. That ultimate goal remains within reach, and with the strength of the farm system the Mariners possess, it's all possible.

Homegrown talent is at a premium in Seattle. Along with Raleigh, Julio Rodriguez is another talent produced in Seattle's system. Homegrown pitchers Logan Gilbert, Bryan Woo, George Kirby and Bryce Miller formed one of the best rotations in baseball, a big reason why Seattle went deep for so long, and all came up in the system together.

PROJECTED 2029 LINEUP

Catcher	Cal Raleigh	32
First Base	Josh Naylor	32
Second Base	Cole Young	25
Third Base	Ben Williamson	28
Shortstop	Colt Emerson	24
Left Field	Randy Arozarena	34
Center Field	Julio Rodriguez	28
Right Field	Michael Arroyo	25
Designated Hitter	Lazaro Montes	25
No. 1 Starter	Bryan Woo	29
No. 2 Starter	Logan Gilbert	32
No. 3 Starter	George Kirby	31
No. 4 Starter	Kade Anderson	25
No. 5 Starter	Ryan Sloan	23
Closer	Andres Muñoz	30

The Mariners acquired Josh Naylor and Eugenio Suarez, two players who didn't come at a low price, at the trade deadline, using a deep farm system to reel in both at the same time.

The fruits of the Mariners' system still loom large.

Former top prospect Cole Young ascended to Seattle, and others aren't too far away. No. 1 prospect Colt Emerson has a chance to contribute to the Mariners in 2026, as does 2025 No. 3 overall pick Kade Anderson.

Seattle has already leveraged its farm system to its advantage, dealing 2021 first-rounder Harry Ford to the Nationals for lefthander Jose Ferrer after the 2025 season—a move that could yield one of the most quietly effective bullpen arms.

Lazaro Montes, Michael Arroyo and Felnin Celesten are all products of the Mariners' international program, one that also identified Rodriguez as well as Noelvi Marte, now on the Reds.

For the Mariners, the path forward is no longer built on hope alone, but on proof. Proof that their development system works. Proof that homegrown stars can thrive on the big stage. And proof that when supplemented with targeted acquisitions, Seattle can stand toe-to-toe with baseball's elite.

The heartbreak of 2025 may linger, but it also clarified something essential: This window isn't closing. It has opened even wider. ■

DEPTH CHART

SEATTLE MARINERS

TOP 2026 ROOKIES	RANK
1. Colt Emerson, SS	1
2. Rhylan Thomas, OF	23

BREAKOUT PROSPECTS	RANK
1. Nick Becker, SS	11
2. Leandro Romero, SS	20
3. Robinson Ortiz, LHP	27

SOURCE OF TOP 30 TALENT

Homegrown	28	Acquired	2
College	14	Trade	2
Junior college	0	Rule 5 draft	0
High school	6	Independent league	0
Undrafted free agent	0	Free agent/waivers	0
International	8		

LF
Jonny Farmelo (6)
Yorger Bautista (12)
Rhylan Thomas (23)

CF
Tai Peete (10)
Korbyn Dickerson (14)
Victor Labrada (25)
Carlos Jimenez

RF
Lazaro Montes (3)
Michael Arroyo (5)
Jared Sundstrom (22)

3B
Josh Hood
Blake Rambusch
Brandon Eike

SS
Colt Emerson (1)
Felnin Celesten (9)
Nick Becker (11)
Leandro Romero (20)
Axel Sanchez

2B
Brock Rodden (16)
Jo Oyama
Kendry Martinez
Charlie Pagliarini

1B
Luis Suisbel (19)
Carson Taylor

C
Luke Stevenson (8)
Grant Knipp (26)
Josh Caron
Grant Jay

LHP

LHSP
Kade Anderson (2)
Jurrangelo Cijntje (7)
Teddy McGraw (15)
Mason Peters (18)

LHRP
Grant Knipp (26)
Robinson Ortiz (27)
Reid VanScoter
Brandon Schaeffer
Nico Tellache

RHP

RHSP
Ryan Sloan (4)
Jurrangelo Cijntje (7)
Griffin Hugus (13)
Michael Morales (17)
Chia-Shi Shen (21)
Marcelo Perez (24)
Brock Moore
Gabriel Sosa

RHRP
Charlie Beilenson (28)
Lucas Kelly (29)
Tyler Cleveland (30)
Jimmy Joyce
Jimmy Kingsbury
Christian Little

SEATTLE MARINERS

1 COLT EMERSON, SS

Born: July 20, 2005. **B-T:** L-R. **HT:** 6-1. **WT:** 195.
Drafted: HS—New Concord, OH, 2023 (1st round).
Signed by: Jackson Laumann.

BA GRADE | **SCOUTING GRADES**
65 Risk: Average | Hit: 60. Power: 50. Run: 45. Field: 55. Arm: 50.
Adjusted grade: 55 | Projected future grades on 20-80 scouting scale

TRACK RECORD: Emerson was one of the youngest players in the 2023 draft when the Mariners selected him 22nd overall, and he quickly established himself as one of the most mature and advanced hitters in their system. He impressed in his pro debut that summer, reaching Low-A Modesto at the end of the year. In 2024 he played at three levels and slashed .263/.393/.376 with nearly as many walks (50) as strikeouts (58). Despite missing 70 games due to a foot fracture, Emerson still earned a promotion to High-A Everett in August and held his own against older competition. Fully healthy in 2025, Emerson showed exactly why he's considered one of baseball's top prospects. Across 124 games between High-A and Double-A, he hit .281/.380/.466 with 14 home runs. He reached Triple-A for six games and went 8-for-22 (.364) with two homers.

SCOUTING REPORT: Emerson's well-balanced lefthanded swing and mature approach impress evaluators. His barrel stays in the zone for a long time, enabling him to hit line drives to all fields. True to the Mariners' strategy of targeting high-contact high school bats, Emerson has long demonstrated consistent bat-to-ball skills. His power, however, has taken significant steps forward. In 2025, Emerson slugged a career-high 16 home runs—quadrupling his previous season's total—and saw his 90th percentile exit velocity improve by 2 mph from 2024 as he continues to physically develop. He could hit upward of 15-20 homers annually in the big leagues. He has added noticeable strength since signing and has begun tapping into power without compromising his high-level plate discipline. His splits were remarkably even in 2025, with an identical .846 OPS against both righties and lefties, though most of his power production came against righties. Emerson's 17.5% strikeout rate nearly mirrored his 2024 output despite facing stiffer competition, though his overall swing and chase rates increased year over year. Emerson's growth wasn't limited to the batter's box. He also showed defensive improvement, particularly in his agility and footwork at shortstop, where he spent most of his time in 2025. He could become an above-average defender thanks to his strong instincts. Coaches noted he looked more confident and fluid, taking a clear step forward, and scouts were impressed with his overall ease of operation. His arm isn't particularly strong but it has enough carry to stick at shortstop.

THE FUTURE: The Mariners aren't an organization that rushes players to the majors, so some extra seasoning at Double-A could be in store for Emerson before a full-time Triple-A residency. He played primarily shortstop, but staying versatile at third base will help his chances of getting into the lineup quicker. His all-around skill set makes him one of the game's best prospects.

BEST TOOLS

BATTING
Best Hitter	Colt Emerson
Best Power Hitter	Lazaro Montes
Best Strike-Zone Discipline	Colt Emerson
Fastest Baserunner	Tai Peete
Best Athlete	Jonny Farmelo

PITCHING
Best Fastball	Jurrangelo Cijntje
Best Curveball	Mason Peters
Best Slider	Teddy McGraw
Best Changeup	Ryan Sloan
Best Control	Kade Anderson

FIELDING
Best Defensive Catcher	Luke Stevenson
Best Defensive Infielder	Colt Emerson
Best Infield Arm	Colt Emerson
Best Defensive Outfielder	Jonny Farmelo
Best Outfield Arm	Lazaro Montes

Year	Age	Club (League)	Level	AVG	G	AB	R	H	2B	3B	HR	RBI	BB	SO	SB	OBP	SLG
2025	19	Everett (NWL)	A+	.281	90	342	58	96	16	5	11	51	54	68	6	.388	.453
2025	19	Arkansas (TL)	AA	.282	34	142	19	40	10	1	3	18	14	31	7	.360	.430
2025	19	Tacoma (PCL)	AAA	.364	6	22	5	8	2	0	2	9	3	6	1	.444	.727
		Minor League Totals		.287	224	871	165	250	55	7	22	128	138	183	37	.398	.442

SEATTLE MARINERS

2 KADE ANDERSON, LHP
FB: 55. **CB:** 60. **SL:** 60. **CH:** 45. **CTL:** 55. **BA Grade:** 60. **Risk:** Average. **Adj:** 50.

Born: July 6, 2004. **B-T:** L-L. **HT:** 6-2. **WT:** 179.
Drafted: LSU, 2025 (1st round). **Signed by:** Derek Miller.
TRACK RECORD: LSU has a track record for developing future big leaguers, and Anderson is on that trajectory. A Louisiana native, Anderson's high school career was cut short by Tommy John surgery that cost him his senior year. After splitting time between LSU's bullpen and rotation as a freshman in 2024, he broke out in 2025. His 180 strikeouts led all Division I pitchers and were the third-most in program history en route to being named the Most Outstanding Player in the College World Series after the Tigers' run to a national title. The Mariners drafted him third overall and signed him for an underslot $8.8 million. He did not make his pro debut.
SCOUTING REPORT: A 6-foot-2 lefty with a strong lower half, Anderson has a smooth delivery and a compact arm action from a high three-quarters slot. In 2025, his mid-80s slider became a key weapon. It regularly flashed plus and generated a 30% whiff rate. He also features a high-spin, upper-70s curveball with depth and a mid-80s changeup that's effective against righties and looked better in 2025. An above-average strike-thrower with feel for all four pitches, Anderson's previous elbow surgery and slighter build are concerns, though he held up over 119 innings in his draft year, and evaluators believe there's some projection remaining. While he didn't make his pro debut, the Mariners focused on developing his strength during his time at the complex.
THE FUTURE: Anderson is a high-probability starter with a blend of strikes and stuff that gives him No. 2 or 3 starter upside. He has the polish and pedigree to move quickly, perhaps even reaching Seattle by the end of 2026, though the Mariners won't need to rush him considering they have one of baseball's best rotations.

Year	Age	Club (League)	Level	W	L	ERA	G	GS	IP	H	HR	BB	SO	BB%	SO%	WHIP	AVG
2025	20	Did not play															

3 LAZARO MONTES, OF
HIT: 40. **POW:** 70. **RUN:** 30. **FLD:** 40. **ARM:** 60. **BA Grade:** 60. **Risk:** High. **Adj:** 45.

Born: October 22, 2004. **B-T:** L-R. **HT:** 6-3. **WT:** 210.
Signed: Cuba, 2022. **Signed by:** Ismael Rosado.
TRACK RECORD: Montes signed in 2022 for $2.5 million out of Cuba, where he trained with Yordan Alvarez's hitting instructor and often drew comparisons to the Astros slugger because of his immense raw power. Montes slimmed down and boosted his athleticism entering 2024, when he slashed .288/.397/.484 with 21 homers across both Class A levels. Montes' power took another leap in 2025, when he bashed 32 homers, the third-most in the minors. His average dropped from .268 in 67 games for High-A Everett to .213 in 64 games for Double-A Arkansas.
SCOUTING REPORT: Montes' calling card is his elite raw power. Every swing is geared to do damage, and the ball often leaves the yard when he connects. He had the highest 90th percentile exit velocity of any Mariners minor leaguer in 2025. However, his aggressive approach leads to swing-and-miss issues, with an overall miss rate that hovered around 38% and plenty of in-zone misses. After experimenting with a more contact-oriented approach in 2024 that suppressed some of his power, the Mariners shifted Montes back to more of a damage-focused philosophy in 2025 that aligns far better with his natural skills and offensive profile. While he strikes out plenty, he also has solid plate discipline and walked at a 14.2% clip in 2025. Defensively, Montes has the strongest arm in the system but is a limited defender in right field. The Mariners are prioritizing improving his mobility and outfield routes in 2026.
THE FUTURE: After finding Double-A more challenging, Montes will likely return to the level to start 2026. He has 30-homer upside in the majors, which should help him find a way into a lineup even if his corner outfield defense comes up short.

Year	Age	Club (League)	Level	AVG	G	AB	R	H	2B	3B	HR	RBI	BB	SO	SB	OBP	SLG
2025	20	Everett (NWL)	A+	.268	67	250	43	67	12	5	18	50	48	83	3	.387	.572
2025	20	Arkansas (TL)	AA	.213	64	240	33	51	7	2	14	39	35	86	4	.319	.433
		Minor League Totals		.273	372	1355	250	370	72	16	76	296	250	447	17	.393	.518

SEATTLE MARINERS

4 RYAN SLOAN, RHP
FB: 60. **SW:** 60. **CH:** 60. **CT:** 50. **CTL:** 55. **BA Grade:** 60. **Risk:** High. **Adj:** 45.

Born: January 29, 2006. **B-T:** R-R. **HT:** 6-5. **WT:** 220.
Drafted: HS—Elmhurst, IL, 2024 (2nd round). **Signed by:** Joe Saunders.
TRACK RECORD: The Mariners made a significant investment in Sloan when they signed him to an overslot $3 million bonus as a second-rounder in 2024. He signed the highest deal for a high school righthander in the class. Paired with first-rounder Jurrangelo Cijntje, the duo represented the first time Seattle used its top two picks on pitchers since 2019—when it landed future big leaguers George Kirby and Brandon Williamson—and bucked their trend of hitter-heavy classes. Sloan made his pro debut in 2025 and was rock solid, posting a 3.73 ERA with 90 strikeouts to just 15 walks over 82 innings with Low-A Modesto. He made three starts with High-A Everett before eye surgery ended his season.
SCOUTING REPORT: Sloan arrived in pro ball as a projectable, high-upside high schooler with tools that hinted at frontline potential. In 2025, he started to deliver on that promise. At 6-foot-5, 220 pounds, he boasts a prototype starter's frame with a clean delivery and a polished arsenal with potential for three plus pitches. In his pro debut, he attacked the zone relentlessly, throwing strikes at a 68% clip. Working from a three-quarters arm slot, Sloan's mid-90s fastball touched 98 mph, but many scouts believe it's not even his best weapon. His sharp, late-breaking sweeper generated a 46% whiff rate, while his fading, low-90s changeup proved to be just as effective. Between his sweeper and changeup, Sloan has two legitimate putaway pitches to complement his velocity. Sloan also worked in an upper-80s cutter at times.
THE FUTURE: Sloan is expected to be healthy for spring training. He will likely return to High-A in 2026 and should reach Double-A by the end of the season, and his stuff and poise give him a chance for front-of-the-rotation upside.

Year	Age	Club (League)	Level	W	L	ERA	G	GS	IP	H	HR	BB	SO	BB%	SO%	WHIP	AVG
2025	19	Modesto (CAL)	A	2	2	3.44	18	18	71	66	2	15	77	5.3	27.1	1.15	.249
2025	19	Everett (NWL)	A+	0	2	5.56	3	3	11	14	3	0	13	0.0	26.5	1.24	.298
		Minor League Totals		2	4	3.73	21	21	82	80	5	15	90	4.5	27.0	1.16	.256

5 MICHAEL ARROYO, OF
HIT: 60. **POW:** 50. **RUN:** 50. **FLD:** 40. **ARM:** 45. **BA Grade:** 50. **Risk:** Mild. **Adj:** 45.

Born: November 3, 2004. **B-T:** R-R. **HT:** 5-8. **WT:** 160.
Signed: Colombia, 2022. **Signed by:** David Brito.
TRACK RECORD: Arroyo signed with the Mariners for $1,375,000 in January 2022. He signed the largest bonus ever awarded to an amateur from Colombia. Touted as a polished hitter, he has more than lived up to expectations as a professional. His 23 home runs in 2024 tied for the most in the minors among teenagers. A year later, the 20-year-old continued his strong production and reached the upper minors for the first time, slashing .262/.401/.433 with 17 homers, 54 RBIs and an .834 OPS between High-A Everett and Double-A Arkansas.
SCOUTING REPORT: Even though he's just 5-foot-8, Arroyo hit 40 home runs in 2024 and 2025 combined because he stands right on top of the plate and uses his quick hands, short levers and balanced stride to deliver the barrel to the baseball. He has advanced plate discipline, excellent plate coverage and impressive bat control. Arroyo can generate above-average exit velocities and has a knack for pulling the baseball, though scouts noted his body might be close to maxed out. He also knows when to pick and choose his spots, makes plenty of contact and chases at roughly a 20% clip. Arroyo thrives against breaking pitches and has solid pitch recognition but can struggle with timing against fastballs. Arroyo played shortstop early in his career before moving to second base exclusively in 2025. He has done well with his agility so far, but he'll have to keep an eye on his body and arm to become an average defender there.
THE FUTURE: After the 2025 season, the Mariners decided to give Arroyo time in the outfield to lessen his defensive demands, take advantage of his average speed and create an avenue to playing time with the organization's crowded infield. Arroyo is expected to return to Double-A to open the 2026 season.

Year	Age	Club (League)	Level	AVG	G	AB	R	H	2B	3B	HR	RBI	BB	SO	SB	OBP	SLG
2025	20	Everett (NWL)	A+	.269	65	242	41	65	14	0	15	39	39	65	3	.422	.512
2025	20	Arkansas (TL)	AA	.255	56	208	37	53	10	1	2	15	30	39	9	.376	.341
		Minor League Totals		.275	351	1308	273	360	77	13	47	193	206	327	42	.408	.462

SEATTLE MARINERS

6 JONNY FARMELO, OF
HIT: 45. **POW:** 45. **RUN:** 70. **FLD:** 55. **ARM:** 50. **BA Grade:** 55. **Risk:** High. **Adj:** 40.

Born: September 9, 2004. **B-T:** L-R. **HT:** 6-2. **WT:** 205.
Drafted: HS—Chantilly, VA, 2023 (1st round supp.). **Signed by:** Ty Holub.
TRACK RECORD: Farmelo made a bit of history before ever stepping on a professional field when the Mariners used the first-ever Prospect Promotion Incentive draft pick to select him 29th overall in 2023. Seattle received the PPI pick after Julio Rodriguez won American League Rookie of the Year in 2022. Farmelo has fared well when healthy, but injuries have limited him to just 75 pro games. He tore the ACL in his right knee in June 2024 after 46 games with Low-A Modesto. He returned to action at High-A Everett in late April 2025, but a stress reaction in his rib put him back on the shelf after a month and limited him to just 29 games. Farmelo was sent to the Arizona Fall League to gain reps and momentum.
SCOUTING REPORT: Farmelo has a somewhat unconventional setup at the plate, featuring a crouched stance that elevates his elbows and bat in the lefthanded batter's box, which leads to a stiffer look. His posture can make him vulnerable to premium velocity, especially up in the zone, where he's occasionally late. His swing-and-miss rates, especially in the strike zone, have raised some concern. He is late on premium velocity and in-between on breaking pitches. Farmelo cut his chase rate in a limited sample size in 2025 and has shown flashes of improved bat speed and barrel control, which the Mariners hope will trend upward with more reps. After returning from injury, his double-plus speed remained intact, allowing him to continue covering ground in center field, where he should be at least a solid-average defender.
THE FUTURE: Farmelo is expected to return to High-A to begin 2026. The Mariners hope he can bounce back after his first full healthy offseason. He profiles as a top-of-the-order threat.

Year	Age	Club (League)	Level	AVG	G	AB	R	H	2B	3B	HR	RBI	BB	SO	SB	OBP	SLG
2025	20	Everett (NWL)	A+	.230	29	113	18	26	6	1	6	16	14	38	2	.318	.460
		Minor League Totals		.251	75	291	57	73	16	4	10	41	50	90	20	.369	.436

7 JURRANGELO CIJNTJE, SHP
FB: 60. **SL:** 60. **CB:** 55. **CH:** 45. **CTL:** 50. **BA Grade:** 55. **Risk:** High. **Adj:** 40.

Born: May 31, 2003. **B-T:** B-B. **HT:** 5-11. **WT:** 200.
Drafted: Mississippi State, 2024 (1st round). **Signed by:** Dan Holcomb.
TRACK RECORD: Born a natural lefthander in the Netherlands, Cijntje grew up in Curacao while teaching himself to throw righthanded using his father's glove. It was his only option, since Mechangelo, a former pro player, didn't have lefthanded gear. That early improvisation laid the foundation for his remarkable athletic versatility and an eventual path to pro ball as a true switch-pitcher. Despite his lefty origins, Cijntje is now better from the right side. The 2024 first-rounder out of Mississippi State debuted in 2025 and worked from both sides while splitting 108.1 innings between High-A and Double-A. He posted a 3.99 ERA with 120 strikeouts and appeared in the Futures Game.
SCOUTING REPORT: The Mariners spent plenty of time pondering how to best deploy Cijntje. Ultimately, they settled on a six-man rotation, where he primarily started games as a righthanded pitcher. Occasionally, he mixed in left-on-left matchups, but the results were mixed and lefthanded batters hit .296 against him when he pitched from the left side in 2025. Cijntje sits in the mid 90s with his fastball and was up to 98 from both sides, though his average lefty fastball velocity was 1-2 mph slower. His best secondary pitch is a firm mid-to-upper-80s slider that has a bit more sweep from the right side, and Cijntje is adept at locating his fastball to his glove side as a righty to set up the slider. He'll also infrequently mix in a low-80s curveball and an upper-80s changeup mostly as a situational pitch against lefties. Much like his arsenal, Cijntje's strike-throwing was much better from the right side.
THE FUTURE: The Mariners will continue to develop Cijntje as a starter, though some scouts wonder how his stuff would play as a reliever. He should return to Double-A Arkansas to begin 2026.

Year	Age	Club (League)	Level	W	L	ERA	G	GS	IP	H	HR	BB	SO	BB%	SO%	WHIP	AVG
2025	22	Everett (NWL)	A+	4	7	4.58	19	16	75	54	14	35	83	11.1	26.4	1.19	.201
2025	22	Arkansas (TL)	AA	1	0	2.67	7	7	34	27	1	16	37	11.0	25.5	1.28	.218
		Minor League Totals		5	7	3.99	26	23	108	81	15	51	120	11.1	26.1	1.22	.207

SEATTLE MARINERS

8 LUKE STEVENSON, C
HIT: 45. **POW:** 55. **RUN:** 40. **FLD:** 60. **ARM:** 60. **BA Grade:** 50. **Risk:** Avg. **Adj:** 40.

Born: July 22, 2004. **B-T:** L-R. **HT:** 6-1. **WT:** 200.
Drafted: North Carolina, 2025 (1st round supp.). **Signed by:** Ty Holub.
TRACK RECORD: Stevenson was born in New Jersey, but he etched his name into North Carolina baseball lore as one of the state's most accomplished catchers. He was a four-year starter at Wake Forest High and led the state in home runs as a senior, then carried that power to college. Stevenson was a two-year mainstay for North Carolina, where he hit 33 homers and walked 19.1% of the time, albeit with just a .267 average. The Mariners drafted Stevenson 35th overall in 2025, and he handled Low-A pitching with ease in his pro debut.
SCOUTING REPORT: Stevenson is a strong defensive catcher whose advanced instincts set him apart. Regarded as one of the premier defensive backstops in his draft class, he brings a natural leadership presence and mature game-calling ability behind the plate. Stevenson's subtle pitch framing consistently earns extra strikes. He persuades umpires to widen the zone with his soft, precise receiving. His quick, quiet hands allow him to pull low pitches into the zone cleanly, giving pitchers confidence to work the edges. At the plate, Stevenson has above-average lefthanded power. There are more questions about his ability to make contact, particularly against premium velocity, which contributed to his draft-day slide out of the first round. Stevenson made an encouraging amount of contact with Low-A Modesto in his pro debut while showing his trademark patience. However, he'll need to show more feel to hit against upper-minors pitchers to eradicate his hitting ability concerns.
THE FUTURE: Stevenson's elite glove, high baseball IQ and power potential provide a strong foundation. He has everyday catcher upside if his contact ability takes a step forward in pro ball. It shouldn't be long before he reaches High-A Everett.

Year	Age	Club (League)	Level	AVG	G	AB	R	H	2B	3B	HR	RBI	BB	SO	SB	OBP	SLG
2025	20	Modesto (CAL)	A	.280	22	75	16	21	4	1	1	14	23	19	1	.460	.400
		Minor League Totals		.280	22	75	16	21	4	1	1	14	23	19	1	.460	.400

9 FELNIN CELESTEN, SS
HIT: 45. **POW:** 50. **RUN:** 60. **FLD:** 55. **ARM:** 50. **BA Grade:** 55. **Risk:** High. **Adj:** 40.

Born: September 15, 2005. **B-T:** B-R. **HT:** 6-1. **WT:** 175.
Signed: Dominican Republic, 2023. **Signed by:** Rafael Mateo.
TRACK RECORD: Celesten was a touted prospect for years before the Mariners signed him for $4.7 million to kick off the 2023 international signing period. He signed the largest bonus for an international amateur in organization history. A hamstring injury delayed Celesten's debut until 2024, when struggles early in extended spring training briefly raised concern. He quickly rebounded in the Arizona Complex League, hitting .352/.431/.568 before a wrist injury ended his season. Celesten stayed healthy in 2025 and handled his first full year of affiliated ball, batting .285/.349/.384 with five home runs for Low-A Modesto before an 11-game look at High-A Everett.
SCOUTING REPORT: Celesten is a constant tinkerer at the plate, frequently experimenting with the depth of his crouch and the size and timing of his leg kick. A switch-hitter, his mechanics are largely consistent from both sides. However, scouts have noted that his lefthanded swing is more fluid. He projects to have at least a fringe-average hit tool, thanks to his ability to let the ball travel in the zone and a mature approach that includes using the opposite field. His pitch recognition is advanced for his age because he tracks pitches deep, rarely expands the zone and shows a strong feel for spin. On the bases, Celesten is a plus runner with long, explosive strides and efficient routes, particularly around the corners. Defensively, he checks every box to stick at shortstop, with quick lateral movements, soft hands and a strong, accurate arm capable of making throws deep in the hole or on the move.
THE FUTURE: Celesten should start the 2026 season back at High-A Everett. He's still young, and the pop could develop more as his body develops. He has what it takes to be a productive everyday player with the right pace.

Year	Age	Club (League)	Level	AVG	G	AB	R	H	2B	3B	HR	RBI	BB	SO	SB	OBP	SLG
2025	19	Modesto (CAL)	A	.285	93	383	52	109	19	2	5	55	37	96	20	.349	.384
2025	19	Everett (NWL)	A+	.158	11	38	6	6	0	1	1	4	9	15	1	.313	.289
		Minor League Totals		.291	136	546	88	159	29	7	9	86	64	139	26	.365	.419

SEATTLE MARINERS

10 TAI PEETE, OF
HIT: 40. POW: 55. RUN: 60. FLD: 55. ARM: 60. BA Grade: 60. Risk: Extreme. Adj: 40.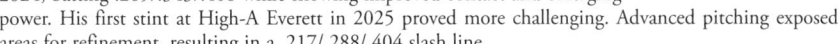

Born: August 11, 2005. **B-T:** L-R. **HT:** 6-2. **WT:** 193.
Drafted: HS—Sharpsburg, GA, 2023 (1st round supp.). **Signed by:** Terry McClure.
TRACK RECORD: Peete emerged as one of the most intriguing two-way talents in Georgia's 2023 high school class, drawing attention for his athleticism and raw tools. The Mariners drafted him 30th overall that year, using its supplemental pick after the first round, betting on his long-term offensive potential. Peete rewarded that confidence in his first full season at Low-A Modesto in 2024, batting .269/.343/.408 while showing improved contact and emerging power. His first stint at High-A Everett in 2025 proved more challenging. Advanced pitching exposed areas for refinement, resulting in a .217/.288/.404 slash line.
SCOUTING REPORT: Peete's lefthanded swing is built for power, and he showed it by hitting 19 home runs—12 more than his previous high—as he grew into his frame. However, swing-and-miss concerns remain a barrier. He struck out 162 times in consecutive seasons. In 2025, that total included a 32% overall miss rate, including 25.3% in-zone and a 27% chase rate. Breaking balls give him the most trouble, though he handles velocity well. Originally a shortstop, he moved around the infield before the Mariners transitioned him to the outfield in 2025—a change he has adapted to well. Defensively, he has improved significantly and is now considered one of the stronger emerging outfielders in the Mariners system.
THE FUTURE: Reducing his whiff rate will be key to Peete unlocking his upside. If he refines his approach, he could see his stock rise in 2026, likely starting in High-A to polish his game before advancing to Double-A.

Year	Age	Club (League)	Level	AVG	G	AB	R	H	2B	3B	HR	RBI	BB	SO	SB	OBP	SLG
2025	19	Everett (NWL)	A+	.217	125	475	58	103	24	4	19	63	46	162	25	.288	.404
		Minor League Totals		.247	264	1042	141	257	54	14	28	154	111	354	76	.318	.406

11 NICK BECKER, SS

HIT: 55. POW: 50. RUN: 60. FLD: 50. ARM: 50. BA Grade: 55. Risk: High. Adj: 40.

Born: December 4, 2006. **B-T:** R-R. **HT:** 6-3. **WT:** 180. **Drafted:** HS—Ramsey, NJ, 2025 (2nd round).
Signed by: David Pepe.
TRACK RECORD: Becker comes from a strong baseball pedigree. His father Jeff played at Duke before spending time in Cleveland's minor league system, and his brother Eric is currently a standout shortstop at Virginia and one of the top college prospects for the 2026 draft. Nick was heralded as one of the top prospects in the Northeast at his New Jersey high school and originally committed to join the Cavaliers as well. The Mariners lured him away in the second round of the 2025 draft with a $2.75 million bonus, a hefty $1.11 million over slot.
SCOUTING REPORT: Becker's athleticism shows up immediately, as he's a plus runner who turned in a 6.65-second 60-yard dash at the 2024 East Coast Pro Showcase. That speed, paired with smooth actions, clean footwork and an average arm, gives him a chance to stick at shortstop. He profiles more as a steady, reliable defender than a flashy one, but should bring consistent, dependable play to the position. Offensively, he offers a clean, efficient swing and the makings of an above-average hit tool. Becker starts from a slightly open stance with good rhythm and an advanced feel for the strike zone, allowing him to control at-bats, lay off close pitches and get on plane for frequent hard contact. His frame and athletic projection leave room for average game power as he physically matures.
THE FUTURE: Becker should start the season in Low-A Inland Empire and is one of the young, bright talents the system has to offer.

Year	Age	Club (League)	Level	AVG	G	AB	R	H	2B	3B	HR	RBI	BB	SO	SB	OBP	SLG
2025	18	Modesto (CAL)	A	.208	6	24	5	5	0	0	0	2	4	9	2	.321	.208
		Minor League Totals		.208	6	24	5	5	0	0	0	2	4	9	2	.321	.208

SEATTLE MARINERS

12 YORGER BAUTISTA, OF
HIT: 35. **POW:** 60. **RUN:** 55. **FLD:** 55. **ARM:** 60. **BA Grade:** 60. **Risk:** Extreme. **Adj:** 40.

Born: September 19, 2007. **B-T:** L-L. **HT:** 6-1. **WT:** 176. **Signed:** Venezuela, 2025. **Signed by:** Luis Martinez.
TRACK RECORD: The Mariners have built a strong track record on the international stage, developing homegrown talent like Michael Arroyo, Lazaro Montes and Felnin Celesten—all of whom have climbed into the organization's Top 10 Prospects. Bautista, a 2025 signee out of Venezuela for $2.1 million, could follow a similar trajectory and was considered one of the top Venezuelan prospects in this year's class. His pro debut came with mixed results. In the Dominican Summer League, Bautista slashed .223/.326/.404 with a 29.8% strikeout rate, but there were flashes of upside, including seven home runs.
SCOUTING REPORT: Standing 6-foot-1, 176 pounds, Bautista is a physical, lefthanded-hitting outfielder with an unconventional uppercut swing that has 25-homer upside. That power, however, comes with swing-and-miss concerns, especially within the strike zone. Scouts found Bautista overaggressive early in counts as he hunted impact, and developing better selectivity will be critical for his growth. Evaluators were also mixed on Bautista's defensive work in the DSL. Some saw enough speed and instincts to stick in center field, while others questioned his mobility and route-running, suggesting a move to a corner outfield spot. Regardless, his plus arm strength rounds out a well-balanced skill set and can handle any outfield spot. He was also 10-for-10 on steals.
THE FUTURE: Bautista has some adjustments to make to tap into his significant upside. Still just 18 years old, he's a candidate to make his stateside debut in the Arizona Complex League in 2026, though a second turn in the DSL is a possibility.

Year	Age	Club (League)	Level	AVG	G	AB	R	H	2B	3B	HR	RBI	BB	SO	SB	OBP	SLG
2025	17	DSL Mariners	Rk	.223	53	193	38	43	8	3	7	25	21	67	10	.326	.404
		Minor League Totals		.223	53	193	38	43	8	3	7	25	21	67	10	.326	.404

13 GRIFFIN HUGUS, RHP
FB: 50. **SL:** 55. **CB:** 45. **CH:** 50. **CTL:** 45. **BA Grade:** 45. **Risk:** Average. **Adj:** 35.

Born: February 25, 2004. **B-T:** L-R. **HT:** 6-2. **WT:** 210. **Drafted:** Miami, 2025 (3rd round). **Signed by:** Bobby Korecky.
TRACK RECORD: Hugus began his career as a two-way player at Cincinnati before shifting to the Bearcats' bullpen full-time as a sophomore. He then returned to his home state when he transferred to Miami as a starter entering 2025. There, he led the staff in starts (17), innings (93) and strikeouts (95), earning second-team All-ACC honors. He also posted a career-best 8.8% walk rate that season. The Mariners drafted Hugus in the third round later that summer. He did not make his pro debut and instead spent the rest of the year at the organization's complex in Arizona.
SCOUTING REPORT: Hugus operates from a high three-quarters slot, paired with a bit of crossfire action at the end of his delivery. Hugus has steadily sharpened his control and now works with a balanced four-pitch mix. His fastball sits 91-94 mph and touches 95. In 2025, his slider gained power and now sits in the mid 80s with strong tilt, and he can adjust its shape to attack both righties and lefties. His mid-70s curveball offers a true 12-6 look, and Hugus showed better definition between the two breakers in 2025. He rounds out his arsenal with a mid-80s split-grip changeup. The Mariners are hopeful that their pitching development program will help Hugus' velocity and pitch shapes tick up.
THE FUTURE: Hugus is set to make his pro debut in the lower minors in 2026 and has the arsenal to settle into the back of a rotation.

Year	Age	Club (League)	Level	W	L	ERA	G	GS	IP	H	HR	BB	SO	BB%	SO%	WHIP	AVG
2025	21	Did not play															

14 KORBYN DICKERSON, OF
HIT: 40. **POW:** 50. **RUN:** 55. **FLD:** 50. **ARM:** 50. **BA Grade:** 45. **Risk:** Average. **Adj:** 35.

Born: October 30, 2003. **B-T:** R-R. **HT:** 6-1. **WT:** 205. **Drafted:** Indiana, 2025 (5th round). **Signed by:** Gabriela Diaz.
TRACK RECORD: Dickerson played his high school ball in Kentucky, but grew up just across the border in Indiana. The Twins selected him in the 20th round in 2022, but he landed at Louisville for a season before transferring to Indiana for the 2025 season. During a breakout junior season with the Hoosiers, he drove in 77 runs—fourth-most in a single season in program history—and blasted 19 home runs, tied for sixth on the Hoosiers' single-season list. Dickerson was drafted in the fifth round, signed for a slot value of $461,000 and debuted at Low-A.
SCOUTING REPORT: Dickerson jumped from zero home runs in 2024 to 19 in 2025, a breakout fueled by added strength to his 6-foot-1, 205-pound frame. That spring at Indiana, he paired a 109.8 mph 90th-percentile exit velocity with a strong 25.6% barrel rate, starting from a crouched, shoulder-tucked

SEATTLE MARINERS

stance before unleashing a quick, powerful swing with natural feel for the barrel. His approach can get overly aggressive, and his 27% chase rate and 82% zone-contact rate in college were both below-average. His 42.1% groundball rate limited some of his impact as well. Still, he runs well, takes efficient routes in the outfield and has room to grow physically. With improved swing decisions and loft, even more damage could be on the way.
THE FUTURE: Dickerson should start 2026 in the lower minors and needs to work on cutting down his chase rate in the pros.

Year	Age	Club (League)	Level	AVG	G	AB	R	H	2B	3B	HR	RBI	BB	SO	SB	OBP	SLG
2025	21	Modesto (CAL)	A	.429	2	7	2	3	1	0	0	1	1	2	0	.556	.571
		Minor League Totals		.429	2	7	2	3	1	0	0	1	1	2	0	.556	.571

15 TEDDY McGRAW, RHP
FB: 50. **SW:** 55. **CH:** 50. **CTL:** 45. **BA Grade:** 55. **Risk:** Extreme. **Adj:** 35.

Born: October 30, 2001. **B-T:** R-R. **HT:** 6-3. **WT:** 210. **Drafted:** Wake Forest, 2023 (3rd round). **Signed by:** Ty Holub.
TRACK RECORD: McGraw already had two Tommy John surgeries on his ledger—one in high school and another while at Wake Forest—when the Mariners drafted him in the third round in 2023, but they believed in McGraw's sheer arm talent. He returned from surgery to log 8.2 innings in 2024 before an elbow flexor injury shut him down. That injury lingered into 2025 and delayed the start of his season until June. McGraw logged 28.1 innings, pitching once a week in short bursts, and struck out 27.5% of batters compared to a 6.7% walk rate.
SCOUTING REPORT: McGraw's calling card in college was a heavy mid-90s sinker that averaged 18 inches of armside movement. It's still part of his three-pitch mix, but in 2025 he leaned on a wicked sweeping mid-80s slider just as often. The pitch averaged roughly 2,800 rpm of spin and almost 17 inches of horizontal break. In a small sample, it was McGraw's best weapon and produced elite whiff and chase rates. He also worked with a separate mid-90s four-seam fastball and a seldom-used 88-91 mph changeup. McGraw was a groundball machine in college and that held true in 2025.
THE FUTURE: The Mariners remain open to exploring McGraw's dynamic arsenal in a starting role, but his checkered medical history might force him to the bullpen so that he can remain healthy. McGraw enters a pivotal 2026 season that he figures to begin back in High-A. If all goes well, he could finish the year in the upper minors.

Year	Age	Club (League)	Level	W	L	ERA	G	GS	IP	H	HR	BB	SO	BB%	SO%	WHIP	AVG
2025	23	ACL Mariners	Rk	0	0	3.00	5	4	9	8	0	4	9	10.8	24.3	1.33	.258
2025	23	Everett (NWL)	A+	0	3	3.26	9	8	19	24	1	4	24	4.8	28.9	1.45	.304
		Minor League Totals		0	3	3.41	18	16	37	41	1	12	41	7.5	25.6	1.43	.287

16 BROCK RODDEN, SS/2B
HIT: 45. **POW:** 50. **RUN:** 55. **FLD:** 50. **ARM:** 50. **BA Grade:** 45. **Risk:** Average. **Adj:** 35.

Born: May 25, 2000. **B-T:** B-L. **HT:** 5-7. **WT:** 170. **Drafted:** Wichita State, 2023 (5th round). **Signed by:** Joe Saunders.
TRACK RECORD: Rodden has bet on himself his whole career. He transferred to Wichita State via the junior college ranks, then broke out in 2022, which led the A's to draft him in the 10th round. Rodden instead returned to school for his senior season and posted a 1.175 OPS, leading the Mariners to select him in the fifth round in 2023. As one of the older players in the draft, Rodden signed an underslot deal worth $200,000. He was excellent for High-A Everett in 2024, but he struggled with Double-A Arkansas in 2025 and was limited to just 41 games by a slew of injuries, including a fractured left hamate. He added 11 Arizona Fall League games to make up for lost time.
SCOUTING REPORT: At 5-foot-7, Rodden has surprising power and belted 14 homers in 2024. While injuries limited him to just five homers in 2025, he still managed an above-average 104.5 mph 90th percentile exit velocity and a 32.4% air-pull rate. A switch-hitter, most of his power comes from the left side. Rodden tends to chase, especially with two strikes, and can be beat by better fastballs. Defensively, he splits time between second, short and third. His average range and a solid arm suggests second base is his natural position, though the added versatility across the infield only helps his cause.
THE FUTURE: If he had stayed healthy, Rodden had a shot to reach the majors in 2025. He should begin 2026 in Triple-A and profiles as a solid utility option.

Year	Age	Club (League)	Level	AVG	G	AB	R	H	2B	3B	HR	RBI	BB	SO	SB	OBP	SLG
2025	25	ACL Mariners	Rk	.273	4	11	1	3	0	0	0	1	3	4	2	.467	.273
2025	25	Arkansas (TL)	AA	.295	37	146	23	43	10	0	5	22	12	49	14	.356	.466
		Minor League Totals		.274	206	806	131	221	48	7	21	107	86	210	47	.352	.429

SEATTLE MARINERS

17 MICHAEL MORALES, RHP
FB: 45. **CB:** 45. **SL:** 40. **CH:** 55. **SW:** 45. **CTL:** 50. **BA Grade:** 45. **Risk:** Average. **Adj:** 35.

Born: August 13, 2002. **B-T:** R-R. **HT:** 6-2. **WT:** 205. **Drafted:** HS—Enola, PA, 2021 (3rd round). **Signed by:** Dave Pepe.
TRACK RECORD: Seattle coughed up an overslot $1.5 million bonus to reel Morales away from his commitment to Vanderbilt as a third-rounder in 2021. He spent 2022 and 2023 in Low-A Modesto, enduring some bumps while posting a 5.22 ERA but also striking out 231 hitters. His development accelerated in Double-A Arkansas, where he sharpened his command and momentum carried into a strong 2024 campaign, finishing with a 3.02 ERA across High-A and Double-A. Offseason elbow inflammation delayed his 2025 start, but he still logged 101.2 innings with a 4.60 ERA in his return to Double-A.
SCOUTING REPORT: Morales' intrigue comes from his diverse arsenal. Despite a fastball that sits in the low 90s, he leaned on a six-pitch mix in 2025 and gave hitters plenty to think about. Morales can land his mid-80s slider in the zone with regularity and then he turns to his upper-70s sweeper and a 12-6 upper-70s curveball to chase swings and misses. Morales' low-80s changeup is early in its development but has above-average upside. He sparingly uses a separate sinker to round out the repertoire. Morales has always been a solid strike-thrower, but his strikeout rate plunged to 16.1% in 2025 and he lost roughly 2 mph of velocity on his fastball.
THE FUTURE: Given that he lacks a true putaway offering, Morales will instead need to hone the sequencing and execution of his deep mix. He should begin 2026 in Triple-A and has back-of-the-rotation potential.

Year	Age	Club (League)	Level	W	L	ERA	G	GS	IP	H	HR	BB	SO	BB%	SO%	WHIP	AVG
2025	22	Arkansas (TL)	AA	4	7	4.60	22	22	102	105	5	37	70	8.5	16.1	1.40	.271
		Minor League Totals		27	20	4.45	98	98	473	478	39	166	449	8.1	22.0	1.36	.261

18 MASON PETERS, LHP
FB: 55. **CB:** 60. **SL:** 45. **CH:** 40. **CTL:** 50. **BA Grade:** 45. **Risk:** Average. **Adj:** 35.

Born: December 18, 2003. **B-T:** L-L. **HT:** 5-11. **WT:** 175. **Drafted:** Dallas Baptist, 2025 (4th round). **Signed by:** Ryan Holmes.
TRACK RECORD: Peters pitched for a Dallas Baptist program that has produced 17 draft picks on the mound since 2020. In his lone season with the Patriots after transferring from Temple (Tex.) JC, Peters pitched to a 4.25 ERA with 58 strikeouts against 16 walks across 42.1 innings. Peters also started four games, including an outing against Liberty when he struck out 10 across six scoreless innings, which set up a combined no-hitter by DBU. The Mariners drafted him in the fourth round in 2025.
SCOUTING REPORT: While Peters throws a 93 mph fastball that can top out at 96 and sets up the rest of his arsenal, his best weapon in 2025 was an upper-70s, high-spin curveball. It's a sharp, diving pitch that has plus potential. Despite its velocity, it's tough for hitters to square up—though his command of it can be inconsistent. Working from a three-quarters arm slot, he brings plenty of intent and some power behind his delivery. He'll show a low-80s slider with more horizontal sweep on occasion, but it's a distant third option behind his fastball-curveball combo. The Mariners believe there's room to shape multiple breaking balls off the look of his curveball. He also has a below-average cutter and could incorporate a sinker into his mix.
THE FUTURE: The Mariners are thin on lefthanded starters in the minors and plan to develop Peters in the rotation. He'll make his pro debut in the lower minors in 2026.

Year	Age	Club (League)	Level	W	L	ERA	G	GS	IP	H	HR	BB	SO	BB%	SO%	WHIP	AVG
2025	21	Did not play															

19 LUIS SUISBEL, 3B/SS
HIT: 45. **POW:** 50. **RUN:** 40. **FLD:** 45. **ARM:** 60. **BA Grade:** 50. **Risk:** High. **Adj:** 35.

Born: May 23, 2003. **B-T:** B-R. **HT:** 6-1. **WT:** 190. **Signed:** Venezuela, 2019. **Signed by:** Illich Salazar.
TRACK RECORD: Suisbel's career has featured its share of peaks and valleys. Signed for $350,000 in July 2019, he didn't debut until 2021 because of the coronavirus pandemic. He struggled early, hitting just .202/.373/.327 with six homers over his first two seasons. He began to turn a corner in 2023, then performed well in a return to Low-A in 2024, slashing .276/.351/.436 with 15 homers. His 2025 campaign brought some regression in contact quality, but he offset it with increased impact, finishing with a career-high 23 homers in High-A Everett.
SCOUTING REPORT: Suisbel's solid power has become a bigger part of his game as he has packed more strength onto his 6-foot-1 frame. The switch-hitter works from an upright stance with a small forward stride and an uppercut swing that plays well on pitches down in the zone. Suisbel feasted on righthanded

pitching in 2025, as 19 of his homers—all of which left the yard to the pull side—came as a lefthanded hitter. Suisbel is a very aggressive hitter who ran an elevated chase rate—mostly against spin—and struck out 27.5% of the time in High-A while producing below-average contact rates. He's a capable defender at third base, though if he continues to get bigger his physicality may eventually push him to first base.
THE FUTURE: Suisbel will need to develop better bat-to-ball skills to maximize his power, and there's pressure on his bat as a corner-only profile. The 22-year-old is ready for the upper minors in 2026.

Year	Age	Club (League)	Level	AVG	G	AB	R	H	2B	3B	HR	RBI	BB	SO	SB	OBP	SLG
2025	22	Everett (NWL)	A+	.211	113	427	62	90	15	1	23	68	48	135	8	.308	.412
		Minor League Totals		.228	267	916	147	209	38	6	41	157	120	308	18	.349	.417

20 LEANDRO ROMERO, SS

HIT: 40. **POW:** 50. **RUN:** 50. **FLD:** 55. **ARM:** 60. **BA Grade:** 55. **Risk:** Extreme. **Adj:** 35.

Born: November 8, 2006. **B-T:** R-R. **HT:** 6-0. **WT:** 170. **Signed:** Dominican Republic, 2024. **Signed by:** Audo Vicente.
TRACK RECORD: Romero signed for $1 million, the second-highest bonus in the Mariners' 2024 international class. He struggled in his Dominican Summer League debut that year, slashing .223/.359/.304 with a 31% strikeout rate. The Dominican shortstop responded with a loud 2025 after adding some muscle to his body, hitting .304/.367/.557 with a .924 OPS. His nine home runs tied for third-most in the circuit.
SCOUTING REPORT: Romero returned to the Mariners' Dominican complex with added moxie in 2025, and it carried over to both his approach and performance. He cut his strikeout rate to 22% and also upped his exit velocities in his second year at the level. Seattle initially asked him to emphasize contact over power, and he adjusted quickly before earning the green light to let it eat. He later attended the Mariners' high-performance camp in Peoria at the end of 2025, where his exit velocities touched 110 mph. Romero can struggle to time up fastballs and tends to be late against premium velocity, and his swing is more geared to do damage at the bottom half of the zone. He's a strong infield defender up the middle with fluid actions, a low center of gravity and a strong arm with a quick, confident release.
THE FUTURE: Romero will make his stateside debut in the Arizona Complex League in 2026. He has second-division regular upside if he can find the right blend of contact and power against better pitching.

Year	Age	Club (League)	Level	AVG	G	AB	R	H	2B	3B	HR	RBI	BB	SO	SB	OBP	SLG
2025	18	DSL Mariners	Rk	.304	42	158	32	48	11	1	9	35	16	35	6	.367	.557
		Minor League Totals		.265	91	306	55	81	19	3	9	48	46	81	10	.363	.435

21 CHIA-SHI SHEN, RHP

FB: 50. **SL:** 55. **CH:** 50. **SW:** 45. **CTL:** 50. **BA Grade:** 50. **Risk:** High. **Adj:** 35.

Born: December 3, 2003. **B-T:** R-R. **HT:** 6-3. **WT:** 185. **Signed:** Taiwan, 2024. **Signed by:** Keith Chiang.
TRACK RECORD: Shen impressed scouts with a mid-90s fastball as a teenager pitching for the New Taipei City baseball team in Taiwan's industrial league. He was slated to sign with the A's in 2022 until that deal fell through. A year later, Shen and the Mariners were close to a deal until he was arrested for drunk driving. Seattle ultimately signed him for $175,000 in July 2024 out of Kainan University in Taoyuan City. He split his 2025 pro debut between the Arizona Complex League and Low-A, pitching to an 18.3% strikeout-to-walk percentage over 69.1 innings.
SCOUTING REPORT: Shen operates from the first base side of the rubber with a traditional three-quarters slot delivery, below-average extension and a smooth leg kick. He's a sinkerballer who sits in the low 90s and ran a 65% strike rate in 2025. Shen's most effective pitch is a low-80s slider that hitters missed nearly 52% of the time, often chasing it out of the zone. He rounds out his arsenal with a mid-80s changeup and dabbled with a separate 80 mph sweeper. Shen is less physical and experienced than a typical 22-year-old righty, though there's some projection remaining in his 6-foot-3 frame.
THE FUTURE: If Shen can add some muscle—and a little more life to his fastball—it will only help as he chases a ceiling of a back-of-the-rotation starter.

Year	Age	Club (League)	Level	W	L	ERA	G	GS	IP	H	HR	BB	SO	BB%	SO%	WHIP	AVG
2025	21	ACL Mariners	Rk	2	1	1.93	7	3	28	19	0	4	34	3.7	31.8	0.82	.186
2025	21	Modesto (CAL)	A	1	4	6.53	9	9	41	49	6	10	34	5.3	18.1	1.43	.290
		Minor League Totals		3	5	4.67	16	12	69	68	6	14	68	4.7	23.1	1.18	.251

SEATTLE MARINERS

22 JARED SUNDSTROM, OF
HIT: 40. **POW:** 55. **RUN:** 55. **FLD:** 50. **ARM:** 50. **BA Grade:** 50. **Risk:** High. **Adj:** 35.

Born: June 21, 2001. **B-T:** R-R. **HT:** 6-3. **WT:** 225. **Drafted:** UC Santa Barbara, 2023 (10th round).
Signed by: Trevor Andresen.
TRACK RECORD: Sundstrom spent his first two college seasons at Santa Rosa JC in California before transferring to UC Santa Barbara, where a breakout junior year in 2023 pushed him into the 10th round, where the Mariners scooped him up. He backed that up with an impressive first full pro season at High-A Everett, hitting .263/.380/.434 with 13 home runs across 112 games. In 2025 at Double-A Arkansas, he hit 12 home runs but also set a career high with 145 strikeouts.
SCOUTING REPORT: Sundstrom's power and encouraging contact results in 2024 should've set him up to have a strong 2025. Instead, he took a step back. Sundstrom still generated above-average exit velocities, but swing-and-miss issues cropped up across the board. His miss, chase and in-zone whiff rates all increased, which led to a career-worst 29.7% strikeout rate. As is often the case with plenty of power-over-hit profiles, Sundstrom has a long swing that causes him to chop over breaking balls and struggle with fastball timing. While he runs well and stole 35 bases on 39 attempts in 2025, Sundstrom spent the bulk of his time in the corners of the outfield.
THE FUTURE: Sundstrom's power potential is appealing, but he'll need to make adjustments in search of more contact to make it work.

Year	Age	Club (League)	Level	AVG	G	AB	R	H	2B	3B	HR	RBI	BB	SO	SB	OBP	SLG
2025	24	Arkansas (TL)	AA	.219	115	438	62	96	22	5	12	53	40	145	35	.297	.374
		Minor League Totals		.240	249	928	148	223	56	8	28	131	115	280	61	.337	.408

23 RHYLAN THOMAS, OF
HIT: 55. **POW:** 30. **RUN:** 55. **FLD:** 50. **ARM:** 40. **BA Grade:** 45. **Risk:** Average. **Adj:** 35.

Born: April 15, 2000. **B-T:** L-L. **HT:** 5-10. **WT:** 170. **Drafted:** Southern California, 2022 (11th round).
Signed by: Rusty McNamara (Mets).
TRACK RECORD: Originally drafted by the Mets in the 11th round in 2022, the Mariners landed Thomas at the 2024 trade deadline for reliever Ryne Stanek. In 2025 with Triple-A Tacoma, Thomas slashed .325/.380/.411 over 134 games and made his MLB debut for the Mariners on May 2, where he recorded a two-run double. He was sent down after three games and spent the rest of the season in Tacoma.
SCOUTING REPORT: If a pitch lands in the strike zone, there's a strong chance Thomas isn't going to miss. Thomas posted elite in-zone contact rates in 2025, and struck out just 5.2% of the time in Triple-A. Thomas doesn't have much power, and his slower bat speed is geared toward a shorter swing and contact-driven approach to spray the ball over the field. Thomas is susceptible to expanding the zone in pursuit of more contact, often trying to poke an outside ball for weak contact. Thomas is an above-average runner who stole 35 bases, but he was also caught 11 times. He's an average outfield defender at all three spots.
THE FUTURE: Thomas is a reliable, contact-oriented bench piece and outfield depth option for the Mariners in 2026.

Year	Age	Club (League)	Level	AVG	G	AB	R	H	2B	3B	HR	RBI	BB	SO	SB	OBP	SLG
2025	25	Tacoma (PCL)	AAA	.325	134	547	105	178	24	1	7	78	46	32	35	.380	.411
2025	25	Seattle (AL)	MLB	.125	3	8	2	1	1	0	0	2	1	0	0	.200	.250
		Minor League Totals		.309	362	1350	231	417	66	3	16	156	128	114	65	.370	.398
		Major League Totals		.125	3	8	2	1	1	0	0	2	1	0	0	.200	.250

24 MARCELO PEREZ, RHP
FB: 45. **SL:** 55. **CH:** 40. **SW:** 55. **CTL:** 50. **BA Grade:** 45. **Risk:** Average. **Adj:** 35.

Born: November 16, 1999. **B-T:** R-R. **HT:** 5-10. **WT:** 195. **Drafted:** Texas Christian, 2022 (11th round).
Signed by: Patrick O'Grady.
TRACK RECORD: Perez's path to pro ball took a few turns. The Angels drafted him in the 20th round in 2021, but he opted to return to Texas Christian for his senior season, then pitched to a 3.23 ERA over a career-high 61.1 innings. The Mariners then came calling in the 11th round in 2022. He performed well in his first full pro season in 2023, but the road got bumpier in 2024, as he struggled to a 6.81 ERA at High-A Everett. He produced better results in 2025 between High-A Everett and Double-A Arkansas, with a 3.44 ERA and improved command.
SCOUTING REPORT: Perez isn't the hardest thrower, but he has always had feel to spin a breaking ball, and in 2025 he created more definition between his 83-87 mph slider with sharp, late gloveside bite and a separate low-80s sweeper that has nearly 16 inches of horizontal break. He's comfortable deploying

both in all counts and he leans heavily on his two sliders. Perez's low-90s fastball velocity backed up by roughly 1 mph compared to 2024 and it's a pitch that doesn't miss many bats. However, he commands it well enough to get ahead in counts. His upper-80s changeup is a distant fourth offering that needs more refinement.
THE FUTURE: Perez uses solid control and plenty of spin to get outs, but he'd benefit from a bit more fastball velocity to become a back-end starter.

Year	Age	Club (League)	Level	W	L	ERA	G	GS	IP	H	HR	BB	SO	BB%	SO%	WHIP	AVG
2025	25	Everett (NWL)	A+	4	2	2.04	8	8	35	28	3	5	34	3.7	25.4	0.93	.222
2025	25	Arkansas (TL)	AA	2	4	4.31	11	11	56	52	7	18	28	7.6	11.9	1.24	.244
		Minor League Totals		9	11	3.41	37	37	166	142	14	47	138	7.0	20.5	1.14	.232

25 VICTOR LABRADA, OF
HIT: 50. **POW:** 40. **RUN:** 60. **FLD:** 50. **ARM:** 50. **BA Grade:** 45. **Risk:** Average. **Adj:** 35.

Born: January 16, 2000. **B-T:** L-L. **HT:** 5-8. **WT:** 195. **Signed:** Dominican Republic, 2019. **Signed by:** Audo Vicente.
TRACK RECORD: Labrada emerged as one of Cuba's brightest young talents, captaining the national team and hitting .350 as its leadoff hitter at the 2018 Pan-American Championships. He left for the Dominican Republic in 2019, and the journey paid off when the Mariners signed him for $350,000 in 2021. The 25-year-old spent all of 2025 split between Double-A and Triple-A and slashed .281/.403/.405 with 44 stolen bases over 128 games.
SCOUTING REPORT: The 5-foot-8 Labrada has a great sense of his strengths and weaknesses. With a game built around speed, he has swiped 172 bases over the last five seasons. His footwork extends to the outfield, where he gets above-average jumps and is a steady defender at all three positions. At the plate, he understands that he's the kind of hitter who thrives by using his solid bat-to-ball skills to hit the ball to the alleys. There's some sneaky power in his bat, too, with a 90th percentile exit velocity that hovers around 103 mph, but his game centers on driving balls into the gaps all over the field rather than swinging for the fences. His zone recognition gains helped him post career bests in walk rate (14.9%) and strikeout rate (16.9%) in 2025.
THE FUTURE: Labrada projects as a fourth outfielder who can serve as a defensive replacement or pinch-runner. He should have a shot at reaching the majors in 2026.

Year	Age	Club (League)	Level	AVG	G	AB	R	H	2B	3B	HR	RBI	BB	SO	SB	OBP	SLG
2025	25	Arkansas (TL)	AA	.295	67	241	40	71	12	1	6	27	42	48	30	.407	.427
2025	25	Tacoma (PCL)	AAA	.265	61	189	40	50	12	3	1	25	37	42	14	.397	.376
		Minor League Totals		.267	508	1846	336	493	96	23	36	219	253	505	172	.365	.402

26 GRANT KNIPP, RHP/C
FB: 55. **CB:** 55. **CH:** 45. **CTL:** 45. **BA Grade:** 50. **Risk:** High. **Adj:** 35.
HIT: 30. **POW:** 55. **RUN:** 40. **FLD:** 40. **ARM:** 70.

Born: November 29, 2001. **B-T:** R-R. **HT:** 6-2. **WT:** 230. **Drafted:** Campbell, 2024 (6th round). **Signed by:** Ty Holub.
TRACK RECORD: If it wasn't for Jurrangelo Cijntje, Knipp may have been the most intriguing selection from the 2024 draft. The Mariners fell in love with him after his draft combine performance and drafted him as a two-way player, even though he took a six-year hiatus from pitching before returning to the mound in his final season at Campbell, where he touched 98 mph. As a catcher for the Camels, he hit .402/.547/1.029 with 18 home runs and 46 RBIs during his junior spring. He missed the 2025 season after having Tommy John surgery during spring training.
SCOUTING REPORT: Offensively, Knipp's biggest selling point is his plus raw power. His swing lacks adjustability, so he can struggle with pitches down or away, but his solid plate discipline helps balance things out. Behind the plate, he shows off a huge arm, though he has a slow transfer, and his receiving and blocking are still works in progress. On the mound, Knipp relies on a straight 93-96 mph fastball with some downward angle and pairs it with a firm 81-84 mph curveball that has good bite. He was a strong strike-thrower in a very limited sample.
THE FUTURE: Scouts preferred Knipp as a pitcher, but the Mariners plan on developing him as a two-way player. He's expected to return during extended spring training.

Year	Age	Club (League)	Level	W	L	ERA	G	GS	IP	H	HR	BB	SO	BB%	SO%	WHIP	AVG
2025	23	Did not play—Injured															

SEATTLE MARINERS

27 ROBINSON ORTIZ, LHP
FB: 60. **SL:** 55. **CH:** 45. **CT:** 50 **CTL:** 50. **BA Grade:** 45. **Risk:** Average. **Adj:** 35.

Born: January 4, 2000. **B-T:** L-L. **HT:** 5-11. **WT:** 175. **Signed:** Dominican Republic, 2017.
Signed by: Luis Marquez/Roman Barinas/Laiky Uribe (Dodgers).
TRACK RECORD: It's hard to label Ortiz a journeyman given how little he has actually pitched. He signed with the Dodgers for $60,000 in 2017, almost a year after first becoming eligible to sign, and has thrown just 238 professional innings since, including just 22.2 innings between 2021 and 2024 as he rehabbed from Tommy John surgery and a separate injury. Ortiz stayed healthy in 2025 and impressed across three levels out of the bullpen. The Dodgers added him to their 40-man roster after the season to prevent him from attaining minor league free agency, then traded him to the Mariners for righthander Tyler Gough.
SCOUTING REPORT: There's nothing particularly flashy about Ortiz's arsenal, but it's effective. He works from the third base side of the rubber from a three-quarter arm slot, finishing with a longer, curling release that adds deception. His fastball is more powerful now than it was before his injuries. It sits 95-96 mph and has been up to 98 with most of its whiffs coming up in the zone. His most-used secondary is a low-80s, high-spin slider that draws plenty of chases, especially from lefties. Ortiz's seldom-used changeup remains a work in progress, and he also added a low-90s cutter into his mix.
THE FUTURE: Ortiz's four-seamer, slider and cutter mix from the left side gives him middle relief upside in the majors, and he should compete for a spot in the Mariners' bullpen out of spring training.

Year	Age	Club (League)	Level	W	L	ERA	G	GS	IP	H	HR	BB	SO	BB%	SO%	WHIP	AVG
2025	25	Great Lakes (MWL)	A+	1	2	3.74	18	0	22	22	3	15	28	15.0	28.0	1.71	.268
2025	25	Tulsa (TL)	AA	3	0	1.69	15	0	21	11	0	9	30	10.5	34.9	0.94	.151
2025	25	Oklahoma City (PCL)	AAA	1	0	2.76	15	1	16	11	1	9	14	13.2	20.6	1.22	.190
		Minor League Totals		17	12	3.48	99	41	238	192	16	109	238	10.8	23.6	1.26	.222

28 CHARLIE BEILENSON, RHP
FB: 50. **SW:** 45. **CH:** 55. **CT:** 50. **CTL:** 55. **BA Grade:** 45. **Risk:** Average. **Adj:** 35.

Born: December 10, 1999. **B-T:** R-R. **HT:** 6-0. **WT:** 215. **Drafted:** Duke, 2024 (5th round). **Signed by:** Ty Holub.
TRACK RECORD: The Mariners spent $7.88 million in 2024 to land pitchers Jurrangelo Cijntje and Ryan Sloan. Beilenson was one of the seniors they selected to balance out their bonus pool allotment, and signed for just $25,000 as a fifth-rounder out of Duke after saving 12 games that year. Beilenson split his first full professional season in 2025 between High-A Everett and Double-A Arkansas working out of the bullpen to the tune of a 28.6% strikeout rate and 4.6% walk rate across 62.2 innings and 44 appearances.
SCOUTING REPORT: Beilenson works exclusively from the stretch, using a compact delivery that hides the ball behind his head before a sharp, deceptive release. He has plenty of pitch shapes to work with. Beilenson has three different variations of his fastball: a 93 mph four-seamer that can touch 98 and plays up thanks to its late life, plus a cutter and a sinker. Beilenson's standout secondary is an 86 mph kick changeup that consistently keeps hitters off-balance. Beilenson's low-80s sweeper also has nearly 18 inches of break, and both secondaries flirted with 38% miss rates. He also has good control, finishing with a 66% strike rate.
THE FUTURE: While Beilenson is already 26, his feel for an unusually deep arsenal makes him a prime candidate for a high-leverage relief role in the big leagues.

Year	Age	Club (League)	Level	W	L	ERA	G	GS	IP	H	HR	BB	SO	BB%	SO%	WHIP	AVG
2025	25	Everett (NWL)	A+	2	1	3.97	20	0	34	28	6	8	48	5.9	35.3	1.06	.224
2025	25	Arkansas (TL)	AA	2	3	4.08	24	0	29	36	4	4	27	3.2	21.4	1.40	.300
		Minor League Totals		4	4	3.93	48	0	66	66	10	17	79	6.1	28.2	1.25	.256

29 LUCAS KELLY, RHP

FB: 55. **SL:** 45. **CH:** 45. **CTL:** 45. **BA Grade:** 45. **Risk:** Average. **Adj:** 35.

Born: July 26, 2003. **B-T:** R-R. **HT:** 6-4. **WT:** 220. **Drafted:** Arizona State, 2025 (6th round). **Signed by:** Ty Bowman.
TRACK RECORD: Kelly originally committed to Texas A&M before transferring to McLennan (Texas) JC in 2024, where he played both ways. He then headed to Arizona State in 2025 and pitched exclusively out of the bullpen. Kelly posted a 4.05 ERA across 26.2 innings with a 27.9% strikeout rate and a 7.4% walk rate. Unlike many draft arms who remain in the complex after being drafted, Kelly went to High-A Everett, where he made his pro debut and logged six innings as a reliever.
SCOUTING REPORT: Kelly works with an unorthodox delivery, starting with his glove low at his torso before reaching back and firing from a sidearm slot. Pitchers with quirky mechanics often rely on deception to offset modest velocity, but Kelly's fastball sat 95-96 mph and touched 99 in college. He threw it

roughly 80% of the time and it generated a 30% miss rate. His main secondary in college was a low-to-mid-80s slider that could be inconsistent, but in his High-A debut he also flashed a mid-80s changeup he could land in the zone with surprising regularity, given the small sample.
THE FUTURE: Kelly's fastball has proven to be effective, but his slider or changeup will need to take a step forward in order for him to be a reliable option in high-leverage situations. He should start in High-A Everett.

Year	Age	Club (League)	Level	W	L	ERA	G	GS	IP	H	HR	BB	SO	BB%	SO%	WHIP	AVG
2025	21	Everett (NWL)	A+	0	0	7.50	5	0	6	4	2	5	6	18.5	22.2	1.50	.182
		Minor League Totals		0	0	7.50	5	0	6	4	2	5	6	18.5	22.2	1.50	.182

30 TYLER CLEVELAND, RHP

FB: 35. **SW:** 50. **CH:** 50. **CT:** 35. **CTL:** 50. **BA Grade:** 45. **Risk:** High. **Adj:** 30.

Born: September 9, 1999. **B-T:** L-R. **HT:** 6-3. **WT:** 185. **Drafted:** Central Arkansas, 2022 (14th round).
Signed by: Dan Holcomb.
TRACK RECORD: Cleveland broke through as Central Arkansas' closer in 2021 and proved he could handle an even bigger role when he moved into the rotation the following year. The Mariners drafted him in the 14th round that year and initially developed him as a starter with Low-A Modesto in 2023 before transitioning him to the bullpen. The 25-year-old was dominant between High-A and Double-A in 2025, posting a 0.87 ERA with 50 strikeouts in 51.2 innings. Cleveland had a 25.5% strikeout rate with an 8.7% walk rate and he did not allow a home run.
SCOUTING REPORT: College programs rarely take walk-ons with mid-80s fastball velocity, yet Cleveland's sinker averaged just 86 mph in 2025. Instead, he gets by on funk and deception. He sets up on the first base side of the rubber with his glove near his chest, then uses a small leg kick before whipping his arm through a sidearm slot, finishing his delivery toward third base. He throws a sinker with nearly 20 inches of run that he isn't afraid to locate in different quadrants of the strike zone. He pairs it with a mid-70s sweeper, a low-80s changeup and the occasional cutter.
THE FUTURE: Cleveland's solid command, deceptive release and a pitch mix that dips and dives in all directions could be enough to help him reach the majors as a low-leverage reliever.

Year	Age	Club (League)	Level	W	L	ERA	G	GS	IP	H	HR	BB	SO	BB%	SO%	WHIP	AVG
2025	25	Everett (NWL)	A+	0	0	0.86	23	0	31	11	0	9	37	7.7	31.6	0.64	.107
2025	25	Arkansas (TL)	AA	3	1	0.89	18	0	20	11	0	8	13	10.1	16.5	0.93	.159
		Minor League Totals		19	8	2.93	103	20	227	184	15	66	213	7.1	22.8	1.10	.219

Junior Caminero

Tampa Bay Rays

BY J.J. COOPER

The Rays enter 2026 in transition, seemingly a few years away from where they want to go.

Tampa Bay returns "home" in 2026, heading back to Tropicana Field after a year at Steinbrenner Field, the Yankees' spring training facility in Tampa. It will do so with a new ownership group led by Patrick Zalupski.

The Rays' long-term home remains uncertain, as attempts to build a new stadium remain fluid. That uncertainty extends to the field as well. For most of the past decade, the Rays entered every year as an American League East contender. Now, they're looking up at much of the rest of the division.

From 2018 to 2023, the Rays had the fourth-best record in MLB. Just three seasons ago, the Rays won 99 games, and this decade they made the World Series (2020) and won 100 games for the first time ever (2021). Now, they are coming off back-to-back losing records and fourth-place finishes. The Rays have figured out ways to surprise before, but the task for 2026 and 2027 looks quite daunting.

So how did the Rays get here? The team has been hit by a variety of unexpected setbacks. The loss of the Trop for a year obviously hurt, but it's one of a number of trials.

Shortstop Wander Franco's 2023 suspension and 2024 arrest in the Dominican Republic on charges of sexual abuse of a minor—Franco was found guilty in a trial, but an appeals court has ordered a new trial—meant the Rays' franchise cornerstone hasn't played in two years.

Franco was a 22-year-old all-star at the time of his suspension. With him, the team had a pair of young hitters, along with Junior Caminero, to build around. Without him, they've had some of the worst offensive production from shortstops in baseball the past two seasons.

A front office brain drain hasn't helped. Andrew Friedman left for the Dodgers more than a decade ago, but other teams have continued to

PROJECTED 2029 LINEUP

Catcher	Nathan Flewelling	22
First Base	Xavier Isaac	25
Second Base	Daniel Pierce	23
Third Base	Junior Caminero	25
Shortstop	Carson Williams	26
Left Field	Chandler Simpson	28
Center Field	Theo Gillen	24
Right Field	Brendan Summerhill	26
Designated Hitter	Jonathan Aranda	31
No. 1 Starter	Brody Hopkins	27
No. 2 Starter	Joe Boyle	29
No. 3 Starter	T.J. Nichols	27
No. 4 Starter	Santiago Suarez	24
No. 5 Starter	Trevor Harrison	24
Closer	Jose Urbina	24

pluck from the Rays.

Three Rays front office officials from as recently as 2019 have become general managers elsewhere: Chaim Bloom (first Red Sox, now Cardinals), James Click (formerly Astros) and Peter Bendix (Marlins). Three coaches working for the Rays in 2019 are now MLB managers: Matt Quatraro with the Royals, Craig Albernaz with the Orioles and Blake Butera with the Nationals. Albernaz and Butera were hired during the 2025 offseason.

The team's drafting and international signings are another issue. Top international signees such as Sandy Gaston, Alejandro Pie, Carlos Colmenarez and Jose Contreras haven't panned out. The international market is full of risk, but the Rays haven't back-filled those misses with low-cost signings, either.

Draft whiffs have also hurt. Brendan McKay, the fourth pick in 2017, saw his career wrecked by shoulder injuries. Taylor Walls proved to be the team's only regular from that class. The 2018 class proved more productive, but it's the exception. The Rays had five top 100 picks in 2019. None have yet had an MLB impact. Ian Seymour is the only remaining hope from 2020.

The system still has solid depth, but it doesn't have the top-tier prospects it had a few years ago, when Shane McClanahan and Caminero were coming up.

In a division that keeps getting better, the Rays have an uphill climb. ∎

DEPTH CHART

TAMPA BAY RAYS

TOP 2026 ROOKIES	RANK
1. Carson Williams, SS	3
2. Dominic Keegan, C	13
3. Ty Johnson, RHP	16

BREAKOUT PROSPECTS	RANK
1. Cooper Flemming, SS	17
2. Taitn Gray, OF	26

SOURCE OF TOP 30 TALENT

Homegrown	21	Acquired	9
College	7	Trade	9
Junior college	1	Rule 5 draft	0
High school	11	Independent league	0
Undrafted free agent	0	Free agent/waivers	0
International	2		

LF
Brendan Summerhill (7)
Taitn Gray (26)
Noah Myers

CF
Theo Gillen (2)
Aidan Smith (8)
Homer Bush Jr. (22)
Maykel Coret

RF
Dean Moss (18)
Brailer Guerrero (20)
James Quinn-Irons (27)
Leonardo Pineda
Mac Horvath

3B
Brayden Taylor (30)

SS
Carson Williams (3)
Daniel Pierce (6)
Adrian Santana (15)
Cooper Flemming (17)
Gregory Barrios (28)
Alberth Palma
Ryan Spikes

2B
Jadher Areinamo (12)
Émilien Pitre (25)
Cooper Kinney

1B
Xavier Isaac (9)
Tre' Morgan (23)
Will Simpson

C
Nathan Flewelling (10)
Dominic Keegan (13)
Tatem Levins
Kenny Piper
J.D. Gonzalez

LHP

LHSP
Joe Rock (29)
Jeremy Pilon
Dominic Fritton

LHRP
Drew Dowd

RHP

RHSP
Brody Hopkins (1)
TJ Nichols (4)
Santiago Suarez (5)
Trevor Harrison (11)
Jose Urbina (14)
Gary Gill Hill (19)
Jackson Baumeister (21)
Marcus Johnson
Owen Wild
Ty Cummings
Logan Workman
Aidan Haugh
Ryan Andrade
Brian Van Belle

RHRP
Ty Johnson (16)
Alex Cook (24)
Evan Reifert
Tommy McCollum
Trevor Martin
Austin Vernon
Luke Jackson
Jacob Kuhn
Dylan Lesko
Moises Palma
Jacob Kisting

TAMPA BAY RAYS

1 BRODY HOPKINS, RHP

Born: January 18, 2002. **B-T:** R-R. **HT:** 6-4. **WT:** 200.
Drafted: Winthrop, 2023 (6th round).
Signed by: Terry McClure (Mariners).

TRACK RECORD: Growing up, Hopkins was always known as TJ's little brother. TJ Hopkins was a star athlete at Summerville (S.C.) High and went on to be a four-year outfield starter at South Carolina. Eventually, he became a major leaguer by spending 25 games with the 2023 Reds. Brody, who is five years younger, quickly made a name for himself as well. He was a baseball and football star—as a big-play wide receiver—in high school before heading to the College of Charleston as an outfielder who also pitched sporadically. After 50 games in the outfield and two on the mound for the Cougars, Hopkins transferred to Winthrop for the 2023 season, focused on pitching and saw his career take off. He was wild as a college pitcher, but his athleticism and stuff enticed the Mariners to draft him in the sixth round in that same year. In July 2024, Seattle sent him to the Rays as part of the return for outfielder Randy Arozarena. Hopkins took a step forward with his control in 2025, and was especially effective over the final two months at Double-A Montgomery. He struck out 32% of batters while allowing just four runs in his final six starts.

SCOUTING REPORT: Hopkins has the best stuff of any Rays minor league starter, with an all-out, all-power, all-the-time approach that is quite unusual for a starting pitcher. There is nothing subtle about Hopkins' stuff, as even his curveball and changeup will flirt with 90 mph. He'll have outings where he doesn't throw a pitch under 88-89 mph. It's an approach seen from very few MLB starters. Jacob Misiorowski and Max Meyer were the only MLB starters in 2025 who averaged 87 mph or harder with every pitch. Hopkins doesn't change speeds much, but he does force hitters to protect the entire strike zone. He's able to work up and down to lefthanded hitters thanks to a 96-97 mph four-seam fastball that touches 100. He throws it from a flat approach angle of less than 4 feet, with enough life to get above bats at the top of the zone. His 89-91 mph changeup gets below hitters' bats with just enough movement to pair with that extreme power, and his 92-93 mph cutter can get in under their hands. He can take that same up-and-down approach with righthanded hitters, but he can also mix in a bigger 87-88 mph power curve. He has also toyed with an 87-88 mph sweeper that runs away from them. Hopkins has a long arm action, which can lead to control issues, but he is athletic enough to repeat his delivery well. His 12% walk rate is high, but his ability to limit hard contact helps make his fringe-average control work.

THE FUTURE: Hopkins carries a bit more reliever risk than some other Rays starters thanks to his still-developing control, but he's made massive strides in just three years. He could develop into a front-of-the-rotation starter if everything clicks, with the kind of arsenal that gives hitters nightmares on a regular basis.

BA GRADE	SCOUTING GRADES
60 Risk: Average	**FB:** 65. **CB:** 70. **CH:** 45. **CT:** 65. **CTL:** 45.
Adjusted grade: **50**	Projected future grades on 20-80 scouting scale

BEST TOOLS

BATTING
Best Hitter	Theo Gillen
Best Power Hitter	Xavier Isaac
Best Strike-Zone Discipline	Theo Gillen
Fastest Baserunner	Homer Bush Jr.
Best Athlete	Brody Hopkins

PITCHING
Best Fastball	Brody Hopkins
Best Curveball	Brody Hopkins
Best Slider	Ty Johnson
Best Changeup	Moises Palma
Best Control	Santiago Suarez

FIELDING
Best Defensive Catcher	Kenny Piper
Best Defensive Infielder	Carson Williams
Best Infield Arm	Carson Williams
Best Defensive Outfielder	Aidan Smith
Best Outfield Arm	Aidan Smith

Year	Age	Club (League)	Level	W	L	ERA	G	GS	IP	H	HR	BB	SO	BB%	SO%	WHIP	AVG
2025	23	Montgomery (SL)	AA	5	7	2.72	25	25	116	85	7	60	141	12.2	28.7	1.25	.204
		Minor League Totals		9	10	2.79	43	43	200	147	9	100	236	11.8	27.8	1.24	.205

TAMPA BAY RAYS

2 THEO GILLEN, OF
HIT: 60. **POW:** 45. **RUN:** 60. **FLD:** 60. **ARM:** 40. **BA Grade:** 60. **Risk:** High. **Adj:** 45.

Born: September 12, 2005. **B-T:** L-R. **HT:** 6-2. **WT:** 195.
Drafted: HS—Austin, TX, 2024 (1st round). **Signed by:** Chris Hom.

TRACK RECORD: Gillen was long viewed as one of the best pure hitters in the 2024 prep draft class, but he was tougher to evaluate because he missed extended time with shoulder and wrist injuries. A strong senior season at Westlake High in Texas helped Gillen rise up draft rankings, and the Rays selected him with the 18th overall pick. Tampa Bay immediately moved him from shortstop to center field as a pro. A calf injury delayed the start of Gillen's 2025 season at Low-A Charleston by a month, but he would have led the Carolina League with a .433 on-base percentage if he had qualified. He missed the final three weeks after injuring his hand sliding into second base.

SCOUTING REPORT: Gillen is an exceptionally polished hitter for a teenager. He crowds the plate with a compact stance, very little pre-pitch movement and a modest load. His stance helps give him excellent plate coverage. His short swing, bat speed and ability to clear his hips allows him to turn on inside pitches, but he's just as comfortable serving the ball to left field when pitchers work him away. Gillen's power is modest, but he should develop into a hitter who hits bushels of line-drive doubles. He's a plus runner with the ability to steal 30-plus bases at a high success rate. Defensively, he made a speedy conversion to the outfield. He has no hesitation to leave his feet, but he does so in a calculated manner that turns doubles into lineouts without turning singles into triples. His old shoulder injury means he has a below-average arm, which is a big reason he moved to the outfield.

THE FUTURE: Gillen's polished lefthanded bat gives him a chance to be an impact regular in center field in an organization that emphasizes outfield defense. His lofty on-base percentages can be expected to dip as he faces better pitching, but his power should tick up as well.

Year	Age	Club (League)	Level	AVG	G	AB	R	H	2B	3B	HR	RBI	BB	SO	SB	OBP	SLG
2025	19	Charleston (CAR)	A	.267	73	243	62	65	12	1	5	18	64	75	36	.433	.387
		Minor League Totals		.257	81	269	66	69	13	1	5	20	72	89	37	.425	.368

3 CARSON WILLIAMS, SS
HIT: 30. **POW:** 60. **RUN:** 60. **FLD:** 65. **ARM:** 65. **BA Grade:** 55. **Risk:** Average. **Adj:** 45.

Born: June 24, 2003. **B-T:** R-R. **HT:** 6-2. **WT:** 180.
Drafted: HS—San Diego, CA, 2021 (1st round). **Signed by:** Jaime Jones.

TRACK RECORD: Williams hit 20 home runs and stole 33 bases for Double-A Montgomery in 2024, but the Rays were aware that he was not a finished product as a hitter. Still, Williams' struggles at Triple-A Durham in 2025 were surprising. His 34% strikeout rate was the second-highest in the International League. After trading away Jose Caballero, waiving Ha-Seong Kim and placing Taylor Walls on the injured list, Williams was called up to Tampa Bay. He hit five homers in 32 games, but it was an all-or-nothing approach that included a 42% strikeout rate.

SCOUTING REPORT: Coming into 2025, there was hope that Williams could be an offensive force as well as a plus defender. Triple-A exposed more issues at the plate, and while there is still hope for offensive improvement, it's more realistic to now project Williams as a strong defender who could hit enough home runs to have value as a bottom-of-the-order bat. If he can get a pitch up in the zone, he can get to his plus power. He has well above-average bat speed, and his 23 Triple-A home runs led all minor league shortstops, but there's little adjustability to his swing. Teams learned that he's almost helpless when pitchers work the bottom of the strike zone, especially with changeups, which he swung over time after time. Defensively, Williams projects as a reliably plus or better defender at shortstop. He is tall and rangy, and he knows how to use his plus arm to full advantage. His hands are soft. He's a plus runner who should steal 15-20 bases a year if he hits at all.

THE FUTURE: Williams has a much wider array of possible outcomes than most players who have already reached the majors. His contact issues could completely derail his career, but as a true shortstop who could hit 20 home runs, he could be a valuable player even with somewhat frightening batting averages if he makes even modest improvements in his contact rate.

Year	Age	Club (League)	Level	AVG	G	AB	R	H	2B	3B	HR	RBI	BB	SO	SB	OBP	SLG
2025	22	Durham (IL)	AAA	.213	111	389	72	83	12	5	23	55	56	154	22	.318	.447
2025	22	Tampa Bay (AL)	MLB	.172	32	99	11	17	3	0	5	12	6	44	2	.219	.354
		Minor League Totals		.247	465	1748	320	431	79	29	85	283	236	637	105	.345	.4713
		Major League Totals		.172	32	99	11	17	3	0	5	12	6	44	2	.219	.354

TAMPA BAY RAYS

4 TJ NICHOLS, RHP
FB: 60. **SL:** 60. **CH:** 40. **CTL:** 60. **BA Grade:** 55. **Risk:** Average. **Adj:** 45.

Born: June 24, 2002. **B-T:** R-R. **HT:** 6-4. **WT:** 190.
Drafted: Arizona, 2023 (6th round). **Signed by:** Brian Oliver.
TRACK RECORD: A standout on the mound and in the classroom at Oakmont High in Roseville, Calif., Nichols was part of coach Jay Johnson's final recruiting class at Arizona. Nichols bounced between the Wildcats' rotation and bullpen for all three years of college. His stuff was exceptional, but he struggled with consistency, largely because of control troubles. The quality of Nichols' stuff made him an enticing sixth-round pick for the Rays in 2023.
SCOUTING REPORT: The Rays are consistently the best organization in baseball in helping pitchers improve their strike-throwing. Nichols is one of the prime beneficiaries. His delivery and arm action were already relatively clean, but the Rays' combination of middle-middle catcher setups and emphasis on pitchers trusting their stuff has led to significant control strides. After walking 10% of batters he faced in college, Nichols slashed that to 6% across High-A and Double-A in 2025. His 68% strike percentage ranked 10th best among all minor league pitchers with 100 innings. Getting ahead of hitters more consistently allowed him to carve them up with his hard slider. If anything, Nichols may be in the zone a bit too much. The majority of the 21 home runs he allowed in 2025 came when he was ahead in the count. His plus fastball and plus slider could be more effective if hitters worried more about chasing them out of the zone. His below-average changeup needs to improve to better attack lefthanded batters, who were responsible for 16 of his 21 homers he allowed.
THE FUTURE: No Rays pitcher has made bigger strides in the past two years than Nichols. He now has a track record of success as a starter, including an 0.97 ERA in 37 innings for Double-A Montgomery to end the season. Nichols will head back there to start 2026. He projects as a midrotation starter.

Year	Age	Club (League)	Level	W	L	ERA	G	GS	IP	H	HR	BB	SO	BB%	SO%	WHIP	AVG
2025	23	Bowling Green (SAL)	A+	10	3	3.63	19	18	97	84	20	21	119	5.4	30.4	1.09	.233
2025	23	Montgomery (SL)	AA	4	0	0.97	6	6	37	22	1	9	37	6.8	28.0	0.84	.182
		Minor League Totals		14	3	2.79	28	26	139	108	21	31	160	5.7	29.5	1.00	.216

5 SANTIAGO SUAREZ, RHP
FB: 55. **CB:** 50. **CT:** 60. **CH:** 40. **CTL:** 70. **BA Grade:** 55. **Risk:** Average. **Adj:** 45.

Born: January 11, 2005. **B-T:** R-R. **HT:** 6-2. **WT:** 175.
Signed: Venezuela, 2022. **Signed by:** Manuel Padron/Clifford Nuitter/Tibaldo Hernandez (Marlins).
TRACK RECORD: A Marlins signee out of Venezuela in 2022, Suarez barely got to get comfortable wearing teal. Miami traded him with Marcus Johnson to the Rays for JT Chargois and Xavier Edwards in 2023. Suarez was impressing at High-A Bowling Green in 2025 when he went down with a sore shoulder in early May. He missed three months. When he returned, the Rays promoted him all the way to Triple-A for his final two starts of the season.
SCOUTING REPORT: The Rays emphasize throwing strikes more than any other organization, but even in a system full of strike-throwers, Suarez's plus-plus control stands out. He walked eight batters in 52 innings all season. By comparison, 10 minor league pitchers walked at least that many in a single start in 2025. He ranked second in the minors in strike percentage in 2025 among pitchers with 50-plus innings. Suarez is no soft-tossing control wizard. His above-average four-seam fastball sits at 94-95 mph and can touch 97, and it has above-average life. His hard, high-80s cutter gives him a plus secondary offering, and he'll use an average, low-80s downer curveball to give lefthanded hitters something to worry about. That curve has been especially important to lefties because Suarez is still exploring changeup grips. His hands are smaller than many pitchers, and he hasn't yet gotten comfortable with any of the multiple changeup grips he has tried.
THE FUTURE: Suarez figures to earn a spot in the Double-A Montgomery rotation in 2026 with a strong spring training. He will be one of the Southern League's younger starters as a 21-year-old. His exceptional control gives him a chance to develop into a midrotation starter, though he may need to learn to expand the zone more often to become more unpredictable.

Year	Age	Club (League)	Level	W	L	ERA	G	GS	IP	H	HR	BB	SO	BB%	SO%	WHIP	AVG
2025	20	Bowling Green (SAL)	A+	0	4	2.88	10	10	41	35	4	6	45	3.8	26.9	1.01	.223
2025	20	Durham (IL)	AAA	0	1	4.09	2	2	11	9	3	2	9	4.7	20.9	1.00	.225
		Minor League Totals		6	8	2.28	38	31	150	129	9	25	144	4.2	24.2	1.03	.230

TAMPA BAY RAYS

6 DANIEL PIERCE, SS
HIT: 45. **POW:** 50. **RUN:** 60. **FLD:** 60. **ARM:** 65. **BA Grade:** 55. **Risk:** High. **Adj:** 40.

Born: August 4, 2006. **B-T:** R-R. **HT:** 6-0. **WT:** 185.
Drafted: HS—Hoschton, GA, (1st round), 2025. **Signed by:** Luke Harrigan.
TRACK RECORD: The son of a high school baseball coach, Pierce seems to always be in control as a defender. But that attribute was likely to carry him only to the late second or third round coming into 2025. Significant improvements at the plate in his senior season pushed Pierce into the first round in a loaded prep shortstop draft class. He showed both more consistent contact and improved power. The Rays drafted him 14th overall and signed him for $4.31 million.
SCOUTING REPORT: The Rays are loaded with plus defenders at shortstop, from Taylor Walls in the majors to Carson Williams, Gregory Barrios and Adrian Santana in the minors. Pierce has a chance to be the equal or better of all of them if everything clicks. He glides around the infield, making the tough plays look easy with a quick first step, hands that erase bad hops and a 65 arm on the 20-to-80 scouting scale that matches Williams as the best in the organization. Offensively, Pierce has more upside than all the Rays' shortstops but Williams. Earlier in his amateur career, he struggled to string together consistent at-bats. He has some noise in his setup that may contribute to that volatility. He cocks the bat and has a big bat waggle at times, but as he filled out, his bat control and contact ability has improved. Pierce has the size and strength to combine average power with a fringe-average hit tool. He's continued to fill out and is already 10 pounds heavier and stronger than he was when the Rays drafted him.
THE FUTURE: Pierce should spend most or all of 2026 at Low-A Charleston, where he can be expected to play excellent defense and provide sneaky power. His defense gives him plenty of chances to develop into a big leaguer, and his power potential gives him a chance to be a star if he can continue to make strides at the plate.

Year	Age	Club (League)	Level	AVG	G	AB	R	H	2B	3B	HR	RBI	BB	SO	SB	OBP	SLG
2025	18	Did not play															

7 BRENDAN SUMMERHILL, OF
HIT: 60. **POW:** 45. **RUN:** 55. **FLD:** 50. **ARM:** 50. **BA Grade:** 50. **Risk:** Average. **Adj:** 40.

Born: November 13, 2003. **B-T:** L-R. **HT:** 6-3. **WT:** 200.
Drafted: Arizona, 2025 (1st round supp.). **Signed by:** Jaime McFarland.
TRACK RECORD: Summerhill was considered one of the top pure hitters in the 2025 college class after producing for average both at Arizona and in the Cape Cod League. He missed a month of his junior season with a broken hand, and the injury may have cost him a spot in the first round. Summerhill was hitting .409/.500/.656 at the time but hit just .263/.412/.434 after he returned. The Rays drafted him with the 42nd overall pick. Summerhill's older brother Colin, an Angels undrafted free agent in 2024, beat Brendan to pro ball by a year.
SCOUTING REPORT: As soon as he signed, Summerhill became one of the Rays' best contact hitters. He's long shown excellent barrel control and adjustability in his swing. There's no one way to pitch him. If a pitcher succeeds in one at-bat, there's little guarantee that the same approach will work the next time. Summerhill's power has always been modest. He could sell out for a few more home runs, but it's more likely he'll settle in as a plus hitter with fringe-average pop. Summerhill played both center and right field in college and eventually fits as a corner outfielder for the Rays. He'll likely get plenty of time in center field for now, because the Rays try to play three center field-capable outfielders most of the time. He's an above-average runner who should be at least average in the corners with a chance to be above-average. He has an average arm.
THE FUTURE: Summerhill's brief pro debut for Low-A Charleston ended early because of an oblique injury, but he should be full speed for spring training. He fits the kind of well-rounded college hitter that the Rays covet in the draft. He should be a key part of the High-A Bowling Green outfield for most of 2026.

Year	Age	Club (League)	Level	AVG	G	AB	R	H	2B	3B	HR	RBI	BB	SO	SB	OBP	SLG
2025	21	Charleston (CAR)	A	.333	10	36	8	12	2	1	0	5	6	5	5	.429	.444
		Minor League Totals		.333	10	36	8	12	2	1	0	5	6	5	5	.429	.444

TAMPA BAY RAYS

8 AIDAN SMITH, OF
HIT: 40. **POW:** 45. **RUN:** 60. **FLD:** 65. **ARM:** 60. **BA Grade:** 50. **Risk:** Average. **Adj:** 40.

Born: July 23, 2004. **B-T:** R-R. **HT:** 6-3. **WT:** 190.
Drafted: HS—Lucas, TX, 2023 (4th round). **Signed by:** Patrick O'Grady (Mariners).
TRACK RECORD: When they traded Randy Arozarena at the 2024 deadline, the Rays knew they needed to nail the deal, because Arozarena was one of the team's best trade chips. A year and a half later, Brody Hopkins is the team's best prospect. Smith, the other prospect in the deal, had a tougher time in 2025. After hitting for average and power in 2024, Smith saw his strikeout rate spike to 31% at High-A Bowling Green while he hit .237 and his power dipped. He went to the Arizona Fall League to try to end the season on an up note. He walked more than he hit in 12 games there. On the bases, Smith has been consistent. He's stolen 41 bases while getting thrown out six times in each of the past two seasons.
SCOUTING REPORT: Smith never seemed to get comfortable at the plate with Bowling Green, and he struggled more with velocity than ever before. He has always been quiet in his setup, but in 2025 he struggled to get in rhythm and get his hands going. When he tried to tweak his stance, his struggles spiraled. He ended up fouling away pitches he should have been pulling for extra-base damage. Smith has a knack for driving the ball in the air when he's synced up. While he struggled more than expected at the plate, there was a much more positive development in 2025 in the field. With the Mariners, Smith was splitting time almost equally between all three outfield spots. The Rays challenged him to focus on center field. He responded by steadily getting better defensively. By the end of the year, he was the Rays' best defensive minor league center fielder. He now projects as a plus center fielder. He's a plus runner with a plus arm.
THE FUTURE: Smith's defensive improvements reduce the pressure on his bat, but he will have to show that his 2025 hitting struggles were a blip more than a trend.

Year	Age	Club (League)	Level	AVG	G	AB	R	H	2B	3B	HR	RBI	BB	SO	SB	OBP	SLG
2025	20	Bowling Green (SAL)	A+	.237	102	397	77	94	14	2	14	59	53	143	41	.331	.388
		Minor League Totals		.257	221	837	175	215	49	6	26	120	127	270	88	.362	.423

9 XAVIER ISAAC, 1B
HIT: 40. **POW:** 60. **RUN:** 50. **FLD:** 50. **ARM:** 50. **BA Grade:** 55. **Risk:** High. **Adj:** 40.

Born: December 17, 2003. **B-T:** L-L. **HT:** 6-4. **WT:** 240.
Drafted: HS—Kernersville, NC, 2022 (1st round). **Signed by:** Landon Lassiter..
TRACK RECORD: After a strong 2023 and first half of 2024, Isaac's career hit a speed bump at Double-A Montgomery. His 2025 season never really got going. A sore elbow sidelined him for the first 10 days, and when he was activated he was limited to DH. He battled a wrist injury, but his season eventually ended for another reason. Isaac announced in November that he had what he described as "life-saving" brain surgery. He is expected to make a full recovery.
SCOUTING REPORT: Isaac's injury issues made him a tough player to evaluate in 2025. He was helpless against lefthanders, which hasn't been an issue in the past, but his power and bat speed were still impressive despite the injuries. No Rays minor leaguer hits the ball harder than Isaac, but he is going to have to make adjustments to get to that power consistently. He has struggled to pull the ball in the air. Fewer than 20% of his fly balls at Double-A were pulled to right field, while 80% of his ground balls in 2025 were pulled. His ability to clear the fence in center and left field has allowed him to get to his power anyway. Isaac's swing is steep. He can drive pitches at the top of the zone but is somewhat helpless against pitchers working down in the zone. He has solid pitch recognition skills, but pitchers can toy with his timing. He is too often tardy on quality fastballs and he struggles to handle changeups, as well. Isaac was an average defender at first base in 2024, but he didn't get on the field in 2025. He is an average runner despite his 6-foot-4, 240-pound frame.
THE FUTURE: Isaac will play the entire 2026 season as a 22-year-old, so he's still on a good timetable, even with a return to Double-A. With his ability to drive the ball and draw walks, he could be productive even with a strikeout rate near 30%. But he needs to get healthy and refine the flaws in his game.

Year	Age	Club (League)	Level	AVG	G	AB	R	H	2B	3B	HR	RBI	BB	SO	SB	OBP	SLG
2025	21	Montgomery (SL)	AA	.201	41	139	21	28	5	1	9	22	34	52	1	.366	.446
		Minor League Totals		.262	250	886	161	232	49	7	46	177	158	292	28	.378	.489

TAMPA BAY RAYS

10 NATHAN FLEWELLING, C
HIT: 45. **POW:** 55. **RUN:** 30. **FLD:** 50. **ARM:** 50. **BA Grade:** 55. **Risk:** High. **Adj:** 40.

Born: November 11, 2006. **B-T:** L-R. **HT:** 6-2. **WT:** 200.
Drafted: HS—Red Deer, AB, 2024 (3rd round). **Signed by:** James Bonnici.
TRACK RECORD: As a 17-year-old catcher coming out of Alberta, Flewelling was not exactly a high-profile, low-risk pick. But the Rays loved his power potential, and they were one of the teams that also believed that he could stick behind the plate. They drafted him in the third round in 2024. Flewelling more than rewarded their faith by being one of the pleasant surprises on the Low-A Charleston club. His surface-level stats (.229/.393/.336) weren't anything special, but his batted-ball data shined while he proved to be a reliable catcher defensively.
SCOUTING REPORT: If Flewelling were a first baseman, his offensive ability would still be intriguing. But he pairs an exceptional batting eye, big power and solid contact ability with work behind the plate to create one of the better sleeper prospects in the game. Flewelling had one of the best chase rates in the Rays' system, and he paired it with above-average power potential. While he hit just six home runs in 2025, he should develop above-average power. His 90th percentile exit velocity of 105 mph is excellent for a teenager. As a catcher, he's already an above-average framer, and he embraces the intellectual aspects of leading the pitching staff. He carries himself like a veteran, rather than one of the youngest players on the team. Flewelling turns in average pop times with plus accuracy, which helped him throw out 27% of basestealers. He caught 75 games in 2025. That topped Ethan Salas' 2024 season as the most games caught by an 18-year-old in pro ball this decade.
THE FUTURE: The Rays haven't produced a homegrown long-term starting catcher at any point in their history. Flewelling has a lot of development left, but his combination of defense, savvy and hitting ability could finally end the three-decade drought.

Year	Age	Club (League)	Level	AVG	G	AB	R	H	2B	3B	HR	RBI	BB	SO	SB	OBP	SLG
2025	18	Charleston (CAR)	A	.229	102	336	46	77	16	1	6	49	89	121	9	.393	.336
2025	18	Bowling Green (SAL)	A+	.250	5	16	2	4	1	1	0	3	5	6	0	.409	.438
		Minor League Totals		.230	107	352	48	81	17	2	6	52	94	127	9	.393	.341

11 TREVOR HARRISON, RHP
FB: 60. **SL:** 55. **CH:** 45. **CTL:** 45. **BA Grade:** 55. **Risk:** High. **Adj:** 40.

Born: August 8, 2005. **B-T:** R-R. **HT:** 6-4. **WT:** 225. **Drafted:** HS—New Port Richey, FL, 2023 (5th round).
Signed by: Brett Foley.
TRACK RECORD: A lifelong Rays fan who grew up just north of Tampa, Harrison was one of the Rays' breakout prospects of 2024. He continued to have success in 2025, but under the hood he demonstrated some issues that will need to be cleaned up if he's going to remain a starter. Harrison worked less than five innings in eight of 22 starts because he's inefficient with his pitch counts. But few Rays starters rival Harrison's stuff and he remained extremely difficult for hitters to square up.
SCOUTING REPORT: Harrison's plus fastball and above-average slider can carve through lineups like a meat cleaver when he's locating. His fastball sits 94-96 mph and can get to 98-99 at his best with enough life to be a swing-and-miss pitch at the top of the zone. Many four-seam pitchers struggle with homers when they miss their spot, but Harrison allowed one homer off his heater all year. His mid-80s slider flashes above-average, although he does struggle to command it at times. His fringe-average changeup is a bigger concern. He showed less feel and confidence for it in 2025, and at times he relied almost exclusively on his fastball against lefties. That worked in Class A, but likely won't as he moves up. He has fringe-average control, but his delivery is clean and he has plenty of mass and muscle to repeat his delivery.
THE FUTURE: Harrison remains one of the Rays' best pitching prospects, but he needs more refinement than his surface-level stats may indicate. His late-season taste of High-A should set him up to be the Hot Rods' ace in 2026.

Year	Age	Club (League)	Level	W	L	ERA	G	GS	IP	H	HR	BB	SO	BB%	SO%	WHIP	AVG
2025	19	Charleston (CAR)	A	7	2	2.61	17	17	83	63	1	36	75	10.7	22.4	1.20	.211
2025	19	Bowling Green (SAL)	A+	1	1	3.33	5	5	24	23	2	13	25	12.4	23.8	1.48	.258
		Minor League Totals		10	5	2.96	30	29	140	118	6	57	139	10.0	24.3	1.25	.232

TAMPA BAY RAYS

12 JADHER AREINAMO, 2B
HIT: 60. **POW:** 45. **RUN:** 45. **FLD:** 60. **ARM:** 50. **BA Grade:** 50. **Risk:** Average. **Adj:** 40.

Born: November 28, 2003. **B-T:** R-R. **HT:** 5-10. **WT:** 201. **Signed:** Venezuela, 2021.
Signed by: Jose Rodriguez/Javier Castillo (Brewers).
TRACK RECORD: Areinamo has never been viewed as the best player on the field throughout his career, but he always produces at a top-tier level. After he won the High-A Midwest League batting title in 2024, the Brewers still sent him back to Wisconsin in 2025. The July trade to the Rays for catcher Danny Jansen gave him a change of scenery and a spot in Double-A. Areinamo's 15 home runs in 2025 were a career high, and then he went out and hit 13 more in his first 36 games in the Venezuelan League.
SCOUTING REPORT: While Areinamo's unorthodox approach yields excellent results, he was never a great fit in a Brewers system full of quality middle infielders. That's because they strongly emphasize plate discipline, and Areinamo swings at everything. Areinamo's 52% swing percentage was among the highest in the minors, but he also posts top-tier contact rates. He has an extremely noisy setup. He lays the bat on his shoulder, brings it off the shoulder, then adds a waggle to start his hands. Somehow it works, thanks to exceptional bat-to-ball skills. His flat swing excels at mashing fastballs at the top of the zone, and he's gotten very good at maximizing his modest power. Defensively, he's a plus defender at second base thanks to excellent hands and baseball savvy, even if he lacks exceptional range. He's playable at third as well thanks to his average arm and those quick hands.
THE FUTURE: Areinamo is a very well-rounded second baseman who could be above-average at the plate and in the field. After being added to the 40-man roster during the offseason, he should be Double-A Montgomery's everyday second baseman. He should reach Triple-A Durham in 2026.

Year	Age	Club (League)	Level	AVG	G	AB	R	H	2B	3B	HR	RBI	BB	SO	SB	OBP	SLG
2025	21	Wisconsin (MWL)	A+	.297	94	367	51	109	24	2	11	51	34	48	15	.355	.463
2025	21	Montgomery (SL)	AA	.255	37	141	18	36	8	0	4	19	12	19	6	.316	.397
		Minor League Totals		.293	457	1731	263	508	108	8	30	233	141	234	80	.349	.417

13 DOMINIC KEEGAN, C
HIT: 35. **POW:** 45. **RUN:** 45. **FLD:** 45. **ARM:** 30. **BA Grade:** 45. **Risk:** Mild. **Adj:** 40.

Born: August 1, 2000. **B-T:** R-R. **HT:** 6-0. **WT:** 205. **Drafted:** Vanderbilt, 2022 (4th round). **Signed by:** Steve Ames.
TRACK RECORD: In his final three seasons at Vanderbilt, Keegan's bat kept him in the lineup, but his struggles catching meant he logged more time at first base than catcher. Keegan's bat wouldn't get him to the majors as a first baseman, but he and the Rays have worked hard to make him a plausible catcher. That's meant he's been on a level-a-year timetable that is slower than most college draftees, but after being held back by an elbow injury early in the season, Keegan was Triple-A Durham's primary catcher in 2025.
SCOUTING REPORT: Keegan's bat isn't a problem—as long as he's catching. He's a mistake hitter who can be beaten by quality pitching despite well above-average bat speed. Keegan's swing has some length, but he looks for sliders, cutters and sweepers he can drive, and he rarely misses a hanging breaking ball. His ability to punish pitchers' mistakes should help him get to 12-15 home runs a year with regular playing time, and he draws enough walks to buttress low batting averages. Defense remains Keegan's biggest question. His arm is well below-average thanks to modest arm strength and a slow exchange. As a pitch framer, he's inconsistent, especially struggling to smoothly steal strikes at the bottom of the zone. He's much more fluid on pitches up, turning pitches just above the zone into called strikes. He has improved to become above-average at blocking balls in the dirt.
THE FUTURE: The Rays added Keegan to the 40-man roster in the offseason. He should head back to Triple-A Durham with a chance to make his MLB debut at some point in 2026. His defensive limitations point toward a more likely outcome as a big league backup with uncommon power and plate discipline.

Year	Age	Club (League)	Level	AVG	G	AB	R	H	2B	3B	HR	RBI	BB	SO	SB	OBP	SLG
2025	24	FCL Rays	Rk	.292	8	24	7	7	2	0	2	4	8	6	0	.469	.625
2025	24	Durham (IL)	AAA	.241	69	266	34	64	16	2	10	36	24	91	0	.306	.429
		Minor League Totals		.276	299	1078	165	298	65	9	36	176	146	287	3	.365	.454

14 JOSE URBINA, RHP
FB: 55. **SL:** 60. **CB:** 40. **CH:** 45. **CTL:** 55. **BA Grade:** 50. **Risk:** Average. **Adj:** 40.

Born: November 2, 2005. **B-T:** R-R. **HT:** 6-3. **WT:** 180. **Signed:** Venezuela, 2023. **Signed by:** Angel Contreras/Juan Castillo.
TRACK RECORD: Urbina had a good frame, but when the Rays signed him at 16 years old he topped out at 90 mph. He has steadily added velocity ever since and did so again in 2025, adding another tick to his fastball in a dominant season at Low-A Charleston.

TAMPA BAY RAYS

SCOUTING REPORT: Urbina's fastball averaged 94 mph in 2023, 95 in 2024 and 96 in 2025 while touching 100 mph. His fastball carry isn't exceptional, but it's still an above-average pitch because of its combination of velocity and flat plane. Urbina largely went away from his big, slower curve, replacing it with a much harder mid-80s cut-slider that tunnels well with his fastball. The slider has plus potential and could get even more powerful as he develops it. He did drop in the below-average high-70s curve from time to time, but he struggled to locate it. His fringe-average changeup needs work. It's a chase pitch for now, and the whiffs it got in Class A are unlikely to continue against better hitters unless he shows he can throw it for strikes. Urbina's control improved from below-average to above-average in 2025 as he better controlled his delivery. He walked zero or one batter in 13 of his 20 starts.

THE FUTURE: Much like a late-season stint in Charleston in 2024 prepped Urbina for 2025, the Rays gave him a one-game sneak peek at High-A Bowling Green to end the season. He'll be at the front of that rotation in 2026 and should be one of the best starters in the South Atlantic League.

Year	Age	Club (League)	Level	W	L	ERA	G	GS	IP	H	HR	BB	SO	BB%	SO%	WHIP	AVG
2025	19	Charleston (CAR)	A	7	2	2.05	19	19	92	68	7	30	96	8.2	26.4	1.06	.207
2025	19	Bowling Green (SAL)	A+	0	0	4.50	1	1	4	4	2	0	5	0.0	31.3	1.00	.250
		Minor League Totals		8	8	3.45	48	40	185	146	21	71	179	9.4	23.6	1.17	.217

15 ADRIAN SANTANA, SS

HIT: 45. **POW:** 20. **RUN:** 70. **FLD:** 60. **ARM:** 55. **BA Grade:** 45. **Risk:** Average. **Adj:** 35.

Born: July 18, 2005. **B-T:** B-R. **HT:** 5-11. **WT:** 155. **Drafted:** HS—Doral, FL, 2023 (1st round supp.).
Signed by: Victor Rodriguez.

TRACK RECORD: Santana is the son of a pro infielder, Osmany Santana, and it shows. His defensive acumen and baseball intelligence stood out throughout his amateur career, but there were many concerns about his small size and lack of physicality. He hit 11 home runs as a high school senior, which alleviated some worries. Those concerns about his size remain. He handled his jump to High-A Bowling Green by showing excellent barrel control, but it's essentially all singles. He had 17 extra-base hits.

SCOUTING REPORT: Santana is an excellent shortstop thanks to an innate understanding of time. He knows when he needs to rush, and when he can slow down. He has an above-average arm, but it's his feet that stand out. He glides across the infield. Santana is more comfortable making plays to his left than to his backhand. As a hitter, he's a bottom-of-the-order slap hitter with 20-grade power. Santana's 12.5% swing-and-miss rate is exceptional, but pitchers don't need to worry if they throw in the zone, and he'll also chase balls out of the zone. He is a plus-plus runner and an excellent basestealing threat.

THE FUTURE: Santana remains a 155-pound shortstop, and at times he's struggled to stay at that weight. His defense has a lot of value, and his basestealing and contact skills give him survival skills offensively, but it will be hard for him to find MLB success as more than a utility infielder unless he adds some power.

Year	Age	Club (League)	Level	AVG	G	AB	R	H	2B	3B	HR	RBI	BB	SO	SB	OBP	SLG
2025	19	Bowling Green (SAL)	A+	.263	89	365	64	96	13	2	2	43	35	49	47	.324	.326
		Minor League Totals		.257	99	404	70	104	15	2	2	46	42	58	50	.325	.319

16 TY JOHNSON, RHP

FB: 55. **SL:** 60. **CTL:** 55. **BA Grade:** 45. **Risk:** Average. **Adj:** 35.

Born: September 25, 2001. **B-T:** R-R. **HT:** 6-6. **WT:** 220. **Drafted:** Ball State, 2023 (15th round).
Signed by: Jacob Williams (Cubs).

TRACK RECORD: One of three players the Rays acquired for Isaac Paredes in a July 2024 trade, Johnson has long been viewed as a future reliever. But it's hard to move a pitcher to the bullpen when he keeps dominating as a starter. He posted the second-best ERA in the Southern League (2.61) with the second-most strikeouts in the league (149) in a standout 2025 season.

SCOUTING REPORT: Johnson's 2025 season was remarkable. He was one of the best starters in the Southern League relying almost entirely on his four-seam fastball and slider. In an age where some starters are using six or seven pitches, Johnson on most nights needs two. Johnson's low slot and delivery make his 91-94 mph above-average fastball play better than its velocity or movement would seem to indicate. Hitters just don't get a good look at the fastball, and his plus 84-86 mph slider is one he can manipulate. He relies on sharp, short-breaking sliders primarily, but he can make it bigger and deeper to run it down and out of the zone to finish off hitters. It generates above-average swings and misses. Despite not having a changeup he trusts, he's been able to handle lefthanded hitters as well as righthanders.

THE FUTURE: Johnson's success as a starter has delayed the transition, but evaluators still believe that Johnson's future lies in the bullpen. His low-slot approach could work in the majors as a one-inning reliever as soon as 2026.

TAMPA BAY RAYS

Year	Age	Club (League)	Level	W	L	ERA	G	GS	IP	H	HR	BB	SO	BB%	SO%	WHIP	AVG
2025	23	Montgomery (SL)	AA	7	6	2.61	26	20	110	66	5	38	149	8.8	34.7	0.94	.174
		Minor League Totals		10	11	2.69	50	33	194	124	7	64	269	8.4	35.3	0.97	.185

17 COOPER FLEMMING, SS

HIT: 50. **POW:** 50. **RUN:** 45. **FLD:** 50. **ARM:** 55. **BA Grade:** 50. **Risk:** High. **Adj:** 35.

Born: August 5, 2006. **B-T:** L-R. **HT:** 6-3. **WT:** 190. **Drafted:** HS—Aliso Viejo, CA, 2025 (2nd round).
Signed by: Jaime Jones.
TRACK RECORD: In 1953, Frederick Flemming played 23 games in the Durham Bulls outfield as part of a four-season minor league career that topped out in Triple-A. Now, more than 70 years later, his grandson Cooper could also play in Durham. The Rays made that possible by drafting the Vanderbilt signee in the second round in 2025 and signing him for $2.297 million. Flemming was a showcase standout who raised his draft stock with an MVP performance at the WWBA 17U National Championship.
SCOUTING REPORT: Flemming has a well-rounded blend of tools and skills, with a solid feel for how to grind out at-bats, run the bases and play defense, even if he doesn't have exceptional power, speed or twitchiness. As a hitter, Flemming's straightforward lefthanded stroke sprays line drives to all fields. He has skinny legs, but should fill out to eventually develop average power. He's a heady baserunner despite fringe-average speed. Defensively, he's an average defender at shortstop. If he gets much bigger, his hands and above-average arm would work at third base as well. He has above-average arm strength, although the length of his arm stroke isn't ideal and can lead to slower transfers.
THE FUTURE: The Rays are stocked with plus defensive shortstops, but Flemming helps them diversify their pool of shortstop prospects. He has more offensive potential than Adrian Santana or Gregory Barrios. Flemming is set to head to Low-A Charleston, where his well-rounded skill set and feel for the game should help him settle into pro ball quickly.

Year	Age	Club (League)	Level	AVG	G	AB	R	H	2B	3B	HR	RBI	BB	SO	SB	OBP	SLG
2025	18	Did not play															

18 DEAN MOSS, OF

HIT: 55. **POW:** 40. **RUN:** 50. **FLD:** 50. **ARM:** 50. **BA Grade:** 50. **Risk:** High. **Adj:** 35.

Born: April 17, 2006. **B-T:** L-R. **HT:** 6-0. **WT:** 180. **Drafted:** HS—Bradenton, FL, 2025 (2nd round supp.).
Signed by: Brett Foley.
TRACK RECORD: Moss has competed against top talent for years. He was named to the 2018 Pan Am Game 12U all-star team at first base, and he played four years at IMG Academy, establishing himself as an above-average hitter in big events. The Rays paid him $2.097 million to forgo his commitment to LSU in 2025.
SCOUTING REPORT: Moss' hitting ability is impressive, as he shows the skills to work counts, draw walks and spray the ball to all fields. He could be an above-average hitter with excellent hand-eye coordination. But he also has to prove that he won't end up as a tweener. His modest below-average power is a tough fit in a corner outfield spot, while his average speed means he's stretched in center. Scouts were mixed in their opinions as to whether Moss can stay in center field long-term in pro ball. The Rays like to have a plus-plus defender in center, but they also are comfortable trading some offensive impact for defense in the corner outfield spots, which makes Moss a potentially useful above-average defender in a corner, even if he's only average in center field.
THE FUTURE: Moss has plenty of experience and polish, but his ability to develop in center field and as a slugger will likely determine his path to the majors. He should be part of a Low-A Charleston team that should have a number of Rays' 2025 draftees.

Year	Age	Club (League)	Level	AVG	G	AB	R	H	2B	3B	HR	RBI	BB	SO	SB	OBP	SLG
2025	19	Did not play															

19 GARY GILL HILL, RHP

FB: 50. **SL:** 50. **CT:** 50. **CH:** 40. **CTL:** 60. **BA Grade:** 45. **Risk:** Average. **Adj:** 35.

Born: September 20, 2004. **B-T:** R-R. **HT:** 6-2. **WT:** 160. **Drafted:** HS—Somers, NY, 2022 (6th round).
Signed by: Zach Clark.
TRACK RECORD: An under-the-radar pitching prospect until his senior year of high school, Gill Hill was an astute sixth-round above-slot find for the Rays in 2022. After struggling in 2023, Gill Hill raised his arm slot and found more velocity in a breakout 2024 season. His 2025 season was a bit rockier, especially early. But his ERA in the second half of the season was two full runs lower than it was in the first half,

and he slashed 100 points off his OPS allowed as well. He's quite durable, throwing 245 innings over the past two seasons.
SCOUTING REPORT: After some adjustments, Gill Hill has settled in as a durable, strike-throwing sinker-baller. He fills the zone with a 68% strike rate, but he doesn't miss a lot of bats (18.8% strikeout rate). His 92-94 mph sinker and his hard 85-88 mph cutter are both best at avoiding barrels and getting early-count grounders. Gill Hill will touch 96-97, but struggles to maintain that sort of velocity. He has some ability to manipulate the shape of his bigger average slider. It will flash depth and bite, and he can add sweep to run away from righthanded hitters. His below-average changeup has backed up, which helps explain why lefties proved a problem in 2025.
THE FUTURE: Gill Hill shows flashes of velocity that would make him a midrotation starter, and the 21-year-old is still young enough to add more strength and stuff. His current arsenal doesn't miss many bats, but his plus control and durability make him a useful back-of-the-rotation arm.

Year	Age	Club (League)	Level	W	L	ERA	G	GS	IP	H	HR	BB	SO	BB%	SO%	WHIP	AVG
2025	20	Bowling Green (SAL)	A+	7	8	3.82	25	25	137	129	17	30	107	5.3	18.8	1.16	.247
		Minor League Totals		12	17	3.80	61	58	286	273	29	76	251	6.4	21.0	1.22	.251

20 BRAILER GUERRERO, OF
HIT: 40. **POW:** 60. **RUN:** 55. **FLD:** 50. **ARM:** 55. **BA Grade:** 55. **Risk:** Extreme. **Adj:** 35.

Born: June 25, 2006. **B-T:** L-R. **HT:** 6-1. **WT:** 215. **Signed:** Dominican Republic, 2023.
Signed by: Daniel Santana/Remmy Hernandez.
TRACK RECORD: Guerrero's $3.7 million bonus was one of the biggest in the 2023 international class, but he has struggled to stay healthy. He played just seven games in 2023 because of a shoulder injury, then played 28 games in 2024 before re-injuring the shoulder. In 2025, he played just 51 games because of an early hamstring injury and subsequent knee injury. The bill for that lost development time came due in the Arizona Fall League, where he hit .077 and was clearly overmatched by more experienced pitchers.
SCOUTING REPORT: Guerrero continues to hit the ball as hard as anyone in the Rays' farm system and generates exceptional exit velocities for a teenager. The lefthanded hitter explodes from a coiled batting stance, and when he connects, he can drive balls far beyond the right field wall. But the rest of his offensive approach needs to catch up to that power. Despite an average batting eye for his age, Guerrero struck out 29.9% of the time because he swings through too many changeups and sliders. Much of this can be attributed to collecting less than 400 plate appearances in three seasons. Guerrero is a well-built right fielder with an above-average arm. He's an above-average runner although his frame suggests he may slow down as he matures.
THE FUTURE: Guerrero needs a full healthy season of at-bats to help him catch up on lost developmental time. His lefthanded power could make him a middle-of-the-lineup cornerstone if he makes more consistent contact. High-A Bowling Green should be a big test in 2026.

Year	Age	Club (League)	Level	AVG	G	AB	R	H	2B	3B	HR	RBI	BB	SO	SB	OBP	SLG
2025	19	FCL Rays	Rk	.000	1	2	0	0	0	0	0	0	1	0	0	.000	.000
2025	19	Charleston (CAR)	A	.251	50	191	22	48	7	2	6	33	25	64	9	.341	.403
		Minor League Totals		.276	86	319	42	88	14	4	8	56	51	103	22	.379	.420

21 JACKSON BAUMEISTER, RHP
FB: 55. **CT:** 50. **CB:** 45. **CH:** 40. **CTL:** 50. **BA Grade:** 50. **Risk:** High. **Adj:** 35

Born: July 10, 2002. **B-T:** R-R. **HT:** 6-4. **WT:** 225. **Drafted:** Florida State, 2023 (2nd round supp.).
Signed by: Eric Robinson (Orioles).
TRACK RECORD: The 63rd pick in the 2023 draft, Baumeister was the Orioles' highest drafted pitcher under Mike Elias until 2025. If he makes the majors, it will be for another team. The O's sent him to Tampa Bay in the 2024 Zach Eflin trade and he is now the Rays' best hope for a useful return on the deal. Mac Horvath has settled into more of an org player while Etzel was traded for Nick Fortes.
SCOUTING REPORT: Baumeister had an eventful 2025 season, with parts he would rather forget. He was shelled to the tune of a 9.95 ERA in April, and after a much better May, he missed two months with a shoulder injury. Returning to action in August, he looked much more like the pitcher the Rays traded for with a sub-1.00 ERA over five starts. His Arizona Fall League stint came to a premature end because he was hit in the head by a 110 mph line drive. Thankfully, he was not seriously injured. Baumeister's lively 93-95 mph fastball gets swings and misses at the top of the zone. He has transformed his slider into a harder 87-89 mph cutter that he can locate in the zone and is average. He now relies much less on his slower curve and the feel for it has backed up. His below-average changeup remains a developing pitch.
THE FUTURE: Baumeister needs more consistency, but at his best, he can carve through a lineup multiple

TAMPA BAY RAYS

times. He will go to spring training competing for a spot in Triple-A Durham. He projects as a No. 4 starter.

Year	Age	Club (League)	Level	W	L	ERA	G	GS	IP	H	HR	BB	SO	BB%	SO%	WHIP	AVG
2025	22	Montgomery (SL)	AA	2	4	4.62	15	15	62	53	6	25	51	9.6	19.5	1.25	.230
		Minor League Totals		5	7	3.33	40	38	162	118	10	73	186	10.8	27.6	1.18	.203

22 HOMER BUSH JR., OF
HIT: 50. **POW:** 20. **RUN:** 70. **FLD:** 65. **ARM:** 30. **BA Grade:** 40. **Risk:** Mild. **Adj:** 35.

Born: October 13, 2001. **B-T:** R-R. **HT:** 6-3. **WT:** 215. **Drafted:** Grand Canyon, 2023 (4th round). **Signed by:** Will Scott (Padres).
TRACK RECORD: The son of seven-year MLB veteran Homer Bush Sr., the Rays acquired Bush from the Padres along with Dylan Lesko and J.D. Gonzalez in the 2024 Jason Adam trade. When acquired, the Rays hoped he could find more power, and Bush worked in the offseason on tweaking his swing to drive the ball more, but there was no sign of it working. He won the Southern League batting crown at .301, but also hit zero home runs.
SCOUTING REPORT: Bush is an athletic, physical specimen at 6-foot-3, 215 pounds who hits like a 150-pound speedster. Of the six homerless MiLB hitters with 450+ plate appearances, Bush outweighed the other five by 35-60 pounds. Bush hits from a very upright stance with a flat swing that doesn't really utilize his lower half, leading to Chandler Simpson-esque exit velocities. Bush's approach could work, but he needs to pair it with a more discerning eye. He has solid contact skills, but he has one of the worst chase rates in the minors. A plus-plus runner, he remarkably has 57 steals in 69 tries each of the past two seasons. Bush is a plus defender in center who relishes turning potential gappers into outs. He makes difficult sliding catches look easy.
THE FUTURE: Bush's ceiling is limited as an over-aggressive singles hitter, since it limits his on-base percentage. But his defense in center and basestealing prowess are useful, especially in an organization that emphasizes run prevention.

Year	Age	Club (League)	Level	AVG	G	AB	R	H	2B	3B	HR	RBI	BB	SO	SB	OBP	SLG
2025	23	Montgomery (SL)	AA	.301	121	472	69	142	12	8	0	45	48	98	57	.375	.360
		Minor League Totals		.296	251	923	155	273	31	8	7	78	98	181	122	.379	.369

23 TRE' MORGAN, 1B
HIT: 55. **POW:** 30. **RUN:** 55. **FLD:** 70. **ARM:** 60. **BA Grade:** 40. **Risk:** Mild. **Adj:** 35.

Born: July 16, 2002. **B-T:** L-L. **HT:** 6-0. **WT:** 215. **Drafted:** LSU, 2023 (3rd round). **Signed by:** Jeff Lavin.
TRACK RECORD: A hero in Baton Rouge for his game-saving defensive play in a dramatic win against Wake Forest in Omaha, Morgan has been a high-average, low-power hitter for three pro seasons. He's a .307 career MiLB hitter, but his career high in home runs is 10.
SCOUTING REPORT: Morgan's unusual profile has generated strong disagreements among scouts. Some see his lack of power as disqualifying for a first baseman, while others believe he can be a solid regular because of his hitting ability and excellent defense. Morgan wasn't awful offensively in 2025, but even his best attributes are average at best. He has below-average bat speed, doesn't drive the ball, has average bat-to-ball skills and average strike-zone discipline. To his credit, his two-strike approach is excellent, which helps him grind out walks. Defensively, Morgan plays first base like a lefthanded shortstop. He doesn't have the quickest first step, but everything else is exceptional. His hands, body control and range make him a Gold Glove candidate. He has a plus arm as well. He's playable in left field.
THE FUTURE: Morgan isn't going to push aside Jonathan Aranda or Yandy Diaz unless he finds more offensive impact. If injuries strike, he's a big-league ready fill-in, but he needs to make significant improvements to be an MLB regular.

Year	Age	Club (League)	Level	AVG	G	AB	R	H	2B	3B	HR	RBI	BB	SO	SB	OBP	SLG
2025	22	Durham (IL)	AAA	.274	92	328	53	90	15	3	8	45	64	77	8	.398	.412
		Minor League Totals		.307	206	749	133	230	40	7	19	119	120	128	32	.408	.455

24 ALEX COOK, RHP

FB: 55. **SL:** 55. **CH:** 40. **CTL:** 60. **BA Grade:** 45. **Risk:** Average. **Adj:** 35.

Born: March 29, 2001. **B-T:** R-R. **HT:** 6-1. **WT:** 230. **Drafted:** Colby (KS) JC, 2022 (12th round). **Signed by:** Matt Alison.
TRACK RECORD: Cook spent a year in the NAIA, then was one of the best starters in junior college baseball for two seasons. The Rays made him a reliever after signing in 2022 before eventually exploring whether he could handle the starting rotation. He was excellent for eight starts in 2024, but his right shoulder didn't enjoy him starting any more than opposing hitters did. He spent the second half of 2024 and the first half of 2025 on the injured list. When he returned, he was back in the bullpen for 13 impressive appearances.
SCOUTING REPORT: Cook is a straightforward four-seam fastball-slider reliever. He tops out at 96-97 mph, but generally sits at 94-95. That's average velocity for an MLB reliever, but he has plus control and command that keeps hitters defensive. Cook got to 0-2 counts five times as often as hitters got to 2-0 in 2025. Cook's mid-80s slider benefits from those pitchers' counts. It flashes above-average and he works it in and below the zone, forcing hitters behind in counts to stay aggressive. Cook uses his below-average changeup sporadically to remind lefties that it exists.
THE FUTURE: The Rays added Cook to the 40-man roster after the season. Despite limited pro experience, he's a good bet to pitch in the majors at some point in 2026 in an up-and-down role. Long-term, he could pitch sixth and seventh innings.

Year	Age	Club (League)	Level	W	L	ERA	G	GS	IP	H	HR	BB	SO	BB%	SO%	WHIP	AVG
2025	24	FCL Rays	Rk	1	0	3.86	4	0	5	4	0	5	10	20.8	41.7	1.93	.211
2025	24	Montgomery (SL)	AA	1	1	2.30	13	0	16	10	1	3	18	5.1	30.5	0.83	.179
		Minor League Totals		11	6	2.62	60	8	124	85	10	44	157	8.9	31.8	1.04	.190

25 EMILIEN PITRE, 2B

HIT: 50. **POW:** 45. **RUN:** 50. **FLD:** 55. **ARM:** 50. **BA Grade:** 45. **Risk:** Average. **Adj:** 35.

Born: October 4, 2002. **B-T:** L-R. **HT:** 5-11. **WT:** 190. **Drafted:** Kentucky, 2024 (2nd round). **Signed by:** Eric Roof.
TRACK RECORD: Pitre has taken an unlikely path to becoming an MLB prospect. He loved baseball, but when the Quebec native first started being recruited by American college coaches, he didn't know that college baseball was even a possibility. A native French speaker, he worked on the English he was learning on recruiting calls. He arrived at Kentucky as a scrawny 135-pound defensive whiz. He left as a 175-pound on-base machine who helped lead the Wildcats to their first College World Series appearance.
SCOUTING REPORT: Pitre has shown more pop than expected as he keeps filling out. He has added 15 more pounds of good weight as a pro. He actually posts above-average exit velocities, but his slashing swing is more geared to spray the ball to left and center field rather than pull it to right. He does a good job of getting the barrel on the ball, and he has long been a grinder who likes to work counts and try to get on base. Pitre is a very reliable defender at second base with above-average range and average hands. His average arm keeps him from being a realistic shortstop option.
THE FUTURE: The Rays have become a haven for Canadian prospects, and while Pitre doesn't have a plus tool, he does a lot of things reasonably well. He could become a useful lefthanded-hitting second baseman in the majors.

Year	Age	Club (League)	Level	AVG	G	AB	R	H	2B	3B	HR	RBI	BB	SO	SB	OBP	SLG
2025	22	Bowling Green (SAL)	A+	.268	118	448	61	120	23	3	9	63	61	107	14	.356	.393
		Minor League Totals		.272	139	525	75	143	29	4	9	77	73	118	21	.363	.394

26 TAITN GRAY, C/OF

HIT: 40. **POW:** 60. **RUN:** 50. **FLD:** 45. **ARM:** 50. **BA Grade:** 50. **Risk:** High. **Adj:** 35.

Born: August 16, 2007. **B-T:** B-R. **HT:** 6-4. **WT:** 220. **Drafted:** HS—Grimes, IA, 2025 (3rd round). **Signed by:** Jeff Lavin.
TRACK RECORD: It's generally difficult for Iowa prep prospects to impress leading up to the draft because their season starts in late May. Gray found a way. He hit the ball harder than anyone at the PBR Super 60 Showcase in February, setting an event max distance record. He then matched college prospects swing for swing at the MLB Draft Combine, posting the third-highest exit velocity (114.5 mph) at the combine. He tossed in a BP homer estimated at over 500 feet for his high school for good measure. He was one of the draft's big risers, as he climbed into the third round, forgoing his Oregon commitment for a $918,300 bonus.
SCOUTING REPORT: While the Rays were willing to draft older high schoolers like Cooper Flemming and Dean Moss in 2025, Gray was one of the youngest players in the draft class. As a slugger from Iowa, patience may be required, but his ability to rotate his trunk generates excellent bat speed and raw power

from both sides of the plate. He loves to lift weights, and already has a chiseled frame. Gray has shown flashes of potential to develop into an average defender behind the plate, in addition to seeing time in the outfield. The Rays seem more likely to develop him in a corner outfield spot. He runs well for his size, turning in average times at his best.
THE FUTURE: Gray will likely move more slowly than some of the older and more polished hitters in the Rays' draft class, but he also has some of the biggest potential if he can handle the massive jump in quality of competition.

Year	Age	Club (League)	Level	AVG	G	AB	R	H	2B	3B	HR	RBI	BB	SO	SB	OBP	SLG
2025	17	Did not play															

27 JAMES QUINN-IRONS, OF
HIT: 40. **POW:** 55. **RUN:** 60. **FLD:** 55. **ARM:** 55. **BA Grade:** 50. **Risk:** High. **Adj:** 35.

Born: June 28, 2003. **B-T:** R-R. **HT:** 6-5. **WT:** 230. **Drafted:** George Mason, 2025 (5th round). **Signed by:** ML Morgan.
TRACK RECORD: Quinn-Irons was a three-year standout at George Mason, finishing his career with a .419/.523/.734 season. His career .371 batting average is second-best in school history, as he showed the ability to hit for average, get on base and drive the ball. Unlike the Rays' prep picks, Quinn-Irons briefly got pro experience in 2025, but went on the IL after 10 days with a minor back injury.
SCOUTING REPORT: At 6-foot-5, 230 pounds, Quinn-Irons looks like a prototypical right fielder with his massive size and athleticism. He has above-average power and plus speed to go with an above-average arm. It all will come down to how much he can hit. While Quinn-Irons was a star in the Atlantic 10, the average fastball he saw there didn't crack 90 mph. He generates plenty of power and leverage with a swing that peppers both power alleys. Quinn-Irons fits what the Rays look for in corner outfielders. He runs well enough and is capable of playing center, but should be an above-average defender in right field with an above-average arm. He bounced among all three outfield spots in his pro debut.
THE FUTURE: Quinn-Irons has more offensive upside than most college fifth-round picks, but there is plenty of risk that he could struggle to adapt to the much higher velocities he'll see in the pro game. He should get settled at High-A Bowling Green in 2026.

Year	Age	Club (League)	Level	AVG	G	AB	R	H	2B	3B	HR	RBI	BB	SO	SB	OBP	SLG
2025	22	Charleston (CAR)	A	.259	8	27	2	7	0	0	0	2	4	10	2	.375	.259
		Minor League Totals		.259	8	27	2	7	0	0	0	2	4	10	2	.375	.259

28 GREGORY BARRIOS, SS
HIT: 30. **POW:** 20. **RUN:** 55. **FLD:** 60. **ARM:** 55. **BA Grade:** 40. **Risk:** Average. **Adj:** 30

Born: April 8, 2004. **B-T:** R-R. **HT:** 6-0. **WT:** 180. **Signed:** Venezuela, 2021.
Signed by: Jose Rodriguez/Fernando Veracierto (Brewers).
TRACK RECORD: The Brewers signed three high-profile Venezuelan shortstops in their 2021 international class. Barrios won't be the star of that trio—Jackson Chourio already locked that up—but he has so far lived up to both expectations and concerns as a plus defender who struggles at the plate. After Barrios hit .325/.367/.429 in the first half of 2024 for High-A Wisconsin, the Brewers traded him to the Rays for Aaron Civale. Barrios missed the first month and a half of 2025 with an elbow injury.
SCOUTING REPORT: That early 2024 stretch in Wisconsin is the only time that Barrios has looked comfortable at the plate as a pro. He's a defensive wizard at shortstop, but few hitters have less impact. Barrios rarely ever swings and misses, but when he hits the ball, it rarely goes anywhere. His 82 mph average exit velocity is bottom of the scale, and outfielders work to take away bloops because he doesn't hit it over their heads. Barrios junked switch-hitting early in his pro career to focus on hitting righthanded. Oddly, it has helped him hit righties, but he has yet to figure out how to hit lefties. Defensively, he has excellent hands and actions. He's a very reliable shortstop with an above-average arm.
THE FUTURE: Barrios and Jadher Areinamo will once again team up in an ex-Brewers reunion for Double-A Montgomery in 2026. Barrios' glove is exceptional, but his lack of impact could doom him to being an on-call Triple-A reserve.

Year	Age	Club (League)	Level	AVG	G	AB	R	H	2B	3B	HR	RBI	BB	SO	SB	OBP	SLG
2025	21	FCL Rays	Rk	.276	11	29	9	8	2	0	0	4	3	1	8	.400	.345
2025	21	Montgomery (SL)	AA	.241	77	274	36	66	7	0	1	27	18	42	28	.292	.277
		Minor League Totals		.244	272	989	149	241	38	5	2	100	76	147	90	.305	.298

TAMPA BAY RAYS

29 JOE ROCK, LHP
FB: 45. **SL:** 45. **CH:** 45. **CTL:** 60. **BA Grade:** 40. **Risk:** Average. **Adj:** 30.

Born: July 29, 2000. **B-T:** L-L. **HT:** 6-6. **WT:** 200. **Drafted:** Ohio, 2021 (1st round supp.). **Signed by:** Ed Santa (Rockies).
TRACK RECORD: The Rays annually make moves to clear 40-man roster spots, trading a player who needs a spot in exchange for a player a year or two away from requiring a protection decision. They acquired Rock in one of those deals, sending Greg Jones to the Rockies during spring training in 2024. Rock made his MLB debut on June 28, 2025 and eventually made three relief appearances scattered across three months.
SCOUTING REPORT: While the Rays love pitchers with plus control, Rock is the rare example where his ability to pitch within the strike zone hasn't yielded consistent outs. In his first year with the Rays, his 69% strike rate was one of the highest in Triple-A, but it also resulted in a league-high 160 hits allowed and .284 opponents' average. Rock tried to expand the zone more often in 2025, especially with his fringe-average changeup and slider. Pitching from a low three-quarters arm slot, the lefthander has long struggled to get lefties out. Rock may need to use his fringe-average 92-94 mph four-seamer less, as hitters tee off on it at times. His sinker doesn't miss bats, but it does stay in the park and generate plenty of ground balls.
THE FUTURE: Rock needs to find another pitch or a new wrinkle to settle into the majors permanently, but his reliability, durability and plus control will keep him viable as an on-call multi-inning reliever/swingman who can start in an emergency.

Year	Age	Club (League)	Level	W	L	ERA	G	GS	IP	H	HR	BB	SO	BB%	SO%	WHIP	AVG
2025	24	Durham (IL)	AAA	3	7	5.21	32	15	97	102	16	39	88	9.3	21.1	1.46	.275
2025	24	Tampa Bay (AL)	MLB	0	0	2.35	3	0	8	7	1	2	11	5.7	31.4	1.17	.226
		Minor League Totals		19	33	4.73	105	82	453	460	59	159	463	8.1	23.6	1.37	.262
		Major League Totals		0	0	2.35	3	0	8	7	1	2	11	5.7	31.4	1.17	.226

30 BRAYDEN TAYLOR, 3B/2B
HIT: 35. **POW:** 40. **RUN:** 50. **FLD:** 50. **ARM:** 50. **BA Grade:** 45. **Risk:** High. **Adj:** 30.

Born: May 22, 2002. **B-T:** L-R. **HT:** 6-0. **WT:** 180. **Drafted:** Texas Christian, 2023 (1st round). **Signed by:** Chris Hom.
TRACK RECORD: What a difference a year makes. Taylor dominated the High-A South Atlantic League in 2024, so his late-season struggles in the Double-A Southern League seemed like a blip. A year later, it seems more like an omen. Taylor hit 12 fewer home runs while being one of the least productive hitters in the league in a season he spent with Montgomery.
SCOUTING REPORT: Taylor's difficulties at the plate seemed to amplify month after month. He struggled at times to clear his body with his hands, and he also got too mechanical as he tried to tweak his approach and swing to halt his long slide. Taylor gets too pull-happy at times. It does mean when he gets the right pitch, he can drive it, but it means he gets a bit predictable and pitchable. Taylor never lost his understanding of the strike zone, and if he can get back to reasonable BABIPs, he could be a productive infielder. Defensively, he's average at second and third base with an average arm. Later in the 2025 season, he focused on third base in deference to Jadher Areinamo, but the Rays will keep his focus on versatility.
THE FUTURE: Taylor's selling point in the past was that he was a well-rounded college hitter with a low risk profile. After one productive season and one in which he hit .173 with a .575 OPS, it's possible that his real talent level lies somewhere in between the extremes. With an offseason mental reset, Taylor will try to prove he can be a useful multi-positional, lefthanded-hitting infielder.

Year	Age	Club (League)	Level	AVG	G	AB	R	H	2B	3B	HR	RBI	BB	SO	SB	OBP	SLG
2025	23	Montgomery (SL)	AA	.173	108	370	47	64	14	2	8	43	61	121	17	.289	.286
		Minor League Totals		.217	247	885	154	192	45	13	33	120	154	296	57	.333	.409

Jack Leiter

Texas Rangers

BY JOSH NORRIS

Two years after winning the World Series, the Rangers suddenly find themselves struggling to fight their way back to the postseason. The 2025 team finished 81-81 and in third place in the American League West, looking up at the Astros and Mariners.

After the season, changes were in store. Out went veteran skipper Bruce Bochy and in came Skip Schumaker. Minor league hitting coordinator Cody Atkinson joined the big league staff in Toronto and assistant farm director Sam Niedorf took over as Houston's farm director.

The Rangers also jettisoned a longtime piece of its infield when Marcus Semien was traded to the Mets for veteran outfielder Brandon Nimmo.

Texas' 2025 club got contributions from some of its youngest talent, but it will need a great deal more consistency to climb back into contention. Jack Leiter and Kumar Rocker combined for 43 starts as part of rotation led by righthander Jacob deGrom, who sipped from the fountain of youth and dominated in ways he hadn't since his mailing address was in Queens.

Wyatt Langford looked like a potential cornerstone, and Evan Carter produced 1.9 bWAR in limited action before hitting the injured list.

In the midst of a sport where plenty of teams are content to play for a next year that never comes, the Rangers were aggressive at the deadline in the hopes of pulling a 2023-style rabbit out of their hat and sneaking into the postseason. They shipped three pitchers to the Diamondbacks for righty Merrill Kelly and spent another minor league arm on Twins reliever Danny Coulombe.

The moves sapped their system of some of its depth. Still, the Rangers' farm is headed by twitchy wunderkind Sebastian Walcott. The 20-year-old shortstop quietly posted one of the better seasons in the Double-A Texas League despite being one of its youngest players. The chain also got a breakout

PROJECTED 2029 LINEUP

Catcher	Malcolm Moore	25
First Base	Jake Burger	33
Second Base	Gavin Fien	22
Third Base	Josh Jung	31
Shortstop	Corey Seager	35
Left Field	Wyatt Langford	27
Center Field	Evan Carter	26
Right Field	Sebastian Walcott	23
Designated Hitter	Brandon Nimmo	39
No. 1 Starter	Jack Leiter	29
No. 2 Starter	Kumar Rocker	29
No. 3 Starter	Caden Scarborough	24
No. 4 Starter	Jose Corniell	26
No. 5 Starter	David Davalillo	26
Closer	Emiliano Teodo	28

year from righty Caden Scarborough, who jumped from interesting high school arm to bat-missing monster at the Class A levels.

In the draft, the Rangers added hitterish high school infielder Gavin Fien to their cache of similar skilled prospects. A few rounds later, they might have scored a player with even more upside in two-way talent Josh Owens.

Initially regarded as more of a shortstop prospect, Owens and his live arm opened scouts' eyes at Low-A and after the season at instructional league. At both stops, he showcased athleticism, projection and a sharp slider with the kind of bite that turns hitters into corkscrews.

Pitching prospect David Davalillo continued quietly dissecting the competition with a bag full of 50-grade pitches and a ton of gumption. The righthander posted sub-3.00 ERAs at High-A and Double-A, vaulting himself into the system's upper tier. Fellow righthander Leandro Lopez got into better shape, repeated his delivery more often and capitalized on the potential he'd teased since his days in the Dominican Summer League.

Walcott should debut by the end of 2026, and Jose Corniell, Winston Santos and Emiliano Teodo could impact the big leagues as well. If they can supplement a roster headed by Langford, Carter and Corey Seager, the path back to the promised land might not be as long as it appears. ∎

DEPTH CHART

TEXAS RANGERS

TOP 2026 ROOKIES — RANK
1. Jose Corniell, RHP — 5
2. Winston Santos, RHP — 9
3. Sebastian Walcott, SS — 1

BREAKOUT PROSPECTS — RANK
1. Izack Tiger, RHP — 16
2. Jack Wheeler, 3B — 20

SOURCE OF TOP 30 TALENT

Homegrown	28	Acquired	2
College	9	Trade	1
Junior college	1	Rule 5 draft	1
High school	7	Independent league	0
Undrafted free agent	0	Free agent/waivers	0
International	11		

LF
Dylan Dreiling (12)

CF
Yeremy Cabrera (14)
Paulino Santana (25)
Anthony Gutierrez (26)
Cameron Cauley (29)

RF
Paxton Kling (21)
Marco Argudin

3B
Jack Wheeler (20)

SS
Sebastian Walcott (1)
Yolfran Castillo (10)
Daniel Rodriguez

2B
Gavin Fien (3)
Devin Fitz-Gerald (8)
Elorky Rodriguez (22)
Curley Martha

1B
Maxton Martin (24)
Abimelec Ortiz
Pablo Guerrero
Marcos Torres
Braylin Morel

C
Malcolm Moore (17)
Josh Springer
Sebastian Baquera
Ian Moller

LHP

LHSP
Dalton Pence (18)

LHRP
Ben Abeldt (27)
Josh Trentadue

RHP

RHSP
Caden Scarborough (2)
Josh Owens (4)
Jose Corniell (5)
David Davalillo (7)
Leandro Lopez (11)
Alejandro Rosario (13)
Izack Tiger (16)
Seong-Jun Kim (23)
Mason McConnaughey
Ismael Agreda

RHRP
AJ Russell (6)
Winston Santos (9)
Emiliano Teodo (15)
Carter Baumler (19)
Paul Bonzagni (28)
Joey Danielson (30)
Jacob Johnson
Marc Church
Kamdyn Perry
Brock Porter

TEXAS RANGERS

1. SEBASTIAN WALCOTT, SS/3B

Born: March 14, 2006. **B-T:** R-R. **HT:** 6-4. **WT:** 190.
Signed: Bahamas, 2023.
Signed by: Jonny Clum.

TRACK RECORD: Walcott signed with the Rangers out of the Bahamas for $3.2 million in 2023 and quickly asserted himself as one of the best prospects not only in Texas' system but in the entire sport. He hit his way from the Dominican Summer League to High-A in his debut season, then reached Double-A at the end of his second year. In 2025, Walcott returned to the Texas League, where he opened the season as the circuit's second-youngest player. He and the Pirates' Konnor Griffin were the only teenagers to finish the year with 15 or more doubles, 10 or more home runs and 30 or more stolen bases and spend any time at Double-A. After 124 games at Frisco, Walcott was assigned to the Arizona Fall League. He played one game before being shut down with a flexor strain in his right elbow. Walcott landed spots in the 2024 and 2025 Futures Games, with the former being played at Texas' home of Globe Life Field.

SCOUTING REPORT: Quietly, Walcott put forth one of the best seasons in the Texas League thanks to a skill set oozing with upside and improved plate discipline and swing decisions. Scouts with history watching Walcott noted that he did a better job laying off the kinds of pitches that would result in weak contact, while more frequently unleashing his best swings on offerings in his happy zone. All of his 13 home runs were hit against pitches located inside or near the middle of the strike zone, and all of them were pulled. Walcott still has improvements to make, and he occasionally will stride in the bucket in an attempt to lift and pull. When his swing is in sync, he creates the kind of contact rarely found in players his age. Among teenagers with 300 or more plate appearances in 2025, Walcott's 90th percentile exit velocity of 106.8 mph ranked fifth. Now, he needs to get to that kind of contact more often. His 46% groundball rate was 11th highest in the Texas League among qualified hitters. Walcott is big, lithe and physical, and may one day grow out of shortstop. He got 17 games of experience at third base in 2025. Walcott committed 24 errors at shortstop, most on wayward throws and misjudged short hops. Some scouts have suggested his double-plus arm might play better in right field, though evaluators aren't convinced he's a sure bet to move off the dirt. Whether the injury that cut short his AFL campaign has any lingering effects will be worth monitoring.

THE FUTURE: Walcott will likely spend the bulk of his 2026 season at Triple-A and has a chance to make his big league debut toward the end of the year. There's no doubt that his tools are star quality, and he's made strides toward turning them into skills. If he can take another couple of steps forward, he has a chance to be the centerpiece of the Rangers' roster.

BA GRADE: 65 / Risk: Average
SCOUTING GRADES
Hit: 50. Power: 70. Run: 55.
Fielding: 50. Arm: 70.

Adjusted grade: **55**

Projected future grades on 20-80 scouting scale

BEST TOOLS

BATTING
Best Hitter	Devin Fitz-Gerald
Best Power Hitter	Sebastian Walcott
Best Strike-Zone Discipline	Devin Fitz-Gerald
Fastest Baserunner	Yeremy Cabrera
Best Athlete	Josh Owens

PITCHING
Best Fastball	Caden Scarborough
Best Curveball	Leandro Lopez
Best Slider	Caden Scarborough
Best Changeup	Brock Porter
Best Control	David Davalillo

FIELDING
Best Defensive Catcher	Ian Moller
Best Defensive Infielder	Yolfran Castillo
Best Infield Arm	Sebastian Walcott
Best Defensive Outfielder	Yeremy Cabrera
Best Outfield Arm	Anthony Gutierrez

Year	Age	Club (League)	Level	AVG	G	AB	R	H	2B	3B	HR	RBI	BB	SO	SB	OBP	SLG
2025	19	Frisco (TL)	AA	.255	124	474	71	121	19	2	13	59	70	108	32	.355	.386
		Minor League Totals		.258	293	1117	167	288	66	15	31	139	146	304	71	.347	.427

TEXAS RANGERS

2 CADEN SCARBOROUGH, RHP
FB: 70. **SW:** 60. **SP:** 45. **CTL:** 55. **BA Grade:** 55. **Risk:** Average. **Adj:** 45.

Born: April 1, 2005. **B-T:** R-R. **HT:** 6-5. **WT:** 200.
Drafted: HS—Harmony, FL, 2023 (6th round). **Signed by:** John Wiedenbauer.
TRACK RECORD: Scarborough's size and athleticism helped him star in both baseball and basketball at Harmony High in Florida. He was skilled enough to earn area player of the year honors in both sports. The Rangers drafted Scarborough in the sixth round in 2023 and used a $515,000 bonus to buy him out of his commitment to Dallas Baptist. He pitched just 10.1 innings in 2024 but was the organization's best pitcher in 2025. Between two Class A stops, the righthander struck out 114 and walked just 21 over 88 innings.
SCOUTING REPORT: Scarborough's game is based around outliers. His fastball, which sits around 94 mph and touched 97, has excellent life through the zone from a low release height. Those traits, plus the fact that he threw the pitch for a strike more than 68% of the time, make it an easy plus offering and the best of its kind in the system. That title was reinforced during the season as he learned to land it in the zone more often. Scarborough complements his fastball with a sweeper that he was able to land in the zone or use to induce empty swings. The pitch got a 44% miss rate, and its strike distribution was nearly 50/50 between called and swinging. Its sharp break makes it a weapon down and away from righties and at the feet of lefties. He completes his mix with a split-changeup that he tinkered with throughout the 2025 season and will be a continuing point of emphasis. Scarborough has added plenty of strength since he's turned pro, which has helped him make his funky delivery more repeatable.
THE FUTURE: Scarborough has a high ceiling thanks to his physical abilities and unique pitch package. If it all comes together, he could pitch in the middle of a rotation. The next steps will include adding more pitches to his mix. He should return to High-A in 2026 and could reach Double-A by midseason.

Year	Age	Club (League)	Level	W	L	ERA	G	GS	IP	H	HR	BB	SO	BB%	SO%	WHIP	AVG
2025	20	Hickory (CAR)	A	2	5	2.88	19	18	75	50	7	19	95	6.5	32.3	0.92	.189
2025	20	Hub City (SAL)	A+	0	0	0.00	3	3	13	6	0	2	19	4.1	38.8	0.62	.133
		Minor League Totals		4	6	2.68	26	22	94	64	7	26	122	7.0	32.7	0.96	.191

3 GAVIN FIEN, SS
HIT: 55. **POW:** 55. **RUN:** 40. **FLD:** 45. **ARM:** 60. **BA Grade:** 55. **Risk:** High. **Adj:** 40.

Born: March 8, 2007. **B-T:** R-R. **HT:** 6-3. **WT:** 200.
Drafted: HS—Temecula, CA, 2025 (1st round). **Signed by:** Jake Vollen/Steve Flores.
TRACK RECORD: Entering the 2025 draft cycle, Fien had earned a reputation as one of the best prep hitters in the class. The California native hit .400/.429/.680 for USA Baseball's 18U National Team in 2024, which included a who's who of the following year's first-rounders. The Rangers drafted Fien 12th overall and used a $4.8 million bonus to sign him away from a commitment to Texas. His official pro debut consisted of 10 games for Low-A Hickory.
SCOUTING REPORT: Part of the reason the Rangers were so comfortable calling Fien's name with their first pick was because of the long history he had developed with area scout Steve Flores. That relationship, plus Fien's stellar track record, made the choice easy. At the plate, he does a good job discerning balls from strikes, limits his chase rate and uses a short, quick swing to help him catch up to premium velocity. As an amateur, Fien drew skepticism from scouts for his swing because of the way he holds his hands and a stiffer bat path than is typical for a player with his kind of production. Defensively, he has plenty of work to do to remain on the infield. Already big and physical at 6-foot-3 and 200 pounds, his frame and footwork could fit better at third base than shortstop. He has a plus arm. Fien also got some experience at first base during his high school career, but he's already been in the lab with Rangers infield coordinator Kenny Holmberg to improve his chances of staying on the left side. Fien is a below-average runner and likely won't be better than fringy no matter where he lands on defense.
THE FUTURE: Fien will likely return to Low-A in 2026 to begin his first full season as a pro but could hit his way to High-A by season's end. His ceiling is as an offensive-minded third baseman who provides most of his value in the batter's box.

Year	Age	Club (League)	Level	AVG	G	AB	R	H	2B	3B	HR	RBI	BB	SO	SB	OBP	SLG
2025	18	Hickory (CAR)	A	.220	10	41	4	9	3	1	0	7	3	11	1	.267	.341
		Minor League Totals		.220	10	41	4	9	3	1	0	7	3	11	1	.267	.341

TEXAS RANGERS

4 JOSH OWENS, RHP/SS

FB: 60. **SL:** 60. **CH:** 45. **CTL:** 50. **BA Grade:** 55. **Risk:** High. **Adj:** 40.
HIT: 50. **POW:** 55. **RUN:** 55. **FLD:** 50. **ARM:** 55.

Born: January 8, 2007. **B-T:** L-R. **HT:** 6-3. **WT:** 185.
Drafted: HS—Johnson City, TN, 2025 (3rd round). **Signed by:** Mike Tidick.
TRACK RECORD: The Rangers looked to the Tennessee high school ranks in 2020 when they drafted Elizabethton's Evan Carter in the second round. Texas again favored the Volunteer State when it chose Owens from neighboring Johnson City in the third round in 2025. A multi-sport athlete who also played football, Owens had legitimate draft stock as both a shortstop and pitcher. The Rangers used $1.1 million to buy him out of his commitment to Georgia Southern.
SCOUTING REPORT: Entering the draft, Owens' future seemed to be veering toward a future as a position player with the potential for average or better tools across the board. After his first taste of pro ball, that's no longer the case. Scouts who saw Owens pitch came away impressed with his blend of athleticism and potentially overwhelming stuff. In instructional league, he showed a 93-96 mph fastball with nasty two-seam life and a well-commanded slider that rode the line between plus and double-plus and was an effective weapon to backfoot against lefthanders. His changeup was an intriguing offering as an amateur but was seldom-used as a pro. Owens' deceptive lower slot and repertoire could help him vault quickly into the top tier of the system's pitchers. Owens has raw power that helped him produce exit velocities of up to 108 mph as an amateur, but scouts believe his swing would need a major overhaul. In eight games for Low-A Hickory he went 2-for-24 with no walks and 11 strikeouts. In the field, his athleticism and above-average speed and arm would help him fit either at shortstop or in center field.
THE FUTURE: Owens is the best athlete in the system and has a variety of ways to produce value in the big leagues one day. After Owens' short stint in pro ball, tapping into his immense upside on the mound might be his best course of action and could one day lead to a spot in the middle of a rotation.

Year	Age	Club (League)	Level	W	L	ERA	G	GS	IP	H	HR	BB	SO	BB%	SO%	WHIP	AVG
2025	18	Hickory (CAR)	A	0	0	0.00	2	2	4	1	0	3	6	20.0	40.0	1.00	.083
		Minor League Totals		0	0	0.00	2	2	4	1	0	3	6	20.0	40.0	1.00	.083

5 JOSE CORNIELL, RHP

FB: 55. **CH:** 55. **CT:** 50. **SW:** 55. **CTL:** 60. **BA Grade:** 45. **Risk:** Mild. **Adj:** 40.

Born: June 22, 2003. **B-T:** R-R. **HT:** 6-3. **WT:** 165.
Signed: Dominican Republic, 2019. **Signed by:** Francisco Rosario (Mariners).
TRACK RECORD: Corniell signed with the Mariners in 2019 but was traded to Texas in 2020 for reliever Rafael Montero. Three seasons later, Corniell's performance at two Class A stops earned him the system's minor league pitcher of the year award. His momentum was stopped halfway through 2024 by an elbow injury that required Tommy John surgery. Once healed, he quickly showed enough at Double-A to warrant a one-game cameo in the big leagues. He made up for some of his lost innings with a turn in the Arizona Fall League.
SCOUTING REPORT: Corniell gets his outs thanks to stellar command of a deep, varied pitch mix led by a full complement of four-seam, sinking and cut fastballs that allows him to attack righties and lefties with velocity and movement. Scouts grade the sinker—which was added during the AFL—as the best of the trio, but the other two variants aren't far behind. The four-seamer would get a bit of a boost if Corniell could command it better toward the top of the zone. Corniell's slider has a sweepier shape than in years past, and it shows above-average potential at its best. Scouts outside the organization believe Corniell's changeup has the same kind of ceiling, but he needs to throw the pitch more often to get it sharp enough to reach that value. The righthander pounds the zone with all his pitches, though the sweeper is designed more for chase swings than to be landed for early-count strikes.
THE FUTURE: After making his MLB debut, Corniell has a chance to reach Arlington again in 2026. If he doesn't land in the Opening Day rotation, he could get back there after a bit more seasoning in Triple-A Round Rock. He has the ceiling of a back-end starter.

Year	Age	Club (League)	Level	W	L	ERA	G	GS	IP	H	HR	BB	SO	BB%	SO%	WHIP	AVG
2025	22	ACL Rangers	Rk	0	0	3.18	4	4	6	7	1	2	7	7.7	26.9	1.59	.304
2025	22	Frisco (TL)	AA	0	1	0.45	6	6	20	5	0	1	20	1.5	30.3	0.30	.078
2025	22	Round Rock (PCL)	AAA	1	1	3.65	3	3	12	11	0	6	14	11.1	25.9	1.38	.234
2025	22	Texas (AL)	MLB	0	1	16.20	1	0	2	3	1	1	1	11.1	11.1	2.40	.375
		Minor League Totals		13	13	4.09	71	43	244	195	28	88	275	8.7	27.1	1.16	.218
		Major League Totals		0	1	16.20	1	0	2	3	1	1	1	11.1	11.1	2.40	.375

TEXAS RANGERS

6 AJ RUSSELL, RHP
FB: 70. **SL:** 50. **CH:** 55. **CTL:** 50. **BA Grade:** 50. **Risk:** Average. **Adj:** 40.

Born: June 29, 2004. **B-T:** R-R. **HT:** 6-6. **WT:** 223.
Drafted: Tennessee, 2025 (2nd round). **Signed by:** Mike Tidick.
TRACK RECORD: After a stellar season in relief at Tennessee in 2023, Russell's sophomore year was stymied by an elbow injury that eventually required surgery to repair his ulnar collateral ligament. He returned in February 2025 for one outing, then came back on a regular basis starting on April 1. In all, he threw 70 innings and made 11 starts during his three seasons in Knoxville. The Rangers drafted Russell with their second-round pick and signed him for $2.6 million. He pitched during instructional league. His selection was the first of back-to-back picks—the second being two-way talent Josh Owens—from the Volunteer State.
SCOUTING REPORT: Russell works with a three-pitch mix led by a potentially double-plus fastball that sits between 92-94 mph and has reached up to 98 with plenty of carry and life through the zone. The pitch showed hard, boring action in on righthanded hitters and got plenty of misses as well. He backs his fastball with a slider that sometimes loses its shape and looks a little bit like a slurve. The Rangers are confident their pitching department can help Russell get to the best version of his breaking ball more often. The physical righthander rounds out his mix with a potentially above-average changeup in the mid 80s that he was confident throwing against both righties and lefties. Russell did a good job filling the zone during his college career and has a chance to have average control.
THE FUTURE: Both in college and as a pro, Russell has shown the type of stuff to be dominant. He'll get plenty of chances to start, but his limited track record and injury might lead him to a future as a reliever who can blow hitters away for an inning or two. His college pedigree might lead to his pro career officially beginning at High-A Hub City.

Year	Age	Club (League)	Level	W	L	ERA	G	GS	IP	H	HR	BB	SO	BB%	SO%	WHIP	AVG
2025	21	Did not play															

7 DAVID DAVALILLO, RHP
FB: 45. **CB:** 50. **SL:** 50. **SW:** 55. **SP:** 55. **CT:** 40. **CTL:** 60. **BA Grade:** 50. **Risk:** Average. **Adj:** 40.

Born: September 21, 2002. **B-T:** R-R. **HT:** 6-1. **WT:** 215.
Drafted: Venezuela, 2022. **Signed by:** Andres Nuñez (Mets).
TRACK RECORD: Davalillo comes from a family bursting with baseball. His brother Gabriel is a catcher who is a top prospect for the Angels. His father David was a longtime coach in the Mets' system. The younger David initially signed with the Mets as well but was released after the 2021 season and signed with Texas. His 1.88 ERA was the lowest in the minor leagues in 2024, and he followed it up with a 2.44 mark in a year split between High-A and the hitter-friendly Texas League.
SCOUTING REPORT: Others in the system have better stuff, but Davalillo is truly the best pitcher in the organization. He doesn't have a plus pitch, but an improved body thanks to a better diet and work in the weight room has helped his stuff tick up. He works with four- and two-seam fastballs, as well as a split-changeup, a curveball, a gyro slider and a newly added sweeper and cutter. The former was added to help him put away righties, while the latter is a bridge between his other fastballs and his offspeeds. Davalillo's splitter is the best pitch in his mix, and in 2025 it drew misses at a rate of better than 50%. Scouts praise his ability to move all his pitches around the zone and execute attack plans against righties and lefties alike. He threw strikes at a clip of 64% in 2025, and his control grades as the best in the system. Davalillo succeeds thanks to an innate ability to repeat his delivery, hand speed that allows him to throw a variety of pitch types and the gumption to pound the strike zone. He fields his position well.
THE FUTURE: Davalillo's lack of a plus pitch limits his ceiling, but he's proved himself throughout the minor leagues and was wily enough in the second half to tame upper-level hitters. He has a chance to make his MLB debut toward the end of the 2026 season, especially after being added to the 40-man roster in November.

Year	Age	Club (League)	Level	W	L	ERA	G	GS	IP	H	HR	BB	SO	BB%	SO%	WHIP	AVG
2025	22	Hub City (SAL)	A+	4	1	2.12	11	11	51	31	2	11	68	5.5	34.0	0.82	.170
2025	22	Frisco (TL)	AA	2	3	2.73	12	11	56	40	4	17	58	7.5	25.7	1.02	.196
		Minor League Totals		15	7	2.35	57	46	241	182	11	65	266	6.7	27.4	1.02	.205

TEXAS RANGERS

8 DEVIN FITZ-GERALD, SS/2B
HIT: 55. **POW:** 50. **RUN:** 40. **FLD:** 45. **ARM:** 40. **BA Grade:** 50. **Risk:** Average. **Adj:** 40.

Born: August 17, 2005. **B-T:** S-R. **HT:** 5-10. **WT:** 185.
Drafted: HS—Parkland, FL, 2024 (5th round). **Signed by:** Tommy Dueñas.
TRACK RECORD: Fitz-Gerald is the son of Todd Fitz-Gerald, the longtime head coach of Stoneman Douglas High, whose big league alumni include Anthony Rizzo, Jesús Luzardo, Roman Anthony and Coby Mayo. The Rangers drafted the younger Fitz-Gerald in the fifth round in 2024 and used a $900,000 bonus to sign him away from a commitment to North Carolina State. In his first season as a pro, Fitz-Gerald was one of the most polished players in the Arizona Complex League before earning a midseason bump to Low-A Hickory. Unfortunately, his time in full-season ball was limited to just 10 games he suffered a left shoulder strain he suffered diving for a ball.
SCOUTING REPORT: Given Fitz-Gerald's background in the game, it's not surprising that he was one of the most polished players in Rookie complex ball. Scouts saw a player without a plus tool but with a wide array of skills. He controls the strike zone well and finished the year with an excellent zone-miss rate of 11.6% and an overall miss rate of just 18.6%, and he hit well from both sides of the plate. Despite a smaller build, Fitz-Gerald has above-average raw power that he could tap into more often with a bit more barrel accuracy and more balls in the air. Defensively, Fitz-Gerald could be fringe-average on the field—most likely at second base—because of limited athleticism and a wider lower half. His speed is likely to wind up as below-average, but he has the kind of instincts that should allow him to steal 12-15 bases a year.
THE FUTURE: After an offseason to recover, Fitz-Gerald will likely return to Low-A Hickory in 2026. He has the skills and polish to be a long-term big leaguer who mostly plays second base but can fill in at third or the outfield.

Year	Age	Club (League)	Level	AVG	G	AB	R	H	2B	3B	HR	RBI	BB	SO	SB	OBP	SLG
2025	19	ACL Rangers	Rk	.318	31	107	25	34	6	0	6	19	17	15	5	.423	.542
2025	19	Hickory (CAR)	A	.250	10	32	8	8	1	0	0	1	11	9	3	.442	.281
		Minor League Totals		.302	41	139	33	42	7	0	6	20	28	24	8	.428	.482

9 WINSTON SANTOS, RHP
FB: 60. **SL:** 40. **CH:** 55. **CTL:** 55. **BA Grade:** 45. **Risk:** Mild. **Adj:** 40.

Born: April 15, 2002. **B-T:** R-R. **HT:** 6-0. **WT:** 160.
Signed: Dominican Republic, 2019. **Signed by:** Willy Espinal.
TRACK RECORD: The Rangers signed Santos in 2019 out of the Dominican Republic, but they had to wait until the sport returned from the pandemic shutdown to get their eyes on him in an official game. Once things resumed, the righthander showed one of the system's more interesting pitch mixes. He broke out during an outstanding 2024 season that included a berth in the Futures Game—played at the Rangers' home ballpark—but was limited by a lingering back injury to just 35.2 frames in 2025 between the regular season and Arizona Fall League.
SCOUTING REPORT: As ever, Santos' profile is driven by his magnificent fastball/changeup combo. The former pitch reached 97 mph during the regular season and touched a couple of ticks hotter in shorter bursts in the AFL. It also showed an average of nearly 18 inches of induced vertical break during the regular season. The righthander's changeup flashes plus in the mid-to-upper 80s and shows fade and bottom at its best. Those two pitches would give him a chance to be a multi-inning reliever. If he can figure out a consistent breaking ball, he could find a way into a rotation. He's working with a fringy, short-breaking version of a slider thrown around 84 mph. At its very best, the pitch has sharp gyro break down and in toward the feet of lefthanders. More often than not, it backs up on him and hangs in the middle of the zone. Santos has the potential for above-average control with perhaps average command. He's done a good job filling up the zone at each of his stops.
THE FUTURE: If Santos can find a breaking ball that plays at least average, he'll have a chance to be a back-end starter. If not, he could use his fastball and changeup to overwhelm hitters for multiple innings out of the bullpen. With a full offseason of rest, he could reach the big leagues in 2026.

Year	Age	Club (League)	Level	W	L	ERA	G	GS	IP	H	HR	BB	SO	BB%	SO%	WHIP	AVG
2025	23	Frisco (TL)	AA	0	0	7.90	5	5	14	19	0	5	22	7.9	34.9	1.76	.328
2025	23	Round Rock (PCL)	AAA	0	0	2.45	1	1	4	3	0	2	4	13.3	26.7	1.36	.231
		Minor League Totals		27	23	4.43	86	78	368	344	39	106	396	6.8	25.4	1.22	.245

TEXAS RANGERS

10 YOLFRAN CASTILLO, SS/3B

HIT: 45. **POW:** 30. **RUN:** 50. **FLD:** 55. **ARM:** 60. **BA Grade:** 45. **Risk:** High. **Adj:** 35.

Born: February 8, 2007. **B-T:** R-R. **HT:** 6-3. **WT:** 165.
Signed: Venezuela, 2024. **Signed by:** Rafic Saab/Willy Espinal/Nelson Muniz.
TRACK RECORD: Castillo signed with Texas in 2024 out of Venezuela and quickly showed exemplary bat-to-ball skills. He lasted just 20 games in the Dominican Summer League—where he hit .414/.552/.471—before the Rangers bumped him to the Arizona Complex League. Although the venue changed, Castillo continued producing at a stellar level. He split his 2025 season between the ACL and Low-A Hickory, where he continued to make plenty of contact but little impact.
SCOUTING REPORT: In 2024, Castillo's body was long and lanky with plenty of room for more strength. Scouts who saw him a year later said he had made some progress in that area, but a large chunk of his future depends on whether he can get even stronger and turn more of his singles into extra-base hits. Castillo's swing is a bit choppy, and he tends to make his contact deeper in the strike zone. Those traits, plus below-average exit velocities, have led to limited offensive success outside of contact abilities. He has just 21 extra-base hits—and only one home run—in 421 career plate appearances. That likely limits his upside to a bottom-of-the-order hitter. Scouts are sold on Castillo sticking at shortstop, and he ranks as the best defensive infielder in the system. He's a smooth fielder with strong instincts, soft hands, plus range and an excellent internal clock. His arm strength is plus, too, and he got 10 games of experience at third base as well. Castillo is an average runner who has stolen 28 bases in 34 career attempts.
THE FUTURE: The next few years will be telling for Castillo. If he can revamp his bat path and add strength, he might be able to hack it as a shortstop who hits toward the bottom of the order. If not, it will be tough to find a path to the big leagues.

Year	Age	Club (League)	Level	AVG	G	AB	R	H	2B	3B	HR	RBI	BB	SO	SB	OBP	SLG
2025	18	ACL Rangers	Rk	.260	60	235	41	61	8	7	1	31	16	52	18	.310	.366
2025	18	Hickory (CAR)	A	.255	28	106	8	27	5	1	0	10	10	17	11	.325	.321
		Minor League Totals		.291	123	471	86	137	18	8	1	67	53	84	39	.365	.369

11 LEANDRO LOPEZ, RHP

FB: 55. **CB:** 55. **SL:** 55. **CH:** 40. **CTL:** 50. **BA Grade:** 45. **Risk:** Average. **Adj:** 35.

Born: June 17, 2002. **B-T:** R-R. **HT:** 6-1. **WT:** 200. **Signed:** Dominican Republic, 2021.
Signed by: Willy Espinal/Jack Marino/Jonny Clum/Anthony Dominguez.
TRACK RECORD: When he signed in 2021, Lopez was immediately tabbed as someone to keep an eye on in the coming years. He made the leap in his second stint in the Dominican Summer League, when he punched out 63 and walked just 18 over 34.1 innings. He flashed potential over the next two seasons, but really broke through in 2025, when he fanned 116 and walked 41 over 101.1 innings in a year when he reached Double-A for the first time. After the season, Lopez was added to the 40-man roster.
SCOUTING REPORT: Lopez has a case as the biggest breakthrough in Texas' system in 2025. He shed fat, added strength and began repeating his delivery much more frequently. Now, his diverse pitch mix is more effective. He works with four- and two-seam fastballs, and backs them with a slider, curveball and changeup. The slider, a new addition to his mix, looks like a cutter but Lopez's high release point makes the pitch appear more slider-ish. The pitch was more effective because of how often he was able to land it for strikes. Having two pitches he could throw in-zone helped the rest of his mix play up. Lopez's split-grip changeup projects as a below-average pitch. Lopez's control gains were more important than anything that happened with one of his pitches, and the improvement stuck after he moved from High-A to Double-A.
THE FUTURE: Now part of the 40-man roster, Lopez has a chance to make his MLB debut in 2026. Despite all but one of his appearances coming in the rotation in 2025, his likely role in the big leagues is as a reliever.

Year	Age	Club (League)	Level	W	L	ERA	G	GS	IP	H	HR	BB	SO	BB%	SO%	WHIP	AVG
2025	23	Hub City (SAL)	A+	2	4	2.19	14	14	66	46	4	26	73	10.0	28.2	1.10	.199
2025	23	Frisco (TL)	AA	1	0	2.78	9	8	36	25	3	15	43	10.6	30.3	1.12	.197
		Minor League Totals		7	13	3.11	68	41	220	154	13	121	297	13.1	32.1	1.25	.195

TEXAS RANGERS

12 DYLAN DREILING, OF
HIT: 45. **POW:** 50. **RUN:** 55. **FLD:** 45. **ARM:** 45. **BA Grade:** 45. **Risk:** Average. **Adj:** 35.

Born: April 17, 2003. **B-T:** L-L. **HT:** 5-11. **WT:** 197. **Drafted:** Tennessee, 2024 (2nd round). **Signed by:** Mike Tidick.
TRACK RECORD: After earning Most Outstanding Player during Tennessee's run to the 2024 College World Series championship, Dreiling had boosted his stock high enough to earn the Rangers' second-round pick and a bonus of $1,287,600. He debuted later that year at High-A Hickory and returned to the level—albeit at Texas' new affiliate in Spartanburg, S.C.—and posted a middling campaign.
SCOUTING REPORT: Dreiling does a strong job controlling the strike zone, but he needs to become more aggressive. His swing rate in 2025 was just 38.7%, among the lowest in the sport among players with 400 or more plate appearances. The Rangers also worked with Dreiling to tweak the mechanics in his lower half, and the results were promising. His August was the best month of the season, and he showed well during the Arizona Fall League. All of Dreiling's exit velocity numbers were promising, including best bolts of better than 111 mph. Despite those numbers, he has a hole on the outer half of the plate that led to a lot of weak contact in 2025. He'll need those positive signs to carry through into 2026 because of a defensive profile that lends itself more toward left field. Even in the corner, Dreiling is unlikely to be more than a fringy defender with similar arm strength.
THE FUTURE: After turning in a strong last few months in regular season and AFL, Dreiling's prospect stock has steadied. He'll begin 2026 at the upper levels and has a future as a second-division left fielder.

Year	Age	Club (League)	Level	AVG	G	AB	R	H	2B	3B	HR	RBI	BB	SO	SB	OBP	SLG
2025	22	Hub City (SAL)	A+	.226	110	420	50	95	21	4	12	62	58	101	15	.319	.381
		Minor League Totals		.221	134	506	62	112	25	4	13	71	77	121	20	.323	.364

13 ALEJANDRO ROSARIO, RHP
FB: 60. **CB:** 55. **SP:** 60. **CTL:** 70. **BA Grade:** 55. **Risk:** Extreme. **Adj:** 35.

Born: January 6, 2002. **B-T:** R-R. **HT:** 6-0. **WT:** 170. **Drafted:** Miami, 2023 (5th round). **Signed by:** Tommy Dueñas.
TRACK RECORD: After watching him for three underwhelming seasons at Miami, the Rangers believed there was much more than met the eye in Rosario's profile. They were right. In 2024, he dominated at two Class A stops and was one of the bigger breakout pitchers in the sport. Unfortunately, his progress was halted in 2025. A torn elbow ligament before spring training required Tommy John surgery, but the operation was delayed until 2026. As a result, he will miss all of the 2026 season as well.
SCOUTING REPORT: The key to Rosario's 2024 breakthrough campaign was the return of a splitter that had been shelved during his career in Coral Gables. The pitch was used as a north-south complement to his four-seamer. The Rangers also moved Rosario to the third-base side of the rubber to help his fastball play up another notch above its 97 mph average velocity. Both of those pitches graded as potential plus offerings, and his curveball checked in a tick lower at a 55-grade offering on the 20-to-80 scouting scale. As if Rosario's pitch mix wasn't impressive enough on its own, he pounded the zone relentlessly and looked like he had a chance to reach double-plus control. He finished the year with a 68% strike rate and got into a 3-0 count just once all year. In addition to the elbow injury, Rosario dealt with a shoulder impingement before the 2024 season.
THE FUTURE: Rosario's standout performance in his lone pro season vaulted him onto the Top 100 Prospects, and a strong encore would have pushed him into a place among the game's elite. Now, his career is on hold until he can recover from a series of issues that will wind up costing him two full seasons.

Year	Age	Club (League)	Level	W	L	ERA	G	GS	IP	H	HR	BB	SO	BB%	SO%	WHIP	AVG
2025	23	Did not play—Injured															
		Minor League Totals		4	5	2.24	18	17	88	69	2	13	129	3.7	36.9	0.93	.207

14 YEREMY CABRERA, OF
HIT: 45. **POW:** 40. **RUN:** 60. **FLD:** 60. **ARM:** 40. **BA Grade:** 45. **Risk:** Average. **Adj:** 35.

Born: July 2, 2005. **B-T:** L-L. **HT:** 5-11. **WT:** 155. **Signed:** Dominican Republic, 2022.
Signed by: Hamilton Sarabia/Jonny Clum.
TRACK RECORD: After signing out of the Dominican Republic in 2022, Cabrera spent the next two seasons in the Dominican Summer League before moving stateside in 2024. He played a career-best 102 games in 2025—all at Low-A Hickory—and posted a .730 OPS.
SCOUTING REPORT: Cabrera is a solid all-around player who does a little of everything but needs a bit more oomph on offense to project as an everyday player. The lefthanded-hitting Cabrera does a solid job controlling the zone and can put a charge into a ball every now and then but mostly fills his slugging percentage with doubles and triples. His best-struck drives have reached 110 mph and he does a solid job

TEXAS RANGERS

pulling the ball in the air, but he needs to show a bit more barrel accuracy in order to get the most out of his strength. He is also a non-factor against lefthanders, against whom he produced a .203/.329/.327 line with just two extra-base hits in 59 at-bats. Cabrera is a plus defender in center field thanks to strong instincts and plus speed and grades as the system's best outfield defender. His arm is below-average, however, and he'll sometimes rush through throws and sacrifice accuracy as a result.

THE FUTURE: Cabrera's next stop will be High-A Hub City. If he can get more out of his hardest-hit balls, his stock will rise in kind. For now, he projects as a hitter who resides toward the bottom of a lineup and provides value on defense and on the bases.

Year	Age	Club (League)	Level	AVG	G	AB	R	H	2B	3B	HR	RBI	BB	SO	SB	OBP	SLG
2025	19	Hickory (CAR)	A	.256	102	383	66	98	12	3	8	52	52	86	43	.364	.366
		Minor League Totals		.259	267	937	199	243	35	16	26	138	159	213	87	.382	.414

15 EMILIANO TEODO, RHP
FB: 70. **SL:** 60. **CH:** 45. **CTL:** 40. **BA Grade:** 45. **Risk:** Average. **Adj:** 35.

Born: February 14, 2001. **B-T:** R-R. **HT:** 6-1. **WT:** 165. **Signed:** Dominican Republic, 2020. **Signed by:** JC Alvarez.

TRACK RECORD: Teodo signed with the Rangers in 2020 but was forced by the pandemic to wait until the following year to make his pro debut. When he finally got on the mound, he showcased one of the system's liveliest arms. After a standout turn in the 2024 Futures Game, it seemed he was on the precipice of the big leagues. A back injury and scattered command scuttled those plans, however, and instead he made his second Arizona Fall League appearance in three seasons.

SCOUTING REPORT: For the first few years of his career, Teodo got by on the sheer velocity of a fastball that routinely touched 100 mph or more. In 2023, while he was in High-A, hitters taught him that the pitch lacked the movement to be effective. He switched to a two-seamer at midseason and saw standout results. Now, he can bully hitters with his fastball, slider and rare changeup. His primary two offerings have a chance to be plus or better, and his changeup could get to fringe-average. Teodo's injury meant he was out of sync all year, and it showed in his inability to throw strikes. He'll need to get back on track in that department to reach the big leagues. The Rangers would also like to see him work back-to-back days, which he did not do in 2025.

THE FUTURE: If he can throw more strikes, Teodo has a chance to be an overwhelming force in the late innings. If not, he might be closer to a low-leverage arm, or someone who rides the shuttle back and forth from Triple-A.

Year	Age	Club (League)	Level	W	L	ERA	G	GS	IP	H	HR	BB	SO	BB%	SO%	WHIP	AVG
2025	24	ACL Rangers	Rk	0	0	0.00	2	0	2	2	0	0	5	0.0	50.0	0.86	.222
2025	24	Frisco (TL)	AA	1	1	5.59	11	0	10	6	0	12	10	25.0	20.8	1.86	.171
2025	24	Round Rock (PCL)	AAA	2	1	9.00	14	0	18	19	4	17	23	18.7	25.3	2.00	.260
		Minor League Totals		20	17	3.52	106	50	292	208	25	174	395	13.8	31.4	1.31	.197

16 IZACK TIGER, RHP
FB: 60. **SL:** 60. **SP:** 55. **CTL:** 45. **BA Grade:** 50. **Risk:** High. **Adj:** 35.

Born: February 8, 2001. **B-T:** R-R. **HT:** 6-2. **WT:** 210. **Drafted:** Butler (KS) JC, 2023 (7th round). **Signed by:** Dustin Smith.

TRACK RECORD: Tiger spent his entire college career in Kansas at Butler JC. He struck out 121 hitters in his final season before the draft, and the Rangers called his name in the seventh round in 2023. He signed for $180,000. He got his first pro experience during Low-A Down East's playoff run. In 2024, Tiger earned a spot in one of Texas' Spring Breakout games, then pitched at three levels in the regular season, peaking at High-A. He pitched 46 innings before a torn ulnar collateral ligament required Tommy John surgery and cost him all of 2025.

SCOUTING REPORT: When healthy, Tiger has one of the most overwhelming pitch mixes in the Rangers' system. His four-seam fastball reached into the upper 90s with plenty of life through the zone. He backed it with a slider in the mid 80s and a split-changeup in the low 90s. The combination allows him to work the strike zone from the top down while drawing plenty of empty swings. At their peak, Tiger's fastball and slider are potential plus pitches. His changeup could get to above-average. He repeats his delivery well and should have fringe-average control once he reaches the big leagues.

THE FUTURE: After a year to recover, Tiger should be ready for spring training. If his stuff returns intact, he has a chance to be a back-end starter or a live-armed force in the back of a bullpen.

Year	Age	Club (League)	Level	W	L	ERA	G	GS	IP	H	HR	BB	SO	BB%	SO%	WHIP	AVG
2025	24	Did not play—Injured															
		Minor League Totals		3	2	2.88	16	13	50	43	4	23	63	11.0	30.1	1.32	.234

TEXAS RANGERS

17 MALCOLM MOORE, C

HIT: 40. **POW:** 40. **RUN:** 30. **FLD:** 40. **ARM:** 45. **BA Grade:** 50. **Risk:** High. **Adj:** 35.

Born: July 31, 2003. **B-T:** L-R. **HT:** 6-2. **WT:** 215. **Drafted:** Stanford, 2024 (1st round). **Signed by:** Gabe Sandy.
TRACK RECORD: After a decorated career at Stanford and with USA Baseball that helped him land a spot on BA's Freshman All-America team, Moore cemented a place among the best catchers in the 2024 draft class. The Rangers selected him with the 30th pick and signed him for $3 million. He got his feet wet at High-A that summer, then returned to the level in 2025. His season was interrupted by a broken finger, and he made up for lost time in the Arizona Fall League.
SCOUTING REPORT: While the disjointed nature of his season didn't help, even when healthy Moore had the look of a player who needed more polish than would be expected of a player with his pedigree. The lefthanded hitter was fairly aggressive and could put a charge into a ball every now and again, but there was much to be desired in terms of barrel accuracy. His season was unsuccessful in general, but he was particularly ineffective against lefthanders, against whom he produced an OPS of just .472 with one extra-base hit in 50 plate appearances. He also needs to find a quicker trigger to help him against premium velocity. Defensively, there's plenty of work to be done as well. He's a slow-twitch athlete and only a fringy receiver with a fringe-average arm. He caught 17.6% of attempted basestealers and had 70 bases stolen on him in just 47 games.
THE FUTURE: Moore's first full pro season was a letdown, but there's at least a partial mulligan required. He has plenty of work to do on both sides of the ball, and will likely head back to High-A to begin 2026. He now looks more like a backup than a starter.

Year	Age	Club (League)	Level	AVG	G	AB	R	H	2B	3B	HR	RBI	BB	SO	SB	OBP	SLG
2025	21	ACL Rangers	Rk	.143	5	14	2	2	0	0	1	5	6	4	1	.381	.357
2025	21	Hub City (SAL)	A+	.198	57	207	25	41	9	0	2	22	20	47	4	.293	.271
		Minor League Totals		.199	87	312	41	62	15	0	6	39	34	80	8	.300	.304

18 DALTON PENCE, LHP

FB: 60. **CB:** 40. **SL:** 55. **SP:** 50. **CTL:** 55. **BA Grade:** 45. **Risk:** Average. **Adj:** 35.

Born: August 28, 2002. **B-T:** L-L. **HT:** 6-2. **WT:** 215. **Drafted:** North Carolina, 2024 (11th round). **Signed by:** Jay Heafner.
TRACK RECORD: Pence redshirted during his first season at North Carolina, then spent the next two seasons pitching mostly out of the bullpen for the Tar Heels. He was used exclusively as a reliever in his draft year, when the Rangers took him in the 11th round and signed him for $350,000. He was shut down after signing, then spent his debut season as a rotation piece at the Class A levels.
SCOUTING REPORT: The Rangers believe Pence has the chops to start. To do so, he'll need a fuller arsenal. Currently, he works with a four-pitch mix led by a low-90s fastball and backed by a slider, splitter and sparsely used curveball. Despite pedestrian velocity, Pence's heater could get to plus thanks to more than 20 inches of induced vertical break and an ability to land it in the zone frequently. His slider—which can look like a cutter—is his most effective offspeed pitch and grades as a potential 55 on the 20-80 scouting scale. The splitter trails as a possible average pitch, and his curveball is a clear fourth option. In 2026, curveball growth will be a point of emphasis in order to give him a wider-breaking pitch as a way to introduce a different look into his mix. Pence had no trouble carving against Class A hitters and could get to above-average control.
THE FUTURE: Pence should reach Double-A in 2026. There, the savvier hitters in the Texas League will let him know just how much more diversity he'll need in his pitch mix to be a starter at the highest level.

Year	Age	Club (League)	Level	W	L	ERA	G	GS	IP	H	HR	BB	SO	BB%	SO%	WHIP	AVG
2025	22	Hickory (CAR)	A	3	1	4.25	17	7	36	25	5	11	52	7.7	36.6	1.00	.195
2025	22	Hub City (SAL)	A+	1	3	1.55	14	11	46	32	0	16	51	8.6	27.6	1.04	.192
		Minor League Totals		4	4	2.73	31	18	82	57	5	27	103	8.3	31.5	1.02	.193

19 CARTER BAUMLER, RHP

FB: 60. **CB:** 60. **SL:** 40. **CTL:** 50. **BA Grade:** 40. **Risk:** Mild. **Adj:** 35.

Born: January 31, 2002. **B-T:** R-R. **HT:** 6-2. **WT:** 210. **Drafted:** HS—West Des Moines, IA, 2020 (5th round). **Signed by:** Scott Thomas (Orioles).
TRACK RECORD: The seventh inning of the 2019 Perfect Game All-American Classic featured a pair of potential future Rangers pitchers. One was Alejandro Rosario. The other was Baumler, who was drafted in the fifth round by the Orioles the next year. The Iowa-bred righthander reached Double-A for the first time in 2025 and then was taken by the Pirates in the Rule 5 draft before being quickly traded to the Rangers.

TEXAS RANGERS

SCOUTING REPORT: Injuries have taken their toll on Baumler, who has thrown just 88.2 innings since signing. The list includes a Tommy John surgery in 2020 that cost him all of the 2021 season. The 39.2 innings he threw in 2025 were a career high. The gem of Baumler's mix is his fastball, which sits in the mid 90s and plays up because of the combination of its life through the zone and the way his delivery works. The righthander backs it up with a mid-80s, two-plane curveball and a slider that averages 89 mph and is rarely thrown. He has a chance to have average control in the big leagues, and he found the zone with both his fastball and curveball at rates of better than 66%. All three of his offerings garnered miss rates of better than 30%.
THE FUTURE: Baumler is a pure relief prospect who will get a chance in spring training to win a shot in Texas' bullpen.

Year	Age	Club (League)	Level	W	L	ERA	G	GS	IP	H	HR	BB	SO	BB%	SO%	WHIP	AVG
2025	23	FCL Orioles	Rk	0	0	3.38	2	0	3	3	0	3	2	23.1	15.4	2.25	.300
2025	23	Aberdeen (SAL)	A+	2	0	2.45	20	0	29	19	0	13	38	11.1	32.5	1.09	.184
2025	23	Chesapeake (EL)	AA	0	0	0.00	6	0	8	3	0	2	6	7.1	21.4	0.65	.115
		Minor League Totals		7	1	3.05	49	10	89	63	3	40	104	11.0	28.7	1.16	.197

20 JACK WHEELER, 3B

HIT: 40. **POW:** 60. **RUN:** 55. **FLD:** 40. **ARM:** 55. **BA Grade:** 50. **Risk:** High. **Adj:** 35.

Born: July 11, 2006. **B-T:** R-R. **HT:** 6-5. **WT:** 205. **Drafted:** HS—Morris, IL, 2025 (6th round). **Signed by:** Mike McCabe.
TRACK RECORD: Wheeler was a two-way player at Illinois' Morris High, where he also played basketball and football. He played with the varsity squad all four years in high school and was drafted by the Rangers in the sixth round in 2025. He signed for an above-slot bonus of $525,000 to keep him from landing on campus at Illinois. He did not play an official game after signing.
SCOUTING REPORT: Despite his potential on the mound, Wheeler's path as a pro will come as a position player only. He's big and physical and moves well for his size. His natural strength and loose swing help him generate premier raw power that should be more than enough to profile at his position. His midwestern roots mean he's a little more raw than prep talents from amateur hotbeds in other parts of the country, and his reaction to spin during instructional league affirmed the idea that patience will be required as Wheeler climbs the ladder. Though he's lithe enough now to handle third base, there's a chance his body might push him to right field as he matures. If that's the case, his above-average arm strength should be more than enough for the position.
THE FUTURE: Wheeler's first official pro reps will come in the Arizona Complex League. If he passes those tests, he has a chance to be a prototype hitter who can profile either at third base or in right field.

Year	Age	Club (League)	Level	AVG	G	AB	R	H	2B	3B	HR	RBI	BB	SO	SB	OBP	SLG
2025	18	Did not play															

21 PAXTON KLING, OF

HIT: 40. **POW:** 55. **RUN:** 60. **FLD:** 50. **ARM:** 55. **BA Grade:** 50. **Risk:** High. **Adj:** 35.

Born: May 28, 2003. **B-T:** R-R. **HT:** 6-2. **WT:** 210. **Drafted:** Penn State, 2025 (7th round). **Signed by:** Carter Lewis.
TRACK RECORD: Kling was a highly regarded prospect out of high school but decided to pull his name from draft consideration and instead enroll at LSU. His time in Baton Rouge did not go according to plan, and he transferred to Penn State after his sophomore season. Things started to click in State College, and Kling finished his lone season with the Nittany Lions with a sparkly 1.102 OPS and 13 home runs. The Rangers selected him in the seventh round in 2025, and he made it to High-A in his pro debut before a collision with Dylan Dreiling closed the curtains on his season.
SCOUTING REPORT: Kling is big and athletic and handles center field well, with mobility to all sectors. His above-average arm strength gives him a weapon that would help him profile in right field if he has to move there at some point. Kling's raw power is evident in his frame, and he did a solid job finding the barrel in his pro debut. His max exit velocities didn't jump off the page, but his 90th percentile mark of 104.2 mph points to consistent flush contact. There were some issues with spin as an amateur, and his miss rates were a little high in a smaller pro sample, so his pure hit tool might not be better than below-average.
THE FUTURE: Kling's pedigrees in the Big Ten and Southeastern conferences should allow him to move quickly through the system. His ceiling is as a masher who can handle center field and make noise on the bases.

Year	Age	Club (League)	Level	AVG	G	AB	R	H	2B	3B	HR	RBI	BB	SO	SB	OBP	SLG
2025	22	Hickory (CAR)	A	.368	10	38	6	14	4	1	1	5	3	9	1	.395	.605
2025	22	Hub City (SAL)	A+	.244	11	45	6	11	3	0	0	2	4	10	1	.320	.311
		Minor League Totals		.301	21	83	12	25	7	1	1	7	7	19	2	.355	.446

TEXAS RANGERS

22 ELORKY RODRIGUEZ, 2B

HIT: 50. **POW:** 40. **RUN:** 50. **FLD:** 40. **ARM:** 40. **BA Grade:** 50. **Risk:** Extreme. **Adj:** 30.

Born: December 26, 2007. **B-T:** L-R. **HT:** 5-10. **WT:** 175. **Signed:** Dominican Republic, 2025.
Signed by: Willy Espinal/Jonny Clum/Jack Marino/Nelson Muniz/Pablo Saviñon.
TRACK RECORD: Rodriguez's $1.1 million bonus was the highest awarded to any of Texas' 2025 international class. He earned that figure based on a well-rounded tool set, and he opened his career in the Dominican Summer League and finished with a .979 OPS and six home runs over 46 games. His year included a berth in the DSL all-star game.
SCOUTING REPORT: On the surface, Rodriguez's professional debut was a success. Under the hood, there's plenty of areas to polish. He took professional at-bats and made sound swing decisions, but his exit velocities were a bit underwhelming. He finished the year with a 90th percentile mark of just 99.5 mph and a max figure of 104.5 mph. Considering his frame lacks much room for projection, there's reason to believe his power numbers might jump much as he gets older. Rodriguez's defense is also a bit of an issue. He split his reps between second base and center field, but scouts are skeptical he has the chops to be more than fringy at either spot. That's especially true if his lower half gets any thicker than its current state.
THE FUTURE: Rodriguez will likely spend most of 2026 in the Arizona Complex League. There, he'll work to up his exit velocities and improve his defense in an effort to stay up the middle.

Year	Age	Club (League)	Level	AVG	G	AB	R	H	2B	3B	HR	RBI	BB	SO	SB	OBP	SLG
2025	17	DSL Rangers Red	Rk	.337	46	178	46	60	10	1	6	48	39	38	9	.473	.506
		Minor League Totals		.337	46	178	46	60	10	1	6	48	39	38	9	.473	.506

23 SEONG-JUN KIM, SS/RHP

FB: 60. **SL:** 50. **CB:** 40. **SP:** 50. **CTL:** 50. **BA Grade:** 50. **Risk:** Extreme. **Adj:** 30.
HIT: 40. **POW:** 40. **RUN:** 50. **FLD:** 50. **ARM:** 60.

Born: May 1, 2007. **B-T:** R-R. **HT:** 6-2. **WT:** 185. **Signed:** South Korea, 2025.
Signed by: Joe Furukawa/Jonny Clum/Andre Park.
TRACK RECORD: After losing out to the Dodgers in the Roki Sasaki sweepstakes, the Rangers had plenty of international pool money to spend. A total of $1.2 million of it went to Kim, an 18-year-old in South Korea with talent on both sides of the ball. He joined the Rangers after graduating from Gwangju Jeil High and spent a few games in the Dominican Summer League. He got 13 plate appearances as a hitter and one inning on the mound. He played both ways as an amateur and had a chance to be picked early in the Korean Baseball Organization draft.
SCOUTING REPORT: The Rangers are planning to let Kim play both ways at the outset of his career, though evaluators believe his stronger path to the big leagues is on the mound. He works with a four-seamer that's peaked at 95 mph as well as a slider and splitter. He's a lithe athlete in the field with the chops to stick at shortstop and the kind of strong arm that's typical of someone who can also get on the mound. He produced limited exit velocity numbers in a small sample in the D.R. before the season ended and he transitioned into instructional league.
THE FUTURE: Kim will get a chance to hit and pitch in his first full season as a professional. The next step will likely be in the Arizona Complex League.

Year	Age	Club (League)	Level	AVG	G	AB	R	H	2B	3B	HR	RBI	BB	SO	SB	OBP	SLG
2025	18	DSL Rangers Red	Rk	.167	3	12	1	2	0	1	0	2	1	3	3	.231	.333
		Minor League Totals		.167	3	12	1	2	0	1	0	2	1	3	3	.231	.333

Year	Age	Club (League)	Level	W	L	ERA	G	GS	IP	H	HR	BB	SO	BB%	SO%	WHIP	AVG
2025	18	DSL Rangers Red	Rk	0	0	0.00	1	1	1	0	0	0	2	0.0	66.7	0.00	.000
		Minor League Totals		0	0	0.00	1	1	1	0	0	0	2	0.0	66.7	0.00	.000

MAXTON MARTIN, OF/1B

HIT: 45. **POW:** 55. **RUN:** 40. **FLD:** 40. **ARM:** 40. **BA Grade:** 40. **Risk:** Average. **Adj:** 30.

Born: May 5, 2005. **B-T:** L-R. **HT:** 6-1. **WT:** 205. **Drafted:** HS—Kennewick, WA, 2023 (11th round).
Signed by: Gary McGraw.
TRACK RECORD: Martin was a two-sport standout in high school in Kennewick, Wash., and was committed to Oregon before the Rangers drafted him in the 11th round in 2023. The younger brother of former Pirates prospect Mason Martin, Maxton spent his first full pro season in the Arizona Complex League. He played most of 2025 at Low-A Hickory before making a season-ending run with High-A Hub City.
SCOUTING REPORT: Martin's calling card is his power, which helped him swat 14 home runs in 2025. His 90th percentile exit velocity was 102 mph, and he maxed out at 111 mph. His raw juice is among the

best in the system, but he'll need to make more contact to use it to its full potential. His miss and chase rates were both worse than 30%, and his in-zone miss rate finished at 21.8%. Most of Martin's defensive reps came in left field, with a few starts in right field and at first base mixed in as well. His arm strength and defense each project to be below-average, which puts plenty of pressure on him to make the offensive adjustments required to squeeze every drop out of his power. Martin is a below-average runner as well, but he showed enough to become one of just two minor leaguers with double-digit home runs and 15 or more stolen bases without getting caught.

THE FUTURE: Martin has a ceiling as a second-division regular who can provide a bit of thump.

Year	Age	Club (League)	Level	AVG	G	AB	R	H	2B	3B	HR	RBI	BB	SO	SB	OBP	SLG
2025	20	Hickory (CAR)	A	.259	102	402	72	104	25	6	12	64	45	101	13	.343	.440
2025	20	Hub City (SAL)	A+	.256	14	43	9	11	2	1	2	3	7	14	2	.385	.488
		Minor League Totals		.251	163	617	119	155	36	9	17	100	75	167	21	.342	.421

25 PAULINO SANTANA, OF

HIT: 40. **POW:** 50. **RUN:** 55. **FLD:** 50. **ARM:** 50. **BA Grade:** 45. **Risk:** High. **Adj:** 30.

Born: November 17, 2006. **B-T:** R-R. **HT:** 6-2. **WT:** 180. **Signed:** Dominican Republic, 2024.
Signed by: Jack Marino/Willy Espinal/Pablo Saviñon.
TRACK RECORD: Santana was the gem of the Rangers' 2024 signing class and opened his career on a strong note in the Dominican Summer League. There, he posted an .829 OPS, finished with more walks (52) than strikeouts (38) and was named the MVP of the league's annual all-star game. The sailing wasn't as smooth stateside, but he made it to Low-A Hickory by season's end.
SCOUTING REPORT: Santana moved to the Arizona Complex League to begin 2025 and produced a middling year. His speed, defense and arm all settled in around average or slightly better, giving him a fair chance to stick in center field. Doing so would be a boon for his future, since his offense is unlikely to profile in a corner. Santana's EV numbers were strong—including 90th percentile and max marks of 103.7 mph and 112.6 mph—but his miss rates were fringy or below-average across the board, and he finished the year with a 30.7% strikeout rate. Scouts chalked up the whiffs to poor swing decisions and general over-aggressiveness against soft stuff. Still, Santana's compact swing and strong body provide hope that he can reach his potential with more refinement.
THE FUTURE: Santana will return to Hickory in 2026. He has the ceiling of a center fielder who hits toward the bottom of a lineup but will take plenty of patience if he is to reach those heights.

Year	Age	Club (League)	Level	AVG	G	AB	R	H	2B	3B	HR	RBI	BB	SO	SB	OBP	SLG
2025	18	ACL Rangers	Rk	.265	56	211	38	56	10	3	5	28	21	65	8	.339	.412
2025	18	Hickory (CAR)	A	.217	18	60	6	13	1	3	0	4	4	29	3	.299	.333
		Minor League Totals		.270	127	466	90	126	17	10	5	62	77	132	31	.392	.382

26 ANTHONY GUTIERREZ, OF

HIT: 40. **POW:** 40. **RUN:** 55. **FLD:** 60. **ARM:** 60. **BA Grade:** 45. **Risk:** High. **Adj:** 30.

Born: November 24, 2004. **B-T:** R-R. **HT:** 6-3. **WT:** 200. **Signed:** Venezuela, 2022. **Signed by:** Rafic Saab/Willy Espinal.
TRACK RECORD: After teasing his tremendous upside in his first pro season, when he was promoted stateside before the close of the Dominican Summer League season, Gutierrez has faced a series of injuries. Those include a fractured finger in 2023, shoulder surgery in 2024 and a hybrid Tommy John surgery in 2025. All told, he hasn't reached the 90-game mark in either of his last two seasons.
SCOUTING REPORT: When healthy, Gutierrez has an ideal body that should produce power and athleticism in equal measure. All the time on the injured list has stunted his development and delayed his path to the big leagues. He's an aggressive swinger who does a good job making contact on pitches in the strike zone but needs to chase at a far lower clip. He hits the ball fairly hard, with max exit velocities up to 109 mph, but needs to improve his barrel accuracy to get the most out of his strength. The 21-year-old Gutierrez still ranks among the best defensive outfielders in the system, and his arm strength—when healthy—is the best in the organization. He is an above-average runner who has been successful on more than 80% of his stolen base attempts in his career.
THE FUTURE: Gutierrez should be ready in time for spring training and should get to Double-A in 2026. When he does, he'll need to become far more selective at the plate to get the most out of his offensive upside. A fully healthy season would go a long way, too.

Year	Age	Club (League)	Level	AVG	G	AB	R	H	2B	3B	HR	RBI	BB	SO	SB	OBP	SLG
2025	20	Hub City (SAL)	A+	.258	89	337	53	87	15	0	2	28	31	79	48	.333	.320
		Minor League Totals		.264	294	1078	169	285	51	9	9	107	89	254	134	.332	.353

TEXAS RANGERS

27 BEN ABELDT, LHP
FB: 60. **SL:** 55. **CH:** 40. **CTL:** 50. **BA Grade:** 45. **Risk:** High. **Adj:** 30.

Born: December 1, 2003. **B-T:** R-L. **HT:** 6-3. **WT:** 210. **Drafted:** TCU, 2025 (5th round). **Signed by:** Takeshi Sakurayama.
TRACK RECORD: Abeldt spent his first two seasons at TCU working almost exclusively out of the bullpen. Abeldt also spent two summers pitching with USA Baseball's Collegiate National Team. He was in line for a spot in the rotation before he tore his ulnar collateral ligament in February and had Tommy John surgery. Instead, he spent the season as the Horned Frogs' informal bullpen coach. The Rangers bet on his upside and drafted him in the fifth round.
SCOUTING REPORT: At his best, Abeldt gets his outs on the strength of three pitches and a funky delivery that features a low slot and a crossfire action. His fastball sits in the low 90s and peaks at 96 with the kind of heavy sink that keeps infielders on their toes. He backs it with a sweepy slider in the 78-82 mph range that drives swings and misses and has above-average potential. He has a low-80s changeup in his back pocket as well, but he threw it just 7.7% of the time in 2024. Despite the high-maintenance delivery, Abeldt did an excellent job in college of pounding the strike zone and should have at least average control in the big leagues.
THE FUTURE: Abeldt should be ready for spring training and could move quickly as a reliever. He profiles as someone who can neutralize lefties, and his stock could tick up if he improves his changeup.

Year	Age	Club (League)	Level	W	L	ERA	G	GS	IP	H	HR	BB	SO	BB%	SO%	WHIP	AVG
2025	20	Did not play															

28 PAUL BONZAGNI, RHP
FB: 60. **SL:** 60. **CH:** 40. **CTL:** 55. **BA Grade:** 45. **Risk:** High. **Adj:** 30.

Born: April 1, 2002. **B-T:** R-R. **HT:** 6-2. **WT:** 200. **Drafted:** Southern Illinois, 2023 (12th round). **Signed by:** Michael Medici.
TRACK RECORD: After two seasons at Weatherford (TX) JC, Bonzagni transferred to Southern Illinois for the second part of his college career. In between, he was part of a talented Cape Cod League team that was loaded with future first-rounders, including 2024 No. 1 overall pick Travis Bazzana. Bonzagni raised his stock with the Salukis, and the Rangers pounced on the chance to draft him in the 12th round. He signed for $150,000 and split his first full pro season between the Class A levels. He pitched just 9.1 innings in 2025 before a torn ulnar collateral ligament required Tommy John surgery.
SCOUTING REPORT: When healthy, Bonzagni is one of the best groundball-drivers in the Rangers' system. That was the case in 2025, when he coaxed grounders at a 66.7% rate before his elbow flared up. At his best, he works with a fastball and slider that each grade as potentially plus offerings, as well as a changeup that was in line for a season of development before the injury. Historically, he's shown a willingness to attack the strike zone with his entire mix and should have at least above-average control.
THE FUTURE: Bonzagni's surgery will likely cost him all of 2026. If his stuff returns in full, he could be a late-game reliever whose pitch mix keeps hitters and infielders on their toes. Starting isn't out of the question, however, and the next step toward that goal will come in 2027.

Year	Age	Club (League)	Level	W	L	ERA	G	GS	IP	H	HR	BB	SO	BB%	SO%	WHIP	AVG
2025	23	Hub City (SAL)	A+	0	1	4.82	3	2	9	11	1	5	15	11.1	33.3	1.71	.282
		Minor League Totals		9	3	3.61	34	18	110	94	8	39	120	8.4	25.9	1.21	.228

29 CAMERON CAULEY, SS/OF
HIT: 30. **POW:** 40. **RUN:** 60. **FLD:** 60. **ARM:** 60. **BA Grade:** 45. **Risk:** High. **Adj:** 30.

Born: February 6, 2003. **B-T:** R-R. **HT:** 5-10. **WT:** 190. **Drafted:** HS—Mont Belvieu, TX, 2021 (3rd round). **Signed by:** Josh Simpson.
TRACK RECORD: Cauley signed for $1 million with Texas after being drafted in the third round in 2021. Injuries stunted his progress in the following seasons, but in 2025 he reached Double-A for the first time and posted a season with middling stats but hints of upside.
SCOUTING REPORT: Cauley is still twitchy and athletic and can put a decent charge into a ball, but he needs plenty of refinement to get the most out of his offensive potential. He handles spin fine, but he was vexed by premium fastballs and changeups. Even so, he got enough out of his contact and plus speed to become one of just nine minor leaguers 22 or younger who finished the year hitting .250 or better with at least 15 home runs and 25 stolen bases. He'd moved back and forth between shortstop and second base, but in 2025 he added center field to his bag of tricks. The results were outstanding. Cauley's quickness and range allowed him to make scads of highlight reel plays, including diving grabs back, forth and side to side while chewing up turf with efficient routes. If that's his future home, he'll provide plenty of value with his glove.

THE FUTURE: Cauley's defensive prowess and versatility gives him a variety of avenues to reach the big leagues. If he can become a more well-rounded hitter, he might tap into the upside the Rangers saw in him five summers ago.

Year	Age	Club (League)	Level	AVG	G	AB	R	H	2B	3B	HR	RBI	BB	SO	SB	OBP	SLG
2025	22	Frisco (TL)	AA	.253	113	435	74	110	26	7	15	51	47	121	28	.325	.448
		Minor League Totals		.240	409	1562	262	375	77	23	44	189	175	497	139	.317	.403

30 JOEY DANIELSON, RHP

FB: 60. **CB:** 50. **SL:** 40. **CT:** 45. **SP:** 40. **CTL:** 40. **BA Grade:** 40. **Risk:** Average. **Adj:** 30.

Born: January 11, 2001. **B-T:** R-R. **HT:** 6-3. **WT:** 235. **Drafted:** North Dakota State, 2024 (17th round).
Signed by: Dustin Smith.

TRACK RECORD: After two seasons as a catcher at North Dakota State, Danielson talked his way into a role as a pitcher. Four seasons later, the Rangers were intrigued enough to call Danielson's name in the 17th round in 2024. He got his feet wet later that summer at Low-A, then zoomed to Double-A in his first full season as a pro. He got a little more work under his belt in the Arizona Fall League.

SCOUTING REPORT: Most pitchers deploy their arsenal differently against righties and lefties, but Danielson takes it to another level. Facing righties, he works with a sinker, sweeper and cutter and delivers from a low three-quarters slot. Against lefties, he works from a much higher slot and utilizes his four-seamer, curveball, splitter and cutter. After annihilating the competition in High-A, the 24-year-old Danielson ran into resistance at Double-A Frisco. He struggled to throw strikes and was crushed by right-handers, who hit .375/.500/.563 against him. Lefties managed an OPS of just .440 against Danielson at Double-A, though he struggled to throw strikes in general. Danielson's fastball is the only plus pitch in his mix. Among his offspeeds, only his curveball grades as average.

THE FUTURE: To land a spot in the big leagues, Danielson will have to drastically improve his control and bring one of his offspeed pitches forward a few clicks. If he can, he could settle in as a low-leverage arm.

Year	Age	Club (League)	Level	W	L	ERA	G	GS	IP	H	HR	BB	SO	BB%	SO%	WHIP	AVG
2025	24	Hub City (SAL)	A+	3	3	3.70	34	0	41	46	4	15	48	8.2	26.1	1.48	.275
2025	24	Frisco (TL)	AA	1	1	6.14	15	0	15	15	2	14	19	20.0	27.1	1.98	.273
		Minor League Totals		4	4	4.34	49	0	56	61	6	29	67	11.4	26.4	1.61	.275

Vladimir Guerrero Jr.

Toronto Blue Jays

BY GEOFF PONTES

After the nightmare that was the Blue Jays' 2024 season, 2025 came as a welcomed change.

Toronto overtook the Yankees for the American League East lead on July 2 and never looked back. The Blue Jays won the division on the last day of the season, clinching the best record in the AL and receiving a first-round bye. Toronto advanced past the Yankees in the Division Series before defeating the Mariners in the Championship Series. The Blue Jays led the World Series three games to two before eventually bowing out to the Dodgers in the 11th inning of Game 7.

A year after it felt nothing could go right for the Blue Jays, everything suddenly seemed to click in 2025.

The team began the season by signing homegrown superstar Vladimir Guerrero Jr. to a 14-year, $500 million extension. Guerrero in turn provided the spark needed in the middle of the lineup, hitting .292/.381/.467 with 23 home runs.

The team also saw breakout seasons from third baseman/outfielder Addison Barger, who established himself as an everyday player by hitting 21 home runs. Bo Bichette bounced back from an injury-plagued 2024 and returned to form by hitting .311 and finishing second in the AL batting race.

The most unexpected twist of the 2025 season was probably the return to peak form for 35-year-old George Springer. The aging outfielder had his best season since 2019 and his best season in a Blue Jays uniform, hitting .309/.399/.560 with 32 home runs over 140 games.

The team's rotation stayed fairly healthy throughout the season as the trio of Kevin Gausman, Chris Bassitt and Jose Berrios each made 30 or more starts.

Things were equally impressive on the farm. The Blue Jays' revamped pitching development under Justin Lehr and Ricky Meinhold led to gains across the organization. The biggest breakout belonged to the team's top prospect and 2024 first-round pick Trey Yesavage. The tall righthander climbed all five levels of the full-season minor leagues in 2025, culminating in a September callup and record-setting 12-strikeout performance against the Dodgers in Game 5 of the World Series. Toronto traded fellow 2024 draftee Khal Stephen to the Guardians for Shane Bieber, who started Game 7 of the World Series.

Besides Yesavage, there were numerous breakouts among Toronto pitching prospects. Johnny King and Gage Stanifer each enjoyed standout seasons. King, a third-round Florida prep lefthander, impressed in the Florida Complex League to earn a promotion to Low-A where he continued his ascent. Stanifer, on the other hand, has been a slow burn. The 19th-round pick out of the Indiana prep ranks in 2022 pitched his way to Double-A by the end of the season, showing significantly improved command.

The Blue Jays drafted heavily from the high school position ranks in 2025. They landed Mississippi shortstop JoJo Parker, Alberta corner infielder Tim Piasentin and speedy Texas outfielder Blaine Bullard. It's a change in approach for a team that previously had been heavily college-focused. This new young core of position talent has a chance to develop into another set of high-upside draft hits for the club. ∎

PROJECTED 2029 LINEUP

Catcher	Alejandro Kirk	30
First Base	Vladimir Guerrero Jr.	30
Second Base	Andres Gimenez	30
Third Base	JoJo Parker	22
Shortstop	Arjun Nimmala	23
Left Field	RJ Schreck	28
Center Field	Jake Cook	25
Right Field	Addison Barger	29
Designated Hitter	Anthony Santander	34
No. 1 Starter	Dylan Cease	33
No. 2 Starter	Trey Yesavage	25
No. 3 Starter	Johnny King	22
No. 4 Starter	Gage Stanifer	25
No. 5 Starter	Ricky Tiedemann	26
Closer	Louie Varland	31

DEPTH CHART

TORONTO BLUE JAYS

TOP 2026 ROOKIES — **RANK**
1. Trey Yesavage, RHP — 1
2. Ricky Tiedemann, LHP — 6
3. RJ Schreck, OF — 8

BREAKOUT PROSPECTS — **RANK**
1. Silvano Hechavarria, RHP — 12
2. Tim Piasentin, 3B — 15
3. Jake Casey, OF — 21

SOURCE OF TOP 30 TALENT

Homegrown	21	Acquired	9
College	7	Trade	7
Junior college	1	Rule 5 draft	2
High school	8	Independent league	0
Undrafted free agent	1	Free agent/waivers	0
International	4		

LF
Yohendrick Pinango (11)
Yeuni Munoz
Yorman Licourt
Eddie Micheletti Jr.

CF
Jake Cook (10)
Victor Arias (13)
Blaine Bullard (14)

RF
RJ Schreck (8)
Jake Casey (21)
Jace Bohrofen
Je'Von Ward

3B
Juan Sanchez (7)
Tim Piasentin (15)
Charles McAdoo (24)
Cutter Coffey
Riley Tirotta

SS
Arjun Nimmala (2)
JoJo Parker (3)
Josh Kasevich (17)
Manuel Beltre
Eric Snow
Cristopher Polanco
Jay Harry

2B
J.R. Freethy
Sam Shaw
Ryan McCarthy
Adrian Pinto

1B
Sean Keys (20)
Jackson Hornung
Damiano Palmegiani
Peyton Williams

C
Brandon Valenzuela (28)
Edward Duran (30)
Aaron Parker
Jaxson West
Franklin Rojas

LHP

LHSP
Johnny King (4)
Ricky Tiedemann (6)
Brandon Barriera (26)
Connor O'Halloran
Jared Spencer

LHRP
Adam Macko (25)
Javen Coleman (29)

RHP

RHSP
Trey Yesavage (1)
Gage Stanifer (5)
Jake Bloss (9)
Silvano Hechavarria (12)
Angel Bastardo (16)
Fernando Perez (18)
Micah Bucknam (19)
Carson Messina (27)
Landen Maroudis
Jackson Wentworth
Austin Cates

RHRP
Spencer Miles (22)
Ryan Jennings (23)
T.J. Brock

TORONTO BLUE JAYS

1 TREY YESAVAGE, RHP

Born: July 28, 2003. **B-T:** R-R. **HT:** 6-4. **WT:** 225.
Drafted: East Carolina, 2024 (1st round).
Signed by: Coulson Barbiche.

BA GRADE: 60 Risk: Mild
Adjusted grade: 55

SCOUTING GRADES
FB: 60. SL: 55.
SP: 70. CTL: 50.
Projected future grades on 20-80 scouting scale

TRACK RECORD: Over three seasons at East Carolina, Yesavage went from a reliever to a key piece of the Pirates' rotation. As a junior in 2024, he went 11-1 with a 2.03 ERA and struck out 145 in 93.1 innings. Late in that season, Yesavage suffered a partially collapsed lung due to an off-field medical procedure. He returned during regionals and outpitched Wake Forest ace Chase Burns. After Yesavage ranked as the No. 11 player in the 2024 class, questions around his medicals dropped him to the Blue Jays at pick No. 20. He signed for a little over $4.75 million and would debut the following spring with Low-A Dunedin. Toronto was deliberate with Yesavage's workload and slowly moved him across each level of the full-season minors before he made his major league debut on Sept. 15. Not only did Yesavage make the Blue Jays' postseason roster, he made five starts during Toronto's run to the World Series. His biggest moment came in Game 5 of the World Series, when he threw seven innings of one-run ball, striking out 12 Dodgers batters to set a World Series rookie record.

SCOUTING REPORT: A physical 6-foot-4 right-hander with a prototypical starter's build, Yesavage employs an unusual operation with a nearly perfect overhand arm slot. Pitching exclusively from the stretch, he gets deep into his back leg as his arm plunges back before he catapults the ball over the top. His vertical arm angle and ability to hide the ball create a deceptive look that keeps opposing hitters off-balance. Yesavage employs a three-pitch mix of four-seam fastball, slider and splitter. The movement on his pitch mix is highly unusual. None of his pitches breaks to his glove side. Yesavage's four-seam fastball is his primary pitch, thrown just under 50% of the time. Due to his over-the-top arm slot, he generates outlier ride on his fastball, averaging nearly 20 inches of induced vertical break in his brief MLB sample. His ride-cut shape and mid-90s velocity create a fearsome combination of traits that drove above-average whiff rates at every level. His slider is used nearly one-for-one to his splitter, and is the harder of his two secondaries, sitting in the upper 80s and touching the low 90s with cutter-like shape. It generates an unusual three inches of armside run. Yesavage's slider is an above-average pitch due to its velocity and unique break, but his splitter is his signature pitch. It sits 83-84 mph with excellent velocity and vertical separation off his fastball. His splitter generates whiffs at elite rates and is a true plus-plus offering. Yesavage shows average control and relies on a heavy dose of chase swings to boost his strike rates.

THE FUTURE: Yesavage enters 2026 as an American League Rookie of the Year frontrunner and key part of the Blue Jays' rotation. He could develop into a No. 2 starter.

BEST TOOLS

BATTING
Best Hitter for Average	Jojo Parker
Best Power Hitter	Juan Sanchez
Best Strike-Zone Discipline	RJ Schreck
Fastest Baserunner	Jake Cook
Best Athlete	Jake Cook

PITCHING
Best Fastball	Trey Yesavage
Best Curveball	Johnny King
Best Slider	Gage Stanifer
Best Changeup	Trey Yesavage
Best Control	Fernando Perez

FIELDING
Best Defensive Catcher	Brandon Valenzuela
Best Defensive Infielder	Arjun Nimmala
Best Infield Arm	Arjun Nimmala
Best Defensive Outfielder	Jake Cook
Best Outfield Arm	Jake Cook

Year	Age	Club (League)	Level	W	L	ERA	G	GS	IP	H	HR	BB	SO	BB%	SO%	WHIP	AVG
2025	21	Dunedin (FSL)	A	3	0	2.43	7	7	33	19	3	8	55	6.3	43.3	0.81	.162
2025	21	Vancouver (NWL)	A+	1	0	1.56	4	4	17	5	2	11	33	15.9	47.8	0.92	.086
2025	21	New Hampshire (EL)	AA	1	1	4.50	8	7	30	21	3	11	46	9.1	38.0	1.07	.198
2025	21	Buffalo (IL)	AAA	0	0	3.63	6	4	17	9	0	11	26	15.3	36.1	1.15	.150
2025	21	Toronto (AL)	MLB	1	0	3.21	3	3	14	13	0	7	16	11.3	25.8	1.43	.236
		Minor League Totals		5	1	3.12	25	22	98	54	8	41	160	10.5	41.1	0.97	.158
		Major League Totals		1	0	3.21	3	3	14	13	0	7	16	11.3	25.8	1.43	.236

TORONTO BLUE JAYS

2 ARJUN NIMMALA, SS
HIT: 45. **POW:** 55. **RUN:** 55. **FLD:** 55. **ARM:** 60. **BA Grade:** 60. **Risk:** High. **Adj:** 45.

Born: October 16, 2005. **B-T:** R-R. **HT:** 6-1. **WT:** 190.
Drafted: HS—Dover, FL, 2023 (1st round). **Signed by:** Brandon Bishoff.
TRACK RECORD: At 17 years old, Nimmala was the youngest player selected in the 2023 draft and debuted in the Florida Complex League months before his 18th birthday. His production was heavily disjointed in his first two full seasons. A rough start in 2024 for Low-A Dunedin led to a stint on the development list after 29 games. Upon his return, Nimmala showed improved posture in his swing and hit .265/.331/.564 over the final 53 games. The 2025 season was the reverse, as Nimmala started hot with High-A Vancouver, hitting .289/.372/.538 over the first 45 games. From June 1 onward, things took a gnarly turn and he hit .184 over the final 75 games.
SCOUTING REPORT: A young shortstop with exciting skills on both sides of the ball, Nimmala still has remaining projection in his broad-shouldered frame. At the plate, he sets up slightly open, deploying a toe-tap timing mechanism. He looks to meet the ball out in front, which at times is to the detriment of his contact quality when he catches the ball off the end of the bat. Nimmala showed improvements to his contact in 2025, which resulted in a drop in strikeout rate. His bat-to-ball skills are fringe-average, which he mitigates with above-average swing decisions. Nimmala showed improved underlying power in 2025 with a jump in exit velocity data, but struggled to pull the ball in the air. Nimmala should be an above-average power hitter due to his plus bat speed, current power and remaining projection. He is an average runner who will show plus run times on jailbreaks to first base. He's an above-average defender at shortstop with a plus arm who looks likely to stick at the position.
THE FUTURE: Nimmala will look to find more consistency at the plate in 2026, and if he does he'll develop into an above-average everyday shortstop. Double-A is next.

Year	Age	Club (League)	Level	AVG	G	AB	R	H	2B	3B	HR	RBI	BB	SO	SB	OBP	SLG
2025	19	Vancouver (NWL)	A+	.224	120	473	70	106	29	3	13	61	55	116	17	.313	.381
		Minor League Totals		.227	219	838	140	190	50	11	30	111	108	244	27	.325	.420

3 JOJO PARKER, SS
HIT: 55. **POW:** 55. **RUN:** 50. **FLD:** 50. **ARM:** 55. **BA Grade:** 60. **Risk:** High. **Adj:** 45.

Born: August 8, 2006. **B-T:** L-R. **HT:** 6-2. **WT:** 200.
Drafted: HS—Purvis, MS, 2025 (1st round). **Signed by:** Don Norris.
TRACK RECORD: In the months leading up to the 2025 draft, no player had more helium than Parker. A four-year varsity starter for Purvis High in Mississippi, his impressive performance at East Coast Pro in 2024 got the hype train to leave the station. The Blue Jays drafted Parker with the eighth overall pick in 2025 and signed him for just under $6.2 million. He didn't debut following the draft but did participate in unofficial bridge league games. Parker's birth name is Joseph, but he goes by JoJo. His twin brother Jacob is an outfielder who played for Purvis and attends Mississippi State.
SCOUTING REPORT: Parker is a physical shortstop who stands 6-foot-2 with a strong, muscular build and room to add more strength. He was one of the older players in the 2025 high school class but shows arguably the best balance of hitting and power among his prep peers. Parker sets up with an open stance and a narrow base. He rests the bat on his shoulder, then engages his load with a leg kick that feeds into an aggressive stride. Parker shows plus bat-to-ball skills and a patient approach. He can get overly passive at times, taking too many hittable pitches in the zone. He does a good job of pulling pitches located on the inner half of the plate and shows plus raw power. His swing is more geared toward hard line drives than lofted fly balls, but he should grow into above-average power at peak. Parker is an average runner who gets out of the box well, but he's unlikely to impact the game much with his speed. Parker is a shortstop at present but is likely to move to third base. He lacks the quick-twitch mechanisms and range needed to play shortstop. He does have a strong internal clock and an above-average arm.
THE FUTURE: Parker projects as an above-average regular at third base who could one day grow into an all-star.

Year	Age	Club (League)	Level	AVG	G	AB	R	H	2B	3B	HR	RBI	BB	SO	SB	OBP	SLG
2025	18	Did not play															

TORONTO BLUE JAYS

4 JOHNNY KING, LHP
FB: 60. **CB:** 60. **CH:** 40. **CTL:** 45. **BA Grade:** 60. **Risk:** High. **Adj:** 45.

Born: July 26, 2006. **B-T:** L-L. **HT:** 6-4. **WT:** 185.
Drafted: HS—Naples, FL, 2024 (3rd round). **Signed by:** Adrian Casanova.
TRACK RECORD: King was just 17 years old on draft day when the Blue Jays selected him in the third round in 2024. A projectable 6-foot-4 lefthander from Naples, Fla., he was one of the brightest performers in Toronto's farm system in 2025. King began in the Florida Complex League, making six appearances and striking out 41 batters to seven walks across 24 innings. He was promoted to Low-A Dunedin on June 29 and made 11 appearances and 10 starts. Over 37.2 innings with Dunedin, King struck out 64 batters to 30 walks, pitching to a 3.35 ERA.
SCOUTING REPORT: King has all the ingredients of a midrotation stalwart. His operation gets deep into his glutes, allowing him to drop and drive with a strong lead leg block. His low three-quarters arm slot creates a deceptive angle for both lefthanded and righthanded batters, though he saw more success in opposite-handed matchups in 2025. King is still learning to repeat his mechanics, something that should help him find more consistency with his release point. King mixes and matches with a four-seam fastball, curveball and changeup. King's fastball is plus and sits 93-95 mph with above-average ride and heavy armside run. King had some of the highest total movement on his fastball of any lefthander in professional baseball in 2025. His most-used secondary pitch is a two-plane curveball that sits 80-82 mph with good depth. His curveball boasted a whiff rate north of 50% in 2025. King's changeup is a clear third pitch and was used sparingly in 2025. King shows fringe-average control and struggled with strike-throwing with Dunedin.
THE FUTURE: King is poised to build on his breakout 2025 on his way to his final destination of midrotation starter.

Year	Age	Club (League)	Level	W	L	ERA	G	GS	IP	H	HR	BB	SO	BB%	SO%	WHIP	AVG
2025	18	FCL Blue Jays	Rk	0	0	1.13	7	5	24	17	0	7	41	7.1	41.8	1.00	.195
2025	18	Dunedin (FSL)	A	1	3	3.35	11	10	38	27	4	30	64	17.9	38.1	1.51	.203
		Minor League Totals		1	3	2.48	18	15	62	44	4	37	105	13.9	39.5	1.31	.200

GAGE STANIFER, RHP
FB: 55. **SL:** 60. **CH:** 45. **CTL:** 45. **BA Grade:** 55. **Risk:** High. **Adj:** 40.

Born: November 18, 2003. **B-T:** R-R. **HT:** 6-3. **WT:** 201.
Drafted: HS—Westfield, IN, 2022 (19th round). **Signed by:** Matt Huck.
TRACK RECORD: Stanifer signed for $125,000 as an Indiana prep pick in the 19th round of the 2022 draft. After spending 2023 in the Florida Complex League and making 19 appearances for Low-A Dunedin in 2024, Stanifer broke out in a big way in 2025. Stanifer spent the first seven weeks of the season as a piggyback starter in tandem with top prospect Trey Yesavage and was promoted to High-A Vancouver alongside him on May 19. He moved into the rotation at High-A and was promoted to Double-A on Sept. 5 and made two starts.
SCOUTING REPORT: Stanifer stands 6-foot-3 with a broad-shouldered, muscular build and little in the way of remaining projection. He works exclusively from the stretch with a high leg lift that contracts into his body before he drives toward the plate. He's a short-strider with a short arm action and releases the ball from a three-quarters arm slot. Stanifer mixes a four-seam fastball, slider and changeup. His four-seam fastball sits 93-96 mph with plus ride and heavy armside run. Despite a lack of extension, Stanifer creates a deceptively flat plane of approach to the plate, leading to impressive whiff rates against the pitch. His primary secondary pitch against righthanders is a low-to-mid-80s slider that looks like a harder curveball with heavy vertical drop. His slider is a plus bat-missing pitch that generated elite whiff rates in 2025. His changeup is his go-to secondary in off-handed matchups. Stanifer shows average feel for his changeup, but its primary function is driving weak grounders, not generating whiffs. Stanifer shows fringe-average control across his arsenal.
THE FUTURE: Stanifer carries a fair amount of relief risk but showed the ability to start over the final three months of the 2025 season and has No. 4 starter upside.

Year	Age	Club (League)	Level	W	L	ERA	G	GS	IP	H	HR	BB	SO	BB%	SO%	WHIP	AVG
2025	21	Dunedin (FSL)	A	4	0	0.69	7	0	26	10	0	12	38	11.7	36.9	0.85	.112
2025	21	Vancouver (NWL)	A+	4	5	3.20	18	14	76	56	2	37	115	11.7	36.5	1.22	.204
2025	21	New Hampshire (EL)	AA	0	1	6.75	2	2	8	5	2	9	8	25.7	22.9	1.75	.192
		Minor League Totals		12	15	4.54	57	40	212	170	12	131	272	14.2	29.5	1.42	.220

TORONTO BLUE JAYS

6 RICKY TIEDEMANN, LHP
FB: 60. **SL:** 60. **CH:** 55. **CTL:** 50. **BA Grade:** 60. **Risk:** Extreme. **Adj:** 40.

Born: August 18, 2002. **B-T:** L-L. **HT:** 6-4. **WT:** 220.
Drafted: Golden West (CA) JC, 2021 (3rd round). **Signed by:** Joey Aversa.
TRACK RECORD: The Blue Jays drafted Tiedemann in the third round out of junior college in 2021 and signed him for $644,800. He dominated in his 2022 debut, starting in Low-A and reaching Double-A in his age-19 season. Tiedemann was limited to just 61.1 innings in 2023 and 2024 because of persistent elbow pain. He had Tommy John surgery in late July 2024 and missed all of 2025. The Blue Jays added Tiedemann to the 40-man roster following the 2025 season and plan to slowly ease him back into game action in 2026.
SCOUTING REPORT: Despite a physical, 6-foot-4 build, Tiedemann has struggled to stay healthy for most of his career. When Tiedemann is healthy and locked in, his arsenal plays up due to his low three-quarters arm slot. His arm swing is long, but it helps him hide the ball, creating deceptive traits. Since his initial elbow injury in 2023, Tiedemann has struggled to consistently repeat his mechanics and release point. He mixes a four-seam fastball, slider and changeup. His fastball sits 94-96 mph with heavy armside run that plays up due to his arm slot. In 2024, Tiedemann generated less armside run on his fastball compared to previous seasons, possibly a product of his lingering elbow injury. Tiedemann's slider is his most-used secondary weapon. It has had varied shapes over the seasons, showing traditional break in 2023 and more sweeper action in 2022 and 2024. When at his best, Tiedemann shows the ability to use his slider against batters of both hands, wearing out the armside half of the plate. His changeup was viewed as his best secondary as an amateur, but it has become less effective in pro ball.
THE FUTURE: Tiedemann will likely see a heavy dose of relief work in 2026 as he builds up his workload, but his midrotation upside remains.

Year	Age	Club (League)	Level	W	L	ERA	G	GS	IP	H	HR	BB	SO	BB%	SO%	WHIP	AVG
2025	22	Did not play—Injured															
		Minor League Totals		5	10	3.02	41	41	140	83	8	68	226	11.9	39.6	1.08	.173

7 JUAN SANCHEZ, SS/3B
HIT: 55. **POW:** 60. **RUN:** 40. **FLD:** 45. **ARM:** 55. **BA Grade:** 60. **Risk:** Extreme. **Adj:** 40.

Born: September 27, 2007. **B-T:** R-R. **HT:** 6-3. **WT:** 180.
Signed: Dominican Republic, 2025. **Signed by:** Sandy Rosario/Jose Natera.
TRACK RECORD: Sanchez signed with the Blue Jays out of the Dominican Republic for $997,500, the second-highest bonus in their 2025 class. He made his debut in the Dominican Summer League a few months later and was one of the standout performers on the circuit. Sanchez hit .341/.439/.565 with eight home runs and ranked as the No. 5 prospect in the league.
SCOUTING REPORT: A large, physical slugger standing 6-foot-3 with plenty of space to add muscle and strength to his frame, Sanchez already shows in-game power with plus bat-to-ball skills. In 2025 he missed pitches in the strike zone just 10.8% of the time and ran solid underlying swing-decision metrics. Sanchez is prone to expanding the zone at times, which leads to whiffs. When he stays inside the zone and looks to do damage on pitches over the plate, he produces hard barrels all over the yard. Sanchez shows plus raw power, having hit a ball 115.8 mph in 2025. Sanchez already shows the ability to pull the ball hard and in the air and produces a high rate of barrel contact. He projects to grow into a plus power hitter at peak with elite high-end exit velocities and the ability to get to them in games. Sanchez is a fringe-average runner who will likely slow down as he matures. His lack of range and questionable actions likely mean a permanent move to third base in the future. He's a natural fit for third base with an above-average arm capable of making all the necessary throws.
THE FUTURE: Sanchez has the tools and requisite bat-to-ball ability and power to grow into an above-average third baseman with peak seasons featuring 30 home runs. He's viewed as one of the top players coming stateside in 2026 and should play in the Florida Complex League.

Year	Age	Club (League)	Level	AVG	G	AB	R	H	2B	3B	HR	RBI	BB	SO	SB	OBP	SLG
2025	17	DSL Blue Jays 2	Rk	.341	56	214	47	73	16	4	8	40	26	44	4	.439	.565
		Minor League Totals		.341	56	214	47	73	16	4	8	40	26	44	4	.439	.565

TORONTO BLUE JAYS

8 RJ SCHRECK, OF

HIT: 60. **POW:** 50. **RUN:** 50. **FLD:** 45. **ARM:** 50. **BA Grade:** 45. **Risk:** Mild. **Adj:** 40.

Born: July 12, 2000. **B-T:** L-R. **HT:** 6-1. **WT:** 205.
Drafted: Vanderbilt, 2023 (9th round). **Signed by:** Dan Holcomb (Mariners).
TRACK RECORD: Schreck struggled as a senior at Duke in 2022 after hitting 18 home runs in 2021 and transferred to Vanderbilt for his graduate student season in 2023. The Mariners drafted Schreck in the ninth round in 2023 and signed him for $75,000. Schreck began the 2024 season with High-A Everett and earned a promotion to Double-A weeks before the 2024 trade deadline. He was traded to the Blue Jays for veteran third baseman Justin Turner. Schreck split his 2025 season between Double-A and Triple-A, hitting a combined .249/.395/.459 with 18 homers across both levels. He missed a month in the middle of the season with a hand injury.
SCOUTING REPORT: A well-rounded player with strong plate skills and the ability to fill in at all three outfield positions, Schreck proved that his contact skills and approach were no flukes in 2024. He replicated his plus zone-contact rate and swing decisions at Double-A and Triple-A in 2025. Schreck rarely expands the zone and uses an aggressive approach on strikes, leading to lots of contact. His ability to discern balls from strikes is his greatest asset, leading to clear plus plate skills. Schreck saw a jump in his exit velocity data in 2025 and hit a career-high max exit velocity of 111.9 mph. He shows the ability to hit the ball hard in the air to his pull side, optimizing his average underlying power. Schreck is likely to hit 15-18 home runs annually while providing solid batting averages and high on-base percentages. Schreck is an average runner who saw time in all three outfield spots in 2025. He is below-average in center field but better suited for a corner, where he is closer to average.
THE FUTURE: Schreck looks like a second-division regular with a bat-driven profile.

Year	Age	Club (League)	Level	AVG	G	AB	R	H	2B	3B	HR	RBI	BB	SO	SB	OBP	SLG
2025	24	FCL Blue Jays	Rk	.167	2	6	2	1	0	0	0	0	2	0	1	.375	.167
2025	24	Dunedin (FSL)	A	.182	4	11	1	2	1	0	0	0	4	2	1	.438	.273
2025	24	New Hampshire (EL)	AA	.266	41	139	27	37	6	1	9	20	26	40	5	.396	.518
2025	24	Buffalo (IL)	AAA	.242	58	186	32	45	7	1	9	33	38	49	2	.392	.435
		Minor League Totals		.251	246	837	149	210	50	4	37	129	158	184	23	.386	.453

9 JAKE BLOSS, RHP

FB: 55. **CB:** 50. **SL:** 45. **SP:** 50. **CTL:** 50. **BA Grade:** 55. **Risk:** High. **Adj:** 40.

Born: June 23, 2001. **B-T:** R-R. **HT:** 6-3. **WT:** 223.
Drafted: Georgetown, 2023 (3rd round). **Signed by:** Bobby St. Pierre (Astros).
TRACK RECORD: After three seasons at Lafayette College, Bloss transferred to Georgetown in 2023 and won Big East Conference pitcher of the year honors. He was drafted by the Astros in the third round in 2023 and began his first full season in 2024 at High-A Asheville. Bloss dominated, earning a promotion to Double-A Corpus Christi by May. After four starts, Houston called Bloss up directly from Double-A on June 21. Bloss exited his MLB debut with shoulder discomfort but returned in early July to make two starts. The Astros traded him to the Blue Jays as a part of the Yusei Kikuchi deal at the 2024 trade deadline. Bloss made six starts for Triple-A Buffalo in 2025 but struggled with his control before requiring season-ending UCL surgery in May.
SCOUTING REPORT: Bloss has a prototypical pitcher's build with the size expected of a starter. He begins from a semi-windup with a high leg lift before driving down the mound with plus extension, which improves the plane on his fastball and allows him to create more ride than expected from his high three-quarters arm slot. Bloss mixes five different pitches, throwing four-seam and two-seam fastball variants, a slider, curveball and splitter. Bloss' four-seam fastball sits 93-95 mph and touches 97 with true ride-cut shape. It's an above-average offering and his most heavily used pitch. Bloss reworked his slider in 2025 by showing a baby sweeper shape with around 7-8 inches of sweep. He ditched his sweeper for a high-70s curveball with heavy two-plane break. He altered his changeup to use a splitter grip in 2025 and added more armside run to the pitch. Bloss struggled with the Triple-A zone but projects for average command.
THE FUTURE: Bloss should return to action in the second half of 2026 and looks like a No. 4 starter.

Year	Age	Club (League)	Level	W	L	ERA	G	GS	IP	H	HR	BB	SO	BB%	SO%	WHIP	AVG
2025	24	Buffalo (IL)	AAA	0	5	6.46	6	6	24	33	3	13	24	11.3	20.9	1.94	.330
		Minor League Totals		5	12	3.71	34	33	136	113	11	61	135	10.7	23.6	1.28	.226
		Major League Totals		0	1	6.94	3	3	12	16	5	3	11	5.5	20.0	1.63	.314

TORONTO BLUE JAYS

10 JAKE COOK, OF
HIT: 55. **POW:** 30. **RUN:** 80. **FLD:** 60. **ARM:** 60. **BA Grade:** 50. **Risk:** High. **Adj:** 35.

Born: July 13, 2003. **B-T:** L-L. **HT:** 6-1. **WT:** 185.
Drafted: Southern Mississippi, 2025 (3rd round). **Signed by:** Don Norris.
TRACK RECORD: Cook redshirted as a freshman at Southern Mississippi and then played sparingly as a two-way player as a sophomore. A lefthanded thrower, he dropped pitching heading into 2025 and put together a strong season as an outfielder, hitting .350/.436/.468 with 19 extra-base hits as one of the toughest players to strike out in college baseball. The Blue Jays drafted Cook in the third round and signed him for $922,500.
SCOUTING REPORT: One of the best athletes in the 2025 draft class, Cook is an excellent mover who made rapid improvements as a hitter in his platform season. He is a lefthanded hitter with an inside-out swing who looks to hit inside the baseball and spray line drives to the opposite field. This approach means Cook rarely swings and misses, and he ran a 4% swinging-strike rate with Southern Miss in 2025. Despite his contact-centric profile, Cook shows above-average on-base skills with a good balance of patience and aggression. His power is well below-average and isn't a major part of his game. He hit three home runs with Southern Miss but has good size and enough bat speed to grow into 8-12 home run power. He'll likely collect a majority of his extra bases hitting the ball to the gaps and using his top-of-the-scale speed. Cook is an 80-grade runner who consistently will show home-to-first run times of 3.8 seconds. However, he is a poor basestealer and was caught on five of eight attempts with Southern Miss. His speed translates to the field, where he's a plus center fielder capable of covering large swaths of ground in the outfield. The former pitcher has a plus arm.
THE FUTURE: Cook has many tools but is more raw than other college draftees. He has the attributes to develop into an everyday center fielder.

Year	Age	Club (League)	Level	AVG	G	AB	R	H	2B	3B	HR	RBI	BB	SO	SB	OBP	SLG
2025	21	Did not play															

11 YOHENDRICK PINANGO, OF
HIT: 55. **POW:** 50. **RUN:** 40. **FLD:** 30. **ARM:** 40. **BA Grade:** 45. **Risk:** Average. **Adj:** 35.

Born: May 7, 2002. **B-T:** L-L. **HT:** 5-11. **WT:** 170. **Signed:** Venezuela, 2018.
Signed by: Julio Figueroa/Hector Ortega/Louie Eljaua (Cubs).
TRACK RECORD: Pinango signed with the Cubs in 2018 for $400,000 out of Venezuela and debuted the following summer. He broke out in 2024 but was traded to the Blue Jays before the trade deadline for righthander Nate Pearson. Pinango began 2025 with Double-A New Hampshire, hitting .298/.406/.522 over 47 games and earning a promotion to Triple-A on June 1st.
SCOUTING REPORT: While Pinango has worked to improve his athleticism and running ability, he's still a bat-first player with physical limitations in the outfield. Pinango shows above-average bat-to-ball skills that are heightened by a selective, almost passive, approach at the plate. He'll take too many hittable pitches down the heart of the plate. This approach leads to walks and Pinango's bat-to-ball skills are such that he shows the ability to flip the switch in two-strike counts, putting the ball in play and avoiding strikeouts. Pinango has plus-plus raw power demonstrated by his outstanding exit velocity data. He has plus-plus bat speed that produced a max exit velocity of 115.4 mph in 2025. Unfortunately Pinango's launch angles are actually flatter on his batted balls clocked at 95+ mph. Adding loft will be imperative to Pinango's future success. If he can there's 25+ home run power to unlock. Pinango is a below-average runner and poor outfielder. He's likely to always be a liability in the field.
THE FUTURE: Pinango is a bat-first player with the ability to hit in the majors but no true defensive position and little value outside his hitting.

Year	Age	Club (League)	Level	AVG	G	AB	R	H	2B	3B	HR	RBI	BB	SO	SB	OBP	SLG
2025	23	New Hampshire (EL)	AA	.298	47	161	18	48	10	1	8	23	27	42	5	.406	.522
2025	23	Buffalo (IL)	AAA	.235	84	293	39	69	19	1	7	47	43	65	1	.335	.379
		Minor League Totals		.265	637	2385	318	631	137	12	49	301	252	445	81	.337	.394

TORONTO BLUE JAYS

12 SILVANO HECHAVARRIA, RHP
FB: 50. **SL:** 55. **CH:** 40. **CTL:** 60. **BA Grade:** 50. **Risk:** High. **Adj:** 35.

Born: March 18, 2003. **B-T:** R-R. **HT:** 6-4. **WT:** 227. **Signed:** Cuba, 2024. **Signed by:** Lorenzo Perez.
TRACK RECORD: Hechavarria signed out of Cuba in 2024 for $240,000. Just four days after signing his contract, he pitched in his first affiliated game in the Dominican Summer League. He moved stateside to begin 2025 and made four appearances in the Florida Complex League before he was promoted to Low-A Dunedin. Hechavarria pitched in 11 games for Dunedin and posted a 1.90 ERA over 47.1 innings with 53 strikeouts to 11 walks.
SCOUTING REPORT: Hechavarria is a tall righthander with a strong lower half and an easy and free moving operation on the mound with a three-quarters slot. His pedestrian three-pitch mix plays up because of his strike-throwing. Hechavarria throws a four-seam fastball, slider and changeup. His fastball sits 93-95 mph and touches 98 with average ride and late, heavy armside run. It's not a huge bat-missing pitch but Hechavarria does a good job getting chases when he elevates it above the zone.he throws an upper-80s cut-slider with ride and heavy cut. His ability to tunnel it off of his four-seam fastball made it a highly successful whiff inducing pitch in 2025. His changeup is a mid-80s splitter-like offering with average vertical separation off the fastball. Hechavarria throws all his pitches for strikes at a well above-average rate and shows plus control.
THE FUTURE: Hechavarria looks like a potential No. 5 starter but will need to prove his average stuff will play at the upper levels.

Year	Age	Club (League)	Level	W	L	ERA	G	GS	IP	H	HR	BB	SO	BB%	SO%	WHIP	AVG
2025	22	FCL Blue Jays	Rk	1	0	2.12	4	3	17	14	2	4	10	5.9	14.7	1.06	.222
2025	22	Dunedin (FSL)	A	1	2	1.90	11	7	47	36	4	11	53	5.9	28.5	0.99	.209
2025	22	Vancouver (NWL)	A+	3	0	3.22	4	4	22	19	1	8	19	8.7	20.7	1.21	.229
		Minor League Totals		10	4	2.12	29	24	136	97	10	39	139	7.2	25.7	1.00	.198

13 VICTOR ARIAS, OF
HIT: 45. **POW:** 50. **RUN:** 70. **FLD:** 50. **ARM:** 40. **BA Grade:** 45. **Risk:** Average. **Adj:** 35.

Born: August 24, 2003. **B-T:** L-L. **HT:** 5-9. **WT:** 150. **Signed:** Venezuela, 2019. **Signed by:** Miguel Leal.
TRACK RECORD: The Blue Jays signed Arias out of Venezuela in August 2019. Over the first five years of his professional career, Arias moved slowly. Assigned to High-A Vancouver out of camp in 2025, Arias hit .294/.381/.437 over the first 66 games before he was promoted to Double-A on July 18. Arias was placed on the injured list in the final week of the regular season with a shoulder injury that required surgery.
SCOUTING REPORT: A diminutive but muscular player, Arias took large steps forward in each of the last two seasons and flashes a variety of exciting tools. He has a fringe-average hit tool with a moderate amount of swing-and-miss in the zone and chase outside of it. A slight improvement to either contact or selectivity would likely push his hit tool to average. Arias is an explosive swinger who produces plus exit velocity data, demonstrated by his 106.5 mph 90th percentile exit velocity in 2025. His in-game power plays down because of a flatter swing and tendency to top-spin everything to his pull side. Arias does show his best angles on balls 95 mph or higher, which is a good sign. For now, Arias has fringe-average game power but could get to average or better with some tweaks. Arias is a plus-plus runner, but that doesn't translate to high stolen base totals. He's an average defender in center field with a lot of range.
THE FUTURE: Arias is most likely a fourth outfielder capable of providing speed and defense. If he adds loft to his swing, there's everyday regular upside.

Year	Age	Club (League)	Level	AVG	G	AB	R	H	2B	3B	HR	RBI	BB	SO	SB	OBP	SLG
2025	21	Vancouver (NWL)	A+	.294	66	279	49	82	15	5	5	36	36	64	12	.381	.437
2025	21	New Hampshire (EL)	AA	.226	36	133	20	30	4	2	2	11	14	38	6	.293	.331
		Minor League Totals		.268	290	1028	179	275	52	14	22	130	158	274	62	.376	.410

14 BLAINE BULLARD, OF
HIT: 50. **POW:** 40. **RUN:** 60. **FLD:** 55. **ARM:** 50. **BA Grade:** 50. **Risk:** High. **Adj:** 35.

Born: August 16, 2006. **B-T:** B-L. **HT:** 6-2. **WT:** 180. **Drafted:** HS—Houston, TX, 2025 (12th round). **Signed by:** Steve Riha.
TRACK RECORD: Bullard was a pop-up name who gained helium late in the spring among Texas area scouts. A Texas A&M commit, Bullard was considered a difficult signing, but the Blue Jays went well over-slot in the 12th round and signed him for just under $1.7 million. Bullard was older at the time of the draft, turning 19 a month after signing.
SCOUTING REPORT: Bullard is a plus-plus athlete who's easy to dream on. His frame suggests strength gains, and his quick-twitch mechanisms shine in all parts of his game. Bullard is a switch-hitter but his

lefthanded swing is far ahead of his righthanded swing. Despite the athletic switch-hitting profile, there's some swing and miss to Bullard's game, particularly on soft stuff. Bullard offsets some of that with a well-balanced approach at the plate. His game is predicated on putting the ball in play and using his speed to push for extra bases. Bullard's game power is projectable despite flatter angles and a general lack of loft in his swing. He will likely hit a lot of ground balls early in his career, but some added strength onto Bullard's 6-foot-2 frame could see him get to 10-14 home runs at peak. A plus runner, Bullard's speed translates to the outfield where he's above-average in center field with an average arm. It's a tooled-up profile with a raw and unrefined hit tool.
THE FUTURE: Bullard has the ceiling of a switch-hitting table-setter with above-average defense in center.

Year	Age	Club (League)	Level	AVG	G	AB	R	H	2B	3B	HR	RBI	BB	SO	SB	OBP	SLG
2025	18	Did not play															

15 TIM PIASENTIN, 3B
HIT: 45. **POW:** 55. **RUN:** 40. **FLD:** 45. **ARM:** 60. **BA Grade:** 50. **Risk:** High. **Adj:** 35.

Born: March 25, 2007. **B-T:** L-R. **HT:** 6-3. **WT:** 200. **Drafted:** HS—Okotoks, BC, 2025 (5th round). **Signed by:** Pat Griffin.
TRACK RECORD: Piasentin was the top Canadian prospect in the 2025 class, and the Blue Jays dialed up some home cooking when they selected him in the fifth round. He signed for $747,500, enough to buy him out of a Miami commitment. Piasentin is one of the more notable prep sluggers from the western provinces, joining Orioles outfielder Tyler O'Neill and Rays catcher Nathan Flewelling.
SCOUTING REPORT: While Piasentin is no standout athlete, he does have a strong and projectable build with fluid movements throughout his game. Piasentin is already physically mature but looks like he could add 10-15 pounds of good weight. Piasentin sets up slightly open at the plate, utilizing a toe-tap mechanism. When he gets into two-strike counts, he shortens up his swing, ditches the toe tap and his stride for a wider base and a quick pivot. Due to the strength of his hands he's still able to drive the ball from his two-strike approach. Piasentin pairs fringy bat-to-ball skills with a fairly passive approach. The power in Piasentin's game is not up for debate. He naturally generates plus-plus bat speed and power, posting impressive exit velocities and hitting majestic fly balls on his best struck drives. Piasentin is a below-average runner who's likely to have little impact in the running game. He's a corner infield profile and there's some question about his ability to stick at third base. Corner outfield could be an alternative where his plus arm strength would play.
THE FUTURE: Piasentin is a high-upside corner infielder who could develop into an everyday regular with above-average power.

Year	Age	Club (League)	Level	AVG	G	AB	R	H	2B	3B	HR	RBI	BB	SO	SB	OBP	SLG
2025	18	Did not play															

16 ANGEL BASTARDO, RHP
FB: 50. **CB:** 40. **SL:** 50. **CH:** 50. **CTL:** 40. **BA Grade:** 45. **Risk:** Average. **Adj:** 35.

Born: June 18, 2002. **B-T:** R-R. **HT:** 6-1. **WT:** 175. **Signed:** Venezuela, 2018.
Signed by: Lenin Rodriguez/Eddie Romero (Red Sox).
TRACK RECORD: The Red Sox signed Bastardo for $35,000 in 2018 out of Venezuela as a raw pitcher who flashed promising traits. He began 2024 with Double-A Portland and pitched better than his ERA, striking out 26% of hitters. On June 4, he blew out his elbow and had season-ending Tommy John surgery. After the Red Sox left Bastardo unprotected for the 2024 Rule 5 draft, the Blue Jays selected him with the sixth overall pick. He did not appear in a game for the Blue Jays in 2025 and is expected to return in 2026.
SCOUTING REPORT: Bastardo is an undersized righthander with big velocity and fringy strike-throwing abilities. He has an athletic operation with some effort in his arm action and throws from a three-quarters slot with a crossfire finish. Bastardo sits 95-98 mph with a four-seamer that has moderate ride but lacks deception. He upped his secondary usage with the Red Sox and throws a mid-80s changeup with good vertical separation from his fastball that he locates well and plays up to its bat-missing upside. Bastardo's primary breaking ball is a low-to-mid-80s gyro slider he shows great feel for that missed a fair amount of bats in Double-A in 2024. The curveball, a clear fourth pitch, sat in the low 80s with downer break and is an effective strike stealer. Bastardo shows below-average control.
THE FUTURE: Bastardo is a bit of a mystery. He was on a starter's trajectory until his injury and now might be headed to the bullpen upon his return.

Year	Age	Club (League)	Level	W	L	ERA	G	GS	IP	H	HR	BB	SO	BB%	SO%	WHIP	AVG
2025	23	Did not play—Injured															
		Minor League Totals		9	21	4.76	78	74	327	303	26	145	357	10.2	25.2	1.37	.243

TORONTO BLUE JAYS

17 JOSH KASEVICH, SS
HIT: 55. **POW:** 40. **RUN:** 55. **FLD:** 55. **ARM:** 40. **BA Grade:** 50. **Risk:** High. **Adj:** 35.

Born: January 17, 2001. **B-T:** R-R. **HT:** 6-1. **WT:** 200. **Drafted:** Oregon, 2022 (2nd round). **Signed by:** Ryan Fox.
TRACK RECORD: Kasevich was a star at Oregon, earning first-team all-Pacific-12 Conference honors as a junior. He was drafted by the Blue Jays in the second round of the 2022 draft, and signed for $1 million. Kasevich's 2025 was delayed by a stress reaction in his lower back. He returned to action in May, but suffered a wrist injury on a rehab assignment and missed the next two months. Kasevich returned to Buffalo in mid-August and struggled over 29 games to end the season. He made up time after the season in the Arizona Fall League.
SCOUTING REPORT: Kasevich's ability to put the bat on the ball has always been his carrying tool. His contact skills remained plus in his injury-plagued 2025 season. He's still a patient hitter who's likely to get on-base at a high rate. The back and wrist injuries clearly impacted Kasevich's ability to impact the ball, as his 90th percentile exit velocity dropped by three mph year-over-year. Kasevich had below-average power to begin with, so the decrease in impact led to worse results. It's possible a fully healthy Kasevich sees his impact return. Though the sample is small, Kasevich's swing added loft during his 2025 sample which will be something to watch early in 2026, if his impact returns. Kasevich is an above-average runner but his speed translates more toward his range in the field than basestealing. Kasevich has an above-average glove but his below-average arm likely means he fits best at second base.
THE FUTURE: Kasevich will look to get back on track in 2026 and prove he's still a potential regular.

Year	Age	Club (League)	Level	AVG	G	AB	R	H	2B	3B	HR	RBI	BB	SO	SB	OBP	SLG
2025	24	FCL Blue Jays	Rk	.357	6	14	0	5	0	0	0	3	5	1	0	.526	.357
2025	24	Dunedin (FSL)	A	.375	7	24	2	9	1	0	0	3	3	3	0	.444	.417
2025	24	Buffalo (IL)	AAA	.173	29	98	6	17	1	0	0	6	13	20	0	.272	.184
		Minor League Totals		.281	289	1097	146	308	53	0	10	133	110	141	24	.350	.356

18 FERNANDO PEREZ, RHP
FB: 40. **CB:** 45. **SL:** 40. **CH:** 50. **CTL:** 70. **BA Grade:** 45. **Risk:** Average. **Adj:** 35.

Born: February 12, 2004. **B-T:** R-R. **HT:** 6-3. **WT:** 170. **Signed:** Nicaragua, 2022. **Signed by:** Daniel Sotelo.
TRACK RECORD: Perez was an under-the-radar $10,000 signing for the Blue Jays in 2022. A native of Nicaragua, Perez was identified after reviewing scouting footage from a tryout where goats roamed around in the background, earning Perez his nickname: "The GOAT." While Perez is unlikely to be mistaken for Tom Brady, he has been productive in four professional seasons. Perez began 2025 with High-A Vancouver, making 20 starts before he was promoted to Double-A on August 15th.
SCOUTING REPORT: One of the best strike-throwers in minor league baseball over the last few seasons, Perez's game is driven by his plus-plus control. Perez's 70.5% strike rate was the third-highest in the minors among pitchers who threw 1,000 or more pitches in 2025. Perez throws four pitches and throws all of them with regularity throughout his starts. Perez mixes a fastball, changeup, slider and curveball. Perez shows excellent command of his fastball allowing it to perform despite its below-average shape and velocity. Added velocity or movement would go a long way in improving Perez's profile. His 81-84 mph changeup is his most frequently thrown pitch and he'll use it against lefties and righties. His slider sits 82-84 mph with gyro shape, and isn't much of a bat-missing pitch but does a good job of driving grounders. Perez's curveball sits in the upper 70s with slurvy break, but he shows great feel for the pitch.
THE FUTURE: Perez is a fringy back-end starter whose below-average stuff plays up due to his plus-plus control.

Year	Age	Club (League)	Level	W	L	ERA	G	GS	IP	H	HR	BB	SO	BB%	SO%	WHIP	AVG
2025	21	Vancouver (NWL)	A+	6	4	3.05	20	20	94	87	6	19	84	4.9	21.8	1.12	.242
2025	21	New Hampshire (EL)	AA	0	3	3.00	6	6	27	26	1	9	21	7.7	17.9	1.30	.243
		Minor League Totals		12	15	3.49	66	65	297	261	18	69	296	5.6	24.2	1.11	.232

19 MICAH BUCKNAM, RHP
FB: 45. **CB:** 50. **SL:** 60. **CH:** 45. **CTL:** 50. **BA Grade:** 45. **Risk:** Average. **Adj:** 35.

Born: August 26, 2003. **B-T:** R-R. **HT:** 6-1. **WT:** 212. **Drafted:** Dallas Baptist, 2025 (4th round). **Signed by:** Brad Jacob.
TRACK RECORD: Born in New Zealand, Bucknam moved to Canada in his youth and was drafted by the Blue Jays out of high school in 2021. He didn't sign and instead made it to campus at LSU, but after two seasons with the Tigers he entered the transfer portal and committed to Dallas Baptist. In his single season at DBU, Bucknam took the role of the Patriots' ace and made 16 starts while striking out 80 batters in 62.1 innings. The Blue Jays selected Bucknam in the fourth round and signed him for $678,300.

SCOUTING REPORT: Bucknam is an undersized righthander with little remaining projection but good strength throughout his frame. He uses a shorter arm action with a higher three-quarters slot. It's a simple operation with few moving parts but some recoil following release. Bucknam mixes four pitches in a four-seam fastball, slider, curveball and changeup. His fastball sits 93-94 mph and touches 96 mph with average ride. It's a fringe-average pitch, and his command of it is also fringy. Bucknam's slider is his best pitch and his most-used pitch against righthanded hitters. The slider is an 86-88 mph gyro that gets into the low 90s and generates bad swings as an effective put-away pitch. Bucknam's curveball sees higher usage against lefties in the 83-85 mph range with more downer shape. He also throws a fringy and firm upper-80s changeup.
THE FUTURE: Bucknam fits the role of a depth starter who feeds hitters a steady diet of secondaries.

Year	Age	Club (League)	Level	W	L	ERA	G	GS	IP	H	HR	BB	SO	BB%	SO%	WHIP	AVG
2025	21	Did not play															

20 SEAN KEYS, 1B/3B
HIT: 50. **POW:** 50. **RUN:** 40. **FLD:** 40. **ARM:** 55. **BA Grade:** 45. **Risk:** Average. **Adj:** 35.

Born: May 26, 2003. **B-T:** L-R. **HT:** 6-2. **WT:** 232. **Drafted:** Bucknell, 2024 (4th round). **Signed by:** Tom Burns.
TRACK RECORD: Keys broke out as a junior at Bucknell and hit .405/.535/.798 with 13 home runs and was named Patriot League player of the year in 2024. The Blue Jays drafted him in the fourth round and signed him for $569,700. He was assigned to High-A Vancouver to begin 2025 and spent the entire season with the Canadians and hit .217/.365/.408 with poor batted-ball luck throughout the season.
SCOUTING REPORT: Keys' bat-first profile didn't translate to his statline in 2025, but the underlying data and scouting feedback tells a different story. Those who saw Keys reported on a player with strong bat-to-ball skills, feel for the strike zone and the ability to impact the baseball. The underlying numbers back the quality of Keys' hit tool as he showed above-average contact and approach in 2025. Keys' hands are fairly stiff, leading to an unusual look to his follow through and at times leads to too steep of angles. The launch comes in handy on Keys' best hit drives, as he shows the ability to hit his hardest balls in play at his best angles. Keys shows above-average underlying power and the ability to hit the ball to his pull side. It's possible Keys breaks out at the plate in 2026. A below-average runner, Keys has limited range at third base and started to see more time at first base in 2025. He has an above-average arm at third.
THE FUTURE: Keys fits into the second-division regular role but he'll need to hit to overcome his lack of defensive value.

Year	Age	Club (League)	Level	AVG	G	AB	R	H	2B	3B	HR	RBI	BB	SO	SB	OBP	SLG
2025	22	Vancouver (NWL)	A+	.217	119	424	67	92	22	1	19	72	86	117	8	.365	.408
		Minor League Totals		.229	141	506	78	116	26	4	20	92	99	138	10	.367	.415

21 JAKE CASEY, OF
HIT: 45. **POW:** 50. **RUN:** 60. **FLD:** 55. **ARM:** 60. **BA Grade:** 50. **Risk:** High. **Adj:** 35.

Born: April 17, 2003. **B-T:** L-R. **HT:** 6-2. **WT:** 190. **Drafted:** Kent State, 2025 (15th round). **Signed by:** Tom Burns.
TRACK RECORD: The son of former three-time all-star Sean Casey, Jake underperformed over his first three seasons at Kent State, and had Tommy John surgery in 2024. He broke out in 2025, hitting .356/.500/.736 with 17 home runs and 20 stolen bases. The Blue Jays selected Casey in the 15th round and signed him for $150,000. He debuted following the draft with Low-A Dunedin and impressed, hitting .281/.439/.531 over 23 games.
SCOUTING REPORT: After three underwhelming seasons with Kent State, Casey broke out in 2025 finding a level of power he had not previously shown. Casey shows average bat-to-ball skills with somewhat passive swing decisions. He is a great fastball hitter but does show some struggles against spin. Casey shows fringe-average power but good launch angles on contact. His ability to hit the ball in the air consistently allows his power to play up to average. Casey is an above-average runner, capable of running plus run times on jailbreaks to first. Casey can play all three outfield positions. He's average in center field but is above-average in a corner. He shows good hands, routes and reactions in the outfield and his plus arm will allow him to make any needed throws while keeping baserunners honest.
THE FUTURE: An underrated senior sign, Casey looks like he could develop into a second-division regular if his hit tool translates.

Year	Age	Club (League)	Level	AVG	G	AB	R	H	2B	3B	HR	RBI	BB	SO	SB	OBP	SLG
2025	22	Dunedin (FSL)	A	.281	23	64	14	18	3	2	3	14	10	19	4	.439	.531
		Minor League Totals	A	.281	23	64	14	18	3	2	3	14	10	19	4	.439	.531

22 SPENCER MILES, RHP

FB: 60. **CB:** 60. **CH:** 40. **CT:** 45. **CTL:** 50. **BA Grade:** 45. **Risk:** High. **Adj:** 30.

Born: July 26, 2000. **B-T:** L-R. **HT:** 6-3. **WT:** 193. **Drafted:** Missouri, 2022 (4th round). **Signed by:** Yancy Ayres (Giants).

TRACK RECORD: Miles showed more promise as a position player in the early days of his amateur career, but quickly blossomed once he started pitching. The Giants drafted Miles in the fourth round in 2022 and signed him for $347,500. He has pitched just 7.1 regular season innings since 2023 thanks to a back injury and then Tommy John surgery. He made up for some of that lost time in the Arizona Fall League. After Miles was left unprotected for the 2025 Rule 5 draft by the Giants, he was selected by the Blue Jays with the 27th overall pick.

SCOUTING REPORT: Miles shows a powerful pitch mix led by four-seam and sinking fastballs in the mid 90s. He backs them with a nasty, downer curveball with 11-to-5 shape that he can bury for chases at the end of at-bats. He also has a changeup, but it mostly takes a back seat to the rest of his mix. He pounded the zone in the Fall League, punching out a dozen and walking just one. Miles' delivery is effortless, and scouts in the AFL noted that he sometimes had trouble driving the ball down in the zone and that his current mechanics might put undue amounts of stress on his shoulder.

THE FUTURE: Miles will work as a one-inning reliever with the stuff to fit in middle relief, but he'll need to stay healthy.

Year	Age	Club (League)	Level	W	L	ERA	G	GS	IP	H	HR	BB	SO	BB%	SO%	WHIP	AVG
2025	24	Did not play—Injury															
		Minor League Totals		2	0	4.30	10	3	15	15	1	5	22	8.1	35.5	1.36	.263

23 RYAN JENNINGS, RHP

FB: 55. **CB:** 50. **SL:** 55. **CH:** 45. **CTL:** 45. **BA Grade:** 40. **Risk:** Average. **Adj:** 30.

Born: June 23, 1999. **B-T:** R-R. **HT:** 6-0. **WT:** 190. **Drafted:** Louisiana Tech, 2022 (4th round). **Signed by:** Chris Curtis.

TRACK RECORD: The Blue Jays signed Jennings for $70,000 in the fourth round out of Louisiana Tech in 2022. He dealt with an elbow injury in 2023 and was limited to 43 innings in his debut. In 2024, after beginning the season as a starter with Vancouver, Jennings was moved to the bullpen late in the season with Double-A New Hampshire. The 2025 season was his first as a full-time reliever. He made 45 appearances between Double-A New Hampshire and Triple-A Buffalo.

SCOUTING REPORT: Jennings was a good strike-thrower over the first few years of his career, but that backed up in 2025 as he struggled to land his pitches in the zone. Now a relief-only prospect, Jennings let it air out in the bullpen as he saw his fastball velocity jump to 95-96 mph with erratic control. Jennings' slider went from a pure gyro slider in 2024 to a harder cutter style slider in 2025. It was a good change for Jennings as he generated lots of whiffs against the slider. He throws a curveball at 83-84 mph with slurvy shape as his third pitch that sees an increase in usage against lefties. Jennings throws a mid-to-high-80s changeup with splitterish traits but it's used infrequently.

THE FUTURE: Jennings will fit into middle relief nicely where he can miss bats with a pair of breaking ball shapes and a mid-90s fastball.

Year	Age	Club (League)	Level	W	L	ERA	G	GS	IP	H	HR	BB	SO	BB%	SO%	WHIP	AVG
2025	26	New Hampshire (EL)	AA	3	1	2.86	11	0	22	16	2	14	28	14.3	28.6	1.36	.200
2025	26	Buffalo (IL)	AAA	1	3	4.25	34	0	36	39	6	29	54	16.2	30.2	1.89	.275
		Minor League Totals		7	11	3.21	73	21	160	139	15	85	201	12.1	28.6	1.40	.233

24 CHARLES McADOO, 3B

HIT: 30. **POW:** 55. **RUN:** 50. **FLD:** 40. **ARM:** 55. **BA Grade:** 45. **Risk:** High. **Adj:** 30.

Born: March 6, 2002. **B-T:** R-R. **HT:** 6-1. **WT:** 210. **Drafted:** San Jose State, 2023 (13th round).
Signed by: Mike Sansoe (Pirates).

TRACK RECORD: McAdoo was first-team All-Mountain West Conference as a sophomore and junior at San Jose State. Questions around his defense and hit tool dropped him to the Pirates in the 13th round in 2023. He broke out in 2024 with High-A Greensboro and was traded to the Blue Jays at that year's trade deadline for Isiah Kiner-Falefa. McAdoo spent all of 2025 with Double-A New Hampshire and started the year in brutal fashion before turning it around over his final 83 games, where he hit .270/.339/.463.

SCOUTING REPORT: McAdoo is a physical slugger who added speed to his repertoire in 2025 as he stole a career-high 34 bases. McAdoo's combination of power and running ability gives him high upside but his unrefined hit tool and aggressive approach cap his in-game power production. McAdoo has well below-average bat-to-ball skills with a fairly aggressive approach. He doesn't chase at a high rate, but he does expand the zone while at times being too passive on strikes. When McAdoo does connect he shows plus

contact quality with strong exit velocities and loft at the point of contact. McAdoo is an average runner but gets excellent jumps and reads on the bases going 34-for-40 in 2025. McAdoo is a below-average defender at third base with an above-average arm.
THE FUTURE: McAdoo could blossom into a second-division regular with a more refined hit tool.

Year	Age	Club (League)	Level	AVG	G	AB	R	H	2B	3B	HR	RBI	BB	SO	SB	OBP	SLG
2025	23	New Hampshire (EL)	AA	.247	121	445	62	110	24	1	16	45	45	137	34	.318	.413
		Minor League Totals		.267	273	992	152	265	54	8	38	147	116	287	60	.349	.453

25 ADAM MACKO, LHP
FB: 40. **CB:** 45. **SL:** 55. **CH:** 40. **CTL:** 45. **BA Grade:** 40. **Risk:** Average. **Adj:** 30.

Born: December 30, 2000. **B-T:** L-L. **HT:** 6-0. **WT:** 170. **Drafted:** HS—Vauxhall, AB, 2019 (7th round).
Signed by: Les McTavish/Alex Ross (Mariners).
TRACK RECORD: Macko grew up in Slovakia and learned to pitch by watching YouTube videos. He moved first to Ireland and then Canada where he entered more formal baseball training. The Mariners drafted him in the seventh round in 2019 and he was traded to the Blue Jays in November 2022. Macko has dealt with numerous injuries over the years and missed the first month of the 2025 season recovering from a torn meniscus in his left knee.
SCOUTING REPORT: Macko is an undersized lefthander with an innate feel for spin and a deceptive arm action. He has a longer arm action and short stride to the plate, raising the release height on his higher three-quarters slot. Macko mixes four pitches in a four-seam fastball, slider, curveball and changeup. His fastball sits 92-94 mph with below-average shape and extension, but he controls the pitch well. Macko's mid-80s cut-slider is his best pitch, as he shows plus feel and ability to generate whiffs against it in and out of the zone. His curveball is purely a chase pitch sitting in the mid 70s with high spin rates and two-plane break. Macko's changeup has good separation off of his fastball but he shows poor command for the pitch.
THE FUTURE: Macko looks like a low-leverage reliever who will throw a high rate of breaking balls.

Year	Age	Club (League)	Level	W	L	ERA	G	GS	IP	H	HR	BB	SO	BB%	SO%	WHIP	AVG
2025	24	FCL Blue Jays	Rk	0	1	3.63	5	4	17	14	0	3	26	4.3	37.1	0.98	.219
2025	24	Buffalo (IL)	AAA	3	8	5.06	18	10	64	61	6	36	65	12.5	22.6	1.52	.253
		Minor League Totals		15	26	4.53	89	73	356	310	29	167	450	10.8	29.2	1.34	.234

26 BRANDON BARRIERA, LHP
FB: 50. **SL:** 60. **CT:** 60. **CH:** 40. **CTL:** 45. **BA Grade:** 50. **Risk:** Extreme. **Adj:** 30.

Born: March 4, 2004. **B-T:** L-L. **HT:** 6-2. **WT:** 180. **Drafted:** HS—Plantation, FL, 2022 (1st round).
Signed by: Adrian Casanova.
TRACK RECORD: The Blue Jays drafted Florida prep star Barriera with the 23rd overall pick in the 2022 draft, signing him for $3.6 million. Considered one of the top lefthanded pitchers in the class, Barriera's professional career is yet to get off the ground. In his three-plus years since turning pro, Barriera has thrown a total of 27.1 innings. After dealing with shoulder, elbow and biceps injuries in 2023, Barriera tore his UCL in his first start of 2024 and had hybrid Tommy John surgery. Barriera returned to action in June of 2025 only to fracture his ulna during his rehab.
SCOUTING REPORT: It's difficult to know how much the injuries over the last three seasons have impacted Barriera. Depending on his health in any given outing his velocity can have wild swings. He's sat between the low- and mid-90s over the last few seasons. Whether or not Barriera can make it through a season healthy is up for some debate. When Barriera was healthy in 2025 his pitch mix looked a little different than it did pre-injury. He came back throwing a low-to-mid-90s cutter as his primary pitch and mixed in his signature mid-to-high-80s slider with moderate sweep. Barriera's four-seam fastball sat 95-96 mph with heavy cut.
THE FUTURE: Barriera still has back-of-the-rotation or high-leverage relief upside. The question is: Can he finish a season healthy?

Year	Age	Club (League)	Level	W	L	ERA	G	GS	IP	H	HR	BB	SO	BB%	SO%	WHIP	AVG
2025	21	FCL Blue Jays	Rk	0	1	14.29	5	5	6	3	0	8	6	28.6	21.4	1.94	.158
		Minor League Totals		0	3	6.59	13	13	27	15	0	18	32	15.5	27.6	1.21	.163

TORONTO BLUE JAYS

27 CARSON MESSINA, RHP
FB: 50. **CB:** 55. **SL:** 50. **CH:** 45. **CTL:** 40. **BA Grade:** 50. **Risk:** Extreme. **Adj:** 30.

Born: April 15, 2006. **B-T:** R-R. **HT:** 6-2. **WT:** 225. **Drafted:** HS—Summerville, SC, 2024 (12th round).
Signed by: Austin Upshaw.
TRACK RECORD: The Messina family had a notable night on draft day in 2024, as Carson and his older brother Cole were both drafted. The Blue Jays selected Carson in the 12th round and signed him for $550,000. Messina was assigned to the Florida Complex League where he made one appearance before going down with right elbow inflammation. Messina missed the rest of the season but was back throwing by the end of the regular season.
SCOUTING REPORT: Messina threw just two innings as a professional and not much has changed in a year. His arm swing is moderate in length as he delivers the ball from a three-quarters slot. Messina mixes four pitches in a fastball, curveball, slider and changeup. The four-seam fastball sits 91-93 mph with ride and some late bite. The curveball is Messina's best pitch and his go-to swing-and-miss weapon. It sits in the low 80s with big downer break and late bite. His mid-to-upper-80s slider is cutter-like and was thrown more his last year as an amateur. Messina's low-80s changeup is a fringe-average pitch that will flash average at its best. Messina's control is below-average and will need to be tightened if he continues to start.
THE FUTURE: Messina has the upside to be a No. 4 starter but will need to prove he can stay healthy and throw enough strikes.

Year	Age	Club (League)	Level	W	L	ERA	G	GS	IP	H	HR	BB	SO	BB%	SO%	WHIP	AVG
2025	19	FCL Blue Jays	Rk	0	0	9.00	1	0	2	3	0	0	2	0.0	22.2	1.50	.333
		Minor League Totals		0	0	9.00	1	0	2	3	0	0	2	0.0	22.2	1.50	.333

28 BRANDON VALENZUELA, C
HIT: 30. **POW:** 45. **RUN:** 30. **FLD:** 60. **ARM:** 55. **BA Grade:** 30. **Risk:** Low. **Adj:** 30.

Born: October 2, 2000. **B-T:** S-R. **HT:** 6-0. **WT:** 225. **Signed:** Mexico, 2017.
Signed by: Bill McLaughlin/Trevor Schumm/Chris Kemp (Padres).
TRACK RECORD: The Padres signed Valenzuela for $100,000 from the Mexican League in July 2017. Valenzuela spent seven seasons in the Padres' system, producing subpar results at the plate. The Padres traded him to the Blue Jays for infielder Will Wagner at the 2025 trade deadline. Valenzuela spent the final two months with Triple-A Buffalo and was added to the Blue Jays 40-man roster after the season.
SCOUTING REPORT: The switch-hitting Valenzuela is a glove-first catcher without a lot of offensive upside. Valenzuela's righthanded swing is better than his lefthanded swing, leading to average results against lefthanded pitching. He shows below-average contact skills with an advanced approach that should lead to at least an average walk rate. There will be a fair amount of strikeouts as Valenzuela is a well below-average contact hitter against righthanded pitching. He hit 15 home runs in 2025 and shows fringe-average game power. To Valenzuela's credit he has average exit velocity data with lofty launch angles. Behind the plate he's a plus defender with an above-average arm that keeps runners in check.
THE FUTURE: Valenzuela has the perfect backup catcher skill set, with split-dependent success and plus defense and provides Toronto catching depth they're sorely lacking. He could see a solid amount of MLB time in 2026 as a ready-made backup catcher and defensive fill-in.

Year	Age	Club (League)	Level	AVG	G	AB	R	H	2B	3B	HR	RBI	BB	SO	SB	OBP	SLG
2025	24	San Antonio (TL)	AA	.229	87	328	42	75	14	1	12	46	40	83	6	.313	.387
2025	24	Buffalo (IL)	AAA	.207	26	92	9	19	6	0	3	12	12	32	0	.295	.370
		Minor League Totals		.242	582	2100	275	509	100	10	47	289	321	568	14	.345	.367

 JAVEN COLEMAN, LHP
FB: 55. **SL:** 50. **SP:** 60. **CTL:** 45. **BA Grade:** 40. **Risk:** Average. **Adj:** 30.

Born: December 3, 2001. **B-T:** L-L. **HT:** 6-2. **WT:** 173. **Signed:** Louisiana State, 2024 (UDFA). **Signed by:** Steve Rivas.
TRACK RECORD: Coleman spent four seasons pitching mostly out of the bullpen for LSU but struggled mightily with command and experienced very little success. The Dodgers drafted him in the 16th round in 2023, but Coleman decided not to sign and headed back to school. Coleman then signed as an undrafted free agent with the Blue Jays in 2024 and made his pro debut in 2025, pitching purely in relief.
SCOUTING REPORT: Coleman is a lefthander power reliever with a three-pitch mix who saw a tremendous improvement with his strike-throwing in 2025. He works entirely from the stretch with a longer arm action and a true three-quarters slot. Coleman mixes three pitches in a four-seam fastball, slider and splitter. Coleman's fastball sits 93-95 mph and touches 97 with 17-19 inches of induced vertical break on average from a 5-foot-6 release height. His fastball was a plus bat-missing pitch in 2025 and generated

lots of swings and misses. Coleman mixes his slider and splitter nearly evenly. He throws the slider versus lefthanded hitters and the splitter versus righties. The slider sits 85-86 mph with cutter shape and he shows average command of the pitch. His splitter sits 82-84 mph with true splitter shape and an element of unpredictability in how it breaks—it's Coleman's best bat-missing pitch.

THE FUTURE: Coleman looks like a one-inning middle reliever.

Year	Age	Club (League)	Level	W	L	ERA	G	GS	IP	H	HR	BB	SO	BB%	SO%	WHIP	AVG
2025	23	Dunedin (FSL)	A	1	1	4.45	20	0	28	23	3	17	45	13.7	36.3	1.41	.223
2025	23	Vancouver (NWL)	A+	1	0	1.40	18	0	26	15	0	6	40	6.1	40.4	0.82	.163
		Minor League Totals		2	1	3.00	38	0	54	38	3	23	85	10.3	38.1	1.13	.195

30 EDWARD DURAN, C

HIT: 45. **POW:** 30. **RUN:** 30. **FLD:** 55. **ARM:** 55. **BA Grade:** 40. **Risk:** Average. **Adj:** 30.

Born: May 29, 2004. **B-T:** R-R. **HT:** 5-11. **WT:** 210. **Signed:** Venezuela, 2021.
Signed by: Henry Sandoval/Fernando Seguignol (Marlins).

TRACK RECORD: The Marlins signed Duran out of Venezuela for $450,000 in January 2021 and the Blue Jays acquired him as the third piece in the Jordan Groshans trade alongside Anthony Bass and Zach Pop. After spending parts of two seasons with Low-A Dunedin in 2023 and 2024, Duran returned to the level in 2025. Duran was promoted to High-A Vancouver after the all-star break and participated in the Arizona Fall League but was unimpressive.

SCOUTING REPORT: A glove-first catcher who took a few years to get his legs under him as a professional, Duran shows average bat-to-ball skills with a fairly aggressive approach in the box. Duran's ability to avoid strikeouts is his carrying tool offensively. He shows below-average exit velocities and flat launch angles, leading to lots of topspin and groundball contact. Duran is not a runner and grades as a 30 runner long term. Behind the plate, Duran shows above-average skills as both a receiver and blocker and he began employing a one-knee stance in 2025. He will show a plus pop time and is quick out of the crouch, but his throwing accuracy is below-average and needs work. Duran's advanced catching and contact skills give him backup catcher upside.

THE FUTURE: Duran fits a quintessential backup catcher's profile with an above-average glove and the ability to make contact.

Year	Age	Club (League)	Level	AVG	G	AB	R	H	2B	3B	HR	RBI	BB	SO	SB	OBP	SLG
2025	21	Dunedin (FSL)	A	.296	66	253	40	75	11	5	5	35	26	62	6	.378	.439
2025	21	Vancouver (NWL)	A+	.230	34	122	15	28	4	0	3	12	16	26	1	.329	.336
		Minor League Totals		.276	202	699	111	193	37	6	10	88	92	140	14	.372	.389

James Wood

Washington Nationals

BY MATT EDDY

Only the Rockies have lost more games in the 2020s than the Nationals.

All that losing serves to amplify the sound of the ticking clock on the Juan Soto trade.

The Nationals traded a 23-year-old Soto to the Padres in August 2022 for a bushel of young talent seldom seen in today's risk-averse environment.

In that one transaction, Washington acquired MacKenzie Gore, CJ Abrams and James Wood, a trio of players that accounted for the Nationals' top three WAR totals in 2025. Righthander and No. 2 prospect Jarlin Susana also was a part of that trade.

As they head into 2026, the Nationals hold just 10 total seasons of club control—out of the 17 they acquired—for the trio of Gore, Abrams and Wood. Now, the 27-year-old Gore is at the same point in his journey that Soto was in 2022: two years away from free agency.

But the man who acquired Gore will not be the one who decides whether to trade him before the 2027 season.

That's because the Nationals fired longtime GM Mike Rizzo, architect of the club's first postseason teams and the 2019 World Series champions, along with manager Dave Martinez on July 6.

Mike DeBartolo assumed GM responsibilities on an interim basis, most notably presiding over the 2025 draft and trade deadline, in which the Nationals traded Alex Call, Michael Soroka and Kyle Finnegan for prospect depth.

After the season, the Nationals hired 35-year-old Red Sox assistant GM Paul Toboni to be president of baseball operations. He retained DeBartolo as an assistant and hired 33-year-old Rays senior director of player development (and former minor league manager) Blake Butera as manager.

Toboni made his name in Boston in amateur scouting and was part of a department that consistently outperformed other clubs, especially beyond the first round, as exemplified by Roman Anthony, Payton Tolle and Connelly Early.

PROJECTED 2029 LINEUP

Catcher	Harry Ford	26
First Base	Brady House	26
Second Base	CJ Abrams	28
Third Base	Seaver King	26
Shortstop	Eli Willits	21
Left Field	Luke Dickerson	23
Center Field	Dylan Crews	27
Right Field	Daylen Lile	26
Designated Hitter	James Wood	26
No. 1 Starter	MacKenzie Gore	30
No. 2 Starter	Jarlin Susana	25
No. 3 Starter	Travis Sykora	25
No. 4 Starter	Alex Clemmey	23
No. 5 Starter	Cade Cavalli	30
Closer	Luis Perales	26

Success in the draft will be critical in reversing the Nationals' fortune. Six straight losing seasons in D.C. have translated to high draft picks and bonus pool dollars galore. Despite this, the Nationals have developed few surefire homegrown contributors.

First-rounders Cade Cavalli (2020), Brady House (2021) and Dylan Crews (2023) played for the 2025 club but haven't hit their stride. Meanwhile, 2021 second-rounder Daylen Lile emerged as a potential right field solution with a strong rookie season, and 26-year-old righthander Brad Lord looks like a dependable innings-eater.

The 2025 draft class, led by No. 1 overall pick Eli Willits, a 17-year-old Oklahoma prep shortstop, represents an inflection point for the franchise. Washington signed Willits for nearly $3 million under slot in order to spread its money around on preps Landon Harmon, Miguel Sime Jr. and Coy James in the third through fifth rounds.

The Nationals rank in the bottom-third of all organizations in terms of talent. In particular, Washington player development has struggled to get the most out of its young hitters. In 2025, Nationals full-season hitters produced a .669 OPS that was second-worst among all 30 organizations.

So for Toboni and company, one thing is clear: Improving the bottom rungs of the organization is the only way to affect change at the top. ■

DEPTH CHART

WASHINGTON NATIONALS

TOP 2026 ROOKIES — RANK
1. Harry Ford, C — 3
2. Andrew Pinckney, OF — 14
3. Andrew Alvarez, LHP — 26

BREAKOUT PROSPECTS — RANK
1. Sam Petersen, OF — 12
2. Marconi German, SS — 17
3. Ronny Cruz, SS — 21

SOURCE OF TOP 30 TALENT

Homegrown	22	Acquired	8
College	11	Trade	7
Junior college	0	Rule 5 draft	1
High school	6	Independent league	0
Undrafted free agent	0	Free agent/waivers	0
International	5		

LF
Phillip Glasser (27)
Browm Martinez

CF
Sam Petersen (12)
Christian Franklin (22)
Nauris De La Cruz (28)
Cristhian Vaquero

RF
Andrew Pinckney (14)
Elijah Green

3B
Coy James (9)
Angel Feliz (10)
Jorgelys Mota (20)
Cayden Wallace

SS
Eli Willits (1)
Seaver King (7)
Ronny Cruz (21)
Brayan Cortesia (29)

2B
Luke Dickerson (8)
Marconi German (17)
Orelvis Martinez

1B
Ethan Petry (13)
Yohandy Morales (16)
Sam Brown

C
Harry Ford (3)
Caleb Lomavita (18)
Sir Jamison Jones
Kevin Bazzell
Daniel Hernandez

LHP

LHSP
Alex Clemmey (6)
Jackson Kent (15)
Andrew Alvarez (26)
Ben Moore

LHRP
Pablo Aldonis
Erik Tolman
Nolan Hughes

RHP

RHSP
Jarlin Susana (2)
Travis Sykora (5)
Landon Harmon (11)
Miguel Sime Jr. (19)
Yoel Tejeda (24)
Riley Cornelio (25)
Tyler Stuart
Davian Garcia
Josh Randall
Darrel Lunar
R.J. Sales
Jose Feliz

RHRP
Luis Perales (4)
Sean Paul Liñan (23)
Griff McGarry (30)
Eriq Swan
Andry Lara
Marquis Grissom Jr.
Robert Cranz
Brayan Romero

WASHINGTON NATIONALS

1 ELI WILLITS, SS

Born: December 9, 2007. **B-T:** B-R. **HT:** 6-1. **WT:** 180.
Drafted: HS—Fort Cobb, OK, 2025 (1st round).
Signed by: Jacorey Boudreaux.

BA GRADE
60 Risk: Average
Adjusted grade: 50

SCOUTING GRADES:
Hit: 55. **Power:** 50. **Run:** 60.
Field: 55. **Arm:** 55.
Projected future grades on 20-80 scouting scale

TOM DIPACE

TRACK RECORD: Willits was originally slated to graduate from Fort-Cobb Broxton High in 2026, but the Oklahoma prep reclassified to become draft eligible in 2025. Doing so made him one of the youngest players available in his draft class, and when the Nationals selected the shortstop first overall, he became the youngest player ever drafted 1-1 based on baseball age. Willits was 17 years, six months and 21 days old on June 30 of his draft year, younger even than the youngest 17-year-old top overall picks such as Ken Griffey Jr., Bryce Harper and Carlos Correa. Willits is the son of former big leaguer Reggie Willits, a switch-hitting outfielder who played six seasons for the Angels. These days, Reggie serves as associate head coach at Oklahoma, where his oldest son Jaxon is the Sooners' shortstop. Eli had committed to Oklahoma before he signed for $8.2 million, which was nearly $2.876 million under slot for the No. 1 pick. Willits got the cachet associated with being drafted first overall; Washington freed up bonus pool money to apply toward signing high schoolers Landon Harmon, Miguel Sime Jr. and Coy James in the third, fourth and fifth rounds. Willits signed on July 19 and saw action in 15 games for Low-A Fredericksburg. He hit .300, drew seven walks and stole two bases while handling shortstop in 14 of his appearances.

SCOUTING REPORT: Willits is a 6-foot-1, 180-pound switch-hitter with a chance to make an impact in every facet of the game with his hitting, running and fielding ability at shortstop. The hallmarks of his offensive game are his bat-to-ball skills—he struck out just a handful of times as a high school senior—and swing decisions that fuel an above-average hit tool. Willits showed sharp zone-contact skills in his pro debut while recognizing pitches and staying in his strike zone with a low chase rate. He hits all different pitch types, while his balanced, line-drive stroke from both sides of the plate allows him to use all fields. If Willits adds good weight to his frame and develops his lower half, he should improve his below-average exit velocities and find at least average power as he learns to hunt his pitch to inflict damage. He is a plus runner who not only poses a basestealing threat but runs the bases efficiently. Willits' body control, range and above-average arm stand out in the field, where he is a no-doubt shortstop. He appears to have the "it" factor and the poise necessary to draw in teammates and emerge as a team leader.

THE FUTURE: Willits' well-rounded profile makes him the Nationals' likely shortstop of the future. That future could arrive as early as at some point during the 2028 season, following two-plus solid development years in the minor leagues. Willits will be just 20 years old in 2028, which, barring an extension, will also be the final season of club control for shortstop CJ Abrams in Washington.

BEST TOOLS

BATTING
Best Hitter — Harry Ford
Best Power Hitter — Andrew Pinckney
Best Strike-Zone Discipline — Harry Ford
Fastest Baserunner — Andrew Pinckney
Best Athlete — Elijah Green

PITCHING
Best Fastball — Jarlin Susana
Best Curveball — Jarlin Susana
Best Slider — Travis Sykora
Best Changeup — Sean Paul Liñan
Best Control — Josh Randall

FIELDING
Best Defensive Catcher — Kevin Bazzell
Best Defensive Infielder — Seaver King
Best Infield Arm — Jorgelys Mota
Best Defensive Outfielder — Cristhian Vaquero
Best Outfield Arm — Andrew Pinckney

Year	Age	Club (League)	Level	AVG	G	AB	R	H	2B	3B	HR	RBI	BB	SO	SB	OBP	SLG
2025	17	Fredericksburg (CAR)	A	.300	15	50	7	15	1	1	0	5	7	12	2	.397	.360
		Minor League Totals		.300	15	50	7	15	1	1	0	5	7	12	2	.397	.360

WASHINGTON NATIONALS

2 JARLIN SUSANA, RHP

FB: 70. **CB:** 60. **SL:** 60. **CH:** 55. **CTL:** 45. **BA Grade:** 60. **Risk:** High. **Adj:** 45.

Born: March 23, 2004. **B-T:** R-R. **HT:** 6-7. **WT:** 283.
Signed: Dominican Republic, 2022. **Signed by:** Trevor Schumm/Chris Kemp (Padres).
TRACK RECORD: The Nationals' Juan Soto trade with the Padres is the gift that keeps giving. CJ Abrams, MacKenzie Gore and James Wood are already established in Washington. Susana is next. He ended 2024 on a roll, with a 2.79 ERA and 123 strikeouts in his final 77.1 innings, mostly for High-A Wilmington. Susana opened 2025 at Double-A Harrisburg but never really got going before he lost nearly three months with a sprained elbow. He looked electric upon his return in July but then injured his right lat and had season-ending surgery in September.
SCOUTING REPORT: Few pitchers can match the electricity of Susana's repertoire. He pitches at 99-100 mph with his four-seam fastball and tops out near 104. The pitch is delivered at a lower release height, which, coupled with its incredible velocity, compensates for ordinary shape. Susana's 99 mph two-seamer tops at 102 and has plus horizontal life. It helps him change batters' eye levels and elicit groundballs. His mid-80s slider has become a devastating pitch as he has harnessed command of it. He manipulates the pitch to produce curveball action at lower speeds and power slider movement up to 91 mph at the other extreme. Susana found a power changeup grip that works in 2025. The pitch has splinker-like action with sink and diving action at 93-94 mph and up to near 97. Susana took major strides with his mental preparation and physical conditioning, and he now throws more quality strikes than ever. He flies open at times and misses east and west, so true command could be elusive.
THE FUTURE: The Nationals' media guide lists Susana at 6-foot-7, 283 pounds, calling to mind a pair of jumbo-sized all-stars: starter Michael Piñeda and closer Felix Bautista. The Nationals will give Susana every chance to start, where his pitch quality could make him a No. 2 or 3 starter. He is expected to be ready to go by midseason at the earliest.

Year	Age	Club (League)	Level	W	L	ERA	G	GS	IP	H	HR	BB	SO	BB%	SO%	WHIP	AVG
2025	21	Wilmington (SAL)	A+	0	2	3.00	3	3	9	6	0	2	16	5.6	44.4	0.89	.176
2025	21	Harrisburg (EL)	AA	1	2	3.61	11	11	47	34	3	32	79	15.4	38.0	1.39	.204
		Minor League Totals		3	17	4.00	58	57	221	171	8	124	306	13.1	32.2	1.34	.215

3 HARRY FORD, C

HIT: 50. **POW:** 50. **RUN:** 60. **FLD:** 40. **ARM:** 50. **BA Grade:** 55. **Risk:** Average. **Adj:** 45.

Born: February 21, 2003. **B-T:** R-R. **HT:** 5-10. **WT:** 200.
Drafted: HS—Kennesaw, GA, 2021 (1st round). **Signed by:** John Wiedenbauer (Mariners).
TRACK RECORD: The Mariners were drawn to Ford's elite athleticism out of high school when they drafted him 12th overall in 2021. Seattle put Ford on a methodical trajectory of a level per year, and he spent almost all of 2025 with Triple-A Tacoma, where he slashed .283/.408/.460 with 16 homers and nearly as many walks (74) as strikeouts (88) before making his big league debut in September. While he got only six at-bats for Seattle, Ford soaked up valuable experience as the Mariners' third catcher through their October postseason run. After the season, Seattle traded Ford and righthander Isaac Lyon to the Nationals for power lefty reliever Jose Ferrer.
SCOUTING REPORT: Ford made a key adjustment at the plate in 2025 by incorporating a toe tap to improve his timing while continuing to use his signature two-hand finish. That change led to the best season of his career. Ford's 16 Triple-A homers were a career high. He posted nearly identical in-zone whiff and chase rates as he did in 2024, while maintaining above-average exit velocities. Ford has long been regarded as a plus runner, which is unusual for a catcher, but he ran less frequently in 2025, stealing just seven bases on 11 attempts after swiping 35 bags in 2024. Ford has long faced questions about his future position, even though he has played just eight games in the outfield as a pro. Scouts noted real defensive progress in 2025 and believe his once-fringy receiving now has a chance to become average. Ford has a strong, albeit sometimes inaccurate, throwing arm and threw out 23% of basestealers in 2025.
THE FUTURE: Ford faced a future in Seattle blocked by all-star Cal Raleigh. Now, he has a much clearer path to playing time in Washington, where he has a good chance to win a share of the catcher job alongside Keibert Ruiz, who is locked into a team-friendly deal through the 2030 season.

Year	Age	Club (League)	Level	AVG	G	AB	R	H	2B	3B	HR	RBI	BB	SO	SB	OBP	SLG
2025	22	Tacoma (PCL)	AAA	.283	97	374	68	106	18	0	16	74	74	88	7	.408	.460
2025	22	Seattle (AL)	MLB	.167	8	6	1	1	0	0	0	1	0	3	0	.250	.167
		Minor League Totals		.266	454	1693	330	450	98	10	52	261	348	441	92	.405	.428
		Major League Totals		.167	8	6	1	1	0	0	0	1	0	3	0	.250	.167

WASHINGTON NATIONALS

4 LUIS PERALES, RHP
FB: 70. **SL:** 45. **CT:** 60. **SP:** 45. **CTL:** 40. **BA Grade:** 60. **Risk:** High. **Adj:** 45.

Born: April 14, 2003. **B-T:** R-R. **HT:** 6-1. **WT:** 198.
Signed: Venezuela, 2019. **Signing scout:** Lenin Rodriguez/Ernesto Gomez/Rollie Pino.
TRACK RECORD: After he signed with the Red Sox for $75,000 out of Venezuela in 2019, Perales quickly started generating buzz thanks to a quick arm that unleashed mid-90s fastballs. His development proceeded slowly in part due to elbow discomfort in both 2021 and 2022, but a solid 2023 campaign served as a prelude to an early breakout in 2024, when a broader mix resulted in a 39% strikeout rate at High-A and Double-A. However, Perales had Tommy John surgery in June. He added significant strength while rehabbing, and when he returned to games in September 2025, he showed triple-digits velocity even as he worked to regain command. In December, the Red Sox traded Perales to the Nationals for 25-year-old lefthander Jake Bennett.
SCOUTING REPORT: Perales has a bazooka. He sat 98-101 mph in his brief return to the mound in 2025, with 17 to 20 inches of ride. His fastball can be a swing-and-miss weapon when he keeps it in the zone, but his ability to do so was inconsistent. He more reliably located his low-90s cutter—a pitch that contributed to his 2024 breakout—and that pitch may end up being his primary offering, with the four-seamer looming as a putaway pitch. His gyro slider and splitter have depth to stretch the zone vertically, but for now his splitter is too often non-competitive below the zone. The development of his splitter as a reliable weapon, not to mention improved control to leave hitters on the defensive, will dictate whether he's a starter or a late-inning reliever.
THE FUTURE: If Perales can harness his stuff in the zone, he has the upside of a No. 3 starter. Otherwise, his future will be as a leverage reliever. He'll compete for a big league bullpen spot in 2026, but more likely will open the year in the Triple-A rotation.

Year	Age	Club (League)	Level	W	L	ERA	G	GS	IP	H	HR	BB	SO	BB%	SO%	WHIP	AVG
2025	22	Portland (EL)	AA	0	0	0.00	1	1	1	0	0	1	0	33.3	0.0	1.00	.000
2025	22	Worcester (IL)	AAA	0	0	13.50	2	0	1	0	0	2	4	33.3	66.7	1.50	.000
		Minor League Totals		6	11	3.31	47	43	163	130	12	86	228	12.3	32.6	1.32	.217

5 TRAVIS SYKORA, RHP
FB: 65. **SL:** 55. **CH:** 55. **CTL:** 50. **BA Grade:** 60. **Risk:** High. **Adj:** 45.

Born: April 28, 2004. **B-T:** R-R. **HT:** 6-6. **WT:** 224.
Drafted: HS—Round Rock, TX, 2023 (3rd round). **Signed by:** Kevin Ham.
TRACK RECORD: Sykora had top-two-rounds talent in the 2023 draft coming out of Round Rock High. When he slipped to the Nationals in round three—but still signed for late first-round money—he used the perceived slight as motivation. Sykora unleashed his fury on Carolina League batters in 2024, leading all Low-A pitchers with 129 strikeouts in 85 innings. He had surgery on the labrum in his hip in the offseason and got a late start in 2025. After Sykora missed time with a triceps injury in July while at Double-A Harrisburg, he later developed a UCL tear in his elbow. Sykora had Tommy John surgery in August.
SCOUTING REPORT: Sykora idolizes Texas pitching icon Nolan Ryan, and like The Ryan Express, he uses a power approach consisting mostly of a high-octane fastball and a devastating breaking pitch. Sykora pitches at 95-96 mph with his four-seam fastball and tops out at 99. He compensates for average fastball shape with strong extension and pure velocity. The pitch should continue to play as Sykora recovers from TJ. He improved the horizontal life on his low-80s slider, which gets up near 87 mph, and he threw the pitch for strikes at a high rate. He also threw it more than his fastball in 2025. Sykora's mid-80s splitter tumbles and fades to his arm side with consistently low spin rates. Sykora needs to tighten up his fastball command to different parts of the zone, but his wandering control is typical for a young power pitcher and will likely improve.
THE FUTURE: Given that he had TJ late in the 2025 season, Sykora probably won't be at full strength again until 2027, when he will still be just 23 years old. His stuff and control make him a candidate to be at least a No. 3 starter.

Year	Age	Club (League)	Level	W	L	ERA	G	GS	IP	H	HR	BB	SO	BB%	SO%	WHIP	AVG
2025	21	FCL Nationals	Rk	0	0	1.80	2	2	5	1	0	1	14	5.9	82.4	0.40	.063
2025	21	Fredericksburg (CAR)	A	0	0	0.00	2	2	6	1	0	2	9	9.5	42.9	0.50	.056
2025	21	Wilmington (SAL)	A+	3	0	1.21	6	6	30	12	0	8	47	7.5	44.3	0.67	.124
2025	21	Harrisburg (EL)	AA	0	1	7.71	2	2	5	4	0	6	9	24.0	36.0	2.14	.211
		Minor League Totals		3	1	1.79	12	12	45	18	0	17	79	10.1	46.7	0.77	.120

WASHINGTON NATIONALS

6 ALEX CLEMMEY, LHP
FB: 60. **SL:** 60. **CH:** 55. **CTL:** 40. **BA Grade:** 55. **Risk:** High. **Adj:** 40.

Born: July 18, 2005. **B-T:** L-L. **HT:** 6-6. **WT:** 223.
Drafted: HS—Warwick, RI, 2023 (2nd round). **Signed by:** Kyle Bamberger (Guardians).
TRACK RECORD: The Guardians drafted Clemmey out of a Rhode Island high school in the second round in 2023, going nearly $1 million over slot to sign him for $2.3 million. Cleveland dealt him to the Nationals at the 2024 trade deadline as part of the package for Lane Thomas. Clemmey logged 116.2 innings in 2025 and led all Nationals minor league pitchers with 136 strikeouts but also 73 walks. He reached Double-A Harrisburg in mid-August and saved his best work for last, when he posted a 2.04 ERA with 15 strikeouts and five walks in his final 17.2 innings.
SCOUTING REPORT: Clemmey's exciting stuff gives him the potential to become a top overall lefthanded pitching prospect. It will come down to control, after he walked more than 14% of batters in 2025 to rank 11th-worst among minor league pitchers with at least 100 innings. The 6-foot-6, long-limbed Clemmey has worked hard to streamline and repeat his mechanics, and his zone and strike rates on his fastball continue to creep upward. Opposing hitters have a hard time seeing his 93-94 mph four-seam fastball that reaches near 98. His arm slot and low release height make his heater difficult to square up for batters of both hands. He upped his sinker usage in 2025 to introduce a new wrinkle. Scouts would like to see him improve his fastball command to his glove side. Clemmey's mid-80s slider has plus potential but wasn't the same type of swing-and-miss weapon as it had been at Low-A in 2024. He threw many more changeups in 2025 to develop the high-80s pitch with above-average potential and good fade to his arm side.
THE FUTURE: Clemmey exudes confidence and is a strong competitor with the athleticism to continue improving his command, which will determine his future role. He has the raw talent to become a No. 3 or 4 starter or potentially a high-leverage relief weapon.

Year	Age	Club (League)	Level	W	L	ERA	G	GS	IP	H	HR	BB	SO	BB%	SO%	WHIP	AVG
2025	19	Wilmington (SAL)	A+	7	4	2.47	19	19	87	56	4	60	113	15.9	30.0	1.33	.182
2025	19	Harrisburg (EL)	AA	0	1	6.44	6	6	29	32	8	13	23	9.9	17.6	1.53	.278
		Minor League Totals		8	10	3.96	50	50	209	155	16	136	259	15.1	28.8	1.39	.208

7 SEAVER KING, SS
HIT: 50. **POW:** 45. **RUN:** 70. **FLD:** 50. **ARM:** 55. **BA Grade:** 50. **Risk:** Average. **Adj:** 40.

Born: April 25, 2003. **B-T:** R-R. **HT:** 6-0. **WT:** 216.
Drafted: Wake Forest, 2024 (1st round). **Signed by:** Bob Hamelin.
TRACK RECORD: King starred at Division II Wingate for two years before the Nationals drafted him 10th overall out of Wake Forest in 2024. In his pro debut, King helped lead Low-A Fredericksburg to the 2024 Carolina League title. He got off to a slow start with High-A Wilmington in 2025 but recovered to reach Double-A Harrisburg on June 3. King showed speed with 30 stolen bases in 125 total games but hit just .244/.294/.337 with six home runs and a 32-to-116 walk-to-strikeout ratio. His bat showed improved life in the Arizona Fall League, where he hit .359/.468/.563 for a 1.031 OPS that ranked 10th in the league.
SCOUTING REPORT: Despite King's poor results in his first full season, scouts remain optimistic about his future because of his overall athleticism and twitch, enhanced by his enthusiasm. Early in the season, he appeared to be selling out for power by trying to pull the ball in the air, which spiked his strikeout rate. King reverted to a more dynamic hitting style by putting aggressive swings on pitches in all parts of the zone and hitting to all fields. He maintained strong exit velocities in 2025, even if hits weren't falling. King has strong bat-to-ball skills but needs to be more selective after an alarming chase rate of 37% in 2025. Some would like to see him move his contact point forward and with a swing coming from a lower slot to avoid excess groundball contact. If he can make things work, King can be a solid-average hitter with fringe power or better. He is a double-plus runner and efficient basestealer. King played more third base and center field at Wake Forest, but he settled in as a reliable everyday shortstop with an above-average arm. He has the athletic ability to adapt at the position and learn its nuances.
THE FUTURE: King has interesting tools and the athleticism to stay up the middle. He could be a few tweaks away from realizing his offensive potential and becoming a solid regular.

Year	Age	Club (League)	Level	AVG	G	AB	R	H	2B	3B	HR	RBI	BB	SO	SB	OBP	SLG
2025	22	Wilmington (SAL)	A+	.263	45	179	28	47	6	3	3	17	9	42	12	.307	.380
2025	22	Harrisburg (EL)	AA	.233	80	326	37	76	13	2	3	26	23	74	18	.287	.313
		Minor League Totals		.250	145	583	80	146	20	8	6	53	41	129	40	.305	.343

WASHINGTON NATIONALS

8 LUKE DICKERSON, SS
HIT: 55. **POW:** 50. **RUN:** 60. **FLD:** 50. **ARM:** 50. **BA Grade:** 55. **Risk:** High. **Adj:** 40.

Born: August 9, 2005. **B-T:** R-R. **HT:** 5-11. **WT:** 203.
Drafted: HS—Rockaway, NJ, 2024 (2nd round). **Signed by:** John Malzone.
TRACK RECORD: The Nationals bet big on Dickerson in the second round of the 2024 draft, taking the New Jersey prep two-sport athlete—he also starred in hockey—in the second round and going way over slot to sign him for $3.8 million. That was nearly double the slot value for the 44th pick. Dickerson debuted in the Florida Complex League in 2025 but stayed just six games before the Nationals promoted him to Low-A Fredericksburg. He hit well for the first 20 games but his production tapered off and he finished his time in the Carolina League with a .204 average, 25% strikeout rate and five home runs in 83 games.
SCOUTING REPORT: The Nationals got an incomplete look at Dickerson in his first full season because he played through a wrist injury. Despite that mitigating factor, he grinded through a full season and showed plus bat speed and aptitude to drive the ball for power to his pull side on occasion. Like many young hitters, Dickerson will need to hone in on his strike zone and make more contact in the zone and avoid chasing out of it. He can get too passive at times. He hits the ball hard enough consistently enough to provide at least average power, while his quality swing decisions should make him an above-average hitter. Dickerson is a solidly-built, 5-foot-11 athlete who moves well on the infield and can convert routine plays at shortstop. He is a plus runner but doesn't have classic shortstop range, and his arm is borderline for the left side of the infield. Dickerson saw time at second base late in the season, and some scouts have floated center field as a possible destination.
THE FUTURE: Scouts who like Dickerson view him as a potential big league second baseman with solid all-around tools with enough hitting ability and power to play regularly.

Year	Age	Club (League)	Level	AVG	G	AB	R	H	2B	3B	HR	RBI	BB	SO	SB	OBP	SLG
2025	19	FCL Nationals	Rk	.273	6	22	5	6	0	0	1	10	4	4	1	.385	.409
2025	19	Fredericksburg (CAR)	A	.204	83	285	34	58	14	2	5	31	41	84	21	.309	.319
		Minor League Totals		.208	89	307	39	64	14	2	6	41	45	88	22	.315	.326

9 COY JAMES, SS
HIT: 55. **POW:** 50. **RUN:** 50. **FLD:** 50. **ARM:** 50. **BA Grade:** 55. **Risk:** High. **Adj:** 40.

Born: February 16, 2007. **B-T:** R-R. **HT:** 6-0. **WT:** 185.
Drafted: HS—Mocksville, NC, 2025 (5th round). **Signed by:** Bob Hamelin.
TRACK RECORD: James is a veteran of USA Baseball who played for the gold medal-winning 15U National Team in 2022 and for the 2023 18U National Team as an underclassman. As a senior in 2025 he won Gatorade North Carolina player of the year honors by hitting .605 with nine home runs for Davie County High. James had top-three rounds talent in the 2025 draft and wound up signing a bonus commensurate with a top 40 overall pick when the Nationals paid him $2.5 million in the fifth round. He worked out at the organization's West Palm Beach, Fla., complex after signing but did not get into an official game.
SCOUTING REPORT: James makes hitting look easy with a loose, whippy righthanded swing and an ability to find the barrel. He makes a ton of hard, line-drive contact with strong hand-eye coordination and a compact swing. James hits velocity and does a good job using all fields to keep defenses guessing. He should grow into 20-homer power based on his feel to hit and present strength, but he doesn't have much projection remaining in his 6-foot, 185-pound frame. James has sure hands in the batter's box and is a reliable shortstop, but he might be stretched to play the position professionally. He's an average runner with ordinary range in the field and an average arm that could be stretched on the left side of the infield. James' time at other positions should increase as he moves up the ladder.
THE FUTURE: Many scouts see James as a bat-first second or third baseman capable of hitting for average, getting on base and delivering average power. The Nationals will have to find playing time for a cadre of young shortstops in 2026 that also includes Luke Dickerson, Angel Feliz and 2025 first overall pick Eli Willits, so it wouldn't be surprising if James begins in the Florida Complex League.

Year	Age	Club (League)	Level	AVG	G	AB	R	H	2B	3B	HR	RBI	BB	SO	SB	OBP	SLG
2025	18	Did not play															

WASHINGTON NATIONALS

10 ANGEL FELIZ, SS

HIT: 50. **POW:** 50. **RUN:** 30. **FLD:** 50. **ARM:** 55. **BA Grade:** 50. **Risk:** High. **Adj:** 40.

Born: November 16, 2006. **B-T:** R-R. **HT:** 6-3. **WT:** 185.
Signed: Dominican Republic, 2024. **Signed by:** Bolivar Pelletier.

TRACK RECORD: The Nationals in recent years have had mixed results in international free agency. They have gotten limited production from Dominican shortstop Armando Cruz and Cuban outfielder Cristhian Vaquero, their top signees in 2021 and 2022, but players from the 2024 and 2025 signing classes offer hope. That includes Feliz, a Dominican shortstop who signed for $1.7 million in 2024. He played well in the Dominican Summer League in his debut, then turned in a fine season in the Florida Complex League in 2025. Feliz finished third in the FCL with 51 hits and seventh with 69 total bases before moving to Low-A Fredericksburg for 31 games to finish his season.

SCOUTING REPORT: Feliz is a strong-bodied, 6-foot-3 shortstop who hits the ball hard for a teenager. His tall, rangy frame could add more good weight as he matures, which, combined with his bat speed, gives him a chance to grow into above-average power. He competes in the box with a slightly open stance and tracks pitches well for his age. Feliz hits the ball where it's pitched on a line but must continue proving himself against velocity, especially on inside pitches. His ability to hit to all fields with authority suggests a future average hit tool or better. Feliz is a well below-average runner who has acceptable range at shortstop as a teenager but could outgrow the position as he matures. His above-average arm would fit at third base if he has to move, and he already has pro experience at second base.

THE FUTURE: Feliz can do a little bit of everything, except run, at a young age, but he risks falling into more of a reserve profile unless his power takes a step forward. The Nationals praise his leadership and poise, so they are optimistic that his game will develop.

Year	Age	Club (League)	Level	AVG	G	AB	R	H	2B	3B	HR	RBI	BB	SO	SB	OBP	SLG
2025	18	FCL Nationals	Rk	.264	53	193	37	51	7	4	1	28	30	44	10	.366	.358
2025	18	Fredericksburg (CAR)	A	.230	31	100	16	23	3	1	3	15	12	27	5	.307	.370
		Minor League Totals		.274	133	464	95	127	19	8	8	63	63	107	42	.359	.401

11 LANDON HARMON, RHP

FB: 70. **SL:** 55. **CH:** 45. **SW:** 50. **CTL:** 50. **BA Grade:** 55. **Risk:** Extreme. **Adj:** 35.

Born: September 9, 2006. **B-T:** R-R. **HT:** 6-5. **WT:** 190.
Drafted: HS—Blue Springs, MS, 2025 (3rd round). **Signed by:** Tommy Jackson.

TRACK RECORD: Harmon threw the best fastball of any high school righthander in the 2025 draft class and trailed only lefthander Jack Bauer among all prep pitchers. Harmon helped pitch East Union High to a Mississippi 2A state title in 2025, the program's second in three years. He was committed to Mississippi State before he aligned with the Nationals in the third round and signed for $2.5 million, a bonus akin to a top 40 overall pick.

SCOUTING REPORT: Harmon is a projectable 6-foot-5 righthander with long limbs and a high-waisted frame. He is tall, lean and flexible with a loose arm that generates easy velocity. Harmon sits in the mid 90s and has been up to 98 mph with riding life and late cutting action to his glove side. His delivery is clean and repeatable, and he throws strikes from a three-quarters arm slot and slight crossfire landing. Harmon's fastball has double-plus potential and could top out at 100 mph one day, but his secondary pitches need more work. He throws a low-80s sweeper and a slider in the high 80s, both of which he can locate well for his age. Refining them into above-average pitches will be a key development goal. He occasionally throws a low-80s changeup that will be another point of emphasis. Adding strength to his frame and testing his stuff against professional hitters are next steps that needs to be tweaked are the next steps.

THE FUTURE: High school righthanders are among the most volatile draft commodities. Harmon has a great foundation for the Nationals to build upon, as they did with Travis Sykora from the 2023 draft, but it will be years before the righthander's full potential comes into focus. The Nationals will likely hold Harmon back in extended spring training, as they did Sykora, before assigning him to the Florida Complex League or Low-A Fredericksburg in 2026.

Year	Age	Club (League)	Level	W	L	ERA	G	GS	IP	H	HR	BB	SO	BB%	SO%	WHIP	AVG
2025	18	Did not play															

WASHINGTON NATIONALS

12 SAM PETERSEN, OF
HIT: 55. **POW:** 55. **RUN:** 55. **FLD:** 50. **ARM:** 40. **BA Grade:** 50. **Risk:** High. **Adj:** 35.

Born: January 20, 2003. **B-T:** R-R. **HT:** 6-0. **WT:** 205. **Drafted:** Iowa, 2024 (8th round). **Signed by:** James Goodwin.
TRACK RECORD: If not for shin splints he contended with as an Iowa junior, Petersen had a chance to be drafted a bit higher than the eighth round in 2024. That's where he landed with the Nationals, who signed him for a slot value bonus of $230,900. Petersen saw action in seven games for Low-A Fredericksburg after signing but got a late start to his 2025 season after dealing with a hamstring injury. He reached High-A Wilmington on June 5 and then played in the Arizona Fall League after the season to add at-bats.
SCOUTING REPORT: Petersen has a strong, 6-foot frame and a hard-nosed playing style. The Nationals have helped coax greater exit velocity out of his righthanded bat, while giving him a chance to prove himself in center field after he played mostly left in college. Petersen hits the ball with authority to all fields with a line-drive approach. He takes aggressive swings and is beginning to take shots to his pull side, with the potential for above-average power. His max exit velocity increased to 110 mph with wood after reaching 109 in 2024 with metal. Petersen does well staying within his zone and keeps strikeouts in check, but his zone-whiff rate of nearly 27% could curtail his production against more advanced pitchers. He is an above-average runner out of the box who is faster underway. His baserunning savvy is apparent in his 18-for-18 showing on stolen bases for Wilmington. Petersen is an average center fielder with a below-average arm that might limit him to left field.
THE FUTURE: Petersen was one of the top performers in the South Atlantic League while healthy, which is notable given that Wilmington suppresses home runs like few minor league parks. He showed the potential to be at least a fourth outfielder and potentially a regular if his power and speed continue to play. Petersen is ready for Double-A.

Year	Age	Club (League)	Level	AVG	G	AB	R	H	2B	3B	HR	RBI	BB	SO	SB	OBP	SLG
2025	22	FCL Nationals	Rk	.387	11	31	11	12	1	0	1	7	6	9	4	.524	.516
2025	22	Fredericksburg (CAR)	A	.250	2	8	2	2	1	0	0	0	0	2	1	.250	.375
2025	22	Wilmington (SAL)	A+	.297	44	145	31	43	6	2	6	21	20	31	18	.398	.490
		Minor League Totals		.316	64	206	50	65	11	3	7	30	27	48	28	.415	.500

13 ETHAN PETRY, OF
HIT: 40. **POW:** 55. **RUN:** 30. **FLD:** 40. **ARM:** 55. **BA Grade:** 45. **Risk:** Average. **Adj:** 35.

Born: June 17, 2004. **B-T:** R-R. **HT:** 6-4. **WT:** 235. **Drafted:** South Carolina, 2025 (2nd round). **Signed by:** Bob Hamelin.
TRACK RECORD: Petry was second-team All-America as a freshman in 2023, when he blasted 23 home runs for South Carolina. That would prove to be his highest single-season total, though he still mashed 54 homers and slugged .661 in three years of Southeastern Conference play. Petry might have topped Justin Smoak's program record of 62 homers had he not missed time as a junior with a shoulder strain. The Nationals drafted Petry in the second round in 2025 and signed him for a slightly above-slot $2.09 million. He got into 24 games for Low-A Fredericksburg and then played in the Arizona Fall League.
SCOUTING REPORT: Petry is a physical, 6-foot-4 righthanded hitter with the plus bat speed to do serious damage when he connects. He is a welcome addition to a Nationals system largely devoid of power. Petry hits the ball as hard as virtually any Washington minor league hitter and could get to plus game power. He has a long swing and had a zone-contact rate of roughly 70% in his pro debut, factors that raise questions about his hitting ability. He does a good job laying off pitches out of the zone and will take his walks. Petry is a left fielder or first baseman all the way, with well below-average speed and merely playable range. He has an above-average arm.
THE FUTURE: Power production will determine Petry's rate of progression and ultimate big league role. The potential for plus power exists if he can dial in his selectivity and contact.

Year	Age	Club (League)	Level	AVG	G	AB	R	H	2B	3B	HR	RBI	BB	SO	SB	OBP	SLG
2025	21	Fredericksburg (CAR)	A	.287	24	87	11	25	3	1	2	10	13	25	1	.386	.414
		Minor League Totals		.287	24	87	11	25	3	1	2	10	13	25	1	.386	.414

14 ANDREW PINCKNEY, OF
HIT: 30. **POW:** 55. **RUN:** 70. **FLD:** 55. **ARM:** 70. **BA Grade:** 40. **Risk:** Mild. **Adj:** 35.

Born: December 7, 2000. **B-T:** R-R. **HT:** 6-4. **WT:** 204. **Drafted:** Alabama, 2023 (4th round). **Signed by:** Tommy Jackson.
TRACK RECORD: The Nationals drafted Pinckney in the fourth round in 2023 following four years at Alabama. He reached Double-A briefly in his first pro summer and spent most of 2024 at the level, reaching Triple-A for 23 games. That season, Pinckney showed speed with 27 stolen bases but struggled to access his raw power and slugged just .362 in 137 games. The tide began to turn in 2025 when Pinckney

hit 20 home runs and stole 34 bases in 125 games for Triple-A Rochester. He was one of just five 20-20 players at Triple-A.
SCOUTING REPORT: Pinckney has a wider array of tools than any Nationals prospect. He is the system's best athlete with double-plus speed, plus raw power and a cannon of an arm. Accessing those tools is going to be the key. Toward that end, Pinckney improved his selective aggression in 2025. He reduced his swing rate and his chase rate, and he hit the ball harder than ever, improving his 90th percentile exit velocity from about 106 mph in 2024 to about 108 in 2025. It's going to come down to the frequency and angle of contact, because Pinckney had high strikeout (29%) and groundball rates (51%) that will inhibit his hit tool. He has double-plus speed to leg out infield hits, take extra bases on gappers and steal efficiently. Pinckney is an adept defender at all three outfield positions and grades as above-average at each spot. His double-plus arm is a deterrent to baserunners. Of the 22 Triple-A outfield throws of 100 mph or faster in 2025, Pinckney made eight of them.
THE FUTURE: Pinckney is a late bloomer who didn't play much during his first two years of college. He stuck with Alabama, though, because he was born in Tuscaloosa and has family there. Now, that determination is beginning to bear fruit in pro ball, where he profiles as an extra outfielder with power, speed and fielding skill.

Year	Age	Club (League)	Level	AVG	G	AB	R	H	2B	3B	HR	RBI	BB	SO	SB	OBP	SLG
2025	24	Rochester (IL)	AAA	.269	125	450	77	121	9	2	20	66	44	148	34	.348	.431
		Minor League Totals		.271	303	1132	181	307	39	7	32	136	106	353	72	.349	.403

15 JACKSON KENT, LHP
FB: 55. **CB:** 40. **SL:** 50. **CH:** 60. **CTL:** 50. **BA Grade:** 45. **Risk:** Average. **Adj:** 40.

Born: February 10, 2003. **B-T:** L-L. **HT:** 6-3. **WT:** 233. **Drafted:** Arizona, 2024 (4th round). **Signed by:** Mitch Sokol.
TRACK RECORD: Kent is a suburban Chicago prep who attended Arizona for two years, moving into the rotation in 2024 as a draft-eligible sophomore. The Nationals drafted him in the fourth round. Kent reached Double-A Harrisburg in the second half of his first pro season, and while his ERA ballooned to 4.61 on the season, he finished third in the Nationals' system with 132 strikeouts and fourth with 123 innings.
SCOUTING REPORT: Kent is a physical 6-foot-3 lefthander who pitches in the low 90s and gets up to 95 mph while throwing one of the better changeups in the system. His velocity is up several ticks from even two years ago, and his four-seamer gets a boost in effectiveness from extension down the mound of nearly 7 feet. The resulting low release height helps make it a trustworthy strike pitch as he moves it around the zone. Kent's low-80s changeup has tremendous fade to his arm side and he sells the pitch effectively. It's a potential plus weapon. He needs to sharpen a low-80s slider and mid-70s curveball to enhance his unpredictability. Kent threw a fastball or changeup about 75% of the time in 2025. He has better feel to command his slider and it could be average with more power. Kent needs to do a better job throwing strike one and working ahead of batters.
THE FUTURE: The Nationals view Kent as perhaps their top competitor on the mound, giving him a good chance to pitch in a rotation one day, most likely toward the back.

Year	Age	Club (League)	Level	W	L	ERA	G	GS	IP	H	HR	BB	SO	BB%	SO%	WHIP	AVG
2025	22	Wilmington (SAL)	A+	5	7	4.31	18	18	94	86	10	25	97	6.5	25.1	1.18	.244
2025	22	Harrisburg (EL)	AA	2	3	5.59	6	6	29	26	4	13	35	10.7	28.7	1.34	.241
		Minor League Totals		7	10	4.61	24	24	123	112	14	38	132	7.5	25.9	1.22	.243

16 YOHANDY MORALES, 1B/3B
HIT: 40. **POW:** 55. **RUN:** 40. **FLD:** 45. **ARM:** 55. **BA Grade:** 45. **Risk:** Average. **Adj:** 35.

Born: October 9, 2001. **B-T:** R-R. **HT:** 6-3. **WT:** 224. **Drafted:** Miami, 2023 (2nd round). **Signed by:** Alex Morales.
TRACK RECORD: Morales' father Andy played for the Cuban national team and reached Double-A as a third baseman for the Red Sox and Yankees. Yohandy starred at Miami for three years, hitting 20 homers as a junior in 2023, when the Nationals drafted him in the second round. He played at four levels during his pro debut that summer but was limited to 75 games in 2024 by a left thumb injury. Fully healthy in 2025, Morales spent most of the season at Triple-A Rochester and led the system with 31 doubles and ranked third with 15 homers and 57 walks.
SCOUTING REPORT: Morales is a physical, 6-foot-3 righthanded hitter with plus raw power and a buggy-whip swing he can use to drive the ball to right field. Many of his extra-base hits are struck to the middle of the field or the other way because he can wait on the ball and let his quick hands take over. He is an aggressive hitter with a longer swing who needs to rein in his chase rate to get the most out of his skills, especially in right-on-right matchups. A high strikeout rate cuts into his productivity. Morales

WASHINGTON NATIONALS

is a below-average runner who has played more first base than third the past two seasons. He can make on-target throws from behind the bag at third base with an above-average arm, but his hands work better at first base.

THE FUTURE: Morales has a power-over-hit corner infield profile that means his outlook is dependent on extra-base production. If he hits at Triple-A, he should get an MLB look in Washington, which has no entrenched first baseman.

Year	Age	Club (League)	Level	AVG	G	AB	R	H	2B	3B	HR	RBI	BB	SO	SB	OBP	SLG
2025	23	Harrisburg (EL)	AA	.315	33	127	19	40	10	2	4	22	11	33	2	.366	.520
2025	23	Rochester (IL)	AAA	.249	95	382	66	95	21	2	11	49	46	131	5	.330	.401
		Minor League Totals		.285	245	944	145	269	60	9	22	144	108	270	13	.362	.438

17 MARCONI GERMAN, SS/2B

HIT: 50. **POW:** 50. **RUN:** 55. **FLD:** 55. **ARM:** 55. **BA Grade:** 50. **Risk:** High. **Adj:** 35.

Born: September 9, 2007. **B-T:** B-R. **HT:** 5-10. **WT:** 170. **Signed:** Dominican Republic, 2025. **Signed by:** Bolivar Pelletier.

TRACK RECORD: German represented one of the best scouting-and-development stories in the Nationals' system in 2025. Signed out of the Dominican Republic for $400,000 in January, he adapted quickly to pro ball as one of the Dominican Summer League's top performers. German batted .283/.479/.513 with eight home runs and 33 stolen bases in 53 games. His steals total ranked seventh in the DSL, while his .992 OPS ranked fourth among qualified 17-year-old peers.

SCOUTING REPORT: German is a 5-foot-10, switch-hitting middle infielder with a well-rounded game. He has a fluid swing from both sides of the plate and a good eye for the strike zone, as demonstrated by him accumulating 43 walks against 42 strikeouts in his DSL debut. German does a good job keeping the ball off the ground and elevating to his pull side when the situation warrants. He's young and untested, but as he adds strength and exit velocity, he could grade as average for hit and power. German is an above-average runner and effective basestealer. His body type should allow him to remain on the middle infield, potentially at shortstop with an above-average arm.

THE FUTURE: German is part of a growing contingent of shortstops at the lower levels of the Nationals' system. He should continue seeing time there and at second base and will be a top candidate to play middle infield in the Florida Complex League in 2026.

Year	Age	Club (League)	Level	AVG	G	AB	R	H	2B	3B	HR	RBI	BB	SO	SB	OBP	SLG
2025	17	DSL Nationals	Rk	.283	53	152	37	43	9	1	8	30	43	42	33	.479	.513
		Minor League Totals		.283	53	152	37	43	9	1	8	30	43	42	33	.479	.513

18 CALEB LOMAVITA, C

HIT: 50. **POW:** 40. **RUN:** 45. **FLD:** 45. **ARM:** 50. **BA Grade:** 45. **Risk:** Average. **Adj:** 35.

Born: November 18, 2002. **B-T:** R-R. **HT:** 5-11. **WT:** 218. **Drafted:** California, 2024 (1st round supp.). **Signed by:** Bryan Byrne.

TRACK RECORD: Lomavita played high school ball in Honolulu before serving as a three-year starter at California, the last two as primary catcher. The Nationals drafted him 39th overall in 2024, using the competitive balance pick they acquired from the Royals for reliever Hunter Harvey. Lomavita helped Low-A Fredericksburg win the Carolina League title in his first pro summer and then spent most of 2025 with High-A Wilmington. He hit just .275/.333/.364 with four home runs in 99 games, playing half his games in a brutal hitter's park, before spending the final three series with Double-A Harrisburg.

SCOUTING REPORT: Lomavita is an athletic catcher who moves well behind the plate but has significant questions to answer about his framing ability and hitting approach. He likes to swing the bat and will follow the pitcher out of the zone, resulting in a lot of groundball contact and easy outs. Lomavita has the average bat speed and raw power to hit 10-plus home runs; it's going to be about identifying pitches to hit and getting off his best swings. Behind the plate, he is a noisy receiver who needs to improve his framing to help gain strikes for his pitchers. He moves well laterally and blocks balls in the dirt. Lomavita has average arm strength that can be improved with more consistent throwing mechanics. He runs well for a catcher and can swipe the occasional base.

THE FUTURE: Lomavita is trending toward a role of bat-first backup catcher, but he has time to iron out his issues. The 2026 season will be just his third as a pro, and it's one likely to be spent primarily at Double-A.

Year	Age	Club (League)	Level	AVG	G	AB	R	H	2B	3B	HR	RBI	BB	SO	SB	OBP	SLG
2025	22	Wilmington (SAL)	A+	.275	99	363	32	100	16	2	4	44	19	83	7	.339	.364
2025	22	Harrisburg (EL)	AA	.273	9	33	3	9	1	0	2	3	4	9	0	.351	.485
		Minor League Totals		.267	125	457	50	122	19	2	6	57	28	105	10	.336	.357

19 MIGUEL SIME JR., RHP

FB: 70. **CB:** 50. **CH:** 50. **CTL:** 40. **BA Grade:** 50. **Risk:** Extreme. **Adj:** 30.

Born: May 8, 2007. **B-T:** R-R. **HT:** 6-4. **WT:** 235. **Drafted:** HS—Brooklyn, NY, 2025 (4th round).
Signed by: Arnold Brathwaite.
TRACK RECORD: Sime grew up in Queens and attended Brooklyn's Poly Prep Country Day School, where he was recognized as the Gatorade New York player of the year as a senior in 2025. Pitching in the MLB Draft League in June, he recorded the first-ever 100 mph pitch in the five-year history of the league. Not that he needed any additional helium. Sime was already regarded as one of the hardest throwers among high school pitchers in the 2025 draft. The Nationals bought him out of an LSU commitment when they drafted him in the fourth round and signed him for $2 million.
SCOUTING REPORT: Sime has a filled-out 6-foot-4, 235-pound frame with broad shoulders and a strong foundation. He looks the part of power pitcher, and that's exactly what he is with consistent upper-90s velocity with a peak of 100 mph. Sime's frame allows him to hold velocity, which he proved in a 100-pitch matchup against SoCal power Corona at the 2025 National High School Invitational. He throws a low-80s curveball that flashes average with 11-to-5 shape and bite. The Nationals like the running, sinking action on Sime's mid-80s changeup and see it as a potential weapon versus lefthanded batters. Sime has an effortless delivery and deep arm action, so maintaining flexibility and keeping his mechanics on line will be key to refining present below-average control.
THE FUTURE: Sime's long trek through the minor leagues begins in 2026. His goals will be building his workload and adapting his repertoire as needed.

Year	Age	Club (League)	Level	W	L	ERA	G	GS	IP	H	HR	BB	SO	BB%	SO%	WHIP	AVG
2025	18	Did not play															

20 JORGELYS MOTA, 3B

HIT: 30. **POW:** 50. **RUN:** 60. **FLD:** 40. **ARM:** 70. **BA Grade:** 50. **Risk:** Extreme. **Adj:** 30.

Born: June 3, 2005. **B-T:** R-R. **HT:** 6-3. **WT:** 215. **Signed:** Dominican Republic, 2022. **Signed by:** Virgilio De Leon.
TRACK RECORD: The Nationals signed Mota out of the Dominican Republic in 2022, and he spent the better part of three seasons in Rookie ball. Assigned to Low-A Fredericksburg out of spring training in 2025, the 20-year-old was the most productive regular on the team and one of the more productive in the pitcher-friendly Carolina League. Mota batted .270/.341/.409 with six home runs and 25 stolen bases in 81 games.
SCOUTING REPORT: Mota is a 6-foot-3 righthanded hitter with broad shoulders and a lanky but strong build. He has a hyper-aggressive hitting approach and likes to swing the bat. He has as much raw power as any Nationals prospect and has the exit velocity data to prove it. Mota's 90th EV of 109 mph was one of the highest in the minor leagues in 2025. But he needs to be more selective to access even average power production, because his 2025 miss rate (39%) and chase rate (34%) are both prohibitive. Those factors contributed to a high groundball rate of 53%. Mota is a plus runner who has begun to amp up his basestealing aggressiveness. He has a chance to become an average defensive third baseman, thanks in part to his double-plus arm.
THE FUTURE: Mota took giant strides in 2025 but still has work to do to become even a second-division third baseman. Enhanced selective aggression would serve him well, because he has obvious 20-homer potential if he can identify which pitches he can drive in the air.

Year	Age	Club (League)	Level	AVG	G	AB	R	H	2B	3B	HR	RBI	BB	SO	SB	OBP	SLG
2025	20	Fredericksburg (CAR)	A	.270	81	296	34	80	17	3	6	42	26	101	25	.341	.409
		Minor League Totals		.253	211	723	102	183	30	9	12	100	60	260	46	.328	.369

21 RONNY CRUZ, SS

HIT: 40. **POW:** 50. **RUN:** 55. **FLD:** 55. **ARM:** 55. **BA Grade:** 50. **Risk:** Extreme. **Adj:** 30.

Born: August 24, 2006. **B-T:** R-R. **HT:** 6-2. **WT:** 170. **Drafted:** HS—Miami, 2024 (3rd round).
Signed by: Ralph Reyes (Cubs).
TRACK RECORD: Cruz is a Dominican Republic native who had an international free agent contract offer fall through. He then moved to Florida and played two prep seasons at Miami Christian School and was still 17 years old when the Cubs drafted him in the third round in 2024. Cruz made his pro debut the following season and batted .270/.314/.431 with two home runs and 10 stolen bases in 48 games in the Arizona Complex League. The Cubs dealt him to the Nationals at the 2025 trade deadline as part of the package for Michael Soroka. Cruz did not play after the trade.
SCOUTING REPORT: Cruz is a lean 6-foot-2 shortstop with room to fill out his frame and add power. He

shows above-average power in batting practice and made plenty of hard contact in his ACL pro debut. He is a pull-oriented hitter who will sometimes leak out on his front side and lose his hitting base. In the field, Cruz has clean actions, an above-average arm and a good internal clock at shortstop. It's possible he outgrows the position and moves to third base. He is an above-average runner who could slow down as he matures.
THE FUTURE: Cruz could develop into a power-over-hit major league infielder, possibly at shortstop, but his development will take time. He should open 2026 at Low-A Fredericksburg, where he will vie for playing time with fellow shortstops Eli Willits and Angel Feliz.

Year	Age	Club (League)	Level	AVG	G	AB	R	H	2B	3B	HR	RBI	BB	SO	SB	OBP	SLG
2025	18	ACL Cubs	Rk	.270	48	174	20	47	10	6	2	21	10	35	10	.314	.431
		Minor League Totals		.270	48	174	20	47	10	6	2	21	10	35	10	.314	.431

22 CHRISTIAN FRANKLIN, OF

HIT: 50. **POW:** 40. **RUN:** 50. **FLD:** 55. **ARM:** 55. **BA Grade:** 40. **Risk:** Average. **Adj:** 30.

Born: November 30, 1999. **B-T:** R-R. **HT:** 5-9. **WT:** 200. **Drafted:** Arkansas, 2021 (4th round). **Signed by:** Ty Nichols (Cubs).
TRACK RECORD: The Cubs drafted Franklin in the fourth round in 2021 after three years at Arkansas. A torn patellar tendon in his left knee the following spring wiped out his season, but he returned in 2023 to play primarily at High-A and then rose to Double-A in 2024. Franklin was playing at Triple-A Iowa in 2025 when the Cubs traded him to the Nationals as part of the package for Michael Soroka. Washington added Franklin to the 40-man roster in November to shield him from the Rule 5 draft.
SCOUTING REPORT: Franklin is an undersized, righthanded-hitting outfielder with good instincts for the game, on-base skills and a likely future as a fourth outfielder. He hits the ball hard with a balanced swing that helps him make steady line-drive contact. He is a contact-oriented hitter who makes pitchers come to him with strong plate discipline and high walk rates. He owns a career .393 OBP in the minors. Franklin would be capable of hitting 10-plus home runs with a full season of play. He is an above-average defender at all three outfield spots with an above-average arm. He is an average runner who can steal the occasional base.
THE FUTURE: Franklin will be 26 years old in 2026 and will be ready for his first taste of the big leagues. He could fill a role similar to the one Alex Call occupied in 2025 as a righthanded-hitting, on-base-oriented extra outfielder.

Year	Age	Club (League)	Level	AVG	G	AB	R	H	2B	3B	HR	RBI	BB	SO	SB	OBP	SLG
2025	25	Iowa (IL)	AAA	.265	86	321	61	85	20	4	8	41	63	80	11	.393	.427
2025	25	Rochester (IL)	AAA	.290	31	124	16	36	3	1	4	23	17	30	8	.382	.427
		Minor League Totals		.264	338	1179	224	311	56	11	30	166	225	319	71	.393	.406

23 SEAN PAUL LIÑAN, RHP

FB: 45. **SL:** 45. **CH:** 70. **CTL:** 45. **BA Grade:** 40. **Risk:** Average. **Adj:** 30.

Born: November 7, 2004. **B-T:** R-R. **HT:** 6-0. **WT:** 185. **Signed:** Colombia, 2022. **Signed by:** Carlos Gonzalez (Dodgers).
TRACK RECORD: Liñan signed with the Dodgers out of Colombia in 2022. He pitched at Rookie ball for two seasons before reaching Low-A in June 2024. He opened back in the California League in 2025 but earned a quick promotion after striking out 44% of batters. Liñan continued pitching effectively at High-A when Los Angeles traded him along with Eriq Swan to the Nationals in the Alex Call deal at the deadline.
SCOUTING REPORT: Liñan is a shorter, stockier righthander with a mediocre fastball but an absolutely deadly offspeed pitch. He throws a high-spin changeup in the low 80s that behaves like a screwball and has been likened to Devin Williams' famous "airbender." It is thrown with an average of more than 2,600 rpm. Class A hitters whiffed at Liñan's changeup on two-thirds of their swings, and it's a highly effective two-strike chase pitch. He takes a long stride and gets great extension while delivering from a three-quarters arm slot, helping his low-90s fastball and mid-80s slider/cutter approach average. He is a fringy strike-thrower and doesn't have a great option to his glove side.
THE FUTURE: Liñan's physique and changeup-driven profile point to a future in the bullpen, where he can air out his fastball and lean more heavily on his change-of-pace.

Year	Age	Club (League)	Level	W	L	ERA	G	GS	IP	H	HR	BB	SO	BB%	SO%	WHIP	AVG
2025	20	Rancho Cucamonga (CAL)	A	2	1	1.21	6	5	30	15	1	10	50	8.8	44.2	0.84	.147
2025	20	Great Lakes (MWL)	A+	1	1	2.65	10	7	37	27	3	14	39	9.0	25.0	1.10	.194
2025	20	Wilmington (SAL)	A+	0	1	9.00	1	1	3	4	0	2	5	14.3	35.7	2.00	.333
2025	20	Oklahoma City (PCL)	AAA	0	1	9.82	2	2	7	8	1	7	12	18.4	31.6	2.05	.286
		Minor League Totals		16	9	3.62	65	26	209	173	15	81	269	9.2	30.5	1.22	.222

24 YOEL TEJEDA, RHP

FB: 60. **SL:** 55. **CH:** 45. **CTL:** 50. **BA Grade:** 45. **Risk:** High. **Adj:** 30.

Born: July 8, 2003. **B-T:** B-R. **HT:** 6-8. **WT:** 217. **Drafted:** Florida State, 2024 (14th round). **Signed by:** Alex Morales.
TRACK RECORD: Tejeda is a South Florida prep who spent one season at Florida and one at Florida State, often working as a reliever, before the Nationals drafted him in the 14th round in 2024. Given his lighter college workload, Tejeda opened his first pro season in 2025 at Low-A Fredericksburg. He struck out 74 in 78.2 innings with a 3.43 ERA over 16 starts. He advanced to High-A Wilmington at the end of July, but his season ended with what the Nationals describe as a minor injury after two starts.
SCOUTING REPORT: Tejeda is an extra-tall, wiry righthander who uses his 6-foot-8 height to his full advantage by getting down the mound with elite extension of more than 7 feet on all his pitch types. He is primarily a fastball/slider pitcher with a three-quarters arm slot and east-west attack that presents a tough look for righthanded batters. Tejeda pitches around 93 mph and topped out at 97 in 2025, with plus tailing action on his four-seamer and sinker. He throws a firm mid-80s slider with good depth and a low-80s sweeper version that features a foot of break. His mid-80s changeup can be an effective weapon versus lefties with its lower spin and fading action. Tejeda is a good strike-thrower despite his long levers.
THE FUTURE: If Tejeda's stuff plays against lefthanded hitters and he can weather a full-season workload, he has the type of profile that could eventually fit as a No. 4 starter.

Year	Age	Club (League)	Level	W	L	ERA	G	GS	IP	H	HR	BB	SO	BB%	SO%	WHIP	AVG
2025	21	Fredericksburg (CAR)	A	4	3	3.43	16	16	79	71	4	21	74	6.5	22.9	1.17	.243
2025	21	Wilmington (SAL)	A+	0	2	9.72	2	2	8	9	2	6	5	15.0	12.5	1.80	.273
		Minor League Totals		4	5	4.03	18	18	87	80	6	27	79	7.4	21.8	1.23	.246

25 RILEY CORNELIO, RHP

FB: 55. **SL:** 55. **CH:** 45. **CTL:** 45. **BA Grade:** 40. **Risk:** Average. **Adj:** 30.

Born: June 6, 2000. **B-T:** R-R. **HT:** 6-3. **WT:** 220. **Drafted:** Texas Christian, 2022 (7th round). **Signed by:** Cody Staab.
TRACK RECORD: Cornelio played high school ball in Colorado before spending three years at Texas Christian. His lone full year in the rotation was 2022, when he led the Horned Frogs in strikeouts. The Nationals drafted Cornelio in the seventh round in 2022, and he plodded through the Class A levels in 2023 and 2024 with high walk rates and bloated ERAs. He reversed course in 2025, finishing second in the system with both 135 strikeouts and 134.1 innings, mostly at Double-A Harrisburg. He reached Triple-A, won the organization's pitcher of the year award and was added to the 40-man roster in November.
SCOUTING REPORT: Cornelio threw nearly 3 mph harder in 2025 than he had the year before, helping to key his breakthrough to the upper levels. He pitched at 94 mph in 2025 and topped out at 98, the result of tweaking his delivery and getting more of his body into his delivery. His four-seamer features riding and running action. Cornelio tightened his mid-80s slider and threw more strikes with it. It's his go-to secondary pitch with cutter action that hitters don't see well. His mid-80s changeup flashes average and helps him compete versus lefthanded hitters. Cornelio is an extreme flyball pitcher with fringy control, and advanced hitters will make him pay when he misses spots.
THE FUTURE: Cornelio could be a late-bloomer with future swingman or bullpen value, perhaps along the lines of what Brad Lord contributed as a rookie in 2025.

Year	Age	Club (League)	Level	W	L	ERA	G	GS	IP	H	HR	BB	SO	BB%	SO%	WHIP	AVG
2025	25	Wilmington (SAL)	A+	1	2	3.03	7	7	33	25	2	16	39	11.6	28.3	1.26	.208
2025	25	Harrisburg (EL)	AA	4	2	2.31	12	11	66	39	3	26	58	10.1	22.6	0.98	.172
2025	25	Rochester (IL)	AAA	1	3	5.35	8	8	35	35	6	13	38	8.7	25.5	1.36	.259
		Minor League Totals		10	15	3.85	49	48	227	207	15	104	221	10.6	22.6	1.37	.240

26 ANDREW ALVAREZ, LHP

FB: 45. **CB:** 50. **SL:** 50. **CH:** 50. **CTL:** 50. **BA Grade:** 40. **Risk:** Average. **Adj:** 30.

Born: June 13, 1999. **B-T:** L-L. **HT:** 6-3. **WT:** 227. **Drafted:** Cal Poly, 2021 (12th round). **Signed by:** Bryan Byrne.
TRACK RECORD: Alvarez pitched for four seasons at Cal Poly before the Nationals drafted him in the 12th round in 2021. He got rocked for a 5.00 ERA in 85 innings in 2022 but rebounded with the organization's pitcher of the year award in 2023. Alvarez's 2024 season was another up-and-down affair, as was his 2025 campaign at Triple-A Rochester, until something seemed to click in the second half. He logged a 3.47 ERA with 59 strikeouts in 57 innings in his final 11 starts to earn a Sept. 1 callup to Washington.
SCOUTING REPORT: Alvarez pitched effectively in four of his five MLB starts as part of the Nationals' homegrown September rotation. Jake Irvin, Mitchell Parker, Brad Lord and Cade Cavalli were the other starters. For Alvarez, it's all about changing speeds, moving the ball around and generating soft,

groundball contact. He pitches at 91-92 mph and does a good job mixing his four-seam fastball with his curveball, slider, sinker and changeup. Righthanded hitters see a lot of breaking stuff from Alvarez. His slider was particularly effective in a small MLB sample, generating an .091 average in at-bats ending with the pitch. He will need to throw strike one more consistently.

THE FUTURE: Without overpowering stuff, Alvarez walks a fine line between success and failure. But he's 27 years old and already has a taste of MLB success, making him a low-risk, moderate-reward option for the 2026 big league pitching staff.

Year	Age	Club (League)	Level	W	L	ERA	G	GS	IP	H	HR	BB	SO	BB%	SO%	WHIP	AVG
2025	26	Rochester (IL)	AAA	3	7	4.10	25	25	123	114	13	52	114	9.8	21.5	1.35	.246
2025	26	Washington (NL)	MLB	1	1	2.31	5	5	23	16	1	10	20	10.2	20.4	1.11	.184
		Minor League Totals		23	30	3.84	112	82	478	440	39	186	459	9.1	22.5	1.31	.242
		Major League Totals		1	1	2.31	5	5	23	16	1	10	20	10.2	20.4	1.11	.184

27 PHILLIP GLASSER, OF/2B

HIT: 55. **POW:** 30. **RUN:** 50. **FLD:** 45. **ARM:** 40. **BA Grade:** 40. **Risk:** Average. **Adj:** 30.

Born: December 3, 1999. **B-T:** L-R. **HT:** 6-0. **WT:** 196. **Drafted:** Indiana, 2023 (10th round). **Signed by:** James Goodwin.

TRACK RECORD: To say that Glasser's path has been unconventional is an understatement. He played five collegiate seasons, three for Youngstown State and two for Indiana, before the Nationals drafted him in the 10th round in 2023 and signed him for $20,000. He was already 24 years old during his first pro season in 2024, when he made the South Atlantic League all-star team after hitting .305 with a .401 OBP for High-A Wilmington. Glasser followed with an all-star nod in 2025 when he led the Double-A Eastern League with 125 hits for Harrisburg.

SCOUTING REPORT: Glasser is a grinder who plays multiple positions and owns a career .301 average and walks as often as he strikes out. He starts with an unusually low handset before launching into a big leg kick while bringing his hands back. He unleashes a lefthanded swing with a slight uppercut that is more about batted-ball angles than pure power. Glasser will run into a home run occasionally but is more about spraying the ball to all fields and finding gaps. He is tough to beat in the zone and rarely strikes out. He is a roughly average runner but gets out of the box well and steals bases because he reads pitchers well. Glasser played shortstop in college but mostly plays corner outfield in pro ball, while seeing some time at second base. He has played corner infield in the past. He is playable at all positions but nothing special.

THE FUTURE: For what Glasser lacks in traditional scouting tools, he makes up for with determination. If he keeps hitting at Triple-A, the Nationals could give him a look.

Year	Age	Club (League)	Level	AVG	G	AB	R	H	2B	3B	HR	RBI	BB	SO	SB	OBP	SLG
2025	25	Harrisburg (EL)	AA	.293	112	427	63	125	18	3	6	41	52	55	30	.379	.391
2025	25	Rochester (IL)	AAA	.391	12	46	8	18	1	1	1	8	8	7	2	.481	.522
		Minor League Totals		.301	250	927	158	279	45	5	16	107	125	136	60	.393	.412

28 NAURIS DE LA CRUZ, OF

HIT: 40. **POW:** 50. **RUN:** 50. **FLD:** 50. **ARM:** 50. **BA Grade:** 50. **Risk:** Extreme. **Adj:** 30.

Born: September 4, 2007. **B-T:** L-L. **HT:** 6-0. **WT:** 160. **Signed:** Dominican Republic, 2025. **Signed by:** Virgilio De Leon.

TRACK RECORD: De La Cruz was part of the Nationals' promising, first-year group in the Dominican Summer League that also included shortstops Marconi German and Brayan Cortesia and catcher Daniel Hernandez. De La Cruz signed for $500,000 out of the Dominican Republic in April 2025 and had a productive DSL debut, batting .294/.448/.450 with two home runs and 15 stolen bases in 39 games. The center fielder drew 30 walks against 17 strikeouts.

SCOUTING REPORT: De La Cruz is a solidly-built, 6-foot outfielder who bats and throws lefthanded. He has a notably mature hitting approach for a 17-year-old, with low rates of chase (18%) and zone whiff (12%). Part of this is simply passivity, as evident by a 38% swing rate that is one of the lowest in the system. De La Cruz has twitchy bat speed and can pull fastballs for power. He could grow into 20-homer power as his body matures and he hits the ball harder. He is an average defensive outfielder who saw most of his time in center in the DSL but could be more of a corner player because of average speed. He stole 15 bases to rank fifth on a DSL Nationals team that liked to run.

THE FUTURE: If De La Cruz develops game power to match his patience, he could emerge as a potential big league corner outfielder or possible center fielder if he retains his speed and athleticism.

Year	Age	Club (League)	Level	AVG	G	AB	R	H	2B	3B	HR	RBI	BB	SO	SB	OBP	SLG
2025	17	DSL Nationals	Rk	.294	39	109	18	32	9	1	2	20	30	17	15	.448	.450
		Minor League Totals		.294	39	109	18	32	9	1	2	20	30	17	15	.448	.450

WASHINGTON NATIONALS

BRAYAN CORTESIA, SS
HIT: 50. **POW:** 40. **RUN:** 55. **FLD:** 50. **ARM:** 50. **BA Grade:** 50. **Risk:** Extreme. **Adj:** 30.

Born: November 14, 2007. **B-T:** R-R. **HT:** 6-2. **WT:** 165. **Signed:** Venezuela, 2025. **Signed by:** Juan Indriago.

TRACK RECORD: The Nationals made Cortesia the headliner of their 2025 international signing class, signing the Venezuelan shortstop for $1.92 million in January. He had a solid pro debut in the Dominican Summer League, batting .317/.440/.358 with 22 stolen bases but just four extra-base hits in 39 games. He drew 25 walks against 25 strikeouts.

SCOUTING REPORT: Cortesia is a well-rounded shortstop who looks to put the ball in play and could grow into power. He has grown several inches in recent years, and the Nationals now list him at 6-foot-2. Cortesia defends the zone with a short, simple, righthanded swing and can put different pitch types into play to all fields. He will take his walks if pitchers don't challenge him. Cortesia has a hit-over-power profile and will require further strength and exit velocity gains to access his fringe power. Cortesia's above-average arm and clean footwork keep him alive at shortstop, and he played second base occasionally in the DSL as well. He is an above-average runner capable of stealing bases, though he was caught 13 times in 35 tries in the DSL.

THE FUTURE: Cortesia projects to do a little of everything—with power production to be determined—but risks falling more on the extra rather than regular side, unless one of his tools emerges as plus.

Year	Age	Club (League)	Level	AVG	G	AB	R	H	2B	3B	HR	RBI	BB	SO	SB	OBP	SLG
2025	17	DSL Nationals	Rk	.317	39	120	26	38	3	1	0	12	25	25	22	.440	.358
		Minor League Totals		.317	39	120	26	38	3	1	0	12	25	25	22	.440	.358

GRIFF McGARRY, RHP
FB: 60. **CB:** 40. **SL:** 60. **SW:** 60. **CTL:** 30. **BA Grade:** 40. **Risk:** Average. **Adj:** 30.

Born: June 8, 1999. **B-T:** R-R. **HT:** 6-2. **WT:** 190. **Drafted:** Virginia, 2021 (5th round). **Signed by:** Kellan McKeon (Phillies).

TRACK RECORD: The Phillies drafted McGarry after four years at Virginia, taking him in the fifth round in 2021. In five pro seasons, he has paired epic strikeout rates with out-of-control walk rates. After McGarry ran up a 6.00 ERA as a starter in 2023, Philadelphia shifted him to the bullpen at Triple-A in 2024. His walk rate ballooned to nearly 25% as he wrestled with the ABS challenge system. Demoted to Double-A and returned to the rotation in 2025, McGarry had his best season with a 3.44 ERA to go with 124 strikeouts in 83.2 innings and a 14% walk rate. The Nationals chose McGarry with the third pick in the Rule 5 draft in December.

SCOUTING REPORT: Stuff models love McGarry. His fastball, sweeper, slider and curveball all grade as above-average to plus pitches, per Stuff+. He sits 94-95 mph and touches 98 on his four-seam fastball with nearly seven feet of extension and a flat vertical approach angle. His sweeper is a one-of-one outlier that sits 83-84 mph with an average of 16-17 inches of horizontal break to generate a 61% strike rate and whiffs and chases aplenty. McGarry's control remains well below-average, but it might be good enough to work in one-inning bursts because he doesn't allow many hits or home runs. In his final start of 2025, he exorcised his Triple-A demons with eight strikeouts and two walks over five one-hit innings.

THE FUTURE: McGarry said that an improved routine he instituted after the 2024 season helped him get on track. Now as a Rule 5 pick, if he pitches well in spring training, he has a good chance to make the Opening Day roster for the rebuilding Nationals.

Year	Age	Club (League)	Level	W	L	ERA	G	GS	IP	H	HR	BB	SO	BB%	SO%	WHIP	AVG
2025	26	Clearwater (FSL)	A	0	1	6.75	3	3	7	8	0	2	13	6.7	43.3	1.50	.308
2025	26	Reading (EL)	AA	1	4	3.25	17	17	72	44	4	45	103	14.8	33.9	1.24	.175
2025	26	Lehigh Valley (IL)	AAA	1	0	1.80	1	1	5	1	1	2	8	10.5	42.1	0.60	.063
		Minor League Totals		10	17	4.14	103	61	287	182	22	202	420	16.3	34.0	1.34	.182

FOREIGN PROFESSIONALS

Beginning with the 2017 Collective Bargaining Agreement, international players who seek to sign with MLB organizations were sorted into two groups: amateurs subject to the bonus pool system or "foreign professionals," who are essentially major league free agents.

The latter group is defined by MLB as players who are at least 25 years of age and have played as a professional in a foreign league—typically in Japan, Korea or Cuba—for a minimum of six seasons.

Beginning in 2024, Baseball America stopped evaluating foreign professionals as prospects, even though they remain eligible for Rookie of the Year awards. Because we still cover these players as rookies, we continue to provide readers with the most accurate scouting reports. What we won't do is rank foreign professionals in organizational Top 30 Prospects rankings or among the Top 100 Prospects.

Geoff Pontes reported and wrote about the top foreign professionals eligible to come to MLB in 2025. ∎

TATSUYA IMAI, RHP

FB: 55. **CB:** 40. **SL:** 60. **CH:** 55. **CTL:** 50. **BA Grade:** 60. **Risk:** Low. **Adjusted:** 60.
Born: May 9, 1998. **B-T:** R-R. **HT:** 5-11. **WT:** 154.

TRACK RECORD: After winning the 2016 Summer Koshien high school tournament with Sakushin Gakuin, Imai made the jump directly to Japanese professional baseball. He was drafted by Seibu with their first pick and spent his debut season with their Eastern League affiliate, the equivalent of Japan's minor leagues. Imai broke in with Seibu in 2018 and saw mixed results over his first three seasons. He established himself as one of the top pitchers in NPB in 2021, earning his first all-star nod. Imai was an all-star twice more in 2024 and 2025 and finished in the top 10 among starters in ERA each of his final two seasons in Japan. Imai helped combine for a Lions no-hitter on April 18, 2025, throwing the first eight innings. On Nov. 18, 2025, Seibu posted Imai to MLB teams.

SCOUTING REPORT: Imai is an undersized righthander who is explosive and mobile on the mound. His low three-quarters slot borders on sidearm and creates a unique approach angle to the plate that creates deception and keeps hitters off-balance. Imai throws four pitches, but his primary mix consists of a four-seam fastball, slider and splitter. His four-seamer sits at 95-97 mph and touches 98-99 with a flat plane of approach and heavy armside run. The fastball is particularly effective when located in the upper third and has been adept at generating swings and misses. Imai's slider is his best pitch and his primary swing-and-miss weapon. It has a gyro shape, sits 85-87 mph and touches 88-89 with late downshift that creates unique armside movement. The combination of Imai's low arm slot, above-average velocity and late armside break make his slider a unique offering. The splitter is Imai's third pitch, and it features good vertical separation off his fastball and heavy armside run to work as a swing-and-miss pitch versus lefthanded hitters. Imai threw a curveball around 2% of the time in 2025, and it featured spin rates in the 2,500-2,600 rpm range along with around 8-9 inches of sweep. There's a real possibility a team adds a sweeper to his arsenal. Imai struggled to throw strikes early in his career, but he has seen consistent gains in that department in each of the last four seasons. He now projects for average control.

THE FUTURE: Imai is a ready-made No. 3 starter who should make an impact immediately.

Year	Age	Club (League)	Level	W	L	ERA	G	GS	IP	H	HR	BB	SO	BB%	SO%	WHIP	AVG
2025	27	Seibu (PL)	NPB	10	5	1.92	24	—	164	101	6	45	178	7.0	27.8	0.89	—
Japanese Major League Totals				58	45	3.15	159	—	964	753	75	468	907	11.5	22.3	1.27	—

MUNETAKA MURAKAMI, 3B

HIT: 40. **POW:** 70. **RUN:** 30. **FLD:** 40. **ARM:** 50. **BA Grade:** 55. **Risk:** Mild. **Adjusted:** 50.
Born: February 2, 2000. **B-T:** L-R. **HT:** 6-2. **WT:** 213.

TRACK RECORD: Nicknamed "Murakami-Sama" as a play on the Japanese word for god (Kami-sama), Murakami is one of the most famous players in Japan. A prodigious power hitter, he was a first-round pick by Yakult who signed for 80 million yen in 2017. He became the youngest Opening Day starter in Swallows team history in 2019 at just 19 years old. Murakami won the Central League MVP award in

Tatsuya Imai

FOREIGN PROFESSIONALS

2021 en route to helping Yakult to their first Japan Series championship in 20 years. In 2022, Murakami set the NPB home run record for a Japanese-born player, topping Sadaharu Oh's single-season mark of 55 on the final day of the season. In the three seasons since he set the home run record, Murakami struggled to replicate his 2022 production. He played just 56 games in 2025 due to an oblique injury.

SCOUTING REPORT: Murakami is a true slugger. His overall profile is driven by his top-of-the-scale raw power, which he's shown an ability to get to in games. Murakami's overall hitting identity falls into the "three true outcomes" bucket. He comes with significant swing-and-miss paired with premium on-base skills. Murakami shows below-average contact rates against nearly every pitch type, but he does a majority of his damage against fastballs. His sample size against premium velocity is limited, but with plus bat speed, he should be able to catch up to top-end MLB fastballs once acclimated. Murakami struggles with offspeed and spin, as evidenced by running whiff rates over 40% against splitters, changeups, curveballs and sliders during his final season in NPB. Splitters, in particular, give Murakami fits. Despite some of the worst contact rates in NPB, he has been one of its most noteworthy sluggers historically. He pairs plus-plus exit velocity data with premium launch angles, hitting majestic home runs and fly balls to all parts of the park. Murakami shows enough contact to get to his power while mitigating some of the risk of his natural swing-and-miss with selective swing decisions. The ability to translate his power into 30-plus home runs annually will be paramount to Murakami's success in MLB. Defensively, he's limited to the infield corners and is a below-average defender at third base and first base. He lacks the speed for an outfield corner, making his most likely path to at-bats at a mix of first base, third base and DH.

THE FUTURE: It will likely take some time for Murakami to adjust to MLB pitching, but when he does, he has the ability to provide middle-of-the-order power with on-base skills.

Year	Age	Club	Level	AVG	G	AB	R	H	2B	3B	HR	RBI	BB	SO	SB	OBP	SLG
2025	25	Yakult (CL)	NPB	.273	56	187	34	51	7	0	22	47	32	64	4	.379	.663
Japanese Major League Totals				.270	892	3117	535	843	146	4	246	647	614	977	59	.394	.557

KAZUMA OKAMOTO, 1B/3B

HIT: 50. **POW:** 55. **RUN:** 40. **FLD:** 55. **ARM:** 55. **BA Grade:** 55. **Risk:** Mild. **Adjusted:** 50.
Born: June 30, 1996. **B-T:** R-R. **HT:** 6-0. **WT:** 212.

TRACK RECORD: Known as the "Young General," Okamoto is a six-time NPB all-star who has led the league in home runs three times, with a high of 41. He made Yomiuri's roster in 2018 after three years in the Eastern League, the equivalent of the Japanese minor leagues. Once breaking in, Okamoto established himself quickly, producing seven consecutive seasons of 25 or more home runs leading up to 2025. He was a key part of Japan's 2023 World Baseball Classic team, hitting .333/.556/.722 over seven games in the tournament. His home run off Kyle Freeland in the fourth inning of the final against the United

FOREIGN PROFESSIONALS

States proved to be the deciding run. Okamoto was limited to 69 games in 2025 after an elbow injury in the first half, but he returned to hit .327/.416/.598 with 15 home runs.

SCOUTING REPORT: One of the most well-rounded players in Japan over the last decade, Okamoto is a highly-skilled player both at the plate and in the field. He combines the ability to hit for power while limiting swing-and-miss with good bat-to-ball skills compared to other sluggers. Okamoto does particular damage against fastballs—he whiffed less than 10% of the time against them in 2025. He has shown strong on-base skills, limiting chase swings and remaining aggressive on pitches inside the zone. His game power is above-average. He combines above-average raw power with the ability to launch the ball to all fields. Okamoto falls into the category of hitters who make consistent hard contact at good angles but with a lack of high-end exit velocity. He will likely settle into the 20-25 home run range with a good supporting batting average and on-base percentage. In the field, he's an above-average defender at third base who has won multiple Gold Gloves. He's a plus-plus defender at first base and offers his signing team defensive versatility.

THE FUTURE: Okamoto should immediately make an impact in MLB thanks to a combination of polished hitting, game power and above-average infield corner defense.

Year	Age	Club	Level	AVG	G	AB	R	H	2B	3B	HR	RBI	BB	SO	SB	OBP	SLG
2025	29	Yomiuri (CL)	NPB	.327	69	251	38	82	21	1	15	49	33	33	1	.416	.598
Japanese Major League Totals				.277	1074	3934	574	1089	212	3	248	717	481	796	13	.361	.521

KONA TAKAHASHI, RHP

FB: 45. **CB:** 40. **SL:** 55. **CT:** 45. **SP:** 55. **CTL:** 55. **BA Grade:** 45. **Risk:** Low. **Adjusted:** 45.

Born: February 3, 1997. **B-T:** R-R. **HT:** 6-2. **WT:** 198.

TRACK RECORD: Takahashi spent parts of four seasons moving between Seibu's Eastern League affiliate and the big league roster. He broke through in 2019 by making 21 starts and going 10-6 with a 4.51 ERA and earning an NPB all-star nod. Takahashi showed improvements over the next two seasons before he broke out in 2022. Across the 2022 and 2023 seasons, he ranked among the NPB leaders in ERA, innings and wins, producing at a level that attracted the interest of MLB teams. Takahashi struggled in 2024, and was demoted to the minors for a stretch. He bounced back slightly in 2025, making 24 starts and going 8-9 with a 3.04 ERA.

SCOUTING REPORT: Takahashi is a control-over-power arm and is unlikely to produce even average strikeout rates in MLB. He mixes five pitches in a four-seam fastball, cutter, slider, curveball and splitter. Takahashi's four-seam fastball sits 92-94 mph with average ride and late run. He generates above-average extension to lower the release height of his high three-quarters arm slot. Takahashi uses his fastball to set up the rest of his arsenal, but it is not a swing-and-miss pitch—it ran a whiff rate of 8% in 2025. His upper-80s splitter is his best-performing pitch, as he shows an ability to continually drive chases against the pitch, leading to some ugly swings. Takahashi's slider is an effective swing-and-miss pitch that sits in the low 80s with sweep. He uses an upper-80s cutter as a bridge pitch between his fastball, splitter and slider. Takahashi will also mix in a curveball in the mid 70s with heavy two-plane break and more depth than his slider. He is an above-average strike-thrower.

THE FUTURE: Takahashi at his best is a strike-throwing innings-eater who mixes five pitch shapes, works efficiently and gets deep into starts. He should be an immediate back-end starter.

Year	Age	Club (League)	Level	W	L	ERA	G	GS	IP	H	HR	BB	SO	BB%	SO%	WHIP	AVG
2025	28	Seibu (PL)	NPB	8	9	3.04	24	—	148	141	10	41	88	6.7	14.3	1.23	—
Japanese Major League Totals				73	77	3.39	196	—	1199	1131	95	423	870	8.3	17.2	1.30	—

FOREIGN PROFESSIONALS

SUNG-MUN SONG, 3B/2B

HIT: 45. **POW:** 45. **RUN:** 55. **FLD:** 50. **ARM:** 55. **BA Grade:** 45. **Risk:** Average. **Adjusted:** 35.
Born: August 29, 1996. **B-T:** L-R. **HT:** 6-0. **WT:** 194.

TRACK RECORD: Song spent parts of seven seasons in the Korea Baseball Organization, only seeing full-time reps with Kiwoom once prior to 2024. As a 27-year-old in that 2024 season, he broke out in a big way, playing in 142 games and hitting .340/.409/.518 with 19 home runs and 21 stolen bases, all career highs. In 2025, Song proved his breakout was no fluke. He hit .315/.387/.530 with 26 homers and 25 steals. Following the season, Kiwoom posted Song for MLB teams. The Padres signed Song to a four-year contract worth $15 million on Dec. 19.

SCOUTING REPORT: A muscular and athletic lefthanded hitter with a steep bat path, Song experienced a power breakout over the last two seasons in Korea and has shown impact hitting ability in KBO. His setup at the plate draws from traditional Japanese hitting traits with a high, drifty leg kick and a lower hand set. Song shows good feel for the strike zone and at least average bat-to-ball skills. While his power began to play in Korea over the last few seasons, he likely will top out at 15-18 home runs in MLB. An above-average runner, Song is a potential basestealing threat who could swipe 20-plus bases annually. A natural third baseman with solid actions and an above-average arm, Song has experience at second base and first base, both positions he may play regularly in MLB.

THE FUTURE: Song is a plug-and-play, lefthanded-hitting utility infielder with second-division regular upside.

Year	Age	Club	Level	AVG	G	AB	R	H	2B	3B	HR	RBI	BB	SO	SB	OBP	SLG
2025	28	Kiwoom	KBO	.315	144	574	103	181	37	4	26	90	68	96	25	.387	.530
Korean Major League Totals				.283	824	2889	410	818	144	22	80	454	294	444	51	.347	.431

2025 RULE 5 DRAFT

The Rule 5 draft occurred on Dec. 10, 2025. Ten players selected rank in their new organizations' Top 30 Prospects, but since all 13 will be in big league spring training camp, we provide thumbnail reports for the three others.

Pick	New Team	Player	Pos	2025 Org	BA Grade/Risk	Page
1.	Rockies	RJ Petit	RHP	Tigers	35/Mild	175
2.	White Sox	Jedixson Paez	RHP	Red Sox	45/High	124
3.	Nationals	Griff McGarry	RHP	Phillies	40/Average	497
4.	Giants	Daniel Susac	C	Athletics	45/Average	412
5.	Rangers	Carter Baumler	RHP	Orioles	40/Mild	460
6.	Red Sox	Ryan Watson	RHP	Giants	40/Average	Not ranked

Watson signed out of Auburn following the five-round 2020 draft. The 28-year-old made 46 appearances for the Giants' Triple-A affiliate in 2025 and pitched to a 4.26 ERA with 64 strikeouts in 50.2 innings. He has a deep pitch mix consisting of a low-90s sinker, an upper-80s cutter, a mid-80s changeup and a low-80s sweeper. He walked just 7% of batters in 2025.

7.	Cardinals	Matt Pushard	RHP	Marlins	40/Average	384
8.	Astros	Roddery Muñoz	RHP	Reds	Not rookie eligible	Not ranked

The 26-year-old Muñoz pitched in the majors in each of the past two seasons, logging a 6.73 ERA in 93.2 innings as a swingman. He mixes five pitches in an upper-80s slider, low-90s cutter, mid-90s sinker, a four-seamer and an occasional changeup. His sinker and slider both grade as above-average. His twin brother Rolddy pitches for the Braves.

9.	Guardians	Peyton Pallette	RHP	White Sox	40/Average	Not ranked

Once upon a time, Pallette was a touted college arm at Arkansas whom the White Sox drafted in the second round in 2022 after he had Tommy John surgery. Moved to the bullpen in 2025, he made 52 appearances and pitched to a 4.06 ERA with 86 strikeouts in 64.1 innings. He mixes a mid-90s four-seam fastball that misses bats with a high-spin, two-plane curveball, a mid-80s slurvy slider and a mid-80s changeup with good vertical separation. The 25-year-old is a plug-and-play reliever.

10.	Blue Jays	Spencer Miles	RHP	Giants	45/High	478
11.	Yankees	Cade Winquest	RHP	Cardinals	40/Mild	332
12.	Phillies	Zach McCambley	RHP	Marlins	40/Average	349
13.	White Sox	Alexander Alberto	RHP	Rays	45/High	125

The White Sox selected two pitchers in the Rule 5 draft: Jedixson Paez (left) and Alexander Alberto.

TOP 50 GRADUATED PROSPECTS

Each fall, Baseball America develops its Top 30 Prospects rankings for the Prospect Handbook.

Recently, we have added a new wrinkle. Now, we evaluate and rank the top overall graduated prospects from last year's Prospect Handbook. The goal is to give prospects-turned-big leaguers their due before we say farewell and turn our attention to the next wave of talent working its way through the minor leagues.

Each graduated prospect is listed here with his updated BA Grade based on what happened in 2025. A Risk assessment deducts points—15 for High, 10 for Average and five for Mild—to determine each prospect's adjusted grade on the 20-80 scale. Players are sorted into tiers and ranked according to their adjusted grade.

Each player's listed age is his baseball age in 2026.

Rk	Name	Pos	Team	Age	BA Grade	Risk	Adjusted	Upside Role
1.	Nick Kurtz	1B	Athletics	23	70	Mild	65	Perennial all-star 1B
2.	Roman Anthony	OF	Red Sox	22	70	Average	60	Perennial all-star RF
3.	Drake Baldwin	C	Braves	25	60	Mild	55	Occasional all-star C
4.	Cade Horton	RHP	Cubs	24	65	Average	55	No. 2 or 3 starter
5.	Chase Burns	RHP	Reds	23	70	High	55	No. 2 starter
6.	Jacob Misiorowski	RHP	Brewers	24	70	High	55	No. 2 starter
7.	Jacob Wilson	SS	Athletics	24	55	Mild	50	Above-average SS
8.	Cam Schlittler	RHP	Yankees	25	60	Average	50	No. 3 starter
9.	Jackson Jobe	RHP	Tigers	23	65	High	50	No. 2 or 3 starter
10.	Cam Smith	OF	Astros	23	55	Average	45	Above-average RF
11.	Colson Montgomery	SS	White Sox	24	55	Average	45	Above-average SS
12.	Matt Shaw	3B	Cubs	24	55	Average	45	Above-average 3B
13.	Marcelo Mayer	SS	Red Sox	23	55	Average	45	Above-average SS or 3B
14.	Roki Sasaki	RHP	Dodgers	24	60	High	45	No. 3 starter or all-star closer
15.	Dylan Crews	OF	Nationals	24	55	Average	45	Above-average CF
16.	Jac Caglianone	1B	Royals	23	60	High	45	Occasional all-star 1B
17.	Luke Keaschall	2B	Twins	23	55	Average	45	Above-average 2B
18.	Kyle Teel	C	White Sox	24	55	Average	45	Above-average C
19.	Chase Dollander	RHP	Rockies	24	60	High	45	No. 3 starter
20.	Dalton Rushing	C	Dodgers	25	55	Average	45	Above-average C
21.	Jakob Marsee	OF	Marlins	25	50	Mild	45	Solid-average CF
22.	Luis Morales	RHP	Athletics	23	60	High	45	No. 3 starter
23.	Carlos Narvaez	C	Red Sox	27	50	Mild	45	Solid-average C
24.	Chad Patrick	RHP	Brewers	27	50	Mild	45	No. 4 starter
25.	Jordan Lawlar	3B	D-backs	23	55	Average	45	Above-average 3B or OF
26.	Kristian Campbell	2B/OF	Red Sox	24	55	High	40	Above-average OF
27.	Jasson Dominguez	OF	Yankees	23	50	Average	40	Solid-average LF
28.	Daylen Lile	OF	Nationals	23	50	Average	40	Solid-average RF
29.	Jack Leiter	RHP	Rangers	26	55	High	40	No. 3 or 4 starter
30.	Hurston Waldrep	RHP	Braves	24	50	Average	40	No. 4 starter
31.	Caleb Durbin	3B	Brewers	26	50	Average	40	Solid-average 3B
32.	Braxton Ashcraft	RHP	Pirates	26	50	Average	40	No. 4 starter
33.	Cade Cavalli	RHP	Nationals	27	55	High	40	No. 3 or 4 starter
34.	Will Warren	RHP	Yankees	27	50	Average	40	No. 4 starter
35.	Coby Mayo	1B	Orioles	24	55	High	40	Above-average 1B
36.	Grant Taylor	RHP	White Sox	24	55	High	40	No. 3 or 4 starter or closer
37.	Brady House	3B	Nationals	23	55	High	40	Above-average 3B
38.	Agustin Ramirez	C	Marlins	24	50	Average	40	Solid-average 1B or DH
39.	CJ Kayfus	1B/OF	Guardians	24	50	Average	40	Solid-average 1B
40.	Kyle Karros	3B	Rockies	23	50	Average	40	Solid-average 3B
41.	Mick Abel	RHP	Twins	24	50	Average	40	No. 4 starter
42.	Cole Young	2B	Mariners	22	50	Average	40	Solid-average 2B
43.	Chandler Simpson	OF	Rays	25	50	Average	40	Solid-average LF
44.	Kumar Rocker	RHP	Rangers	26	55	High	40	No. 3 or 4 starter or closer
45.	Shane Smith	RHP	White Sox	26	55	High	40	No. 3 or 4 starter
46.	Denzel Clarke	OF	Athletics	26	50	Average	40	Solid-average CF
47.	Noah Cameron	LHP	Royals	26	50	Average	40	No. 4 starter
48.	Isaac Collins	OF	Royals	28	45	Mild	40	Platoon or extra OF
49.	Chase Meidroth	2B/SS	White Sox	24	45	Mild	40	Second-division 2B or UT
50.	Ronny Mauricio	3B	Mets	25	55	High	40	Above-average 3B

SIGNING BONUSES

2025 DRAFT — TOP THREE ROUNDS

FIRST ROUND

No.	Team: Player, Pos	Bonus
1.	Nationals: Eli Willits, SS	$8,200,000
2.	Angels: Tyler Bremner, RHP	$7,689,525
3.	Mariners: Kade Anderson, LHP	$8,800,000
4.	Rockies: Ethan Holliday, SS	$9,000,000
5.	Cardinals: Liam Doyle, LHP	$7,250,000
6.	Pirates: Seth Hernandez, RHP	$7,250,000
7.	Marlins: Aiva Arquette, SS	$7,149,900
8.	Blue Jays: JoJo Parker, SS	$6,197,500
9.	Reds: Steele Hall, SS	$5,747,500
10.	White Sox: Billy Carlson, SS	$6,235,900
11.	Athletics: Jamie Arnold, LHP	$5,985,100
12.	Rangers: Gavin Fien, SS	$4,800,000
13.	Giants: Gavin Kilen, SS	$5,247,500
14.	Rays: Daniel Pierce, SS	$4,310,600
15.	Red Sox: Kyson Witherspoon, RHP	$5,000,000
16.	Twins: Marek Houston, SS	$4,497,500
17.	Cubs: Ethan Conrad, OF	$3,563,100
18.	D-backs: Kayson Cunningham, SS	$4,581,900
19.	Orioles: Ike Irish, C	$4,418,400
20.	Brewers: Andrew Fischer, 3B	$3,500,000
21.	Astros: Xavier Neyens, SS	$4,120,000
22.	Braves: Tate Southisene, SS	$2,622,500
23.	Royals: Sean Gamble, OF	$3,997,500
24.	Tigers: Jordan Yost, SS	$3,247,500
25.	Padres: Kruz Schoolcraft, LHP	$3,606,600
26.	Phillies: Gage Wood, RHP	$3,000,000
27.	Guardians: Jace LaViolette, OF	$4,000,000

SUPPLEMENTAL FIRST ROUND

No.	Team: Player, Pos.	Bonus
28.	Royals (PPI): Josh Hammond, SS	$3,197,500
29.	D-backs (1C): Patrick Forbes, RHP	$3,000,000
30.	Orioles (1C): Caden Bodine, C	$3,110,800
31.	Orioles (1C): Wehiwa Aloy, SS	$3,040,300
32.	Brewers (1C): Brady Ebel, SS	$2,750,000
33.	Red Sox (CBA): Marcus Phillips, RHP	$2,500,000
34.	Tigers (CBA): Michael Oliveto, C	$2,447,500
35.	Mariners (CBA): Luke Stevenson, C	$2,800,000
36.	Twins (CBA): Riley Quick, RHP	$2,692,000
37.	Orioles (CBA): Slater de Brun, OF	$4,000,000
38.	Mets (CBA): Mitch Voit, 2B/RHP	$1,750,000
39.	Yankees: Dax Kilby, SS	$2,797,500
40.	Dodgers: Zach Root, LHP	$2,197,500
41.	Dodgers (CBA): Charles Davalan, OF	$1,997,500
42.	Rays (CBA): Brendan Summerhill, OF	$1,997,500
43.	Marlins (CBA): Cam Cannarella, OF	$2,277,425

SECOND ROUND

No.	Team: Player, Pos.	Bonus
44.	White Sox: Jaden Fauske, OF	$2,997,500
45.	Rockies: J.B. Middleton, RHP	$2,071,900
46.	Marlins: Brandon Compton, OF	$2,000,000
47.	Angels: Chase Shores, RHP	$2,077,200
48.	Athletics: Devin Taylor, OF	$2,500,000
49.	Nationals: Ethan Petry, OF	$2,090,000
50.	Pirates: Angel Cervantes, RHP	Did not sign
51.	Reds: Aaron Watson, RHP	$2,747,500
52.	Rangers: A.J. Russell, RHP	$2,600,000
53.	Rays: Cooper Flemming, SS	$2,297,500
54.	Twins: Quentin Young, SS	$1,761,600
55.	Cardinals: Ryan Mitchell, OF	$2,250,000
56.	Cubs: Kane Kepley, OF	$1,400,000
57.	Mariners: Nick Becker, SS	$2,750,000
58.	Orioles: Joseph Dzierwa, LHP	$1,497,500
59.	Brewers: JD Thompson, LHP	$1,560,200
60.	Braves: Alex Lodise, SS	$1,297,500
61.	Royals: Michael Lombardi, RHP	$1,297,500
62.	Tigers: Malachi Witherspoon, RHP	$1,448,700
63.	Phillies: Cade Obermueller, LHP	$1,197,500
64.	Guardians: Dean Curley, SS	$1,733,905
65.	Dodgers: Cam Leiter, RHP	$1,346,600

SUPPLEMENTAL SECOND ROUND

No.	Team: Player, Pos.	Bonus
66.	Guardians (CBB): Aaron Walton, OF	$1,100,000
67.	Rays (2C): Dean Moss, OF	$2,097,500
68.	Brewers (2C): Frank Cairone, LHP	$1,097,500
69.	Orioles (CBB): JT Quinn, RHP	$1,147,500
70.	Guardians (CBB): Will Hynes, RHP	$950,000
71.	Royals (CBB): Justin Lamkin, LHP	$1,161,200
72.	Cardinals (CBB): Tanner Franklin, RHP	$1,145,900
73.	Pirates (CBB): Murf Gray, 3B	$997,500
74.	Rockies (CBB): Max Belyeu, OF	$1,111,000
75.	Red Sox (2C): Henry Godbout, SS	$1,093,800

THIRD ROUND

No.	Team: Player, Pos.	Bonus
76.	White Sox: Kyle Lodise, SS	$922,500
77.	Rockies: Ethan Hedges, 3B	$950,000
78.	Marlins: Max Williams, OF	$897,500
79.	Angels: Johnny Slawinski, LHP	$2,497,500
80.	Nationals: Landon Harmon, RHP	$2,500,000
81.	Blue Jays: Jake Cook, OF	$922,500
82.	Pirates: Easton Carmichael, C	$977,000
83.	Reds: Mason Morris, RHP	$897,500
84.	Rangers: Josh Owens, SS/RHP	$1,100,000
85.	Giants: Trevor Cohen, OF	$847,500
86.	Rays: Taitn Gray, C	$918,300
87.	Red Sox: Anthony Eyanson, RHP	$1,750,000
88.	Twins: James Ellwanger, RHP	$1,000,000
89.	Cardinals: Jack Gurevitch, 1B	$879,000
90.	Cubs: Dominick Reid, RHP	$649,125
91.	Mariners: Griffin Hugus, RHP	$640,000
92.	D-backs: Brian Curley, RHP	$700,000
93.	Orioles: RJ Austin, OF	$823,900
94.	Brewers: Jacob Morrison, RHP	$697,500
95.	Astros: Ethan Frey, OF	$997,500
96.	Braves: Cody Miller, SS	$297,500
97.	Royals: Cameron Millar, RHP	$1,497,500
98.	Tigers: Ben Jacobs, LHP	$722,500
99.	Padres: Ryan Wideman, OF	$650,000
100.	Phillies: Cody Bowker, RHP	$700,000
101.	Guardians: Nolan Schubart, OF	$730,000
102.	Mets: Antonio Jimenez, SS	$564,000
103.	Yankees: Kaeden Kent, SS	$741,900
104.	Dodgers: Landyn Vidourek, OF	$552,750
105.	Angels (3C): Nate Snead, RHP	$597,500

SIGNING BONUSES

2024 DRAFT — TOP THREE ROUNDS

FIRST ROUND

No.	Team: Player, Pos	Bonus
1.	Guardians: Travis Bazzana, 2B	$8,950,000
2.	Reds: Chase Burns, RHP	$9,250,000
3.	Rockies: Charlie Condon, OF	$9,250,000
4.	Athletics: Nick Kurtz, 1B	$7,000,000
5.	White Sox: Hagen Smith, LHP	$8,000,000
6.	Royals: Jac Caglianone, 1B/LHP	$7,497,500
7.	Cardinals: JJ Wetherholt, SS	$6,900,000
8.	Angels: Christian Moore, 2B	$4,997,500
9.	Pirates: Konnor Griffin, SS	$6,532,025
10.	Nationals: Seaver King, SS	$5,150,000
11.	Tigers: Bryce Rainer, SS	$5,797,500
12.	Red Sox: Braden Montgomery, OF	$5,000,000
13.	Giants: James Tibbs III, OF	$4,747,500
14.	Cubs: Cam Smith, 3B	$5,070,700
15.	Mariners: Jurrangelo Cijntje, SHP	$4,880,900
16.	Marlins: PJ Morlando, OF	$3,400,000
17.	Brewers: Braylon Payne, OF	$3,440,000
18.	Rays: Theo Gillen, OF	$4,370,000
19.	Mets: Carson Benge, OF	$3,997,500
20.	Blue Jays: Trey Yesavage, RHP	$4,175,000
21.	Twins: Kaelen Culpepper, SS	$3,934,400
22.	Orioles: Vance Honeycutt, OF	$4,000,000
23.	Dodgers: Kellon Lindsey, SS	$3,297,500
24.	Braves: Cam Caminiti, LHP	$3,553,800
25.	Padres: Kash Mayfield, LHP	$3,442,100
26.	Yankees: Ben Hess, RHP	$2,747,500
27.	Phillies: Dante Nori, OF	$2,497,500
28.	Astros: Walker Janek, C	$3,130,000
29.	D-backs: Slade Caldwell, OF	$3,087,000
30.	Rangers: Malcolm Moore, C	$3,000,000

SUPPLEMENTAL FIRST ROUND

No.	Team: Player, Pos	Bonus
31.	D-backs (PPI): Ryan Waldschmidt, OF	$2,904,000
32.	Orioles (PPI): Griff O'Ferrall, SS	$2,697,500
33.	Twins (1C): Kyle DeBarge, SS	$2,400,000
34.	Brewers (CBA): Blake Burke, 1B	$2,100,000
35.	D-backs (CBA): JD Dix, SS	$2,150,000
36.	Guardians (CBA): Braylon Doughty, RHP	$2,569,200
37.	Pirates (CBA): Levi Sterling, RHP	$2,508,900
38.	Rockies (CBA): Brody Brecht, RHP	$2,700,000
39.	Nationals (CBA): Caleb Lomavita, C	$2,325,000

SECOND ROUND

No.	Team: Player, Pos	Bonus
40.	Athletics: Tommy White, 3B	$3,000,000
41.	Royals: David Shields, LHP	$2,300,000
42.	Rockies: Jared Thomas, OF	$2,000,000
43.	White Sox: Caleb Bonemer, SS	$2,997,500
44.	Nationals: Luke Dickerson, SS	$3,800,000
45.	Angels: Chris Cortez, RHP	$1,597,500
46.	Mets: Jonathan Santucci, LHP	$2,031,700
47.	Pirates: Wyatt Sanford, SS	$2,497,500
48.	Guardians: Jacob Cozart, C	$2,050,000
49.	Tigers: Owen Hall, RHP	$1,747,500
50.	Red Sox: Payton Tolle, LHP	$2,000,000
51.	Reds: Tyson Lewis, SS	$3,047,500
52.	Padres: Boston Bateman, LHP	$2,500,000
53.	Yankees: Bryce Cunningham, RHP	$2,297,500
54.	Cubs: Cole Mathis, 3B	$1,681,200
55.	Mariners: Ryan Sloan, RHP	$3,000,000
56.	Marlins: Carter Johnson, SS	$2,800,000
57.	Brewers: Bryce Meccage, RHP	$2,500,000
58.	Rays: Emilien Pitre, 2B	$1,522,700
59.	Blue Jays: Khal Stephen, RHP	$1,116,750
60.	Twins: Billy Amick, 3B	$1,453,700
61.	Orioles: Ethan Anderson, C	$1,172,500
62.	Braves: Carter Holton, LHP	$1,347,500
63.	Phillies: Griffin Burkholder, OF	$2,497,500
64.	D-backs: Ivan Luciano, C	$990,000
65.	Rangers: Dylan Dreiling, OF	$1,287,600

SUPPLEMENTAL SECOND ROUND

No.	Team: Player, Pos	Bonus
66.	Rays (CBB): Tyler Bell, SS	Did not sign
67.	Brewers (CBB): Chris Levonas, RHP	Did not sign
68.	White Sox (CBB): Blake Larson, LHP	$1,397,500
69.	Twins (CBB): Dasan Hill, LHP	$1,997,500
70.	Marlins (CBB): Aiden May, RHP	$900,000
71.	Reds (CBB): Luke Holman, RHP	$997,500
72.	Tigers (CBB): Ethan Schiefelbein, LHP	$1,797,500
73.	Athletics (CBB): Gage Jump, LHP	$2,000,000
74.	Angels (2C): Ryan Johnson, RHP	$1,747,500

THIRD ROUND

No.	Team: Player, Pos	Bonus
75.	Athletics: Josh Kuroda-Grauer, SS	$1,043,900
76.	Royals: Drew Beam, RHP	$1,097,500
77.	Rockies: Cole Messina, C	$1,011,900
78.	White Sox: Nick McLain, OF	$800,000
79.	Nationals: Kevin Bazzell, C	$980,300
80.	Cardinals: Brian Holiday, RHP	$800,000
81.	Angels: Ryan Prager, LHP	Did not sign
82.	Mets: Nate Dohm, RHP	$797,500
83.	Pirates: Josh Hartle, LHP	$850,000
84.	Guardians: Joey Oakie, RHP	$2,000,000
85.	Tigers: Josh Randall, RHP	$697,500
86.	Red Sox: Brandon Neely, RHP	$700,000
87.	Reds: Mike Sirota, OF	$863,300
88.	Padres: Cobb Hightower, SS	$852,300
89.	Yankees: Thatcher Hurd, RHP	$836,400
90.	Cubs: Ronny Cruz, SS	$620,000
91.	Mariners: Hunter Cranton, RHP	$50,000
92.	Marlins: Gage Miller, 2B	$800,800
93.	Brewers: Jaron DeBerry, RHP	$25,000
94.	Rays: Nathan Flewelling, C	$774,000
95.	Blue Jays: Johnny King, LHP	$1,247,500
96.	Twins: Khadim Diaw, C	$597,500
97.	Orioles: Austin Overn, OF	$847,500
98.	Dodgers: Chase Harlan, 3B	$1,747,500
99.	Braves: Luke Sinnard, RHP	$735,300
100.	Phillies: John Spikerman, SS	$672,500
101.	Astros: Ryan Forcucci, RHP	$997,500
102.	D-backs: Daniel Eagen, RHP	$650,000
103.	Rangers: Casey Cook, OF	$700,000

SIGNING BONUSES

2023 DRAFT

TOP THREE ROUNDS

FIRST ROUND

No.	Team: Player, Pos	Bonus
1.	Pirates: Paul Skenes, RHP	$9,200,000
2.	Nationals: Dylan Crews, OF	$9,000,000
3.	Tigers: Max Clark, OF	$7,697,500
4.	Rangers: Wyatt Langford, OF	$8,000,000
5.	Twins: Walker Jenkins, OF	$7,144,200
6.	Athletics: Jacob Wilson, SS	$5,500,000
7.	Reds: Rhett Lowder, RHP	$5,700,000
8.	Royals: Blake Mitchell, C	$4,897,500
9.	Rockies: Chase Dollander, RHP	$5,716,900
10.	Marlins: Noble Meyer, RHP	$4,500,000
11.	Angels: Nolan Schanuel, 1B	$5,253,000
12.	D-backs: Tommy Troy, SS	$4,400,000
13.	Cubs: Matt Shaw, SS	$4,848,500
14.	Red Sox: Kyle Teel, C	$4,000,000
15.	White Sox: Jacob Gonzalez, SS	$3,900,000
16.	Giants: Bryce Eldridge, OF/RHP	$3,997,500
17.	Orioles: Enrique Bradfield Jr., OF	$4,169,700
18.	Brewers: Brock Wilken, 3B	$3,150,000
19.	Rays: Brayden Taylor, SS	$3,877,600
20.	Blue Jays: Arjun Nimmala, SS	$3,000,000
21.	Cardinals: Chase Davis, OF	$3,618,200
22.	Mariners: Colt Emerson, SS	$3,800,000
23.	Guardians: Ralphy Velazquez, C	$2,500,000
24.	Braves: Hurston Waldrep, RHP	$2,997,500
25.	Padres: Dillon Head, OF	$2,800,000
26.	Yankees: George Lombard Jr., SS	$3,300,000
27.	Phillies: Aidan Miller, SS	$3,100,000
28.	Astros: Brice Matthews, SS	$2,478,200

SUPPLEMENTAL FIRST ROUND

No.	Team: Player, Pos	Bonus
29.	Mariners (PPI): Jonny Farmelo, OF	$3,200,000
30.	Mariners (CBA): Tai Peete, SS	$2,500,000
31.	Rays (CBA): Adrian Santana, SS	$2,002,950
32.	Mets (CBA): Colin Houck, SS	$2,750,000
33.	Brewers (CBA): Josh Knoth, RHP	$2,000,000
34.	Twins (CBA): Charlee Soto, RHP	$2,481,400
35.	Marlins (CBA): Thomas White, LHP	$4,100,000
36.	Dodgers (CBA): Kendall George, OF	$1,847,500
37.	Tigers (CBA): Kevin McGonigle, SS	$2,847,500
38.	Reds (CBA): Ty Floyd, RHP	$2,097,500
39.	Athletics (CBA): Myles Naylor, 3B	$2,202,500

SECOND ROUND

No.	Team: Player, Pos	Bonus
40.	Nationals: Yohandy Morales, 3B	$2,600,000
41.	Athletics: Ryan Lasko, OF	$1,700,000
42.	Pirates: Mitch Jebb, SS	$1,647,500
43.	Reds: Sammy Stafura, SS	$2,497,500
44.	Royals: Blake Wolters, RHP	$2,800,000
45.	Tigers: Max Anderson, 2B	$1,429,650
46.	Rockies: Sean Sullivan, LHP	$1,700,000
47.	Marlins: Kemp Alderman, OF	$1,400,000
48.	D-backs: Gino Groover, 3B	$1,783,000
49.	Twins: Luke Keaschall, 2B	$1,500,000
50.	Red Sox: Nazzan Zanetello, SS	$3,000,000
51.	White Sox: Grant Taylor, RHP	$1,659,800
52.	Giants: Walker Martin, SS	$2,997,500
53.	Orioles: Mac Horvath, OF	$1,400,000
54.	Brewers: Mike Boeve, 3B	$1,250,000
55.	Rays: Colton Ledbetter, OF	$1,297,500
56.	Mets: Brandon Sproat, RHP	$1,474,500
57.	Mariners: Ben Williamson, 3B	$600,000
58.	Guardians: Alex Clemmey, LHP	$2,300,000
59.	Braves: Drue Hackenberg, RHP	$1,997,500
60.	Dodgers: Jake Gelof, 3B	$1,334,400
61.	Astros: Alonzo Tredwell, RHP	$1,497,500

SUPPLEMENTAL SECOND ROUND

No.	Team: Player, Pos	Bonus
62.	Guardians (CBB): Andrew Walters, RHP	$955,275
63.	Orioles (CBB): Jackson Baumeister, RHP	$1,605,100
64.	D-backs (CBB): Caden Grice, LHP	$1,250,000
65.	Rockies (CBB): Cole Carrigg, C	$1,300,000
66.	Royals (CBB): Carson Roccaforte, OF	$897,500
67.	Pirates (CBB): Zander Mueth, RHP	$1,797,500
68.	Cubs (2C): Jaxon Wiggins, RHP	$1,401,500
69.	Giants (2C): Joe Whitman, LHP	$805,575
70.	Braves (2C): Cade Kuehler, RHP	$1,045,000

THIRD ROUND

No.	Team: Player, Pos	Bonus
71.	Nationals: Travis Sykora, RHP	$2,600,000
72.	Athletics: Steven Echavarria, RHP	$3,000,000
73.	Pirates: Garret Forrester, 3B	$772,500
74.	Reds: Hunter Hollan, LHP	$597,500
75.	Royals: Hiro Wyatt, RHP	$1,497,500
76.	Tigers: Paul Wilson, LHP	$1,697,500
77.	Rockies: Jack Mahoney, RHP	$925,000
78.	Marlins: Brock Vradenburg, 1B	$916,000
79.	Angels: Alberto Rios, 3B	$847,500
80.	D-backs: Jack Hurley, OF	$887,500
81.	Cubs: Josh Rivera, SS	$725,000
82.	Twins: Brandon Winokur, OF	$1,500,000
83.	Red Sox: Antonio Anderson, SS	$1,500,000
84.	White Sox: Seth Keener, RHP	$800,000
85.	Giants: Cole Foster, SS	$747,500
86.	Orioles: Kiefer Lord, RHP	$760,000
87.	Brewers: Eric Bitonti, SS	$1,750,000
88.	Rays: Tre' Morgan, 1B	$781,300
89.	Blue Jays: Juaron Watts-Brown, RHP	$1,002,785
90.	Cardinals: Travis Honeyman, OF	$700,000
91.	Mets: Nolan McLean, RHP/OF	$747,600
92.	Mariners: Teddy McGraw, RHP	$600,000
93.	Guardians: C.J. Kayfus, OF	$700,000
94.	Braves: Sabin Ceballos, SS	$597,500
95.	Dodgers: Brady Smith, RHP	$703,000
96.	Padres: J.D. Gonzalez, C	$550,000
97.	Yankees: Kyle Carr, LHP	$692,500
98.	Phillies: Devin Saltiban, SS	$602,500
99.	Astros: Jake Bloss, RHP	$497,500
100.	Orioles: Tavian Josenberger, OF	$603,000
101.	Mets: Kade Morris, RHP	$666,500

INDEX

A

Abeldt, Ben (Rangers)	464
Abeyta, Blane (Braves)	64
Acosta, Maximo (Marlins)	272
Adamczewski, Josh (Brewers)	280
Adams, Luke (Brewers)	282
Adams, Mason (White Sox)	122
Aguiar, Julian (Reds)	138
Aita, Blake (Red Sox)	96
Alberto, Alexander (White Sox)	125
Alcantara, Kevin (Cubs)	103
Aldegheri, Samuel (Angels)	235
Alderman, Kemp (Marlins)	263
Alfonzo, Omar (Pirates)	362
Aloy, Wehiwa (Orioles)	73
Alvarez, Andrew (Nationals)	495
Alvarez, Carlos (Padres)	400
Alvarez, Hayden (Angels)	237
Alvarez, Kevin (Astros)	199
Anderson, Ethan (Orioles)	80
Anderson, Kade (Mariners)	421
Anderson, Max (Tigers)	183
Andujar, Ashly (Rockies)	173
Anthony, Keaton (Phillies)	351
Antonacci, Sam (White Sox)	120
Aponte, Liberts (Reds)	142
Aracena, Wellington (Orioles)	79
Arana, Luis (Marlins)	267
Araujo, Anderson (Phillies)	350
Areinamo, Jadher (Rays)	442
Arguellas, Cristian (Rockies)	173
Arias, Franklin (Red Sox)	85
Arias, Victor (Blue Jays)	474
Armas, Ariel (Cubs)	113
Arnold, Jamie (Athletics)	37
Arquette, Aiva (Marlins)	261
Arronde, Felix (Royals)	217
Arroyo, Edwin (Reds)	135
Arroyo, Michael (Mariners)	422
Avant, Corey (Athletics)	47
Avila, Luinder (Royals)	216
Avina, Jace (Yankees)	335
Ayers, Owen (Cubs)	108
Azocar, Enddy (Red Sox)	90

B

Baez, Henry (Athletics)	42
Baez, Jesus (Cardinals)	379
Baez, Joshua (Cardinals)	374
Balcazar, Leo (Reds)	139
Ballesteros, Moises (Cubs)	100
Balzer, Bryan (Padres)	399
Barco, Hunter (Pirates)	360
Barnett, Mason (Athletics)	43
Baro, Boston (Mets)	317
Barr, Matt (Twins)	300
Barreto, Yulian (Giants)	417
Barriera, Brandon (Blue Jays)	479
Barrios, Gregory (Rays)	448
Basallo, Samuel (Orioles)	68
Bastardo, Angel (Blue Jays)	475
Bateman, Boston (Orioles)	74
Batista, Aldrin (White Sox)	124
Baumann, Garrett (Braves)	56
Baumeister, Jackson (Rays)	445
Baumler, Carter (Rangers)	460
Bautista, Yorger (Mariners)	426
Bazzana, Travis (Guardians)	148
Beam, Drew (Royals)	216
Beavers, Dylan (Orioles)	69
Becker, Nick (Mariners)	425
Beidelschies, Landon (Braves)	60
Beilenson, Charlie (Mariners)	432
Belyeu, Max (Rockies)	167
Benge, Carson (Mets)	309
Benitez, Keyner (Marlins)	268
Bennett, Jake (Red Sox)	87
Bergolla, William (White Sox)	122
Bernal, Leonardo (Cardinals)	377
Bernard, Derek (Rockies)	176
Birdsell, Brandon (Cubs)	106
Bitonti, Eric (Brewers)	285
Black, Mason (Royals)	222
Black, Tyler (Brewers)	287
Blanco Jr., Tony (Pirates)	369
Bleis, Miguel (Red Sox)	92
Bloss, Jake (Blue Jays)	472
Blubaugh, A.J. (Astros)	199
Bodine, Caden (Orioles)	75
Bohorquez, Adrian (Twins)	299
Boles, Grayson (Royals)	221
Bolte, Henry (Athletics)	39
Bonemer, Caleb (White Sox)	117
Bonzagni, Paul (Rangers)	464
Bostick, Josh (Giants)	413
Boughton, Matthew (White Sox)	129
Bowker, Cody (Phillies)	345
Bradfield Jr., Enrique (Orioles)	72
Bragg, Braxton (Orioles)	73
Brannigan, Jack (Pirates)	368
Bratt, Mitch (D-backs)	28
Braun, Lucas (Braves)	55
Brecht, Brody (Rockies)	166
Bremner, Tyler (Angels)	228
Bresnahan, Jacob (Giants)	406
Briceño, Josue (Tigers)	182
Brito, Anderson (Astros)	197
Brito, Juan (Guardians)	155
Brito, Roldy (Rockies)	166
Brown, McCade (Rockies)	175
Bucknam, Micah (Blue Jays)	476
Bullard, Blaine (Blue Jays)	474
Burke, Blake (Brewers)	283
Burkhalter, Blake (Braves)	58
Burkholder, Griffin (Phillies)	347
Burns, Connor (Reds)	145
Bush, Ky (White Sox)	122
Bush, Will (Astros)	205
Bush Jr., Homer (Rays)	446

C

Caba, Starlyn (Marlins)	265
Cabada, Juan (Cubs)	109
Cabrera, Jean (Phillies)	350
Cabrera, Yeremy (Rangers)	458
Caceres, Juneiker (Guardians)	153
Cairone, Frank (Brewers)	286
Caissie, Owen (Cubs)	101
Calaz, Robert (Rockies)	168
Calcaño, Warren (Royals)	220
Caldwell, Slade (D-backs)	22
Callihan, Tyler (Reds)	140
Caminiti, Cam (Braves)	52
Cannarella, Cam (Marlins)	263
Carey, Owen (Braves)	65
Carlson, Billy (White Sox)	118
Carmichael, Easton (Pirates)	368
Carr, Kyle (Yankees)	331
Carrigg, Cole (Rockies)	167
Casey, Jake (Blue Jays)	477
Castellanos, Santiago (Twins)	300
Castillo, Haritzon (Twins)	303
Castillo, Yolfran (Rangers)	457
Castro, Allan (Red Sox)	96
Castro, Jose (Marlins)	273
Cauley, Cameron (Rangers)	464
Cayama, Argenis (Giants)	409
Cebert, Jack (Yankees)	332
Celesten, Felnin (Mariners)	424
Cepeda, Angel (Cubs)	109
Cespedes, Yoeilin (Red Sox)	93
Chace, Moises (Phillies)	344
Chalas, Yordin (D-backs)	33
Chandler, Bubba (Pirates)	357
Chourio, Jaison (Guardians)	152
Chourio, Kendry (Royals)	213
Church, Nathan (Cardinals)	379
Cijntje, Jurrangelo (Mariners)	423
Clark, Max (Tigers)	181
Clarke, Brandon (Cardinals)	375
Clemmey, Alex (Nationals)	487
Cleveland, Tyler (Mariners)	433
Clifford, Ryan (Mets)	311
Clohisy, Patrick (Braves)	64
Cohen, Harrison (Yankees)	333
Cohen, Trevor (Giants)	408
Cole, Zach (Astros)	202
Coleman, Carson (Yankees)	337
Coleman, Javen (Blue Jays)	480
Colleran Jr., Dennis (Royals)	224
Collier, Cam (Reds)	136
Colon, Edgar (Reds)	144
Compton, Brandon (Marlins)	264
Condon, Charlie (Rockies)	165
Conrad, Ethan (Cubs)	102
Contreras, Freddy (Royals)	224
Cook, Alex (Rays)	447
Cook, Jake (Blue Jays)	473
Copen, Patrick (Dodgers)	253
Coppola, Pierce (Cubs)	112
Cornelio, Riley (Nationals)	495
Corniell, Jose (Rangers)	454
Coronil, Deivid (Padres)	398
Cortesia, Brayan (Nationals)	497
Cortez, Chris (Angels)	234
Cova, Luis (Marlins)	266
Cox, Jackson (Rockies)	168
Cozart, Jacob (Guardians)	154
Craig, Gabe (Phillies)	348
Crawford, Justin (Phillies)	341
Crisantes, Demetrio (D-backs)	21
Crooks, Jimmy (Cardinals)	376
Cross, Gavin (Royals)	220
Crossland, Cade (Cardinals)	380
Crow, Coleman (Brewers)	289
Cruz, Humberto (Padres)	391
Cruz, Ronny (Nationals)	493
Cruz, Trei (Tigers)	188
Culpepper, Kaelen (Twins)	293
Cunningham, Bryce (Yankees)	327
Cunningham, Kayson (D-backs)	21
Curet, Yoniel (Phillies)	352
Curley, Brian (D-backs)	29
Curley, Dean (Guardians)	154
Curtis, Khristian (Pirates)	363

D

Dalis, Wilder (Rockies)	170
Danielson, Joey (Rangers)	465
Davalan, Charles (Dodgers)	247
Davalillo, David (Rangers)	455
Davalillo, Gabriel (Angels)	230
Davidson, Bo (Giants)	405
Davis, Braden (Cardinals)	382
Davis, Chase (Cardinals)	384
Davis, Gabe (White Sox)	128
de Brun, Slater (Orioles)	74
De La Cruz, Jhoan (Padres)	397
De La Cruz, Nauris (Nationals)	496
De La Cruz, Wilfri (Orioles)	78
De La Rosa, Carlos (Giants)	415
De La Torre, Luis (Giants)	412
De Leon, Luis (Orioles)	70
De Los Santos, Angel (Tigers)	190
De Los Santos, Deyvison (Marlins)	273
De Los Santos, Johan (Pirates)	369
De Paula, Josue (Dodgers)	245
De Paula, Yilver (Angels)	239
De Vries, Leo (Athletics)	36
Dean, Nick (Cubs)	113
Debarge, Kyle (Twins)	304
Defrank, Kevin (Marlins)	262
De Grandpre, Cedric (Braves)	61
DeLauter, Chase (Guardians)	149
Delzine, Sadbiel (Red Sox)	95
DeMartini, Carson (Phillies)	346
Diaw, Khadim (Twins)	302
Dickerson, Korbyn (Mariners)	426
Dickerson, Luke (Nationals)	488
Dickinson, Daniel (Brewers)	289
Dinges, Marco (Brewers)	280
Dishmey, Eliazar (Marlins)	271
Dix, JD (D-backs)	24
Dohm, Nate (Cardinals)	383
Dorchies, Ethan (Brewers)	283
Dotel, Wilber (Pirates)	361
Doughty, Braylon (Guardians)	151
Doyle, Liam (Cardinals)	373
Drake, Isaiah (Braves)	63
Drake, Kohl (D-backs)	26
Dreiling, Dylan (Rangers)	458
Drohan, Shane (Red Sox)	91
Dubanewicz, Jayden (Brewers)	288
Dumesnil, Nick (Tigers)	190
Duno, Alfredo (Reds)	133
Duran, Edward (Blue Jays)	481
Dzierwa, Joseph (Orioles)	77

E

Eagen, Daniel (D-backs)	23
Early, Connelly (Red Sox)	85
Ebel, Brady (Brewers)	282
Echavarria, Steven (Athletics)	43
Ehrhard, Zach (Dodgers)	253
Eldridge, Bryce (Giants)	404
Elissalt, Frank (Cardinals)	382
Elliott, Clark (Athletics)	47
Ellwanger, James (Twins)	300
Emerson, Colt (Mariners)	420
Encarnacion, Handelfry (Brewers)	288
Encarnacion, Kifraidy (Marlins)	271
Escobar, Aroon (Phillies)	342
Espino, Daniel (Guardians)	156
Espinosa, Romeli (Phillies)	350
Essenburg, Conor (Braves)	59
Estrada, Aron (Orioles)	74
Ewing, A.J. (Mets)	311
Eyanson, Anthony (Red Sox)	90

F

Facundo, Allen (Yankees)	336
Fajardo, Yhoiker (Red Sox)	88
Farmelo, Jonny (Mariners)	423
Farris, Mitch (Angels)	240
Fauske, Jaden (White Sox)	119
Feliz, Angel (Nationals)	489
Fernandez, Dauri (Guardians)	159
Ferrebus, Alirio (Phillies)	347
Ferris, Jackson (Dodgers)	246
Fien, Gavin (Rangers)	453
Fischer, Andrew (Brewers)	281
Fisher, Matthew (Phillies)	344
Fitz-Gerald, Devin (Rangers)	456
Flemming, Cooper (Rays)	444
Fleury, Jose (Astros)	206
Flewelling, Nathan (Rays)	441
Florentino, Edward (Pirates)	357
Florentino, Jostin (Cubs)	107
Flores, Juan (Angels)	236
Flores, Rafael (Pirates)	359
Forbes, Patrick (D-backs)	23
Forcucci, Ryan (Astros)	201
Ford, Harry (Nationals)	485
Forret, Michael (Orioles)	72
Fountain, Kale (Padres)	393
Francisca, Welbyn (Guardians)	155
Franco, Jose (Reds)	138
Franklin, Christian (Nationals)	494
Franklin, Tanner (Cardinals)	375
Freeland, Alex (Dodgers)	247
Frey, Ethan (Astros)	198
Fuentes, Didier (Braves)	53

G

Gallagher, Ryan (Twins)	302
Gamble, Sean (Royals)	215
Garcia, Brandyn (D-backs)	27
Garcia, Jhostynxon (Pirates)	358
Garcia, Johanfran (Red Sox)	97
Gasser, Robert (Brewers)	282
Genao, Angel (Guardians)	150
George, Kendall (Dodgers)	249
George, Nate (Orioles)	70
German, Marconi (Nationals)	492
German, Nestor (Orioles)	75
Gibson, Trey (Orioles)	69
Gil, John (Braves)	58
Gill Hill, Gary (Rays)	444
Gillen, Theo (Rays)	437
Glasser, Philip (Nationals)	496
Godbout, Henry (Red Sox)	89
Gomez, Franklin (Mets)	318
Gomez, Yorman (Guardians)	157
Gonzales, Justin (Red Sox)	87
Gonzalez, Asbel (Royals)	219
Gonzalez, Gabriel (Twins)	297
Gonzalez, Jacob (White Sox)	127
Gonzalez, Josuar (Giants)	405
Gordon, Austin (Angels)	240
Gordon, RJ (Mets)	319
Gourson, Duce (Pirates)	365
Gray, CJ (Angels)	236
Gray, Murf (Pirates)	368
Gray, Taitn (Rays)	447
Gregory-Alford, Trey (Angels)	232
Griffin, Konnor (Pirates)	356
Grinsell, Grayson (Tigers)	193
Groover, LuJames (D-backs)	27
Guedez, Breyson (Athletics)	46
Guerrero, Brailer (Rays)	445
Gurevitch, Jack (Cardinals)	382

Gutierrez, Anthony (Rangers)	463
Gutierrez, Carlos (Giants)	410
Gutierrez, Daiverson (Mets)	319
Gutierrez, Luis (Padres)	399
Guzman, Denzer (Angels)	232
Guzman, Randy (Mets)	317

H

Hagaman, David (D-backs)	22
Haley, Talon (Angels)	233
Hall, Owen (Tigers)	186
Hall, Ryan (Tigers)	187
Hall, Steele (Reds)	134
Halpin, Petey (Guardians)	158
Hamilton, River (Tigers)	191
Hammond, Josh (Royals)	214
Hampton, Chase (Yankees)	329
Harber, Parks (Giants)	411
Hardin, Tyson (Brewers)	281
Harlan, Chase (Dodgers)	249
Harmon, Landon (Nationals)	489
Harrington, Thomas (Pirates)	364
Harris, Hayden (Braves)	59
Harris, Trent (Giants)	414
Harrison, Trevor (Rays)	441
Hartle, Josh (Guardians)	159
Hartman, Eric (Braves)	63
Hartshorn, Josiah (Cubs)	106
Harvey, Ty (Padres)	391
Hawkins, Garrett (Padres)	398
Haynes, Jagger (Padres)	393
Head, Dillon (Marlins)	266
Hechavarria, Silvano (Blue Jays)	474
Hedges, Ethan (Rockies)	170
Hence, Tink (Cardinals)	378
Henderson, Ixan (Cardinals)	376
Henderson, Logan (Brewers)	278
Hernandez, Cristian (Cubs)	107
Hernandez, Herick (Braves)	57
Hernandez, Seth (Pirates)	358
Herrera, Welinton (Rockies)	169
Herrera, Yujanyer (Rockies)	177
Herring, Griffin (Rockies)	170
Hertzler, Cole (Astros)	208
Hess, Ben (Yankees)	326
Heuer, Mac (Yankees)	330
Heyman, Luke (Red Sox)	97
Hicks, James (Astros)	206
Hill, Dasan (Twins)	295
Hjerpe, Cooper (Cardinals)	380
Hodge, Landon (White Sox)	126
Hoglund, Gunnar (Athletics)	42
Holliday, Ethan (Rockies)	164
Holman, Luke (Reds)	142
Holobetz, John (Red Sox)	91
Honeycutt, Vance (Orioles)	81
Honeyman, Travis (Cardinals)	385
Hope, Zyhir (Dodgers)	246
Hopkins, Brody (Rays)	436
Houston, Marek (Twins)	296
Huang, Chung-Hsiang (D-backs)	33
Huezo, Anthony (Astros)	203
Huggins, Kenya (Athletics)	48
Hughes, Gabriel (Rockies)	174
Hugus, Griffin (Mariners)	426
Hurd, Thatcher (Yankees)	328
Hurt, Kyle (Dodgers)	254
Hurtado, Joel (Angels)	238
Hynes, Will (Guardians)	161

I

Ingle, Cooper (Guardians)	153
Iriarte, Jairo (White Sox)	126
Irish, Ike (Orioles)	71
Isaac, Xavier (Rays)	440
Izzi, Ashton (D-backs)	26

J

Jacobs, Ben (Tigers)	188
James, Coy (Nationals)	488
Janek, Walker (Astros)	200
Jarvis, Jim (Braves)	64
Jasso, Dylan (Yankees)	335
Jenkins, Walker (Twins)	292
Jennings, Ryan (Blue Jays)	478
Jensen, Carter (Royals)	212
Jimenez, Antonio (Mets)	317
Jimenez, Enrique (Twins)	304
Johnson, Ryan (Angels)	229
Johnson, Seth (Phillies)	348
Johnson, Termarr (Pirates)	359
Johnson, Ty (Rays)	443
Jones, Brendan (Yankees)	330
Jones, Druw (D-backs)	28
Jones, Spencer (Yankees)	327
Jordan, Blaze (Cardinals)	385
Jordan, Dakota (Giants)	407
Jordan, Dylan (Angels)	233
Jorge, Carlos (Reds)	144
Jump, Gage (Athletics)	37

K

Karpathios, Braedon (Padres)	394
Kasevich, Josh (Blue Jays)	476
Keegan, Dominic (Rays)	442
Kelly, Antwone (Pirates)	360
Kelly, Jaitoine (D-backs)	31
Kelly, Lucas (Mariners)	432
Kelly, Riley (Rockies)	175
Kemp, Kannon (Padres)	397
Kempner, William (Marlins)	271
Kent, Barrett (Angels)	234
Kent, Jackson (Nationals)	491
Kent, Kaeden (Yankees)	331
Kepley, Kane (Cubs)	103
Keys, Sean (Blue Jays)	477
Kilby, Dax (Yankees)	325
Kilen, Gavin (Giants)	408
Kim, Seong-Jun (Rangers)	462
King, Johnny (Blue Jays)	470
King, Seaver (Nationals)	487
King Jr., Lamar (Padres)	394
Klassen, George (Angels)	229
Klein, John (Twins)	302
Kling, Paxton (Rangers)	461
Knipp, Grant (Mariners)	431
Knoth, Josh (Brewers)	287
Ko, Ching-Hsien (Dodgers)	252
Kohn, Pico (Yankees)	332
Kopp, Ronan (Dodgers)	256
Kudrna, Ben (Royals)	218
Kuncl, Trevor (Reds)	144
Kuroda-Grauer, Joshua (Athletics)	40
Kussow, Peter (Mets)	321

L

Labrada, Victor (Mariners)	431
LaCombe, Mathias (White Sox)	121
LaCourse, Luke (Angels)	241
Lagrange, Carlos (Yankees)	326
Lalane, Henry (Yankees)	333
Lamkin, Justin (Royals)	220
Lantigua, Arnaldo (Reds)	143
Lara, Jhancarlos (Braves)	62
Lara, Luis (Brewers)	279
Laroche, Alberto (Giants)	416
Larson, Blake (White Sox)	126
Lasko, Ryan (Athletics)	46
LaViolette, Jace (Guardians)	151
Leach, Hudson (Astros)	208
Lee, Hao-Yu (Tigers)	183
Leiter, Cam (Dodgers)	255
Letson, Bishop (Brewers)	278
Level, Jhonny (Giants)	406
Levenson, Zach (Cardinals)	384
Lewis, Dillon (Yankees)	328
Lewis, Tyson (Reds)	134
Lin, Sheng-En (Reds)	139
Lin, Wei-En (Athletics)	38
Lin, Yu-Min (D-backs)	31
Liñan, Sean Paul (Nationals)	494
Lindsey, Kellon (Dodgers)	251
Liranzo, Joshua (Orioles)	80
Liranzo, Thayron (Tigers)	188
Livingston, Dean (D-backs)	32
Lizarraga, Victor (Padres)	401
Lodise, Alex (Braves)	55
Lodise, Kyle (White Sox)	121
Lomavita, Caleb (Nationals)	492
Lombard Jr., George (Yankees)	324
Lombardi, Michael (Royals)	219
Long, Jonathon (Cubs)	104
Lopez, Leandro (Rangers)	457
Lowder, Rhett (Reds)	133
Luciano, Ivan (D-backs)	30
Lugo, Joswa (Angels)	231
Luis, Jansel (D-backs)	26

M

Mack, Joe (Marlins)	262
Macko, Adam (Blue Jays)	479
Madden, Ty (Tigers)	191
Made, Jesus (Brewers)	276
Madonna, Truitt (Padres)	396
Maldonado, Cam (Giants)	414
Maldonado, Gerelmi (Giants)	417
Marinez, Stiven (Yankees)	334
Marquez, Ramon (Phillies)	346
Marriott, Mason (D-backs)	31
Marte, Yunior (Giants)	416
Martin, Maxton (Rangers)	462
Martin, Riley (Cubs)	109
Martinez, Jeter (Pirates)	367
Martinez, Keyner (Giants)	407
Martinez, Liomar (Marlins)	269
Martinez, Stiven (Orioles)	80
Mathews, Quinn (Cardinals)	374
Mathis, Cole (Cubs)	104
Matthews, Brice (Astros)	198
Mautz, Brycen (Cardinals)	381
Maxwell, Zach (Reds)	140
Mayea, Brando (Yankees)	336
Mayer, Bryce (Astros)	201
Mayfield, Kash (Padres)	389
McAdoo, Charles (Blue Jays)	478
McCabe, David (Braves)	61
McCambley, Zach (Phillies)	349
McCullough, Brody (Cubs)	112
McDonald, Trevor (Giants)	411
McDougal, Tanner (White Sox)	119
McFarlane, Alex (Phillies)	348
McGarry, Griff (Nationals)	497
McGonigle, Kevin (Tigers)	180
McGraw, Teddy (Mariners)	427
McKenzie, Briggs (Braves)	54
McLean, Nolan (Mets)	308
Meccage, Bryce (Brewers)	286
Medina, Ramcell (Royals)	221
Mejia, Esteban (Orioles)	71
Melton, Jacob (Astros)	196
Mena, Cristian (D-backs)	25
Mendez, Hendry (Twins)	298
Mendez, Miguel (Padres)	390
Meola, Lorenzo (Giants)	413
Messick, Parker (Guardians)	150
Messina, Carson (Blue Jays)	480
Messina, Cole (Rockies)	174
Meyer, Noble (Marlins)	269
Middleton, J.B. (Rockies)	169
Milbrandt, Karson (Marlins)	264
Miles, Spencer (Blue Jays)	478
Millar, Cameron (Royals)	223
Miller, Aidan (Phillies)	340
Miller, Cody (Braves)	61
Miller, Cole (Athletics)	48
Miller, Jake (Tigers)	190
Miller, Noah (Dodgers)	254
Mitchell, Blake (Royals)	214
Mitchell, Jase (Astros)	204
Mitchell, Ryan (Cardinals)	378
Mitchell, Xavier (Angels)	238
Mogollon, Javier (White Sox)	123
Monistere, Nick (Astros)	207
Montero, Edgar (Athletics)	39
Montes, Lazaro (Mariners)	421
Montgomery, Braden (White Sox)	117
Montilla, Franyerber (Tigers)	184
Moore, Malcolm (Rangers)	460
Morabito, Nick (Mets)	314
Morales, Emil (Dodgers)	248
Morales, Michael (Mariners)	428
Morales, Yohandy (Nationals)	491
Morel, Darell (Pirates)	364
Morgan, Tre' (Rays)	446
Morii, Shotaro (Athletics)	41
Morillo, Jirvin (Reds)	141
Morlando, PJ (Marlins)	268
Morris, Andrew (Twins)	298
Morris, Kade (Athletics)	42
Morris, Mason (Reds)	141
Moss, Dean (Rays)	444
Mota, Jorgelys (Nationals)	493
Mozzicato, Frank (Royals)	224
Mueth, Zander (Pirates)	367
Mullins, Hayden (Red Sox)	94
Muñoz, Rolddy (Braves)	60
Murphy, Owen (Braves)	54
Murphy, Shane (White Sox)	128
Musgrove, Tucker (Padres)	394

N

Navarro, Reinold (Pirates)	363
Nett, Braden (Athletics)	38
Neville, Mason (Reds)	140
Neyens, Xavier (Astros)	197
Nezuh, Jackson (Astros)	204
Nichols, TJ (Rays)	438
Nieves, Marlon (Dodgers)	255
Nikhazy, Doug (Guardians)	160
Nimmala, Arjun (Blue Jays)	469
Nori, Dante (Phillies)	343
Nunez, Anthony (Orioles)	78
Nuñez, Eduarnel (Athletics)	45

O

Oakie, Joey (Guardians)	154
Obermueller, Cade (Phillies)	345
Olejnik, Peyton (Angels)	240
Olivares, Jose (Twins)	301
Oliveto, Michael (Tigers)	185
Oppor, Christian (White Sox)	120
Ornelas, Tirso (Padres)	399
Ortiz, Deniel (Cardinals)	381
Ortiz, Robinson (Mariners)	432
Overn, Austin (Orioles)	76
Owens, Josh (Rangers)	454
Ozuna, Darwing (Athletics)	49
Ozuna, Sandy (Rockies)	177
Padilla, Yairo (Cardinals)	377
Paez, Jedixson (White Sox)	124
Painter, Andrew (Phillies)	341
Palmquist, Carson (Rockies)	172

P

Panzini, Shane (Royals)	223
Parker, JoJo (Blue Jays)	469
Patick, Sterling (Dodgers)	257
Patteson, Hunter (Royals)	222
Payne, Braylon (Brewers)	284
Payne, Nate (Marlins)	270
Peck, John (Tigers)	187
Pecko, Ethan (Astros)	200
Peete, Tai (Mariners)	425
Peña, Elian (Mets)	314
Peña, Francis (Padres)	400
Peña, Luis (Brewers)	277
Pence, Dalton (Rangers)	460
Penney, Jack (Tigers)	189
Perales, Luis (Nationals)	486
Perez, Fernando (Blue Jays)	476
Perez, Jeral (White Sox)	124
Perez, Junior (Athletics)	45
Perez, Marcelo (Mariners)	430
Peters, Mason (Mariners)	428
Peterson, Sam (Nationals)	490
Petit, RJ (Rockies)	175
Petry, Ethan (Nationals)	490
Petty, Chase (Reds)	135
Phillips, Marcus (Red Sox)	89
Piasentin, Tim (Blue Jays)	475
Pierce, Daniel (Rays)	439
Pinango, Yohendrick (Blue Jays)	473
Pinckney, Andrew (Nationals)	490
Pintaro, Jonathan (Mets)	318
Pitre, Emilien (Rays)	447
Pitts, Eli (Reds)	142
Plaz, Axiel (Pirates)	365
Potter, Nick (Astros)	208
Pratt, Cooper (Brewers)	277
Prielipp, Connor (Twins)	294
Pushard, Matt (Cardinals)	384

Q

Quero, Jeferson (Brewers)	279
Quick, Riley (Twins)	297
Quinn, JT (Orioles)	79
Quinn-Irons, James (Rays)	448
Quintana, Jorge (Padres)	390
Quintero, Eduardo (Dodgers)	244
Quintero, Marlon (Angels)	239

R

Rada, Nelson (Angels)	230
Rainer, Bryce (Tigers)	181
Ramirez, German (Astros)	209
Ramirez, Pedro (Cubs)	105
Ramirez, Ramon (Royals)	215
Ramos, Hector (Red Sox)	95
Ray, Dylan (D-backs)	29
Raya, Marco (Twins)	301
Reid, Dominick (Cubs)	106
Reimer, Jacob (Mets)	312
Reyes, Luis (White Sox)	127
Ricardo, Yandel (Royals)	217
Riggio, Roc (Rockies)	171
Rincon, Bryan (Phillies)	353
Rincones Jr., Gabriel (Phillies)	343
Ritchie, JR (Braves)	53
Rivas, Harold (Red Sox)	93
Rivas, Xavier (Yankees)	334
Robinson, Kyle (Athletics)	48
Roby, Tekoah (Cardinals)	378
Roccaforte, Carson (Royals)	218
Rock, Joe (Rays)	449
Rodden, Brock (Mariners)	427
Rodriguez, Bradgley (Padres)	392
Rodriguez, Cris (Tigers)	184
Rodriguez, Elmer (Yankees)	325
Rodriguez, Elorky (Rangers)	462
Rodriguez, Emmanuel (Twins)	293
Rodriguez, Erian (Cubs)	111
Rodriguez, Gabriel (Guardians)	160
Rodriguez, Gerardo (Red Sox)	95
Rodriguez, Hector (Reds)	136
Rodriguez, Jeremy (Mets)	320
Rodriguez, Jesus (Giants)	412
Rodriguez, Jose (Dodgers)	257
Rodriguez, Jose M. (Yankees)	337
Rodriguez, Manuel (Brewers)	288
Rodriguez, Rainiel (Cardinals)	373
Rodriguez, Raudi (Angels)	237
Rodriguez, Yobal (White Sox)	129
Rojas, Jefferson (Cubs)	102
Rojas, Kendry (Twins)	296
Romero, Leandro (Mariners)	429
Romero, Mikey (Red Sox)	93
Root, Zach (Dodgers)	248
Rosario, Alejandro (Rangers)	458
Rosario, Alfonsin (Guardians)	159
Rosario, Kala'i (Twins)	305
Ross, Dylan (Mets)	320
Russell, AJ (Rangers)	455
Ryan, River (Dodgers)	250

S

Salas, Andrew (Marlins)	266
Salas, Ethan (Padres)	388
Salcedo, Kelvis (Tigers)	185
Salina, Michael (Padres)	395
Saltiban, Devin (Phillies)	349
Samaniego, Tyler (Red Sox)	94
Sanabria, Romeo (Padres)	395
Sanchez, Adolfo (Reds)	138
Sanchez, Carlos (Reds)	143
Sanchez, Jordan (Orioles)	78
Sanchez, Juan (Blue Jays)	471
Sanders, Will (Cubs)	110
Sandlin, David (Red Sox)	90
Sanford, Wyatt (Pirates)	362
Santa, Alimber (Astros)	209
Santana, Adrian (Rays)	443
Santana, Paulino (Rangers)	463
Santos, Winston (Rangers)	456
Santucci, Jonathan (Mets)	313
Scarborough, Caden (Rangers)	453
Schlaffer, Tyler (Cubs)	112
Schlesinger, Rafe (Guardians)	161
Schoolcraft, Kruz (Padres)	389
Schreck, RJ (Blue Jays)	472
Schubart, Nolan (Guardians)	157
Schultz, Noah (White Sox)	116
Sears, Andrew (Tigers)	186
Sears, Brett (Braves)	65
Selvidge, Brock (Yankees)	330
Serna, Jared (Marlins)	272
Serrano, Teilon (Twins)	304
Serrano III, Eli (Mets)	316
Serwinowski, Adam (Dodgers)	250
Shen, Chia-Shi (Mariners)	429
Shepardson, Grant (Marlins)	270
Shields, David (Royals)	213
Shores, Chase (Angels)	234
Sime Jr., Miguel (Nationals)	493
Sinnard, Luke (Braves)	56
Sirota, Mike (Dodgers)	245
Slawinski, Johnny (Angels)	231
Sloan, Ryan (Mariners)	422
Smith, Aidan (Rays)	440
Smith, Cade (Yankees)	329
Smith, Dylan (Tigers)	189
Smith, Hagen (White Sox)	118
Smith, Parker (Astros)	205
Snead, Nate (Angels)	236
Snelling, Robby (Marlins)	261
Snyder, Trey (Mets)	320
Soler, Yassel (D-backs)	30
Sosa, Thomas (Orioles)	77
Soto, Charlee (Twins)	295
Soto, Dorian (Red Sox)	88
Soto, Ubaldo (Angels)	238
Southisene, Tate (Braves)	58
Southisene, Ty (Cubs)	110
Spence, Lucas (Astros)	202
Sproat, Brandon (Mets)	310
Stafura, Sammy (Pirates)	362
Stanifer, Gage (Blue Jays)	470
Stephen, Khal (Guardians)	152
Sterling, Levi (Pirates)	366
Stevenson, Luke (Mariners)	424
Steward, Casey (Phillies)	352
Stewart, Sal (Reds)	132
Strong, Jackson (Tigers)	192
Su, Lan-Hong (Padres)	396
Suarez, Santiago (Rays)	438
Suero, Chris (Mets)	314
Suisbel, Luis (Mariners)	428
Sullivan, Joseph (Astros)	203
Sullivan, Sean (Rockies)	171
Summerhill, Brendan (Rays)	439
Sundstrom, Jared (Mariners)	430
Susac, Daniel (Giants)	412
Susana, Jarlin (Nationals)	485
Sykora, Travis (Nationals)	486

T

Tait, Eduardo (Twins)	294
Tallon, James (Phillies)	353
Taylor, Brayden (Rays)	449
Taylor, Devin (Athletics)	40
Taylor, Zane (Athletics)	44
Tears, Kavares (Tigers)	396
Tejeda Jr., Yoel (Nationals)	495
Teodo, Emiliano (Rangers)	459
Teran, Saul (Phillies)	351
Thach, Tanner (Rockies)	176

Thomas, Jared (Rockies)	165
Thomas, Rhylan (Mariners)	430
Thompson, JD (Brewers)	285
Thompson, Sterlin (Rockies)	173
Thornton, Zach (Mets)	315
Tibbs III, James (Dodgers)	255
Tidwell, Blade (Giants)	410
Tiedemann, Ricky (Blue Jays)	471
Tiger, Izack (Rangers)	459
Tilly, Cam (Mets)	321
Tolle, Payton (Red Sox)	84
Tomas, Juan (Cubs)	111
Tong, Jonah (Mets)	309
Torin, Cristofer (D-backs)	25
Tornes, Diego (Braves)	57
Torres, Bryan (Cardinals)	383
Torres, Stharlin (Reds)	137
Travieso, Jesus (Pirates)	366
Tredwell, Alonzo (Astros)	207
Triantos, James (Cubs)	105
Trimble, Fenwick (Marlins)	265
Troy, Tommy (D-backs)	24
Tunink, Brendan (Dodgers)	252
Tur, Yunior (Athletics)	46
Turley, Gavin (Athletics)	44
Uberstine, Tyler (Red Sox)	92

U

Ullola, Miguel (Astros)	202
Urbina, Jose (Rays)	442
Ureña, Walbert (Angels)	235

V

Valdez, Esmerlyn (Pirates)	361
Valencia, Eduardo (Tigers)	192
Valencia, Esmil (Marlins)	267
Valenzuela, Brandon (Blue Jays)	480
Valera, Juan (Red Sox)	86
Vargas, Joendry (Dodgers)	251
Vargas, Marco (Mets)	316
Vasquez, Daury (D-backs)	32
Veen, Zac (Rockies)	172
Velasquez, Diego (Giants)	414
Velazquez, Ralphy (Guardians)	149
Verdugo, Rosman (Padres)	401
Vidourek, Landyn (Dodgers)	256
Villarroel, Jancel (Astros)	205
Villoria, Geremy (Twins)	303
Vilorio, Francisco (Yankees)	334
Virahonda, Carlos (D-backs)	29
Voit, Mitch (Mets)	313

W

Walcott, Sebastian (Rangers)	452
Waldschmidt, Ryan (D-backs)	20
Walters, Andrew (Guardians)	156
Walton, Aaron (Guardians)	158
Watson, Aaron (Reds)	137
Watson, Kahlil (Guardians)	157
Watson, Will (Mets)	315
Watts-Brown, Juaron (Orioles)	76
Wells, Levi (Orioles)	76
Wenninger, Jack (Mets)	312
West, Aidan (Dodgers)	253
Wetherholt, JJ (Cardinals)	372
Wheeler, Jack (Rangers)	461
Whisenhunt, Carson (Giants)	409
White, Josh (Marlins)	269
White, Thomas (Marlins)	260
White, Tommy (Athletics)	41
Whitman, Joe (Giants)	415
Wideman, Ryan (Padres)	392
Wiggins, Jaxon (Cubs)	101
Wilken, Brock (Brewers)	284
Williams, Carson (Rays)	437
Williams, Dixon (Braves)	62
Williams, Henry (Royals)	225
Williams, Jett (Mets)	310
Willits, Eli (Nationals)	484
Wilson, Paul (Tigers)	192
Wing, Kaleb (Cubs)	108
Winokur, Brandon (Twins)	299
Winquest, Cade (Yankees)	332
Witherspoon, Kyson (Red Sox)	86
Witherspoon, Malachi (Tigers)	186
Wolkow, George (White Sox)	123
Wolters, Blake (Royals)	222
Wood, Gage (Phillies)	342
Worley, Reid (Giants)	416

Y

Yesavage, Trey (Blue Jays)	468
Yoho, Craig (Brewers)	285
Yorke, Nick (Pirates)	365
Yost, Jordan (Tigers)	182
Young, Quentin (Twins)	298
Youngerman, Sean (Phillies)	346

Z

Zazueta, Christian (Dodgers)	250
Zhuang, Chen-Zhong Ao (Athletics)	49
Ziehl, Gage (White Sox)	125
Zobac, Steven (Royals)	218